Educational Policy and The Law

Cases and Materials

David L. Kirp

Graduate School of Public Policy
and School of Law
University of California (Berkeley)

Mark G. Yudof

School of Law
University of Texas

Foreword by

Nathan Glazer

McCutchan Publishing Corporation
2526 Grove Street
Berkeley, California 94704

© 1974 by McCutchan Publishing Corporation
all rights reserved

Library of Congress Catalog Card no. 73-17609
ISBN 0-8211-1015-2

Printed in the United States of America

To

Lauren,

Judy,

and our parents

Contents

CHAPTER SEVEN. EQUAL EDUCATIONAL OPPORTUNITY AND STUDENT CLASSIFICATION   644

Table of Cases

[Note: quoted cases are indicated by italics.]

Table of
Secondary Authorities

[Note: quoted authorities are indicated by italics.]

)

Foreword

Educational Policy and the Law is one of a new breed of law textbooks. Indeed, one is uncertain whether to call it a "casebook" or even to consider it a "textbook," despite its traditional format of cases embedded in an analytical text that addresses questions on the law to students. The first of its kind is always more than a textbook or casebook: it is a way of wording—of conceptualizing—a new field. And the new breed of lawbooks I have in mind deals with rapidly evolving fields of social policy.

Of course, the law has dealt with issues such as aid for the poor, housing, and education for hundreds of years. However, the 1960s in this country introduced a revolution in social policy and a revolution in the relationship of law to social policy. Legal rights in Anglo-Saxon countries have for centuries concentrated on the protection of person and property and on the limits of governmental power. This power has rapidly expanded to include the social services—education, welfare rights, housing, medical care. It is not likely that this expansion of the law is merely temporary, since it follows the lead of public opinion, the executive branch, and the legislature, rather than—as in education—leading from case opinions. The law, the courts, and the law schools will never be the same. To contracts and torts have been added education and many other specific fields.

In responding to this revolution, the lawbook has had to become a very different thing indeed. When we deal with education (and with the other fields of social policy) we deal not only with rights, but also with the problem of knowledge guiding power—of effectiveness. The judge who decrees that a fortune belongs to one claimant rather than another need not (one assumes would not) consider whether claimant A will be corrupted by the money or claimant B will put it to good use. Of course, in education cases, too, we deal with a strict and sheer determination of rights, regardless of effects or consequences. But, inevitably, when we deal with social policy, we must also consider the *ends* of policy, and these are never only equity or justice: they are also effectiveness in light of the specific objective of the policy. To consider effectiveness we must extend our concern to include the findings of the social sciences—economics, sociology, political science, psychology, and anthropology. It is no accident that *Brown v Board of Education*, the case that opened up expansion of the law into education, controversially made use of social science findings. Presumably the justices could have avoided all questions of the *effects* of segregated education, but they did not. Thus, a marriage was forged between the social sciences and the law. What was the effect of segregated education? Did its effect differ in the North and the South? Did de facto segregation differ from de jure? What were the effects of different proportions of racial mixtures in school populations? What role did local support of integrated schooling play in its effectiveness? From the few brief references in *Brown* to various social science studies, we have come to the point where huge research projects on the effectiveness of schooling, such as the Coleman Report, are again and again—wisely or not, with understanding or not—brought into litigation.

Not only in questions of segregation and integration—dealt with in chapter 4 of this book—are legal issues raised, at least in part, on the basis of data developed by the social scientists. The problem of sex-based discrimination (discussed in chapter 5) has also raised questions that call for recourse to social scientists. What is the effect of education in single-sex schools? At different levels? In classrooms limited to one sex? How does sex affect the qualification of teachers specialized in certain areas? What are sound tests of discrimination? How are they to be distinguished from concern for the needs of one sex or another?

The question of the equalization of educational resources, raised in chapter 6, also inevitably involves social scientists, because much of the litigation concerns the causes of differential resources, which are themselves difficult to trace, and the effectiveness of different resources in affecting educational outcomes.

The first three chapters of this book deal with more traditional topics. They concern the limits that may be imposed on the state in its requirement and support of schooling, and they discuss the rights of parents, students, and teachers. These topics provide the setting of classic issues of liberty, out of which our newer concerns with effectiveness have developed.

The law, we have said, has had to go to the social scientist as it moves into fields of social policy; the social scientist, on the other hand, has increasingly found it necessary to go to the law. Litigation, based as it is on the conflict of strongly held views as to the right, has generated a remarkable amount of research. Thus, much of what we know now about the history of districting schools has been developed in response to the needs of lawsuits challenging the districting that made for de facto segregated schools. The Coleman Report itself was a response to the needs of the law: It was called for by the Civil Rights Act of 1964 as an effort to deal with the complex issues raised by the *Brown* decision and the desegregation of the schools. Thus the law has found it necessary to call upon the social sciences, and the social sciences have found that much of their agenda is set by the law. This book bears witness to the complex and fruitful interaction that is now developing between these two great realms of knowledge.

Nathan Glazer
*Professor of Education
and Sociology
Harvard University*

Introduction

During the past two decades, lawmakers have reshaped the realm of educational policy. Courts have reviewed a wide range of issues—including the behavior of students and teachers, and the permissibility of differentiation in terms of race, sex, and access to educational resources—that historically have been resolved by school administrators and boards of education. New mandates have also emerged from Congress, traditionally removed from the education fray, and from state legislatures. This casebook examines that emergent law and attempts to assess its impact on American schooling policy and practice.

Educational Policy and the Law is not a traditional "school law" book. We have sacrificed certain topics that are typically featured, such as the tort and contract liability of school districts, in an effort to address fully issues that appear to have greater vitality. The casebook does not treat "the law" as an isolated entity, but rather focuses on the interaction between legal decisions and educational practice. As the index of sources suggests, it borrows liberally from a wealth of social science material, ranging from historical studies of compulsoriness to survey data concerning the relationship between school resources and educational outcomes. That material serves in part to afford greater understanding of problems that become legal issues. It identifies factors that promote present patterns of behavior and the institutional and social demands that the behavior satisfies. Social science material is also used to assess the effects, both positive and negative, of legal change.

To the education student and administrator, this approach affords a means of understanding the law as something other than a series of disjointed and arbitrary happenings, *deus ex machina* that disturb the lives of schoolmen and, on occasion, the values of society. Sufficient material on the techniques of legal analysis is included so that the person unschooled in the law can read finely nuanced court decisions and statutes with some confidence. To the law student, this approach provides at least a rudimentary sense of the education policy issues that the law reaches. It reveals that there are notable, if sometimes inadvertent, pedagogical and political consequences of legal action.

The first three chapters of the casebook treat questions of student and teacher liberty. The book begins with the underlying issue: Can the state compel all children to attend some school? To what extent can it regulate their education? That inquiry, which includes a discussion of alternatives to the present scheme, identifies tensions among the interests of the state, the family, and the child in education, concerns that recur throughout the text. It also frames the background for a related set of questions, addressed in the second and third chapters: In what ways may the government regulate the lives of children and their teachers? What are the bounds of permissible governmental socialization or indoctrination of students? What "academic freedoms" does the public school teacher bring to the classroom? The effects of relatively recent phenomena—the student rights movement and the growth of teachers' unions—upon these issues, as well as conflicts between the interests of students and those of their teachers, are also considered.

Chapters 4-6 reverse the focus, examining the legal and policy implications of claims that students may press on the school. These chapters disentangle several quite different concepts of equal educational opportunity. Chapter 4 traces the evolution of the constitutional definition of equal opportunity in the racial context; while its primary emphasis is on the development of the obligation to desegregate schools, the chapter assesses the political ramifications of this issue, and considers more recently posed questions, such as the demand for preferential quotas and community-run schools. Chapter 5 looks at a less frequently noted phenomenon, sex differentiation in school, considering the nature of the problem, the constitutional challenges that have thus far been leveled at practices alleged to discriminate against women, and the likely effects of judicial intervention. Chapter 6 treats equal educational opportunity in terms of school resources and outcomes, focusing on the consequences of adopting—as a matter of either policy or constitutional law—any of several quite different standards of dollar or outcome equity. The final chapter brings together the two parts of the text: it examines the applicability of equal opportunity doctrine to issues that arise when schools seek to distinguish among their students on the basis of academic performance or potential, for example, by grouping them according to ability. Throughout the casebook, most of the materials concern primary and secondary education, but higher education issues are treated where they are germane to a broader policy or legal problem.

The casebook can be covered, in its entirety, in a one-semester course meeting three hours each week, by an instructor who believes in intellectual jogging. For the teacher with less time to teach the material, or one who prefers to inquire more closely into a limited number of issues, we suggest that chapters 5, 7, and 3—in that order—may be skipped without fatally affecting the structure of the book. These chapters present issues that either have not reached full legal maturity (those in chapters 5 and 7) or focus on a group that, while obviously essential to the schooling process, has rights and interests only tangentially linked to the balance of the discussion.

The format of the casebook requires brief explanation. The materials have been edited, sometimes drastically, to bring them within reasonable page limitations. We have retained the footnote numbers of our original sources, so that readers wishing to examine the unexpurgated text may more easily find their way. Each major selection is followed by notes that offer background information and raise the questions we have found most difficult and most challenging to confront.

The authors have amassed considerable debts, intellectual and otherwise, in preparing this casebook. Work began on the venture four years ago, when both of us were associated with the Harvard Center for Law and Education. Our initial contact with educational policy and law was as advocates: each of us participated in a number of the cases and legislative matters that have found their way into this book, and that involvement helped shape our views of the field. Equally important was our association with the educational policy community at Harvard. The influence of such men as David Cohen, Christopher Jencks, and Nathan Glazer at the Graduate School of Education; Frank Michelman and Abram Chayes at the Law School; and Thomas Pettigrew in the Department of Social Relations, is too pervasive for ready pinpointing. During the past two years, the handsome financial support provided by the Ford Foundation and Carnegie Corporation to the Project on Childhood and Government at Berkeley, and the suggestions of Berkeley colleagues John Coons, Stephen Sugarman, and Robert Mnookin, and of Albert Alschuler at Texas both aided and extended the process of revision. Without the research help of Susan Appleton, Steven Knudsen, James Martin, Carl Milofsky, Donald Brodsky, Hunter Harrison, and Alice Word, the text would have had notable gaps; without the editorial help of Loralee Lowe and the extraordinary secretarial efforts of Julie F. Isen, the casebook might never have appeared at all.

chapter one
Schooling and the State

I. The "*Pierce* Compromise" and Its Implications for Education Governance

In all but two states, American children are legally obliged to attend school. Most of them attend publicly run schools whose policies are determined by state and local officials. In many states private schools are also governmentally regulated. These bare-bones facts of American schooling are familiar to most citizens. Less generally understood are such matters as how this pattern came to be; its implications for children, educators, and society; the nature and scope of legitimate governmental interest; and, most significantly for our purposes, the constitutional and statutory bases of the structure. Consideration of such questions is essential to intelligent comprehension of the relationship between educational policy and law.

Pierce v Society of Sisters establishes the basic constitutional framework within which the states regulate schooling. The power of the state to compel attendance at a school is unquestioned; but, as the case indicates, the state cannot employ that power to eliminate all educational choice. *Pierce* embodies the tension between state and individual that is revealed throughout this chapter.

PIERCE v SOCIETY OF SISTERS
268 US 510 (1925)

Mr. Justice McReynolds delivered the opinion of the court.

These appeals are from decrees, based upon undenied allegations, which granted preliminary orders restraining appellants from threatening or attempting to enforce the Compulsory Education Act (Ore Gen Laws, ch 1, p 9 (1923))[1] adopted November 7, 1922, under the initiative provision of her constitution by the voters of Oregon. Judicial Code § 266 (Comp St § 1243) . . . .

---

1. *Be it enacted by the people of the state of Oregon:*
Section 1. That section 5259, Oregon Laws, be and the same is hereby amended so as to read as follows:
Section 5259. *Children Between the Ages of Eight and Sixteen Years.* Any parent, guardian or other person in the state of Oregon, having control or charge or custody of a child under the age of sixteen years and of the age of eight years or over at the commencement of a term of public school of the district in which said child resides, who shall fail or neglect or refuse to send such child to a public school for the period of time a public school shall be held during the current year in said district, shall be guilty of a misdemeanor and each day's failure to send such child to a public school shall constitute a separate offense; provided, that in the following cases, children shall not be required to attend public schools:
(a) *Children Physically Unable.* Any child who is abnormal, subnormal or physically unable to attend school.

The challenged act, effective September 1, 1926, requires every parent, guardian, or other person having control or charge or custody of a child between eight and sixteen years to send him "to a public school for the period of time a public school shall be held during the current year" in the district where the child resides; and failure to do so is declared a misdemeanor . . . . The manifest purpose is to compel general attendance at public schools by normal children, between eight and sixteen, who have not completed the eighth grade. And without doubt enforcement of the statute would seriously impair, perhaps destroy, the profitable features of appellees' business and greatly diminish the value of their property.

Appellee the Society of Sisters is an Oregon corporation, organized in 1880, with power to care for orphans, educate and instruct the youth, establish and maintain academies or schools, and acquire necessary real and personal property. It has long devoted its property and effort to the secular and religious education and care of children, and has acquired the valuable goodwill of many parents and guardians. It conducts interdependent primary and high schools and junior colleges, and maintains orphanages for the custody and control of children between eight and sixteen. In its primary schools many children between those ages are taught the subjects usually pursued in Oregon public schools during the first eight years. Systematic religious instruction and moral training according to the tenets of the Roman Catholic Church are also regularly provided. All courses of study, both temporal and religious, contemplate continuity of training under appellee's charge; the primary schools are essential to the system and the most profitable. It owns valuable buildings, especially constructed and equipped for school purposes. The business is remunerative—the annual income from primary schools exceeds $30,000—and the successful conduct of this requires long-time contracts with teachers and parents. The Compulsory Education Act of 1922 has already caused the withdrawal from its schools of children who would otherwise continue, and

(b) *Children Who Have Completed the Eighth Grade.* Any child who has completed the eighth grade, in accordance with the provisions of the state course of study.

(c) *Distance from School.* Children between the ages of eight and ten years, inclusive, whose place of residence is more than one and one-half miles, and children over ten years of age whose place of residence is more than three miles, by the nearest traveled road, from a public school; provided, however, that if transportation to and from school is furnished by the school district, this exemption shall not apply.

(d) *Private Instruction.* Any child who is being taught for a like period of time by the parent or private teacher such subjects as are usually taught in the first eight years in the public school; but before such child can be taught by a parent or a private teacher, such parent or private teacher must receive written permission from the county superintendent, and such permission shall not extend longer than the end of the current school year. Such child must report to the county school superintendent or some person designated by him at least once every three months and take an examination in the work covered. If, after such examination, the county superintendent shall determine that such child is not being properly taught, then the county superintendent shall order the parent, guardian or other person, to send such child to the public school the remainder of the school year.

If any parent, guardian, or other person having control or charge or custody of any child between the ages of eight and sixteen years, shall fail to comply with any provision of this section, he shall be guilty of a misdemeanor, and shall, on conviction thereof, be subject to a fine of not less than $5, nor more than $100, or to imprisonment in the county jail not less than two nor more than thirty days, or by both such fine and imprisonment in the discretion of the court.

This act shall take effect and be and remain in force from and after the first day of September, 1926.

their income has steadily declined. The appellants, public officers, have proclaimed their purpose strictly to enforce the statute.

After setting out the above facts, the society's bill alleges that the enactment conflicts with the right of parents to choose schools where their children will receive appropriate mental and religious training, the right of the child to influence the parents' choice of a school, the right of schools and teachers therein to engage in a useful business or profession, and is accordingly repugnant to the Constitution and void. And, further, that unless enforcement of the measure is enjoined the corporation's business and property will suffer irreparable injury.

Appellee Hill Military Academy is a private corporation organized in 1908 under the laws of Oregon, engaged in owning, operating, and conducting for profit an elementary college preparatory, and military training school for boys between the ages of five and twenty-one years . . . . It owns considerable real and personal property, some useful only for school purposes. The business and incident goodwill are very valuable. In order to conduct its affairs, long time contracts must be made for supplies, equipment, teachers, and pupils. Appellants, law officers of the state and county, have publicly announced that the act of November 7, 1922, is valid and have declared their intention to enforce it. By reason of the statute and threat of enforcement appellee's business is being destroyed and its property depreciated; parents and guardians are refusing to make contracts for the future instruction of their sons, and some are being withdrawn.

The academy's bill states the foregoing facts and then alleges that the challenged act contravenes the corporation's rights guaranteed by the Fourteenth Amendment and that unless appellants are restrained from proclaiming its validity and threatening to enforce it irreparable injury will result. The prayer is for an appropriate injunction.

No answer was interposed in either cause, and after proper notices they were heard by three judges (Judicial Code §266 [Comp St §1243]) on motions for preliminary injunctions upon the specifically alleged facts. The court ruled that the Fourteenth Amendment guaranteed appellees against the deprivation of their property without due process of law consequent upon the unlawful interference by appellants with the free choice of patrons, present and prospective. It declared the right to conduct schools was property and that parents and guardians, as a part of their liberty, might direct the education of children by selecting reputable teachers and places. Also, that these schools were not unfit or harmful to the public, and that enforcement of the challenged statute would unlawfully deprive them of patronage and thereby destroy their owners' business and property. Finally, that the threats to enforce the act would continue to cause irreparable injury; and the suits were not premature.

No question is raised concerning the power of the state reasonably to regulate all schools, to inspect, supervise and examine them, their teachers and pupils; to require that all children of proper age attend some school, that teachers shall be of good moral character and patriotic disposition, that certain studies plainly essential to good citizenship must be taught, and that nothing be taught which is manifestly inimical to the public welfare.

The inevitable practical result of enforcing the act under consideration would be destruction of appellees' primary schools, and perhaps all other private primary schools for normal children within the state of Oregon. These parties are engaged in a kind of undertaking not inherently harmful, but long regarded as useful and meritorious. Certainly there is nothing in the present records to indicate that they have failed to discharge their obligations to patrons, students, or the state. And there are no peculiar circumstances or present emergencies which demand extraordinary measures relative to primary education . . . .

[W] e think it entirely plain that the act of 1922 unreasonably interferes with the liberty of parents and guardians to direct the upbringing and education of children under their control. As often heretofore pointed out, rights guaranteed by the Constitution may not be abridged by legislation which has no reasonable relation to some purpose within the competency of the state. The fundamental theory of liberty upon which all governments in this Union repose excludes any general power of the state to standardize its children by forcing them to accept instruction from public teachers only. The child is not the mere creature of the state; those who nurture him and direct his destiny have the right, coupled with the high duty, to recognize and prepare him for additional obligations.

Appellees are corporations, and therefore, it is said, they cannot claim for themselves the liberty which the Fourteenth Amendment guarantees. Accepted in the proper sense, this is true . . . . . But they have business and property for which they claim protection. These are threatened with destruction through the unwarranted compulsion which appellants are exercising over present and prospective patrons of their schools. And this court has gone very far to protect against loss threatened by such action . . . .

The courts of the state have not construed the act, and we must determine its meaning for ourselves. Evidently it was expected to have general application and cannot be construed as though merely intended to amend the charters of certain private corporations, as in *Berea College v Kentucky,* 211 US 45. No argument in favor of such view has been advanced.

Generally, it is entirely true, as urged by counsel, that no person in any business has such an interest in possible customers as to enable him to restrain exercise of proper power of the state upon the ground that he will be deprived of patronage. But the injunctions here sought are not against the exercise of any *proper* power. Plaintiffs asked protection against arbitrary, unreasonable, and unlawful interference with their patrons and the consequent destruction of their business and property. Their interest is clear and immediate, within the rule approved in *Truax v Raich* 239 US 33 (1915), *Truax v Corrigan* 257 US 312 (1921), and *Terrace v Thompson* 263 US 197 (1923), and many other cases where injunctions have issued to protect business enterprises against interference with the freedom of patrons or customers. . . .

The suits were not premature. The injury to appellees was present and very real, not a mere possibility in the remote future. If no relief had been possible prior to the effective date of the act, the injury would have become irreparable. Prevention of impending injury by unlawful action is a well-recognized function of courts of equity.

The decrees below are affirmed.

Notes and Questions

1. Historical Background

The requirement that Oregon's children attend public schools was unique among the American states. It had been adopted after a referendum campaign organized and promoted primarily by the Ku Klux Klan and the Oregon Scottish Rite Masons as part of a strategy to "Americanize" the schools: if the campaign was successful, a dozen other states were next in line. Bans on the teaching of Darwinism and foreign languages and requirement of teacher loyalty oaths and inoffensive textbooks were all part of a larger assault on pluralism in education and society. As one Klansman noted: "Somehow these mongrel hordes must be Americanized; failing that, deportation is the only remedy." Oregon's public school teachers also supported the bill, apparently fearing that its rejection would be taken as a rejection of public schooling. Parochial schools were the most numerous private schools in the state, and anti-Catholicism—"religious revenge," as the Portland *Telegram* put it—helped sway voters' minds. The bill's opponents—among them churchmen who denied that "sectarianism" was "unpatriotic," businessmen fearing increased school taxes, minority groups and civil rights organizations concerned about constitutional and religious liberties—objected to state monopoly over education. But the referendum narrowly carried, splitting political party lines; one Oregon newspaper editor commented that "politics has simply gone mad." How might that background have influenced the *Pierce* decision? For a more extended discussion of the Oregon experience, see David Tyack, "The Perils of Pluralism: The Background of the Pierce Case," 74 *Amer Hist Rev* 74 (1968).

The requirement that children attend some school, public or private, was not new. The common school—locally run and financed and open without tuition to all children—had been energetically and successfully promoted by reformers such as Massachusetts' Horace Mann since the early nineteenth century. In the view of some school officials the taxation of property for the support of schools created a "reciprocal obligation" on the part of the state to ensure that all enjoyed the benefits of education. But the uneducated and unassimilated immigrant proletariat resisted this new venture; they badly needed the income their children's labor secured. As the Pennsylvania Board of State Charities saw the issue: "It is precisely those children whose parents or guardians are unable or indisposed to provide them with an education . . . for whom the state is most interested to provide and secure it." Education was simply too important, in the eyes of its promoters, to be left to the caprice of parental choice; it was a good imposed on the benighted by the more "enlightened" members of the community. As historian Michael Katz notes:

> If everyone was taxed for school support, if this was justified by the necessity of schooling for the preservation of urban social order, if the beneficial impact of schooling required the regular and prolonged attendance of *all* children, and, finally, if persuasion and a variety of experiments had failed to bring all the children to school—then, clearly, education had to be compulsory. (M. Katz, *Class, Bureaucracy, and Schools* 48 (1971).)

Massachusetts passed the first compulsory education law in 1852, requiring that all children between the ages of eight and fourteen attend school for at least twelve weeks a year; twenty-eight states passed similar legislation in the years following the Civil War. But compulsory education, although legally required, did not immediately become social fact. The resistance of some educators affords one explanation of this phenomenon. Auburn New York's school superintendent, B. B. Snow, voiced a not uncommon sentiment: "The compulsory attendance of the element attempted to be reached by law would be detrimental to the well-being of any respectable school." In many school systems, there was insufficient space to accommodate this class of youngsters: in Illinois, for instance, school buildings could house only one-third of all eligible schoolchildren, while in New York City the average elementary school class enrolled seventy-five pupils. The insatiable demand for cheap labor continued to be satisfied by the hiring of school-age youngsters, and officials—many of whom believed that the education of workers' children was a waste of time— often ignored these violations of the law. An 1884 report drafted by Charles Peck, New York Commissioner of Statistics of Labor, pronounced the compulsory education statute a "dead letter." In the South, compulsory attendance laws were not enforced until well into the twentieth century, and the educational needs of black children were given lowest priority.

By the end of the nineteenth century, however, the principle of compulsory schooling was generally accepted, and by the time of the *Pierce* decision almost every child had at least an elementary education. For a compilation of compulsory attendance laws, see A. Steinhilber & C. Sokolowski, *State Law on Compulsory Attendance* (1966). No thorough history of compulsory schooling in America has been written; for discussion of the phenomenon, see F. Ensign, *Compulsory School Attendance and Child Labor* (1921) and brief treatments in J. Felt, *Hostages of Fortune: Child Labor Reform in New York State* (1965); M. Katz, *Class, Bureaucracy, and Schools* 45-48 (1971); R. Welter, *Popular Education and Democratic Thought in America* 100-102 (1962).

2. The Constitutional Standard: Family versus State?

The *Pierce* court could conceivably have adopted any of three standards. It could have upheld the right of the state to compel public school attendance, or it could have struck down compulsory attendance laws (an issue which was not, however, raised in the litigation), giving complete control over the child's education to the family. The formula it adopted was a compromise between these two positions: the state may compel attendance at some school, but it is the parents' right to choose between public and private schools. That result required the court to balance the claims made by competing interests—the state, the family (speaking, at least nominally, for the child), and the private schools. Is the balance clearly correct?

3. Option 1: State Monopoly over Education

What argument might the state make to justify compulsory public schooling? For example, might the state claim that all children should be treated equally and, thus, receive the same education? Might the argument be made that the state has an obligation to instill certain common values, such as love of country and responsibilities of the citizen, and that this function can be performed most successfully through universal public education? How are such assertions to be treated by a court? Are they "arbitrary, unreasonable"—the language used in *Pierce*?

A century before *Pierce*, Jacksonian Frances Wright proposed that all parents be taxed for the "protective care and guardianship of the state." Their children would be registered at birth and shortly thereafter placed in public nurseries and schools where they would live, work, and study together "in pursuit of the same object— their own and each other's happiness—say! would not such a race, when arrived at manhood and womanhood, work out the reform of society, perfect the free institutions of America?" If adopted, Wright's proposal would have constricted the family's role far more than the Oregon legislation struck down in *Pierce.* Is the proposal unwise, as a matter of policy, or clearly unconstitutional, after *Pierce*? Is it relevant to either query that some societies have adopted a version of Wright's scheme with considerable success? See, e.g., M. Spiro, *Children of the Kibbutz* (1965); B. Bettelheim, *The Children of the Dream* (1969).

4. Option 2: The *"Pierce* Compromise"

How does the *Pierce* court balance the several conflicting interests? It recognizes the private schools' interest in maintaining their business and property, but how does that interest differ from the claim that any private concern (an airline not certified by the Civil Aeronautics Board, for example) might advance against particular governmental actions that limit or curtail its market? Since *Pierce*, the court has abandoned aggressive use of the due process clause as a vehicle for overturning social and economic legislation. "[I]f our recent decisions mean anything, they leave debatable issues as respects business, economic, and social affairs to legislative decision." *Day-Brite Lighting v Missouri* 342 US 421, 425 (1952). In light of such statements, do the interests of the private schools seem constitutionally persuasive today?

The *Pierce* decision is most often cited as authority for the proposition that parents have a constitutional right to educate their children in private schools. Why should parents have such a right? As a policy or constitutional matter, should parental values concern us less than the state's values? Does *Pierce* suggest that where the wishes of parent and child with respect to schooling conflict, the parents' view routinely prevails? See *Wisconsin v Yoder* 406 US 205 (1972) and subsequent notes for a more detailed discussion of this issue.

The source of this parental right is almost as difficult to fathom as its justification: some justices have based it on the first amendment right to freedom of speech (see, e.g., *Griswold v Connecticut* 381 US 479 (1965) (Douglas, J, concurring)), while others view the due process clause of the Fourteenth Amendment as its proper constitutional basis (see, e.g., *Abington School Dist v Schempp* 374 US 203, 230 (1963) (Brennan, J, concurring)). Still others regard *Pierce* as a suit upholding the free exercise of religion, thus limiting its scope to issues of religious liberty (see, e.g., *Board of Educ v Allen* 392 US 236 (1968)).

Which textual argument seems most persuasive? What is the nexus between the constitutional right to freedom of speech and the parents' desire to educate their children in private schools? These questions are of more than lawyerly interest; the very scope of the *Pierce* compromise hinges on whether one views religion or speech as critical to the decision.

John Stuart Mill's classic essay, *On Liberty,* advances a quite different compromise between state and parental interest:

> Is it not almost a self-evident axiom, that the state should require and compel the education, up to a certain standard, of every human being who is born its citizen? Yet .... hardly anyone indeed will deny that it is one of the most sacred duties of the parents ... after summoning a human being into the world, to give to that being an education fitting him to perform his part well in life towards others and towards himself. But while this is unanimously

declared to be the father's duty, scarcely anybody, in this country, will bear to hear of obliging him to perform it . . . .

Were the duty of enforcing universal education once admitted there would be an end to the difficulties about what the state should teach, and how it should teach . . . . If the government would make up its mind to require for every child a good education, it might save itself the trouble of providing one. It might leave to parents to obtain the education where and how they pleased, and content itself with helping to pay the school fees of the poorer classes of children, and defraying the entire school expenses of those who have no one else to pay for them. The objections which are urged with reason against state education do not apply to the enforcement of all education by the state, but to the state's taking upon itself to direct that education; which is a totally different thing . . . . A general state education is a mere contrivance for molding people to be exactly like one another . . . . An education established and controlled by the state should exist, if it exists at all, as one among many competing experiments, carried on for the purpose of example and stimulus, to keep the others up to a certain standard of excellence. (J. Mill, "On Liberty," in *The Utilitarians* 586-87 (1961).)

Mill attempts to disentangle the question of compulsoriness from the matter of who operates schools, striking a balance of interests differing from both *Pierce* (which presumes that public schooling will be the typical, if not universal, mode of education) and the more radical education critics; his proposal is in many respects similar to the education voucher plan (discussed in section IV of this chapter). How would you compare its merits with, for example, Frances Wright's suggested compulsory nursery school for all American youngsters? Is Mill's approach preferable to the *Pierce* court's alternative? Is it a constitutionally conceivable approach?

Does the state's interest in compelling children to attend school give rise to any rights on the part of students subject to the compulsion: are they, for example, entitled to equitable treatment by the public schools? (For discussion of this concept, see chapters 4-6.) May they exercise their rights of free speech and of expression in the fullest fashion consistent with the constraint of compulsoriness? (See chapter 2.) Can those exempted from the requirement of compulsory attendance—those who, in the words of the Oregon legislation, are "abnormal, subnormal, or physically unable to attend school"—make a legal claim that they are entitled to state-provided educational services (see chapter 7), or does the state's interest in compelling "educable" youngsters to attend school carry with it no corollary obligations to those youngsters?

5. Option 3: Abolishing Compulsory Education

No litigant in *Pierce* challenged Oregon's compulsory attendance law, and the court did not seriously entertain the proposition. Indeed, not until the 1960s were any notable objections to compulsory education voiced in this country. A 1959 UN General Assembly "Declaration of the Rights of the Child" confirmed what had not been questioned for a century: "The child is entitled to receive education, which shall be free and *compulsory*, at least in the elementary stages." (Emphasis added.)

Leo Tolstoy's claim that "the compulsory structure of the school excludes the possibility of all progress," has been vigorously pressed in recent years. In *Compulsory Mis-Education* (1964), Paul Goodman declared: "The compulsory system has become a universal trap, and it is no good. Very many of the youth, both poor and middle class, might be better off if the system simply did not exist, even if they then had no formal schooling at all." Ivan Illich has urged that the society be "deschooled" and that "radical alternative[s] . . . the total prohibition of legislative attendance, and the transfer of control over tax funds from benevolent institutions to the individual person" be adopted. "The first article of a bill of rights for a modern, humanist society would correspond to the First Amendment of the US Constitution: 'The State shall make no law with respect to the establishment of education.' There shall be no ritual obligatory for all." See, e.g., I. Illich, *Deschooling Society* (1970) and I. Illich, "After Deschooling, What?" 2 *Social Policy* 5 (September/October 1971).

These assaults on compulsory education are not merely criticisms of unhappy experiences in urban schools (for a sample of such criticisms, see *Radical School Reform,* B. & R. Gross, eds (1969) and chapter 2, *infra*); they are political criticisms of all required schooling, whether pleasant or oppressive. The critics reject the argument that the state can best provide for the individual's education and point to the historic failure of public schools to alter social status relations or benefit poor and nonwhite children. See, e.g., C. Greer, *The Great School Legend* (1972). They view as illegitimate the state's asserted interest in shaping the political and social attitudes of children through schooling. In short, both as a matter of policy and as a matter of law, these critics prefer a pluralist educational and social system; they stress the interests of the individual, discounting the notion of collective or societal interests.

At this point agreement among the critics of compulsory schooling ends. Paul Goodman's preferred alternatives include " 'no school at all' for a few classes"; "decentraliz[ing] an urban school . . . into small units"; "us[ing] appropriate *unlicensed* adults of the community—the druggist, the storekeeper, the mechanic—as the proper educators . . . [emphasis added]"; and "send[ing] children to economically marginal farms for a couple of months of the year," none of which is necessarily inconsistent with general compulsory education laws. Ivan Illich's views are avowedly more political, directly linked to redistribution of other social resources. Educator John Holt views compulsoriness as but one of many restrictions on children's freedom that should be abolished; his dream is the autonomous child, not the restructured state. See J. Holt, *Freedom and Beyond* (1972).

These proposals raise questions of both policy and law. Would an end to compulsoriness be desirable of itself? What would be likely to happen if laws requiring school attendance were repealed and no other changes were made either in schools or elsewhere in the society? In other words, would the social functions presently performed by schools disappear if the requirement of school attendance disappeared? Would alternative forms of education routinely emerge? If the response to these queries is "no," does that suggest that abolishing compulsoriness would have no effect? Or that it would affect only those who chose—perhaps because of economic necessity—to exercise the option of not attending schools? Might such a pattern of choice actually widen disparities between rich and poor?

The ultimate goal of many contemporary critics of compulsory education is the substitution of a pluralistic society (in which, in philosopher Thomas Green's terms, "there are available institutions through which people can give concrete expression to a multiplicity of different, even incompatible values") for an achievement society (in which schools function "as the channel of access for manpower and a primary agency to 'fit' the human resources to the requirements of technological and military institutions"). But can changes in schools "change the social order," as educator John Dewey once hoped? Which changes first, the society or the schools? Green posits five conditions necessary to insure pluralism: (1) the society must contain institutions designed to permit, or even encourage, the expression of different value commitments in specific behavior; (2) alternative value choices must be available everywhere in the society; (3) such value choices must be available to people of roughly equal legal status and approximately equal educational opportunity; (4) the choices available to members of the society must be fundamental enough to produce significant differences between people in their attitudes and outlook on the world; and (5) those differences must not be so fundamental as to be divisive. (T. Green, "Schools as Communities," 39 *Harv Educ Rev* 221 (1969).) To Green such value commitments represent political, not pedagogical, decisions; he considers them unlikely "in a society committed to mass education of a managerial type." Do you share that assessment?

Constitutional challenges to compulsory schooling are treated in *Wisconsin v Yoder* 406 US 205 (1972) and the notes following. In light of this discussion, what effect on educational policy—or, more broadly, on social policy—might a successful constitutional assault have?

II. Compulsory Schooling, Public Policy, and the Constitution

WISCONSIN v YODER
406 US 205 (1972)

Mr. Chief Justice Burger delivered the opinion of the court.

On petition of the State of Wisconsin, we granted the writ of certiorari in this case to review a decision of the Wisconsin Supreme Court holding that respondents' convictions of violating the state's compulsory school attendance law were invalid under the free exercise clause of the First Amendment to the United States Constitution made applicable to the states by the Fourteenth Amendment. For the reasons hereafter stated we affirm the judgment of the Supreme Court of Wisconsin.

Respondents Jonas Yoder and Wallace Miller are members of the Old Order Amish religion, and respondent Adin Yutzy is a member of the Conservative Amish Mennonite Church.* They and their families are residents of Green County, Wisconsin. Wisconsin's compulsory school attendance law required them to cause their children to attend public or private school until reaching age sixteen but the respondents declined to send their children, ages fourteen and fifteen, to public school after they completed the eighth grade. The children were not enrolled in any private school, or within any recognized exception to the compulsory attendance law, and they are conceded to be subject to the Wisconsin statute.

On complaint of the school district administrator for the public schools, respon-

---

*There is some question as to the correct religious affiliation of plaintiffs Yutzy and Miller. In the Wisconsin Supreme Court report, 49 Wis2d 430, 182 NW2d 539 (1971), Miller is listed as a member of the Conservative Mennonite Church, while Yutzy is labeled an Old Order Amish. These affiliations are also given in the unofficial report, 32 L Ed 2d 15 (1971), but conflict with the official US version given above.

dents were charged, tried, and convicted of violating the compulsory attendance law in Green County Court and were fined the sum of $5 each.[3] Respondents defended on the ground that the application of the compulsory attendance law violated their rights under the First and Fourteenth Amendments. The trial testimony showed that respondents believed, in accordance with the tenets of the Old Order Amish communities generally, that their children's attendance at high school, public or private, was contrary to the Amish religion and way of life. They believed that by sending their children to high school, they would not only expose themselves to the danger of the censure of the church community, but, as found by the county court, endanger their own salvation and that of their children. The state stipulated that respondents' religious beliefs were sincere.

In support of their position, respondents presented as expert witnesses scholars on religion and education whose testimony is uncontradicted. They expressed their opinions on the relationship of the Amish belief concerning school attendance to the more general tenets of their religion, and described the impact that compulsory high school attendance could have on the continued survival of Amish communities as they exist in the United States today. The history of the Amish sect was given in some detail, beginning with the Swiss Anabaptists of the sixteenth century who rejected institutionalized churches and sought to return to the early, simple, Christian life deemphasizing material success, rejecting the competitive spirit, and seeking to insulate themselves from the modern world. As a result of their common heritage, Old Order Amish communities today are characterized by a fundamental belief that salvation requires life in a church community separate and apart from the world and worldly influence. This concept of life aloof from the world and its values is central to their faith.

A related feature of Old Order Amish communities is their devotion to a life in harmony with nature and the soil, as exemplified by the simple life of the early Christian era that continued in America during much of our early national life. Amish beliefs require members of the community to make their living by farming or closely related activities. Broadly speaking, the Old Order Amish religion pervades and determines the entire mode of life of its adherents. Their conduct is regulated in great detail by the *Ordnung,* or rules, of the church community. Adult baptism, which occurs in late adolescence, is the time at which Amish young people voluntarily undertake heavy obligations, not unlike the bar mitzvah of the Jews, to abide by the rules of the church community.

3. Prior to trial, the attorney for respondents wrote the state superintendent of public instruction in an effort to explore the possibilities for a compromise settlement. Among other possibilities, he suggested that perhaps the state superintendent could administratively determine that the Amish could satisfy the compulsory attendance law by establishing their own vocational training plan similar to one that has been established in Pennsylvania . . . . Under the Pennsylvania plan, Amish children of high school age are required to attend an Amish vocational school for three hours a week, during which time they are taught such subjects as English, mathematics, health, and social studies by an Amish teacher. For the balance of the week, the children perform farm and household duties under parental supervision, and keep a journal of their daily activities. The major portion of the curriculum is home projects in agriculture and homemaking. See generally, Hostetler and Huntington, *Children in Amish Society* (1971); *Socialization and Community Education* c5 (1971). A similar program has been instituted in Indiana. *Ibid.* See also Iowa Code §299.24; Kansas Stats Ann §72-1111 (Supp 1971).

The superintendent rejected this proposal on the ground that it would not afford Amish children "substantially equivalent education" to that offered in the schools of the area . . . .

Amish objection to formal education beyond the eighth grade is firmly grounded in these central religious concepts. They object to the high school and higher education generally because the values they teach are in marked variance with Amish values and the Amish way of life; they view secondary school education as an impermissible exposure of their children to a "worldly" influence in conflict with their beliefs. The high school tends to emphasize intellectual and scientific accomplishments, self-distinction, competitiveness, worldly success, and social life with other students. Amish society emphasizes informal learning through doing, a life of "goodness," rather than a life of intellect, wisdom, rather than technical knowledge, community welfare rather than competition, and separation from rather than integration with contemporary worldly society.

Formal high school education beyond the eighth grade is contrary to Amish beliefs not only because it places Amish children in an environment hostile to Amish beliefs with increasing emphasis on competition in classwork and sports and with pressure to conform to the styles, manners and ways of the peer group, but because it takes them away from their community, physically and emotionally, during the crucial and formative adolescent period of life. During this period, the children must acquire Amish attitudes favoring manual work and self-reliance and the specific skills needed to perform the adult role of an Amish farmer or housewife. They must learn to enjoy physical labor. Once a child has learned basic reading, writing, and elementary mathematics, these traits, skills, and attitudes admittedly fall within the category of those best learned through example and "doing" rather than in a classroom. And, at this time in life, the Amish child must also grow in his faith and his relationship to the Amish community if he is to be prepared to accept the heavy obligations imposed by adult baptism. In short, high school attendance with teachers who are not of the Amish faith—and may even be hostile to it—interposes a serious barrier to the integration of the Amish child into the Amish religious community. Dr. John Hostetler, one of the experts on Amish society, testified that the modern high school is not equipped, in curriculum or social environment, to impart the values promoted by Amish society.

The Amish do not object to elementary education through the first eight grades as a general proposition because they agree that their children must have basic skills in the "three Rs" in order to read the Bible, to be good farmers and citizens and to be able to deal with non-Amish people when necessary in the course of daily affairs. They view such a basic education as acceptable because it does not significantly expose their children to worldly values or interfere with their development in the Amish community during the crucial adolescent period. While Amish accept compulsory elementary education generally, wherever possible they have established their own elementary schools in many respects like the small local schools of the past. In the Amish belief higher learning tends to develop values they reject as influences that alienate man from God.

On the basis of such considerations, Dr. Hostetler testified that compulsory high school attendance could not only result in great psychological harm to Amish children, because of the conflicts it would produce, but would also, in his opinion, ultimately result in the destruction of the Old Order Amish church community as it exists in the United States today. The testimony of Dr. Donald A. Erickson, an expert witness on education, also showed that the Amish succeed in preparing their high school age children to be productive members of the Amish community. He described their system of learning through doing the skills directly relevant to their adult roles in the Amish community as "ideal" and perhaps superior to ordinary high school education. The evidence also showed that the Amish have an excellent record as law-abiding and generally self-sufficient members of society.

Although the trial court in its careful findings determined that the Wisconsin compulsory school attendance law "does interfere with the freedom of the defendants to act in accordance with their sincere religious belief" it also concluded that the requirement of high school attendance until age sixteen was a "reasonable and constitutional" exercise of governmental power, and therefore denied the motion to dismiss the charges. The Wisconsin Circuit Court affirmed the convictions. The Wisconsin Supreme Court, however, sustained respondents' claim under the free exercise clause of the First Amendment and reversed the convictions. A majority of the court was of the opinion that the state had failed to make an adequate showing that its interest in "establishing and maintaining an education system overrides the defendants' right to the free exercise of their religion." 49 Wis2d 430, 447, 182 NW2d 539, 547 (1971).

I

There is no doubt as to the power of a state, having a high responsibility for education of its citizens, to impose reasonable regulations for the control and duration of basic education. See, e.g., *Pierce v Society of Sisters* 268 US 510, 534 (1925). Providing public schools ranks at the very apex of the function of a state. Yet even this paramount responsibility was, in *Pierce,* made to yield to the right of parents to provide an equivalent education in a privately operated system. There the court held that Oregon's statute compelling attendance in a public school from age eight to age sixteen unreasonably interfered with the interest of parents in directing the rearing of their offspring including their education in church-operated schools . . . . Thus, a state's interest in universal education, however highly we rank it, is not totally free from a balancing process when it impinges on fundamental rights and interests, such as those specifically protected by the free exercise clause of the First Amendment and the traditional interest of parents with respect to the religious upbringing of their children so long as they, in the words of *Pierce,* "prepare [them] for additional obligations." 268 US at 535.

It follows that in order for Wisconsin to compel school attendance beyond the eighth grade against a claim that such attendance interferes with the practice of a legitimate religious belief, it must appear either that the state does not deny the free exercise of religious belief by its requirement, or that there is a state interest of sufficient magnitude to override the interest claiming protection under the free exercise clause . . . .

II

We come then to the quality of the claims of the respondents concerning the alleged encroachment of Wisconsin's compulsory school attendance statute on their rights and the rights of their children to the free exercise of the religious beliefs they and their forebears have adhered to for almost three centuries. In evaluating those claims we must be careful to determine whether the Amish religious faith and their mode of life are, as they claim, inseparable and interdependent. A way of life, however virtuous and admirable, may not be interposed as a barrier to reasonable state regulation of education if it is based on purely secular considerations; to have the protection of the religion clauses, the claims must be rooted in religious belief.

Although a determination of what is a "religious" belief or practice entitled to constitutional protection may present a most delicate question, the very concept of ordered liberty precludes allowing every person to make his own standards on matters of conduct in which society as a whole has important interests. Thus, if the Amish asserted their claims because of their subjective evaluation and rejection of the contemporary secular values accepted by the majority, much as Thoreau rejected the social values of his time and isolated himself at Walden Pond, their claim would not rest on a religious basis. Thoreau's choice was philosophical and personal rather than religious, and such belief does not rise to the demands of the religion clauses.

Giving no weight to such secular considerations, however, we see that the record in this case abundantly supports the claim that the traditional way of life of the Amish is not merely a matter of personal preference, but one of deep religious conviction, shared by an organized group, and intimately related to daily living. That the Old Order Amish daily life and religious practice stems from their faith is shown by the fact that it is in response to their literal interpretation of the biblical injunction from the Epistle of Paul to the Romans, "Be not conformed to this world . . . ." This command is fundamental to the Amish faith. Moreover, for the Old Order Amish, religion is not simply a matter of theocratic belief. As the expert witnesses explained, the Old Order Amish religion pervades and determines virtually their entire way of life, regulating it with the detail of the talmudic diet through the strictly enforced rules of the church community.

The record shows that the respondents' religious beliefs and attitude toward life, family, and home have remained constant—perhaps some would say static—in a period of unparalleled progress in human knowledge generally and great changes in education. The respondents freely concede, and indeed assert as an article of faith, that their religious beliefs and what we would today call "life-style" have not altered in fundamentals for centuries. Their way of life in a church-oriented community, separated from the outside world and "worldly" influences, their attachment to nature and the soil, is a way inherently simple and uncomplicated, albeit difficult to preserve against the pressure to conform. Their rejection of telephones, automobiles, radios, and television, their mode of dress, of speech, their habits of manual work do indeed set them apart from much of contemporary society; these customs are both symbolic and practical.

As the society around the Amish has become more populous, urban, industrialized, and complex, particularly in this century, government regulation of human affairs has correspondingly become more detailed and pervasive. The Amish mode of life has thus come into conflict increasingly with requirements of contemporary society exerting a hydraulic insistence on conformity to majoritarian standards. So long as compulsory education laws were confined to eight grades of elementary basic education imparted in a nearby rural schoolhouse, with a large proportion of students of the Amish faith, the Old Order Amish had little basis to fear that school attendance would expose their children to the worldly influence they reject. But modern compulsory secondary education in rural areas is now largely carried on in a consolidated school, often remote from the student's home and alien to his daily homelife. As the record so strongly shows, the values and programs of the modern secondary school are in sharp conflict with the fundamental mode of life mandated by the Amish religion; modern laws requiring compulsory secondary education have accordingly engendered great concern and conflict. The conclusion is inescapable that secondary schooling, by exposing Amish children to worldly influences in terms of attitudes, goals, and values contrary to beliefs, and by substantially interfering with the religious development of the Amish child and his integration into the way of life of the Amish faith community at the crucial adolescent state of development, contravenes the basic religious tenets and practice of the Amish faith, both as to the parent and the child.

The impact of the compulsory attendance law on respondents' practice of the Amish religion is not only severe, but inescapable, for the Wisconsin law affirmatively compels them, under threat of criminal sanction, to perform acts undeniably at odds with fundamental tenets of their religious beliefs. See *Braunfeld v Brown* 366 US 599, 605 (1961). Nor is the impact of the compulsory attendance law confined to grave interference with important Amish religious tenets from a subjective point of view. It carries with it precisely the kind of objective danger to the free exercise of religion that the First Amendment was designed to prevent. As the record shows, compulsory school attendance to age sixteen for Amish children carries with it a very real threat of undermining the Amish community and religious practice as they exist today; they must either abandon belief and be assimilated into society at large, or be forced to migrate to some other and more tolerant region.[9]

In sum, the unchallenged testimony of acknowledged experts in education and religious history, almost 300 years of consistent practice, and strong evidence of a sustained faith pervading and regulating respondents' entire mode of life support the claim that enforcement of the state's requirement of compulsory formal education after the eighth grade would gravely endanger if not destroy the free exercise of respondents' religious beliefs.

III

Neither the findings of the trial court nor the Amish claims as to the nature of their faith are challenged in this court by the State of Wisconsin. Its position is that the state's interest in universal compulsory formal secondary education to age sixteen is so great that it is paramount to the undisputed claims of respondents that their mode of preparing their youth for Amish life, after the traditional elementary education, is an essential part of their religious belief and practice. Nor does the state undertake to meet the claim that the Amish mode of life and education is inseparable from and a part of the basic tenets of their religion—indeed, as much a part of their religious belief and practices as baptism, the confessional, or a sabbath may be for others.

Wisconsin concedes that under the religion clauses religious beliefs are absolutely free from the state's control, but it argues that "actions," even though religiously grounded, are outside the protection of the First Amendment.[10] But our decisions

---

9. Some states have developed working arrangements with the Amish regarding high school attendance. See n3, *supra*. However, the danger to the continued existence of an ancient religious faith cannot be ignored simply because of the assumption that its adherents will continue to be able, at considerable sacrifice, to relocate in some more tolerant state or country or work out accommodations under threat of criminal prosecution. Forced migration of religious minorities was an evil that lay at the heart of the religion clauses. See, e.g., *Everson v Board of Educ* 330 US 1, 9-10 (1947); J. Madison, "Memorial and Remonstrance Against Religious Assessments," 2 *Writings of James Madison* 183 (G. Hunt ed 1901).

10. That has been the apparent ground for decision in several previous state cases rejecting claims for exemption similar to that here. See, e.g., *State v Garber* 197 Kan 567, 419 P2d 896

have rejected the idea that religiously grounded conduct is always outside the protection of the free exercise clause . . . .

Nor can this case be disposed of on the grounds that Wisconsin's requirement for school attendance to age sixteen applies uniformly to all citizens of the state and does not, on its face, discriminate against religions or a particular religion, or that it is motivated by legitimate secular concerns. A regulation neutral on its face may, in its application, nonetheless offend the constitutional requirement for governmental neutrality if it unduly burdens the free exercise of religion . . . .

We turn, then to the state's broader contention that its interest in its system of compulsory education is so compelling that even the established religious practices of the Amish must give way. Where fundamental claims of religious freedom are at stake, however, we cannot accept such a sweeping claim; despite its admitted validity in the generality of cases, we must searchingly examine the interests that the state seeks to promote by its requirement for compulsory education to age sixteen, and the impediment to those objectives that would flow from recognizing the claimed Amish exemption . . . .

The state advances two primary arguments in support of its system of compulsory education. It notes, as Thomas Jefferson pointed out early in our history, that some degree of education is necessary to prepare citizens to participate effectively and intelligently in our open political system if we are to preserve freedom and independence. Further, education prepares individuals to be self-reliant and self-sufficient participants in society. We accept these propositions.

However, the evidence adduced by the Amish in this case is persuasively to the effect that an additional one or two years of formal high school for Amish children in place of their long-established program of informal vocational education would do little to serve those interests. Respondents' experts testified at trial, without challenge, that the value of all education must be assessed in terms of its capacity to prepare the child for life. It is one thing to say that compulsory education for a year or two beyond the eighth grade may be necessary when its goal is the preparation of the child for life in modern society as the majority live, but it is quite another if the goal of education be viewed as the preparation of the child for life in the separated agrarian community that is the keystone of the Amish faith . . . .

The state attacks respondents' position as one fostering "ignorance" from which the child must be protected by the state. No one can question the state's duty to protect children from ignorance but this argument does not square with the facts disclosed in the record. Whatever their idiosyncrasies as seen by the majority, this record strongly shows that the Amish community has been a highly successful social unit within our society even if apart from the conventional "mainstream." Its members are productive and very law-abiding members of society; they reject public welfare in any of its usual modern forms. The Congress itself recognized their self-sufficiency by authorizing exemption of such groups as the Amish from the obligation to pay social security taxes.

It is neither fair nor correct to suggest that the Amish are opposed to education beyond the eighth grade level. What this record shows is that they are opposed to conventional formal education of the type provided by a certified high school because it comes at the child's crucial adolescent period of religious development.

(1966), *cert denied*, 389 US 51 (1967); *State v Hershberger* 103 Ohio App 188, 144 NE2d 693 (1955); *Commonwealth v Beiler*, 168 Pa Super 462, 79 A2d 134 (1951).

Dr. Donald Erickson, for example, testified that their system of learning by doing was an "ideal system" of education in terms of preparing Amish children for life as adults in the Amish community, and that "I would be inclined to say they do a better job in this than most of the rest of us do." As he put it: "These people aren't purporting to be learned people, and it seems to me the self-sufficiency of the community is the best evidence I can point to—whatever is being done seems to function well."[12]

We must not forget that in the Middle Ages important values of the civilization of the Western world were preserved by members of religious orders who isolated themselves from all worldly influences against great obstacles. There can be no assumption that today's majority is "right" and the Amish and others like them are "wrong." A way of life that is odd or even erratic but interferes with no rights or interests of others is not to be condemned because it is different.

The state, however, supports its interest in providing an additional one or two years of compulsory high school education to Amish children because of the possibility that some such children will choose to leave the Amish community, and that if this occurs they will be ill-equipped for life. The state argues that if Amish children leave their church they should not be in the position of making their way in the world without the education available in the one or two additional years the state requires. However, on this record, that argument is highly speculative. There is no specific evidence of the loss of Amish adherents by attrition, nor is there any showing that upon leaving the Amish community Amish children, with their practical agricultural training and habits of industry and self-reliance would become burdens on society because of educational shortcomings. Indeed, this argument of the state appears to rest primarily on the state's mistaken assumption, already noted, that the Amish do not provide any education for their children beyond the eighth grade, but allow them to grow in "ignorance." To the contrary, not only do the Amish accept the necessity for formal schooling through the eighth grade level, but continue to provide what has been characterized by the undisputed testimony of expert educators as an "ideal" vocational education for their children in the adolescent years.

There is nothing in this record to suggest that the Amish qualities of reliability, self-reliance, and dedication to work would fail to find ready markets in today's society. Absent some contrary evidence supporting the state's position, we are unwilling to assume that persons possessing such valuable vocational skills and habits are doomed to become burdens on society should they determine to leave the Amish faith, nor is there any basis in the record to warrant a finding that an additional one or two years of formal school education beyond the eighth grade would serve to eliminate any such problem that might exist.

Insofar as the state's claim rests on the view that a brief additional period of formal education is imperative to enable the Amish to participate effectively and intelligently in our democratic process, it must fall. The Amish alternative to formal

---

12. Dr. Erickson had previously written "Many public educators would be elated if their programs were as successful in preparing students for productive community life as the Amish system seems to be. In fact, while some public schoolmen strive to outlaw the Amish approach, others are being forced to emulate many of its features." D. Erickson, "Showdown at an Amish Schoolhouse: A Description and Analysis of the Iowa Controversy," in *Public Controls for Nonpublic Schools* 15, 53 (D. Erickson ed 1969). And see F. Littell, "Sectarian Protestantism and the Pursuit of Wisdom: Must Technological Objective Prevail?" *id* at 61.

secondary school education has enabled them to function effectively in their day-to-day life under self-imposed limitations on relations with the world, and to survive and prosper in contemporary society as a separate, sharply identifiable and highly self-sufficient community for more than 200 years in this country. In itself this is strong evidence that they are capable of fulfilling the social and political responsibilities of citizenship without compelled attendance beyond the eighth grade at the price of jeopardizing their free exercise of religious belief. When Thomas Jefferson emphasized the need for education as a bulwark of a free people against tyranny, there is nothing to indicate he had in mind compulsory education through any fixed age beyond a basic education. Indeed, the Amish communities singularly parallel and reflect many of the virtues of Jefferson's ideal of the "sturdy yeoman" who would form the basis of what he considered as the ideal of a democratic society. Even their idiosyncratic separateness exemplifies the diversity we profess to admire and encourage.

The requirement for compulsory education beyond the eighth grade is a relatively recent development in our history. Less than sixty years ago, the educational requirements of almost all of the states were satisfied by completion of the elementary grades, at least where the child was regularly and lawfully employed.[15] The independence and successful social functioning of the Amish community for a period approaching almost three centuries and more than 200 years in this country are strong evidence that there is at best a speculative gain, in terms of meeting the duties of citizenship, from an additional one or two years of compulsory formal education. Against this background it would require a more particularized showing from the state on this point to justify the severe interference with religious freedom such additional compulsory attendance would entail.

We should also note that compulsory education and child labor laws find their historical origin in common humanitarian instincts, and that the age limits of both laws have been coordinated to achieve their related objectives. In the context of this case, such considerations, if anything, support rather than detract from respondents' position. The origins of the requirement for school attendance to age sixteen, an age falling after the completion of elementary school but before completion of high school, are not entirely clear. But to some extent such laws reflected the

---

15. See US Dep't of Interior, Bureau of Educ, Bull No 47, *Digest of State Laws Relating to Public Education* 527-559 (1916); *Joint Hearings on S 2475 and HR 7200 Before the Senate Comm on Education and the House Comm on Labor,* 75th Cong, 1st Sess, pt 2, at 416.

Even today, an eighth-grade education fully satisfies the educational requirements of at least six states. See Ariz Rev Stat Ann §15-321 (B)(4) (1956); Ark Stat Ann §80-1504 (1947); Iowa Code §299.2 (1971); SD Comp Laws Ann §13-27-1 (1967); Wyo Stat Ann §21.1-48 (Supp 1971). (Mississippi has no compulsory education law.) A number of other states have flexible provisions permitting children aged fourteen or having completed the eighth grade to be excused from school in order to engage in lawful employment. E.g., Colo Rev Stat Ann §§123-20-5, 80-6-1—80-6-12 (1963); Conn Gen Stat Rev §§10-184, 10-189 (1964); DC Code Ann §§31-202, 36-201—36-228 (1967); Ind Ann Stat §§28-505—28-506, 28-519 (1948); Mass Gen Laws Ann, c76, §1 (Supp 1972) and c149, §86 (1971); Mo Rev Stat §§167.031, 294.051 (1969); Nev Rev Stat §392.110 (1968); NM Stat Ann §77-10-6 (1968).

An eighth-grade education satisfied Wisconsin's formal education requirements until 1933. See Wis Laws 1927, c425, §97; Laws 1933, c143. (Prior to 1933, provision was made for attendance at continuation or vocational schools by working children past the eighth grade, but only if one was maintained by the community in question.) For a general discussion of the early development of Wisconsin's compulsory education and child labor laws, see F. Ensign, *Compulsory School Attendance and Child Labor* 203-230 (1921).

movement to prohibit most child labor under age sixteen that culminated in the provisions of the Federal Fair Labor Standards Act of 1938. It is true, then, that the sixteen-year child labor age limit may to some degree derive from a contemporary impression that children should be in school until that age. But at the same time, it cannot be denied that, conversely, the sixteen-year education limit reflects, in substantial measure, the concern that children under that age not be employed under conditions hazardous to their health, or in work that should be performed by adults.

The requirement of compulsory schooling to age sixteen must therefore be viewed as aimed not merely at providing educational opportunities for children, but as an alternative to the equally undesirable consequence of unhealthful child labor displacing adult workers, or, on the other hand, forced idleness. The two kinds of statutes—compulsory school attendance and child labor laws—tend to keep children of certain ages off the labor market and in school; this regimen in turn provides opportunity to prepare for a livelihood of a higher order than that which children could pursue without education and protects their health in adolescence.

In these terms, Wisconsin's interest in compelling the school attendance of Amish children to age sixteen emerges as somewhat less substantial than requiring such attendance for children generally. For, while agricultural employment is not totally outside the legitimate concerns of the child labor laws, employment of children under parental guidance and on the family farm from age fourteen to age sixteen is an ancient tradition that lies at the periphery of the objectives of such laws. There is no intimation that the Amish employment of their children on family farms is in any way deleterious to their health or that Amish parents exploit children at tender years. Any such inference would be contrary to the record before us. Moreover, employment of Amish children on the family farm does not present the undesirable economic aspects of eliminating jobs that might otherwise be held by adults.

IV

Finally, the state, on authority of *Prince v Massachusetts* 321 US 158 (1944), argues that a decision exempting Amish children from the state's requirement fails to recognize the substantive right of the Amish child to a secondary education, and fails to give due regard to the power of the state as *parens patriae* to extend the benefit of secondary education to children regardless of the wishes of their parents. Taken at its broadest sweep, the court's language in *Prince,* might be read to give support to the state's position. However, the court was not confronted in *Prince* with a situation comparable to that of the Amish as revealed in this record; this is shown by the court's severe characterization of the evils that it thought the legislature could legitimately associate with child labor, even when performed in the company of an adult. 321 US at 169-170. The court later took great care to confine *Prince* to a narrow scope in *Sherbert v Verner,* when it stated:

> On the other hand, the court has rejected challenges under the free exercise clause to governmental regulation of certain overt acts prompted by religious beliefs or principles, "for even when the action is in accord with one's religious convictions, [it] is not totally free from legislative restrictions." *Braunfeld v Brown* 366 US 599, 603 (1961). The conduct or actions so regulated have invariably posed some substantial threat to public safety, peace or order.

See, e.g., *Reynolds v US* 98 US 145; *Jacobson v Massachusetts* 197 US 11; *Prince v Massachusetts* 321 US 158. . . . (374 US 398, 402-403 (1963).)

This case, of course, is not one in which any harm to the physical or mental health of the child or to the public safety, peace, order, or welfare has been demonstrated or may be properly inferred. The record is to the contrary, and any reliance on that theory would find no support in the evidence.

Contrary to the suggestion of the dissenting opinion of Mr. Justice Douglas, our holding today in no degree depends on the assertion of the religious interest of the child as contrasted with that of the parents. It is the parents who are subject to prosecution here for failing to cause their children to attend school, and it is their right of free exercise, not that of their children, that must determine Wisconsin's power to impose criminal penalties on the parent. The dissent argues that a child who expresses a desire to attend public high school in conflict with the wishes of his parents should not be prevented from doing so. There is no reason for the court to consider that point since it is not an issue in the case. The children are not parties to this litigation. The state has at no point tried this case on the theory that respondents were preventing their children from attending school against their expressed desires, and indeed the record is to the contrary. The state's position from the outset has been that it is empowered to apply its compulsory attendance law to Amish parents in the same manner as to other parents—that is, without regard to the wishes of the child. That is the claim we reject today.

Our holding in no way determines the proper resolution of possible competing interests of parents, children, and the state in an appropriate state court proceeding in which the power of the state is asserted on the theory that Amish parents are preventing their minor children from attending high school despite their expressed desires to the contrary. Recognition of the claim of the state in such a proceeding would, of course, call into question traditional concepts of parental control over the religious upbringing and education of their minor children recognized in this court's past decisions. It is clear that such an intrusion by a state into family decisions in the area of religious training would give rise to grave questions of religious freedom comparable to those raised here and those presented in *Pierce v Society of Sisters* 268 US 510 (1925). On this record we neither reach nor decide those issues.

The state's argument proceeds without reliance on any actual conflict between the wishes of parents and children. It appears to rest on the potential that exemption of Amish parents from the requirements of the compulsory education law might allow some parents to act contrary to the best interests of their children by foreclosing their opportunity to make an intelligent choice between the Amish way of life and that of the outside world. The same argument could, of course, be made with respect to all church schools short of college. There is nothing in the record or in the ordinary course of human experience to suggest that non-Amish parents generally consult with children up to ages fourteen through sixteen if they are placed in a church school of the parents' faith.

Indeed it seems clear that if the state is empowered, as *parens patriae*, to "save" a child from himself or his Amish parents by requiring an additional two years of compulsory formal high school education, the state will in large measure influence, if not determine, the religious future of the child. Even more markedly than in *Prince,* therefore, this case involves the fundamental interest of parents, as contrasted with that of the state, to guide the religious future and education of their children. The history and culture of western civilization reflect a strong tradition of parental concern for the nurture and upbringing of their children. This primary role of the parents in the upbringing of their children is now established beyond debate as an enduring American tradition . . . .

However read, the court's holding in *Pierce* stands as a charter of the rights of parents to direct the religious upbringing of their children. And, when the interests of parenthood are combined with a free exercise claim of the nature revealed by this record, more than merely a "reasonable relation to some purpose within the competency of the state" is required to sustain the validity of the state's requirement under the First Amendment. To be sure, the power of the parent, even when linked to a free exercise claim, may be subject to limitation under *Prince* if it appears that parental decisions will jeopardize the health or safety of the child, or have a potential for significant social burdens. But in this case, the Amish have introduced persuasive evidence undermining the arguments the state has advanced to support its claims in terms of the welfare of the child and society as a whole. The record strongly indicates that accommodating the religious objections of the Amish by forgoing one, or at most two, additional years of compulsory education will not impair the physical or mental health of the child, or result in an inability to be self-supporting, or to discharge the duties and responsibilities of citizenship, or in any other way materially detract from the welfare of society.

In the face of our consistent emphasis on the central values underlying the religion clauses in our constitutional scheme of government, we cannot accept a *parens patriae* claim of such all-encompassing scope and with such sweeping potential for broad and unforeseeable application as that urged by the state.

V

For the reasons stated we hold, with the Supreme Court of Wisconsin, that the First and Fourteenth Amendments prevent the state from compelling respondents to cause their children to attend formal high school to age sixteen. Our disposition of this case, however, in no way alters our recognition of the obvious fact that courts are not school boards or legislatures, and are ill equipped to determine the "necessity" of discrete aspects of a state's program of compulsory education. This should suggest that courts must move with great circumspection in performing the sensitive and delicate task of weighing a state's legitimate social concern when faced with religious claims for exemption from generally applicable educational requirements. It cannot be overemphasized that we are not dealing with a way of life and mode of education by a group claiming to have recently discovered some "progressive" or more enlightened process for rearing children for modern life.

Aided by a history of three centuries as an identifiable religious sect and a long history as a successful and self-sufficient segment of American society, the Amish in this case have convincingly demonstrated the sincerity of their religious beliefs, the interrelationship of belief with their mode of life, the vital role that belief and daily conduct play in the continued survival of Old Order Amish communities and their religious organization, and the hazards presented by the state's enforcement of a statute generally valid as to others. Beyond this, they have carried the even more difficult burden of demonstrating the adequacy of their alternative mode of continuing informal vocational education in terms of precisely those overall interests that the state advances in support of its program of compulsory high school education. In light of this convincing showing, one that probably few other religious groups or sects could make, and weighing the minimal difference between what the state would require and what the Amish already accept, it was incumbent on the state to show with more particularity how its admittedly strong interest in compulsory education would be adversely affected by granting an exemption to the Amish . . . .

Nothing we hold is intended to undermine the general applicability of the state's compulsory school attendance statutes or to limit the power of the state to promulgate reasonable standards that, while not impairing the free exercise of religion, provide for continuing agricultural vocational education under parental and church guidance by the Old Order Amish or others similarly situated. The states have had a long history of amicable and effective relationships with church-sponsored schools, and there is no basis for assuming that, in this related context, reasonable standards cannot be established concerning the content of the continuing vocational education of Amish children under parental guidance, provided always that state regulations are not inconsistent with what we have said in this opinion.

Affirmed . . . .

(The separate concurring opinion of Mr. Justice Stewart, joined by Mr. Justice Brennan, is omitted.)

Mr. Justice White, with whom Mr. Justice Brennan and Mr. Justice Stewart join, concurring.

. . . In the present case, the state is not concerned with the maintenance of an educational system as an end in itself, it is rather attempting to nurture and develop the human potential of its children, whether Amish or non-Amish: to expand their knowledge, broaden their sensibilities, kindle their imagination, foster a spirit of free inquiry, and increase their human understanding and tolerance. It is possible that most Amish children will wish to continue living the rural life of their parents, in which case their training at home will adequately equip them for their future role. Others, however, may wish to become nuclear physicists, ballet dancers, computer programmers, or historians, and for these occupations, formal training will be necessary. There is evidence in the record that many children desert the Amish faith when they come of age. A state has a legitimate interest not only in seeking to develop the latent talents of its children, but also in seeking to prepare them for the life style that they may later choose or at least to provide them with an option other than the life they have led in the past. In the circumstances of this case, although the question is close, I am unable to say that the state has demonstrated that Amish children who leave school in the eighth grade will be intellectually stultified or unable to acquire new academic skills later. The statutory minimum school attendance age set by the state is, after all, only sixteen.

Decision in cases such as this and the administration of an exemption for Old Order Amish from the state's compulsory school attendance laws will inevitably involve the kind of close and perhaps repeated scrutiny of religious practices, as is exemplified in today's opinion, which the court has heretofore been anxious to avoid. But such entanglement does not create a forbidden establishment of religion where it is essential to implement free exercise values threatened by an otherwise neutral program instituted to foster some permissible, nonreligious state objective. I join the court because the sincerity of the Amish religious policy here is uncontested, because the potentially adverse impact of the state requirement is great and because the state's valid interest in education has already been largely satisfied by the eight years the children have already spent in school.

Mr. Justice Douglas, dissenting in part.

I

I agree with the court that the religious scruples of the Amish are opposed to the education of their children beyond the grade schools, yet I disagree with the court's conclusion that the matter is within the dispensation of parents alone. The court's analysis assumes that the only interests at stake in the case are those of the Amish parents on the one hand, and those of the state on the other. The difficulty with this approach is that, despite the court's claim, the parents are seeking to vindicate not only their own free exercise claims, but also those of their high-school-age children.

It is argued that the right of the Amish children to religious freedom is not presented by the facts of the case, as the issue before the court involves only the Amish parents' religious freedom to defy a state criminal statute imposing upon them an affirmative duty to cause their children to attend high school.

First, respondents' motion to dismiss in the trial court expressly asserts, not only the religious liberty of the adults, but also that of the children, as a defense to the prosecutions. It is, of course, beyond question that the parents have standing as defendants in a criminal prosecution to assert the religious interests of their children as a defense. Although the lower courts and the majority of this court assume an identity of interest between parent and child, it is clear that they have treated the religious interest of the child as a factor in the analysis.

Second, it is essential to reach the question to decide the case not only because the question was squarely raised in the motion to dismiss, but also because no analysis of religious liberty claims can take place in a vacuum. If the parents in this case are allowed a religious exemption, the inevitable effect is to impose the parents' notions of religious duty upon their children. Where the child is mature enough to express potentially conflicting desires, it would be an invasion of the child's rights to permit such an imposition without canvassing his views. As in *Prince v Massachusetts* 321 US 158 (1944), it is an imposition resulting from this very litigation. As the child has no other effective forum, it is in this litigation that his rights should be considered. And, if an Amish child desires to attend high school, and is mature enough to have that desire respected, the state may well be able to override the parents' religiously motivated objections.

Religion is an individual experience. It is not necessary, nor even appropriate, for every Amish child to express his views on the subject in a prosecution of a single adult. Crucial, however, are the views of the child whose parent is the subject of the suit. Frieda Yoder has in fact testified that her own religious views are opposed to high school education. I therefore join the judgment of the court as to respondent Jonas Yoder. But Frieda Yoder's views may not be those of Vernon Yutzy or Barbara Miller. I must dissent, therefore, as to respondents Adin Yutzy and Wallace Miller as their motion to dismiss also raised the question of their children's religious liberty.

II

This issue has never been squarely presented before today. Our opinions are full of talk about the power of the parents over the child's education . . . . And we have in the past analyzed similar conflicts between parent and state with little regard for the views of the child. See *Prince v Massachusetts, supra.* Recent cases, however, have clearly held that the children themselves have constitutionally protectable interests.

These children are "persons" within the meaning of the Bill of Rights. We have so held over and over again . . . .

On this important and vital matter of education, I think the children should be entitled to be heard. While the parents, absent dissent, normally speak for the entire family, the education of the child is a matter on which the child will often have decided views. He may want to be a pianist or an astronaut or an oceanographer. To do so he will have to break from the Amish tradition.[2]

It is the future of the student, not the future of the parents, that is imperiled by today's decision. If a parent keeps his child out of school beyond the grade school, then the child will be forever barred from entry into the new and amazing world of diversity that we have today. The child may decide that that is the preferred course, or he may rebel. It is the student's judgment, not his parents', that is essential if we are to give full meaning to what we have said about the Bill of Rights and of the right of students to be masters of their own destiny. If he is harnessed to the Amish way of life by those in authority over him and if his education is truncated, his entire life may be stunted and deformed. The child, therefore, should be given an opportunity to be heard before the state gives the exemption which we honor today.

The views of the two children in question were not canvassed by the Wisconsin courts. The matter should be explicitly reserved so that new hearings can be held on remand of the case.

III

I think the emphasis of the court on the "law and order" record of this Amish group of people is quite irrelevant. A religion is a religion irrespective of what the misdemeanor or felony records of its members might be. I am not at all sure how the Catholics, Episcopalians, the Baptists, Jehovah's Witnesses, the Unitarians, and my own Presbyterians would make out if we were subjected to such a test . . . .

Action, which the court deemed to be antisocial, could be punished even though it was grounded on deeply held and sincere religious convictions. What we do today, at least in this respect, opens the way to give organized religion a broader base than it has ever enjoyed . . . .

In another way, however, the court retreats when in reference to Henry Thoreau it says his "choice was philosophical and personal rather than religious, and such belief does not rise to the demands of the religion clause." That is contrary to what we held in *US v Seeger* 380 US 163, where we were concerned with the meaning of the words "religious training and belief" in the Selective Service Act, which were the basis of many conscientious objector claims. We said:

> Within that phrase would come all sincere religious beliefs which are based upon a power or being, or upon a faith, to which all else is subordinate or upon which all else is ultimately dependent. The test might be stated in these

---

2. A significant number of Amish children do leave the Old Order. Professor Hostetler notes that "the loss of members is very limited in some Amish districts and considerable in others." *Children in Amish Society* 226. In one Pennsylvania church, he observed a defection rate of 30 percent. Ibid. Rates up to 50 percent have been reported by others. Casad, "Compulsory High School Attendance and the Old Order Amish: A Commentary on *State v Garber*," 16 *Kan L Rev* 423, 434 n51 (1968).

words: A sincere and meaningful belief which occupies in the life of its possessor a place parallel to that filled by the god of those admittedly qualifying for the exemption comes within the statutory definition. This construction avoids imputing to Congress an intent to classify different religious beliefs, exempting some and excluding others, and is in accord with the well-established congressional policy of equal treatment for those whose opposition to service is grounded in their religious tenets. (380 US at 176.)

Welsh v US 398 US 333, was in the same vein, the court saying:

In this case, Welsh's conscientious objection to war was undeniably based in part on his perception of world politics. In a letter to his local board, he wrote: "I can only act according to what I am and what I see. And I see that the military complex wastes both human and material resources, that it fosters disregard for (what I consider a paramount concern) human needs and ends; I see that the means we employ to 'defend' our 'way of life' profoundly change that way of life. I see that in our failure to recognize the political, social, and economic realities of the world, we, *as a nation,* fail our responsibility *as a nation.*" (398 US at 342.)

The essence of Welsh's philosophy on the basis of which we held he was entitled to an exemption was in these words:

I believe that human life is valuable in and of itself; in its living; therefore I will not injure or kill another human being. This belief (and the corresponding "duty" to abstain from violence toward another person) is not "superior to those arising from any human relation." On the contrary: *it is essential to every human relation.* I cannot, therefore, conscientiously comply with the government's insistence that I assume duties which I feel are immoral and totally repugnant. (398 US at 343.)

I adhere to these exalted views of "religion" and see no acceptable alternative to them now that we have become a nation of many religions and sects, representing all of the diversities of the human race . . . .

Notes and Questions

1. Historical Background

Conflicts between the 30,000 American Amish and the government have existed since the Amish arrived in the United States in 1720; in recent years, disputes over schooling have predominated. The adventures of the Amish in Iowa are the best known and documented. The difficulties of the plain folk began with an effort in 1961 to unify the Hazelton and Olwein school districts. The Amish, who operated two private one-room schools in the Hazelton district, held the swing vote in the unification campaign. After high-echelon school officials promised to provide public schools tailored to their needs, the Amish voted for district reorganization. Many Hazelton residents were upset both by voter approval of the unification plan and by the Amish role in the affair. That, and a more general anti-Amish sentiment, led the school officials to renege on their promise to the Amish and to declare that the Amish schools would stay open no longer than two years and that—after fifteen years of doing so—no effort would be made to fit school instruction to Amish needs. The Amish retaliated with the announcement that they would no longer permit state-certified teachers to instruct in Amish schools. Already highly irritated, neighbors of the Amish demanded that the Amish be prosecuted for failure to send their children to schools with certified teachers. Amish fathers were accordingly fined and, when they refused to pay, sentenced to three days in jail. Newspaper pictures of Amish women visiting their jailed husbands elicited national sympathy for the plain folk and resulted in volumes of disparaging mail to Iowa officials.

After the routine of Amish fathers' driving their buggies to town to appear in court and then faithfully refusing to pay their fines grew tiresome, state and local school officials attempted, without success, to arrange a compromise with the Amish. Then they announced that the Amish were truants and would be bused to public school. One November morning in 1965 a school bus departed for Amish country, followed by carloads of newspaper men. No children were to be found at their homes, but some were discovered at the local school. Before the distraught children filed out of the one-room school, the superintendent announced to the newspapermen that the children would board the bus and be driven to school. But it was not to be. An unidentified individual yelled "run," and the children scattered through the barbed wire fence and into the corn fields. Cameras clicked and pictures of small, frightened Amish children climbing the cornfield fence found their way into national newspapers. School officials captured one screaming six-year-old girl and a weeping thirteen-year-old boy who had been unable to keep up with their classmates.

In 1966 Governor Harold Hughes decided to intervene and push for a settlement. In its 1967 session the state legislature, strongly influenced by outside parties, exempted the Amish from the state's minimum educational standards laws. The state superintendent of education was given discretion to fix educational requirements. Thus far he has allowed the Amish schools to remain open under the direction of uncertified Amish teachers. School districts west of Hazelton provide the Amish with rural schools staffed by certified teachers sympathetic to Amish ways. See D. Erickson, "Showdown in an Amish Schoolhouse," in *Public Controls for Nonpublic Schools* 53 (Erickson ed 1969).

Pennsylvania was the first state to attempt to compel the Amish children to attend public school. After initial embarrassments not unlike those suffered by Iowa school officials, the Pennsylvania code was reinterpreted to permit the Amish to manage their own schools. The school day of the Amish school is like that of public schools, and attendance is taken. Beyond these two aspects, however, the Amish school in Pennsylvania is essentially unregulated: teachers, for example, are not required to be certified. Eighth-grade graduates may enter "vocational high schools" where they perform farm and household chores under parental supervision and attend classes a few hours a week.

In Ohio, Amish schools operate in defiance of the state school code but school officials, perhaps learning from the Iowa and Pennsylvania experiences, have chosen to ignore the situation.

2. The Constitutional Standard

Yoder raises the question not explicitly posed in *Pierce*: Are there constitutional interests of parents and children that outweigh the state's interest in compelling all youngsters to attend school? The question is one of extreme difficulty; as the

Yoder decision notes, the contending interests are of the "highest order." Parental direction of the religious upbringing of their children has a "high place in our society," the court declares. The values underlying the constitutional protections of religious freedom have been "zealously protected, sometimes even at the expense of other interests of admittedly high social importance." Compulsory education laws, the court notes, "demonstrate our recognition of the importance of education to our democratic society." How is the court meaningfully to evaluate and balance such imponderables? What judicial controls are imposed on the balance?

a. The Amish Interest in Religious Freedom. The majority opinion notes that the Amish have "convincingly demonstrated the sincerity of their religious beliefs." What factors does the court consider in reaching that judgment? Should the court attempt to assess religious sincerity?

Would the result in *Yoder* have been the same had the court not concluded that the Amish faith and mode of life are inseparable and interdependent? Compare the result in *Yoder* with that reached in *Braunfeld v Brown* 366 US 599 (1961). In *Braunfeld* the plaintiff, an Orthodox Jew who closed his business on Saturday in accordance with the precepts of his faith, alleged he would be forced to shut down his business and thereby lose his capital investment unless he were permitted to open his store in contravention of Pennsylvania's compulsory Sunday closing law. He further stipulated that "one who does not observe the Sabbath cannot be an Orthodox Jew." 366 US at 602. The court held that the Pennsylvania statute did not abridge the plaintiff's right of free exercise. How is *Braunfeld,* where the compulsory closing law forced the plaintiff to abandon either his belief or his business, to be distinguished from *Yoder*, where the compulsory school attendance law compelled the plaintiff to abandon either his faith or his farm? In which case is the state's interest the more compelling?

Does *Yoder* affect the result of the following cases where no infringement on religious freedom was found and the child forced to attend public school? *Commonwealth v Bey* 166 Pa Super 136, 70 A2d 693 (1950) (Muslim parents refused to send their child to public school on Friday, the sacred day of their religion); *In re Currence* 42 Misc2d 418, 248 NYS2d 251 (King's County Fam Ct, 1963) (parents belonging to the Ancient Divine Order of Melchizedek kept their child out of public school on a Wednesday-through-Thursday sabbath); *Commonwealth v Renfrew* 332 Mass 492, 126 NE2d 109 (1955) (Buddhist parents who did not wish their child exposed to the tenets of the Christian faith taught their child at home); *Application of Auster* 198 Misc 1055, 100 NYS2d 60 (Sup Ct 1950) (an Orthodox Jew sought to send his son to an unaccredited yeshiva; his belief that secular secondary education was forbidden by the laws of Orthodox Jewry was disputed in court by both his estranged wife and two rabbis).

How credible is the *Yoder* assertion that "compulsory school attendance to age sixteen for Amish children carried with it a very real threat of undermining the Amish community and religious practice as it exists today"? Consider the following comment:

> Amish parents have remarkable control over their children, and neither parents nor children, much as they might wish it to be otherwise, live entirely separate from our world. Amish children ride in cars, hear radios, read newspapers and magazines and books, perhaps even sneak off to the movies.

Amish children know a great deal more of the outside world than their parents might wish; certainly even without schools, they are exposed to it frequently. Yet the majority of them remain in the faith and join the church. And it may be unrealistic, as well as futile, to argue to the courts that the existence of their religion depends on judicial exemptions for their children from compulsory education laws. (Note, "The Right Not To Be Modern Men: The Amish and Compulsory Education," 53 *Va L Rev* 925, 950 (1967).)

Is the threat rendered more plausible by the fact that the years in issue are the child's "formative years"?

How important to the decision is the fact that the Amish religion countenanced school attendance until the eighth grade? What would be the result if only a sixth-grade education were permitted? What would be the result if a particular sect permitted no formal schooling at all, but the good citizenship and economic self-reliance of its members were unquestioned? What if the members of a religious sect demanding no formal education after the eighth grade held unimpeachable religious beliefs but were not always "very law abiding"?

b. Parental Rights. "However read," Chief Justice Burger states, "the court's holding in *Pierce* stands as a charter of the rights of parents to direct the religious upbringing of their children." 406 US at 233. Is that the proposition for which *Pierce* stands?

In *Prince v Massachusetts* 321 US 158 (1944), nine-year-old Betty, under the supervision of her aunt and custodian, Mrs. Prince, sold religious literature on the street in violation of Massachusetts' child labor laws. Both Betty and Mrs. Prince were Jehovah's Witnesses and believed it their religious duty to do this work. The court held for the state; in its opinion it discussed the "harmful possibilities" that the legislature sought to prevent and then noted: "Parents may be free to become martyrs themselves. But it does not follow they are free to make martyrs of their children before they have reached the age of full and legal discretion when they can make the choice themselves." 321 US at 170. *Prince* is characterized in *Yoder* as a case in which the conduct regulated posed a substantial threat to public safety and on that basis is distinguishable from the Amish situation. How satisfactory is that distinction? Should *Prince* have been overruled? Was the danger to the physical or mental health of the child in *Prince* any more than the danger that might be "properly inferred" in *Yoder*?

c. Interests of the State. Wisconsin suggested two justifications for compulsory education: the preparation of the child for political citizenship and the development of economic self-reliance. Are these concerns satisfied, as the *Yoder* decision suggests, by eight years of schooling?

The answer to that query may turn on whether Amish youngsters remain in the Amish community or choose a quite different life style. As Justice White notes in his concurring opinion: "It is possible that most Amish children will wish to continue living the rural life of their parents, in which case their training at home will adequately equip them for their future role. Others, however, may wish to become nuclear physicists, ballet dancers, computer programmers, or historians, and for these occupations, formal training will be necessary." 406 US at 239. Does the state have a legitimate interest in providing maximum educational opportunities to all youngsters?

If in fact few Amish youngsters deserted their community for the larger society, the interest might be dismissed as of trivial practical significance. But is that the case? Compare the discussions of Justices Burger, White, and Douglas on this point. And consider the conclusion reached by the Wisconsin Supreme Court in *Yoder*: "[T]his harm to the Amish [is not] justified because on speculation some Amish children may after reaching adulthood leave their religion. To force a worldly education on all Amish children, the majority of whom do not want or need it, in order to confer a dubious benefit on the few who might later reject their religion is not a compelling interest." *State v Yoder* 49 Wis2d 430, 440, 182 NW2d 539, 543 (1971). What does that statement assume with respect to the wishes of Amish children (see d, *infra*)? Compare the position of the dissent in the same case: "The state's interest and obligation runs to each and every child in the state. In the context of the public law of the state, no child's education is below the concern of the law." 49 Wis2d at 451, 182 NW2d at 549.

The state argues that the Amish faith fosters ignorance. The court's response speaks to the "productive and very law-abiding" nature of the Amish. Does the response confront the question? The court also notes that the Amish community provides "valuable vocational skills and habits." Just how valuable are these skills likely to be outside of the religious community? How might the black parent—or any parent, for that matter—respond if his child were compelled to attend a vocational school?

The last paragraph of the majority opinion suggests the state may require Amish children to attend an "Amish vocational school" or at least regulate the content of continuing vocational training provided by Amish parents. One commentator asserts: "It is not simply public school to which [the Amish] object, but *all* schooling above the eighth grade." S. Arons, "Compulsory Education: the Plain People Resist," *Saturday Review,* 15 January 1972, p 53. After *Yoder,* what is the likely outcome of a suit by Amish plaintiffs alleging that any type of school at all beyond the eighth grade is inconsistent with their faith?

d. The Interests of Amish Children. The possibility of a clash between Amish youngsters and their parents is skirted by the court, which notes that the children were not parties to the litigation. Since children must be represented in court by an adult (typically, but not necessarily, by a parent or legal guardian), how might the Amish youngsters make themselves parties to the litigation? The court also denies the likelihood of a parent-child conflict, noting that "there is nothing in the record or in the ordinary course of human experience to suggest that non-Amish parents generally consult with children up to ages fourteen through sixteen if they are placed in a church school of their parents' faith." 406 US at 232. Is the observation correct? Can the Amish community be analogized to an extended parochial school?

If the views of the Amish children do bear consideration, how should they be expressed? Should the court appoint a guardian explicitly to represent the children? Should the children be canvassed, as Justice Douglas' dissent suggests? What impact would such a venture have on the Amish child? On the Amish community? Any device designed to identify the independent interest of Amish youngsters necessarily intrudes into family and community life, imposing both political and legal costs. Is the child's right to be heard of sufficient importance to justify such an intrusion?

The *Yoder* decision preserves the religious and community interests of the

Amish, but in so doing denies Amish children the opportunity of acquiring sufficient education to choose for themselves whether to stay in the community; a
decision compelling these children to attend school would seriously affect the
future viability of the Amish religion. Is there a resolution of the issue less far-
reaching in its consequences than either of these alternatives?

The rights of the child against both his parents and the potential role of the state
as *parens patriae* have frequently presented perplexing problems to the courts. In *In
re Green* 448 Pa 338, 292 A2d 38 (1972), parents refused on religious grounds to
permit blood transfusion preparations necessary to proceed with a spinal operation
on a sixteen-year-old boy. The Pennsylvania Supreme Court found that where the
situation was not one of life-or-death urgency, the state interest in the well-being of
the child did not outweigh the interests of the parents in religious freedom. The
court, however, reserved its decision in the light of a possible parent-child conflict
and remanded the case for a hearing to determine the child's views.

> [T] he ultimate question . . . is whether a parent's religious beliefs are para-
> mount to the possibly adverse decision of the child. . . . It would be most
> anomalous to ignore [the child] in this situation when we consider the prefer-
> ence of an intelligent child of sufficient maturity in determining custody . . . .
> Moreover, we have held that a child of the same age can waive consti-
> tutional rights and receive a life sentence. . . . Indeed, minors can now
> bring a personal injury action in Pennsylvania against their parents. (292
> A2d at 392.)

The dissent took issue with the majority's disposition of the case.

> I do not believe that sending the case back to allow Ricky to be heard is an
> adequate solution. We are herein dealing with a young boy who has been
> crippled most of his life, consequently, he has been under the direct control
> of his parents for that time. To now presume that he could make an indepen-
> dent decision as to what is best for his welfare and health is not reasonable.
> (292 A2d at 395.)

See also *State v Perricone* 37 NY 463, 181 A2d 751, *cert denied,* 371 US 890
(1962); *Raleigh Fitkin-Paul Morgan Memorial Hosp v Anderson* 42 NJ 421, 201
A2d 537, *cert denied,* 377 US 985 (1964). Can *Green* be reconciled with *Yoder*? Is
the only difference between the two situations one of the foreseeability of serious
injury to the child? Is this difference sufficient to justify the conclusion in *Yoder*
that the education of the child is for the parents alone to determine? Note in the
Green case that there was apparently no showing of actual conflict between parent
and child. Nonetheless, the Pennsylvania court considered the child's opinion essential and thus in essence adopted the approach of Justice Douglas in *Yoder*. Consider
in this context the criticism of the dissent in *Green*. Does it apply with equal
validity to the opinion of Justice Douglas?

May a child ever assert his own interest in educational liberty? In *In re Mario*
317 NYS2d 659, 65 Misc2d 708 (Fam Ct 1971), the New York family court upheld
the assignment of a thirteen-year-old boy, "beyond parental control in regard to his
school attendance," to Warwick State Training School, a residential "rehabilitative"
institution. The respondent asserted that such placement "imposes a restraint on his
liberty." The court found the restraint constitutional,

because reasonable rehabilitative measures are justified by respondent's truancy. . . . the state has the power to perform the parental role of insuring the child's education and training, when the parent is unable to control him sufficiently to perform it. If children were permitted the same freedom of choice as adults, they might well be unequipped when they attain adulthood to exercise any freedom of choice—specifically, without any education or training, they would be unable to choose to work in a job for which they in fact have the potential. (317 NYS2d at 668.)

Is the state's interest more compelling in *Mario* than in *Yoder?* How would the *Yoder* majority (or Justice Douglas) resolve this issue?

3. The Scope of the *Yoder* Decision

a. A Broad Challenge to Compulsoriness? The *Yoder* court notes that the Amish way of life has come "into conflict increasingly with the requirements of contemporary society . . . . There can be no assumption that today's majority is 'right,' and that the Amish and others like them are 'wrong.' " 406 US at 223. Are these "others" only religious sects, as the court's opinion intimates? Why should the children of a contemporary Thoreau, whose objections to schooling derive not from a religion but from a philosophy of life, be forced to submit to socialization in debatable political and social values? Does freedom of religion have a higher claim to constitutional protection than freedom of expression? One commentator notes:

> That socialization of children is basic to the state's attempt to include the Amish in its captive audience raises the most serious question about the preservation of social pluralism . . . . The state may forbid the exclusion of any group from a public program; but as soon as it can compel the *inclusion* of some group in a program whose inevitable effect is to mold opinion and values, the entire basis of individual freedom has been eroded. The court has already ruled once (in *Yoder*) that such logic cannot justify compelling all children to attend public school; now it must decide the issue of standardization anew. (S. Arons, "Compulsory Education: the Plain People Resist," *Saturday Review*, 15 January 1972, p 54.)

Does the *Yoder* opinion in fact raise this range of questions, undercutting the *Pierce* premise that the state may compel children to attend some form of school?

b. Compulsoriness and Equal Educational Opportunity. In re Skipwith 14 Misc2d 325, 180 NYS2d 852 (Dom Rel Ct 1958) poses a quite different constitutional challenge to compulsoriness. In *Skipwith,* parents refused to send their children to ghetto schools, which they alleged were inferior to predominantly white schools. In a suit brought by the board of education to compel attendance, the parents introduced testimony of educators and psychologists concerning the harmful impact of racial segregation, and evidence that the school in question had unlicensed teachers filling forty-three of eighty-five positions, a proportion substantially greater than the citywide average (see chapter 4 for a discussion of racial discrimination and equal educational opportunity). Is it appropriate—as a matter either of policy or constitutional law—to keep children from school as a means of addressing the inequalities asserted by the *Skipwith* parents? See also *Dobbins v Commonwealth* 198 Va 697, 96 SE2d 154 (1957).

III. The Scope of Governmental Regulation of Nonpublic Schools

A. State Regulation of Nonpublic Schools

FARRINGTON v TOKUSHIGE
273 US 284 (1926)

Mr. Justice McReynolds delivered the opinion of the court.

The circuit court of appeals affirmed [11 F2d 710] an interlocutory decree rendered by the United States District Court of Hawaii July 21, 1925, which granted a temporary injunction forbidding petitioners—governor, attorney general and superintendent of public instruction of that territory—from attempting to enforce the provisions of Act 30, Special Session 1920, Legislature of Hawaii, entitled, "An Act relating to foreign language schools and teachers thereof," as amended by Act 171 of 1923 and Act 152 of 1925, and certain regulations adopted by the department of public instruction June 1, 1925. The interlocutory decree was granted upon the bill and affidavits presented by both sides. No answer has been filed. In these circumstances we only consider whether the judicial discretion of the trial court was improperly exercised.

Respondents claimed below and maintain here that enforcement of the challenged act would deprive them of their liberty and property without due process of law contrary to the Fifth Amendment. Petitioners insist that the entire act and the regulations adopted thereunder are valid; that they prescribe lawful rules for the conduct of private foreign language schools necessary for the public welfare; also that if any provision of the statute transcends the power of the legislature it should be disregarded and the remaining ones should be enforced. . . .

There are one hundred sixty-three foreign language schools in the territory. Nine are conducted in the Korean language, seven in the Chinese and the remainder in the Japanese. Respondents are members of numerous voluntary unincorporated associations conducting foreign language schools for instruction of Japanese children. These are owned, maintained and conducted by upwards of five thousand persons; the property used in connection therewith is worth two hundred fifty thousand dollars; the enrolled pupils number twenty thousand; and three hundred teachers are employed. These schools receive no aid from public funds. All children residing within the territory are required to attend some public or equivalent school; and practically all who go to foreign language schools also attend public or such private schools. It is affirmed by counsel for petitioners that Japanese pupils in the public and equivalent private schools increased from one thousand, three hundred twenty in 1900 to nineteen thousand, three hundred fifty-four in 1920, and that out of a total of sixty-five thousand, three hundred sixty-nine pupils of all races on December 31, 1924, thirty thousand, four hundred eighty-seven were Japanese.

The challenged enactment declares that the term, "foreign language school," as used therein, "shall be construed to mean any school which is conducted in any language other than the English language or Hawaiian language, except Sabbath schools." And, as stated by the circuit court of appeals, the following are its more prominent and questionable features:

> No such school shall be conducted in the territory unless under a written permit therefor from the department of public instruction, nor unless the fee

therefor shall have been paid as therein provided, and such permit shall be kept exposed in a prominent place at the school so as to be readily seen and read by visitors thereat.

The fee prescribed is one dollar per pupil on the estimated average attendance of pupils at the school during the period during which such school was conducted during the next preceding school year, or if such school was not conducted during any part of such preceding school year, then at the same rate at [sic] the estimated average attendance during the school year or unexpired part thereof in question, in which latter case the amount shall be adjusted to conform to the estimated average attendance during such year or part thereof . . . .

No person shall teach in a foreign language school unless and until he shall have first applied to and obtained a permit so to do from the department and this shall also be construed to include persons exercising or performing administrative powers at any school. No permit to teach in a foreign language school shall be granted unless and until the department is satisfied that the applicant for the same is possessed of the ideals of democracy; knowledge of American history and institutions, and knows how to read, write and speak the English language.

It is the declared object of the act to fully and effectively regulate the conducting of foreign language schools and the teaching of foreign languages, in order that the Americanism of the pupils may be promoted, and the department is directed to carry out the provisions of the act in accordance with its spirit and purpose.

Before issuing a permit to conduct a foreign language school or to teach in any such school the department shall require the applicant for such permit to sign a pledge that the applicant will, if granted a permit to teach in such a school, abide by and observe the terms of the act, and the regulations and orders of the department, and will, to the best of his ability, so direct the minds and studies of pupils in such schools as will tend to make them good and loyal American citizens, and will not permit such students to receive instructions in any way inconsistent therewith.

No foreign language school shall be conducted in the morning before the school hours of the public schools or during the hours while the public schools are in session, nor shall any pupil attend any foreign language school for more than one hour each day, nor exceeding six hours in any one week, nor exceeding thirty-eight weeks in any school year; provided, however, the department may in its discretion and with the approval of the governor, modify this provision.

The department shall have full power from time to time to prescribe by regulations the subjects and courses of study of all foreign language schools, and the entrance and attendance prerequisites or qualifications of education, age, school attainment, demonstrated mental capacity, health and otherwise, and the textbooks used in any foreign language school.

Until otherwise provided by the department, the following regulations are in effect: Up to September 1, 1923, every pupil shall have first satisfactorily completed the American public school first grade, or a course equivalent thereto, before attending or being allowed to attend any foreign language school. Beginning September 1, 1923, and thereafter, every pupil shall have satisfactorily completed the American public school first and second grades, or courses equivalent thereto, before attending or being allowed to attend any foreign language school. Beginning September 1, 1923, and thereafter, for grades one, two and three, and beginning September 1, 1924, and thereafter, for grades four and above, all new textbooks used in elementary foreign language schools shall be based upon the principle that the pupil's normal medium of expression is English and shall contain, as far as practicable, English equivalents for foreign words and idioms.

The department is authorized to prepare, or cause to be prepared, or procure or arrange for procuring suitable textbooks for the teaching of foreign languages in the foreign language schools and to enter into an agreement or agreements for the publishing and sale of the same . . . .

If the department shall at any time become satisfied that any holder of a permit to conduct a foreign language school or to teach therein does not possess the qualifications required by the act, or shall have violated or failed to observe any of the provisions of the act or of the regulations or orders of the department, the department may then and thereupon revoke the permit theretofore granted and the same shall thereupon be and become null and void.

Any person who shall conduct or participate in conducting a foreign language school or who shall teach in a foreign language school contrary to the provisions of the act, or who shall violate or participate in violating any of the provisions thereof, or any of the regulations or orders of the department, shall be guilty of a misdemeanor, and upon conviction thereof shall be punished by a fine not to exceed twenty-five dollars, and each day's violation shall be deemed a separate offense . . . .

On June 1, 1925, the department of public instruction adopted, and the governor approved, certain regulations which undertook to limit the pupils who might attend foreign language schools to those who regularly attended some public school or approved private school, or had completed the eighth grade, or were over fourteen years of age. Also, to designate the textbooks which foreign language schools should use in their primary grades . . . .

[T]he school act and the measures adopted thereunder go far beyond mere regulation of privately supported schools where children obtain instruction deemed valuable by their parents and which is not obviously in conflict with any public interest. They give affirmative direction concerning the intimate and essential details of such schools, intrust their control to public officers, and deny both owners and patrons reasonable choice and discretion in respect of teachers, curriculum and textbooks. Enforcement of the act probably would destroy most, if not all, of them; and, certainly, it would deprive parents of fair opportunity to procure for their children instruction which they think important and we cannot say is harmful. The Japanese parent has the right to direct the education of his own child without unreasonable restrictions; the Constitution protects him as well as those who speak another tongue.

Upon the record and the arguments presented, we cannot undertake to consider the validity of each separate provision of the act and decide whether, dissociated from the others, its enforcement would violate respondents' constitutional rights. Apparently all are parts of a deliberate plan to bring foreign language schools under a strict governmental control for which the record discloses no adequate reason. Here, the enactment has been defended as a whole. No effort has been made to discuss the validity of the several provisions. In the trial court the cause proceeded upon the theory that petitioners intended to enforce all of them.

The general doctrine touching rights guaranteed by the Fourteenth Amendment to owners, parents and children in respect of attendance upon schools has been announced in recent opinions. [Citing *Pierce v Society of Sisters,* among other cases] . . . .

We of course appreciate the grave problems incident to the large alien population of the Hawaiian Islands. These should be given due weight whenever the validity of any governmental regulation of private schools is under consideration; but the limitations of the Constitution must not be transcended.

It seems proper to add that when petitioners present their answer the issues may become more specific and permit the cause to be dealt with in greater detail.

We find no abuse of the discretion lodged in the trial court. The decree of the circuit court of appeals must be

Affirmed.

EXCERPTS FROM THE FARRINGTON BRIEFS, SUMMARIZED IN THE COURT'S OPINION

Mr. William B. Lymer, Attorney General of the Territory of Hawaii, with whom Marguerite K. Ashford, First Deputy Attorney General, was on the brief, for the petitioners.

These laws do not violate the Constitution. *Pierce v Society of Sisters* 268 US 510 (1925) . . . concern[s] prohibitory legislation alone, and not purely regulatory measures such as those involved in this case, which attempt rather to supervise and control than to abolish foreign language schools.

It would be a sad commentary on our system of government to hold that the territory must stand by, impotent, and watch its foreign-born guests conduct a vast system of schools of American pupils, teaching them loyalty to a foreign country and disloyalty to their own country, and hampering them during their tender years in the learning of the home language in the public schools,—to hold that the territory could not by mere regulatory measures even alleviate these evils to a moderate extent while not interfering in the least with the proper maintenance of these schools or the teaching of foreign languages in them, but on the contrary making them more efficient for this their declared object.

The state has authority over such schools for at least two reasons: (1) that as *parens patriae* it has extensive power with respect to infants; and (2) that it is vitally interested in the quality of its citizenship . . . .

Private schools are a proper subject of regulation. *State v Bailey* 157 Ind 324, 61 NE 730 (1901). Compulsory education statutes do not require attendance at public schools alone, but at either public or private schools. Necessarily, in order to meet the requirements in respect of the period of years and the field of knowledge to be covered, it must be within the power of the legislature to regulate within reasonable limits the qualifications of the teachers, the subjects to be covered, the instruction to be given and how and to what extent—within the limits of the power—other instruction should be forbidden. The right to regulate private schools in Hawaii has long been unquestioned . . . .

Mr. Joseph Lightfoot, with whom Mr. Joseph B. Poindexter was on the brief, for respondents.

The statute unreasonably interferes with the fundamental right of parents and guardians to direct the upbringing and education of children under their control . . . .

The Hawaiian statute . . . takes from the parent of a child attending a foreign language school, all control and direction of the education of his child. Complete control of these schools is given to the department of education. The effect is to make them public schools in all but the name, though the public contributes nothing to their support. They are prohibited from employing a teacher, teaching a subject, using a book, admitting a pupil, or engaging in any activity of any nature, unless approved by the department of education. Nor can such a school be conducted until a permit is granted and an exorbitant fee paid—a condition not imposed on any other private school in the territory.

In the public schools all are taught the same lessons of Americanism and democratic ideals, which are considered sufficient for a majority of the pupils, yet the minority of the pupils, whose parents desire to fit them for the battle of life by teaching them a language which will be of great benefit to them in their after careers, attend the foreign language schools where they are further regulated, controlled, taxed, and this, too, in the face of the admitted fact that nothing un-American is taught in the foreign language schools, and the Americanism of the pupils is advanced, not retarded in them.

The sole purpose of the law is the Americanization of the pupils of these schools, though it is admitted that nothing un-American is taught in them. . . .

STATE v WILLIAMS
253 NC 337, 117 SE2d 444 (1960)

Moore, Justice.

Defendant is indicted pursuant to the provisions of GS § 115-253. This section is a part of Article 31, Chapter 115, of the General Statutes of North Carolina, which provides for the regulation of business, trade, and correspondence schools—private schools. The first seven sections of the article deal, almost entirely, with the regulation of such schools located in North Carolina. General Statutes § 115-253 requires persons soliciting students within the state for schools "located within or without the state" to secure a license annually from the state board of education. The license fee is five dollars. When application is made for a license by a solicitor certain information must be furnished with the application. If the board approves the instructional program and the solicitor, license will be issued. If license is issued to a solicitor for an out-of-state school, the solicitor shall execute and file a bond in each county in which students are solicited. Nonresident schools employing solicitors shall be responsible for the acts, representations and contracts made by their solicitors. "Any person soliciting students for any such school without first having secured a license from the state board of education and without having executed the bond . . . shall be guilty of a misdemeanor . . . ." General Statutes § 115-252 imposes the duty on out-of-state schools to see that their solicitors are licensed and bonded. General Statutes §115-254 provides that contracts, notes and evidences of debt obtained by unlicensed solicitors shall be null and void.

Allegro Bryant, a high school teacher, resident of Craven County, received through the mail a card addressed to boxholder. The card had been placed in the mail by Citizens Training Service, Inc., a Virginia corporation, having its principal office and place of business in Danville, Virginia. It conducts a correspondence school for preparation for civil service careers—federal, state and municipal. Bryant mailed the card to the school indicating an interest in certain courses. She promptly received certain forms to be held by her until a canvasser called. On 16 January 1960 defendant contacted her and as a consequence, she signed a contract for instruction designed to prepare her to take examinations for civil service employment as teacher, social worker and junior professional assistant. The fee for the course was $135. Bryant paid $20 in cash and signed a promissory note for $115, to be due 25 February 1960. The contract, according to its terms, was not to be complete until accepted at the business office in Danville. Bryant testified that defendant represented to her that a job was guaranteed. The written contract is to the contrary. Bryant received by mail a book containing twenty-five or more lessons. She completed and sent in only one assignment. She made no payment on the note. Defendant was not licensed or bonded under the provisions of GS §115-253.

Defendant's testimony clearly states her position in this case: "My plea of not guilty and my defense in this prosecution is based solely on the grounds that the provisions of GS §115-253 are unconstitutional. If the provisions of this statute are constitutional, I am guilty of violating such provisions of the statute. Otherwise I am not . . . ."

The primary purpose of article 31, of which the challenged section is a part, is to control and regulate certain private schools—specifically business, trade and correspondence schools. The article is entitled, "Business, Trade and Correspondence Schools." As an incident to such control, GS §115-253 undertakes to regulate solicitors and canvassers for such schools. It seems clear that the provision for regulation of solicitors is to enable the state board of education to indirectly extend its control and supervision to correspondence schools located beyond the borders of the state that solicit and instruct students in North Carolina . . . .

[I]t is the intent of the enactment that the state board of education pass upon the adequacy of the equipment, curricula and instructional personnel of the schools and protect students from fraud and breach of contract on the part of the schools and their agents and representatives.

The Constitution of North Carolina provides that "schools and means of education shall forever be encouraged." Art IX, §1. Further, the state board of education shall have the power and duty "generally to supervise and administer the free *public* school system of the state and make all needful rules and regulations in relation thereto." Art IX, §9 (emphasis added). The constitutional authority of the state board of education to make regulations for and supervise and administer schools is confined to *public* schools and activities substantially affecting public schools and the public school system. It may have and exert only such authority in the supervision and control of private schools and their agents and representatives as is conferred by the general assembly in the proper exercise of the police power of the state . . . .

The state has the power and authority to establish minimum standards for, and to regulate in a reasonable manner, private schools giving instruction to children of compulsory school age. This is necessarily true because such schools affect the public school system . . . .

The courts stress the proposition that the regulation of private schools under the police power of the state must be reasonable and in response to a manifest present public need or emergency.

The Court of Appeals of Maryland, in *Schneider v Pullen* 198 Md 64, 81 A2d 226, 229 (1951) upheld the constitutionality of a statute providing for the regulation of certain private schools, including trade schools. The case involved a barber school. It is suggested that the regulatory act was necessary "because many mushroom schools of various characters sprang up in order to take advantage of government subsidies given to veterans of World War II." The New York Supreme Court held constitutional a statute which provided that private schools be licensed, and that no license should issue if it appeared that the instruction to be given included the doctrine that organized government should be overthrown by force, violence or unlawful means. *People v American Socialist Soc'y* 202 App Div 640, 195 NYS 801, 806 (1922). The court declared:

> There can be little question but that it is within the power of the legislature to enact statutes for the self-preservation of the state, and to prevent the teaching of doctrine advocating the destruction of the state by force . . . . [I]t seems to us that the act in question is well within the proper exercise of the police power of the state, and that for the purpose of protecting the peace, public safety, and security of the citizens of the state the legislature had the right to enact the statute.

On the other hand, the courts have stricken down as unconstitutional many legislative enactments affecting, or seeking to restrict or regulate, private schools, for want of any manifest need therefor by reason of the public morals, health, peace, safety or security, or because of the arbitrary and unreasonable character of the regulation. Instances are: Provision that certain trade schools may not be established in a county without a favorable vote of the electors. *Columbia Trust Co v Lincoln Inst of Ky* 138 Ky 804, 129 SW 113 (1910); prohibition against teaching other than the English language to children below the ninth grade, *Meyer v Nebraska* 262 US 390. Requisite for issuance of license to trade school that its tuition charge be approved by commissioner of education. *Grow System School v Board of Regents* 277 App Div 122, 98 NYS2d 834. . . .

A New York statute provided that no private nursery, kindergarten or elementary schools should be established or maintained unless registered under regulations prescribed by the board of regents of the university of the state. The act was declared unconstitutional. *Packer Collegiate Inst v University* 298 NY 184, 81 NE2d 80 (1948). The court explained the holding:

> Private schools have a constitutional right to exist, and parents have a constitutional right to send their children to such schools. [Citing *Pierce v Society of Sisters, supra.*] The legislature, under the police power, has a limited right to regulate such schools in the public interest. [Citing authorities.] Such being the fundamental law of the subject, it would be intolerable for the legislature to hand over to any official or group of officials, an unlimited, unrestrained, undefined power to make such regulations as he or they shall desire, and to grant or refuse licenses to such schools, depending on their compliance with such regulation . . . .

Beyond all question the state may exercise its police power to regulate salesmen in the public interest. But the regulations must be clearly necessary to protect a substantial public interest and must be reasonable and nondiscriminatory.

The class of salesmen most often regulated is peddlers. Statutes and ordinances requiring those who hawk and peddle from door to door to be licensed have been held constitutional . . . . In upholding such regulations the courts are careful to explain the need for the legislation. It is stated that peddlers often have no fixed places of abode and no established business site. They are here today and gone tomorrow. The regulations seek to protect the public against cheats, frauds and even thievery which often attends the activities of peddlers. Though there are significant exceptions, their goods are generally inferior in quality and exorbitant in price. Peddlers are generally strangers to their customers. Thus, the courts emphasize need for regulation. The regulatory statutes usually contain, in preamble, a full statement of the purpose and necessity for regulation . . . .

In summary, the state has a limited right, under the police power, to regulate private schools and their agents and solicitors, provided: (1) there is a manifest present need which affects the health, morals, or safety of the public generally, (2) the regulations are not arbitrary, discriminatory, oppressive or otherwise unreasonable, and (3) adequate legislative standards are established. *State v Warren* 252 NC 690, 114 SE2d 660 (1960); *State v Harris* 216 NC 746, 6 SE2d 854, . . .

The showing of need, in the instant case, is meager at best. In GS § 115-249 it is declared, with reference to the supervision of the specified schools by the state board of education: "[T]he object of said supervision being to protect the public welfare by having the licensed business, trade, or correspondence schools maintain proper school quarters, equipment, and teaching staff and to have the school carry out its advertised promises and contracts made with its students and patrons." This is the only statement of purpose or need which appears. The need is not declared but, if any exists, must be inferred. For the most part the curricula of the schools sought to be regulated are outside the scope and purpose of instruction given in public schools, colleges, and universities. It does not appear, nor is there any publicly accepted thesis known to us, that the instruction by such schools is inadequate in the areas of learning in which they profess to teach. The law proposes to protect students from fraudulent practices and breaches of contract. If fraud exists in this field, it does not appear that it is widespread and affects a large segment of the population. Besides, no special legislation is necessary for this purpose. The courts of this state are open at all times to redress such wrongs, under laws and procedures long established. However, our decision does not rest upon the lack of public need for the regulation. "The legislative department is the judge, within reasonable limits, of what the public welfare requires . . . ." *State v Warren,* supra, 252 NC at 696, 114 SE2d at 666. But it should be remembered that, though the schools involved are not of equal dignity with many old and revered private institutions of learning in our state, the same law applies to all. The principles the legislature may follow in regulating one, it may apply to all. Standardization and regimentation in the field of learning is contrary to the American concept of individual liberty. It would be difficult to overestimate the contribution of private institutions of learning to the initiative, progress and individualism of our people. Regulation should never be resorted to unless the need is compellingly apparent.

General Statutes §115-253 contains the following provisions:

> When application is made for such license by a solicitor, he shall submit to said board (state board of education) for its approval a copy of each type of contract offered prospective students and used by his said school, together with such advertising material and other representations as are made by said school to its students or prospective students, and such instructional material as requested by the board to enable it to evaluate the instructional program, as well as the sales methods. If the board approves the instructional program and the solicitor, it shall issue to the solicitor a license . . . .

The legislature has set no standards for evaluating the contract, advertising material or instructional program. Furthermore, no test or rule of any kind has been established for determining the fitness of the solicitor. All of these matters are left to the unlimited discretion of the administrative body—a body which, most likely, has little familiarity with the operation of schools of this type. Such unlimited delegation of authority is beyond the bounds of valid legislation . . . .

Packer Collegiate Inst v University, supra, deals with a statute of the State of New York providing that no private nursery, kindergarten or elementary school might be established or maintained without a certificate of registration under regulations prescribed by the board of regents of the university. On the question of legislative standards, the court concluded:

> The quoted statute is, we think, patently unconstitutional as being an attempted delegation of legislative power . . . . The statute before us is nothing less than an attempt to empower an administrative officer . . . to register and license, or refuse to register and license, private schools, under regulations to be adopted by him, with no standards or limitations of any sort . . . [T]here must be a clearly delimited field of action and, also, standards for action therein . . . . This is not really a question of what powers of control over private schools may validly be delegated by the legislature. It is here impossible to discover what authority was intended to be turned over . . . [T]he statute's validity must be judged not by what has been done under it but "by what is possible under it."

These quotations from the *Packer* case aptly state the principles applicable to the case at bar.

General Statutes §115-253 is clearly an unwarranted delegation of legislative power, and defendant's conviction and punishment under the criminal provisions thereof violate the "law of the land" section of the Constitution of North Carolina. Art I, §17. . . .

Reversed.

Notes and Questions

1. The Courts and Private School Regulation

a. The *Pierce* decision leaves states free "reasonably to regulate all schools, to inspect, supervise and examine them, their teachers and pupils; require . . . that certain studies plainly essential to good citizenship must be taught, and that nothing be taught that is manifestly inimical to the public welfare"; and *Yoder* does not, on its face, withdraw this authority. If such regulation were not constitutionally permitted, how would the *Pierce* compromise have been affected? Could the state effectively compel the education of all children at a "school," if any private enterprise could refer to itself by that name?

Pierce gives states considerable latitude in the scope of regulation. Might a state exercise that right to adopt regulations so intrusive that they either make all private schools exactly like their public counterparts or drive nonpublic education out of business? How should the balance between competing interests be struck in this context?

b. In *Meyer v Nebraska* 262 US 390 (1923), the Supreme Court struck down a Nebraska statute that imposed criminal penalties on public or private school teachers who taught in any language except English or who taught languages other than English to students below high school level. The legislation in *Meyer,* as in *Farrington,* was born of the animosity against alien groups aroused by World War I; in Nebraska, the target was Germans generally, and the German language in particular. The Supreme Court concluded that the legislation interfered with both the language instructor's right to engage in his profession and the parents' right to encourage such instruction. It rejected the state's claim that such legislation was needed to "promote civic development," noting that while the "desire of the legislature to foster a homogeneous people with American ideals" was understandable, the particular measure did "violence to both the letter and spirit of the constitution."

c. Farrington v Tokushige does not indicate which provisions of the Hawaii legislation it finds objectionable. If the Hawaii legislature wished to redraft the bill to render it constitutionally acceptable, which provisions should be stricken? Why? Note that by the terms of the Hawaii statute the foreign language schools can only provide a supplementary education; they are not permitted to provide full instruction. Is that feature of the legislation constitutionally invalid? If Japanese-American students attend public or state-approved private schools during the normal school day, should the state be permitted to impose any regulations on after-school instruction? Could the state, for example, regulate the content of instruction in after-school church-run classes? In classes run by the Communist party? Suppose after-school instruction was structured explicitly to identify and rebut the alleged ideological bias of the public school; could such an enterprise be prohibited or regulated by the state?

d. State v Williams is typical of the relatively few post-*Farrington* decisions concerning the constitutionality of private school regulation. It does not directly consider whether state regulation of such schools interferes with the free speech or due process rights of school proprietors, parents, or students, but rejects the legislation as "an unwarranted delegation of legislative power," a constitutional doctrine seldom invoked in recent years. Courts have long recognized that legislatures often cannot fix precise standards for regulating conduct, and necessarily leave such standard setting to administrative agencies. Why might the *Williams* court have focused on the delegation issue? What more precise standards might the North Carolina legislature set?

e. May the state permit voters in local election districts to determine whether a private school may operate in that community? See *Columbia Trust Co v Lincoln*

Inst of Ky 138 Ky 804, 129 SW 113 (1910). But see *Valtierra v James* 402 US 137 (1971).

2. State Statutory Regulation of Nonpublic Schools

In light of the court's holding in *Farrington* consider the following example of contemporary regulation of private schools:

SOUTH DAKOTA COMPILED LAWS, 1967 (SUPP 1972)

13-4-1. Conformity to state course of study required—Approval supervision and visitation by state superintendent—Revocation of approval. All private kindergartens and nursery schools and all private and parochial instruction accepted in lieu of public school instruction shall conform with the state course of study and must be approved by the state superintendent of public instruction, who shall exercise supervision over such schools and such instruction and shall exercise the right of visitation and inspection thereof. The superintendent may revoke his approval of such instruction at any time for failure to conform with state law.

13-33-4. Instruction on United States and state constitutions required—Years when given. In all public and private schools located within the state there shall be given regular courses of instruction in the constitutions of the United States and the state of South Dakota. Such instruction shall begin not later than the opening of the eighth grade and shall continue in the high school course to an extent to be determined by the state board of education.

13-33-5. Patriotic instruction required. In addition to other prescribed branches, special instruction shall be given in all public and private elementary and secondary schools in the state in patriotism, including the singing of patriotic songs, the reading of patriotic addresses, and a study of the lives and history of American patriots.

13-33-6. Moral instruction required. In addition to other prescribed branches, there shall be given in all public and private elementary and secondary schools in the state, special moral instruction intended to impress upon the minds of students the importance of truthfulness, temperance, purity, public spirit, patriotism, respect for honest labor, obedience to parents, respect for the contributions of minority and ethnic groups to the heritage of South Dakota, and due deference to old age.

13-33-7. Required instruction on alcohol and controlled substances. In addition to other prescribed branches, special instruction shall be given in all public and private elementary and secondary schools in the state in the nature of alcoholic drinks, narcotics, depressants, stimulants, hallucinogens and other controlled substances which have a potential abuse because of their depressant or stimulant effect on the central nervous system or alteration of its normal function.

13-33-11. Instruction to promote mastery of English language. Instruction in any elementary school, high school, academy, college or higher institution of learning shall be such that it promotes a mastery of the English language in oral and written communications.

13-42-2. Teaching in private school without certificate as misdemeanor—Penalty —Revocation of certificate—Disposition of fines. Any person teaching in any private school in this state any of the branches prescribed to be taught in the public schools of this state who is not the holder of a certificate authorizing him to teach the same branches in the public schools of this state shall be guilty of a misdemeanor and upon conviction thereof shall be punished by a fine of not less than $25 nor more than $100. Such violation shall also be sufficient grounds for revocation by the state superintendent of public instruction of any teachers certificate held by such person.

All fines collected under this section shall be paid to the county treasurer and by him credited to the county general school fund.

How do the provisions of the South Dakota legislation regulating nonpublic schools differ from the Hawaii legislation struck down in *Farrington*? Does the prevalence of such legislation indicate that *Farrington,* although not expressly overruled, is nonetheless no longer good law? That there is little interest in creating schools that differ significantly from public schools? That enforcement of the laws is considerably more lenient than the letter of the legislation?

In "State Regulation of Nonpublic Schools: The Legal Framework," in *Public Controls for Nonpublic Schools* 103, 133 D. Erickson, ed (1969), John Elson summarizes the policy rationales for state regulation:

Nonpublic school regulations are intended to promote five main policies. First and most important, minimum curriculum and teacher certification laws are enacted to make school attendance requirements effective. Second, statutes more common in recent years are designed to prevent the teaching of ideas considered socially dangerous. Third, regulations are intended to promote cultural unity, although this concept is less popular since the 1920s and is now apparent in only a few states. Fourth, voluntary accreditation statutes are enacted to provide criteria by which to choose quality nonpublic schooling. Finally, in all states, laws applicable to nonpublic schools as well as to any private business are designed to protect the public from dangerous business, health, and building practices . . . .

Do *Farrington* and *Meyer* call into question the constitutionality of any of these legislative goals? Is there a constitutionally significant difference between a requirement that certain subjects be taught and a ban on certain subjects? Are the policy objectives of the two types of legislation—Elson's first two categories—similar?

Consider the following hypothetical statute: "Every family shall devote one hour each day to activities conducive to good citizenship, including reading about public issues from state-approved journals and participation in community activities. Training that fosters respect for the legal system, and awareness of the dangers of alcohol and other drugs, shall also be provided regularly by the family." Such legislation is simply inconceivable—but why? What considerations justify differentiating the private school from the family or the child from the adult?

3. State Regulation of Nonpublic Schools: The Problem of Discretion

Consider the following passage:

J. Elson
"STATE REGULATION OF NONPUBLIC SCHOOLS:
THE LEGAL FRAMEWORK" in
PUBLIC CONTROLS FOR PUBLIC SCHOOLS, edited by D. Erickson
120-133 (1969)

Nonpublic school laws vary widely in the degree to which they specify substantive standards and enforcement procedures. One of the few examples of detailed statutory prescription is the California Education Code which requires instruction in the subjects of public safety and accident prevention, physical education, fire prevention, the effects of alcohol and narcotics, and others.

Illustrative of statutes granting wide discretion in the implementation of legislative policy is the Nebraska provision empowering the state board of education to "establish standards and procedures for classifying, approving and accrediting schools, including the establishment of minimum standards and procedures for approving the opening of new schools, the continued legal operation of all schools . . . ."

Most nonpublic school statutes fall between these two extremes in prescribing substantive standards that still required the exercise of considerable discretion in their implementations.

The most common and troublesome instructional standard requires nonpublic schools to have courses of instruction equivalent to those in public schools. Typical expressions of this standard provide that nonpublic school instruction shall "be equivalent to that provided in the public schools," teach "subjects comparable to those taught in the public schools," and equal "in thoroughness and efficiency and in the progress made therein to that in the public schools . . . ."

Considerable discretion is necessary to implement these mandates, since their language gives little indication of how the legislature wants them-construed. One administrator might reasonably find that failure to provide courses in home economics violates the equivalency standard, while another might just as reasonably find nonequivalency only when nonpublic school instruction is virtually without educational value . . . .

Statutory vagueness may result not only in administrative and judicial confusion but also in the failure even to attempt implementation of statutory purposes. The seriousness of this problem is evidenced by the report that fifteen states take no steps to enforce statutory instructional requirements. The Michigan nonpublic school laws exemplify how statutory ambiguity can result in nonimplementation of legislative intentions.

The Michigan superintendent of public instruction is granted "supervision of all the private, denominational and parochial schools of this state in such matters and manner as is hereinafter provided . . . ." The statute specifies the purpose of this delegation of authority: "It is the intent of this act that the sanitary conditions of such schools, the course of study therein and the qualifications of the teachers thereof shall be of the same standard as provided by the general school laws of the state." It then requires that all nonpublic school teachers be certified, that nonpublic schools in violation of state law shall be closed, and, finally, that nonpublic schools must both teach "subjects comparable to those taught in the public schools" and comply with all provisions of the act, in order that their students may comply with the compulsory attendance requirement. Despite the twice-stated statutory intention that nonpublic schools have curriculum standards equivalent to public schools, the Michigan Department of Education reported that its grant of power is too vague to permit regular enforcement of the equivalent instruction requirement.

Legislatures could vastly improve nonpublic school regulation if they would define specifically the regulatory purpose and all the precise standards and procedures to be used in fulfilling that purpose. However, few legislatures even attempt to eliminate vagueness through detailed statutory definition, and none has ever succeeded.

Inept draftsmanship and political opposition often contribute to this failure. But the primary and unavoidable reason is that legislatures cannot possibly foresee and stipulate all the detailed, changing circumstances which a good administrator must consider in effectuating legislative policy . . . .

In applying a statutory mandate to dissimilar situations, individual judgment must have leeway to avoid inappropriate implementation of legislative policy. An especially wide grant of discretion would seem necessary for effective regulation of nonpublic schools since the variations in both the educational approachs of non-public schools and the character of the communities they serve defy sound classification by statutory formula. One questions the fairness and social value of statutes that prescribe the same compulsory standards for an Amish school, a Montessori school, and a mission school, or for an Exeter, a military academy, and a special school for slow learners and problem children.

The legislature, unlike an administrative agency, cannot devote sufficient time to the study of all the regulatory problems raised by these different types of schools and the communities they serve. Nor has it time to work out detailed solutions and review them in the light of changing circumstances. Unlike an administrative agency, it cannot develop increasingly better regulations through the accumulation of specialized knowledge in its rule-making and rule-enforcing functions. Only a department of education vested with ample discretion to make and enforce rules can reconcile legislative policy with the problems and purposes of each type of non-public school.

This approach is subject to the criticism that the result of giving any agency discretion to make and enforce its own rules will be sweeping and harsh controls exercised by administrators who want maximum extension of their jurisdiction.

The argument against expanding agency discretion does recognize, however, that the dangers from abuse of discretion vary in proportion to the degree of delegation of rule-making and rule-enforcing power. Although the inability of many state departments to impose serious restrictions may allow nonpublic schools to continue substandard teaching, it also prevents the departments from imposing harsh requirements not contemplated by the legislature. Perhaps in states where substandard nonpublic schools are not considered a danger, a lax system of enforcement is the best way to protect the independent role of the nonpublic school without completely abdicating state control in the face of extreme deficiencies. Where substandard nonpublic schools do jeopardize the welfare of society, however, there is an urgent need for ways to compel their compliance with instructional standards without subjecting them to unreasonable administrative demands.

Many state courts . . . attempt to curb administrative abuse of power by requiring all statutes delegating rule-making authority to specify standards for the agency to follow. The requirement has largely been futile and has been abandoned by several state courts. The inescapable difficulty in using statutory standards to check agency power is that standards effective in curbing abuse preclude needed discretionary authority, while standards allowing sufficient discretion are too vague and general to prevent abuse . . . .

In fifteen states administrative procedure acts have been enacted to provide safeguards for the rule-making and adjudicating functions. Two provisions are usually considered of greatest importance: first, that all interested parties after notice of rule making be given reasonable opportunity to present their own views to the rule-making officials; and second, that parties contesting enforcement of rules against them be given a hearing in which they can present evidence and arguments on all issues involved . . . .

The crux of the problem lies in providing safeguards against abuse of an agency's power to make comprehensive rules. The inescapable dilemma in this attempt is that on the one hand, the rule-making discretion needed to implement legislative policy is undermined by inflexible procedural safeguards, while, on the other hand, if that discretion is not safeguarded the administrator can largely pursue his own policy, regardless of legislative intent . . . .

Although the success of legislative policy often depends on enlightened rule making, there are no safeguards that can guarantee the making of wise rules. However, certain procedures, such as the requirement of an open hearing, can promote sound rule making. The hearing requirement is based on the assumption that through exchanging ideas with all the regulated parties the rule maker can more fully understand the position of those parties and, consequently, write wiser and fairer rules. It is an attempt to put into practice the salutary jurisprudential principal [sic] that decisions can be made in the public interest only to the extent that all the interests affected are first fully considered.

For reasons peculiar to the field of education the policy of considering all views before making rules is vital to effective nonpublic school regulation. The constant intellectual ferment in educational thought precludes the possibility that anyone can make rules to meet all school situations solely on the basis of his own belief in certain enduring principles of sound education. Traditional theories are being supplemented, amended, or discredited so rapidly that unswerving reliance on long-accepted, unreexamined ideas inevitably sacrifices the best for the easiest solutions.

Equally as important as willingness to consider different ideas is the predisposition to consider ideas from different people. More than in most areas of governmental regulation, in education valuable insights are not limited to persons with professional qualifications. They can come from anyone of intelligence, seriously concerned with educational problems, especially if they are his own.

The harm resulting from a rule maker's refusal seriously to consider challenging ideas from different sources is aggravated where the conflict between regulator and regulated stems from differences in cultural attitudes toward the proper social function of nonpublic schools. It seems a reasonable probability that where the two antagonistic parties join in a good faith discussion of the reasons behind their respective positions, mutual understanding will be promoted and will contribute to improved rule making and rule abiding . . . .

The bare hearing requirement is clearly insufficient to bring these small but important nonpublic school groups into communication with the rule makers. Hearings are often cumbersome, costly, and excessively time-consuming. Successful interchange with nonpublic groups requires a department of education to try a wide variety of tactics.

The most effective procedure for this purpose is to draft tentative rules and then submit them to the interested parties for written comments. A department of education can also sponsor periodic statewide nonpublic school conventions or hold smaller, more specialized conferences. Space in its bulletin or journal can be devoted to views of nonpublic school officials. It can initiate informal contacts through questionnaires, telephone calls, or personal consultations . . . . advisory committees made up of professional educators, religious leaders, and community spokesmen of various types could be the source of valuable ideas in proposing and reviewing rules governing nonpublic schools. The agency could also promote consideration of divergent views by employing people with diverse school backgrounds. Finally, inviting detailed criticism of the statutory scheme and agency practices by various nonagency experts could facilitate periodic reevaluation of the department's success in regulating nonpublic schools.

Although these tactics could stimulate illuminating exchanges of ideas, the legislature would be ill advised to require an agency to use them. Their success depends on the administrator's personal judgment of the type of issue involved, the proper timing, the dispositions of the parties, and the agency's past experiences. A statute cannot tell an administrator the proper time to hold a conference or consult outside advisors. It cannot estimate which problems could be best solved by soliciting suggestions from knowledgeable parties. The simple requirement of holding a hearing before rule making, Professor Davis points out, can cause much wasted effort when the rules being made concern minor matters such as parking in the agency lot or amending printers' errors in published regulations.

The costs in administrative efficiency must, thus, be carefully measured before binding agency discretion by procedural requirements. But even if the legislature is willing to sacrifice administrative efficiency for procedural protections, it has been noted that there are no safeguards that can require agencies to make wise and fair rules. Legislative oversight in the present condition of most state legislatures is virtually nonexistent. Judicial review is almost always available, but judges are usually reluctant to substitute their own ideas of wisdom and fairness for those of the agencies.

For wise and fair treatment under statutes delegating broad rule-making powers nonpublic schools must rely primarily on the intelligence and goodwill of government officials. Even assuming a high-caliber staff, it may be argued with some force that agency fair-mindedness is a product of happenstance, the luck to have a particular person in a particular position, and therefore cannot be depended upon for real protection. However, on deeper analysis it is apparent that government fairness in making and enforcing regulations originates in popular respect for the educational competence and social contributions of nonpublic schools. Without the support of public opinion, as it is reflected in the attitude of state officials, the only substantial protection against harsh nonpublic school controls is the defeat of the legislation authorizing the controls. In view of the harm done children educated in substandard nonpublic schools, this decision to preclude effective regulation is a difficult one to make. It would be far better for government and nonpublic school officials to avoid such an impasse by entering into a continuing dialogue to find common bases for constructive work together and practical methods for cooperative settlement of differences . . . .

Kenneth Culp Davis begins his discussion of "discretionary justice" with this observation: "[W]e should eliminate much unnecessary discretionary power and . . . should do much more than we have been doing to confine, to structure, and to check necessary discretionary power. The goal is not the maximum degree of confining, structuring, and checking; the goal is to find the optimum degree for each power in each set of circumstances." *Discretionary Justice: A Preliminary Inquiry* 3,4 (1969). Does Elson's analysis of appropriate regulatory policy satisfy this admittedly elusive standard? In contrasting alternative regulatory schemes, what choices among policy desiderata does Elson make? Is it possible to construct a workable regulatory scheme that relies less heavily on the wise exercise of discretion? Income tax laws and regulations represent perhaps the best-known example of a legal structure designed to minimize the exercise of discretion; is it conceivable, or sensible, to develop similarly detailed standards for nonpublic school regulation?

4. Problem: The Santa Fe School

The New Mexico State Board of Education, on the recommendation of the state department of education, has disapproved the secondary school program of the Santa Fe Community School (SFCS), a nonprofit, tax-exempt corporation that began three years ago. The state apparently disagrees with the "educational philosophy" of the school. Yet the school has attracted national attention, including descriptions in leading national publications and in John Holt's *What Do I Do Monday?* Beyond its own confines, the SFCS is helping to develop guidelines for cooperation among community schools in the Rio Grande area through the Rio Grande Educational Association, of which it is a founding member. The state's disapproval and accompanying threat of enforcement of the compulsory school attendance act against parents of SFCS school children raise significant constitutional issues concerning the limits of a state's right to regulate private education.

The disapproval was ostensibly based on alleged failures of the school to meet minimum state standards for private schools. Substantially identical to those for public schools, they fix requirements for teacher certification (there must be a certified teacher for each of thirty different required subjects), number and type of courses, and minimum enrollment (there must be fifty pupils per grade). They also contain a licensing procedure that obligates each new private school to obtain state approval before opening.

A new uniform-testing regulation subjects the SFCS and its patrons to additional burdens contrary to their educational principles by requiring all students in public and private schools to submit to periodic standardized testing. The costs of the program in public schools are met by the state; in nonpublic schools, they are paid for by the schools themselves.

The Santa Fe Community School has an accredited elementary school program for about forty children. Its high school had thirteen students last year and expected as many or more this year. After the state department released unfavorable publicity about the school's disapproved secondary program, however, only six high school students enrolled for this year. The school employed two certified teachers for the high school last year, a ratio of one teacher to seven students. But the two teachers were not certified in each of the thirty required areas.

Other private schools in the state have received waivers of several of the requirements for accreditation, including teacher certification and minimum class and library size. The exceptions are made for the leading preparatory schools in the state.

Assume that both the Santa Fe Community School and the parents of children attending that school have filed a lawsuit in a federal district court against the New

Mexico State Board of Education and the New Mexico State Department of Education. (This problem is taken from a prelitigation memorandum drawn up by attorneys for SFCS and the parents; therefore the facts are cast in terms favorable to them.) Are the actions of the state board and state department against the SFCS legal and constitutional under state and federal law? What additional legal material, if any, do you need in order fully to answer that question? What effect will the new portions of §77-10-2 have on the SFCS?

CONSTITUTION OF NEW MEXICO
ARTICLE XII
EDUCATION

Section 1. [Free public schools]
A uniform system of free public schools sufficient for the education of, and open to, all the children of school age in the state shall be established and maintained.
Sec. 5. [Compulsory school attendance]
Every child of school age and of sufficient physical and mental ability shall be required to attend a public or other school during such period and for such time as may be prescribed by law.
Sec. 6. [State department of public education—State board of education]
A. There is hereby created a "state department of public education" and a "state board of education." The state board of education shall determine public school policy and vocational educational policy and shall have control, management and direction of all public schools, pursuant to authority and powers provided by law. The board shall appoint a qualified, experienced educational administrator to be known as the superintendent of public instruction, who shall, subject to the policies established by the board, direct the operation of the state department of public education.
B. The members of the state board of education shall be elected at the general election next following the adoption of this amendment . . . .

NEW MEXICO PUBLIC SCHOOL CODE (Interim Supp 1972)
Article 2—State Board of Education

77-2-2. State board—Duties. Without limiting those powers granted to the state board pursuant to section 77-2-1 NMSA 1953, the state board shall perform the following duties:
A. properly and uniformly enforce the provisions of the Public School Code;
B. determine policy for the operation of all public schools and vocational education programs in the state; . . .
D. purchase and loan instructional material to students pursuant to the Instructional Material Law;
E. designate courses of instruction to be taught in all schools in the state to which instructional material is distributed pursuant to the Instructional Material Law;
F. adopt standards for the operation of business colleges, commercial departments of public schools, and for private schools and issue certificates of recognition to those colleges or schools meeting these standards;

G. prescribe courses of instruction in industrial and vocational education, including courses in domestic science, manual training and agriculture;

H. determine the qualifications for and issue a certificate to any person teaching, assisting teachers, supervising an instructional program, counseling, providing special instructional services or administering in public schools according to law and according to a system of classification adopted and published by the state board;

I. suspend or revoke a certificate held by a certified school instructor or administrator according to law for incompetency, immorality, or for any other good and just cause; . . .

K. prescribe courses of instruction, requirements for graduation and standards for all schools subject to its jurisdiction;

L. adopt regulations for the administration of all public schools and bylaws for its own administration;

M. require periodic reports on forms prescribed by it from all schools and their officials coming within the provisions of the Public School Code; . . .

P. require all accrediting agencies for schools in the state to act with its approval; . . .

R. require prior approval for any educational program in a public school which is to be conducted, sponsored, carried on or caused to be carried on by a private organization or agency; . . .

W. assess and evaluate for accreditation purposes at least one-third of all public schools each year through visits by department personnel to investigate the adequacy of pupil gain in standard required subject matter, adequacy of pupil activities, functional feasibility of public school and school district organization, adequacy of staff preparation and other matters bearing upon the education of qualified students;

X. provide for management and other necessary personnel to operate any public school or school district which has failed to meet requirements of law, state board standards or state board regulations; Provided, that such operation of the public school or district shall not include any consolidation or reorganization without the approval of the local board of such district.

Article 8—Certified School Personnel

77-8-1. Certificate requirement—Types of certificates—Forfeiture of claim—Exception.

A. Any person teaching, supervising an instructional program, counseling, providing special instructional services or administering in a public school shall hold a valid certificate authorizing the person to perform that function.

B. All certificates issued by the state board shall be standard certificates except that the state board may issue substandard and substitute certificates under certain circumstances. If a local school board certifies to the state board that an emergency exists in the hiring of a qualified person, the state board may issue a substandard certificate to a person not meeting the requirements for a standard certificate. The state board may also issue a substitute certificate to a person not meeting the requirements for a standard certificate to enable the person to perform the functions of a substitute teacher pursuant to the regulations of the state board. All substandard and substitute certificates issued shall be effective for only one school year. No person under the age of eighteen years shall hold a valid certificate, whether a standard, substandard or substitute . . . .

Article 10—Compulsory School Attendance and School Census

77-10-2. Compulsory school attendance—Responsibility.

A. Any person attaining six years of age prior to September 1 of a school year and until attaining seventeen years of age shall attend a public school, a private school maintaining courses of instruction approved by the state board, or a program of instruction offered by a state institution. At the request of the parent, guardian, or person having custody and control of the person to be enrolled, a person may be enrolled in a public school if his sixth birth date falls between September 1 and January 1 of the school year. A person may be excused from this requirement if:

(1) the person is specifically exempted by law from the provisions of this section;

(2) the person has graduated from a high school approved by the department of education;

(3) with consent of the parent, guardian, or person having custody and control of the person to be excused, the person is excused from the provisions of this section by the superintendent of schools of the school district in which the person is a resident, and such person is under eight years of age;

(4) the person is a high school student and has passed the general educational development test;

(5) the person is a high school student and can prove to the local school board that he is not personally benefiting from a high school program or has a justifiable reason for not attending school;

(6) the person is a high school student and can prove to the local school board that he has a plan for pursuing educational interest that the school is not satisfying; or

(7) the person is judged, based on standards and procedures adopted by the state board of education, to be unable to benefit from instruction because of mental, physical or emotional conditions.

B. A person subject to the provisions of the Compulsory School Attendance Law [77-10-1—77-10-7] shall attend school for at least the length of time of the school year that is established in the school district in which the person is a resident.

C. Any parent, guardian or person having custody and control of a person subject to the provisions of the Compulsory School Attendance Law is responsible for the school attendance of that person.

Before 1972, §77-10-2 read as follows:

A. Any person attaining six years of age prior to January 1 of a school year and until attaining seventeen years of age shall attend a public school, a private school maintaining courses of instruction approved by the state board, or a school offered by a state institution, unless:

(1) the person is specifically exempted by law from the provisions of this section;

(2) the person has graduated from a high school approved by the department of education;

(3) the person is physically incapable of attending or mentally incompetent to attend public school; or

(4) the person is excused from the provisions of this section by the superintendent of schools of the school district in which the person is a resident, and such person is under nine years of age.

B. State Regulation of Parentally Directed Education

Most states do not expressly permit parents to educate their own children. Indeed, the rise of the common school more than a century ago reflected, at least in part, a belief that parentally directed education was too haphazard an enterprise to satisfy state needs. States that do allow the child's formal education to take place in the home usually impose specific conditions. California requires that the parent have a teaching credential. Cal Educ Code §§13286, 13287 (West Supp 1972). New Jersey and New York both require that home instruction be "equivalent" to that provided in the public school. NY Educ Law §3204 (McKinney 1970); NJ Stats Ann §18A: 38-25 (West 1968). The two New Jersey cases presented below attempt to define equivalency.

STEPHENS v BONGART
15 NJM 80, 189 Atl 131 (Juv & Dom Rel Ct 1937)

Siegler, Judge

Helen Stephens, attendance officer of the school district of the town of West Orange in the county of Essex, filed her complaint against Gertrude R. Bongart and Benno Bongart, the defendants in this action, charging that they reside within the school district of the town of West Orange, and being the parents and having custody and control of William Bongart, aged twelve, and Robert Bongart, aged eleven, their children, have since the 5th day of April, 1936, failed to cause their said children regularly to attend the public schools of the school district of the said town of West Orange; further charging said defendants having neither caused said children to attend a day school in which there is given instruction equivalent to that provided in the public schools for children of similar grades and attainments, nor have they received equivalent instruction elsewhere than at school . . . .

The act upon which these proceedings are based, chapter 307 of the Laws of 1931 (NJ St Annual 1931, §185-165c), reads as follows:

> Every parent, guardian or other person having custody and control of a child between the ages of seven and sixteen years shall cause such child regularly to attend the public schools of such district or to attend a day school in which there is given instruction equivalent to that provided in the public schools for children of similar grades and attainments or to receive equivalent instruction elsewhere than at school unless such child is above the age of fourteen years . . . . Such regular attendance shall be during all the days and hours that the public schools are in session in said school district, unless it shall be shown to the satisfaction of the board of education of said school district that the mental condition of the child is such that he or she cannot benefit from instruction in the school or that the bodily condition of the child is such as to prevent his or her attendance at school.
>
> . . . .

The first point raised by the defendants is that the statute under which these proceedings are brought; to wit, chapter 307 of the Laws of 1931 is invalid because it invades the Fourteenth Amendment of the United States Constitution. The problem for determination is whether the statute, as construed and applied, unreasonably infringes the liberty guaranteed to the defendants by the Fourteenth Amendment: "No state shall . . . deprive any person of life, liberty, or property, without due process of law." This statute is a legitimate exercise of the police power of the state. The object of the legislation was to create an enlightened American citizenship in sympathy with our principles and ideals, and to prevent children reared in America from remaining ignorant and illiterate. If it is within the police power of the state to regulate wages, to legislate respecting housing conditions in crowded cities, to prohibit dark rooms in tenement houses, to compel landlords to place windows in their tenements which will enable their tenants to enjoy the sunshine, it is within the police power of the state to compel every resident of New Jersey so to educate his children that the light of American ideals will permeate the life of our future citizens . . . .

The defendants rely upon the authority of . . . *Pierce v Society of Sisters* . . . for support of their contention that the legislation under consideration is unconstitutional. The issue in the *Pierce* case . . . was not that involved here. There the court was considering property rights of the appellees; the right to engage in the business of conducting a school for the instruction of children; but throughout the whole case the question of the right of the state to require children to attend school was not challenged; this right appeared to be conceded . . . .

In *State v Hoyt* 84 NH 38, 146 A 170, 171 in dealing with the constitutional validity of the compulsory attendance statute, in substance like the statute in New Jersey, Chief Justice Peaslee said:

> The constitutionality of the compulsory school attendance statute . . . has not been considered to be an open question in this state . . . . "Free schooling furnished by the state is not so much a right granted to pupils as a duty imposed upon them for the public good. If they do not voluntarily attend the schools provided for them, they may be compelled to do so". . . . The defendants' claim that the federal guaranty of liberty enables them to set at defiance any attempt of the state to prescribe the means for ascertaining the sufficiency of educational facilities furnished and to be furnished as a substitute for the public school, goes far beyond anything that has been decided to be the law.
>
> . . . .

The second point for determination is whether or not the defendants provided instruction for their children equivalent to that provided in the public schools for children of similar grades and attainments.

This necessitates an analysis of the testimony. The proof is that the defendants' children, William, twelve, and Robert, eleven, were in the sixth and fifth grades, respectively, in the Washington Street School, West Orange, until April 3, 1936. From that date, these children failed to attend a public or day school, although proper notice was served upon the defendants to return the children to a school. The defendants admit they caused the children's withdrawal from the Washington School.

Since that time, the defendants claim that they instructed their children in their own home in the subjects taught in the fifth and sixth grades. This instruction, they claim, is equivalent to that provided in the public schools for children of similar grades and attainments. The case turns on this factual situation. 2 *Words and Phrases, Second Series* 312, defines the word *equivalent* as follows: "*Equivalent* means 'equal in worth or value, force, power, effect, import and the like.'"

. . . .

Quite definitely, the term refers to the giving of instruction equal in value and effect to that given in a public school. In determining this question, consideration must be given, first, to the matter of the ability of the parents to provide equivalent instruction, and, secondly, to a comparison of the quality, character, and methods of teaching employed by the defendants and that of the West Orange public school system. Mrs. Bongart was graduated from the Eastern District High School, New York City, in 1911. In 1917 she was a special student at Hunter College, evening course. This required three or four evenings a week, which she carried on for only two years. She studied economics, psychology, art, portrait work, charcoal work and painting; she majored in home economics. Mrs. Bongart had no teaching experience. She was married about fifteen years ago, and her chief employment was that of housewife. Mr. Bongart is a graduate of the University of Strassbourg, in the field of electrical and mechanical engineering. He never trained for teaching, but did have employment as a teacher at the New York Aerial School, Newark Technical School, and the Newark Junior High School until recently. He taught subjects in mechanical drawing and electrical engineering. The teachers in the elementary grades of the public schools, particularly the fifth and sixth grades in the West Orange school system, must have at least a high school education and three years at an approved normal school in the state of New Jersey.

The normal school curriculum includes a type of training and education intended to qualify students to teach in the elementary class in the subjects of English, history, science, sociology, civics, mathematics, hygiene, geography, art, music, and physical education. The major aim is to give the teachers training in techniques of presentation of material to elementary school students. That involves the proper selection of material, knowledge of children, and the organization of their work, so that every teacher should know the results which must be achieved in terms of knowledge, habits, skills, attitudes, and appreciations. Her training should qualify her to develop individuality and the personality of each child under her supervision. One of the major aims of our public school today is to teach the way in which the individual must fit into the social group. The evidence establishes that the teachers in the fifth and sixth grades of Washington School possess this training and qualify in these courses.

It is clear, upon comparison, that there is a substantial variance between the training, qualifications, and experience of the defendants and those obtaining in the public school system of West Orange.

Now, what was the instruction given by the defendants at their home? The children assemble, one in the dining room and the other in the front room, each morning at 9 o'clock, and continue until 12; they resume at 1 o'clock, and recess at 3 in the afternoon. They receive instruction in arithmetic, spelling, history, geography, language, and music. In the evening, the father instructs them in science between 7 and 9 o'clock.

In the study of arithmetic a textbook is used by Stone and Millis, dated 1914. There were no textbooks for spelling, language, music, civics, hygiene, and art;

while the textbooks used were outmoded and outdated, the latest published in 1921 and the oldest in 1881, and all certainly of questionable value in the instruction of children. Spelling was taught without a book, the mother giving twenty words at random each week, which the children had to learn and place in a notebook. The other subjects were taught by assigning periods of thirty or thirty-five minutes for each. Language was largely taught through the reading of the newspapers, the Literary Digest and the Saturday Evening Post. Poetry was principally taught by the use of an occasional piece of poetry out of the Sunday Times and the New York Daily News, a tabloid newspaper. No poems were memorized. Music was taught by listening to radio concerts. There were no song books or singing exercises. Mechanical drawing and current events were given by the father in the evening. The Newark Evening News and some other periodicals were sources from which current events were drawn for discussion. The Bible was read once in a while. The flag of the country was exhibited in front of the house on patriotic occasions. The mother spoke to them about hygiene and the danger of alcoholic beverages, but no hygiene textbook was used. There were no instructions in observance of patriotic holidays, and no observance of Arbor Day. There was no physical training except that which they got outside in the ordinary course of their play. They had membership in the YMCA, but failed to attend during September and October. Of this default the parents had no knowledge.

The instruction was interrupted from time to time by the mother's household duties, occasional shopping tours, and house callers. The defendants had no definite schedule for daily instruction. The evidence indicates that the boys obtained from children in school, periodically, information as to the subjects they were studying in school, and transmitted that information to their mother, who guided herself in instructing the children, to some extent, by it. They had no marks for their work. There were no daily work papers, tests, or examinations; at least, there were none presented in evidence. In fact, the mother admits she had no standard by which to determine whether the children were absorbing the instruction she was attempting to give. There was no organized supervision over the teaching the defendants gave; the work of the children, and the results accomplished, were never submitted to any other competent authority for supervision, criticism, or approval.

A summary of the methods of instruction at the Washington School of West Orange will be useful for comparative purposes. The elementary grades are supervised by a specially trained person, who has complete supervision over the courses of study, the textbooks used, and the methods employed by the teachers in transmitting knowledge and the building and developing of the personalities of the children. The school is organized as a miniature community center, a sort of city, where each child considers himself a citizen, with duties toward the community as is required on the outside. The educational structure thus developed is in the nature of a group enterprise, where the children work together for the common good. The teacher creates the atmosphere and becomes the guiding influence. A high discipline is maintained by strict attention to the development of habits, skills and attitudes. There is group discussion. The children bring in articles from the outside. They study the biographies of great men, and discuss their achievements. In the fifth and sixth grades, reading, writing, spelling, arithmetic, English, history, geography, civics, hygiene, safety education, music, art, and penmanship are taught. The children are taught to use the dictionary. The norm for instruction may be found in several monographs on each subject, provided by the state board of education, and strict adherence is required. In the fifth grade, there are seven textbooks in daily use to cover the subjects. In the sixth grade, there are also seven textbooks, supplemented by thirteen reference and reading books used in connection with their courses, and, in addition, the school library is available to them. Every text, reading, and reference book, twenty-six in number, produced in evidence, is carefully selected in accordance with the regulations of the state board of education and approved by the supervisor of the elementary grades and by the board of education of West Orange. There is a student schedule for the fifth and sixth grades, which provides for instruction from 8:45 a.m. until 3 p.m. from Monday to Friday, inclusive. The curriculum provides for instruction in the development of abilities, habits, and skills. Instruction is also given by way of travel lectures, picture studies, art and music, so that every child has something to talk about. Thus, an audience situation is created for the children, where each child is required to rise and speak to the entire group. This creates self-confidence, and tends to adjust the child to the social group.

One poem a week, and appreciation for the beauties of nature and literature are taught. Besides teaching arithmetic from texts, they instruct in practical matters requiring arithmetic. Geography is taught to meet life situations by creating interest in world travel and training the children to visualize, in their reading, places that they have studied. In music, each child is allowed to develop whatever talent he may possess. In art, each child learns the harmony of color in dress, interior decoration, and everyday life. Every morning the children have a reading from the Bible and recite the Lord's prayer. They salute the flag and sing patriotic songs. They observe Arbor Day and all patriotic holidays. A course in safety education and fire prevention is pursued. The month of June is devoted to review. They have physical education four periods each week under a special supervisor. In the civics course, the children are on the lookout for all material in current events. There are three school magazines. Washington School has a monthly newspaper, and all children are eligible to participate in its columns . . . .

From this comparison and analysis of the evidence, I find (1) that the education, training, and equipment of the defendants are substantially inadequate, as compared with those of the public school teacher; (2) that the schedule of study and the program of activities of the defendants are irregular, uncertain, and without form, while the public school curriculum is definite and allots a specified time and, in most cases, a special teacher for every subject studied in the fifth and sixth grades; (3) that the instruction given by the defendants is without proper or modern textbooks, lacks supervision by competent authorities of pupil and teacher, lacks a method, standard, or other means of determining the progress or attainments of the child; none of which deficiencies are present in the public school; (4) that the teaching of discipline and health habits lacks plan and a trained method, fixing responsibility on the child for its execution; while, at the school, it is part of a definite program of character education; (5) that the defendants cannot provide for group or class teaching, and lack the ability to develop attitudes and create a social setting so that the children may be trained to deal with their playmates and friends as a part of a social group; (6) that the public school system provides such social groups and lays emphasis on its development, and stresses the adjustment of the child to group life and group activity and a course of living that he will be required to follow and meet as he goes out into the world.

The primary function of education is to get an understanding and interpretation of modern civilization. In the early days of the Republic, the idea that an educated citizenship lies at the very foundation of a democratic government has defined our philosophy of national development. For these reasons, the maintenance of an adequate system of public education for youth is a fundamental responsibility of any commonwealth. The public school system of New Jersey embodies the highest ideals of American democracy, and has developed a program which offers unusual opportunities to the children of our state. All citizens have a deep interest in our public schools, and should take pride in the high rank which they occupy in the nation. To deny children instruction seems as unnatural as to withhold their necessary subsistence. Education is brought, as it were, to the very door of all classes of society, and ignorance is quite inexcusable. The failure of the parents to provide the child with the benefits of that opportunity should be a matter of great concern when at issue. The education of youth is of such vast importance and of such singular utility in the journey of life that it obviously carries its own recommendation with it, for on it, in a great measure, depends all that we ever hope to be; every perfection that a generous and well-disposed mind would gladly arrive at. It is this that usually renders one man preferable to another. And, as the great end of learning is to teach man to know himself and to fit him for life, so he who knows most is enabled to practice best and to be an example for those who know but little.

The schools, whose function frequently is thought of solely in material terms, have a far more important responsibility. They must aid parents, not simply in the training of their children for the trades and professions, whose criterion of success too often is the amount of money they can make, but, rather, the training and development of men and women of character; men and women whose minds have been trained to the understanding of basic principles and ideals, with the courage and strength of will to live up to and apply them in their daily lives.

I incline to the opinion that education is no longer concerned merely with the acquisition of facts; the instilling of worthy habits, attitudes, appreciations, and skills is far more important than mere imparting of subject matter. A primary objective of education today is the development of character and good citizenship. Education must impart to the child the way to live. This brings me to the belief that, in a cosmopolitan area such as we live in, with all the complexities of life, and our reliance upon others to carry out the functions of education, it is almost impossible for a child to be adequately taught in his home. I cannot conceive how a child can receive in the home instruction and experiences in group activity and in social outlook in any manner or form comparable to that provided in the public school. To give him less than that is depriving the child of the training and development of the most necessary emotions and instincts of life. I cannot accept the theory asserted by Mr. Bongart that, "I am not interested in method, but in results." That theory is archaic, mechanical, and destructive of the finer instincts of the child. It does seem to me, too, quite unlikely that this type of instruction could produce a child with all the attributes that a person of education, refinement, and character should possess.

I have carefully observed the defendants' children in court, their demeanor, their responses under examination, and their reaction to the proceedings while in court, and there is clear evidence that it is their belief that they are on a "grand holiday," free from the restraints, discipline, and responsibility of other children in school attendance. All of this seems to me to be attributable to the course adopted and pursued by the parents. I have also carefully examined all the evidence and exhibits, and it is my opinion that the defendants have failed to give their children instruction equivalent to that provided in the public schools in the fifth and sixth grades, but, rather, have engaged in a haphazard and hit-or-miss kind of instruction, not calculated to conform with the provisions of the statute, and that both defendants actively and independently participated in causing their children not to go to the public school or a day school. I have been satisfied beyond a reasonable doubt by the evidence of the guilt of both defendants as charged. Both defendants are hereby deemed to be disorderly persons.

STATE v MASSA
95 NJ Super 382, 231 A2d 252 (Morris County Ct 1967)

Collins, J. C. C.

This is a trial *de novo* on appeal from the Pequannock Township Municipal Court. Defendants were charged and convicted with failing to cause their daughter Barbara, age twelve, regularly to attend the public schools of the district and further for failing to either send Barbara to a private school or provide an equivalent education elsewhere than at school, contrary to the provisions of NJSA 18:14-14. The municipal magistrate imposed a fine of $2490 for both defendants.

Mr. and Mrs. Massa appeared *pro se*. Mrs. Massa conducted the case; Mr. Massa concurred.

The state presented two witnesses who testified that Barbara had been registered in the Pequannock Township School but failed to attend the sixth grade class from April 25, 1966, to June 1966 and the following school year from September 8, 1966, to November 16, 1966—a total consecutive absence of eighty-four days.

Mrs. Massa testified that she had taught Barbara at home for two years before September 1965. Barbara returned to school in September 1965, but began receiving her education at home again on April 25, 1966.

Mrs. Massa said her motive was that she desired the pleasure of seeing her daughter's mind develop. She felt she wanted to be with her child when the child would be more alive and fresh. She also maintained that in school much time was wasted and that at home a student can make better use of her time.

Mrs. Massa is a high school graduate. Her husband is an interior decorator. Neither holds a teacher's certificate. However, the state stipulated that a child may be taught at home and also that Mr. or Mrs. Massa need not be certified by the state of New Jersey to so teach. The sole issue in this case is one of equivalency. Have defendants provided their daughter with an education equivalent to that provided by the Pequannock Township School System?

Mrs. Massa introduced into evidence nineteen exhibits. Five of these exhibits, in booklet form, are condensations of basic subjects, are concise and seem to contain all the basic subject material for the respective subjects. Mrs. Massa also introduced textbooks which are used as supplements to her own compilations as well as for test material and written problems.

Mrs. Massa introduced English, spelling and mathematics tests taken by her daughter at the Pequannock School after she had been taught for two years at home. The lowest mark on these tests was a B . . . .

There is also a report by an independent testing service of Barbara's scores on standard achievement tests. They show that she is considerably higher than the national median except in arithmetic.

Mrs. Massa satisfied this court that she has an established program of teaching and studying. There are definite times each day for the various subjects and recreation. She evaluates Barbara's progress through testing. If Barbara has not learned something which has been taught, Mrs. Massa then reviews that particular area.

Barbara takes violin lessons and attends dancing school. She also is taught art by her father, who has taught this subject in various schools.

Mrs. Massa called Margaret Cordasco as a witness. She had been Barbara's teacher from September 1965 to April 1966. She testified basically that Barbara was bright, well behaved and not different from the average child her age except for some trouble adjusting socially.

The state called as a witness David MacMurray, the assistant superintendent of Pequannock Schools. He testified that the defendants were not giving Barbara an equivalent education. Most of his testimony dealt with Mrs. Massa's lack of certification and background for teaching and the lack of social development of Barbara because she is being taught alone.

He outlined procedures which Pequannock teachers perform, such as evaluation sheets, lesson plans and use of visual aids. He also stressed specialization since Pequannock schools have qualified teachers for certain specialized subjects. He did not think the defendants had the specialization necessary to teach all basic subjects. He also testified about extra-curricular activity, which is available but not required.

The state placed six exhibits in evidence. These included a more recent mathematics book than is being used by defendants, a sample of teacher evaluation, a list of visual aids, sample schedules for the day and lesson plans, and an achievement testing program . . . .

NJSA 18:14-14 provides:

Every parent, guardian or other person having custody and control of a child between the ages of six and sixteen years shall cause such child regularly to attend the public schools of the district or a day school in which there is given instruction equivalent to that provided in the public schools for children of similar grades and attainments *or to receive equivalent instruction elsewhere than at school.* (Emphasis added.)

State v Vaughn 44 NJ 142, 207 A2d 537 (1965), interpreted the above statute to permit the parent having charge and control of the child to elect to substitute one of the alternatives for public school. It is then incumbent upon the parent to introduce evidence showing one of the alternatives is being substituted. "If there is such evidence in the case, then the ultimate burden of persuasion remains with the state.". . .

NJSA 18:14-39 provides for the penalty for violation of NJSA 18:14-14:

A parent, guardian or other person having charge or control of a child between the ages of six and sixteen years, who shall fail to comply with any of the provisions of this article relating to his duties shall be deemed a disorderly person and shall be subject to a fine of not more than $5 for a first offense and not more than $25 for each subsequent offense, in the discretion of the court. . . .

This case presents two questions on the issue of equivalency for determination.

What does the word *equivalent* mean in the context of NJSA 18:14-14? And, has the state carried the required burden of proof to convict defendants?

In *Knox v O'Brien* 7 NJ Super 608, 72 A2d 389 (1950), the county court interpreted the word *equivalent* to include not only academic equivalency but also the equivalency of social development. This interpretation appears untenable in the face of the language of our own statute and also the decisions in other jurisdictions.

If the interpretation in *Knox* were followed, it would not be possible to have children educated outside of school. Under the *Knox* rationale, in order for children to develop socially it would be necessary for them to be educated in a group. A group of students being educated in the same manner and place would constitute a de facto school. Our statute provides that children may receive an equivalent education elsewhere than at school. What could have been intended by the legislature by adding this alternative?

The legislature must have contemplated that a child could be educated alone provided the education was equivalent to the public schools. Conditions in today's society illustrate that such situations exist. Examples are the child prodigy whose education is accelerated by private tutoring, or the infant performer whose education is provided by private tutoring. If group education is required by our statute, then these examples as well as all education at home would have to be eliminated . . . .

Faced with exiguous precedent in New Jersey and having reviewed the above cited cases in other states, this court holds that the language of the New Jersey statute, NJSA 18:14-14, providing for "equivalent education elsewhere than at school," requires only a showing of academic equivalence. As stated above, to hold that the statute requires equivalent social contact and development as well would emasculate this alternative and allow only group education, thereby eliminating private tutoring or home education. A statute is to be interpreted to uphold its validity in its entirety if possible . . . . This is the only reasonable interpretation available in this case which would accomplish this end.

Having determined the intent of the legislature as requiring only equivalent academic instruction, the only remaining question is whether the defendants provided their daughter with an education equivalent to that available in the public schools. After reviewing the evidence presented by both the state and the defendants, this court finds that the state has not shown beyond a reasonable doubt that defendants failed to provide their daughter with an equivalent education.

The majority of testimony of the state's witnesses dealt with the lack of social development.

The other point pressed by the state was Mrs. Massa's lack of teaching ability and techniques based upon her limited education and experience. However, this court finds this testimony to be inapposite to the actual issue of equivalency under the New Jersey statute and the stipulations of the state. In any case, from my observation of her while testifying and during oral argument, I am satisfied that Mrs. Massa is self-educated and well qualified to teach her daughter the basic subjects from grades one through eight. . . .

It is the opinion of this court that defendants' daughter has received and is receiving an education equivalent to that available in the Pequannock public schools. There is no indication of bad faith or improper motive on defendants' part. Under a more definite statute with sufficient guidelines or a lesser burden of proof, this might not necessarily be the case. However, within the framework of the existing law and the nature of the stipulations by the state, this court finds the defendant not guilty and reverses the municipal court conviction. . . .

Notes and Questions

1. Contrasting *Bongart* and *Massa*

Note the curt treatment the *Bongart* court gives to the argument that New Jersey's compulsory attendance law impinges on Bongart's liberty. Is its analysis satisfactory?

The *Bongart* definition of equivalency renders compulsory education synonymous with compulsory schooling. "[I]n a cosmopolitan area such as we live in . . . it is almost inconceivable for a child to be adequately taught in his home . . . ." 15 NJM at 92, 189 A at 137. Is the conclusion empirically defensible? Is it a justifiable interpretation of a statute that expressly permits equivalent instruction to take place "elsewhere than the school"?

Massa defines equivalency in a manner that permits parents to educate their own children at home. But is the process by which the court attempts to match fact situation to statutory requirement different in the two cases? How does the court in each case determine whether the parent is qualified to serve as teacher? Whether the curriculum provided at home is adequate? Whether social as well as academic development should be treated as part of the definition of equivalency?

The statutory "equivalency" language appears to compel the same analysis that these questions implicitly criticize. How might one draft legislation to render more manageable the task of regulating home instruction? Are the issues identical to those posed by the task of developing legislation to regulate nonpublic schools?

2. Problem: Too Bright Children

The state of California compels children not otherwise excused to attend either a public or state-approved private school, or to receive instruction from a tutor holding a state teaching credential. One California family, unhappy with the poor progress that its children were making in school, decided to educate them at home. The children were enrolled in a correspondence course, where they did astoundingly well: the youngsters covered as much as five years of work in eighteen months. Suit was brought against the youngsters, charging them with habitual truancy. During the trial, the state introduced a school psychologist's report that, while admitting the children were "of better than average intelligence" and "well adjusted," concluded that they would be better off "in school [where] each individual child would be in his own age group and would have a better chance to compete and to learn by hearing the others go over the same class work." The family introduced evidence of the children's academic progress. What result? See *Shinn v People* 16 Cal Rptr 165 (4th Dist 1961). But see *State v Paterman* 32 Ind App 655, 70 NE 550 (1904); *Sheppart v State* 306 P2d 346 (Okla Crim App 1957). In these cases, the courts had no "equivalency" legislation on which to rest a decision. Do parents have a constitutional right to provide equivalent education? Should the court inquire in specific cases, such as *Shinn*, whether the purposes of the compulsory education laws are satisfied, even if the way in which those purposes have been satisfied deviates from legal requirements?

Cases such as *Bongart* and *Shinn* are relatively rare legal events. Does that fact suggest that few parents wish to educate their children at home? That most school districts are not interested in enforcing compulsory school legislation? Mr. Shinn asserted that the trial judge in his case was "under pressure." What sort of pressure might exist in cases like *Shinn*?

IV. Education Vouchers

A. An Alternative Model for the Regulation of Education

Center for the Study of Public Policy,
EDUCATION VOUCHERS (1970)

1. An Overview

The system of education vouchers . . . would make it possible for parents to translate their concern for their children's education into action. If they did not like the education their child was getting in one school (or if the child did not like it), he could go to another. By fostering both active parental interest and educational variety, a voucher system should improve all participating schools, both public and private.

Under the proposed voucher system, a publicly accountable agency would issue a voucher for a year's schooling for each eligible child. This voucher could be turned over to any school which had agreed to abide by the rules of the voucher system. Each school would turn in its vouchers for cash. Thus, parents would no longer be forced to send their children to the school around the corner simply because it was around the corner. If the school was attractive and desirable, it would not be seriously affected by the institution of a voucher plan. If not, attendance might fall, perhaps forcing the school to improve.

Even if no new schools were established under the voucher system, the responsiveness of existing schools would probably increase. But new schools will be established. Some parents will get together to create schools reflecting their special perspectives or their children's special needs. Educators with new ideas—or old ideas that are now out of fashion in the public schools—will also be able to set up their own schools. Entrepreneurs who think they can teach children better and cheaper than the public schools will also have an opportunity to do so.

None of this ensures that every child will get the education he needs, but it does make such a result more likely than at present . . . .

[Education voucher plans raise innumerable questions.] Who would be eligible for vouchers? How would their value be determined? Would parents be allowed to supplement the vouchers from their own funds? What requirements would schools have to meet before cashing vouchers? What arrangements would be made for the children whom no school wanted to educate? Would church schools be eligible? Would schools promoting unorthodox political views be eligible? Once the advocates of vouchers begin to answer such questions, it becomes clear that the catch-phrase around which they have united stands not for a single panacea, but for a multitude of controversial programs, many of which have little in common.

These diverse voucher schemes can be viewed merely as different approaches to the regulation of the educational marketplace. Some schemes propose no regulation at all, counting on the "hidden hand" to ensure that the sum total of private choices promotes the public good. Others involve considerable economic regulation, aimed at offsetting differences in parental income and at providing schools with incentives to educate certain kinds of children. Still other schemes involve not only economic regulation, but administrative regulations aimed at ensuring that schools which receive public money do not discriminate against disadvantaged children. Finally, some schemes would establish extensive regulations to ensure that schools provided the public with usable information about what the school was trying to do and how well it was succeeding in doing it . . . .

[A] voucher plan should have two objectives:

—To improve the education of children, particularly disadvantaged children;
—To give parents, and particularly disadvantaged parents, more control over the kind of education their children get . . . .

These broad generalizations require some elaboration. First, it is important to decide whether "improving the education of the disadvantaged" means improvement relative to the education offered advantaged children today. We believe that, at least in education, closing the gap between the advantaged and disadvantaged is of paramount importance. This conviction is central to our proposals for regulating the educational marketplace, so the reasons for it require explanation . . . .

[I]f the upheavals of the 1960s have taught us anything, it should be that merely increasing the gross national product, the absolute level of government spending, and the mean level of educational attainment will not solve our basic economic, social and political problems. These problems do not arise because the nation as a whole is poor or ignorant. They arise because the benefits of wealth, power, and knowledge have been unequally distributed and because many Americans believe that these inequalities are unjust. A program which seeks to improve education must therefore focus on inequality, attempting to close the gap between the disadvantaged and the advantaged.

Having said that regulatory machinery ought to help close the gap between the advantaged and the disadvantaged, we must also say something about how this might be done.

First, America must *reallocate educational resources* so as to expose "difficult" children to their full share of the bright, talented, sensitive teachers, instead of exposing them to less than their share, as at present . . . .

Second, America must alter *enrollment patterns* so that disadvantaged children have more advantaged classmates . . . .

All this implies that a competitive market is unlikely to help disadvantaged children unless it is regulated so as to:

—provide substantially more money to schools that enroll disadvantaged children than to schools which enroll only advantaged children; and
—prevent an increase in segregation by race, income, ability, and "desirable" behavior patterns.

The second general requirement of a regulatory system is that it give parents more control than they now have over the kind of education their children receive. We assume that increasing parents' sense of control over their environment and over their children's life chances is an end in itself both because it makes parents' lives less frustrating and because it makes them more effective advocates of their family's interest in noneducational areas.

Increasing parents' control over the kind of education their children receive should, however, also increase the chances that their children get a good education. The more control parents have over what happens to their children, the more responsible they are likely to feel for the results. This could easily make them take a more active role in educating their children at home. In addition, parents tend to care more than public servants about making sure that their child gets whatever he needs. The intensity of the typical parent's concern is, of course, often partially or entirely offset by his naivete about what would actually be good for his child or by his inability to get what he thinks the child needs. Nonetheless, we think that on the average parents are unlikely to make choices that are any worse than what their public schools now offer.

For parental choice to make a difference, however, genuine alternatives must really be available. "Good" education will always be in short supply, even if the parents are given money to buy it. Most (though not all) disadvantaged parents will want the same kinds of education as advantaged parents. When the two groups apply to the same "good" schools, disadvantaged children will not normally get their share of places. If disadvantaged parents are to feel that they also have control over the kinds of education their children receive, the market must be regulated in such a way that disadvantaged children have a fair chance of being admitted to the school of their choice.

The foregoing criteria do not exhaust the possible yardsticks for evaluating alternative regulatory systems. Before presenting our proposals it may therefore be useful to review the principal objections that others have raised to vouchers as a device for promoting competition and choice.

First, integrationists fear that vouchers would make it harder to achieve racial integration. This might result in a voucher system's being declared unconstitutional, as has already happened in four Southern states. Even if the system were not declared unconstitutional, it would be undesirable if it intensified rather than alleviated racial separation.

Second, civil libertarians fear that vouchers would break down the separation of church and state. Again, this might result in a voucher scheme's being declared unconstitutional. Even if it did not, it could unleash a series of bitter political struggles from which American has in the past been relatively exempt.

Third, egalitarians have emphasized that an unregulated market would increase the expenditures of the rich more than it increased those of the poor, exacerbating present resource inequalities instead of reducing them.

Fourth, public school men have feared that the public schools would become the "schools of last resort" and hence dumping grounds for students no other schools wanted.

Finally, some educators have argued that parents are not qualified to decide how their children should be educated and that giving parents a choice would encourage the growth of bad schools, not good ones . . . .

[A]n additional voucher system which [might resolve these problems] would work in the following manner:

1. An Educational Voucher Agency (EVA) would be established to administer the vouchers. Its governing board might be elected or appointed, but in either case

it should be structured so as to represent minority as well as majority interests. The EVA might be an existing local board of education, or it might be a new agency with a larger or smaller geographic jurisdiction. The EVA would receive all federal, state, and local education funds for which children in the area were eligible. It would pay this money to schools only in return for vouchers. (In addition, it would pay parents for children's transportation costs to the school of their choice.)

2. The EVA would issue a voucher to every family in its district with school-age children. The value of the basic voucher would initially equal the per pupil expenditure of the public schools in the area. Schools which took children from families with below-average incomes would receive additional payments, on a scale that might, for example, make the maximum payment for the poorest child double the basic voucher.

3. In order to become an "approved voucher school," eligible to cash vouchers, a school would have to:

a. accept a voucher as full payment of tuition;

b. accept any applicant so long as it had vacant places;

c. if it had more applicants than places, fill at least half these places by picking applicants randomly and fill the other half in such a way as not to discriminate against ethnic minorities;

d. accept uniform standards established by the EVA regarding suspension and expulsion of students;

e. agree to make a wide variety of information about its facilities, teachers, program, and students available to the EVA and to the public;

f. maintain accounts of money received and disbursed in a form that would allow both parents and the EVA to determine whether a school operated by a board of education was getting the resources to which it was entitled on the basis of its vouchers, whether a school operated by a church was being used to subsidize other church activities, and whether a school operated by a profit-making corporation was siphoning off excessive amounts to the parent corporation;

g. meet existing state requirements for private schools regarding curriculum, staffing, and the like.

Control over policy in an approved voucher school might be vested in an existing local school board, a PTA, or any private group. No governmental restrictions would be placed on curriculum, staffing, and the like except those established for all private schools in a state.

4. Just as at present, the local board of education (which might or might not be the EVA) would be responsible for ensuring that there were enough places in publicly managed schools to accommodate every school-age child who did not want to attend a privately managed school. If a shortage of places developed for some reason, the board of education would have to open new schools or create more places in existing schools. (Alternatively, it might find ways to encourage privately managed schools to expand, presumably by getting the EVA to raise the value of the voucher.)

5. Every spring, each family would submit to the EVA the name of the school to which it wanted to send each of its school-age children next fall. Any child already enrolled in voucher school would be guaranteed a place, as would any sibling of a child enrolled in a voucher school. So long as it had room, a voucher school would

be required to admit all students who listed it as a first choice. If it did not have room for all applicants, a school could fill half its places in whatever way it wanted, choosing among those who listed it as a first choice. It could not, however, select these applicants in such a way as to discriminate against racial minorities. It would then have to fill remaining places by a lottery among the remaining applicants. All schools with unfilled places would report these to the EVA. All families whose children had not been admitted to their first choice school would then choose an alternative school which still had vacancies. Vacancies would then be filled in the same manner as in the first round. This procedure would continue until every child had been admitted to a school.

6. Having enrolled their children in a school, parents would give their vouchers to the school. The school would send the vouchers to the EVA and would receive a check in return. . . .

[A] system of the kind just described would avoid the dangers usually ascribed to a tuition voucher scheme.

—it should increase the share of the nation's educational resources available to disadvantaged children.
—it should produce at least as much mixing of blacks and whites, rich and poor, clever and dull, as the present system of public education.
—it should ensure advantaged and disadvantaged parents the same chance of getting their children into the school of their choice.
—it should provide parents (and the organizations which are likely to affect their decisions) whatever information they think they need to make intelligent choices among schools.
—it should avoid conflict with both the Fourteenth Amendment prohibition against racial discrimination and with First Amendment provisions regarding church and state . . . .

2. Seven Alternative Economic Models

[This discussion considers] seven alternative education voucher plans, i.e., sets of ground rules for distributing money to voucher schools . . . . [T]he plans resemble one another in that per pupil spending in the voucher schools would at least equal what was spent in the public schools in the district before the voucher plan went into effect. The plans, however, regulate schools' efforts to get money in different ways. . . .

1. Unregulated Market Model. Perhaps the simplest and certainly the commonest proposal for vouchers is to provide every child with a flat grant or tax credit which his family could use to pay tuition at the school of its choice. The amount of the grant would be determined by legislators, but most advocates of the plan assume that the grant would be roughly equal to the present level of expenditure in the public schools. Most advocates also assume that public schools would continue to exist, and that they would charge tuition equal to the amount of the grant. This is the version of vouchers advocated by Milton Friedman and others.[1] . . .

2. Unregulated Compensatory Model. In order to protect the poor against an unregulated marketplace, some advocates of vouchers have proposed making the value of vouchers higher for children from low-income families.

---

1. See M. Friedman, *Capitalism and Freedom* chap 6 (1962).

Theodore Sizer and Phillip Whitten have proposed one version of this plan.[2] Families with income below $2,000 would receive $1,500 vouchers. The value of the voucher would decline to zero as the family's income approached the national average. Families with incomes above the national average would receive no subsidy. Sizer and Whitten clearly do not envisage this plan as an *alternative* to the present system, but rather as a *supplement* to it. They do not explain whether a child who stayed in an existing public school would bring that school the full value of his voucher, or whether he would only bring the difference between his voucher and what the public school was already receiving from other public sources for the student. Were publicly controlled schools to receive the voucher *in addition* to other public monies, it would be extraordinarily difficult for privately controlled schools to compete. We will therefore assume that the value of the voucher would be reduced by the amount of current tax subsidy to any given school, putting publicly and privately controlled schools on the same footing.

If this were done, the Sizer proposal would have the effect of giving the poor some opportunity to buy their way into privately controlled schools, just as the rich now do. It would *not* give the middle classes such an opportunity, since they would receive little or no subsidy and would not be able to pay $1,000 or $1,500 tuition from their own resources . . . .

3. Compulsory Private Scholarship Model. The compulsory scholarship model resembles the unregulated market in that schools would be allowed to charge whatever tuition they wished. But they would also be required to provide enough scholarships so that no applicant's family had to pay more than it could afford. Several well-endowed private schools follow this policy, as do a number of wealthy private colleges. The colleges calculate parents' ability to pay from formulas developed by the College Scholarship Service (CSS). They then guarantee every successful applicant enough financial aid from one source or another so that he can pay tuition, room, and board without getting any more help from home than required by the CSS formula.

If a scheme like this were adopted as public policy, legislative bodies would presumably establish formulas equivalent to those of the CSS. In theory, any public or private voucher school would apply these formulas to raise additional funds from its more affluent parents. If this money were allocated evenly to all sort of pupils, the effect would be to "overcharge" the rich and "undercharge" the poor, relative to costs . . . .

4. The Effort Voucher. While it seems to be impractical to force schools to subsidize needy students from their own receipts, it might be possible to establish a system in which the EVA did so. At first glance the simplest way to do this is for each family to pay what it can afford, based on some official formula, and for the EVA to pay the rest. The difficulty with this is that if a family's liability for tuition depends exclusively on its income and not at all on what the school spends, the market no longer puts any check on school expenditures. Schools will raise tuition higher and higher in an effort to improve their programs, but parents will pay a fixed amount of tuition based on their income. The rising cost of education will therefore be absorbed entirely from the public treasury. At this point legislators

2. T. Sizer & P. Whitten, "A Proposal for a Poor Children's Bill of Rights," *Psychology Today* (August 1968).

will almost certainly intervene and put upper limits on what tuition a school can charge.

The most practical approach to this problem is probably the one outlined by John Coons and his associates.[3] The Coons model gives every school a choice between four different levels of expenditure, ranging from roughly the present public school level to two-to-three times that level. Schools at the lowest level would be almost subsidized by the state, although at each level parents are expected to pay at least a token charge. The size of their contribution would depend *both* on the family's ability to pay *and* on the cost of the school the family chose. The government would contribute the difference between what a family paid and what the school spent per pupil . . . .

5. "Egalitarian" Model. What we have called the "egalitarian" approach to vouchers would provide vouchers of equal value to all children and would prohibit any school which cashed the vouchers from charging tuition beyond the value of the voucher. It seems reasonable to assume that the value of vouchers would resemble the present and projected levels of per pupil expenditure in public schools . . . .

6. Achievement Model. All of the foregoing models assume that the value of a voucher is determined by the characteristics of the family of the child receiving it. There is another possible approach, however, under which the value of a voucher is determined not by how much the school "needs" to educate the child, nor by how much the parents "want to spend" on the child, but by whether the school actually succeeds in teaching the child what the state (or the parent) wants taught . . . .

7. Regulated Compensatory Model. The regulated compensatory model resembles the egalitarian model in that every child would receive a voucher roughly equal to the cost of the public schools of his area. No voucher school would be allowed to charge tuition beyond the value of the voucher. If schools wanted to increase their expenditure per pupil beyond the level of the vouchers, they could seek subventions from churches or from federal agencies and foundations for special purposes. They could also increase their incomes by enrolling additional children who were in some way disadvantaged. The extra costs of educating these children would be defrayed by the EVA. The EVA would pay every school a special "supplementary education fee" for every child with special educational problems.

Notes and Questions

1. Vouchers and State Regulation

All of the voucher plans described in the preceding excerpt ostensibly provide parents and children with greater choice concerning education than does the present system. To that extent, they make it financially feasible for all families to use the *Pierce*-guaranteed right to attend nonpublic schools. They also provide assurance of financial support to the several hundred "free schools" that have emerged in recent years as alternatives to public and traditional private institutions.

3. J. Coons, W. Clune & S. Sugarman, *Private Wealth and Public Education* (1970). . . . [See also Coons & Sugarman, "Family Choice in Education: A Model State System for Vouchers," 59 *Calif L Rev* 321 (1971), which develops model legislation incorporating the "effort" or—in the words of the authors—"family power equalizing" concept.]

See A. Graubard, *Free the Children: Radical Reform and the Free School Movement* (1972).

The "price" of such a system is that all schools participating in a voucher plan would become "public," in the sense that they would be subject to government regulation. Do the preceding sections of this chapter suggest the kind of regulations states might adopt under a voucher scheme? Do they cast doubt on the educational diversity likely under such a scheme?

2. The Market Assumptions of a Voucher Scheme

In order for a voucher plan to succeed—that is, to provide maximum educational choices consistent with the constitutional principles discussed in the preceding notes—parents must be given detailed and useful information about the school options available to them. In other words, parents must become knowledgeable buyers of educational services. But buyer knowledge cannot ensure success for a voucher plan. In addition, the schools must meet the demands of the newly empowered parents; they must be willing and varied sellers. How likely is it that either condition will be satisfied? What kinds of parents might be expected to take most advantage of the choices open to them? What kinds of schools might be created if a voucher arrangement were adopted?

3. Vouchers and Politics

Because they call for drastically new educational arrangements, voucher proposals create both uncertainty and opposition. The objections of those concerned about racial segregation and aid to parochial schools have already been noted. The most frequently expressed position has been that a voucher approach would destroy the public schools, a point made by both public school officials and representatives of teachers' unions. Is that result actually foreseeable? In assessing the likelihood that a voucher plan might be generally adopted, is the political perception of threat to public schools more important than the possibility that the feared result would actually occur?

[S]tructural aspects of American education have conspired against implementation of a voucher demonstration: complexity caused by the number of actors [state officials, including school boards, administrators, citizens' group leaders; and courts] who must virtually simultaneously approve educational change; the inability of any person or group to muster sufficient power to impose change, and the direct threat to the already limited power of professionals posed by vouchers. McCann, "The Politics and Ironies of Educational Change: The Case of Vouchers," 2 *Yale Rev of Law & Social Action* 374, 383.

Does the analysis seem politically plausible? If so, how might these considerable obstacles be overcome? What structural changes in the voucher model might be required to gain additional political support or, at least, to neutralize presently vocal opposition?

4. The Experience with Vouchers

The Office of Economic Opportunity, which sponsored the education vouchers study excerpted above, was unable for several years to persuade a state or school district to try out a voucher scheme on an experimental basis (such a plan was approved for the state of New Hampshire in spring 1973). The OEO did, however, grant the Alum Rock California school district (a 50 percent Mexican-American, 10 percent black district) $2.2 million for a public school voucher plan. Under that plan, parents whose children were previously assigned to one of six schools in the district could use a voucher at any of the six schools; private schools were excluded from the arrangement. While it is too early to evaluate the Alum Rock experience in any detail, certain developments are worth noting. There has been a sharp reduction in truancy and absenteeism; parents have turned out in record numbers at parent-teacher association meetings; the six participating schools have adopted a wide assortment of educational programs, some experimental and some traditional; and the staffs of seven additional schools have voted to join the experiment (OEO has approved an additional grant of $4.6 million to finance this expansion). Civil rights groups that initially opposed the project are "still suspicious," but "can't say it's proven to be no good." See Lublin, "Buying Your School With a Voucher Looks Like a Good Deal So Far," *Wall Street Journal,* 4 June 1973.

What criteria would you use to evaluate the Alum Rock experience? Suppose such an evaluation concluded that parents and students expressed more positive attitudes toward schooling, but that the students' academic achievement showed no change or a slight decline. What would you make of that result?

B. Vouchers, Religion, and Race

COMMITTEE FOR PUBLIC EDUCATION & RELIGIOUS LIBERTY
v NYQUIST
37 L Ed 2d 948 (1973)

Mr. Justice Powell delivered the opinion of the court.

This case raises a challenge under the establishment clause of the First Amendment to the constitutionality of a recently enacted New York law which provides financial assistance, in several ways, to nonpublic elementary and secondary schools in that state. The case involves an intertwining of societal and constitutional issues of the greatest importance. . . .

I

The first section of the challenged enactment, entitled "Health and Safety Grants for Nonpublic School Children," provides for direct money grants from the state to "qualifying" nonpublic schools to be used for the "maintenance and repair of . . . school facilities and equipment to ensure the health, welfare and safety of enrolled pupils." A "qualifying" school is any nonpublic, nonprofit elementary or secondary school which "has been designated during the [immediately preceding] year as serving a high concentration of pupils from low-income families for purposes of Title IV of the Federal Higher Education Act of 1965 (20 USC §425)." Such schools are entitled to receive a grant of thirty dollars per pupil per year, or forty dollars per pupil per year if the facilities are more than twenty-five years old. Each school is required to submit to the commissioner of education an audited statement of its expenditures for maintenance and repair during the preceding year, and its grant may not exceed the total of such expenses. The commissioner is also required to ascertain the average per-pupil cost for equivalent maintenance and repair services in the public schools, and in no event may the grant to nonpublic qualifying schools exceed 50 percent of that figure. . . .

The remainder of the challenged legislation—§§2-5—is a single package captioned the "Elementary and Secondary Education Opportunity Program." It is composed, essentially, of two parts, a tuition grant program and a tax benefit program. Section 2 establishes a limited plan providing tuition reimbursements to parents of children attending elementary or secondary nonpublic schools. To qualify under this section the parent must have an annual taxable income of less than $5,000. The amount of reimbursement is limited to $50 for each grade school child and $100 for each high school child. Each parent is required, however, to submit to the commissioner of education a verified statement containing a receipted tuition bill, and the amount of state reimbursement may not exceed 50 percent of that figure. No restrictions are imposed on the use of the funds by the reimbursed parents.

This section, like §1, is prefaced by a series of legislative findings designed to explain the impetus for the state's action. Expressing a dedication to the "vitality of our pluralistic society," the findings state that a "healthy competitive and diverse alternative to public education is not only desirable but indeed vital to a state and nation that have continually reaffirmed the value of individual differences." The findings further emphasize that the right to select among alternative educational systems "is diminished or even denied to children of lower-income families, whose parents, of all groups, have the least options in determining where their children are to be educated." Turning to the public schools, the findings state that any "precipitous decline in the number of nonpublic school pupils would cause a massive increase in public school enrollment and costs," an increase that would "aggravate an already serious fiscal crisis in public education" and would "seriously jeopardize the quality education for all children." Based on these premises, the statute asserts the state's right to relieve the financial burden of parents who send their children to nonpublic schools through this tuition reimbursement program. . . .

The remainder of the "Elementary and Secondary Education Opportunity Program," contained in §§3, 4, and 5 of the challenged law, is designed to provide a form of tax relief to those who fail to qualify for tuition reimbursement. Under these sections parents may subtract from their adjusted gross income for state income tax purposes a designated amount for each dependent for whom they have paid at least fifty dollars in nonpublic school tuition. If the taxpayer's adjusted gross income is less than $9,000 he may subtract $1,000 for each of as many as three dependents. As the taxpayer's income rises, the amount he may subtract diminishes. . . . The amount of the deduction is not dependent upon how much the taxpayer actually paid for nonpublic school tuition, and is given in addition to any deductions to which the taxpayer may be entitled for other religious or charitable contributions. . . .

Although no record was developed in this case, a number of pertinent generalizations may be made about the nonpublic schools which would benefit from these enactments. . . . Some 700,000 to 800,000 students, constituting almost 20 percent of the state's entire elementary and secondary school population, attend over 2,000 nonpublic schools, approximately 85 percent of which are church-affiliated. And while "all or practically all" of the 280 schools entitled to receive "maintenance and repair" grants "are related to the Roman Catholic Church and teach Catholic religious doctrine to some degree," . . . institutions qualifying under the remainder of the statute include a substantial number of Jewish, Lutheran, Episcopal, Seventh Day Adventist, and other church-affiliated schools. . . .

II

The history of the establishment clause has been recounted frequently and need not be repeated here. See *Everson v Board of Educ* 330 US 1 (Black, J, opinion of the court), 28 (Rutledge, J, dissenting) (1947); *McCollum v Board of Educ* 333 US 203, 212 (1948) (Frankfurter, J, separate opinion); *McGowan v Maryland* 366 US 420 (1961); *Engel v Vitale* 370 US 421 (1962). It is enough to note that it is now firmly established that a law may be one "respecting the establishment of religion" even though its consequence is not to promote a "state religion," *Lemon v Kurtzman* 403 US 602, 612 (1971), and even though it does not aid one religion more than another but merely benefits all religions alike. . . . It is equally well established, however, that not every law that confers an "indirect," "remote," or "incidental" benefit upon religious institutions is, for that reason alone, constitutionally invalid . . . *Walz v Tax Comm'n* 397 US 664, 671-672, 674-675 (1970). What our cases require is careful examination of any law challenged on establishment grounds with a view to ascertaining whether it furthers any of the evils against which that clause protects. Primary among those evils have been "sponsorship, financial support, and active involvement of the sovereign in religious activity." . . .

Most of the cases coming to this court raising establishment clause questions have involved the relationship between religion and education. Among these religion-education precedents, two general categories of cases may be identified: those dealing with religious activities within the public schools[29] and those involving public aid in varying forms to sectarian educational institutions.[30] While the New York legislation places this case in the latter category its resolution requires consideration not only of the several aid-to-sectarian-education cases but also of our other education precedents and of several important noneducation cases. For the now well-defined three-part test that has emerged from our decisions is a product of considerations derived from the full sweep of the establishment clause cases. Taken together these decisions dictate that to pass muster under the establishment clause the law in question, first, must reflect a clearly secular legislative purpose, e.g., *Epperson v Arkansas* 393 US 97 (1968), second, must have a primary effect that neither advances nor inhibits religion, e.g., . . . *School Dist of Abington Township v Schempp* 374 US 203 (1963), and, third, must avoid excessive government entanglement with religion. . . .

In applying these criteria to the three distinct forms of aid involved in this case, we need touch only briefly on the requirement of a "secular legislative purpose." As the recitation of legislative purposes appended to New York's law indicates, each measure is adequately supported by legitimate, nonsectarian state interests. . . . [W] e do not doubt—indeed, we fully recognize—the validity of the state's interests

---

29. *McCollum v Board of Educ, supra* ("release time" from public education for religious education); *Zorach v Clauson* 343 US 306 (1952) (also a "release time" case); *Engel v Vitale* 370 US 421 (1962) (prayer reading in public schools); *School Dist of Abington Township v Schempp* 374 US 203 (1963) (Bible reading in public schools); *Epperson v Arkansas* 393 US 97 (1968) (antievolutionary limitation on public school study).

30. *Everson v Board of Educ, supra* (bus transportation); *Board of Educ v Allen* 392 US 236 (1968) (textbooks); *Lemon v Kurtzman, supra* (teachers' salaries, textbooks, instructional materials); *Earley v DiCenso* 403 US 602 (1971) (teachers' salaries); *Tilton v Richardson,* 403 US 672 (1971) (secular college facilities).

in promoting pluralism and diversity among its public and nonpublic schools. Nor do we hesitate to acknowledge the reality of its concern for an already overburdened public school system that might suffer in the event that a significant percentage of children presently attending nonpublic schools should abandon those schools in favor of the public schools.

But the propriety of a legislature's purposes may not immunize from further scrutiny a law which either has a primary effect that advances religion, or which fosters excessive entanglements between church and state. Accordingly, we must weigh each of the three aid provisions challenged here against these criteria of effect and entanglement.

A

The "maintenance and repair" provisions of §1 authorize direct payments to nonpublic schools, virtually all of which are Roman Catholic schools in low-income areas. . . . [I] t simply cannot be denied that this section has a primary effect that advances religion in that it subsidizes directly the religious activities of sectarian elementary and secondary schools. . . .

B

New York's tuition reimbursement program also fails the "effect" test. . . .

There can be no question that these grants could not, consistently with the establishment clause, be given directly to sectarian schools . . . In the absence of an effective means of guaranteeing that the state aid derived from public funds will be used exclusively for secular, neutral, and nonideological purposes, it is clear from our cases that direct aid in whatever form is invalid. . . . The controlling question here, then, is whether the fact that the grants are delivered to parents rather than schools is of such significance as to compel a contrary result. The state and intervenor-appellees rely on *Everson* and *Allen* for their claim that grants to parents, unlike grants to institutions, respect the "wall of separation" required by the Constitution. It is true that in those cases the court upheld laws that provided benefits to children attending religious schools and to their parents: . . . [I] n *Everson* parents were reimbursed for bus fares paid to send children to parochial schools, and in *Allen* textbooks were loaned directly to the children. But those decisions make clear that, far from providing a per se immunity from examination of the substance of the state's program, the fact that aid is disbursed to parents rather than to the schools is only one among many factors to be considered.

In *Everson*, the court found the bus fare program analogous to the provision of services such as police and fire protection, sewage disposal, highways, and sidewalks for parochial schools . . . . Such services, provided in common to all citizens, are "so separate and so indisputably marked off from the religious function," . . . that they may fairly be viewed as reflections of a neutral posture toward religious institutions. *Allen* is founded upon a similar principle. The court there repeatedly emphasized that upon the record in that case there was no indication that textbooks would be provided for anything other than purely secular courses. "Of course books are different from buses. Most bus rides have no inherent religious significance, while religious books are common. However, the language of [the law under consideration] does not authorize the loan of religious books, and the state claims no right to distribute religious literature . . . . Absent evidence, we cannot assume that school authorities . . . are unable to distinguish between secular and religious books or that they will not honestly discharge their duties under the law." 392 US at 244-45.[38]

The tuition grants here are subject to no such restrictions. There has been no endeavor "to guarantee the separation between secular and religious educational functions and to ensure that State financial aid supports only the former." . . . Indeed, it is precisely the function of New York's law to provide assistance to private schools, the great majority of which are sectarian. By reimbursing parents for a portion of their tuition bill, the state seeks to relieve their financial burdens sufficiently to assure that they continue to have the option to send their children to religion-oriented schools. And while the other purposes for that aid—to perpetuate a pluralistic educational environment and to protect the fiscal integrity of overburdened public schools—are certainly unexceptionable, the effect of the aid is unmistakably to provide desired financial support for nonpublic, sectarian institutions. . . .[39]

Although we think it clear, for the reasons above stated, that New York's tuition grant program fares no better under the "effect" test than its maintenance and repair program, in view of the novelty of the question we will address briefly the subsidiary arguments made by the state officials and intervenors in its defense.

First, it has been suggested that it is of controlling significance that New York's program calls for *reimbursement* for tuition already paid rather than for direct contributions which are merely routed through the parents to the schools, in advance of or in lieu of payment by the parents. The parent is not a mere conduit, we are told, but is absolutely free to spend the money he receives in any manner he wishes. There is no element of coercion attached to the reimbursement, and no assurance that the money will eventually end up in the hands of religious schools. The absence of any element of coercion, however, is irrelevant to questions arising under the establishment clause. . . . Whether the grant is labeled a reimbursement, a reward or a subsidy, its substantive impact is still the same. . . .

Finally, the state argues that its program of tuition grants should survive scrutiny

---

38. *Allen* and *Everson* differ from the present case in a second important respect. In both cases the class of beneficiaries included *all* school children, those in public as well as those in private schools. . . . We do not agree with the suggestion in the dissent of the chief justice that tuition grants are an analogous endeavor to provide comparable benefits to all parents of school children whether enrolled in public or nonpublic schools. . . . The grants to parents of private school children are given in addition to right that they have to send their children to public schools "totally at state expense." And in any event, the argument proves too much, for it would also provide a basis for approving through tuition grants the *complete subsidization* of all religious schools on the ground that such action is necessary if the state is fully to equalize the position of parents who elect such schools—a result wholly at variance with the establishment clause.

Because of the manner in which we have resolved the tuition grant issue, we need not decide whether the significantly religious character of the statute's beneficiaries might differentiate the present case from a case involving some form of public assistance (e. g., scholarships) made available generally without regard to the sectarian-nonsectarian, or public-nonpublic nature of the institution benefitted. See *Wolman v Essex* 342 F Supp 399, 412-413 (SD Ohio 1972), aff'd, 409 US 808 (1972). Thus, our decision today does not compel, as appellees have contended, the conclusion that the educational assistance provisions of the "GI Bill," 38 USC § 1651, impermissibly advance religion in violation of the establishment clause. . . .

39. Appellees, focusing on the term *principal or primary effect* which this court has utilized in expressing the second prong of the three-part test . . . , have argued that the court must decide in this case whether the "primary" effect of New York's tuition grant program is to

because it is designed to promote the free exercise of religion. . . . [T] his court repeatedly has recognized that tension inevitably exists between the free exercise and the establishment clauses . . . and that it may often not be possible to promote the former without offending the latter. As a result of this tension, our cases require the state to maintain an attitude of "neutrality," neither "advancing" nor "inhibiting" religion. In its attempt to enhance the opportunities of the poor to choose between public and nonpublic education, the state has taken a step which can only be regarded as one "advancing" religion. . . .

C

Sections 3, 4, and 5 establish a system for providing income tax benefits to parents of children attending New York's nonpublic schools. . . .

[A] taxpayer's benefit under these sections is unrelated to, and not reduced by, any deductions to which he may be entitled for charitable contributions to religious institutions.[49]

In practical terms there would appear to be little difference, for purposes of determining whether such aid has the effect of advancing religion, between the tax benefit allowed here and the tuition grant allowed under §2. The qualifying parent under either program receives the same form of encouragement and reward for sending his children to nonpublic schools. The only difference is that one parent receives an actual cash payment while the other is allowed to reduce by an arbitrary amount the sum he would otherwise be obliged to pay over to the state. . . .

Appellees . . . place their strongest reliance on *Walz v Tax Comm'n,* in which New York's property tax exemption for religious organizations was upheld. We think that *Walz* provides no support for appellees' position. Indeed, its rationale plainly compels the conclusion that New York's tax package violates the establishment clause.

Tax exemptions for church property enjoyed an apparently universal approval in this country both before and after the adoption of the First Amendment. . . . We know of no historical precedent for New York's recently promulgated tax relief program. . . .

But historical acceptance without more would not alone have sufficed. . . . It was the reason underlying that long history of tolerance of tax exemptions for religion that proved controlling. A proper respect for both the free exercise and the establishment clauses compels the state to pursue a course of "neutrality" toward religion. Yet governments have not always pursued such a course, and oppression has taken many forms, one of which has been taxation of religion. Thus, if taxation was regarded as a form of "hostility" toward religion, "exemption constitute[d] a

---

subsidize religion or to promote these legitimate secular objectives. . . . . We do not think that such metaphysical judgments are either possible or necessary. Our cases simply do not support the notion that a law found to have a "primary" effect to promote some legitimate end under the state's police power is immune from further examination to ascertain whether it also has the direct and immediate effect of advancing religion. . . .

Such secular objectives, no matter how desirable and irrespective whether judges might possess sufficiently sensitive calipers to ascertain whether the secular effects outweigh the sectarian benefits. cannot serve today any more than they could 200 years ago to justify such a direct and substantial advancement of religion. . . .

49. Since the program here does not have the elements of a genuine tax deduction, such as for charitable contributions, we do not have before us, and do not decide, whether that form of tax benefit is constitutionally acceptable under the "neutrality" test in *Walz.*

reasonable and balanced attempt to guard against those dangers. . . ." Special tax benefits, however, cannot be squared with the principle of neutrality established by the decisions of this court. To the contrary, insofar as such benefits render assistance to parents who send their children to sectarian schools, their purpose and inevitable effect are to aid and advance those religious institutions.

Apart from its historical foundations, *Walz* is a product of the same dilemma and inherent tension found in most government-aid-to-religion controversies. To be sure, the exemption of church property from taxation conferred a benefit, albeit an indirect and incidental one. Yet that "aid" was a product not of any purpose to support or to subsidize, but of a fiscal relationship designed to minimize involvement and entanglement between church and state. . . . The granting of the tax benefits under the New York statute, unlike the extension of an exemption, would tend to increase rather than limit the involvement between church and state.

One further difference between tax exemptions for church property and tax benefits for parents should be noted. The exemption challenged in *Walz* was not restricted to a class composed exclusively or even predominantly of religious institutions. Instead the exemption covered all property devoted to religious, educational or charitable purposes. As the parties here must concede, tax reductions authorized by this law flow primarily to the parents of children attending sectarian, nonpublic schools. Without intimating whether this factor alone might have controlling significance in another context in some future case, it should be apparent that in terms of the potential divisiveness of any legislative measure the narrowness of the benefited class would be an important factor. . . .

III

Because we have found that the challenged sections have the impermissible effect of advancing religion, we need not consider whether such aid would result in entanglement of the state with religion in the sense of "[a] comprehensive, discriminating, and continuing state surveillance." *Lemon v Kurtzman* 403 US at 619. But the importance of the competing societal interests implicated in this case prompts us to make the further observation that, apart from any specific entanglement of the state in particular religious programs, assistance of the sort here involved carries grave potential for entanglement in the broader sense of continuing political strife over aid to religion. . . .

The court recently addressed this issue specifically and fully in *Lemon v Kurtzman*. After describing the political activity and bitter differences likely to result from the state programs there involved, the court said: "The potential for political divisiveness related to religious belief and practice is aggravated in these two statutory programs by the need for continuing annual appropriations and the likelihood of larger and larger demands as costs and population grow." 403 US at 623.[54]

The language of the court applies with peculiar force to the New York statute now before us. Section 1 (grants for maintenance) and §2 (tuition grants) will require continuing annual appropriations. Sections 3, 4, and 5 (income tax relief)

---

54. The court in *Lemon* further emphasized that political division along religious lines is to be contrasted with the political diversity expected in a democratic society: "Ordinarily political debate and division, however vigorous or even partisan, are normal and healthy manifestations of our democratic system of government, but political division along religious lines was one of the principal evils against which the First Amendment was intended to protect. Freund, Comment, "Public Aid to Parochial Schools," 82 *Harv L Rev* 1680, 1692 (1969)." 403 US at 622.

will not necessarily require annual reexamination, but the pressure for frequent enlargement of the relief is predictable. . . . But we know from long experience with both federal and state governments that aid programs of any kind tend to become entrenched, to escalate in cost, and to generate their own aggressive constituencies. And the larger the class of recipients, the greater the pressure for accelerated increases. Moreover, the state itself, concededly anxious to avoid assuming the burden of educating children now in private and parochial schools, has a strong motivation for increasing this aid as public school costs rise and population increases. In this situation, where the underlying issue is the deeply emotional one of church-state relationships, the potential for serious divisive political consequences needs no elaboration. And while the prospect of such divisiveness may not alone warrant the invalidation of state laws that otherwise survive the careful scrutiny required by the decisions of this court, it is certainly a "warning signal" not to be ignored. . . .

Our examination of New York's aid provisions, in light of all relevant considerations, compels the judgment that each, as written, has a "primary effect that advances religion" and offends the constitutional prohibition against laws "respecting the establishment of religion." We therefore affirm the three-judge court's holding as to § § 1 and 2, and reverse as to § § 3, 4, and 5.

It is so ordered.

Mr. Chief Justice Burger, joined in part by Mr. Justice White, and joined by Mr. Justice Rehnquist, concurring in part and dissenting in part.

I join in that part of the Court's opinion in *Committee for Public Education and Religious Liberty v Nyquist, ante,* which holds the New York "maintenance and repair" provision unconstitutional under the establishment clause because it is a direct aid to religion. I disagree, however, with the court's decisions . . . to strike down the . . . tuition grant programs and the New York tax relief provisions. I believe the court's decisions on those statutory provisions ignore the teachings of *Everson v Board of Educ* 330 US 1 (1947) and *Board of Educ v Allen* 392 US 236 (1968), and fail to observe what I thought the court had held in *Walz v Tax Comm'n* 397 US 664 (1970). . . .

While there is no straight line running through our decisions interpreting the establishment and free exercise clauses of the First Amendment, our cases do, it seems to me, lay down one solid, basic principle: that the establishment clause does not forbid governments, state or federal, from enacting a program of general welfare under which benefits are distributed to private individuals, even though many of those individuals may elect to use those benefits in ways that "aid" religious instruction or worship. Thus, in *Everson* the court held that a New Jersey township could reimburse *all* parents of school-age children for bus fares paid in transporting their children to school. . . .

Twenty-one years later, in *Board of Educ v Allen* 392 US 236 (1968), the court again upheld a state program that provided for direct aid to the parents of all school children including those in private schools. The statute there required "local public school authorities to lend textbooks free of charge to all students in grades seven through twelve; students attending private schools [were] included." Recognizing that *Everson* was the case "most nearly in point," the *Allen* court interpreted *Everson* as holding that "the establishment clause does not prevent a state from extending the benefits of state laws to all citizens without regard to their religious affiliation . . . ." Applying that principle to the statute before it, the *Allen* court stated:

> . . . Appellants have shown us nothing about the necessary effects of the statute that is contrary to its stated purpose. The law merely *makes available to all children* the benefits of a general program to lend school books free of charge. Books are furnished at the request of the pupil and ownership remains, at least technically, in the state. *Thus no funds or books are furnished to parochial schools, and the financial benefit is to the parents and children, not to schools.* . . .

The court's opinions in both *Everson* and *Allen* recognized that the statutory programs at issue there may well have facilitated the decision of many parents to send their children to religious schools. . . . Notwithstanding, the court held that such an indirect or incidental "benefit" to the religious institutions that sponsored parochial schools was not conclusive indicia of a "law respecting an establishment of religion." . . .

The essence of all these decisions, I suggest, is that government aid to individuals generally stands on an entirely different footing from direct aid to religious institutions. . . .

This fundamental principle which I see running through our prior decisions in this difficult and sensitive field of law, and which I believe governs the present cases, is premised more on experience and history than on logic. It is admittedly difficult to articulate the reasons why a state should be permitted to reimburse parents of private school children—partially at least—to take into account the state's enormous savings in not having to provide schools for those children, when a state is not allowed to pay the same benefit directly to sectarian schools on a per-pupil basis. In either case, the private individual makes the ultimate decision that may indirectly benefit church-sponsored schools; to that extent the state involvement with religion is substantially attenuated. The answer, I believe, lies in the experienced judgment of various members of this court over the years that the balance between the policies of free exercise and establishment of religion tips in favor of the former when the legislation moves away from direct aid to religious institutions and takes on the character of general aid to individual families. This judgment reflects the caution with which we scrutinize any effort to give official support to religion and the tolerance with which we treat general welfare legislation. . . .

The tuition grant and tax relief programs now before us are, in my view, indistinguishable in principle, purpose and effect from the statutes in *Everson* and *Allen*. . . . The only discernible difference between the programs in *Everson* and *Allen* and these cases is in the method of the distribution of benefits: here the particular benefits of the Pennsylvania and New York statutes are given only to parents of private school children, while in *Everson* and *Allen* the statutory benefits were made available to parents of both public and private school children. But to regard that difference as constitutionally meaningful is to exalt form over substance. It is beyond dispute that the parents of public school children in New York and Pennsylvania presently receive the "benefit" of having their children educated totally at state expense; the statutes enacted in those states and at issue here merely attempt to equalize that "benefit" by giving to parents of private school children, in the form of dollars or tax deductions, what the parents of public school children receive in kind. It is no more than simple equity to grant partial relief to parents who support the public schools they do not use.

The court appears to distinguish the Pennsylvania and New York statutes from *Everson* and *Allen* on the ground that here the state aid is not apportioned between the religious and secular activities of the sectarian schools attended by some recipients, while in *Everson* and *Allen* the state aid was purely secular in nature. . . . There are at present many forms of government assistance to individuals that can be used to serve religious ends, such as social security benefits or "GI Bill" payments, which are not subject to nonreligious use restrictions. Yet, I certainly doubt that today's majority would hold those statutes unconstitutional under the establishment clause.

Since I am unable to discern in the court's analysis of *Everson* and *Allen* any neutral principle to explain the result reached in these cases, I fear that the court has in reality followed the unsupportable approach of measuring the "effect" of a law by the percentage of the recipients who choose to use the money for religious, rather than secular, education. . . .

With all due respect, I submit that such a consideration is irrelevant to a constitutional determination of the "effect" of a statute. For purposes of constitutional adjudication of that issue, it should make no difference whether 5 percent, 20 percent, or 80 percent of the beneficiaries of an educational program of general application elect to utilize their benefits for religious purposes. The "primary effect" branch of our three-pronged test was never, at least to my understanding, intended to vary with the *number* of churches benefitted by a statute under which state aid is distributed to private citizens. . . .

Mr. Justice White joins this opinion insofar as it relates to the . . . tuition grant . . . and tax relief statute[s].

Mr. Justice White, joined in part by the chief justice and Mr. Justice Rehnquist, dissenting. [omitted].

Mr. Justice Rehnquist, with whom the chief justice and Mr. Justice White concur, dissenting in part. . . .

I find both the court's reasoning and result all but impossible to reconcile with *Walz v Tax Comm'n* 397 US 664 (1970), decided only three years ago. . . .

I

The opinions in *Walz* . . . make it clear that tax deductions and exemptions, even when directed to religious institutions, occupy quite a different constitutional status under the religion clauses of the First Amendment than do outright grants to such institutions. . . . Mr. Justice Brennan in his concurring opinion amplified the distinction between tax benefits and direct payments in these words:

> Tax exemptions and general subsidies, however, are qualitatively different. Though both provide economic assistance, they do so in fundamentally different ways. A subsidy involves the direct transfer of public monies to the subsidized enterprise and uses resources exacted from taxpayers as a whole. An exemption, on the other hand, involves no such transfer. . . . Tax exemptions, accordingly, constitute mere passive state involvement with religion and not the affirmative involvement characteristic of outright governmental subsidy. . . .

Here the effect of the tax benefit is trebly attenuated as compared with the outright exemption considered in *Walz*. There the result was a complete forgiveness of taxes, while here the result is merely a reduction in taxes. There the ultimate benefit was available to an actual house of worship, while here even the ultimate benefit redounds only to a religiously sponsored school. There the churches themselves received the direct reduction in the tax bill, while here it is only the parents of the children who were sent to religiously sponsored schools who receive the direct benefit.

The court seeks to avoid the controlling effect of *Walz* by comparing its historical background to the relative recency of the challenged deduction plan; by noting that in its historical context, a property tax exemption is religiously neutral, whereas the educational cost deduction here is not; and by finding no substantive difference between a direct reimbursement from the state to parents and the state's abstention from collecting the full tax bill which the parents would otherwise have had to pay.

While it is true that the court reached its result in *Walz* in part by examining the unbroken history of property tax exemptions for religious organizations in this country, there is no suggestion in the opinion that only those particular tax exemption schemes that have roots in pre-Revolutionary days are sustainable against an establishment clause challenge. . . .

[I]f long-established use of a particular tax exemption scheme leads to a holding that the scheme is constitutional, that holding should extend equally to newly devised tax benefit plans which are indistinguishable in principle from those long established.

The court's statement that "special tax benefits, however, cannot be squared with the principle of neutrality established by decisions of this court," . . . and that "insofar as such benefits render assistance to parents who send their children to sectarian schools, their purpose and inevitable effect are to aid and advance those religious institutions," . . . are impossible to reconcile with *Walz*. Who can doubt that the tax exemptions which that case upheld were every bit as much of a "special tax benefit" as the New York tax deduction plan here, or that the benefits resulting from the exemption in *Walz* had every bit as much tendency to "aid and advance . . . religious institutions" as did New York's plan here? . . .

Notes and Questions

1. Nonpublic School Vouchers, Tax Credits, and the Church-State Question: Constitutional Issues

   a. The "Secular Purpose" Test. The court in *Committee for Public Education and Religious Liberty* (hereafter *PERL*) concludes that both the voucher and tax credit legislation reflect a "clearly secular legislative purpose." Is the court simply referring to the formal justifications for the legislation that were advanced both before its passage and during oral argument before the court? Is it likely that the legislators had *both* a secular and religious purpose in adopting this legislation? Is that fact relevant to the court's analysis?

   b. The "Primary Effect" Test. The court notes that "the effect of the [voucher] aid is unmistakably to provide desired financial support for nonpublic, sectarian institutions." Does that fact alone render it unconstitutional? Does the court successfully distinguish *PERL* from *Everson v Board of Educ* 330 US 1 (1947) and *Board of Educ v Allen* 392 US 236 (1968), which upheld aid legislation—transportation and textbooks—benefitting "nonpublic, sectarian institutions?" Would $100 "tuition supplements" paid to parents whose children attended public as well as private schools survive judicial scrutiny after *PERL*?

In *Barrera v Wheeler* 475 F2d 1338 (8th Cir 1973), a divided circuit court held that Title I of the Elementary and Secondary Education Act of 1965, 20 USC §§241a-241m, 242-244 (1972), requires "a program for educationally deprived nonpublic school children that is comparable in quality, scope and opportunity, which may or may not necessarily be equal in dollar expenditures to that provided in the public schools." 475 F2d at 1344. The court declined to consider whether providing such support violates the First Amendment. "[W]e determine that it would be improper for us to pass on the constitutionality of an abstract program of remedial teaching services which are not properly before us." 475 F2d at 1353, 1354. After *PERL* how would the Supreme Court decide the *Barrera* issue? See chapter 6 for a discussion of Title I, ESEA.

In dissent, Chief Justice Burger notes: "I fear that the court has in reality followed the insupportable approach of measuring the 'effect' of a law by the percentage of the recipients who choose to use the money for religious, rather than secular, education." Is that in fact what the *PERL* court does? If so, is it constitutionally "insupportable"?

How does the court reconcile its decision to strike down tax credits for nonpublic schools with *Walz v Tax Comm'n* 397 US 664 (1970), which permitted states to exempt church property from taxation? Are tax credits less "neutral"—or less likely to aid sectarian institutions—than property tax exemptions?

c. The "Entanglement" Test. By providing vouchers and tax credits, which could be used for any public school activity, New York sought to avoid "a comprehensive, discriminating, and continuing state surveillance" of sectarian schools. *Lemon v Kurtzman* 403 US 602, 619 (1971). Yet the tax credit and voucher schemes do permit public money to be spent for sectarian purposes, a factor that strongly influenced the *PERL* decision. Can one construct state legislation that avoids the Scylla of entanglement and the Charybdis of financing religion?

d. Higher versus Lower Education. In *Hunt v McNair* 93 S Ct 2868 (1973), decided the same day as *PERL,* the Supreme Court upheld state legislation that provided financial assistance for higher education construction; secular as well as sectarian institutions are eligible for the assistance. The court thus reaffirmed a distinction, first advanced in *Tilton v Richardson* 403 US 672 (1971), between aid that benefits sectarian institutions of higher education and aid that benefits sectarian primary and secondary schools. The court suggests that the former are likely to promote genuinely secular ends, while the latter seek to indoctrinate their students with religious values. Is the distinction factually correct? Is it a distinction of constitutional dimension? Would legislation combining aid to institutions of higher and lower education fare better before the court than did the voucher and tax credit legislation overturned in *PERL*?

e. References. The constitutional issues discussed in *PERL* have been extensively debated by legal commentators. See Choper, "The Establishment Clause and Aid to

Parochial Schools," 56 *Cal L Rev* 260 (1968); Duffy, "A Review of Supreme Court Decisions on Aid to Nonpublic Elementary and Secondary Education," 23 *Hastings LJ* 966 (1972), Freund, "Public Aid to Parochial Schools," 82 *Harv L Rev* 1680 (1969); Giannella, "Religious Liberty, Nonestablishment, and Doctrinal Development," 81 *Harv L Rev* 513 (1968); King, "Rebuilding the 'Fallen House'—State Tuition Grants for Elementary and Secondary Education," 84 *Harv L Rev* 1057 (1971).

2. The Education Voucher Plan and *Committee for Public Instruction and Religious Instruction v Nyquist*

The New York voucher legislation struck down by the court would have provided funds for those students attending private schools. By contrast, the education voucher plan (discussed above), or the scheme proposed by Professors Coons and Sugarman ("Family Choice in Education: A Model State System for Vouchers," 59 *Cal L Rev* 321 (1971)), would make most schools—both public and private—"voucher" schools. The vast majority of students would receive vouchers, which could be used at any participating school, secular or sectarian. See 38 USC 1651 (the "GI bill"). Would a system-wide voucher stand a better chance of success if challenged in court? What, if any, are the pertinent constitutional distinctions? If sectarian schools were excluded from such a voucher plan, could parents desiring a religious education for their children raise constitutional objections, arguing that such a policy demonstrated "state hostility" toward religion? See Note, "Education Vouchers: the Fruit of the *Lemon* Tree," 24 *Stan L Rev* 687 (1972).

3. Should Sectarian Schools Receive Public Subsidies?

In 1965-1966, 6,304,772 students attended nonpublic schools. Of these, 86.9 percent were enrolled in Catholic schools, 7.7 percent in other denomination schools, and 5.4 percent in sectarian schools. National Catholic Educational Association, *State Aid to Nonpublic Schools* 1 (1971). Thus, the primary beneficiaries of legislation such as New York's voucher and tax credit plans are the parochial schools. As a matter of policy, should they receive financial support? That issue has been debated by government commissions (compare President's Commission on School Finance, *Schools, People, and Money* 53-57 (1972) with 1 *Report of the New York State Commission on the Quality, Cost and Financing of Elementary and Secondary Education* 389-92 (1972)) and commentators (see Swomley, "Who Wants Catholic Schools?" 211 *The Nation* 14 December 1970, p 627; Friedman & Binzen, "Politics and Parochiaid," 164 *The New Republic* 23 January 1971, p 12; Walinsky, "Aid to Parochial Schools," *The New Republic* 7 October 1972.) Consider the following discussion of the "myths" of parochial school financing:

> The major myth in the debate [over public aid to parochial schools] centers on tuition . . . All [aid proposals] are based on the false premise that enrollments are falling because Catholic parents cannot afford to pay tuition charges to Catholic schools. . . .
> The real reason why enrollment is dropping is that Catholic parents—for many reasons—simply are not choosing to send their children to Catholic schools . . . Increasingly, Catholic families moving to the suburbs are choosing public schools, which often have attractive physical facilities . . . that Catholic schools can't afford. . . .

[N]ot even substantial amounts of new income from . . . the government are going to help the Catholic schools until church leaders stop concentrating their efforts on keeping schools open that will close in a few years anyway. Instead of continuing to preserve buildings, church leaders should begin to preserve the option of Catholic education itself . . . . One reason why church leaders have not consolidated the schools is that they are depending on promises of public aid to keep the system going . . . but public aid will [not] stop the decline in enrollments. . . .

The final myth is that, no matter how much it might cost to aid the Catholic schools, it would cost much more if most of the pupils in those schools were transferred into the public system. The fact is, however, that projected enrollment declines in most public elementary schools would make room for most transfers at a cost that makes this a viable public policy option. . . . Gary & Cole, "The Politics of Aid—And a Proposal for Reform," *Saturday Review* 22 July 1972.

If, as the authors suggest, the financial crisis of parochial education would only be eased, not resolved, by public support, does that fact negate any policy justification for supporting these institutions? Putting to one side the constitutional issues, would an aid scheme designed to "preserve the option of Catholic education"—by compelling, for example, consolidation of parochial schools—constitute appropriate government policy?

4. Vouchers and Racial Segregation

a. The Constitutional Question. If a voucher scheme increases racial segregation, either by design or effect, it is vulnerable to constitutional attack as a denial of equal educational opportunity to black students. The issue has arisen in several Southern states that sought to close their public schools and provide vouchers as a means of avoiding judicial mandates to desegregate. In Louisiana, for example, a three-judge district court overturned a statute which would have permitted counties to close their public schools, sell or lease them to others, and then provide "tuition vouchers" that could be cashed in by the "private schools." *Hall v St. Helena Parish School Bd* 197 F Supp 649 (ED La 1961), *aff'd per curiam,* 368 US 515 (1962). A subsequent Louisiana statute sought to accomplish the same end. Its rationale was framed in terms of the right of the parent to decide "on the type of education ultimately received by the child. . . ;" no mention of race was made in the legislation. The court, noting Louisiana's long history of resistance to desegregation, concluded that "the law was designed to establish and maintain a system of segregated schools" and had the effect of maintaining segregation. *Poindexter v Louisiana Financial Assistance Comm'n* 275 F Supp 833 (ED La 1967), *aff'd per curiam,* 389 US 571 (1968). See also *Coffey v State Educ Fin Comm'n* 296 F Supp 1389 (SD Miss 1969); *Lee v Macon County Bd* 267 F Supp 458 (MD Ala 1967), *aff'd per curiam, sub nom, Wallace v US* 389 US 215 (1967). The Supreme Court recently held unconstitutional Mississippi legislation that provided free textbooks to segregated private schools. *Norwood v Harrison* 93 S Ct 2804 (1973). The complex political and constitutional questions concerning racial discrimination in education are addressed in chapter 4.

b. The Policy Question. The history of voucher plans in the South has made the approach suspect to liberals and blacks, who equate vouchers with increased segregation. See McCann, "The Politics and Ironies of Educational Changes: The Case of Vouchers," 2 *Yale Rev of Law & Social Action* 374, 377-78 (1972). But would a voucher plan increase the racial segregation of students? That answer is likely to turn on such factors as the present level of segregation, the extent to which the racial composition of a school influences parental choice, and the number of parents who prefer integrated schools.

A voucher scheme can be structured to increase school desegregation: For example, information about the racial composition of the school can be withheld from parents; where a given school has more student applications than places, some or all of its students can be selected by lottery (a feature of the education vouchers proposal excerpted above); racial quotas can be fixed; and minority children can be provided with larger grants to make them more attractive to voucher schools. How effective would each of these approaches be? Do they sacrifice other goals of the voucher scheme?

7. Problem: Constitutional Right to a Voucher

Amy Indigent has long wished to send her children to a private school, because she feels that only private school will fully develop her children's intellectual and creative potential. Amy's neighbor sends her youngsters to private schools, but, unlike Amy, she can afford to pay both school taxes and private school fees. Amy believes that her predicament may have constitutional implications. She feels the First Amendment rights of her children are restricted because they can learn only what the state chooses to teach. She also contends that the "right" to attend nonpublic schools, guaranteed by *Pierce* and available to wealthier parents, is denied her because of her indigence. Does Amy have a legal case? If she were willing to send her children to attend a public school in a district other than the one in which she lives, would her case be strengthened? See *Board of Educ of Ind School Dist No 2 v Maris* 458 P2d 305 (Okla 1969). If Amy's concern were predicated on a desire to provide religious education for her children, could she argue that her constitutional interest in "free exercise of religion" entitles her to state assistance in financing such an education? See *Jackson v California* 460 F2d 282 (9th Cir 1972); *Brusca v Board of Education* 332 F Supp 275 (ED Mo 1971), *aff'd per curiam*, 405 US 1050 (1972).

chapter two
Life in Schools: Students

I. Introduction

A. Student Rights and Socialization

Chapter 1 focused on the legal requirement that children attend some public or private school. That requirement, virtually unchallenged except in the *Yoder* case, is premised on a number of asserted state interests: preparing the individual for citizenship, inculcating values, imparting skills, assuring the economic self-sufficiency of the individual, and preserving the security of the state. But beyond compulsoriness and the reasons for its existence, there lies an equally fundamental issue: how may the state regulate and supervise the children who attend its schools in order to accomplish these goals? How may the conduct of students be limited? What punishments may be meted out for misbehavior? What procedural safeguards must be observed before sanctions are imposed? What courses may the state require a student to take? What may a student be required to read? What values may be inculcated? What ritual acts may students be required to perform? What "rights" do students have? In short, how may the state socialize children in the public schools to particular norms that it deems desirable?

Many of the issues of state control and regulation of private schools were taken up in chapter 1. There is an integral relationship between the *Pierce* guaranteed parental right to send children to private schools and the degree of control that the state may assert over those schools and the children who attend them. If the state's power over private schools were not subject to limitation, private schools might quickly be regulated out of existence or be rendered indistinguishable from public schools. Such concerns are not apparent in court decisions when the issue is the scope of state regulation of public schools, and the courts have taken the position that the state has broader power over public schools than over private schools. See, e.g., *Meyer v Nebraska* 262 US 390, 402 (1923)(dictum). Why this should be the case is not at all clear. Whether the parental interest in raising children as they see fit is characterized as a concern for parental speech, religion, or privacy, protection of that interest seems as essential in the public school as in its private counterpart. The *Pierce* compromise is almost proprietary in its resolution of the legal and policy dilemma. Where private persons own and operate an educational institution, and where it is supported by private tuition payments, the scope of constitutionally permissible state control is narrow. Where, however, an education institution is controlled by elected or appointed public officials, supported by public tax dollars, and operated by paid public employees, the state has much greater latitude in overriding other interests.

Section II of this chapter deals with the broad question of political and religious socialization of public school students. The materials attempt to give the reader a sense of student life in public schools, and the impact of the school environment. Although most aspects of the socialization process have never been the subject of legal challenge, leading curriculum, textbook, school prayer, and flag salute cases will be explored. See generally E. Fulbright and E. Bolmeier, *Courts and the Curriculum* (1964); Reutter, "The Law and the Curriculum," 20 *Law & Contemp Prob* 91 (1955). The problem as it relates to teaching is explored in chapter 3.

Sections III and IV raise issues that may be conceptualized in two ways. From one perspective, they are concerned with the rights of students to resist socialization to undemocratic institutional norms, what Professor Ladd calls the Puritan model of educational governance. Ladd, "Regulating Student Behavior without Ending Up in Court," 54 *Phi Delta Kappan* 304 (1973). Students assert a right to distribute and publish newspapers, speak out on public issues, secure a hearing before suspension, and protect their persons or lockers from searches, notwithstanding traditional notions of school governance that place all these matters exclusively in the hands of school authorities. In short, the institutional authority structure and the norm of unquestioning obedience by students are challenged. From another perspective, students are asserting a right to socialize their peers and teachers, urging values that are inconsistent with the school's or community's values. Students opposed to the Vietnam War or to the principal's policies attempt to persuade others of the rightness of their position. In a sense, they, like the state, are attempting to take advantage of the compulsoriness of schooling to communicate and to instill values. See Nahmod, "First Amendment Protection for Learning and Teaching: The Scope of Judicial Review," 18 *Wayne L Rev* 1479, 1482 (1972). However, the source of the students' "right" to engage in such conduct lies in the constitutional value we place on freedom of speech, whereas the state's right is premised on all the interests underlying compulsory education. Just as the inability of the state to regulate private schools would destroy the *Pierce* compromise, so the inability to socialize public school students would destroy the raison d'etre of compulsory schooling. Much of the legal doctrine developed in students' rights cases has been an attempt to resolve this underlying tension.

B. "State Action"

The power of the state to control and supervise children in the public school may be approached from still another perspective. Where the state punishes students for disobeying school rules, the state has engaged in "state action," which is subject to the prohibitions contained in the First and Fourteenth Amendments. The nub of this legal doctrine is that constitutional guarantees such as freedom of speech and religion, equal protection of the laws, and due process of law apply only to acts of the state and not to private acts. For example, private schools may suspend students without a hearing to determine whether a school rule has been offended. See, e.g., *Bright v Isenbarger* 314 F Supp 1382 (ND Ind 1970), *aff'd*, 445 F2d 412 (7th Cir 1971); *Blackburn v Fisk Univ* 443 F2d 121 (6th Cir 1971). Public schools may not. *Dixon v Alabama State Bd of Educ* 294 F2d 150 (5th Cir 1961). The result presents a rather complex picture. Where the state seeks to regulate the lives of students in private schools, its regulations are subject to constitutional attack. Where, however, the private school itself—without the intervention of the state—seeks to control and supervise students, those restrictions are not subject to constitutional challenge by students and parents. In public schools, every administrative act must be tested against constitutional restrictions. Thus, the permissible scope of state regulation of private schools is less than the scope of regulation of public schools, but the scope of judicially protected individual rights is far greater in public than in private institutions.

The line between public and private schools—in practice, the distinction between schools operated by the government and those that are not—is not identical to the separation between state action and private action in constitutional litigation. See, e.g., *Coleman v Wagner College* 429 F2d 1120 (2d Cir 1970). It has been argued that all schools are "public" in the sense that they perform a public service and that they often receive state support for school lunches, transportation, or disadvantaged children. Moreover, if state regulation is the earmark of publicness, all schools, as chapter 1 demonstrates, are "public" schools. Without fully exploring the complex legal problems behind the various state action arguments, the functional question is simply, when may the courts require private institutions to adhere to the same constitutional norms that apply to public schools? See *Bright v Isenbarger, supra*. With the possible exception of cases involving racial discrimination (see Black, "State Action, Equal Protection, and California's Proposition 14," 81 *Harv L Rev* 69 (1967)), the courts have tended to accept the position taken by Judge Friendly in *Powe v Miles* 407 F2d 73, 81 (2d Cir 1968), a litigation in which students attacked the disciplinary procedures of a private university:

> The contention that [there is state action in this case] overlooks the essential point—that the state must be involved not simply with some activity of the institution alleged to have inflicted injury upon a plaintiff but with the activity that caused the injury. . . . When the state bans a subject from the curriculum of a private school, as in *Meyer* [*v Nebraska* 262 US 390] . . . its responsibility needs no elucidation. State action would be similarly present here . . . if New York had undertaken to set policy for the control of demonstrations in all private universities . . . . But the fact that New York has exercised some regulatory powers over the standard of education offered by Alfred University does not implicate it generally in Alfred's policies toward demonstrations and discipline. (407 F2d at 81.)

See also *Grafton v Brooklyn Law School* 478 F2d 1137 (2d Cir 1973); *Coleman v Wagner College* 429 F2d 1120, 1126 (2d Cir 1970) (Friendly, J, concurring); *Browns v Mitchell* 409 F2d 593 (10th Cir 1969); H. Friendly, *The Dartmouth College Case and the Public-Private Penumbra* (1968); O'Neill, "Private Universities and Public Law," 19 *Buff L Rev* 155 (1970). Thus, barring direct state regulation of private schools with respect to the very decision that is challenged, it should not be assumed that the constitutional doctrines developed in this and subsequent chapters have any application to privately operated educational institutions. Those doctrines, however, embody societal notions of fairness and equity as the judiciary perceives them, and the very fact that they are law may influence private institutions to abide by them voluntarily.

II. Political and Religious Socialization

A. Socialization and Social Science Research

POLITICAL SOCIALIZATION

R. Dawson and K. Prewitt

5-6, 146-166 (1969)

A nation's political life is linked closely to the moods, manners, and values of its people. What citizens believe and feel about politics both reflect and shape the politics of their nation. . . .

These are, of course, not completely new notions in political studies. A very perceptive nineteenth-century French visitor to the United States, Alexis de Tocqueville, analyzed the social foundations of democratic processes in America, emphasizing just these relationships. His explanation is as instructive today as it was 130 years ago. Tocqueville singled out the special attitudes and values of the American people. The country's physical conditions and legal structures were important, he allowed, but the manners and customs of the inhabitants were of the greatest import:

> These three great causes serve, no doubt, to regulate and direct American democracy; but if they were to be classed in their proper order, I should say that physical circumstances are less efficient than the laws, and the laws less so than the customs of the people. I am convinced that the most advantageous situation and the best possible laws cannot maintain a constitution in spite of the customs of a country; while the latter may turn to some advantage the most unfavorable positions and the worst laws. The importance of customs is a common truth to which study and experience incessantly direct our attention. [Citing Alexis de Tocqueville, *Democracy in America* 322 (1960).] . . .

The "common truth" that political customs "regulate and direct" political life is an assumption political socialization theory shares with Tocqueville. Working with this assumption, students of politics are asking about the sources of political customs and values: What social mechanisms provide a nation with its peculiar political customs? Part of the answer to this question, as we attempt to make clear in this essay, is found in political socialization. "Political socialization" is the name given the processes through which a citizen acquires his own view of the political world. The school child pledging allegiance to the flag each morning or learning from experiences with teachers that authorities command obedience is being politically socialized. Social experiences of a wide variety become relevant for the ways in which the child, the adolescent, and the adult will view political matters. Viewed from another perspective, political socialization is the way in which one generation passes on political standards and beliefs to succeeding generations. "Cultural transmission" is the phrase that best describes this process. Through both deliberate official political education programs and the passing on of political norms in less deliberate and more informal groups such as the family and peer groups, societies ensure intergenerational continuity in political attitudes and values. . . .

In modern societies a major portion of political learning takes place in the classroom. It is through this agency that the most comprehensive and deliberate efforts are made by modern and modernizing politics to shape the political outlooks of new citizens. Within the classroom the formal curriculum of instruction, various ritual activities, and the activities of the teacher all help to shape the political development of youngsters.

1. *The Curriculum.* The curriculum is potentially one of the major instruments of political socialization. . . . Nationalistic values, in particular, permeate the entire school curriculum. Courses in national history tend to be selective: "those episodes that redound most to our national glory receive emphasis; and the picture of the past is deficient in cracks and crevices." [Citing V. O. Key, *Public Opinion and American Democracy* 317 (1961).] Formal instruction in civics and government is designed to acquaint the adolescent citizen with the nature and the glory of the established order. The use of literature reflects favorably on the nation's past and forecasts great things for its future. Such portrayals are presented for citizenship training. Generally political leaders and educators explicitly view the curriculum as an appropriate agency for transmitting knowledge and values conducive to good citizenship.

A distinction can be made between the two types of formal political instruction: civic education and political indoctrination. The distinction is ambiguous, but will serve the purpose at hand. Following the suggestion of Coleman, we call "civic training" that part of political education which emphasizes how a good citizen participates in the political life of his nation. Political indoctrination, on the other hand, concerns the learning of a specific political ideology which is intended to rationalize and justify a particular regime. Civic training acquaints the student with a political unit toward which loyalty is assumed. Political indoctrination inculcates loyalty to the nation. All educational curricula contain a mixture of both of these objectives. . . .

. . . . There is no doubt that citizenship training is a part of most school curricula. There is some doubt about the influence of such programs. Some commentators, sensitive to the gap between what is taught in the school and what the child learns outside the classroom, play down the influence of such attempts at civic training. . . .

Laurence Wylie reports that the core curriculum in the local school includes various civics courses. [L. Wylie, *Village in the Vauvcluse* 206-8 (1957).] Students memorize sentences which stress the benevolent, disinterested nature of the government. But parents and teachers speak a different language when they talk about the government. The attitude caught when the children overhear adults "is in direct conflict with what the children are taught in school." From listening to the grown-ups, children learn that government is made up of "weak, stupid, selfish, ambitious men." No matter what image the children read about in their civics textbooks, they "constantly hear adults referring to government as a source of evil and to the men who run it as instruments of evil." They further learn that it is the "duty of the citizen *not* to cooperate with these men, as the civics books would have people do, but rather to hinder them, to prevent them in every possible way from increasing their power over individuals and over families." This is a picture of incongruity, in which the content of the formal school curriculum is probably superseded by informal learning experiences.

For most students the discrepancy between curriculum materials, other political cues, and actual political experiences is not as severe. When the textbook portrays a political world which is confirmed by his own observation, or by what is transmitted by other socialization agents, the student is likely to be more receptive to its political lessons. A study of civic training in several American high schools confirms this notion. [Citing Litt, "Civic Education, Community Norms, and Political Indoctrination," 28 *Amer Soc Rev* 9 (1963).] This study, conducted by Edgar Litt, found that the curriculum did affect the kinds of political values developed by students. The influence was accelerated when the values being taught were in harmony with those articulated by other socialization agents. It was attenuated, however, where the textbook values were out of line with the norms of other, more powerful, agents of political learning.

However, the influence of the civics curriculum is quite different if the student is a Negro. Negroes who take civics courses do alter many of their political views. This suggests an important generalization for political socialization theory. For the white student, the material presented in a civics course is more or less redundant; he has heard it all before. For many Negro students, on the other hand, the material is new and presents them with political images and ideas that have not yet been part of their socialization experiences.

. . . . All school systems carry on some form of political indoctrination. The myths and legends from the past, the policies and programs of the present, and the goals and aspirations of the future are taught selectively. Consciously or not, textbooks and other teaching materials justify and rationalize political practices. The goals and means of political indoctrination through classroom materials, however, are more obvious in some nations than in others. Children in different nations receive varying doses of slanted material. Political authorities permit varying degrees of honest criticism to appear in course materials.

. . . . However, knowing that a school's curriculum includes a certain type of lesson tells us little about its influence. The articulation of a particular value in a classroom is not presumptive evidence that the value is internalized by the student. Students rarely become perfect replicas of the model citizen portrayed in such political indoctrination. In some instances political indoctrination efforts in the classroom, like some attempts at civic education, may be quite ineffective.

2. *Classroom Ritual Life.* Political values are also transmitted to the child through the ritual life of the classroom—saluting the flag, singing patriotic songs, honoring national heroes and events, and being exposed to patriotic symbols such as pictures and sayings of leaders. With greater or lesser self-consciousness, schools throughout the world append to the normal curriculum numerous ceremonial expressions of devotion to the nation. Educational policy makers assume that systematic exposure to such symbols will produce greater attachment and respect to the nation and its institutions. Patriotic feelings are formed and cemented by participation in ritual acts.

A major indicator of the importance placed on ritual exercises is the amount of time and resources allocated to them. Teachers are compelled, by social norms if not always by law, to spend valuable school hours and scarce resources on classroom activities and programs which stress national patriotism.

The fact that ritual experiences are stressed in the classroom and that they are deemed an important part of political indoctrination programs by most regimes, however, does not give a clear picture of what is contained in them, how effective they are, and how important they are in relation to other socialization methods. A clear statement on these issues must await much more research. We can, however, suggest two possible implications of the students' ritual life.

(a) In one sense rituals are the acting out of one's sense of awe toward what is symbolized by the ritual. Basic feelings of patriotism and loyalty are reinforced as one acts out his devotion to the state. In their report on American school children, Hess and Torney comment: "The feelings of respect for the pledge and the national anthem are reinforced daily and are seldom questioned by the child." The authors continue by pointing out that the very gestures and words associated with the acts suggest submission, respect, and dependence. They conclude that the rituals "establish an emotional orientation toward country and flag even though an understanding of the meaning of the words and actions has not been developed. These seem to be indoctrinating acts that cue and reinforce feelings of loyalty and patriotism. . . ." [Citing R. Hess and J. Torney, *The Development of Political Attitudes in Children* 108 (1967).]

(b) *Rituals also emphasize the collective nature of patriotism.* Saluting the flag, singing the anthems, and honoring national figures are group activities. Group experiences can be very compelling, especially to the impressionable mind of the child. Consider the difference between the classroom and the family as settings for acquiring emotional attachment to the country. In the family, the child may learn to be patriotic because he recognizes that this orientation is highly valued by adults he tries to imitate. Patriotism in the classroom, in contrast, is *acted out* in the rituals, and acted out by the individual in a group he has come to be closely related with. In an attenuated way, the classroom approximates the "we-feeling" that is an important part of the political culture. The rituals lay the groundwork for adult political activity—most of which is necessarily group activity. Nationalism, partisanship, and identification with a social or political movement are orientations more meaningful when experienced as part of a collectivity. The ritual life of the school often involves such collective experiences.

3. *The Teacher.* The third way in which the classroom affects political socialization is through the teacher. Because of the special role he has in society and the direct contact he has with youth during the formative years, the teacher has considerable influence on the child's political orientations. . . . The evidence about the public school teacher in the United States forms a consistent picture. Teachers are expected to, and do, propagate political views and beliefs appropriately labeled "consensus values." Teachers should not, and generally do not, use the classroom as a forum for discussion of "partisan values" and controversial positions. Democracy, the two-party system, free enterprise, basic freedoms, and so forth, are not only permissible subjects in the classroom; the teacher is expected to urge these beliefs on his students. Liberal or conservative positions, foreign policy views, party allegiances, on the other hand, are seen as partisan values; and the teacher generally is expected to avoid particular interpretations of such issues.

The teacher, then, is expected simultaneously to be very political in some senses, and apolitical in others. The evidence suggests that the American public school teacher is generally adroit in balancing these two demands. A similar state exists among public school teachers throughout the world. A polity cannot afford to have its school system rent by partisan debates; but neither can it afford a public education system negligent in transmitting the basic political norms of the society. This is the general pattern for public school systems. The picture may be quite different for some private and parochial schools. In such schools one of the major objectives may be to inculcate particular partisan or group values, some of which might be at odds with the general consensus values of the larger society.

The teacher's role as conveyor of consensus values is so widely assumed that few students of political socialization have investigated it. One major reason why teachers operate so effectively in this connection is that they are products of the same political socialization for which they serve as agents. Teachers generally do not need to be taught to laud the virtues of the nation. Their own political selves have been shaped in accordance with the very consensus values they now transmit. This condition is more prevalent in older, established nations than in newer, developing ones. In the latter teachers are frequently sent through accelerated courses designed to teach them the new "consensus values."

The extent to which consensus and patriotic values are part of the orientations of American school teachers is indicated in a survey of high school teachers. Forty-two percent of the teachers sampled considered the following statement to be fact rather than opinion: "The American form of government may not be perfect, but it is the best type of government yet devised by man." All but 3 percent of these teachers, whether they considered the statement fact or opinion, felt it was a view which could be freely expressed in the classroom.

. . . .

We conclude this section with an observation Hess and Torney made after reporting on extensive data comparing teachers' views and students' attitudes. They find that teachers and students are more alike in their attitudes in areas where there is consensus in the society (e.g., the behavior of the good citizen) and less similar in attitudes which lack such consensus (political parties). This finding offers strong support for the ideas we have developed in this section. Teachers communicate to their students the political consensus values of society. They appear to have some influence. Teachers do not talk as often about partisan values. There is more discrepancy between teacher and student and among the students on these issues. Partisan or group values are acquired elsewhere and generally are not affected by the school classroom.

(b) *The teacher and the learning culture.* The teacher also affects the political development of the student by establishing some sort of "learning culture" or "social system" in the classroom. The elementary school teacher with whom millions of children the world over have daily contact is institutionally defined as superior to the child. He knows more about the subject matter, establishes and interprets school rules, is looked up to as a behavioral model, and is publicly labeled a representative of society's authority over the young. In a normal day the elementary teacher will have more than 10,000 exchanges with the student through which he will transmit numerous cultural values. Some of these values, as discussed above, will have specific political content; others will have latent political meaning. As the first person to represent to the child the large, impersonal society beyond the personal family circle, the elementary teacher cannot avoid influencing the impressionable child in ways beyond the formal curriculum. We can illustrate this in two areas of politically relevant learning: obedience and competitiveness.

. . . .

Evidence from American elementary school children links the "lesson of obedience" more closely with political learning. Elementary teachers place more emphasis on compliance to rules and authority than any other "political" topic. Second- and third-grade teachers consider the obligation of the child to conform to school rules and laws of the community a more important lesson than reading and arithmetic. This concern with compliance appears to be characteristic of teachers of all elementary grades. At the same time that teachers emphasize compliance, they underemphasize the right of citizens to participate in government. Hess and Torney conclude that "much of what is called citizenship training in the public schools does not teach the child about the city, state, or national government, but is an attempt to teach regard for the rules and standards of conduct of the school."

Competitiveness is another politically meaningful orientation learned in the classroom. The authors of a leading textbook on education in the United States write: "The child learns that it is serious to fail, important to succeed, that the society disapproves of slow people and rewards fast ones." A simple fourth-grade spelling contest conveys this lesson. Whether the student masters the intricacies of spelling or not, he internalizes the cultural value of competitiveness and success.

With these examples and notions in mind, we can turn to the aspect of the teacher's role in the classroom considered most important to political socialization: the authoritarian or democratic atmosphere of the classroom. Classrooms are said to be more or less democratic (or authoritarian) depending on how the teacher handles his role as authority figure. He may stress disciplined learning of the material presented, rigid adherence to rules, and a deferential attitude toward himself as the authority. Student participation may be kept to a minimum. Or, the teacher may assume an opposite stance. More student participation may be encouraged. School rules may be few and relaxed. The teacher may require less deference from students.

The crucial notion for political socialization is that these conditions affect the political outlook of the students. Democratic leadership by the teacher fosters attitudes and skills consonant with democratic values. The authoritarian teacher induces his charges to think according to hierarchy and deference to power. This notion has two variants: One line of reasoning stresses the teacher as a role model, the other concerns the importance of student participation for learning.

Notes and Questions

1. Socialization and the Courts

Is the socialization process described by Dawson and Prewitt amenable to judicial limitation? Should it be? How would a court enforce its decree? Is it realistic to believe that one branch of government, the courts, will impose limits on a process designed to secure the survival of the government? If political socialization is inherent in the educational process, does this argue for a rethinking of the *Pierce* compromise? Was John Stuart Mill correct in his opposition to state-operated educational institutions? Can any modern nation afford to accept the Mill position?

2. Constitutional Issues

What constitutional arguments other than the free exercise of religion would you make to attack the socialization process? Is it a speech problem? Do the freedoms of expression and belief imply that parents and students should have the "right" to prevent the state from influencing children's values?

3. Socialization and "Quality Education"

Is political socialization inconsistent with "quality education"? Is it inconsistent with learning to think for oneself and approach problems critically? Would you, as a matter of policy, wish to limit schools to the task of imparting skills? Consider these comments by Michael B. Katz:

> It must be emphasized that, opinion to the contrary notwithstanding, people ask no more of schools today than they did 125 years ago. Even then the schools were asked to do the impossible. As we have seen, the purpose of the school people has been more the development of attitudes than of intellect, and this continues to be the case. It is true, and this point must be stressed, of radical reformers as well as of advocates of law and order. The latter want the schools to stop crime and check immorality by teaching obedience to authority, respect for the law, and conformity to conventional standards. The former want the schools to reform society by creating a new sense of community through turning out warm, loving, noncompetitive people.
>
> The moral should be clear. Educational reformers should begin to distinguish between what formal schooling can and cannot do. They must separate the teaching of skills from the teaching of attitudes, and concentrate on the former. In actual fact, it is of course impossible to separate the two; attitudes adhere in any form of practice. But there is a vast difference between leaving the formation of attitudes untended and making them the object of education. ("The Present Moment in Educational Reform," 41 *Harv Educ Rev* 342 (1971).)

In light of your answers to the questions in note 1, has Katz proposed a feasible policy alternative? Is Katz responding more to the failure of socialization to alter values and conduct than to its undesirability? If so, is his assumption consistent with the conclusions of Dawson and Prewitt?

4. Socialization and Totalitarianism

How do you distinguish between the socialization that takes place in American schools and the propagandizing that allegedly occurs in schools in totalitarian countries. Is the concept of political socialization inconsistent with democratic values? Is it simply a question of the acceptability of the means employed to accomplish the socialization objective? See F. Wirt and M. Kirst, *The Political Web of American Schools* 24-26 (1972).

B. Sectarian Socialization

ABINGTON SCHOOL DISTRICT v SCHEMPP
374 US 203 (1963)

Mr. Justice Clark delivered the opinion of the court.

Once again we are called upon to consider the scope of the provision of the First Amendment to the United States Constitution which declares that "Congress shall make no law respecting an establishment of religion, or prohibiting the free exercise thereof . . . ." These companion cases present the issues in the context of state action requiring that schools begin each day with readings from the Bible. While raising the basic questions under slightly different factual situations, the cases permit of joint treatment. In light of the history of the First Amendment and of our cases interpreting and applying its requirements, we hold that the practices at issue and the laws requiring them are unconstitutional under the establishment clause, as applied to the states through the Fourteenth Amendment.

I

The Facts in Each Case: No. 142. The Commonwealth of Pennsylvania by law, 24 Pa Stat § 15-1516, as amended, Pub Law 1928 (Supp 1960) December 17, 1959, requires that "At least ten verses from the Holy Bible shall be read, without comment, at the opening of each public school on each school day. Any child shall be excused from such Bible reading, or attending such Bible reading, upon the written request of his parent or guardian." The Schempp family, husband and wife and two of their three children, brought suit to enjoin enforcement of the statute, contending that their rights under the Fourteenth Amendment to the Constitution of the United States are, have been, and will continue to be violated unless this statute be declared unconstitutional as violative of the provisions of the First Amendment . . . . A three-judge statutory District Court for the Eastern District of Pennsylvania held that the statute is violative of the establishment clause of the First Amendment as applied to the states by the due process clause of the Fourteenth Amendment and directed that appropriate injunctive relief issue. . . .

The appellees Edward Lewis Schempp, his wife Sidney, and their children, Roger and Donna, are of the Unitarian faith and are members of the Unitarian Church in Germantown, Philadelphia, Pennsylvania, where they as well as another son, Ellory, regularly attend religious services. The latter was originally a party but having graduated from the school system *pendente lite* was voluntarily dismissed from the action. The other children attend the Abington Senior High School, which is a public school operated by appellant district.

On each school day at the Abington Senior High School between 8:15 and 8:30 a.m., while the pupils are attending their home rooms or advisory sections, opening exercises are conducted pursuant to the statute. The exercises are broadcast into each room in the school building through an intercommunications system and are conducted under the supervision of a teacher by students attending the school's radio and television workshop. Selected students from this course gather each morning in the school's workshop studio for the exercises, which include readings by one of the students of ten verses of the Holy Bible, broadcast to each room in the building. This is followed by the recitation of the Lord's Prayer, likewise over the intercommunications system, but also by the students in the various classrooms, who are asked to stand and join in repeating the prayer in unison. The exercises are closed with the flag salute and such pertinent announcements as are of interest to the students. Participation in the opening exercises, as directed by the statute, is voluntary. The student reading the verses from the Bible may select the passages and read from any version he chooses, although the only copies furnished by the school are the King James version, copies of which were circulated to each teacher by the school district. . . . The students and parents are advised that the student may absent himself from the classroom or, should he elect to remain, not participate in the exercises. . . .

At the first trial Edward Schempp and the children testified as to specific religious doctrines purveyed by a literal reading of the Bible "which were contrary to the religious beliefs which they held and to their familial teaching." . . . The children testified that all of the doctrines to which they referred were read to them at various times as part of the exercises. Edward Schempp testified at the second trial that he had considered having Roger and Donna excused from attendance at the exercises but decided against it for several reasons, including his belief that the children's relationship with their teachers and classmates would be adversely affected.[3]

No. 119. In 1905 the Board of School Commissioners of Baltimore City adopted a rule pursuant to Art 77, §202 of the Annotated Code of Maryland. The rule provided for the holding of opening exercises in the schools of the city, consisting primarily of the "reading, without comment, of a chapter in the Holy Bible and/or the use of the Lord's Prayer." The petitioners, Mrs. Madalyn Murray and her son, William J. Murray III, are both professed atheists. Following unsuccessful attempts to have the respondent school board rescind the rule, this suit was filed for mandamus to compel its rescission and cancellation. It was alleged that William was a student in a public school of the city and Mrs. Murray, his mother, was a taxpayer therein; that it was the practice under the rule to have a reading on each school morning from the King James version of the Bible; that at petitioners' insistence the rule was amended to permit children to be excused from the exercise on request of the parent and that William had been excused pursuant thereto; that nevertheless the rule as amended was in violation of the petitioners' rights "to freedom of religion under the First and Fourteenth Amendments" and in violation of "the principle of separation between church and state, contained therein. . . ." The petition particularized the petitioners' atheistic beliefs and stated that the rule, as practiced, violated their rights

> in that it threatens their religious liberty by placing a premium on belief as against nonbelief and subjects their freedom of conscience to the rule of the majority; it pronounces belief in God as the source of all moral and spiritual values, equating these values with religious values, and thereby renders sinister, alien and suspect the beliefs and ideals of your petitioners, promoting doubt and question of their morality, good citizenship and good faith.

The respondents demurred and the trial court, recognizing that the demurrer admitted all facts well pleaded, sustained it without leave to amend. The Maryland

---

3. The trial court summarized his testimony as follows:

"Edward Schempp, the children's father, testified that after careful consideration he had decided that he should not have Roger or Donna excused from attendance at these morning ceremonies. Among his reasons were the following. He said that he thought his children would be 'labeled as "odd balls" ' before their teachers and classmates every school day; that children, like Roger's and Donna's classmates, were liable 'to lump all particular religious difference[s] or religious objections [together] as "atheism" ' and that today the word 'atheism' is often connected with 'atheistic communism,' and has 'very bad' connotations, such as 'un-American' or 'anti-Red,' with overtones of possible immorality. Mr. Schempp pointed out that due to the events of the morning exercises following in rapid succession, the Bible reading, the Lord's Prayer, the Flag Salute, and the announcements, excusing his children from the Bible reading would mean that probably they would miss hearing the announcements so important to children. He testified also that if Roger and Donna were excused from Bible reading they would have to stand in the hall outside their 'homeroom' and that this carried with it the imputation of punishment for bad conduct."

Court of Appeals affirmed, the majority of four justices holding the exercise not in violation of the First and Fourteenth Amendments, with three justices dissenting. 228 Md 239, 179 A2d 698. . . .

Before examining [the] "neutral" position in which the establishment and free exercise clauses of the First Amendment place our government it is well that we discuss the reach of the amendment under the cases of this court.

First, this court has decisively settled that the first amendment's mandate that "Congress shall make no law respecting an establishment of religion, or prohibiting the free exercise thereof" has been made wholly applicable to the states by the Fourteenth Amendment. . . .

Second, this court has rejected unequivocally the contention that the establishment clause forbids only governmental preference of one religion over another. Almost twenty years ago in *Everson* [*v Board of Educ* 330 US 1 (1947)], the court said that "neither a state nor the federal government can set up a church. Neither can pass laws which aid one religion, aid all religions, or prefer one religion over another. . . ."

In *Everson v Board of Educ* . . . this court, through Mr. Justice Black, stated that the "scope of the First Amendment . . . was designed forever to suppress" the establishment of religion or the prohibition of the free exercise thereof. In short, the court held that the amendment "requires the state to be a neutral in its relations with groups of religious believers and nonbelievers; it does not require the state to be their adversary. State power is no more to be used so as to handicap religions than it is to favor. them." 330 US at 18. And Mr. Justice Jackson, in dissent, declared that public schools are organized "on the premise that secular education can be isolated from all religious teaching so that the school can inculcate all needed temporal knowledge and also maintain a strict and lofty neutrality as to religion. The assumption is that after the individual has been instructed in worldly wisdom he will be better fitted to choose his religion." 330 US at 23-24. . . .

Finally, in *Engel v Vitale,* only last year, these principles were so universally recognized that the court, without the citation of a single case and over the sole dissent of Mr. Justice Stewart, reaffirmed them. The Court found the twenty-two-word prayer used in "New York's program of daily classroom invocation of God's blessing as prescribed in the Regents' prayer [to be] a religious activity. 370 US 421, 424 (1962). It held that "it is no part of the business of government to compose official prayers for any group of the American people to recite as a part of a religious program carried on by government." 370 US at 425. . . .

[I]n both cases the laws require religious exercises and such exercises are being conducted in direct violation of the rights of the appellees and petitioners. Nor are these required exercises mitigated by the fact that individual students may absent themselves upon parental request, for that fact furnishes no defense to a claim of unconstitutionality under the establishment clause. . . . Further, it is no defense to urge that the religious practices here may be relatively minor encroachments on the First Amendment. The breach of neutrality that is today a trickling stream may all too soon become a raging torrent and, in the words of Madison, "it is proper to take alarm at the first experiment on our liberties. . . ."

It is insisted that unless these religious exercises are permitted a "religion of secularism" is established in the schools. We agree of course that the state may not establish a "religion of secularism" in the sense of affirmatively opposing or showing hostility to religion, thus "preferring those who believe in no religion over those who do believe." . . . We do not agree, however, that this decision in any sense has that effect. In addition, it might well be said that one's education is not complete without a study of comparative religion or the history of religion and its relationship to the advancement of civilization. It certainly may be said that the Bible is worthy of study for its literary and historic qualities. Nothing we have said here indicates that such study of the Bible or of religion, when presented objectively as part of a secular program of education, may not be effected consistently with the First Amendment. But the exercises here do not fall into those categories. They are religious exercises, required by the states in violation of the command of the First Amendment that the government maintain strict neutrality, neither aiding nor opposing religion.

Finally, we cannot accept that the concept of neutrality, which does not permit a state to require a religious exercise even with the consent of the majority of those affected, collides with the majority's right to free exercise of religion.[10] While the free exercise clause clearly prohibits the use of state action to deny the rights of free exercise to *anyone,* it has never meant that a majority could use the machinery of the state to practice its beliefs.

The place of religion in our society is an exalted one, achieved through a long tradition of reliance on the home, the church and the inviolable citadel of the individual heart and mind. We have come to recognize through bitter experience that it is not within the power of government to invade that citadel, whether its purpose or effect be to aid or oppose, to advance or retard. In the relationship between man and religion, the state is firmly committed to a position of neutrality.

[Concurring opinions by Justices Douglas and Goldberg are omitted.]

Mr. Justice Brennan, concurring.

A too literal quest for the advice of the Founding Fathers upon the issues of these cases seems to me futile and misdirected for several reasons: First, on our precise problem the historical record is at best ambiguous, and statements can readily be found to support either side of the proposition. The ambiguity of history is understandable if we recall the nature of the problems uppermost in the thinking of the statesmen who fashioned the religious guarantees; they were concerned with far more flagrant intrusions of government into the realm of religion than any that our century has witnessed. While it is clear to me that the Framers meant the establishment clause to prohibit more than the creation of an established federal church such as existed in England, I have no doubt that, in their preoccupation with the imminent question of established churches, they gave no distinct consideration to the particular question whether the clause also forbade devotional exercises in public institutions.

Second, the structure of American education has greatly changed since the First Amendment was adopted. In the context of our modern emphasis upon public education available to all citizens, any views of the eighteenth century as to whether the exercises at bar are an "establishment" offer little aid to decision. Education,

---

10. We are not of course presented with and therefore do not pass upon a situation such as military service, where the government regulates the temporal and geographic environment of individuals to a point that, unless it permits voluntary religious services to be conducted with the use of government facilities, military personnel would be unable to engage in the practice of their faiths.

as the Framers knew it, was in the main confined to private schools more often than not under strictly sectarian supervision. Only gradually did control of education pass largely to public officials. It would, therefore, hardly be significant if the fact was that the nearly universal devotional exercises in the schools of the young Republic did not provoke criticism; even today religious ceremonies in church-supported private schools are constitutionally unobjectionable.

Third, our religious composition makes us a vastly more diverse people than were our forefathers. They knew differences chiefly among Protestant sects. Today the nation is far more heterogeneous religiously, including as it does substantial minorities not only of Catholics and Jews but as well of those who worship according to no version of the Bible and those who worship no god at all. See *Torcaso v Watkins* 367 US 488, 495. In the face of such profound changes, practices which may have been objectionable to no one in the time of Jefferson and Madison may today be highly offensive to many persons, the deeply devout and the nonbelievers alike.

Whatever Jefferson or Madison would have thought of Bible reading or the recital of the Lord's Prayer in what few public schools existed in their day, our use of the history of their time must limit itself to broad purposes, not specific practices. By such a standard, I am persuaded, as is the court, that the devotional exercises carried on in the Baltimore and Abington schools offend the First Amendment because they sufficiently threaten in our day those substantive evils the fear of which called forth the establishment clause of the First Amendment. It is "*a constitution* we are expounding," and our interpretation of the First Amendment must necessarily be responsive to the much more highly charged nature of religious questions in contemporary society.

Fourth, the American experiment in free public education available to all children has been guided in large measure by the dramatic evolution of the religious diversity among the population which our public schools serve. The interaction of these two important forces in our national life has placed in bold relief certain positive values in the consistent application to public institutions generally, and public schools particularly, of the constitutional decree against official involvements of religion which might produce the evils the Framers meant the establishment clause to forestall. The public schools are supported entirely, in most communities, by public funds—funds exacted not only from parents, nor alone from those who hold particular religious views, nor indeed from those who subscribe to any creed at all. It is implicit in the history and character of American public education that the public schools serve a uniquely *public* function: the training of American citizens in an atmosphere free of parochial, divisive, or separatist influences of any sort—an atmosphere in which children may assimilate a heritage common to all American groups and religions. See *Illinois ex rel McCollum v Board of Educ* 333 US 203. This is a heritage neither theistic nor atheistic, but simply civic and patriotic. See *Meyer v Nebraska* 262 US 390, 400-403.

Attendance at the public schools has never been compulsory; parents remain morally and constitutionally free to choose the academic environment in which they wish their children to be educated. The relationship of the establishment clause of the First Amendment to the public school system is preeminently that of reserving such a choice to the individual parent, rather than vesting it in the majority of voters of each state or school district. The choice which is thus preserved is between a public secular education with its uniquely democratic values, and some form of private or sectarian education, which offers values of its own. In my judgment the First Amendment forbids the state to inhibit that freedom of choice by diminishing the attractiveness of either alternative—either by restricting the liberty of the private schools to inculcate whatever values they wish, or by jeopardizing the freedom of the public schools from private or sectarian pressures. The choice between these very different forms of education is one—very much like the choice of whether or not to worship—which our Constitution leaves to the individual parent. It is no proper function of the state or local government to influence or restrict that election. The lesson of history—drawn more from the experiences of other countries than from our own—is that a system of free public education forfeits its unique contribution to the growth of democratic citizenship when that choice ceases to be freely available to each parent.

Mr. Justice Stewart, dissenting.

I think the records in the two cases before us are so fundamentally deficient as to make impossible an informed or responsible determination of the constitutional issues presented. Specifically, I cannot agree that on these records we can say that the establishment clause has necessarily been violated.[1] But I think there exist serious questions under both that provision and the free exercise clause—insofar as each is imbedded in the Fourteenth Amendment—which require the remand of these cases for the taking of additional evidence.

The First Amendment declares that "Congress shall make no law respecting an establishment of religion, or prohibiting the free exercise thereof . . . ." It is, I think, a fallacious oversimplification to regard these two provisions as establishing a single constitutional standard of "separation of church and state," which can be mechanically applied in every case to delineate the required boundaries between government and religion. We err in the first place if we do not recognize, as a matter of history and as a matter of the imperatives of our free society, that religion and government must necessarily interact in countless ways. Secondly, the fact is that while in many contexts the establishment clause and the free exercise clause fully complement each other, there are areas in which a doctrinaire reading of the establishment clause leads to irreconcilable conflict with the free exercise clause.

As a matter of history, the First Amendment was adopted solely as a limitation upon the newly created national government. The events leading to its adoption strongly suggest that the establishment clause was primarily an attempt to insure that Congress not only would be powerless to establish a national church, but would also be unable to interfere with existing state establishments. See *McGowan v Maryland* 366 US 420, 440-41. Each state was left free to go its own way and pursue its own policy with respect to religion. Thus Virginia from the beginning pursued a policy of disestablishmentarianism. Massachusetts, by contrast, had an established church until well into the nineteenth century.

So matters stood until the adoption of the Fourteenth Amendment, or more accurately, until this court's decision in *Cantwell v Connecticut* in 1940. 310 US 296. In that case the court said: "The First Amendment declares that Congress shall make no law respecting an establishment of religion or prohibiting the free exercise

---

1. It is instructive, in this connection, to examine the complaints in the two cases before us. Neither complaint attacks the challenged practices as "establishments." What both allege as the basis for their causes of actions are, rather, violations of religious liberty.

thereof. The Fourteenth Amendment has rendered the legislatures of the states as incompetent as Congress to enact such laws."

Since the *Cantwell* pronouncement in 1940, this court has only twice held invalid state laws on the ground that they were laws "respecting an establishment of religion" in violation of the Fourteenth Amendment. *McCollum v Board of Educ* 333 US 203; *Engel v Vitale* 370 US 421. On the other hand, the court has upheld against such a challenge laws establishing Sunday as a compulsory day of rest, *McGowan v Maryland* 366 US 420, and a law authorizing reimbursement from public funds for the transportation of parochial school pupils. *Everson v Board of Educ* 330 US 1.

Unlike other First Amendment guarantees, there is an inherent limitation upon the applicability of the establishment clause's ban on state support to religion. That limitation was succinctly put in *Everson v Board of Educ* 330 US 1, 18: "State power is no more to be used so as to handicap religions than it is to favor them." And in a later case, this court recognized that the limitation was one which was itself compelled by the free exercise guarantee.

It is this concept of constitutional protection embodied in our decisions which makes the cases before us such difficult ones for me. For there is involved in these cases a substantial free exercise claim on the part of those who affirmatively desire to have their children's school day open with the reading of passages from the Bible.

It has become accepted that the decision in *Pierce v Society of Sisters* 268 US 510, upholding the right of parents to send their children to nonpublic schools, was ultimately based upon the recognition of the validity of the free exercise claim involved in that situation. It might be argued here that parents who wanted their children to be exposed to religious influences in school could, under *Pierce*, send their children to private or parochial schools. But the consideration which renders this contention too facile to be determinative has already been recognized by the court: "Freedom of speech, freedom of the press, freedom of religion are available to all, not merely to those who can pay their own way." *Murdock v Pennsylvania* 319 US 105, 111.

It might also be argued that parents who want their children exposed to religious influences can adequately fulfill that wish off school property and outside school time. With all its surface persuasiveness, however, this argument seriously misconceives the basic constitutional justification for permitting the exercises at issue in these cases. For a compulsory state educational system so structures a child's life that if religious exercises are held to be an impermissible activity in schools, religion is placed at an artificial and state-created disadvantage. Viewed in this light, permission of such exercises for those who want them is necessary if the schools are truly to be neutral in the matter of religion. And a refusal to permit religious exercises thus is seen, not as the realization of state neutrality, but rather as the establishment of a religion of secularism, or at the least, as government support of the beliefs of those who think that religious exercises should be conducted only in private.

Notes and Questions

1. The Constitutional Standard

What constitutional standard did the court apply in *Schempp*? Does the prohibition of school prayers follow from the proposition that the state may not establish a church? Is the history of the First Amendment or of the early relationship between public schools and religion of any relevance to this issue? See generally Corwin, "The Supreme Court as National School Board," 14 *Law & Contemp Prob* 3 (1949); L. Pfeffer, *Church, State, and Freedom* 118-59 (1953). Why cannot the state seek neutrality by treating equally all religions, preferring none? Would such a standard raise insurmountable difficulties with respect to the definition of "religion"? Would atheists have a claim to engage in some ritual in the school? In the light of the discussion in chapter 1, should a distinction be drawn between state financial aid to church schools and the inclusion of religious ceremonies in public schools? Which is more dangerous in terms of the policies underlying the First Amendment requirement of separation of church and state? See generally Brown, "Quis Custodiet Ipso Custodes?—The School Prayer Cases," 1963 *Sup Ct Rev* 1.

2. Socialization

Justice Brennan observes in *Abington* that public schools serve the public function of creating "an atmosphere in which children may assimilate a heritage common to all American groups and religions. . . . This is a heritage neither theistic nor atheistic, but simply civic and patriotic." Are these remarks consistent with the court's holding? What justifies the distinction between sectarian and nonsectarian socialization? See *US v Ballard* 322 US 78, 92 (1944) (Jackson, J, dissenting). In this regard, consider these comments written almost forty years ago by Howard Beale:

> Americans . . . generally are as determined to keep irreligion out of the schools as to exclude sectarianism. An overwhelming majority of citizens believe that teachers with at least a mild interest in religion "have a better influence" on children than those of no religion . . . . Religion makes children "better children." It gives them something that even parents who have discarded it wish them to have . . . . "Christian" in ordinary parlance is an adjective of commendation.
>
> . . . . Furthermore, if the purpose of schools is to instill "patriotic" attitudes, correct economic views, and conformity to political, social, and business practices of the community . . . , why should not the community religious beliefs also be implanted in children: agnostic attitudes where they prevail, the Protestant faith where it prevails, and Catholic dogmas where Catholics predominate? (H. Beale, *Are American Teachers Free?* 210, 217 (1936).)

Does this hostility to irreligion merit constitutional protection? Does Beale's comment support Justice Stewart's contention that the court's decision impedes the free exercise of religion? Compare *Donahoe v Richards* 38 Me 376 (1854).

3. Remedy

Why did the court reject the remedy of excusal of the plaintiff's children from the objectionable exercises? Compare *West Virginia State Bd of Educ v Barnette* 319 US 624 (1943). Does the text of the establishment clause make such a remedy mandatory? Would the plaintiffs be entitled to the same relief if their constitutional attack were grounded in the free exercise clause? Does the court adopt the more sweeping remedy because it fears that nonparticipating children will be stigmatized or abused? Does it fear that these pressures toward conformity would emasculate a constitutional holding that voluntary prayers in the schools were permissible? Would the result in the case have changed if the prayers had taken place before and after school and if no student were required to participate? See *Vaughn v Reed* 313 F Supp 431 (WD Va 1970).

4. Scope of the Decision

Is religious instruction in public schools permissible after *Schempp*? What is the distinction between ritual worship and instruction? Does instruction imply an objective treatment of many religions and a range of religious and nonreligious values? Does it imply a descriptive, nonevaluative approach? In terms of the fears of the plaintiffs, does ritual worship or instruction pose a greater threat to their children?

5. Reaction of Politicians and Schoolmen

None of the justices writing in *Schempp* expresses concern for judicial interference with the political process. However, as the following discussion by Professor Washby demonstrates, the political reaction to *Schempp* was complex, and compliance with the court's judgment was far from immediate:

THE IMPACT OF THE SUPREME COURT
Wasby, 129-133 (1970)

Reaction to the school prayer decisions in Congress was [strong].... Over one hundred congressmen (more Republicans than Democrats, with most of the latter being from the South and from rural constituencies) introduced amendments to the Constitution on the subject.... "Political leaders and a number of spontaneous citizens' organizations opposed the decision so strongly that they were willing to alter the words of the First Amendment to gain a reversal." It should be noted that the reaction to *Engel,* involving a state-written prayer in one state, was far greater, at least in terms of immediate emotional outburst, than to *Schempp,* affecting a majority of the states. This may have occurred because the first decision was read to be far broader than it was, as saying what the second actually did, and because people were prepared for (or resigned to) the *Schempp* ruling.

[T]he Becker Amendment on school prayer failed in the House when Becker could muster only 167 of the necessary 218 signatures for a discharge petition to get the bill out of the Judiciary Committee, where it was opposed by committee chairman Emanuel Celler, who had also vehemently opposed the Tuck Bill. ...

The campaign for the amendment to the Constitution came to an end ... quickly.... One key reason may be that there was [no] mass of follow-up litigation ... and resistance tended to be a local or community-by-community matter. To be sure, national leaders spoke out. Within the churches, "The Jewish community welcomed [*Schempp*], Protestant leaders were divided but the overwhelming majority of the national leaders approved the decision, and the Catholic Church was firmly opposed to the decisions. Particular groups of clergymen and other church leaders in particular places made statements and passed resolutions on both sides of the decision. ...

The Governors Conference in 1962 called for a constitutional amendment allowing Bible reading in the schools. And there was some litigation: ... lower courts struck down Bible reading in five states shortly after *Schempp,* although the Florida Supreme Court upheld practices conflicting with the ruling. Some attempts by parents to evade the ruling, by substituting voluntary prayers, ended up in court. When prayers occurred before and after the school day in one town, the judge only prohibited the ringing of the school bell to designate the period, while upholding the prayer itself. When parents in a New York community wanted a prayer with the milk and cookies, the practice was blocked, with the judges holding that the state is not required to permit student-initiated prayers.

On the whole, however, the battle was fought out elsewhere than in the courts. And not all noncompliance was resisted, by any means. Where one religion predominated in an area, or where religious sentiment was relatively homogeneous, those in the minority may have been unwilling to subject themselves to obloquy by attacking the practices, particularly as their children may have been ostracized at school. The school officials whose responsibility it might be considered to comply with "the law" may have been hesitant to move against practices firmly supported by the school boards to which they were directly responsible, or by interests in the community to whom they looked for approval. . . .

We do have a relatively broad picture of compliance and noncompliance with the school prayer rulings as a result of several surveys, both national and within particular states. Surveys by the state superintendent of education in Kentucky, and by the Indiana School Board Association, both showed low compliance; only 61 of 204 school districts in Kentucky had discontinued prayers and Bible reading, and 121 superintendents had unwritten policies permitting both, while in Indiana fewer than 6 percent of the boards had changed policies to come into compliance with the court. In Texas, in a survey conducted by the Council of Churches, the change was negligible, and few responding said they agreed in principle with the decisions. . . .

In line with other research, Dierenfield found major regional differences both in frequency of the practice and degree of compliance. Thus, in comparing the responses he found in 1960 with those in 1966 concerning regular devotional services, he found 8 percent of the reporting districts in 1966 showed all schools in the system with such services, where the comparable figure in 1960 had been over 33 percent; the drop for districts reporting some schools having services was from 17 percent to 10.7 percent. With respect to devotional Bible reading in the schools, we find a shift nationally from almost 42 percent Yes (have the practice) to just below 14 percent. However, the 42 percent figure (1960) covers up vast regional differences—from 11 percent in the western states and 18 percent in the Midwest to more than 75 percent in the South and more than two thirds in the East. By 1966, except for the South, the regional variation had decreased; western, midwestern, and eastern were all below 5 percent, although the South still showed more than half retaining the practices. Dierenfield's work also shows variation by size of unit, but the spread is not as great as for regions. In 1960, almost 31 percent of communities from 500 to 2,500 had the practices, as did 54 percent of the largest communities (100,000+). In 1966, the largest units still were the ones where the practice would be most frequently found (almost 30 percent), but existence of the Bible reading had dropped to under 10 percent in the smallest communities.

If we shift from the units involved to teachers, we can find out other factors relevant to compliance with the school prayer cases. To test the impact of the *Schempp* and *Murray* decisions, Way conducted a national survey, using a random sample of 2,320 public elementary schoolteachers (in 464 schools). He found noticeable shifts in classroom practices concerning prayers and Bible reading. Whereas more than 60 percent of the teachers had had classroom prayers at the time of the decisions, by 1964-65, this had dropped to 28 percent, most of whom were involved in daily prayer practices; with respect to Bible reading, the percentage dropped from 48 percent to 22 percent. "The average teacher," Way asserts, "did feel the impact of the Supreme Court's decisions." While teachers did have much discretion in what they did and while their personal religious views had an effect on their compliance, the policy under which they operated also had a marked effect. When asked about school policy on prayers, 155 said that some prayers were favored, 494 said they were opposed, and by far the largest number, 1,011, said there was no policy, that it was left to the teacher's discretion, or that they did not know of a policy. The figures for Bible reading are much the same. The effect is shown by the fact that only 4 percent of the teachers in schools opposing the prayers did say them, while 43 percent of those in schools favoring the prayers did so. Having no policy or teacher discretion was equivalent to having a policy in favor of prayer, as 40 percent of the "others" had prayer exercises in their classrooms. For Bible reading, 91 percent of those in schools favoring the policy had the practice, but only 3 percent of those in schools opposed did; here, only 25 percent of the "others" had the practice.

C. Nonsectarian Socialization

1. Compulsory Flag Salute Laws

WEST VIRGINIA STATE BOARD OF EDUCATION v BARNETTE
319 US 624 (1943)

Mr. Justice Jackson delivered the opinion of the court.

Following the decision by this court on June 3, 1940, in *Minersville School Dist v Gobitis* 310 US 586, the West Virginia legislature amended its statutes to require all schools therein to conduct courses of instruction in history, civics, and in the Constitutions of the United States and of the state "for the purpose of teaching, fostering and perpetuating the ideals, principles and spirit of Americanism, and increasing the knowledge of the organization and machinery of the government." Appellant board of education was directed, with advice of the state superintendent of schools, to "prescribe the courses of study covering these subjects" for public schools. The act made it the duty of private, parochial and denominational schools to prescribe courses of study "similar to those required for the public schools."

The board of education on January 9, 1942, adopted a resolution containing recitals taken largely from the court's *Gobitis* opinion and ordering that the salute to the flag become "a regular part of the program of activities in the public schools," that all teachers and pupils "shall be required to participate in the salute honoring the nation represented by the flag; provided, however, that refusal to salute the flag be regarded as an act of insubordination, and shall be dealt with accordingly."

The resolution originally required the "commonly accepted salute to the flag" which it defined. Objections to the salute as "being too much like Hitler's" were raised by the Parent and Teachers Association, the Boy and Girl Scouts, the Red Cross, and the Federation of Women's Clubs. Some modification appears to have been made in deference to these objections, but no concession was made to Jehovah's Witnesses. What is now required is the "stiff-arm" salute, the saluter to keep the right hand raised with palm turned up while the following is repeated: "I pledge allegiance to the flag of the United States of America and to the Republic for which it stands; one nation, indivisible, with liberty and justice for all."

Failure to conform is "insubordination" dealt with by expulsion. Readmission is denied by statute until compliance. Meanwhile the expelled child is "unlawfully absent" and may be proceeded against as a delinquent. His parents or guardians are liable to prosecution, and if convicted are subject to fine not exceeding $50 and jail term not exceeding thirty days.

Appellees, citizens of the United States and of West Virginia, brought suit in the United States District Court for themselves and others similarly situated asking its injunction to restrain enforcement of these laws and regulations against Jehovah's Witnesses. The Witnesses are an unincorporated body teaching that the obligation imposed by law of God is superior to that of laws enacted by temporal government. Their religious beliefs include a literal version of Exodus, chapter 20, verses 4 and 5, which says: "Thou shalt not make unto thee any graven image, or any likeness of anything that is in heaven above, or that is in the earth beneath, or that is in the water under the earth; thou shalt not bow down thyself to them nor serve them." They consider that the flag is an "image" within this command. For this reason they refuse to salute it.

The freedom asserted by these appellees does not bring them into collision with rights asserted by any other individual. It is such conflicts which most frequently require intervention of the state to determine where the rights of one end and those of another begin. But the refusal of these persons to participate in the ceremony does not interfere with or deny rights of others to do so. Nor is there any question in this case that their behavior is peaceable and orderly. The sole conflict is between authority and rights of the individual. The state asserts power to condition access to public education on making a prescribed sign and profession and at the same time to coerce attendance by punishing both parent and child. The latter stand on a right of self-determination in matters that touch individual opinion and personal attitude.

As the present Chief Justice said in dissent in the *Gobitis* case, the state may "require teaching by instruction and study of all in our history and in the structure and organization of our government, including the guaranties of civil liberty, which tend to inspire patriotism and love of country." 310 US at 604. Here, however, we are dealing with a compulsion of students to declare a belief. They are not merely made acquainted with the flag salute so that they may be informed as to what it is or even what it means. The issue here is whether this slow and easily neglected route to aroused loyalties constitutionally may be short-cut by substituting a compulsory salute and slogan. . . .

[T]he compulsory flag salute and pledge require affirmation of a belief and an attitude of mind. It is not clear whether the regulation contemplates that pupils forgo any contrary convictions of their own and become unwilling converts to the prescribed ceremony or whether it will be acceptable if they simulate assent by words without belief and by a gesture barren of meaning. It is now a commonplace that censorship or suppression of expression of opinion is tolerated by our Constitution only when the expression presents a clear and present danger of action of a kind the state is empowered to prevent and punish. It would seem that involuntary affirmation could be commanded only on even more immediate and urgent grounds than silence. But here the power of compulsion is invoked without any allegation that remaining passive during a flag salute ritual creates a clear and present danger that would justify an effort even to muffle expression. To sustain the compulsory flag salute we are required to say that a Bill of Rights which guards the individual's right to speak his own mind, left it open to public authorities to compel him to utter what is not in his mind.

Whether the First Amendment to the Constitution will permit officials to order observance of ritual of this nature does not depend upon whether as a voluntary exercise we would think it to be good, bad or merely innocuous. Any credo of nationalism is likely to include what some disapprove or to omit what others think essential, and to give off different overtones as it takes on different accents or interpretations. If official power exists to coerce acceptance of any patriotic creed, what it shall contain cannot be decided by courts, but must be largely discretionary with the ordaining authority, whose power to prescribe would no doubt include power to amend. Hence validity of the asserted power to force an American citizen publicly to profess any statement of belief or to engage in any ceremony of assent to one, presents questions of power that must be considered independently of any idea we may have as to the utility of the ceremony in question.

Nor does the issue as we see it turn on one's possession of particular religious views or the sincerity with which they are held. While religion supplies appellees' motive for enduring the discomforts of making the issue in this case, many citizens who do not share these religious views hold such a compulsory rite to infringe constitutional liberty of the individual. It is not necessary to inquire whether nonconformist beliefs will exempt from the duty to salute unless we first find power to make the salute a legal duty.

The *Gobitis* decision, however, *assumed,* as did the argument in that case and in this, that power exists in the state to impose the flag salute discipline upon school children in general. The court only examined and rejected a claim based on religious beliefs of immunity from an unquestioned general rule. The question which underlies the flag salute controversy is whether such a ceremony so touching matters of opinion and political attitude may be imposed upon the individual by official authority under powers committed to any political organization under our Constitution. . . .

It was also considered in the *Gobitis* case that functions of educational officers in states, counties and school districts were such that to interfere with their authority "would in effect make us the school board for the country." 310 US at 598.

The Fourteenth Amendment, as now applied to the states, protects the citizen against the state itself and all of its creatures—boards of education not excepted. These have, of course, important, delicate, and highly discretionary functions, but none that they may not perform within the limits of the Bill of Rights. That they are educating the young for citizenship is reason for scrupulous protection of Constitutional freedoms of the individual, if we are not to strangle the free mind at its source and teach youth to discount important principles of our government as mere platitudes.

Such boards are numerous and their territorial jurisdiction often small. But small and local authority may feel less sense of responsibility to the Constitution, and agencies of publicity may be less vigilant in calling it to account. The action of Congress in making flag observance voluntary and respecting the conscience of the objector in a matter so vital as raising the army contrasts sharply with these local regulations in matters relatively trivial to the welfare of the nation. There are village tyrants as well as village Hampdens, but none who acts under color of law is beyond reach of the Constitution.

The *Gobitis* opinion reasoned that this is a field "where courts possess no marked and certainly no controlling competence," that it is committed to the legislatures as well as the courts to guard cherished liberties and that it is constitutionally appropriate to "fight out the wise use of legislative authority in the forum of public opinion and before legislative assemblies rather than to transfer such a contest to the judicial arena," since all the "effective means of inducing political changes are left free." 310 US at 597-98, 600.

The very purpose of a Bill of Rights was to withdraw certain subjects from the vicissitudes of political controversy, to place them beyond the reach of majorities and officials and to establish them as legal principles to be applied by the courts. One's right to life, liberty, and property, to free speech, a free press, freedom of worship and assembly, and other fundamental rights may not be submitted to vote; they depend on the outcome of no elections. . . .

Lastly, and this is the very heart of the *Gobitis* opinion, it reasons that "National unity is the basis of national security," that the authorities have "the right to select appropriate means for its attainment," and hence reaches the conclusion that such compulsory measures toward "national unity" are constitutional. 310 US at 595. Upon the verity of this assumption depends our answer in this case.

National unity as an end which officials may foster by persuasion and example is not in question. The problem is whether under our Constitution compulsion as here employed is a permissible means for its achievement.

Struggles to coerce uniformity of sentiment in support of some end thought essential to their time and country have been waged by many good as well as by evil men. Nationalism is a relatively recent phenomenon but at other times and places the ends have been racial or territorial security, support of a dynasty or regime, and particular plans for saving souls. As first and moderate methods to attain unity have failed, those bent on its accomplishment must resort to an ever-increasing severity. As governmental pressure toward unity becomes greater, so strife becomes more bitter as to whose unity it shall be. Probably no deeper division of our people could proceed from any provocation than from finding it necessary to choose what doctrine and whose program public educational officials shall compel youth to unite in embracing.

The case is made difficult not because the principles of its decision are obscure but because the flag involved is our own. Nevertheless, we apply the limitations of the Constitution with no fear that freedom to be intellectually and spiritually diverse or even contrary will disintegrate the social organization. To believe that patriotism will not flourish if patriotic ceremonies are voluntary and spontaneous instead of a compulsory routine is to make an unflattering estimate of the appeal of our institutions to free minds.

If there is any fixed star in our constitutional constellation, it is that no official, high or petty, can prescribe what shall be orthodox in politics, nationalism, religion, or other matters of opinion or force citizens to confess by word or act their faith therein. If there are any circumstances which permit an exception, they do not now occur to us.

We think the action of the local authorities in compelling the flag salute and pledge transcends constitutional limitations on their power and invades the sphere of intellect and spirit which it is the purpose of the First Amendment to our Constitution to reserve from all official control.

Affirmed.

[Concurring opinions of Justices Black, Douglas, and Murphy are omitted.]

Mr. Justice Frankfurter, dissenting. . . .

Not so long ago we were admonished that "the only check upon our own exercise of power is our own sense of self-restraint. For the removal of unwise laws from the statute books appeal lies not to the courts but to the ballot and to the processes of democratic government. . . ."

The reason why from the beginning even the narrow judicial authority to nullify legislation has been viewed with a jealous eye is that it serves to prevent the full play of the democratic process. The fact that it may be an undemocratic aspect of our scheme of government does not call for its rejection or its disuse. But it is the best of reasons, as this court has frequently recognized, for the greatest caution in its use. . . .

Under our constitutional system the legislature is charged solely with civil concerns of society. If the avowed or intrinsic legislative purpose is either to promote or to discourage some religious community or creed, it is clearly within the constitutional restrictions imposed on legislatures and cannot stand. But it by no means follows that legislative power is wanting whenever a general nondiscriminatory civil regulation in fact touches conscientious scruples or religious beliefs of an individual or a group. Regard for such scruples or beliefs undoubtedly presents one of the most reasonable claims for the exertion of legislative accommodation. It is, of course, beyond our power to rewrite the state's requirement, by providing exemptions for those who do not wish to participate in the flag salute or by making some other accommodations to meet their scruples. That wisdom might suggest the making of such accommodations and that school administration would not find it too difficult to make them and yet maintain the ceremony for those not refusing to conform, is outside our province to suggest. . . .

This is no dry, technical matter. It cuts deep into one conception of the democratic process—it concerns no less the practical differences between the means for making these accommodations that are open to courts and to legislatures. A court can only strike down. It can only say "This or that law is void." It cannot modify or qualify, it cannot make exceptions to a general requirement. And it strikes down not merely for a day. . . .

The constitutional protection of religious freedom terminated disabilities, it did not create new privileges. It gave religious equality, not civil immunity. Its essence is freedom from conformity to religious dogma, not freedom from conformity to law because of religious dogma. Religious loyalties may be exercised without hindrance from the state, not the state may not exercise that which except by leave of religious loyalties is within the domain of temporal power. Otherwise each individual could set up his own censor against obedience to laws conscientiously deemed for the public good by those whose business it is to make laws.

The essence of the religious freedom guaranteed by our Constitution is therefore this: no religion shall either receive the state's support or incur its hostility. Religion is outside the sphere of political government. This does not mean that all matters on which religious organizations or beliefs may pronounce are outside the sphere of government. Were this so, instead of the separation of church and state, there would be the subordination of the state on any matter deemed within the sovereignty of the religious conscience. Much that is the concern of temporal authority affects the spiritual interests of men. But it is not enough to strike down a nondiscriminatory law that it may hurt or offend some dissident view. It would be too easy to cite numerous prohibitions and injunctions to which laws run counter if the variant interpretations of the Bible were made the tests of obedience to law. The validity of secular laws cannot be measured by their conformity to religious doctrines. It is only in a theocratic state that ecclesiastical doctrines measure legal right or wrong.

An act compelling profession of allegiance to a religion, no matter how subtly or tenuously promoted, is bad. But an act promoting good citizenship and national allegiance is within the domain of governmental authority and is therefore to be judged by the same considerations of power and of constitutionality as those involved in the many claims of immunity from civil obedience because of religious scruples.

Parents have the privilege of choosing which schools they wish their children to attend. And the question here is whether the state may make certain requirements that seem to it desirable or important for the proper education of those future citizens who go to schools maintained by the states, or whether the pupils in those schools may be relieved from those requirements if they run counter to the consciences of their parents. Not only have parents the right to send children to schools of their own choosing but the state has no right to bring such schools "under a strict governmental control" or give "affirmative direction concerning the intimate and essential details of such schools, entrust their control to public officers, and deny both owners and patrons reasonable choice and discretion in respect of teachers, curriculum, and textbooks." *Farrington v Tokushige* 273 US 284, 298 (1926). Why should not the state likewise have constitutional power to make reasonable provisions for the proper instruction of children in schools maintained by it? . . .

We are told that a flag salute is a doubtful substitute for adequate understanding of our institutions. The states that require such a school exercise do not have to justify it as the only means for promoting good citizenship in children, but merely as one of diverse means for accomplishing a worthy end. We may deem it a foolish measure, but the point is that this court is not the organ of government to resolve doubts as to whether it will fulfill its purpose. Only if there be no doubt that any reasonable mind could entertain can we deny to the states the right to resolve doubts their way and not ours. . . .

One's conception of the Constitution cannot be severed from one's conception of a judge's function in applying it. The court has no reason for existence if it merely reflects the pressures of the day. Our system is built on the faith that men set apart for this special function, freed from the influences of immediacy and from the deflections of worldly ambition, will become able to take a view of longer range than the period of responsibility entrusted to Congress and legislatures. We are dealing with matters as to which legislators and voters have conflicting views. Are we as judges to impose our strong convictions on where wisdom lies? That which three years ago had seemed to five successive courts to lie within permissible areas of legislation is now outlawed by the deciding shift of opinion of two justices. What reason is there to believe that they or their successors may not have another view a few years hence? Is that which was deemed to be of so fundamental a nature as to be written into the Constitution to endure for all times to be the sport of shifting winds of doctrine? Of course, judicial opinions, even as to questions of constitutionality, are not immutable. As has been true in the past, the court will from time to time reverse its position. But I believe that never before these Jehovah's Witnesses cases (except for minor deviations subsequently retraced) has this court overruled decisions so as to restrict the powers of democratic government. Always heretofore, it has withdrawn narrow views of legislative authority so as to authorize what formerly it had denied.

In view of this history it must be plain that what thirteen justices found to be within the constitutional authority of a state, legislators can not be deemed unreasonable in enacting. Therefore, in denying to the states what heretofore has received such impressive judicial sanction, some other tests of unconstitutionality must surely be guiding the court than the absence of a rational justification for the legislation. But I know of no other test which this court is authorized to apply in nullifying legislation. . . .

The uncontrollable power wielded by this court brings it very close to the most sensitive areas of public affairs. As appeal from legislation to adjudication becomes more frequent, and its consequences more far-reaching, judicial self-restraint becomes more and not less important, lest we unwarrantably enter social and political domains wholly outside our concern. I think I appreciate fully the objections to the law before us. But to deny that it presents a question upon which men might reasonably differ appears to me to be intolerance. And since men may so reasonably differ, I deem it beyond my constitutional power to assert my view of the wisdom of this law against the view of the state of West Virginia. . . .

Notes and Questions

1. The Constitutional Standard

Is *Barnette* a case about free exercise of religion or free speech? Do Justice Frankfurter and the majority join issue on this point? Might the necessity to distinguish *Minersville School Dist v Gobitis* 310 US 586 (1940), explain the majority's choice of constitutional doctrine? Viewed as a free exercise case, are the arguments in favor of the Jehovah's Witnesses stronger? Are there dangers in such an approach? Can we allow individuals, even on the basis of religious conviction, to flout the civil law? Does it depend on which law they choose to disregard—for example, a flag salute law rather than a burglary statute? Is this too slippery a line for sound and predictable judicial administration? Would the motivation of the legislature—

whether "it was out to get" a particular religious group—be relevant to the free exercise issue? Could the Jehovah's Witnesses reasonably argue that the flag salute violates the establishment clause? Does the addition of the words "under God" to the Pledge of Allegiance make this conclusion inevitable?

As a speech case, *Barnette* assumes that there is a critical relationship between freedom of expression, belief, and the coerced declaration of belief. In this regard, consider this analysis of *Barnette* by Professor Emerson:

> The full protection extended to the right of belief in the *Barnette* case is essential to an effective system of freedom of expression. Forcing public expression of a belief is an affront of personal integrity. It can indeed be considered an invasion of the constitutional right to privacy, established in *Griswold v Connecticut,* as well as an abridgment of freedom of expression. Beyond that it is designed to instill a disposition to conformity and to substitute the will of the state for the free expression of the citizen. It establishes the psychological tone of a closed society. And nothing of social value is gained. Whatever outward conformity is achieved is undoubtedly more than offset by the inward hostility engendered. As Justice Jackson remarked, "Compulsory unification of opinion achieves only the unanimity of the graveyard." (T. Emerson, *The System of Freedom of Expression* 30 (1970).)

How does the coerced recitation of particular words interfere with a person's beliefs and values? Is the case better understood as protecting the "freedom not to speak"? Does our legal system generally protect this "freedom" in the absence of an assertion of privilege against self-incrimination as to the commission of a crime?

Is *Barnette* a privacy case, as Professor Emerson suggests? Privacy, of course, has many definitions: it may refer to protection against physical intrusion (in the human body, home, office, etc.), freedom from surveillance (e.g., wiretapping), freedom from state regulation of private conduct (e.g., use of contraceptives), protection against the publication and dissemination of facts about one's private life, etc. Which of these definitions, if any, is applicable to *Barnette*? Is it the "affront to personal integrity" inherent in a compulsory flag salute that justifies the court's decision? What does this mean? Is it an aspect of privacy?

The court alludes to the "clear and present danger" test as the appropriate criterion for determining whether speech is protected, and states "that involuntary affirmation could be commanded only on even more immediate and urgent grounds than silence." When would silence lead to a more immediate threat than a "clear and present danger"? What is a "clear and present danger" in the school context? Is this the test Justice Jackson actually applied? See Emerson, *System of Freedom of Expression* 29. In this regard, consider the following problem: Three high school students refuse to recite the pledge of allegiance because they assert that the words *with liberty and justice for all* are not true in America. They also refuse to stand or to leave the classroom when the pledge is being recited by the other students. The students are suspended, but a lower court orders their readmission. Subsequently, fifty other students join in their protest. On appeal the school district urges "that permitting a student to remain seated during the pledge could be a real threat to the maintenance of discipline and would be pedagogically foolhardy." What result should the appellate court reach? Is *Barnette* dispositive? See *Frain v Baron* 307 F Supp 27 (ED NY 1969). See also *Goetz v Ansell,* 477 F2d 636 (2d Cir 1973).

2. Scope of the Decision

How does the compulsory flag salute differ from compulsory instruction in American civics or history? Should *Barnette* be extended to these courses? Do they interfere with privacy, belief, and expression? Is the opportunity to remain silent in the classroom or to dispute the propositions asserted by the teacher a critical difference? Which is more "dangerous" to the Jehovah's Witnesses: compulsory instruction or compulsory ritual? Does the flag salute fail because it is a less efficient form of political socialization?

Would *Barnette* require excusing children whose parents objected from singing the national anthem? See *Sheldon v Fannin* 221 F Supp 766 (D Ariz 1963). From patriotic exercises that celebrate Memorial Day or Lincoln's Birthday? Schools often close for religious or patriotic holidays (Christmas, Thanksgiving, etc.). Could parents reasonably argue after *Barnette* that nonattendance is usually interpreted as an affirmation of belief in the religious or patriotic values underlying the observance of the holiday? Should a court require the schools to remain open on these days?

Consider a related problem, addressed in *Nistad v Board of Educ* 61 Misc2d 60, 304 NYS 2d 971 (Sup Ct 1969), where the New York City School Board issued a statement advising teachers and students that they would be permitted to participate in a Vietnam war moratorium. The schools would remain open, but each individual, as a matter of conscience, would be responsible for choosing whether or not to attend. The court, relying on *Barnette,* held that teachers and students were being deprived of their constitutional rights by being compelled to declare their support or opposition to the Vietnam War:

> Those people who are strongly against this country's Vietnam involvement have a constitutional right to remain silent; some of them might prefer to attend school . . . rather than participate in any visible demonstration favoring their position. Yet their school attendance could be interpreted as supporting the very view they oppose. Similarly, those who support the government's present Vietnam stance are not required to make their views known. 304 NYS 2d at 974.

Is *Barnette* dispositive of *Nistad*? Should the courts distinguish between the coerced declaration of beliefs contrary to the speaker's actual beliefs and the coerced declaration of beliefs consistent with the speaker's actual beliefs? Between required attendance and permissive nonattendance? Even after *Barnette,* are not the children of Jehovah's Witnesses who are obliged either to participate or not to participate in flag salute ceremonies being compelled to declare their beliefs?

Suppose in *Nistad* that the school board had not issued a policy statement, that many students and teachers attended the Vietnam war moratorium, and that their absences were recorded as unexcused. If students punished for these unexcused absences brought a court challenge, would the *Nistad* court have upheld their right to absent themselves from school under *Barnette*? Compare *Ferriter v Tyler* 48 Vt 444 (1876). If so, does the *Nistad* decision rest on the proposition that "the prestige and power of the board of education may not be used to support, influence or condone on [controversial] matters of this nature." Is this proposition defensible policy or constitutional law? Is it consistent with the widespread observance of religious and patriotic holidays?

2. Curriculum and Textbooks

Historically, selections of texts and curriculum subjects have been primary instruments in the political and religious socialization of children in the public schools. Educators did not view themselves as value-neutral. They were charged, not only with imparting skills, but also with training "citizens in character and proper principles." R. Elson, *Guardians of Tradition* 1 (1964). These "principles" derived from the community's political persuasion, social sensibilities, and religious preferences.

Before the American Revolution, the curriculum of most public schools included the three Rs, all taught from a strongly religious perspective. Educators did their best to ensure that religious values permeated courses and texts ostensibly devoted to these basic subjects. For example, early "spellers" (textbooks from which spelling was taught) included *popery* and *heresy* among the lists of words to be memorized. Elson, *Guardians of Tradition*, 2, 5. By 1825, however, the dominance of the church over public schools had declined. The state—urging allegiance to nonsectarian, national values—became the most significant influence on textbook and curriculum choices. Geography and grammar were added to the curriculum, and American history courses began to appear in the 1830s, although they were not generally required until after the Civil War. *Guardians of Tradition*, 5. Both curricula and textbooks emphasized patriotism, loyalty to government, and the protestant ethic. The widespread establishment of free public schools and the passage of compulsory attendance laws (events roughly coincident with the increased state role in determining curricula) greatly expanded the potential for political socialization by the state. Ruth Elson, in her treatise on nineteenth-century American textbooks, aptly summarized the tenor of public school education in the last century:

> The world created in nineteenth-century schoolbooks is essentially a world of fantasy . . . . It is an ideal world, peopled by ideal villains as well as ideal heroes. Nature is perfectly if sometimes inscrutably planned by God for the good of man, with progress as its first and invariable law. . . . Individuals are to be understood in terms of easily discernible, inherent characteristics of their race and nationality as much as in terms of their individual character. Virtue is always rewarded, vice punished. And one can achieve virtue and avoid vice by following a few simple rules. . . .
>
> . . . . The value judgment is their stock in trade: love of country, love of God, duty to parents, the necessity to develop habits of thrift, honesty and hard work in order to accumulate property, the certainty of progress, the perfection of the United States. . . . (*Guardians of Tradition*, 337-38.)

World War I and the postwar period saw even greater emphasis on nationalistic values in textbooks and curricula in the public schools. The anti-British bias of much of American history was replaced by an effort "to blacken the national character of the Germans and to minimize what modern civilization owes to Teutonic influence." H. Beale, *Are American Teachers Free?* 182 (1936). The American Revolution was blamed on the Germans in history texts: "There was no English tyranny over America . . . until a German king had tricked his colonists into hating his ministry . . . . So the American Revolution was a contest between German tyranny and English freedom. . . ." *Are American Teachers Free?* 183. Many states enacted laws requiring that English be the language of instruction in public and private schools or excluding all foreign languages or only German. *Are American Teachers Free?* 332-35. See *Meyer v Nebraska* 262 US 390 (1923). In 1918, South Dakota enacted a law requiring a public school course devoted "to the teaching of patriotism, the singing of patriotic songs, the reading of patriotic addresses and a study of the lives and history of American patriots." B. Pierce, *Public Opinion and the Teaching of History* 74 (1926). A similar law was enacted in Texas without the requisite number of readings in the legislature, because "the fact that this nation is now at war with a foreign foe . . . creates an emergency. . . ." *Public Opinion,* 75. In 1918 the New York legislature enacted the infamous Lusk Law, which required instruction in patriotism and citizenship, and authorized the New York State commissioner of education to withhold state funds from school districts that failed to comply with the law. Between 1917 and 1926 a total of forty-three states enacted statutes requiring patriotic instruction. A similar trend was evident with respect to textbook laws. For example, a 1925 Wisconsin law provided that "no history or other textbook shall be adopted for use . . . which falsifies the facts regarding the War of Independence, or the War of 1812 or which defames our nation's founders or misrepresents the ideals and causes for which they struggled and sacrificed, or which contains propaganda favorable to any foreign government." *Public Opinion,* 101. Many other states followed suit.

Other social, political, and economic values were carefully regulated in the public schools during this period. Criticisms of presentations of sexual materials in hygiene or biology courses were frequent. A biology reference book entitled *Devils, Drugs, and Doctors* was removed from an Iowa school as unfit for students. H. Beale, *Are American Teachers Free?* 338 (1936). Mandatory instruction in temperance and the "evils of tobacco" was made a part of the curriculum. *Are American Teachers Free?* 324, 326. John J. Tigert, appointed United States commissioner of education in 1921, vowed "to crush out of the schools communism, bolshevism, socialism, and all persons who did not recognize the sanctity of private property and 'the right of genius to its just awards.' " *Are American Teachers Free?* 108-9. Teachers often were disciplined for discussing the Soviet Union or for espousing public ownership of industry. Issues of race relations were perhaps the most volatile, often resulting in violence if views offensive to the community were communicated. A 1920 Mississippi law forbade teachers to suggest that "social equality or marriage between the white and Negro races" was desirable. *Are American Teachers Free?* 146. The ideological biases of public school curricula and textbooks remain generally unchanged today, although the bias may be expressed somewhat less forthrightly. Professors Wirt and Kirst describe the modern curriculum and textbook in the following terms:

THE POLITICAL WEB OF AMERICAN SCHOOLS
F. Wirt and M. Kirst 29-31 (1972)

What is offered in American public school is formalistically descriptive, weakly linked to reality, devoid of analytical concepts except legalistic ones, highly prescriptive in tone—and, as a direct consequence of all this, noncontroversial. [There have been] few changes in a half-century of social studies offerings: civics in the ninth grade, world history in the tenth, American history in the eleventh, and some government or social problems in the senior year. The curriculum contains little of the recent behavioral developments, comparative analysis, or international studies, and almost no sociology, anthropology, or psychology.

From elementary to secondary education, the instruction proceeds from emphasis on indirect and symbolic patriotism to explicit but shaded use of facts about American history and government. In the elementary school child's world, . . . classroom symbols and rituals, for example, pledging allegiance, showing the flag or pictures of important events or men, singing patriotic songs [are commonplace]. With the child's increasing interest in institutions rather than persons, more attention is given in successive years to specific political institutions. This curriculum content has special empirical and normative perspectives. Empirically, it ignores events and conditions that contradict the ideal descriptions of the political system. The normative content emphasizes compliance with rules and authority while skimping citizens' rights to participate in their government (other than by voting), which leads to a deemphasis on parties, interest groups, and partisan behavior.

At the secondary level, although more information is provided the student, it bears little relationship to the world portrayed by social scientists. . . .

Today's high school student studies about government in much the same way that his parents studied government. Current high school civic and government courses continue to be based upon legalistic descriptions and ethical prescriptions. The social foundations of political behavior and the cultural forces that shape political roles and decisions are neglected. The relationships between certain kinds of political behavior and socioeconomic status, ethnic identity, or primary and secondary group memberships are ignored. Little or nothing is said about basic concepts of current political science such as political culture, political socialization, status, role, reference groups, and function. . . . The political world presented . . . bears little resemblance to the world of the politician.

The major elements of distinguishing the perceptions of politician and teacher is the absence of controversy in the teacher's world. The clamor over issues about which contemporary Americans sharply divide rarely enters the classroom; even those issues which divided our ancestors may still be handled gingerly. Characteristically, American history courses leave little time for the current scene; sometimes it is not even reached, as the course fuzzes away somewhere between World Wars I and II.

The blandness of the curriculum may be attributable to two major kinds of fault—lack of teacher competence to handle controversy and pressures upon teachers, textbook publishers, and school boards by interest groups. . . . Textbooks are obviously another major instrument for political socialization. They played a powerful role in the decades after the Civil War in citizenship training in history and patriotism, when the textbook was "Teacher to America." Indeed, the perspective of the Southern white saturated the national perspective of Reconstruction because of the dominance of some Southern historians whose ideas dominated secondary textbooks. But even in more recent decades, the historical function of citizenship training still dominates those books.

Again, the findings are much like those for the total curriculum—textbooks are characteristically as bland as the curriculum they serve. Noncontroversial, offering few conceptual and analytical tools for understanding political reality, jingoistic and narrowly moralistic (only the rare book mentions any mistake the United States has ever made in domestic policy and none in foreign affairs), naive in descriptions of the political process, overly optimistic about the system's ability to handle future problems—the criticisms of such books are repetitive and insistent. Instructional methods are not much more useful. At a chapter's end appear questions for review that stress formal facts. The naturalist fallacy pervades such instruction, that is, by assembling enough empirical facts, one can make value judgments.

One illustration of such textbook blandness is the treatment of minorities. Despite the past and present highly minoritarian basis of American social life, until very recently what students might learn about this social fact in their school books was scant and stereotyped. Jews, Negroes, and other immigrants, as well as Indians, were often not presented at all, or only as picturesque "human interest" facets of history. They were never shown having an impact on American history. The "melting pot" thesis of such books is the implicit reason for not presenting such historical evidence; somehow, the immigrant stepped off the boat and into a giant social fondue. Often explicit was this view of the harmony in which all groups were said to have lived, except for the regrettable aberration of the Civil War. Negroes disappeared from history textbooks after that war, except for an occasional patronizing reference to George Washington Carver—but rarely to Frederick Douglass and never to William Du Bois. Indians were presented as quaint natives who sometimes caused "trouble" that was quickly put down. America was "discovered" by an Italian or a Swede but never by Indians. It is hard to parody such a narrow view of the pluralistic basis of American history; the actual presentations do so on their face.

Yet, at the end of the second third of this century, as a result of political and educational protest, minorities began receiving more realistic treatment of their roles in history. A comparison of textbooks from 1949 to 1960 found some improvement for Jews, but still little for Negroes and immigrants of other races. By the late 1960s, however, a fuller exposition of the Negro's role—including changing references to the "black" role—as well as removal of offensive characterizations, were widely evident in these books. Pressure from the urban centers by the increasingly politicized blacks was a major force in this change. The rate of adoption of these textbooks, however, was still very slow by 1970.

KELLEY v FERGUSON
95 Neb 63, 144 NW 1039 (1914)

The petitioner alleges: That prior to December 17, 1912, plaintiff had instructed his daughter Eunice Kelley

> not to go to the class in domestic science; that said class was conducted in a building more than a mile distant from the Saratoga school which she was attending, and that the time consumed by said class was almost a half day, thereby causing the said Eunice Kelley to fall behind in her other studies for lack of time; that the respondents wrongfully and unlawfully and against the protests of relator required said Eunice Kelley to take said course in domestic science, and on the 17th day of December 1912 the respondents wrongfully,

unlawfully, and without cause therefor dismissed said Eunice Kelley from said school and refused and have ever since refused to allow her to attend school of said district, although since said time relator has several times made demand upon the said school board and its officers to reinstate her.

The issue presented by the pleadings and decided by the district court is clean-cut and raises the single question: Can the parent of a child in a city grade school decide the question as to whether or not such child shall be required to carry any particular study which has been prescribed by the board of education; or does the power to make such decision rest entirely in such board? Or, to state it another way, has the parent a right to make a reasonable selection from the prescribed studies for his child to pursue, and, having done so, must this selection be respected by the board of education? If the parent has such right, the judgment in this case must be affirmed, for we do not think a case could be presented where a selection made by a parent would more clearly be a reasonable selection than the one attempted to be made in this case. The relator's child was a girl twelve years of age. She was in the sixth grade. The study which the relator directed her not to take was that of cooking, which is required under the subject of domestic science. The other studies which she was required to take and was taking were reading, spelling, arithmetic, geography, general lessons, drawing, and writing. The testimony of the father is that at the time the disagreement arose the daughter was studying music, which required not less than two hours a day. If the relator desired to have his daughter study music, he had the unquestionable right to have her do so, and if he thought that the taking of lessons in music in addition to the studies she was taking in school, as above set out, was all she was able to carry, then, if he had a right to make a selection at all, it must be conceded that it was reasonable for him to select the lesson domestic science, which took substantially one-tenth of her entire school time, as the lesson to be dropped, in order that she might continue her music. It is contended that this selection was not made by the relator in good faith but was made because of the fact that the school authorities declined to permit his daughter, at the close of the cooking lesson at the Capital school, to which the class were taken in a body by the teacher from the Saratoga school, to return to her home on the Seventeenth street car line instead of requiring her to return with the entire class to the Saratoga school and to be there dismissed. We do not think this fact, even if it were the cause which finally impelled relator to make his attempted selection, is very material. The important question to the school board and to parents generally is that of the right of a parent to make a reasonable selection from the prescribed studies for his child to pursue.

The question is not a new one. It was considered and decided by this court in *State v School Dist* 31 Neb 552, 48 NW 393. In that case the father expressed a desire to have his daughter study grammar instead of rhetoric. His wish was respected and the change made. Subsequently he objected to her studying grammar and demanded that she be excused from continuing the study. When asked what reason he had for not wanting his daughter to pursue the study, he informed the board "that said study was not taught in said school as he had been instructed when he went to school." That was the only reason he would offer for not wanting his daughter to pursue the study. Under his direction the daughter refused to pursue the study, and as a result of such refusal she was expelled. An original application for mandamus was made in this court, and the writ awarded. The syllabus holds:

The school trustees of a high school have authority to classify and grade the scholars in the district and cause them to be taught in such departments as they may deem expedient; they may also prescribe the courses of study and textbooks for the use of the school and such reasonable rules and regulations as they may think needful. They may also require prompt attendance, respectful deportment, and diligence in study. The parent, however, has a right to make a reasonable selection from the prescribed studies for his child to pursue, and this selection must be respected by the trustees, as the right of the parent in that regard is superior to that of the trustees and the teachers.

In discussing the regulations referred to in the syllabus, Judge Maxwell in the opinion says (31 Neb 555, 48 NW 394):

Such regulations are for the benefit of all and tend to promote a common interest and the efficiency of the school. Neither has a parent any right to require that the interests of other children shall be sacrificed for the interests of his children. Therefore he cannot insist that his child or children shall be placed in a particular class, when by so doing other pupils will be retarded in the advancement they would otherwise make; neither can he require that his children be taught branches different from those in the prescribed course of the school, or be allowed to use textbooks different from those required by the trustees, nor will he be allowed to adopt methods of study for his children which interfere with methods adopted by the trustees, because, in order to secure efficiency in the school, it is necessary that the different classes work in harmony and cooperate together. A high school is designed for scholars who have passed through the primary grades and are supposed to be able to read, write, and spell correctly and to be familiar with other branches which need not be noticed. Many, if not most, of the high schools of this state are in fact preparatory schools for the university, and the course of study determined with a regard to that object. The testimony tends to show that Ann Sheibley is about fifteen years of age; that she is pursuing studies outside of those taught in the school which occupy a portion of her time. Now who is to determine what studies she shall pursue in school, a teacher, who has a mere temporary interest in her welfare, or her father, who may reasonably be supposed to be desirous of pursuing such course as will best promote the happiness of his child? The father certainly possesses superior opportunities of knowing the physical and mental capabilities of his child .... The right of the parent, therefore, to determine what studies his child shall pursue is paramount to that of the trustees or teacher. Schools are provided by the public in which prescribed branches are taught, which are free to all within the district between certain ages. But no pupil attending the school can be compelled to study any prescribed branch against the protest of the parent that the child shall not study such branch, and any rule or regulation that requires the pupil to continue such studies is arbitrary and unreasonable. There is no good reason why the failure of one or more pupils to study one or more prescribed branches should result disastrously to the proper discipline, efficiency, and well-being of the school. Such pupils are not idle but merely devoting their attention to other branches; and so long as the failure of the students, thus excepted, to study all the branches of the prescribed course does not prejudice the equal rights of other students, there is no cause for complaint.

Wherever education is most general, there life and property are the most safe, and civilization of the highest order. The public school is one of the main bulwarks of our nation, and we would not knowingly do anything to undermine it; but we should be careful to avoid permitting our love for this noble institution to cause us to regard it as "all in all" and destroy both the god-given and constitutional right of a parent to have some voice in the bringing up and education of his children. We believe in the doctrine of the greatest good to the greatest number, and that the welfare of the individual must give away to the welfare of society in general. The whole current of modern thought and agitation is "onward." The people are beginning to realize as never before that, if we continue to jog along in the ruts our fathers before us have made, little will be accomplished in the way of national and social improvement. The state is more and more taking hold of the private affairs of individuals and requiring that they conduct their business affairs honestly and with due regard for the public good. All this is commendable and must receive the sanction of every good citizen. But in this age of agitation, such as the world has never known before, we want to be careful lest we carry the doctrine of governmental paternalism too far, for, after all is said and done, the prime factor in our scheme of government is the American home.

TODD v ROCHESTER COMMUNITY SCHOOLS
41 Mich App 320, 200 NW2d 90 (1972)

Before BRONSON, PJ, and V. J. BRENNAN and O'HARA, JJ
BRONSON, Presiding Judge.

On March 24, 1971, plaintiff, Bruce Livingston Todd, filed a complaint for a writ of mandamus against the defendant, Rochester Community Schools, in the Oakland County Circuit Court. Mr. Todd's complaint alleged that one of his minor children was enrolled in a course of instruction referred to as "Current Literature" which was being taught in a Rochester public high school. Plaintiff averred that part of the curriculum in said course was the study of *Slaughterhouse-Five* or *The Children's Crusade*, a novel by the contemporary American author, Kurt Vonnegut, Jr.

The gravamen of plaintiff's complaint was that *Slaughterhouse-Five* "contains and makes reference to religious matters" and, therefore, "the use of such book as a part or in connection with any course of instruction by a public school district or system is illegal and contrary to the laws of the land; namely, the First and Fourteenth Amendments of the United States Constitution." Predicated on these factual allegations, Mr. Todd requested that the Oakland County Circuit Court issue a writ of mandamus compelling the defendant school district to cease utilizing *Slaughterhouse-Five* "as a part of a course of instruction in the Rochester community schools." In his complaint, Mr. Todd did not allege that *Slaughterhouse-Five* was obscene nor that it had no literary value.

On March 31, 1971, defendant answered plaintiff's complaint. In its pleading the Rochester community schools affirmatively stated that the novel at issue, along with several others, "is used in connection with a general secular course of instruction entitled 'Current Literature' and the fact that the same might incidentally refer to religious matters does not render its use in violation of the First and Fourteenth

Amendments of the Constitution of the United States." Defendant further contended that the selection of books to be used in its course of instruction was a matter exclusively within its administrative powers and not subject to judicial supervision nor review. . . .[3]

. . . . On June 9, 1971, a final opinion and order granting plaintiff a judgment of mandamus was issued. . . .

Plaintiff's complaint specifically pleads only that *Slaughterhouse-Five* is used in a public school and "contains and makes reference to religious matters." We have been cited to no authority, nor has our own research uncovered any, which holds that *any* portion of *any* constitution is violated simply because a novel, utilized in a public school "contains and makes reference to religious matters." This concept is legally repugnant to what we believe is the time-tested rationale underlying the First and Fourteenth Amendments. By couching a personal grievance in First Amendment language, one may not stifle freedom of expression. Vigorously opposed to such a suggestion, we stand firm in rendering plaintiff's theory constitutionally impermissible.

If plaintiff's contention was correct, then public school students could no longer marvel at Sir Galahad's saintly quest for the Holy Grail, nor be introduced to the dangers of Hitler's *Mein Kampf* nor read the mellifluous poetry of John Milton and John Donne. Unhappily, Robin Hood would be forced to forage without Friar Tuck and Shakespeare would have to delete Shylock from *The Merchant of Venice.** Is this to be the state of our law? Our Constitution does not command ignorance; on the contrary, it assures the people that the state may not relegate them to such a status and guarantees to all the precious and unfettered freedom of pursuing one's own intellectual pleasures in one's own personal way.

We hasten to point out that plaintiff did not allege that the Rochester public schools were intentionally taking action which was derogatory to Christianity. Nor did plaintiff aver that defendant was attempting to "establish" any specific religious sect in preference over another; nor one over all others; nor none at all. Had plaintiff's complaint suggested such a state of affairs, the question before the court would be substantially different. But in this case the evidence is undisputed that the novel in question, and the Bible, were being utilized as literature. There is no allegation nor proof that *Slaughterhouse-Five* was being taught subjectively, or that the religious or antireligious view contained therein were espoused by the teachers. . . .

In rendering his decision the trial court relied solely upon *Abington v Schempp*

---

3. The "Current Literature" course offered by the Rochester community schools was not part of the prescribed curriculum but was an elective. Some of the other literature which was required reading for the course was: *Arsenic and Old Lace, The Detective Story,* Herman Hesse's *Steppenwolf, The American Dream,* short stories by J. D. Salinger, and selected poetry by James Dickey, Allen Ginsberg, Lawrence Ferlinghetti, and Howard Nemerov. The supplemental reading list for the course included: *Love Story* by Erich Segal, *Walden II* by B. F. Skinner, *Catch-22* by Joseph Heller, *Waiting for Godot* by Samuel Beckett, *Catcher in the Rye* by J. D. Salinger, *The Andromeda Strain* by Michael Crichton, *Who's Afraid of Virginia Woolf?* by Edward Albee and *The Power and the Glory* by Graham Greene. Since plaintiff apparently did not find these writings to violate the First and Fourteenth Amendments, we express no judicial opinion as to their constitutional validity. Nor is such necessary.

*The use of *The Merchant of Venice* and *Oliver Twist* in the New York City public schools was unsuccessfully challenged in *Rosenberg v Board of Education* (Sup Ct NY 1949). In that case, plaintiffs alleged "that the two books are objectionable because they tend to engender hatred of the Jew as a person and as a race."—Eds.

374 US 203 (1963). *Schempp* held that a statute requiring daily Bible reading without comment in public schools violated the First Amendment, even though participation by each pupil was voluntary. *Schempp* is totally dissimilar to the case at bar. *Schempp* turned upon the fact that reciting a prayer in public schools had no connection whatsoever with secular education. Saying the prayer was an end in itself. Such conduct had as its primary purpose the advancement of religion; the relationship between prayer and education was nonexistent. This cannot be said about *Slaughterhouse-Five*. In our opinion, Mr. Vonnegut's novel is an antiwar allegory which dwells on the horror of the Allied fire-bombing of Dresden and which makes ancillary use of religious matter only for literary reasons. . . .

Obscenity, although not raised in the pleadings, and declared not to be at issue in the trial court's June 9, 1971, judgment, is pervasive in the lower court's opinion.

In his findings of fact, the trial judge did indeed cite many words which, if standing alone, would offend some person's sensibilities. Yet each and every example advanced by the trial court was taken totally out of context. . . .

We are constrained to hold that *Slaughterhouse-Five* is clearly not obscene under present constitutional tests.

Defendant and amicus curiae urge that the real issue underlying this case is that a circuit judge, or any government official, has no lawful right to impose his own particular value judgments on our citizenry in matters which are traditionally protected by the penumbra of the First Amendment. They argue that that is what happened here and meticulously cite the trial record for factual support. . . .

. . . .

In his May 11, 1971, opinion, the trial judge stated:

> The court did read the book as requested for determination of factual matters and issues of law alike, and unfortunately did thus waste considerable time. At points, the court was deeply disgusted. How any educator entrusted during school hours with the educational, emotional and moral welfare and healthy growth of children could do other than reject such cheap, valueless reading material, is incomprehensible. Its repetitive obscenity and immorality, merely degrade and defile, teaching nothing. Contemporary literature, of real educational value to youth abounds, contains scientific, social and cultural facts, of which youth need more to know, today.
>
> Certainly, it is unnecessary for any school system to search out and select obscenity, pornography, or deviated immorality in order to teach modern literature. . . .

While the May 11, 1971, opinion was subsequently superseded by a later one, the former is instructive insomuch as it allows this court the opportunity to follow the trial judge's judicial thought process. Clearly, the trial judge found *Slaughterhouse-Five* to be a "bad" book, totally worthless and utterly lacking in any merit, literary or otherwise. But as Shakespeare reminds us in language antedating almost all of our sacred precedent, "There is nothing either good or bad, but thinking makes it so." (*Hamlet*, act II, scene 2, line 259). This court cannot, in good conscience, nor in adherence to our constitutional oath of office, allow a noneducational public official the right, in absence of gross constitutional transgressions, to regulate the reading material to which our students are exposed. Our Constitution will tolerate no supreme censor nor allow any man to superimpose his judgment on that of

others so that the latter are denied the freedom to decide and choose for themselves.

Reversed. Summary judgment of no cause of action is entered in this court in
favor of defendant Rochester Community Schools.

O'Hara, Judge (concurring in result).

Judge Brennan and I concur only in the result reached by Judge Bronson. We are
not prepared to endorse his opinion.

We feel the basic point involved here is not whether the book in question is per
se obscene or pornographic as those terms have been judicially defined by the
United States Supreme Court. . . .

There is no doubt, as the trial court noted, that certain *characters* in the novel
express sentiments that are derogatory of the religious beliefs of a very sizable
segment of our society. However, the novel in question is merely listed as one of a
number of books reflective of a current literary style. It is not alleged that the
teacher of the course advocated, approved or promulgated concepts offensive to
established religious beliefs or organized religious sects.

This, of course, is precisely the point. Writings, contemporary as well as of ages
past, have attributed to characters beliefs and expressions highly antagonistic to
established religious beliefs. Manifestly, many of these writings have attained classical status. As we view the constitutional test, a public educational institution cannot espouse as part of its teaching program such expressions of belief pro or contra
as representative of the beliefs of the institution. In the presentation of reading
material, the public institution is well within its teaching function to list the particular books the faculty regards as valuable to the full exposure of the student to
conflicting views of religious beliefs. To advocate the views doctrinally as those of
the institution is quite another thing. It is not alleged that defendant in this case
espoused any antireligious views as opposed merely to making available course
material.

We find no violation of the establishment clause of the First Amendment. . . .

Notes and Questions

1. *Ferguson:* The Legal Standard

What legal theory did the *Ferguson* court employ to reach the result that Eunice
Kelley need not attend the domestic science class? Did it rely on statutory or
constitutional provision? Did it simply reach its own independent policy judgment?
Did it rely on common law notions about the rights of parents to direct the
upbringing of their children? Do the compulsory attendance laws implicitly reject
such notions? See *School Bd Dist No 18, Garvin County v Thompson* 103 P 578
(Okla 1909). Compare *Mitchell v McCall* 143 So2d 629 (Ala 1962). What if Mr.
Kelley (a) removed Eunice from the basic arithmetic, English, and history courses,
or (b) demanded a course in Irish history not currently offered at the Saratoga
school? Would the result be different in either case?

2. *Todd:* The Legal Standard

What standard of constitutional review did the school district propose in *Todd*?
What standard of constitutional review did the *Todd* court adopt? If the Vonnegut
novel is objectionable to some religious groups, is it sufficient that other books

in the curriculum present contrary religious views? Is it sufficient if the teacher refrains from endorsing Vonnegut's views? Does the court imply that school districts have a constitutional right of expression and that plaintiff was seeking to interfere with that right? Do you find this theory persuasive? Would *Schempp* survive such a constitutional test? Is the real issue the literature teacher's right to assign and teach what she deems educationally appropriate? Would *Todd* have been decided the same way if the teacher had adopted the Vonnegut book without the permission of the school district, the district had found the book objectionable and dismissed her, and the teacher had challenged her dismissal as a violation of her First Amendment rights? See *Parducci v Rutland* 316 F Supp 352 (MD Ala 1970).

3. Reconciling the Cases

Are *Ferguson* and *Todd* consistent? If a parent may remove his child from a domestic science class, why can he not prevent his child from being exposed to an objectionable book? Did the plaintiff in *Todd* err in seeking broad relief, which would have affected many children, not just his own child? Would the *Todd* court have been more sympathetic to the plaintiff's grievance if he had sought only to absent his child from the objectionable aspects of the literature course? See *Hopkins v Handen Bd of Educ* 29 Conn Sup 397, 289 A2d 914 (Ct CP 1971). Compare *Vaughn v Reed* 313 F Supp 431 (WD Va 1970).

4. The Propriety of Judicial Intervention

The court in *Ferguson* notes that Mr. Kelley's objections to the domestic science course were based primarily on his preference for music instruction and on the inconvenience that attendance of the domestic science course occasioned. The court also refers to *State v School Dist* 31 Neb 552, 48 NW 393 (1891), in which a parent objected to his daughter's study of grammar on the ground "that said study was not taught in said school as he had been instructed when he went to school." Are these reasons compelling? Should the courts give weight to such idiosyncratic arguments? From this perspective, is the *Todd* case a more appropriate setting for judicial intervention? Should more weight be given to objections deriving from the First Amendment? See *Hardwicke v Board of School Trustees* 54 CA 696, 205 P 49 (1921). But see *Hamilton v Regents of the Univ of Cal* 293 US 245 (1934). Could the plaintiffs' arguments in *State v School District* and *Ferguson* be framed reasonably in such constitutional terms? Would *Pierce v Society of Sisters* have been of any assistance in this regard if it had been decided earlier?

5. Sex Education

Sex education courses have been a subject of considerable controversy, and many parents have objected, usually unsuccessfully, to their inclusion in the curriculum on the grounds of violation of the free exercise or establishment clauses, unlawful delegations of legislative authority, invasion of privacy, or, more generally, interference with the rights of parents to direct the sex education of their children. See, e.g., *Cornwell v State Bd of Educ* 428 F2d 471 (4th Cir 1970); *Hopkins v Hamden Bd of Educ* 29 Conn Sup 397, 289 A2d 914 (1971). The accepted rationale for these decisions is that sex education courses are "public health measures" necessitated by pregnancies among unmarried students and the spread of venereal disease. Some state sex education laws exempt children whose parents request that they be excused. See *Medeiros v Kiyosaki* 478 P2d 314 (Hawaii 1970). Should such exemptions be constitutionally required? Is *Ferguson* distinguishable?

6. Problems: Textbooks and Parent Choice

Consider the following situations:

(a) After a number of parent protests, a New York City community school board voted to remove all copies of the novel *Down These Mean Streets* by Piri Thomas from junior high school libraries. The book is an autobiographical account of a Puerto Rican youth growing up in Spanish Harlem in New York City and depicts many sordid and depressing events. It refers explicitly to criminal violence, sexual acts, and drug addiction. The community school district is predominantly white and middle class, but a number of parents and organizations believe that it is important for such children to understand "the bitter realities facing their contemporaries in Manhattan's Spanish Harlem." Suit has been filed to require the school district to return the novel to the junior high school libraries. At the trial, the plaintiffs introduce expert psychological testimony to the effect that "the book is valuable and [has] no adverse effect on the development of the children of the district." What result should the court reach? How does the case differ from *Todd*? See *Presidents Council, Dist 25 v Community School Bd No 25* 457 F2d 289 (2d Cir 1972).

(b) In the Burch County Unified School District (California), the school board is responsible for approving textbooks for public elementary and secondary schools. An eleventh grade supplementary American history text, *The Burdens of Manifest Destiny*, approved for the 1972-73 academic year, describes American Indians as "noble savages, prone to drunkenness, who dutifully raise sheep and cultivate crops." The textbook further notes that Chief Joseph, a revered figure in Indian history, supplied the early white settlers with food, shelter, and clothing, but that subsequent Indian leaders "turned on the settlers and engaged in murder, rape, and arson, until they were subdued by military forces in 1881."

Indian parents in the district acknowledge that alcoholism is a major social problem among California Indians and that most Burch County Indians are farmers. They assert, however, that these facts are not explained "sympathetically" and that, in any event, the history of white-Indian relations is distorted because it fails to mention the "atrocities" committed by whites against Indians. The Indian parents petition the school board to adopt *Bury My Heart at Wounded Knee* as a substitute for *The Burdens of Manifest Destiny*. The school board refuses for the following reasons:

(i) The school district is contractually obligated to the Eclectic Publishing Company to purchase 1,000 copies of *Burdens of Manifest Destiny*. If the district purchased another book, it would be subject to a suit for breach of contract.

(ii) *Bury My Heart at Wounded Knee* is too expensive for use in the public schools, costing almost twice as much as an average history textbook.

(iii) *Bury My Heart at Wounded Knee* expresses values that are antithetical to the overwhelming majority of Burch County taxpayers. "Since the taxpayers pay the cost of the public schools, they are entitled to determine the type of education their children receive." (Indians comprise only 3 percent of Burch County's population, but 5 percent of all school children are Indian.)

(iv) The viewpoint of *Bury My Heart at Wounded Knee* is unacceptably biased. The Indian parents wish to bring a lawsuit attacking the board's decision. What legal arguments should they make? What remedy should be sought? Would the following section of the California Education Code be of any assistance?

Removal for sectarianism, propaganda, or bias in portrayal of contributions of ethnic groups, entrepreneurs and labor

When in the judgment of the state board of education, there exists sufficient evidence that a textbook offered and sold by a publisher for use as a textbook in any public high school in the state contains sectarian or denominational doctrine contrary to law or contains propaganda injurious to the welfare of the public schools, the board shall cause the book to be investigated by a committee of impartial experts. The committee shall be constituted and shall conduct its investigation under such rules and regulations as may be prescribed by the state board of education. If, in the opinion of the committee, the textbook does contain sectarian or denominational doctrine contrary to law or does contain propaganda injurious to the welfare of the public schools, or does not correctly portray the role and contribution of the American Negro and members of other ethnic groups and the role of the entrepreneur and labor in the total development of the United States and of the state of California, the board of education may order that the publisher shall cease to offer and sell such textbook for use as a textbook in any public high school in the state. If the state board of education shall make such an order, it shall be illegal for any district to purchase copies of such textbook for use as a textbook in any high school or to continue the use of the book as a textbook beyond the close of the current school year. Cal Educ Code §9959 (West 1970).

7. Problem: Textbooks and Local Autonomy

Suppose a state adopts a law designed to ensure that textbook selection is made uniform in all school districts. A state textbook commission is established, and the commission draws up a list of approved textbooks from which local districts must choose. A school district challenges the law on the ground that "the act denies local self-government. . . . the people have an inherent fundamental and vested right to administer their own local affairs as the people of each county and district shall deem right and proper." See generally McBain, "The Doctrine of an Inherent Right to Local Self-Government," 16 *Col L Rev* 190 (1916); Baton, "The Right to Local Self-Government," 13 *Harv L Rev* 441 (1900). Is there any legal basis for a district to assert a "right" to resist the socialization of its children by the state? Is a uniform textbook law wise as a matter of policy? What is the state's interest in such a law? Is the state's argument stronger if it subsidizes local districts from state revenues?

3. The Hidden Curriculum

The public schools, in their role as ongoing social institutions that have a defined constituency and purpose, must establish rules and procedures for organizing the educational process and for managing the flow of social traffic. See Jackson, "The Student's World," 66 *Elementary School J* 345 (1966). In this respect, schools resemble hospitals, prisons, cafeterias, factories, and other public and private institutions that must create an organizational framework within which to carry out their assigned tasks. In the case of schools, this framework is often ignored, perhaps because we are so accustomed to the institutional ways of schools that we do not find them exceptional. Professor Sarason has suggested another reason for popular ignorance of the structure of schools:

> [W]e learn, formally or informally, to think and act in terms of what goes on inside the heads of individuals. In the process it becomes increasingly difficult to become aware that individuals operate in various social settings that have a structure not comprehensible by our existing theories of individual personality. In fact, in many situations it is likely that one can predict an individual's behavior far better on the basis of knowledge of the social structure and his position in it than one can on the basis of his personal dynamics.
>
> . . . when we say a setting is "organized," or that cultures differ from each other, we mean, among other things, that there is a distinct structure or pattern that . . . governs roles and interrelationships within that setting. What is implied, in addition, is that structure antedates any one individual and will continue in the absence of the individual. It may well be that it is precisely because one cannot *see* structure in the same way that one sees an individual that we have trouble grasping and acting in terms of its existence. (S. Sarason, *The Culture of the School and the Problem of Change* 12 (1971).)

What are the distinct patterns of schools, what Professor Sarason calls "existing regularities?" Some of the more interesting and significant include:

(1) For five days a week, schools are densely populated, while for two days they are empty. Sarason, *Culture of the School,* 63-64.

(2) The schools include adults, most of whom instruct, and children, who receive instruction. The children are divided according to age and assigned to classrooms in groups of thirty to thirty-five with one adult teacher.

(3) The teacher is the dominant figure in the classroom, standing while the children remain seated. In the average half-hour of class time, the teacher will ask the students 45 to 150 questions, while the children will ask the teacher fewer than 2 questions. Sarason, *Culture of the School,* 74. Children are not allowed to speak while the teacher is speaking, and no more than one child may speak at a time. Periodically, this regularity is not observed, and the offending children are reprimanded. The teacher, by virtue of her position, expertise, and maturity, decides what will be discussed and what children will do in the classroom. See generally W. Waller, *The Sociology of Teaching* 6-13 (1965).

(4) Children seated in the back of a classroom tend to behave differently from those seated in the front. Sarason, *Culture of the School,* 183.

(5) The adults evaluate the classroom performance of the children, but the converse does not occur, at least not formally.

(6) The school day is segmented by instructional topics: history is taught at one hour, mathematics at another, etc. In junior and senior high schools a change of topics usually involves a change of classrooms.

(7) There are separate lunchroom and bathroom facilities for adults and children. Bathroom facilities are segregated by sex.

(8) During "preparation periods" and lunch, the adults are either alone or in the company of a small number of other adults. This is rarely true for children; even their recess and lunch periods are carefully supervised by adults.

(9) The children are required to line up and wait for lunch or dismissal. Jackson, "Student's World."

The importance of these regularities lies not only in their alleged necessity for the safe and efficient operation of the school, but also in the values they implicitly communicate to students. These institutional patterns socialize children to particular norms, whether school authorities intend that result or not. See Bowles and Gintis, "IQ in the Class Structure," 3 *Social Policy* 65 (Nov/Dec 1972-Jan/Feb 1973). This socialization process is not an explicit part of the curriculum but, as Professor Jackson suggests, a "hidden curriculum."

The hidden curriculum values communicated include delay, denial, and interruption:

> Consider for a moment the frequency of delay. When we examine the details of classroom life carefully, it is surprising to see how much of the student's time is spent in waiting. In the elementary school, the students often line up for recess, for lunch, and for dismissal, and they frequently have to wait for the lines to be straight before they move. During individual seat-work they wait for the teacher to come around to their desk to inspect their work. When the whole class is working together, there is the waiting for the slower pupil to finish the work that the faster ones have completed. During discussion there is the waiting for fellow students to answer the teacher's query. When motion pictures or slides are shown, there is usually a delay as the room and the equipment are made ready. As time for the bell approaches, students are waiting for it to ring, even though they may still have their eyes on the teacher.
>
> No one knows for sure how much of the student's time is spent in neutral, as it were, but it is certainly a memorable portion. . . .
>
> The denial of desire is a commonplace in school, and likely it has to be. Not everyone who wants to speak can be heard, not all the students' queries can be answered to their satisfaction, not all their requests can be granted. It is true that, considered individually, most of these denials are psychologically trivial, but considered cumulatively, their significance increases. Part of learning how to live in school involves learning how to give up desire as well as waiting for its fulfillment.
>
> Typically, things happen on time in school, and, as a result, activities are often begun before interest is aroused and terminated before interest wanes. Once again, there is probably no alternative to this unnatural state of affairs. If we were to wait until students requested a history class on their own, as an instance, we would have a long wait. Similarly, if we allowed students to remain in their physical education classes until they grew tired of the game, there likely would not be time for other things. There seems to be no alternative, therefore, but to stop and start things on time, even though it means constantly interrupting the natural flow of interest and desire for at least some students. . . .
>
> Interruptions in the classroom are not confined to the beginning and ending of subject matter periods. There are also more subtle ways in which activities are broken into. The irrelevant comment during class discussion, as an instance, often breaks the spell created by the relevant remarks that have

preceded it. When the teacher is working individually with a student while others are present—a common arrangement in elementary school classrooms— petty interruptions, in the form of minor misbehavior or students coming to the teacher for advice, are the rule rather than the exception. In countless small ways the bubble of reality created during the teaching session is punctured, and much of the teacher's energy is spent in patching up the holes, just as much of the student's energy is spent in attempting to ignore them. Students are constantly "turning back" to their studies after their attention has been momentarily drawn elsewhere. (Jackson, "Student's World," 66 *Elementary School J* 345, 349-350 (1966).)

The relationship between the hidden curriculum and the regular curriculum is vital to an understanding of the socialization process in schools. Professor Jackson describes this relationship in the following terms:

Two or three important observations might be made about the relationship between these two curriculums. One is that the reward system of the school is tied to both. Indeed, many of the rewards and punishments that sound as if they are being dispensed on the basis of academic success and failure are really more closely related to the mastery of the hidden curriculum. Consider, as an instance, the common teaching practice of giving a student credit for trying. What do teachers mean when they say a student tries to do his work? They mean, in essence, that he complies with the procedural expectations of the institution. He does his homework (though incorrectly), he raises his hand during class discussion (though he usually comes up with the wrong answer), he keeps his nose in his book during free study period (though he does not turn the page very often). He is, in other words, a "model" student, though not necessarily a good one. . . .

The point is simply that in schools, as in prisons, good behavior pays off. . . .

Just as conformity to institutional expectations can lead to praise, so can the lack of it lead to trouble. As a matter of fact, the relationship of the hidden curriculum to student difficulties is even more striking than is its relationship to student success. Consider, as an instance, the conditions that lead to disciplinary action in the classroom. Why do teachers scold students? Because the student has given the wrong answer? Or because, try as he may, he fails to grasp the intricacies of long division? Not usually. A student is more likely to be scolded for coming into the room late or for making too much noise or for not listening to the teacher's directions or for pushing while in line. The teacher's wrath, in other words, is commonly triggered by violations of institutional regulations and routines rather than by the student's intellectual deficiencies.

Even with the more serious difficulties that clearly entail academic failure, the demands of the hidden curriculum lurk in the shadows. When Johnny's parents are summoned to school because their son is not doing too well in arithmetic, what explanation will be given for their son's poor performance? More than likely blame will be placed on motivational deficiencies in Johnny rather than on his intellectual shortcomings. The teacher may even go so far as to say that Johnny is unmotivated during arithmetic period. But what does this mean? It means, in essence, that Johnny does not even try. And not trying, as we have seen, often boils down to a failure to comply with institutional expectations, a failure to master the hidden curriculum.

There is a further question that must be asked about the relationship between the official and the unofficial curriculums in our schools: To what extent does the mastery of one interfere with the mastery of the other? In other words, how do the demands of intellectual achievement relate to the demands of institutional conformity? Are they complementary or contradictory?

We have already seen that many features of classroom life call for patience, at best, and resignation, at worst. As the student learns to live in school, he learns to subjugate his own desires to the will of the teacher and to subdue his own actions in the interest of the common good. He learns to be passive and to acquiesce to the network of rules, regulations, and routines in which he is imbedded. He learns to tolerate petty frustrations and to accept the plans and the policies of higher authorities, even when their rationale is unexplained and their meaning unclear. Like the inhabitants of other institutional settings he learns that he must frequently shrug and say, "That's the way the ball bounces."

But the personal qualities that play a role in intellectual mastery are of a very different order from those that characterize the Company Man. Curiosity, as an instance, that most fundamental of all scholarly traits, calls forth the kind of probing, poking, and exploring that is almost antithetical to the attitude of passivity that has just been described. The productive scholar must develop the habit of challenging authority and of questioning the value of tradition. He must insist on explanations for things that are unclear. The scholar must certainly be a disciplined man, but his discipline is developed in the service of his scholarship, rather than in the service of other people's wishes and desires. In short, intellectual mastery calls for sublimated forms of aggression rather than submission to constraints. (Jackson, "Student's World" at 353-355.)

In light of the analyses by Professors Sarason and Jackson, consider these examples of the impact of the hidden curriculum on students:

"IS THIS WHAT SCHOOLS ARE FOR?"
Noyes and McAndrew
Saturday Review, 21 December 1968

[We interviewed] another boy [who] picked up the "system" theory. "School is like roulette or something. You can't just ask: Well, what's the point of it?" he explained. "The point of it is to do it, to get through and get into college. But you have to figure the system or you can't win, because the odds are all on the house's side. I guess it's a little like the real world in that way. The main thing is not to take it personal, to understand that it's just a system and it treats you the same way it treats everybody else, like an engine or a machine or something mechanical. Our names get fed into it—*we* get fed into it—when we're five years old, and if we catch on and watch our step, it spits us out when we're seventeen or eighteen, ready for college.

"But some kids never understand this, and they get caught, chewed up, or pushed out. I'll give you an example: The other day this other guy and I had to make up an English test we'd missed because we were absent. The English teacher said she'd give it to us at 8 o'clock in the morning before school begins. Well I knew that if the test made me late for my homeroom period at 8:30, that teacher would send down an absent slip on me to the office. So I went to my homeroom at five of 8 and wrote a note on the blackboard to the teacher, telling her where I was and that I might be late.

"This other guy, though, he didn't know enough to do that. He hasn't studied the system. So we go and make up our test and sure enough before we are through the late bell rings for homeroom period. I can see he's nervous and he doesn't know what to do, so he tries to hurry up and finish the test so he can get to his homeroom before the absent slips get sent down. He tears through the test and probably marks half the multiple-choices wrong. Then he takes off just as the first bell for first period is ringing.

"I saw him later in the day and he was all shook up. He couldn't catch the absent slips so he had to go down to the dean of boys' office to explain that he wasn't really tardy or absent. But the dean's office had a long line, and while the guy's waiting in line, the late bell for first period rings. So now he's halfway out of his mind, you know? By the time he gets up to the dean of boys, he really *is* late for first period and another absent slip about him is already on its way down from *that* teacher. The dean of boys tells him to come in for detention after school, one hour."

Our narrator stopped and laughed uproariously and then went on. "Well, the guy gets all uptight and tries to explain why he now has two absent slips going when he wasn't even tardy. He loses his cool and says some things and the dean says some things and the next thing you know, the guy's got *two* hours detention, for being rude and smart-alecky. But wait, it gets worse. I swear he hasn't got a brain, that kid. Anyway, as it happens, the day he was absent and missed the English test, he also missed a math test. And he's scheduled to make that one up after school, when he's supposed to be in the detention hall. If he misses the math test, it won't be given again, and he doesn't know if his grade can stand a zero for this marking period. But if he misses detention, he might be suspended and have three days' worth of stuff to make up when he gets back.

"I don't know what he did, finally. Probably just had a nervous breakdown. It was really pathetic. But the point is that he should have foreseen all that and made arrangements for it. I'll be surprised if he makes it through school. He just doesn't understand the system."

The speaker obviously did; he had learned well. The only question is, is that what he went to school to learn?

THE STUDENT AS NIGGER
J. Farber (1970)

Students are niggers. When you get that straight, our schools begin to make sense. . . .

Let's look at the role students play in what we like to call education. At Cal State LA, where I teach, the students have separate and unequal dining facilities. If

I take them into the faculty dining room, my colleagues get uncomfortable, as though there were a bad smell. If I eat in the student cafeteria, I become known as the educational equivalent of a nigger-lover. In at least one building there are even rest rooms which students may not use. At Cal State, also, there is an unwritten law barring student-faculty lovemaking. Fortunately, this antimiscegenation law, like its Southern counterpart, is not 100 percent effective.

Students at Cal State are politically disenfranchised. They are in an academic Lowndes County. Most of them vote in national elections—their average age is about twenty-six—but they have no voice in the decisions which affect their academic lives. The students are, it is true, allowed to have a toy government run for the most part by Uncle Toms and concerned primarily with trivia. The faculty and administrators decide what courses will be offered; the students get to choose their own Homecoming Queen. . . .

A student at Cal State is expected to know his place. He calls a faculty member "Sir" or "Doctor" or "Professor"—and he smiles and shuffles some as he stands outside the professor's office waiting for permission to enter. The faculty tell him what courses to take (in my department, English, even electives have to be approved by a faculty member); they tell him what to read, what to write, and, frequently, where to set the margins on his typewriter. They tell him what's true and what isn't. Some teachers insist that they encourage dissent but they're almost always jiving and every student knows it. Tell the man what he wants to hear or he'll fail your ass out of the course.

Even more discouraging than the master-slave approach to education is the fact that the students take it. They haven't gone through twelve years of public school for nothing. They've learned one thing and perhaps only one thing during those twelve years. They've forgotten their algebra. They've grown to fear and resent literature. They write like they've been lobotomized. But, Jesus, can they follow orders! Freshmen come up to me with an essay and ask if I want it folded, and whether their name should be in the upper right hand corner. And I want to cry and kiss them and caress their poor tortured heads.

Students don't ask that orders make sense. They give up expecting things to make sense long before they leave elementary school. Things are true because the teacher says they're true. At a very early age we all learn to accept "two truths," as did certain medieval churchmen. Outside of class, things are true to your tongue, your fingers, your stomach, your heart. Inside class things are true by reason of authority. And that's just fine because you don't care anyway.

IN RE WILSON
Commissioner of Education, State of New York, No 8421 (1972)

[Commissioner Nyquist:]

The infant petitioner, Sandra Wilson, formerly attended Ditmas Junior High School, which is under the jurisdiction of Community School Board No. 20, Kings County. She graduated from that school in June 1971 but was not permitted to participate in the school's ninth-grade graduation exercise for the reasons indicated below.

Approximately two weeks before the date set for graduation, petitioner's mother received a form letter indicating that the "privilege of participating in graduation" would be withheld from petitioner and other "selected students whose records show a consistent lack of good citizenship during the past three years." . . .

Petitioner was told that she would receive a diploma and would be advanced to the tenth grade in the 1971-72 school year. The initial pleadings before me indicate this understanding. However, at the time of oral argument of this appeal, it was asserted by respondent that petitioner was not entitled to a diploma because of unsatisfactory academic achievement, but that she would nevertheless be given a certificate of attendance and would be advanced to the tenth grade on this basis.

Petitioner alleges, in substance, that she has been illegally deprived of her right to participate in the graduation ceremony because of a unilateral determination of "bad citizenship," predicated upon records which were unavailable to her or to her parents. . . .

The record before me indicates that Sandra Wilson, during the school years 1969-70 and 1970-71, during which she was enrolled at this junior high school, was a habitual truant, was irregular in school attendance, was insubordinate and disorderly, was abusive to her teachers, used obscene language, did not tell the truth, consistently refused to abide by the rules of the school and was a disruptive and disturbing influence in the school.

Specifically, the record indicates that during 1970-71 her teachers reported to the principal that she was absent from class forty-five times and frequently left the school without permission. Consequently, on May 6, 1971, a conference was held in the principal's office at which the student, her mother, their family minister and a friend of the family were present. At this conference all the problems involved were discussed with the mother, and as a result the minister at that time undertook to help Sandra adjust to school. On the day following this conference, however, Sandra again absented herself and failed to attend her classes. Under the circumstances the principal then sought to have Sandra transferred to another school.

Another conference was held thereafter with Sandra and her mother, at which Sandra lied, to the knowledge of the principal, her statements being contrary to statements made by Sandra's father to the principal.

After still further acts of insubordination, a third conference was held with the girl and her mother on May 17, 1971, at which, according to the principal's affidavit, the mother defended the girl's "right" to leave classrooms at will.

The record further shows acts by the student which may or may not have been brought to the mother's attention and which undoubtedly were a part of the basis for the board's action. Among these are the repeated writing of vulgar language on a desk on March 31, 1971, the use of vulgar and obscene language and various other acts of insubordination, such as roaming the school building and other classrooms at will.

Petitioner's cumulative record reflects many incidents which might have served as a predicate for specific disciplinary action either by way of the five-day administrative suspension or otherwise. Respondent, however, did not exercise its discretion to take some form of corrective disciplinary action, but instead relied upon a disciplinary technique which I feel is educationally inappropriate. While there can be circumstances in which the denial of participation in a graduation ceremony would be warranted, it is generally an educationally unsound practice to deny a student the opportunity to appear at graduation where he has successfully completed the academic requirements therefor.

Further, disciplinary action should not be predicated upon so nebulous a finding as "lack of good citizenship," a term which is undefined by respondent and which may be interpreted by reasonable men in completely different ways. It is of course a major responsibility of the school system to inculcate in students a basic respect for and adherence to the principles of good citizenship. This is an essential portion of the learning process. However, it is educationally unsound for a school system to brand an individual with the label of "poor citizen." The placing of such a label upon a student is not a proper function of a school system. . . .

It appears from the record that the petitioner is not entitled to a diploma as a result of her failure to satisfy the academic conditions specified in General Circular 13 (1966-1967). Consequently, that relief may not be afforded here. She is, however, entitled . . . to [an] order expunging all references in her cumulative file to the determination of lack of good citizenship and of respondent's refusal to permit her to participate in the graduation exercises.

The appeal is sustained to the extent indicated. It is so ordered.

Notes and Questions

1. "Hidden Curriculum"

Is *Wilson* a "hidden curriculum" case? Recalling Professor Jackson's analysis, was it Sandra Wilson's failure to abide by rules relating to delay, interruption, and denial that resulted in the punitive action taken against her? Could a school continue to operate efficiently and safely if there were many Sandra Wilsons in the student body? Did Sandra pose a challenge to the authority structure of the school?

2. Basis of the Decision

Why did Commissioner Nyquist sustain Wilson's appeal? Did he deny the authority of the school district to ensure that Sandra Wilson abided by the requirements of the hidden curriculum? Did he view the punishment as inappropriate? Would the commissioner have upheld punishment premised on specific acts of disobedience and disruption? Did Miss Wilson have inadequate notice that she was transgressing school rules?

3. Judicial Role

Cases such as *Wilson* are quite rare, for nearly all student challenges to school discipline assert some constitutional deprivation or the lack of statutory authority of the school district under state law. Could such arguments have been reasonably made in *Wilson*? Do you foresee greater problems with respect to judicial interference with the "hidden curriculum" than with respect to judicial interference with the regular curriculum, (school prayers, textbooks, and flag salutes)? What standards could the courts evolve? How would the courts enforce their decrees?

III. Student Rights

A. Introduction: Democratization of Schools?

In earlier casebooks and treatises on "school law," a short chapter entitled "Student Control" typically subsumed all questions relating to the disciplining of students. The treatment of the subject was brief, both because there were few cases that denied to school authorities the power to regulate the school activities of their charges, and because it was generally accepted that constitutional guarantees applicable to adults were not to be extended to students. See, e.g., *Hodgkins v Rockport* 105 Mass 875 (1870). Since the mid-1960s, however, much of this has changed. Courts are regularly called on to resolve disputes between students and school administrators, and, while the former do not always prevail, little remains of the traditional notions about the unreviewability of school disciplinary actions. In this process the label "student control" has gradually yielded to the more volatile term "student rights."

The conflict over student rights is not purely—or even primarily—legal; the combatants assert social, political, and pedagogical reasons for expanding or limiting the freedom of students in the public schools. Many parents lament what they perceive as the breakdown of discipline in the schools, the decline of adult authority. See "Crisis in the High Schools: The *Life* Poll," *Life* 16 May 1969, p 22. They point to increases in school vandalism and crime, which they assert are part and parcel of a rampant permissiveness that is eroding the structure and values of American society. These parents, joined by some educators and courts, emphasize the immaturity of school children, the need for restrictions in the special environment of the school, and the relationship between order and attainment of the educational goals of compulsory schooling. See, e.g., *Ferrell v Dallas Independent School Dist* 392 F2d 697 (5th Cir 1968); *Robinson v Sacramento City Unified School Dist* 53 Cal Rptr 781 (1966). Critics perceive the schools as authoritarian institutions that promote order for its own sake, stifling the free creative development of children. See, e.g., C. Silberman, *Crisis in the Classroom* (1970); G. Dennison, *The Lives of Children* (1969). They look to the courts to redress both the inhumanity and the educational futility of conditions in the modern public school. These critics have also found their allies in the communities of educators, judges, and lawyers.

In many ways, as Professor Ladd has noted, the student rights debate centers on the choice of governance models for public education. Ladd, "Regulating Student Behavior without Ending Up in Court," 54 *Phi Delta Kappan* 304 (1973). See also Ladd, "Alleged Disruptive Student Behavior and the Legal Authority of Public School Officials," 19 *J Pub Law* 209, 218-22 (1970). Schools have traditionally chosen what Ladd terms a Puritan governance model. That model asserts that authority in the schools should reside in the administrative structure, that students—because of their immaturity—should be afforded privileges but not rights, and that coercion is an acceptable way of compelling students to conform to standards imposed by adults. The state, through adult educators, knows what is best both for society and the child, and thus it may justifiably reduce the scope of student rights and comforts. See Rhea, "Institutional Paternalism in High School," 2 *Urban Rev* 13 (1968). Discipline and order are an inherent part of pedagogy. See H. Rickover, *Education and Freedom* 136-37 (1959). The alternative governance model finds its genesis in traditional democratic and progressive theory. It views students as having particular rights and responsibilities, and holds that authority imposed from above should be limited to the minimum necessary to make possible the achievement of educational goals.

It is no mere chance that most student rights cases are brought in federal courts by lawyers arguing from the Bill of Rights, for federal courts and civil liberties lawyers represent in general a quite distinct and different system of governance. This system, also going far back into our history, indeed into the history of England, is the Madisonian system of governance embodied in our federal constitution and interpreted over the years by our federal courts. In it the rights of individuals, far from being left out, are central: Everyone has certain important rights, including the rights to freedom of speech and the press, to a degree of privacy, and to due process of law. (Ladd, "Regulating Student Behavior," 307.)

Proponents of this model urge that learning can take place more efficiently in a democratic environment in which "the intrinsic activities and needs . . . of the given individual to be educated" are respected. J. Dewey, *Democracy and Education* 106 (1966). To be sure, educational progressives such as Dewey did not insist on democratization of the schools; teachers and administrators still would retain ultimate authority. But, since schooling must be pleasant and not highly restrictive if educational progress is to occur, detailed and extensive regulation of student conduct have little place in schools.

In the dispute over educational governance, our Constitution and traditions are not neutral. Generally, the society protects free speech, privacy, and the like, because we think that such rights protect democratic processes, preserve the individual's integrity, and prevent change by violent means. See generally T. Emerson, *Toward a General Theory of the First Amendment* (1966). These values seem particularly important in the public school context, since it is there that society attempts to socialize its children to democratic values. See Brennan, "Comment: Education and the Bill of Rights," 113 *U Pa L Rev* 219, 225 (1964). This legal perspective requires that student rights receive broad protection unless there are important policy reasons for not doing so.

There appear to be five plausible bases for limiting the speech and privacy rights of students:

(1) The students will learn better.

(2) The students must be socialized to social, political, and religious norms.

(3) In a compulsory school setting, the student body must be protected from communications that parents or school officials find objectionable.

(4) The students and the school must be protected from violence and destruction of property.

(5) Traffic regulations, relating to the orderly movement of students and faculty and to the harmonization of competing individual demands for facilities or instruction, are necessary to the efficient operation of the school.

Reasons (2) and (3) are closely interrelated with the problems of socialization, discussed in section II, and reasons (4) and (5) resurrect notions of institutional values discussed in the section on the "hidden curriculum." Reason (1) links particular educational policies and the academic performance of students, a set of issues considered in some detail in chapters 4-6. As the reader proceeds through the materials in this section, the five justifications for circumscribing otherwise protected student speech and conduct should be kept in mind and applied to the various fact situations.

Each court decision presents several other recurring issues. Which justification did the court rely on? Is that justification legitimate in the light of the relevant

policy considerations and the constitutional framework? Does the rule of law announced in the case respond adequately to the asserted justification? Does it unnecessarily invade the student's interest in privacy or free speech? On whom was
the burden of persuasion cast with respect to proving that some substantial or
insubstantial state interest was at stake? What kind of proof was sufficient to carry
that burden? How much deference was accorded the policy decisions of school
officials? What is the likely impact of the court's decision on the operation of the
public schools?

B. Historical Note on Student Rights Litigation

Before *Tinker v Des Moines Independent Community School Dist,* 393 US 503
(1969), nearly all challenges to the disciplinary authority of school officials were
litigated in state courts. State courts, relying on statutory and common law
grounds, almost invariably ruled in favor of school authorities and against objecting
parents and students. Berkman, "Students in Court: Free Speech and the Functions
in Schooling in America," 40 *Harv Educ Rev* 567 (1970). In one famous case, an
Arkansas court upheld the reasonableness of the expulsion of an eighteen-year-old
female high school student for wearing talcum powder. *Pugsley v Sellmeyer* 158
Ark 247, 250 SW 538 (1923). In *Tanton v McKenney* 226 Mich 245, 197 NW 510
(1924), a state court upheld the suspension of an Ypsilanti State Teachers' College
female student for smoking in public, riding in a car in the lap of a young man, and
airing her grievances in public. The court held that the only constraint on the
school's power to "define the offenses for which . . . the punishment of exclusion . . . may be imposed" was impermissible arbitrariness, and that the power of
expulsion was not limited to previously adopted rules:

> In the school, as in the family, there exists on the part of the pupils the
> obligation of obedience to lawful commands, subordination and civil deport-
> ment, respect for the rights of others, and fidelity to duty.
>   The Dean of Women, Mrs. Priddy . . . showed every consideration for this
> plaintiff and displayed a motherly interest in her. She urged upon plaintiff's
> older sister the imperative necessity of getting plaintiff out of the rut she was
> traveling in. . . . [P]laintiff, after consulting her older sister, proceeded to air
> her defiance of discipline in the public press. This of itself was sufficient
> grounds for refusing her readmission. 197 NW at 512-513.

The rationales of the early student rights decisions usually took one of the
following forms: First, local school boards operate under broad statutory provisions
that allow them wide discretion in determining the rules and regulations governing
pupil conduct. As long as this discretion is not exercised in bad faith—meaning that
the objective of a regulation is a legitimate educational goal—the courts should not
attempt to supersede the judgment of elected authorities. Compare *Healy v James*
408 US 169, 189 n20 (1972). Second, in the absence of clear legislative pronouncements, any reasonable, nonarbitrary exercise of power by a school board or school
administrator should be affirmed by the courts. See *Tanton v McKenney, supra.*
The burden of proof under the standard clearly rested on the plaintiff student who
alleged that a particular regulation was capricious. Third, students have no "right"
to attend a public school. School attendance is a privilege bestowed by the state,
and as such, it can attach whatever conditions it pleases to its largesse, even if those

conditions are discriminatory or arbitrary. *Hamilton v Regents of the Univ of Cal* 293 US 245 (1934). Fourth, particularly where a private school or college is involved, the relationship between the student and the educational institution he attends is governed by the law of contracts. If the particular rule or penalty in question has been provided for under the contract between the student and his parents and the school, the courts are obliged to uphold the action of school authorities. See "Developments in the Law—Academic Freedom," 81 *Harv L Rev* 1045-47 (1968). Finally, school authorities, as the agents of the parents, have the same rights as parents to prescribe rules for children during the portion of the day that the children are in their charge. Thus courts may interfere with the schools' treatment of students only if they have exceeded the bounds of parental discretion. Given the scope of parental authority at common law, rarely could such overstepping of authority be demonstrated. This rule was called the in loco parentis doctrine, and strangely enough, it often operated under circumstances where the parents expressly denied that they had authorized school officials to act. See, e.g., *Beaty v Randall* 79 Mo App 226 (1899). See generally, Goldstein, "The Scope and Sources of School Board Authority to Regulate Student Conduct and Status: A Nonconstitutional Analysis," 117 *U Pa L Rev* 373 (1969).

Anthony v Syracuse Univ 224 App Div 487, 231 NYS 435 (1928), although a nonpublic school case, is an interesting example of the traditional attitude of the courts toward student rights. Beatrice Anthony, a home economics student at Syracuse University, was dismissed from the university without either a statement of reasons or a hearing. School authorities apparently had heard rumors about her: "She had caused a lot of trouble," and she was not "a typical Syracuse girl." University regulations stated that attendance was a privilege and not a right. The university had "the right to request the withdrawal of any student whose presence is deemed detrimental." The New York court held that the regulation was within the discretion of the university and that the dismissal was within the terms of the contract. Further, it placed the burden of proof on the plaintiff and concluded that she had failed to prove—even in the absence of stated reasons—that she was dismissed on legally inadequate grounds.

Professor Goldstein is highly critical of the standard of judicial review adopted in cases such as *Anthony*; he proposes a more flexible and functional alternative:

> Some courts, having determined that the school board was purporting to base its rule on a proper school board concern, have concluded that their review function is terminated or, at best, is limited to the "reasonableness" or "nonarbitrariness" of the rule. But the analysis suggested here requires further judicial inquiry. The fact that the school board is acting out of proper interest is a necessary but not a conclusive element in determining the validity of a rule. General enabling acts should not be construed to allow school board regulation of all matters properly of concern to them regardless of any conflict with other social interests. Rather, the general enabling acts should be construed to allow school board regulation to predominate over other social concerns if, and only if, the school board interest is the paramount one involved. (Goldstein, "Scope and Sources of School Board Authority," 425-26.)

Notes and Questions

1. Judicial Deference

To what extent may the traditional nonconstitutional student rights cases be explained by judicial deference to elected officials in a sensitive area of public policy? If communities, through their elected officials, have chosen the authoritarian model of school governance and have elected to emphasize order and discipline in the learning process, is it appropriate for judges to interfere with those choices? Is there any rational basis for judicial interference in the absence of a constitutional claim, e.g., the lack of authority of school officials under the relevant enabling legislation?

2. Balancing Interests: Nonconstitutional Contest

a. Has the Balance Been Drawn? Is Professor Goldstein correct when he argues that it is not enough that a school board is motivated by educational concerns, but that the consequences of its actions must be weighed against other social concerns? Compare *Tinker v Des Moines Independent Community School Dist, infra* (Justice Harlan dissenting). How does Professor Goldstein conclude that general legislative grants of authority should be limited by a balancing of the social interests involved? Has not the legislature already struck the balance in favor of the school's interests? Does Professor Goldstein's position impose a constitutional analysis in nonconstitutional cases?

b. How Is the Balance Struck? How does Professor Goldstein's balancing test operate? Should a regulation be upheld whenever there is a "reasonable likelihood of serious harm to the moral health of other students?" See Goldstein, "Scope and Sources of School Board Authority," 373. Is the "moral health" formulation anything more than a restatement of the conflict over socialization in the schools? Does it help resolve that conflict? Does it imply some legitimate and fixed values? Would a formulation that sustained school regulations necessary to the "efficient operation of school activities" offer more guidance? Goldstein, "Scope and Sources of School Board Authority," 377. See *Tinker v Des Moines Independent Community School Dist,* below.

3. On-Campus—Off-Campus

Should the courts in nonconstitutional cases draw a distinction between the punishment of students for on-campus and off-campus conduct? Do the traditional rationales for those decisions demand such a distinction? See Van Alstyne, "The Student as University Resident," 45 *Denver LJ* 482 (1968) and cases cited. But see *Kinzer v Directors of Independent School Dist of Marion* 129 Iowa 441, 105 NW 686 (1906).

C. First Amendment Rights

TINKER v DES MOINES INDEPENDENT COMMUNITY SCHOOL DISTRICT
393 US 503 (1969)

Mr. Justice Fortas delivered the opinion of the court.

Petitioner John F. Tinker, fifteen years old, and petitioner Christopher Eckhardt, sixteen years old, attended high schools in Des Moines, Iowa. Petitioner Mary Beth Tinker, John's sister, was a thirteen-year-old student in junior high school.

In December 1965, a group of adults and students in Des Moines held a meeting at the Eckhardt home. The group determined to publicize their objections to the hostilities in Vietnam and their support for a truce by wearing black armbands during the holiday season and by fasting on December 16 and New Year's Eve. Petitioners and their parents had previously engaged in similar activities, and they decided to participate in the program.

The principals of the Des Moines schools became aware of the plan to wear armbands. On December 14, 1965, they met and adopted a policy that any student wearing an armband to school would be asked to remove it, and if he refused he would be suspended until he returned without the armband. Petitioners were aware of the regulation that the school authorities adopted.

On December 16, Mary Beth and Christopher wore black armbands to their schools. John Tinker wore his armband the next day. They were all sent home and suspended from school until they would come back without their armbands. They did not return to school until after the planned period for wearing armbands had expired—that is, until after New Year's Day.

This complaint was filed in the United States District Court by petitioners, through their fathers, under §1983 of Title 42 of the United States Code. It prayed for an injunction restraining the respondent school officials and the respondent members of the board of directors of the school district from disciplining the petitioners, and it sought nominal damages. After an evidentiary hearing the district court dismissed the complaint. It upheld the constitutionality of the school authorities' action on the ground that it was reasonable in order to prevent disturbance of school discipline. 258 F Supp 971 (1966). The court referred to but expressly declined to follow the fifth circuit's holding in a similar case that the wearing of symbols like the armbands cannot be prohibited unless it "materially and substantially interfere[s] with the requirements of appropriate discipline in the operation of the school." *Burnside v Byars* 363 F2d 744, 749 (1966).[1]

On appeal, the Court of Appeals for the Eighth Circuit considered the case *en banc*. The court was equally divided, and the district court's decision was accordingly affirmed, without opinion. 383 F2d 988 (1967). . . .

The district court recognized that the wearing of an armband for the purpose of expressing certain views is the type of symbolic act that is within the free speech clause of the First Amendment . . . . As we shall discuss, the wearing of armbands in the circumstances of this case was entirely divorced from actually or potentially disruptive conduct by those participating in it. It was closely akin to "pure speech" which, we have repeatedly held, is entitled to comprehensive protection under the First Amendment. Cf. *Cox v Louisiana* 379 US 536, 555 (1965); *Adderley v Florida* 385 US 39 (1966).

[3, 4] First Amendment rights, applied in light of the special characteristics of

---

1. In *Burnside*, the Fifth Circuit ordered that high school authorities be enjoined from enforcing a regulation forbidding students to wear "freedom buttons." It is instructive that in *Blackwell v Issaquena County Bd of Educ* 363 F2d 749 (1966), the same panel on the same day reached the opposite result on different facts. It declined to enjoin enforcement of such a regulation in another high school where the students wearing freedom buttons harassed students who did not wear them and created much disturbance.

the school environment, are available to teachers and students. It can hardly be argued that either students or teachers shed their constitutional rights to freedom of speech or expression at the schoolhouse gate. This has been the unmistakable holding of this court for almost fifty years. . . . On the other hand, the court has repeatedly emphasized the need for affirming the comprehensive authority of the states and of school officials, consistent with fundamental constitutional safeguards, to prescribe and control conduct in the schools. See *Epperson v Arkansas* [393 US 104 (1968)]; *Meyer v Nebraska* [262 US 390, 402 (1923)]. Our problem lies in the area where students in the exercise of First Amendment rights collide with the rules of the school authorities.

The problem posed by the present case does not relate to regulation of the length of skirts or the type of clothing, to hair style, or deportment. Cf. *Ferrell v Dallas Independent School Dist* 392 F2d 697 (5th Cir 1968); *Pugsley v Sellmeyer* 158 Ark 247, 250 SW 538 (1923). It does not concern aggressive, disruptive action or even group demonstrations. Our problem involves direct, primary First Amendment rights akin to "pure speech."

The school officials banned and sought to punish petitioners for a silent, passive expression of opinion, unaccompanied by any disorder or disturbance on the part of petitioners. There is here no evidence whatever of petitioners' interference, actual or nascent, with the schools' work or of collision with the rights of other students to be secure and to be let alone. Accordingly, this case does not concern speech or action that intrudes upon the work of the schools or the rights of other students.

Only a few of the 18,000 students in the school system wore the black armbands. Only five students were suspended for wearing them. There is no indication that the work of the schools or any class was disrupted. Outside the classrooms, a few students made hostile remarks to the children wearing armbands, but there were no threats or acts of violence on school premises.

The district court concluded that the action of the school authorities was reasonable because it was based upon their fear of a disturbance from the wearing of the armbands. But, in our system, undifferentiated fear or apprehension of disturbance is not enough to overcome the right to freedom of expression. Any departure from absolute regimentation may cause trouble. Any variation from the majority's opinion may inspire fear. Any word spoken, in class, in the lunchroom, or on the campus, that deviates from the views of another person may start an argument or cause a disturbance. But our Constitution says we must take this risk, *Terminiello v Chicago* 337 US 1 (1949); and our history says that it is this sort of hazardous freedom—this kind of openness—that is the basis of our national strength and of the independence and vigor of Americans who grow up and live in this relatively permissive, often disputatious, society.

In order for the state in the person of school officials to justify prohibition of a particular expression of opinion, it must be able to show that its action was caused by something more than a mere desire to avoid the discomfort and unpleasantness that always accompany an unpopular viewpoint. Certainly where there is no finding and no showing that engaging in the forbidden conduct would "materially and substantially interfere with the requirements of appropriate discipline in the operation of the school," the prohibition cannot be sustained. *Burnside v Byars, supra,* 363 F2d at 749.

In the present case, the district court made no such finding, and our independent examination of the record fails to yield evidence that the school authorities had reason to anticipate that the wearing of the armbands would substantially interfere with the work of the school or impinge upon the rights of other students. Even an official memorandum prepared after the suspension that listed the reasons for the ban on wearing the armbands made no reference to the anticipation of such disruption.[3]

On the contrary, the action of the school authorities appears to have been based upon an urgent wish to avoid the controversy which might result from the expression, even by the silent symbol of armbands, of opposition to this nation's part in the conflagration in Vietnam.[4] It is revealing, in this respect, that the meeting at which the school principals decided to issue the contested regulation was called in response to a student's statement to the journalism teacher in one of the schools that he wanted to write an article on Vietnam and have it published in the school paper. (The student was dissuaded.)

It is also relevant that the school authorities did not purport to prohibit the wearing of all symbols of political or controversial significance. The record shows that students in some of the schools wore buttons relating to national political campaigns, and some even wore the Iron Cross, traditionally a symbol of nazism. The order prohibiting the wearing of armbands did not extend to these. Instead, a particular symbol—black armbands worn to exhibit opposition to this nation's involvement in Vietnam—was singled out for prohibition. Clearly, the prohibition of expression of one particular opinion, at least without evidence that it is necessary to avoid material and substantial interference with schoolwork or discipline, is not constitutionally permissible.

In our system, state-operated schools may not be enclaves of totalitarianism. School officials do not possess absolute authority over their students. Students in school as well as out of school are "persons" under our Constitution. They are possessed of fundamental rights which the state must respect, just as they themselves must respect their obligations to the state. In our system, students may not be regarded as closed-circuit recipients of only that which the state chooses to communicate. They may not be confined to the expression of those sentiments that are officially approved. In the absence of a specific showing of constitutionally valid reasons to regulate their speech, students are entitled to freedom of expression of their views. . . .

---

3. . . . The testimony of school authorities at trial indicates that it was not fear of disruption that motivated the regulation prohibiting the armbands; the regulation was directed against "the principle of the demonstration" itself. School authorities simply felt that "the schools are no place for demonstrations," and if the students "didn't like the way our elected officials were handling things, it should be handled with the ballot box and not in the halls of our public schools."

4. The district court found that the school authorities, in prohibiting black armbands, were influenced by the fact that "the Vietnam War and the involvement of the United States therein has been the subject of a major controversy for some time. When the armband regulation involved herein was promulgated, debate over the Vietnam War had become vehement in many localities. A protest march against the war had been recently held in Washington, D.C. A wave of draft card burning incidents protesting the war had swept the country. At that time two highly publicized draft card burning cases were pending in this court. Both individuals supporting the war and those opposing it were quite vocal in expressing their views." 258 F Supp at 972-73.

In *Keyishian v Board of Regents* 385 US 589 . . . Mr. Justice Brennan, speaking for the court, said: " 'The vigilant protection of constitutional freedoms is nowhere more vital than in the community of American schools.' *Shelton v Tucker* [364 US 479], at 487. The classroom is peculiarly the 'marketplace of ideas.' The nation's future depends upon leaders trained through wide exposure to that robust exchange of ideas which discovers truth 'out of a multitude of tongues, [rather] than through any kind of authoritative selection.' "

The principle of these cases is not confined to the supervised and ordained discussion which takes place in the classroom. The principal use to which the schools are dedicated is to accommodate students during prescribed hours for the purpose of certain types of activities. Among those activities is personal intercommunication among the students.[6] This is not only an inevitable part of the process of attending school; it is also an important part of the educational process. A student's rights, therefore, do not embrace merely the classroom hours. When he is in the cafeteria, or on the playing field, or on the campus during the authorized hours, he may express his opinions, even on controversial subjects like the conflict in Vietnam, if he does so without "materially and substantially interfer[ing] with the requirements of appropriate discipline in the operation of the school" and without colliding with the rights of others. *Burnside v Byars, supra,* 363 F2d at 749. But conduct by the student, in class or out of it, which for any reason—whether it stems from time, place, or type of behavior—materially disrupts classwork or involves substantial disorder or invasion of the rights of others is, of course, not immunized by the constitutional guarantee of freedom of speech. . . .

As we have discussed, the record does not demonstrate any facts which might reasonably have led school authorities to forecast substantial disruption of or material interference with school activities, and no disturbances or disorders on the school premises in fact occurred. These petitioners merely went about their ordained rounds in school. Their deviation consisted only in wearing on their sleeve a band of black cloth, not more than two inches wide. They wore it to exhibit their disapproval of the Vietnam hostilities and their advocacy of a truce, to make their views known, and, by their example, to influence others to adopt them. They neither interrupted school activities nor sought to intrude in the school affairs or the lives of others. They caused discussion outside of the classrooms, but no interference with work and no disorder. In the circumstances, our Constitution does not permit officials of the state to deny their form of expression.

We express no opinion as to the form of relief which should be granted, this being a matter for the lower courts to determine. We reverse and remand for further proceedings consistent with this opinion.

Reversed and remanded.

Mr. Justice Stewart, concurring.

Although I agree with much of what is said in the court's opinion, and with its judgment in this case, I cannot share the court's uncritical assumption that, school

6. In *Hammond v South Carholina State College* 272 F Supp 947 (DSC 1967), District Judge Hemphill had before him a case involving a meeting on campus of 300 students to express their views on school practices. He pointed out that a school is not like a hospital or a jail enclosure. Cf. *Cox v Louisiana* 379 US 536 (1965); *Adderley v Florida* 385 US 39 (1966). It is a public place, and its dedication to specific uses does not imply that the constitutional rights of persons entitled to be there are to be gauged as if the premises were purely private property. . . .

discipline aside, the First Amendment rights of children are coextensive with those of adults. Indeed, I had thought the court decided otherwise just last term in *Ginsberg v New York* 390 US 629. I continue to hold the view I expressed in that case: "[A] state may permissibly determine that, at least in some precisely delineated areas, a child—like someone in a captive audience—is not possessed of that full capacity for individual choice which is the presupposition of First Amendment guarantees." Id., at 649-50 (concurring in result). Cf. *Prince v Massachusetts* 321 US 158.

Mr. Justice White, concurring.

While I join the court's opinion, I deem it appropriate to note, first, that the court continues to recognize a distinction between communicating by words and communicating by acts or conduct which sufficiently impinges on some valid state interest; and, second, that I do not subscribe to everything the court of appeals said about free speech in its opinion in *Burnside v Byars* 363 F2d 744, 748 (5th Cir 1966), a case relied upon by the court in the matter now before us.

Mr. Justice Black, dissenting.

The court's holding in this case ushers in what I deem to be an entirely new era in which the power to control pupils by the elected "officials of state-supported public schools" in the United States is in ultimate effect transferred to the Supreme Court. The court brought this particular case here on a petition for certiorari urging that the First and Fourteenth Amendments protect the right of school pupils to express their political views all the way "from kindergarten through high school." Here the constitutional right to "political expression" asserted was a right to wear black armbands during school hours and at classes in order to demonstrate to the other students that the petitioners were mourning because of the death of United States soldiers in Vietnam and to protest that war which they were against. Ordered to refrain from wearing the armbands in school by the elected school officials and the teachers vested with state authority to do so, apparently only seven out of the school system's 18,000 pupils deliberately refused to obey the order. One defying pupil was Paul Tinker, eight years old, who was in the second grade; another, Hope Tinker, was eleven years old and in the fifth grade; a third member of the Tinker family was thirteen, in the eighth grade; and a fourth member of the same family was John Tinker, fifteen years old, an eleventh-grade high school pupil. Their father, a Methodist minister without a church, is paid a salary by the American Friends Service Committee. Another student who defied the school order and insisted on wearing an armband in school was Christopher Eckhardt, an eleventh-grade pupil and a petitioner in this case. His mother is an official in the Women's International League for Peace and Freedom.

As I read the court's opinion it relies upon the following grounds for holding unconstitutional the judgment of the Des Moines school officials and the two courts below. First, the court concludes that the wearing of armbands is "symbolic speech" which is "akin to 'pure speech' " and therefore protected by the First and Fourteenth Amendments. Secondly, the court decides that the public schools are an appropriate place to exercise "symbolic speech" as long as normal school functions are not "unreasonably" disrupted. Finally, the court arrogates to itself, rather than to the state's elected officials charged with running the schools, the decision as to which school disciplinary regulations are "reasonable."

Assuming that the court is correct in holding that the conduct of wearing armbands for the purpose of conveying political ideas is protected by the First Amendment, cf., e.g., *Giboney v Empire Storage & Ice Co* 336 US 490 (1949), the crucial remaining questions are whether students and teachers may use the schools at their whim as a platform for the exercise of free speech—"symbolic" or "pure"—and whether the courts will allocate to themselves the function of deciding how the pupils' school day will be spent. While I have always believed that under the First and Fourteenth Amendments neither the state nor the federal government has any authority to regulate or censor the content of speech, I have never believed that any person has a right to give speeches or engage in demonstrations where he pleases and when he pleases.

While the record does not show that any of these armband students shouted, used profane language, or were violent in any manner, detailed testimony by some of them shows their armbands caused comments, warnings by other students, the poking of fun at them, and a warning by an older football player that other, nonprotesting students had better let them alone. There is also evidence that a teacher of mathematics had his lesson period practically "wrecked" chiefly by disputes with Mary Beth Tinker, who wore her armband for her "demonstration." Even a casual reading of the record shows that this armband did divert students' minds from their regular lessons, and that talk, comments, etc., made John Tinker "self-conscious" in attending school with his armband. While the absence of obscene remarks or boisterous and loud disorder perhaps justifies the court's statement that the few armband students did not actually "disrupt" the classwork, I think the record overwhelmingly shows that the armbands did exactly what the elected school officials and principals foresaw they would, that is, took the students' minds off their classwork and diverted them to thoughts about the highly emotional subject of the Vietnam War. And I repeat that if the time has come when pupils of state-supported schools, kindergartens, grammar schools, or high schools, can defy and flout orders of school officials to keep their minds on their own schoolwork, it is the beginning of a new revolutionary era of permissiveness in this country fostered by the judiciary. The next logical step, it appears to me, would be to hold unconstitutional laws that bar pupils under twenty-one or eighteen from voting, or from being elected members of the boards of education.

I deny, therefore, that it has been the "unmistakable holding of this court for almost fifty years" that "students" and "teachers" take with them into the "schoolhouse gate" constitutional rights to "freedom of speech or expression." Even *Meyer* did not hold that. It makes no reference to "symbolic speech" at all; what it did was to strike down as "unreasonable" and therefore unconstitutional a Nebraska law barring the teaching of the German language before the children reached the eighth grade. One can well agree with Mr. Justice Holmes and Mr. Justice Sutherland, as I do, that such a law was no more unreasonable than it would be to bar the teaching of Latin and Greek to pupils who have not reached the eighth grade. In fact, I think the majority's reason for invalidating the Nebraska law was that it did not like it or in legal jargon that it "shocked the court's conscience," "offended its sense of justice, or" was "contrary to fundamental concepts of the English-speaking world," as the court has sometimes said. . . .

In my view, teachers in state-controlled public schools are hired to teach there. Although Mr. Justice McReynolds may have intimated to the contrary in *Meyer v Nebraska, supra,* certainly a teacher is not paid to go into school and teach subjects the state does not hire him to teach as a part of its selected curriculum. Nor are public school students sent to the schools at public expense to broadcast political or any other views to educate and inform the public. The original idea of schools, which I do not believe is yet abandoned as worthless or out of date, was that children had not yet reached the point of experience and wisdom which enabled them to teach all of their elders. It may be that the nation has outworn the old-fashioned slogan that "children are to be seen not heard," but one may, I hope, be permitted to harbor the thought that taxpayers send children to school on the premise that at their age they need to learn, not teach. . . .

But even if the record were silent as to protests against the Vietnam War distracting students from their assigned class work, members of this court, like all other citizens, know, without being told, that the disputes over the wisdom of the Vietnam War have disrupted and divided this country as few other issues ever have. Of course students, like other people, cannot concentrate on lesser issues when black armbands are being ostentatiously displayed in their presence to call attention to the wounded and dead of the war, some of the wounded and the dead being their friends and neighbors. It was, of course, to distract the attention of other students that some students insisted up to the very point of their own suspension from school that they were determined to sit in school with their symbolic armbands.

Change has been said to be truly the law of life but sometimes the old and the tried and true are worth holding. The schools of this nation have undoubtedly contributed to giving us tranquility and to making us a more law-abiding people. Uncontrolled and uncontrollable liberty is an enemy to domestic peace. We cannot close our eyes to the fact that some of the country's greatest problems are crimes committed by the youth, too many of school age. School discipline, like parental discipline, is an integral and important part of training our children to be good citizens—to be better citizens. Here a very small number of students have crisply and summarily refused to obey a school order designed to give pupils who want to learn the opportunity to do so. One does not need to be a prophet or the son of a prophet to know that after the court's holding today some students in Iowa schools and indeed in all schools will be ready, able, and willing to defy their teachers on practically all orders. This is the more unfortunate for the schools since groups of students all over the land are already running loose, conducting break-ins, sit-ins, lie-ins, and smash-ins. Many of these student groups, as is all too familiar to all who read the newspapers and watch the television news programs, have already engaged in rioting, property seizures, and destruction. They have picketed schools to force students not to cross their picket lines and have too often violently attacked earnest but frightened students who wanted an education that the pickets did not want them to get. Students engaged in such activities are apparently confident that they know far more about how to operate public school systems than do their parents, teachers, and elected school officials. It is no answer to say that the particular students here have not yet reached such high points in their demands to attend classes in order to exercise their political pressures. Turned loose with lawsuits for damages and injunctions against their teachers as they are here, it is nothing but wishful thinking to imagine that young, immature students will not soon believe it is their right to control the schools rather than the right of the states that collect the taxes to hire the teachers for the benefit of the pupils. This case, therefore, wholly without constitutional reasons in my judgment, subjects all the public schools in the country to the whims and caprices of their loudest-mouthed, but maybe not their brightest, students. I, for one, am not fully persuaded that school pupils are wise enough, even with this court's expert help from Washington, to run the 23,390 public school systems in our fifty states. I wish, therefore, wholly to disclaim any purpose on my part to hold that the federal Constitution compels the teachers, parents, and elected school officials to surrender control of the American public school system to public school students. I dissent.

Mr. Justice Harlan, dissenting.

I certainly agree that state public school authorities in the discharge of their responsibilities are not wholly exempt from the requirements of the Fourteenth Amendment respecting the freedoms of expression and association. At the same time I am reluctant to believe that there is any disagreement between the majority and myself on the proposition that school officials should be accorded the widest authority in maintaining discipline and good order in their institutions. To translate that proposition into a workable constitutional rule, I would, in cases like this, cast upon those complaining the burden of showing that a particular school measure was motivated by other than legitimate school concerns—for example, a desire to prohibit the expression of an unpopular point of view, while permitting expression of the dominant opinion.

Finding nothing in this record which impugns the good faith of respondents in promulgating the armband regulation, I would affirm the judgment below.

Notes and Questions

1. Symbolic Speech

Tinker presumes that the wearing of armbands is a symbolic act, "closely akin to 'pure speech'." Is that presumption debatable? With respect to the former, consider the views by Professor Haskell:

> There are, however, bases for questioning the soundness of the *Tinker* decision. *Tinker* was concerned with the symbolic expression of an anti-Vietnam War position, which is in the nature of an assertion, as distinguished from reasoned discourse. It is not clear what such symbolic assertion contributes to the world of ideas and, consequently, what weight should be attributed to it in balancing the private interest in speaking out against the public interest in operating an efficient educational institution for young people. The limited intellectual significance of the symbolic expression involved in *Tinker* was not considered by the court. It should also be noted that an oral assertion of an anti-Vietnam position in a mathematics class would undoubtedly be constitutionally proscribable, though it seems that, under *Tinker,* the nonprotesting student in the mathematics class cannot complain of the symbolic expression which is in his line of vision. . . . (Haskell, "Student Expression in the Public Schools: *Tinker* Distinguished," 59 *Geo LJ* 37, 51 (1970).)

Should the court have afforded less protection to the message conveyed by the Tinker children because that message was inarticulate and insufficiently intellectual? Must protected communications invite "reasoned discourse?" How do you respond to Professor Haskell's notion that symbolic expression may be protected in circumstances where verbal or written expression would not be? Has the court created a constitutional rule that protects unobtrusive, probably ineffectual speech, while denying protection to speech that may persuade or cause others to act?

2. Rights of Children

The *Tinker* majority views students as citizens entitled to protection under the First Amendment. Justice Stewart disagrees, noting that children are "not possessed of that full capacity for individual choice which is the presupposition of First Amendment guarantees." *Tinker v Des Moines Independent Community School Dist* 393 US 503, 515 (1969). Which view seems preferable? Should immature adults be afforded fewer constitutional rights than mature adults? Is rational choice-making ability a condition to the protection of expression? Might Justice Stewart simply be saying that the state's interest in socializing and protecting children from injury is greater than its interest in socializing and protecting adults? Is this a defensible position?

3. The *Tinker* Standards

If the First Amendment is deemed applicable to student speech, the critical issue then becomes its appropriate application "in light of the special characteristics of the school environment." What standard did the court announce? Did the court create a single standard of constitutional review? Consider these excerpts from the opinion:

[i.] [W]earing of armbands in the circumstances of this case was entirely divorced from actually or potentially disruptive conduct by those participating in it.

[ii.] There is here no evidence whatever of petitioners' interference, actual or nascent, with the schools' work or of collision with the rights of other students to be secure and to be let alone.

[iii.] Any word spoken, in class, in the lunchroom, or on the campus, that deviates from the views of another person may start an argument or cause a disturbance. But our Constitution says we must take this risk. . . .

[iv.] Certainly where there is no finding and no showing that engaging in the forbidden conduct would "materially and substantially interfere with the requirements of appropriate discipline in the operation of the school," the prohibition cannot be sustained.

[v.] But conduct by the student . . . which for any reason . . . materially disrupts classwork . . . is, of course, not immunized by the constitutional guarantee of freedom of speech.

[vi.] [T]he record does not demonstrate any facts which might reasonably have led school authorities to forecast substantial disruption or material interference with school activities. . . .

Are these different formulations consistent with each other? What is the difference between interfering with the school's work and interference with discipline? What rights do other students have to be secure and left alone? Has the court stated with precision the educational interest of the state? Do the vagaries of the *Tinker* opinion invite lower federal courts to decide cases based on their own perceptions of acceptable student conduct? See, e.g., *Guzick v Drebus* 431 F2d 594 (6th Cir

1970). Do they invite disobedience by school officials? Should the court have created per se rules to protect defined categories of student speech? If not, how would you draft a rule of law which more clearly embodied the court's position? Does the importance of *Tinker* lie in its articulation of a rule of law or in its symbolic message to school officials that they do not have unfettered discretion to control student conduct. See Denno, "Mary Beth Tinker Takes the Constitution to School," 38 *Fordham L Rev* 35 (1969).

4. The "Disruption" Standard

a. Definition. Does the court require an actual disruption or simply a reasonable forecast of disruption? If a forecast is sufficient, is the standard consistent with the rights usually afforded adults? What is the difference between "undifferentiated fear or apprehension of disturbance" and a "forecast [of] substantial disruption"? Does the court offer any guidance concerning the meaning of "substantial disruption"? Is noise a disruption? Disobedience? Distraction? Inattentiveness? A verbal disagreement between students or between a student and a teacher? Is not the purpose of speech to bring the attention of listeners to the speaker's message? See generally Ladd, "Allegedly Disruptive Student Behavior and the Legal Authority of Public School Officials," 19 *J Pub Law* 209, 212-18 (1970).

b. The Hecklers' Veto. In order to justify limiting student speech, must the disruption arise from the student speaker's conduct? Is it sufficient if others react to the speaker's message in a disruptive fashion? See *Fowler v State* 93 SE2d 183 (Ga Ct App 1956). In *Ferrell v Dallas Independent School Dist* 392 F2d 697 (5th Cir 1968), a case involving the suspension of male students for their failure to abide by school regulations on hair length, Judge Tuttle, in dissenting from the majority's decision in favor of the school district, addressed himself to this issue:

> These boys were not barred from school because of any actions carried out by them which were of themselves a disturbance of the peace. They were barred because it was anticipated, by reason of previous experiences, that their fellow students in some instances would disrupt the serenity or calm of the school. It is these acts which should be prohibited, not the expressions of individuality by the suspended students. 392 F2d at 706.

See also Nahmod, "Controversy in the Classroom: The High School Teacher and Freedom of Expression," 39 *Geo Wash L Rev* 1032, 1039-41 (1971). Should it ever be permissible to silence the speaker? Should the courts require a showing by school district officials that they attempted to control the disruption? That there were no feasible alternatives to silencing the speaker? How should a school district handle this situation: in a recently integrated school, where racial tensions are high, a white student comes to school garbed in a Ku Klux Klan hood?

c. Disruption and the Tinker *Record.* In the light of the disruptive standard adopted in *Tinker,* consider these excerpts from the record:

> [1] A former student of one of our high schools was killed in Vietnam. Some of his friends are still in school, and it was felt that if any kind of demonstration existed, it might evolve into something which would be difficult to control.
> [2] I [John Tinker] felt self-conscious about wearing the arm band . . .

some of the other students talked to me about the arm band and asked why I was wearing it. I told them why and some of them didn't think I should do this. . . . This discussion took place on and off during the class period.

[3] After gym some students were making fun of me [John Tinker] for wearing it. . . . Two or three boys made remarks in the locker room that were not very friendly. This lasted for perhaps three or four minutes. They did not threaten me with any physical harm.

[4] [In the lunchroom] there was one student . . . who was making smart remarks for about ten minutes. There were four or five people with him standing milling around. There were quite a few other students standing and milling around the lunchroom. To my knowledge there were no threats to hit me or anything like that. At no time was I in fear that they might attack me or hit me in the student center because there were too many people there. . . . A football player named Joe Thompson told the kids to leave me alone; that everyone had their own opinions.

Do these facts contradict the majority's characterization of the armband protest? Do they help define the majority's concept of disruption? Do they support Justice Black's dissent? Could the court have employed the disruption standard and decided the case in favor of the school authorities? In this regard, is it relevant that the school authorities may not have been aware of the disruption standard when the protest took place? Consider these remarks made by the school principal to John Tinker at the time of his suspension: ". . . . I personally felt that there were appropriate times for us to mourn our war dead, including this event [Veteran's Day] and Memorial Day, and it did not seem appropriate or necessary to me to mourn them as he was doing at this time. I told him that I was a veteran of World War II and the Korean War." *Tinker v Des Moines Independent School Dist* 393 US 503 (1969) (Brief for Petitioner, p 8). With the advantage of hindsight, was this frank admission by the principal a tactical mistake? Compare *Breen v Kahl* 296 F Supp 702, 705 n3 (WD Wisc 1969). In future student rights cases, how would you advise school officials to defend their actions?

d. Proof of Disruption. What evidence is necessary to prove substantial disruption? Will the uncorroborated testimony of school officials suffice? Must past instances of material disruption resulting from similar speech or conduct be brought to the attention of the court? Empirical studies? Compare *Breen v Kahl, supra,* with *Ferrell v Dallas Independent School Dist, supra.* Expert witnesses? See *Bannister v Paradis* 316 F Supp 185 (DNH 1970). Which party bears the burden of persuasion? Must the school board prove that the speech did or probably would have resulted in material disruption, or must the student prove that such consequences did not or were unlikely to occur? Is the answer to this question likely to affect the outcome of student rights cases? Should it? See *Healy v James* 408 US 169 (1972).

5. *Tinker* and Verbal Communication

In *Goldberg v Regents of the Univ of Cal* 248 CA2d 867, 57 Cal Rptr 463 (1967), decided before *Tinker*, a number of University of California at Berkeley students were dismissed or suspended for their protest activities in the spring of 1965. Essentially they were charged with using obscene language repeatedly in speeches before rallies in front of campus buildings including the student union, reading aloud passages from D. H. Lawrence's *Lady Chatterley's Lover* that contained numerous references to the same term, manning a fund-raising table that displayed the words "Fuck Fund" in large letters, and leading cheers "consisting of first spelling and then shouting the word *fuck*." A special ad hoc university committee appointed to hear the charges against the students concluded that "the loud use and prominent display of the words in question in a public place such as the Sproul-Student Union Plaza is a violation" of university regulations. 248 CA2d at 873, 57 Cal Rptr at 468. The court upheld the dismissals and suspensions: "The irresponsible activity of plaintiffs seriously interfered with the university's interest in preserving proper decorum in campus assemblages. . . . Conduct involving rowdiness, rioting, the destruction of property, the reckless display of impropriety or any unjustifiable disturbance of the public order on or off campus is indefensible. . . ." 57 Cal Rptr at 473. In the light of the *Tinker* decision, is *Goldberg* still good law? In order to make this determination, would it be necessary to gather evidence of whether the plaintiffs materially interfered with the classroom work of the other students? Should a distinction be drawn between political speech and obscenity? See Justice Rehnquist's dissent in *Papish v Board of Curators*, page 163 *infra.* Would the plaintiffs' speech be protected if it were less loud and prominent? If the rallies had been held when no instruction was taking place? If the rallies had been held in some remote part of the campus instead of in front of the student union? Does *Tinker* address itself to these time, place, and manner distinctions? Should it?

Goldberg is one of the few decided cases in which students are punished for verbal rather than symbolic or written communication. Why is this so? Does it indicate that freedom of verbal communication is so well entrenched that school administrators rarely challenge it? Might it suggest that when administrators object to verbal communication, they find a different and more widely acceptable rationale for punishment? If the latter hypothesis is correct, what does it auger for the eventual impact of *Tinker* on the operation of public educational institutions?

6. *Tinker* and School Newspapers

The court notes that the meeting at which the principals decided to ban armbands was prompted by a student's request to publish an article on Vietnam in the school newspaper. The student ultimately was dissuaded. What if the student had insisted on his "right" to publish the article? Does *Tinker* command access to school publications as well as to the school building? Would the critical question be whether the article might be disruptive? Obscene? Is the fact that the school newspaper had previously published advertisements or articles relating to political subjects relevant to the inquiry? See *Zucker v Panitz* 299 F Supp 102 (SDNY 1969). Is it pertinent that the school is under no obligation to publish a newspaper? If such an article had been published, what disciplinary action, if any, could be taken? See *Dickey v Alabama State Bd of Educ* 273 F Supp 613 (MD Ala 1967); *Eisner v Stamford Bd of Educ*, page 157 *infra.*

7. Socialization

Did the court give adequate consideration to the attempt by the Tinker children to change their classmates' perception of the Vietnam war? The *Tinker* record notes that the "principals [of the five senior high schools in Des Moines] felt that since the schools are made up of a captive audience, the other students should not be forced to view the demonstrations of a few." Are the principals subject to their own criticism? See 4c above. Do the principals implicitly deny that political socialization takes place in schools? Does the *Tinker* decision undermine the constitutional legitimacy of the school's interest in political socialization? Consider this hypothetical case: Colonel Rogers is a former prisoner of war who was released by North Vietnam in early 1973. He is a resident of Des Moines, and is a genuinely beloved, popular hero in that city. After his arrival in Des Moines, many parades, banquets, and other functions were held to honor him. Subsequently, the superintendent of the Des Moines public schools asked him to speak to an assembly of students at each of the senior high schools. Colonel Rogers accepted, and he plans to talk about the necessity for the war effort, the atrocities committed in the prison camps in North Vietnam, and the role that peace demonstrators played in prolonging the war and delaying the release of American prisoners. A number of "antiwar" parents object to Colonel Rogers' proposed presentation. What legal action might they take? Is it likely that a court would prevent Colonel Rogers from speaking? Might the parents persuade the court that the speech would disrupt the operation of the school? Can only school officials make this judgment? Should a court compel the school district to excuse the children of objecting parents from attendance at the Rogers assembly? Could the parents rely on *Tinker* for the proposition that an antiwar speaker must be included on the program? Must that speaker be a student in the school? Could armbands or buttons protesting the Rogers speech be banned on the basis of a "reasonable forecast of disruption"?

8. *Tinker* and Speaker Bans

In the state university context, courts have unanimously held that once the university's doors are open to off-campus speakers, the university may not engage in political censorship by banning speakers with politically objectionable views. See, e.g., *Pickings v Bruce* 430 F2d 595 (8th Cir 1970); *Brooks v Auburn Univ* 296 F Supp 188 (MD Ala 1969). Compare *Dunkel v Elkins* 325 F Supp 1235 (D Md 1971) (statute authorizing exclusion of "outsiders" from university campus). See generally Wright, "The Constitution on the Campus," 22 *Vand L Rev* 1027, 1050-52 (1969); Van Alstyne, "Political Speakers at State Universities: Some Constitutional Considerations," 111 *U Pa L Rev* 328 (1963). Does *Tinker* command this result? Might a speaker be banned from a university campus if there was some likelihood of a substantial disruption? Or is the *Tinker* standard applicable only to primary and secondary school students?

GUZICK v DREBUS
431 F2d 594 (6th Cir 1970)

Before: Weick, Circuit Judge, and McAllister and O'Sullivan, Senior Circuit Judges.

O'Sullivan, Senior Circuit Judge. Plaintiff-Appellant, Thomas Guzick, Jr.,—prosecuting this action by his father and next friend, Thomas Guzick—appeals from dismissal of his complaint in the United States District Court for the Northern District of Ohio, Eastern Division. . . .

The complaint charged that Thomas Guzick, Jr., a seventeen-year-old, eleventh-grade student at Shaw High School, had been denied the right of free speech guaranteed to him by the United States Constitution's First Amendment. He asserted that this right had been denied him when he was suspended for refusing to remove, while in the classrooms and the school premises, a button which solicited participation in an antiwar demonstration that was to take place in Chicago on April 5. The legend of the button was:

April 5 Chicago
GI - Civilian
Anti-War
Demonstration
Student Mobilization Committee

On March 11, 1969, young Guzick and another student, Havens, appeared at the office of defendant Drebus, principal of the high school, bringing with them a supply of pamphlets which advocated attendance at the same planned Chicago antiwar demonstration as was identified by the button. The boys were denied permission to distribute the pamphlets, and were also told to remove the buttons which both were then wearing. Guzick said that his lawyer, counsel for him in this litigation, told him that a United States Supreme Court decision entitled him to wear the button in school. Principal Drebus directed that he remove it and desist from wearing it in the school. Being told by Guzick that he would not obey, the principal suspended him and advised that such suspension would continue until Guzick obeyed. The other young man complied, and returned to school. Guzick did not, and has made no effort to return to school. This lawsuit promptly followed on March 17. The complaint prayed that the school authorities be required to allow Guzick to attend school wearing the button, that it be declared that Guzick had a constitutional right to do so, and that damages of $1,000 be assessed for each day of school missed by Guzick as a result of the principal's order. . . .

Plaintiff insists that the facts of this case bring it within the rule of *Tinker v Des Moines Independent School Dist* 393 US 503 (1969). We are at once aware that unless *Tinker* can be distinguished, reversal is required. We consider that the facts of this case clearly provide such distinction.

The rule applied to appellant Guzick was of long-standing—forbidding all wearing of buttons, badges, scarves and other means whereby the wearers identify themselves as supporters of a cause or bearing messages unrelated to their education. Such things as support the high school athletic teams or advertise a school play are not forbidden. The rule had its genesis in the days when fraternities were competing for the favor of the students and it has been uniformly enforced. The rule has continued as one of universal application and usefulness. While controversial buttons appeared from time to time, they were required to be removed as soon as the school authorities could get to them.

Reciting the history of the no-button or symbol rule, and the fact that the current student population of Shaw High School is 70 percent black and 30 percent white, the district judge observed:

> The rule was created in response to a problem which Shaw has had over a period of many years. At the time high school fraternities were in vogue, the various fraternities at Shaw were a divisive and disruptive influence on the school. They carved out portions of the school cafeteria in which only mem-

bers of a particular fraternity were permitted to sit. The fraternities were competitive and engaged in activities which disrupted the educational process at Shaw. There were fights between members of the individual fraternities and often strong feelings between the members.

The same problem was encountered with the informal clubs, which replaced high school fraternities and sororities. The problem again exists as a result of the racial mixture at Shaw. Buttons, pins, and other emblems have been used as identifying "badges." They have portrayed and defined the divisions among students in the school. They have fostered an undesirable form of competition, division and dislike. The presence of these emblems, badges and buttons are taken to represent, define and depict the actual division of the students in various groups.

The buttons also encourage division among the students, for they portray and identify the wearer as a member of a particular group or the advocate of a particular cause. This sets the wearer apart from other students wearing different buttons or without buttons. It magnifies the differences between students, encourages emphasis on these differences, and tends to polarize the students into separate, distinct, and unfriendly groups. In addition, there have been instances in which students have attempted to force other students to wear a particular manner of dress or to wear their particular insignia or expressive button. For those reasons, Shaw High officials have enforced the antibutton rule and have prohibited the wearing of such indicia.

The rule has acquired a particular importance in recent years. Students have attempted to wear buttons and badges expressing inflammatory messages inscribed thereon. "White is right"; "Say it loud, Black and Proud"; "Black Power." Other buttons have depicted a mailed black fist, commonly taken to be the symbol of black power.

There have been occasions when the wearing of such insignia has led to disruptions at Shaw and at Kirk Junior High. A fight resulted in the cafeteria when a white student wore a button which read "Happy Easter, Dr. King." (Dr. Martin Luther King was assassinated in the Easter season.) (305 F Supp at 467-77.)

From the total evidence, including that of educators, school administrators and others having special relevant qualifications, the district judge concluded that abrogation of the rule would inevitably result in collisions and disruptions which would seriously subvert Shaw High School as a place of education for its students, black and white.[1] . . .

Contrasting with the admitted long standing and uniform enforcement of Shaw's no-symbol rule, the majority opinion in *Tinker* was careful to point out,

It is also relevant that the school authorities [in *Tinker*] did not purport to prohibit the wearing of all symbols of political or controversial significance. The record shows that students in some of the schools wore buttons relating to national political campaigns, and some even wore the Iron Cross,

---

1. He concluded that this was so even though he did not find the message of the particular button inflammatory, per se. "Although there was evidence that the message conveyed in this particular button might be such as to inflame some of the students at Shaw High, the court does not feel that such a result is likely." 305 F Supp at 479.

traditionally a symbol of nazism. The *order prohibiting the wearing of arm-bands did not extend to these.* Instead, a particular symbol—black armbands worn to exhibit opposition to this nation's involvement in Vietnam—was singled out for prohibition. (393 US at 510-11.)

The armband demonstration in *Tinker* was a one-time affair, with a date for its ending fixed in its original plan. . . .

Further distinguishing *Tinker* from our case are their respective settings. No potential racial collisions were background to *Tinker,* whereas here the changing racial composition of Shaw High from all white to 70 percent black, made the no-symbol rule of even greater good than had characterized its original adoption. In our view, school authorities should not be faulted for adhering to a relatively nonoppressive rule that will indeed serve our ultimate goal of meaningful integration of our public schools. Such was the command of *Brown v Board of Educ* 347 US 483 (1954). . . .

In *Tinker* the court concluded that a regulation forbidding expressions opposing the Vietnam conflict anywhere on school property would violate the students' constitutional rights, "at least *if it could not be justified* by a showing that the students' activities would materially and substantially disrupt the work and discipline of the school." 393 US at 513.

The Supreme Court then went on to say that the district judge in *Tinker* made no such finding. . . .

But in the case at bar, the district judge, upon a valid appraisal of the evidence, did find that "if all buttons are permitted or if any buttons are permitted, a serious discipline problem will result, racial tensions will be exacerbated, and the educational process will be significantly and substantially disrupted." 305 F Supp at 478. . . .

We will not attempt extensive review of the many great decisions which have forbidden abridgment of free speech. We have been thrilled by their beautiful and impassioned language. They are part of our American heritage. None of these masterpieces, however, were composed or uttered to support the wearing of buttons in high school classrooms. We are not persuaded that enforcement of such a rule as Shaw High School's no-symbolic proscription would have excited like judicial classics. Denying Shaw High School the right to enforce this small disciplinary rule could, and most likely would, impair the rights of its students to an education and the rights of its teachers to fulfill their responsibilities.

Mr. Justice Douglas spoke for a majority of the court in *Terminiello v Chicago* 337 US 1 (1949) which had to do with utterances made at a public meeting in a Chicago auditorium. Describing the nature of free speech, he said:

[A] function of free speech under our system of government is to invite dispute. It may indeed best serve its high purpose when it induces a condition of unrest, creates dissatisfaction with conditions as they are, or even stirs people to anger. Speech is often provocative and challenging. It may strike at prejudices and preconceptions and have profound unsettling effects as it presses for acceptance of an idea. (337 US at 4.)

However correct such language when applied to an open public protest meeting, we doubt the propriety of protecting in a high school classroom such aggressive and colorful use of free speech. We must be aware in these contentious times that America's classrooms and their environs will lose their usefulness as places in which to educate our young people if pupils come to school wearing the badges of their respective disagreements, and provoke confrontations with their fellows and their teachers. The buttons are claimed to be a form of speech. Unless they have some relevance to what is being considered or taught, a school classroom is no place for the untrammeled exercise of such right. . . .

The complaint's contention that Guzick was denied equal protection of the law is not argued to this court; neither is it now asserted that he was denied due process of law in the method by which the relevant discipline was imposed.

Judgment affirmed.

McAllister, Senior Circuit Judge, dissenting. When a few students noticed the button which appellant was wearing, and asked him "what it said," appellant's explanation resulted only in a casual reaction; and there was no indication that the wearing of the button would disrupt the work and discipline of the school.

I am of the opinion that the judgment of the district court should be reversed and the case dismissed upon the authority of *Tinker v Des Moines Independent School Dist* 393 US 503 (1969). . . .

Notes and Questions

1. Distinguishing *Tinker*

a. Disruption. The record in *Guzick* indicates that the plaintiff wore the objectionable button for an entire school day without causing disruption. He was suspended on the day after he requested permission from the principal to distribute leaflets. The district court, in effect, took note of these facts in finding that it was unlikely that students would be inflamed by the message on the button. If this is the case, can *Guzick* be reconciled with *Tinker*? Does the vagueness of the *Tinker* disruption formulation invite decisions like *Guzick*?

b. Other Factors. The court refers to a number of factors that assertedly distinguish *Tinker*:

i. The antibutton rule is of long standing and is uniformly applied.

ii. Shaw High School is racially integrated (70 percent black, 30 percent white), and the nonenforcement of the antibutton rule would lead to racial disturbances. On one occasion a fight broke out between black and white students with respect to a "Happy Easter, Dr. King" button.

iii. Nonenforcement of the rule might defeat the goal of "meaningful integration of our public schools."

Do you find these distinctions persuasive? Was the antibutton rule uniformly applied? What is the relevance of its long standing or the racial composition of the school? Did the button contain a racially antagonistic message? Compare *Melton v Young* 465 F2d 1332 (6th Cir 1972). Was the evidence of the previous racial disturbance probative as to the disposition of *Guzick*?

2. Administrative Convenience

Is a total ban on buttons justified by the difficulty in distinguishing disruptive from nondisruptive buttons? Do these administrative difficulties outweigh the plaintiff's interest in free expression? What weight does *Tinker* accord to administrative convenience?

3. *Tinker* Rejected?

Is the heart of Judge O'Sullivan's position his fundamental disagreement with the *Tinker* majority? Is *Guzick* an example of a rebellion by lower federal courts against a Supreme Court decision? Did *Tinker* invite such a rebellion? Judge O'Sullivan states that "America's classrooms and their environs will lose their usefulness as places in which to educate our young people if pupils come to school wearing the badges of their respective disagreements, and provoke confrontations with their fellows and their teachers. . . . Unless they have some relevance to what is being considered or taught, a school classroom is no place for the untrammeled exercise of [free speech] . . . ." *Guzick v Drebus* 431 F2d 594, 600-601 (6th Cir 1970). Is this statement consistent with *Tinker*? Were not the *Tinker* armbands "badges of [the students'] respective disagreements?" Did they not provoke confrontation and disagreement? Was that not their purpose? Were the armbands "relevant" to the instructional process? Does *Guzick* adopt a pedagogical and school governance model inconsistent with that adopted in *Tinker*? Is it the business of courts—rather than of parents and elected officials—to make such choices? Compare Justice Black's dissent in *Tinker, supra,* p. 144.

EISNER v STAMFORD BOARD OF EDUCATION
440 F2d 803 (2d Cir 1971)

Kaufman, Circuit Judge:

The Board of Education of the City of Stamford, Connecticut, on November 18, 1969, adopted the following "policy":

Distribution of Printed or Written Matter

The board of education desires to encourage freedom of expression and creativity by its students subject to the following limitations:

No person shall distribute any printed or written matter on the grounds of any school or in any school building unless the distribution of such material shall have prior approval by the school administration.

In granting or denying approval, the following guidelines shall apply.

No material shall be distributed which, either by its content or by the manner of distribution itself, will interfere with the proper and orderly operation and discipline of the school, will cause violence or disorder, or will constitute an invasion of the rights of others.

Plaintiffs are students at Rippowam High School in Stamford. They wish to distribute free of the restraint imposed by the quoted policy, or of any other similar restraint, a mimeographed newspaper of their own creation and other printed and written literature. The district court agreed with their contention that the board's policy violates their right to freedom of expression. Limiting the issue to the constitutional validity of the requirement that the *contents* of "the literature be submitted to school officials for approval prior to distribution" (the validity of reasonable regulation concerning time, place, and manner of distribution being conceded by plaintiffs), the court reasoned that the policy imposed a "prior restraint" on student speech and press, invalid under *Near v Minnesota ex rel Olson* 283 US 697 (1931), in the absence of even "a scintilla of proof which would justify" the restraint. As an independent ground for granting plaintiffs' and denying defendants' motions for summary judgment, the court found the policy fatally defective for lack of "procedural safeguards," citing *Freedman v Maryland* 380 US 51 (1965). . . .

We affirm the decision below, 314 F Supp 832 (1970), insofar as it declares unconstitutional and enjoins the enforcement of the board's policy of November 18, 1970, but we do so, as will shortly appear, with some reservations and for reasons significantly different from those advanced by the court below. In sum, we agree that *Freedman v Maryland* delineates precisely why the policy here is defective. We do not agree with the district court, however, that reasonable and fair regulations which corrected those defects but nevertheless required prior submission of material for approval, would in all circumstances be an unconstitutional "prior restraint."

Consideration of the judicial interpretations enunciated over the years in this highly complex free speech-press area are a necessary backdrop to our discussion. In *Near,* the Supreme Court struck down a statute which if analogized to the instant case would place a prior restraint upon distribution of literature by any student who had in the past regularly distributed material deemed by school authorities to be obscene, lewd, and lascivious, or malicious, scandalous, and defamatory. The law held unconstitutional in *Near* permitted such a broad restraint to be imposed by county courts upon publishers of newspapers and periodicals in the state of Minnesota. The court considered such a scheme to be "of the essence of censorship" and in strong terms, gave expression to the enmity reflected in the first amendment toward "previous restraints upon publication." 283 US at 713. The court's particular concern was directed at that aspect of the law under which crusading newspaper publishers would hazard not only libel actions, but the utter abatement of their publications and consequently the squelching of their campaigns, if they should attempt systematically to expose the derelictions of public officials. But Chief Justice Hughes made it clear that his opinion was not to be read as invalidating all "previous restraints." He took pains to catalogue several varieties of "exceptional cases" which would justify a "previous restraint." Thus, it was well established then as it is now that "[t]he constitutional guaranty of free speech does not 'protect a man from an injunction against uttering words that may have all the effect of force'." Nor did it question that "the primary requirements of decency may be enforced against obscene publications." 283 US at 716, . . .

We agree with appellants that we need not and should not concern ourselves with the content or disruptive potential of the specific issue of the newspaper which plaintiffs sought unsuccessfully to distribute on school property. The students are challenging the policy "on its face" and not as applied to their particular publication.

Moreover, we cannot ignore the oft-stressed and carefully worded dictum in the leading precedent, *Tinker v Des Moines School Dist* 393 US 503 (1969), that protected speech in public secondary schools may be forbidden if school authorities reasonably "forecast substantial disruption of or material interference with school activities. . . ."

The potential "evil," the school board urges, is the disruption of the effort by the state of Connecticut through its system of public schooling, to give its children "opportunities for growth into free and independent well-developed men and citizens. . . ." A public school is undoubtedly a "marketplace of ideas." Early involvement in social comment and debate is a good method for future generations of adults to learn intelligent involvement. But we cannot deny that Connecticut has authority to minimize or eliminate influences that would dilute or disrupt the effectiveness of the educational process as the state conceives it. The task of judging the actual effects of school policy statements and regulations is a delicate and difficult one. But, to the extent that the board's policy statement here merely vests school officials under state law with authority which under *Tinker* they may constitutionally exercise, it is on its face unexceptionable. Unless the policy, therefore, purports to delegate greater power to restrain the distribution of disruptive matter than *Tinker* allows, or unless it otherwise unreasonably burdens students' first amendment activity, it is valid.

The policy criteria by which school authorities may prevent students from distributing literature on school property departs in no significant respect from the similarly very general and broad instruction of *Tinker* itself. Although the policy does not specify that the foreseeable disruption be either "material" or "substantial" as *Tinker* requires, we assume that the board would never contemplate the futile as well as unconstitutional suppression of matter that would create only an immaterial disturbance. Thus, the regulation tracks the present state of the authoritative constitutional law, and while we realize this does not end the matter it does save the regulation from the charge that it is on its face fatally overbroad, since the policy statement does not purport to authorize suppression of a significant class of protected activity. . . .

Absence of overbreadth, of course, does not in itself absolve the policy statement of the plaintiffs' charge that it is also unduly vague. The phrase "invasion of the rights of others" is not a model of clarity or preciseness. But several factors present here lessen or remove the familiar dangers to first amendment freedoms often associated with vague statutes. Thus, the statement does not attempt to authorize *punishment* of students who publish literature that under the policy may be censored by school officials. If it did, students would be left to guess at their peril the thrust of the policy in a specific case and the resultant chill on First Amendment activity might be intolerable. See *Keyishian v Board of Regents* 385 US 589, 604 (1967). Also, because any ban that school authorities may impose would apply only to students *on school property,* the policy statement does not threaten to foreclose, e.g., from the publisher of a newspaper, a significant market or block of potential buyers should the publisher guess wrongly as to the kind of literature that a school principal will tolerate under particular circumstances. Cf. *Interstate Circuit v City of Dallas* 390 US 676 (1968). The policy does not in any way interfere with students' freedom to disseminate and to receive material outside of school property; nor does it threaten to interfere with the predominate responsibility of *parents* for their children's welfare. The statement is, therefore, in many ways narrowly drawn to achieve its permissible purposes, and indeed may fairly be characterized as a regulation of speech, rather than a blanket prior restraint.[5]

---

5. Because of such factors as the larger size of university campuses, and the tendency of students to spend a greater portion of their time there, the inhibitive effect of a similar policy

In sum, we believe that the board's policy statement is neither overbroad nor unconstitutionally vague, so far as it prescribes *criteria* by which school officials may prevent the distribution on secondary school property of written or printed matter.

Since, however, the policy statement is in other ways constitutionally deficient, it would not be remiss for us to observe that greater specificity in the statement would be highly desirable. The board would in no way shackle school administrators if it attempted to confront and resolve in some fashion, prior to court intervention, some of the difficult constitutional issues that will almost inevitably be raised when so broad a rule is applied to particular cases. For example, to what extent and under what circumstances does the board intend to permit school authorities to suppress criticism of their own actions and policies? See Berkman, "Students in Court: Free Speech & the Functions of Schooling in America," 40 *Harv Educ Rev* 567, 589 (1970); cf. *New York Times Co v Sullivan* 376 US 254 (1964). Similarly, does the board anticipate that school officials will take reasonable measures to minimize or forestall potential disorder and disruption that might otherwise be generated in reaction to the distribution of controversial or unpopular opinions, before they resort to banishing the ideas from school grounds? See *Terminiello v City of Chicago* 337 US 1 (1949). The board might also undertake to describe the kinds of disruptions and distractions, and their degree, that it contemplates would typically justify censorship, as well as other distractions or disorders that it would consider do not justify suppression of students' attempts to distribute literature. At the same time it would be wise for the board to consider the areas of school property where it would be appropriate to distribute approved material.

Refinements of the sort we mention would lessen the possibility that the policy statement under attack here because of its tendency to overgeneralization, will be administered arbitrarily, erratically, or unfairly . . . . By grappling with some of the difficult issues suggested, the board might also succeed in demonstrating its conscientious intent to formulate policy not only within the outer limits of constitutional permissibility, but also with a sensitivity to some of the teaching reflected in relevant constitutional doctrine and to the dangers lurking in improper and unconstitutional administration of a broad and general standard.

Finally, greater specificity might reduce the likelihood of future litigation and thus forestall the possibility that federal courts will be called upon again to intervene in the operation of Stamford's public schools. It is to everyone's advantage that decisions with respect to the operation of local schools be made by local officials. The greater the generosity of the board in fostering—not merely tolerating—students' free exercise of their constitutional rights, the less likely it will be that local officials will find their rulings subjected to unwieldy constitutional litigation.

Although the board's regulation passes muster as authorizing prior restraints, we believe it is constitutionally defective in its lack of procedure for prior *submission* by students for school administration approval of written material before "distribution." In *Freedman v Maryland* 380 US 51 (1965), the court instructed that strict procedural formalities must be observed whenever a state attempts to enforce a requirement that motion picture exhibitors submit a film to a state board of

statement might be greater on the campus of an institution of higher education than on the premises of a secondary school and the justifications for such a policy might be less compelling in view of the greater maturity of the students there.

censors for clearance before the film is shown to the public. In order "to obviate the dangers of a censorship system" the state must:

(1) assume the burden of proving that a film is obscene in the constitutional sense and hence unprotected by the First Amendment;

(2) secure a judicial determination of the film's obscenity before it may "impose a valid final restraint"; and

(3) reach a final decision whether to restrain the showing of the film "within a specified brief period." 380 US at 58-59.

For the reasons we have already set forth, we do not regard the board's policy as imposing nearly so onerous a "prior restraint" as was involved in *Freedman*. Also, we believe that it would be highly disruptive to the educational process if a secondary school principal were required to take a school newspaper editor to court every time the principal reasonably anticipated disruption and sought to restrain its cause. Thus, we will not require school officials to seek a judicial decree before they may enforce the board's policy.[7] As for the burden of proof, *Tinker* as well as other fundamental cases, e.g., *Blackwell v Isaquena County Bd of Educ* 363 F2d 749 (5th Cir 1966), and a companion case cited with approval in *Tinker, Burnside v Byars* 363 F2d 744 (5th Cir 1966), establish that, if students choose to litigate, school authorities must demonstrate a reasonable basis for interference with student speech, and that courts will not rest content with officials' bare allegation that such a basis existed. We believe that this burden is sufficient to satisfy the intent of *Freedman* in the special context of a public secondary school. Of course, this standard is a matter for courts to enforce and need not be reflected in the policy statement.

We see no good reason, however, why the board should not comply with *Freedman* to the extent of ensuring an expeditious review procedure. The policy as presently written is wholly deficient in this respect for it prescribes no period of time in which school officials must decide whether or not to permit distribution. To be valid, the regulation must prescribe a definite brief period within which review of submitted material will be completed.

The policy is also deficient in failing to specify to whom and how material may be submitted for clearance. Absent such specifications, students are unreasonably proscribed by the terms of the policy statement from distributing *any* written material on school property, since the statement leaves them ignorant of clearance procedures. Nor does it provide that the prohibition against distribution without prior approval is to be inoperative until each school has established a screening procedure.

Finally, we believe that the proscription against "distributing" written or printed material without prior consent is unconstitutionally vague. We assume that by *distributing* the board intends something more than one student passing to a fellow student his copy of a general newspaper or magazine. Indeed, this assumption underpins most of our discussion concerning the constitutional validity of the

---

7. Nor do we find any basis for holding, as the district court suggested, that the school officials must in every instance conduct an adversary proceeding before they may act to prevent disruptions, although the thoroughness of any official investigation may in a particular case influence a court's retrospective perception of the reliability and rationality of officials' fear of disruption.

policy statement, apart from the deficiencies we describe here. If students are to be required to secure prior approval before they may pass notes to each other in the hallways or exchange *Time, Newsweek,* or other periodicals among themselves, then the resultant burden on speech might very likely outweigh the very remote possibility that such activities would ever cause disruption. We assume, therefore, that the board contemplates that it will require prior submission only when there is to be a *substantial* distribution of written material, so that it can reasonably be anticipated that in a significant number of instances there would be a likelihood that the distribution would disrupt school operations. . . .

We therefore affirm and remand the case to the district court for entry of an appropriate judgment in accordance with this opinion.

Notes and Questions

1. Armbands and Underground Newspapers

Should the *Tinker* standard be extended to the more than 1,000 underground student newspapers published in America? If armbands are protected by the First Amendment, does it necessarily follow that the distribution of newspapers is similarly protected? Can it be reasonably argued that the distribution of newspapers on school grounds or in school buildings is per se disruptive? Should student newspapers receive less protection than official school publications or the *New York Times*?

2. Prior Restraints

The *Eisner* court held that prior restraints requiring official approval before distribution of underground student newspapers are constitutional. See also *Shanley v Northeast Independent School Dist* 462 F2d 960 (5th Cir 1972); *Baughman v Freienmuth* 478 F2d 1345 (4th Cir 1973). Did the court adequately distinguish *Near v Minnesota*? Does not the Stamford board of education seek to "censor" student publications? Should students be encouraged to "expose the derelictions of public [school] officials"? Does *Tinker,* by asserting that a forecast of disruption is sufficient to limit student expression, inevitably lead to the approval of prior restraints on underground newspapers? Does this suggest that *Tinker* generally affords much narrower constitutional protections to students than to adults? Is the difference between distribution on a street corner or in the public school of constitutional significance?

3. Problem: When Is Prior Restraint Justified?

If the asserted authority to approve student newspapers before distribution is constitutional, when would a principal be justified in refusing permission to distribute on the ground that the content was objectionable? Consider the following cases:

a. Two students plan to sell a publication entitled "Grass High." The newspaper replies to a school publication sent to parents, and urges students not to deliver such "propaganda" to their parents in the future. It refers to the dean as having a "sick mind" and notes that "oral sex may prevent tooth decay." See *Scoville v Board of Educ* 425 F2d 10 (7th Cir 1970).

b. A high school student plans to distribute a newspaper calling for a student strike to protest the lengthening of the school day. The principal is called a "King Louis," "a big liar," and a "racist." See *Schwartz v Schuker* 298 F Supp 238 (EDNY 1969).

c. Students at a state university plan to distribute a newspaper containing the following comments:

> It's been a long quarter, hasn't it? And an interesting one too . . . This has been a quarter . . . wherein the administration has forbidden girls to wear the latest fashions . . . ; a quarter wherein the administration fired some poor student from his job at the library because he grew a beard; . . . a quarter wherein women's social rules were maintained at a level of liberality [prevailing] when Queen Victoria was young; . . . a quarter where the administration bureaucracy achieved new heights of rudeness, inefficiency, and intolerance.
>
> And how has the . . . student body reacted: have they precipitated a revolution like French students? . . . Have they seized buildings and raised havoc . . . ?—No. . . .
>
> Maybe students will get some sense and learn . . . to stand up and fight . . . When we move against them, remember, like the man says, "Put up or shut up." (See *Norton v Discipline Comm of E Tenn State Univ* 419 F2d 194, 201 (6th Cir 1969).)

Is the issue in these cases, properly framed, one of disruption? Obscenity? Should the courts take into account the challenge to existing authority? Should a distinction be drawn between communications about national political issues and "student advocacy of disregard of school rules and procedures and student ridicule of school administrators and teachers"? See Haskell, "Student Expression in the Public Schools: *Tinker* Distinguished," 59 *Geo LJ* 37, 57 (1970). Compare Nahmod, "Beyond Tinker: The High School as an Educational Public Forum," 5 *Harv Civ Rights—Civ Lib L Rev* 278 (1970). If so, what standard should be applied in each situation?

4. *Papish:* "indecent speech"

In *Papish v Board of Curators of Univ of Mo* 35 L Ed2d 618, 93 S Ct 1197 (1973), *per curiam,* a graduate journalism student was expelled for distributing a campus newspaper that contained "indecent speech." On the front cover of the newspaper, there was a political cartoon depicting policemen raping the Statue of Liberty and the Goddess of Justice. Inside, there was an article entitled "Mother Fucker Acquitted," which discussed the trial and acquittal on an assault charge of a member of an organization known as "Up Against the Wall, Mother Fucker." The court overturned the expulsion:

> We think . . . it [is] clear that the mere dissemination of ideas—no matter how offensive to good taste—on a state university campus may not be shut off in the name alone of "conventions of decency." Other recent precedents of this court make it equally clear that neither the political cartoon nor the headline story involved in this case can be labeled as constitutionally obscene or otherwise unprotected. . . . There is language in the opinion below which suggests that the university's action here could be viewed as an exercise of its

legitimate authority to enforce reasonable regulations as to the time, place, and manner of speech and its dissemination. While we have repeatedly approved such regulatory authority . . . , the facts show clearly that petitioner was dismissed because of the disapproved *content* of the newspaper rather than the time, place, or manner of its distribution.

"It is true . . . that the district court emphasized that the newspaper was distributed near the university's memorial tower and concluded that petitioner was engaged in "pandering." The opinion makes clear, however, that the reference to "pandering" was addressed to the content of the newspaper . . . rather than to the manner in which the newspaper was disseminated. . . . Moreover, the majority [of the court of appeals] quoted without disapproval petitioner's verified affidavit that "no disruption of the university's functions occurred in connection with the distribution.". . . Thus, in the absence of any disruption of campus order or interference with the rights of others, the sole issue was whether a state university could proscribe this form of expression.

Since the First Amendment leaves no room for the operation of a dual standard in the academic community with respect to the content of speech, and because the state university's action here cannot be justified as a nondiscriminatory application of reasonable rules governing conduct, the judgments of the courts below must be reversed. . . . (35 L Ed 2d at 622.)

Are *Papish* and *Eisner* consistent? Are *Papish* and *Goldberg* consistent? Does *Papish* countenance the censoring of the content of a student newspaper in order to avoid disruption or to protect students from obscenity? Does *Papish* implicitly reject the *Tinker* formulation, which permits limitations on speech if there is a reasonable forecast of material disruption? Does the *Papish* standard apply to public elementary and secondary schools? In this regard, consider Justice Rehnquist's dissent in *Papish*:

. . . . A state university is an establishment for the purpose of educating the state's young people, supported by the tax revenues of the state's citizens. The notion that the officials lawfully charged with the governance of the university have so little control over the environment for which they are responsible that they may not prevent the public distribution of a newspaper on campus which contained the language described in the court's opinion is quite unacceptable to me . . . . This is indeed a case where the observation of a unanimous court in *Chaplinski* [*v New Hampshire* 315 US 568 (1942)] that "such utterances are no essential part of any exposition of ideas and are of such slight social value as a step to truth that any benefit that may be derived from them is clearly outweighed by the social interest in order and morality" applies with compelling force.

[A] wooden insistence on equating, for constitutional purposes, the authority of the state to criminally punish with its authority to exercise even a modicum of control over the university which it operates, serves neither the Constitution nor public education well. . . . [Public universities] must have something more than the grudging support of taxpayers and legislators. But one can scarcely blame the latter, if told by the court that their only function is to supply tax money for the operation of the university, the "disenchantment" may reach such a point that they doubt the game is worth the candle. (35 L Ed 2d at 626.)

Are Justice Rehnquist's arguments more forceful as applied to elementary and secondary schools?

5. Solicitation

School authorities often are concerned when students attempt to solicit money from each other for political, personal, or other purposes. Often underground newspapers are not distributed free, and students are asked to pay for copies in order to defray publication costs. In the light of *Eisner* and *Papish,* would a complete ban on solicitations in public primary and secondary schools be constitutional? See *Katz v McAulay* 438 F2d 1058 (2d Cir 1971). Should the courts require more narrowly drawn bans, focusing on disruption and extortion? What is the relationship between the right to distribute nondisruptive underground newspapers and the ability to charge for them?

In *New Left Educ Project v Board of Regents* 326 F Supp 158 (WD Tex 1971), *vacated and remanded,* 404 US 541 (1971), the University of Texas Board of Regents had adopted the following rule:

Commercial solicitations will not be authorized on the campus of any component institution of the University of Texas system, except as otherwise provided in this section. Commercial solicitations include the sale, disposition of or contract to dispose of any item of personal property . . . ; or the solicitation of funds or personal property. The following commercial solicitations are permissible:

(1) commercial solicitations in a student union building that have been approved by the board of directors . . . ;

(2) the sale of any authorized student publication or any publication authorized by an agency of a component institution;

(3) any commercial solicitation made pursuant to a contract or agreement between the administration of a component institution and the vendor. . . . (326 F Supp at 162.)

What interests was the University of Texas seeking to further by the adoption of this rule? If you were legal counsel to the university, how would you advise them to redraft the rule in order to avoid constitutional infirmities? See note 7 below. Would you rely on *Katz v McAulay* which forbade solicitations on a public high school campus?

6. "Lawful" Objections

Assuming that the distribution of a particular student newspaper is constitutionally protected, is the student required to challenge unconstitutional censorship by "lawful" means? Even if the "unlawful" means do not result in disruption? Consider these passages from *Sullivan v Houston Independent School Dist* 475 F2d 1071, 1075-76 (5th Cir 1973):

. . . Paul defied Mr. Cotton's request that he stop selling the newspapers, persisted in returning to the campus during the initial six-day suspension period, and twice shouted profanity at Mr. Cotton within the hearing of others. Paul's reappearance on the campus and continued sale of the newspapers . . . served only to exacerbate the situation.

Moreover, Paul never once attempted to comply with the prior submission rule . . . . Had Paul submitted the newspaper prior to distribution and had it been disapproved, then he could have promptly sought relief in the courts without having been first suspended from school.

Considering Paul's flagrant disregard of established school regulations, his open and repeated defiance of the principal's request, and his resort to profane epithet, we cannot agree that the school authorities were powerless to discipline Paul simply because his action did not materially and substantially disrupt school activities.

How do you explain *Sullivan*? Is it consistent with *Tinker, Eisner,* and *Papish*? Does *Sullivan* suggest that insubordination or disobedience is distinct from the constitutional issues involved in the distribution of student newspapers. See also *Schwartz v Schuker* 298 F Supp 238 (EDNY 1969). Might the court have reasonably distinguished between Paul's disregard of the order to cease distributing the newspaper and his violation of other school rules? Does *Sullivan* stand for the proposition that students must obey all instructions from administrators and teachers, even if they are later declared to be unconstitutional? If so, was *Tinker* properly decided?

7. Vagueness and Overbreadth

The *Eisner* court discusses the problem of vagueness and overbreadth in school regulations. This doctrine was well-described in *Sullivan v Houston Independent School Dist* 307 F Supp 1328 (SD Tex 1969), an earlier round of the litigation discussed in note 6:

The Supreme Court's "void-for-vagueness" doctrine has developed two distinct concepts. A statute is scrutinized first to determine if it is "overbroad"; could a reasonable application of its sanctions include conduct protected by the Constitution? . . . See generally, Amsterdam, "The Void for Vagueness Doctrine," 109 *U Pa L Rev* 67 (1960).

A statute must also satisfy the "vagueness" standard of *Connally v General Constr Co* 269 US 385 (1926): "[A] statute which either forbids or requires the doing of an act in terms so vague that men of common intelligence must necessarily guess at its meaning and differ as to its application violates the first essential of due process. . . ." See *Zwickler v Koota* 389 US 241 (1967).

In their General Order on Student Discipline, 45 FRD 133, 146-47 (WD Mo 1968), the judges of the Western District of Missouri adopted the following view on this issue: "The legal doctrine that a prohibitory statute is void if it is overly broad or unconstitutionally broad does not, in the absence of exceptional circumstances, apply to standards of student conduct. The validity of the form of standards of student conduct, relevant to the lawful missions of higher education, ordinarily should be determined by recognized educational standards."

However, in the case of *Soglin v Kauffman* 295 F Supp 978, 990 (WD Wis 1968) the court expressly rejected this view: "The constitutional doctrines of vagueness and overbreadth are applicable, in some measure, to the standard or standards to be applied by the university in disciplining its students, and that a regime in which the term "misconduct" serves as the sole standard violates the due process clause of the Fourteenth Amendment by reason of its vagueness, or, in the alternative, violates the First Amendment as embodied in the Fourteenth by reason of its vagueness and overbreadth. . . ."

This court is persuaded by the *Soglin* decision. And in this court's judgment, these fundamental concepts of constitutional law must be applied "in some measure" even to high schools. The "measure" should reach only to rules the violation of which could result in expulsion or suspension for a substantial period of time. When faced with such drastic consequences, a high school student has no less a right to a clear, specific normative statement which does not infringe on free expression than does a university student or possibly even the accused in a criminal case. If the punishment could be this severe, there is no question but that a high school student as well as a university student might well suffer more injury than one convicted of a criminal offense. School rules probably do not need to be as narrow as criminal statutes but if school officials contemplate severe punishment they must do so on the basis of a rule which is drawn so as to reasonably inform the student what specific conduct is prescribed. Basic notions of justice and fair play require that no person shall be made to suffer for a breach unless standards of behavior have first been announced, for who is to decide what has been breached?

It is also clear that severe punishment may not be based on a rule which could reasonably be construed to embrace conduct protected by the first amendment. . . .

At the conclusion of the evidentiary hearing in this case the parties entered the following stipulation: "The only written rule or regulation of the Houston Independent School District concerning the private publication and distribution of written material by students in secondary schools newspapers which are not published in the name of the school and which do not purport to be published under the auspices of any school is as follows: 'The school principal may make such rules and regulations that may be necessary in the administration of the school and in promoting its best interests. He may enforce obedience to any reasonable and lawful command. . . .' "

Little can be said of a standard so grossly overbroad as "in the best interests of the school." *Soglin v Kauffman* 295 F Supp 978, 991 (WD Wis 1968). It cannot be contended that it supplies objective standards by which a student may measure his behavior or by which an administrator may make a specific ruling in evaluation of behavior. *Shuttlesworth v Birmingham* 382 US 87 (1965). It patently "sweeps within its broad scope activities that are constitutionally protected free speech and assembly." *Cox v Louisiana* 379 US 586, 592 (1965).

This is not meant as criticism of defendants. Generalities such as this one have been accepted for years as the proper sort of standard for our "unique educational environment." However, *Tinker* has tolled the beginnings of change. . . . 307 F Supp at 1343-46.

What policy reasons support the application or nonapplication of the vagueness and overbreadth doctrines to public schools? Are *Soglin* and *Sullivan* consistent with *Eisner*? Is the formulation "interference with the proper and orderly operation and discipline of the school" less broad or vague than "in the best interests of the school" or "misconduct"? Was it proper for the *Eisner* court to read the words "material" and "substantial" into the Stamford school board's policy statement? If the reason for applying of the vagueness doctrine in the school setting is to require notice to students of what conduct will lead to suspension, is the constitutional issue what the school board intended to say or what was actually conveyed to the students?

In *Eisner,* the court suggests greater specificity in the school board's rules while not requiring it as a matter of constitutional obligation. What measures does it suggest? Is the core problem the vagueness of the policy statement or the vagueness of the *Tinker* doctrine?

HEALY v JAMES
408 US 169 (1972)

Mr. Justice Powell delivered the opinion of the court.

Petitioners are students attending Central Connecticut State College (CCSC), a state-supported institution of higher learning. In September 1969 they undertook to organize what they then referred to as a "local chapter" of SDS. Pursuant to procedures established by the college, petitioners filed a request for official recognition as a campus organization with the Student Affairs Committee, a committee composed of four students, three faculty members, and the dean of student affairs. The request specified three purposes for the proposed organization's existence. It would provide "a forum of discussion and self-education for students developing an analysis of American society"; it would serve as "an agency for integrating thought with action so as to bring about constructive changes"; and it would endeavor to provide "a coordinating body for relating the problems of leftist students" with other interested groups on campus and in the community. The committee, while satisfied that the statement of purposes was clear and unobjectionable on its face, exhibited concern over the relationship between the proposed local group and the national SDS organization. In response to inquiries, representatives of the proposed organization stated that they would not affiliate with any national organization and that their group would remain "completely independent."

In response to other questions asked by Committee members concerning SDS' reputation for campus disruption, the applicants made the following statements, which proved significant during the later stages of these proceedings:

"Q. How would you respond to issues of violence as other SDS chapters have?

"A. Our action would have to be dependent upon each issue.

"Q. Would you use any means possible?

"A. No I can't say that; would not know until we know what the issues are.

. . . .

"Q. Could you envision the SDS interrupting a class?

"A. Impossible for me to say."

By a vote of six to two the committee ultimately approved the application and recommended to the president of the college, Dr. James, that the organization be accorded official recognition. In approving the application, the majority indicated that its decision was premised on the belief that varying viewpoints should be represented on campus and that since the Young Americans for Freedom, the Young Democrats, the Young Republicans, and the Liberal Party all enjoyed recognized status, a group should be available with which "left-wing" students might identify. The majority also noted and relied on the organization's claim of independence. Finally, it admonished the organization that immediate suspension would be considered if the group's activities proved incompatible with the school's policies against interference with the privacy of other students or destruction of property.

The two dissenting members based their reservation primarily on the lack of clarity regarding the organization's independence.

Several days later, the president rejected the committee's recommendation, and issued a statement indicating that petitioners' organization was not to be accorded the benefits of official campus recognition. His accompanying remarks . . . indicate several reasons for his action. He found that the organization's philosophy was antithetical to the school's policies, and that the group's independence was doubtful. He concluded that approval should not be granted to any group that "openly repudiates" the college's dedication to academic freedom.

Denial of official recognition posed serious problems for the organization's existence and growth. Its members were deprived of the opportunity to place announcements regarding meetings, rallies, or other activities in the student newspaper; they were precluded from using various campus bulletin boards; and—most importantly—nonrecognition barred them from using campus facilities for holding meetings. This latter disability was brought home to petitioners shortly after the president's announcement. Petitioners circulated a notice calling a meeting to discuss what further action should be taken in light of the group's official rejection. The members met at the coffee shop in the student center ("Devils' Den") but were disbanded on the president's order since nonrecognized groups were not entitled to use such facilities.

Their efforts to gain recognition having proved ultimately unsuccessful, and having been made to feel the burden of nonrecognition, petitioners resorted to the courts. They filed a suit in the United States District Court for the District of Connecticut, seeking declaratory and injunctive relief against the president of the college, other administrators, and the state board of trustees. Petitioners' primary complaint centered on the denial of First Amendment rights of expression and association arising from denial of campus recognition. . . .

The court concluded, first, that the formal requisites of procedural due process had been complied with, second, that petitioners had failed to meet their burden of showing that they could function free from the national organization, and, third, that the college's refusal to place its stamp of approval on an organization whose conduct it found "likely to cause violent acts of disruption" did not violate petitioners' associational rights. 319 F Supp 113, 116.

Petitioners appealed to the Court of Appeals for the Second Circuit where, by a two-to-one vote, the district court's judgment was affirmed. . . .

Among the rights protected by the First Amendment is the right of individuals to associate to further their personal beliefs. While the freedom of association is not explicitly set out in the amendment, it has long been held to be implicit in the freedoms of speech, assembly, and petition. See, e. g., *Baird v State Bar of Ariz* 401 US 1, 6 (1971); *NAACP v Button* 371 US 415, 430 (1963); *Louisiana ex rel Gremillion v NAACP* 366 US 293, 296 (1961); *NAACP v Alabama ex rel Patterson* 357 US 449 (1958) (Harlan, J, for a unanimous court). There can be no doubt that denial of official recognition, without justification, to college organizations burdens or abridges that associational right. The primary impediment to free association flowing from nonrecognition is the denial of use of campus facilities for meetings and other appropriate purposes. . . .

Petitioners' associational interests also were circumscribed by the denial of the use of campus bulletin boards and the school newspaper. If an organization is to remain a viable entity in a campus community in which new students enter on a regular basis, it must possess the means of communicating with these students. Moreover, the organization's ability to participate in the intellectual give-and-take of campus debate, and to pursue its stated purposes, is limited by denial of access to the customary media for communicating with the administration, faculty members, and other students.[8] Such impediments cannot be viewed as insubstantial. . . .

The opinions below . . . assumed that petitioners had the burden of showing entitlement to recognition by the College. While petitioners have not challenged the procedural requirement that they file an application in conformity with the rules of the college, they do question the view of the courts below that final rejection could rest on their failure to convince the administration that their organization was unaffiliated with the national SDS. For reasons to be stated later in this opinion, we do not consider the issue of affiliation to be a controlling one. But, apart from any particular issue, once petitioners had filed an application in conformity with the requirements, the burden was upon the college administration to justify its decision of rejection. See, e. g., *Law Students Civil Rights Research Council v Wadmond* 401 US 154, 162-63 (1971); *US v O'Brien* 391 US 367, 376-77 (1968); *Speiser v Randall* 357 US 513 (1958). It is to be remembered that the effect of the college's denial of recognition was a form of prior restraint, denying to petitioners' organization the range of associational activities described above. While a college has a legitimate interest in preventing disruption on the campus, which under circumstances requiring the safeguarding of that interest may justify such restraint, a "heavy burden" rests on the college to demonstrate the appropriateness of that action. See *Near v Minnesota* 283 US 697, 713-16 (1931); *Organization for a Better Austin v Keefe* 402 US 415, 418 (1971); *Freedman v Maryland* 380 US 51, 57 (1965).

These fundamental errors—discounting the existence of a cognizable First Amendment interest and misplacing the burden of proof—require that the judgments below be reversed. But we are unable to conclude that no basis exists upon which nonrecognition might be appropriate. . . . Four possible justifications for nonrecognition, all closely related, might be derived from the record and his statements. Three of those grounds are inadequate to substantiate his decision: a fourth, however, has merit.

From the outset the controversy in this case has centered in large measure around the relationship, if any, between petitioners' group and the national SDS. The Student Affairs Committee meetings, as reflected in its minutes, focused considerable attention on this issue; the court-ordered hearing also was directed primarily to this question. Despite assurances from petitioners and their counsel that the local group was in fact independent of the national organization, it is evident that President James was significantly influenced by his apprehension that there was a connection. Aware of the fact that some SDS chapters had been associated

---

8. It is unclear on this record whether recognition also carries with it a right to seek funds from the school budget. Petitioners' counsel at oral argument indicated that official recognition entitled the group to "make application for use of student funds." Tr of Oral Arg 4. The first district court opinion, however, states flatly that "[r]ecognition does not thereby entitle an organization to college financial support." 311 F Supp 1275, 1277. Since it appears that, at the least, recognition only entitles a group to *apply* for funds, and since the record is silent as to the criteria used in allocating such funds, we do not consider possible funding as an associational aspect of nonrecognition in this case.

with disruptive and violent campus activity, he apparently considered that affiliation itself was sufficient justification for denying recognition.

Although this precise issue has not come before the court heretofore, the court has consistently disapproved governmental action imposing criminal sanctions or denying rights and privileges solely because of a citizen's association with an unpopular organization. See, e. g., *US v Robel* 389 US 258 (1967); *Keyishian v Board of Regents* 385 US at 605-610; *Elfbrandt v Russell* 384 US 11 (1966); *Scales v US* 367 US 203 (1961). In these cases it has been established that "guilt by association alone, without [establishing] that an individual's association poses the threat feared by the government," is an impermissible basis upon which to deny First Amendment rights. . . . The government has the burden of establishing a knowing affiliation with an organization possessing unlawful aims and goals, and a specific intent to further those illegal aims.

Students for a Democratic Society, as conceded by the college and the lower courts, is loosely organized, having various factions and promoting a number of diverse social and political views, only some of which call for unlawful action. Not only did petitioners proclaim their complete independence from this organization, but they also indicated that they shared only some of the beliefs its leaders have expressed. On this record it is clear that the relationship was not an adequate ground for the denial of recognition.

Having concluded that petitioners were affiliated with, or at least retained an affinity for, national SDS, President James attributed what he believed to be the philosophy of that organization to the local group. He characterized the petitioning group as adhering to "some of the major tenets of the national organization," including a philosophy of violence and disruption. Understandably, he found that philosophy abhorrent. . . .

The mere disagreement of the president with the group's philosophy affords no reason to deny it recognition. As repugnant as these views may have been, especially to one with President James' responsibility, the mere expression of them would not justify the denial of First Amendment rights. Whether petitioners did in fact advocate a philosophy of "destruction" thus becomes immaterial. The college, acting here as the instrumentality of the state, may not restrict speech or association simply because it finds the views expressed by any group to be abhorrent. . . .

As the litigation progressed in the district court, a third rationale for President James' decision—beyond the questions of affiliation and philosophy—began to emerge. His second statement, issued after the court-ordered hearing, indicates that he based rejection on a conclusion that this particular group would be a "disruptive influence at CCSC.". . .

If this reason, directed at the organization's activities rather than its philosophy, were factually supported by the record, this court's prior decisions would provide a basis for considering the propriety of nonrecognition. The critical line heretofore drawn for determining the permissibility of regulation is the line between mere advocacy and advocacy "directed to inciting or producing imminent lawless action and . . . likely to incite or produce such action." *Brandenburg v Ohio* 395 US 444, 447 (1969) (unanimous *per curiam* opinion). . . . In the context of the "special characteristics of the school environment," the power of the government to prohibit "lawless action" is not limited to acts of a criminal nature. Also prohibitable are actions which "materially and substantially disrupt the work and discipline of the school." *Tinker v Des Moines Independent School Dist* 393 US 503, 513 (1969). Associational activities need not be tolerated where they infringe reasonable campus rules, interrupt classes, or substantially interfere with the opportunity of other students to obtain an education.

The "Student Bill of Rights" at CCSC, upon which great emphasis was placed by the president, draws precisely this distinction between advocacy and action. It purports to impose no limitations on the right of college student organizations "to examine and discuss *all* questions of interest to them." (Emphasis supplied.) But it also states that students have no right (1) "to deprive others of the opportunity to speak or be heard," (2) "to invade the privacy of others," (3) "to damage the property of others," (4) "to disrupt the regular and essential operation of the college," or (5) "to interfere with the rights of others." The line between permissible speech and impermissible conduct tracks the constitutional requirement, and if there were an evidential basis to support the conclusion that CCSC-SDS posed a substantial threat of material disruption in violation of that command the president's decision should be affirmed.[20]

The record, however, offers no substantial basis for that conclusion. The only support for the view expressed by the president, other than the reputed affiliation with national SDS, is to be found in the ambivalent responses offered by the group's representatives at the Student Affairs Committee hearing, during which they stated that they did not know whether they might respond to "issues of violence" in the same manner that other SDS chapters had on other campuses. Nor would they state unequivocally that they could never "envision . . . interrupting a class." Whatever force these statements might be thought to have is largely dissipated by the following exchange between petitioners' counsel and the dean of student affairs during the court-ordered hearing:

Counsel: ". . . I just read the document that you're offering [minutes from Student Affairs Committee meeting] and I can't see that there's anything in it that intimates that these students contemplate any illegal or disruptive practice."

Dean: "No. There's no question raised to that, counselor . . . ." App 73-74.

Dean Judd's remark reaffirms, in accord with the full record, that there was no substantial evidence that these particular individuals acting together would constitute a disruptive force on campus. Therefore, insofar as nonrecognition flowed from such fears, it constituted little more than the sort of "undifferentiated fear or apprehension of disturbance [which] is not enough to overcome the right to freedom of expression.". . .

These same references in the record to the group's equivocation regarding how it might respond to "issues of violence" and whether it could ever "envision . . . inter-

20. It may not be sufficient merely to show the existence of a legitimate and substantial state interest. Where state action designed to regulate prohibitable action also restricts associational rights—as nonrecognition does—the state must demonstrate that the action taken is reasonably related to protection of the state's interest and that "the incidental restriction on alleged First Amendment freedoms is no greater than is essential to the furtherance of that interest." *United States v O'Brien* 391 US 367, 377 (1968). . . . On this record, absent a showing of any likelihood of disruption or unwillingness to recognize reasonable rules governing campus conduct, it is not necessary for us to decide whether denial of recognition is an appropriately related and narrow response.

rupting a class," suggest a fourth possible reason why recognition might have been denied to these petitioners. These remarks might well have been read as announcing petitioners' unwillingness to be bound by reasonable school rules governing conduct. The college's Statement of Rights, Freedoms, and Responsibilities of Students contains, as we have seen, an explicit statement with respect to campus disruption. The regulation, carefully differentiating between advocacy and action, is a reasonable one, and petitioners have not questioned it directly. Yet their statements raise considerable question whether they intend to abide by the prohibitions contained therein. . . .

Petitioners may, if they so choose, preach the propriety of amending or even doing away with any or all campus regulations. They may not, however, undertake to flout these rules. . . . Just as in the community at large, reasonable regulations with respect to the time, the place, and the manner in which student groups conduct their speech-related activities must be respected. A college administration may impose a requirement, such as may have been imposed in this case, that a group seeking official recognition affirm in advance its willingness to adhere to reasonable campus law. Such a requirement does not impose an impermissible condition on the students' associational rights. Their freedom to speak out, to assemble, or to petition for changes in school rules is in no sense infringed. It merely constitutes an agreement to conform with reasonable standards respecting conduct. This is a minimal requirement, in the interest of the entire academic community, of any group seeking the privilege of official recognition.

Petitioners have not challenged in this litigation the procedural or substantive aspects of the college's requirements governing applications for official recognition. Although the record is unclear on this point, CCSC may have, among its requirements for recognition, a rule that prospective groups affirm that they intend to comply with reasonable campus regulations. Upon remand it should first be determined whether the college recognition procedures contemplate any such requirement. If so, it should then be ascertained whether petitioners intend to comply. Since we do not have the terms of a specific prior affirmation rule before us, we are not called on to decide whether any particular formulation would or would not prove constitutionally acceptable. Assuming the existence of a valid rule, however, we do conclude that the benefits of participation in the internal life of the college community may be denied to any group that reserves the right to violate any valid campus rules with which it disagrees. . . .

Reversed and remanded.

Notes and Questions

1. Association

Suppose that Central Connecticut State College refused to recognize or allow the use of college facilities to all student organizations? Would this be an unconstitutional exercise of power? Is *Healy*, like the speaker ban cases, better understood as requiring equal treatment when a college chooses to open its door to particular activities and organizations? What if a public high school student joined an organization that met during school hours, and he was charged with truancy? Could he reasonably argue that compulsory attendance laws violate his right of association?

2. Prior Constraint

Does the court's treatment of *Near v Minnesota* 283 US 697 (1931) vindicate the position of the Court of Appeals in *Eisner*? Does *Healy* in fact involve a prior restraint?

3. Penalties

Was the penalty imposed in *Healy* severe? Should the severity of the penalty influence the court's decision on the associational issues raised in the case? Should the court have awaited a student expulsion for violation of the recognition rules?

4. Disruption

President James argued that the SDS chapter would be a "disruptive influence." How can the mere existence of an organization be disruptive, apart from the activities it undertakes? Was President James engaging in the prediction that the organization would engage in disruptive activities if it is permitted recognition and access to facilities. If so, what is the difference between the allegation that the SDS chapter is or might be disruptive, which the court rejects, and the allegation that it may not have agreed to abide by "reasonable school rules governing conduct," for which the court remands the case?

5. Fraternity Bans

A number of states and school districts have forbidden public school students from joining fraternal organizations. In the light of *Healy*, would these prohibitions violate the First Amendment? See *Waugh v Board of Trustees* 237 US 589 (1915); *Webb v State Univ of NY* 125 F Supp 910 (NDNY 1954). But see *Wright v Board of Educ* 246 SW 43 (Mo 1922). See generally Comment, "Public Education: Judicial Protection of Student Individuality," 42 *So Cal L Rev* 126 (1969). Should the courts distinguish social and political organizations for constitutional purposes? Are political organizations deserving of more protection? Is the ban on joining fraternities more objectionable than nonrecognition in *Healy*, because the former extends beyond campus?

6. *Healy* and Student Gatherings

Suppose a state university adopts a rule that "the student body or any part of the student body is not to celebrate, parade, or demonstrate on the campus at any time without the approval of the office of the president." No distinction is drawn between disruptive and nondisruptive demonstrations. After *Healy*, is this university rule unconstitutional? See *Hammond v South Carolina St College* 272 F Supp 947 (DSC 1967). Compare *Esteban v Central Mo St College* 415 F2d 1077 (8th Cir 1969) (Blackmun, CJ). What if the rule forbade only demonstrations inside buildings? See *Grossner v Trustees of Columbia Univ* 287 F Supp 535 (SDNY 1968). Does it follow from *Healy* that the right to assemble peacefully should be afforded students in public elementary and secondary schools? Would such assemblies be disruptive per se? See *Dunn v Tyler Independent School Dist* 460 F2d 137 (5th Cir 1972).

D. Privacy and Related Rights

MOORE v STUDENT AFFAIRS COMMITTEE
OF TROY STATE UNIVERSITY
284 F Supp 725 (MD Ala 1968)

Johnson, Chief Judge.

On February 28, 1968, plaintiff, Gregory Gordon Moore, was a student in good standing at Troy State University and resided in a dormitory on the campus which he rented from the school. A search of his room on that day, conducted by the dean of men and two agents of the state of Alabama Health Department, Bureau of Primary Prevention, in plaintiff's presence, revealed a substance which, upon analysis, proved to be marijuana. Following a hearing on March 27, 1968, by the Student Affairs Committee of Troy State University, plaintiff was "indefinitely suspended" from that institution on March 28. . . .

On the morning of February 23, 1968, the dean of men of Troy State University was called to the office of the chief of police of Troy, Alabama, where a conference was held regarding "the possibility of there being marijuana on the campus." Two narcotics agents, the chief of police, and two students were present. A second meeting was held later that morning at which a list was procured of the names of students whose rooms the officers desired permission to search. This information came from unnamed but reliable informers. About 1 p.m., the officers received additional information that some of the subjects they were interested in were packing to leave the campus for a break following the end of an examination period. Upon receipt of this information, and fearing a "leak," two narcotics agents, accompanied by the dean of men, searched six dormitory rooms in two separate residence halls. The search of the room which plaintiff occupied alone occurred between approximately 2:30 and 2:45 p.m., in his presence, but without his permission.

At the second hearing before the Student Affairs Committee, the following stipulation was entered concerning the search:

> That no search warrant was obtained in this case, that no consent to search was given by the defendant, that the search was not incidental to a legal arrest, that no other offense was committed by the defendant in the arresting officers' presence, that Troy State University had in force and effect at the time of the search and subsequent arrest of the defendant the following regulation: "The college reserves the right to enter rooms for inspection purposes. If the administration deems it necessary the room may be searched and the occupant required to open his personal baggage and any other personal material which is sealed.". . .
>
> It is further stipulated that the defendant's room was searched at the invitation or consent of Troy State University by the law enforcement officials acting under the above quoted regulations.

The search revealed a matchbox containing a small amount of vegetable matter, which a state toxicologist who examined it testified was marijuana. All this testimony was received over plaintiff's objection that the evidence was seized as a result of a search in violation of the Fourth Amendment. He also challenges the constitutionality, facially and as applied, of the regulation under which the search was conducted. . . .

College students who reside in dormitories have a special relationship with the college involved. Insofar as the Fourth Amendment affects that relationship, it does not depend on either a general theory of the right of privacy or on traditional property concepts. The college does not stand, strictly speaking, in loco parentis to its students, nor is their relationship purely contractual in the traditional sense. The relationship grows out of the peculiar and sometimes the seemingly competing interests of college and student. A student naturally has the right to be free of unreasonable search and seizures, and a tax-supported public college may not compel a "waiver" of that right as a condition precedent to admission. The college, on the other hand, has an "affirmative obligation" to promulgate and to enforce reasonable regulations designed to protect campus order and discipline and to promote an environment consistent with the educational process. The validity of the regulation authorizing search of dormitories thus does not depend on whether a student "waives" his right to Fourth Amendment protection or on whether he has "contracted" it away; rather, its validity is determined by whether the regulation is a reasonable exercise of the college's supervisory duty. In other words, if the regulation—or, in the absence of a regulation, the action of the college authorities— is necessary in aid of the basic responsibility of the institution regarding discipline and the maintenance of an "educational atmosphere," then it will be presumed facially reasonable despite the fact that it may infringe to some extent on the outer bounds of the Fourth Amendment rights of students. . . .

The student is subject only to reasonable rules and regulations, but his rights must yield to the extent that they would interfere with the institution's fundamental duty to operate the school *as an educational institution*. A reasonable right of inspection is necessary to the institution's performance of that duty even though it may infringe on the outer boundaries of a dormitory student's Fourth Amendment rights. *People v Overton* 20 NY2d 360, 283 NYS2d 22, 229 NE2d 596 (1967).[10] The regulation of Troy State University in issue here is thus facially reasonable.

The regulation was reasonably applied in this case. The constitutional boundary line between the right of the school authorities to search and the right of a dormitory student to privacy must be based on a reasonable belief on the part of the college authorities that a student is using a dormitory room for a purpose which is illegal or which would otherwise seriously interfere with campus discipline. Upon this submission, it is clear that such a belief existed in this case.

This standard of "reasonable cause to believe" to justify a search by college administrators—even where the sole purpose is to seek evidence of suspected violations of law—is lower than the constitutionally protected criminal law standard of

10. That case deals with the right of a high school principal to give consent to a search of a high school student's locker for marijuana over the student's objection. While there are obviously functional differences between the disciplinary requirements of high school and college students, no distinction can be drawn between the fundamental duties of educators at both levels to maintain appropriate campus discipline. A reasonable right of inspection of school property and premises—even though it may have been set aside for the exclusive use of a particular student—is necessary to carry out that duty. . . .

"probable cause." This is true because of the special necessities of the student-college relationship and because college disciplinary proceedings are not criminal proceedings in the constitutional sense.

Assuming that the Fourth Amendment applied to college disciplinary proceedings, the search in this case would not be in violation of it. It is settled law that the Fourth Amendment does not prohibit reasonable searches when the search is conducted by a superior charged with a responsibility of maintaining discipline and order or of maintaining security. A student who lives in a dormitory on campus which he "rents" from the school waives objection to any reasonable searches conducted pursuant to reasonable and necessary regulations such as this one. . . .

In accordance with the foregoing, it is the order, judgment and decree of this court that plaintiff's claims for relief be and are, in each instance, hereby denied. It is ordered that this cause be and the same is hereby dismissed. . . .

PIAZZOLA v WATKINS
316 F Supp 624 (MD Ala 1970)

Johnson, Chief Judge.

The petitioners were indicted by a grand jury of Pike County, Alabama, for the offense of illegal possession of marijuana. After pleas of not guilty were interposed, trials were had, and petitioner Piazzola was convicted on April 25, 1968, and petitioner Marinshaw on April 26, 1968. The convictions were affirmed by the Alabama Court of Criminal Appeals. The matter is presented to this court upon a habeas corpus petition filed April 24, 1970. The basis for the petition is that the convictions violate the Fourth Amendment to the Constitution of the United States.

On the morning of February 28, 1968, the dean of men of Troy State University was called to the office of the chief of police of Troy, Alabama, to discuss "the drug problem" at the university. Two state narcotic agents and two student informers from Troy State University were also present. Later on that same day, the dean of men was called to the city police station for another meeting; at this time he was informed by the officers that they had sufficient evidence that marijuana was in the dormitory rooms of certain Troy State students and that they desired the cooperation of university officials in searching these rooms. The police officers were advised by the dean of men that they would receive the full cooperation of the university officials in searching for the marijuana. The informers, whose identities have not yet been disclosed, provided the police officers with names of students whose rooms were to be searched. Still later on that same day (which was during the week of final examinations at the university and was to be followed by a week-long holiday) the law enforcement officers, accompanied by some of the university officials, searched six or seven dormitory rooms located in two separate residence halls. The rooms of both Piazzola and Marinshaw were searched without search warrants and without their consent. Present during the search of the room occupied by Marinshaw were two state narcotic agents, the university security officer, and a counselor of the residence hall where Marinshaw's room was located. Piazzola's room was searched twice. Present during the first search were two state narcotic agents and a university official; no evidence was found at this time. The second search of Piazzola's room, which disclosed the incriminating evidence, was conducted solely by the state and city police officials.

At the time of the seizure the university had in effect the following regulation: "The college reserves the right to enter rooms for inspection purposes. If the administration deems it necessary, the room may be searched and the occupant required to open his personal baggage and any other personal material which is sealed." Each of the petitioners was familiar with this regulation. After the search of the petitioners' rooms and the discovery of the marijuana, they were arrested, and the state criminal prosecutions and convictions ensued. The basic question presented is whether the evidence that formed the basis for the petitioners' convictions and present incarceration was obtained as a result of an unreasonable search and seizure within the meaning of the Fourth Amendment to the Constitution of the United States. As justification for the search and seizure, the respondents rely almost entirely upon this court's opinion in *Moore v Student Affairs Comm of Troy St Univ* 284 F Supp 725 (MD Ala). The *Moore* case involved judicial review of the constitutional validity of university administrative proceedings which resulted in the suspension of Gary Moore from Troy University. The suspension in the *Moore* case was based upon a search of Moore's dormitory room by university officials and the discovery of marijuana in his room. Upon the facts presented in *Moore,* this Court held that the university regulation authorizing the search of dormitory rooms was a reasonable exercise of university supervisory duties. . . .

This court does not find *Moore* applicable in the case *sub judice.* Here, the search was instigated and in the main executed by state police and narcotic bureau officials. The only part the university officials played in the search of the petitioners' dormitory rooms was at the request of and under the direction of the state law enforcement officers. Under such circumstances the state of Alabama, upon the petitioners' motion to suppress, had the burden of showing probable cause for the search of petitioners' rooms. The standard of "reasonable cause to believe" laid down by this court in *Moore* as a justification for a search by college officials that resulted in school disciplinary proceedings cannot be the justification for a search by a police officer for the sole purpose of gathering evidence for criminal prosecutions. . . .

No other evidence was offered by the state in justification of the search, except . . . that the officers "had information," that they believed that information, and that implied by the testimony, there were some unnamed informers whose information or credibility as informers was never discussed.

The state's evidence on the question of probable cause failed completely. Under the circumstances that existed in this case, in order to establish probable cause the state police officers must give the underlying facts or circumstances upon which they base their conclusions. Furthermore, when officers contend that they searched upon information from an informer, they must show that the informer was reliable, and the evidence must also reflect some factual basis for the informant's conclusions. . . .

The state argues, in support of its warrantless search, that the petitioners consented to the search indirectly by reason of the university regulation. This argument cannot stand. As stated earlier, this was not a university-initiated search for university purposes, but rather a police-initiated search for criminal prosecution purposes. The fact that the university officials agreed to the search gives it no validity. As this court emphasized in *Moore,* students and their college share a special relationship, which gives to the college certain special rights including the right to enter into and inspect the rooms of its students under certain situations. However, the fact that the college has this right—for a restricted purpose—does not mean that the college may exercise the right by admitting a third party. . . . This means, therefore, that, even though the special relationship that existed between these petitioners and Troy University officials conferred upon the university officials the right to enter and search petitioners' dormitory rooms, that right cannot be expanded and used for purposes other than those pertaining to the special relationship. . . .

Since there was no warrant, no probable cause for searching without a warrant, and no waiver or consent, the search of petitioners' dormitory rooms by state law enforcement officers, including narcotic agents and Troy city police officers, on February 28, 1968, was in violation of the petitioners' rights as guaranteed by the Fourth Amendment to the Constitution of the United States. It follows that the convictions of the petitioners, having been based solely upon the fruits of such search, are likewise illegal and cannot stand. . . .

Notes and Questions

1. Distinguishing *Moore* and *Piazzola*

How do you distinguish *Moore* and *Piazzola*? In what ways did the nature of the searches differ? Was there a waiver in *Moore* but not in *Piazzola*? Should *Piazzola* apply to high school students whose lockers are searched? See *People v Overton* 20 NY2d 360, 283 NYS2d 22, 229 NE2d 596 (1967); *Mercer v Donaldson* 269 CA2d 509, 75 Cal Rptr 220 (1969). Do you accept the proposition that Fourth Amendment guarantees against unreasonable searches and seizures should apply only to criminal prosecutions and not to suspensions and expulsions from public schools? Is Judge Johnson's position consistent with *Tinker* and the majority opinion in *Healy*? Is a student entitled to privacy vis-à-vis other students, but not school officials? See *State v Stein* 203 Kan 638, 456 P2d 1 (1969) *cert den*, 397 US 947. Would the result in *Moore* change if there had been no specific rule authorizing "inspections" of student rooms? If school authorities had inspected the rooms on their own initiative, without the presence of police offers, and then turned the incriminating evidence over to the police? See *Mercer v Texas* 450 SW2d 715 (Ct Civ App 1970). Does the *Moore* result hinge on the conclusion that marijuana is harmful to students or at least that school officials could reasonably reach this conclusion? Would a similar search for liquor or for a forbidden hot plate be reasonable? Can it be reasonably argued that the *Piazzola* inspection regulation is unconstitutionally vague and overbroad?

2. Double Jeopardy?

Suppose that Piazzola had been convicted on the basis of evidence found at his off-campus apartment pursuant to a properly issued search warrant? Can Troy State lawfully expel him on the ground that its students should not be exposed to a convicted criminal? Is this "double jeopardy?" Would you differentiate between classes of crime in deciding whether exclusion was proper? Between arson and driving while intoxicated? Between heroin possession and possession of marijuana? What if a student had been arrested and indicted but not convicted? See *R.R. v Board of Educ* 109 NJ Super 337, 263 A2d 180 (1970).

3. Privacy and Semitotal Institutions

Social scientists have characterized public schools, particularly elementary and secondary schools, as "semitotal institutions." J. Nelson and F. Besag, *Sociological Perspectives in Education: Models for Analysis* 67 (1970). By this term, they intend to describe an institution which, "during the six hours a day that the child is in school, the influence exerted on the child is sufficient to force him to conform to the patterns prescribed by the school or accept the consequences: he is forced to become a member of the institution." Ibid. Compare E. Goffman, *Asylums* (1961). To what extent is membership in such an institution inconsistent with the privacy normally afforded individuals in our society? Consider the following legal challenges to school rules and practices:

a. Parents object to filling out a registration form that requires them to state their occupations and the child's physical history.

b. A student argues that the system of bathroom permission slips employed at his school is an invasion of his right to privacy.

c. A student challenges a hair and dress code as violating his personal right to dress and wear his hair as he wishes within the limits of decency. See *Richards v Thurston* 424 F2d 1281 (1st Cir 1970). But see *Karr v Schmidt* 460 F2d 609 (5th Cir 1972) (en banc). See generally H. Punke, *Social Implications of Lawsuits over Student Hairstyles* (1973); Ladd, "Assessing the Reasonableness of School Disciplinary Actions: Haircut Cases Illuminate the Problem," 22 *Buff L Rev* 545 (1973).

d. A student seeks to compel a school board to divulge the names and addresses of his classmates in order to prepare his defense in a pending criminal prosecution.

e. A student sues a school board for libel for mailing this announcement to the general public:

> At a special public meeting to be held Tuesday, November 24, 1959, ... the Caruthers High School Board of Trustees ... will bring the public in full focus of the serious violation of manners, morals and discipline that occurred in Los Angeles as the direct result of the interference by the Elder and Fries boys who are now suspended from school.

See *Elder v Anderson* 205 CA2d 326, 328, 23 Cal Rptr 48 (1962).

f. High school students seek to restrain school officials from transmitting the following letter to universities to which they have applied for admission:

> This letter is submitted to supplement the information we have furnished concerning _____. He/she was one of twenty-two seniors who wore armbands at our commencement exercises bearing the legend *"Humanize Education"* as an indication of his/her concern regarding certain aspects of our educational program.
>
> These students wore armbands even though they had been requested not to wear any insignia that deviated from the formal graduation attire. There was no disorder at the commencement exercises.

See *Einhorn v Maus* 300 F Supp 1169, 1170 (ED Pa 1969).

g. Unmarried state university students challenge a rule requiring them to live and eat in campus dormitories. See *Pratz v Louisiana Polytechnic Inst* 316 F Supp 872 (WD La 1970), *aff'd,* 401 US 1004 (1971). But see *Mollere v Southeastern Louisiana College* 304 F Supp 826 (ED La 1969).

h. State college students object to university and local police forces' paying informers and undercover agents to spy on students and keeping files or dossiers on members of the university community. See Brest, "Intelligence Gathering on the Campus," in *Law and Discipline on Campus,* 197 (G. Holmes ed 1971).

E. Compliance with Student Rights Court Decisions

Lawyers traditionally have viewed their task as complete once a court renders a decision in favor of their client. The impact of the decision, the social result, or the organizational changes it occasioned lay outside the lawyer's scope of concern. In part, the lawyer's myopia was caused by the nature of the common law advocacy system: the lawyer, within ethical limits, represented the client's interest as the client perceived it. Unless the client required it, the lawyer did not reflect on the rightness of the cause or the ultimate consequences of a favorable decision. So too, the lawyer was concerned primarily with the case at hand. His job was to secure the readmission of his client to a public high school or to protect his right to refuse to participate in flag salute exercises or his right to join a fraternity. Whether these rights were afforded to other students in the same school or in other schools or school districts was, strictly speaking, irrelevant. In greater part, however, the lawyer's ignorance of social consequences derived from his legal training; his perception of society and social change was filtered through the selective screen of appellate decisions. In school law students were taught what the law "is" and what it "ought" to be, and they were taught to speculate as to policy consequences. There was—and for the most part still is—no interdisciplinary training in the impact of legal rules on individual and institutional behavior.

In recent years, lawyers have begun to move away from the formalistic decisional approach to law to a more functional, impact-oriented perspective. Two interrelated factors—the advent of interdisciplinary courses at law schools and the rise of the "movement" lawyer whose dedication is more to a "cause" than to an individual client—encouraged this altered viewpoint. Lawyers and social scientists have posed the essential questions: What happens after a judge has ruled? How does the institution, subject to the court's order, respond? How do similar institutions, not involved in the litigation, respond? While most people undoubtedly are aware of the enforcement agonies accompanying school desegregation (see chapter 4) after the decision in *Brown v Board of Educ* 347 US 483 (1954), there has been a paucity of careful research on the relationship between court decisions and social change. See, e.g., *The Supreme Court as Policy-Maker: Three Studies on the Impact of Judicial Decisions* (D. Everson ed 1965); S. Wasby, *The Impact of the United States Supreme Court* (1970); *The Impact of Supreme Court Decisions* (T. Becker ed 1969). See generally Mandel, "The Impact of the Judicial Process upon Organizational Change in Public Schools," *School Review,* in press. Many of the studies sacrifice rigor for anecdotes, and nearly all pertain exclusively to the Supreme Court, completely omitting state and lower federal courts. With respect to student rights issues, there is only one study of compliance with court decisions, undertaken by the New York Civil Liberties Union for the years 1971-1972. The NYCLU's report is not encouraging:

The [Student Rights] Project was launched in New York City against a backdrop of official policy toward students rights which had as many versions as there were schools in the system. Students were punished—or threatened— in one school for an officially disapproved newspaper article, in another for hair fashionably long, in another for distributing an underground newspaper, in another for not wearing the proper gym uniform. To note that students in other schools were not similarly punished was not to say that in those schools students had "rights." Rather it was to confirm that throughout the school system students were permitted to do only that which the principal allowed them to do. . . .

This began to change at the beginning of the school year 1969-70 when the board of education . . . enacted provisions affording students certain procedural rights when suspended. Substantive rights, pertaining to personal appearance, free expression, and participation in school governance, were outlined in a statement on rights and responsibilities promulgated at the end of the school year. . . .

The rights promulgated by the board of education, and those established by judicial and administrative decisions, were won over the passionate opposition of school administrators. It was, therefore, to be expected that much of the project's work would be involved in forcing resistant school officials to recognize those rights which had already been won. . . .

Although students now had a clearly established right to hand out literature on school property, distribution of the NYCLU's Student Rights Handbook, which advised students of that right, was itself prohibited at many high schools . . . . One [principal] said that it incited students to exercise their rights.

The project wrote to the chancellor protesting the prohibitions and never received an answer. A lawsuit followed which has been resolved by a stipulation authorizing distribution of the handbook. . . .

Given a board which had agreed to the policies only reluctantly and was willing to do little more to make them a reality, and given a network of school officials who had never agreed to them, even reluctantly, and were willing to do a great deal to prevent them from becoming a reality, a major part of the project's work became enforcement of rights which purportedly students already enjoyed. (New York Civil Liberties Union, *Student Rights Project: Report on the First Two Years 1971-1972* (hereafter *NYCLU Report*).)

See also Glasser and Levine, "Bringing Student Rights to New York City's School System," 1 *J Law & Educ* (1972). Despite the new school board policy statement and extensive previous litigation, the NYCLU reported that many suits were filed to protect student rights, including one case in which a student was suspended for distributing antiwar literature. *NYCLU Report,* 70-90.

To some extent, the lack of compliance reported by the NYCLU may be explained by its own zealousness in expanding the scope of student rights; inevitably there will be disagreements about the application of relatively broad standards to concrete situations. Ignorance of the law may also be an explanation. But the enforcement difficulties reported by the NYCLU cannot be explained away so easily. Individual schools chose to ignore or disregard explicit normative rules embodied in court decisions and school board policies. How can such behavior be explained?

Professor Mandel, while decrying the lack of systematically collected data, generalizes from the report and other studies of compliance with court decisions to explain this phenomenon:

> While there is no conceptually coherent framework for understanding the dynamics of compliance by school organizations with court decisions, the available evidence indicates that the decision to comply or not to comply with a court decision that affects an organization is, in significant measure, a group decision influenced by social-psychological forces, particularly the group's evaluation of whether compliance or noncompliance is most consistent with the group's needs and goals. If group members engage in noncompliant behavior, they tend to develop norms, values, and defenses to support their decision. (Mandel, "Impact of the Judicial Process.")

Administrators and teachers will resist student rights decisions if they perceive those decisions as educationally counterproductive, a threat to their authority, inconsistent with their professional status and self-image, and at odds with community and institutional values. This is particularly true if the sanctions for noncompliance are perceived as less burdensome than judicial interference "with the group's needs and goals."

Professor Sarason, speaking to the broader issue of change in the public schools, perceives other impediments to compliance with student rights decisions. These impediments derive not so much from the psychology of teachers and administrators—individually or as a group—as from the cultural framework of the school.

> The fact is that we simply do not have adequate descriptive data on the ways in which change is conceived, formulated, and executed within a school system. Obviously, there are many different ways in which it comes about, with differing degrees of success and failure, but it has hardly been studied. We are frequently, therefore, in a position analogous to that of interpreting the data from an experiment without any clear idea of the procedures employed. We lack adequate knowledge of the natural history of change processes within the school culture. . . .
>
> . . . . Any attempt to introduce an important change in the school culture requires changing existing regularities to produce intended outcomes. In practice, the regularities tend not to be changed and the intended outcomes, therefore cannot occur; that is, the more things change the more they remain the same.
>
> . . . . It is probably true that the most important attempts to introduce change into the school culture require changing existing teacher-child regularities. When one examines the natural history of the change process it is precisely these regularities that remain untouched. (S. Sarason, *The Culture of the School and the Problem of Change* 20, 86-87 (1971).)

The Sarason analysis suggests two factors that may inhibit compliance with student rights decisions. First, in the absence of a coherent model of educational change, hortatory appeals by courts are not likely to produce significant change. Words must be translated into actions that produce intended outcomes. Second, a change in the attitudes of teachers and administrators will not ensure change; the existing patterns or regularities of the teacher-student relationship must be altered. See 134-137, *supra*. Thus, adherence to student rights decrees implies substantial interference with the organizational and authority structures of public schools.

Resistance to student rights decisions may take many forms, and there is an unfortunate tendency to view compliance or noncompliance strictly in terms of student suspension and expulsion policies. Apart from official school policies, in each classroom there is an informal "constitution, verbalized or unverbalized, consistent or inconsistent . . . that governs behavior." Sarason, *Culture of the School*, 175. This constitution as well as school rules may be enforced by suspension or exclusion. It may also be enforced by corporal punishment, grade reductions, assignment of "demerits," exclusion from extracurricular activities, transfer to another class or school, or unfavorable notations on the student's school record. See, e.g., *Ware v Estes* 328 F Supp 657 (ND Tex 1971), *aff'd*, 458 F2d 1360 (5th Cir 1972); *Madera v New York City Bd of Educ* 386 F2d 778 (2d Cir 1967); *Hagopian v Knowlton* 470 F2d 201 (1972); *In re Wilson* (NY Comm'r of Educ, Feb 1972). More subtle punishments may also be applied, as an educator indicates in his advice to young secondary school teachers:

> Let us suppose you locate a troublemaker who is deliberately provoking a situation. What do you do? . . . [H]ere are some positive suggestions with additional comments:
>
> 1. At the end of the period talk to him privately. Let him know by the tone of your voice and your manner that you have no intention of tolerating his nonsense. *Be careful that you do not permit yourself to become involved in defending your actions to him.*
>
> 2. Change his seat to one directly in front of you. If he shows the slightest indication of getting out of line, speak to him in a low voice, as if you were his confidential friend warning him of trouble ahead. This technique often works magic, especially with younger teen-agers.
>
> 3. Make out a special disciplinary card that you keep in your files for future reference. Let the class as well as the troublemaker know that you are keeping a record. A variation of this technique is established in many schools by having an official blue or pink card made out that is sent to the discipline supervisor's office. A formal, carefully written complaint is frequently a strong deterrent to future outbursts.
>
> 4. Immediately send the troublemaker to your department office. Take the precaution to write a special pass *in ink*. Put the time when the pass is issued and request that the time be noted when the student arrives in the office. The youngster is to wait there until the end of the period when you can go to thrash the matter out with him. This procedure has the advantage of getting the troublemaker out of your classroom so that you may proceed with your lesson.
>
> 5. If school regulations do not permit you to send him to the department office, keep him in your room, but have him stand in the rear away from supporting walls or desks. The gesture is that he is not considered a part of

your class until disciplinary measures have been taken. A variation of this technique is to have him stand in the hall outside your room. Often, however, this last procedure is frowned upon by supervisors who feel that a student— especially if misbehaving—should always be under a teacher's observation.

6. Inform the guidance counselor. Be careful to give him an exact account. If possible, arrange a meeting with him, the troublemaker, and yourself.

7. Go to your subject supervisor. Usually he has the experience to be of definite help. In addition, he customarily wants his department to function smoothly. Of course be explicit in your charges.

8. Telephone to the parent, preferably the father in most cases, that evening. If there is no phone, and your supervisor doesn't object, write a letter *that afternoon* with a full account. Ask for the parent to see you in school to discuss the matter, stating the time when you have a free period. Cooperation of the home is important in disciplinary matters.

9. Contact the supervisor in charge of discipline. Be specific, giving *exact* and *all* details of your complaint. The completeness of your report is important because when the parent comes into school, the discipline supervisor will have your version at hand. You cannot expect him to support you if you file inaccurate reports.

10. In extreme cases, especially if there are indications of violence, send to the discipline supervisor's office for immediate help. Also, as soon as you perceive that the situation has slipped beyond your control, be careful of what you say and do.

11. On succeeding days keep a sharp eye on him. Call on him frequently, but *don't bear a grudge*. Remind yourself that you are trying to correct a youngster's attitude, not persecute him. As soon as he begins to cooperate, ease up. Strive earnestly to work with him. If he makes a good contribution, praise him. The trite saying, "More flies are caught with honey than vinegar," applies here. (Keene, *Beginning Secondary School Teacher's Guide* 98-103 (1969).)

School officials may also resort to persuasion rather than punishment. Large-group assemblies, principal-student meetings, superintendent-student meetings, student discussion groups, and community consultation are commonly employed methods of dealing with student activism. Havighurst, Smith, and Wilder, "A Profile of the Large-City High School," *Nat'l Ass'n of Secondary School Principals Bull,* January 1971, at 1, 84.

The fact that students may in some instances no longer be suspended for constitutionally protected activities is by no means a sufficient indicator that schools have accepted or endorsed the exercise of student rights. Moreover, a student's classmates may discourage him, for as Professor Keene implies, the most potent weapon of the teacher may be her ability to isolate a student from his peers and to cause them to exert pressure on the student to conform.

Viewed from the perspective of strict adherence to law, the student rights cases demonstrate the inability of courts to impose on complex social organizations values and purposes inconsistent with institutional norms and individual and bureaucratic perceptions. This inability to change schools, reach into the minds of administrators and teachers, monitor each classroom, and review the myriad minor punishments applied to nonconforming students might be viewed as arguing for judicial abstention. The futility of "paper decrees" and the uncertainty over the propriety of judicial interference with democratic educational policy choices are powerful arguments for judicial restraint. See Kurland, "Equal Educational Opportunity: The Limits of the Constitutional Jurisprudence Undefined," 35 *U Chi L Rev* 583 (1968). On the other hand, courts, particularly the Supreme Court, occupy a sensitive position in public policy making, a position that often allows them to influence policy choices in subtle and desirable ways:

> The distinction between the instrumental and symbolic functions of courts is crucial in evaluating the courts' role:
> We readily perceive that acts of officials, legislative enactments, and court decisions often affect behavior . . . through a direct influence on the actions of people. . . . The instrumental function of such laws lies in their enforcement; unenforced they have little effect. Symbolic aspects of law and government do not depend on enforcement for their effect. They are symbolic in a sense close to that used in literary analysis. The symbolic act "invites consideration rather than overt reaction." . . .
> . . . . Law can thus be seen as symbolizing the public affirmation of social ideals and norms as well as a means of direct social control. (Gusfield, "Moral Passage: The Symbolic Process in Public Designations of Deviance," in *Law and the Behavioral Sciences* 308, 309 (L. Friedman and S. Macaulay eds (1969).)

The symbolic affirmation of values and the designation of certain activities as deviant help create the consensus critical to the enforcement of equal protection decisions. Many commentators have noted the role of the courts, particularly the Supreme Court, as educational bodies, or the "ultimate interpreter[s] of the American code" of social ideals and morality. As "symbols of an ancient sureness and a comforting stability," the courts play a significant part in the formulation of public policy. A court decision often represents an appeal to the public conscience or to public idealism that may be accorded enormous weight in the legislative and political processes. . . . As Paul Freund once stated, "The moral quality of law is itself a force toward compliance and the change of attitudes."

A court decision that serves a symbolic function has another value, for a symbolic victory may have significant consequences for a political group at a particular point in time. In the absence of tangible benefits the morale of an organization working for governmental reform may depend on judicial success, a reaffirmation of the "rightness" of their position. The symbolic utterances of the courts have an impact not only on the culture at large but also on specific constituencies that are working for reform. (Yudof, "Equal Educational Opportunity and the Courts," 51 *Tex L Rev* 411, 414-16 (1973); see J. Skolnick, *Justice without Trial* 230-45 (1966).)

If this analysis of the symbolic role of the courts is correct (and there is much discussion and little empirical research to corroborate it), it yields a number of hypotheses about the impact of the student rights decisions:

1. Those decisions may bring forth a redefinition of what is deviant student behavior. Although teachers and administrators may be far from enthusiastic about student armbands, the courts, in effect, have sanctioned them and given them some legitimacy. Even if armbands continue to be prohibited, school officials may begin to view their interference as illegitimate or inconsistent with moral and social ideals. Over time this perception may make them less likely to interfere, or at least less sanguine about it.

2. Adult views of students may gradually change. In the wake of *Tinker*, students are—at least symbolically—no longer completely subject to school authority. They have become persons with rights: citizens who, with the assistance of their parents, can bring lawsuits and cause much trouble. Implicit in the concept of student rights is a rejection of the authoritarian model, regardless of whether students win or lose in particular litigations. Notwithstanding judicial assertions to the contrary, this change in adult perception of students moves the schools closer to a legal, democratic model of school governance and a progressive pedagogy. See generally Howarth, "On the Decline of in Loco Parentis," 52 *Phi Delta Kappan* 626 (1972).

3. The possibility of litigation may lead school administrators to minimize their risks, and that affects the culture of the school. In some instances, they may fail to take action for fear of reprisal in the courts. In others, they may resort to persuasion or milder sanctions to bring students into conformity with institutional norms. Where skilled legal counsel is available to administrators, they may carefully frame their actions in the light of prevailing judicial sentiment. For example, a principal who ideologically objects to the antiwar message in a student newspaper or finds the distribution of the newspaper to be a challenge to his authority may couch his decision to ban the newspaper in "disruption" terms. In this sense, student rights decisions alter the language of school decisions, if not their substance.

4. Judicial intervention may undermine the traditional paternal relationship between principal and student or teacher and student. While school officials previously attempted to deal with student misbehavior on an individual basis—often disregarding official policy and reducing sanctions—they may now choose to refer the student to his legal remedies. This pattern may be particularly evident where nonpolitical misbehavior is at issue.

5. In response to judicial pressures, the impetus against professionalism and in favor of teacher organization may accelerate in order to offset political gains made by students.

6. Organizations and individuals working for educational change may be strengthened and made more aggressive by student rights litigations that reaffirm the rightness of their positions. Recall the New York Civil Liberties Union Student Rights Project, established after a number of favorable judicial and school board decisions, and Thomas Guzick's declaration, ultimately shown to be wrong, that "a United States Supreme Court decision entitled him to wear the button in school." *Guzick v Drebus* 431 F2d 594 (6th Cir 1970). This effect on discrete constituencies is highly dependent on the amount of publicity surrounding student rights decisions; people must know about court decisions before they can modify their behavior in response to them. See Kirp, "The Role of Law in Educational Policy," *Social Policy*, September/October 1971.

Notes and Questions

1. Individual Fairness and Systemic Change

Is there some inconsistency between deciding an individual student rights case in accordance with notions of fairness and equity and creating sound and practical system-wide solutions? Is it illegitimate for a court to look beyond the individual result, the readmission of a single student, to the broader policy dimensions? Is the broader view consistent with the common law tradition described in the note?

2. Corporal Punishment

Is the preceding note relevant to the problem of corporal punishment? See *Ware v Estes* 328 F Supp 657 (ND Tex 1971), *aff'd,* 458 F2d 1360 (5th Cir 1972); *Sims v Board of Educ* 329 F Supp 678 (DNM 1971). But see Note, "Corporal Punishment in the Public Schools," 6 *Harv Civ Rights—Civ Lib L Rev* 583 (1971). Is it a sound reason for upholding corporal punishment that angered and frustrated teachers are likely to strike children irrespective of school rules? Are there advantages in not institutionalizing corporal punishment? See J. Kozol, *Death at an Early Age* 9-19 (1967). Would you require the parents' permission? Suppose that social scientists concluded that (a) corporal punishment was appropriate for those children who do not respond to more subtle punishments, and (b) for those children, fairly meted out corporal punishment improves academic performance. Would there be any basis for denying the constitutionality of corporal punishment?

3. Records

One of the least discussed but most significant punishments available to school authorities is the notation on a student's permanent record. As the report of the New York Civil Liberties Union Student Rights Project noted: "Used correctly, the maintenance of personal and educational records about a child is an important way for the school system to learn of a child's abilities and needs and to individualize instruction as he progresses from class to class. Used incorrectly, they can have a pernicious and far-reaching impact on a student's ability to succeed in school, get into college and even get a job." *NYCLU Report,* at 34. The NYCLU found a number of what it viewed as improper notations. One child was described as a "bed wetter." Another's record noted that his father was a "black militant." Anecdotes relating to minor misconduct were common. Still another child was described as a "real sickie—abs, truant, stubborn, & very dull." *NYCLU Report,* 34-35. Should any limits be placed on what may be recorded on a child's record? Should the parents and child be permitted to attach "their side of the story?" Is the problem cured by simply allowing parents to have access to school records? See *Van Allen v McCleary* 211 NYS2d 501 (Sup Ct 1961). Should such access be determined by the parents' purpose (e.g., whether they intend to embarrass the school)? Should school records be treated like any other public document? What impact would free access by parents have on record keeping? Is that effect desirable? If schools were barred from keeping the sorts of records scored by the Civil Liberties Union, would the type of information they contain continue to circulate informally? If so, would that be preferable to the present system?

4. The Therapeutic Approach

Some educators reject the "restrictive-punitive" style described in the note in favor of a therapeutic approach. They make the following assumptions:

1. That objectionable behavior is an abnormal, and in that sense an unnecessary, occurrence, stemming from a sickness or pathology in the child. ("There are no problem children," as a popular educational slogan has it, "only children with problems.")

2. That it is part of the job of school personnel to diagnose the unmet needs of a misbehaver, whatever they may be, and to try to meet them; and that this can be done, because:

a. Those who control schools will allow the personnel who deal with children to establish and maintain effective therapeutic or quasi-therapeutic relationships with them—as against purely didactic or autocratic ones—and to maintain these as long as there is hope that they can achieve the desired results;

b. School personnel can and will learn to work with children in such a relationship; and

c. Whenever school persons who thus intervene in the inner lives of children for whose behavior they have responsibility must choose between meeting the needs of the children and meeting their own needs or the demands of the school as an institution, they will stand by the children.

3. That objectionable behavior which resists elimination by this approach derives from pathology so serious as to require therapy by a specialist. (Ladd, "Disciplinary Principles and Behavior Changing Drugs," 8 *Inequality in Educ* (June 1971).)

Does the therapeutic approach in any way affect the arguments for or against judicial intervention in student rights cases? Does it make compliance with student rights decisions more or less likely? Does the therapeutic model justify the use of behavior altering drugs in the public schools? Does the answer to this question depend on whether qualified medical doctors approve and administer the drug to the students? Is parent approval (or student approval) necessary? See Ireland and Dimond, "Drugs and Hyperactivity: Process Is Due," 8 *Inequality in Educ* 19 (June 1971).

5. Student Lawlessness

To what extent may the student rights decisions have contributed to lawlessness in the schools by undermining the authority of school officials to deal with student misconduct? A study at large city high schools concluded that:

The most striking aspect of the large city high school is conflict among students and between students and faculty. This was reported for 53 percent of the schools during the two-year period from 1967-1969. The conflict took various forms: 29 percent of the schools were disrupted for a half-day or more; there were student strikes in 31 percent of the schools; and picketing or protest marches took place in 27 percent. At least moderate damage was done to the school building or its contents in 30 percent of the schools. . . . (Havighurst, Smith, and Wilder, "A Profile of the Large-City High School," *Nat'l Ass'n of Secondary School Principals Bull,* January 1971, at 100.)

Is lawlessness a response to court decisions, or do both emanate from more fundamental social causes?

6. Student Codes

In light of the discussion in the note, would the purposes of school administrators, teachers, and students be better served by the adoption of detailed student codes on student rights and responsibilities? What interests would be served by their adoption? Is there a danger in further legalization of dispute resolution in schools by increasingly detailed rule making? Should the student body ratify the code? What impact would such ratification have on enforcement? Would the code appear to be internally adopted rather than externally imposed? Suppose a school board asked you to draft a student code. In the light of the cases studied in this chapter, how would you go about performing that task? What provisions would you include?

IV. Due Process for Students

DIXON v ALABAMA BOARD OF EDUCATION
294 F2d 150 (5th Cir 1961)

Before Rives, Cameron and Wisdom, Circuit Judges.
Rives, Circuit Judge.

The question presented by the pleadings and evidence, and decisive of this appeal, is whether due process requires notice and some opportunity for hearing before students at a tax-supported college are expelled for misconduct. We answer that question in the affirmative.

The misconduct for which the students were expelled has never been definitely specified. Defendant Trenholm, the president of the college, testified that he did not know why the plaintiffs and three additional students were expelled and twenty other students were placed on probation. The notice of expulsion which Dr. Trenholm mailed to each of the plaintiffs assigned no specific ground for expulsion, but referred in general terms to "this problem of Alabama State College."

The acts of the students considered by the state board of education before it ordered their expulsion are described in the opinion of the district court reported in 186 F Supp 945, 947, from which we quote in the margin.[3]

---

3. On the 25th day of February 1960, the six plaintiffs in this case were students in good standing at the Alabama State College for Negroes in Montgomery, Alabama . . . . On this date, approximately twenty-nine Negro students, including these six plaintiffs, according to a prearranged plan, entered as a group a publicly owned lunch grill located in the basement of the county courthouse in Montgomery, Alabama, and asked to be served. Service was refused; the lunchroom was closed; the Negroes refused to leave; police authorities were summoned; and the Negroes were ordered outside where they remained in the corridor of the courthouse for approximately one hour. On the same date, John Patterson, as governor of the state of Alabama and as chairman of the state board of education, conferred with Dr. Trenholm, a Negro educator and president of the Alabama State College, concerning this activity on the part of some of the students. Dr. Trenholm was advised by the governor that the incident should be investigated, and that if he were in the president's position he would consider expulsion and/or

As shown by the findings of the district court, just quoted in footnote 3, the only demonstration which the evidence showed that *all* of the expelled students took part in was that in the lunch grill located in the basement of the Montgomery County Courthouse. The other demonstrations were found to be attended "by several if not all of the plaintiffs." We have carefully read and studied the record, and agree with the district court that the evidence does not affirmatively show that *all* of the plaintiffs were present at any but the one demonstration.

Only one member of the state board of education assigned the demonstration attended by all of the plaintiffs as the sole basis for his vote to expel them. . . .

The district court found the general nature of the proceedings before the state board of education, the action of the board, and the official notice of the expulsion given to the students as follows:

Investigations into this conduct were made by Dr. Trenholm, as president of the Alabama State College, the director of public safety for the state of Alabama under directions of the governor, and by the investigative staff of the attorney general for the state of Alabama.

On or about March 2, 1960, the state board of education met and received reports from the governor of the state of Alabama, which reports embodied the investigations that had been made and which reports identified these six plaintiffs, together with several others, as the 'ring leaders' for the group of students that had been participating in the above-recited activities. During this meeting, Dr. Trenholm, in his capacity as president of the college reported to the assembled members of the state board of education that the action of these students in demonstrating on the college campus and in certain downtown areas was having a disruptive influence on the work of the other students at the college and upon the orderly operation of the college in general. Dr. Trenholm further reported to the board that, in his opinion, he as president of the college could not control future disruptions and demonstrations. There were twenty-nine of the Negro students identified as the core of the organization that was responsible for these demonstrations. This group of twenty-nine included these six plaintiffs. After hearing these reports and recommendations and upon the recommendation of the governor as chairman

---

other appropriate disciplinary action. On February 26, 1960, several hundred Negro students from the Alabama State College, including several if not all of these plaintiffs, staged a mass attendance at a trial being held in the Montgomery County courthouse, involving the perjury prosecution of a fellow student. After the trial these students filed two by two from the courthouse and marched through the city approximately two miles back to the college. On February 27, 1960, several hundred Negro students from this school, including several if not all of the plaintiffs in this case, staged mass demonstrations in Montgomery and Tuskegee, Alabama. On this same date, Dr. Trenholm advised all of the student body that these demonstrations and meetings were disrupting the orderly conduct of the business at the college and were affecting the work of other students, as well as the work of the participating students. Dr. Trenholm personally warned plaintiffs Bernard Lee, Joseph Peterson and Elroy Embry, to cease these disruptive demonstrations immediately, and advised the members of the student body at the Alabama State College to behave themselves and return to their classes. . . . On or about March 1, 1960, approximately six hundred students in the Alabama State College engaged in hymn singing and speech making on the steps of the state capitol. Plaintiff Bernard Lee addressed students at this demonstration, and the demonstration was attended by several if not all of the plaintiffs. Plaintiff Bernard Lee at this time called on the students to strike and boycott the college if any students were expelled because of these demonstrations.

of the board, the board voted unanimously, expelling nine students, including these six plaintiffs, and placing twenty students on probation. This action was taken by Dr. Trenholm as president of the college, acting pursuant to the instructions of the state board of education. Each of these plaintiffs, together with the other students expelled, was officially notified of his expulsion on March 4 or 5, 1960. No formal charges were placed against these students and no hearing was granted any of them prior to their expulsion. . . . *Dixon v Alabama Bd of Educ* 186 F Supp 945, 948-49 (MD Ala 1960).

The evidence clearly shows that the question for decision does not concern the sufficiency of the notice or the adequacy of the hearing, but is whether the students had a right to any notice or hearing whatever before being expelled. After careful study and consideration, we find ourselves unable to agree with the conclusion of the district court that no notice or opportunity for any kind of hearing was required before these students were expelled. . . .

Whenever a governmental body acts so as to injure an individual, the Constitution requires that the act be consonant with due process of law. The minimum procedural requirements necessary to satisfy due process depend upon the circumstances and the interests of the parties involved. . . .

It is not enough to say, as did the district court in the present case, "The right to attend a public college or university is not in and of itself a constitutional right." 186 F Supp at 950. That argument was emphatically answered by the Supreme Court in the Cafeteria and Restaurant Workers Union case, *supra,* [81 S Ct 1748] when it said that the question of whether

> summarily denying Rachel Brawner access to the site of her former employment violated the requirements of the due process clause of the Fifth Amendment . . . cannot be answered by easy assertion that, because she had no constitutional right to be there in the first place, she was not deprived of liberty or property by the superintendent's action. "One may not have a constitutional right to go to Bagdad, but the government may not prohibit one from going there unless by means consonant with due process of law." As in that case, so here, it is necessary to consider the nature both of the private interest which has been impaired and the governmental power which has been exercised.

The appellees urge upon us that under a provision of the board of education's regulations the appellants waived any right to notice and a hearing before being expelled for misconduct.

> Attendance at any college is on the basis of a mutual decision of the student's parents and of the college. Attendance at a particular college is voluntary and is different from attendance at a public school where the pupil may be required to attend a particular school which is located in the neighborhood or district in which the pupil's family may live. Just as a student may choose to withdraw from a particular college at any time for any personally-determined reason, the college may also at any time decline to continue to accept responsibility for the supervision and service to any student with whom the relationship becomes unpleasant and difficult.

We do not read this provision to clearly indicate an intent on the part of the student to waive notice and a hearing before expulsion. If, however, we should so assume, it nonetheless remains true that the state cannot condition the granting of even a privilege upon the renunciation of the constitutional right to procedural due process. . . . Only private associations have the right to obtain a waiver of notice and hearing before depriving a member of a valuable right. And even here, the right to notice and a hearing is so fundamental to the conduct of our society that the waiver must be clear and explicit. . . .

The precise nature of the private interest involved in this case is the right to remain at a public institution of higher learning in which the plaintiffs were students in good standing. It requires no argument to demonstrate that education is vital and, indeed, basic to civilized society. Without sufficient education the plaintiffs would not be able to earn an adequate livelihood, to enjoy life to the fullest, or to fulfill as completely as possible the duties and responsibilities of good citizens.

There was no offer to prove that other colleges are open to the plaintiffs. If so, the plaintiffs would nonetheless be injured by the interruption of their course in midterm. It is most unlikely that a public college would accept a student expelled from another public college of the same state. Indeed, expulsion may well prejudice the student in completing his education at any other institution. Surely no one can question that the right to remain at the college in which the plaintiffs were students in good standing is an interest of extremely great value.

Turning then to the nature of the governmental power to expel the plaintiffs, it must be conceded, as was held by the district court, that that power is not unlimited and cannot be arbitrarily exercised. Admittedly, there must be some reasonable and constitutional ground for expulsion or the courts would have a duty to require reinstatement. The possibility of arbitrary action is not excluded by the existence of reasonable regulations. There may be arbitrary application of the rule to the facts of a particular case. Indeed, that result is well nigh inevitable when the board hears only one side of the issue. In the disciplining of college students there are no considerations of immediate danger to the public, or of peril to the national security, which should prevent the board from exercising at least the fundamental principles of fairness by giving the accused students notice of the charges and an opportunity to be heard in their own defense. Indeed, the example set by the board in failing so to do, if not corrected by the courts, can well break the spirits of the expelled students and of others familiar with the injustice, and do inestimable harm to their education. . . .

It was not a case denying any hearing whatsoever but one passing upon the adequacy of the hearing, which provoked from Professor Warren A. Seavey of Harvard the eloquent comment:

> At this time when many are worried about dismissal from public service, when only because of the overriding need to protect the public safety is the identity of informers kept secret, when we proudly contrast the full hearings before our courts with those in the benighted countries which have no due process protection, when many of our courts are so careful in the protection of those charged with crimes that they will not permit the use of evidence illegally obtained, our sense of justice should be outraged by denial to students of the normal safeguards. It is shocking that the officials of a state

educational institution, which can function properly only if our freedoms are preserved, should not understand the elementary principles of fair play. It is equally shocking to find that a court supports them in denying to a student the protection given to a pickpocket. "Dismissal of Students: 'Due Process,' " 70 *Harv L Rev* 1406, 1407.

We are confident that precedent as well as a most fundamental constitutional principle support our holding that due process requires notice and some opportunity for hearing before a student at a tax-supported college is expelled for misconduct.

For the guidance of the parties in the event of further proceedings, we state our views on the nature of the notice and hearing required by due process prior to expulsion from a state college or university. They should, we think, comply with the following standards. The notice should contain a statement of the specific charges and grounds which, if proven, would justify expulsion under the regulations of the board of education. The nature of the hearing should vary depending upon the circumstances of the particular case. The case before us requires something more than an informal interview with an administrative authority of the college. By its nature, a charge of misconduct, as opposed to a failure to meet the scholastic standards of the college, depends upon a collection of the facts concerning the charged misconduct, easily colored by the point of view of the witnesses. In such circumstances, a hearing which gives the board or the administrative authorities of the college an opportunity to hear both sides in considerable detail is best suited to protect the rights of all involved. This is not to imply that a full-dress judicial hearing, with the right to cross-examine witnesses, is required. Such a hearing, with the attending publicity and disturbance of college activities, might be detrimental to the college's educational atmosphere and impractical to carry out. Nevertheless, the rudiments of an adversary proceeding may be preserved without encroaching upon the interests of the college. In the instant case, the student should be given the names of the witnesses against him and an oral or written report on the facts to which each witness testifies. He should also be given the opportunity to present to the board, or at least to an administrative official of the college, his own defense against the charges and to produce either oral testimony or written affidavits of witnesses in his behalf. If the hearing is not before the board directly, the results and findings of the hearing should be presented in a report open to the student's inspection. If these rudimentary elements of fair play are followed in a case of misconduct of this particular type, we feel that the requirements of due process of law will have been fulfilled.

The judgment of the district court is reversed and the cause is remanded for further proceedings consistent with this opinion. . . .

Notes and Questions

1. Scope of Due Process

Why should due process hearing requirements attach to the dispensation of school punishments? Does the importance of education argue for procedural protections for those whom the school wishes to exclude, even temporarily? Does the demise of the in loco parentis doctrine make obligatory the extension of due process rights to students? See Van Alstyne, "The Judicial Trend Toward Student Academic Freedom," 20 *U Fla L Rev* 290 (1968). Are ad hoc decisions more likely to produce unjust outcomes than due process hearings? Do hearings appear fairer to the student than "informal justice?" Is school exclusion sufficiently punitive to require due process guarantees? See generally Kirp, "Schools as Sorters: The Constitutional and Policy Implications of Student Classification," 121 *U Pa L Rev* 705, 776-78 (1973).

Would these same considerations apply to short-term suspensions, for example, three days? See, e.g., *Dunn v Tyler Independent School Dist* 460 F2d 137 (5th Cir 1972); *Banks v Board of Pub Instruction* 450 F2d 1103 (5th Cir 1971). Should a hearing be required before after-school detentions are imposed? Before demerits are assessed? See *Hagopian v Knowlton* 470 F2d 201 (2d Cir 1972). Before noting on a student's permanent record that she cheated on a test? See *In re Goldwyn* 54 Misc2d 94, 281 NYS2d 899 (Sup Ct 1967). What if the student is subjected to an "educational" rather than a "punitive" decision, e.g., transfer to a special school? See *Madera v Board of Educ* 267 F Supp 356 (SDNY 1967), rev'd, 386 F2d 778 (2d Cir 1967). For consideration of due process requirements in the context of such educational classifications, see chapter 7. Would it be accurate to say that due process rights attach to all of these school decisions, but that the gravity of the punishment determines the extent to which formal procedures are required? See *Board of Regents v Roth* 408 US 564, 570 n8 (1972).

2. The Hearing Requirement

Courts repeatedly note that due process is "an elusive concept" whose "content varies according to specific factual contexts." *Hannah v Larche* 363 US 420, 442 (1960). What are the elements of a fair hearing for a long-term suspension or expulsion? See generally Buss, "Procedural Due Process for School Discipline: Probing the Constitutional Outline," 119 *U Pa L Rev* 545 (1971). Consider the following hypothetical cases:

a. Cross-examination. A high school student was suspended for an assault on other female students as they were walking home after classes. At her hearing, the school vice-principal offers to testify and to subject himself to cross-examination. Statements written by student witnesses are introduced into evidence, but these statements are unsigned and the witnesses themselves are unavailable for cross-examination. The witnesses, according to school authorities "were in terror of retaliation." The suspended student's lawyer objects to the proceeding as a denial of the due process of law to which his client is entitled. What result? See *Tibbs v Board of Educ* 114 NJ Super 287, 276 A2d 165 (1971).

b. Counsel. Ten students were expelled or suspended from a state university for their alleged participation in campus disturbances. At the disciplinary hearing, the students request that their retained counsel be permitted to participate in the proceedings. This request is denied. The prosecution of the cases, however, is conducted by a senior law school student. Have the students been denied due process of law? See *French v Bashful* 303 F Supp 1333 (ED La 1969); Wright, "The Constitution on the Campus," 22 *Vand L Rev* 1027, 1075-76 (1969). Would your answer change if the university had not employed a lawyer or law student to prosecute the case? See *Zanders v Louisiana Bd of Educ* 281 F Supp 747 (WD La 1968); Sherry, "Governance of the University: Rules, Rights, and Responsibilities," 54 *Cal L Rev* 23, 37 (1966). But see *Wasson v Trowbridge* 382 F2d 807, 812 (2d Cir 1967).

c. Record. A student is expelled, and a full hearing is held by school officials. The student requests that a stenographic record of the proceedings be kept. The request is refused. Is such a record an integral part of a fair hearing? See *Due v Florida A & M Univ* 233 F Supp 396, 403 (ND Fla 1963). What if the student offers to pay for the stenographic record? See *Charles S. v Board of Educ* 20 CA3d 83, 97 Cal Rptr 422 (1971).

d. Impartiality. A student is suspended for using profanity toward the school's principal and violating a direct order from the principal. The student is afforded a hearing, which is conducted by the principal. The student's attorney argues that the principal must disqualify himself since he is not impartial, but the argument is rejected. Has the student been denied due process of law? See *Sullivan v Houston Independent School Dist* 475 F2d 1071 (5th Cir 1973). See also *Murray v West Baton Rouge Parish School Bd* 472 F2d 438 (5th Cir 1973). Compare *Keene v Rodgers* 316 F Supp 217 (ND Me 1970). What if school rules provide for subsequent de novo hearings before impartial tribunals? Would this cure the procedural defect in the original hearing? See *Sullivan v Houston Independent School Dist, supra; Speake v Grantham* 440 F2d 1351 (5th Cir 1971)(per curiam).

e. Hearing Before Suspension. A student was suspended on January 21, 1970, the day after he allegedly stabbed a fifteen-year-old girl off school grounds, until the next scheduled meeting of the board of education. The board met on February 10, conducted a full hearing, and decided to continue the suspension. The student alleges that he was denied due process because he was afforded no hearing before his suspension. What result? See *R.R. v Board of Educ* 109 NJ Super 337, 263 A2d 180 (1970). What would be the elements of such an interim hearing? Would they differ from what is required at the board's hearing on February 10?

3. Costs and Benefits

In answering the questions in notes 2 and 3, the costs and benefits associated with increased proceduralization of school decisions affecting students merit consideration. Professor O'Neill identifies the interests that are generally served by due process hearings: (a) accuracy and fairness; (b) accountability; (c) visibility and impartiality; (d) consistency; and (e) administrative integrity. O'Neill also notes several governmental interests inconsistent with such hearings: (a) collegiality and informality; (b) flexibility in the dispensation of benefits; (c) agency initiative; (d) discretion and confidentiality; and (e) minimization of costs. O'Neill, "Justice Delayed and Justice Denied," 1970 *Sup Ct Rev* 161, 184-95. How should a court take these competing interests into account?

4. Judicial Acceptance

While the issues surrounding substantive student rights have provoked mixed judicial reactions, since *Dixon* no court has seriously questioned that students are entitled to significant procedural guarantees when severe sanctions are imposed on them. How do you explain this phenomenon? Is the development of procedural safeguards easier for courts because of the judicial experience with such matters in other contexts? See Buss, "Procedural Due Process for School Discipline: Probing the Constitutional Outline," 119 *U Pa L Rev* 545, 571 (1971).

5. Impact

Does general judicial acceptance of due process standards presage widespread compliance with both letter and spirit of due process requirements? Or are school personnel—unhappy about the diversion of time and energy that due process requires—likely to retaliate in subtle ways against the student who is sufficiently intrepid to demand a hearing before discipline can be imposed? Assume that under the facts of note 2a above the student is ordered readmitted to school. The school (a) assigns him to the principal's office for "permanent study hall"; (b) requires that he be escorted between classes by a guard who is posted outside the door while he is attending class; (c) assigns him to a school for "disciplinary problems"; or (d) places him on home instruction. Does the student have legal basis for challenging each of these alternative school actions? Would adoption of any of these school actions serve as a signal to other students? Given the facts of note 2a, are these "irrational" actions, in either the legal or commonsense meaning of that word?

6. Judicial Review

If a school or school district holds a disciplinary hearing in conformity with judicial requirements, what standard of review should the courts apply to the factual findings of the hearing body? In "General Order on Judicial Standards of Procedure and Substance in Review of Student Discipline in Tax-supported Institutions of Higher Education," 45 FRD 133 (WD Mo 1968)(en banc), the court held that the due process clause required "that no disciplinary action be taken on grounds which are not supported by any substantial evidence." 45 FRD at 147. See also Wright, "The Constitution on the Campus," 22 *Vand L Rev* 1027, 1071-72 (1969). Is such a limited standard of review appropriate where the student alleges violation of First Amendment rights? See generally Nahmod, "First Amendment Protection for Learning and Teaching: The Scope of Judicial Review," 18 *Wayne L Rev* 1479 (1972).

chapter three
Life in Schools: Teachers

I. Introduction

In many respects the legal rights of teachers may be viewed as indistinguishable from those of students. In a public institution dedicated to teaching skills and values to the young, the teacher, like the student, often must put aside her personal preferences and interests in order to conform to the bureaucratic and institutional demands of a goal-oriented enterprise.* From this perspective, the teacher is neither more nor less able than the student to disrupt the educational process or challenge the policy decisions of administrators or elected school officials. Thus there are many cases in which teachers have challenged school regulations that have also provoked objections from the student population. For example, in *Finot v Pasadena Bd of Educ* 58 Cal Rptr 520 (Ct App 1967), a teacher attacked a grooming regulation that, according to the school's principal, forbade any teacher to grow a beard. The principal argued, among other things, that a beard would be "disruptive of the educational program of the school," but the attack was successful. Compare *Blanchet v Vermillion Parish School Bd* 220 So2d 534 (La Ct App 1969). Similarly, in *James v Board of Educ* 461 F2d 566 (2d Cir 1972), a teacher successfully challenged an armband regulation that was similar to the prohibition involved in *Tinker v Des Moines Independent Community School Dist,* 393 US 503 (1969). In *Russo v Central School Dist No 1* 469 F2d 623 (2d Cir 1972), the United States Court of Appeals for the Second Circuit held that a high school teacher could not be dismissed for her silent refusal to participate in flag salute ceremonies. Compare *West Virginia v Barnette* 319 US 624 (1943).

Despite these similarities, there are many respects in which the position of the teacher differs from that of the student, and these differences do not relate only to the fact that the teacher is one step higher in a rigidly stratified institution. Some, but not all, of these factors suggest the propriety of affording teachers greater personal autonomy than students.

1. The age, experience, and maturity of teachers argue for a more expansive definition of their rights in the schools. In contrast to the arguments made by critics of student rights, there is no doubt that teachers should be afforded the same constitutional prerogatives as other adults, subject to whatever limitations are necessitated by the special characteristics of the school environment. Moreover, teachers bring an educational expertise to the schooling process that rivals or exceeds that possessed by those with whom they are likely to be in conflict: students, parents, other teachers, administrators, and school board members.

---

*Since most elementary and secondary teachers are female, feminine pronouns will be used unless the context requires otherwise.

2. Notwithstanding traditional perceptions of the apolitical nature of schools and teachers, teachers cannot simply be viewed as dedicated public servants; they are also employees with their own coherent set of interests, values, and needs. This is not to say that the roles of employee and pedagogue must conflict, but merely that the teacher's function must be viewed more broadly. Teachers may feel compelled to accommodate themselves to the dominant political and social coalition in the community, and they are obliged to maintain a working relationship with peers and superiors. Moreover, teachers assert claims for adequate compensation, decent working conditions, and collective bargaining, and this further differentiates them from the position of the students.

3. Further, the nature of the teacher's job is vital to analysis of the appropriate legal constraints on her conduct and speech. Teachers are paid to communicate, to pass on knowledge to the young, to explore issues critically, and to promote understanding. In this sense, the job of teaching is closely connected to the freedoms of speech, belief, and association: a connection often referred to by the vague phrase "academic freedom." While academic freedom may simply provide a label for a result without articulated reasons, it should bring to mind a number of independent policy reasons for expanding teacher rights: reasons that must be weighed against the advantages to be derived from circumscribing those rights. See generally R. Hofstadter & W. Metzger, *The Development of Academic Freedom in the United States* (1955); R. Kirk, *Academic Freedom* (1955); D. Rubin, *The Rights of Teachers* (1972); "Developments in the Law—Academic Freedom," 81 *Harv L Rev* 1045 (1968).

4. The compulsoriness of education distinguishes the positions of student and teacher. The teacher who voluntarily seeks and obtains employment may not be in the same position as a student to demand freedom from institutional constraints; ethically, if not legally, the student may assert a right to a particular quality of institutional life in exchange for the sacrifice of his freedom to do or go elsewhere. Without attempting to resurrect the discarded lawyers' distinction between rights and privileges (see pp 134-37), the teacher's claim to liberty may be less persuasive because she is free to seek employment elsewhere. In addition, the compulsory nature of schooling may itself argue for limiting the independence of teachers. Since most parents cannot remove their children from public school, it is particularly important that those schools be governed by the will of the parents or community rather than the whim and prejudices of individual teachers. The teacher has a captive audience and arguably should not be permitted to abuse a position of power and trust that was not created for her benefit.

5. Teachers function in a compulsory school environment as models for student conduct and attitudes; they are a primary instrument in the schools' effort to socialize students (see chapter 2). For that reason it is generally expected they will influence students in a manner acceptable to parents, elected officials, and the community. Teachers have been dismissed for in-class conduct ranging from the assignment of allegedly obscene materials to the endorsement of political candidates. Out-of-school activities such as adultery, homosexuality, alcoholism, and gambling have also provided the cause for termination. While students may also influence their peers with respect to values and conduct, the legitimate and authoritative position of adult teachers may argue for more stringent limitations on the latter. This is amply reflected in the common law tradition that regularly permitted

sanctions against teachers for out-of-school conduct but rarely did so with respect to students.

This chapter explores these five themes in the specific context of the litigations in which they have arisen: the permissible scope of teacher conduct and speech inside and outside the classroom, tenure, the procedural rights of teachers, and the right to organize and scope of collective bargaining. Throughout this chapter, however, two important caveats must be kept in mind:

1. The convenient separation of students and teachers with respect to their treatment under the law is defensible in terms of their distinct positions and interests, but the line is not always as clear as it first appears. For example, to speak of academic freedom as exclusively relevant to teachers—without reference to its importance to students—is to distort analysis of the problem.

2. A statement of legal rights in a judicial opinion is not necessarily a mirror of what will happen in the public schools after the date of decision. School districts not directly affected by the decision may choose to disregard it or may not be aware of its existence. Organized teacher groups may use the opinion in a number of unanticipated ways, including the bargaining away of their legal rights for some other concession from administrators. School systems may choose to employ informal or subtle sanctions to ensure adherence to institutional norms at odds with the court decision. Thus, each case must be examined not only in terms of what it theoretically demands of school systems in their treatment of teachers, but also in terms of its likely impact on teachers' lives in schools.

THE COMING REVOLUTION IN PUBLIC SCHOOL MANAGEMENT
Donald H. Wollett
67 *Mich L Rev* 1017, 1018 (1969)

School boards and superintendents have considered it perfectly legitimate . . . to exercise strict control over the teacher's behavior, his method of instruction, or both. In part, this reflects the tradition of emphasizing the role of the teacher as an "employee" of the "community" to which the board and superintendent are "responsible." Thus, teachers, individually and collectively, are expected to tailor their expectations and behavior to fit the limits tolerable to the community in which they are employed—or, more precisely, to organized groups which have political leverage within that community. If the teachers exceed those limits, the school board and the superintendent will predictably stand with the community rather than with the faculty, even though the quality of education may suffer as a result. The rationale for choosing sides in this way is self-preservation: the community not only pays taxes to support the public educational establishment, but also retains the ultimate power to dismiss unresponsive boards of education and superintendents. Educational policy that is set in response to such pressure from community groups often does not satisfy the legitimate educational needs of the community's children . . . .

However, teachers do not have authority within local school systems commensurate with their responsibilities. They frequently lack a meaningful voice in determining the content of the courses they are teaching or in selecting appropriate textbooks. Often they are not free to formulate their own lesson plans or to modify them if they do not produce desirable classroom responses. Seldom, if ever, do they share a role in overall curricular planning. A teacher who maintains rigorous performance standards for his pupils or strict rules of eligibility to participate in extracurricular activities for which he is responsible may be supported by his school board in the teeth of parental complaints. But it is more likely that he will be forced to relax his standards under threat of an adverse performance rating, a transfer to the boondocks, or discharge. Teachers are frequently told that they should accept responsibility for their colleagues who "beat the clock" or who are otherwise guilty of untoward behavior. Yet, teachers typically have no voice in recruiting new colleagues or in promotion and tenure decisions. The on-the-job freedom and authority of classroom teachers has been seriously curtailed by standardization of teaching procedures which are regimentally enforced. Most teachers have inadequate office space (if indeed they have an office at all), and they have little or no secretarial help. Faculty libraries are virtually unknown. Teachers are seldom involved in decisions about the design or rehabilitation of physical plant or about the mix of technology and manpower to be employed in the teaching process . . . .

Teachers must submit weekly lesson plans for the approval of supervisors who frequently do not even take the trouble to read them. Considerable time is devoted to minor clerical chores such as taking attendance, filling out forms, and keeping records. Teachers are required to direct traffic in hallways between classes, and they are importuned never to sit down while teaching a class. Supervisors roam the halls during class changes and peer into classroom windows to enforce both of these rules strictly. Worse, the principal maintains an informal espionage system wherein teachers are encouraged to report on the activities of their fellow teachers by the prospect of relief from unwanted nonteaching duties such as cafeteria supervision.

Notes and Questions

1. Quality Education and Professional Control

Is it inappropriate for school authorities to compel teachers to conform to the community's education values? Professor Wollett suggests that there may be some inconsistency between the satisfaction of the educational needs of children and the interference by community groups in the day-to-day operation of the public schools. Do you agree? Does his suggestion ignore the essentially political nature of many public school decisions? Is it enough to answer that teachers, by virtue of their education and experience, are better equipped to make curricular, performance, and hiring decisions than laymen? See D. Kirp, "Collective Bargaining in Education: Professionals as a Political Interest Group," 21 *J Pub L* 323, 334-38 (1972). Is there necessarily any connection between the improvement of the status and working conditions of teachers and improvement of the educational process?

2. Teacher Grievances and the Courts

Is litigation an appropriate method of ameliorating the undesirable aspects of the teacher's plight? Are courts likely to alter the political balance between teachers on one side and school officials and the community on the other?

THE POLITICAL LIFE OF AMERICAN TEACHERS
H. Zeigler
29-30 (1967)

This [study] undertook to discover if male and female teachers react to the teaching experience in markedly different patterns. The evidence is that they do, and that the patterns are typified in the behaviors respectively of high-income females and low-income males. The high-income females have the greater satisfaction with their jobs, the lesser need for respect, the lesser opposition to change, the more conservative political opinions, [but] the lesser tendency to radical conservatism. They are also the more educationally progressive. The low-income males are the less satisfied with their jobs, have the greater need for respect, and are more likely to oppose change. They are more liberal politically than females, but the most radically conservative of teachers are in this group. They are less educationally progressive than women.

Between these two extreme patterns fall the behavior of high-income males, who seem to have more in common with low-income males than with high-income females, and of low-income females, whose values seem at times closer to low-income males and at other times closer to high-income females. That is to say, for male teachers the clearest congruence of values is with those of other males, whereas females have a less exclusive tendency to adopt the values of other females. Granted that income is important for the males, it does not seem to provide a set of identifications as viable and permanent as simply being a male. Maleness emerges as the essential variable and the male high school teacher is, in a sense, the underclass of the teaching profession, a rebel in a female system.

Notes and Questions

1. Feminine Dominance

Statistically, women make up the overwhelming majority of elementary school faculties, while men predominate in high schools. The entrance of men into the teaching profession, however, is a relatively recent phenomenon, apparently the result of "elaborate inducements" offered on the assumption that men are superior authority figures in the classroom. Zeigler, *Political Life* 11-12. The overall character of the teaching profession, notwithstanding the influx of men, remains feminine: "it does not offer men the stature of a fully legitimate male role. The American masculine conviction that education and culture are feminine concerns is thus confirmed . . . . In a certain constricted sense, the male teacher may be respected, but he is not 'one of the boys.' " R. Hofstadter, *Anti-Intellectualism in American Life* 320 (1963).

2. Feminine Dominance and Change

What do the sexual composition of the school and the dominancy of the female character portend with respect to changes in the school environment that Professor Wollett might advocate? Do they alter the relationship between teacher and community? Teacher and administration?

3. Feminine Dominance and Socialization

What impact might Professor Zeigler's conclusions have on the role of teachers as socializers of the young? Would that impact make interference by the community in school affairs more or less likely?

II. Academic Freedom: The Classroom

PARDUCCI v RUTLAND
316 F Supp 352 (MD Ala 1970)

Johnson, Chief Judge.

On April 21, 1970, plaintiff assigned as outside reading to her junior English classes a story, entitled "Welcome to the Monkey House." The story, a comic satire, was selected by plaintiff to give her students a better understanding of one particular genre of western literature—the short story. The story's author, Kurt Vonnegut, Jr., is a prominent contemporary writer who has published numerous short stories and novels, including *Cat's Cradle* and a recent best seller, *Slaughterhouse-Five*.

The following morning, plaintiff was called to Principal Rutland's office for a conference with him and the associate superintendent of the school system. Both men expressed their displeasure with the content of the story, which they described as "literary garbage," and with the "philosophy" of the story, which they construed as condoning, if not encouraging, "the killing off of elderly people and free sex." They also expressed concern over the fact that three of plaintiff's students had asked to be excused from the assignment and that several disgruntled parents had called the school to complain. They then admonished plaintiff not to teach the story in any of her classes.

Plaintiff retorted that she was bewildered by their interpretation of and attitude toward the story, that she still considered it to be a good literary work, and that, while not meaning to cause any trouble, she felt that she had a professional obligation to teach the story . . . .

On May 6, the school board notified plaintiff that she had been dismissed from her job for assigning materials which had a "disruptive" effect on the school and for refusing "the counseling and advice of the school principal." The school board also advised the plaintiff that one of the bases for her dismissal was "insubordination" by reason of a statement that she made to the principal and associate superintendent that "regardless of their counseling" she "would continue to teach the eleventh-grade English class at the Jeff Davis High School by the use of whatever material" she wanted "and in whatever manner" she thought best. . . .

At the outset, it should be made clear that plaintiff's teaching ability is not in issue. The principal of her school has conceded that plaintiff was a good teacher and that she would have received a favorable evaluation from him at the end of the year but for the single incident which led to her dismissal.

Plaintiff asserts in her complaint that her dismissal for assigning "Welcome to the Monkey House" violated her First Amendment right to academic freedom.

That teachers are entitled to First Amendment freedoms is an issue no longer in dispute. "It can hardly be argued that either students or teachers shed their constitutional rights to freedom of speech or expression at the schoolhouse gate." *Tinker v Des Moines Independent Community School Dist* 393 US 503, 506 (1969). . . . These constitutional protections are unaffected by the presence or absence of tenure under state law. . . .

Although academic freedom is not one of the enumerated rights of the First Amendment, the Supreme Court has on numerous occasions emphasized that the right to teach, to inquire, to evaluate and to study is fundamental to a democratic society.[3] In holding a New York loyalty oath statute unconstitutionally vague, the court stressed the need to expose students to a robust exchange of ideas in the classroom:

> Our nation is deeply committed to safeguarding academic freedom, which is of transcendant value to all of us and not merely to the teachers concerned. That freedom is therefore a special concern of the First Amendment, which does not tolerate laws that cast a pall of orthodoxy over the classroom . . . . The classroom is peculiarly the "marketplace of ideas."[4]

Furthermore, the safeguards of the First Amendment will quickly be brought into play to protect the right of academic freedom because any unwarranted invasion of this right will tend to have a chilling effect on the exercise of the right by other teachers. . . .

The right to academic freedom, however, like all other constitutional rights, is not absolute and must be balanced against the competing interests of society. This court is keenly aware of the state's vital interest in protecting the impressionable minds of its young people from *any* form of extreme propagandism in the classroom.

> A teacher works in a sensitive area in a schoolroom. There he shapes the attitudes of young minds towards the society in which they live. In this, the state has a vital concern.[5]

While the balancing of these interests will necessarily depend on the particular facts before the court, certain guidelines in this area were provided by the Supreme Court in *Tinker v Des Moines Independent Community School District, supra.* The court there observed that in order for the state to restrict the First Amendment right of a student, it must first demonstrate that: "[T]he forbidden conduct would '*materially* and *substantially* interfere with the requirements of appropriate discipline in the operation of the school.' ". . .

Thus, the first question to be answered is whether "Welcome to the Monkey House" is inappropriate reading for high school juniors. While the story contains several vulgar terms and a reference to an involuntary act of sexual intercourse, the court, having read the story very carefully, can find nothing that would render it obscene either under the standards of *Roth v US*[8] or under the stricter standards for minors as set forth in *Ginsberg v New York.*[9]

The slang words are contained in two short rhymes which are less ribald than

---

3. See, e.g., *Sweezy v New Hampshire by Wyman* 354 US 234 (1957); *Wieman v Updegraff* 344 US 183 (1952).

4. *Keyishian v Board of Regents, etc.* 385 US 589, 603 (1967). Cf. *Meyer v Nebraska* 262 US 390 (1923).

5. *Shelton v Tucker* 364 US 479, 485 (1960).

8. 354 US 476 (1957).

9. 390 US 629 (1968).

those found in many of Shakespeare's plays. The reference in the story to an act of sexual intercourse is no more descriptive than the rape scene in Pope's *Rape of the Lock*. As for the theme of the story, the court notes that the anthology in which the story was published was reviewed by several of the popular national weekly magazines, none of which found the subject matter of any of the stories to be offensive. It appears to the court, moreover, that the author, rather than advocating the "killing off of old people," satirizes the practice to symbolize the increasing depersonalization of man in society.

The court's finding as to the appropriateness of the story for high school students is confirmed by the reaction of the students themselves. Rather than there being a threatened or actual substantial disruption to the educational processes of the school, the evidence reflects that the assigning of the story was greeted with apathy by most of the students. Only three of plaintiff's students asked to be excused from the assignment. On this question of whether there was a material and substantial threat of disruption, the principal testified at the school board hearing that there was no indication that any of plaintiff's other eighty-seven students were planning to disrupt the normal routine of the school. . . .

A recent First Circuit case lends further support to this court's conclusion. There a high school teacher was suspended for assigning and discussing a magazine article which contained several highly offensive words. The court, finding the article to be well written and thought-provoking, formulated the issues thusly,

> Hence the question in this case is whether a teacher may, for demonstrated educational purposes, quote a "dirty" word currently used in order to give special offense, or whether the shock is too great for high school seniors to stand. If the answer were that the students must be protected from such exposure, we would fear for their future. We do not question the good faith of the defendants in believing that some parents have been offended. With the greatest of respect to such parents, their sensibilities are not the full measure of what is proper education. [10]

Since the defendants have failed to show either that the assignment was inappropriate reading for high school juniors, or that it created a significant disruption to the educational processes of this school, this court concludes that plaintiff's dismissal constituted an unwarranted invasion of her First Amendment right to academic freedom. . . .

With these several basic constitutional principles in mind it inevitably follows that the defendants in this case cannot justify the dismissal of this plaintiff under the guise of insubordination. The facts are clear that plaintiff's "insubordination" was not insubordination in any sense and was not, in reality, a reason for the school board's action. *Dickey v Alabama State Bd of Educ* 273 F Supp 613 (DC Ala 1967).

In accordance with the foregoing, it is the order, judgment and decree of this court that the plaintiff be reinstated as a teacher for the duration of her contract, with the same rights and privileges which attached to her status prior to her illegal suspension.

It is further ordered that plaintiff be paid her regular salary for both the period during which she was suspended and for the remaining period of her contract.

---

10. *Keefe v Geanakos* 418 F2d 359, 361-62 (1st Cir 1969).

It is further ordered that defendants expunge from plaintiff's employment record and transcripts any and all references relating to her suspension and dismissal. . . .

Notes and Questions

1. Appropriate Literature for High School Students

Consider these sample passages from "Welcome to the Monkey House": "The pills were so effective that you could blindfold a man who had taken one, tell him to recite the Gettysburg Address, kick him in the balls while he was doing it, and he wouldn't miss a syllable . . . ." "Virgin hostess, death's recruiter, / Life is cute, but you are cuter. / Mourn my pecker, purple daughter, / All it passed was sky-blue water."

Do you agree with the court's conclusion that such passages are appropriate for high school juniors? Compare *Parker v Board of Educ* 348 F2d 464 (4th Cir 1965). If a parent does not wish his child to be exposed to such literature, why should the teacher not respect that judgment? Are judges, by virtue of their method of selection or their training and experience, better able to determine the appropriateness of such literature than school officials? Than parents?

2. Standard of Review

What standard should courts employ to evaluate the materials a teacher presents to her class? Is the appropriateness formulation simply a restatement of the *Tinker* disruption test? Are "dirty words" disruptive per se? Should a court permit the firing of a teacher for assigning books by Charles Dickens or George Eliot if the students protest the lack of "relevancy" of their novels?

3. Academic Freedom

Judge Johnson relies on the doctrine of academic freedom to justify the result in the *Parducci* case and cites a number of Supreme Court opinions that pay homage to that doctrine. Professor Thomas Emerson describes academic freedom as an elaborate system of principles and procedures, imported in the nineteenth century from German universities:

> The German notions of academic freedom—essentially freedom of the teacher within the university but not outside, and freedom of the student from administrative coercion in the form of a required curriculum—underwent substantial changes as they developed in the United States. The rights claimed as academic freedom in this country during the latter part of the nineteenth century and the early part of the twentieth century involved freedom of the faculty member as teacher and scholar within the university and as a citizen of the outside community.
>
> The heart of the system consists in the right of the faculty member to teach, carry on research, and publish without interference from the government, the community, the university administration, or his fellow faculty members. (T. Emerson, *The System of Freedom of Expression* 593-94 (1970).)

Should the doctrine of academic freedom, traditionally applied to university teachers, be extended to elementary and secondary public school teachers such as

Mrs. Parducci? Is the compulsoriness of schooling relevant here? Is it pertinent that most public school teachers are not as well educated as university professors, do not engage in scholarly research, and most often limit themselves to the transmission of knowledge rather than its discovery? Is the maturity of the students also pertinent?

4. Academic Freedom and the Constitution

Is the doctrine of academic freedom simply the First Amendment by another name? Or does it stand for a range of interests that must be taken into account when the scope of teacher expression in the classroom is to be weighed under the First Amendment? Professor Emerson argues that academic freedom, despite the multitude of judicial encomiums, has never been established as an independent constitutional right. *Freedom of Expression* 610. Should it be so established? Is there any sound basis for affording teachers a greater claim to freedom of speech than other persons? See R. Kirk, *Academic Freedom* 5 (1955). Are teachers the "priests of our democracy"? *Wieman v Updegraff* 344 US 183, 195-96 (1952) (Frankfurter, J, concurring).

5. Limits of Academic Freedom

In order to test the limits of the doctrine of academic freedom, consider what results a court should reach in the following hypothetical situations:

a. A teacher is fired for assigning a poem entitled "Ballad of the Landlord," because it was not in the course of study and because "no poem . . . by any Negro author can be considered permissible if it involves suffering." The school in which the teacher is employed is predominantly Negro, and the teacher argues that the poem is a "good poem" that means a great deal to him and his pupils. See J. Kozol, *Death at an Early Age* 195-203 (1967).

b. A teacher is fired for failing to eliminate noise from the classroom. See *Johns v Jefferson Davis Parish School Bd* 154 So2d 581 (La Ct App 1963).

c. A teacher of trainable mentally handicapped children is dismissed for a number of reasons: her teaching activities are largely limited to baby-sitting instead of the promotion of educational growth, she refuses to follow the recommendations of school psychologists, and she keeps an inadequate record of the behavior of the students. See *Wells v Board of Education* 85 Ill App 2d 312, 230 NE2d 6 (1967).

d. Mrs. Rabbel is a tenured teacher who taught English for 28 years at all-black Wadling High School and two years ago was transferred to Rodney High School, a formerly all-white school, now integrated. Throughout her teaching career it has been Mrs. Rabbel's practice to give 50 percent of her first semester English classes Ds or lower, a practice she has continued at Rodney. There were never any complaints at Wadling, but the uproar from parents, students, and administrators at Rodney is deafening. Mrs. Rabbel defends her practice as a valuable method by which she forces students to work diligently during the second semester. The school administrator objects to the arbitrariness of her rule and points out that she is ultimately harming each student's competitive position vis-à-vis other students. The school board fires Mrs. Rabbel. See *Raney v Board of Trustees* 239 CA2d 256, 48 Cal Rptr 555 (1966); *Barnstable Teachers Ass'n v Barnstable School Comm*, Educators Negotiating Services, case no 1130-0043-68, 2 December 1968 (Fallon, arbitrator).

e. Rosebud High School has been the center of great controversy. Several students published an issue of the *Purple Albatross* using a series of explicit sexual references. They were suspended. The following morning, faculty and students coming to school found a huge sign bearing an "offensive" four letter word on the front lawn. Everyone in school has seen it, and workmen have been called to remove it. The school is buzzing with conversation over its presence. Mr. Post is teaching a mathematics class, but it is clear that the students are supremely uninterested in what he is saying. Post decides to discuss the presence of the sign and the reasons for the controversy. The incident forms the basis for Post's dismissal. Would it affect your response if Mr. Post were a civics teacher?

f. A teacher who was hired to teach "black history" in a black community-controlled public high school in New York City decides to teach a standard American history course to his students. The school board fires him for insubordination.

6. Impact of Academic Freedom Decisions

If academic freedom, however defined, is important to the health of educational institutions, what impact will court decisions such as *Parducci* have on those institutions? Is a successful challenge to the dismissal of a teacher for her exercise of academic freedom likely to encourage other teachers to speak more freely? Does the resistance by school authorities in the courts make it clear to the more timid precisely where the school administration stands and the lengths to which it will go to defend its policies? Or is the school system less likely to fire teachers and bear the costs of litigation when the prospect of winning is small? Is the disapproval of the community, peers, and superiors a potent force against academic freedom notwithstanding the legalities of lawyers and judges? Is it "professional" to seek to change internal school policies through the intercession of outside legal agencies? With respect to the last two questions, consider the following excerpt:

THE POLITICAL LIFE OF AMERICAN TEACHERS
H. Zeigler
130-34 (1967)

[I]t appears that the participants in the educational system—the societal subsystem charged with the duty of transmitting cultural norms—do not look upon the community as a source of severe danger. Contrast this perception with the description of attacks upon the schools by patriotic groups that are said to exert unremitting pressure against the school system. At practically every convention attended by school administrators or other educationists, a panel discussion of pressure groups and the schools is a standard event. Yet to the teachers themselves, so-called pressure groups are a small threat compared to parents, superintendents, school board members, and principals. . . .

The exceedingly repressive perception of administrators can be explained to some extent by the fact that school administrators generally are very cautious, anxious to avoid clashes with the community. They may let it be known to the teaching staff, in a subtle fashion, that the successful teacher is the cautious teacher. The principal is an exception to these generalizations. He ranks very high on the list of potential sanctioning agents, but teachers believe that principals are likely to be relatively mild sanctioners, less severe than other teachers as a matter of fact. Principals sanction on as many or more issues than the other high-ranking sanctioners, but in a very mild fashion. The other sanctioners of high rank are perceived as being considerably more tenacious and severe. Students are perceived to be more vicious in their sanctions than principals.

The teacher perception of the principal that emerges seems to be one of a benevolent authority—the principal will undertake punitive action in the same fashion that a father would discipline a mischievous child. The principal is accepted as the supreme authority in the school, but his basic function is to support, not sanction, the teacher, especially in cases of parental interference. But being an agent of support, the principal has a powerful sanction weapon: refusal to support a teacher in critical situations. His most effective sanction may simply be to do nothing. As the administrative officer for the school, the principal has at his disposal other relatively undramatic but nevertheless quite effective sanctioning techniques. He has the authority to distribute unpleasant extra duties among his teachers. He also controls the use of various equipment and the assigning of rooms. Some rooms have better lights than others; certain equipment never works properly. The principal's control over such trivial affairs can be a very basic resource for sanctions. The following comment, as reported by Becker, illustrates this point. A teacher was asked what might happen if she disobeyed a principal. The teacher replied:

> There were lots of things she could do. She had charge of assigning children to their new rooms when they passed. If she didn't like you she could really make it tough for you. You'd get all the slow children and all the behavior problems, the dregs of the school. After six months of that, you really know what work meant. She had methods like that.

Since the principal controls the day-to-day life of the teacher, the sanctions which he can impose are more annoying than dangerous, but administered in a cumulative manner they can be quite effective.

The principal is not likely to kick up much of a public fuss, but a superintendent lacking recourse to the principal's resources might. Part of the conflict between teachers and administrators is attributable to their differing role perceptions of the proper role of the teacher. Administrators tend to look upon teachers as serving a liaison role between school and community whereas teachers regard themselves as transmitters of basic societal norms to children.

Some conflict between teachers and administrators is inevitable because of the different demands of the position that each occupies, but such conflict is mild compared to the conflict of parents with teachers . . . . Although they both have the interest of the child at heart, the fundamental conflict between parents and teachers occurs because each has a legitimate yet competing claim for the child's obedience. The teacher can lay claim to a special competence built by professional training. The parent has no such competence and, according to the teacher, cannot thoroughly understand the problems of education. Therefore, parents are considered to have no legitimate right to interfere with schoolwork.

Because they do have a legitimate claim for authority over their child, parents are likely to challenge the teacher. The challenge of parents becomes especially crucial because the classroom authority of the teacher is already slipping. Thus, the basic fear that teachers have of parents stems from two sources; first, they resent nonprofessional advice on how to do their jobs; second and more important, they fear that an intrusion by the parents will damage their authority position. The ideal world for the teacher would be a world without parents. . . .

The nonprofessional aspects of the parent-teacher relationship are also present in the perceptions of school board members by teachers. School board members, like parents, are representative of the lay community. Like parents, they are more threatening than either the superintendent or the principal, both of whom symbolize the professional system. The potential control of the lay community might be described as even more illegitimate than that of parents, since it originates more obviously from outsiders. As outsiders, they do not necessarily share the norms of the educational establishment. Lay school boards are less likely to be educationally progressive than are principals or superintendents. Hence, the demand for a return to the three R's could easily originate from a school board, but would probably not originate from professional administrators.

There are almost no reciprocal sanctions that teachers can impose on teachers, school board members, superintendents, or parents. Teachers can sanction their principal, however. Becker points out that if enough teachers request transfers to another school in the system, the attention of higher authorities will focus upon the principal. In some cases, teachers may use their connections in the community to create antagonism toward the principal. None of these possibilities really exists with regard to the school board, superintendent, or the parents. The principal is, in a sense, the weakest of all the sanctioning agents whose positions are superior to that of the teachers. . . .

Colleagues, whose position is one of peer rather than one of subordinate or superordinate are another source of possible sanction for teachers. Presumably, teachers should be expected to cooperate with one another and to defend themselves against attacks from outsiders, whether these outsiders be superintendents or parents. Teachers should be expected to avoid directly endangering one another's authority. Most of these rules of conduct deal with the problem, as expected, of authority. Teachers are not supposed to disagree with one another in front of their pupils, for example. But according to teachers, their colleagues can be rather difficult to get along with. If teachers were to go on strike, or to express personal preferences for a presidential candidate, or to speak in favor of socialism or to allow an atheist to address the class, or take part in racial demonstrations, they believe their colleagues would not only disapprove but would do something about it. Thus, the relative quiescence of teachers is not only imposed upon them from above by the members of the school board and the superintendent, it is also established by means of peer group norms. All groups establish norms and punish deviants. The group norm of teachers, as they describe it, is the avoidance of controversy.

See generally H. Beale, *Are American Teachers Free* (1936).

EPPERSON v ARKANSAS
393 US 97 (1968)

Mr. Justice Fortas delivered the opinion of the court.

I.

This appeal challenges the constitutionality of the "anti-evolution" statute which the state of Arkansas adopted in 1928 to prohibit the teaching in its public schools and universities of the theory that man evolved from other species of life. The statute was a product of the upsurge of "fundamentalist" religious fervor of the twenties. The Arkansas statute was an adaptation of the famous Tennessee "monkey law" which that state adopted in 1925 [Tenn Code Ann § 49-1922, repealed 1967 (Supp 1972)]. The constitutionality of the Tennessee law was upheld by the Tennessee Supreme Court in the celebrated *Scopes* case in 1927.[2]

The Arkansas law makes it unlawful for a teacher in any state-supported school or university "to teach the theory or doctrine that mankind ascended or descended from a lower order of animals," or "to adopt or use in any such institution a textbook that teaches" this theory. Violation is a misdemeanor and subjects the violator to dismissal from his position. . . .

The Chancery Court, in an opinion by Chancellor Murray O. Reed, held that the statute violated the Fourteenth Amendment to the United States Constitution. The court noted that this amendment encompasses the prohibitions upon state interference with freedom of speech and thought which are contained in the First Amendment. Accordingly, it held that the challenged statute is unconstitutional because, in violation of the First Amendment, it "tends to hinder the quest for knowledge, restrict the freedom to learn, and restrain the freedom to teach." In this perspective, the act, it held, was an unconstitutional and void restraint upon the freedom of speech guaranteed by the Constitution.

On appeal, the Supreme Court of Arkansas reversed. Its two-sentence opinion is set forth in the margin.[7] It sustained the statute as an exercise of the state's power to specify the curriculum in public schools. It did not address itself to the competing constitutional considerations. . . .

[T]he law must be stricken because of its conflict with the constitutional prohibition of state laws respecting an establishment of religion or prohibiting the free exercise thereof. The overriding fact is that Arkansas' law selects from the body of knowledge a particular segment which it proscribes for the sole reason that it is deemed to conflict with a particular religious doctrine; that is, with a particular interpretation of the Book of Genesis by a particular religious group. . . .

The earliest cases in this court on the subject of the impact of constitutional guarantees upon the classroom were decided before the court expressly applied the specific prohibitions of the First Amendment to the states. But as early as 1923, the court did not hesitate to condemn under the due process clause "arbitrary"

---

2. *Scopes v Tennessee* 154 Tenn 105, 289 SW 363 (1927). The Tennessee court, however, reversed Scopes' conviction on the ground that the jury and not the judge should have assessed the fine of $100. Since Scopes was no longer in the state's employ, it saw "nothing to be gained by prolonging the life of this bizarre case." It directed that a *nolle prosequi* be entered in the interests of "the peace and dignity of the state." 154 Tenn at 121, 289 SW at 367.

7. "Per Curiam. Upon the principal issue, that of constitutionality, the court holds that Initiated Measure No 1 of 1928, Ark Stat Ann §80-1627 and §80-1628 (Repealed 1960), is a valid exercise of the state's power to specify the curriculum in its public schools. The court expresses no opinion on the question whether the act prohibits any explanation of the theory of evolution or merely prohibits teaching that the theory is true; the answer not being necessary to a decision in the case, and the issue not having been raised.

"The decree is reversed and the cause dismissed.

"Ward, J, concurs. Brown, J, dissents.

"Paul Ward, Justice, concurring. I agree with the first sentence in the majority opinion.

"To my mind, the rest of the opinion beclouds the clear announcement made in the first sentence."

restrictions upon the freedom of teachers to teach and of students to learn. In that year, the court, in an opinion by Justice McReynolds, held unconstitutional an act of the state of Nebraska making it a crime to teach any subject in any language other than English to pupils who had not passed the eighth grade. The state's purpose in enacting the law was to promote civic cohesiveness by encouraging the learning of English and to combat the "baneful effect" of permitting foreigners to rear and educate their children in the language of the parents' native land. The court recognized these purposes, and it acknowledged the state's power to prescribe the school curriculum, but it held that these were not adequate to support the restriction upon the liberty of teacher and pupil. The challenged statute it held, unconstitutionally interfered with the right of the individual, guaranteed by the due process clause, to engage in any of the common occupations of life and to acquire useful knowledge. *Meyer v Nebraska* 262 US 390 (1923). See also *Bartels v Iowa* 262 US 404 (1923).

For purposes of the present case, we need not reenter the difficult terrain which the court, in 1923, traversed without apparent misgivings. We need not take advantage of the broad premise which the court's decision in *Meyer* furnishes, nor need we explore the implications of that decision in terms of the justiciability of the multitude of controversies that beset our campuses today. Today's problem is capable of resolution in the narrower terms of the First Amendment's prohibition of laws respecting an establishment of religion or prohibiting the free exercise thereof. . . .

While the study of religions and of the Bible from a literary and historic viewpoint, presented objectively as part of a secular program of education, need not collide with the First Amendment's prohibition, the state may not adopt programs or practices in its public schools or colleges which "aid or oppose" any religion. *Abington School Dist v Schempp* 374 US 203, 225 (1963). This prohibition is absolute. It forbids alike the preference of a religious doctrine or the prohibition of a theory which is deemed antagonistic to a particular dogma. As Mr. Justice Clark stated in *Joseph Burstyn, Inc v Wilson,* "the state has no legitimate interest in protecting any or all religions from views distasteful to them . . . ." 343 US 495, 505 (1952). The test was stated as follows in *Abington School Dist v Schempp* 374 US at 222, "[W]hat are the purpose and the primary effect of the enactment? If either is the advancement or inhibition of religion then the enactment exceeds the scope of legislative power as circumscribed by the Constitution."

These precedents inevitably determine the result in the present case. The state's undoubted right to prescribe the curriculum for its public schools does not carry with it the right to prohibit, on pain of criminal penalty, the teaching of a scientific theory or doctrine where that prohibition is based upon reasons that violate the First Amendment. It is much too late to argue that the state may impose upon the teachers in its schools any conditions that it chooses, however restrictive they may be of constitutional guarantees. *Keyishian v Board of Regents* 385 US 589, 605-6 (1967).

In the present case, there can be no doubt that Arkansas has sought to prevent its teachers from discussing the theory of evolution because it is contrary to the belief of some that the Book of Genesis must be the exclusive source of doctrine as to the origin of man. No suggestion has been made that Arkansas' law may be justified by considerations of state policy other than the religious views of some of its citizens. It is clear that fundamentalist sectarian conviction was and is the law's reason for existence. . . .

Reversed.

Mr. Justice Black, concurring. . . .

It seems to me that in this situation the statute is too vague for us to strike it down on any ground but that: vagueness. Under this statute as construed by the Arkansas Supreme Court, a teacher cannot know whether he is forbidden to mention Darwin's theory at all or only free to discuss it as long as he refrains from contending that it is true. It is an established rule that a statute which leaves an ordinary man so doubtful about its meaning that he cannot know when he has violated it denies him the first essential of due process. See, e.g., *Connally v General Constr Co* 269 US 385, 391 (1926). Holding the statute too vague to enforce would not only follow long-standing constitutional precedents but it would avoid having this court take unto itself the duty of a state's highest court to interpret and mark the boundaries of the state's laws. And, more important, it would not place this court in the unenviable position of violating the principle of leaving the states absolutely free to choose their own curriculums for their own schools so long as their action does not palpably conflict with a clear constitutional command. . . .

A second question that arises for me is whether this court's decision forbidding a state to exclude the subject of evolution from its schools infringes the religious freedom of those who consider evolution an antireligious doctrine. If the theory is considered antireligious, as the court indicates, how can the state be bound by the federal Constitution to permit its teachers to advocate such an "antireligious" doctrine to schoolchildren? The very cases cited by the court as supporting its conclusion hold that the state must be neutral, not favoring one religious or antireligious view over another. The Darwinian theory is said to challenge the Bible's story of creation; so too have some of those who believe in the Bible, along with many others, challenged the Darwinian theory. Since there is no indication that the literal Biblical doctrine of the origin of man is included in the curriculum of Arkansas schools, does not the removal of the subject of evolution leave the state in a neutral position toward these supposedly competing religious and antireligious doctrines? Unless this court is prepared simply to write off as pure nonsense the views of those who consider evolution an antireligious doctrine, then this issue presents problems under the establishment clause far more troublesome than are discussed in the court's opinion.

I am also not ready to hold that a person hired to teach school children takes with him into the classroom a constitutional right to teach sociological, economic, political, or religious subjects that the school's managers do not want discussed. This court has said that the rights of free speech "while fundamental in our democratic society, still do not mean that everyone with opinions or beliefs to express may address a group at any public place and at any time." *Cox v Louisiana* 379 US 536, 554; *Cox v Louisiana* 379 US 559, 574. I question whether it is absolutely certain, as the court's opinion indicates, that "academic freedom" permits a teacher to breach his contractual agreement to teach only the subjects designated by the school authorities who hired him.

Certainly the Darwinian theory, precisely like the Genesis story of the creation of man, is not above challenge. In fact the Darwinian theory has not merely been criticized by religionists but by scientists, and perhaps no scientist would be willing to take an oath and swear that everything announced in the Darwinian theory is unquestionably true. The court, it seems to me, makes a serious mistake in bypassing the plain, unconstitutional vagueness of this statute in order to reach out and decide this troublesome, to me, First Amendment question. However wise this court may be or may become hereafter, it is doubtful that, sitting in Washington, it can successfully supervise and censor the curriculum of every public school in every hamlet and city in the United States. I doubt that our wisdom is so nearly infallible.

. . . .

[Mr. Justice Harlan's concurring opinion is omitted.]

Mr. Justice Stewart, concurring in the result.

The states are most assuredly free "to choose their own curriculums for their own schools." A state is entirely free, for example, to decide that the only foreign language to be taught in its public school system shall be Spanish. But would a state be constitutionally free to punish a teacher for letting his students know that other languages are also spoken in the world? I think not.

It is one thing for a state to determine that "the subject of higher mathematics, or astronomy, or biology" shall or shall not be included in its public school curriculum. It is quite another thing for a state to make it a criminal offense for a public school teacher so much as to mention the very existence of an entire system of respected human thought. That kind of criminal law, I think, would clearly impinge upon the guarantees of free communication contained in the First Amendment, and made applicable to the states by the Fourteenth. . . .

Notes and Questions

1. Constitutional Standard: Religious Motivation

How does the majority reach the conclusion that the Arkansas "Monkey Law" is unconstitutional? Does the court rely on the religious motivation of the Arkansas legislature? How does the court determine motive? Why is it relevant? See generally, Ely, "Legislative and Administrative Motivation in Constitutional Law," 79 *Yale LJ* 1205 (1970). Is motive decisive in determining whether a law is in "aid of or in opposition" to religion? Is the impact of the "Monkey Law" "proreligion"? Is the teaching of evolution "antireligion"? Does not nearly every aspect of schooling have a favorable or unfavorable impact on some religion? Would you accept the argument that Saturday and Sunday school holidays are favorable to Jews and Christians? Is it the nature of the debate over the policy issue in question that determines its constitutionality?

2. Constitutional Standard: Free Speech

Should the majority have rested its decision on "freedom of speech and thought" as the chancery court did? If so, how do you answer Justice Black? Consider Professor Van Alstyne's response to the Black concurrence:

THE CONSTITUTIONAL RIGHTS OF TEACHERS AND PROFESSORS
1970 *Duke LJ* 841, 855

The difficulty, however, is not stated with complete fairness when presented in such broad dilemmatic terms. One may readily concede that the contending preferences of teacher, students, parents, and the members of an elected board of education must necessarily be distilled into overall curricular decisions by some group with ultimate responsibility; among these groups, authority to make such decisions logically devolves upon the more democratically accountable board or, as a general recourse, upon the legislature. They, at least, are subject to the orderly and formal check of the electoral process, the informal influences of various groups including PTAs, student organizations, professional education associations and teacher unions, and the admonitions of the federal Constitution such as the establishment clause of the First Amendment. Moreover, the school classroom and, albeit to a distinctly lesser extent, the university classroom are not at all free and voluntary forums in which the remunerated teacher may appropriately assert the same full measure of his own freedom of speech available to him as a citizen in private life. Students compelled by law to attend classes constitute a wholly captive audience neither free to depart if offended by, or in disagreement with, the teacher's utterances nor free even genuinely to offer dissenting views against the presumed authority of the teacher, armed with his command of sanctions over classroom decorum, the awarding of grades, and the dispensing of personal recommendations. The teacher receives a salary for his hired service; he is employed for a specific task; and he is insulated within his classroom even from the immediate competition of differing views held by others equally steeped in the same academic discipline. Indeed, the use of his classroom by a teacher or a professor deliberately to proselytize for a personal cause or knowingly to emphasize only that selection of data best conforming to his own personal biases is far beyond the license granted by the freedom of speech and furnishes precisely the just occasion to question his fitness to teach.

If these considerations are sufficient to forbid the teacher to impose his own orthodoxy upon his students, however, they apply with equal force when the prescription for biased treatment of a given subject or the mandate to use the classroom as an instrument of ideological proselytism is fashioned by a legislature or a school board instead—a legislature or school board that so rigidly determines the exact and preselected details of each course that in fact it employs the teacher as a mere mechanical instrument of its impermissible design. For instance, it may be relatively unimportant that Commager's high school text on American history is uniformly purchased in bulk and prescribed as the basic text in high school civics in lieu of a text by Jones or Smith unless its particular selection *plus* detailed proscriptions of any classroom reference to other texts, other impressions, and other historical ideas cumulatively combined to describe a process of unfree education and academic indoctrination. Indeed, arbitrary restrictions on alternative sources of information or opinion, resulting not from understandable budgetary constraints or the restraints upon the time available for study by teachers and students, are precisely what the First Amendment disallows. Against a school board decree requiring the inculcation of one theory and forbidding mention or examination of another, for instance, a mere taxpayer should have standing to contest his compelled financial support for the propagation of ideas to which he is opposed: "[I] can think of few plainer, more direct abridgments of the freedoms of the First Amendment than to compel persons to support . . . ideologies or causes that they are against." Against a state law provision that a student might be disciplined for consulting any source of education save that prescribed in regimented detail, the student could also succeed on a First Amendment claim. "In our system students may not be regarded as the closed-circuit recipients of only that which the state chooses to communicate." Correspondingly, neither must teachers or professors endure similar arbitrary restrictions in the course of their own inquiries or *upon their own communicated classroom references*. One may not, as a condition of his employment, be made an implement of governmental practices which are themselves violative of the First Amendment. Accordingly, a teacher violating a statutory restriction forbidding reference to, or consideration of, a source of opinion or information otherwise within the proper compass of his subject should be as much shielded by the First Amendment from prosecution or dismissal as a social worker refusing to conduct a midnight search forbidden to the state by the Fourth Amendment. Concurring in *Epperson,* Mr. Justice Stewart more nearly recognized the presence of important First Amendment issues beyond the valid but limited reach of the religious establishment clause:

> It is one thing for a state to determine that "the subject of higher mathematics, or astronomy, or biology" shall or shall not be included in its public school curriculum. It is quite another thing for a state to make it a criminal offense for a public school teacher so much as to mention the very existence of an entire system of respected human thought. That kind of criminal law, I think, would clearly impinge upon the guarantees of free communication contained in the First Amendment . . . . (*Epperson v Arkansas* 393 US 97, 116 (1968).)

3. Applying the Van Alstyne Standard

A high school teacher made the following assignment to his class for oral and written discussion of Shakespeare's *Romeo and Juliet*:

Some Interpretations of Romeo and Juliet
1. Story of a feud between two families
2. Conquest of love over hate or conquest of hate over love
3. Destruction of love by a cruel society
4. Rise, decline, and fall of Romeo's sex drive
5. Moderation (nothing in excess) as a principle in guiding one's life
6. Romeo's rise to maturity
7. Juliet as an innocent nymph
8. Juliet as a sexpot

A school board member's daughter showed the assignment to her father, who took it to a meeting of the school board that same night. After circulation of the sheet, the board asked the superintendent to investigate. The next day the superintendent called the teacher out of his class and told him, "I have had enough of you. You can either leave quietly or make a fuss about it, but you are going to leave." The teacher was then fired. How do you assess the constitutionality of the dismissal in light of Professor Van Alstyne's remarks quoted in note 2? See also *Dunham v Crosby* 435 F2d 1177 (1st Cir 1970).

III. Teacher Freedom outside the Classroom

Mr. Justice Burton, speaking for the Supreme Court in *Beilan v Board of Educ* 357 US 399, 406 (1958) said: "We find no requirement in the federal Constitution that a teacher's classroom conduct be the sole basis for determining his fitness. Fitness for teaching depends on a broad range of factors." If most teachers and courts find some restriction and regulation of teacher classroom conduct tolerable in mutual pursuit of educational excellence, how far should the teacher's out-of-school conduct be subordinated to the will of the school? To what extent is a teacher's behavior away from the school building relevant to her performance in class? To what extent is it relevant to her working relationships with administrators and other teachers? This section explores the limits of schools' attempts to censure, limit, or supervise such behavior. See generally H. Beale, *Are American Teachers Free?* (1936).

KAY v BOARD OF HIGHER EDUCATION
173 Misc 943, 18 NYS2d 821 (Sup Ct 1940)

McGeehan, Justice.

In this application . . . , the petitioner seeks to review the action of the board of higher education in appointing Bertrand Russell to the chair of philosophy at City College. Petitioner contends that the action of the board of higher education was illegal and an abuse of such powers as the board of higher education had in making such appointments, because (a) Bertrand Russell was not a citizen and had not declared his intention to become a citizen; (b) the appointment did not comply with Article V, section 6, of the Constitution of the State of New York with reference to appointments in civil service on the basis of merit and fitness; and, finally, (c) because the appointment was against public policy because of the teachings of Bertrand Russell and his immoral character . . . .

Petitioner contends, in the first place, that section 550 of the Education Law requires that, "No person shall be employed or authorized to teach in the public schools of the state who is: . . . . not a citizen. The provisions of this subdivision shall not apply, however, to an alien teacher now or hereafter employed, provided such teacher shall make due application to become a citizen and thereafter within the time prescribed by law shall become a citizen." It is conceded that Bertrand Russell is not a citizen and that he has not applied to become a citizen. . . .

The section applies generally to "teachers and pupils" and is not limited to elementary and secondary schools, and the court therefore holds that Bertrand Russell is not qualified to teach by reason of the provisions of this section, but the decision herein made is not based solely upon this ground.

The second contention of the petitioner is that no examination of any kind was given to Bertrand Russell at the time of his appointment, and this is borne out by the minutes of the administrative committee of the City College of the City of New York and of the board of higher education at the time of his appointment. . . .

While it is not necessary for this court to adjudicate the action of the board of higher education in proceeding by assuming that a competitive examination for the position of professor of philosophy in City College was impracticable, such assumption on the part of the board of higher education is held to be unwarranted, arbitrary and capricious and in direct violation of the plain mandate of the Constitution of the State of New York. If there were only one person in the world who knew anything about philosophy and mathematics and that person was Mr. Russell, the taxpayers might be asked to employ him without examination, but it is hard to believe, considering the vast sums of money that have been spent on American education, that there is no one available, even in America, who is a credit both to learning and to public life. Other universities and colleges, both public and private, seem to be able to find American citizens to employ and to say that the College of the City of New York could not employ a professor of philosophy by an examination of some sort, is an assumption by the board of higher education of the power which was denied to them by the people of the state of New York in the constitution and no legislature and no board can violate this mandate.

The foregoing reasons would be sufficient to sustain the petition and to grant the relief prayed for but there is a third ground on which the petitioner rests and which, to the court, seems most compelling. The petitioner contends that the appointment of Bertrand Russell has violated the public policy of the state and of the nation because of the notorious immoral and salacious teachings of Bertrand Russell and because the petitioner contends he is a man not of good moral character.

It has been argued that the private life and writings of Mr. Russell have nothing whatsoever to do with his appointment as a teacher of philosophy. It has also been argued that he is going to teach mathematics. His appointment, however, is to the Department of Philosophy in City College . . . .

The contention of the petitioner that Mr. Russell has taught in his books immoral and salacious doctrines, is amply sustained by the books conceded to be the writings of Bertrand Russell, which were offered in evidence. It is not necessary to detail here the filth which is contained in the books. It is sufficient to record the following: from *Education and the Modern World,* pages 119 and 120: "I am sure that university life would be better, both intellectually and morally, if most university students had temporary childless marriages. This would afford a solution of the sexual urge neither restless nor surreptitious, neither mercenary nor casual, and of such a nature that it need not take up time which ought to be given to work." From *Marriage and Morals,* pages 165 and 166:

> For my part, while I am quite convinced that companionate marriage would be a step in the right direction, and would do a great deal of good, I do not think that it goes far enough. I think that all sex relations which do not involve children should be regarded as a purely private affair, and that if a man and a woman choose to live together without having children, that should be no one's business but their own. I should not hold it desirable that either a man or a woman should enter upon the serious business of a marriage intended to lead to children without having had previous sexual experience. . . .

It is contended that Bertrand Russell is extraordinary. That makes him the more dangerous. The philosophy of Mr. Russell and his conduct in the past is in direct conflict and in violation of the Penal Law of the state of New York. When we consider how susceptible the human mind is to the ideas and philosophy of teaching professors, it is apparent that the board of higher education either disregarded the probable consequences of their acts or were more concerned with advocating a cause that appeared to them to present a challenge to so-called "academic freedom" without according suitable consideration of the other aspects of the problem before them. While this court would not interfere with any action of the board insofar as a pure question of "valid" academic freedom is concerned, it will not tolerate academic freedom being used as a cloak to promote the popularization in the minds of adolescents of acts forbidden by the Penal Law. This appointment affects the public health, safety and morals of the community and it is the duty of the court to act. Academic freedom does not mean academic license. It is the freedom to do good and not to teach evil . . . .

The appointment of Dr. Russell is an insult to the people of the city of New York and to the thousands of teachers who were obligated upon their appointment to establish good moral character and to maintain it in order to keep their positions. Considering the instances in which immorality alone has been held to be sufficient basis for removal of a teacher and mindful of the aphorism "As a man thinketh in his heart, so he is," the court holds that the acts of the Board of Higher Education of the City of New York in appointing Dr. Russell to the Department of Philosophy of the City College of the City of New York, to be paid by public funds, is in effect establishing a chair of indecency and in doing so has acted arbitrarily, capriciously, and in direct violation of the public health, safety and morals of the people and of the petitioner's rights herein, and the petitioner is entitled to an order revoking the appointment of the said Bertrand Russell and discharging him from his said position, and denying to him the rights and privileges and the powers appertaining to his appointment. . . .

Notes and Questions

1. Relevance of Beliefs to Teaching Fitness

Consider the following comment on the Russell cause célèbre:

At one end [Judge McGeehan] sets down passages from *What I Believe* and *Education and the Modern World.* . . . At the other he places provisions of the criminal code . . . which outlaw "abduction" and "rape." Then he undertakes to span the yawning gulf with a dialectical bridge. . . . The statutes which outlaw rape and abduction seek to protect chaste females under eighteen. As report has it there are at City College no chaste females, over eighteen years of age or under; even worse, there are no females at all. . . . It is unfortunate that the argument peters out at this point that the judge does not strip naked the process of corruption by which the teacher's mind corrodes the morals of his pupils. It is however, not impossible to supply the links essential to the unbroken chain. The student body at City College consists of males, chaste or unchaste, some of them over eighteen, with morals poised so delicately that, if Bertrand Russell expounds mathematics or philosophy, they are impelled to abduct and rape, while if he does not appear in their midst, woman's virtue knows no peril. In the modern world such an Eden of innocence as City College is too precious to allow the serpent to intrude. (W. Hamilton, "Trial by Ordeal, New Style," 46 *Yale LJ* 670, 778, 784 (1941).)

How would you respond to Professor Hamilton's criticism of Judge McGeehan's opinion? Is it irrational to perceive some connection between a man's views and his likely actions? Might students become aware of Russell's concept of morality even if it is not expressed openly in the mathematics class?

2. Scholarship and Teaching Fitness

What significance do you attach to the fact that Russell's ideas were expressed in scholarly books? Does this pose issues of academic freedom that might not be applicable in other settings? Compare *Pickering v Board of Educ* 391 US 563 (1968). Is *Kay* consistent with *Parducci*? Should courts distinguish between the failure to employ a teacher and the dismissal of a teacher after she has been employed? If the board of higher education denied Russell his appointment on the ground that his writings were mediocre, would this raise a constitutional issue?

3. Standing to Challenge Teaching Appointment

Is it wise to allow any member of the community to challenge the credentials of an appointee to a teaching position in a public institution? One commentator noted that *Kay* "appears to be the first reported American decision which treats the qualifications of an appointed teacher as presenting an issue justiciable at the insistence of any citizen." Note, "The Bertrand Russell Case: The History of a Litigation," 53 *Harv L Rev* 1192 (1940). See also Note, 8 *U Chi L Rev* 316 (1941). What alternatives to a court challenge are available to a citizen who objects to a particular teaching appointment? If these alternatives are essentially political in nature, should the courts seek to intervene in that process?

PICKERING v BOARD OF EDUCATION
391 US 563 (1968)

Mr. Justice Marshall delivered the opinion of the court.

Appellant Marvin L. Pickering, a teacher in Township High School District 205, Will County, Illinois, was dismissed from his position by the appellee board of education for sending a letter to a local newspaper in connection with a recently proposed tax increase that was critical of the way in which the board and the district superintendent of schools had handled past proposals to raise new revenue for the schools. Appellant's dismissal resulted from a determination by the board, after a full hearing, that the publication of the letter was "detrimental to the efficient operation and administration of the schools of the district" and hence, under the relevant Illinois statute, Ill Rev Stat c 122, §10-22.4 (1963), that "interests of the schools require[d] [his dismissal]." . . .

In May of 1964 a proposed increase in the tax rate to be used for educational purposes was submitted to the voters by the board and was defeated. Finally, on September 19, 1964, a second proposal to increase the tax rate was submitted by the board and was likewise defeated. It was in connection with this last proposal of the school board that appellant wrote the letter to the editor . . . that resulted in his dismissal.

Prior to the vote on the second tax increase proposal a variety of articles attributed to the District 205 teachers' organization appeared in the local paper. These articles urged passage of the tax increase and stated that failure to pass the increase would result in a decline in the quality of education afforded children in the district's schools. A letter from the superintendent of schools making the same point was published in the paper two days before the election and submitted to the voters in mimeographed form the following day. It was in response to the foregoing material, together with the failure of the tax increase to pass, that appellant submitted the letter in question to the editor of the local paper.

The letter constituted, basically, an attack on the school board's handling of the 1961 bond issue proposals and its subsequent allocation of financial resources between the schools' educational and athletic programs. It also charged the super-intendent of schools with attempting to prevent teachers in the district from op-posing or criticizing the proposed bond issue.

The board dismissed Pickering for writing and publishing the letter. Pursuant to Illinois law, the board was then required to hold a hearing on the dismissal. At the hearing the board charged that numerous statements in the letter were false and that the publication of the statements unjustifiably impugned the "motives, hon-esty, integrity, truthfulness, responsibility and competence" of both the board and the school administration. The board also charged that the false statements dam-aged the professional reputations of its members and of the school administrators, would be disruptive of faculty discipline, and would tend to foment "controversy, conflict, and dissension" among teachers, administrators, the board of education, and the residents of the district . . . .

The Illinois courts reviewed the proceedings solely to determine whether the board's findings were supported by substantial evidence and whether, on the facts as found, the board could reasonably conclude that appellant's publication of the letter was "detrimental to the best interests of the schools." Pickering's claim that his letter was protected by the First Amendment was rejected on the ground that his acceptance of a teaching position in the public schools obliged him to refrain from making statements about the operation of the schools "which in the absence of such position he would have an undoubted right to engage in.". . .

To the extent that the Illinois Supreme Court's opinion may be read to suggest that teachers may constitutionally be compelled to relinquish the First Amendment rights they would otherwise enjoy as citizens to comment on matters of public interest in connection with the operation of the public schools in which they work, it proceeds on the premise that has been unequivocally rejected in numerous prior decisions of this court. E.g., *Wieman v Updegraff* 344 US 183 (1952); *Shelton v Tucker* 364 US 479 (1960); *Keyishian v Board of Regents* 385 US 589 (1967). "[T] he theory that public employment which may be denied altogether may be subjected to any conditions, regardless of how unreasonable, has been uniformly rejected." *Keyishian v Board of Regents, supra,* at 605-606. At the same time it cannot be gainsaid that the state has interests as an employer in regulating the speech of its employees that differ significantly from those it possesses in connec-tion with regulation of the speech of the citizenry in general. The problem in any case is to arrive at a balance between the interests of the teacher, as a citizen, in commenting upon matters of public concern and the interest of the state, as an employer, in promoting the efficiency of the public services it performs through its employees.

The board contends that "the teacher by virtue of his public employment has a duty of loyalty to support his superiors in attaining the generally accepted goals of education and that, if he must speak out publicly, he should do so factually and accurately, commensurate with his education and experience." Appellant, on the other hand, argues that the test applicable to defamatory statements directed against public officials by persons having no occupational relationship with them, namely, that statements to be legally actionable must be made "with knowledge that [they were] . . . false or with reckless disregard of whether [they were] . . . false or not" (*New York Times Co v Sullivan* 376 US 254, 280 (1964)), should also be applied to public statements made by teachers. . . .

An examination of the statements in appellant's letter objected to by the board reveals that they, like the letter as a whole, consist essentially of criticism of the board's allocation of school funds between educational and athletic programs, and of both the board's and the superintendent's methods of informing, or preventing the informing of, the district's taxpayers of the real reasons why additional tax revenues were being sought for the schools. The statements are in no way directed toward any person with whom appellant would normally be in contact in the course of his daily work as a teacher. Thus no question of maintaining either discipline by immediate superiors or harmony among coworkers is presented here. Appellant's employment relationships with the board and, to a somewhat lesser extent, with the superintendent are not the kind of close working relationships for which it can persuasively be claimed that personal loyalty and confidence are necessary to their proper functioning. Accordingly, to the extent that the board's position here can be taken to suggest that even comments on matters of public concern that are substantially correct, . . . may furnish grounds for dismissal if they are sufficiently critical in tone, we unequivocally reject it.[3]

We next consider the statements in appellant's letter which we agree to be false. The board's original charges included allegations that the publication of the letter damaged the professional reputations of the board and the superintendent and would foment controversy and conflict among the board, teachers, administrators, and the residents of the district. However, no evidence to support these allegations was introduced at the hearing. So far as the record reveals, Pickering's letter was greeted by everyone but its main target, the board, with massive apathy and total disbelief. The board must, therefore, have decided, perhaps by analogy with the law of libel, that the statements were per se harmful to the operation of the schools.

However, the only way in which the board could conclude, absent any evidence of the actual effect of the letter, that the statements contained therein were per se detrimental to the interest of the schools was to equate the board members' own interests with that of the schools. Certainly an accusation that too much money is being spent on athletics by the administrators of the school system . . . cannot reasonably be regarded as per se detrimental to the district schools . . . .

In addition, the fact that particular illustrations of the board's claimed undesirable emphasis on athletic programs are false would not normally have any necessary impact on the actual operation of the schools, beyond its tendency to anger the board. For example, Pickering's letter was written after the defeat at the polls of the second proposed tax increase. It could, therefore, have had no effect on the ability of the school district to raise necessary revenue, since there was no showing that there was any proposal to increase taxes pending when the letter was written.

More importantly, the question whether a school system requires additional funds is a matter of legitimate public concern on which the judgment of the school

---

3. It is possible to conceive of some positions in public employment in which the need for confidentiality is so great that even completely correct public statements might furnish a permissible ground for dismissal. Likewise, positions in public employment in which the relationship between superior and subordinate is of such a personal and intimate nature that certain forms of public criticism of the superior by the subordinate would seriously undermine the effectiveness of the working relationship between them can also be imagined. We intimate no views as to how we would resolve any specific instances of such situations, but merely note that significantly different considerations would be involved in such cases.

administration, including the school board, cannot, in a society that leaves such questions to popular vote, be taken as conclusive. On such a question free and open debate is vital to informed decision making by the electorate. Teachers are, as a class, the members of a community most likely to have informed and definite opinions as to how funds allotted to the operation of the schools should be spent. Accordingly, it is essential that they be able to speak out freely on such questions without fear of retaliatory dismissal.

In addition, the amounts expended on athletics which Pickering reported erroneously were matters of public record on which his position as a teacher in the district did not qualify him to speak with any greater authority than any other taxpayer. The board could easily have rebutted appellant's errors by publishing the accurate figures itself, either via a letter to the same newspaper or otherwise. We are thus not presented with a situation in which a teacher has carelessly made false statements about matters so closely related to the day-to-day operations of the schools that any harmful impact on the public would be difficult to counter because of the teacher's presumed greater access to the real facts. Accordingly, we have no occasion to consider at this time whether under such circumstances a school board could reasonably require that a teacher make substantial efforts to verify the accuracy of his charges before publishing them.[4]

What we do have before us is a case in which a teacher has made erroneous public statements upon issues then currently the subject of public attention, which are critical of his ultimate employer but which are neither shown nor can be presumed to have in any way either impeded the teacher's proper performance of his daily duties in the classroom[5] or to have interfered with the regular operation of the schools generally. In these circumstances we conclude that the interest of the school administration in limiting teachers' opportunities to contribute to public debate is not significantly greater than its interest in limiting a similar contribution by any member of the general public. . . .

In sum, we hold that, in a case such as this, absent proof or false statements knowingly or recklessly made by him,[6] a teacher's exercise of his right to speak on issues of public importance may not furnish the basis for his dismissal from public employment. Since no such showing has been made in this case regarding appellant's letter . . . his dismissal for writing it cannot be upheld and the judgment of the Illinois Supreme Court must, accordingly, be reversed and the case remanded for further proceedings not inconsistent with this opinion. . . .

Mr. Justice White, concurring in part and dissenting in part.

The court holds that truthful statements by a school teacher critical of the school board are within the ambit of the First Amendment. So also are false

4. There is likewise no occasion furnished by this case for consideration of the extent to which teachers can be required by narrowly drawn grievance procedures to submit complaints about the operation of the schools to their superiors for action thereon prior to bringing the complaints before the public.

5. We also note that this case does not present a situation in which a teacher's public statements are so without foundation as to call into question his fitness to perform his duties in the classroom. In such a case, of course, the statements would merely be evidence of the teacher's general competence, or lack thereof, and not an independent basis for dismissal.

6. Because we conclude that appellant's statements were not knowingly or recklessly false, we have no occasion to pass upon the additional question whether a statement that was knowingly or recklessly false would if it were neither shown nor could reasonably be presumed to have had any harmful effects, still be protected by the First Amendment. See also n5, *supra*.

statements innocently or negligently made. The state may not fire the teacher for making either unless, as I gather it, there are special circumstances, not present in this case, demonstrating an overriding state interest, such as the need for confidentiality or the special obligations which a teacher in a particular position may owe to his superiors.[1]

The core of today's decision is the holding that Pickering's discharge must be tested by the standard of *New York Times Co v Sullivan* 376 US 254 (1964). To this extent I am in agreement.

The court goes on, however, to reopen a question I had thought settled by *New York Times* and the cases that followed it, particularly *Garrison v Louisiana* 379 US 64 (1964). The court devotes several pages to reexamining the facts in order to reject the determination below that Pickering's statements harmed the school system, *ante,* at 570-73, when the question of harm is clearly irrelevant given the court's determination that Pickering's statements were neither knowingly nor recklessly false and its ruling that in such circumstances a teacher may not be fired even if the statements are injurious. The court then gratuitously suggests that when statements are found to be knowingly or recklessly false, it is an open question whether the First Amendment still protects them unless they are shown or can be presumed to have caused harm. *Ante,* at 574, n6. Deliberate or reckless falsehoods serve no First Amendment ends and deserve no protection under that amendment. The court unequivocally recognized this in *Garrison,* where after reargument the court said that "the knowingly false statement and the false statement made with reckless disregard of the truth, do not enjoy constitutional protection." 379 US at 75. The court today neither explains nor justifies its withdrawal from the firm stand taken in *Garrison.* As I see it, a teacher may be fired without violation of the First Amendment for knowingly or recklessly making false statements regardless of their harmful impact on the schools. As the court holds, however, in the absence of special circumstances he may not be fired if his statements were true or only negligently false, even if there is some harm to the school system. . . .

Nor can I join the court in its findings with regard to whether Pickering knowingly or recklessly published false statements. Neither the state in presenting its evidence nor the state tribunals in arriving at their findings and conclusions of law addressed themselves to the elements of the new standard which the court holds the First Amendment to require in the circumstances of this case. Indeed, the state courts expressly rejected the applicability of both *New York Times* and *Garrison.* I find it wholly unsatisfactory for this court to make the initial determination of knowing or reckless falsehood from the cold record now before us. It would be far more appropriate to remand this case to the state courts for further proceedings in light of the constitutional standard which the court deems applicable to this case, once the relevant facts have been ascertained in appropriate proceedings.

---

1. See *ante,* at 569-570, 572 and nn3, 4. The court does not elaborate upon its suggestion that there may be situations in which, with reference to certain areas of public comment, a teacher may have special obligations to his superiors. It simply holds that in this case, with respect to the particular public comment made by Pickering, he is more like a member of the general public and, apparently, too remote from the school board to require placing him into any special category. Further, as I read the court's opinion, it does not foreclose the possibility that under the First Amendment a school system may have an enforceable rule, applicable to teachers, that public statements about school business must first be submitted to the authorities to check for accuracy.

Notes and Questions

1. Duty of Loyalty

Is there any merit to the school board's contention that teachers have a duty of loyalty to their superiors? If so, has not the court saddled already burdened administrators with an additional source of conflict and controversy? Is there a conflict between the just resolution of Mr. Pickering's case and the creation of wise and workable public policy with respect to teacher speech?

2. Types of Teacher Speech

Consider the following classifications of teacher speech outside of the school:

a. True statements that do not disrupt the educational process

b. True statements that disrupt the educational process

c. False statements that are negligently made without malice and do not disrupt the educational process

d. False statements that are negligently made without malice and do disrupt the educational process

e. False statements that are knowingly and maliciously made and do not disrupt the educational process

f. False statements that are knowingly and maliciously made and do disturb the educational process.

Which categories of speech would the majority protect? Which categories would Mr. Justice White protect? Does it make any sense to test the right to speak by the speaker's state of mind at the time of his utterance? How does a court determine whether a person was reckless or malicious? Is not the impact of the speech more critical? Can the speaker's motivation be determined, at least in part, by his impact? *Tinker* was decided after *Pickering*. In a subsequent case raising *Pickering* issues should the Supreme Court abandon the *Pickering* formulations in favor of a *Tinker* disruption standard? Can speech outside the school ever be disruptive of the educational process? Under what circumstances? Is there a difference between "disruption" as the term is used in *Tinker* and interference with a "working relationship"?

3. Disruptive Teacher Speech

Assume that disruption as defined by *Tinker* is the appropriate standard for testing the constitutionality of teacher speech outside the school. How would you decide the following hypothetical cases?

a. The facts are the same as *Pickering,* except that the letter was written before the defeat of the second proposed tax increase, and school board members testified that, in their opinion, the letter contributed to the defeat of the proposal.

b. The facts are the same as *Pickering,* except that Mr. Pickering is director of the athletic program.

c. The facts are the same as *Pickering,* except that Mr. Pickering is assistant superintendent for academic affairs.

d. The facts are the same as *Pickering,* except that Mr. Pickering, at a public meeting, accused the superintendent of being a liar. See *Jones v Battles* 315 F Supp 601 (D Conn 1970).

e. Mr. Renough is a tenured black teacher at Oakville High School. Integration of Oakville has led to a heightening of racial tensions. The principal of Oakville, Mr. Smyth, is known to be hostile to the demands for more black faculty members. He has particular difficulty dealing with Mr. Renough, who is an effective advocate for increased black participation in the administrative and instructional process. The philosophical disagreement between Renough and Smyth is exacerbated as racial tensions rise. Smyth finally fires Renough, claiming that they simply cannot get along: all work, supervision, and contact between the two is impossible. Renough argues that he has been fired for speaking out on educational policy issues. Smyth admits that the conflict between the two men is philosophical but asserts that it is unabridgeable, "one or the other must go." Renough files suit for reinstatement. See *Roberts v Lake Central School Corp* 317 F Supp 63 (ND Ind 1970); La Stat Ann §17: 443 (1963).

f. A teacher is fired who played an instrumental role in attempting to have the school superintendent dismissed. See *Watts v Seward School Bd* 395 P2d 372 (Alas 1964), vacated 381 US 126 (1965), on remand 421 P2d 586 (Alas 1966), rehearing denied 423 P2d 678 (Alas 1967), vacated 391 US 592 (1968), on remand, 454 P2d 732 (Alas 1969).

g. The facts are the same as *Pickering* except Mr. Pickering is not discharged but is transferred to a less desirable vocational school. Compare *Springston v King* 340 F Supp 314 (WD Va 1972).

4. Impact of *Pickering*

Is it likely that *Pickering* will have a significant impact on school operations? How would you advise a school board to handle those whom it regarded as trouble-makers? Should it be as forthright in giving reasons for the firing as the school board in *Pickering*? Could not the board muster a stronger case for disruption? What if the teacher's record is already blemished by lateness, failure to attend PTA meetings, failure to stand in the doorway when classes are changing, or other violations of school rules? See *Johnson v Branch* 364 F2d 177 (4th Cir 1966). Should teachers with good records be afforded wider latitude in criticizing school policies than other teachers? Would a teacher critical of school policies be likely to retain his unblemished record? Does the complexity of determining the real reasons for discharge argue against judicial intervention or for an equally complex judicial review procedure?

5. Insubordination

Insubordination is the first cousin of disruption of the professional relationship between teachers and administrators:

A board of education is entrusted with the conduct of the schools under its jurisdiction, their standards of education, and the moral, mental, and physical welfare of the pupils during school hours. An important part of the education of any child is the instilling of a proper respect for authority and obedience to necessary discipline. Lessons are learned from example as well as from precept. The example of a teacher who is continually insubordinate and who refuses to recognize constituted authority may seriously affect the discipline in a school, impair its efficiency, and teach children lessons they should not learn. Such conduct may unfit a teacher for service in a school even though her other qualifications may be sufficient. *Johnson v Taft School Dist* 19 CA2d 405, 408, 65 P2d 912, 913 (1937).

Do you find this argument persuasive? If so, does *Pickering* afford realistic protection for teachers? See *Reed v Board of Educ* 333 F Supp 816 (ED Mo 1971), *rev'd*, 460 F2d 824 (8th Cir 1972); *Calvin v Rupp* 334 F Supp 358 (ED Mo 1970). But see *Puentes v Board of Educ of Union Free School Dist #21* 24 NY2d 996, 250 NE2d 232, 302 NYS2d 824 (1969).

6. Teacher Morality

School districts and the populace have traditionally insisted that school teachers be morally unimpeachable citizens of the community. See generally H. Beale, *Are American Teachers Free?* (1936). In 1898, a Massachusetts superintendent of schools was dismissed because of an indictment for adultery in another state. The Massachusetts' Supreme Judicial Court held that "schools will suffer if those who conduct them are open to general and well-grounded suspicion of this kind. . . . [N]ot merely good character, but good reputation, is essential to the greatest usefulness in such a position as that of superintendent of schools." *Freeman v Town of Bourne* 170 Mass 289, 49 NE 435, 437 (1898). The standard of good reputation did not disappear at the turn of the century. As with insubordination, it has been held proper for the schools to demand that teachers be held to a standard that presupposes that they teach by precept and example, and the requirement of exemplary conduct is not confined to school hours. In *Bradford v School Dist #20* 364 F2d 185 (4th Cir 1966), a teacher was fired for public drunkenness and assaulting an officer. Teachers have been dismissed for being intoxicated at a private party. *Bowman v Ray* 118 Ky 110, 80 SW 516 (1904). Unmarried female teachers have been dismissed for being seen with married men. See, e.g., *In re Schwer's Appeal,* 36 Pa D&C 531 (Clinton County 1939). Male teachers have been discharged for committing homosexual acts for which they were arrested. *Sarac v State Bd of Educ* 249 CA2d 58, 57 CR 69 (1967); cf. *Morrison v State Bd of Educ* 1 C3d 214, 82 Cal Rptr 175 (1969); *Neal v Bryant* 159 So2d 529 (Fla 1962). See generally Horenstein, "Homosexuals in the Teaching Profession," 20 *Cleveland St L Rev* 125 (1971). Does *Pickering* cast doubt on the constitutionality of such dismissals?

7. Teacher Loyalty: The Scope of Supreme Court Decisions

THE SYSTEM OF FREEDOM OF EXPRESSION
T. Emerson
600-604, 616 (1970)

[T]he Supreme Court has dealt with matters touching on academic freedom in cases of loyalty regulations involving educational institutions. These decisions [will be discussed only with reference to academic freedom.] . . . .

The first case in which the Supreme Court had occasion to consider the impact of a loyalty program upon the schools was *Adler v Board of Education* [342 US 485 (1952)], when it upheld the New York Feinberg Law and other loyalty regulations for teachers. Justice Minton's majority opinion took the view that teachers were in no better position than other government employees, so far as a loyalty program was concerned. In fact he indicated there were reasons for applying more stringent loyalty requirements to teachers than to others:

> A teacher works in a sensitive area in a schoolroom. There he shapes the attitude of young minds toward the society in which they live. In this, the state has a vital concern. It must preserve the integrity of the schools. That the school authorities have the right and the duty to screen the officials, teachers, and employees as to their fitness to maintain the integrity of the schools as a part of ordered society, cannot be doubted.[13]

Justice Douglas in dissent, joined by Justice Black, expressed a wholly different concept of the educational process. Invoking the principles of academic freedom he urged that loyalty regulations were particularly repressive in an academic setting:

> What happens under this law is typical of what happens in a police state. Teachers are under constant surveillance; their pasts are combed for signs of disloyalty; their utterances are watched for clues to dangerous thoughts. A pall is cast over the classrooms. There can be no real academic freedom in that environment where suspicion fills the air, and holds scholars in line for fear of their jobs; there can be no exercise of the free intellect. Supineness and dogmatism take the place of inquiry. A "party line"—as dangerous as the "party line" of the Communists—lays hold. It is the "party line" of the orthodox view, of the conventional thought, of the accepted approach. A problem can no longer be pursued with impunity to its edges. Fear stalks the classroom. The teacher is no longer a stimulant to adventurous thinking; she becomes instead a pipeline for safe and sound information. A deadening dogma takes the place of free inquiry. Instruction tends to become sterile; pursuit of knowledge is discouraged; discussion often leaves off where it should begin.[14]

Shortly afterward, in *Wieman v Updegraff*, the Supreme Court held invalid an Oklahoma loyalty oath that had been challenged by faculty members of Oklahoma A & M College. The majority opinion, finding the oath violated due process in penalizing "innocent" as well as "knowing" membership in an organization, placed no emphasis on the fact that an educational institution was involved. But Justice Frankfurter, in a concurring opinion which Justice Douglas joined, gave express recognition to the principles of academic freedom. After declaring that "inhibition of freedom of thought . . . in the case of teachers brings the safeguards [of the First Amendment] vividly into operation," he went on:

> To regard teachers—in our entire educational system, from the primary grades to the university—as the priests of our democracy is therefore not to indulge in hyperbole. It is the special task of teachers to foster those habits of open-mindedness and critical inquiry which alone make for responsible citizens, who, in turn, make possible an enlightened and effective public opinion. Teachers must fulfill their function by precept and practice, by the very atmosphere which they generate; they must be exemplars of open-mindedness and free inquiry. They cannot carry out their noble task if the conditions for

---

13. *Adler v Board of Educ* 342 US 485, 493 (1952). . . .
14. 342 US at 510.

the practice of a responsible and critical mind are denied to them. They must have the freedom of responsible inquiry, by thought and action, into the meaning of social and economic ideas, into the checkered history of social and economic dogma. They must be free to sift evanescent doctrine, qualified by time and circumstance, from that restless, enduring process of extending the bounds of understanding and wisdom, to assure which the freedoms of thought, of speech, of inquiry, of worship are guaranteed by the Constitution of the United States against infraction by national or state government.[15]

The case in which the theme of academic freedom was most prominent is *Sweezy v New Hampshire,* decided in 1957. The attorney general of New Hampshire, acting as a legislative investigating committee, had questioned Paul M. Sweezy about the contents of a lecture on socialism that he had given at the University of New Hampshire. Sweezy refused to answer and was cited for contempt. The Supreme Court reversed the conviction by a vote of six to two. Chief Justice Warren, writing also for Justices Black, Douglas, and Brennan, stressed the significance of academic freedom:

> The essentiality of freedom in the community of American universities is almost self-evident. No one should underestimate the vital role in a democracy that is played by those who guide and train our youth. To impose any strait jacket upon the intellectual leaders in our colleges and universities would imperil the future of our nation. No field of education is so thoroughly comprehended by man that new discoveries cannot yet be made. Particularly is that true in the social sciences, where few, if any, principles are accepted as absolutes. Scholarship cannot flourish in an atmosphere of suspicion and distrust. Teachers and students must always remain free to inquire, to study and to evaluate, to gain new maturity and understanding; otherwise our civilization will stagnate and die.[16]

Chief Justice Warren concluded, however, that he did not need to reach "fundamental questions of state power to decide this case." He ended by holding that the authority of the attorney general to propound the questions had not been sufficiently established.[17]

Justice Frankfurter, joined by Justice Harlan, concurred in the result on First Amendment grounds. Applying the balancing test he gave predominant weight to "the grave harm resulting from governmental intrusion into the intellectual life of a university...."

The potential of *Sweezy,* however, was not extended further in the *Barenblatt* case, decided two years later. Barenblatt had been a graduate student and teaching fellow at the University of Michigan, and an instructor in psychology at Vassar until shortly before his appearance before the House Committee on Un-American Activities. His refusal to answer questions about Communist party membership resulted in a conviction for contempt. On appeal to the Supreme Court both Barenblatt and the American Association of University Professors as amicus curiae relied heavily upon academic freedom arguments. They were, however, unsuccessful, the Supreme Court upholding the conviction five to four. Justice Harlan, writing the majority

---

15. *Wieman v Updegraff* 344 US 183, 195, 196-97 (1952).
16. *Sweezy v New Hampshire* 354 US 234, 250 (1957).
17. 354 US at 251.

opinion, applied the balancing test. He recognized the academic freedom element in the case: "Of course, broadly viewed, inquiries cannot be made into the teaching that is pursued in any of our educational institutions. When academic teaching-freedom and its corollary learning-freedom, so essential to the well-being of the nation, are claimed, this court will always be on the alert against intrusion by Congress into this constitutionally protected domain." But he proceeded: "We think that investigatory power in this domain [Communist activities] is not to be denied Congress solely because the field of education is involved." Concluding that the investigation was not "directed at controlling what is being taught at our universities rather than at overthrow" of government, he resolved the balance against Barenblatt.[19]

The dissenting opinion of Justice Black, joined by Chief Justice Warren and Justice Douglas, proceeded upon straight First Amendment grounds, with little reference to academic freedom. Justice Brennan's dissenting opinion likewise did not rely upon academic freedom.

A majority of the court returned to the emphasis upon academic freedom some years later in *Keyishian v Board of Regents*. Reviewing again the New York loyalty requirements for teachers, this time in a case brought by a group of faculty members at the State University of New York in Buffalo, the court overruled *Adler* and struck down the key provisions of the loyalty program as vague and overbroad. Justice Brennan, writing for the majority of five, supported his position with another strong statement on academic freedom:

> Our nation is deeply committed to safeguarding academic freedom, which is of transcendent value to all of us and not merely to the teachers concerned. That freedom is therefore a special concern of the First Amendment, which does not tolerate laws that cast a pall of orthodoxy over the classroom. . . . The classroom is peculiarly the "marketplace of ideas." The nation's future depends upon leaders trained through wide exposure to that robust exchange of ideas which discovers truth "out of a multitude of tongues, [rather] than through any kind of authoritative selection." *US v Associated Press* 52 F Supp 362, 372. . . .[20]

The decisions of the Supreme Court until now . . . have not utilized the First Amendment in any unique way in the academic freedom area. Apart from *Tinker,* the decisions have been concerned largely with governmental restrictions of the loyalty variety. Their approach has been a simple, not to say a superficial, one. The court has confined itself to eloquent but isolated statements on the significance of academic freedom, considering the academic freedom element of the case as one factor in a balancing test (*Sweezy, Barenblatt*), or as a reason for stricter applica-

19. *Barenblatt v US* 360 US 109, 112, 129, 130 (1959). . . .

20. *Keyishian v Board of Regents of the University of New York* 385 US 589, 603 (1967). See also *Whitehill v Elkins* 389 US 54, 59-60, 62 (1967). In other loyalty cases involving educational institutions the court did not make any express reference to the academic freedom theme. See *Slochower v Board of Higher Educ of New York City* 350 US 551 (1956); *Beilan v Board of Public Educ* 357 US 399 (1958); *Baggett v Bullitt* 377 US 360 (1964); *Elfbrandt v Russell* 384 US 11 (1966) . . . . Discussion of the court's treatment of academic freedom in the loyalty cases may be found in William P. Murphy, "Academic Freedom—An Emerging Constitutional Right," 28 *Law & Contemp Prob* 447 (1963); Arval A. Morris, "Academic Freedom and Loyalty Oaths," 28 *Law & Contemp Prob* 487 (1963); Note, "Loyalty Oaths," 77 *Yale LJ* 739 (1968).

tion of peripheral rules such as vagueness or overbreadth (*Shelton, Keyishian*). The potentialities of such an approach seem limited.

IV. Tenure

Tenure laws and regulations seek to make a faculty member secure in her position by severely limiting the circumstances in which she can be discharged. Generally, they provide for a specified probationary period, usually from three to seven years, after which the teacher is evaluated and either given or denied tenure status. In institutions of higher education, the faculty tends to be deeply involved in this evaluation. In elementary and secondary schools, administrators and school board members make such decisions without faculty participation. In theory, at least, tenure is not a form of absolute job security; a tenured teacher may be dismissed before retirement for a variety of reasons: adequate cause, gross misconduct, neglect of duty, mental or physical incapacity, moral turpitude, or financial emergency. The teacher expects, however, to serve until retirement, barring extraordinary circumstances. Forty-five states have adopted tenure laws, but most statutes cover only elementary and secondary school teachers and do not extend to university instructors.

Tenure is often thought to be intimately tied to notions of academic freedom. As Professor Emerson has stated: "The institution of tenure is designed to guard the faculty against dismissal for political or other inadmissible reasons, a fact often hard for him to prove, and to assure him economic security in which he can carry on his search for truth in his teaching and research." T. Emerson, *The System of Freedom of Expression* 595 (1970). However, the concept of tenure has increasingly come under attack as a mechanism for retaining "deadwood" on faculties, for denying junior teachers permanent positions, and for straining the financial resources of educational institutions. These arguments should be kept in mind while reading the materials in this section and the next on the procedural protections afforded teachers. Consider also whether the results in *Parducci* and *Pickering* would be altered in any respect by the tenure status of the teachers challenging their dismissals.

SHOULD COLLEGES RETAIN TENURE?
Kingman Brewster Jr.
Wall Street Journal, 2 October 1973

How, it is asked, can we talk glibly about the knowledge explosion or the exponential rate of change—with all its risks of rapid intellectual obsolescence—and at the same time lock ourselves into lifetime obligations to people in their mid-thirties? Not only do we risk becoming stuck with the obsolete, but we remove the most popularly understood incentive to higher levels of performance. Furthermore, since even in financially easy times university resources are finite, every "slot" mortgaged for a full professor's lifetime blocks the hope for advancement by some promising members of oncoming generations. When resources are so tight that the faculty must be pruned, because of tenure most of the pruning is at the expense of the junior faculty. Many juniors are more up to date in their command of new methods and problems in fast-moving fields, and many of them are more talented than are some of the elders.

The AAUP's Position

The Association of American University Professors—the organized guardian of academic freedom and tenure—has recently taken some pains to make it clear that tenure is not an absolute protection against dismissal. They say that a person can be fired for gross misconduct or neglect of duty. They assert that even a person with tenure may be terminated for financial reasons. Such termination is permissible in their eyes, however, only by a process which puts the burden of proof upon the university and in which the victim's faculty peers are both judge and jury, subject to final disposition by the trustees.

The practical fact in most places, and the unexceptional rule at Yale, is that tenure is for all normal purposes a guarantee of appointment until retirement age. Physical or mental incapacity, some chronic disability, some frightful act of moral turpitude, or persistent neglect of all university responsibilities have on a very few occasions in the past resulted in "negotiated" termination settlements. However, even in extreme circumstances there is a deep reluctance to compromise the expectations of tenure.

The defense of tenure usually falls into two categories: the need for job security, in order to draw good people into underpaid academic life; and the need to protect the academic freedom of the faculty.

Both of these points are valid; but put this simply, both grossly understate the significance of tenure to the quality of a first-rate university.

The argument based on the recruitment of faculty is underscored by the simple fact that as long as most institutions grant tenure then any single institution must go along in order to remain competitive.

The job security argument arose when university faculty were grossly underpaid in comparison with other professional callings. They were even more disadvantaged when compared with the marts of trade and finance. This is still true, especially at both ends of the ladder: the bottom rungs of starting salaries and the higher rungs of top management compensation. In the middle range, however, academic salaries at a place like Yale are not grossly lower than the earnings of other professional callings. So, the use of job security as bait to persuade people to take a vow of "academic poverty" is not a sufficient argument. (It still has persuasive merit, however, for those institutions which pay substandard salaries. Such institutions are the proper concern of not only the AAUP but should be the concern of a society which has an enormous stake in attracting a sufficient number of people into careers devoted to the higher education of the young and the advancement of knowledge and understanding.)

The rationale of academic tenure, however, is somewhat different from job security in the industrial world, especially in an institution which wants its teachers to be engaged in pushing forward the frontiers of learning. This lies in the fact that contributions to human knowledge and understanding which add something significant to what has gone before involve a very high risk and a very long-term intellectual investment. This is true especially of those whose life is more devoted to thought, experimentation and writing than it is to practice.

Teachers as Scholars

If teaching is to be more than the retailing of the known, and if research is to seek real breakthroughs in the explanation of man and the cosmos, then teachers must be scholars, and scholarship must be more than the refinement of the inherited stock of knowledge. If scholarship is to question assumptions and to take the risk of testing new hypotheses, then it cannot be held to a timetable which demands proof of pay-out to satisfy some review committee. . . .

The second, and most highly touted, rationale for tenure is academic freedom. This concern, traditionally, has focused on the privilege of immunity from "outside" interference. Within the memory of those still active, "McCarthyism" is the most telling nightmare. . . .

This struggle to preserve the integrity of the institution and the freedom of its faculty members from external coercion is never over. However, despite the winds of controversy in a troubled time, whetted occasionally by demagogic desire to make academia the scapegoat for society's ills, the ability of a strong university to give its faculty convincing protection against such threats will depend more on the steadfastness of the institution as a whole than it will on tenure.

The dramatic image of the university under siege from taxpayers, politicians, or even occasional alumni is a vivid but not the most difficult aspect of the pressures which tend to erode academic freedom. The more subtle condition of academic freedom is that faculty members, once they have proved their potential during a period of junior probation, should not feel beholden to *anyone,* especially department chairmen, deans, provosts, or presidents, for favor, let alone for survival. In David Riesman's phrase teachers and scholars should, insofar as possible, be truly "inner directed"—guided by their own intellectual curiosity, insight and conscience. In the development of their ideas they should not be looking over their shoulders either in hope of favor or in fear of disfavor from anyone other than the judgment of an informed and critical posterity.

In strong universities assuring freedom from intellectual conformity coerced *within* the institution is even more of a concern than is the protection of freedom from external interference.

This spirit of academic freedom within the university has a value which goes beyond protecting the individual's broad scope of thought and inquiry. It bears crucially upon the distinctive quality of the university as a community. If a university is alive and productive, it is a place where colleagues are in constant dispute; defending their latest intellectual enthusiasm, attacking the contrary views of others. From this trial by intellectual combat emerges a sharper insight, later to be blunted by other, sharper minds. It is vital that this contest be uninhibited by fear of reprisal. Sides must be taken only on the basis of the merits of a proposition. Jockeying for favor by trimming the argument because some colleague or some group will have the power of academic life or death in some later process of review would falsify and subvert the whole exercise.

I have not been able to devise, nor have I heard of, any regime of periodic review with the sanction of dismissal which would not have disastrous effect. It would both dampen the willingness to take long-term intellectual risks and inhibit, if not corrupt, the free and spirited exchanges upon which the vitality of a community of scholars depends. This, not the aberrational external interference, is the threat to the freedom of the academic community which tenure seeks to mitigate.

Also, I do not think the costs of tenure are very high for a first-rate university. Those who gain tenure at Yale do not rest in happy security on their professional laurels. Indeed, in my relatively brief experience, almost without exception it is the elders who are productive up to and well beyond retirement. They are the ones affected with the migraine headaches and other forms of psychosomatic traumae, lest their life should ebb away without the completion of their great work.

THE FUTURE OF TENURE
Robert Nisbet
Change (April 1973):27, 30-31

[L]et us turn to the justification of tenure we knew in our deepest minds President Brewster would find his way to, the only element of suspense being, as is always the case in these matters, which specific way. If freedom from external threat and academic poverty are not sufficient justifications of a policy that confers security for life upon a person in his twenties or thirties, what is? The answer—and I do not deny that it is put with grace and feeling—lies in the ideal of the academic community. The essence of this ideal is boldness of mind, creative discovery, avoidance of "riskless footnote gathering" and a high measure of "curiosity, insight and conscience" on the part of the faculty. Above all, scholarship and science, of the kind that requires not only the qualities I have just mentioned but also long periods for their gestation and relative freedom from the marketplace, must be seen as the reason-for-being of both the academic community and tenure. . . .

What are we to say to this fresh proof of the necessity of God? Let us pay no attention to the testimony of souls of the departed, trying to remind us from some heavenly eminence that the history of Western thought is full of long-term risk-taking and nonconforming by those who, from the days of the ancient Greeks, have known neither university nor tenure. Let us not stop here to heed the voices of those who could prove that even in our own day there is often more boldness of mind to be found outside the academy than in. . . .

No, let us push these considerations aside, compelling as they must be to a great many humane and gentle minds, and say that President Brewster has given us an attractive justification of tenure, all right, but one, alas, that has very little pertinence to the American university as we know it today. What is at fault is not so much his reasoning as the image of the academic community to which the reasoning is directed. It is as though the president of Yale saw still around him the university of yore, one composed overwhelmingly of "locals" instead of "cosmopolitans," of men of light and leading still motivated in largest part by qualities of "curiosity, insight and conscience" buoyed up by what is rooted in one's members of the community within the walls.

He does not see the American university as it has so largely become since World War II, the university infinitely more responsive to the norms, incentives, rewards and, not least, pressures generated today by government bureau, foundation and industry, all of which, emanating from centers of power and affluence and status hundreds or even thousands of miles away from the local community, have been eagerly sought out by faculty members themselves. He does not see the heavy inroads made upon "curiosity, insight and conscience" by the higher capitalists and their management of literally billions of dollars, from Berkeley to Harvard, during this past quarter of a century. He does not see his cherished inner-directed scholar or scientist elbowed aside by the other-directed, those who find greater inspiration in federal grant than in natural curiosity. He does not see the new men of power on the campus, those who move with practiced ease from professorship to assistant secretaryship in Washington and then back again and whose management of institute, bureau and center has its nearest counterpart in Washington or Detroit. . . .

But taking the American university as history has recently shaped it and giving due weight to projections into the future of this same university by its most powerful academic spokesmen, I see little reason for persisting in the view, the romantic, nostalgic view, taken of the academic community in our time by President Brewster. He is describing an institution uniquely *different* from anything to be found in the rest of American society. What is only too evident today, however, is an institution increasingly *like* the rest of society in its now favored roles, norms and operations . . . .

Why can we not be honest in our defense of academic tenure? There is one, and one only, honest justification of tenure: It is there! It has been there a long time. Tenure, not freedom, is academic man's most cherished idol. No president could last in office a week if he sought to abolish academic tenure. At very best, the ancient rule of conservatism applies: If it is not necessary to change, it is not necessary to change. From how much cant, fustian and banality we would be spared if that defense of tenure were accepted for what it is.

Notes and Questions

1. Scope of Tenure

How relevant are the arguments in favor of and against tenure to the elementary or secondary school teacher? How do you explain the fact that tenure laws often exclude university teachers from their coverage? Does it make sense in terms of the policy reasons supporting tenure?

2. Sanctions Other than Dismissal

Should tenured teachers be protected against sanctions that fall short of dismissal, such as assignment to a vocational school? See, e.g., Ariz Rev Stat Ann §15-257 (1956); Colorado Rev Stat Ann §123-18-14 (Supp 1970). Is such protection wise in view of the flexibility often needed to devise new and innovative educational programs? How should those interests be reconciled?

3. Constitutional Tenure?

Do decisions such as *Parducci* and *Pickering* create a form of constitutional tenure? Is this wise? Might other remedies for the violation of academic freedom be less harmful to the offending institution?

4. Impact of Judicial Enforcement of Tenure

If the courts rigidly enforce tenure laws, what would be the likely impact on educational institutions? Does judicial enforcement of tenure conflict with the underlying policy bases for its adoption? See generally L. Joughin, ed, *Academic Freedom and Tenure* (1967).

5. Impact of Abolishing Tenure

What impact would the abolition of tenure have on teacher organization? Would such organizations be strengthened or weakened? Would contractual negotiations assume even greater importance? Would teacher strikes become more likely?

V. Due Process Rights of Teachers

BOARD OF REGENTS v ROTH
408 US 564 (1972)

Mr. Justice Stewart delivered the opinion of the court.

In 1968 the respondent, David Roth, was hired for his first teaching job as assistant professor of political science at Wisconsin State University-Oshkosh. He was hired for a fixed term of one academic year. The notice of his faculty appointment specified that his employment would begin on September 1, 1968, and would end on June 30, 1969.[1] The respondent completed that term. But he was informed that he would not be rehired for the next academic year.

The respondent had no tenure rights to continued employment. Under Wisconsin statutory law a state university teacher can acquire tenure as a "permanent" employee only after four years of year-to-year employment. Having acquired tenure, a teacher is entitled to continued employment "during efficiency and good behavior." A relatively new teacher without tenure, however, is under Wisconsin law entitled to nothing beyond his one-year appointment.[2] There are no statutory or administrative standards defining eligibility for reemployment. State law thus clearly leaves the decision whether to rehire a nontenured teacher for another year to the unfettered discretion of university officials.

The procedural protection afforded a Wisconsin State University teacher before he is separated from the university corresponds to his job security. As a matter of statutory law, a tenured teacher cannot be "discharged except for cause upon written charges" and pursuant to certain procedures.[3] A nontenured teacher, similarly, is protected to some extent *during* his one-year term. Rules promulgated by the board of regents provide that a nontenured teacher "dismissed" before the end of the year may have some opportunity for review of the "dismissal." But the rules provide no real protection for a nontenured teacher who simply is not reemployed for the next year. He must be informed by February first "concerning retention or

---

1. The respondent had no contract of employment. Rather, his formal notice of appointment was the equivalent of an employment contract. . . .

2. Wis Stat 1967, §37.31(1), in force at the time, provided in pertinent part that: "All teachers in any state university shall initially be employed on probation. The employment shall be permanent, during efficiency and good behavior, after four years of continuous service in the state university system as a teacher."

3. Wis Stat §37.31(1) further provided that:

"No teacher who has become permanently employed as herein provided shall be discharged except for cause upon written charges. Within thirty days of receiving the written charges, such teacher may appeal the discharge by a written notice to the president of the board of regents of state colleges. The board shall cause the charges to be investigated, hear the case and provide such teacher with a written statement as to their decision."

nonretention for the ensuing year." But "no reason for nonretention need be given. No review or appeal is provided in such case."[4]

In conformance with these rules, the president of Wisconsin State University-Oshkosh informed the respondent before February 1, 1969, that he would not be rehired for the 1969-1970 academic year. He gave the respondent no reason for the decision and no opportunity to challenge it at any sort of hearing.

The respondent then brought this action in a federal district court alleging that the decision not to rehire him for the next year infringed his Fourteenth Amendment rights. . . . First, he alleged that the true reason for the decision was to punish him for certain statements critical of the university administration, and that it therefore violated his right to freedom of speech.[5] Second, he alleged that the failure of university officials to give him notice of any reason for nonretention and an opportunity for a hearing violated his right to procedural due process of law.

The district court granted summary judgment for the respondent on the procedural issue, ordering the university officials to provide him with reasons and a hearing. 310 F Supp at 972. The court of appeals, with one judge dissenting, affirmed this partial summary judgment. 446 F2d at 806. We granted certiorari. 404 US 909. The only question presented to us at this stage in the case is whether the respondent had a constitutional right to a statement of reasons and a hearing on the university's decision not to rehire him for another year.[6] We hold that he did not.

I

The requirements of procedural due process apply only to the deprivation of interests encompassed by the Fourteenth Amendment's protection of liberty and property. When protected interests are implicated the right to some kind of prior hearing is paramount. But the range of interests protected by procedural due process is not infinite.

The district court decided that procedural due process guarantees apply in this

---

4. The rules, promulgated by the board of regents in 1967, provide:

"RULE I—February 1st is established throughout [the] State University system as the deadline for written notification of nontenured faculty concerning retention or nonretention for the ensuing year. The president of each university shall give such notice each year on or before this date.

"RULE II—During the time a faculty member is on probation, no reason for nonretention need be given. No review or appeal is provided in such case.

"RULE III—'Dismissal' as opposed to 'Nonretention' means termination of responsibilities during an academic year. When a nontenured faculty member is dismissed he has no right under Wisconsin Statutes to a review of his case or to appeal. The president may, however, in his discretion, grant a request for a review within the institution, either by a faculty committee or by the president, or both. Any such review would be informal in nature and would be advisory only.

"RULE IV—When a nontenured faculty member is dismissed he may request a review by or hearing before the board of regents. Each such request will be considered separately and the board will, in its discretion, grant or deny same in each individual case."

5. While the respondent alleged that he was not rehired because of his exercise of free speech, the petitioners insisted that the nonretention decision was based on other, constitutionally valid grounds. The district court came to no conclusion whatever regarding the true reason for the university president's decision. "In the present case," it stated, "it appears that a determination as to the actual bases of the decision must await amplification of the facts at trial. . . . Summary judgment is inappropriate." 310 F Supp at 982.

6. The courts that have had to decide whether a nontenured public employee has a right to a statement of reasons or a hearing upon nonrenewal of his contract have come to varying

case by assessing and balancing the weights of the particular interests involved. It concluded that the respondent's interest in reemployment at the Wisconsin State University-Oshkosh outweighed the university's interest in denying him reemployment summarily. 310 F Supp at 977-979. Undeniably, the respondent's reemployment prospects were of major concern to him—concern that we surely cannot say was insignificant. And a weighing process has long been a part of any determination of the *form* of hearing required in particular situations by procedural due process.[8] But to determine whether due process requirements apply in the first place, we must look not to the "weight" but to the *nature* of the interest at stake. . . . We must look to see if the interest is within the Fourteenth Amendment's protection of liberty and property.

"Liberty" and "property" are broad and majestic terms. They are among the "great [constitutional] concepts . . . purposely left to gather meaning from experience. . . . [T]hey relate to the whole domain of social and economic fact, and the statesmen who founded this nation knew too well that only a stagnant society remains unchanged." *National Ins Co v Tidewater Co* 337 US 582, 646 (Frankfurter, J, dissenting). For that reason the court has fully and finally rejected the wooden distinction between "rights" and "privileges" that once seemed to govern the applicability of procedural due process rights.[9] The court has also made clear that the property interests protected by procedural due process extend well beyond actual ownership of real estate, chattels, or money.[10] By the same token, the court has required due process protection for deprivations of liberty beyond the sort of formal constraints imposed by the criminal process.[11]

Yet, while the court has eschewed rigid or formalistic limitations on the protection of procedural due process, it has at the same time observed certain boundaries.

---

conclusions. Some have held that neither procedural safeguard is required. E.g., *Orr v Trinter* 444 F2d 128 (6th Cir); *Jones v Hopper* 410 F2d 1323 (10th Cir); *Freeman v Gould Special School Dist* 405 F2d 1153 (8th Cir). At least one court has held that there is a right to a statement of reasons but not a hearing. *Drown v Portsmouth School Dist* 435 F2d 1182 (1st Cir). And another has held that both requirements depend on whether the employee has an "expectancy" of continued employment. *Ferguson v Thomas* 430 F2d 852, 856 (5th Cir).

8. "The formality and procedural requisites for the hearing can vary, depending upon the importance of the interest involved and the nature of the subsequent proceedings." *Boddie v Connecticut* 401 US 371, 378. See, e.g., *Goldberg v Kelly* 397 US 254, 263; *Hannah v Larche* 363 US 420. The constitutional requirement of opportunity for *some* form of hearing before deprivation of a protected interest, of course, does not depend upon such a narrow balancing process. . . .

9. In a leading case decided many years ago, the Court of Appeals for the District of Columbia Circuit held that public employment in general was a "privilege," not a "right," and that procedural due process guarantees therefore were inapplicable. *Bailey v Richardson* 182 F2d 46 (DC Cir 1950), aff'd by an equally divided court, 341 US 918 (1951). The basis of this holding has been thoroughly undermined in the ensuing years. For, as Mr. Justice Blackmun wrote for the court . . . , "this court now has rejected the concept that constitutional rights turn upon whether a governmental benefit is characterized as a 'right' or a 'privilege.'" *Graham v Richardson* 403 US 365, 374. See, e.g., *Morrissey v Brewer* 408 US 471, 482 (1972); *Bell v Burson* 402 US 535, 539; *Goldberg v Kelly* 397 US 254, 262; *Shapiro v Thompson* 394 US 618, 627 n6; *Pickering v Board of Educ* 391 US 563, 568; *Sherbert v Verner* 374 US 398, 404.

10. See, e.g., *Connell v Higgenbotham* 403 US 207, 208; *Bell v Burson* 402 US 535; *Goldberg v Kelly* 397 US 254.

11. "Although the court has not assumed to define 'liberty' [in the Fifth Amendment's due process clause] with any great precision, that term is not confined to mere freedom from bodily restraint." *Bolling v Sharpe* 347 US 497, 499. See, e.g., *Stanley v Illinois* 405 US 645.

For the words "liberty" and "property" in the due process clause of the Fourteenth Amendment must be given some meaning.

II

"While this court has not attempted to define with exactness the liberty . . . guaranteed [by the Fourteenth Amendment] the term has received much consideration, and some of the included things have been definitely stated. Without doubt, it denotes not merely freedom from bodily restraint but also the right of the individual to contract, to engage in any of the common occupations of life, to acquire useful knowledge, to marry, establish a home and bring up children, to worship God according to the dictates of his own conscience, and generally to enjoy those privileges long recognized . . . as essential to the orderly pursuit of happiness by free men." *Meyer v Nebraska* 262 US 390, 399 (1923). In a constitution for a free people, there can be no doubt that the meaning of "liberty" must be broad indeed. See, e.g., *Bolling v Sharpe* 347 US 497, 499-500 (1954); *Stanley v Illinois* 405 US 645.

There might be cases in which a state refused to reemploy a person under such circumstances that interests in liberty would be implicated. But this is not such a case.

The state, in declining to rehire the respondent, did not make any charge against him that might seriously damage his standing and associations in his community. It did not base the nonrenewal of his contract on a charge, for example, that he had been guilty of dishonesty, or immorality. Had it done so, this would be a different case. For "[w]here a person's good name, reputation, honor or integrity is at stake because of what the government is doing to him, notice and an opportunity to be heard are essential." *Wisconsin v Constantineau* 400 US 433, 437. . . . See *Cafeteria Workers v McElroy* 367 US 886, 898. In such a case, due process would accord an opportunity to refute the charge before university officials.[12] In the present case, however, there is no suggestion whatever that the respondent's interest in his "good name, reputation, honor or integrity" is at stake.

Similarly, there is no suggestion that the state, in declining to reemploy the respondent, imposed on him a stigma or other disability that foreclosed his freedom to take advantage of other employment opportunities. The state, for example, did not invoke any regulations to bar the respondent from all other public employment in state universities. Had it done so, this, again, would be a different case. For "to be deprived not only of present government employment but of future opportunity for it certainly is no small injury. . . ." *Joint Anti-Fascist Refugee Comm v McGrath* 310 F Supp 185 (Jackson, J, concurring). See *Truax v Raich* 239 US 33, 41.[13]

---

12. The purpose of such notice and hearing is to provide the person an opportunity to clear his name. Once a person has cleared his name at a hearing, his employer, of course, may remain free to deny him future employment for other reasons.

13. The district court made an *assumption* "that nonretention by one university or college creates concrete and practical difficulties for a professor in his subsequent academic career." 310 F Supp at 979. And the court of appeals based its affirmance of the summary judgment largely on the premise that "the substantial adverse effect nonretention is likely to have upon the career interests of an individual professor" amounts to a limitation on future employment opportunities sufficient to invoke procedural due process guarantees. 446 F2d at 809. But even assuming *arguendo,* that such a "substantial adverse effect" under these circumstances would constitute a state imposed restriction on liberty, the record contains no support for these assumptions. There is no suggestion of how nonretention might affect the respondent's future employment prospects. Mere proof, for example, that his record of nonretention in one job,

To be sure, the respondent has alleged that the nonrenewal of his contract was based on his exercise of his right to freedom of speech. But this allegation is not now before us. The district court stayed proceedings on this issue, and the respondent has yet to prove that the decision not to rehire him was, in fact, based on his free speech activities.[14]

Hence, on the record before us, all that clearly appears is that the respondent was not rehired for one year at one university. It stretches the concept too far to suggest that a person is deprived of "liberty" when he simply is not rehired in one job but remains as free as before to seek another. *Cafeteria Workers v McElroy*, ...

III

The Fourteenth Amendment's procedural protection of property is a safeguard of the security of interests that a person has already acquired in specific benefits. These interests—property interests—may take many forms.

Thus the court has held that a person receiving welfare benefits under statutory and administrative standards defining eligibility for them has an interest in continued receipt of those benefits that is safeguarded by procedural due process. *Goldberg v Kelly* 397 US 254. See *Flemming v Nestor* 363 US 603, 611. Similarly, in the area of public employment, the court has held that a public college professor dismissed from an office held under tenure provisions (*Slochower v Board of Educ* 350 US 551 (1956)), and college professors and staff members dismissed during the terms of their contracts (*Wieman v Updegraff* 344 US 183 (1952)) have interests in continued employment that are safeguarded by due process. Only last year, the court held that this principle "proscribing summary dismissal from public employment without hearing or inquiry required by due process" also applied to a teacher recently hired without tenure or a formal contract, but nonetheless with a clearly implied promise of continued employment. *Connell v Higgenbotham* 403 US 207, 208.

Certain attributes of "property" interests protected by procedural due process

taken alone, might make him somewhat less attractive to some other employers would hardly establish the kind of foreclosure of opportunities amounting to a deprivation of "liberty. . . . ."

14. See n5, *infra*. The court of appeals, nonetheless, argued that opportunity for a hearing and a statement of reasons were required here "as a *prophylactic* against nonretention decisions improperly motivated by exercise of protected rights." 446 F2d at 810 (emphasis supplied). While the court of appeals recognized the lack of a finding that the respondent's nonretention was based on exercise of the right of free speech, it felt that the respondent's interest in liberty was sufficiently implicated here because the decision not to rehire him was made "with a background of controversy and unwelcome expressions of opinion." *Ibid.*

When a state would directly impinge upon interests in free speech or free press, this court has on occasion held that opportunity for a fair adversary hearing must precede the action, whether or not the speech or press interest is clearly protected under substantive First Amendment standards. Thus we have required fair notice and opportunity for an adversary hearing before an injunction is issued against the holding of rallies and public meetings. *Carroll v Princess Anne* 393 US 175. Similarly, we have indicated the necessity of procedural safeguards before a state makes a large-scale seizure of a person's allegedly obscene books, magazines, and so forth. *A Quantity of Books v Kansas* 378 US 205; *Marcus v Search Warrant* 367 US 717. See *Freedman v Maryland* 380 US 51; *Bantam Books v Sullivan* 372 US 58. See generally Monaghan, "First Amendment 'Due Process,'" 83 *Harv L Rev* 518.

In the respondent's case, however, the state has not directly impinged upon interests in free speech or free press in any way comparable to a seizure of books or an injunction against meetings. Whatever may be a teacher's rights of free speech, the interest in holding a teaching job at a state university, *simpliciter*, is not itself a free speech interest.

emerge from these decisions. To have a property interest in a benefit, a person clearly must have more than an abstract need or desire for it. He must have more than a unilateral expectation of it. He must, instead, have a legitimate claim of entitlement to it. It is a purpose of the ancient institution of property to protect those claims upon which people rely in their daily lives, reliance that must not be arbitrarily undermined. It is a purpose of the constitutional right to a hearing to provide an opportunity for a person to vindicate those claims.

Property interests, of course, are not created by the Constitution. Rather, they are created and their dimensions are defined by existing rules or understandings that stem from an independent source such as state laws—rules or understandings that secure certain benefits and that support claims of entitlement to those benefits. Thus the welfare recipients in *Goldberg v Kelly, supra,* had a claim of entitlement to welfare payments that was grounded in the statute defining eligibility for them. The recipients had not yet shown that they were, in fact, within the statutory terms of eligibility. But we held that they had a right to a hearing at which they might attempt to do so.

Just as the welfare recipients' "property" interest in welfare payments was created and defined by statutory terms, so the respondent's "property" interest in employment at the Wisconsin State University-Oshkosh was created and defined by the terms of his appointment. Those terms secured his interest in employment up to June 30, 1969. But the important fact in this case is that they specifically provided that the respondent's employment was to terminate on June 30. They did not provide for contract renewal absent "sufficient cause." Indeed, they made no provision for renewal whatsoever.

Thus the terms of the respondent's appointment secured absolutely no interest in reemployment for the next year. They supported absolutely no possible claim of entitlement to reemployment. Nor, significantly, was there any state statute or university rule or policy that secured his interest in reemployment or that created any legitimate claim to it.[16] In these circumstances, the respondent surely had an abstract concern in being rehired, but he did not have a *property* interest sufficient to require the university authorities to give him a hearing when they declined to renew his contract of employment.

IV

Our analysis of the respondent's constitutional rights in this case in no way indicates a view that an opportunity for a hearing or a statement of reasons for nonretention would, or would not, be appropriate or wise in public colleges and universities.[17] For it is a written Constitution that we apply. Our role is confined to interpretation of that Constitution.

We must conclude that the summary judgment for the respondent should not have been granted, since the respondent has not shown that he was deprived of liberty or property protected by the Fourteenth Amendment. The judgment of the

16. To be sure, the respondent does suggest that most teachers hired on a year-to-year basis by the Wisconsin State University-Oshkosh are, in fact, rehired. But the district court has not found that there is anything approaching a "common law" of reemployment (see *Perry v Sindermann* 408 US 602) so strong as to require university officials to give the respondent a statement of reasons and a hearing on their decision not to rehire him.

17. See, e.g., Report of Committee A on Academic Freedom and Tenure, "Procedural Standards in the Renewal or Nonrenewal of Faculty Appointments," 56 *AAUP Bull* 21 (Spring 1970).

court of appeals, accordingly, is reversed and the case is remanded for further proceedings consistent with this opinion.

It is so ordered.

Mr. Justice Powell took no part in the decision of this case.

Mr. Justice Douglas, dissenting.

Respondent Roth, like Sindermann in the companion case, had no tenure under Wisconsin law and, unlike Sindermann, he had had only one year of teaching at Wisconsin State University-Oshkosh—where during 1968-69 he had been assistant professor of political science and international studies. Though Roth was rated by the faculty as an excellent teacher, he had publicly criticized the administration for suspending an entire group of ninety-four black students without determining individual guilt. He also criticized the university's regime as being authoritarian and autocratic. He used his classroom to discuss what was being done about the black episode; and one day, instead of meeting his class, he went to the meeting of the board of regents. . . .

No more direct assault on academic freedom can be imagined than for the school authorities to be allowed to discharge a teacher because of his or her philosophical, political, or ideological beliefs. The same may well be true of private schools, if through the device of financing or other umbilical cords they become instrumentalities of the state. . . .

When a violation of First Amendment rights is alleged, the reasons for dismissal or for nonrenewal of an employment contract must be examined to see if the reasons given are only a cloak for activity or attitudes protected by the Constitution. A statutory analogy is present under the National Labor Relations Act, 29 USC § 151 *et seq.* While discharges of employees for "cause" are permissible (*Fibreboard Corp v NLRB* 379 US 203, 217), discharges because of an employee's union activities are banned by § 8(a)(3), 29 USC § 158(a)(3). So the search is to ascertain whether the stated ground was the real one or only a pretext. See *J. P. Stevens & Co v NLRB* 380 F2d 292, 300 (1967).

In the case of teachers whose contracts are not renewed, tenure is not the critical issue. In the *Sweezy* case, the teacher, whose First Amendment rights we honored, had no tenure but was only a guest lecturer. In the *Keyishian* case, one of the petitioners (Keyishian himself) had only a "one-year-term contract" that was not renewed. 385 US at 592. In *Shelton v Tucker* 364 US 479, one of the petitioners was a teacher whose "contract for the ensuing school year was not renewed" (364 US at 483) and two others who refused to comply were advised that it made "impossible their reemployment as teachers for the following school year." 364 US at 484. The oath required in *Keyishian* and the affidavit listing memberships required in *Shelton* were both, in our view, in violation of the First Amendment rights. Those cases mean that conditioning renewal of a teacher's contract upon surrender of First Amendment rights is beyond the power of a state.

There is sometimes a conflict between a claim for First Amendment protection and the need for orderly administration of the school system, as we noted in *Pickering v Board of Educ* 391 US 563, 569. That is one reason why summary judgments in this class of cases are seldom appropriate. Another reason is that careful factfinding is often necessary to know whether the given reason for nonrenewal of a teacher's contract is the real reason or a feigned one. . . .

If this nonrenewal implicated the First Amendment, then Roth was deprived of constitutional rights because his employment was conditioned on a surrender of First Amendment rights and apart from the First Amendment he was denied due process when he received no notice and hearing of the adverse action contemplated against him. Without a statement of the reasons for the discharge and an opportunity to rebut those reasons—both of which were refused by petitioners—there is no means short of a lawsuit to safeguard the right not to be discharged for the exercise of First Amendment guarantees. . . .

Mr. Justice Marshall, dissenting . . . .

In my view, every citizen who applies for a government job is entitled to it unless the government can establish some reason for denying the employment. This is the "property" right that I believe is protected by the Fourteenth Amendment and that cannot be denied "without due process of law." And it is also liberty—liberty to work—which is the "very essence of the personal freedom and opportunity" secured by the Fourteenth Amendment. . . .

Employment is one of the greatest, if not the greatest, benefits that governments offer in modern-day life. When something as valuable as the opportunity to work is at stake, the government may not reward some citizens and not others without demonstrating that its actions are fair and equitable. And it is procedural due process that is our fundamental guarantee of fairness, our protection against arbitrary, capricious, and unreasonable government action. . . .

We have often noted that procedural due process means many different things in the numerous contexts in which it applies. See, e.g., *Goldberg v Kelly* 397 US 254 (1970); *Bell v Burson* 402 US 535 (1971). Prior decisions have held that an applicant for admission to practice as an attorney before the United States Board of Tax Appeals may not be rejected without a statement of reasons and a chance for a hearing on disputed issues of fact;[4] that a tenured teacher could not be summarily dismissed without notice of the reasons and a hearing;[5] that an applicant for admission to a state bar could not be denied the opportunity to practice law without notice of the reasons for the rejection of his application and a hearing;[6] and even that a substitute teacher who had been employed only two months could not be dismissed merely because she refused to take a loyalty oath without an inquiry into the specific facts of her case and a hearing on those in dispute.[7] I would follow these cases and hold that respondent was denied due process when his contract was not renewed and he was not informed of the reasons and given an opportunity to respond.

It may be argued that to provide procedural due process to all public employees or prospective employees would place an intolerable burden on the machinery of government. Cf. *Goldberg v Kelly, supra.* The short answer to that argument is that it is not burdensome to give reasons when reasons exist. Whenever an application for employment is denied, an employee is discharged, or a decision not to rehire an employee is made, there should be some reason for the decision. It can scarcely be argued that government would be crippled by a requirement that the reason be communicated to the person most directly affected by the government's action.

Where there are numerous applicants for jobs, it is likely that few will choose to

---

4. *Goldsmith v Board of Tax Appeals* 270 US 117 (1926).
5. *Slochower v Board of Higher Educ* 350 US 551 (1956).
6. *Willner v Committee on Character* 373 US 96 (1963).
7. *Connell v Higgenbotham* 403 US 207 (1971).

demand reasons for not being hired. But, if the demand for reasons is exceptionally great, summary procedures can be devised that would provide fair and adequate information to all persons. As long as the government has a good reason for its actions it need not fear disclosure. It is only where the government acts improperly that procedural due process is truly burdensome. And that is precisely when it is most necessary.

It might also be argued that to require a hearing and a statement of reasons is to require a useless act, because a government bent on denying employment to one or more persons will do so regardless of the procedural hurdles that are placed in its path. Perhaps this is so, but a requirement of procedural regularity at least renders arbitrary action more difficult. Moreover, proper procedures will surely eliminate some of the arbitrariness that results not from malice, but from innocent error. "Experience teaches . . . that the affording of procedural safeguards, which by their nature serve to illuminate the underlying facts, in itself often operates to prevent erroneous decisions on the merits from occurring." *Silver v New York Stock Exch* 373 US 341, 366 (1963). When the government knows it may have to justify its decisions with sound reasons, its conduct is likely to be more cautious, careful, and correct. . . .

Accordingly, I dissent.

PERRY v SINDERMANN
408 US 593 (1972)

Mr. Justice Stewart delivered the opinion of the court.

From 1959 to 1969 the respondent, Robert Sindermann, was a teacher in the state college system of the state of Texas. After teaching for two years at the University of Texas and four years at San Antonio Junior College, he became a professor of government and social science at Odessa Junior College in 1965. He was employed at the college for four successive years, under a series of one-year contracts. He was successful enough to be appointed, for a time, the cochairman of his department.

During the 1968-69 academic year, however, controversy arose between the respondent and the college administration. The respondent was elected president of the Texas Junior College Teachers Association. In this capacity, he left his teaching duties on several occasions to testify before committees of the Texas legislature, and he became involved in public disagreements with the policies of the college's board of regents. In particular, he aligned himself with a group advocating the elevation of the college to four-year status—a change opposed by the regents. And, on one occasion, a newspaper advertisement appeared over his name that was highly critical of the regents.

Finally, in May 1969, the respondent's one-year employment contract terminated and the board of regents voted not to offer him a new contract for the next academic year. The regents issued a press release setting forth allegations of the respondent's insubordination.[1] But they provided him no official statement of the reasons for the nonrenewal of his contract. And they allowed him no opportunity for a hearing to challenge the basis of the nonrenewal.

---

1. The press release stated, for example, that the respondent had defied his superiors by attending legislative committee meetings when college officials had specifically refused to permit him to leave his classes for that purpose.

The respondent than brought this action in federal district court. He alleged primarily that the regents' decision not to rehire him was based on his public criticism of the policies of the college administration and thus infringed his right to freedom of speech. He also alleged that their failure to provide him an opportunity for a hearing violated the Fourteenth Amendment's guarantee of procedural due process. The petitioners—members of the board of regents and the president of the college—denied that their decision was made in retaliation for the respondent's public criticism and argued that they had no obligation to provide a hearing. On the basis of these bare pleadings and three brief affadavits filed by the respondent, the district court granted summary judgment for the petitioners. It concluded that the respondent had "no cause of action against the [petitioners] since his contract of employment terminated May 31, 1969, and Odessa Junior College has not adopted the tenure system."

The court of appeals reversed the judgment of the district court. 430 F2d 939 (5th Cir). First, it held that, despite the respondent's lack of tenure, the nonrenewal of his contract would violate the Fourteenth Amendment if it in fact was based on his protected free speech. Since the actual reason for the regents' decision was "in total dispute" in the pleadings, the court remanded the case for a full hearing on this contested issue of fact: 430 F2d at 942-943. Second, the court of appeals held that, despite the respondent's lack of tenure, the failure to allow him an opportunity for a hearing would violate the constitutional guarantee of procedural due process if the respondent could show that he had an "expectancy" of reemployment. It, therefore, ordered that this issue of fact also be aired upon remand. 430 F2d at 943-944. We granted a writ of certiorari, 403 US 917, and we have considered this case along with *Board of Regents v Roth, ante.* . . .

I

The first question presented is whether the respondent's lack of a contractual or tenure right to reemployment, taken alone, defeats his claim that the nonrenewal of his contract violated the First and Fourteenth Amendments. We hold that it does not.

For at least a quarter century, this court has made clear that even though a person has no "right" to a valuable governmental benefit and even though the government may deny him the benefit for any number of reasons, there are some reasons upon which the government may not rely. It may not deny a benefit to a person on a basis that infringes his constitutionally protected interests—especially, his interest in freedom of speech. For if the government could deny a benefit to a person because of his constitutionally protected speech or associations, his exercise of those freedoms would in effect be penalized and inhibited. This would allow the government to "produce a result which [it] could not command directly." *Speiser v Randall* 357 US 513, 526. Such interference with constitutional rights is impermissible. . . .

Thus the respondent's lack of a contractual or tenure "right" to reemployment for the 1969-70 academic year is immaterial to his free speech claim. Indeed, twice before, this court has specifically held that the nonrenewal of a nontenured public school teacher's one-year contract may not be predicated on his exercise of First and Fourteenth Amendment rights. *Shelton v Tucker* 364 US 479; *Keyishian v Board of Regents* 385 US 589. We reaffirm those holdings here.

In this case of course, the respondent has yet to show that the decision not to renew his contract was, in fact, made in retaliation for his exercise of the constitutional right of free speech. The district court foreclosed any opportunity to make this showing when it granted summary judgment. Hence, we cannot now hold that the board of regents' action was invalid.

But we agree with the court of appeals that there is a genuine dispute as to "whether the college refused to renew the teaching contract on an impermissible basis—as a reprisal for the exercise of constitutionally protected rights." 430 F2d at 943. The respondent has alleged that his nonretention was based on his testimony before legislative committees and his other public statements critical of the regents' policies. And he has alleged that this public criticism was within the First and Fourteenth Amendment's protection of freedom of speech. Plainly, these allegations present a bona fide constitutional claim. For this court has held that a teacher's public criticism of his superiors on matters of public concern may be constitutionally protected and may, therefore, be an impermissible basis for termination of his employment. *Pickering v Board of Educ* 391 US 563.

For this reason we hold that the grant of summary judgment against the respondent, without full exploration of this issue, was improper.

II

The respondent's lack of formal contractual or tenure security in continued employment at Odessa Junior College, though irrelevant to his free speech claim, is highly relevant to his procedural due process claim. But it may not be entirely dispositive.

We have held today in *Board of Regents v Roth* 408 US 564, that the Constitution does not require opportunity for a hearing before the nonrenewal of a nontenured teacher's contract, unless he can show that the decision not to rehire him somehow deprived him of an interest in "liberty" or that he had a "property" interest in continued employment, despite the lack of tenure or a formal contract. In *Roth* the teacher had not made a showing on either point to justify summary judgment in his favor.

Similarly, the respondent here has yet to show that he has been deprived of an interest that could invoke procedural due process protection. As in *Roth,* the mere showing that he was not rehired in one particular job, without more, did not amount to a showing of a loss of liberty.[5] Nor did it amount to a showing of a loss of property.

But the respondent's allegations—which we must construe most favorably to the respondent at this stage of the litigation—do raise a genuine issue as to his interest in continued employment at Odessa Junior College. He alleged that this interest, though not secured by a formal contractual tenure provision, was secured by a no less binding understanding fostered by the college administration. In particular, the respondent alleged that the college had a de facto tenure program, and that he had tenure under that program. He claimed that he and others legitimately relied upon an unusual provision that had been in the college's official faculty guide for many years:

---

5. The court of appeals suggested that the respondent might have a due process right to some kind of hearing simply if he *asserts* to college officials that their decision was based on his constitutionally protected conduct. 430 F2d at 944. We have rejected this approach in *Board of Regents v Roth* 408 US at 575, n14.

Teacher Tenure: Odessa College has no tenure system. The administration of the college wishes the faculty member to feel that he has permanent tenure as long as his teaching services are satisfactory and as long as he displays a cooperative attitude toward his coworkers and his superiors, and as long as he is happy in his work.

Moreover, the respondent claimed legitimate reliance upon guidelines promulgated by the Coordinating Board of the Texas College and University System that provided that a person, like himself, who had been employed as a teacher in the state college and university system for seven years or more has some form of job tenure.[6] Thus the respondent offered to prove that a teacher, with his long period of service, at this particular state college had no less a "property" interest in continued employment than a formally tenured teacher at other colleges, and had no less a procedural due process right to a statement of reasons and a hearing before college officials upon their decision not to retain him. . . .

A written contract with an explicit tenure provision clearly is evidence of a formal understanding that supports a teacher's claim of entitlement to continued employment unless sufficient "cause" is shown. Yet absence of such an explicit contractual provision may not always foreclose the possibility that a teacher has a "property" interest in reemployment. For example, the law of contracts in most, if not all, jurisdictions long has employed a process by which agreements, though not formalized in writing, may be "implied." 3 Corbin, *Contracts* §§561-572A (1960). Explicit contractual provisions may be supplemented by other agreements implied from "the promisor's words and conduct in the light of the surrounding circumstances." Ibid., §562. And, "the meaning of [the promisor's] words and acts is found by relating them to the usage of the past." Ibid.

A teacher, like the respondent, who has held his position for a number of years, might be able to show from the circumstances of this service—and from other relevant facts—that he has a legitimate claim of entitlement to job tenure. Just as this court has found there to be a "common law of a particular industry or of a

---

6. The relevant portion of the guidelines, adopted as "Policy Paper 1" by the coordinating board on October 16, 1967, reads:

"A. Tenure

"Tenure means assurance to an experienced faculty member that he may expect to continue in his academic position unless adequate cause for dismissal is demonstrated in a fair hearing, following established procedures of due process.

"A specific system of faculty tenure undergirds the integrity of each academic institution. In the Texas public colleges and universities, this tenure system should have these components:

"(1) Beginning with appointment to the rank of full-time instructor or a higher rank, the probationary period for a faculty member shall not exceed seven years, including within this period appropriate full-time service in all institutions of higher education. This is subject to the provision that when, after a term of probationary service of more than three years in one or more institutions, a faculty member is employed by another institution, it may be agreed in writing that his new appointment is for a probationary period of not more than four years (even though thereby the person's total probationary period in the academic profession is extended beyond the normal maximum of seven years) . . . .

"(3) Adequate cause for dismissal for a faculty member with tenure may be established by demonstrating professional incompetence, moral turpitude, or gross neglect of professional responsibilities." The respondent alleges that, because he has been employed as a "full-time instructor" or professor within the Texas College and University System for ten years, he should have "tenure" under these provisions.

particular plant" that may supplement a collective-bargaining agreement, *Steelworkers v Warrior & Gulf Co* 363 US 574, 579, so there may be an unwritten "common law" in a particular university that certain employees shall have the equivalent of tenure. This is particularly likely in a college or university, like Odessa Junior College, that has no explicit tenure system even for senior members of its faculty, but that nonetheless may have created such a system in practice. See Byse & Joughin, *Tenure in American Higher Education* 17-28 (1959).[7]

In this case, the respondent has alleged the existence of rules and understandings, promulgated and fostered by state officials, that may justify his legitimate claim of entitlement to continued employment absent "sufficient cause." We disagree with the court of appeals insofar as it held that a mere subjective "expectancy" is protected by procedural due process, but we agree that the respondent must be given an opportunity to prove the legitimacy of his claim of such entitlement in light of "the policies and practices of the institution." 430 F2d at 943. Proof of such a property interest would not, of course, entitle him to reinstatement. But such proof would obligate college officials to grant a hearing at his request, where he could be informed of the grounds for his nonretention and challenge their sufficiency.

Therefore, while we do not wholly agree with the opinion of the court of appeals, its judgment remanding this case to the district court is

Affirmed.

Mr. Justice Powell took no part in the decision of this case.

Mr. Chief Justice Burger, concurring.

I concur with the court's judgments and opinions in *Perry* and *Roth,* but there is one central point in both decisions that I would like to underscore since it may have been obscured in the comprehensive discussion of the cases. That point is that the relationship between a state institution and one of its teachers is essentially a matter of state concern and state law. The court holds today only that a state-employed teacher who has a right to reemployment under state law, arising from either an express or implied contract, has, in turn, a right guaranteed by the Fourteenth Amendment to some form of prior administrative or academic hearing on the cause for nonrenewal of his contract. Thus [the issue] hinges on a question of state law. The court's opinion makes this point very sharply: "Property interests . . . are created and their dimensions are defined by existing rules or understandings that stem from an independent source such as state law. . . ." *Board of Regents v Roth. . . .*

Because the availability of the Fourteenth Amendment right to a prior administrative hearing turns in each case on a question of state law, the issue of abstention will arise in future cases contesting whether a particular teacher is entitled to a hearing prior to nonrenewal of his contract. If relevant state contract law is unclear, a federal court should, in my view, abstain from deciding whether he is constitutionally entitled to a prior hearing, and the teacher should be left to resort to state courts on the questions arising under state law.

---

7. We do not now hold that the respondent has any such legitimate claim of entitlement to job tenure. For "property interests . . . are not created by the Constitution. Rather, they are created and their dimensions are defined by existing rules or understandings that stem from an independent source such as state law. . . ." *Board of Regents v Roth.* If it is the law of Texas that a teacher in the respondent's position has no contractual or other claim to job tenure, the respondent's claim would be defeated.

Mr. Justice Brennan, joined by Mr. Justice Douglas, dissenting in part. [Opinion omitted.]

Mr. Justice Marshall, dissenting in part. [Opinion omitted.]

Notes and Questions

1. Distinguishing *Roth* and *Sindermann*

What distinguishes the *Roth* and *Sindermann* cases? Was Sindermann's dismissal more stigmatizing than Roth's? Did Sindermann have a more reasonable expectancy of reemployment than Roth? Why was the university's practice with respect to other teachers irrelevant to Roth but relevant to Sindermann? What is the difference between a contract for continued employment implied from the conduct of the parties and a reasonable expectancy of reemployment? Would a teacher's expectancy of reemployment be reasonable unless the school or university indicated its intention to continue the employment relationship?

2. The Test

Is the problem, as Justice Stewart suggests, largely definitional rather than one of balancing institutional and individual interests? Did Roth lose because his claim did not fall within acceptable definitions of "property" or "liberty"? How did Justice Douglas define those terms? How should they be defined? Does not the term "property" convey a myriad of legal meanings depending on the context of litigation? Might it mean a right to exclusive enjoyment over competing private interests? A right to compensation or some legal process when governmental deprivation takes place? If the latter meaning is appropriate to the *Roth* and *Sindermann* cases, is Justice Stewart's formulation of the problem defensible? See generally Reich, "The New Property," 73 *Yale LJ* 733 (1964).

3. Interests of the School

If you used a functional approach to the problem of hearings for nontenured teachers, what interests of the school would you take into account? Does the school have an interest in secrecy? If a school dismisses a teacher for personal reasons, *e.g.*, the teacher is contentious or discourteous, are these legitimate reasons that should not be publicized? Is it adequate to argue that the teacher should have an option to demand reasons and a hearing and should bear the consequences of her choice? Might the formality of providing reasons and a hearing discourage educational institutions from making hard personnel decisions? Does a hearing subtly shift the burden of persuasion to the school? What of the expenses of a hearing? Should the dismissed teacher be required to pay part of the costs?

4. Interests of the Teacher

What are the interests of the dismissed teacher that you would take into account? Might the absence of reasons for dismissal lead prospective employers to think that she was fired for academic incompetence or immorality, even if her firing had no such cause? Will required formalities of hearing and reasons alter substantive decisions? Correct arbitrary or erroneous behavior? Might a hearing make universities less likely to dismiss a teacher for the exercise of first amendment rights?

5. Legalization of Dispute Resolution

Are there dangers in legalizing the methods of conflict resolution in educational institutions with respect to personnel decisions? Is legalization consistent with the interests at stake? Would you distinguish between due process for students and for teachers? See chapter 2.

6. Applying *Roth* and *Sindermann*

The Supreme Court's decisions in *Roth* and *Sindermann* give rise to a number of practical problems with respect to advising dismissed teachers as to the appropriate avenue for seeking legal redress. Consider the following hypothetical case:

Mr. Jones is the local chairman of the American Association of University Professors on the faculty of State University. He is also an assistant professor in the English department. As AAUP chairman, Jones has often criticized the conduct of the president of State University whom he considers unsympathetic to academic freedom. Jones also attacked him for his treatment of students who participated in anti-Vietnam demonstrations. The university has a published rule stating that an instructor has tenure after he has completed four years of service. Jones has completed three years at the university and is sent a fourth annual contract stating that his employment will be terminated at the end of the year. Jones crosses out the termination clause, signs the contract, and returns it. Jones completes his fourth year and is dismissed. The university, contending that Jones is not tenured, refuses to divulge the reasons for the dismissal. Nonetheless, it offers Jones a hearing "in order to be fair," not because it is obligated to do so. The hearing is to take place before the tenured members of the English faculty, who previously had voted to grant Jones tenure but were overruled by the president. The decision of the faculty will be reviewed by the university deans, the president, and finally by the university board of governors.

What advice would you give Jones? What are the legal and tactical difficulties with his position? Consider these questions:

(a) Does Jones' situation fall within the *Roth* or the *Sindermann* decisions? Does he have an implied contract of reemployment? In accordance with Chief Justice Burger's concurring opinion in *Sindermann,* would it be appropriate for a federal district court to abstain from deciding the due process issue until a state court has passed on the state law contract issues raised by the case? Would you be concerned by the delay in the proceeding which abstention might occasion? If so, would you advise Jones to waive his due process claim to a statement of reasons and a hearing and ask the federal district court to adjudicate only his claim that he was dismissed on impermissible first amendment grounds?

(b) What of the fact that the university has already offered a hearing? Why not simply accept that offer to obviate the issue? What sense does a hearing make when the teacher has not been advised of the reasons for firing? Is the university likely to introduce any evidence at the hearing other than the notice of dismissal? If this Kafkaesque proceeding seems unappealing, are there dangers in declining the university's offer? Might a federal judge hold that Jones failed to exhaust his administrative remedies and therefore dismiss his case? At the very least, might a judge be unimpressed with the sincerity of Jones' claim to a due process hearing when he has declined the university's offer? Would your acceptance of the university's hearing be a waiver of any objections to defects in that proceeding? Would it be wise simply to use the proffered hearing as an opportunity to build a record for review by the federal courts?

(c) Is this series of events likely: Jones is heard before the English department three months after his dismissal, and they vote to reinstate him and grant him tenure. The deans of the university reverse this decision. Six weeks later, the president affirms the deans' decision. Three months later the board of governors affirms the president's decision. Jones files a suit in federal court alleging denial of due process and first amendment rights. After a hearing in federal court, the judge rules that he must abstain pending a state court resolution of the contract issues. One year later, the state supreme court rules that Jones had tenure. The matter returns to the federal district court which remands to the university for a hearing. One month later, the members of the English department convene and vote to reinstate Jones. The deans reverse, finding that Jones has engaged in gross misconduct in his criticisms of the president. Six weeks later, the president affirms the deans, and four months later, the board of governors once again affirms the president. Jones returns to the federal district court, and that court rules in his favor on the first amendment issues. State University appeals to the United States Court of Appeals, and the district court's judgment is affirmed. In all, almost three years have elapsed since the date of his original dismissal. Would you advise Jones zealously to pursue his due process claim? What advice would you give the university?

7. University and Elementary and Secondary School Teachers

With respect to a hearing and statement of reasons before the dismissal of nontenured teachers, would you draw any distinction between public university instructors and public elementary and secondary school instructors?

8. Dismissal Procedures

With few exceptions, most tenure statutes require lengthy and detailed procedures before dismissal. Alabama's statutory provisions are typical. Ala Code tit 52, §§ 351-61 (Cum Supp 1971). A dismissed teacher must be notified of her dismissal, and is entitled to a statement of the reasons for the dismissal. If the dismissed teacher indicates her desire for a hearing, the school administration is required to conduct one. The hearing may be public or private at the teacher's discretion; she has the rights to counsel, to present evidence and witnesses, to cross-examine witnesses, and to subpoena witnesses. The hearing is held before the board of education, and a majority of the board must vote to dismiss the teacher for her removal to be effective. Provision is made for appeal to the state tenure commission, which reviews the record made before the board of education. The decision of the state commission is final.

In Colorado, the hearing is held before a three-member board, one member chosen by the teacher, one by the school board, and the third member (the chairman) chosen by the other two. In Michigan all hearings are originally heard by the state tenure commission, composed of two classroom teachers, one school board member, one school superintendent, and one public member. Nevada provides for a hearing by a professional review committee of forty-two citizens, hearing cases in five-member panels. See generally National Education Association, *Teacher Tenure and Contracts* (1971). Is the majority in *Roth* and *Sindermann* open to the charge that they have chosen to protect only those who are not in need of protection?

9. Requirements for a Fair Hearing

For an analysis of what constitutes a fair hearing, see chapter 2, pages 190-97. See also *Duke v North Texas State Univ* 469 F2d 829 (5th Cir 1972). Should the requirements as to an impartial judge, legal counsel, cross-examination, etc., be different for teachers than for students?

VI. Teacher Organization and Collective Bargaining

A. The Background

"UNITED STATES," in TEACHER UNIONS AND ASSOCIATIONS
M. Moskow and R. Doherty
295 (A. Blum ed, 1969)

Teacher organizations in the United States have undergone a dramatic change since 1962. They have turned to collective bargaining or variations thereof as methods of making demands to their employers for determining salaries and working conditions. In prior years, state teacher organizations concentrated most of their efforts in lobbying, while local teacher organizations did little more than present proposals to their boards of education. Now the trend is for local organizations to negotiate formal written collective bargaining agreements with boards of education and for state and national affiliates to lobby for legislation requiring boards of education to negotiate. The affiliates also continue to supply research and personnel services to the local organizations. From 1965 to 1967, nine state statutes were passed requiring boards of education to engage in collective bargaining with teacher organizations; only one, Wisconsin, had a negotiation statute prior to 1965. The number of teacher strikes reached an all time high in 1967 and 1968. New York City teachers strikes involved over 40,000 teachers, and a statewide strike closed most of Florida's schools for almost two weeks. . . .

There are two national organizations representing teachers in the United States: The National Education Association (NEA) and the American Federation of Teachers (AFT). . . .

National Education Association

At the national level is the National Education Association with over one million members consisting of "classroom teachers, school administrators, and specialists in schools, colleges, and educational agencies which are both public and private." Classroom teachers in public schools constitute over 85 percent of the total membership. One of the major beliefs of the NEA, however, is that since education is a profession unique unto itself, membership in associations should not be limited to classroom teachers. Therefore, most state and local affiliates accept both teachers and administrators as members. In fact, several state associations will not accept local affiliates unless they are open to both classroom teachers and administrators.

According to the *NEA Handbook*:

The NEA is an independent, voluntary nongovernmental organization available to all professional teachers. It believes that all educators, regardless of position, rank, or authority, are workers in a common cause. It cooperates with all groups in American life who seek to improve education. It works for better schools and, to further that end, for the improvement of the professional status of teachers. Under such policies, the National Education Association has become the largest professional organization in the world and the only overall professional association for teachers in the United States.

The NEA has thirty-three departments . . . , twenty-five commissions and committees, seventeen headquarters divisions, and a staff of over 900 persons to carry out its policies. . . .

The thirty-three departments reflect the wide diversity of the activities of the NEA. The largest is the Department of Classroom Teachers which includes approximately 800,000 teachers in elementary and secondary schools. School administrators are members of departments such as the American Association of School Administrators, the National Association of Secondary-School Principals, and the Department of Elementary School Principals. Other departments include art education, educational research, foreign languages, and speech.

The American Federation of Teachers

With approximately 450 local affiliates, the AFT has approximately 140,000 members most of whom are concentrated in large cities. The AFT permits locals to decide on an individual basis whether they will accept principals as members; school superintendents are prohibited from membership by a constitutional provision. Separate locals for administrators are now prohibited, but prior to 1966 they were permitted providing the local AFT affiliate approved. The AFT constantly emphasizes that it is the only organization specifically devoted to the interests of the classroom teacher.

Although the NEA and the AFT have been in competition since 1919 the struggle gained new impetus in December 1961, when the United Federation of Teachers, a local affiliate of the AFT, was elected bargaining agent for 44,000 New York City public school teachers. The UFT received nearly three times as many votes as the NEA's hastily formed contender—the Teachers' Bargaining Organization. More important though, was the fact that for the first time the labor movement gave active support, in the form of personnel and financial resources, to a local of the AFT. Shortly after the victory, the AFT joined the Industrial Union Department of the AFL-CIO, which had been the major contributor to the UFT. . . .

After its overwhelming victory, the UFT immediately began negotiating with the school board. When negotiations broke down in April 1962, the UFT called a strike and over 20,000 teachers refused to work. The work stoppage lasted only one day, however, and after the mayor of the city and the governor of the state became involved, a salary agreement was reached. By the end of August, the parties had negotiated a forty-page written agreement which has been surpassed in its detailed provisions only by the later 1963 and 1965 agreements reached between the same parties.

Changes in NEA Policy

While the UFT was negotiating its written agreement in the summer of 1962, the NEA was holding its annual convention in Denver. Dr. William Carr, executive secretary of the NEA entitled his address "The Turning Point" which aptly describes the dramatic changes that took place in the NEA's policy toward collective negotiations at this convention.

In earlier years, the NEA had on occasion spoken about the necessity for group action by teachers, but they had no organized program and issued no guidelines or directives for implementation. At the 1962 convention the NEA's official policy on negotiations was formulated. Objecting to the term "collective bargaining," the NEA passed a resolution emphasizing the need for "professional negotiation." This was the first time the NEA used the term "negotiation" and it ended the search for a suitable substitute to "collective bargaining."

In reality "professional negotiations" is a generic term which the NEA uses to refer to a wide variety of different relationships between school boards and local teacher associations. For example, a local affiliate is considered to have a Level I professional negotiations agreement if the school board has made a written statement (which may be in the minutes of the board meeting) that it recognizes the association as the representative of all teachers in the district or even merely as the representative of its own members. Level II agreements consist of recognition and establishment of a negotiations procedure. If a means for settling impasses is added, the agreement is then considered Level III. Level IV agreements include terms and conditions of employment. When an impasse arises, it provides for various forms of third-party intervention most of which consist of modified forms of mediation and fact finding. At no time, however, do Level IV agreements provide for the utilization of state labor relations agencies or state mediation agencies since, in the NEA's opinion, disputes should always be settled through "educational channels." In extreme cases or when agreement cannot be reached, the association will resort to sanctions which may range from publicizing unfavorable teaching conditions in a particular school district to a mass refusal to sign contracts by all teachers employed in the district. At its 1967 convention, the NEA took an even more militant stand by voting to support local affiliates who had gone on strike. . . .

AFT Policy on Collective Bargaining

The AFT makes no effort to distinguish its approach to teacher-board relations from the collective bargaining process carried on in private industry. Delegates to the 1963 National Convention passed a resolution which recognized the right of locals to strike under certain circumstances and urged "the AFL-CIO and affiliated international unions to support such strikes when they occur." This resolution constituted a change in AFT policy since in prior years it had no official strike policy, even though locals had been supported when they had gone on strike. . . .

Until recently, the AFT has displayed no clear understanding of exactly what collective bargaining for teachers would entail. In fact the confusion over the AFT's definition of collective bargaining is quite similar to that exhibited by the NEA on professional negotiations. For example, although the AFT claimed to have approximately twelve written agreements between school boards and teachers' unions in

1964, only four of them included terms and conditions of employment, while the others were merely recognition agreements. In addition, several agreements did not provide for exclusive recognition, and in two cases the school boards signed written agreements with both the NEA local and the AFT local.

The agreement negotiated by the United Federation of Teachers, in New York, however, rapidly became the model for agreements later negotiated in other cities. By 1967, AFT locals had won representation rights for teachers in many of the large city school systems in the United States such as Baltimore, Boston, Chicago, Cleveland, Philadelphia, and Washington, D.C. They had negotiated collective bargaining agreements covering over 20 percent of the teachers in the United States even though they enrolled less than 10 percent of the teaching staff as members.

Causal Factors in the Emergence of Collective Bargaining in Public Education

Why did this movement begin in the past few years, roughly twenty-five years after the big organizing drives in private employment, and beyond that, what caused the movement to grow so rapidly once it had begun? Certainly the evidence is not all in at this stage, but there is enough to allow us to hazard a few observations. One thing does seem to be clear: The two essential ingredients for social change, pressure for change and the opportunity for change, were noticeably present in public school employment arrangements in the 1960s.[20]

The pressures stemmed from an apparently increasing dissatisfaction with employment conditions in public education, the changing ratio between male and female teachers, and the intense, sometimes bitter, rivalry between the two teacher organizations. We have said that teacher dissatisfaction is *apparently* on the increase only because there is no hard evidence to support this contention. We conclude merely that the increasing number of strikes, strike threats, sanctions, and slowdowns is a reasonably good barometer of how a great many teachers feel about their working conditions. On the other hand, it should be pointed out that teachers were better off, at least superficially, in the 1960s than ever before in their history. Salaries had increased by over 100 percent between 1950 and 1965, as compared to a 90 percent increase for industrial production workers; class size was not so great a problem; teachers were performing fewer clerical and subprofessional chores; and autocratic rule and administrative favoritism were probably less pronounced than they had been in earlier years.

Teachers *were* troubled by the decline in "psychic income," which had set in in many school districts, particularly in urban areas. Many teachers were complaining about meaningless bureaucratic intransigence. There was less opportunity to exercise one's initiative in the classroom. They also complained about the growing problem of unruly and academically disinterested students. The cities were being abandoned by the upwardly mobile, self-disciplined middle-class students, and many of the new and remaining students were hostile to the schools and to the teachers and were unwilling to conform to normal classroom routines. School administrations, it is alleged, have been reluctant to make adjustments either in the

---

20. For a more detailed explanation of these causal factors see Robert E. Doherty and Walter E. Oberer, *Teachers, School Boards and Collective Bargaining* (Ithaca, N.Y.: State School of Industrial and Labor Relations, 1967) and Myron Lieberman and Michael H. Moskow, *Collective Negotiations for Teachers* (Chicago: Rand McNally & Co., 1966).

curriculum or in discipline procedures to accommodate to this change. In a relatively short period of time, according to some teachers, a professional calling had been reduced to a job which was often boring, always difficult, and sometimes perilous. It is not surprising that under these circumstances the trade union approach should begin to have a great deal of appeal to teachers.

At the same time that disenchantment was setting in among public school teachers, men were joining the teaching ranks in significant numbers. . . .

It is a curious irony that while men teachers appear to be far less certain than women that they have made the correct occupational choice (34.4 percent would definitely choose teaching again as against 60 percent for women, according to a recent NEA survey), they seem at the same time to have a much stronger commitment to teaching as a career. Eighty percent of men teachers questioned in a New York City survey by Rabinowitz and Crawford saw teaching as a lifetime career, while only 40 percent of women teachers planned to continue teaching indefinitely.

If these surveys indeed represent a mood of a substantial number of male teachers, the picture they portray is that of a great number of men, resentful over their occupational choice but helpless to escape it. Collective bargaining may not erase this sense of bitterness and frustration, but it does present an opportunity to act upon it. . . .

Yet these two developments, the evident decline in job satisfaction and the emergence of a substantial percentage of men teachers, do not in themselves constitute sufficient pressure to launch a teacher bargaining drive on a scale such as the one that has developed. Teacher organizations must also be motivated to enroll new members, to try strenuously to achieve bargaining rights, and to press hard for their demands at the bargaining table.

If one were to attempt to locate the single event that stimulated teacher organizations around the country to greater activity, it would have to be the collective bargaining agreement negotiated by the United Federation of Teachers and the New York City Board of Education in 1962. Since the agreement provided for substantial improvements in working conditions for New York City teachers (at least it was generally agreed that there would have been fewer improvements in the absence of bargaining), AFT affiliates in other school systems began to push for bargaining rights. NEA affiliates, most of which had heretofore been reluctant to become involved in collective bargaining, were pressed to do likewise or stand to lose a considerable portion of their membership. Thus in many school systems the initiative began to come from NEA affiliates, many of them evidently feeling that if they did not represent the teachers at the bargaining table the AFT surely would. This rivalry has been almost as important a reason for bargaining activity as dissatisfaction with teaching conditions.

. . . [T] he pressure for bilateral determination of employment conditions has in several states been happily coupled with opportunity. Indeed, the statutes providing teachers with collective bargaining rights, most of which were enacted initially in response to public employee demands for such legislation, had in several states become a very important *cause* for bargaining activity. Once these laws were passed, a great many teacher organizations which had not sought a change in the informal method of dealing with boards of education began to bargain vigorously with their employers. It is probably fair to say that in some instances legislation *created* dissatisfaction. For example, there had been no pervasive or profound feeling of teacher discontent in Connecticut prior to June of 1965, when the Connecticut teacher bargaining statute went into effect. General teaching conditions in that state were, in fact, considered to be among the best in the nation. Yet within six months after the governor had signed the bill into law 50 percent of the state's 300,000 teachers were covered by collective agreements. Truly, opportunity had stimulated a need which a great many teachers barely knew existed.

By 1968, however, neither opportunity nor pressure were serving as the essential stimulants. The question most teachers sitting on the sidelines had been asking—does it work, does collective bargaining really bring about significant improvements in employment conditions?—had been answered in the affirmative. It had become clear even to the most cautious of NEA affiliates, that school boards were, under bargaining conditions, granting teacher concessions which were often far in excess of what they would have granted on their own. Nor could these teachers have helped but notice that demands backed by a strike threat or an actual strike usually resulted in even more concessions. It is not very likely, for example, that the Detroit School Board would have increased its teachers' starting salary from $5,800 to $7,500 yearly, reduced class size, and shortened the school year, had it not been faced with a strike and a determined group of teacher representatives sitting across the bargaining table. . . .

It should be emphasized that not all, or even a majority, of the state legislatures have been persuaded that a teacher bargaining statute is necessary. In some cases they have yet to be persuaded that teacher bargaining itself is in the public good. In fact, as of March 1968, school boards in Alabama, Georgia, North Carolina, and South Carolina—to name but a few states—were forbidden either by statute, court ruling, or attorney general opinion to enter into collective bargaining arrangements with their employees. In a handful of states it was illegal for public employees even to join labor organizations.

In still other states, such as New Jersey, Pennsylvania, Ohio, Indiana, Illinois, the legislatures have been silent on the matter of collective negotiations in public education. But while governments in these states do not grant to teachers the right to bargain collectively, neither do they disallow the right. Thousands of public school teachers are covered by comprehensive collective agreements in such cities as Newark, Philadelphia, Cleveland, South Bend, and Chicago, all of which are located in states without negotiations legislation.

Situated somewhere between the above category and the grouping of states with statutes mandating some form of bargaining are those states having what has come to be called "permissive" legislation—Alaska (1959), New Hampshire (1955), Florida (1965), Nebraska (1967). In essence, these statutes permit, but do not require, school boards and/or public employers generally to negotiate collectively, with their employees. The Alaska statute, for example, states that while a school district "may enter into a contract with a labor organization" nothing in the act "requires" the board to enter into such an agreement. Similarly, the Nebraska statute provides that "no board of education . . . shall be required to meet or confer with represent-atives of an organization of certificated school employees unless a majority of members of such board determines to recognize such an organization." As of March 1968, relatively few school districts in the so-called permissive states were involved in collective bargaining nor were there many teachers in these states covered by collective agreements.

Notes and Questions

1. Legal Protection and Teacher Militancy

Can the rise of militancy of teacher organizations in collective bargaining be explained, at least in part, by the failure of the legal system to protect teachers from arbitrary rules and loss of academic freedom, tenure, and procedural fairness? In this regard, consider the remarks of Albert Shanker, president of the United Federation of Teachers of New York City:

"ASPIRATIONS OF THE EMPIRE STATE FEDERATION OF TEACHERS," in EMPLOYER-EMPLOYEE RELATIONS IN THE PUBLIC SCHOOLS (R. Doherty ed, 1967)

Perhaps the biggest burr for the average teacher in terms of working conditions involves the internal politics of a school or a school system. The most cursory visit to any teacher lunchroom will bring this home clearly. Teachers suspect that the method of making school assignments is not based on a sense of justice or on ability so much as on favoritism or discrimination. There is widespread belief, with more than passing justification, that perhaps Mr. Jones receives the most difficult class year after year because he dared be critical of the school principal at a faculty conference or because of some other "unprofessional" criteria, teachers are just as convinced that a certain Mrs. Brown is given added cafeteria and patrol duties simply because the principal does not like her. Or was favoritism responsible when a teacher new to the school with no training in guidance was made acting guidance counselor, while other teachers possessed both training and years of experience.

Thus a major part of the efforts to secure a first-class citizenship must be directed to establishing equitable procedures, rules, and regulations which would reduce (if not eliminate) this sub rosa system of favoritism and discrimination current in school systems. Necessarily, nondiscriminatory procedures would have to be based upon principles of seniority, rotation, and objective qualifications. These procedures are not designed to *replace* the administrative and supervisory echelon, but to provide a system of checks and balances whereby whimsical administrative decisions may be appealed.

Similarly, in disputed cases involving teachers and the board of education or between a teacher and her principal the decision on the merits of the dispute should not be imposed by either the board or the principal who are in fact parties to the dispute. Machinery to resolve disputes in a fair manner must shy from vesting all the decision-making power in the hands of administrators or in boards of education. Final decision must rest with a neutral third party.

Finally there is the question of the "civil rights" of teachers. There are two million teachers in the United States who yearly inculcate the values and virtues of democracy while they experience less of what is meant by democracy in their respective schools than any substantial segment of our society.

There are basic civil rights which are not enjoyed by teachers in New York State or the United States at present. Teachers simply do not enjoy the right of free speech and assembly. A probationary teacher who may want to join the union rather than the association may not have his job the following year. This is not exaggeration. And how can teachers lay claim to first-class citizenship in the face of this situation?

2. Professionalism and Teacher Unions

Might not the rise of teachers' unions be attributed to a reaction against "professional" conceptions of the teachers' role that ignored their position as paid employees with their own discrete economic interests? Mr. Shanker also addressed himself to this problem:

> The economic citizenship of teachers deserves special emphasis because the teacher is first an employee. This seemingly obvious fact is frequently ignored or glossed over. For example, very few discussions of teacher salaries make a point that teachers have much the same right as any other segment in society to evidence a healthy concern with their own economic well-being; rather this concern is chalked up as being unprofessional. A healthy self-interest in economic well-being has erroneously become equated with a lack of concern with students. This prevalent view—this myth in fact—is one which a teacher's union aims to dispel.
>
> There is no conflict between professional concern and economic self-interest and well-being; rather than being mutually exclusive, professionalism and economic interest truly complement one another—one cannot be found without the other.
>
> Other professions are very much concerned with their clients yet they do not experience this supposed conflict. Doctors are expected to show great devotion to the welfare of their patients yet they do not find it improper to lobby actively and strenuously for legislation which in effect will ensure a high economic standard for the medical profession.
>
> It is vital to realize that teachers are *employees in a school system*—working under uniform salary schedules, under uniform pension plans, and under uniform policies and regulations respecting sick leaves, holidays, transfers, discharge, and the like—and that they cannot gain any productive insight into their economic plight through a concept of "professionalism" applicable to the doctor, the lawyer, or the dentist. One is self-employed, the other is not. Little similarity exists between the necessary structure to provide sound economic status and first-class economic citizenship for salaried, employed, professionals on the one hand and self-employed, fee-taking professionals on the other.
>
> Salary improvement then becomes a prime goal.
>
> Economic well-being, however, is not confined to salary. It entails vacations, holidays, how many classes to teach per week, the size of class registers, and so on. It is this area—the so-called area of working conditions—that has been traditionally the province of unilateral determination on the part of paternalistic (at best) and tyrannical (at worst) school boards. Decisions to lengthen the school year or the school day or to increase class size have traditionally been made not only without agreement on the part of teachers affected but without even bothering to solicit that consensus. (At times this operates on a more subtle level when boards go through pro forma rituals of consultation with teachers when in fact they are merely securing a ready

acceptance of fait accompli.) Teaching must be the largest occupation in the country where such basic economic decisions are made on a unilateral basis from above.

Despite Mr. Shanker's assertions to the contrary, do you see any inconsistency between sound educational planning and the economic demands of teacher organizations? Are these demands consistent with democratic control over the direction of public education? Is there any connection between the educational interests of the community and the economic interests of the teachers? If the democratic process surrounding the governance of the public schools is viewed not simply as control by the ballot but as a confrontation between various active and legitimate groups in the community, is there anything undemocratic about teacher unionization? In this regard, consider the position taken by Professors Wellington and Winter:

THE LIMITS OF COLLECTIVE BARGAINING IN PUBLIC EMPLOYMENT
78 *Yale LJ* 1107, 1123-24 (1969)

Although the market does not discipline the union in the public sector to the extent that it does in the private, the paradigm case, nevertheless, would seem to be consistent with what Robert A. Dahl has called the " 'normal' American political process," which is "one in which there is a high probability that an active and legitimate group in the population can make itself heard effectively at some crucial stage in the process of decision," for the union may be seen as little more than an "active and legitimate group in the population." With elections in the background to perform, as Mr. Dahl tells us, "the critical role . . . in maximizing political equality and popular sovereignty," all seems well, at least theoretically, with collective bargaining and public employment.

But there is trouble even in the house of theory if collective bargaining in the public sector means what it does in the private. The trouble is that if unions are able to withhold labor—to strike—as well as to employ the usual methods of political pressure, they may possess a disproportionate share of effective power in the process of decision. Collective bargaining would then be so effective a pressure as to skew the results of the " 'normal' American political process."

One should straightway make plain that the strike issue is not *simply* the essentiality of public services as contrasted with services or products produced in the private sector. This is only half of the issue, and in the past the half truth has beclouded analysis. The services performed by a private transit authority are neither less nor more essential to the public than those that would be performed if the transit authority were owned by a municipality. A railroad or a dock strike may be much more damaging to a community than "job action" by teachers. This is not to say that governmental services are not essential. They are, both because the demand for them is inelastic and because their disruption may seriously injure a city's economy and occasionally the physical welfare of its citizens. Nevertheless, essentiality of governmental services is only a necessary part of, rather than a complete answer to, the question: What is wrong with strikes in public employment?

What is wrong with strikes in public employment is that because they disrupt essential services, a large part of a mayor's political constituency will press for a quick end to the strike with little concern for the cost of settlement. The problem is that because market restraints are attenuated and because public employee strikes cause inconvenience to voters, such strikes too often succeed. Since other interest groups with conflicting claims on municipal government do not, as a general proposition, have anything approaching the effectiveness of this union technique—or at least cannot maintain this relative degree of power over the long run—they are put at a significant competitive disadvantage in the political process. Where this is the case, it must be said that the political process has been radically altered. And because of the deceptive simplicity of the analogy to collective bargaining in the private sector, the alteration may take place without anyone realizing what has happened.

Therefore, while the purpose and effect of strikes by public employees may seem in the beginning merely designed to establish collective bargaining or to "catch up" with wages and fringe benefits in the private sector, in the long run strikes must be seen as a means to redistribute income, or, put another way, to gain a subsidy for union members, not through the employment of the usual types of political pressure, but through the employment of what might appropriately be called political force.

How might Mr. Shanker respond to the Wellington and Winter argument?

3. *Board of Education v Shanker*

In light of Mr. Shanker's remarks, consider this quotation from *Board of Educ v Shanker* 54 Misc2d 941, 283 NYS2d 548, 552-53 (Sup Ct 1967):

> The testimony adduced . . . demonstrates overwhelmingly . . . that the defendant union and its president, Albert Shanker . . . have deliberately, willfully and contumaciously flouted the clear mandate of the court which restrained them from engaging in or assisting in any work stoppage against . . . the board of education . . . .
>
> From time immemorial, it has been a fundamental principle that a government employee may not strike. . . .
>
> Transcending in importance defendant's violation of our statutes is the fact that in doing so they have deliberately defied the lawful mandate of the court. The defendant union, powerful though it may be, is nevertheless insufficiently powerful to disdain, with impunity, the law and the court. Our existence as a free people is dependent on a healthy respect for law and order. . . . Ironic indeed is the fact that this basic lesson in elementary civics must be taught anew to, of all pupils, the very persons to whom we daily entrust our tender offspring for training and development as the leaders of tomorrow.

4. Teacher Organization and Political Pressure

Can one persuasively argue that the increased activism of teacher organizations is a response to the increase in external political pressure on schools, a type of "countervailing power"? See D. Wollett, "The Coming Revolution in Public School Management," 67 *Mich L Rev* 1017 (1969). But see excerpt from Zeigler, *Political Life of American Teachers, supra* at 208-10.

5. Teacher Organization: Wages and Working Conditions

Many commentators suggest the primary impetus to teacher organization and collective bargaining is the desire to increase wages and improve working conditions. If so, how do you account for the relatively late development of such activities among teachers? Do you find the Moskow and Doherty explanation persuasive? Economists have long and inconclusively debated whether unionization results in higher wages for employees. Does the fact that teacher unions bargain with public agencies give them greater bargaining leverage than their nonpublic counterparts? Professors Wellington and Winter have addressed themselves to this problem in the broader context of all public employment ("Limits of Collective Bargaining in Public Employment," 78 *Yale LJ* 1107, 1114-22):

> [In the private sector] union power is frequently constrained by the fact that consumers react to a relative increase in the price of a product by purchasing less of it. As a result any significant real financial benefit, beyond that justified by an increase in productivity, which accrues to workers through collective bargaining, may well cause significant unemployment among union members. Because of this employment-benefit relationship, the economic costs imposed by collective bargaining as it presently exists in the private sector seem inherently limited. . . .
>
> In the public sector, the trade-off between benefits and employment seems much less important. Government does not generally sell a product the demand for which is closely related to price. There usually are not close substitutes for the products and services provided by government and the demand for them is inelastic. Such market conditions are, as we have seen, favorable to unions in the private sector because they permit the acquisition of benefits without the penalty of unemployment, subject to the restraint of nonunion competitors, actual or potential. But no such restraint limits the demands of public employee unions. Because much government activity is, and must be, a monopoly, product competition, nonunion or otherwise, does not exert a downward pressure on price and wages. Nor will the existence of a pool of labor ready to work for a wage below union scale attract new capital and create a new, and competitively less expensive, governmental enterprise. The fear of unemployment, however, can serve as something of a restraining force in two situations. First, if the cost of labor increases, the city may reduce the quality of the service it furnishes by reducing employment. For example, if teachers' salaries are increased, it may decrease the number of teachers and increase class size. However, the ability of city government to accomplish such a change is limited not only by union pressure, but also by the pressure of other affected interest groups in the community. Political considerations, therefore, may cause either no reduction in employment or services, or a reduction in an area other than that in which the union members work. Both the political power exerted by the beneficiaries of the services, who are also voters, and the power of the public employee union as a labor organization, then, combine to create great pressure on political leaders either to seek new funds or to reduce municipal services of another kind. Second, if labor costs increase, the city may, even as a private employer would, seek to replace

labor with machines. The absence of a profit motive, and a political concern for unemployment, however, may be a deterrent in addition to the deterrent of union resistance. The public employer which decides it must limit employment because of unit labor costs will likely find that the politically easiest decision is to restrict new hires, rather than to lay off current employees.

Even if we are right that a close relationship between increased economic benefits and unemployment does not exist as a significant deterrent to unions in the public sector, might not the argument be made that in some sense the taxpayer is the public sector's functional equivalent of the consumer? If taxes become too high, the taxpayer can move to another community. While it is generally much easier for a consumer to substitute products than for a taxpayer to substitute communities, is it not fair to say that, at the point at which a tax increase will cause so many taxpayers to move that it will produce less total revenue, the market disciplines or restrains union and public employer in the same way and for the same reasons that the market disciplines parties in the private sector? Moreover, does not the analogy to the private sector suggest that it is legitimate in an economic sense for unions to push government to the point of substitutability?

Several factors suggest that the answer to this latter question is at best indeterminate, and that the question of legitimacy must be judged not by economic, but by political criteria.

In the first place, there is no theoretical reason—economic or political—to suppose that it is desirable for a government entity to liquidate its taxing power, to tax up to the point where another tax increase will produce less revenue because of the number of people it drives to different communities. In the private area, profit maximization is a complex concept, but its approximation generally is both a legal requirement and socially useful as a means of allocating resources. The liquidation of taxing power seems neither imperative nor useful.

Second, consider the complexity of the tax structure and the way in which different kinds of taxes (property, sales, income) fall differently upon a given population. Consider, moreover, that the taxing authority of a particular governmental entity may be limited (a municipality may not have the power to impose an income tax). What is necessarily involved, then, is principally the redistribution of income by government rather than resource allocation, and questions of income redistribution surely are essentially political questions.

For his part, the mayor in our paradigm case will be disciplined not by a desire to maximize profits, but by a desire—in some cases at least—to do a good job (to effectuate his programs), and in virtually all cases either to be reelected or to move to a better elective office. What he gives to the union must be taken from some other interest group or from taxpayers. His is the job of coordinating these competitive claims while remaining politically viable. And that coordination will be governed by the relative power of the competing interest groups. . . .

6. Merger of Teacher Organizations

The recent merger of the New York State Teachers Association (NEA) and the United Teachers of New York (AFT) raises the prospect that both national organizations will merge in the near future. If merged, the resultant union would become the largest in the country. For a discussion of the problems and prospects for the merger, see M. Lieberman, "The Union Merger Movement—Will 3,500,000 Teachers Put It All Together?" *Saturday Review* 24 June 1972, p. 50. What would be the impact of such a merger on teacher organization? Would statewide contracts become the norm? Would uniformity between school districts be unavoidable?

B. The Constitutional Issues

McLAUGHLIN v TILENDIS
398 F2d 287 (7th Cir 1968)

Cummings, Circuit Judge.

This action was brought under Section 1 of the Civil Rights Act of 1871 (42 USC §1983)[1] by John Steele and James McLaughlin who had been employed as probationary teachers by Cook County, Illinois, School District No. 149. Each sought damages of $100,000 from the superintendent of School District No. 149 and the elected members of the board of education of that district.

Steele was not offered a second-year teaching contract and McLaughlin was dismissed before the end of his second year of teaching. Steele alleged that he was not rehired and McLaughlin alleged that he was dismissed because of their association with Local 1663 of the American Federation of Teachers, AFL-CIO. Neither teacher had yet achieved tenure.

In two additional counts, Local 1663 and the parent union, through their officers and on behalf of all their members, sought an injunction requiring the defendants to cease and desist from discriminating against teachers who distribute union materials and solicit union membership.

The district court granted the defendants' motion to dismiss the complaint, holding that plaintiffs had no First Amendment rights to join or form a labor union, so that there was no jurisdiction under the Civil Rights Act. . . . Concluding that the First Amendment confers the right to form and join a labor union, we reverse on the ground that the complaint does state a claim under section 1983.

It is settled that teachers have the right of free association, and unjustified interference with teachers' associational freedom violates the due process clause of the Fourteenth Amendment. *Shelton v Tucker* 364 US 479, 485-487. Public employment may not be subjected to unreasonable conditions, and the assertion of First Amendment rights by teachers will usually not warrant their dismissal. *Keyishian v Board of Regents* 385 US 589, 605-606; *Garrity v New Jersey* 385 US 493, 500; *Pickering v Board of Educ* 391 US 563. Unless there is some illegal intent, an individual's right to form and join a union is protected by the First Amendment. . . . As stated in *NAACP v Alabama* 357 US 449, 460: "It is beyond debate that freedom to engage in association for the advancement of beliefs and ideas is an inseparable aspect of the 'liberty' assured by the due process clause of the Fourteenth Amendment, which embraces freedom of speech."

---

1. Section 1983 of Title 42 of the US Code provides: "Every person who, under color of any statute, ordinance, regulation, custom, or usage, of any state or territory, subjects, or causes to be subjected, any citizen of the United States or other person within the jurisdiction thereof to the deprivation of any rights, privileges, or immunities secured by the Constitution and laws, shall be liable to the party injured in an action at law, suit in equity, or other proper proceedings for redress."

Even though the individual plaintiffs did not yet have tenure, the Civil Rights Act of 1871 gives them a remedy if their contracts were not renewed because of their exercise of constitutional rights. . . .

There is no showing on this record that plaintiffs' activities impeded "[the] proper performance of [their] daily duties in the classroom." [Citing *Pickering v Board of Educ* 391 US 563.] If teachers can engage in scathing and partially inaccurate public criticism of their school board, surely they can form and take part in associations to further what they consider to be their well-being.

The trial judge was motivated by his conclusion that more than free speech was involved here, stating:

> The union may decide to engage in strikes, to set up machinery to bargain with the governmental employer, to provide machinery for arbitration, or may seek to establish working conditions. Overriding community interests are involved. The very ability of the governmental entity to function may be affected. The judiciary, and particularly this court, cannot interfere with the power or discretion of the state in handling these matters.

It is possible of course that at some future time plaintiffs may engage in union-related conduct justifying their dismissal. But the Supreme Court has stated that: "Those who join an organization but do not share its unlawful purposes and who do not participate in its unlawful activities surely pose no threat, either as citizens or as public employees." *Elfbrandt v Russell* 384 US 11, 17. Even if this record disclosed that the union was connected with unlawful activity, the bare fact [of] membership does not justify charging members with their organization's mis-deeds. . . . A contrary rule would bite more deeply into associational freedom than is necessary to achieve legitimate state interests, thereby violating the First Amendment.

Illinois has not prohibited membership in a teacher's union, and defendants do not claim that the individual plaintiffs engaged in any illegal strikes or picketing.[3] Moreover, collective bargaining contracts between teachers' unions and school districts are not against the public policy of Illinois. *Chicago, etc., Educ Ass'n v Board of Educ* 76 Ill App2d 456, 222 NE2d 243 (1966). Illinois even permits the automatic deduction of union dues from the salaries of employees of local governmental agencies. Ill Rev Stats 1967, ch 85, sec 472. These very defendants have not adopted any rule, regulation, or resolution forbidding union membership. Accordingly, no paramount public interest of Illinois warranted the limiting of Steele's and McLaughlin's right of association. Of course, at trial defendants may show that these individuals were engaging in unlawful activities or were dismissed for other proper reasons, but on this record we hold that the complaint sufficiently states a justifiable claim under section 1983. There is nothing anomalous in protecting teachers' rights to join unions. Other employees have long been similarly protected by the National Labor Relations Act. See *NLRB v Jones & Laughlin* 301 US 1, 33 . . . .

The judgment of the district court is reversed and the cause is remanded for trial.

---

3. In Illinois, strikes and certain picketing by public employees are enjoinable. *Board of Educ of Community Unit School Dist. No 2 v Redding* 32 Ill2d 567, 207 NE2d 427 (1965).

Notes and Questions

1. Constitutional Issues: Organization

Does *McLaughlin* suggest that state statutes prohibiting public employees, including teachers, from joining labor organizations are unconstitutional? See generally H. Wellington and R. Winter, *The Unions and the Cities* chap 5 (1971). Would the result have been different if the union had engaged in illegal strike or picketing activities? Would the court require that the plaintiffs personally participate in such illegal activities before upholding their dismissals?

2. Security Clauses

Suppose a teachers' union negotiates a contract with the school board that requires all teachers to become members of the union within thirty days of their employment, or by September 4 if they are presently employed in the school system. The penalty for failing to join is that nonunion members do not receive any salary increases negotiated by the union. Would such a security clause violate the First Amendment rights of nonunion members? See *Benson v School Dist No 1* 136 Mont 77, 344 P2d 117 (1959). What if the school board argued that union members were more competent teachers? See *Magenheim v Board of Educ* 347 SW2d 409 (Mo Ct App 1961). Can one argue that teachers who benefit from union services should pay for them even if they do not wish to become union members? See *Smigel v Southgate Community School Dist* 24 Mich App 179, 180 NW2d 215 (1970).

3. Organizational Activities on School Grounds

Should teacher unions' and associations' organizational activities on school grounds be constitutionally protected as an aspect of teachers' First Amendment associational rights? What if a school board forbids the circulation of a union petition in faculty rooms during free periods? See *Los Angeles Teachers Union v Los Angeles City Bd of Educ* 71 CA2d 551, 78 Cal Rptr 723 (1969). What of a school board rule forbidding the use of faculty mail boxes to disseminate union materials? See *Friedman v Union Free School Dist No 1* 314 F Supp 223 (EDNY 1970). Recall the discussion in chapter 2 of student-distributed materials. Should the same constitutional test be applicable to teacher union activities?

4. Constitutional Issues: Strikes and Collective Bargaining

Prohibitions on strike and collective bargaining by public employees, including teachers, have not been thought to raise constitutional issues:

THE UNIONS AND THE CITIES
H. Wellington and R. Winter
73-74 (1971)

Whatever may be the constitutional power of the state to control freedom to associate, its power to control group action is a different—if ultimately related—matter. For the state must be in a position to protect itself and its citizens from oppression by private groups. Some regulation is surely permissible where organizations dedicated to violence are concerned. And the due process clause does not prevent the state from controlling the activities of trade associations or labor unions. In the absence of federal statutory law, the strike, for example, if it is coercive, may be barred; for that matter, so may the establishment of wages and working conditions through collective bargaining.

In the private sector, strikes have not been generally prohibited, as they have in the public. Indeed, in the public sector, attempting restrictions on the right of association rest in large part on a fear of strikes by organized employees. Yet it has been argued, with respect to strikes that do not create a threat to public health and welfare, that the equal protection clause of the Fourteenth Amendment forbids a state from distinguishing between public and private employment. If employees in the private sector may strike, so may public employees. This argument is without merit. The test, under the equal protection clause, is whether the distinction between public and private employment is rational. And it plainly is, . . . because of the relative inelasticity of demand for public services and the relative vulnerability of the municipal employer, strikes in the public sector have effects different from strikes in the private. The Constitution surely does not prevent the states from taking these very real differences into account.

Do you find this argument persuasive? Would a ban on strikes under particular circumstances, rather than a blanket prohibition, raise fewer constitutional concerns?

C. The Scope of Bargaining and Enforcement of the Collective Bargaining Agreement

JOINT SCHOOL DISTRICT NO 8 v WISCONSIN EMPLOYMENT RELATIONS BOARD
37 Wisc 2d 483, 155 NW2d 78 (1967)

Hallows, Justice.

It is provided in [Wisc Stat Ann] §111.70 (2) that municipal employees shall have ". . . the right to be represented by labor organizations of their own choice in conferences and in negotiations with their municipal employers or their representatives on questions of wages, hours, and conditions of employment. . . ."

The question is whether the school calendar is a question "of wages, hours and conditions of employment" and thus a subject of conferences and negotiations under §111.70(2). The WERB found and the circuit court agreed that the school calendar affecting teachers in the employ of the school board "has a direct and intimate relationship to their salaries and working conditions," because it established the number and dates of the teaching days and of the inservice days including the dates of the beginning and end of the school year. We think the language of §111.70(2) is sufficiently broad to cover the items constituting the school calendar. The days on which teachers must teach or be in service have a significant relationship to the "hours and conditions," if not the salary, of teachers and render the school calendar negotiable. The United States Supreme Court has construed the language "wages, hours and other terms and conditions of employment" under the National Labor Relations Act §8(d), to include the particular days of the week on which the employees are required to work. In addressing itself to the problem of whether a collective bargaining agreement violated the Sherman Antitrust Act, the Supreme Court said in *Local 189, Amalgamated Meat Cutters v Jewel Tea Co* 381 US 676, 691 (1965): "Contrary to the court of appeals, we think that the particular hours of the day and the particular days of the week during which employees shall be required to work are subjects well within the realm of 'wages, hours, and other terms and conditions of employment' about which employers and unions must bargain." . . .

The brief on behalf of Wisconsin Association of School Boards, Inc. as amicus curiae makes it plain that they do not contend that conferences and negotiations between school boards and employee units are precluded in all areas but only that the school board may not be required by legislation to bargain or submit to fact finding on basic educational-policy determinations. This argument assumes the school calendar is a basic educational-policy determination and that the negotiation of such calendar violates Art. X, §§1 and 3, of the Wisconsin Constitution. The state constitution by Art. X, §1, provides the supervision of the educational policy for public schools is vested in the state superintendent and such other officers as are designated by the legislature. . . .

We need not decide whether the determination of a school calendar is a major educational-policy determination. While its determination is for the school board, we do not consider it to be immunized for that reason from the scope of §111.70(2). Many items and restrictions in a school calendar are established by statute. School year, term and session are defined in §40.01. In §40.45 the requirements for a school month are set forth and certain holidays are designed as nonteaching days and others as only special observance days. In §40.22(12) a school board is given power to fix the length of time school shall be taught and in §40.30(17m) a board may establish rules scheduling the hours of each school day. These items determined by statute, of course, cannot be changed by negotiation. But what is left to the school boards in respect to the school calendar is subject to compulsory discussion and negotiation. . . .

The contents of the curriculum would be a different matter. Subjects of study are within the scope of basic educational policy and additionally are not related to wages, hours and conditions of employment. It is admitted, however, the school calendar is a permissively negotiable subject. It is stated the number of days an individual teacher works in a school term is negotiable with the teacher in the individual teacher contract. But if the number of teaching days may be negotiated with an individual teacher, it may be negotiated through representation on behalf of all the teachers.

But it is argued that if the school board were to negotiate the school calendar it would surrender its power as a municipal corporation and would be delegating its legislative powers to the negotiating process and ultimately to the fact-finding proceeding. . . .

We think if the ultimate responsibility for decision is solely that of the school board, the legislative authority is not limited or delegated. . . . However, under §111.70 the school board need neither surrender its discretion in determining calendar policy nor come to an agreement in the collective-bargaining sense. The board must, however, confer and negotiate and this includes a consideration of the suggestions and reasons of the teachers. But there is no duty upon the school board to agree against its judgment with the suggestions and it is not a forbidden practice for the school board to determine in its own judgment what the school calendar should be even though such course of action rejects the teachers wishes. . . .

Judgment Affirmed

PORCELLI v TITUS
108 NJ Super 301, 261 A2d 364 (App Div 1969)

Lewis, J.A.D.

Plaintiffs, ten members of the teaching staff of the Newark Board of Education (herein Newark board), appeal . . . from a final determination of the New Jersey State Board of Education (herein state board). The latter affirmed a decision of the commissioner of education which held that the action of the Newark board, in suspending its promotional procedure and its eligibility lists and in instituting a new policy for promotions, was a lawful exercise of discretionary authority.

Plaintiffs here urge that the Newark board (1) is bound by the terms of an outstanding employment agreement with the Newark Teachers' Association (herein NTA), the exclusive bargaining agent for all teachers in the Newark school district, and (2) may not lawfully disregard or modify by unilateral action the terms of that agreement.

The teachers' contract under review, dated June 19, 1967, covers the period from February 1, 1967, to February 1, 1970, and provides in pertinent part:

Article X. PROMOTIONS
A. The positions of principal, vice principal, . . . shall be filled in order of numerical ranking from the appropriate list, which ranking shall be determined by written and oral examination. . . .

. . . .

Article XXII. GENERAL

. . . .

F. The board hereby amends its rules and regulations to the extent necessary to give effect to the provisions of this agreement.

. . . .

Article XXIV. MUTUALITY OF OBLIGATION
The board and the association will make every good faith effort to carry out the spirit as well as the letter of this agreement, subject to law. . . .

Subsequently, on June 30, 1967, Newark board adopted an amendment to its rules and regulations, §505.4 thereof, to conform to Article X of the agreement and to provide specifically that "all promotional lists shall expire after four years."

On May 28, 1968, after a public hearing, the Newark board passed a resolution suspending the making of any appointments to the positions of principal or vice-principal from promotional lists "pending an evaluation by the board of education of the present procedure for making such appointments, effective after October 1, 1968." Thereafter no appointments for the positions of principal or vice-principal were made from promotional lists.

On August 22, 1968, defendant Franklyn Titus, superintendent of schools of the City of Newark (herein superintendent), proposed to the Newark board that written examinations and numerical listings according to any test scorings be abolished and replaced by a general pool of qualified candidates selected by a screening committee, from which appointments would be made by the superintendent. The recommendations were adopted by the Newark board on that date.

Prior to that August meeting, the numerical ranking lists included three plaintiffs for the position of principal and three plaintiffs for the position of vice-principal. The remaining four plaintiffs had passed written examinations during the 1967-68 school year for the position of principal or vice-principal but because of the suspension resolution they had no opportunity to take the oral part of the examination. All plaintiffs, however, were placed in the general pool of qualified candidates but lost the advantage they had acquired by being on the eligibility lists.

At this juncture we note that plaintiffs also filed suit in the United States District Court, District of New Jersey, against defendants superintendent and the Newark board alleging a violation of their civil rights under 42 USCA § 1983 in that defendants, acting under color of law, abolished an established examinational procedure in order to appoint Negroes to positions for which they would not otherwise be eligible and made appointments to such positions solely on the basis of race, and that plaintiffs were thereby discriminated against solely because they are white. . . . Their complaint was dismissed with prejudice. *Porcelli v Titus* 302 F Supp 726 (DNJ 1969) [*aff'd* 431 F2d 1254 (3d Cir 1970)] .

In the instant proceedings plaintiffs, in substance, demand a rescission of the challenged action of the Newark board and an enforcement of the promotional system prescribed by the agreement of June 19, 1967. They argue on appeal, as they did before the state agencies, that the Newark board, in changing its procedure for promotions, violated its own rules and regulations and unlawfully breached its negotiated contractual obligations with the NTA.

There can be no doubt, as plaintiffs contend in their brief, that the teachers in the Newark school system, as public employees, had the right to organize and, through organizational representation, the right to make proposals which could be effectuated by an enforceable agreement between the school board and its organized employees. . . .

Thus, the critical issue before us is whether the Newark board had the right to adopt unilaterally an educational policy relating to promotions which was inconsistent with the procedure contemplated by agreement voluntarily entered into with its employees. We need not for purpose of this opinion consider the issue as to what extent a board of education may contractually bind its successor board or boards, since here the commissioner found specifically that the contract in question was authorized by the Newark board in 1967 and ratified by its 1968 and 1969 successor boards.

Defendants justify their action on the grounds of statutory authority and educational necessity. They refer to the constitutional requirement that the legislature provide for a thorough and efficient system of free public schools, NJ Const (1947) Art VIII §IV, ¶1; the legislative implementation thereof delegating the operation of public schools to local boards of education, NJSA 18A:10-1; the broad discretionary powers vested in such boards with respect to the day-to-day functioning of the schools within their jurisdiction, NJSA 18A:11-1; and the board's authority enunciated under NJSA 18A:27-4:

> Each board of education may make rules, not inconsistent with the provisions
> of this title, governing the employment, terms and tenure of employment,

promotion and dismissal, and salaries and time and mode of payment thereof of teaching staff members for the district, *and may from time to time change, amend or repeal the same,* and the employment of any person in any such capacity and his rights and duties with respect to such employment shall be dependent upon and governed by the rules in force with reference thereto. [Emphasis added.]

. . .

The argument of defendants then runs that the action of the Newark board on May 28 and August 22 was in accord with its Rule 103.28 which reads: "Any rule of the board may be suspended by a two-third vote of the entire board. . . ." Therefore, since plaintiffs are employed under board rules which, as provided by law, may be changed, amended or repealed from time to time, and their employment contract of June 19, 1967, sets forth in its terms that it would become part of the board's rules and expressly provides that the agreement is "subject to law," the decision to suspend and modify the promotional system was consonant with the statutory powers with which the Newark board was vested.

In considering those contentions the commissioner properly observed that:

the law is not to be construed to imply that a board of education is not legally and morally bound to comply in good faith with the terms of any agreement consummated with its employees. Nor is a board permitted to enter into such an agreement with the implicit reservation that it can abrogate the terms thereof on any pretext. Such drastic, unilateral action can be sustained only in the face of *a real threat or obstacle* to the proper operation of the school system, or in an emergency of equal importance. [Emphasis added.]

He found that the Newark board deemed it essential to alter its method of selecting and appointing administrative and supervisory personnel for the reason that the educational needs and aspirations of the school children and the local community were being thwarted by the dearth of representation by Negro staff members in the leadership councils of the schools. Also, it was found that defendants endeavored, without success, to accomplish the desired result within the framework of the existing agreement; the dilemma that confronted the board was expressed in these words:

It could abide by its agreement and make no deviation of any kind in its rules and ignore public demand for change, or it could respond to what it conceived to be the needs of the school system and the desires of the community by modifying a part of its agreement against the wishes of a majority of the teachers' association. Faced with such a Hobson's choice the board made its decision in terms of its overriding obligation to serve the needs of the children and the community.

It is significant that the challenged action of defendants eventuated after the period between July 13 and 17, 1967, when the city of Newark was violently shaken by widespread civil disorders. . . . It is only reasonable to assume that the city and state school authorities were seriously concerned about the impact of such disturbances upon the students and their parents, the community at large, and the general administration of the school system throughout the city. . . .

In [the] federal proceeding it was stipulated that in September 1968 the school census was 75,876 with a Negro student population of 72.5 percent. It was also stipulated that of the seventy-two positions of principal in existence prior to August 22, 1968, none were held by Negroes, and with respect to the sixty-four vice-principal positions only three were held by Negroes. . . .

The commissioner held that the subject agreement, "whatever it may be labeled," could not constitute a surrender by the Newark board of its responsibility under the law to conduct the schools under its charge "in the best interests of the children to be served." . . .

We endorse the principle as did the court in *Kemp v Beasley* 389 F2d 178, 189 (8th Cir 1968), that "faculty selection must remain for the broad and sensitive expertise of the school board and its officials," and this we do notwithstanding an existing employment agreement where subsequent conditions make impossible a literal performance of all of its terms. The essence of the modern defense of impossibility is that the promised performance was at the making of the contract, or thereafter became impracticable owing to some extreme or unreasonable difficulty or the like "rather than it is scientifically or actually impossible." 6 Williston, *Contracts* §1931, p 5410 (rev ed 1938). Cf. 6 Corbin, *Contracts* §1336, p 384 (1962).

As approvingly noted in *Newark v North Jersey Dist Water Sup Comm* 106 NJ Super 88, 106, 254 A2d 313 (Ch Div 1968), affirmed o.b. 54 NJ 258, 255 A2d 193 (1969), "A thing is impossible in legal contemplation when it is not practicable; and a thing is impracticable when it can only be done at an excessive or unreasonable cost" (quoted from 1 Beach, *Contracts* § 216, p 269 (1896)). A fortiori, the concept of impossibility should prevail where a particular provision in a school contract is rendered impracticable by subsequent events demanding changes in an educational program in order to give meaningful effect to an overriding public policy. . . .

Implicit in the agency's decision here under review are findings that the Newark board was in fact faced with "a real threat or obstacle" to the proper administration of its school system. The record before us, and the attendant public events that may be judicially noticed, support the findings of the commissioner that the ex parte adoption of new promotional rules by the Newark board, notwithstanding lack of approval by a majority of the NTA, was "warranted and appropriate."

The determination of the state board that the Newark board acted lawfully, in the particular circumstances of this case, is affirmed.

Notes and Questions

1. Subjects for Bargaining

In *Wisconsin Employment Relations Board*, how does the court distinguish bargaining over the school calendar from bargaining over curriculum? Is it true, as the court asserts, that a decision can be reached in the case without deciding "whether the determination of a school calendar is a major educational policy determination?" Is the school calendar preserved as a subject of negotiation because of the limited power of school boards to alter it? Is it appropriate for the court to cite the *Jewel Tea Co* case, which arose in the private sector?

Which of the following subjects, if any, should be subject to collective negotiation and agreement: Class size? Physical facilities? Penalties for student misbe-havior? Admission of emotionally disturbed children to regular classes? Curriculum changes? Compensatory education programs? See Wellington and Winter, *The Unions and the Cities* 137-41 (1971).

2. Distinguishing *Porcelli* and *Wisconsin Employment Relations Board*

Are *Porcelli* and *Wisconsin Employment Relations Board* consistent? Is it sen-sible to hold that a particular subject is within the scope of bargaining but cannot be included as an enforceable part of the collective bargaining agreement? Is this what the *Porcelli* court held? Do you distinguish between personnel decisions and school calendar decisions? If the issue in *Porcelli* is the legal discretion of the board of education to make and implement educational policy decisions, do not all col-lective bargaining agreements abridge that discretion? Could not a board always argue that it had an "overriding obligation to serve the needs of the children and community?" Is the position of the commissioner of education that there was " 'a real threat or obstacle' to the proper administration of its school system" a realistic limitation on the board's power to overturn collective bargaining agreements?

3. Sovereignty and Illegal Delegation

Historically, limitations on collective bargaining in the public sector have been articulated in terms of the "sovereignty of the state" and the "illegal delegation of power." The former refers to the limitations a collective bargaining agreement places on the state's power to conduct its affairs as it sees fit. In the present context, it would refer to a board's inability to make policy decisions that conflict with its contractual arrangement with a teachers' organization. This concept has been roundly criticized:

Sovereignty must also seem to the critics too elusive and too remote a concept to be of practical significance in the fashioning of labor policy. The issue is not, they say, whether government's power is "supreme," but how government as an employer ought to exercise that power. And the concept of sovereignty, while it locates the source of ultimate authority, does not seem to speak to that issue. (H. Wellington and R. Winter, "The Limits of Collec-tive Bargaining in Public Employment," 78 *Yale LJ* 1107, 1109 (1969).)

"The doctrine of illegal delegation of power refers to the notion that an agency of the state, charged with particular responsibilities, may not delegate its authority to others." If state constitutional and statutory provisions charge school boards with particular educational policy decisions, they may not share their authority with teacher organizations.

4. Explaining *Porcelli*

If the contract theory espoused by the *Porcelli* court is difficult to defend, can the decision be justified on the basis of the traditional illegal delegation doctrine? In this regard, consider Professor Goldstein's comments on the *Porcelli* case:

The issue of the scope of permissible subjects of collective bargaining and contract resolution is more complex. It essentially is the issue of the old delegation doctrine—a doctrine that is being repudiated and, I believe, proper-ly so, in terms of its absolutist legal theory which could preclude all teacher collective bargaining in the absence of explicit legislative authorization. But the doctrine has an underlying core of validity in that it requires that those who have been selected by a given process and from a given constituency retain the power to make ultimate policy decisions and override decisions made by others. In terms of teacher collective bargaining there may be some subjects—acutely sensitive and quantitatively, if not qualitatively, removed from wages and hours—about which school boards cannot contractually bind themselves for an extended period of time.

In addition, a recent decision in New Jersey suggests the development of a doctrine limiting the effect of nonmandatory collective bargaining without reliance on a rigid delegation approach. . . . [In upholding the board's position, the court in *Porcelli v Titus* relied on the] contract doctrine of impossibility of performance.

This reliance on the private contract doctrine of impossibility is questionable contract law, to say the least. Moreover, the decision is unclear as to the perimeters of the doctrine enunciated and the theory, if any, of its public law basis. These and other aspects of the decision are quite troublesome. However, the practical effect of the approach of *Porcelli* is quite attractive in light of the concerns I have expressed herein. *Porcelli* does not, of course, address itself to the concern of the nature of the negotiating and contracting process. It does, however, limit the effect of a school board being bound by a contract on sensitive issues during dynamic times. Moreover, it does so in a way that minimizes the theoretical and practical problems of the unrestrained delegation doctrine.

Both the education commissioner and the court emphasized the normally binding effect of collective bargaining agreements and treated the board's action here as highly exceptional. The action was upheld on the basis of the persuasive need of Newark to do something to obtain a greater number of minority group principals. Although the existence and effect of the need did not seem to have been subject to significant review either by the education commissioner or the court in this case, the court did suggest that their doctrine requires review of the school board's determination of necessity in such cases.

Even if outside review of the school board's determination of necessity is minimal or nonexistent, the *Porcelli* doctrine is more protective of collective bargaining than is the old delegation doctrine. Under *Porcelli* the school board must act to set aside the contractual provision in question. The delegation doctrine allows outside groups to attack and enjoin enforcement of agreements. While it may be argued that an outside group would not gain anything by enjoining a contract provision that the school board wants to honor, this argument misses the real dynamics involved. It is much easier for an outside group to attack an agreement and the school board not to honor it after it has been enjoined from enforcing the contract, than it is for the school board itself to initiate abrogation of an agreement which it has signed. Not only is there the restraint of a school board's keeping its word generally, but the board has an ongoing relationship with the union that requires it to adhere to contracts except in the most extreme situations. The *Porcelli* rationale thus affords the school board an escape clause for extreme situations. It thus may present a practical compromise between the old delegation doctrine and one of no restraint on permissible subjects of bargaining or the duration of contractually binding agreements. (Goldstein, "Book Review," 22 *Buff L Rev* 603, 608-10 (1972).)

Do you agree with Professor Goldstein that the *Porcelli* approach is less "rigid" than the traditional delegation approach? Might it not be too flexible? What are the functional problems to which both *Porcelli* and the delegation doctrine are addressed? Does either label add much to the resolution of those problems?

5. Alternatives

Are there alternatives to traditional bipartite collective bargaining that might be more responsive to the peculiar demands of public schools? Should representatives of the parents and community be invited to participate? Student groups? What of a public referendum on the collective bargaining agreement? See D. Kirp, "Collective Bargaining in Education: Professionals as a Political Interest Group," 21 *J Pub Law* 323, 337 (1972).

6. Other Questions

In addition to the scope of bargaining and enforcement of agreements, there are many other questions about teacher organization. These include procedures for bargaining unit determination, elections to determine representation, certification of union representatives, grievance procedures, and arbitration. These matters generally are treated in traditional labor law courses. See, e.g., A. Cox and D. Bok, *Labor Law* (1965). For a discussion of these problems with respect to educational institutions, see P. Carlton and H. Goodwin, eds, *The Collective Dilemma: Negotiations in Education* (1969); Elam, Lieberman, and Moskow, eds, *Readings on Collective Negotiations in Public Education* (1967); Wollett, "The Coming Revolution in Public School Management," 67 *Mich L Rev* 1017 (1969).

D. The Power to Strike

State courts have often upheld the legality of prohibitions on strikes by public employees. See, e.g., *In re Block* 50 NJ 494, 236 A2d 589 (1967); *Zeluck v Board of Educ* 62 Misc2d 274, 307 NYS2d 329 (Sup Ct 1970). Compare *Board of Educ v Public School Employees Local #63* 233 Minn 144, 45 NW2d 797 (1951). They have also held that public employees can be accorded the right to strike only where there is an express legislative mandate. See, e.g., *Anderson Federation of Teachers, Local 519 v School City of Anderson* 252 Ind 558, 254 NE2d 329 (1970). State courts also have had no difficulty in treating "mass resignations" as the functional equivalent of a strike. See, e.g., *Board of Educ of New York v Shanker* 54 Misc2d 941, 283 NYS2d 548 (Sup Ct 1967). The live issues are complex and delicate policy problems. Is it wise to allow teachers' organizations to strike? If not, how can local governments avoid or end illegal strikes?

The temptation, of course, is to carry over concepts of collective bargaining from the private sector to the public sector. If bricklayers and factory employees may strike to press their demands on an unwilling employer, why may not teachers resort to similar tactics in order to coerce their employer to make concessions? As

Professor Goldstein has noted, if inequality in bargaining power on the part of individual employees is a substantial reason for unionization and resort to collective strike tactics, is not the teacher in as unenviable a position as employees in the private sector? See Goldstein, "Book Review," 22 *Buff L Rev* 603, 606 (1972). The teacher's training is not readily transferable to private industry, and the private school market is quite small and has comparatively lower salaries. Moreover, to deprive teacher unions of the power to strike may render them powerless in negotiations with school boards. See, Kheel, "Strikes and Public Employment," 67 *Mich L Rev* 931 (1969).

The answer to these lines of argument, if they are answerable at all, must be in the impact of strikes on the educational and political processes of the community. Professors Wellington and Winter assert that there are three reasons for circumscribing the power of public employees, including teachers, to strike. First, disruption of the service may be detrimental to public health and safety. Second, the demand for public services is usually inelastic, and therefore increases in wages and the price of the service will not lead to lower public consumption. This means that there is no effective economic check on the union's demands and little likelihood of nonunion entrants into the labor market. Finally, a strike that disrupts a vital public service such as education seriously inconveniences parents and other citizens who have the power to punish political leadership. In turn, vulnerable politicians may yield to short-term political expediency, sacrificing more long-term policy considerations. See Wellington and Winter, *The Unions and the Cities* 29-32 (1971).

To this list of the consequences of strikes by public employees, Professor Goldstein would add one item peculiar to teachers: they do not lose working time or wages as a result of their strike. Most states require a minimum number of school days for public school students; thus, in most instances, teachers will make up the lost time and be paid for their efforts. See Goldstein, 22 *Buff L Rev* 603, 606 (1972). Obviously, this argument assumes a strike of relatively short duration, for a long strike might well overlap into the next academic year or, at a minimum, leave insufficient time for makeup. In addition, outside income derived from employment over holidays and summer months would be lost if those days were used for makeup purposes.

If a legislature were to find the arguments against teacher strikes persuasive, the next issue to be faced is enforcement of the prohibitory legislation, for it is not clear what impact such legislation has on the actual conduct of teacher organizations. If the laws are to be something more than hortatory, effective sanctions must be found for punishing those who engage in illegal strikes:

> In some situations . . . the incarceration of a union leader for contempt [of a judicial order to refrain from striking] will turn that leader into a martyr and stiffen support for the strike. . . .
> Harsh penalties automatically invoked, moreover, run the risk of converting an economic strike into a strike for amnesty that will be difficult to settle without openly abandoning the law. The harsher the penalties, the less the strikers will feel they have to lose, and the effect may be to extend rather than end the strike. These considerations suggest gradually escalating sanctions that seek to make the cost of continuing the strike at any point . . . greater than the cost of ending it.

Other problems exist as well. To what extent should sanctions be directed against the organization, its leaders, or its members? The answer to this question depends in part upon the prevalence of wildcat strikes, and may also be influenced by what has come to be known as the ratification problem; that is, the increasing frequency with which union members turn down negotiated settlements. (Wellington and Winter, *The Unions and the Cities* 186-87.)

See, e.g., *New York State Teachers' Ass'n v Helsby* 57 Misc2d 1066, 294 NYS2d 38 (Sup Ct 1968).

Notes and Questions

1. Sanctions

In the light of the difficulties in enforcing teacher strike bans, would it be wiser to accept the "inevitable" and permit them? If not, what sanctions might a court or legislature apply? Revocation of teaching certificates? Fines levied against the union treasury? Fines levied against the leadership or membership?

2. Impact on the Political System

Do you agree with Wellington and Winter that strikes by public employees are harmful to the political system? Consider this description of a recent strike in Philadelphia:

TIME
12 March 1973, p 78

"I'm thrilled," said Philadelphia's Mayor Frank L. Rizzo. "Now I can walk around without some teachers jumping out at me."

What thrilled the onetime cop, who had vowed never to give in to the teachers' "arrogance" was that President Nixon's chief negotiator, Assistant Secretary of Labor Willie Usery, had just settled the second-longest teacher strike in the nation's history. It had lasted eleven weeks and two days (two days short of the 1971 Newark walkout) of mounting bitterness that will not soon die. "I don't think we'll even try to talk to the scabs," said fifth-grade teacher Anne Philips.

The issues were the familiar ones. The teachers wanted a 34 percent salary increase, smaller classes, and fewer teaching hours in proportion to preparation time. The school board, then operating on a $52 million deficit, claimed union demands would cost $1 billion. When the board offered a pay raise of only 3 percent, the strike was on.

Court of Common Pleas Judge D. Donald Jamieson issued an injunction to end the walkout. When the teachers ignored him, the confrontation got rougher. Some 317 teachers were arrested for picketing and will be arraigned for trial next week. Union negotiators Frank Sullivan and John Ryan were jailed for contempt but were permitted to emerge each morning to continue negotiations, then returned behind bars at night. Teachers who continued to work (about 3,500 of the 13,000) suffered tire slashings and other harassment.

In the background was the intractable division between blacks and whites. Philadelphia's teachers are 70 percent white, but 65 percent of the city's 285,000 public school pupils are black: of the city's 240,000 white children, more than half go to parochial schools, among them four children of union negotiator Ryan.

Throughout the long controversy, the city tried to maintain an appearance of business as usual. Some 260 of the 285 schools officially remained open part-time, local television stations broadcast supplementary lessons and eight special "learning centers" were opened for college-bound seniors. Even the part-time education reached only about half the students. One senior, Marilyn Etkins, 17, got 1,500 student signatures on a petition protesting the poor quality of the substitute education, but nobody at city hall would accept it.

The final pressure came from other unions, which said that their 100,000 members would shut down Philadelphia for a "day of conscience" if the strike was not settled by last Wednesday. At that, Usery closeted himself and the negotiators in a room on the seventh floor of the Penn Square Building. Fifty-two hours later, the room was a shamble of sandwich wrappers and coffee cups—and there was a settlement. The terms: $99.5 million over four years. Mayor Rizzo, who had promised not to increase taxes, said he would raise the money through "a conglomerate of new taxes that won't affect the workingman."

"Everybody won," he insisted.

"And the children who missed two months of school?" a reporter wondered.

"I agree," said Rizzo. "Everybody lost."

3. Professors' Strikes

Consider these comments on professorial strikes by Professor Kadish:

"THE STRIKE AND THE PROFESSORIATE"
54 AAUP Bull 160, 163-65 (1968)

Of course, there are a variety of strikes differing in the nature of their objectives, the time, place, and manner of their calling, and in other ways. But to start let us consider the kind of strike which is being urged upon professors by the American Federation of Teachers as a standard policy—the economic strike as a final effort to prevail on issues of wages and working conditions when collective bargaining reaches impasse. Let me identify five professional values which are imperiled by strikes of this kind: *the service ideal; the moral basis of professional claims; the commitment to shared and co-operative decision making; the commitment to reason; and the pursuit of distinction*. . . .

[W]hat the economic strike amounts to is that the professor holds his services ransom for his own benefit. And what further adds to its inappropriateness is the way in which pressure is brought. The shutting down of the university poses no direct economic threat to the administration or the governing board, or in the case of a public university, to the state. The pressure on these groups is the pressure that comes from their accountability for providing the services of the university and the public's expectation that they will meet it. Yet, providing the services of the university is a pivotal element of the professor's professionalism. The irony of the economic strike is that it operates through the professors' cutting off the service that both they and the governing boards are responsible for providing on the premise that the boards will yield before the professors do to the pressures to continue that service. . . .

What is involved in the regularized use of the strike in a collective bargaining relationship—not entirely but in important part—is shifting the basis of professorial claims from common commitment and moral entitlement to the play of power in a competitive context. The move from academic senates to collective bargaining backed by the strike is a move to the marketplace, and the spirit of the marketplace is that you are entitled to what you can exact, and what you can exact is what you're entitled to. . . .

[I] nsistence upon independence in planning, performing and judging work may be regarded principally as either a demand in the employee interest or a claim resting on the requirements of the effective rendering of the services and on its high social importance. What gives the professor's claim to autonomy its moral legitimacy and persuasiveness in the latter sense is his primary commitment to the service of research and education. To the extent that the professor is prepared to subordinate this service ideal to his employee self-interest and to relegate the determination of what he is to be accorded to the play of power in a competitive relationship, he has compromised the moral legitimacy of his claim. And the same may be said for other claims, such as that to academic freedom. . . .

The next danger is closely related to that just described. I have in mind the potential destructiveness of the collective bargaining strike to cooperative and shared decision making between the faculty and the administration and governing board of the university. For what is imperiled by such action is the system of university government which holds the greatest promise for the effective progress of the main business of research and education. In many essential respects, decisions taken by the administration in American universities in those matters within its special competence make as necessary a contribution to research and education as the decisions the faculty makes within its sphere. And administrative decisions often have an acutely direct bearing upon the faculty's own professional contributions. In a word, there is in fact a closely meshed interdependence between the university's faculty and its administrators, which indeed provides the rationale of shared decision-making authority.

I would think that the injection of the collective bargaining strike, both in threat and in fact, might prove a formidable obstacle to that salutary pattern of governance. Annual contract time could become annual battle time, with the community divided between the faculty and the administrators and each side assigning its men to their battle stations. The natural strategy is to get as much as you can from the other side with a minimum of loss to your own. Exaggerated claims and overstated positions have become the currency of compromise. At the worst, high emotion and distrust are the by-products. I don't say all this must necessarily be in its worst form. Quite possibly a union of professors negotiating with university administrators, even against the backdrop of a strike threat, would produce an atmosphere different from that which prevails in industrial collective bargaining. But situational pressures have their own logic and momentum and it would be surprising if something of this atmosphere were not created. . . .

As university professors, we are charged preeminently and constitutionally with the advancement of and instruction in the uses of reason. More so than any other group in the community. This entails many things, but at least it entails commitment to noncoercive argument and persuasion, and skepticism of self-interested judgments. To an important extent the strike is inconsistent with such commitments. . . .

Effective collective action, such as a strike, requires mass support and this is attainable over the long run by appealing to mass interest. This entails a constant quest for political solidarity even as against academic principle and practices. For example, protection of the employee against discharge or nonrenewal whenever his case is arguable, or sometimes even when it is not; salary increases controlled by automatic formulas rather than by professional judgments of merit; timidness in the face of damaging or irresponsible behavior by faculty members. In a word, the push for distinction tends to be redirected, simply by the dynamics of collective action, toward solidarity, with consequent loss to the educational enterprise. . . .

Do you find Professor Kadish's arguments persuasive? Are any of his arguments applicable to elementary and secondary school teachers?

chapter four
Equal Educational Opportunity and Race

I. Introduction

Chapters 1-3 focus primarily on the ways in which the public education system constrains the freedom of its two most important constituent groups: students and teachers. In the next four chapters, we turn to other issues and focus on what educational opportunities the individual can demand of the state. These demands may be affirmative, asserting an entitlement to a minimum educational opportunity, equal access to the schooling process, or a specified educational outcome, or they may be framed negatively, asserting a right to be free of race, sex, or class discrimination in the operation of the public schools.

This chapter deals with the fully matured and litigated definition of equal educational opportunity: the rights of minority students to be free of racial discrimination. Of necessity, the chapter is organized primarily along historical lines. The complex issues presented by segregation in both North and South, the scope of the constitutional duty to desegregate, the Civil Rights Act of 1964, the emergence (and apparent demise) of community control and the demand for preferential treatment of minority groups can best be understood against the backdrop of historical changes in social attitudes and in governmental policy. In addition, the materials examine the ethical and policy implications of racial discrimination. Why is state-created segregation constitutionally repugnant? What is the impact of segregation on the educational achievement of minority and white students? What ethical, social, and economic costs attach to the alternative means of undoing racial segregation in the schools?

Finally, this chapter raises sensitive issues of federalism and democracy. It examines the relationship between the federal courts, Congress, and the president in the context of school desegregation. It analyzes the relationship between the federal courts, the Department of Health, Education, and Welfare, and the thousands of school districts that have been compelled to desegregate their schools. More importantly, it seeks to assess the role of the judiciary in carrying out what now—two decades after the landmark *Brown* decision—appears to have been a social revolution of mammoth proportions.

II. The Judicial Response to School Segregation: 1896-1954

A. The "Separate But Equal" Doctrine

PLESSY v FERGUSON

163 US 537 (1896)

Mr. Justice Brown, after stating the case, delivered the opinion of the court. This case turns upon the constitutionality of an act of the general assembly of the state of Louisiana, passed in 1890, providing for separate railway carriages for the white and colored races. Acts 1890, No 111, p 152.

The first section of the statute enacts

that all railway companies carrying passengers in their coaches in this state, shall provide equal but separate accommodations for the white, and colored races, by providing two or more passenger coaches for each passenger train, or by dividing the passenger coaches by a partition so as to secure separate accommodations: *Provided,* That this section shall not be construed to apply to street railroads. No person or persons, shall be admitted to occupy seats in coaches, other than, the ones assigned to them on account of the race they belong to.

By the second section it was enacted

that the officers of such passenger trains shall have power and are hereby required to assign each passenger to the coach or compartment used for the race to which such passenger belongs; any passenger insisting on going into a coach or compartment to which by race he does not belong, shall be liable to a fine of twenty-five dollars, or in lieu thereof to imprisonment for a period of not more than twenty days in the parish prison, and any officer of any railroad insisting on assigning a passenger to a coach or compartment other than the one set aside for the race to which said passenger belongs, shall be liable to a fine of twenty-five dollars, or in lieu thereof to imprisonment for a period of not more than twenty days in the parish prison; and should any passenger refuse to occupy the coach or compartment to which he or she is assigned by the officer of such railway, said officer shall have power to refuse to carry such passenger on his train, and for such refusal neither he nor the railway company which he represents shall be liable for damages in any of the courts of this state.

The third section provides penalties for the refusal or neglect of the officers, directors, conductors and employees of railway companies to comply with the act, with a proviso that "nothing in this act shall be construed as applying to nurses attending children of the other race." The fourth section is immaterial.

The information filed in the criminal district court charged in substance that Plessy, being a passenger between two stations within the state of Louisiana, was assigned by officers of the company to the coach used for the race to which he belonged, but he insisted upon going into a coach used by the race to which he did not belong. Neither in the information nor plea was his particular race or color averred.

The petition for the writ of prohibition averred that petitioner was seven-eighths Caucasian and one-eighth African blood; that the mixture of colored blood was not discernible in him, and that he was entitled to every right, privilege and immunity secured to citizens of the United States of the white race; and that, upon such theory, he took possession of a vacant seat in a coach where passengers of the white race were accommodated, and was ordered by the conductor to vacate said coach and take a seat in another assigned to persons of the colored race, and having refused to comply with such demand he was forcibly ejected with the aid of a police officer, and imprisoned in the parish jail to answer a charge of having violated the above act.

The constitutionality of this act is attacked upon the ground that it conflicts both with the Thirteenth Amendment of the Constitution, abolishing slavery, and the Fourteenth Amendment, which prohibits certain restrictive legislation on the part of the states.

1. That it does not conflict with the Thirteenth Amendment, which abolished slavery and involuntary servitude, except as a punishment for crime, is too clear for argument. Slavery implies involuntary servitude—a state of bondage; the ownership of mankind as a chattel, or at least the control of the labor and services of one man for the benefit of another, and the absence of a legal right to the disposal of his own person, property and services. . . .

A statute which implies merely a legal distinction between the white and colored races—a distinction which is founded in the color of the two races, and which must always exist so long as white men are distinguished from the other race by color—has no tendency to destroy the legal equality of the two races, or reestablish a state of involuntary servitude. Indeed, we do not understand that the Thirteenth Amendment is strenuously relied upon by the plaintiff in error in this connection.

2. By the Fourteenth Amendment, all persons born or naturalized in the United States, and subject to the jurisdiction thereof, are made citizens of the United States and of the state wherein they reside; and the states are forbidden from making or enforcing any law which shall abridge the privileges or immunities of citizens of the United States, or shall deprive any person of life, liberty or property without due process of law, or deny to any person within their jurisdiction the equal protection of the laws.

The proper construction of this amendment was first called to the attention of this court in the *Slaughter-house cases,* 16 Wall 36, which involved, however, not a question of race, but one of exclusive privileges. The case did not call for any expression of opinion as to the exact rights it was intended to secure to the colored race, but it was said generally that its main purpose was to establish the citizenship of the Negro; to give definitions of citizenship of the United States and of the states, and to protect from the hostile legislation of the states the privileges and immunities of citizens of the United States, as distinguished from those of citizens of the states.

The object of the amendment was undoubtedly to enforce the absolute equality of the two races before the law, but in the nature of things it could not have been intended to abolish distinctions based upon color, or to enforce social, as distinguished from political equality, or a commingling of the two races upon terms unsatisfactory to either. Laws permitting, and even requiring, their separation in places where they are liable to be brought into contact do not necessarily imply the inferiority of either race to the other, and have been generally, if not universally, recognized as within the competency of the state legislatures in the exercise of their police power. The most common instance of this is connected with the establishment of separate schools for white and colored children, which has been held to be a valid exercise of the legislative power even by courts of states where the political rights of the colored race have been longest and most earnestly enforced.

One of the earliest of these cases is that of *Roberts v City of Boston* 5 Cush 198, in which the Supreme Judicial Court of Massachusetts held that the general school committee of Boston had power to make provision for the instruction of colored children in separate schools established exclusively for them, and to prohibit their attendance upon the other schools. . . . It was held that the powers of the committee extended to the establishment of separate schools for children of different ages, sexes and colors, and that they might also establish special schools for poor and neglected children, who have become too old to attend the primary school, and yet have not acquired the rudiments of learning, to enable them to enter the ordinary schools. Similar laws have been enacted by Congress under its general power of legislation over the District of Columbia, Rev Stat DC §§281-283, 310, 319, as well as by the legislatures of many of the states, and have been generally, if not uniformly, sustained by the courts. . . .

The distinction between laws interfering with the political equality of the Negro and those requiring the separation of the two races in schools, theatres and railway carriages has been frequently drawn by this court. Thus in *Strauder v West Virginia* 100 US 303, it was held that a law of West Virginia limiting to white male persons, twenty-one years of age and citizens of the state, the right to sit upon juries, was a discrimination which implied a legal inferiority in civil society, which lessened the security of the right of the colored race, and was a step toward reducing them to a condition of servility. Indeed, the right of a colored man that, in the selection of jurors to pass upon his life, liberty and property, there shall be no exclusion of his race, and no discrimination against them because of color, has been asserted in a number of cases. . . .

So far, then, as conflict with the Fourteenth Amendment is concerned, the case reduces itself to the question whether the statute of Louisiana is a reasonable regulation, and with respect to this there must necessarily be a large discretion on the part of the legislature. In determining the question of reasonableness it is at liberty to act with reference to the established usages, customs and traditions of the people, and with a view to the promotion of their comfort, and the preservation of the public peace and good order. Gauged by this standard, we cannot say that a law which authorizes or even requires the separation of the two races in public conveyances is unreasonable, or more obnoxious to the Fourteenth Amendment than the acts of Congress requiring separate schools for colored children in the District of Columbia, the constitutionality of which does not seem to have been questioned, or the corresponding acts of state legislatures.

We consider the underlying fallacy of the plaintiff's argument to consist in the assumption that the enforced separation of the two races stamps the colored race with a badge of inferiority. If this be so, it is not by reason of anything found in the act, but solely because the colored race chooses to put that construction upon it. The argument necessarily assumes that if, as has been more than once the case, and is not unlikely to be so again, the colored race should become the dominant power in the state legislature, and should enact a law in precisely similar terms, it would thereby relegate the white race to an inferior position. We imagine that the white race, at least, would not acquiesce in this assumption. The argument also assumes that social prejudices may be overcome by legislation, and that equal rights cannot be secured to the negro except by an enforced commingling of the two races. We cannot accept this proposition. If the two races are to meet upon terms of social equality, it must be the result of natural affinities, a mutual appreciation of each other's merits and a voluntary consent of individuals. . . .

The judgment of the court below is, therefore,

Affirmed.

Mr. Justice Harlan dissenting.

[W] e have before us a state enactment that compels, under penalties, the separation of the two races in railroad passenger coaches, and makes it a crime for a citizen of either race to enter a coach that has been assigned to citizens of the other race. . . .

However apparent the injustice of such legislation may be, we have only to consider whether it is consistent with the Constitution of the United States. . . .

In respect of civil rights, common to all citizens, the Constitution of the United States does not, I think, permit any public authority to know the race of those entitled to be protected in the enjoyment of such rights. Every true man has pride of race, and under appropriate circumstances when the rights of others, his equals before the law, are not to be affected, it is his privilege to express such pride and to take such action based upon it as to him seems proper. But I deny that any legislative body or judicial tribunal may have regard to the race of citizens when the civil rights of those citizens are involved. Indeed, such legislation, as that here in question, is inconsistent not only with that equality of rights which pertains to citizenship, national and state, but with the personal property enjoyed by every one within the United States.

The Thirteenth Amendment does not permit the withholding or the deprivation of any right necessarily inhering in freedom. It not only struck down the institution of slavery as previously existing in the United States, but it prevents the imposition of any burdens or disabilities that constitute badges of slavery or servitude. It decreed universal civil freedom in this country. This court has so adjudged. But that amendment having been found inadequate to the protection of the rights of those who had been in slavery, it was followed by the Fourteenth Amendment, which added greatly to the dignity and glory of American citizenship, and to the security of personal liberty, by declaring that "all persons born or naturalized in the United States, and subject to the jurisdiction thereof, are citizens of the United States and of the state wherein they reside," and that "no state shall make or enforce any law which shall abridge the privileges or immunities of citizens of the United States; nor shall any state deprive any person of life, liberty or property without due process of law, nor deny to any person within its jurisdiction the equal protection of the laws." These two amendments, if enforced according to their true intent and meaning, will protect all the civil rights that pertain to freedom and citizenship. Finally, and to the end that no citizen should be denied, on account of his race, the privilege of participating in the political control of his country, it was declared by the Fifteenth Amendment that "the right of citizens of the United States to vote shall not be denied or abridged by the United States or by any state on account of race, color or previous condition of servitude."

These notable additions to the fundamental law were welcomed by the friends of liberty throughout the world. They removed the race line from our governmental systems. They had, as this court has said, a common purpose, namely, to secure

to a race recently emancipated, a race that through many generations have been held in slavery, all the civil rights that the superior race enjoy. . . .

The words of the amendment, it is true, are prohibitory, but they contain a necessary implication of a positive immunity, or right, most valuable to the colored race—the right to exemption from unfriendly legislation against them distinctively as colored—exemption from legal discriminations, implying inferiority in civil society, lessening the security of their enjoyment of the rights which others enjoy, and discriminations which are steps towards reducing them to the condition of a subject race.

It was, consequently, adjudged that a state law that excluded citizens of the colored race from juries, because of their race and however well-qualified in other respects to discharge the duties of jurymen, was repugnant to the Fourteenth Amendment. *Strauder v West Virginia* 100 US 303, 306-307.

It was said in argument that the state of Louisiana does not discriminate against either race but prescribes a rule applicable alike to white and colored citizens. But this argument does not meet the difficulty. Everyone knows that the statute in question had its origin in the purpose, not so much to exclude white persons from railroad cars occupied by blacks, as to exclude colored people from coaches occupied by or assigned to white persons. Railroad corporations of Louisiana did not make discrimination among whites in the matter of accommodation for travelers. The thing to accomplish was, under the guise of giving equal accommodation for whites and blacks, to compel the latter to keep to themselves while traveling in railroad passenger coaches. No one would be so wanting in candor as to assert the contrary. The fundamental objection, therefore, to the statute is that it interferes with the personal freedom of citizens. . . . If a white man and a black man choose to occupy the same public conveyance on a public highway, it is their right to do so, and no government, proceeding alone on grounds of race, can prevent it without infringing the personal liberty of each. . . .

The white race deems itself to be the dominant race in this country. And so it is, in prestige, in achievements, in education, in wealth and in power. So, I doubt not, it will continue to be for all time, if it remains true to its great heritage and holds fast to the principles of constitutional liberty. But in view of the Constitution, in the eye of the law, there is in this country no superior, dominant, ruling class of citizens. There is no caste here. Our Constitution is color-blind, and neither knows nor tolerates classes among citizens. In respect of civil rights, all citizens are equal before the law. The humblest is the peer of the most powerful. The law regards man as man, and takes no account of his surroundings or of his color when his civil rights as guaranteed by the supreme law of the land are involved. It is, therefore, to be regretted that this high tribunal, the final expositor of the fundamental law of the land, has reached the conclusion that it is competent for a state to regulate the enjoyment by citizens of their civil rights solely upon the basis of race. . . .

The destinies of the two races, in this country, are indissolubly linked together, and the interests of both require that the common government of all shall not permit the seeds of race hate to be planted under the sanction of law. What can more certainly arouse race hate, what more certainly create and perpetuate a feeling of distrust between these races, than state enactments, which, in fact, proceed on the ground that colored citizens are so inferior and degraded that they cannot be allowed to sit in public coaches occupied by white citizens? That, as all will admit, is the real meaning of such legislation as was enacted in Louisiana.

This question is not met by the suggestion that social equality cannot exist between the white and black races in this country. That argument, if it can be properly regarded as one, is scarcely worthy of consideration; for social equality no more exists between two races when traveling in a passenger coach or a public highway than when members of the same races sit by each other in a street car or in the jury box, or stand or sit with each other in a political assembly, or when they use in common the streets of a city or town, or when they are in the same room for the purpose of having their names placed on the registry of voters, or when they approach the ballot box in order to exercise the high privilege of voting. . . .

I do not deem it necessary to review the decisions of state courts to which reference was made in argument. Some, and the most important, of them are wholly inapplicable, because rendered prior to the adoption of the last amendments of the Constitution, when colored people had very few rights which the dominant race felt obliged to respect. Others were made at a time when public opinion, in many localities, was dominated by the institution of slavery; when it would not have been safe to do justice to the black man; and when, so far as the rights of blacks were concerned, race prejudice was, practically, the supreme law of the land. Those decisions cannot be guides in the era introduced by the recent amendments of the supreme law, which established universal civil freedom, gave citizenship to all born or naturalized in the United States and residing here, obliterated the race line from our systems of governments, national and state, and placed our free institutions upon the broad and sure foundation of the equality of all men before the law. . . .

For the reasons stated, I am constrained to withhold my assent from the opinion and judgment of the majority. . . .

Notes and Questions

1. Distinction between "Social" and "Political" Equality

The court's analysis of the constitutionality of "separate but equal" facilities relies on the distinction between social and political equality. Does this distinction have a foundation in the Constitution: do the Thirteenth and Fourteenth Amendments apply exclusively to political aspects of life? Does the distinction suggest that the court has two alternative paths to follow in race cases—a hands-off approach with respect to social behavior and close judicial supervision in the political sphere—and that the outcomes and policy implications of future race cases will depend on the court's determination of the nature of the activity involved? If transportation is a "social activity," why must racially separate transportation facilities be equal?

Are there situations in which "social" and "political" activities overlap? Should the court have distinguished between racial discrimination in social activities expressly condoned by the state and purely private discrimination? Consider *Moose Lodge v Irvis* 407 US 163 (1972) in which a private Pennsylvania club was permitted to refuse service to the black guest of one of its white members.

The court held that a state-granted liquor license did not constitute sufficient state action to bring the discrimination within the ambit of the Fourteenth Amendment. See chapter 2, pp 86-87. Justice Douglas' dissent contains some reflections on the social/political dichotomy:

> As the first Justice Harlan, dissenting in the *Civil Rights Cases* 102 US 1, 59, said: "I agree that government has nothing to do with social, as distinguished from technically legal, rights of individuals. No government has ever brought or ever can bring, its people into social intercourse against their wishes. Whether one person will permit and maintain social relations with another is a matter with which government has no concern. . . . What I affirm is that no state, nor the officers of any state, nor any corporation or individual wielding power under state authority for the public benefit or the public convenience, can consistently . . . with the freedom established by the fundamental law . . . discriminate against freemen or citizens, in those rights, because of their race. . . ." The regulation governing this liquor license has in it that precise infirmity. (407 US at 175.)

How do the following remarks by sociologist Joseph Gusfield bear on the distinctions that *Plessy* makes between social and political rights and Justice Douglas makes between private and publicly sanctioned discrimination? Do they suggest a role for the court in adjudicating questions of "social" rights or "position in the status order?"

> The enhancement or defense of a position in the status order is as much an interest as the protection or expansion of income or economic power. The activities of government . . . confer respect upon a given style of life or directly upon a specific group. For this reason questions of institutional support of tastes, morals, and other aspects of life styles have consequences for the prestige of persons. . . . Government is a prestige-granting agency. (J. Gusfield, *Symbolic Crusade,* 175-76 (1963).)

2. The Court's Reliance on Psychological Evidence

In studying *Brown v Board of Education* you will consider the significance of the role of social science evidence in the court's reasoning. Does *Plessy* foreshadow such a judicial technique when it generalizes that blacks have construed (wrongly, so the majority thinks) separation to connote inferiority or when the court predicts that "enforced commingling" of the races will not eradicate social prejudices? Does that statement represent a finding of fact? Is the court taking judicial notice of something that "everyone knows?"

3. The Separate-But-Equal Standard and Public Education

The *Plessy* standard subsequently was extended to public schooling. In *Gong Lum v Rice* 275 US 78, 85-86 (1927), the Supreme Court, almost without analysis, treated the separate but equal rule as an orthodox constitutional principle applicable to public education:

> The question here is whether a Chinese citizen of the United States is denied equal protection of the laws when he is classed among the colored races and furnished facilities for education equal to that offered to all,

whether white, brown, yellow, or black. Were this a new question, it would call for full argument and consideration, but we think that it is the same question which has been many times decided to be within the constitutional power of the state legislature to settle without intervention of the federal courts under the federal Constitution. . . .

In *Plessy v Ferguson* . . . in upholding the validity under the Fourteenth Amendment of a statute of Louisiana requiring the separation of the white and colored races in railway coaches, a more difficult question than this, this court, speaking of permitted race separation, said: "The most common instance of this is connected with the establishment of separate schools, which has been held to be a valid exercise of the legislative power. . . ." 275 US at 81.

See also *Cumming v Richmond County Board of Educ* 175 US 528 (1899). Is this extension of the separate but equal doctrine to education logical? Are transportation and education sufficiently similar to warrant applying rules adopted in one context to the other? Does the application of the separate but equal doctrine to education presuppose that education is a social as opposed to a political right? In the light of chapters 1 and 2, does this seem an appropriate view of education?

4. *Plessy* and Majority Social and Political Values

Might the Supreme Court's refusal to invalidate segregation laws be a reflection of widely shared values of the times? Consider Professor Peltason's observation:

For the Supreme Court to have declared segregation unconstitutional in 1896 would have been unthinkable. Most Negroes did not aspire to enter the "white man's world." The Negro was considered by many whites, North and South, to be a depraved, comic, childlike, or debased person. Southern political leaders openly and unapologetically espoused white supremacy. In 1896 one Negro was lynched every fifty-six hours; few citizens, black or white, raised a voice in protest. (Peltason, *58 Lonely Men*, 248 (1961).)

Might the court have feared that a contrary decision in *Plessy* would be widely flouted and that such a decision would place the Supreme Court in institutional disrepute? Is it legitimate for the court to take such factors into account in deciding cases?

B. Note on Legal Developments from *Plessy* to *Brown*

The National Association for the Advancement of Colored People (NAACP) initiated its attack on *Plessy* in *Missouri ex rel Gaines v Canada* 305 US 337 (1938). Gaines, a black law school applicant, was obliged by Missouri to attend a law school outside the state because Missouri had not yet established a separate law school for blacks. Missouri would have defrayed Gaines' out-of-state tuition fees. The court held that the separate but equal doctrine required Missouri to provide its black citizens with an educational opportunity equal to that of its white citizens, and that the availability of services in adjacent states did not meet its obligation. A director of the NAACP Legal Defense and Education Fund explained why that organization began its assault on *Plessy* with higher education litigation:

> [I] nequality in higher education could be proved with [greater] ease [since] there were virtually no public Negro graduate and professional schools in the South, and judges would readily understand the shortcomings of separate legal education. . . . [Moreover] , since it would be financially impossible to furnish true equality—both tangible and intangible—desegregation would be the only practicable way to fulfill the constitutional obligation of equal protection for students in graduate and professional schools. The policy of starting at the college level seemed wise to the NAACP strategists from still another angle. Their assessment of Southern white psychology had convinced them that resistence to integration at that level would be far less determined than with respect to elementary schools.
>
> (Thurgood Marshall thought he detected something of a paradox in the relative equanimity with which the South contemplated the possibility that graduate and professional schools would be integrated. "Those racial supremacy boys somehow think," he said, "that little kids of six or seven are going to get funny ideas about sex and marriage just from going to school together, but for some equally funny reasons youngsters in law school aren't supposed to feel that way." He added: "We didn't get it but we decided that if that was what the South believed, then the best thing for the moment was to go along.). . . .
>
> [T] wo other factors [supported the focus on higher education] : "Small numbers of mature students were involved, undercutting opposing arguments based on violence and widespread social revolution. Finally, Negro leadership would be augmented whether there was desegregation or enriched separate schools." (Berman, *It Is So Ordered,* 32-33 (1966) (with footnotes partially reprinted here as part of the text).)

Such considerations undoubtedly lay behind the next education cases prosecuted before the Supreme Court by the NAACP: *Sipuel v Board of Regents of the Univ of Okla* 322 US 631 (1948), and *Sweatt v Painter* 339 US 629 (1950), both of which concerned law school admissions. The opinion in *Sweatt* is especially noteworthy, for in addition to comparing the tangible factors of Texas' separate law schools, it recognizes that intangibles—such as prestige, faculty reputation, and experience of the administration—must be part of the equality determination. "Moreover," said the court,

> the law school, the proving ground for legal learning and practice, cannot be effective in isolation from the individuals and institutions with which the law interacts. Few students and no one who has practiced law would choose to study in an academic vacuum, removed from the interplay of ideas and the exchange of views with which the law is concerned. The law school to which Texas is willing to admit petitioner excludes from its student body members of the racial groups which number 85 percent of the population of the state and include most of the lawyers, witnesses, jurors, judges and other officials with whom petitioner will inevitably be dealing when he becomes a member of the Texas bar. (339 US at 634.)

McLaurin v Oklahoma State Regents for Higher Educ 339 US 637 (1950), the companion case to *Sweatt,* applied this reasoning to graduate programs other than legal education; it also examined the treatment received by black students within the formerly white institutions. The court found that McLaurin, having been admitted to the state university, was virtually quarantined in his activities there: only certain portions of the library, a certain row of desks in the classroom, and an isolated table in the cafeteria were accessible to him. The court found that McLaurin was "handicapped in his pursuit of effective graduate instruction," by what may be described as intangible factors, such as the inability for "intellectual commingling" with other students. 339 US 637, 641.

Two features of this historical sketch stand out with special clarity: (1) the Supreme Court increasingly recognized that interaction with others was part of the learning process itself rather than merely a social byproduct, and (2) the NAACP strategy obliged the court to focus on the "equal" provision of the *Plessy* rule, compelling it to determine whether separateness might carry with it subtle and unquantifiable inequalities. See generally Ransmier, "The Fourteenth Amendment and the 'Separate But Equal' Doctrine," 50 *Mich L Rev* 203 (1951); Roche, "Education, Segregation and the Supreme Court—A Political Analysis," 99 *U Pa L Rev* 949 (1951). The next logical step was to extend such reasoning to the primary and secondary schools.

C. *Brown 1:* Legal and Policy Implications

BROWN v BOARD OF EDUCATION
347 US 483 (1954)

Mr. Chief Justice Warren delivered the opinion of the court.

These cases come to us from the states of Kansas, South Carolina, Virginia, and Delaware. They are premised on different facts and different local conditions, but a common legal question justifies their consideration together in this consolidated opinion.[1]

---

1. In the Kansas case, *Brown v Board of Education,* the plaintiffs are Negro children of elementary school age residing in Topeka. They brought this action in the United States District Court for the District of Kansas to enjoin enforcement of a Kansas statute which permits, but does not require, cities of more than 15,000 population to maintain separate school facilities for Negro and white students. Kan Gen Stat 1949, §72-1724. Pursuant to that authority, the Topeka Board of Education elected to establish segregated elementary schools. Other public schools in the community, however, are operated on a nonsegregated basis. The three-judge district court convened under 28 USC §§2281 and 2284, 28 USCA §§2281, 2284, found that segregation in public education has a detrimental effect upon Negro children, but denied relief on the ground that the Negro and white schools were substantially equal with respect to buildings, transportation, curricula, and educational qualifications of teachers. 93 F Supp 797. The case is here on direct appeal under 28 USC §1253, 28 USCA §1253.

In the South Carolina case, *Briggs v Elliott,* the plaintiffs are Negro children of both elementary and high school age residing in Clarendon County. They brought this action in the United States District Court for the Eastern District of South Carolina to enjoin enforcement of provisions in the state constitution and statutory code which require the segregation of Negroes and whites in public schools. SC Const Art XI, §7; SC Code 1942, §5377. The three-judge district court, . . . denied the requested relief. The court found that Negro schools were inferior to the white schools and ordered the defendants to begin immediately to equalize the facilities. But the court sustained the validity of the contested provisions and

In each of the cases, minors of the Negro race, through their legal representatives, seek the aid of the courts in obtaining admission to the public schools of their community on a nonsegregated basis. In each instance, they have been denied admission to schools attended by white children under laws requiring or permitting segregation according to race. This segregation was alleged to deprive the plaintiffs of the equal protection of the laws under the Fourteenth Amendment. In each of the cases other than the Delaware case, a three-judge federal district court denied relief to the plaintiffs on the so-called separate but equal doctrine announced by this court in *Plessy v Ferguson* 163 US 537. Under that doctrine, equality of treatment is accorded when the races are provided substantially equal facilities, even though these facilities be separate. In the Delaware case, the Supreme Court of Delaware adhered to that doctrine, but ordered that the plaintiffs be admitted to the white schools because of their superiority to the Negro schools.

The plaintiffs contend that segregated public schools are not "equal" and cannot be made "equal," and that hence they are deprived of the equal protection of the laws. Because of the obvious importance of the question presented, the court took jurisdiction. Argument was heard in the 1952 term, and reargument was heard this term on certain questions propounded by the court.

Reargument was largely devoted to the circumstances surrounding the adoption of the Fourteenth Amendment in 1868. It covered exhaustively consideration of the amendment in Congress, ratification by the states, then existing practices in racial segregation, and the views of proponents and opponents of the amendment. This discussion and our own investigation convince us that, although these sources cast some light, it is not enough to resolve the problem with which we are faced. At best, they are inconclusive. The most avid proponents of the postwar amendments undoubtedly intended them to remove all legal distinctions among "all persons born or naturalized in the United States." Their opponents,

---

denied the plaintiffs admission to the white schools during the equalization program. 98 F Supp 529. This court vacated the district court's judgment and remanded the case for the purpose of obtaining the court's views on a report filed by the defendants concerning the progress made in the equalization program. 342 US 350. On remand, the district court found that substantial equality had been achieved except for buildings and that the defendants were proceeding to rectify this inequality as well. 103 F Supp 920. The case is again here on direct appeal under 28 USC 1253, ...

In the Virginia case, *Davis v County School Board*, the plaintiffs are Negro children of high school age residing in Prince Edward County. They brought this action in the United States District Court for the Eastern District of Virginia to enjoin enforcement of provisions in the state constitution and statutory code which require the segregation of Negroes and whites in public schools. Va Const §140, Va Code 1950, §22-221. The three-judge district court, ... denied the requested relief. The court found the Negro school inferior in physical plant, curricula, and transportation, and ordered the defendants forthwith to provide substantially equal curricula and transportation and to "proceed with all reasonable diligence and dispatch to remove" the inequality in physical plant. But, as in the South Carolina case, the court sustained the validity of the contested provisions and denied the plaintiffs admission to the white schools during the equalization program. 103 F Supp 337. The case is here on direct appeal under 28 USC §1253.

In the Delaware case, *Gebhart v Belton*, the plaintiffs are Negro children of both elementary and high school age residing in New Castle County. They brought this action in the Delaware Court of Chancery to enjoin enforcement of provisions in the state constitution and statutory code which require the segregation of Negroes and whites in public schools. Del Const, Art X, §2; Del Rev Code §2631 (1935). The chancellor gave judgment for the

just as certainly, were antagonistic to both the letter and the spirit of the amendments and wished them to have the most limited effect. What others in Congress and the state legislatures had in mind cannot be determined with any degree of certainty.

An additional reason for the inconclusive nature of the amendment's history, with respect to segregated schools, is the status of public education at that time. In the South, the movement toward free common schools, supported by general taxation, had not yet taken hold. Education of white children was largely in the hands of private groups. Education of Negroes was almost nonexistent, and practically all of the race were illiterate. In fact, any education of Negroes was forbidden by law in some states. Today, in contrast, many Negroes have achieved outstanding success in the arts and sciences as well as in the business and professional worlds. It is true that public school education at the time of the amendment had advanced further in the North, but the effect of the amendment on northern states was generally ignored in the congressional debates. Even in the North, the conditions of public education did not approximate those existing today. The curriculum was usually rudimentary; ungraded schools were common in rural areas; the school term was but three months a year in many states; and compulsory school attendance was virtually unknown. As a consequence, it is not surprising that there should be so little in the history of the Fourteenth Amendment relating to its intended effect on public education.

In the first cases in this court construing the Fourteenth Amendment, decided shortly after its adoption, the court interpreted it as proscribing all state-imposed discriminations against the Negro race. The doctrine of separate but equal did not make its appearance in this court until 1896 in the case of *Plessy v Ferguson, supra,* involving not education but transportation.[6] American courts have since labored with the doctrine for over half a century. In this court, there have been six cases involving the separate but equal doctrine in the field of public education. In *Cumming v Board of Educ of Richmond County* 175 US 528 and *Gong Lum v Rice* 275 US 78, the validity of the doctrine itself was not challenged. In more recent cases, all on the graduate school level, inequality was found in that specific benefits enjoyed by white students were denied to Negro students of the same educational qualifications. *State of Mo ex rel Gaines v*

plaintiffs and ordered their immediate admission to schools previously attended only by white children, on the ground that the Negro schools were inferior with respect to teacher training, pupil-teacher ratio, extracurricular activities, physical plant, and time and distance involved in travel. 87 A2d 862. The chancellor also found that segregation itself results in an inferior education for Negro children (see note 10, *infra*), but did not rest his decision on that ground. 87 A2d at 865. The chancellor's decree was affirmed by the Supreme Court of Delaware, which intimated, however, that the defendants might be able to obtain a modification of the decree after equalization of the Negro and white schools had been accomplished. 91 A2d 137, 152. The defendants, contending only that the Delaware courts had erred in ordering the immediate admission of the Negro plaintiffs to the white schools, applied to this court for certiorari. The writ was granted, 344 US 891. The plaintiffs, who were successful below, did not submit a cross-petition.

6. The doctrine apparently originated in *Roberts v City of Boston* 5 Cush 198, 59 Mass 198, 206; upholding school segregation against attack as being violative of a state constitutional guarantee of equality. Segregation in Boston public schools was eliminated in 1855. Mass Acts 1855, c 256. But elsewhere in the North segregation in public education has persisted in some communities until recent years. It is apparent that such segregation has long been a nationwide problem, not merely one of sectional concern.

Canada 305 US 337; *Sipuel v Board of Regents of Univ of Okla* 332 US 631; *Sweatt v Painter* 339 US 629; *McLaurin v Oklahoma State Regents* 339 US 637. In none of these cases was it necessary to reexamine the doctrine to grant relief to the Negro plaintiff. And in *Sweatt v Painter, supra,* the court expressly reserved decision on the question whether *Plessy v Ferguson* should be held inapplicable to public education.

In the instant cases, that question is directly presented. Here, unlike *Sweatt v Painter,* there are findings below that the Negro and white schools involved have been equalized, or are being equalized, with respect to buildings, curricula, qualifications and salaries of teachers, and other "tangible" factors. Our decision, therefore, cannot turn on merely a comparison of these tangible factors in the Negro and white schools involved in each of the cases. We must look instead to the effect of segregation itself on public education.

In approaching this problem, we cannot turn the clock back to 1868 when the amendment was adopted, or even to 1896 when *Plessy v Ferguson* was written. We must consider public education in the light of its full development and its present place in American life throughout the nation. Only in this way can it be determined if segregation in public schools deprives these plaintiffs of the equal protection of the laws.

Today, education is perhaps the most important function of state and local governments. Compulsory school attendance laws and the great expenditures for education both demonstrate our recognition of the importance of education to our democratic society. It is required in the performance of our most basic public responsibilities, even service in the armed forces. It is the very foundation of good citizenship. Today it is a principal instrument in awakening the child to cultural values, in preparing him for later professional training, and in helping him to adjust normally to his environment. In these days, it is doubtful that any child may reasonably be expected to succeed in life if he is denied the opportunity of an education. Such an opportunity, where the state has undertaken to provide it, is a right which must be made available to all on equal terms.

We come then to the question presented: Does segregation of children in public schools solely on the basis of race, even though the physical facilities and other "tangible" factors may be equal, deprive the children of the minority group of equal educational opportunities? We believe that it does.

In *Sweatt v Painter, supra,* in finding that a segregated law school for Negroes could not provide them equal educational opportunities, this court relied in large part on "those qualities which are incapable of objective measurement but which make for greatness in a law school." In *McLaurin v Oklahoma State Regents, supra,* the court, in requiring that a Negro admitted to a white graduate school be treated like all other students, again resorted to intangible considerations: "his ability to study, to engage in discussions and exchange views with other students, and, in general, to learn his profession." Such considerations apply with added force to children in grade and high schools. To separate them from others of similar age and qualifications solely because of their race generates a feeling of inferiority as to their status in the community that may affect their hearts and minds in a way unlikely ever to be undone. The effect of this separation on their educational opportunities was well stated by a finding in the Kansas case by a court which nevertheless felt compelled to rule against the Negro plaintiffs:

Segregation of white and colored children in public schools has a detrimental effect upon the colored children. The impact is greater when it has the sanction of the law; for the policy of separating the races is usually interpreted as denoting the inferiority of the Negro group. A sense of inferiority affects the motivation of a child to learn. Segregation with the sanction of law, therefore, has a tendency to retard the educational and mental development of Negro children and to deprive them of some of the benefits they would receive in a racial[ly] integrated school system.

Whatever may have been the extent of psychological knowledge at the time of *Plessy v Ferguson,* this finding is amply supported by modern authority.[11] Any language in *Plessy v Ferguson* contrary to this finding is rejected.

We conclude that in the field of public education the doctrine of separate but equal has no place. Separated educational facilities are inherently unequal. Therefore, we hold that the plaintiffs and others similarly situated for whom the actions have been brought are, by reason of the segregation complained of, deprived of the equal protection of the laws guaranteed by the Fourteenth Amendment. This disposition makes unnecessary any discussion whether such segregation also violates the due process clause of the Fourteenth Amendment.

Because these are class actions, because of the wide applicability of this decision, and because of the great variety of local conditions, the formulation of decrees in these cases presents problems of considerable complexity. On reargument, the consideration of appropriate relief was necessarily subordinated to the primary question—the constitutionality of segregation in public education. We have now announced that such segregation is a denial of the equal protection of the laws. In order that we may have the full assistance of the parties in formulating decrees, the cases will be restored to the docket, and the parties are requested to present further argument on questions 4 and 5 previously propounded by the court for the reargument this term.[13] The attorney general of

11. K. B. Clark, *Effect of Prejudice and Discrimination on Personality Development* (Midcentury White House Conference on Children and Youth, 1950); Witmer and Kotinsky, *Personality in the Making* c 6 (1952); Deutscher and Chein, "The Psychological Effects of Enforced Segregation: A Survey of Social Science Opinion," 26 *J Psychol* 259 (1948); Chein, "What Are the Psychological Effects of Segregation under Conditions of Equal Facilities?" 3 *Int J Opinion and Attitude Res* 229 (1949); Brameld, *Educational Costs, in Discrimination and National Welfare,* 44-48 (MacIver ed 1949); Frazier, *The Negro in the United States,* 674-81 (1949). And see generally Myrdal, *An American Dilemma* (1944).

13. "Assuming it is decided that segregation in public schools violates the Fourteenth Amendment

"(a) would a decree necessarily follow providing that, within the limits set by normal geographic school districting, Negro children should forthwith be admitted to schools of their choice, or

"(b) may this court, in the exercise of its equity powers, permit an effective gradual adjustment to be brought about from existing segregated systems to a system not based on color distinctions?

"5. On the assumption on which questions 4(a) and (b) are based, and assuming further that this court will exercise its equity powers to the end described in question 4(b),

"(a) should this court formulate detailed decrees in these cases;

"(b) if so, what specific issues should the decrees reach;

"(c) should this court appoint a special master to hear evidence with a view to recommending specific terms for such decrees;

the United States is again invited to participate. The attorneys general of the states requiring or permitting segregation in public education will also be permitted to appear as amici curiae upon request to do so . . . .

It is so ordered.

Notes and Questions

1. Debate about the "Original Meaning" of the Fourteenth Amendment

The oral arguments in *Brown* reveal that one of the fundamental issues in the case was the intended scope of the Fourteenth Amendment. The NAACP attorneys contended that congressional debates from the era in which the amendment was enacted demonstrate that it was designed to operate "as a prohibition against the imposition of any racial classification in respect to civil rights." Counsel for the Southern school districts argued that such a reading misread and distorted the words and history of the amendment. In their eyes, the abolitionist movement's sole target had been slavery, and banning slavery does not reach the question of mixed or segregated schools. The court concludes that the legislative history is ambiguous on the issue raised by the parties. Does the language of the amendment, and its presence in conjunction with the Thirteenth Amendment, favor either side of this debate? How important should legislative history be in constitutional interpretation and application? Should the courts treat the history surrounding enactment of a constitutional amendment similarly to the history surrounding legislation? Is the greater "permanence" of an amendment justification for less emphasis on its history?

2. *Brown 1* and the Separate But Equal Doctrine

Did the court's position in *Sweatt* presage its decision in *Brown?* Did *Brown* explicitly repudiate *Plessy* when it held that "in the field of public education the doctrine of separate but equal has no place?" Or is it more accurate to say that *Brown*, like *Sweatt,* was decided within the ambit of the *Plessy* rule but that the court simply found that in the context of public education, "separate educational facilities are inherently unequal." Is Professor Cahn's observation that, "[In *Brown*] Chief Justice Warren had, in effect, to snatch the cloth of reasoning from under the *Plessy* case without spilling the content of its holding," correct? Cahn, "Jurisprudence," 30 *NYU L Rev* 150, 153 (1955). If so, why did the court choose not to overrule *Plessy* directly?

3. *Brown 1*: A Case about Education or a Case about Race?

a. Education. Is *Brown* most appropriately described as a case about education? In other words is the central thrust of *Brown* the idea that all children must be afforded equal educational opportunities and that segregated schooling is antithetical to that policy, just as inferior textbooks or teachers might be? Certainly, the encomium to education in the *Brown* opinion gives support to this view. Does treating *Brown* as a case primarily concerned with educational equality

---

"(d) should this court remand to the courts of first instance with directions to frame decrees in these cases, and if so what general directions should the decrees of this court include and what procedures should the courts of first instance follow in arriving at the specific terms of more detailed decrees?"

imply that all school segregation—adventitious as well as deliberate—is constitutionally defective? Does it imply that the court is treating the student peer group as an educational resource? See generally Cohen, "Defining Racial Equality in Education," 16 *UCLA L Rev* 255 (1969). Does the *Brown* focus on education and equality imply that nonracial educational inequalities would be similarly treated? (See chapters 6 and 7.) That racial separation with respect to other governmental services would be treated differently?

b. Race. Is *Brown* more aptly described as a case primarily concerned with racial constraints and freedom of association? If so, does the holding in *Brown* become applicable to any situation in which racial segregation occurs, provided, of course, that the requisite governmental involvement can be demonstrated? Historic judicial hostility to state-imposed racial classification, and the numerous per curiam extensions of *Brown,* striking down racial separation in noneducation areas, suggest that race may have been the critical factor. See, e.g., *Watson v Memphis* 373 US 526 (1963); *New Orleans City Park Improvement Ass'n v Detiege* 358 US 54 (1958).

c. Race and Education. Is *Brown* best treated as both an education and a race case: that is, one that posits a relationship between unconstrained racial association, equality of educational resources, and equality of opportunity, with the benefits of equality seen as following from school desegregation?

4. Ethical Principles and Social Science Evidence

a. Quality of Social Science Evidence in Brown. The social science evidence that *Brown* relied on to assess the effects of segregation has been roundly attacked on methodological and interpretive grounds. See, e.g., Cahn, "A Dangerous Myth in the School Segregation Cases," 30 *NYU L Rev* 150 (1955); Garfinkel, "Social Science Evidence and the School Desegregation Cases," 21 *J Pol* 37 (1959); Van Den Haag, "Social Science Testimony in the Desegregation Cases—A Reply to Professor Kenneth Clark," 6 *Vill L Rev* 69 (1960). In this regard, consider the following excerpts from the social scientists' amicus brief in *Brown,* which epitomizes the type of empirical data that confronted the Supreme Court;

> [T]he opinion stated by a large majority (90 percent) of social scientists who replied to a questionnaire concerning the probable effects of enforced segregation under conditions of equal facilities [is] . . . that, regardless of the facilities which are provided, enforced segregation is psychologically detrimental to the members of the segregated group [here, the blacks].
> . . . .
> The available scientific evidence indicates that much, perhaps all, of the observable differences among various racial and national groups may be adequately explained in terms of environmental differences.
> . . . .
> Comprehensive reviews of . . . instances [of desegregation] clearly establish the fact that desegregation has been carried out successfully in a variety of situations although outbreaks of violence had been commonly predicted.

Is this survey really evidence at all? Dr. Kenneth B. Clark, one of the moving forces behind the introduction of empirical data in the *Brown* case, has commented: "By providing such evidence, the social scientists made it possible to avoid the need to obtain proof of individual damage and to avoid assessment of the equality of facilities in each individual school situation. The assumption of inequality could now be made wherever segregation existed." Clark, "The Social Scientists, the Brown Decision, and Contemporary Confusion," in *Argument*, xxxvii (L. Friedman ed. 1969). Might the appellants have submitted empirical evidence of greater probative force without resorting to a school-by-school survey of each district involved in the litigation? Do you agree with Clark's conclusion? Should the lawyers for appellants in *Brown* be faulted for relying on such inconclusive data? See Greenberg, "Social Scientists Take the Stand," 54 *Mich L Rev* 953 (1956). In this regard, consider these remarks by Jerome Frank about the adversary process:

> ... the lawyer aims at winning in the fight, not in aiding the court to discover the facts. He does not want the trial court to reach a sound educated guess, if it is likely to be contrary to his client's interests. Our present trial method is thus the equivalent of throwing pepper in the eyes of a surgeon when he is performing an operation. (J. Frank, *Courts on Trial* 85 (1945).)

Did the decision in *Plessy*, which rejected the argument that segregation might be stigmatic or otherwise injurious, invite reliance on psychological and sociological data by the court and appellants in *Brown*? See J. Peltason, *58 Lonely Men* 49 (1961). Might this reliance be explained by the necessity to give a controversial decision an aura of legitimacy by demonstrating that it was consistent with both a constitutional and empirical calculus?

b. The Controversy. Apart from criticisms of the specific evidence submitted in *Brown*, scholars have sharply debated the propriety of reliance on social science to justify the desegregation decisions. Professor Frank Goodman has observed that "constitutional scholars, whatever their views as to the correctness of the decision, have been reluctant to believe that the court relied to any great extent on the 'modern authorities' cited in its opinion." Goodman, "De Facto Segregation: A Constitutional and Empirical Analysis," 60 *Calif L Rev* 275, 279 (1972). See also Cahn, "Jurisprudence," 30 *NYU L Rev* 150 (1955); Black, "The Lawfulness of the Segregation Decisions," 69 *Yale LJ* 421 (1960); Heyman, "The Chief Justice, Racial Segregation, and the Friendly Critics," 49 *Calif L Rev* 104 (1961). Other scholars have attributed great importance to the court's suggestion that the social science evidence indicated that blacks were injured by segregation in the schools. See, e.g., Fiss, "Racial Imbalance in the Public Schools: The Constitutional Concepts," 78 *Harv L Rev* 564, 569-70 (1965); Clark, "Law and Social Science," 5 *Vill L Rev* 224 (1959); Honnold, Book Review, 33 *Ind LJ* 612 (1958). With respect to this controversy, consider these remarks by Professor Yudof:

EQUAL EDUCATIONAL OPPORTUNITY AND THE COURTS
M. Yudof
51 Tex L Rev 411, 437-39 (1973)

Explaining Footnote 11 and All That

The *Brown* court's troublesome references to educational and psychological harm have been explained in various ways. Some have viewed the findings as unessential to the result. According to this view the court "did not need the cold empirical foundation that would have been required had constitutional imperatives truly hinged upon them." This explanation is the simplest, and may be the soundest. It may also be argued that the findings of harm were self-evident and thus subject to judicial notice. [Goodman, "De Facto Segregation: A Constitutional and Empirical Analysis," 60 *Calif L Rev* 275, 280 (1972).]

This view, however, is unpersuasive. It should be clear that virtually nothing about the educational process is self-evident. The theory of self-evident injury may rely upon empirically unverifiable notions as to how a just society should function, and thus amount to little more than a statement of ethical preferences grounded in history.

Finally, the findings may have been a way of saying that the state had drawn a racial classification and failed to meet its burden of showing that racial separation is consistent with equality. According to this explanation, the state could survive the strict scrutiny of racial classifications only by showing that racially segregated education was totally harmless to the members of the minority group, an impossible task that the defendants did not even attempt. Under this analysis, where the evidence is vague or dubious, the state loses. [This view was first] espoused by Professor Pollak in his brilliant draft of an "adequate" opinion for *Brown*. [Pollak, "Racial Discrimination and Judicial Integrity: A Reply to Professor Wechsler, 108 *U Pa L Rev* 1 (1959).] . . .

[W]hy should the burden of justifying segregation be shifted to the state? . . . Perhaps those seeking to change the educational system should bear the burden of demonstrating the need for the change. Casting the analysis of desegregation cases in the formalistic legal mold of burdens of proof obfuscates the critical underlying social and political issues. . . .

[T]he whole suspect classification argument is premised on unarticulated concepts of equality. . . . Like the self-evident harm thesis, the shifting of burdens approach ultimately reduces to the proposition that segregation is somehow ethically unacceptable. If this is the case, then the first reading of *Brown* is vindicated—the references to social science literature and to psychological and academic harm must be viewed as unessential to the result.

The post-*Brown* judicial experience confirms this hypothesis: the courts have consistently and adamantly refused to countenance, in Judge Wisdom's words, "the popular myth that *Brown* was decided for sociological reasons." [*Jackson Munic Separate School Dist v Evers* 357 F2d 653, 654 (5th Cir 1966).] With rare exceptions [e.g., *Stell v Savannah-Chatham County Bd of Educ* 255 F Supp 88 (SD Ga 1966)] . . . . courts have not allowed school boards or white intervenors to introduce social science data and testimony to contradict the *Brown* result. They have simply not been interested in proof suggesting that integration is injurious or that segregation is not harmful.

c. Ethical Principles. If the social science evidence was not essential to the *Brown* decision, on what constitutional or ethical basis may the case be defended? Consider these additional comments by Professor Yudof:

> The difficulties inherent in defining equal educational opportunity in terms of benefit and injury lead me to believe that *Brown* and its progeny are fundamentally based on ethical principles. As used here, ethical principles are defined as normative, or mixed normative and factual, statements

about how a just society should function. Ethical principles or social ideals may be explicitly adopted as legal principles, or they may exist independent of legal institutions. Basic ethical principles assert the truth of facts that cannot be proven; in other words, barring the most extraordinary advances in learning, even the most scientific among us must rely upon rather unscientific interpretations of historical experience. Indeed because ethical principles are not necessarily dependent on empirical verification, they can operate as standards that relieve courts of the obligation to reweigh social science data in every case. If desegregation decisions are to be stable, consistent, and manageable, courts have little choice but to rely on ethical principles. The cases can be explained only by reference to such principles. . . .

According to one formulation, the desegregation cases rest on the simple proposition that the state may not treat blacks differently from whites in the operation of the public schools merely because of their race. [Citing, inter alia, Hyman and Newhouse, "Desegregation of the Schools: Present Legal Situation," 14 Buffalo L Rev 208, 218 (1964); Kaplan, "Segregation, Litigation, and the Schools—Part II: The General Northern Problem," 58 NWU L Rev 157, 172 (1965).] In the words of Judge Sobeloff,

> Certainly Brown had to do with the equalization of educational opportunity; but it stands for much more. Brown articulated the truth that Plessy chose to disregard: that relegation of blacks to separate facilities represents a declaration by the state that they are inferior and not to be associated with. [Brunson v Board of Trustees 429 F2d 820, 825 (1970).]

An affirmation by the state that whites are superior to blacks is ethically unacceptable, regardless of any particular harm that may result: it simply does not comport with widely shared notions as to how a just society should function. This principle is in part grounded in historical experience. The history of separatist legislation indicates that it was designed to relegate blacks to an inferior position in society, and in fact school segregation did operate as a vital component of a larger caste system. [Citing, inter alia, Black, "The Lawfulness of the Segregation Decisions," 69 Yale LJ 421, 424-25 (1960); J. Franklin, From Slavery to Freedom 338-43 (1969).] The principle has been adopted as a rule of law by the courts in many fields. Classification by race has been held to violate the constitutional imperative of equality under the laws in areas unrelated to public schooling, ranging from public golf courses and parks to public beaches, without reference to the "specifically hurtful character of segregation, as a net matter in the life of each segregated individual." (51 Tex L Rev, at 446-47.)

Does the Brown opinion support Professor Yudof's interpretation? Is the court better equipped to articulate ethical principles than to pass on social science controversies? Can the formulation of values be separated from the empirical evidence of their impact on individuals and society? In a democratic society, should the court assume the role of interpreter of ethical principles? See Rostow, "The Democratic Character of Judicial Review," in Judicial Review and the Supreme Court, 74-90 (L. Levy ed 1967); Lerner, "The Supreme Court as Republican Schoolmaster," 1967 Sup Ct Rev 127.

5. Neutral Principles

Professor Herbert Wechsler, a proponent of neutrality in judicial decision making, describes a "principled decision" as "one that rests on reasons with respect to all the issues in the case, reasons that in their generality and their neutrality transcend any immediate result that is involved." Wechsler, "Toward Neutral Principles," 73 *Harv L Rev* 1, 15 (1959). But see Mueller and Schwartz, "The Principle of Neutral Principles," 7 *UCLA L Rev* 571, 588 (1960); Wright, "Professor Bickel, The Scholarly Tradition and the Supreme Court," 84 *Harv L Rev* 769, 775-83 (1971). According to Wechsler, adherence to such a view of the judicial process is necessary to guard against a court's becoming a partisan instrument. Wechsler concludes that the two principles at issue in the school desegregation cases were "denial by the state of freedom to associate, a denial that impinges in the same way on any groups or races that may be involved," and the individual's competing right not to associate with certain members of society. He further asserts that the court has not applied these principles in a neutral fashion since blacks are legally entitled to associate with whites or other blacks, but whites cannot legally choose to associate with whites only. How do you respond to Professor Wechsler's criticism of *Brown*? Does the problem lie in his designation of the principles involved in *Brown*? Suppose the underlying principle is that the state may not classify its citizens according to race in the operation of the public schools? Has not this principle been applied by the *Brown* court in an evenhanded fashion? See Pollak, "Racial Discrimination and Judicial Integrity: A Reply to Professor Wechsler," 180 *U Pa L Rev* 1 (1959). Can the principle itself be attacked as not being neutral even if it is neutrally applied? Does the Fourteenth Amendment contain its own biases in this regard?

If one treats *Brown* as grounded in a right of association, as Professor Wechsler suggests, can it be persuasively argued that the denial of the rights of blacks and whites to associate with members of the opposite race is a greater detriment to blacks than whites, because blacks are deprived of the opportunity to associate with 90 percent of the population, while whites are deprived only of the right to associate with 10 percent of the population?

Consider a variant of Wechsler's associational formulation: the state may not interfere with the voluntary associational choices of *any* of its citizens? Does the Harlan dissent in *Plessy* suggest this rationale? Does this mean that white and black parents must choose integration or segregation? How could a court determine whether these choices were voluntary? Suppose that the blacks choose integrated schools while the whites choose segregated schools? See generally Kirp, "Community Control, Public Policy, and the Limits of the Law," 68 *Mich L Rev* 1355 (1970).

6. *Brown* and *Plessy*: Evolving Equal Protection Standards

Are the contrasting results in *Plessy* and *Brown* accurately described as reflections, at different times, of an evolving standard of what "equal protection of the laws" means? Since "the very idea of classification is that of inequality," the mere fact that a law classifies or distinguishes among different groups of people is not sufficient to render it unconstitutional under the equal protection clause. Tussman and tenBroek, "Equal Protection of the Laws," 37 *Calif L Rev* 341,

344 (1949). Historically, the threshold requirement demanded by the Fourteenth Amendment of any classification or unequal treatment is that of reasonableness. Reasonableness is a function of both the purpose or aim of the law and the fashion in which it is administered or applied. In this context, recall that the *Plessy* court described the primary issue in that case as simply "the question whether the statute of Louisiana is a reasonable regulation." Does *Brown* suggest that a subsequent reconsideration of analogous facts resulted in a finding that racial classifications are irrational? Or did the *Brown* court invoke a different equal protection test?

More recent equal protection cases have in particular instances supplemented the requirement of reasonableness. When a state-fostered distinction is based on a "suspect trait" such as race or when the classification jeopardizes a so-called fundamental right (interstate travel, privacy, criminal process), the state has been held to a more rigorous test of justification. A "compelling state interest" must be demonstrated, and the burden of proof clearly rests on the state. Some members of the Supreme Court, notably the late Justice Harlan, have criticized this "new equal protection approach" as a verbal manipulation by which the court labels or defines a "right" or a "trait" according to the standard by which the interests in question can be vindicated. *Shapiro v Thompson* 394 US 618, 655 (1970) (Harlan, J, dissenting). See generally chapter 6.

7. The Remedy Question

What remedy did plaintiffs' counsel envision when *Brown* was prosecuted? In the pre-*Brown* education cases (*Gaines, Sipuel, Sweatt,* and *McLaurin*), judicial intervention consisted simply of a prohibition against segregation. Thurgood Marshall's oral argument before the Supreme Court indicates that he sought a similar remedy in *Brown*:

> The only thing that we ask for is that the state-imposed racial segregation be taken off, and to leave the county school board, the county people, the district people, to work out their own solution of the problem to assign children on any reasonable basis they want to assign them on.
>
> . . . .
>
> I think, sir [addressing Justice Frankfurter], that the decree would be entered which would enjoin the school officials from one, enforcing the statute [which required segregation]; two, from segregating on the basis of race or color. Then I think whatever district lines they draw, if it can be shown that those lines are drawn on the basis of race or color, then I think they would violate the injunction. If the lines are drawn on a natural basis, without regard to race or color, then I think that nobody would have any complaint.
>
> For example, the colored child that is over here in this school would not be able to go to that school. But the only thing that would come down would be the decision that whatever rule you set in, if you set in, it shall not be on race, either actually or by any other way.

How does one make the transition, in a logical sense, from the elimination of state-fostered segregation to affirmative remedies, such as busing, the use of racial quotas, and the rearrangement of districts or attendance zones, which more recent Supreme Court decisions require? Might the seeds of such a transition and its accompanying problems be discerned in what Marshall describes as "lines . . . drawn on a natural basis?" Cannot black children be described in many ways (e.g., in terms of the neighborhoods in which they live) that would result in racial segregation under a superficially neutral standard of pupil assignment?

8. *Bolling v Sharpe*

Bolling v Sharpe 347 US 497 (1954), was the companion case to *Brown*, applying that decision to the District of Columbia (not a "state" under the Fourteenth Amendment). The nucleus of the opinion is the court's statement that "in view of our decision that the Constitution prohibits the states from maintaining racially segregated public schools, it would be unthinkable that the same Constitution would impose a lesser duty on the federal government." The legal underpinnings of the statement suggest what might be called a type of "inverse incorporation": the prohibition against discrimination that is embodied in the Fourteenth Amendment is applicable to the federal government because "discrimination may be so unjustifiable as to be violative of [the Fifth Amendment] due process."

D. *Brown 2*: The Scope of Relief

BROWN v BOARD OF EDUCATION
349 US 294 (1955)

Mr. Chief Justice Warren delivered the opinion of the court.

These cases were decided on May 17, 1954. The opinions of that date, declaring the fundamental principle that racial discrimination in public education is unconstitutional, are incorporated herein by reference. All provisions of federal, state, or local law requiring or permitting such discrimination must yield to this principle. There remains for consideration the manner in which relief is to be accorded.

Because these cases arose under different local conditions and their disposition will involve a variety of local problems, we requested further argument on the question of relief. . . .

These presentations were informative and helpful to the court in its consideration of the complexities arising from the transition to a system of public education freed of racial discrimination. The presentations also demonstrated that substantial steps to eliminate racial discrimination in public schools have already been taken, not only in some of the communities in which these cases arose, but in some of the states appearing as amici curiae, and in other states as well. Substantial progress has been made in the District of Columbia and in the communities in Kansas and Delaware involved in this litigation. The defendants in the cases coming to us from South Carolina and Virginia are awaiting the decision of this court concerning relief.

Full implementation of these constitutional principles may require solution of varied local school problems. School authorities have the primary responsibility for elucidating, assessing, and solving these problems; courts will have to consider whether the action of school authorities constitutes good faith implementation of the governing constitutional principles. Because of their proximity to local conditions and the possible need for further hearings, the courts which originally heard these cases can best perform this judicial appraisal. Accordingly, we believe it appropriate to remand the cases to those courts.

In fashioning and effectuating the decrees, the courts will be guided by equitable principles. Traditionally, equity has been characterized by a practical flexibility in shaping its remedies and by a facility for adjusting and reconciling public and private needs. These cases call for the exercise of these traditional attributes of equity power. At stake is the personal interest of the plaintiffs in admission to public schools as soon as practicable on a nondiscriminatory basis. To effectuate this interest may call for elimination of a variety of obstacles in making the transition to school systems operated in accordance with the constitutional principles set forth in our May 17, 1954, decision. Courts of equity may properly take into account the public interest in the elimination of such obstacles in a systematic and effective manner. But it should go without saying that the vitality of these constitutional principles cannot be allowed to yield simply because of disagreement with them.

While giving weight to these public and private considerations, the courts will require that the defendants make a prompt and reasonable start toward full compliance with our May 17, 1954, ruling. Once such a start has been made, the courts may find that additional time is necessary to carry out the ruling in an effective manner. The burden rests upon the defendants to establish that such time is necessary in the public interest and is consistent with good faith compliance at the earliest practicable date. To that end, the courts may consider problems related to administration, arising from the physical condition of the school plant, the school transportation system, personnel, revision of school districts and attendance areas into compact units to achieve a system of determining admission to the public schools on a nonracial basis, and revision of local laws and regulations which may be necessary in solving the foregoing problems. They will also consider the adequacy of any plans the defendants may propose to meet these problems and to effectuate a transition to a racially nondiscriminatory school system. During this period of transition, the courts will retain jurisdiction of these cases.

The judgments below, except that in the Delaware case, are accordingly reversed and the cases are remanded to the district courts to take such proceedings and enter such orders and decrees consistent with this opinion as are necessary and proper to admit to public schools on a racially nondiscriminatory basis with all deliberate speed the parties to these cases. The judgment in the Delaware case—ordering the immediate admission of the plaintiffs to schools previously attended only by white children—is affirmed on the basis of the principles stated in our May 17, 1954, opinion, but the case is remanded to the Supreme Court of Delaware for such further proceedings as that court may deem necessary in light of this opinion.

It is so ordered.

Notes and Questions

1. "All Deliberate Speed:" An Unusual Remedy?

The "all deliberate speed" standard describes an unspecified remedy that would take effect in an undefined interval of time. That standard differs from the typically precise formulations of relief that usually require immediate implementation. As Professor Bickel points out:

> In the vast majority of cases—barring those that are dismissed outright as not suitable for adjudication—the normal and expected judgment of the court is a crisp and specific writing which tells one of the parties exactly what he must do, such as pay a judgment, deliver certain real estate, cease from doing something, or, indeed, go to jail. The equivalent in these cases would have been a decree ordering the named children, and perhaps, since these were class actions, all children in the five school districts affected who were similarly situated, to be admitted forthwith to the white schools of their choice. (Bickel, *The Least Dangerous Branch* 247 (1962).)

See also McKay, " 'With All Deliberate Speed'—A Study of School Desegregation," 31 *NYU L Rev* 991 (1956). Does the court's approach minimize the legal significance of the injury suffered by the actual plaintiffs who initiated *Brown 1*? Did the court, in characterizing *Brown* as a test case of broad dimensions, submerge the claims of the individual plaintiffs into the hypothesized claims of the black race as a whole—with the consequence that an eventual remedy ("with all deliberate speed") for all blacks would ultimately benefit the particular parties who had brought the suit? See Hartman, "The Right to Equal Educational Opportunities as a Personal and Present Right," 9 *Wayne L Rev* 424 (1963); Lusky, "The Stereotype: Hard Core of Racism," 13 *Buff L Rev* 450, 458 (1964). In this sense, is "all deliberate speed" analogous to "prospective overruling"? Typically a prospective decree that a particular precedent has been overruled is joined with a refusal to apply the new law in the instant case. As a result, the overruled law—that is, the old law—is held to govern the parties to the case in which the new law was made. See Comment, "Prospective Overruling and Retroactive Application in the Federal Courts," 71 *Yale LJ* 907 (1962). Was the *Brown* court consciously striving for such a result? Or does the "all deliberate speed" standard spring from practical problems in implementation rather than from considerations of more abstract principles of justice?

If a more straightforward and forceful standard, as urged by the NAACP, had been embraced by the court's decree, would actual desegregation have occurred more quickly? Justice Black once stated that the "deliberate speed" formula "delayed the process of outlawing segregation" and that "the court should have forced its judgment on the counties it affected that minute." W. Lockhart, Y. Kamisar, and J. Choper, *Constitutional Law* 1208-9 (1970). Might such a decree have engendered even more hostile resistance than that which greeted the "all deliberate speed" mandate? See pp 307-47. In this context, consider the relevance of Justice Frankfurter's apparently realistic appraisal of the competing problems confronting the court: "Nothing could be worse from my point of view than for this court to make an abstract declaration that segregation is bad and then to have it evaded by tricks."

Did the court's choice of remedy, by necessary implication, call on other governmental agencies for help in implementation? Consider these remarks by Professor Bickel:

> The formula [of "all deliberate speed"] does not signify that the process of judicial review will involve itself in finding expedient compromises for a

difficult situation. It means only that the court, having announced its principle, and having required a measure of initial compliance, resumed its posture of passive receptiveness to the complaints of litigants. . . . The court placed itself in position to engage in a continual colloquy with political institutions, leaving it to them to tell the court what expedients of accommodation and compromise they deemed necessary. The court would reply in the negative—and did eventually once so reply [*Cooper v Aaron* 358 US 1]—only when a suggested expedient amounted to the abandonment of a principle. On the other hand, the court would not approve, let alone itself work out, agreeable compromises, though the lower federal courts might take a hand. More typically, the passive devices of the colloquy precede, and prepare or avoid, the moment of constitutional judgment. . . . In the *Segregation Cases* the deliberate speed formula opened a colloquy following judgment and called for employment of the passive devices to ease the way to its acceptance and effectuation. (Bickel, *The Least Dangerous Branch*, 254 (1962).)

2. *Brown 2* and the Lower Federal Courts

Because the court placed responsibility for school desegregation in the hands of federal district courts and local school boards, delay in the implementation of *Brown* was inevitable. See generally H. Rodgers and C. Bullock, *Law and Social Change*, chap 4 (1972); G. Orfield, *The Reconstruction of Southern Education* 15-18 (1969). The court had not developed adequate guidelines for school desegregation, and thus much time was to be wasted in lower courts converting nebulous doctrine into understandable and administrable constitutional law. See Carter, "Equal Educational Opportunities for Negroes—Abstraction or Reality," 1968 *U Ill LF* 160, 177-80. These delays were confounded by the open-endedness of the "all deliberate speed" formula. Thurgood Marshall aptly expressed the fear that such problems would emasculate the *Brown* decision:

> What is needed . . . is a firm hand. . . . A district court properly instructed by [the Supreme] Court will supply the firm hand. . . . But the Supreme Court must arm the district judges and appellate judges with authority. If no time is set, [the defendants are] going to argue in any event the same way they've argued here, which is nothing. . . . If no time limit is included the district judges will be placed in the legislative field—their duties are merely to tell the state what it can't do." J. Peltason, *58 Lonely Men* (1961).

Moreover, many federal district court judges were unenthusiastic about or openly hostile to *Brown*. G. Orfield, *The Reconstruction of Southern Education* 18 (1969). They often were isolated from their communities, subjected to social ostracism if they acted contrary to the community's views on segregation, and unaided either by the national administration (which may have appointed them) or local and state governmental authorities. See generally Peltason, *58 Lonely Men* (1961).

What alternative courses of action might the court have pursued in 1954-55 to speed the course of desegregation? See Leflar and Davis, "Segregation in the Public Schools—1953," 67 *Harv L Rev* 377 (1954). Was delay inevitable in any judicial solution as long as Congress and the president refrained from acting? Was the failure of the other branches of government to act one of the long-range consequences of *Plessy*?

III. The Civil Rights Act: Background, Scope, and Impact

A. The Progress of School Desegregation

1. Southern Resistance. From 1954 until 1964, progress in the desegregation of southern school districts was miniscule. In 1964, in seven of the eleven states, only 2.14 percent of black students attended desegregated schools. H. Horowitz and K. Karst, *Law, Lawyers, and Social Change* 239 (1969). As Professors Horowitz and Karst have noted, in the decade after *Brown* "the desegregation of southern school districts was not characterized by speed, deliberate or otherwise. . . . The fact is that most of the putative beneficiaries of the legal principle declared in *Brown* [were] frustrated in the vindication of their rights." Ibid, 239-40 (1969).

The modes of southern resistance were varied. On March 12, 1956, ninety-six congressmen from the South issued a manifesto in which they promised to use "all lawful means" to maintain segregation and "commended those states which have declared the intention to resist." Popular opposition to school desegregation, supported by political leaders playing on the race issue, often resulted in massive resistance to the enforcement of *Brown*. See *Bush v Orleans Parish School Bd* 187 F Supp 42 (SD La 1960), *aff'd,* 365 US 569 (1961). The myriad new pupil assignment laws, "interposition" plans, and other ingenious schemes demonstrated the truth of the popular saying, "as long as we can legislate, we can segregate." See generally Meador, "The Constitution and the Assignment of Pupils to Public Schools," 45 *Va L Rev* 517 (1969); Bickel, "The Decade of School Desegregation: Progress and Prospects," 64 *Colum L Rev* 193 (1964); B. Muse, *Ten Years of Prelude: The Story of Integration Since the Supreme Court's 1954 Decision* (1964). The most important of these devices was the pupil assignment law, which purported to assign pupils to schools on the basis of considerations and characteristics other than race. In practice such laws perpetuated one-race schools. (See the Mobile, Alabama, case history below.) On one occasion, the Supreme Court affirmed a three-judge court decision upholding a pupil placement act. *Shuttlesworth v Birmingham Bd of Educ* 358 US 101 (1958). See Johnson, "School Desegregation Problems in the South: An Historical Perspective," 54 *Minn L Rev* 1157 (1970). A popular variation of pupil assignment laws was the "minority to majority transfer" arrangement. After formally desegregating, a Southern school district would grant to any students who constituted a racial minority in their new school the option of transferring back to their old school in which their race was a majority. In *Goss v Board of Educ* 373 US 683 (1963), the Supreme Court struck down such plans as in violation of *Brown*: "Here the right of transfer, which operates solely on the basis of a racial classification, is a one-way ticket leading to but one destination, i.e., the majority race of the transferee and continued segregation." 373 US at 687.

Another device southern legislatures used was support for private, segregated schools, where desegregation of the public schools seemed likely. Tuition grants to students and private institutions were employed, but both practices were declared unconstitutional as a method of avoiding *Brown. Hall v St Helena Parish School Bd* 197 F Supp 649 (ED La 1961), *aff'd,* 368 US 515 (1962); *Aaron v McKinley* 173 F Supp 944 (ED Ark), *aff'd sub nom, Faubus v Aaron* 361 US 1972 (1959); *Poindexter v Louisiana Assistance Corp* 389 US 571 (1961). See also *Norwood v Harrison* 93 S Ct 2804 (1973) (textbooks).

2. Examples of Southern Resistance

a. Little Rock, Arkansas, *Cooper v Aaron* 358 US 1 (1958). Soon after *Brown,* the Little Rock District School Board issued a public statement of its intention to comply with the Supreme Court's order; a group of black plaintiffs, seeking rapid compliance, filed suit in federal district court. Pursuant to this statement, the board and the superintendent of schools formulated a plan by which to implement the policy of desegregation in a gradual, yet apparently satisfactory, fashion. Other state authorities sought to resist this course of action. The Arkansas Constitution was hastily amended in 1956 to command statewide opposition to *Brown.* In September 1957, when 9 black students were scheduled to enter Central High School to integrate the student body of 2000, Governor Orval Faubus dispatched the Arkansas National Guard to prevent the plan's execution.

Confronted with this show of force, the school board requested that black students not attend Central High. However, the district court, reviewing that action, concluded that the presence of military guards, summoned by state authorities, was not a sufficient reason for the board to discontinue its program. The school board and the superintendent were ordered to proceed with integration as planned.

Compliance with the district court's mandate was thwarted by units of the Arkansas National Guard, which, "acting pursuant to the Governor's order, stood shoulder to shoulder at the school grounds and thereby forcibly prevented the nine Negro students . . . from entering" for a period of three weeks. 156 F Supp 220, 225 (ED Ark 1957) The district court responded by enjoining both the governor and the national guard from further interference. As a result, the children were able to enter the school, but only under the protection of the Little Rock and Arkansas State Police. More trouble ensued, and the president of the United States dispatched federal troops to Central High School.

The issue that brought the case to the Supreme Court concerned the efforts of the board and the superintendent to seek postponement of the original plan for desegregation. "Their position in essence was that because of extreme public hostility, which they stated had been engendered largely by the official attitudes and actions of the governor and the legislature, the maintenance of a sound educational program at Central High School, with the Negro students in attendance, would be impossible." 358 US 1, 12 (1958).

While sympathetic to the board's explanation that its good faith efforts had been undercut by public resentment and official defiance, the court declared that " 'important as is the preservation of the public peace, this aim cannot be accomplished by laws or ordinances which deny rights created or protected by the federal Constitution.' *Buchanan v Warley* 245 US 60, 81. Thus law and order are not here to be preserved by depriving the Negro children of their constitutional rights." 358 US at 16.

As Professors Horowitz and Karst note:

[*Cooper v Aaron*] is an unusual case in many ways: the timing of the action of the various courts was accelerated in order to permit disposition of the case to be completed before the school term began; the opinion was signed by all nine of the justices; the opinion lectures Governor Orval Faubus in a rather personal way, although it does not name him; and the opinion goes out of its way to announce the adherence of three new members of the court to the *Brown* decision. *Cooper v Aaron* is notable also in a doctrinal sense, . . . [because of the way in which it reinforces the supremacy of the federal Constitution and the judicial interpretations thereunder]. But the confrontation in Little Rock had an importance far beyond the judicial decision in this case. The sight, on national television, of a handful of black children, walking into school down a path cleared by police through a mob of screaming adults, solidified public opinion outside the south. Furthermore, the defiance of a federal court order prodded a hitherto reluctant federal executive branch into its first important action supporting desegregation. (*Law, Lawyers, and Social Change,* 241-42 (1969).)

b. Mobile, Alabama

"THE ROAD TO SWANN: MOBILE COUNTY CRAWLS TO THE BUS"
L. Powe
51 *Tex L Rev* 505, 506-11 (1973)

The Mobile County school system is large, both in numbers of students and in area; and it is divided into an urban and a rural system. Through the 1962-63 school year, the system was entirely segregated. During the years of the desegregation process, the number of students in the system averaged about 75,000. The ratio of white to black students, and white to black teachers, was approximately sixty-to-forty, although the white-black ratio in the urban system approached fifty-fifty. As the desegregation process progressed the interstate highway system was begun; the completion of I-65 created a man-made barrier conforming to the racial patterns of the urban area. The vast majority of the urban blacks lived east of I-65; the school population there was 62 percent black to 38 percent white, while the white-black ratio west of I-65 was 88:12. . . .

While Alabama did not greet *Brown* with wild public rejoicing, neither did it respond with the massive resistance that occurred in Arkansas, Louisiana, and Virginia. The legislature quickly enacted a pupil placement act designed to govern school board actions. [Ala Code tit 52, §61 (1960).] The act clearly dismissed any immediate desegregation; instead, it suggested more flexible and selective procedures that were designed to further the economy and maintain public support for public schools. "Pending further studies"—which were never made—the legislature rejected "any general or arbitrary reallocation of pupils . . . according to any rigid rule of proximity of residence or in accordance solely with request on behalf of the pupil. . . ."

School boards were without authority to accede to transfer demands from *any* source unless the local board found, as to each individual pupil, that the transfer would be consistent with public and educational policy. The indefinite guidelines contained in the act provided a convenient justification for refusing to transfer any child to a particular school. Further, section 8 used the following language to ensure that segregation would remain the norm for those who desired it: "Any other provisions of law notwithstanding, no child shall be compelled to attend any school in which the races are commingled when a written objection of the parent or guardian has been filed with the board of education." A final fail safe device provided for a hearing and appeal procedure, thus utilizing the requirement of exhaustion of remedies to moot an individual case.

The act was first challenged while the controversy in Little Rock was raging; unlike the result in Arkansas, the challenge in Alabama failed. The Pupil Placement Act was still inoperative and only the facial validity of the act was challenged. Unanimously upholding the act, the three-judge district court stated:

> The School Placement Law furnishes the legal machinery for an orderly administration of the public schools in a constitutional manner by the admission of qualified pupils upon a basis of individual merit without regard to their race or color. We must presume that it will be so administered. If not, in some future proceeding it is possible that it may be declared unconstitutional in its application. The responsibility rests primarily upon the local school boards, but ultimately upon all the people of the state. [*Shuttlesworth v Birmingham Bd of Educ* 162 F Supp 372, 384 (ND Ala 1958).]

The black plaintiffs appealed directly to the Supreme Court, and only two months after the ringing reaffirmation of *Brown* in *Cooper v Aaron* [358 US 1 (1958)], the court meekly affirmed the district court without argument. [*Shuttlesworth v Birmingham Bd of Educ* 358 US 101 (1958).]

It is hard to account for the court's action. On the basis of section 8 alone, the law was unquestionably unconstitutional, and the case is still the only school desegregation case decided by the Supreme Court in which the black plaintiffs have not prevailed. Writing in 1964, Alexander Bickel suggested a plausible explanation:

> But this was at a time when the outlook in Alabama might have seemed ambiguous; Alabama was in any event not yet writhing in the grip of massive resistance, and it happened to be the moment when the crises in both Arkansas and Virginia were at their height. This was a peak of political struggle, and the court, not unnaturally, was holding its breath. [Bickel, "The Decade of School Desegregation," 64 *Colum L Rev* 193, 204 (1964).]

Following the court's decision no serious efforts were made to desegregate Alabama schools. [A surprisingly long period of time elapsed before suits were filed in Mobile and other parts of Alabama. This delay was partially the result of the protracted litigation resulting from the state's efforts to ban the NAACP.] *Brown* was decided, but schooling went on as if *Plessy* were still the law. . . .

The initial attempts to desegregate the Mobile schools began almost a year in advance of the target date set by the black plaintiffs—the 1963-64 school year. Resulting negotiations, however, proved futile, and in March 1963 a class action was filed before Judge Daniel H. Thomas in the Southern District of Alabama. Shortly after this suit was filed, plaintiffs requested a preliminary injunction and Judge Thomas gave the school district approximately a month to respond. Plaintiffs unsuccessfully attempted to set aside the order as an abuse of discretion.

Ruling on the preliminary injunction, Judge Thomas found it administratively impossible to make the changes necessary to desegregate prior to the start of the 1963-64 school year. Additionally, he suggested that the Alabama Pupil Placement Act itself might constitute an adequate desegregation plan, even though no one had attempted to implement it. Judge Thomas then reminded the Fifth Circuit "of that 'area of discretion in the desegregation process [left] to the district courts.' " [219 F Supp 542, 545 (SD Ala 1963).] Concluding, he stated that if no one pushed too hard or too fast "the mandate of the court will be honestly, conscientiously, and fairly carried out with the least possible, if not complete absence of, unfortunate incidents." Trial on the merits, aiming at the 1964-65 school year, was then set for mid-November.

An appeal was filed immediately. The school board argued that any token integration would be detrimental to 99 percent of the black students. Furthermore, this action would seriously delay the much needed improvement of the black schools in Mobile. In July 1963 the Fifth Circuit reversed Judge Thomas, finding his reasons inadequate since the school board had known of the problem for almost a year, and since the system was 100 percent segregated, nothing in the record indicated that forbearance would produce results. [322 F2d 356 (5th Cir), *cert denied*, 375 US 895 (1963).] This latter conclusion was underscored by the school board's contention that plaintiffs had failed to state a claim for relief.

The panel ordered the district court to require the school board to comply with *Brown 2* and to submit a plan by August 1, 1963, for desegregating the first grade and at least one successively higher grade for each following school year. Later, the court modified its order by requiring the school board to submit a plan for an immediate start in desegregation and after the initial start to continue by applying the Alabama Pupil Placement Act to all grades without racial discrimination. [*Armstrong v Board of Educ* 323 F2d 333 (5th Cir 1963), *cert denied*, 376 US 908 (1964).] The Mobile School Board then requested a stay from an incredulous Justice Black who denied the motion, stating: "It is difficult to conceive of any administrative problems which could justify the Board in failing in 1963 to make a start toward ending the racial discrimination in the public schools which is forbidden by the equal protection clause of the Fourteenth Amendment, as authoritatively determined by this court in *Brown* nine years ago." [*Board of School Comm'rs v Davis* 84 S Ct 10, 12 (1963) (Black, CJ).]

The school board responded by disavowing the existence of racial discrimination; it continued by introducing evidence purporting to show that black students were intellectually inferior to whites. The first assertion was a knowing falsehood, and the second contention had been rejected by the Fifth Circuit five months earlier. [Citing *Stell v Savannah-Chatham County Bd of Educ* 318 F2d 425 (5th Cir 1963), *cert denied*, 376 US 908 (1964).]

At the end of the hearing required by the Fifth Circuit, the district court approved a plan that applied the Pupil Placement Act to the twelfth grade of the urban system while leaving the rural system untouched. A year later the Fifth Circuit took the case on the merits and ruled that the plan must provide for swifter desegregation and that the Pupil Placement Act must function without any cumbersome administrative procedure. [333 F2d 53 (5th Cir), *cert denied*, 379 US 844 (1964).] The court also demanded the abolition of dual attendance zones.

The district judge immediately made certain modifications, and during the 1964-65 school year sixteen black children went to school with whites for the first time in their lives.

Notes and Questions

1. Lessons from Little Rock and Mobile

What lessons should be drawn from the desegregation experiences in Little Rock and Mobile? Do they indicate the futility of the "all deliberate speed" doctrine? Was the Supreme Court simply not aggressive enough in securing compliance with *Brown*? How do you explain the court's decision in *Shuttlesworth v Birmingham Bd of Educ* 358 US 101 (1958)? In the light of the contrasting reactions to *Brown* in Little Rock and Mobile, was massive resistance or "exhaustion" of the legal process a better way to avoid desegregation? How can or should the court deal with rebellious district court judges? Was delay inherent as plaintiffs and judges were compelled to take the time to understand the complexities of school administration?

2. Judicial Frustration

To what extent does the Mobile experience portend judicial frustration (at least in appellate courts) with the progress of desegregation in school districts in which no good faith efforts are made to comply with *Brown 2*? Will appellate courts feel compelled to give district courts and school boards less and less discretion, ultimately leading to the adoption of per se rules? What per se rules might an appellate court adopt? Should the development of such rules be encouraged? What are the dangers?

c. Prince Edward County

GRIFFIN v COUNTY SCHOOL BOARD OF PRINCE EDWARD COUNTY
377 US 218 (1964)

Mr. Justice Black delivered the opinion of the court.

This litigation began in 1951 when a group of Negro school children living in Prince Edward County, Virginia, filed a complaint in the United States District Court for the Eastern District of Virginia alleging that they had been denied admission to public schools attended by white children and charging that Virginia laws requiring such school segregation denied complainants the equal protection of the laws in violation of the Fourteenth Amendment. . . .

Efforts to desegregate Prince Edward County's schools met with resistance. In 1956 Section 141 of the Virginia Constitution was amended to authorize the general assembly and local governing bodies to appropriate funds to assist students to go to public or to nonsectarian private schools, in addition to those owned by the state or by the locality. The general assembly met in special session and enacted legislation to close any public schools where white and colored children were enrolled together, to cut off state funds to such schools, to pay tuition grants to children in nonsectarian private schools, and to extend state retirement benefits to teachers in newly created private schools. The legislation closing mixed schools and cutting off state funds was later invalidated by the Supreme Court of Appeals of Virginia, which held that these laws violated the Virginia Constitution. *Harrison v Day* 200 Va 439, 106 SE2d 636 (1959). In April 1959 the general assembly abandoned "massive resistance" to desegregation and turned instead to what was called a "freedom of choice" program. The assembly repealed the rest of the 1956 legislation, as well as a tuition grant law of January 1959, and enacted a new tuition grant program. At the same time the assembly repealed Virginia's compulsory attendance laws and instead made school attendance a matter of local option.

In June 1959, the United States Court of Appeals for the Fourth Circuit directed the federal district court (1) to enjoin discriminatory practices in Prince Edward County schools, (2) to require the county school board to take "immediate steps" toward admitting students without regard to race to the white high school "in the school term beginning September 1959," and (3) to require the board to make plans for admissions to elementary schools without regard to race. *Allen v County School Bd of Prince Edward County* 266 F2d 507, 511 (4th Cir 1959). Having as early as 1956 resolved that they would not operate public schools "wherein white and colored children are taught together," the supervisors of Prince Edward County refused to levy any school taxes for the 1959-1960 school year, explaining that they were "confronted with a court decree which requires the admission of white and colored children to all the schools of the county without regard to race or color." As a result, the county's public schools did not reopen in the fall of 1959 and have remained closed ever since, although the public schools of every other county in Virginia have continued to operate under laws governing the state's public school system and to draw funds provided by the state for that purpose. A private group, the Prince Edward School Foundation, was formed to operate private schools for white children in Prince Edward County and, having built its own school plant, has been in operation ever since the closing of the public schools. An offer to set up private schools for colored children in the county was rejected, the Negroes of Prince Edward preferring to continue the legal battle for desegregated public schools, and colored children were without formal education from 1959 to 1963, when federal, state, and county authorities cooperated to have classes conducted for Negroes and whites in school buildings owned by the county. During the 1959-1960 school year the foundation's schools for white children were supported entirely by private contributions, but in 1960 the general assembly adopted a new tuition grant program making every child, regardless of race, eligible for tuition grants of $125 or $150 to attend a nonsectarian private school or a public school outside his locality, and also authorizing localities to provide their own grants. The Prince Edward board of supervisors then passed an ordinance providing tuition grants of $100, so that each child attending the Prince Edward School Foundation's schools received a total of $225 if in elementary school or $250 if in high school. In the 1960-1961 session the major source of financial support for the foundation was in the indirect form of these state and county tuition grants, paid to children attending foundation schools. At the same time, the county board of supervisors passed an ordinance allowing property tax credits up to 25 percent for contributions to any "nonprofit, nonsectarian private school" in the county.

In 1964 petitioners here filed a supplemental complaint, adding new parties and seeking to enjoin the respondents from refusing to operate an efficient system of public free schools in Prince Edward County and to enjoin payment of public funds to help support private schools which excluded students on account of race. The district court, finding that "the end result of every action taken by that body [board of supervisors] was designed to preserve separation of the races in the schools of Prince Edward County," enjoined the county from paying tuition grants or giving tax credits so long as public schools remained closed. *Allen v County School Bd of Prince Edward County* 198 F Supp 497, 503 (ED Va 1961). At this time the district court did not pass on whether the public schools of the county could be closed but abstained pending determination by the Virginia courts of whether the constitution and laws of Virginia required the public schools to be kept open. Later, however, without waiting for the Virginia courts to decide the question, the district court held that "the public schools of Prince Edward County may not be closed to avoid the effect of the law of the land as interpreted by the Supreme Court, while the Commonwealth of Virginia permits other public schools to remain open at the expense of the taxpayers." *Allen v County School Bd of Prince Edward County* 207 F Supp 349, 355 (ED Va 1962). Soon thereafter a declaratory judgment suit was brought by the county board of supervisors and the county school board in a Virginia circuit court. Having done this, these parties asked the federal district court to abstain from further proceedings until the suit in the state courts had run its course, but the district court declined; it repeated its order that Prince Edward's public schools might not be closed to avoid desegregation while the other public schools in Virginia remained open. The court of appeals reversed, Judge Bell dissenting, holding that the district court should have abstained to await state court determination of the validity of the tuition grants and the tax credits, as well as the validity of the closing of the public schools. *Griffin v Board of Supervisors of Prince Edward County* 322 F2d 332 (4th Cir 1963). For reasons to be stated, we agree with the district court that, under the circumstances here, closing the Prince Edward County schools while public schools in all the other counties of Virginia were being maintained denied the petitioners and the class of Negro students they represent the equal protection of the laws guaranteed by the Fourteenth Amendment.

Virginia law, as here applied, unquestionably treats the school children of Prince Edward differently from the way it treats the school children of all other Virginia counties. Prince Edward children must go to a private school or none at all; all other Virginia children can go to public schools. Closing Prince Edward's schools bears more heavily on Negro children in Prince Edward County since white children there have accredited private schools which they can attend, while colored children until very recently have had no available private schools, and even the school they now attend is a temporary expedient. Apart from this expedient, the result is that Prince Edward County school children, if they go to school in their own county, must go to racially segregated schools which, although designated as private, are beneficiaries of county and state support.

A state, of course, has a wide discretion in deciding whether laws shall operate statewide or shall operate only in certain counties, the legislature "having in mind the needs and desires of each." *Salsburg v Maryland, supra,* 346 US at 552. A state may wish to suggest, as Maryland did in *Salsburg,* that there are reasons why one county ought not to be treated like another. 346 US at 553-54. But the record in the present case could not be clearer that Prince Edward's public schools were closed and private schools operated in their place with state and county assistance, for one reason, and one reason only: to ensure, through measures taken by the county and the state, that white and colored children in Prince Edward County would not, under any circumstances, go to the same school. Whatever nonracial grounds might support a state's allowing a county to abandon public schools, the object must be a constitutional one, and grounds of race and opposition to desegregation do not qualify as constitutional. . . .

We come now to the question of the kind of decree necessary and appropriate to put an end to the racial discrimination practiced against these petitioners under authority of the Virginia laws. That relief needs to be quick and effective. The parties defendant are the board of supervisors, school board, treasurer, and division superintendent of schools of Prince Edward County, and the state board of education and the state superintendent of education. All of these have duties which relate directly or indirectly to the financing, supervision, or operation of the schools in Prince Edward County. The board of supervisors has the special responsibility to levy local taxes to operate public schools or to aid children attending the private schools now functioning there for white children. The district court enjoined the county officials from paying county tuition grants or giving tax exemptions and from processing applications for state tuition grants so long as the county's public schools remained closed. We have no doubt of the power of the court to give this relief to enforce the discontinuance of the county's racially discriminatory practices. For the same reasons the district court may, if necessary to prevent further racial discrimination, require the supervisors to exercise the power that is theirs to levy taxes to raise funds adequate to reopen, operate, and maintain without racial discrimination a public school system in Prince Edward County like that operated in other counties in Virginia.

The district court held that "the public schools of Prince Edward County may not be closed to avoid the effect of the law of the land as interpreted by the Supreme Court, while the Commonwealth of Virginia permits other public schools to remain open at the expense of the taxpayers." *Allen v County School Bd of Prince Edward County* 207 F Supp 349, 355 (ED Va 1962). At the same time the court gave notice that it would later consider an order to accomplish this purpose if the public schools were not reopened by September 7, 1962. That day has long passed, and the schools are still closed. On remand, therefore, the court may find it necessary to consider further such an order. An order of this kind is within the court's power if required to assure these petitioners that their constitutional rights will no longer be denied them. The time for mere "deliberate speed" has run out, and that phrase can no longer justify denying these Prince Edward County school children their constitutional rights to an education equal to that afforded by the public schools in the other parts of Virginia.

The judgment of the court of appeals is reversed, the judgment of the district court is affirmed, and the cause is remanded to the district court with directions to enter a decree which will guarantee that these petitioners will get the kind of education that is given in the state's public schools. And, if it becomes necessary to add new parties to accomplish this end, the district court is free to do so.

It is so ordered.

Mr. Justice Clark and Mr. Justice Harlan disagree with the holding that the federal courts are empowered to order the reopening of the public schools in Prince Edward County, but otherwise join in the court's opinion.

Notes and Questions

1. Injury

What legal injury did the court find that merited the relief granted? Was the injury suffered only by the black children in Prince Edward County, or does the opinion suggest that all children in that county were denied equal protection of the laws? See Kurland, "Equal in Origin and Equal in Title to the Legislative and Executive Branches of the Government," 78 *Harv L Rev* 143, 157 (1964).

2. Territorial Discrimination

Does *Griffin* suggest that a county may not close its public schools when public schools in other counties remain open? Would this be true if the case arose in a nonracial context? Is there any constitutional significance to whether the state ordered a county school system to close or whether it enacted local option legislation pursuant to which a county decided to close its schools? Might the court's characterization of the importance of the service make any difference? See *Palmer v Thompson* 403 US 217 (1971)(swimming pools).

Consider Professor Shoettle's observation:

> Substantially the same rationale that underlies the *Brown* decision was reiterated in *Griffin v County School Board,* in which the court struck down the decision of Prince Edward County, Virginia, to close its public schools rather than submit to court-ordered integration. Despite the court's apparent reliance upon the racially discriminatory purpose of the closings as a principal ground of decision, at least two members of the court [Marshall and Brennan dissenting in *Dandridge v Williams* 397 US 471, 508, 519 (1970)] have subsequently cited the case for the far more sweeping proposition that "the state may not, in the provision of important services or the distribution of governmental payments, supply benefits to some individuals while denying them to others who are similarly situated." (Shoettle, "The Equal Protection Clause in Public Education," 71 *Colum L Rev* 1355, 1364 (1971).)

See also F. Michelman and T. Sandalow, *Government in Urban Areas*, 238-42 (1971).

3. Racial Motivation

Griffin considers not only the unconstitutional effect of the school closing decision, but also the racial factors motivating that decision. This inquiry represents a departure from normal Supreme Court practice.

The established view is that inquiries into motive are not open to the Supreme Court. "There is a wise and ancient doctrine," said Mr. Justice Cardozo, "that a court will not inquire into the motives of a legislative body or assume them to be wrongful." "The process of psychoanalysis," he remarked, must not be carried into such "unaccustomed fields." This is the position that was taken from the first, if without reference to the newer arts. Marshall, ... stated it quite early in *Fletcher v Peck* [10 US 87]. (Bickel, *The Least Dangerous Branch,* 208 (1962).)

Is this departure from tradition justifiable? Consider these remarks by Professor Ely:

In *Griffin v County School Board of Prince Edward County,* decided in 1964, the Supreme Court, speaking the language of motivation, invalidated Virginia's closing of Prince Edward County's public schools, which had been ordered integrated ... [T]he reference to motivation was quite in order. A decision to close the schools in only that county where integration has been ordered can fairly be taken, in the absence of rebuttal evidence, to have been motivated by a desire to continue segregation. And that motivation should, in turn, trigger a demand for a rational and nonracial defense of the choice of that county—a defense which almost certainly would not be, and in the event was not, forthcoming. Indeed, should a state close *all* its schools under circumstances clearly revealing that it has done so in order to preserve segregation, the same theory would apply. (Ely, "Legislative and Administrative Motivation in Constitutional Law," 79 *Yale LJ* 1207, 1295 (1970).)

4. *Palmer v Thompson*

New interest in the subject of racial motivation has been sparked by a more recent constitutional decision, *Palmer v Thompson* 403 US 217 (1971). The case held that the closing of Jackson, Mississippi's public swimming pools, on the heels of an order to desegregate them, was not unconstitutional:

Mr. Justice Black's opinion for the court gave short shrift to the petitioners' argument that the closing of the pools was unconstitutionally motivated. He asserted that the court has never "held that a legislative act may violate equal protection solely because of the motivations of the men who voted for it," distinguishing *Griffin v Prince Edward County School Board* and *Gomillion v Lightfoot* [377 US 218 (1964)—an apportionment case] on the ground that "the focus in those cases was on the actual effect." (Brest, *"Palmer v Thompson:* An Approach to the Problem of Unconstitutional Legislative Motive," 1971 *Sup Ct Rev* 98.)

Professor Brest disputes Justice Black's attempt to distinguish *Palmer* from *Griffin*: "Mr. Justice Black's assertion that *Griffin v County School Board* ... turned solely on effect rather than on motivation is untenable." He cites the *Griffin* statement that "Whatever nonracial grounds might support a state's allowing a county to abandon public schools, the object must be a constitutional one, and grounds of race and opposition to desegregation do not qualify as unconstitutional." 1971 *Sup Ct Rev* at 99. Can Mr. Justice Black's position be defended? On what basis?

5. The Courts' Power to Order the Levying of Taxes

Did the Supreme Court have the power to order the levying of taxes, if necessary, in order to reopen Prince Edward County's schools? Justices Clark and Harlan seem to have thought not. Professor Kurland considers the question to be one of institutional embarrassment rather than of inherent lack of power:

> The case represents one of the many factual situations that compels the court to resort to unbecoming and unfortunate methods of assuring that its will is done. Certainly, if the discrimination were deemed to result from the fact that schools in Prince Edward County were closed while others in the state were open, the usual mandate that would follow from a finding of equal protection would offer the alternatives of closing all public schools or opening public schools in Prince Edward County. Such a decree could have assured that public schools did not become private schools in name only. Indeed, one of the great advantages that the equal protection clause has had over the due process clause is the possibility of more limited interference with the prerogatives of the states. The choice under the equal protection clause normally leaves to the state the decision whether to broaden the class or eliminate the regulation entirely. It is certainly unfortunate that the behavior of the state in the *Prince Edward County* case compelled the court to undertake to make the choice for it. (Kurland, "Equal in Origin and Equal in Title to the Legislative and Executive Branches of the Government," 78 *Harv L Rev* 143, 158 (1964).

Does the quotation help explain *Palmer v Thompson* 403 US 217 (1971)?

B. Measuring the Impact of *Brown*

In the light of this history of noncompliance, the ultimate question is whether *Brown* was wisely decided. Although empirical proof of the proposition is lacking and likely to remain so, the symbolic consequences of *Brown*, transcending the immediate difficulties in securing compliance, contributed significantly to the creation of a political and social environment in which racial justice became possible. See, e.g., W. Murphy & J. Tanenhaus, *The Study of Public Law*, 38 (1972); Frantz, "Is The First Amendment Law?—A Reply to Professor Mendelson," in *Judicial Review and the Supreme Court* 161 (L. Levy ed 1967). The costs of *Brown* in terms of social dislocation, controversy, delay, and judicial energy were great: one commentator has noted that *Brown* was "costly indeed, if it convinced libertarians that the judicial process is an effective tool of libertarianism." Mendelson, "On the Meaning of the First Amendment: Absolutes in the Balance," 50 *Calif L Rev* 821, 828 n39 (1962). None of the factors necessary for the enforcement of the court's mandate were present when the decision was announced, and the early gains were negligible. Yet there has been tremendous progress in achieving racial equality in the almost twenty years since *Brown*. See generally, *The Struggle for Racial Equality* (H. Commager ed 1967); L. Woodward, *The Strange Career of Jim Crow* (1966). This progress has manifested itself not only in the integration of the public schools, but also in voting, employment, and housing. There has been increasing public acquiescence in the *Brown* principle, and a mounting racial pride among blacks who formerly accepted the inferiority of their race. Woodward, *The Strange Career of Jim Crow* 67-109.

Too often judges and lawyers ignore a fundamental truth that is obvious to laymen and politicians: regardless of the formal rules of constitutional adjudication, a judicial declaration that a state law is constitutional is likely to enshrine it as the recommended solution of a difficult question of public policy. Certainly, *Plessy v Ferguson* serves as a constant reminder of this proposition. Although certainly not a golden age of race relations, the early post-Reconstruction years saw a clumsy search for accommodation between the "old heritage of slavery and the new and insecure heritage of legal equality." It was a time of experimentation and testing in which blacks found a place in society they had never before enjoyed. Yet as the twentieth century approached, the trend reversed, heralded by widespread adoption of Jim Crow legislation and the Supreme Court's refusal to uphold the civil rights of blacks. Woodward, *The Strange Career of Jim Crow* 67-109. The culmination was *Plessy v Ferguson*, in which the Supreme Court legitimated the abandonment of black rights, placing the judicial seal of approval on a racial ostracism that reached all phases of life. The court not only created a doctrinal justification for racist policies, but also symbolically affirmed that whites were indeed superior to blacks. This judicial coup de grace certainly accounts, at least in part, for the lack of progress toward racial justice in the decades after *Plessy*. A reaffirmation of *Plessy* in *Brown* might well have portended a similar blow to racial equality and the civil rights movement—not only in the courts, but also in the legislatures, the voting booths, the universities, and the job and housing markets.

On the other hand, the judicial declaration that discrimination by race in pupil assignment was unconstitutional ultimately may have helped to mold public opinion and prod the legislative and executive branches of government into action. Certainly governmental hopes for racial justice preceded the *Brown* decision. Under the separate but equal doctrine the Supreme Court had struck down a number of racially discriminatory practices in the late post-*Plessy* period, and in 1948 President Truman had courageously declared: "We shall not . . . finally achieve the ideals for which this nation was founded so long as any American suffers discrimination as a result of his race, or religion, or color, or the land of origin of his forefathers." Numerous private groups, including the NAACP, worked forcefully for the protection of Negro rights, and the political consciousness of blacks rose dramatically. The combination of private and public movement toward racial justice may well have enabled the Supreme Court to do in 1954 what it was apparently incapable of doing in 1896. But cause and effect merge; whatever the forces that brought *Brown* into being, those forces were strengthened by the decision itself. In the early years after *Brown*, reform proposals that would have allowed the attorney general to sue local school boards that engaged in segregationary practices were seriously considered. Proposals for federal aid to education that would have strengthened the dual school system were defeated. Secretary of Health, Education, and Welfare Abraham Ribicoff inserted nondiscrimination clauses in contracts with colleges participating in National Defense Education Act programs. Federal funds were denied to local school districts that forced children living on military bases to attend segregated schools.

Perhaps the most immediate result of *Brown* was to arouse black organizations and their white liberal allies: "*Brown* . . . awakened a new consciousness of group identity among blacks and a fresh awareness of the possibilities of removing the discrepancy between their supposed and actual rights." W. Murphy and J. Tanenhaus, *The Study of Public Law* 38 (1972). In turn this effect may have led to the confrontations between the civil rights groups and the southern political leadership. The impact of those dramas on American public opinion and on the federal leadership was profound, ultimately leading to the adoption of the 1964 Civil Rights Act, the greatest blow to southern resistance to desegregation. G. Orfield, *The Reconstruction of Southern Education* 2-3, 33-46 (1969).

To say that *Brown* caused this change in public opinion, in social behavior, and in the role of the federal government is simplistic. Many complex factors led to the civil rights revolution, but it would be foolish to deny the role of the Supreme Court:

> Can one doubt . . . the immensely constructive influence of the series of decisions in which the court is slowly asserting the right of Negroes to vote and to travel, live, and have a professional education without segregation? These decisions have not paralyzed or supplanted legislative and community action. They have precipitated it. . . . The cycle of decisions in these cases . . . have played a crucial role in leading public opinion and encouraging public action. . . . The Negro does not yet have equality in American society or anything approaching it. But his position is being improved, year by year. And the decisions and opinions of the Supreme Court are helping immeasurably in that process. (Rostow, "The Democratic Character of Judicial Review," in *Judicial Review and the Supreme Court* 74, 88-89 (L. Levy ed 1967).

C. The Civil Rights Act of 1964

While the ambiguity of the court's pronouncements and the reluctance of lower federal courts and school boards had much to do with the delay in implementing *Brown 2*, the failure of the Congress and the president to support the court also proved a significant contributing factor. See G. Orfield, *The Reconstruction of Southern Education* 15-22 (1969); J. Vander Zanden, *Race Relations in Transition* 88-94 (1966). Because of the awesome political ramifications of *Brown*, the dual school system could be dismantled only with the active assistance of the other branches of government. This support did not materialize in the early years after *Brown*. Apart from the isolated Little Rock incident, President Eisenhower never responded affirmatively to the desegregation mandate of the court. Perhaps President Eisenhower's attitude is best revealed by a statement he made in 1958 to Anthony Lewis of the *New York Times*, who asked what his personal attitude was toward school desegregation:

> Now, I am sworn to one thing, to defend the Constitution of the United States, and execute its laws. Therefore, for me to weaken public opinion by discussion of separate cases, where I might agree or might disagree, seems to me to be completely unwise and not a good thing to do.
> I have an oath; I expect to carry it out. And the mere fact that I could disagree very violently with a decision, and would so express myself, then

my own duty would be much more difficult to carry out I think. (*Public Papers of the Presidents: Dwight D. Eisenhower, 1958,* 625 (1959).)

Significant progress toward desegregation in the South came only with what has been characterized as the "administrative-judicial era" (H. Rodgers and C. Bullock, *Law and Social Change* 18 (1972)), which came into being with the passage of the Civil Rights Act of 1964. 42 USC §§2000c, d (1970). See generally, G. Orfield, *The Reconstruction of Southern Education* (1969). This legislation empowered the Department of Health, Education, and Welfare to withhold federal funds from school districts that continued to discriminate against blacks and gave the attorney general authority to file desegregation suits on the complaint of private citizens. 42 USC §§2000c-6, d-1 (1970). See generally Note, "The Courts, HEW, and Southern School Desegregation," 77 *Yale LJ* 321, 356-64 (1967). Under the Civil Rights Act of 1964, HEW promulgated guidelines requiring school districts to make a good faith start toward desegregation. US Office of Education, HEW, "General Statement of Policies under Title VI of the Civil Rights Act of 1964 Respecting Desegregation of Elementary and Secondary Schools (1965)," reprinted in *Price v Denison Independent School Dist Bd of Educ* 348 F2d 1010, 1015 (1965). See also US Office of Education, HEW, "Revised Statement of Policies for School Desegregation Plans under Title VI of the Civil Rights Act of 1964," 45 CFR §181 (1967). The complex relationships between the HEW guidelines and developing constitutional standards, and between the judiciary and the other branches of government who participated in desegregation efforts will be explored in this section.

TITLE IV
42 USC §2000c (1970)

§2000c. Definitions
As used in this subchapter—
    (a) "Commissioner" means the Commissioner of Education.
    (b) "Desegregation" means the assignment of students to public schools and within such schools without regard to their race, color, religion, or national origin, but "desegregation" shall not mean the assignment of students to public schools in order to overcome racial imbalance.
    (c) "Public school" means any elementary or secondary educational institution, and "public college" means any institution of higher education or any technical or vocational school above the secondary school level, provided that such public school or public college is operated by a state, subdivision of a state, or governmental agency within a state, or operated wholly or predominantly from or through the use of governmental funds or property, or funds or property derived from a governmental source.
    (d) "School board" means any agency or agencies which administer a system of one or more public schools and any other agency which is responsible for the assignment of students to or within such system.
Pub L 88-352, Title IV, §401, July 2, 1964, 78 Stat 246.
§2000c-2. Technical assistance in preparation, adoption, and implementation of
        plans for desegregation of public schools
    The commissioner is authorized, upon the application of any school board, state, municipality, school district, or other governmental unit legally responsible for operating a public school or schools, to render technical assistance to such

applicant in the preparation, adoption, and implementation of plans for the desegregation of public schools. Such technical assistance may, among other activities, include making available to such agencies information regarding effective methods of coping with special educational problems occasioned by desegregation, and making available to such agencies personnel of the Office of Education or other persons specially equipped to advise and assist them in coping with such problems.

Pub L 88-352, Title IV, §403, July 2, 1964, 78 Stat 247.

§2000c-4. Grants for inservice training in dealing with and for employment of specialists to advise in problems incident to desegregation. . . .

(a) The commissioner is authorized, upon application of a school board, to make grants to such board to pay, in whole or in part, the cost of—

(1) giving to teachers and other school personnel inservice training in dealing with problems incident to desegregation, and

(2) employing specialists to advise in problems incident to desegregation.

(b) In determining whether to make a grant, and in fixing the amount thereof and the terms and conditions on which it will be made, the commissioner shall take into consideration the amount available for grants under this section and the other applications which are pending before him; the financial condition of the applicant and the other resources available to it; the nature, extent, and gravity of its problems incident to desegregation; and such other factors as he finds relevant.

Pub L 88-352, Title IV, §405, July 2, 1964, 78 Stat 247.

§2000c-6. Civil actions by the attorney general . . . .

(a) Whenever the attorney general receives a complaint in writing—

(1) signed by a parent or group of parents to the effect that his or their minor children, as members of a class of persons similarly situated, are being deprived by a school board of the equal protection of the laws, or

(2) signed by an individual, or his parent, to the effect that he has been denied admission to or not permitted to continue in attendance at a public college by reason of race, color, religion, or national origin,

and the attorney general believes the complaint is meritorious and certifies that the signer or signers of such complaint are unable in his judgment, to initiate and maintain appropriate legal proceedings for relief and that the institution of an action will materially further the orderly achievement of desegregation in public education, the attorney general is authorized, after giving notice of such complaint to the appropriate school board or college authority and after certifying that he is satisfied that such board or authority has had a reasonable time to adjust the conditions alleged in such complaint, to institute for or in the name of the United States a civil action in any appropriate district court of the United States against such parties and for such relief as may be appropriate, and such court shall have and shall exercise jurisdiction of proceedings instituted pursuant to this section, provided that nothing herein shall empower any official or court of the United States to issue any order seeking to achieve a racial balance in any school by requiring the transportation of pupils or students from one school to another or one school district to another in order to achieve such racial balance, or otherwise enlarge the existing power of the court to insure compliance with constitutional standards. The attorney general may implead as defendants such additional parties as are or become necessary to the grant of effective relief hereunder. . . .

(b) The attorney general may deem a person or persons unable to initiate and maintain appropriate legal proceedings within the meaning of subsection (a) of this section when such person or persons are unable, either directly or through other interested persons or organizations, to bear the expense of the litigation or to obtain effective legal representation; or whenever he is satisfied that the institution of such litigation would jeopardize the personal safety, employment, or economic standing of such person or persons, their families, or their property. . . .

§2000c-8. Personal suits for relief against discrimination in public education

Nothing in this subchapter shall affect adversely the right of any person to sue for or obtain relief in any court against discrimination in public education.

Pub L 88-352, Title IV, §409, July 2, 1964, 78 Stat 249.

§2000c-9. Classification and assignment

Nothing in this subchapter shall prohibit classification and assignment for reasons other than race, color, religion, or national origin.

Pub L 88-352, Title IV, §410, July 2, 1964, 78 Stat 249.

TITLE VI
42 USC §2000d (1970)

§2000d. Prohibition against exclusion from participation in, denial of benefits of, and discrimination under federally assisted programs on ground of race, color, or national origin

No person in the United States shall, on the ground of race, color, or national origin, be excluded from participation in, be denied the benefits of, or be subjected to discrimination under any program or activity receiving federal financial assistance.

Pub L 88-352, Title VI, §601, July 2, 1964, 78 Stat 252.

§2000d-1. Federal authority and financial assistance to programs or activities by way of grant, loan, or contract other than contract of insurance or guaranty. . . . rules and regulations; approval by president; compliance with requirements; reports to congressional committees; effective date of administrative action

Each federal department and agency which is empowered to extend federal financial assistance to any program or activity, by way of grant, loan, or contract other than a contract of insurance or guaranty, is authorized and directed to effectuate the provisions of section 2000d of this title with respect to such program or activity by issuing rules, regulations, or orders of general applicability which shall be consistent with achievement of the objectives of the statute authorizing the financial assistance in connection with which the action is taken. No such rule, regulation, or order shall become effective unless and until approved by the president. Compliance with any requirement adopted pursuant to this section may be effected (1) by the termination of or refusal to grant or to continue assistance under such program or activity to any recipient as to whom there has been an express finding on the record, after opportunity for hearing, of a failure to comply with such requirement, but such termination or refusal shall be limited to the particular political entity, or part thereof, or other recipient as to whom such a finding has been made and, shall be limited in its effect to the particular program, or part thereof, in which such noncompliance has been so found, or (2) by any other means authorized by law: *Provided, however,* that no such action shall be taken until the department or agency concerned has advised the appropriate person or persons of the failure to comply with the requirement and has determined that compliance cannot be secured by voluntary means. In the case of any action terminating, or refusing to grant or continue, assistance because of failure to comply with a requirement imposed pursuant to this section, the head of the federal department or agency shall file with the committees of the House and Senate having legislative jurisdiction over the program or activity involved a full written report of the circumstances and the grounds for such action. No such action shall become effective until thirty days have elapsed after the filing of such report.

Pub L 88-352, Title VI, §602, July 2, 1964, 78 Stat 252.

§2000d-3. Construction of provisions not to authorize administrative action with respect to employment practices except where primary objective of Federal financial assistance is to provide employment

Nothing contained in this subchapter shall be construed to authorize action under this subchapter by any department or agency with respect to any employment practice of any employer, employment agency, or labor organization except where a primary objective of the federal financial assistance is to provide employment.

Pub L 88-352, Title VI, §604, July 2, 1964, 78 Stat 253.

§2000d-5. Prohibited deferral of action on applications by local educational agencies seeking federal funds for alleged noncompliance with Civil Rights Act

The commissioner of education shall not defer action or order action deferred on any application by a local educational agency for funds authorized to be appropriated by this act, by the Elementary and Secondary Education Act of 1965, by the Act of September 30, 1950 (Public Law 874, Eighty-first Congress), by the Act of September 23, 1950 (Public Law 815, Eighty-first Congress), or by the Cooperative Research Act, on the basis of alleged noncompliance with the provisions of this subchapter for more than sixty days after notice is given to such local agency of such deferral unless such local agency is given the opportunity for a hearing as provided in section 2000d-1 of this title, such hearing to be held within sixty days of such notice, unless the time for such hearing is extended by mutual consent of such local agency and the commissioner, and such deferral shall not continue for more than thirty days after the close of any such hearing unless there has been an express finding on the record of such hearing that such local educational agency has failed to comply with the provisions of this subchapter: *Provided,* that, for the purpose of determining whether a local educational agency is in compliance with this subchapter, compliance by such agency with a final order or judgment of a federal court for the desegregation of the school or school system operated by such agency shall be deemed to be compliance with this subchapter, insofar as the matters covered in the order or judgment are concerned.

§2000d-6. Policy of United States as to application of nondiscrimination provisions in schools of local educational agencies—Declaration of uniform policy [1972 Supp]

(a) It is the policy of the United States that guidelines and criteria established pursuant to title VI of the Civil Rights Act of 1964 and section 182 of the Elementary and Secondary Education Amendments of 1966 dealing with conditions of segregation by race, whether de jure or de facto, in the schools of the local educational agencies of any state shall be applied uniformly in all regions of the United States whatever the origin or cause of such segregation.

(b) Such uniformity refers to one policy applied uniformly to de jure segregation wherever found and such other policy as may be provided pursuant to law applied uniformly to de facto segregation wherever found.

(c) Nothing in this section shall be construed to diminish the obligation of responsible officials to enforce or comply with such guidelines and criteria in order to eliminate discrimination in federally assisted programs and activities as required by title VI of the Civil Rights Act of 1964.

(d) It is the sense of the Congress that the Department of Justice and the Department of Health, Education, and Welfare should request such additional funds as may be necessary to apply the policy set forth in this section throughout the United States.

EXECUTIVE ORDER NO. 11247
Sept 24, 1965, 30 FR 12327
Coordination of Enforcement

WHEREAS the departments and agencies of the federal government have adopted uniform and consistent regulations implementing Title VI of the Civil Rights Act of 1964 [sections 2000d to 2000d−4 of this title] and, in cooperation with the President's Council on Equal Opportunity, have embarked on a coordinated program of enforcement of the provisions of that title;

WHEREAS the issues hereafter arising in connection with coordination of the activities of the departments and agencies under that title will be predominantly legal in character and in many cases will be related to judicial enforcement; and

WHEREAS the attorney general is the chief law officer of the federal government and is charged with the duty of enforcing the laws of the United States:

NOW, THEREFORE, by virtue of the authority vested in me as president of the United States by the Constitution and laws of the United States, it is ordered as follows:

Section 1. The attorney general shall assist federal departments and agencies to coordinate their programs and activities and adopt consistent and uniform policies, practices, and procedures with respect to the enforcement of Title VI of the Civil Rights Act of 1964. He may promulgate such rules and regulations as he shall deem necessary to carry out his functions under this order.

Sec. 2. Each federal department and agency shall cooperate with the attorney general in the performance of his functions under this order and shall furnish him such reports and information as he may request. . . .

Lyndon B. Johnson

Notes and Questions

1. Sections 2000c-2, 2000c-4

What is the purpose of §§2000c-2 and 2000c-4, which offer technical assistance and grants in aid to desegregating school districts? To ease the course of desegregation? To bribe local school districts into accepting desegregation? Is there a danger that the technical assistance may take on a coercive character as federal officials involve themselves in local affairs?

How should desegregation funds be used? Can you think of any uses that are or should be impermissible?

The Emergency School Assistance Act (1971) provided additional funds to desegregating districts. This act was widely opposed by civil rights groups, who were concerned that the new monies would not be spent for the benefit of black children.

2. Section 2000c-6

a. Purpose and Significance. What is the purpose of §2000c-6, which authorizes civil rights actions by the attorney general? To reduce the financial burdens imposed on individuals and civil rights groups? To place the power and prestige of the federal government behind the desegregation movement? Is the attorney general likely to be more successful than private litigants in particular litigations? For what reasons? Greater resources? Greater judicial sympathy?

b. Relationship to Private Litigations. What role does §2000c-6 envision for private litigants? See also §2000c-8. Would it permit both private parties and the attorney general to participate in the same litigation, even if the attorney general and the private parties disagree on the theory of the suit or the appropriateness of a particular remedy? What difficulties might this pose for courts? Should the attorney general be permitted to intervene in private suits? See 42 USC §2000h-2 (1970).

c. Complaint Procedures. What is the difference between paragraphs (a)(1) and (a)(2) of §2000c-6 with respect to complaint procedures? Does (a)(1) apply to all denials of equal protection, whether or not segregation is involved? If so, how does the complaint procedure embodied in this section differ from that in (a)(2), which explicitly applies to denials of admissions based on race? Under both sections, the attorney general must determine whether a complaint is "meritorious" before he acts. How should he determine this? What standards should he employ? Should complainants have a right to a hearing before a complaint is rejected? To an appeal process through the department of justice? What about the determination of whether an individual is "unable to initiate and maintain appropriate legal proceedings?" Is it appropriate, as section 2000c-6(b) indicates, to look to the willingness of organizations to defray litigation expenses for a complainant? Does this section shed any light on the purposes of the Civil Rights Act (see note 2a)?

d. Enforcement of Brown. What impact might §2000c-6 have on the course of desegregation in the South? If the issue is one of securing compliance with court decrees, overcoming the recalcitrance of federal district courts, and resolving the ambiguity of Supreme Court decisions, how would the addition of the United States as a party resolve any of these difficulties? Does the importance of the attorney general's activities lie in the symbolic affirmation by the national government of the rightness of desegregation? Does the combined prestige of all three branches of the federal government make compliance in the future more likely?

3. Section 2000d

Does section 2000d restate the principle embodied in *Brown 1* and *2*? What is the difference between discrimination and the denial of benefits? Might a person be denied benefits who was not discriminated against on the basis of race?

Why did Congress limit governmental review under this section to programs receiving federal assistance? Is the scope of section 2000d's coverage dictated by a prior judgment as to the appropriate remedy?

4. Section 2000d-1

a. Sections 2000d-1 and 2000c-2, 2000c-4 Compared. How does §2000d-1 complement §§2000c-2 and 2000c-4. Is it intended to provide the punishment (fund cutoffs), in a reward (federal aid) or punishment approach to school desegregation? In 1965, Congress passed the Elementary and Secondary Education Act, which enormously expanded federal assistance to local school districts. 20 USC §241 a-m (1970). What impact would that act have on the application of §2000d-1?

b. Administration of §2000d-1. The process of identifying a violation of §2000d is left to existing federal agencies, but their regulations must be approved by the president. Why might Congress have adopted this approach? In the interest of uniformity between federal agencies? See Executive Order No. 11247, above. To prevent embarrassment of the president by reluctant or overly aggressive federal agencies? To ensure that the president would be associated with school desegregation, thereby spreading the political risks among Congress, the president, and the courts?

c. Fund Cutoffs. Why did Congress limit the fund cutoff for noncompliance with §2000d "to the particular program, or part thereof, in which such noncompliance has been so found. . . ."? See *Board of Pub Instruction of Taylor County, Fla v Finch* 414 F2d 1068 (5th Cir 1969).

If the purpose of this section was to promote desegregation of the schools and the elimination of discrimination in other areas, would not the threat of a cutoff of all federal funding be more likely to bring positive results?

While funding cutoffs have been rare, the threat of such cutoffs has been thought to be the strongest weapon against local officials in the fight to desegregate public schools. See generally, G. Orfield, *The Reconstruction of Southern Education*, 252-58 (1969). Compare Badger and Browning, "Title I and Comparability: Recent Developments," 7 *Clearinghouse Rev* 263 (1973); *Natonabah v Board of Educ* 355 F Supp 716 (DNM 1973). Would this be true in all districts? Suppose a district were composed largely of black students, most of whom qualified for assistance to disadvantaged children under Title I of the Elementary and Secondary Education Act. 20 USC §241a-m (1970). Who would be the greater loser as a result of a fund cutoff? Does this particular weapon run the risk of dividing private litigants and the federal government, with the former opposing a fund cutoff and the latter advocating it?

d. Alternative to Fund Cutoffs

In addition to allowing the administering agency to achieve compliance by terminating or refusing aid to recipients who refuse to comply with desegregation requirements, Title VI also empowers the agency to proceed "by any other means authorized by law." This represents an effort to provide an alternative to the severe step of denying all federal aid. One such alternative, which would entail reliance on the courts, is suggested by the standard paragraph in the form all recipients must sign which states that the appropriate assurance of compliance "is given in consideration of and for the purpose of obtaining any and all federal grants, loans, contract, property, discounts or other federal financial assistance. . . . The applicant recognizes and agrees that such federal financial assistance will be extended in reliance on the representations and agreements made in the assurance and that the United States or the state agency . . . jointly or severally shall have the right to seek enforcement of this assurance."

HEW included this wording with the specific intent of making assurances enforceable in a court action asking for specific performance. The agency has not extensively explored the possibility of such an alternative yet, however. High HEW officials have only expressed an intent to use such legal alternatives in the future "as the program proceeds." . . . (Note, "The Courts, HEW and Southern School Desegregation," 77 *Yale L Rev* 321 (1967).)

Does this approach seem preferable to cutoffs? Why might HEW not have employed it?

5. Enforcement of the Civil Rights Act: 1964-66

The primary responsibility for enforcing Title VI of the Civil Rights Act was given to the Office of Education within the Department of Health, Education, and Welfare. Historically the United States Office of Education had been a powerless agency, without any policy-making functions, whose sole responsibility was to collect educational statistics and publish reports. The impotency of the Office of Education derived from traditional American adherence to localism in educational matters, the office's small staff, and its total dependence on local and state education officials. G. Orfield, *The Reconstruction of Southern Education*, 9 (1969). Needless to say, the Office of Education, even under the able leadership of Francis Keppel, was not prepared for the monumental task that confronted it after the enactment of the Civil Rights Act of 1964. Vast institutional and staffing changes were required, chaos in the early months of the "administrative judicial era" was not uncommon, but despite these problems, substantial progress was made in desegregating Southern schools. Professor Orfield summarizes the experience of this era:

THE RECONSTRUCTION OF SOUTHERN EDUCATION
G. Orfield
147-50 (1969)

Confronting the task of enforcing a revolutionary change in southern schools, the commissioner of education recognized very early that a staff independent of the grant programs was essential. The establishment of the Equal Educational Opportunities Program was a recognition of the fact that the most important constituency of the program officials was composed of state and local schoolmen, and that the same men could not run effective programs that depended on local cooperation and simultaneously enforce a revolution in the local social order. Given the determination to enforce the law, it became necessary to establish a new staff and to expand it as it began to define its job.

A handful of men can administer a social revolution without great difficulty if the revolution is just waiting to happen, as was the case with the public accommodations section of the Civil Rights Act. At first, Title VI officials assumed that local school districts would readily propose adequate means of complying with the new law. As it became evident that school desegregation would be bitterly resisted, it became essential for [the] tiny staff to organize itself and to construct a system of threats sufficiently credible to persuade local officials to undertake hated changes. The program was forced to define its goals in terms that could be understood by thousands of worried local officials and administered in a mass-production bureaucratic process. This necessity gave rise to the school desegregation guidelines. . . .

The summer transformed the abstract principles of the guidelines into thousands of plans molded by contacts with local school officials. The summer also saw an attempt by civil rights groups to make desegregation plans work in the Deep South, an attempt that generated a division within the staff on the issue of the program's proper constituency and the nature of its constituency relationships. The activists on the staff, those who viewed the program as an extension of the civil rights movement, saw the Negro community and the civil rights leaders as natural allies and the natural constituency of the program. [Commissioner] Keppel, however, recognized that such a stance would be politically impossible within the Office of Education. The only real alternative to allowing local school officials to receive primary consideration in formation of Title VI policy was to turn to the courts and to impartially enforce standards derived from federal court decisions. This decision, however, left the program with no external supporting constituency, thus attempting to play a neutral role by balancing between school officials and civil rights groups.

The frantic effort of summer 1965 was a major achievement. Almost all southern districts promised to implement plans that would have been seen as completely intolerable a year earlier. A major psychological breakthrough had been achieved. Under a good deal of political pressure, the administration held firm, and integration in the South had increased by more than 100 percent.

In important ways, however, the initial effort was a failure. Many of the apparently impressive plans proved to be nothing but "paper compliance." Local officials commonly abused the spirit of the freedom-of-choice plan. By the end of 1965 it was obvious that the original guidelines would never be able to eliminate the dual school system.

With the broad issue of the program's constituency settled, the policy debates on the revision of the guidelines [began].

The new guidelines were to provide a charter for a second summer of change across the South. When the second September under the guidelines arrived, classrooms in the states of the old Confederacy revealed that the new authority written into the revised guidelines had been sufficient to continue at an accelerated pace the revolution set in motion in 1965. The barrier of total faculty integration fell in the great majority of districts, and student integration increased from 6 percent to 16 percent in the 11 states where less than one Negro child in 100 had attended an integrated school when the Civil Rights Act was passed. A long step had been taken toward the destruction of the separate school systems of the South, but a longer, steeper road remained.

Freedom-of-choice plans and the HEW guidelines are discussed below.

UNITED STATES v JEFFERSON COUNTY BOARD OF EDUCATION
372 F2d 836 (5th Cir 1966),
aff'd, 380 F2d 385 (5th Cir 1967) (en banc)

Wisdom, Circuit Judge:

I

"No army is stronger than an idea whose time has come." Ten years after *Brown,* came the Civil Rights Act of 1964. Congress decided that the time had come for a sweeping civil rights advance, including national legislation to speed up desegregation of public schools and to put teeth into enforcement of desegregation. Titles IV and VI together constitute the congressional alternative to court-supervised desegregation. These sections of the law mobilize in aid of desegregation the United States Office of Education and the nation's purse.

A. Title IV authorizes the Office of Education to give technical and financial assistance to local school systems in the process of desegregation.[18] Title VI requires all federal agencies administering any grant-in-aid program to see to it that there is no racial discrimination by any school or other recipient of federal financial aid.[19] School boards cannot, however, by giving up federal aid, avoid the policy that produced this limitation on federal aid to schools: Title IV authorizes the attorney general to sue, in the name of the United States, to desegregate a public school or school system.[20] More clearly and effectively than either of the other two coordinate branches of government, Congress speaks as the voice of the nation. *The national policy is plain: formerly de jure segregated public school systems based on dual attendance zones must shift to unitary, nonracial systems—with or without federal funds. . . .*

In April 1965 Congress for the first time in its history adopted a law providing general federal aid—a billion dollars a year—for elementary and secondary schools.[24] It is a fair assumption that Congress would not have taken this step had Title VI not established the principle that schools receiving federal assistance must meet uniform national standards for desegregation.[25]

To make Title VI effective, the Department of Health, Education, and Welfare (HEW) adopted the regulation, "Nondiscrimination in federally assisted pro-

18. 78 Stat 246-99, 42 USC §2000c (1964).

19. 78 Stat 252-53, 42 USC §2000d (1964). . . .

20. 78 Stat 246-49, 42 USC §2000c (1964). In addition, Title IX authorizes the attorney general to intervene in private suits where persons have alleged denial of equal protection of the laws under the Fourteenth Amendment where he certifies that the case is of "general public importance." 78 Stat 266, Title IX §902, 42 USC §2000h-2 (1964).

24. The Elementary and Secondary Education Act of 1965, 79 Stat 27.

25. "The Elementary and Secondary Education Act of 1965 greatly increased the amount of federal money available for public schools, and did so in accordance with a formula that pumps the lion's share of the money to low-income areas such as the Deep South. Consequently, Title VI of the Civil Rights Act of 1964 has become the main instrument for accelerating and completing the desegregation of Southern public schools." A. Bickel, in *The New Republic,* 9 April 1966.

grams."[26] This regulation directs the commissioner of education to approve applications for financial assistance to public schools only if the school or school system agrees to comply with a court order, if any, outstanding against it, or submits a desegregation plan satisfactory to the commissioner.[27]

To make the regulation effective, by assisting the Office of Education in determining whether a school qualifies for federal financial aid and by informing school boards of HEW requirements, HEW formulated certain standards or guidelines. In April 1965, nearly a year after the act was signed, HEW published its first *Guidelines*, "General Statement of Policies under Title VI of the Civil Rights Act of 1964 Respecting Desegregation of Elementary and Secondary Schools."[28] These *Guidelines* fixed the fall of 1967 as the target date for total desegregation of all grades. In March 1966 HEW issued *"Revised Guidelines"* to correct most of the major flaws revealed in the first year of operation under Title VI.[29]

B. The HEW guidelines raise the question: To what extent should a court, in determining whether to approve a school desegregation plan, give weight to the HEW guidelines? We adhere to the answer this court gave in four earlier cases. The HEW guidelines are "minimum standards", representing for the most part standards the Supreme Court and this court established *before the guidelines were promulgated.* Again we hold, "we attach great weight" to the *guidelines....*

II

We read Title VI as a congressional mandate for change—change in pace and method of enforcing desegregation. The 1964 act does not disavow court-supervised desegregation. On the contrary, Congress recognized that to the courts belongs the last word in any case or controversy.[31] But Congress was dissatisfied with the slow progress inherent in the judicial adversary process. Congress therefore fashioned a new method of enforcement to be administered not on a case-by-case basis as in the courts but generally, by federal agencies operating on a national scale and having a special competence in their respective fields. Congress looked to these agencies to shoulder the additional enforcement burdens resulting from the shift to high gear in school desegregation.

A. Congress was well aware that it was. time for a change. In the decade following *Brown,* court-supervised desegregation made qualitative progress: Responsible Southern leaders accepted desegregation as a settled constitutional

---

26. 45 CFR Part 80, 4 December 1964, 64 FR 12539.

27. "Every application for federal financial assistance to carry out a program to which this part applies ... shall, as a condition to its approval ..., contain or be accompanied by an assurance that the program will be conducted or the facility operated in compliance with all requirements imposed by or pursuant to this part. ... 45 CFR §80-4(a) (1964).

28. US Department of Health, Education and Welfare, Office of Education, General Statement of Policies under Title VI of the Civil Rights Act of 1964 Respecting Desegregation of Elementary and Secondary Schools, April, 1965. It is quoted in full in *Price v Denison Independent School Dist* 348 F2d at 1010 (5th Cir 1965).

29. Revised Statement of Policies for School Desegregation Plans Under Title VI of the Civil Rights Act of 1964 (March 1966).

31. Title IV, §407, 42 USC §2000c-6 authorizing the attorney general to bring suit, on receipt of a written complaint, would seem to imply this conclusion. Section 409 preserves the right of individual citizens "to sue for or obtain relief" against discrimination in public education. HEW regulations provide: "In any case in which a final order of a court of the United States for the desegregation of such school or school system is entered after submission of such a plan, such a plan shall be revised to conform to such final order, including any future modification of such order." 45 CFR §80.4(c) (1964).

principle. Quantitively, the results were meagre. The statistics speak eloquent-
ly. . . . In 1965 the public school districts in the consolidated cases now before
this court had a school population of 155,782 school children, 59,361 of whom
were Negro. Yet under the existing court-approved desegregation plans, only 110
Negro children in these districts, 0.19 percent of the school population, attend
formerly "white" schools. In 1965 there was no faculty desegregation in any of
these school districts; indeed, none of the 30,500 Negro teachers in Alabama,
Louisiana, and Mississippi served with any of the 65,400 white teachers in those
states. In the 1963-64 school year, the eleven states of the Confederacy had 1.17
percent of their Negro students in schools with white students. In 1964-65,
undoubtedly because of the effect of the 1964 act, the percentage doubled,
reaching 2.25. For the 1965-66 school year, this time because of HEW guidelines,
the percentage reached 6.01 percent. In 1965-66 the entire region encompassing
the Southern *and border states* had 10.9 percent of their Negro children in
school with white children; 1,555 biracial school districts out of 3,031 in the
Southern and border states were still fully segregated; 3,101,043 Negro children
in the region attended all-Negro schools. Despite the impetus of the 1964 act,
the states of Alabama, Louisiana, and Mississippi, still had less than 1 percent of
their Negro enrollment, attending schools with white students.

The dead hand of the old past and the closed fist of the recent past account
for some of the slow progress. There are other reasons—as obvious to Congress as
to courts. (1) Local loyalties compelled school officials and elected officials to
make a public record of their unwillingness to act. But even school authorities
willing to act have moved slowly because of uncertainty as to the scope of their
duty to act affirmatively. This is attributable to (a) a misplaced reliance on the
Briggs [*v Elliott* 132 F Supp 776, 777 (EDSC 1955)] dictum that the Constitution "does not require integration," (b) a misunderstanding of the *Brown 2*
mandate, desegregate with "all deliberate speed", and (c) a mistaken notion that
transfers under the pupil placement laws satisfy desegregation requirements. (2)
Case-by-case development of the law is a poor sort of medium for reasonably
prompt and uniform desegregation. There are natural limits to effective legal
action. Courts cannot give advisory opinions, and the disciplined exercise of the
judicial function properly makes courts reluctant to move forward in an area of
the law bordering the periphery of the judicial domain. (3) The contempt power
is ill-suited to serve as the chief means of enforcing desegregation. Judges naturally shrink from using it against citizens willing to accept the thankless, painful
responsibility of serving on a school board. (4) School desegregation plans are
often woefully inadequate; they rarely provide necessary detailed instructions and
specific answers to administrative problems. And most judges do not have sufficient competence—they are not educators or school administrators—to know the
right questions, much less the right answers. (5) But one reason more than any
other has held back desegregation of public schools on a large scale. This has
been the lack, until 1964, of effective congressional statutory recognition of
school desegregation as the law of the land.

"Considerable progress has been made. . . . Nevertheless, in the last decade it
has become increasingly clear that progress has been too slow and that national
legislation is required to meet a national need which becomes ever more ob-

vious."[44] Title VI of the Civil Rights Act of 1964, therefore, was not only appropriate and proper legislation under the Thirteenth and Fourteenth Amendments; it was necessary to rescue school desegregation from the bog in which it had been trapped for ten years. . . .

C. We must therefore cooperate with Congress and the executive in enforcing Title VI. The problem is: Are the HEW guidelines within the scope of the congressional and executive policies embodied in the Civil Rights Act of 1964. We hold that they are.

The guidelines do not purport to be a rule or regulation or order. They constitute a statement of policy under section 80.4(c) of the HEW regulations issued after the president approved the regulations December 3, 1964. HEW is under no statutory compulsion to issue such statements. It is, however, of manifest advantage to school boards throughout the country and to the general public to know the criteria the commissioner uses in determining whether a school meets the requirements for eligibility to receive financial assistance. . . .

D. Because our approval of a plan establishes eligibility for federal aid, our standards should not be lower than those of HEW. Unless judicial standards are substantially in accord with the guidelines, school boards previously resistent to desegregation will resort to the courts to avoid complying with the minimum standards HEW promulgates for schools that desegregate voluntarily. . . .

The announcement in HEW regulations that the commissioner would accept a final school desegregation order as proof of the school's eligibility for federal aid prompted a number of schools to seek refuge in the federal courts. Many of these had not moved an inch toward desegregation. In Louisiana alone twenty school boards obtained quick decrees providing for desegregation according to plans greatly at variance with the guidelines.

We shall not permit the courts to be used to destroy or dilute the effectiveness of the congressional policy expressed in Title VI. There is no bonus for foot dragging.

E. The experience this court has had in the last ten years argues strongly for uniform standards in court-supervised desegregation.

The first school case to reach this Court after *Brown v Board of Education* was *Brown v Rippy* 233 F2d 796 (5th Cir 1956). Since then we have reviewed forty-one other school cases, many more than once. The district courts in this circuit have considered 128 school cases in the same period. Reviewing these cases imposes a taxing, time-consuming burden on the courts not reflected in statistics. An analysis of the cases shows a wide lack of uniformity in areas where there is no good reason for variations in the schedule and manner of desegregation. In some cases there has been a substantial time lag between this court's opinions and their application by the district courts. In certain cases—cases we consider unnecessary to cite—there has even been a manifest variance between this court's decision and a later district court decision. . . .

III

The defendants contend that the guidelines require integration, not just desegregation; that school boards have no affirmative duty to integrate. They say

44. HR Rep No 914, 88th Cong, 1st Sess.

that in this respect the guidelines are contrary to the provisions of the Civil Rights Act of 1964 and to constitutional intent expressed in the act. . . . [Discussion of the "affirmative duty to integrate" will be undertaken in conjunction with *Green v County School Board, infra.* This portion of the opinion of Judge Wisdom is omitted.]

IV

We turn now to the specific provisions of the Civil Rights Act on which the defendants rely to show that HEW violates the congressional intent. These provisions are the amendments to Title IV and VI added in the Senate. The legislative history of these amendments is sparse and less authoritative than usual because of the lack of committee reports on the amended version of the bill.

A. Section 401(b) defines desegregation: " 'Desegregation' means the assignment of students to public schools and within such schools without regard to their race, color, religion, or national origin, but 'desegregation' shall not mean the assignment of students to public schools in order to overcome racial imbalance."

The affirmative portion of this definition, down to the "but" clause, describes the assignment provision necessary in a plan for conversion of a de jure dual system to a unitary, integrated system. The negative portion, starting with "but", excludes assignment to overcome racial imbalance, that is acts to overcome de facto segregation. As used in the act, therefore, "desegregation" refers only to the disestablishment of segregation in de jure segregated schools. Even if a broader meaning should be given to "assignment . . . to overcome racial imbalance", section 401 would not mean that such assignments are unlawful:

> The intent of the statute is that no funds and no technical assistance will be given by the United States commissioner of education with respect to plans for the assignment of students to public schools in order to overcome racial imbalance. The statute may not be interpreted to mean that such assignment is illegal or that reasonable integration efforts are arbitrary or unlawful.

The prohibition against assignment of students to overcome racial imbalance was added as an amendment during the debates in the House to achieve the same result as the antibusing provision in section 407. Some of the difficulty in understanding the act and its legislative history arises from the statutory use of the undefined term "racial imbalance." It is clear however from the hearings and debates that Congress equated the term, as do the commentators, with "de facto segregation" that is, nonracially motivated segregation in a school system based on a single neighborhood school for all children in a definable area.[92] . . .

The neighborhood school system is rooted deeply in American culture. Whether its continued use is constitutional when it leads to grossly imbalanced schools

---

92. For example, "Racial imbalance" and "de facto segregation" are "used synonymously [to] refer to a situation where a school is predominantly composed of Negro students not as a result of state action but rather as the end product of segregated housing and adherence to the neighborhood school plan." *Gillmor and Gosule* 46 *BU L Rev* 45, 46 (1966). The term "de facto segregation" has become accepted as denoting nonracially motivated separation of the races as opposed to "de jure segregation" denoting deliberate separation of the races by law. . . .

is a question some day to be answered by the Supreme Court, but that question is not present in any of the cases before this court. . . . we have many instances of a heavy concentration of Negroes or whites in certain areas, but always that type of imbalance has been superimposed on total school separation. And always the separation originally was racially motivated and sanctioned by law in a system based on two schools within a neighborhood or overlapping neighborhoods, each school serving a different race. The situations have some similarity but they have different origins, create different problems, and require different corrective action.[94]

In the 1964 act (and again in 1966 during consideration of amendments to the Elementary and Secondary Education Act of 1965) Congress, within the context of debates on aid to de facto segregated schools declined to decide just what should be done about imbalanced neighborhood schools.[94a] The legislative solution, if there is one to this problem, will require a carefully conceived and thoroughly debated comprehensive statute. In the 1964 act Congress simply directed that the federal assistance provided in Title IV, §§403-5 was not to be used for developing plans to assign pupils to overcome racial imbalance. Similarly, Congress withheld authorizing the attorney general, in school desegregation actions, to ask for a court order calling for busing pupils from one school to another to "achieve a racial balance."[96]

B. Section 407(a)(2) of Title IV authorizing the attorney general to file suit to desegregate, contains the "antibusing" proviso:

". . . nothing herein shall empower any official or court of the United States to issue any order seeking to achieve a racial balance in any school by requiring the transportation of pupils or students from one school to another or one school district to another in order to achieve such racial balance, or otherwise enlarge the existing power of the court to insure compliance with constitutional standards."

---

94. For some idea of the number and complexity of the administrative problems school officials face in dealing with de facto segregation, see Kaplan, "Segregation Litigation and the Schools—Part II: The General Northern Problem," 58 *NWU L Rev* 157, 182-86 (1963).

94a. The question of providing special, earmarked federal funds for school districts that were trying to correct imbalanced neighborhood schools came up again in connection with the 1966 amendments to the Elementary and Secondary Education Act of 1965. The House committee recommended special priority for applications under Title III of the act from local school districts which sought help with problems of overcrowding, obsolescence, or racial imbalance. The House withdrew priority for dealing with problems of racial imbalance and added an amendment to section 604 of the act to the effect that nothing in the act be construed to "require the assignment or transportation of students or teachers in order to overcome racial imbalance." The Senate went along with both actions. The debate makes clear that Congress was once again talking about racial imbalance in the context of de facto, not de jure, school segregation. See particularly *Cong Rec* 24538-9, 24541-3 (daily record Oct. 6, 1966). See also 1966 USC Cong & Admin News, pp. 3865-66, for language in House committee report recommending the priority position of applications to deal with racial imbalance.

96. This restriction appears in §407 of the act. In its context it seems clearly to restrict the attorney general to requesting only such relief as is constitutionally compelled. In other words, the act is *not* to be construed as authorizing a statutory duty to reduce imbalance by bussing. Certainly the language of §407 does not call for a construction that prohibits a court order directing that school boards abandon racially discriminatory practices which violate the Constitution. Nor does it suggest that the attorney general is precluded from requesting court orders to end racial imbalance resulting from unconstitutional practices.

First, it should be noted that the prohibition applies only to transportation; and only to transportation across school lines to achieve racial balance. The furnishing of transportation as part of a freedom of choice plan is not prohibited. Second, the equitable powers of the courts exist independently of the Civil Rights Act of 1964. It is not contended in the instant cases that the act conferred new authority on the courts. And this court has not looked to the act as a grant of new judicial authority.

Section 407(a)(2) might be read as applying only to orders issued in suits filed by the attorney general under Title IV. However, Senator, now Vice President Humphrey, floor manager in the Senate, said it was his understanding that the provision applied to the entire bill. In particular, he said that it applies to any refusal or termination of federal assistance under Title VI since the procedure for doing so requires an order approved by the president. . . .

C. Section 601 states the general purpose of Title VI of the act: "No person in the United States shall, on the ground of race, color, or national origin, be excluded from participation in, *be denied the benefits of,* or be subjected to discrimination under any program or activity receiving federal financial assistance." (Emphasis added.) This is a clear congressional statement that racial discrimination against the beneficiaries of federal assistance is unlawful. Children attending schools which receive federal assistance are of course among the beneficiaries.

D. Section 604 of the act, 42 USC §2000d-3 is the section the defendants principally rely upon and the section most misunderstood.[97] It provides: "Nothing contained in this title shall be construed to authorize action under this title by any department or agency *with respect to any employment practice of any employer,* employment agency, or labor organization except where a primary objective of the federal financial assistance is to provide employment." (Emphasis added.) The defendants contend that this section bars any action requiring desegregation of faculties and school personnel.

Section 604 was not a part of the original House bill. Senator Humphrey, while introducing the act explained: "[The] commissioner might also be justified in requiring elimination of racial discrimination in employment or assignment of teachers, at least where such discrimination affected the educational opportunities of students. See *Braxton v Board of Pub Instruction of Duval County* 326 F2d 616 (5th Cir 1964)." 110 *Cong Rec* 6345. That was in March 1964. In June 1964, in explaining the amendments, Senator Humphrey said, "This provision is in line with the provisions of section 602 and serves to spell out more precisely the declared scope of coverage of the title." In the same speech he stated (110 *Cong Rec* 12714): "We have made no changes of substance in Title VI." This explanation plainly indicates that the amendment was not intended as a statutory bar to faculty integration in schools receiving federal aid.

However, in the interval between these two explanations the attorney general, in response to a letter from Senator Cooper, stated that section 602 would not apply to federally aided employers who discriminated in employment practices: "Title VI is limited . . . to discrimination against the beneficiaries of federal assist-

---

97. See *Hearings on HR 826 Before the House Comm on Rules,* 89th Cong 2d Sess, 24-26, 37-40 (1966).

ance programs. . . . Where, however, employees are the intended beneficiaries of a program, Title VI would apply." He gave as an example accelerated public works programs. It was after the receipt of the attorney general's letter that the amended Senate bill was passed. The school boards argue therefore that section 604 was enacted, because of the attorney general's interpretation, to exclude interference with employment practices of schools.

In its broadest application this argument would allow racial discrimination in the hiring, discharge, and assignment of teachers. In its narrowest application this argument would allow discrimination in hiring and discharging but not in assigning teachers, an inexplicable anomaly. There is no merit to this argument. Section 604 and the attorney general's letter are not inconsistent, since under section 601 it is the school children, not the teachers (employees), who are the primary beneficiaries of federal assistance to public schools. Faculty integration is essential to student desegregation. To the extent that teacher discrimination jeopardizes the success of desegregation, it is unlawful wholly aside from its effect upon individual teachers. . . .

Collaterally to their argument on section 604, the defendants cite section 701(b) of Title VII, covering equal employment. Opportunities, which specifically excepts a "state or political subdivision thereof". This section has no application to schools. Section 701(b), defines "employer" as "a person engaged in an industry affecting commerce who has twenty-five or more employees . . . ."

Section 604 was never intended as a limitation on desegregation of schools. If the defendants' view of section 604 were correct the purposes of the statute would be frustrated, for one of the keys to desegregation is integration of faculty. As long as a school has a Negro faculty it will always have a Negro student body. As the District Court for the Western District of Virginia put it in *Brown v County School Bd of Frederick County* 245 F Supp 549, 560 (1965): "[T]he presence of all Negro teachers in a school attended solely by Negro pupils in the past denotes that school a 'colored school' just as certainly as if the words were printed across its entrance in six-inch letters."

As far as possible federal courts must carry out congressional policy. But we must not overlook the fact that "we deal here with constitutional rights and not with those established by statute". The right of Negro students to be free from racial discrimination in the form of a segregated faculty is part of their broader right to equal educational opportunities. The "mandate of *Brown* . . . forbids the discriminatory consideration of race in faculty selection just as it forbids it in pupil placement." *Chambers v Hendersonville City Bd of Educ* 364 F2d 189 (4th Cir 1966).

In *Brown 2* the Supreme Court specifically referred to the reallocation of staff as one of the reasons permitting desegregation "with all deliberate speed." In determining the additional time necessary "courts may consider problems related to administration, arising from . . . *personnel* . . . . (Emphasis added.) 349 US at 300. For ten years, however, this court and other circuit courts had approved district courts' postponing hearings on faculty desegregation. *Bradley v School Bd of the City of Richmond* 382 US 103 (1965) put an end to this practice. In *Bradley* the Supreme Court held that faculty segregation had a direct impact on desegregation plans. The court summarily remanded the case to the district court holding that it was improper for that court to approve a desegregation plan without considering, at a full evidentiary hearing, the impact of faculty allocation on a racial basis. The court said, "[There is] no merit to the suggestion that relation between faculty allocation on an alleged racial basis and the adequacy of the desegregation plans are entirely speculative." Moreover, "Delays in desegregating school systems are no longer tolerable." 382 US at 105. In *Rogers v Paul* 382 US 198, 200 (1965), the Supreme Court held that Negro students in grades not yet desegregated were entitled to an immediate transfer to a white high school. They "plainly had standing" to sue on two theories: (1) "that *racial allocation of faculty denies them equality of educational opportunity without regard to* segregation of pupils; and (2) that it renders inadequate an otherwise constitutional pupil desegregation plan soon to be applied to their grades." . . . We cannot impute to Congress an intention to repudiate Senator Humphrey's explanation of section 604 and to change the substance of Title VI, tearing the vitals from the statutory objective. Integration of faculty is indispensable to the success of desegregation plan. Nor can we impute to Congress the intention to license, unconstitutionally, discrimination in the employment and assignment of teachers, a conspicuous badge of de jure segregated schools.

E. As we construe the act and its legislative history, Congress, because of its hands-off attitude on bona fide neighborhood school systems, qualified its broad policy of nondiscrimination by precluding HEW's requiring the busing of children across district lines or requiring compulsory placement of children in schools to strike a balance when the imbalance results from de facto, that is, nonracially motivated segregation. As Congressman Cramer said, "De facto segregation is racial imbalance." But *there is nothing in the language of the act or in the legislative history that equates corrective acts to desegregate or to integrate a dual school system initially based on de jure segregation with acts to bring about a racial balance in a system based on bona fide neighborhood schools.*

Congress recognized that HEW's requirements for qualifying for financial assistance are one thing and the courts' constitutional and judicial responsibilities are something else again. The act states, therefore, that it did not enlarge the court's existing powers to ensure compliance with constitutional standards. *But neither did it reduce the courts' power.*

V

The HEW guidelines agree with decisions of this circuit and of the similarly situated Fourth and Eighth Circuits. And *they stay within the congressional mandate.* There is no cross-district or cross-town busing requirement. There is no provision requiring school authorities to place white children in Negro schools or Negro children in white schools for the purpose of striking a racial balance in a school or school district proportionate to the racial population of the community or school district.[105] The provision referring to percentages is a general rule of

---

105. The present commissioner of education, Harold Howe II, in a congressional hearing declared: "The guidelines do not mention and do not require 'racial balance' or the correction of racial 'imbalance.' Nor have we in the administration of our obligations under Title VI sought to establish 'racial balance.' They deal only with desegregation plans designed to eliminate the dual school systems for whites and Negroes, systems being operated in violation of the 1954 Supreme Court ruling. . . . Racial imbalance certainly means the notion of trying to establish some proportion of youngsters that must be in each and every school. We are not about such an enterprise. We are trying to give the effect of free choices to enter

thumb or objective administrative guide for measuring progress in desegregation rather than a firm requirement that must be met.[106] ... Good faith in compliance should be measured by performance, not promises.

In reviewing the effectiveness of an approved plan it seems reasonable to use some sort of yardstick or objective percentage guide. The percentage requirements in the guidelines are modest, suggesting only that systems using free choice plans for at least two years should expect 15 to 18 percent of the pupil population to have selected desegregated schools. This court has frequently relied on percentages in jury exclusion cases. Where the percentage of Negroes on the jury and jury venires is disproportionately low compared with the Negro population of a county, a prima facie case is made for deliberate discrimination against Negroes. Percentages have been used in other civil rights cases. A similar inference may be drawn in school desegregation cases, when the number of Negroes attending school with white children is manifestly out of line with the ratio of Negro school children to white school children in public schools. Common sense suggests that a gross discrepancy between the ratio of Negroes to white children in a school and the HEW percentage guides raises an inference that the school plan is not working as it should in providing a unitary, integrated system. ... The guidelines were adopted for the entire country. However, they have been formulated in a context sympathetic with local problems. Sections 403-5 of the 1964 Civil Rights Act provide that, upon request, the commissioner of education may render technical assistance to public school systems engaged in desegregation. The commissioner may also establish training institutes to counsel school personnel having educational problems occasioned by desegregation; and the commissioner may make grants to school boards to defray the costs of providing inservice training on desegregation. In short, the commissioner may assist those school boards who allege that they will have difficulty complying with the guidelines. When desegregation plans do not meet minimum standards, the school authorities

into, or to allow free choices in having pupils enter into whatever school they may wish to attend. I do not believe that free choice plans were ever intended by the courts or by us to be an arrangement whereby the dual school system could continue without support of law. But rather an arrangement by which over a period of time we would gradually have one school system rather than two separate school systems. I do not see that we are engaged in any way in establishing procedures for balance." *Hearings on HR 26 before the House Comm on Rules,* 89th Cong 2d Sess, 32-34 (1966). . . .

106. In a letter addressed to Members of Congress and Governors, dated April 9, 1966, and given wide publicity in the press, John W. Gardner, Secretary of Health, Education and Welfare explained the purpose of the percentages:

"The second area of concern involves the percentages mentioned in the guidelines. Some have contended that this portion of the guidelines imposes a formula of 'racial balance.' This contention misconceives the purpose of the percentages. The prevailing method of desegregation is what is called the 'free choice' plan. Under such a plan, students select their schools instead of being assigned to them on a geographic basis. Courts have expressly conditioned their approval of such plans on affirmative action by school boards to insure that 'free choice' actually exists. It is our responsibility to review such plans to insure that the choice is, in fact, free and to indicate to school districts what procedures should be used to assure true freedom of choice.

"In seeking appropriate criteria to guide us in review of free choice plans, we have adopted the objective criteria applied by the courts in similar situations. One such criterion is the distribution of students by race in the various schools of a system after the students have made their choices. If substantial numbers of Negro children choose and go to previous-

should ask HEW for assistance. And district courts should invite HEW to assist by giving advice on raising the levels of the plans and by helping to coordinate a school's promises with the school's performance. In view of the competent assistance HEW may furnish schools, there is a heavy burden on proponents of the argument that their schools cannot meet HEW standards. . . .

The court reverses the judgments below and remands each case to the district court for further proceedings in accordance with this opinion.

[Dissent of Judge Cox omitted.]

Notes and Questions

1. Eligibility for Federal Aid and Court Orders

a. Proof of Compliance with Title VI. Why do the HEW regulations and guidelines require the government to accept a court order as proof that a district is desegregated? Does Title VI itself compel this result? Is there a danger that HEW might impose one set of requirements on school districts while the courts would impose another? Is there a danger that unsympathetic lower court judges could emasculate Title VI by issuing decrees that were inconsistent with appellate court decisions? What is meant by the requirement that the court order be a "final" one? That the appellate process has been exhausted? That the litigation is over? That the lower court no longer retains jurisdiction over the case?

b. Impact on Constitutional Standards. Under HEW guidelines, judicial decisions determine both the constitutional obligation of segregated school systems and the eligibility of such school systems for federal aid. What impact is this interconnection likely to have on the evolution of constitutional doctrines? Is it likely to make judges more cautious? To make them bolder, by giving them a weapon to achieve compliance that is not normally within the power of federal judges? In this regard, might Title VI have greater impact on the development of remedies than on constitutional standards?

2. What Is a Guideline?

What effect does Judge Wisdom give to the HEW guidelines? Does he treat them as law? As sound advice? How do guidelines differ from regulations? Is there any suggestion that legislative hearings were held by HEW before the adoption of the guidelines? Note that §2000d-1 requires the president's approval before any "rule, regulation, or order" can be effectuated. The guidelines do not carry that formal approval. Is this a violation of the statute? Does it suggest how the courts should treat the guidelines? Does it suggest that the decision to issue

ly all-white schools, the choice system is clearly operating freely. If few or none choose to do so in a community where there has been a pattern of segregation, then it is appropriate that the free choice plan be reviewed and other factors considered to determine whether the system is operating freely.

"*With more than 2,000 separate districts to consider, such percentages are thus an administrative guide which helps us to determine those districts requiring further review. Such review in turn will determine whether or not the freedom of choice plan is in fact working fairly.*" *New York Times*, April 12, 1966, p 1. Printed in *Hearings on HR826 Before the House Committee on Rules*, 89th Cong 2d Sess, 31 (1966). Commissioner Howe reaffirmed Secretary Gardner's policies as stated in the letter. See Ibid, 30-33.

guidelines was prompted in part by a desire not to commit the president to HEW's actions? If so, what does this portend for the desegregation process? For a history of the evolution of the HEW guidelines, see G. Orfield, *The Reconstruction of Southern Education,* chap 2 (1969).

3. Implementation of *Brown 1* and *2* and the Civil Rights Act

a. Reasons for Noncompliance. What reasons does Judge Wisdom give for the difficulties encountered by the judiciary in enforcing *Brown*? Which of these reasons relate to the ambiguities of evolving constitutional standards? To the handicaps of case-by-case enforcement of the law? See Orfield, *Reconstruction of Southern Education* 21. If case-by-case adjudication is inappropriate "for reasonably prompt and uniform desegregation," is this an indication that the courts have stepped well beyond their traditional role? Is this a further indication that the desegregation decisions involve group rights more than individual rights? See generally Hartman, "The Right to Equal Educational Opportunities as a Personal and Present Right," 9 *Wayne L Rev* 424 (1963); Comment, "The Class Action Device in Antisegregation Cases," 20 *U Chi L Rev* 577 (1953); "Class Actions—A Study of Group Interest Litigation," 1 *Race Rel L Rep* 991 (1956).

b. Judicial and Administrative Competence Compared. In a portion of the *Jefferson County* case not reproduced here, Judge Wisdom remarked that "a national effort, bringing together Congress, the executive, and the judiciary may be able to make meaningful the right of Negro children to equal educational opportunities. *The courts acting alone have failed.*" US v Jefferson County Bd of Educ 372 F2d 836, 847 (5th Cir 1966). (Emphasis added.) Is this an assessment of the relative competency of the courts? Does it imply that the Congress, HEW, and the courts *will* succeed where the courts alone have failed? Consider these remarks by a perceptive commentator:

NOTE, "THE COURTS, HEW, AND
SOUTHERN SCHOOL DESEGREGATION"
77 Yale LJ 321, 339-56 (1967)

Both in the substantive standards adopted and the method of administration employed the *Jefferson* opinion represents the tendency of at least one circuit to look more and more toward Washington in discharging its duty to assure plaintiffs their constitutional right to a desegregated education. The opinion indicates that this deference by the courts arises from more than a mere wish to see that court orders do not become a route in a few cases for evasion of Title VI. Judge Wisdom also argues in terms of an assessment of the supposed relative institutional competence of the two institutions. The failure of litigation in other circuits to follow a similar pattern suggests other courts see the comparison differently—perhaps, as will be explored later, for reasons more practical than conceptual.

Expertise: The Question of Substantive Standards

In cases requiring a court order directing the desegregation of a school system the judge has the option either to rely on the Office of Education or to tailor his own special plan for the districts. If his plan is sufficiently demanding this latter approach need not be inconsistent with efforts to prevent use of the courts as a way to avoid Title VI requirements.

Deference to HEW standards is found in all circuits but most commonly it occurs in the Fifth. Numerous cases, even before *Jefferson,* adopted the HEW plans without explanation. Reliance on the HEW guidelines in such cases might result in simply an order for the parties to adopt any plan approved by the Office of Education under present, or in a few cases, future standards.

Technically such reliance in this last instance on the guidelines makes the school district subject to Office of Education requirements in a way Title VI never contemplated. Under such a solution the school district must follow government requirements whether it chooses to receive federal aid or not and whether the court has reviewed them or not. This therefore gives to the Office of Education powers beyond those found in the Civil Rights Act. Such court orders, in effect delegating power to the Office of Education to write and rewrite the court decree, are certainly examples of unusually complete judicial deference to an administrative agency. It is qualified only by the district court judge's power to decide at any moment to modify his decree so as not to require conformity with present or future guidelines. One dissenting judge has seen in such practices problems of constitutional dimension. Since HEW professes to base its guidelines only on constitutional requirements as evolved by the courts, there is also a danger of complete stasis in the system should all courts decide to rely on HEW guidelines.

One justification for such practices, found in *Jefferson* and a few circuit court cases, is based on a belief in the greater expertise of the Office of Education. In the *Jefferson* opinion Wisdom refers to "experts in education and school administration," mentions "their day-to-day experience with thousands of school systems," notes that "it is evident to anyone that the guidelines were carefully formulated by educational authorities," and contrasts such qualifications with judicial ignorance. "[M]ost judges," he asserts, "do not have sufficient competence—they are not educators or school administrators—to know the right questions, much less the right answers." . . . [B]rief examination of the actual character of the Office of Education expertise suggests the issue to be at least more complicated than Judge Wisdom suggests. The civil rights effort at the Office of Education has been in the past directed by a division charged with responsibility for the Equal Educational Opportunity Program (EEOP). In fiscal year 1967 Congress appropriated for HEW's entire civil rights enforcement effort $3,385,000 and established a personnel ceiling of 278. As a result, EEOP in fiscal year 1967 actually employed sixty-five professional staff members, of whom only forty-three were assigned to eleven states in the deep South. . . .

Given the size and immensity of the problem HEW in Washington could obviously never give direction reflecting local difficulties in all 5,146 school districts. Originally the Office of Education had hoped that at least some of the state departments of education would take the lead in administering Title VI at the state level in order to prevent the full burden from falling solely on Washington. The office planned to rely solely on the regulations, leaving the state to work out the details with local school boards. At first the state departments of education sought to avoid their obligation by submitting "dirty" statements of compliance stipulating that the state would not insist that local school districts receiving federal money desegregate. Ultimately all capitulated. However, while a few state departments of education, notably North Carolina in 1965 and Florida in 1966, have taken the lead in helping school boards desegregate, the majority have been no help.

Unaided by the state, the local school boards proved unable to do the job on their own. Commissioner Howe has said that the Office of Education "would have been perfectly willing to leave it up to local school districts" to carry out their obligations under Title VI and the regulations. "In practice, however, local school authorities raised so many questions or made so little progress that the Office of Education found it necessary to issue guidelines establishing minimum desegregation standards."

The burden of directing each school district as it moved toward desegregation thus fell on the Office of Education alone, whether the agency thought it advisable or not. At first it issued only a quarter-page description of the type of plan that would be acceptable, accompanying it with a general statement warning that "no tersely stated or vague plan will be approved" and that "the real question for any district is the extent to which it wishes to risk disapproval of its plans." However, the local school districts, confessing themselves still unable to take the initiative and draft acceptable plans, sought further aid from the Office of Education. The earlier general statement was pronounced too vague to be of any help, and the argument was made that local popular acceptance of a plan could not be secured until Washington put in concrete terms what was required. The result was the guidelines, for given the centralization of the task in Washington, the government obviously had no choice but to seek to formulate advice which could be applied in all cases. It had neither the time, the staff, nor the detailed knowledge to draft specific advice for each school district that requested help. The guidelines were originally intended not to have the force of law but merely to serve as a "reasonable and understandable administrative device" to explain to school districts what was expected of them. The inevitable need, however, for a quick efficient administrative device meant that they came to be relied on almost exclusively. But now they are widely viewed by educators as having the status of law.

The Office of Education thus solved its administrative problems by extensive reliance on the simplicity of uniformity. Such an approach has its price. By specifically stating the minimum acceptable standard, the Office of Education assured that the minimum would also be the maximum for most school districts. The Office of Education thereby denied itself the opportunity to require more of Maryland than of Mississippi.

By opting for a procedure that could be quickly and easily administered without detailed knowledge of a particular school district, the Office of Education also had to emphasize in the guidelines those standards which were susceptible to such an approach. The attention paid faculty desegregation has been dictated partly by the ease with which the problem may be spotted and the relative speed with which the situation may be rectified as compared with the question of the assignment of the students themselves.

The inclusion in the revised guidelines of stated minimum percentages of desegregation that would be accepted resulted from similar limitations. The Office of Education is too centralized and too understaffed to analyze conditions in each school district and to determine as a result the appropriate speed at which each district should move toward complete desegregation. It therefore adopted the percentages with the intent that they serve only as an administrative touch-stone to measure the amount of good faith compliance being made by each school district. Inevitably, however, heavy reliance on the percentages has aroused much opposition from those who see or want to see in them a require-ment of racial balance. . . .

Elaborating on the theme of judicial inadequacy, Wisdom refers to "the slow progress inherent in the judicial adversary process," citing a committee report that had emphasized the burden court suits place on Negro plaintiffs. He points to the inability of courts to give advisory opinions; the tendency of the problems to be outside the immediate judicial scope of a particular case; the inappropriate-ness of the only means courts have to enforce their orders, contempt proceed-ings. He also reiterates Judge Tuttle's worries about the inevitable time lag be-tween the court of appeals' decision and application by the district court.

Courts have never considered the bar against advisory opinions and the canons of judicial restraint to be rigid when constitutional considerations demand flexi-bility. The all-inclusive nature of the *Jefferson* opinion itself demonstrates that to a resourceful court such doctrines need not impede the judiciary from addressing itself with adequate breadth to the problems before it. The argument has even less force on the district court level. A court of equity has vast powers in framing its decree to "go beyond the matters immediately underlying its equita-ble jurisdiction and decide whatever other issues and give whatever other relief may be necessary under the circumstances."

The argument that contempt powers are inappropriate as means of enforcing desegregation is difficult to understand. Wisdom's theory is that a court should not impose such severe sanctions on those who have accepted the thankless and difficult task of running schools in areas where popular feeling is strongly against desegregation and where state laws designed to avoid desegregation further handi-cap local efforts to obey the Constitution. The existence of laws that prevent local school officials from complying with a court order would seem a fact within a court's discretion to consider when deciding whether to cite the defend-ant for contempt. Furthermore, a court faced with such a problem could attack the problem directly by reviewing the constitutionality of the state law. The Office of Education faced with a similar problem may well be powerless. . . . If the judges' attitude toward the Office of Education is actually inspired by a legitimate fear of overwork and therefore inability to devote sufficient time to each case, the solution is not to pretend that the administrative agency can do a better job but to state the problem clearly and hope for larger judicial appropria-tions. . . .

Evidence suggests that despite any institutional limitations courts are still as well equipped procedurally as the Office of Education to enforce the desegrega-tion of a particular school district once that school district has come before the court.

Applying sanctions in the form of termination of aid can be a long cumber-some process indeed. HEW regulations prescribe an elaborate procedure that must be followed. At the hearing itself the government cannot rely simply on a school district's failure to observe guideline requirements but must affirmatively prove that the officials are not making a good faith effort to desegregate as rapidly as possible. Many school districts have not contested the proceedings, but a concerted effort to thwart the administrative process by all school districts taking full advantage of all their procedural rights would at least delay the effectiveness of the enforcement proceedings, given the smallness of the Office of Education litigation staff. There is no comparison with the speed with which a court may grant a temporary injunction or move to enforce its own order if not complied with. Even after the administrative process is completed and steps are taken to enforce Title VI by ending federal aid, desegregation itself has still not been enforced. . . .

The Office of Education's efforts to assure observance of the programs adopted by school officials are also hampered by other institutional shortcomings. With only a limited staff it is obvious that HEW may never learn of any but the most notorious violations of the guidelines until too late. For instance, the government has not been able to check harassment and intimidation of Negroes seeking to register at a formerly white school. While HEW may well not have done all it could, a truly successful campaign to halt such practices would require a staff far larger than Congress seems likely to approve in the near future.

The Office of Education presently relies heavily on the circumstantial evidence provided by the actual number of transfers accomplished. Even this monitoring process, however, occurs too long after the fact to have any immediate effect on progress in the school district. By the time reports are received from all the school districts and the complicated factual evaluations made, it is often too late for the Office of Education to require the school board to offer another free choice period for the same school term.

A court, in contrast, can receive a report from the school district on the results of the free choice period and react in time to order immediate remedial measures before the opening of school. Furthermore, because he is close to the problem, because he can rely on the self-interest of the parties to the suit, and because he can have immediate recourse to the injunctive powers, a district court judge stands a better chance of learning about and stopping irregularities before any harm is done.

Neither courts nor administrative agencies such as the Office of Education have solved the problems of assuring swift, effective enforcement of steps ordered in the name of justice. While Judge Wisdom and Judge Tuttle argue with some merit that courts are procedurally ill equipped for the task of enforcing the law in a particular school district, their opinions do not fully substantiate their position and fail to take into account the difficulties these same problems cause the Office of Education.

Do these remarks contradict the often-asserted conclusion that the Civil Rights Act of 1964 greatly accelerated the pace of desegregation? Does the author properly take into account the symbolic consequences of all the branches of government joining forces to ensure school desegregation? Does his analysis suggest that in *Jefferson County* it was the judiciary coming to the aid of HEW rather than the converse? Does HEW suffer from political disadvantages not suffered by the courts? Does *Jefferson County* complete a cycle in which responsibility for desegregation first rested with the courts, then shifted to HEW, then moved back to the courts for judicial approval of HEW actions, and then back to HEW for uniform enforcement?

4. Model Decree

In *Jefferson County,* the Fifth Circuit for the first time promulgated a model decree that was binding on all district courts in the circuit. How does this development relate to the passage of the Civil Rights Act of 1964? Is it made necessary by the exception for court orders under Title VI? Does it indicate an independent change in judicial policy caused by the unsympathetic treatment given to desegregation cases by lower courts? Note that after *Jefferson County* a three-judge federal court in the Fifth Circuit issued a statewide injunction ordering ninety-nine districts in Alabama to desegregate. *Lee v Macon County Bd of Educ* 267 F Supp 458 (MD Ala 1967), *aff'd sub nom Wallace v US,* 389 US 215 (1967). How does this relief differ from the relief afforded in *Jefferson County?* Does it indicate that the cooperation between HEW and the courts evidenced by *Jefferson County* was not sufficient to bring about desegregation?

5. Section 2000d-3 and Desegregation of Faculties

Section 2000d-3 provides that employment discrimination is not a violation of Title VI unless "a primary objective of the federal financial assistance is to provide employment." The defendants in *Jefferson County* alleged that this barred HEW from requiring faculty desegregation in its guidelines because teachers and administrators were not the primary beneficiaries of federal education grants. How does Judge Wisdom respond to this argument? Do you accept his construction of Senator Humphrey's remarks? In any event, are those remarks dispositive in the light of the specific language of § 2000d-3? What weight should be attached to the letter from the attorney general—secured before the passage of Title VI—which made no reference to faculty desegregation? Note that in 1965 the Supreme Court had declared that faculty desegregation was a vital component in the promulgation of adequate desegregation plans for students. *Bradley v School Bd of Richmond* 382 US 103 (1965); *Rogers v Paul* 382 US 198 (1965). Was Judge Wisdom suggesting that if § 2000d-3 forbade faculty desegregation, it would be unconstitutional? How does the desegregation of faculties relate to the underlying basis of the *Brown* decision?

6. Civil Rights Act of 1964 and Racial Balance

Judge Wisdom discusses the distinction between de jure and de facto segregation, a distinction that has built great complexity into desegregation law (for a detailed analysis in connection with *Keyes v School Dist No 1, Denver,* 93 S Ct 2686 (1973), *supra* p 410). He asserts that the former involves purposeful or deliberate school segregation, while the latter involves nonracially motivated segregation resulting from a neutral assignment policy such as neighborhood attendance zones. This distinction is drawn to distinguish the provisions of Title IV that prohibit federal officials from ordering or seeking a court order to achieve racial balance in the public schools. In other words, the defendants in *Jefferson* assert that HEW and the courts were insisting on a particular ratio of blacks and whites in each school and not simply the admission of blacks to schools they were otherwise eligible to attend and from which they were unlawfully excluded.

Judge Wisdom, in reply, argues that this prohibition applies only to de facto segregation and not to de jure segregation. Apart from the constitutional and policy ramifications of this debate, is Judge Wisdom's position supportable as a matter of statutory construction?

In this context consider the following exchange from the Congressional Record:

> Mr. Byrd of West Virginia: Can the Senator from Minnesota assure the Senator from West Virginia that under Title VI school children may not be bused from one end of the community to another end of the community at the taxpayers' expense to relieve so-called racial imbalance in the schools?
>
> Mr. Humphrey: I do.
>
> Mr. Byrd of West Virginia: Will the Senator from Minnesota cite the language in Title VI which would give the Senator from West Virginia such assurance?
>
> Mr. Humphrey: That language is to be found in another title of the bill [Title IV], in addition to the assurance to be gained from a careful reading of Title VI itself. . . . I should like to make one . . . reference to the Gary case. [*Bell v School Dist* 213 F Supp 819 (ND Ind 1963).] The thrust of this case provided the substance of the quoted portion of the statute. The case was affirmed at 324 F2d 209 (7th Cir 1963). This case makes it quite clear that while the Constitution prohibits segregation, it does not require integration. The busing of children to achieve racial balance would be an act to effect the integration of schools. In fact, if the bill were to compel it, it would be a [constitutional] violation, because it would be handling the matter on the basis of race and we would be transporting children because of race. The bill does not attempt to integrate the schools, but it does attempt to eliminate segregation in the school system. (110 *Cong Rec* 12715, 12717 (1964).)

Does the prohibition in §2000c-6(a)(2) of Title IV apply to HEW guidelines promulgated under Title VI? That is, does the same standard of racial balance apply to federal fund cutoffs as to the attorney general when he files aa desegregation suit? What if §2000c-6(a)(2) were construed as a limitation on the courts' power to remedy segregation? Would it be unconstitutional?

IV. Desegregation: Evolution of a Constitutional Standard

A. Freedom of Choice

GREEN v COUNTY SCHOOL BOARD
391 US 430 (1968)

Mr. Justice Brennan delivered the opinion of the court.

The question for decision is whether, under all the circumstances here, respondent school board's adoption of a "freedom-of-choice" plan which allows a pupil to choose his own public school constitutes adequate compliance with the board's responsibility "to achieve a system of determining admission to the public schools on a nonracial basis . . . ." *Brown v Board of Educ* 349 US 294, 300-1 (*Brown 2*).

Petitioners brought this action in March 1965 seeking injunctive relief against respondent's continued maintenance of an alleged racially segregated school system. New Kent County is a rural county in Eastern Virginia. About one-half of its population of some 4,500 are Negroes. There is no residential segregation in the county; persons of both races reside throughout. The school system has only two schools, the New Kent school on the east side of the county and the George W. Watkins school on the west side. In a memorandum filed May 17, 1966, the district court found that the "school system serves approximately 1,300 pupils, of which 740 are Negro and 550 are white. The school board operates one white combined elementary and high school [New Kent], and one Negro combined elementary and high school [George W. Watkins]. There are no attendance zones. Each school serves the entire county." The record indicates that twenty-one school buses—eleven serving the Watkins school and ten serving the New Kent school—travel overlapping routes throughout the county to transport pupils to and from the two schools.

The segregated system was initially established and maintained under the compulsion of Virginia constitutional and statutory provisions mandating racial segregation in public education, Va Const, Art IX, §140 (1902); Va Code §22-221 (1950). These provisions were held to violate the Federal Constitution in *Davis v County School Board of Prince Edward County,* decided with *Brown v Board of Educ* 347 US 483, 487 (*Brown 1*). The respondent school board continued the segregated operation of the system after the *Brown* decisions, presumably on the authority of several statutes enacted by Virginia in resistance to those decisions. Some of these statutes were held to be unconstitutional on their face or as applied. One statute, the Pupil Placement Act, Va Code §22-232.1 *et seq.* (1961), not repealed until 1966, divested local boards of authority to assign children to particular schools and placed that authority in a state pupil placement board. Under that act children were each year automatically reassigned to the school previously attended unless upon their application the state board assigned them to another school; students seeking enrollment for the first time were also assigned at the discretion of the state board. To September 1964, no Negro pupil had applied for admission to the New Kent school under this statute and no white pupil had applied for admission to the Watkins school.

The school board initially sought dismissal of this suit on the ground that petitioners had failed to apply to the state board for assignment to New Kent school. However on August 2, 1965, five months after the suit was brought, respondent school board, in order to remain eligible for federal financial aid, adopted a "freedom-of-choice" plan for desegregating the schools. Under that plan, each pupil, except those entering the first and eighth grades, may annually choose between the New Kent and Watkins schools and pupils not making a choice are assigned to the school previously attended; first- and eighth-grade pupils must affirmatively choose a school. After the plan was filed the district court denied petitioners' prayer for an injunction and granted respondent leave to submit an amendment to the plan with respect to employment and assignment of teachers and staff on a racially nondiscriminatory basis. The amendment was duly filed and on June 28, 1966, the district court approved the "freedom-of-choice" plan as so amended. The Court of Appeals for the Fourth Circuit, *en banc,* 382 F2d 338, affirmed the district court's approval of the "freedom-of-choice" provisions of the plan but remanded the case to the district court for entry of an order regarding faculty "which is much more specific and more comprehensive" and which would incorporate in addition to a "minimal, objective time table" some of the faculty provisions of the decree entered by the Court of Appeals for the Fifth Circuit in *US v Jefferson County Bd of Educ* 372 F2d 836, *aff'd en banc*, 380 F2d 385 (1967). Judges Sobeloff and Winter concurred with the remand on the teacher issue but otherwise disagreed, expressing the view "that the district court should be directed . . . also to set up procedures for periodically evaluating the effectiveness of the [board's] 'freedom of choice' [plan] in the elimination of other features of a segregated school system." *Bowman v County School Bd of Charles City County*, 382 F2d 326, at 330. We granted certiorari, 389 US 1003.

The pattern of separate "white" and "Negro" schools in the New Kent County school system established under compulsion of state laws is precisely the pattern of segregation to which *Brown 1* and *Brown 2* were particularly addressed, and which *Brown 1* declared unconstitutionally denied Negro school children equal protection of the laws. Racial identification of the system's schools was complete, extending not just to the composition of student bodies at the two schools but to every facet of school operations—faculty, staff, transportation, extracurricular activities and facilities. In short, the state, acting through the local school board and school officials, organized and operated a dual system, part "white" and part "Negro."

It was such dual systems that fourteen years ago *Brown 1* held unconstitutional and a year later *Brown 2* held must be abolished; school boards operating such school systems were *required* by *Brown 2* "to effectuate a transition to a racially nondiscriminatory school system." 349 US at 301. It is of course true that for the time immediately after *Brown 2* the concern was with making an initial break in a long-established pattern of excluding Negro children from schools attended by white children. The principal focus was on obtaining for those Negro children courageous enough to break with tradition a place in the "white" schools. See, e.g., *Cooper v Aaron* 358 US 1. Under *Brown 2* that immediate goal was only the first step, however. The transition to a unitary, nonracial system of public education was and is the ultimate end to be brought about; it was because of the "complexities arising from the transition to a system of public education freed of racial discrimination" that we provided for "all deliberate speed" in the implementation of the principles of *Brown 1*. 349 US at 299-301.

It is against this background that thirteen years after *Brown 2* commanded the abolition of dual systems we must measure the effectiveness of respondent school board's "freedom-of-choice" plan to achieve that end. The school board contends that it has fully discharged its obligation by adopting a plan by which every student, regardless of race, may "freely" choose the school he will attend. The board attempts to cast the issue in its broadest form by arguing that its "freedom-of-choice" plan may be faulted only by reading the Fourteenth Amendment as universally requiring "compulsory integration," a reading it insists the wording of the amendment will not support. But that argument ignores the thrust of *Brown 2*. In the light of the command of that case, what is involved here is the question whether the board has achieved the "racially nondiscriminatory school system" *Brown 2* held must be effectuated in order to remedy the established unconstitutional deficiencies of its segregated system. In the context of the state-imposed segregated pattern of long standing, the fact that in 1965 the Board opened the doors of the former "white" school to Negro children and of the "Negro" school to white children merely begins, not ends, our inquiry whether the board has taken steps adequate to abolish its dual, segregated system. *Brown 2* was a call for the dismantling of well-entrenched dual systems tempered by an awareness that complex and multifaceted problems would arise which would require time and flexibility for a successful resolution. School boards such as the respondent then operating state-compelled dual systems were nevertheless clearly charged with the affirmative duty to take whatever steps might be necessary to convert to a unitary system in which racial discrimination would be eliminated root and branch. See *Cooper v Aaron, supra,* at 7; *Bradley v School Bd* 382 US 103; cf *Watson v City of Memphis* 373 US 526. The constitutional rights of Negro school children articulated in *Brown 1* permit no less than this; and it was to this end that *Brown 2* commanded school boards to bend their efforts.

In determining whether respondent school board met that command by adopting its "freedom-of-choice" plan, it is relevant that this first step did not come until some eleven years after *Brown 1* was decided and ten years after *Brown 2* directed the making of a "prompt and reasonable start." This deliberate perpetuation of the unconstitutional dual system can only have compounded the harm of such a system. Such delays are no longer tolerable, for "the governing constitutional principles no longer bear the imprint of newly enunciated doctrine." . . .

The burden on a school board today is to come forward with a plan that promises realistically to work, and promises realistically to work *now.*

The obligation of the district courts, as it always has been, is to assess the effectiveness of a proposed plan in achieving desegregation. There is no universal answer to complex problems of desegregation; there is obviously no one plan that will do the job in every case. The matter must be assessed in light of the circumstances present and the options available in each instance. It is incumbent upon the school board to establish that its proposed plan promises meaningful and immediate progress toward disestablishing state-imposed segregation. It is incumbent upon the district court to weigh that claim in light of the facts at hand and in light of any alternatives which may be shown as feasible and more promising in their effectiveness. Where the court finds the board to be acting in good faith and the proposed plan to have real prospects for dismantling the state-imposed dual system "at the earliest practicable date," then the plan may be said to provide effective relief. Of course, the availability to the board of other more promising courses of action may indicate a lack of good faith; and at least it places a heavy burden upon the board to explain its preference for an apparently less effective method. Moreover, whatever plan is adopted will require evaluation in practice, and the court should retain jurisdiction until it is clear that state-imposed segregation has been completely removed. See . . . *Raney v Board of Education* . . . .

We do not hold that "freedom of choice" can have no place in such a plan. We do not hold that a "freedom-of-choice" plan might of itself be unconstitutional, although that argument has been urged upon us. Rather, all we decide today is that in desegregating a dual system a plan utilizing "freedom of choice" is not an end in itself. As Judge Sobeloff has put it,

> "Freedom of choice" is not a sacred talisman; it is only a means to a constitutionally required end—the abolition of the system of segregation and its effects. If the means prove effective, it is acceptable, but if it fails to undo segregation, other means must be used to achieve this end. The school officials have the continuing duty to take whatever action may be necessary to create a "unitary, nonracial system" (*Bowman v County School Bd* 382 F2d 326, 333 (4th Cir 1967) (concurring opinion).)

Accord, *Kemp v Beasley* 389 F2d 178 (8th Cir 1968); *US v Jefferson County Bd of Educ, supra*. Although the general experience under "freedom of choice" to date has been such as to indicate its ineffectiveness as a tool of desegregation,[5] there may well be instances in which it can serve as an effective device. Where it offers real promise of aiding a desegregation program to effectuate conversion of a state-imposed dual system to a unitary, nonracial system there might be no objection to allowing such a device to prove itself in operation. On the other hand, if there are reasonably available other ways, such for illustration as zoning, promising speedier and more effective conversion to a unitary, nonracial school system, "freedom of choice" must be held unacceptable.

The New Kent School Board's "freedom-of-choice" plan cannot be accepted as a sufficient step to "effectuate a transition" to a unitary system. In three years of operation not a single white child has chosen to attend Watkins school and although 115 Negro children enrolled in New Kent school in 1967 (up from 35 in 1965 and 111 in 1966) 85 percent of the Negro children in the system still attend the all-Negro Watkins school. In other words, the school system remains a dual system. Rather than further the dismantling of the dual system, the plan has operated simply to burden children and their parents with a responsibility which *Brown 2* placed squarely on the school board. The board must be required to formulate a new plan and, in light of other courses which appear open to the

---

5. The views of the United States commissioner on civil rights, which we neither adopt nor refuse to adopt, are as follows:

"Freedom-of-choice plans, which have tended to perpetuate racially identifiable schools in the Southern and border states, require affirmative action by both Negro and white parents and pupils before such disestablishment can be achieved. There are a number of factors which have prevented such affirmative action by substantial numbers of parents and pupils of both races:

"(a) Fear of retaliation and hostility from the white community continue to deter many Negro families from choosing formerly all-white schools;

"(b) During the past school year [1966-67], as in the previous year, in some areas of the South, Negro families with children attending previously all-white schools under free choice plans were targets of violence, threats of violence and economic reprisal by white persons and Negro children were subjected to harassment by white classmates notwithstanding conscientious efforts by many teachers and principals to prevent such misconduct.

"(c) During the past school year, in some areas of the South public officials improperly influenced Negro families to keep their children in Negro schools and excluded Negro children attending formerly all-white schools from official functions;

"(d) Poverty deters many Negro families in the South from choosing formerly all-white schools. Some Negro parents are embarrassed to permit their children to attend such schools without suitable clothing. In some districts special fees are assessed for courses which are available only in the white schools;

board, such as zoning, fashion steps which promise realistically to convert promptly to a system without a "white" school and a "Negro" school, but just schools.

The judgment of the court of appeals is vacated insofar as it affirmed the district court and the case is remanded to the district court for further proceedings consistent with this opinion.

It is so ordered.

Notes and Questions

1. *Green* and *Brown*

In the first line of the *Green* opinion, Justice Brennan states that the question for decision is whether the school board has complied with *Brown v Board of Education* by "determining admission to the public schools on a nonracial basis." If this is the issue, how can the result in the case be defended? Did the defendants assign students according to their race? Were the assignments not made on the basis of racially neutral choices made by black and white parents?

Justice Brennan attempts to deal with these problems by arguing that the original thrust of *Brown 2* was the assignment of black youngsters to white schools from which they were excluded solely because of their race, but that now the goal is the "transition to a unitary, nonracial system of public education." Is this consistent with Justice Brennan's formulation of the question for decision? What basis is there for this change in purpose? What is a unitary school system? Is it, as the defendants suggest, a euphemism for "compulsory integration"? Is this view supported by the court's reference to the fact that 85 percent of the black children in the district still attend all-black schools, and its conclusion that, under such circumstances, the defendants have not met their obligation to create a unitary school system?

a. Racial Classification Ethic and Remedies. If prohibition of racial classifications underlies the desegregation cases, and if the constitutional wrong identified in those cases is the exclusion of blacks from white schools, the logical remedy, apparently contemplated in *Brown,* is the admission of black students to the schools from which they were excluded because of their race. See Bickel, "The Decade of School Desegregation: Progress and Prospects," 64 *Colum L Rev* 193, 212 (1964). Yet, in *Green* the court apparently sought to abolish racially identifiable schools by integrating black and white students throughout the system. How can this inconsistency between wrong and remedy be explained?

b. The "Bad Faith" Argument. Proponents of the racial neutrality principle have attempted to explain the integration remedy by focusing on the bad faith of many school boards in implementing *Brown.* In *Green,* for example, the school board had not taken any steps to eliminate segregation until 1965, eleven years after *Brown 1.* According to this theory, the duty to integrate "might be justified as a prophylactic, a way of making certain that a school board's policy of

---

"(e) Improvements in facilities and equipment . . . have been instituted in all-Negro schools in some districts in a manner that tends to discourage Negroes from selecting white schools." *Southern School Desegregation, 1966-1967,* 88 (1967). Ibid, 45-69; *Survey of School Desegregation in the Southern and Border States 1965-1966,* 30-44, 51-52 (US Comm'n on Civil Rights 1966).

racial segregation has in fact been discarded." Goodman, "De Facto Segregation: A Constitutional and Empirical Analysis," 60 *Calif L Rev* 275, 293 (1972). Is there any language in *Green* that supports this approach? Does the prophylactic theory really impose an analytical legal framework, or is it simply a description of the dynamics of judicial psychology when judges are confronted with unco-operative litigants? If only racial classifications are forbidden, and a school board has abandoned its policy of making such classifications, of what relevance is its good or bad faith? Has the offensive conduct not been cured? Is it not circular reasoning to infer bad faith from the failure to achieve integration?

c. Elimination of Discriminatory Effects of Past Segregation. A more cogent explanation of the integration remedy in *Green* is that integration is necessary to eliminate the discriminatory effects of past practices. See Hearings on School Busing Before Subcomm No 5 of the House Comm on the Judiciary, 92d Cong 2d Sess, ser 32, pt 3, at 1631-32 (1972) (statement of Professor Wright); Cox, "The Role of Congress in Constitutional Determinations," 40 *U Cin L Rev* 199, 258 (1971). Integration is not a substantive entitlement; rather it stands as a remedy to cure past instances of racial discrimination in the public schools. Is there any support for this position in the *Green* opinion? What is the relationship between the past discrimination in *Green* and the unacceptability of the freedom-of-choice plan?

i. Can it be argued that the prior dual school system has influenced the current assignment choices of black and white parents? Do courts normally examine such decisions to determine the prejudices, fears, and values that underlie them?

ii. Was *Green* premised on the view that the choices of blacks were dictated by economic and physical threats made against them? How do you explain footnote 5, which appears to reject this rationale? Might the difficulties of a case-by-case search for coercion have led the court to adopt a per se rule against freedom-of-choice plans? Is there any language in the opinion to support this position?

iii. Might *Green* rest on the principle that any form of segregation is particularly injurious in previously de jure school districts, because the past discrimination may have "helped to shape the attitudes of the community, both black and white, toward Negroes and Negro schools." Goodman, "De Facto Segregation: A Constitutional and Empirical Analysis," 60 *Calif L Rev* 275, 295 (1972). Is this approach realistic? Is the stigma of assignment to an all-black school limited to previously de jure systems? Will integration necessarily change these perceptions? See generally Yudof, "Equal Educational Opportunity and the Courts," 51 *Tex L Rev* 411, 449-55 (1973).

3. Discretionary Remedies?

If integration is a remedial and not a substantive requirement, does this suggest that federal district court judges have the discretion to decide whether this particular remedy is appropriate under the circumstances? Does *Green* support this view?

4. Waiver of the Integration Remedy

Assuming that the plaintiffs in *Green* were entitled to an integration remedy, did they not effectively waive their right to that remedy when they declined to choose white schools for their children? While the courts require the state to meet a heavy burden of proof, the waiver of constitutional rights is often permitted where the waiver was knowingly and intelligently exercised. See *Overmyer v Frick Co* 405 US 174, 185 (1972). Is this not even more the case when the right waived is remedial and not substantive? Does the waiver issue bring us back to the problems raised in note 2c?

5. Unitary School System

What is a unitary school system? Must each school reflect the racial composition of the entire school population? For both students and faculty? How precise must the racial balance be in each school? Can any one-race schools remain? See Powe, "The Road to *Swann*: Mobile County Crawls to the Bus," 51 *Tex L Rev* 505, 526 n98 (1973); Goodman, "De Facto Segregation: A Constitutional and Empirical Analysis," 60 *Calif L Rev* 275 (1972).

6. Scope of Green

New Kent County is a rural and residentially integrated county. For that reason, school desegregation could be instituted with less busing of students than had characterized the dual system. Does that fact limit the applicability of *Green* in situations where residential segregation exists and the costs of transporting students to eliminate school segregation would be greater? That question, among others, is raised in *Swann v Charlotte-Mecklenburg Board of Education.*

B. Dismantling the Dual School System: Scope of the Obligation

SWANN v CHARLOTTE-MECKLENBURG BOARD OF EDUCATION
402 US 1 (1971)

Mr. Chief Justice Burger delivered the opinion of the court.

We granted certiorari in this case to review important issues as to the duties of school authorities and the scope of powers of federal courts under this court's mandates to eliminate racially separate public schools established and maintained by state action. . . .

This case and those argued with it arose in states having a long history of maintaining two sets of schools in a single school system deliberately operated to carry out a governmental policy to separate pupils in schools solely on the basis of race. That was what *Brown v Board of Education* was all about. These cases present us with the problem of defining in more precise terms than heretofore the scope of the duty of school authorities and district courts in implementing *Brown 1* and the mandate to eliminate dual systems and establish unitary systems at once. Meanwhile district courts and courts of appeals have struggled in hundreds of cases with a multitude and variety of problems under this court's general directive. Understandably, in an area of evolving remedies, those courts had to improvise and experiment without detailed or specific guidelines. This court, in *Brown 1* appropriately dealt with the large constitutional principles; other federal courts had to grapple with the flinty, intractable realities of day-to-day implementation of those constitutional commands. Their efforts, of necessity, embraced a process of "trial and error," and our effort to formulate guidelines must take into account their experience. . . .

I

The Charlotte-Mecklenburg school system, the forty-third largest in the nation, encompasses the city of Charlotte and surrounding Mecklenburg County, North Carolina. The area is large—550 square miles—spanning roughly twenty-two miles east-west and thirty-six miles north-south. During the 1968-69 school year the system served more than 84,000 pupils in 107 schools. Approximately 71 percent of the pupils were found to be white and 29 percent Negro. As of June 1969 there were approximately 24,000 Negro students in the system, of whom 21,000 attended schools within the city of Charlotte. Two-thirds of those 21,000—approximately 14,000 Negro students—attended twenty-one schools which were either totally Negro or more than 99 percent Negro.

This situation came about under a desegregation plan approved by the district court at the commencement of the present litigation in 1965, 243 F Supp 667 (WDNC), aff'd, 369 F2d 29 (4th Dist 1966), based upon geographic zoning with a free-transfer provision. The present proceedings were initiated in September 1968 by petitioner Swann's motion for further relief based on Green v County School Bd 391 US 430 (1968), and its companion cases. All parties now agree that in 1969 the system fell short of achieving the unitary school system that those cases require. . . .

In April 1969 the district court ordered the school board to come forward with a plan for both faculty and student desegregation. . . . [I] n February 1970, the district court was presented with two alternative pupil assignment plans—the finalized "board plan" and the "finger plan.". . .

The Board Plan

. . . The plan . . . provided racially mixed faculties and administrative staffs, and modified its free-transfer plan into an optional majority-to-minority transfer system.

The board plan proposed substantial assignment of Negroes to nine of the system's ten high schools, producing 17 percent to 36 percent Negro population in each. The projected Negro attendance at the tenth school, Independence, was 2 percent.

As for junior high schools, the board plan rezoned the twenty-one school areas so that in twenty the Negro attendance would range from 0 percent to 38 percent. The other school, located in the heart of the Negro residential area, was left with an enrollment of 90 percent Negro.

The board plan with respect to elementary schools relied entirely upon gerrymandering of geographic zones. More than half of the Negro elementary pupils were left in nine schools that were 86 percent to 100 percent Negro; approximately half of the white elementary pupils were assigned to schools 86 percent to 100 percent white.

The Finger Plan

The plan submitted by the court-appointed expert, Dr. Finger, adopted the school board zoning plan for senior high schools with one modification: it required that an additional 300 Negro students be transported from the Negro residential area of the city to the nearly all-white Independence High School.

The Finger plan for the junior high schools employed much of the rezoning plan of the board, combined with the creation of nine "satellite" zones. Under the satellite plan, inner-city Negro students were assigned by attendance zones to nine outlying predominately white junior high schools, thereby substantially desegregating every junior high school in the system.

The Finger plan departed from the board plan chiefly in its handling of the system's seventy-six elementary schools. Rather than relying solely upon geographic zoning, Dr. Finger proposed use of zoning, pairing, and grouping techniques, with the result that student bodies throughout the system range from 9 percent to 38 percent Negro. . . .

On February 5, 1970, the district court adopted the board plan, as modified by Dr. Finger, for the junior and senior high schools, 311 F Supp 265. The court rejected the board elementary school plan and adopted the Finger plan as presented. . . .

On appeal the court of appeals affirmed the district court's order as to faculty desegregation and the secondary school plans, but vacated the order respecting elementary schools. While agreeing that the district court properly disapproved the board plan concerning these schools, the court of appeals feared that the pairing and grouping of elementary schools would place an unreasonable burden on the board and the system's pupils. The case was remanded to the district court for reconsideration and submission of further plans. . . .

II

Nearly seventeen years ago this court held, in explicit terms, that state-imposed segregation by race in public schools denies equal protection of the laws. At no time has the court deviated in the slightest degree from that holding or its constitutional underpinnings. None of the parties before us challenges the court's decision [in *Brown 1* and *2*].

Over the sixteen years since *Brown 2*, many difficulties were encountered in implementation of the basic constitutional requirement that the state not discriminate between public school children on the basis of their race. Nothing in our national experience prior to 1955 prepared anyone for dealing with changes and adjustments of the magnitude and complexity encountered since then. Deliberate resistance of some to the court's mandates has impeded the good-faith efforts of others to bring school systems into compliance. The detail and nature of these dilatory tactics have been noted frequently by this court and other courts.

By the time the court considered *Green v County School Bd* 391 US 430, in 1968, very little progress had been made in many areas where dual school systems had historically been maintained by operation of state laws. In *Green*, the court was confronted with a record of a freedom-of-choice program that the district court had found to operate in fact to preserve a dual system more than a decade after *Brown 2*. While acknowledging that a freedom-of-choice concept could be a valid remedial measure in some circumstances, its failure to be effective in *Green* required that: "The burden on a school board today is to come forward with a plan that promises realistically to work *now* . . . until it is clear that state-imposed segregation has been completely removed." *Green, supra*, at 439.

This was plain language, yet the 1969 term of court brought fresh evidence of the dilatory tactics of many school authorities. *Alexander v Holmes County Bd of Educ* 396 US 19, restated the basic obligation asserted in *Griffin v County School Bd* 377 US 218, 234 (1964), and *Green, supra,* that the remedy must be implemented *forthwith.*

The problems encountered by the district courts and courts of appeals make plain that we should now try to amplify guidelines, however incomplete and imperfect, for the assistance of school authorities and courts. The failure of local authorities to meet their constitutional obligations aggravated the massive problem of converting from the state-enforced discrimination of racially separate school systems. This process has been rendered more difficult by changes since 1954 in the structure and patterns of communities, the growth of student population, movement of families, and other changes, some of which had marked impact on school planning, sometimes neutralizing or negating remedial action before it was fully implemented. Rural areas accustomed for half a century to the consolidated school systems implemented by bus transportation could make adjustments more readily than metropolitan areas with dense and shifting population, numerous schools, congested and complex traffic patterns.

III

. . . . In seeking to define even in broad and general terms how far this remedial power extends it is important to remember that judicial powers may be exercised only on the basis of a constitutional violation. Remedial judicial authority does not put judges automatically in the shoes of school authorities whose powers are plenary. Judicial authority enters only when local authority defaults.

School authorities are traditionally charged with broad power to formulate and implement educational policy and might well conclude, for example, that in order to prepare students to live in a pluralistic society each school should have a prescribed ratio of Negro to white students reflecting the proportion for the district as a whole. To do this as an educational policy is within the broad discretionary powers of school authorities; absent a finding of a constitutional violation, however, that would not be within the authority of a federal court. As with any equity case, the nature of the violation determines the scope of the remedy. In default by the school authorities of their obligation to proffer acceptable remedies, a district court has broad power to fashion a remedy that will assure a unitary school system.

The school authorities argue that the equity powers of federal district courts have been limited by Title IV of the Civil Rights Act of 1964, 42 USC §2000c et seq. The language and the history of Title IV show that it was enacted not to limit but to define the role of the federal government in the implementation of the *Brown 1* decision. . . . [T]he provisions of Title IV of the Civil Rights Act of 1964 [do not demonstrate] an intention to restrict [official] powers or withdraw from courts their historic equitable remedial powers. The legislative history of Title IV indicates that Congress was concerned that the act might be read as creating a right of action under the Fourteenth Amendment in the situation of so-called de facto segregation, where racial imbalance exists in the schools but with no showing that this was brought about by discriminatory action of state authorities. In short, there is nothing in the act that provides us material assistance in answering the question of remedy for state-imposed segregation in violation of *Brown 1*. The basis of our decision must be the prohibition of the Fourteenth Amendment that no state shall "deny to any person within its jurisdiction the equal protection of the laws."

IV

We turn now to the problem of defining with more particularity the responsibilities of school authorities in desegregating a state-enforced dual school system in light of the equal protection clause. Although the several related cases before us are primarily concerned with problems of student assignment, it may be helpful to begin with a brief discussion of other aspects of the process.

In *Green,* we pointed out that existing policy and practice with regard to faculty staff transportation, extracurricular activities, and facilities were among the most important indicia of a segregated system. 391 US at 435. Independent of student assignment, where it is possible to identify a "white school" or a "Negro school" simply by reference to the racial composition of teachers and staff, the quality of school buildings and equipment, or the organization of sports activities, a prima facie case of violation of substantive constitutional rights under the equal protection clause is shown.

When a system has been dual in these respects, the first remedial responsibility of school authorities is to eliminate invidious racial distinctions. With respect to such matters as transportation, supporting personnel, and extracurricular activities, no more than this may be necessary. Similar corrective action must be taken with regard to the maintenance of buildings and the distribution of equipment. In these areas, normal administrative practice should produce schools of like quality, facilities, and staffs. Something more must be said, however, as to faculty assignment and new school construction.

In the companion *Davis* case, 402 US 33, the Mobile school board has argued that the Constitution requires that teachers be assigned on a "color-blind" basis. It also argues that the Constitution prohibits district courts from using their equity power to order assignment of teachers to achieve a particular degree of faculty desegregation. We reject that contention.

In *United States v Montgomery County Bd of Educ* 395 US 225 (1969), the district court set as a goal a plan of faculty assignment in each school with a ratio of white to Negro faculty members substantially the same throughout the system. This order was predicated on the district court finding that:

> The evidence does not reflect any real administrative problems involved in immediately desegregating the substitute teachers, the student teachers, the night school faculties, and in the evolvement of a really legally adequate program for the substantial desegregation of the faculties of all schools in the system commencing with the school year 1968-69. (Quoted at 395 US at 232.)

The district court in *Montgomery* then proceeded to set an initial ratio for the whole system of at least two Negro teachers out of each twelve in any given school. The court of appeals modified the order by eliminating what it regarded as "fixed mathematical" ratios of faculty and substituted an initial requirement of *"substantially or approximately"* a five-to-one ratio. With respect to the future, the court of appeals held that the numerical ratio should be eliminated and that compliance should not be tested solely by the achievement of specified proportions. 395 US at 234.

We reversed the court of appeals and restored the district court's order in its entirety, holding that the order of the district judge

> was adopted in the spirit of this court's opinion in *Green* . . . in that his plan 'promises realistically to work, and promises realistically to work *now.*' The modifications ordered by the panel of the court of appeals, while of course not intended to do so, would, we think, take from the order some of its capacity to expedite, by means of specific commands, the day when a completely unified, unitary, nondiscriminatory school system becomes a reality instead of a hope. . . . We also believe that under all the circumstances of this case we follow the original plan outlined in *Brown 2* . . . by accepting the more specific and expeditious order of [District] Judge Johnson . . . . 395 US at 235-236.

The principles of *Montgomery* have been properly followed by the district court and the court of appeals in this case.

The construction of new schools and the closing of old ones are two of the most important functions of local school authorities and also two of the most complex. They must decide questions of location and capacity in light of population growth, finances, land values, site availability, through an almost endless list of factors to be considered. The result of this will be a decision which, when combined with one technique or another of student assignment, will determine the racial composition of the student body in each school in the system. Over the long run, the consequences of the choices will be far-reaching. People gravitate toward school facilities, just as schools are located in response to the needs of people. The location of schools may thus influence the patterns of residential development of a metropolitan area and have important impact on composition of inner-city neighborhoods.

In the past, choices in this respect have been used as a potent weapon for creating or maintaining a state-segregated school system. In addition to the classic pattern of building schools specifically intended for Negro or white students, school authorities have sometimes, since *Brown,* closed schools which appeared likely to become racially mixed through changes in neighborhood residential patterns. This was sometimes accompanied by building new schools in the areas of white suburban expansion farthest from Negro population centers in order to maintain the separation of the races with a minimum departure from the formal principles of "neighborhood zoning." Such a policy does more than simply influence the short-run composition of the student body of a new school. It may well promote segregated residential patterns which, when combined with "neighborhood zoning," further lock the school system into the mold of separation of the races. Upon a proper showing a district court may consider this in fashioning a remedy.

In ascertaining the existence of legally imposed school segregation, the existence of a pattern of school construction and abandonment is thus a factor of great weight. In devising remedies where legally imposed segregation has been established, it is the responsibility of local authorities and district courts to see to it that future school construction and abandonment are not used and do not serve to perpetuate or reestablish the dual system. When necessary, district courts should retain jurisdiction to assure that these responsibilities are carried out. Cf *US v Board of Pub Instruction* 395 F2d 66 (5th Dist 1968); *Brewer v School Bd* 397 F2d 37 (4th Dist 1968).

V

The central issue in this case is that of student assignment, and there are essentially four problem areas:

(1) to what extent racial balance or racial quotas may be used as an implement in a remedial order to correct a previously segregated system;

(2) whether every all-Negro and all-white school must be eliminated as an indispensable part of a remedial process of desegregation;

(3) what the limits are, if any, on the rearrangement of school districts and attendance zones, as a remedial measure; and

(4) what the limits are, if any on the use of transportation facilities to correct state-enforced racial school segregation.

(1) Racial Balances or Racial Quotas

. . . . We are concerned in these cases with the elimination of the discrimination inherent in the dual school systems, not with myriad factors of human existence which can cause discrimination in a multitude of ways on racial, religious, or ethnic grounds. . . . We do not reach in this case the question whether a showing that school segregation is a consequence of other types of state action, without any discriminatory action by the school authorities, is a constitutional violation requiring remedial action by a school desegregation decree. This case does not present that question and we therefore do not decide it.

Our objective in dealing with the issues presented by these cases is to see that school authorities exclude no pupil of a racial minority from any school, directly or indirectly, on account of race; it does not and cannot embrace all the problems of racial prejudice, even when those problems contribute to disproportionate racial concentrations in some schools.

In this case it is urged that the district court has imposed a racial balance requirement of 71 percent to 29 percent on individual schools. The fact that no such objective was actually achieved—and would appear to be impossible—tends to blunt that claim, yet in the opinion and order of the district court of December 1, 1969, we find that court directing

> that efforts should be made to reach a 71 : 29 ratio in the various schools so that there will be no basis for contending that one school is racially different from the others . . . . [t]hat no school [should] be operated with an all-black or predominantly black student body, [and] [t]hat pupils of all grades [should] be assigned in such a way that as nearly as practicable the various schools at various grade levels have about the same proportion of black and white students.

The district judge went on to acknowledge that variation "from that norm may be unavoidable." This contains intimations that the "norm" is a fixed mathematical racial balance reflecting the pupil constituency of the system. If we were to read the holding of the district court to require, as a matter of substantive constitutional right, any particular degree of racial balance or mixing, that approach would be disapproved and we would be obliged to reverse. The constitutional command to desegregate schools does not mean that every school in every community must always reflect the racial composition of the school system as a whole.

As the voluminous record in this case shows, the predicate for the district court's use of the 71 percent to 29 percent ratio was twofold: first, its express finding, approved by the court of appeals and not challenged here, that a dual school system had been maintained by the school authorities at least until 1969; second, its finding, also approved by the court of appeals, that the school board had totally defaulted in its acknowledged duty to come forward with an acceptable plan of its own . . . .

We see therefore that the use made of mathematical ratios was no more than a starting point in the process of shaping a remedy, rather than an inflexible requirement. From that starting point the district court proceeded to frame a decree that was within its discretionary powers, as an equitable remedy for the particular circumstances. As we said in *Green,* a school authority's remedial plan or a district court's remedial decree is to be judged by its effectiveness. Awareness of the racial composition of the whole school system is likely to be a useful starting point in shaping a remedy to correct past constitutional violations. In sum, the very limited use made of mathematical ratios was within the equitable remedial discretion of the district court.

(2) One-Race Schools

The record in this case reveals the familiar phenomenon that in metropolitan areas minority groups are often found concentrated in one part of the city. In some circumstances certain schools may remain all or largely of one race until new schools can be provided or neighborhood patterns change. Schools all or predominantly of one race in a district of mixed population will require close scrutiny to determine that school assignments are not part of state-enforced segregation.

In light of the above, it should be clear that the existence of some small number of one-race, or virtually one-race, schools within a district is not in and of itself the mark of a system that still practices segregation by law. The district judge or school authorities should make every effort to achieve the greatest possible degree of actual desegregation and will thus necessarily be concerned with the elimination of one-race schools. No *per se* rule can adequately embrace all the difficulties of reconciling the competing interests involved; but in a system with a history of segregation the need for remedial criteria of sufficient specificity to assure a school authority's compliance with its constitutional duty warrants a presumption against schools that are substantially disproportionate in their racial composition. Where the school authority's proposed plan for conversion from a dual to a unitary system contemplates the continued existence of some schools that are all or predominately of one race, they have the burden of showing that such school assignments are genuinely nondiscriminatory. The court should scrutinize such schools, and the burden upon the school authorities will be to satisfy the court that their racial composition is not the result of present or past discriminatory action on their part. . . .

(3) Remedial Altering of Attendance Zones

The maps submitted in these cases graphically demonstrate that one of the principal tools employed by school planners and by courts to break up the dual school system has been a frank—and sometimes drastic—gerrymandering of school districts and attendance zones. An additional step was pairing, "clustering," or "grouping" of schools with attendance assignments made deliberately to accomplish the transfer of Negro students out of formerly segregated Negro schools and transfer of white students to formerly all-Negro schools. More often than not, these zones are neither compact nor contiguous; indeed they may be on opposite ends of the city. As an interim corrective measure, this cannot be said to be beyond the broad remedial powers of a court.

Absent a constitutional violation there would be no basis for judicially ordering assignment of students on a racial basis. All things being equal, with no history of discrimination, it might well be desirable to assign pupils to schools nearest their homes. But all things are not equal in a system that has been deliberately constructed and maintained to enforce racial segregation. The remedy for such segregation may be administratively awkward, inconvenient, and even bizarre in some situations and may impose burdens on some; but all awkwardness and inconvenience cannot be avoided in the interim period when remedial adjustments are being made to eliminate the dual school systems.

No fixed or even substantially fixed guidelines can be established as to how far a court can go, but it must be recognized that there are limits. The objective is to dismantle the dual school system. "Racially neutral" assignment plans proposed by school authorities to a district court may be inadequate; such plans may fail to counteract the continuing effects of past school segregation resulting from discriminatory location of school sites or distortion of school size in order to achieve or maintain an artificial racial separation. When school authorities present a district court with a "loaded game board," affirmative action in the form of remedial altering of attendance zones is proper to achieve truly nondiscriminatory assignments. In short, an assignment plan is not acceptable simply because it appears to be neutral.

In this area, we must of necessity rely to a large extent, as this court has for more than sixteen years, on the informed judgment of the district courts in the first instance and on courts of appeals.

We hold that the pairing and grouping of noncontiguous school zones is a permissible tool and such action is to be considered in light of the objectives sought. . . .

(4) Transportation of Students

The scope of permissible transportation of students as an implement of a remedial decree has never been defined by this court and by the very nature of the problem it cannot be defined with precision. No rigid guidelines as to student transportation can be given for application to the infinite variety of problems presented in thousands of situations. Bus transportation has been an integral part of the public education system for years, and was perhaps the single most important factor in the transition from the one-room schoolhouse to the consolidated school. Eighteen million of the nation's public school children, approximately 39 percent were transported to their schools by bus in 1969-70 in all parts of the country.

The importance of bus transportation as a normal and accepted tool of educational policy is readily discernible in this and the companion case *Davis, supra.* The Charlotte school authorities did not purport to assign students on the basis of geographically drawn zones until 1965 and then they allowed almost unlimited transfer privileges. The district court's conclusion that assignment of children to the school nearest their home serving their grade would not produce an effective dismantling of the dual system is supported by the record.

Thus the remedial techniques used in the district court's order were within that court's power to provide equitable relief; implementation of the decree is well within the capacity of the school authority.

The decree provided that the buses used to implement the plan would operate on direct routes. Students would be picked up at schools near their homes and transported to the schools they were to attend. The trips for elementary school pupils average about seven miles and the district court found that they would take "not over thirty-five minutes at the most." This system compares favorably with the transportation plan previously operated in Charlotte under which each day 23,600 students on all grade levels were transported an average of fifteen miles one way for an average trip requiring over an hour. In these circumstances, we find no basis for holding that the local school authorities may not be required to employ bus transportation as one tool of school desegregation. Desegregation plans cannot be limited to the walk-in school.

An objection to transportation of students may have validity when the time or distance of travel is so great as to either risk the health of the children or significantly impinge on the educational process. District courts must weigh the soundness of any transportation plan in light of what is said in subdivisions (1), (2), and (3) above. It hardly needs stating that the limits on time of travel will vary with many factors, but probably with none more than the age of the students. The reconciliation of competing values in a desegregation case is, of course, a difficult task with many sensitive facets but fundamentally no more so than remedial measures courts of equity have traditionally employed.

VI

The court of appeals, searching for a term to define the equitable remedial power of the district courts, used the term "reasonableness." In *Green, supra*, this court used the term "feasible" and by implication, "workable," "effective," and "realistic" in the mandate to develop "a plan that promises realistically to work, and . . . to work *now*." On the facts of this case, we are unable to conclude that the order of the district court is not reasonable, feasible and workable. However, in seeking to define the scope of remedial power or the limits on remedial power of courts in an area as sensitive as we deal with here, words are poor instruments to convey the sense of basic fairness inherent in equity. Substance, not semantics, must govern, and we have sought to suggest the nature of limitations without frustrating the appropriate scope of equity.

At some point, these school authorities and others like them should have achieved full compliance with this court's decision in *Brown 1*. The systems would then be "unitary" in the sense required by our decisions in *Green* and *Alexander*.

It does not follow that the communities served by such systems will remain demographically stable, for in a growing, mobile society, few will do so. Neither school authorities nor district courts are constitutionally required to make year-by-year adjustments of the racial composition of student bodies once the affirmative duty to desegregate has been accomplished and racial discrimination through official action is eliminated from the system. This does not mean that federal courts are without power to deal with future problems; but in the absence of a showing that either the school authorities or some other agency of the state has deliberately attempted to fix or alter demographic patterns to affect the racial composition of the schools, further intervention by a district court should not be necessary.

For the reasons herein set forth, the judgment of the court of appeals is affirmed as to those parts in which it affirmed the judgment of the district court. The order of the district court, dated August 7, 1970, is also affirmed. It is so ordered.

Judgment of court of appeals affirmed in part; order of district court affirmed.

Notes and Questions

1. *Swann* and the Discretion of District Courts

While *Swann* alone might be read as merely upholding the broad discretionary powers of an equity court, the Supreme Court's decision in a companion case (*Davis v Board of School Comm'rs* 402 US 33 (1971)) casts doubt on this interpretation. Chief Justice Burger, who wrote the opinion on behalf of a unanimous court, saw the fundamental issue in *Davis* as the court of appeals' failure to consider the possible use of busing and split zoning in its desegregation order for Mobile. Apparently, that court had "felt constrained to treat the eastern part of metropolitan Mobile in isolation from the rest of the school system." 402 US at 38. Citing *Swann*, Burger pointed out that

> "neighborhood school zoning," whether based strictly on home-to-school distance or on "unified geographic zones," is not the only constitutionally permissible remedy; nor is it per se adequate to meet the remedial responsibilities of local boards. Having once found a violation, the district judge or school authorities should make every effort to achieve the greatest possible degree of actual desegregation, taking into account the practicalities of the situation. A district court may and should consider the use of all available techniques including restructuring of attendance zones and both contiguous and noncontiguous attendance zones. . . . The measure of any desegregation plan is its effectiveness. (402 US at 37.)

Is Chief Justice Burger's reference to the "effectiveness" standard consistent with his assertion that busing is a remedy that the lower courts have the discretionary power to order? Consider these remarks by Professor Powe:

> The . . . language [of *Davis*] is ambiguous. What is meant by "inadequate consideration" of busing and split zoning? Who gave the "inadequate consideration"? The court observed that a "district court may and should consider the use of all available techniques" of desegregation. Yet that was just what Judge Thomas [the district court judge] did. . . . His order . . . was explicit; since the Supreme Court had not mandated racial balance, he was not going to order busing across [an interstate highway]. . . .
>
> The Supreme Court in effect underscored the following language first used in the *Green* trilogy: "The measure of any desegregation plan is its

effectiveness." District judges may well have large discretion in choosing a remedy, as *Swann* suggests, but it is a one-way discretion and must be used to facilitate integration. . . . Judge Thomas erred not by failing to consider busing, but by rejecting it. . . ." (Powe, "The Road to Swann: Mobile County Crawls to the Bus," 51 *Tex L Rev* 505, 523-25 (1973).)

If Professor Powe is correct, how do you explain the ambiguity of *Swann*? Why did the court not say what it intended?

2. *Swann* and Racial Quotas

While *Swann* does not approve the use of racial quotas, it recognizes the appropriateness of such quotas as a starting point for judicial analysis. But what weight should this "starting point" be given? If the measure of a desegregation plan is its effectiveness, may quotas be used to calculate that effectiveness? Although the opinion in *Swann* disavows the requirement of racial balance, do the results in *Swann* and *Davis* suggest that plans that substantially vary from such balance are ineffective and hence constitutionally inadequate?

Does the following analysis accurately reflect the *Swann-Davis* treatment of the racial quota issue?

the court approved the use of quotas not as rigid guidelines, but only as flexible starting points. . . . District judges are thus left with only polar guidelines regarding the racial composition of schools. If schools are one-race, that may require correction; yet if school population throughout the district is forced to mirror overall racial ratios, that may well be an abuse of discretion. Anything in between may be permissible. ("The Supreme Court, 1970 Term," 85 *Harv L Rev* 3, 78 (1971).)

3. *Swann* and One-Race Schools

While not requiring the elimination of all one-race schools, the *Swann* opinion places on the school board the burden of demonstrating that they are "genuinely nondiscriminatory." *Davis* suggests that the burden is a heavy one. Presumably, the feasibility of desegregating those schools is also an appropriate factor for the district court to consider. Under what circumstances would one-race schools be permissible?

4. *Swann* and the Remedial Theory

Swann orders extensive busing to integrate the public schools in Charlotte-Mecklenburg, a largely urban area with substantial neighborhood segregation. If, as the opinion suggests, this step was taken to remedy past de jure segregation and not to achieve racial balance per se, then some nexus between past discrimination and the present neighborhood segregation in the school must be demonstrated. In this regard, consider these remarks by Professor Yudof:

The difficulty with the remedial interpretation of *Swann* is that it is theoretically plausible but empirically speculative. There is no evidence that segregated schools materially influenced racial isolation by neighborhood in southern communities. Where the whole structure of society reflects the inferior status assigned to blacks, it is difficult to say that any particular practice or institution caused segregated neighborhoods. Additionally, segregated housing is far more prevalent in the North where officially sanc-tioned school segregation was relatively rare. Only when the burden of persuasion is placed upon school boards that previously discriminated against blacks can it be presumed that there is some connection between that past discrimination and segregation resulting from neighborhood assign-ment plans. This "is a frail basis on which to construct a remedial duty of such mammoth proportions." [Goodman, "De Facto Segregation: A Consti-tutional and Empirical Analysis," 60 *Calif L Rev* 275, 295 (1972).] (Yudof, "Equal Educational Opportunity and the Courts," 51 *Tex L Rev* 411 (1973).)

Do these remarks suggest that the court in *Swann* was moving toward an integra-tionist position? Is this consistent with the court's references to the remedial powers of lower courts to fashion decrees in segregation cases? With its assertion that "we do not reach in this case the question whether a showing that school segregation is a consequence of other types of state action, without any discrimi-natory action by the school authorities, is a constitutional violation requiring remedial action by a school desegregation decree." Consider these remarks by Professor Fiss:

THE CHARLOTTE-MECKLENBURG CASE: ITS SIGNIFICANCE
FOR NORTHERN SCHOOL DESEGREGATION
Owen Fiss
38 U Chi L Rev 697 (1971)

[T]hese causal connections between past discrimination and present segregation are no more than theoretical possibilities and obviously involve significant elements of conjecture. The court's response [in *Swann*] was to announce an evidentiary presumption that in effect resolves all the uncertainties against the school board. The court quite consciously avoided holding that segregated student attendance patterns are, in themselves, a denial of equal protection, and instead emphasized the role that past discriminatory conduct might have played in causing those patterns. . . . But the court also said that it was prepared to presume an imper-missible cause from the mere existence of segregation. . . . Concededly, the school board has the opportunity to show that the consequence—segregated schools—is not caused by its discriminatory action and that it is therefore not responsible for the segregation. In that sense the distinction between cause and consequence is preserved. But the distinction is likely to become blurred because the burden cast on the board is a heavy one. The burden cannot be discharged simply by showing that the school segregation is produced, given the segregated residential patterns, by assigning students on the basis of a criterion other than race, such as geographic proximity. The school board will also have to show that its past discriminatory conduct—involving racial designation of schools, site selection, and determination of school size—is not a link in the causal chain producing the segregation. This will be very difficult to do, and the difficulty of overcoming a presumption will tend to accentuate the fact that gives rise to it, namely, the segregated patterns, and this will be reflected in the board's assignment policies. Greater attention will be paid to the segregated patterns. . . .

These . . . doctrinal advances of *Charlotte-Mecklenburg* occurred in response to a situation, not readily found in the North, in which a school board had maintained a "dual school system" in the recent past. . . . In time, however, the legacy of past discrimination may become so attenuated that it will be unrealistic to presume the existence of any causal connection between it and the present school segregation.

Nevertheless, it should be emphasized that this concern with recent past discrimination does not confine *Charlotte-Mecklenburg* to the South. Until a few years ago, southern school districts openly maintained dual school systems, and therefore the existence of past discriminatory practices can be established by admission. In northern systems, there is no such admission. But that, of course, does not mean that the past discriminatory practices of the *Charlotte-Mecklenburg* type did not occur. It only means that they are most difficult, though not impossible to prove. In my judgment, a very close, hard look at the construction policies of northern school systems would reveal numerous instances in which school boards in the recent past have chosen sites and determined capacity with an eye toward serving racially homogeneous areas—often called "neighborhoods. . . ."

[O]ne cannot simply say that *Charlotte-Mecklenburg* "outlaws" the school segregation of the North. Because of its focus on past discrimination, the case does not lend itself in a blanket judgment about the North, as it does with respect to the South. The net effect of *Charlotte-Mecklenburg* is to move school desegregation doctrine further along the continuum toward a result oriented approach. But the progression is not complete. Additional steps are required. It seems to me, however, that over time this move will probably be made and that, in retrospect, *Charlotte-Mecklenburg* will then be viewed, like *Green*, as a way station to the adoption of a general approach to school segregation which, by focusing on the segregated patterns themselves, is more responsive to the school segregation of the North.

This forecast is based in part on my view that the court will want to avoid the appearance of picking on the South. This appearance is derived from the fact that segregated patterns of student attendance are no less severe in northern cities than in southern ones. Under *Charlotte-Mecklenburg,* southern school systems are obliged to eliminate those patterns and to achieve the greatest possible degree of integration. But there is no similar blanket judgment about those patterns in the North . . . no national institution can afford to be unresponsive to the popular pressures likely to be engendered by an appearance of differential treatment of certain regions of the country. . . .

The forecast is based also on my view that predominant concern of the court in *Charlotte-Mecklenburg* is in fact the segregated pattern of student attendance, rather than the causal role played by past discriminatory practices . . . the court made no serious attempt either to determine or even to speculate on the degree to which it contributes to present segregation. Nor did the court attempt to tailor the remedial order to the correction of that portion of the segregation that might reasonably be attributable to past discrimination. The court moved from (a) the undisputed existence of past discrimination to (b) the possibility or *likelihood* that the past discrimination played some *causal* role in producing segregated patterns to (c) an order requiring the complete elimination of those patterns. The existence of past discrimination was thus used as a "trigger"—and not for a pistol, but for a cannon. Such a role cannot be defended unless the primary concern of the court is the segregated patterns themselves, rather than the causal relation of past discrimination to them. The attention paid to past discrimination can be viewed as an attempt by the court to preserve the continuity with *Brown* and to add a moral quality to its decision.

Does Professor Fiss attribute too little significance to the fact that the defendants in *Swann* had practiced de jure segregation? Does Fiss suggest that the court's reference to school construction and site location policies expands the definition of de jure segregation? Does the fact that school location policies reinforce existing segregation prove that they were motivated by that concern? Is there any suggestion in *Swann* that the court intended to attack all forms of segregation in the public schools, North and South?

5. Alternative Theories

If the integration remedies adopted in *Green* and *Swann* are difficult to justify in terms of the prohibition on racial classification embodied in *Brown*, how might those decisions be explained? There are essentially two approaches. First, integration may be justified, as a matter of policy if not of constitutional law, on the ground that it is educationally, psychologically, or socially desirable. This sociological interpretation of the desegregation decisions rests on empirical assumptions about the relationship between integration and desirable social outcomes. Second, integration may be premised, morally if not legally, on the ethical assertion that a just society is an integrated society. This view finds its roots in liberal intellectual traditions and in historical experience and is not subject, at least in the short run, to rigorous scientific proof.

a. The Sociological Approach. In *Brown v Board of Educ* 357 US 483 (1954), the court referred to segregation as generating "a feeling of inferiority [among blacks] as to their status in the community that may affect their hearts and minds in a way unlikely ever to be undone." And it quoted with favor the finding of the lower court that "segregation with the sanction of law . . . has a tendency to [retard] the educational and mental development of Negro children. . . ." 357 US at 494. And in the now-famous footnote 11, the court cited what it called modern authority on the effects of segregation on black children. These references have given support to a sociological interpretation of the desegregation cases.

Professor Fiss is perhaps the most eloquent spokesman for this position. See "Racial Imbalance in the Public Schools: The Constitutional Concepts," 78 *Harv L Rev* 564, 604-7 (1965). Fiss argues that the constitutional case against racially imbalanced schools, whether a result of de jure or de facto segregation, must rest on a claim that the educational opportunities afforded black children forced to attend such schools are unequal to those afforded children attending other public schools. Racially imbalanced schools harm black children in a number of ways: there is "a lessening of motivation, alienation of the child from the educational institution, distortion of personal relationships, and various forms of antisocial behavior." 78 *Harv L Rev* at 569. Fiss also asserts that segregated schools are academically inferior, concluding that "this academic inadequacy seriously impairs the Negro's ability to compete in society and deprives society of an appreciable amount of talent." Finally, he argues that segregation may perpetuate social barriers between the races. 78 *Harv L Rev* at 570.

Professor Fiss's arguments necessarily rely on an empirical demonstration that segregation is harmful and that integration cures those harms. In fact, social scientists have sharply debated these propositions.

The *Equal Educational Opportunities Survey* (popularly known as the Coleman Report) indicated that the percentage of white students in a school had only a modest impact on school achievement; the social background of the child and his fellow students proved far more significant. An evaluation of seven northern busing programs (METCO, A Better Chance, in Boston; White Plains, NY; Ann Arbor, Mich; Riverside, Cal; and Hartford, Conn) whose conclusions are set forth below, confirms, and amplifies the Coleman Report findings.

"THE EVIDENCE ON BUSING"
D. Armor
28 The Public Interest 90-126 (Summer 1972)

The Findings: Achievement

None of the studies were able to demonstrate conclusively that integration has had an effect on academic achievement as measured by standardized tests. Given the results of the Coleman study and other evaluations of remedial programs (e.g., Head Start), many experts may not be surprised at this finding. To date there is no published report of *any* strictly educational reform which has been proven substantially to affect academic achievement; school integration programs are no exception.

The changes in reading achievement for elementary and secondary students in the METCO program . . . show . . . grade-equivalent gains for bused third and fourth graders after one year somewhat greater than those for the [nonbused] control group (.4 to .3), but this is not a statistically significant difference. For grades five and six the situation is reversed; the control group outgained the bused group (.7 and .5), but again the difference is not significant. We can see that the control group is somewhat higher initially for both grade levels, but this difference, too, is not significant.

In the case of high school students, the bused group scores somewhat higher than the control groups initially (but not significantly so). Nonetheless, the gain scores present no particular pattern. While the bused junior high students increased their grade-equivalent score from 7.5 to 7.7, the control group improved from 7.4 to 7.5; the bused gain is not significantly different from that for the control group. For senior high students the effect is reversed; the control students gain more than the bused students (nine percentile points compared to four points), but again the gains are not statistically significant for either group.

The results for reading achievement are substantially repeated in a test of arithmetic skills; the bused students showed no significant gains in arithmetic skills compared to the control group, and there were no particular patterns in evidence.

The White Plains, Ann Arbor, and Riverside studies also found no significant changes in achievement level for bused students in the elementary grades when comparisons were made with control groups. . . .

Studies in the fifth program, Project Concern, showed mixed results. A study of the Hartford students compared bused black students who received special supportive assistance with nonbused inner-city black students. . . .

The bused students showed significant IQ gains only in grades two and three; the gains in kindergarten and grades one, four, and five were either insignificant or, in two cases, favored the control group. In a study of New Haven students, second- and third-grade students were randomly assigned to bused and nonbused conditions and were given reading, language, and arithmetic tests in October 1967 (when the busing began) and again in April 1968.

Of the six comparisons possible (three tests and two grades), only two showed significant differences favoring the bused students.

While none of these studies are flawless, their consistency is striking. Moreover, their results are not so different from the results of the massive cross-sectional studies. An extensive reanalysis of the Coleman data showed that the *best* that integration could do would be to move the average black group from the second percentile to the seventh percentile (on the *white* scale, where the average white group is at the fiftieth percentile). But the social class differences of integrated black students in the Coleman study could easily explain a good deal of even this small gain. Other investigators, after examining a number of studies, have come to similar conclusions.

While there are no important gains for the METCO group in standardized test scores, there were some important differences in school grades. Even though the bused secondary school students have somewhat higher test scores than the control group, the bused group was about half a grade point *behind* the control group in 1969, and the bused students dropped even further behind by 1970. The average control student is able to maintain a grade average at above a B− level in the central city, while the average bused student in the suburbs is just above a C average. . . . The average white student *academic* grade average (i.e., excluding nonacademic courses—an exclusion not made for the black students) [is] about 2.45, or between a B− and C+ average.

Again, if we take into account the Coleman findings, we should not be too surprised. Since black students of the same age are, on average, behind white students in all parts of the country with respect to academic achievement, we should expect their grades to fall when they are taken from the competition in an all-black school to the competition in a predominantly white school. In addition, the bused students may not be adequately prepared for this competition, at least in terms of the higher standards that may be applied in the suburban schools.

Aspiration and Self-concept

In the METCO study we found that there were no increases in educational or occupational aspiration levels for bused students; . . . on the contrary, there was a significant decline for the bused students, from 74 percent wanting a college degree in 1968 to 60 percent by May 1970. . . .

Since the other cities in our review included only elementary students, they do not provide data on regular educational or occupational aspirations. But two of the studies did examine a concept closely related to aspirations—"motivation for achievement." The findings of the Ann Arbor and Riverside studies corroborate the pattern of high aspirations for black children in both the pre- and postintegration periods. In addition, the Ann Arbor researchers concluded that the overly high aspiration of black boys may have been lowered by the integration experience. The Riverside study, on the other hand, concluded that there were no significant changes in achievement motivation.

In the METCO study we also found some important differences with respect to academic self-concept. . . . The students were asked to rate how bright they were in comparison to their classmates. While there were some changes in both the bused and control groups, the important differences are the gaps between the bused students and controls at each time period. The smallest difference is 15 percentage points in 1970 (11 points for the full cross-section), with the control students having the higher academic self-concept. Again, this finding makes sense if we recall that the academic performance of the bused students falls considerably when they move from the black community to the white suburbs. In rating their intellectual ability, the bused students may simply be reflecting the harder competition in suburban schools. . . .

Race Relations

One of the central sociological hypotheses in the integration policy model is that integration should reduce racial stereotypes, increase tolerance, and generally improve race relations. Needless to say, we were quite surprised when our data failed to verify this axiom. Our surprise was increased substantially when we discovered that, in fact, the converse appears to be true. The data suggest that, under the circumstances obtaining in these studies, integration heightens racial identity and consciousness, enhances ideologies that promote racial segregation, and reduces opportunities for actual contact between the races.

There are several indicators from the METCO study that point to these conclusions. The question which speaks most directly to the 50 percent racial balance standard suggested by the Civil Rights Commission asked: "If you could be in any school you wanted, how many students would be white?" . . . While both the control and the bused students started out fairly close together in 1968 (47 percent and 51 percent, respectively), two school years later the bused students were 15 percentage points *more* in favor of attending *nonwhite* schools than the controls (81 percent compared to 66 percent), although the differential change is not statistically significant. The changes for the controls (both the panel and the full cross-sections) indicate that the black community as a whole may be changing its attitudes toward school integration, but the bused students appear to be changing at a more rapid rate. Ironically, just as white America has finally accepted the idea of school integration.

The changes do not appear to be in ideology alone. From 1969 to 1970 the bused students reported less friendliness from whites, more free time spent with members of their own race, more incidents of prejudice, and less frequent dating with white students . . . . In other words, the longer the contact with whites, the fewer the kinds of interracial experiences that might lead to a general improvement in racial tolerance.

To what extent might these changes be a result of negative experiences with white students in the schools? We do not doubt that there has been considerable hostility shown by certain groups of white students. Nonetheless, although the evidence is not complete, what we have indicates that the white students themselves were negatively affected by the contact. Support for the busing program was generally high among white sophomores in the eight high schools studied, especially among middle-class students in the college preparatory tracks . . . . For example, 46 percent of all students were "very favorable" to METCO (only 11 percent were "not favorable"); 73 percent felt METCO should be continued; and 52 percent agreed that there should be more METCO students (20 percent disagreed and 27 percent were not sure). But those students who had direct classroom contact with bused black students showed *less* support for the busing program than those without direct contact. In fact, the kind of students who were generally the most supportive—the middle-class, high-achieving students— showed the largest decline in support as a result of contact with bused black students. This finding is based on cross-sectional data and does not indicate a change over time, but it is suggestive of the possibility that a general polarization has occurred for both racial groups. . . .

The Riverside data support the conclusion that integration heightens racial identity and solidarity. Data from a test in which children rate pictures of faces portraying various ethnic and racial groups showed that fewer cross-racial choices were made after integration than before integration. For example, one rating task required that the children choose the face that they would "most like for a friend." Both black and white children tended to choose their own race to a greater extent after one year of integration than before integration. The Riverside study also concluded that these effects were stronger with increasing age; that is, the cross-racial choices declined more in the later grades than in the earlier grades.

To avoid any misinterpretation of these findings, we should caution that the measures discussed here do not necessarily indicate increased *overt* racial hostility or conflict. This may occur to some extent in many busing programs, but our impression based on the METCO program is that overt racial incidents initiated by black or white students are infrequent. The polarization that we are describing, and that our instruments assess, is characterized by ideological solidarity and behavioral withdrawal. Our inferences pertain to a lack of racial togetherness rather than to explicit racial confrontations or violence. While it is conceivable that a connection may exist between these ideological shifts and open racial conflicts, such a connection is not established by the studies reviewed.

There are two other qualifications we must place on the interpretation of these data. First, as of 1970 the *majority* of the bused METCO students still supported general integration ideology. Only 40 percent of the METCO students would ideally prefer schools with a majority of black students (compared to 28 percent of the controls); 60 percent of METCO students believe that "once you really get to know a white person, they can be as good a friend as anyone else" (compared to 78 percent of the controls); and 58 percent of METCO students do not agree that "most black people should live and work in black areas, and most whites should live and work in white areas" (compared to 71 percent of the control students).

The main point we are making is that the integration policy model predicts that integration should cause these sentiments to *increase,* while the evidence shows they actually *decrease,* leaving the bused students *more opposed* to integration than the nonbused students. Only further research can determine whether this trend will continue until the majority of bused students shifts to a general anti-integration ideology.

Second, group averages tend to obscure important differences between individual students. While we do not deny the existence of racial tension and conflict for some students, other students and families (both black and white) have had very meaningful relationships with one another, relationships made possible only through the busing program. It is very difficult, indeed, to weigh objectively the balance of benefit and harm for the group as a whole. The main point to be made is that a change in a group average does not necessarily reflect a change in every individual group member.

Long-term Educational Effects

In view of the fact that most of the short-term measures do not conclusively demonstrate positive effects of busing in the area of achievement, aspirations, self-concept, and race relations, it becomes even more important to consider possible longer term changes that may relate to eventual socioeconomic parity between blacks and whites. Since no busing program has been in operation for more than seven years or so, this area, obviously, has not been studied extensively. There are, however, some preliminary findings on long-term educational effects. Specifically, two studies have investigated the effects of integration on college attendance, and some tentative conclusions have emerged.

Seniors from the 1970 graduating class in the METCO program, as well as the seniors in the 1970 control group, formed samples for a follow-up telephone interview in the spring of 1972. Approximately two-thirds of both groups were contacted, resulting in college data for thirty-two bused students and sixteen control group students. The results of the follow-up are striking. The bused students were very much more likely to start college than the control group (84 percent compared to 56 percent), but by the end of the second year the bused students resembled the control group (59 percent compared to 56 percent). In other words, the METCO program seems to have had a dramatic effect upon the impetus for college, and many more of the bused students actually started some form of higher education. But the bused drop-out rate was also substantially higher, so that towards the end of the sophomore year the bused students were not much more likely to be enrolled full-time in college than the control group.

In spite of this higher drop-out rate, the bused students were still enrolled in what are generally considered higher quality institutions. That is, 56 percent of the bused students were in regular four-year colleges, compared to 38 percent for the control group. An even greater difference was found for those enrolled in full universities (which include a graduate school). The figures are 47 percent and 12 percent for bused and control students, respectively. . . .

  . . . .

. . . It is possible that there are psychological consequences of [the] increased competition [in integrated schools] that may be harmful to black children. Being moved from an environment where they are above average to one in which they are average or below may be frustrating and discouraging. It might be one of the reasons why the bused black students have become less supportive of the program and more supportive of black separatism.

We tested this latter possibility by examining the relationship between support for the Black Panthers and academic grades in our 1970 sample from METCO .... Consistent with our findings, the bused students are more favorable to the Panthers than the control group. But among the bused students we find that the METCO group which has college aspirations but which has a C average or below stands out clearly as more pro-Panther than the other groups. In other words, the increased militancy and anti-integration sentiments among the bused students may arise partly from the fact that their aspirations remain at a very high level even though their performance declines to the point where they may question their ability to compete with whites at the college level. The fact that this group is proportionally a large one (about 25 percent of the total bused group compared to 13 percent for the analogous control group) may be an indication of a potentially serious problem.

The integration policy model predicted that integration should raise black aspirations. Again, our studies reveal no evidence for such an effect. Unlike poor achievement, however, low aspirations do not appear to be much of a problem. The black students in our busing program seem to have aspirations as high as or higher than white students. If anything, given their academic records in high school, these aspirations may be unrealistic for some students. The emphasis on equality of educational opportunity may be pushing into college many black students whose interests and abilities do not warrant it. The fact that only half of the 1970 METCO seniors are still enrolled in four-year colleges (after over 80 percent had started) may attest to this possibility. . . .

. . . .

Why has the integration policy model failed to be supported by the evidence on four out of five accounts? . . . we believe that there may be . . . reasons as well having to do with (1) inadequate research designs, (2) induced versus "natural" factors, and (3) changing conditions in the black cultural climate.

Most of the methodological procedures which have been used to develop various components of the integration policy model are not adequate. The single most important limitation is that they have been cross-sectional designs. That is, the studies have measured aspects of achievement or race relations at a single point in time, with causal inferences being drawn from comparisons of integrated groups with segregated groups. Such inferences are risky at best, since the cross-sectional design cannot control for self-selection factors. For example, the Coleman study showed that integrated black students had slightly higher achievement than segregated students, but it is more than likely that families of higher achieving students move to integrated neighborhoods in the first place (for reasons of social class or other issues involving opportunity). . . .

The second reason for our findings in the race relations realm may have to do with the relatively contrived nature of current school integration programs. In all of the programs reviewed, the integration has been induced by the actions of state or local agencies: it has not occurred in a more natural way through individual voluntary actions. The use of busing, the relatively instantaneous transition from an all-black to an all-white environment, the fact of being part of a readily identifiable group in a new and strange setting, may all combine to enhance racial solidarity and increase separatist tendencies for black students. (We might find a very different picture for black families that move into predominantly white neighborhoods and allow their children some time to adjust to the new environment.) On the other hand, this set of mechanisms would not explain why white student attitudes in the receiving schools also tended to become less favorable to black students, as shown in the Ann Arbor, Riverside, and METCO studies. Moreover, these mechanisms—if they are, in fact, operating—do not invalidate our evaluation of those current policies that focus precisely on induced school integration.

The final major reason why the integration policy model may fail is that the racial climate has changed drastically in the years since the Allport work and the Supreme Court decision [*Brown v Board of Educ* 347 US 483 (1954)]. The most noteworthy change, of course, has been in the attitudes of black people. Although the majority of blacks may still endorse the concept of integration, many younger black leaders deemphasize integration as a major goal. Black identity, black control, and black equality are seen as the real issues, and integration is regarded as important only insofar as it advances these primary goals. Some black leaders, albeit the more militant ones, feel that integration might actually defeat attainment of these goals by dispersing the more talented blacks throughout the white community and thereby diluting their power potential. Integration is also seen as having white paternalistic overtones and as the means whereby the white man allays his guilty conscience while ignoring reform on the really important issues. Given these sentiments, school integration programs are seen by blacks not as a fulfillment of the goal of joining white society, but only as a means of obtaining better educational opportunities, which would ultimately lead to a more competitive position in the occupational and economic market.

Integrated schools per se are not the real issue; if schools in the black community provided education of the same quality as those in white communities, blacks would not be so interested in busing programs. In fact, when we asked students in the METCO program this question, almost 75 percent said they would prefer to attend their own community school if it were as good as the suburban schools.

Not surprisingly, Professor Armor's research and conclusions were attacked by other social scientists. Consider this reply to Armor:

"BUSING: A REVIEW OF 'THE EVIDENCE'"
T. Pettigrew, E. Useem, C. Normand, and M. Smith
30 The Public Interest 88-114 (Winter 1973)

David Armor's "The Evidence on Busing," presented a distorted and incomplete review of this politically charged topic. We respect Armor's right to publish his views against "mandatory busing." But we challenge his claim that these views are supported by scientific evidence. A full discussion of our reading of the relevant research would be too lengthy and technical for the nonspecialist. We must limit ourselves here to outlining and discussing briefly our principal disagreements with Armor, which center on four major points.

First, his article begins by establishing unrealistically high standards by which to judge the success of school desegregation. "Busing," he claims, works only if it leads—in *one* school year—to increased achievement, aspirations, self-esteem, interracial tolerance, and life opportunities for black children. And "busing" must meet these standards in *all* types of interracial schools; no distinction is made between *merely desegregated* and *genuinely integrated* schools.

This "integration policy model," as it is labeled, is *not* what social scientists who specialize in race relations have been writing about over the past generation. Indeed, Armor's criteria must surely be among the most rigid ever employed for the evaluation of a change program in the history of public education in the United States.

Second, the article presents selected findings from selected studies as "*the* evidence on busing." The bias here is twofold. On the one hand, the few studies mentioned constitute an incomplete list and are selectively negative in results. Unmentioned are at least seven investigations—from busing programs throughout the nation—that meet the methodological criteria for inclusion and report *positive* achievement results for black students. These seven studies are widely known.

On the other hand, only cursory descriptions are provided of the few investigations that are reviewed. Mitigating circumstances surrounding black responses to desegregation are not discussed. For example, we are not told that educational services for the transported black pupils were actually *reduced* with the onset of desegregation in three of the cited cities. In addition, negative findings consistent with the paper's antibusing thesis are emphasized, while positive findings from these same cities are either obscured or simply ignored. Newer studies from three of the cited cities showing more positive results are not discussed.

Positive findings are also obscured by the utilization of an unduly severe standard. The achievement gains of black students in desegregated schools are often compared with white gains, rather than with the achievement of black students in black schools. But such a standard ignores the possibility that *both* racial groups can make more meaningful educational advances in interracial schools. Indeed, this possibility actually occurs in three of the cities mentioned by Armor. Yet he does not inform us of this apparent dual success of desegregation; instead, "busing" is simply rated a failure because the black children did not far outgain the improving white children.

Third, the paper's antibusing conclusions rest primarily on the findings from one short-term study conducted by Armor himself. This investigation focused on a voluntary busing program in metropolitan Boston called METCO. Yet this study is probably the weakest reported in the paper. Our reexamination of its data finds that it has extremely serious methodological problems.

Two major problems concern deficiencies of the control group. To test the effects of "busing" and school desegregation, a control group should obviously consist exclusively of children who neither are "bused" nor attend desegregated schools. But our check of this critical point reveals that this is not the case. Among the eighty-two control students used to test the achievement effects of METCO at all ten grade levels, we obtained records on fifty-five. Only twenty-one of these fifty-five actually attended segregated schools in the tested year of 1968-69. Many of the thirty-four (62 percent) desegregated children by necessity utilized buses and other forms of transportation to get to school.

Incredible as it sounds, then, Armor compared a group of children who were bused to desegregated schools with another group of children which included many who *also* were bused to desegregated schools. Not surprisingly, then, he found few differences between them. But this complete lack of adequate controls renders his METCO research of no scientific interest in the study of "busing" and school desegregation. Since this METCO investigation furnished the chief "evidence" against "busing," Armor's conclusions are severely challenged by this point alone.

Serious, too, is an enormous nonresponse rate in the second test administration, a problem alluded to by Armor only in a footnote. For the elementary students, only 51 percent of the eligible METCO students and 28 percent of the eligible "control" students took part in both of the achievement test sessions. The achievement results for junior and senior high students are also rendered virtually meaningless by the participation of only 44 percent of the eligible METCO students and 20 percent of the eligible "control" students. Compare these percentages to the survey standard of 70 to 80 percent, and one can appreciate the magnitude of the possible selection bias introduced into the METCO results by the widespread lack of student participation. Efforts to compensate for these high nonresponse rates through the use of cross-sectional samples that also suffer from extensive nonresponse are insufficient.

There are other problems in the METCO study. Some children were included who initially performed as well as the test scoring allowed and therefore could not possibly demonstrate "improvement"; in fact, these pupils comprise one-sixth of all the junior high pupils tested for achievement gains in reading. Moreover, the conditions for the third administration of the attitude tests were different for the METCO students and the "controls": The former took the tests at school and the latter took them at home with their parents as proctors. Even apart from the severe control group problems, then, the faulty research design makes any conclusion about differences in racial attitudes between the two groups hazardous.

The inadequate discussion of the METCO study in Armor's article makes it virtually impossible for even the discerning reader to evaluate it properly. We uncovered its many errors only from unpublished earlier materials and from reanalyzing the data ourselves. The METCO discussion is inadequate in other ways. Differential statistical standards are employed, with less rigorous standards applied to findings congruent with the article's antibusing thesis; attitude differences among METCO schools are not shown; and misleading claims of consistency with other research findings are made.

From this assortment of "evidence," Armor concludes authoritatively that "busing" fails on four out of five counts. It does not lead, he argues, to improved achievement, grades, aspirations, and racial attitudes for black children; yet, despite these failures, he admits that desegregated schools do seem somehow to lead more often to college enrollment for black students.

The picture is considerably more positive, as well as more complex, than Armor paints it. For example, when specified school conditions are attained, research has repeatedly indicated that desegregated schools improve the academic performance of black pupils. Other research has demonstrated that rigidly high and unrealistic aspirations actually deter learning; thus, a slight lowering of such aspirations by school desegregation can lead to better achievement and cannot be

regarded as a failure of "busing." Moreover, "militancy" and "black consciousness and solidarity" are not negative characteristics, as Armor's article asserts,
and their alleged development in desegregated schools could well be regarded as a
further success, not a failure, of "busing." Finally, the evidence that desegregated
education sharply expands the life opportunities of black children is more extensive than he has indicated.

Consequently, Armor's sweeping policy conclusion against "mandatory busing" is neither substantiated nor warranted. Not only does it rely upon impaired
and incomplete "evidence," but in a real sense his paper is not about "busing" at
all, much less "mandatory busing." Three of the cities discussed—among them
Boston, the subject of Armor's own research—had *voluntary*, not "mandatory
busing." "Busing" was never cited as an independent variable, and many of the
desegregation studies discussed involved some children who were not bused to
reach their interracial schools. Indeed, in Armor's own investigation of METCO,
some of the METCO children were not bused while many of the controls were.
Fourth, objections must be raised to the basic assumptions about racial change
that undergird the entire article. Public school desegregation is regarded as largely
a technical matter, a matter for social scientists more than for the courts. Emphasis is placed solely on the adaptive abilities of black children rather than on
their constitutional rights. Moreover, the whole national context of individual
and institutional racism is conveniently ignored, and interracial contact under any
conditions is assumed to be "integration."

Now we wish to pursue these basic points in more detail.

The use of white control groups is inadequate and often misleading. The
contention that black children will learn more in integrated than in segregated
schools is not tested when black data are compared with those of white control
groups. Moreover, the use of a desegregated white control group ignores the
possibility that *both* whites and blacks could benefit significantly from integration without "the racial gap" in achievement closing at all. As a matter of fact,
precisely this possibility occurs in Riverside, Berkeley, and Ann Arbor—though
this is not mentioned by Armor and is allowed to mask black gains in desegregated schools. . . .

This point represents a crucial difference between our perspective and Armor's. We believe it to be unrealistic to expect any type of educational innovation to close most of the racial differential in achievement while gross racial
disparities, especially economic ones, remain in American society. Furthermore,
we know of no social scientists who ever claimed school desegregation alone
could close most of the differential. We are pleased to note the many instances
where effective desegregation has apparently benefited the achievement of both
black and white children, and where over a period of years it appears to close
approximately a fourth of the differential.

But to insist that "mandatory busing" must close most of the achievement
differential by itself in a short time or be abolished is, to understate the case, an
extreme position. Indeed, Armor himself has wavered on this point. In *The
Public Interest* he wrote: "The ideal control group, of course, would consist of
black students who are identical to the integrated students in every way except
for the integrated experience" . . . , though white students in the same school
constituted an "adequate" control. Later, however, while testifying in support of

antibusing legislation before the Senate Subcommittee on Education, he used white pupils as the critical comparison. This stern criterion leads to some strange conclusions. A desegregation program that dramatically raises the achievement levels of both racial groups is judged a failure when it does not close most of the racial disparity, but another desegregation program that entirely closes the gap by raising the blacks' scores and *lowering* the whites' scores would have to be deemed a success!

III

The achievement effects of "busing" are more complex and positive than reported. Armor concludes that "busing" fails on four of the five standards he alone sets for it. One of these alleged failures concerns the academic achievement of black students. From the selected findings of selected studies, Armor concludes that desegregation research throughout the nation has typically found no statistically significant enhancement of black achievement. Further, he claims that the METCO results support this conclusion. But we have noted how this conclusion was reached through the omission of at least seven busing investigations with positive black achievement results and through serious weaknesses in the METCO research.

This is not the place for a complete review of the relevant research literature. But our evaluation of the available evidence points to a more encouraging, if more tentative and complex set of conclusions. First, the academic achievement of both white and black children is not lowered by the types of racial desegregation so far studied. Second, the achievement of white and especially of black children in desegregated schools is generally higher when some of the following critical conditions are met: equal racial access to the school's resources; *classroom*—not just school—desegregation; . . . the initiation of desegregation in the early grades; interracial staffs; substantial rather than token student desegregation; the maintenance of or increase in school services and remedial training; and the avoidance of strict ability grouping.

Shifts in aspirations and "academic self-image" during desegregation are positive in meaning. Armor further contends that "busing" fails because it lowers both the aspirations and academic self-concept of black children. Several qualifications are briefly discussed initially . . . but when the conclusions are drawn, this METCO "finding" has become unqualifiedly one of the four failures of "busing". . . .

The key to understanding the apparent paradox of reduced aspirations combined with increased achievement is the well-known psychological principle that achievement motivation and aspiration level are by no means identical. Researchers have repeatedly found that moderate motivational levels are best for learning and achievement . . . . Some of this motivational research directly concerns black children. Katz ["The Socialization of Academic Motivation in Minority Group Children," in *Nebraska Symposium on Motivation* (R. O'Reilly ed 1967)], for example, has demonstrated experimentally how unduly high aspirations can doom black students to serious learning difficulties. In his view, desegregation benefits learning among black children by lowering their aspirations to more effective and realistic levels.

If METCO had drastically curtailed black ambitions to low levels, this would have been a negative result. But METCO reduced these ambitions only slightly, for they remained as high or higher than the ambitions of white students in METCO schools. In short, when desegregation lowers rigidly high aspirations of black students to moderate, effective levels, it should be considered a positive, not a negative effect. . . .

The firm policy conclusion against "mandatory busing" is not substantiated by the evidence presented. For the many reasons discussed above, the evidence does not justify Armor's unqualified conclusion: "The available evidence on busing, then, seems to lead to two clear policy conclusions. One is that mandatory busing for purposes of improving student achievement and interracial harmony is not effective and should not be adopted at this time" . . . . Interestingly, this conclusion was added to the final version after considerable publicity concerning Armor's paper had been generated by its repeated leaks to the mass media. An earlier draft had concluded only that "the data may fail to support mandatory busing as it is currently justified . . . ."

Armor also concludes that "voluntary busing" should continue for those who still believe in it and for the sake of social science research. Yet he never demonstrated, nor do we detect it when reviewing the evidence, that "mandatory" and "voluntary" desegregation lead to different effects. "Mandatory busing" is condemned out of hand even though his article rests most heavily on a voluntary program's effects, and rests entirely, except for Berkeley, upon token programs with small numbers and percentages of black children, while most "mandatory" programs involve larger numbers and percentages of black children in southern cities excluded from consideration.

In a real sense, Armor's article does not concern itself with "busing" at all, save for its title and its conclusions. It does not provide us with direct evidence on the "busing" of school children for racial desegregation, for it never treats "busing" as an independent variable. Rather, his article is an attack upon the racial desegregation of public schools that often, but not always, involves "busing." Large numbers of the children in the few studies cited by Armor attend desegregated schools without "busing." And we have noted that in his own METCO study many of his so-called controls, who were supposed to be "unbused" and segregated, were in fact "bused" and desegregated. Furthermore, a check on his METCO sample finds that a substantial number were *not* bused. Armor was apparently aware of these problems, for he admitted in his court testimony for segregation in Detroit that "a more accurate title would be 'The Effects of Induced School Integration.' "

To our knowledge, there is actually no evidence whatsoever that "busing" for desegregation harms children. This is fortunate, since over 40 percent of all school children in the United States are "bused" daily (though only 3 percent are "bused" for purposes of achieving racial desegregation). Only one of the investigations mentioned in Armor's article actually utilized "busing" as an independent variable. It found, though this was also omitted, that black pupils in Evanston who were bused to desegregated schools attained significantly higher test score gains than those who either remained in or walked to desegregated schools . . . . This result may be an artifact of selection, but it at least indicates that "busing" per se did not impair achievement. . . .

IV

The article's basic assumptions about racial change are unjustified. To this point, our critique has answered Armor's argument within the narrow confines of his view of the process of racial desegregation of the public schools. But here we wish to break out of these confines and to challenge the basic assumptions about racial change that undergird his entire article. Armor's thesis is predicated on viewing school desegregation as a technical matter, an inconvenient intervention whose merit must be judged solely by how well *black* children manage to adapt to it. Blacks are once again the "object" whose reactions should determine "what is good for them." The conditions faced by black children go unmeasured and ignored, and the whole context of American race relations is conveniently forgotten. All interracial contact is assumed to constitute "integration." No mention whatsoever is made of white racism, individual and institutional, which the Kerner Commission maintained was at the root of the problem . . . . Nor is there any discussion of the strong argument that genuine integration is necessary primarily for its potential effects on *white* Americans and *their* racial attitudes.

Instead, the whole issue is portrayed as the creation of "liberal educators" who are "so intent on selling integration to reluctant white communities that they risk the danger of ignoring the opinion of the black community." . . . Forgotten is the fact that the issue was the creation of black America, from Charles Hamilton Houston to Roy Wilkins, and that it has been continuously opposed by white America with every conceivable means.

Data from the limited METCO sample are generalized to the whole black community . . . . The antibusing resolution of the National Black Political Convention held in Gary, Indiana, in March 1972 is emphasized, but the paradoxical fact that the same convention also passed a strong "probusing" resolution is not cited. While it is acknowledged that "many black leaders favor school integration . . ." and that "the *majority* of blacks *may still* endorse the *concept* of integration . . ."; the full range of support for school integration (not merely desegregation) in the black community is never revealed. "Would you like to see the children in your family go to school with white children or not?" When asked this question at the time of the METCO research in 1969, 78 percent of a national sample of black Americans (*up* from 70 percent three years before) chose "go with whites," as opposed to 9 percent "not with whites" and 14 percent "unsure" . . . . Thus not just a majority but an overwhelming portion of black America still opts for school integration. If any further evidence were needed, the immediate and hostile public reactions of many blacks to the initial newspaper stories concerning Armor's paper should have supplied it. This is not to deny that there are strong doubts among blacks, especially the young, as to whether white America will ever allow genuine integration to become the national norm, doubts that are only reinforced by the assumptions upon which Armor's article is based.

Armor asserts that the burden must fall upon those who support school integration to prove that it works. Given America's unhappy racial history, we believe that the burden of proof rests with those who wish to maintain racial segregation. But actually such contentions miss the point. The courts' interpretation of the Fourteenth Amendment of the United States Constitution, and not social scientists' opinions about black responses, ultimately governs the racial desegregation of the public schools and court-ordered transportation which may be needed to achieve it.

i. Controversy over Evidence. Which side has the better argument with respect to the adequacy of the Armor data? How does one proceed to answer that query?

Does the Pettigrew criticism of Armor's control group weaken the validity of his conclusions? Of what relevance is the fact that the data is drawn from a relatively short period (typically two years)?

It may well be that many of the issues discussed in the Armor-Pettigrew debate cannot be definitively answered unless a carefully controlled social experiment is undertaken. Such experimentation is rare in education, largely because parents resist the coercion (and possible educational injury) that experimentation implies. Is the resolution of this issue of sufficient social importance to justify such compulsion? Does your response to that query turn in part on how likely a given experiment is to provide definitive answers? Better answers than are presently available?

ii. The Sociological Approach and the Evidence. In the light of the controversy over the impact of integration, can Professor Fiss's sociological position be defended? On whom should the legal burden of proof of injury rest? Is it necessary for black litigants to prove that integration favorably affects academic performance, racial attitudes, or psychological well-being before a court may order integration? Is it fair to cast this burden on school officials, thereby mandating integration unless school officials can prove that integration is harmful or has no positive effects? Should the constitutionality of segregation turn, wholly or in part, on allocations of burdens of proof?

iii. Social Science Evidence and Constitutional Decisions. What weight should the courts attach to studies of social integration? How do constitutional decisions and social science evidence relate to each other? Should constitutional decisions change as new social science evidence is uncovered? Is there a danger that court decisions will be unstable and the law will be in a constant state of flux if this occurs? Are Pettigrew and his colleagues correct in asserting that: "The courts' interpretation of the Fourteenth Amendment of the United States Constitution, and not social scientists' opinions about black responses, ultimately governs the racial desegregation of the public schools and court-ordered transportation which may be needed to achieve it."

iv. Brown and the Social Science Evidence. Does the Armor study cast doubt on whether Brown was correctly decided?

v. Other Studies. The social science literature on the effects of integration is immense. For the interested reader, the following books and articles afford a useful starting place: Clark, "Desegregation: An Appraisal of the Evidence," 9 J Social Issues 2 (1953); Coleman et al, Equality of Educational Opportunity (1966); Crain, "School Integration and Occupational Achievement of Negroes," 75 Amer J Soc'y 593 (1971); Frary and Goolsby, "Achievement of Integrated and Segregated Negro and White First Graders in a Southern City," 8 Integrated Educ 48 (1970); Katz, "Review of Evidence Relating to Effects of Desegregation on the Intellectual Performance of Negroes," 19 Amer Psych 318 (1964); Katz, "The Socialization of Academic Motivation in Minority Group Children," Nebraska Symposium on Motivation (D. Levine ed 1967); Klesling, "The Value to Society of Integrated Education and Compensatory Education," 61 Geo L J 857 (1973); Racial and Social Class Isolation in the Schools (R. O'Reilly ed 1970); On Equality of Educational Opportunity (F. Mosteller and P. Moynihan eds

1970); St. John, "Desegregation and Minority Group Performance," 40 *Rev Educ Research* 111 (1970).

b. The Universalist Ethic. Professor Yudof advocates a principle different from both the sociological approach and the racial classification ethic:

"EQUAL EDUCATIONAL OPPORTUNITY AND THE COURTS"
M. Yudof
51 *Tex L Rev* 411, 456-59 (1973)

[T]he actions of the court in the desegregation decisions seem curiously evocative of the liberal, progressive intellectual tradition that demands a universal society undiminished by racially identifiable institutions [Fein, "Community Schools and Social Theory: The Limits of Universalism," in *Community Control of Schools* 67, 88-90 (H. Levin ed 1970)]. The cornerstone of the liberal, progressive thinking is what might be called a universalist ethic, the basic premise of which is that a stable, just society, without violence, alienation, and social discord, must be an integrated society. Segregation of the races in public institutions, employment, and housing will inevitably lead to conflict and the destruction of democratic values and institutions. In short, the goal is a shared culture in which all segments of the population participate.

To be sure, the universalist principle fails as a photograph of reality. [Citing N. Glazer and D. Moynihan, *Beyond the Melting Pot* (1963); C. Greer, *The Great School Legend* (1972).] Rather it is a statement of a social ideal—some would say a utopian vision—and as such ignores the debate over the extent of actual assimilation of minorities. It is also a controversial ideal. It does not rest on the consent of the minorities . . . .

The very choice of the public schools as the arena for the Supreme Court's most significant thrust in integration and the sustained emphasis on this thrust in the years after *Brown* suggest the operation of the universalist principle. The public schools historically have been the primary focus of those committed to the universalist ideal. Horace Mann, the "father of American public education," envisioned the common school, the school common to all people, as the instrument for creating a new sense of community and a new common value system shared by all Americans in which diversity might flourish. [Citing L. Cremin, *The Transformation of the School* (1961).] Moreover, universalism was inherent in progressive educational theories, which stressed the need to create schools that were small democratic communities in which children of all classes and ethnic backgrounds would be brought together. It is no accident that John Dewey's major work was entitled *Democracy and Education.*

In large part the universalists' and the court's attraction to the schools may simply reflect the popular mystique surrounding public education—"the great school legend"—that schooling can cure all of society's ills. There may be another reason: if an integrated society is the desired end, the schools were the most logical as well as the most traditional place to begin the process of integration. The public schools touch virtually every child: schooling is compulsory and free. Most children spend twelve or more years in the public schools, a significant portion of a person's life. Integration of the schools therefore would involve more people over a greater period of time than the integration of virtually any other public or private institution: it probably would accomplish more toward the creation of an integrated society than any other single measure. In addition, the preadult years are a peculiarly appropriate time to attempt integration. The assumption is that the schools may be able to influence the social behavior of children, who are more flexible, more malleable, and less captive of prejudice than adults whose value systems are relatively fixed. There is some empirical evidence to support this assumption. [Citing A. Morrison and D. McIntyre, *Schools and Socialization* 106-25 (1971).] Less charitably, adults may wish to hold children to a social ideal with which the adults are incapable of complying— before the children become old enough to challenge it. Finally, despite the many difficulties over the years in enforcing desegregation decisions, integration of the public schools may be more manageable than integration in housing and employment, the other logical starting places toward an integrated society. Both housing and employment exact a price—either dollars or ability. They are both affected by principles of supply and demand that often compel denials of access, and they are both diffuse in the sense that they involve millions of decisionmakers. The public schools, in theory at least, are available to all, regardless of wealth or ability, and they are managed by a relatively small number of decisionmakers.

i. Universalism and the Supreme Court. Do you agree with Professor Yudof's conclusion? If so, how do you explain the apparent shift from the racial classification to the universalist position? Was there simply an ideological shift in the Supreme Court's thinking? Did the difficulties in enforcing *Brown* push the court toward a per se integration rule? In 1954, might the court have presumed that a prohibition of racial classifications would lead to integration: a presumption that required reevaluation in the light of subsequent developments?

ii. Universalism and the Decision. Is the universalist ethic consistent with what the court stated in *Swann* and *Green*? Does the court make specific reference to it? Might the court be justly accused of misleading the public as to its true intentions? Why might the court have done this?

iii. Universalism, Compulsoriness, and Socialization. Is the universalist ethic consistent with *Pierce v Society of Sisters,* discussed in chapter 1? With *West Virginia v Barnette, Abington School District v Schempp,* and the other socialization cases discussed in chapter 2? What is the relationship between the socialization of children to national (universal?) values and the universalist ethic?

iv. Racial Balance. Is the universalist ethic simply another name for racial balance? Does it destroy the de jure/de facto distinction? If so, is there any stopping point in its application? Would Mexican-Americans, Chinese-Americans, Italian-Americans, etc., have to be represented in each school in accordance with their share of the total school population? Are there historic or other reasons for applying the universalist ethic to only some groups, e.g., blacks and Mexican-Americans? See Rosenfelt, "Indian Schools and Community Control," 25 *Stan L Rev* 489, 544-50 (1973). What of the development of community consciousness and group identity, which many racial and ethnic groups seek to foster? Is it defensible for courts to deny these impulses? Is it sound to apply an ethical principle that engenders widespread opposition, is opposed by many of those that it is designed to aid, and finds little support in the social science literature?

See generally M. Novak, *The Rise of the Unmeltable Ethnics* (1972), and the discussion at pp 455-60.

c. Choice Between Racial Classification and Universalist Principles. How does one compare the social and political costs of the racial classification and universalist principles? If they are essentially ethical propositions, can the the marginal costs be computed? Does each principle involve an ethical cost in that it violates the other principle? Should the balance be drawn in favor of the fewest institutional and social adjustments, i.e., the status quo? Is the consideration of marginal costs for some long-range benefit a part of the moral decision itself? What value should be placed on community sentiment against busing or racial balance? On pluralism? On the liberty of parents to make schooling choices? Consider these excerpts from a perceptive article by Professor Glazer:

"IS BUSING NECESSARY?"
53 Commentary 39 (March 1972)

The desegregation of schools is the most divisive of American domestic issues. Two large points of view can be discerned as to how this has happened. To the reformers and professionals who have fought this hard fight—the civil rights lawyers, the civil rights organizations, the government officials, the judges—the fight is far from over, and even to review the statistics of change may seem an act of treason in the war against evil. Indeed, if one is to take committed supporters of civil rights at their word, there is nothing to celebrate. A year ago the Civil Rights Commission, the independent agency created by the Civil Rights Act of 1957 to review the state of civil rights, attacked the government in a massive report on the civil rights enforcement effort. "Measured by a realistic standard of results, progress in ending inequity has been disappointing. . . . In many areas in which civil rights laws afford pervasive legal protection—education, employment, housing—discrimination persists, and the goal of equal opportunity is far from achievement." And the report sums up the gloomy picture of southern school segregation, sixteen years after *Brown*: "Despite some progress in southern school desegregation . . . a substantial majority of black school children in the South still attend segregated schools." Presumably, then, when a majority of Negro children attended schools in which whites were the majority, success by one measure should have been reported. But in its follow-up report one year later, this measure of success in southern school desegregation was not even mentioned. The civil rights enforcement effort in elementary and secondary schools, given a low "marginal" score for November 1970 (out of four possibilities, "poor," "marginal," "adequate," and "good"), is shown as having regressed to an even *lower* "marginal" score by May 1971, after HEW's most successful year in advancing school integration!

But from the point of view of civil rights advocates, desegregation as such in the South is receding as a focus of attention. A second generation of problems has come increasingly to the fore: dismissal or demotion of black school principals and teachers as integration progresses and their jobs are to be given to whites; expulsions of black students for disciplinary reasons; the use of provocative symbols (the Confederate flag, the singing of "Dixie"); segregation within individual schools based on tests and ability grouping; and the rise of private schools in which whites can escape desegregation.

But alongside these new issues, there is the reality that the blacks of the North and West are also segregated, not to mention the Puerto Ricans, Mexican Americans, and others. The civil-rights movement sees that minorities are concentrated in schools that may be all or largely minority, sees an enormous agenda of desegregation before it, and cannot pause to consider a success which is already in its mind paltry and inconclusive. The struggle must still be fought, as bitterly as ever.

There is a second point of view as to why desegregation, despite its apparent success, is no success. This is the southern point of view, and now increasingly the northern point of view. It argues that a legitimate, moral, and constitutional effort to eliminate the unconstitutional separation of the races (most southerners now agree with this judgment of *Brown*), has been turned into something else— an intrusive, costly, painful, and futile effort to regroup the races in education by elaborate transportation schemes. The southern congressmen who for so long tried to get others to listen to their complaints now watch with grim satisfaction the agonies of northern congressmen faced with the crisis of mandatory, court-imposed transportation for desegregation. . . .

As a massive wave of antagonism to transportation for desegregation sweeps the country, the liberal congressmen and Democratic presidential aspirants who have for so long fought for desegregation ask themselves whether there is any third point of view: whether they must join with the activists who say that the struggle is endless and they must not flag, even now; or whether they must join with the southerners. To stand with the courts in their latest decisions is, for liberal congressmen, political suicide. A Gallup survey last October revealed that 76 percent of respondents opposed busing, almost as many in the East (71 percent), Midwest (77 percent), and West (72 percent), as in the South (82 percent); a majority of Muskie supporters (65 percent) as well as a majority of Nixon supporters (85 percent). Even more blacks oppose busing than support it (47 to 45 percent). But if to stand with the further extension to all the northern cities and suburbs of transportation for desegregation is suicide, how can the liberal congressmen join with the South and with what they view as northern bigotry in opposing busing? Is there a third position, something which responds to the wave of frustration at court orders, and which does not mean the abandonment of hope for an integrated society?

How have we come from a great national effort to repair a monstrous wrong to a situation in which the sense of right of great majorities is offended by policies which seem continuous with that once noble effort? . . .

Busing has often been denounced as a false issue. Until busing was decreed for the desegregation of southern cities, it was. As has been pointed out again and again, buses in the South regularly carried black children past white schools to black schools, and white children past black schools to white schools. When "freedom of choice" failed to achieve desegregation and geographical zoning was imposed, busing sometimes actually declined. In any case, when the school systems were no longer allowed to have buses for blacks and buses for whites, certainly the busing system became more efficient. After 1970, busing for desegregation replaced the busing for segregation.

But this was not true when busing came to Charlotte, North Carolina, and many other cities of the South, in 1971, after the key Supreme Court decision in

Swann v Charlotte-Mecklenburg County Board of Education. The city of Charlotte is 64 square miles, larger than Washington, D.C., but it is a part of Mecklenburg County, with which it forms a single school district of 550 square miles, which is almost twice the size of New York City. Many other southern cities (Mobile, Nashville, Tampa) also form part of exceptionally large school districts. While 29 percent of the schoolchildren of Mecklenburg County are black, almost all live in Charlotte. Owing to the size of the county, 24,000 of 84,500 children were bused, for the purpose of getting children to schools beyond walking distance. School zones were formed geographically, and the issue was, could all-black and all-white schools exist in Mecklenburg County, if a principle of neighborhood school districting meant they would be so constituted?

The Supreme Court ruled they could not, and transportation could be used to eliminate black and white schools. The court did not argue that there was a segregative intent in the creation of geographical zones—or that there was not—and referred to only one piece of evidence suggesting an effort to maintain segregation, free transfer. There are situations in which free transfer is used by white children to get out of mostly black schools, but if this had been the problem, the court could have required a majority-to-minority transfer only (in which one can only transfer from a school in which one's race is a majority, and to a school in which one's race is a minority), as is often stipulated in desegregation plans. Instead the court approved a plan which involved the busing of some 20,000 additional children, some for distances of up to fifteen miles, from the center of the city to the outer limits of the county, and vice versa.

Two implications of the decision remain uncertain, but they may lead to a reorganization of all American education. If Charlotte, because it is part of the school district of Mecklenburg County, can be totally desegregated with each school having a roughly 71 : 29 white to black proportion, should not city boundaries be disregarded in other places and larger school districts of the Mecklenburg County scale be created wherever such action would make integration possible? A district judge has already answered this question in the affirmative for Richmond, Virginia.

But the second implication is: If Charlotte is—except for the background of a dual school system—socially similar to many northern cities, and if radical measures can be prescribed to change the pattern that exists in Charlotte, should they not also be prescribed in the North? And to that question also a federal judge, ruling in a San Francisco case, has returned an affirmative answer.

I believe that three questions are critical here. First, do basic human rights, as guaranteed by the Constitution, require that the student population of every school be racially balanced according to some specified proportion, and that no school be permitted a black majority? Second, whether or not this is required by the Constitution, is it the only way to improve the education of black children? Third, whether or not this is required by the Constitution, and whether or not it improves the education of black children, is it the only way to improve relations between the races?

These questions are in practice closely linked. What the court decides is constitutional is very much affected by what it thinks is good for the nation. If it thinks that the education of black children can only be improved in schools with black minorities, it will be very much inclined to see situations in which there are schools with black majorities as unconstitutional. If it thinks race relations can only be improved if all children attend schools which are racially balanced, it will be inclined to find constitutional a requirement to have racial balance.

This is not to say that the courts do not need authority in the Constitution for what they decide. But this authority is broad indeed and it depends on a doctrine of judicial restraint—which has not been characteristic of the Supreme Court and subordinate federal courts in recent years—to limit judges in demanding what they think is right as well as what they believe to be within the Constitution. Indeed, it was in part because the Supreme Court believed that Negro children *were* being deprived educationally that it ruled as it did in *Brown*. . . .

While much has been made of the point that the court ruled as it did because of the evidence and views of social scientists as to the effects of segregation on the capacity of black children to learn, the fact is that the basis of the decision was that distinctions by race had no place in American law and public practice, neither in the schools, nor, as subsequent rulings asserted, in any other area, whether in waiting rooms or golf courses. This was clearly a matter of the "equal protection of the laws." It was more problematic as to what should be done to insure the "equal protection of the laws" when such protection had been denied for so long by dual school systems. But remedies were eventually agreed upon, and the court has continued to rule unanimously—as it did in *Brown*—on these remedies down through *Swann v Charlotte-Mecklenburg Board of Education*. . . .

We are engaged here in a great enterprise to determine what the "equal protection of the laws" should concretely mean in a multiracial and multiethnic society, and one in which various groups have suffered differing measures of deprivation. The blacks have certainly suffered the most, but the Chinese have suffered too, as have the Spanish-speaking groups, and some of the white ethnic groups. Is it "equal protection of the laws" to prevent Chinese-American children from attending nearby schools in their own community, conveniently adjacent to the afternoon schools they also attend? It is "equal protection of the laws" to keep Spanish-speaking children from attending school in which their numerical dominance has led to bilingual classes and specially trained teachers? Can the Constitution possibly mean that?

One understands that the people do not vote on what the Constitution means. The judges decide. But it is one thing for the Constitution to say that, despite how the majority feels, it must allow black children into the public schools of their choice; and it is quite another for the Constitution to say, in the words of its interpreters, that some children, owing to their race or ethnic group alone, may not be allowed to attend the schools of their choice, even if their choice has nothing to do with the desire to discriminate racially. When, starting with the first proposition, one ends up with the second, as one has in San Francisco, one wonders if the Constitution can possibly have been interpreted correctly.

Again and again, reading the briefs and the transcripts and the analyses, one finds the words "escape" and "flee." The whites must not escape. They must not flee. Constitutional law often moves through strange and circuitous paths, but perhaps the strangest yet has been the one whereby, beginning with an effort to expand freedom—no Negro child shall be excluded from any public school because of his race—the law has ended up with as drastic a restriction of freedom as we have seen in this country in recent years. No child, of any race or group, may "escape" or "flee" the experience of integration. No school district may facilitate such an escape. Nor may it even . . . fail to take action to close the loopholes permitting anyone to escape. . . .

There is unfortunately a widespread feeling, strong among liberals who have fought so long against the evil of racial segregation, that to stop now—before busing and expanded school districts are imposed on every city in the country—would be to betray the struggle for an integrated society. They are quite wrong. They have been misled by the professionals and specialists—in this instance, the government officials, the civil rights lawyers, and the judges—as to what integration truly demands, and how it is coming about. Professionals and specialists inevitably overreach themselves, and there is no exception here. . . .

There is a third path for liberals now agonized between the steady imposition of racial and ethnic group quotas on every school in the country—a path of pointlessly expensive and destructive homogenization—and surrender to the South. It is a perfectly sound American path, one which assumes that groups are different and will have their own interests and orientations, but which insists that no one be penalized because of group membership, and that a common base of experience be demanded of all Americans. It is the path that made possible the growth of the parochial schools, not as a challenge to a common American society, but as one variant within it. It is a path that, to my mind, legitimizes such developments as community control of schools and educational vouchers permitting the free choice of schools. There are as many problems in working out the details of this path as of the other two, but it has one thing to commend it as against the other two: it expands individual freedom, rather than restricts it.

One understands that the Constitution sets limits to the process of negotiation and bargaining even in a multiracial and multiethnic setting. But the judges have gone far beyond what the Constitution can reasonably be thought to allow or require in the operation of this complex process. The judges should now stand back, and allow the forces of political democracy in a pluralist society to do their proper work.

i. Costs. On what basis does Professor Glazer object to court-ordered racial balance in the public schools? Is it undemocratic to interfere with community school assignment choices? If so, why does he support court-ordered prohibition of racial classifications? Does racial balance unduly interfere with the freedom of parents to make educational choices for their children? To move to a particular neighborhood in order to take advantage of educational opportunities afforded there? Is this freedom of choice consistent with the *Pierce* compromise and the notion of compulsory education? With the socialization function of schools described in chapter 2? Does Glazer argue that busing is harmful per se? That popular opposition to busing somehow harms the society?

ii. *Swann.* Do you agree with Professor Glazer's contention that *Swann* supports a theory of racial balance in the North and South? Does his contention differ materially from those of Professors Fiss and Yudof? What weight does Professor Glazer give to the remedial theory which the court articulated in *Green* and *Swann*?

iii. Civil Rights Movement. Do you agree with Professor Glazer that the transition from a racial classification to a universalist ethic was triggered by the overzealousness of civil rights groups? Are there other explanations for the court's behavior? See note 5b(i), above.

iv. Segregation for Integration? Professor Glazer alludes favorably to the goal of an integrated society, the underlying basis of the universalist ethic. Does he intend to suggest that the racial classification ethic will lead to integration more quickly than the universalist ethic? Is he saying that integration for the long run will be furthered by segregation in the short run? How can this be so? Is this a political prediction that immediate movement toward integration will backfire and ultimately retard integration, whereas a prohibition of racial classification, being politically acceptable, might more readily achieve the goals of the integrationist?

6. Reaction to *Swann*

a. Congressional Reaction. At least fifty-nine constitutional amendments addressed to school desegregation and busing were proposed in Congress in 1972. See *Hearings on School Busing Before Subcomm No 5 of the House Comm on the Judiciary,* 92d Cong, 2d Sess, ser 32, pt 3, at xii-xiii (1972). Congress, rejecting an administration proposal that would have effectively banned busing for integration below the seventh grade, enacted a busing moratorium as part of the Education Amendments of 1972:

TITLE VIII—GENERAL PROVISIONS RELATING TO THE ASSIGNMENT OR TRANSPORTATION OF STUDENTS

Prohibition against Assignment or Transportation of Students to Overcome Racial Imbalance

Section 801. No provision of this act shall be construed to require the assignment or transportation of students or teachers in order to overcome racial imbalance.

Prohibition against Use of Appropriated Funds for Busing

Sec. 802(a). No funds appropriated for the purpose of carrying out any applicable program may be used for the transportation of students or teachers (or for the purchase of equipment for such transportation) in order to overcome racial imbalance in any school or school system, or for the transportation of students or teachers (or for the purchase of equipment for such transportation) in order to carry out a plan of racial desegregation of any school or school system, except on the express written voluntary request of appropriate local school officials. No such funds shall be made available for transportation when the time or distance of travel is so great as to risk the health of the children or significantly impinge on the educational process of such children, or where the educational opportunities available at the school to which it is proposed that any such student be transported will be substantially inferior to those opportunities offered at the school to which such student would otherwise be assigned under a nondiscriminatory system of school assignments based on geographic zones established without discrimination on account of race, religion, color, or national origin.

(b) No officer, agent, or employee of the Department of Health, Education, and Welfare (including the Office of Education), the Department of Justice, or any other federal agency shall, by rule, regulation, order, guideline, or otherwise (1) urge, persuade, induce, or require any local education agency, or any private nonprofit agency, institution, or organization to use any funds derived from any state or local sources for any purpose, unless constitutionally required, for which federal funds appropriated to carry out any applicable program may not be used, as provided in this section, or (2) condition the receipt of federal funds under any federal program upon any action by any state or local public officer or employee which would be prohibited by clause (1) on the part of a federal officer or employee. No officer, agent, or employee of the Department of Health, Education, and Welfare (including the Office of Education) or any other federal agency shall urge, persuade, induce, or require any local education agency to undertake transportation of any student where the time or distance of travel is so great as to risk the health of the child or significantly impinge on his or her educational process; or where the educational opportunities available at the school to which it is proposed that such student be transported will be substantially inferior to those offered at the school to which such student would otherwise be assigned under a nondiscriminatory system of school assignments based on geographic zones established without discrimination on account of race, religion, color, or national origin.

(c) An applicable program means a program to which the General Education Provisions Act applies.

Provision Relating to Court Appeals

Sec. 803. Notwithstanding any other law or provision of law, in the case of any order on the part of any United States district court which requires the transfer or transportation of any student or students from any school attendance area prescribed by competent state or local authority for the purposes of achieving a balance among students with respect to race, sex, religion, or socioeconomic status, the effectiveness of such order shall be postponed until all appeals in connection with such order have been exhausted or, in the event no appeals are taken, until the time for such appeals has expired. This section shall expire at midnight on January 1, 1974.

Provision Authorizing Intervention in Court Orders

Sec. 804. A parent or guardian of a child, or parents or guardians of children similarly situated, transported to a public school in accordance with a court order, may seek to reopen or intervene in the further implementation of such court order, currently in effect, if the time or distance of travel is so great as to risk the health of the student or significantly impinge on his or her educational process.

Provision Requiring that Rules of Evidence Be Uniform

Sec. 805. The rules of evidence required to proved that state or local authorities are practicing racial discrimination in assigning students to public schools shall be uniform throughout the United States.

Application of Proviso of §407(a) of the Civil Rights Act of 1964 to the Entire United States

Sec. 806. The proviso of §407(a) of the Civil Rights Act of 1964 providing in substance that no court or official of the United States shall be empowered to issue any order seeking to achieve a racial balance in any school by requiring the transportation of pupils or students from one school to another or one school district to another in order to achieve such racial balance, or otherwise enlarge the existing power of the court to insure compliance with constitutional standards shall apply to all public school pupils and to every public school system, public school and public school board, as defined by title IV, under all circumstances and conditions and at all times in every state, district, territory, Commonwealth, or possession of the United States regardless of whether the residence of such public school pupils or the principal offices of such public school system, public school or public school board is situated in the northern, eastern, western, or southern part of the United States. (41 USLW 46-47 (1972).)

i. Busing Moratorium and Civil Rights Act of 1964. What does the busing moratorium add to the prohibitions contained in the Civil Rights Act of 1964? See pp 320-47. What of the prohibition on the use of ›federal funds for busing to achieve racial balance? What of the provision postponing all busing orders until all appeals have been exhausted?

ii. Statutory Interpretation. In the light of the *Swann* and *Jefferson County* decisions, was the use of the "racial balance" language in the busing moratorium calculated to prevent the integration of public schools in previously de jure school systems? Why did Congress not say more clearly what it intended? In fact, the Supreme Court viewed the busing moratorium as limited to de facto segregation, rendering it consistent with the *Jefferson County* and *Swann* decisions. See Powell, J, order in *Drummond v Acree* 93 S Ct 18 (1972).

iii. Busing Moratorium and Congressional Power. If the courts had interpreted the busing moratorium as a limitation on the power of federal courts to remedy unconstitutional segregation, would this law be constitutional? In other words, to what extent can Congress define the scope of the equal protection clause by limiting the range of judicial remedies?

A detailed response would take the reader well beyond the subject matter of this casebook. In simplified terms, Congress may have the power under §5 of the Fourteenth Amendment, which empowers "Congress . . . to enforce, by appropriate legislation, the provisions of this article," or under article III, which empowers Congress to regulate the jurisdiction of the federal courts. In any event, the question is whether the exercise of power under either of these provisions interferes with the constitutional power vested in the federal courts to apply and enforce the Constitution. In this regard, Professor Bickel offers the following observation:

> [T] he argument in behalf of [busing control measures] , whatever its trappings, necessarily boils down to the claim that Congress always has plenary power to suspend enforcement of constitutional rights. But the "judicial power of the United States" is vested by article III of the Constitution in the courts, not in Congress, and ever since John Marshall's decision in *Marbury v Madison,* the judicial power has been held to be supreme over the legislative, so far as the application and enforcement of the Constitution is concerned. There is no evidence that §5 of the Fourteenth Amendment, empowering Congress to enforce its first four sections, was meant to alter the relationship between the judicial and legislative functions as established by *Marbury v Madison.* (Bickel, "What's Wrong with Nixon's Busing Bills?" *The New Republic* 19, 20 (April 22, 1972).)

See also *North Carolina State Bd of Educ v Swann* 402 US 43 (1971); *Oregon v Mitchell* 400 US 112, 128-29 (1972); *Katzenbach v Morgan* 384 US 641 (1966); *McCulloch v Maryland* 17 US 316 (1819); *Marbury v Madison* 1 Cranch 137 (1803); *Ex Parte McCardle* 74 US 506 (1869); Cox, "The Supreme Court, 1965 Term, Foreward: Constitutional Adjudication and the Promotion of Human Rights," 80 *Harv L Rev* 91 (1966); Cox, "The Role of Congress in Constitutional Determinations," 40 *U Cin L Rev* 199, 253, 257-61 (1971); *Hearings on School Busing Before Subcomm No 5 of the House Comm on the Judiciary,* 92d Cong, 2d Sess, ser 32, pt 3, at 1631-32 (1972)(statement of Professor Wright).

iv. Busing Moratorium and Northern Desegregation. Do §§804 and 806 of the statute indicate that the busing moratorium was enacted because of the fear that court-ordered busing would be extended to the North? Is *Swann* (or the numerous lower court decisions finding de jure segregation in the North, see pp 401-29) the cause of this concern?

b. *Executive Reaction.* President Nixon, even as a presidential candidate, consistently opposed busing to achieve racial balance. See generally G. Orfield, *The Reconstruction of Southern Education* 345-46 (1969). After his election, significant changes were made in the federal role in civil rights enforcement. In *Alexander v Holmes County Bd of Educ* 396 US 19 (1969), the Supreme Court rejected the administration's request for a one-year delay in school integration in southern school districts and ordered the immediate integration of previously de jure school districts. That case marked the first split between the government and the NAACP since passage of the Civil Rights Act. See also *Carter v West Feliciana Parish School Bd* 396 US 290 (1970). Subsequently, a joint HEW and Department of Justice statement on school desegregation was made public; while noteworthy for its lack of clarity, it was widely interpreted as signifying a slowdown in the integration process. H. Rodgers and C. Bullock, *Law and Social Change* 89-90 (1972). After *Swann,* in addition to the submission of the antibusing bill to Congress, the president made even clearer his opposition to school busing:

> The Justice Department is today announcing the government's decision to take an appeal on limited constitutional grounds in the case of United

States v Austin Independent School District, involving school desegregation.

The attorney general advises me that he must appeal the district court's decision that the school board's plan to bus children periodically for interracial experiences eliminates the dual school system, because that decision is inconsistent with recent rulings of the United States Supreme Court. The Justice Department is not appealing to impose the HEW plan. In the process of the appeal, the Justice Department will disavow that plan on behalf of the government.

I would also like to restate my position as it relates to busing. I am against busing as that term is commonly used in school desegregation cases. I have consistently opposed the busing of our nation's schoolchildren to achieve a racial balance, and I am opposed to the busing of children simply for the sake of busing. Further, while the executive branch will continue to enforce the orders of the court, including court-ordered busing, I have instructed the attorney general and the secretary of Health, Education and Welfare that they are to work with individual school districts to hold busing to the minimum required by law.

Finally, I have today instructed the secretary of Health, Education and Welfare to draft and submit today to the Congress an amendment to the proposed Emergency School Assistance Act that will expressly prohibit expenditure of any of those funds for busing. (*New York Times,* 4 August 1971, p 15, col 1.)

The president's opposition to school busing was further evidenced in the administration of Title VI of the Civil Rights Act of 1964 by the Department of Health, Education and Welfare. Civil rights groups charged that the Nixon administration had relaxed its standards with respect to school desegregation by refusing to threaten or employ the ultimate sanction of a cutoff of federal funds in noncomplying districts. Suit was filed against the secretary of Health, Education and Welfare, and in an extraordinary decision, the United States Court of Appeals for the District of Columbia ordered HEW to take "appropriate action to end segregation in public educational institutions receiving federal funds." *Adams v Richardson* 356 F Supp 92 (DDC 1973), *aff'd per curiam* (DC Cir June 12, 1973). Compare *Lee v Macon County Bd of Educ* 270 F Supp 859 (MD Ala 1967)(three-judge court).

ADAMS v RICHARDSON
356 F Supp 92 (DDC 1973)

The district court found appellants' performance to fall below that required of them under Title VI, and ordered them to (1) institute compliance procedures against ten state-operated systems of higher education, (2) commence enforcement proceedings against seventy-four secondary and primary school districts found either to have reneged on previously approved desegregation plans or to be otherwise out of compliance with Title VI, (3) commence enforcement proceedings against forty-two districts previously deemed by HEW to be in presumptive violation of the Supreme Court's ruling in *Swann v Charlotte-Mecklenburg Bd of Educ* 402 US 1 (1971), (4) demand of eighty-five other secondary and primary districts an explanation of racial disproportion in apparent violation of *Swann,* (5) implement an enforcement program to secure Title VI compliance with respect to vocational and special schools, (6) monitor all school districts under court desegregation orders to the extent that HEW resources permit, and (7) make periodic reports to appellees on their activities in each of the above areas.[3]

We modify the injunction concerning higher education and affirm the remainder of the order. . . .

Appellants rely almost entirely on cases in which courts have declined to disturb the exercise of prosecutorial discretion by the attorney general or by United States attorneys. *Georgia v Mitchell* 450 F2d 1317 (DC Cir 1971); *Peek v Mitchell* 419 F2d 575 (6th Cir 1970); *Powell v Katzenbach* 359 F2d 234 (DC Cir 1965); *Moses v Katzenbach* 342 F2d 931 (DC Cir 1965). Those cases do not support a claim to *absolute* discretion and are, in any event, distinguishable from the case at bar. Title VI not only requires the agency to enforce the act, but also sets forth specific enforcement procedures. The absence of similar special legislation requiring particular action by the attorney general was one factor upon which this court relied in *Powell v Katzenbach* 359 F2d 234, 235 (1965), to uphold the exercise of discretion in that case.

More significantly, this suit is not brought to challenge HEW's decisions with regard to a few school districts in the course of a generally effective enforcement program. To the contrary, appellants allege that HEW has consciously and expressly adopted a general policy which is in effect an abdication of its statutory duty. We are asked to interpret the statute and determine whether HEW has correctly construed its enforcement obligations.

A final important factor distinguishing this case from the prosecutorial discretion cases cited by HEW is the nature of the relationship between the agency and the institutions in question. HEW is actively supplying segregated institutions with federal funds, contrary to the expressed purposes of Congress. It is one thing to say the Justice Department lacks the resources necessary to locate and prosecute every civil rights violator; it is quite another to say HEW may affirmatively continue to channel federal funds to defaulting schools. The anomaly of this latter assertion fully supports the conclusion that Congress's clear statement of an affirmative enforcement duty should not be discounted.

Appellants attempt to avoid the force of this argument by saying that, although enforcement is required, the means of enforcement is a matter of absolute agency discretion, and that they have chosen to seek voluntary compliance in most cases. This position is untenable in light of the plain language of the statute. . . .

The act sets forth two alternative courses of action by which enforcement may be effected. In order to avoid unnecessary invocation of formal enforcement procedures, it includes the proviso that the institution must first be notified and given a chance to comply voluntarily. Although the act does not provide a specific limit to the time period within which voluntary compliance may be sought, it is clear that a request for voluntary compliance, if not followed by responsive action on the part of the institution within a reasonable time, does

---

3. The district court found that HEW lacks authority to recapture funds already disbursed to institutions not in compliance or to terminate previously authorized funds during pendency of enforcement proceedings. This issue has not been pursued on appeal.

not relieve the agency of the responsibility to enforce Title VI by one of the two alternative means contemplated by the statute. A consistent failure to do so is a dereliction of duty reviewable in the courts.[4]. . .

The injunction does not direct the termination of any funds, nor can any funds be terminated prior to a determination of noncompliance. In this suit against the agency, in contrast to actions brought against individual school systems, our purpose, and the purpose of the district court order as we understand it, is not to resolve particular questions of compliance or noncompliance.[5] It is, rather, to assure that the agency properly construes its statutory obligations, and that the policies it adopts and implements are consistent with those duties and not a negation of them. . . .

[The portion of the opinion dealing with higher education is omitted.]

We do not understand the district court's order to require close surveillance by HEW of all court-order districts, nor that HEW shall be accountable for more than the resources available to it from time to time permit in the good faith performance of its general obligation not to allow federal funds to be supportive of illegal discrimination. Presumably that good faith would call for a special effort in those instances where significant noncompliance is brought to its attention. So viewed, we do not find this aspect of the district court's injunction to be unwarranted.

The injunction issued by the district court relating to state-operated systems of higher education is modified as set forth above. In all other respects, the judgment appealed from is

Affirmed.

i. The Executive and Enforcement of *Swann.* Has the antibusing position of the president made the enforcement of *Swann* less likely? Why might this be so? Does the president's opposition to busing have an independent effect on public opinion with respect to integration? Will lower federal courts be reluctant to order racial integration unless assured that the executive will aid them in the enforcement of their decrees? What symbolic impact will the demise of the alliance between the executive and the courts have on the progress of integration?

ii. *Adams v Richardson.* Should private parties be permitted to file lawsuits to compel an administrative agency to comply with its own guidelines and regulations? If HEW is reluctant to seek fund cutoffs, what impact will *Adams* have on its policies? Did the *Adams* court order any fund cutoffs? What is the likely

---

4. HEW's decision to rely primarily upon voluntary compliance is particularly significant in view of the admitted effectiveness of fund termination proceedings in the past to achieve the Congressional objective.

5. Far from dictating the final result with regard to any of these districts, the order merely requires initiation of a process which, excepting contemptuous conduct, will then pass beyond the district court's continuing control and supervision. The school districts must be notified of the purpose to terminate and be given a hearing. 45 CFR §80.8(c). At the hearing conducted by a hearing examiner, the district enjoys the usual protections of an adjudicatory proceeding, including the right to counsel, the right to introduce all relevant evidence, and the right to cross-examine witnesses. The examiner's decision can be appealed to a reviewing authority, then to the secretary, and finally to the courts. 45 CFR §§80.10, 80.11; 42 USC 2000d-2. 28 USC §1391 gives the school districts and states petitioning for such judicial review a choice of venue, including the judicial district in which the plaintiff resides.

effect of ordering an administrative agency to be diligent and to act in good faith in administering a law? Why might civil rights groups consider *Adams* to be an important victory?

c. Public Reaction. The outcry against forced busing was probably greater after *Swann* than at any time in the post-*Brown* era; elections in both the North and South were waged (and quite probably won or lost) on the issue.

A Gallup poll found that 76 percent of the respondents opposed school busing for racial balance. The black community was ambivalent on the issue. Popular opposition was heightened by a number of lower court desegregation decisions that threatened to bring court-ordered busing to the North. See, e.g., *Kelly v Guinn* 456 F2d 100 (9th Cir 1972), *infra,* at pp 401-7; *Davis v School Dist* 443 F2d 573 (6th Cir 1971). How do you explain this popular reaction? Does it imply that a ban on racial classification is a more acceptable legal and ethical proposition than an affirmative obligation to integrate? Was the public reacting to the greater costs of integration discussed by Professor Glazer? Was the *Swann* decision, despite its careful remedial language, popularly interpreted as mandating busing for racial balance? What other explanations might be posited? Is it relevant

"ACTUALLY, SERVING AS CLASS PRESIDENT ISN'T
MY ONLY INVOLVEMENT IN POLITICS ——
I RIDE THE SCHOOL BUS, TOO."

"Tell It Like It Is" by Ralph Dunagin
Courtesy of Publishers-Hall Syndicate

that as the courts rejected token integration and extended their decrees to more and more districts, much greater numbers of people were affected?

V. School Segregation and Government Responsibility: An Emerging National Standard

A. Evolution of a Constitutional Standard

Racial segregation in the public schools is not a phenomenon limited to the South. In 1967, the United States Commission on Civil Rights found that in fifteen major northern cities, roughly three in four black students attended majority black schools. In nine of the fifteen cities, more than half of the black students attended 90 to 100 percent black schools. United States Commission on Civil Rights, *Racial Isolation in the Public Schools* (1967). In 1970, the Department of Health, Education and Welfare reported that 57.6 percent of all black students in thirty-two northern and western states attended 80 to 100 percent minority schools. Dimond, "School Segregation in the North: There Is But One Constitution," 7 *Harv Civil Rights—Civil Liberties L Rev* 1 (1972).

The causes of northern racial segregation are complex, interrelated, and often debated. In some school districts in the North, purposeful segregation of the southern variety was apparent:

[I]n some places in the North . . . laws and policies explicitly authorized segregation by race. State statutes authorizing separate but equal public schools were on the books in Indiana until 1959, in New Mexico and Wyoming until 1954, and in New York until 1938. Other northern states authorized such segregation after the Civil War and did not repeal their authorizing statutes until early in the twentieth century. (United States Commission on Civil Rights, *Racial Isolation in the Public Schools* (1967).)

See also *Becket v School Bd* 308 F Supp 1274, 1311-15 (ED Va 1969). The division of many metropolitan areas into a large number of school districts, each serving distinct racial and socioeconomic groups, has contributed to the phenomenon. Demographic trends (with blacks concentrated in urban areas and whites divided between cities and suburbs), disparities in personal income between the races, segregation in housing (sometimes encouraged by federal, state, and local policies), and the availability of nearly all-white private schools, have reinforced racial segregation resulting from school district organization and neighborhood school assignment policies. See also F. Tauber, *Negroes in Cities* (1965).

Constitutional attacks on school segregation in the North have met with varied judicial responses. In an early case arising in Gary, Indiana, the Court of Appeals for the Seventh Circuit upheld a neighborhood plan that assigned two-thirds of all black students to schools that were 99 to 100 percent black. The court reviewed the history of student and teacher assignment policies and school construction decisions in Gary and concluded that the resultant racial segregation was not unconstitutional:

BELL v SCHOOL CITY OF GARY
324 F2d 209 (7th Cir 1963), *cert denied,* 377 US 924 (1964)

Duffy, Circuit Judge:

The Negro population in Gary is concentrated in the "central district" which occupies roughly the south half of the cross-bar of the "T" from east to west and is bounded on the north by the Wabash Railroad and on the south by the city limits and the Little Calumet River. Approximately 70,000 Negroes including 23,000 Negro school children live in this district which comprises about one-third of the area of the city.

The city of Gary was organized in 1906. Originally, eight school districts were laid out, and as the school population required, one large school was built in each of the eight districts. As the school population expanded, elementary schools were built. At the same time, attendance zones were drawn for such elementary schools and as the students completed the course in the elementary school to which they were assigned, they then went to the high school in the district in which they resided for the completion of their public school education.

The school staff has been integrated. A Negro occupies the position of assistant superintendent of schools. He is one of three assistant superintendents, all of whom have equal rank. The coordinator of secondary education is a Negro as is the supervisor of special education, the mathematics consultant, a coordinator in the food services department and a member of the special services department who devotes a large part of his time to the problem of proper boundary lines for attendance areas. There are eighteen Negro principals and thirty-eight white principals. On the teaching staff, there are 798 Negro teachers, 833 white teachers and 3 Orientals. All schools with the exception of one small elementary school have at least one Negro teacher on the staff. All but five of the forty-two schools have at least one white teacher.

Those in charge of the administration of the Gary schools have had a difficult problem for more than a decade in maintaining facilities for the rapidly expanding school population. Twenty-two new schools or additions have been built in the last ten years and classrooms have been more than doubled. . . .

In addition to building new school buildings, the board of trustees and the school administration have rented churches, storerooms, and utilized such buildings as armories and park buildings for the purpose of providing class rooms for children. Some schools have been operated on a two-shift basis. Roosevelt is predominantly a Negro school. It operates as a senior high school in the morning and as a junior high school in the afternoon. It should be noted that Wallace, an all-white school, is operated in precisely the same manner. . . .

Pursuant to the policy of transferring students from overcrowded schools, 123 students, 92 of whom are Negroes, were transferred from Tolleston, a predominantly Negro school to Mann, a predominantly white school. Eighty-seven Negro students were transferred from Tolleston to Edison, a predominantly white school. One hundred forty students of whom one hundred twenty are Negroes, were transferred from Froebel, a predominantly Negro school to Chase, a predominantly white school.

The transfer of students from one school to another is handled on an individual basis. There is no transfer as a matter of right from one school to the other. However, no racial characteristics are considered in allowing or disallowing a transfer.

The school board has consistently followed the policy requiring students to attend the school designated to serve the district in which they live regardless of race. This was in accord with the Indiana statute which provides that all students in the public schools are to be admitted ". . . in the public or common school in their districts in which they reside without regard to race, creed or color, class or national origin . . . ." §28-5159 Burns Ind Stats.

Plaintiffs' position is grounded on their fundamental theory that their right to be integrated in school is such an overriding purpose that little, if any, consideration need to be given to the safety of the children, convenience of pupils and their parents, and costs of the operation of the school system. There was testimony that under plaintiffs' plan, at least six thousand pupils would have to be transported on each school day, presumably by bus, and that the cost of operating one bus was twenty dollars per day.

We approve also of the statement in the district court's opinion, "Nevertheless, I have seen nothing in the many cases dealing with the segregation problem which leads me to believe that the law requires that a school system developed on the neighborhood school plan, honestly and conscientiously constructed with no intention or purpose to segregate the races, must be destroyed or abandoned because the resulting effect is to have a racial imbalance in certain schools where the district is populated almost entirely by Negroes or whites. . . .

Notes and Questions

1. The De Facto-De Jure Distinction

The *Bell* reasoning was adopted by the Sixth and Tenth Circuit Courts of Appeal. *Deal v Cincinnati Bd of Educ* 369 F2d 55 (6th Cir 1966), *cert denied*, 380 US 914 (1965). Compare *Clemons v Board of Educ* 228 F2d 853 (6th Cir 1956), *cert denied*, 350 US 1006 (1956).

The *Bell* plaintiffs argued that segregation, whatever its cause, is inherently harmful, and therefore unconstitutional. They did not attempt to prove specific harm. Compare *Barksdale v Springfield School Comm* 237 F Supp 543 (D Mass 1965), *vacated on other grounds*, 348 F2d 261 (1st Cir 1965). Is the argument constitutionally sound? Does it make policy sense? Is a black child who finds himself in a segregated school likely to care whether his racial isolation is purposeful or not? See A. Bickel, *The Supreme Court and the Idea of Progress*, 119 (1970).

The *Bell* decision sharply distinguished fortuitous or de facto segregation and segregation which was a result of deliberate board policies. See generally Kaplan, "Segregation Litigation and the Schools—Part III: The Gary Litigation," 59 *Nw U L Rev* 121 (1964). The plaintiffs apparently lost the case, because "although they had shown that the board *could* have acted from improper motives, they had failed to show that the board in fact did so," 59 *Nw U L Rev* at 142, but argued instead that segregation, whatever its cause, was inherently harmful and therefore unconstitutional. How should a court determine whether there has been improper racial motivation? Is it relevant to this inquiry that Gary had explicitly required racially separate schools until 1947? 59 *Nw U L Rev* at 124-25. If a school board, which has wide discretionary power to assign students and faculty and to determine sites for school construction, adopts policies that lead to segregation, is this not a significant indication of its motive? Is it constitutional to adopt assignment policies, knowing that the result of those policies will be to increase racial isolation, even though that was not their purpose? In the former case, is the failure to act a form of state action? Is it clear that the plaintiffs should bear the burden of proving improper motive when there is substantial school segregation? These considerations, among others, led other northern courts to reject the *Bell* rationale. See, e.g., *Taylor v Board of Educ* 294 F2d 36 (2d Cir 1961), *cert denied,* 368 US 940 (1961); *Henry v Goodsell* 165 F Supp 87 (ED Mich 1958). But see *Blocker v Board of Educ* 226 F Supp 208 (EDNY 1964); *Branche v Board of Educ* 204 F Supp 150 (EDNY 1962).

More recently, and especially since the Supreme Court's decision in *Swann,* more and more federal courts have ruled that northern segregation violates the Fourteenth Amendment. See, e.g., *Davis v School Dist* 309 F Supp 734 (ED Mich 1970), *aff'd,* 443 F2d 573 (6th Cir); *Johnson v San Francisco Unified School Dist* 339 F Supp 1315 (ND Cal 1971); *US v Board of School Comm'rs* 474 F2d 81 (7th Cir 1973). Compare *Cisneros v Corpus Christi Independent School Dist* 467 F2d 142, 148 (5th Cir 1972)(en banc). Many of these decisions implicitly overruled earlier de facto precedents. See, e.g., *US v School Dist 151* 404 F2d 1125 (7th Cir 1968). They did so not by repudiating the de jure/de facto distinction, but by expanding the scope of de jure segregation. *Kelly v Guinn* typifies this phenomenon.

KELLY v GUINN
456 F2d 100 (9th Cir 1972)

Browning, Circuit Judge:

The district court held that elementary schools in the Clark County (Nevada) School District, which includes the City of Las Vegas, were racially segregated. The court ordered implementation of a so-called Sixth Grade Center Plan to desegregate the schools. Defendant school officials appeal, asserting that no constitutional violation was established. Plaintiffs cross-appeal, contending that the Sixth Grade Center Plan is inadequate.... We affirm on both appeals....

In 1954, when *Brown v Board of Educ* 347 US 483 was decided, there were only three schools in the Westside area. All had racially mixed enrollments. After 1954 the population of Westside increased rapidly and became increasingly black in racial composition.

In 1956, to avoid racial segregation in junior and senior high schools, the school district announced that no new junior and senior high schools would be built in Westside. Thereafter, Westside pupils were bused to junior and senior high schools outside the area. At these grade levels the Clark County school system was, and is, completely integrated.

In contrast, between 1956 and 1966, four new elementary schools were constructed in Westside and one of the two existing schools was extensively renovated to accommodate additional students. The first of the four new elementary schools opened the same year the school district decided to open no new secondary schools in the area to avoid racial segregation at those grade levels. When the complaint was filed in 1968, black student enrollment in each of the six Westside elementary schools exceeded 97 percent.

During the same period, in 1965, the school district closed two predominately white schools on the fringe of Westside, between black and white neighborhoods. If these schools had not been closed, their enrollment would now be about half

white students and half black.[2] At about the same time, the school district built
a new elementary school in a more distant white residential area.[3]

When the complaint was filed, 102 of the 1359 teachers in Clark County
elementary schools were black. Of the 102 black teachers, 83 were assigned to
Westside schools, and only 19 to schools outside the area. These figures appear
to be representative of prior years.[4]

Defendants argue that under *Swann v Charlotte-Mecklenburg Bd of Educ,
supra,* 402 US 1 a school district is required to integrate racially imbalanced
schools only if the school district caused the racial imbalance. Defendants contend that the segregated conditions in Clark County's elementary schools do not
result from discriminatory acts or omissions of the school district. They maintain
that the school district is simply adhering to a neighborhood school policy under
which children are assigned to schools nearest their homes. They claim that
whatever imbalance exists stems not from any official action of the school district but rather from the racial composition of the Westside population, which is
almost completely black.

Defendants point out that the *Swann* case involved a school district "having a
long history of maintaining two sets of schools in a single school system deliberately operated to carry out a governmental policy to separate pupils in schools
solely on the basis of race." 402 US at 5-6. Defendants claim that there has been
no finding that the segregated condition in Clark County elementary schools are
a result of such official action. Therefore, since no constitutional violation by the
school district has been established, and since, under *Swann,* there is no legal
requirement that racial balance exist in every school (see 402 US at 24), they
conclude that they have no affirmative duty to integrate Clark County schools.

We agree with defendants that it is clear from *Swann* that a court has no
power to order a school district to take steps to integrate its schools unless the
court first finds that the schools have been operated in a manner violative of the
Constitution. 402 US at 16. Defendants are incorrect, however, in saying that the
district court found no official action on their part constituting a constitutional
violation.

In its judgment of December 2, 1970, the district court referred to the fact

---

2. The school district points out that counsel stipulated that these schools were closed
because of their physical condition. But counsel did not stipulate that this was the sole
reason for the closings. Defendant Guinn, superintendent of schools, testified that the
schools were closed in part because it was foreseen that the student body would become
increasingly black due to changing residential patterns. The reply brief filed on behalf of the
school district agrees that this was one reason for the closings. It is not suggested that these
schools could not have been renovated for continued elementary school use, as other schools
in Westside were. Both schools are still used for special classes and other educational purposes.

3. The present policy of Clark County School District is to phase out "neighborhood"
elementary schools in Westside. No new elementary schools have been built in Westside since
1966.

4. Plaintiffs argue that the evidence also shows (1) that white students were bused to
white schools although Westside black schools were closer to their homes; (2) that efforts of
Westside black students to transfer to white schools were frustrated; (3) that attendance
zones were manipulated to perpetuate black segregation in Westside schools; (4) that only
Westside schools were treated as "neighborhood" schools, and busing was common outside
Westside. However, either the facts asserted or their significance are disputed. The district
court did not resolve these disputes either by express findings or by clear implication.

that the school district had adopted a construction policy with respect to junior and senior high schools that effectively eliminated segregation at those grade levels. . . .

This is a clear finding that the school board furthered racial segregation by official conduct beyond the mere adoption and administration of a neutral, neighborhood school policy.[7] This finding is supported by the record, and establishes a constitutional violation.

Not surprisingly, the record contains no express mandate or sanction by any state agency of racial segregation in Clark County elementary schools. Historically, racial segregation has rarely been required by law in northern and western states. There was other evidence, however, to support the district court's ultimate finding that the Clark County School District used its official powers to further the maintenance of segregated schools.

1. The existence of almost total segregation of the races in the elementary schools of racially mixed Clark County School District is itself a relevant factor. As Chief Justice Burger said in *Swann v Charlotte-Mecklenburg Bd of Educ, supra,* 402 US at 25-26: "Schools all or predominately of one race in a district of mixed population will require close scrutiny to determine that school assignments are not part of state-enforced segregation."

2. The almost completely black composition of the teaching staffs of Westside schools when the complaint was filed, combined with the district's methods of placing teachers (see note 8), established a prima facie case of violation of substantive constitutional rights.

This is settled by *Swann.* There the court stated, "where it is possible to identify a 'white school' or a 'Negro school' simply by reference to the racial composition of teachers and staff . . . a *prima facie* case of violation of substantive constitutional rights under the equal protection clause is shown." 402 US at 18. See *Green v County School Bd* 391 US 430, 435 (1968).

This is not to say that racially balanced faculties are constitutionally required, for they are not. See *US v Montgomery County Bd of Educ* 395 US 225, 236 (1969). Rather, teacher assignment is so clearly subject to the complete

---

7. We do not mean to suggest that we would agree with plaintiffs' assumption that the Constitution is not violated by implementation of a "neighborhood school" policy in a school district having racially segregated residential patterns when the foreseeable result [is] segregation of the races in the district's schools. That question remains open. It has been argued with some force that a school authority cannot ignore the obvious fact of racially segregated residential patterns in making decisions regarding school attendance zones, and that if it elects to impose so-called neighborhood school attendance zones upon racially segregated residential areas it is responsible for the racially segregated schools that are the readily foreseeable consequences of its conduct. Fiss, "The Charlotte-Mecklenburg Case—Its Significance for Northern School Desegregation," 38 *U Chi L Rev* 697, 706-7 (1971); Fiss, "Racial Imbalance in the Public Schools," 78 *Harv L Rev* 564, 584-88 (1965); see *Bradley v Milliken* 338 F Supp 582, 592 (ED Mich 1971).

Of course, under *Swann* any racially motivated manipulation of attendance zones violates the Constitution. See Dimond, "Segregation Northern Style," 9 *Inequality in Education* (Harvard Center for Law & Education) 17, 19-20 (1971). [See also Dimond, "School Segregation in the North: There Is But One Constitution," 7 *Harv Civil Rights—Civil Liberties L Rev* 1 (1972).] The Supreme Court also pointed out that choices made by a school authority in locating schools may contribute to the creation of the residential segregation itself, making the school authority responsible for the school segregation resulting from the residential segregation. 402 US at 20-21.

control of school authorities, unfettered by such extrinsic factors as neighbor-hood residential composition or transportation problems, that the assignment of an overwhelmingly black faculty to black schools is strong evidence that racial considerations have been permitted to influence the determination of school policies and practices. "[T]he school district's obvious regard for race in assign-ing faculty members and administrators is a factor which may be considered in assessing motives underlying past decisions which resulted in segregation." *Davis v School Dist* 443 F2d 573, 576 (6th Cir 1971).[8]

3. The prima facie case of constitutional violation established by proof of virtually complete racial segregation of teachers in Clark County elementary schools was buttressed by the evidence showing that segregation of pupils by race was aggravated by the school district's practices in building new schools and abandoning old ones. As we have seen, while the Clark County School District built new elementary schools in the black residential area and in a distant white residential area, at the same time it closed existing schools in the fringe areas, in part to avoid their integration.

Like assignment of faculty by race, school construction policies that create or aggravate racial segregation are among the "important indicia of a segregated system." *Swann v Charlotte-Mecklenburg Bd of Educ, supra,* 402 US at 18. . . .

4. Finally, the school district's decision to continue a "neighborhood" school policy at the elementary level while abandoning it at the secondary level for the very reason that the policy patently furthered racial segregation lends weight to the inference that the school district's purpose in constructing, renovating, and abandoning schools was to limit integration at the elementary level.

For these reasons we conclude that there was ample evidence to support the district court's finding that the Clark County School District used its power to aggravate segregation in elementary schools in violation of the Constitution.

A constitutional violation having been established, the district court properly called upon the Clark County School District to come forward with a plan to eliminate the vestiges of state-imposed segregation. The school district was "clear-ly charged with the affirmative duty to take whatever steps might be necessary to convert to a unitary system in which racial discrimination would be eliminated root and branch." *Green v County School Bd, supra,* 391 US at 437-38. . . .

The district court also properly rejected the school district's "freedom-of-choice" plan after a year's trial. "[A] school authority's remedial plan . . . is to be judged by its effectiveness," *Swann v Charlotte-Mecklenburg Bd of Educ,*

8. During oral argument in this court, defendants' counsel offered the suspiciously tardy suggestion that the school district may have acted on the theory that black students would respond better to black teachers, see *Keyes v School Dist No 1* 445 F2d 990, 1007 (10th Cir 1971), *cert granted,* 30 L Ed 2d 728 (1972). Counsel's suggestion is no substitute for proof in the trial court.

The inference of racial motivation is not weakened by the fact that teacher assignments were made primarily on the basis of requests by the principal of each school, or by the teachers themselves. Since the power to assign teachers clearly belonged to school author-ities, the principals, or teachers, must be viewed as acting as agents of the school district in exercising that power, particularly when, as here, the power is exercised over a long period of time in a way that is obviously racially influenced. . . . While the school district could independently assign black teachers to schools outside Westside, the statistics reveal that this has seldom been done. . . .

supra, 402 US at 25, and the freedom-of-choice plan proved entirely inadequate. . . .

The school district's initial plan having failed, the district court's power and duty to enter a remedial decree was clear. . . . However, both the school district and plaintiffs criticize the specific remedy approved by the district court.

The parties join in opposing the provision of the December 2 judgment "that the black enrollment in any elementary school in the Clark County District shall not exceed 50 percent of the total enrollment in such grade."[12]

The school board's objection rests upon statements in *Swann* that the Constitution does not require a particular racial balance or mixture of races in public schools, and that the existence of a small number of one-race schools does not in and of itself establish a constitutional violation. 402 US at 22-29.

In these passages, the court was speaking only of the proof necessary to establish the existence of the constitutional violation that is a prerequisite to any judicial remedy at all. Once a constitutional violation has been found, different considerations apply. Then both the school district and the court are obliged to take all necessary steps to eliminate the past violation and its continuing effects. The Supreme Court specifically approved use of a mathematical ratio as "a useful starting point in shaping a remedy to correct past constitutional violations," 402 US at 25, and warned that whenever a proposed remedial plan contemplated the continuance of schools all or predominately of one race, "The court should scrutinize such schools, and the burden upon the school authorities will be to satisfy the court that their racial composition is not the result of present or past discriminatory action on their part." 402 US at 26. . . .

Plaintiffs argue that the district court did not go far enough—that the court should have ordered the school district "to avoid schools substantially disproportionate to the system-wide racial enrollment"; and that a "50 percent black school in Las Vegas is substantially disproportionate." . . .

We are satisfied that "the very limited use made of mathematical ratios was within the equitable remedial discretion of the district court." *Swann v Charlotte-Mecklenburg Bd of Educ, supra*, 402 US at 25. . . . The present decree is the beginning, not the end, of the remedial process. No doubt it will be modified and adjusted in the light of progress made in the elimination of effects of segregation. . . .

Affirmed.

Notes and Questions

1. *Guinn* and *Bell*

Can *Guinn* be distinguished from *Bell* on its facts? Is the neighborhood segregation in the central district in *Bell* distinguishable from the segregation in Westside in *Guinn*? Did the *Bell* court use the same standard as the *Guinn* court in determining whether there was faculty segregation? Is there more evidence of improper motive—with respect to school construction, closing, and neighborhood

---

12. The district court later orally amended the judgment to make it clear that enrollment in any single *class* was not to be more than 50 percent black. By the terms of the amended judgment of February 8, 1971, the 50 percent requirement did not apply in those "special classes involving federal or other remedial or experimental programs of the school district."

assignment policies—in *Guinn* than in *Bell*? How did the *Guinn* and *Bell* courts allocate the burden of proving discriminatory intent?

2. Purposeful and Knowing Conduct

In note 7, although it does not pass on the question, the court suggests that a neighborhood school policy in a district with racially segregated housing patterns may be unconstitutional. In other words, school officials know, even if they do not intend, that their policies will result in substantial segregation. If this reasoning is sound, what remains of the de jure/de facto distinction? Is there such a thing as de facto segregation, under *Guinn*? Does *Bell* have continuing value as a precedent? Is the type of discrimination involved in *Guinn* as invidious as the discrimination in *Brown*? Would different remedies be in order? Compare Fiss, "The *Charlotte-Mecklenburg* Case: It Significance for Northern School Desegregation," 48 *U Chi L Rev* 697 (1971).

3. *Guinn* and *Swann*

To what extent does the *Guinn* court rely on *Swann*? Is that reliance justifiable? Was the *Swann* declaration that one-race schools require close scrutiny for constitutional infirmity intended to apply to cities like Las Vegas? Is the court correct in relying on *Swann* for the proposition that whenever there are segregated teaching staffs, the burden of proving that there has been no discrimination is shifted to school authorities?

4. Remedy

Why did the court of appeals affirm the lower court's order that black enrollment may not exceed 50 percent in each grade when blacks apparently constitute a much smaller proportion of the system-wide school population? Was the court simply relying on *Swann* for the proposition that district courts have wide remedial discretion in desegregation cases? Does the court allude to any factors—for example, safety, convenience, or transportation costs—that might justify the lower court's order? Suppose the district court had set a 75 percent figure? Of what significance is the amended judgment of February 8, 1971, which provided that no single class could contain more than 50 percent black students? Does this make any sense? Is it consistent with a constitutional prohibition of racial classifications? Is this also within the remedial discretion of district courts? Compare the discussion of racial representation in special education programs, chapter 7.

5. De Facto Segregation and Public Policy

A coherent analysis of the constitutional status of northern school segregation is difficult to discern from the case law. Rather, a variety of interrelated theories, all of constitutional dimension, begin to take shape. Professor Goodman's recent examination of de facto segregation considers five distinct arguments for invalidating racial imbalance:

(1) "The racially specific effects rationale." The Supreme Court found de jure segregation unconstitutional because of the educational and psychological harm it inflicted on blacks; since de facto segregation inflicts the same harms, it too should be invalidated.

(2) "The linkage of neutral state action with private racial action: neighborhood school and private discrimination in housing." Where race determines the location of one's residence because of discrimination in the housing market, neighborhood school policies become unconstitutional "racial classification[s] once removed" on the part of the state.

(3) "The linkage of neighborhood schooling and state-induced housing discrimination—the collateral state action argument." Where the state can be shown to have played some role in the existence of segregated housing patterns, then that fact coupled with a neighborhood school policy would present a strong case against the constitutionality of de facto segregation.

(4) "The neighborhood school as an incubator of prejudice." Neighborhood school policies, by exacerbating racial isolation, foster racism and encourage discrimination. Since, in other contexts, state action with such effects has been held unconstitutional, de facto segregation in the schools should be treated likewise by the courts.

(5) "Equal educational opportunity as a fundamental right." If segregated schools are educationally inferior, then regardless of the state's role in their existence, the state must alter the neighborhood school policy in order to comply with the equal protection clause unless it can show a compelling interest for not doing so. Goodman, "*De Facto* School Segregation: A Constitutional and Empirical Analysis," 60 *Cal L Rev* 275, 298-374 (1972).

How would you evaluate the cogency of these arguments? Do they exhaust the legal possibilities? Which of these arguments depends on empirical showing of educational harm to pupils attending racially imbalanced schools? How does each divide procedural burdens, and with what likely consequences? See Kaplan, "Segregation Litigation and the Schools—Part III: The Gary Litigation," 59 *Nw U L Rev* 121, 142-43 (1964).

6. Proving State-Enforced Segregation in the North

"SCHOOL SEGREGATION IN THE NORTH:
THERE IS BUT ONE CONSTITUTION"
P. Dimond
7 Harv Civil Rights—Civil Liberties L Rev 1, 20-27 (1972)

School authorities have considerable discretion in assigning teachers and pupils to schools, constructing and locating schools and attendance boundaries, choosing initial student assignments, and setting transfer policies and enforcing them. Careful examination will reveal choices and practices, and their effects, which operate to segregate schools on a racial basis.

Teacher Hiring and Assignment. Perhaps the most obvious evidence concerns teacher hiring and assignment. Where there are disproportionately few black faculty in any community's public schools, relative to the adult racial mix, there is a substantial question of racial discrimination in hiring. More telling is a pattern of black teachers assigned primarily to schools with high concentrations of black students, and white teachers primarily to schools with predominantly white student bodies. Schools are thereby identified as black or white by faculty assignment, and inference of racial discrimination in teacher assignment is appropriate. . . .

Pupil Assignment. Assignment of pupils to various schools often involves many processes. Where schools rely on geographic zoning for pupil assignment, the drawing of boundaries, policing of the assignments, size of schools, grade structure, construction and location of new schools, additions to old ones, and placement of portable classrooms all help to determine which students attend particular schools. Pupil composition of schools is further affected by exceptions to strict reliance on geographic zoning. These include transfer policies ("optional zones," "free transfer," "free choice," "open enrollment," "majority to minority"), transportation practices, and school plant use.

Exceptions to Geographic Zoning. This set of practices often reveals how acts of school authorities create and perpetuate school segregation. Optional zones usually straddle the edges of geographic attendance zones to permit students to attend either school. When optional zones exist between a predominantly black and a predominantly white school, their purpose is usually to allow whites to flee from the black school to the white one. The consistent result is that whites "choose" to attend the white school and blacks, with a few exceptions, the black school. In many instances, constraints on choice inherent in the existence of the optional zone, and the identifiability of the schools, are further accentuated by the hostility that school authorities show the few students who attempt to opt for the school of the opposite race. If such optional zones are maintained primarily in areas of racial mix or transition while strict geographical zoning is the rule in areas of high black or white concentration, an inference of official intent to impose segregation throughout the school systems is appropriate.

Similarly, "free transfer" and "open enrollment" policies, even with transportation provided and space guaranteed at receiving schools, often operate to intensify school segregation. While these policies theoretically allow any student to transfer from his school of geographic assignment to any other school, purely racial reasons often can be shown to govern the transfer choice. In other instances, subtle pressure by school authorities may promote a white flight from black schools, while discouraging a similar transfer by black students into white schools. Invariably, such policies increase segregation: many whites flee geographically assigned schools that are perceived as black; no whites transfer into black schools; few blacks transfer into white schools; and some blacks "transfer" from white to black schools. "Hardship," and even "majority-to-minority," transfer policies must also be closely examined, for in practice they may be manipulated to segregate schools.

Regardless of a system's transfer policies, the actual transportation of children may show how school authorities segregate schools. Black children may be bused to black schools past, or away from, predominantly white schools with space available, or white students may be transported to white schools past, or away from, predominantly black schools with space available, or both. Such busing sometimes occurs under the guise of relieving overcrowding and maximizing the efficient use of the school plant.

The pattern of school plant utilization may also provide proof of state-imposed segregation. Black schools may be overcrowded while white schools have space. Or black elementary and white secondary schools may be overcrowded, while white elementary and black secondary schools are undercrowded. Or there may be a mix of black and white schools over- and undercrowded. In each case, school authorities are faced with the choice of equalizing school plant use to integrate, or to segregate schools, or not to equalize plant use at all and thereby perpetuate segregation. When over- and undercrowding are clear and consistent over a period of time, failure to integrate by equalizing use of school plant constitutes an affirmative choice by public school authorities to impose segregation. It is the election of an option that intensifies segregation. . . .

Manipulation of Geographic Zones. To examine geographic zoning as a basis for school assignment is necessarily to examine the relationship between attendance areas, actual school assignments, and residential patterns. These relationships must be subjected to searching judicial scrutiny. Assertions that school segregation results from a neighborhood school policy and housing patterns over which the school board has no control should not be idly accepted. . . .

When courts do examine school officials' actions, school compositions, and housing patterns, the following practices and patterns of state-imposed school segregation often appear:

—contiguous school attendance zones contain black and white children in separate schools.

—school boundaries trace a sharp demarcation between white and black residential areas.

—railroad tracks (or other similar barriers) are used as school boundary lines when only blacks live on the "other side", but attendance boundaries cross the tracks freely when blacks and whites live on both sides.

—school attendance zones generally follow residential patterns that maximize school segregation.

—when black residential areas expand, school boundaries are altered or maintained to perpetuate the containment of blacks and whites in separate schools.

—where pockets of one race reside within a large area of the other race, attendance zones coincide with the pocket and students living there are assigned to a noncontiguous school of their own race, or to a school within the pocket just large enough to serve the students living there.

—where attendance zones encompass a mixed population, whites are allowed to slip into other schools. The failure to enforce zone lines strictly may make every attendance area an "optional zone" for whites who wish to escape from a black school.

—despite the variety of other manipulations, the school attendance zones of predominantly white residential areas are never altered to feed into a black school.

—school capacities vary with the racial composition of residential areas in a district. Large schools may serve vast areas that are predominantly black or white, but at the edges between areas, smaller schools may minimize interracial education. Or school size may be finely tuned to meet the exclusive needs of a particular racial pocket.

—the grade structure of schools may be varied to segregate schools. Because the area served by a school varies with the number of grades it serves, schools may be structured so that all schools in an area are predominantly of one race. An alternative grade structure might lead to substantial integration in the very same schools.

—the size and location of new schools throughout a district, in conjunction with attendance boundaries, grade structures, and teacher assignments, frequently create schools that open and remain predominantly white or black.

In view of the vast range of options available to school officials in each decision, a pattern of predominantly one-race schools is strong evidence of the "quantum" of discriminatory state action compelling judicial intervention to enforce the Constitution in the face of default by public officials.

Is it likely that any northern school district could prove that pupil segregation is fortuitous or de facto in the light of the searching factual inquiry that Mr. Dimond suggests? If not, is that a criticism of Dimond's approach?

B. Northern School Segregation and the Supreme Court

KEYES v SCHOOL DISTRICT NO 1
93 S Ct 2686 (1973)

Mr. Justice Brennan delivered the opinion of the court.

This school desegregation case concerns the Denver, Colorado, school system. That system has never been operated under a constitutional or statutory provision that mandated or permitted racial segregation in public education. Rather, the gravamen of this action, brought in June 1969 in the District Court for the District of Colorado by parents of Denver school children, is that respondent school board alone, by use of various techniques such as the manipulation of student attendance zones, school site selection and a neighborhood school policy, created or maintained racially or ethnically (or both racially and ethnically) segregated schools throughout the school district, entitling petitioners to a decree directing desegregation of the entire school district.

The boundaries of the school district are coterminus with the boundaries of the city and county of Denver. There were in 1969 119 schools with 96,580 pupils in the school system. In early 1969, the respondent school board adopted three resolutions, Resolutions 1520, 1524, and 1531, designed to desegregate the schools in the Park Hill area in the northeast portion of the city. Following an election which produced a broad majority opposed to the resolutions, the resolutions were rescinded and replaced with a voluntary student transfer program. Petitioners then filed this action, requesting an injunction against the rescission of the resolutions and an order directing that the respondent school board desegregate and afford equal educational opportunity "for the school district as a whole." The district court found that by the construction of a new, relatively small elementary school, Barrett, in the middle of the Negro community west of Park Hill, by the gerrymandering of student attendance zones, by the use of so-called optional zones, and by the excessive use of mobile classroom units, among other things, the respondent school board had engaged over almost a decade after 1960 in an unconstitutional policy of deliberate racial segregation with respect to the Park Hill schools. The court therefore ordered the board to desegregate those schools through the implementation of the three rescinded resolutions. 303 F Supp 279 (1969); 303 F Supp 289 (1969).

Segregation in Denver schools is not limited, however, to the schools in the Park Hill area, and not satisfied with their success in obtaining relief for Park Hill, petitioners pressed their prayer that the district court order desegregation of all segregated schools in the city of Denver, particularly the heavily segregated schools in the core city area. But that court concluded that its finding of a purposeful and systematic program of racial segregation affecting thousands of students in the Park Hill area did not, in itself, impose on the school board an affirmative duty to eliminate segregation throughout the school district. Instead, the court fractionated the district and held that petitioners must make a fresh showing of de jure segregation in each area of the city for which they seek relief. Moreover, the district court held that its finding of intentional segregation in Park Hill was not in any sense material to the question of segregative intent in other areas of the city. Under this restrictive approach, the district court concluded that petitioners' evidence of intentionally discriminatory school board action in areas of the district other than Park Hill was insufficient to "dictate the conclusion that this is de jure segregation which calls for an all-out effort to desegregate. It is more like de facto segregation, with respect to which the rule is that the court cannot order desegregation in order to provide a better balance." 313 F Supp 61, 73 (1970).

Nevertheless, the district court went on to hold that the proofs established that the segregated core city schools were educationally inferior to the predominantly "white" or "Anglo" schools in other parts of the district—that is, "separate facilities . . . unequal in the quality of education provided." 313 F Supp at 83. Thus, the court held that, under the doctrine of *Plessy v Ferguson* 163 US 537 (1896), respondent school board constitutionally "must at a minimum . . . offer an equal educational opportunity," . . . and, therefore, although all-out desegregation "could not be decreed, . . . the only feasible and constitutionally acceptable program—the only program which furnishes anything approaching substantial equality—is a system of desegregation and integration which provides compensatory education in an integrated environment." 313 F Supp at 90, 96. The district court then formulated a varied remedial plan to that end which was incorporated in the final decree.

Respondent school board appealed, and petitioners cross-appealed, to the Court of Appeals for the Tenth Circuit. That court sustained the district court's finding that the board engaged in an unconstitutional policy of deliberate racial segregation with respect to the Park Hill schools and affirmed the final decree in that respect. As to the core city schools, however, the court of appeals reversed the legal determination of the district court that those schools were maintained in violation of the Fourteenth Amendment because of the unequal educational opportunity afforded, and therefore set aside so much of the final decree as required desegregation and educational improvement programs for those schools. 445 F2d at 990. . . .

I

Before turning to the primary question we decide today, a word must be said about the district court's method of defining a "segregated" school. Denver is a tri-ethnic, as distinguished from a biracial, community. The overall racial and ethnic composition of the Denver public schools is 66 percent Anglo, 14 percent Negro and 20 percent Hispano. The district court, in assessing the question of de jure segregation in the core city schools, preliminarily resolved that Negroes and Hispanos should not be placed in the same category to establish the segregated character of a school. 313 F Supp at 69. Later, in determining the schools that were likely to produce an inferior educational opportunity, the court concluded that a school would be considered inferior only if it had "a concentration of either Negro or Hispano students in the general area of 70 to 75 percent." 313 F Supp at 77. We intimate no opinion whether the district court's 70 to 75 percent requirement was correct. The district court used those figures to signify educationally inferior schools, and there is no suggestion in the record that those same figures were or would be used to define a "segregated" school in the de jure context. What is or is not a segregated school will necessarily depend on the facts of each particular case. In addition to the racial and ethnic composition of a school's student body, other factors such as the racial and ethnic composition of faculty and staff and the community and administration attitudes toward the school must be taken into consideration. . . .

We conclude, however, that the district court erred in separating Negroes and Hispanos for purposes of defining a "segregated" school. We have held that Hispanos constitute an identifiable class for purposes of the Fourteenth Amendment. *Hernandez v Texas* 347 US 475 (1954). . . . [T]here is . . . much evidence that in the southwest Hispanos and Negroes have a great many things in common. The United States Commission on Civil Rights has recently published two reports on Hispano education in the southwest.[7] Focusing on students in the states of Arizona, California, Colorado, New Mexico, and Texas, the commission concluded that Hispanos suffer from the same educational inequities as Negroes and American Indians.[8] In fact, the district court itself recognized that "one of the things which the Hispano has in common with the Negro is economic and cultural deprivation and discrimination." 313 F Supp at 69. This is agreement that, though of different origins, Negroes and Hispanos in Denver suffer identical discrimination in treatment when compared with the treatment afforded Anglo students. In that circumstance, we think petitioners are entitled to have schools with a combined predominance of Negroes and Hispanos included in the category of "segregated" schools.

II

In our view, the only other question that requires our decision at this time is . . . whether the district court and the court of appeals applied an incorrect legal standard in addressing petitioners' contention that respondent school board engaged in an unconstitutional policy of deliberate segregation in the core city schools. Our conclusion is that those courts did not apply the correct standard in addressing that contention.[9]

---

7. United States Commission on Civil Rights, Mexican-American Education Study, *Ethnic Isolation of Mexican-Americans in the Public Schools of the Southwest* (April 1971); United States Commission on Civil Rights, Mexican-American Education Series, *The Unfinished Education* (October 1970).

8. The Commission's first report, on p. 41, summarizes its findings:

"The basic finding of this report is that minority students in the Southwest—Mexican-Americans, blacks, American Indians—do not obtain the benefits of public education at a rate equal to that of their Anglo classmates."

9. . . . But at this stage, we have no occasion to review the factual findings concurred in

Petitioners apparently concede for the purposes of this case that in the case of a school system like Denver's, where no statutory dual system has ever existed, plaintiffs must prove not only that segregated schooling exists but also that it was brought about or maintained by intentional state action. Petitioners proved that for almost a decade after 1960 respondent school board had engaged in an unconstitutional policy of deliberate racial segregation in the Park Hill schools. Indeed, the district court found that "between 1960 and 1969 the board's policies with respect to those northeast Denver schools show an undeviating purpose to isolate Negro students" in segregated schools "while preserving the Anglo character of [other] schools." 303 F Supp at 294. This finding did not relate to an insubstantial or trivial fragment of the school system. On the contrary, respondent school board was found guilty of following a deliberate segregation policy at schools attended, in 1969, by 37.69 percent of Denver's total Negro school population, including one-fourth of the Negro elementary pupils, over two-thirds of the Negro junior high pupils, and over two-fifths of the Negro high school pupils. In addition, there was uncontroverted evidence that teachers and staff had for years been assigned on a minority teacher to minority school basis throughout the school system. Respondent argues, however, that a finding of state-imposed segregation as to a substantial portion of the school system can be viewed in isolation from the rest of the district, and that even if state-imposed segregation does exist in a substantial part of the Denver school system, it does not follow that the district court could predicate on that fact a finding that the entire school system is a dual system. We do not agree. We have never suggested that plaintiffs in school desegregation cases must bear the burden of proving the elements of de jure segregation as to each and every school or each and every student within the school system. Rather, we have held that where plaintiffs prove that a current condition of segregated schooling exists within a school district where a dual system was compelled or authorized by statute at the time of our decision in *Brown v Board of Educ* 347 US 483 (1954) (*Brown 1*), the state automatically assumes an affirmative duty "to effectuate a transition to a racially nondiscriminatory school system," *Brown v Board of Educ* 349 US 294, 301 (1955) (*Brown 2*), see also *Green v County School Bd*, 391 US 430, 437-38 (1968), that is, to eliminate from the public schools within their school system "all vestiges of state-imposed segregation." *Swann v Charlotte-Mecklenburg Bd of Educ* 402 US 1, 15 (1971).[11]

by the two courts below . . . We address only the question whether those courts applied the correct legal standing in deciding the case as it affects the core city schools.

11. Our brother Rehnquist argues in dissent that *Brown v Board of Education* did not impose an "affirmative duty to integrate" the schools of a dual school system but was only a "prohibition against discrimination" "in the sense that the assignment to a child of a particular school is not made to depend on his race . . . ."

That is the interpretation of *Brown* expressed 18 years ago by a three-judge court in *Briggs v Elliott* 132 F Supp 776, 777 (1955): "The Constitution, in other words, does not require integration. It merely forbids discrimination." But *Green v County School Bd* 391 US 430, 438 (1968), rejected that interpretation insofar as *Green* expressly held that "School boards . . . operating state-compelled dual systems were nevertheless clearly charged [by *Brown 2*] with the affirmative duty to take whatever steps might be necessary to convert to a unitary system in which racial discrimination would be eliminated root and branch." *Green* remains the governing principle. *Alexander v Holmes County Bd of Educ* 396 US 19 (1969); *Swann v Charlotte-Mecklenburg Bd of Educ* 402 US 1, 15 (1971). See also *Kelley v Metropolitan County Bd of Educ* 317 F Supp 980, 984 (1970).

This is not a case, however, where a statutory dual system has ever existed. Nevertheless, where plaintiffs prove that the school authorities have carried out a systematic program of segregation affecting a substantial portion of the students, schools, teachers and facilities within the school system, it is only common sense to conclude that there exists a predicate for a finding of the existence of a dual school system. Several considerations support this conclusion. First, it is obvious that a practice of concentrating Negroes in certain schools by structuring attendance zones or designating "feeder" schools on the basis of race has the reciprocal effect of keeping other nearby schools predominantly white.[12] Similarly, the practice of building a school—such as the Barrett Elementary School in this case—to a certain size and in a certain location, "with conscious knowledge that it would be a segregated school," 303 F Supp at 285, has a substantial reciprocal effect on the racial composition of other nearby schools. So also, the use of mobile classrooms, the drafting of student transfer policies, the transportation of students, and the assignment of faculty and staff, on racially identifiable bases, have the clear effect of earmarking schools according to their racial composition, and this, in turn, together with the elements of student assignment and school construction, may have a profound reciprocal effect on the racial composition of residential neighborhoods within a metropolitan area, thereby causing further racial concentration within the schools. We recognized this in *Swann* . . . .

In short, common sense dictates the conclusion that racially inspired school board actions have an impact beyond the particular schools that are the subjects of those actions. This is not to say, of course, that there can never be a case in which the geographical structure of or the natural boundaries within a school district may have the effect of dividing the district into separate, identifiable and unrelated units. Such a determination is essentially a question of fact to be resolved by the trial court in the first instance, but such cases must be rare. In the absence of such a determination, proof of state-imposed segregation in a substantial portion of the district will suffice to support a finding by the trial court of the existence of a dual system. . . .

III

Although petitioners had already proved the existence of intentional school segregation in the Park Hill schools, this crucial finding was totally ignored when attention turned to the core city schools. Plainly, a finding of intentional segregation as to a portion of a school system is not devoid of probative value in assessing the school authorities' intent with respect to other parts of the same school system. On the contrary, where, as here, the case involves one school board, a finding of intentional segregation on its part in one portion of a school system is highly relevant to the issue of the board's intent with respect to other segregated schools in the system. This is merely an application of the well-settled evidentiary principle that "the prior doing of other similar acts, whether clearly a part of a scheme or not, is useful as reducing the possibility that the act in question was done with innocent intent." 2 Wigmore, *Evidence* §200 (3d ed 1940). . . .

---

12. . . . Judge Wisdom has recently stated: "Infection at one school infects all schools. To take the most simple example, in a two-school system, all blacks at one school means all or almost all whites at the other." *US v Texas Educ Agency* 467 F2d 848, 888 (5th Cir 1972).

Applying these principles in the special context of school desegregation cases, we hold that a finding of intentionally segregative school board actions in a meaningful portion of a school system, as in this case, creates a presumption that other segregated schooling within the system is not adventitious. It establishes, in other words, a prima facie case of unlawful segregative design on the part of school authorities, and shifts to those authorities the burden of proving that other segregated schools within the system are not also the result of intentionally segregative actions. This is true even if it is determined that different areas of the school district should be viewed independently of each other because, even in that situation, there is high probability that where school authorities have effectuated an intentionally segregative policy in a meaningful portion of the school system, similar impermissible considerations have motivated their actions in other areas of the system. We emphasize that the differentiating factor between de jure segregation and so-called de facto segregation to which we referred in *Swann* is *purpose* or *intent* to segregate. Where school authorities have been found to have practiced purposeful segregation in part of a school system, they may be expected to oppose system-wide desegregation, as did the respondents in this case, on the ground that their purposefully segregative actions were isolated and individual events, thus leaving plaintiffs with the burden of proving otherwise. But at that point where an intentionally segregative policy is practiced in a meaningful or significant segment of a school system, as in this case, the school authorities cannot be heard to argue that plaintiffs have proved only "isolated and individual" unlawfully segregative actions. In that circumstance, it is both fair and reasonable to require that the school authorities bear the burden of showing that their actions as to other segregated schools within the system were not also motivated by segregative intent.

This burden-shifting principle is not new or novel. There are no hard and fast standards governing the allocation of the burden of proof in every situation. The issue, rather, "is merely a question of policy and fairness based on experience in the different situations." 9 Wigmore, *Evidence* §2486 (3d ed 1940). In the context of racial segregation in public education, the courts, including this court, have recognized a variety of situations in which "fairness" and "policy" require state authorities to bear the burden of explaining actions or conditions which appear to be racially motivated. Thus, in *Swann, supra,* 402 US at 18, we observed that in a system with a "history of segregation," "where it is possible to identify a 'white school' or a 'Negro school' simply by reference to the racial composition of teachers and staff, the quality of school buildings and equipment, or the organization of sport activities, a prima facie case of violation of substantive constitutional rights under the equal protection clause is shown." Again, in a school system with a history of segregation, the discharge of a disproportionately large number of Negro teachers incident to desegregation "thrust[s] upon the school board the burden of justifying its conduct by clear and convincing evidence." *Chambers v Hendersonville Bd of Educ* 364 F2d 189, 192 (4th Cir 1966) (*en banc*). . . .

Nor is this burden-shifting principle limited to former statutory dual systems. See, e.g., *Davis v School Dist* 309 F Supp 734, 743-44 (ED Mich 1970), *aff'd,* 443 F2d 573 (6th Cir 1971); *US v School Dist No 151* 301 F Supp 201, 228 (ND Ill 1969), *modified on other grounds,* 432 F2d 1147 (7th Cir 1970). . . .

In discharging that burden, it is not enough, of course, that the school authorities rely upon some allegedly logical, racially neutral explanation for their actions. Their burden is to adduce proof sufficient to support a finding that segregative intent was not among the factors that motivated their actions. The courts below attributed much significance to the fact that many of the board's actions in the core city area antedated our decision in *Brown*. We reject any suggestion that remoteness in time has any relevance to the issue of intent. If the actions of school authorities were to any degree motivated by segregative intent and the segregation resulting from those actions continues to exist, the fact of remoteness in time certainly does not make those actions any less "intentional."

This is not to say, however, that the prima facie case may not be met by evidence supporting a finding that a lesser degree of segregated schooling in the core city area would not have resulted even if the board had not acted as it did. In *Swann*, we suggested that at some point in time the relationship between past segregative acts and present segregation may become so attenuated as to be incapable of supporting a finding of de jure segregation warranting judicial intervention. 402 US at 31-32. See also *Hobson v Hansen* 269 F Supp 401, 495 (DC 1967), aff'd sub nom, *Smuck v Hobson*, 132 U S App DC 372, 408 F2d 175 (1969). We made it clear, however, that a connection between past segregative acts and present segregation may be present even when not apparent and that close examination is required before concluding that the connection does not exist. Intentional school segregation in the past may have been a factor in creating a natural environment for the growth of further segregation. Thus, if respondent school board cannot disprove segregative intent, it can rebut the prima facie case only by showing that its past segregative acts did not create or contribute to the current segregated condition of the core city schools.

The respondent school board invoked at trial its "neighborhood school policy" as explaining racial and ethnic concentrations within the core city schools, arguing that since the core city area population had long been Negro and Hispano, the concentrations were necessarily the result of residential patterns and not of purposefully segregative policies. We have no occasion to consider in this case whether a "neighborhood school policy" of itself will justify racial or ethnic concentrations in the absence of a finding that school authorities have committed acts constituting de jure segregation. It is enough that we hold that the mere assertion of such a policy is not dispositive where, as in this case, the school authorities have been found to have practiced de jure segregation in a meaningful portion of the school system by techniques that indicate that the "neighborhood school" concept has not been maintained free of manipulation. . . .

The judgment of the court of appeals is modified to vacate instead of reverse the parts of the final decree that concern the core city schools, and the case is remanded to the district court for further proceedings consistent with this opinion.[18]

It is so ordered.

18. We therefore do not reach and intimate no view upon the merits of the holding of the district court, premised upon its erroneous finding that the situation "is more like de facto segregation," 313 F Supp at 73, that nevertheless, although all-out desegregation "could not be decreed, . . . the only feasible and constitutionally acceptable program . . . is a system of desegregation and integration which provides compensatory education in an integrated environment." 313 F Supp at 96.

Mr. Chief Justice Burger concurs in the result.

Mr. Justice White took no part in the decision of this case.

Mr. Justice Douglas.

While I join the opinion of the court, I agree with my brother Powell that there is, for the purposes of the equal protection clause of the Fourteenth Amendment as applied to the school cases, no difference between de facto and de jure segregation. The school board is a state agency and the lines that it draws, the locations it selects for school sites, the allocation it makes of students, the budgets it prepares are state action for Fourteenth Amendment purposes. . . . If a "neighborhood" or "geographical" unit has been created along racial lines by reason of the play of restrictive covenants that restrict certain areas to "the elite," leaving the "undesirables" to move elsewhere, there is state action in the constitutional sense because the force of law is placed behind those covenants.

There is state action in the constitutional sense when public funds are dispersed by urban development agencies to build racial ghettoes. . . .

When a state forces, aids, or abets, or helps create a racial "neighborhood," it is a travesty of justice to treat that neighborhood as sacrosanct in the sense that its creation is free from the taint of state action.

The Constitution and Bill of Rights have described the design of a pluralistic society. The individual has the right to seek such companions as he desires. But a state is barred from creating by one device or another ghettoes that determine the school one is compelled to attend.

Mr. Justice Powell concurring in part and dissenting in part.

I concur in the remand of this case for further proceedings in the district court, but on grounds that differ from those relied upon by the court.

This is the first school desegregation case to reach this court which involves a major city outside the South. It comes from Denver, Colorado, a city and a state which have not operated public schools under constitutional or statutory provisions which mandated or permitted racial segregation. . . .

The situation in Denver is generally comparable to that in other large cities across the country in which there is a substantial minority population and where desegregation has not been ordered by the federal courts. There is segregation in the schools of many of these cities fully as pervasive as that in southern cities prior to the desegregation decrees of the past decade and a half. The focus of the school desegregation problem has now shifted from the South to the country as a whole. Unwilling and footdragging as the process was in most places, substantial progress toward achieving integration has been made in southern states. No comparable progress has been made in many nonsouthern cities with large minority populations primarily because of the de facto/de jure distinction nurtured by the courts and accepted complacently by many of the same voices which denounced the evils of segregated schools in the south. But if our national concern is for those who attend such schools, rather than for perpetuating a legalism rooted in history rather than present reality, we must recognize that the evil of operating separate schools is no less in Denver than in Atlanta.

I

In my view we should abandon a distinction which long since has outlived its time, and formulate constitutional principles of national rather than merely regional application. When *Brown v Board of Educ* 347 US 483 (1954), was decided, the distinction between de jure and de facto segregation was consistent with the limited constitutional rationale of that case. The situation confronting the court, largely confined to the southern states, was officially imposed racial segregation in the schools extending back for many years and usually embodied in constitutional and statutory provisions.

The great contribution of *Brown 1* was its holding in unmistakable terms that the Fourteenth Amendment forbids state-compelled or authorized segregation of public schools. 347 US at 488, 493-95. Although some of the language was more expansive, the holding in *Brown 1* was essentially negative: It was impermissible under the Constitution for the states, or their instrumentalities, to force children to attend segregated schools. The forbidden action was de jure, and the opinion in *Brown 1* was construed—for some years and by many courts—as requiring only state neutrality, allowing "freedom of choice" as to schools to be attended so long as the state itself assured that the choice was genuinely free of official restraints.

But the doctrine of *Brown 1,* as amplified by *Brown 2,* 349 US 294 (1955), did not retain its original meaning. In a series of decisions extending from 1954 to 1971 the concept of state neutrality was transformed into the present constitutional doctrine requiring affirmative state action to desegregate school systems. The keystone case was *Green v County School Bd* 391 US 430, 438 (1968) where school boards were declared to have "the affirmative duty to take whatever steps might be necessary to convert to a unitary system in which racial discrimination would be eliminated root and branch." The school system before the court in *Green* was operating in a rural and sparsely settled county where there were no concentrations of white and black populations, no neighborhood school system (there were only two schools in the county), and none of the problems of an urbanized school district. The court properly identified the freedom-of-choice program there as a subterfuge, and the language in *Green* imposing an affirmative duty to convert to a unitary system was appropriate on the facts before the court. There was, however, reason to question to what extent this duty would apply in the vastly different factual setting of a large city with extensive areas of residential segregation, presenting problems and calling for solutions quite different from those in the rural setting of New Kent County, Virginia.

But the doubt as to whether the affirmative duty concept would flower into a new constitutional principle of general application was laid to rest by *Swann v Board of Educ* 402 US 1 (1971), in which the duty articulated in *Green* was applied to the urban school system of metropolitan Charlotte, North Carolina. . . .

Whereas *Brown 1* rightly decreed the elimination of state-imposed segregation in that particular section of the country where it did exist, *Swann* imposed obligations on southern school districts to eliminate conditions which are not regionally unique but are similar both in origin and effect to conditions in the rest of the country. As the remedial obligations of *Swann* extend far beyond the elimination of the outgrowths of the state-imposed segregation outlawed in *Brown,* the rationale of *Swann* points inevitably towards a uniform, constitutional approach to our national problem of school segregation.

II

The court's decision today, while adhering to the de jure/de facto distinction, will require the application of the *Green/Swann* doctrine of "affirmative duty" to the Denver School Board despite the absence of any history of state-mandated school segregation. The only evidence of a constitutional violation was found in various decisions of the school board. I concur in the court's position that the public school authorities are the responsible agency of the state, and that if the affirmative duty doctrine is sound constitutional law for Charlotte, it is equally so for Denver. I would not, however, perpetuate the de jure/de facto distinction nor would I leave to petitioners the initial tortuous effort of identifying "segregative acts" and deducing "segregatory intent." I would hold, quite simply, that where segregated public schools exist within a school district to a substantial degree, there is a prima facie case that the duly constituted public authorities (I will usually refer to them collectively as the "school board") are sufficiently responsible to impose upon them a nationally applicable burden to demonstrate they nevertheless are operating a genuinely integrated school system.

A

The principal reason for abandonment of the de jure/de facto distinction is that, in view of the evolution of the holding in *Brown 1* into the affirmative duty doctrine, the distinction no longer can be justified on a principled basis. In decreeing remedial requirements for the Charlotte/Mecklenburg school district, *Swann* dealt with a metropolitan, urbanized area in which the basic causes of segregation were generally similar to those in all sections of the country, and also largely irrelevant to the existence of historic, state-imposed segregation at the time of the *Brown* decision. Further, the extension of the affirmative duty concept to include compulsory student transportation went well beyond the mere remedying of that portion of school segregation for which former state segregation laws were ever responsible. Moreover, as the court's opinion today abundantly demonstrates, the facts deemed necessary to establish de jure discrimination present problems of subjective intent which the courts cannot fairly resolve. . . .

. . . . In the evolutionary process since 1954, decisions of this court have added a significant gloss to [*Brown*]. Although nowhere expressly articulated in these terms, I would now define it as the right, derived from the equal protection clause, to expect that once the state has assumed responsibility for education, local school boards will operate *integrated school systems* within their respective districts. This means that school authorities, consistent with the generally accepted educational goal of attaining quality education for all pupils, must make and implement their customary decisions with a view toward enhancing integrated school opportunities.

The term "integrated school system" presupposes, of course, a total absence of any laws, regulations or policies supportive of the type of "legalized" segregation condemned in *Brown*. A system would be integrated in accord with constitutional standards if the responsible authorities had taken appropriate steps to (i) integrate faculties and administration; (ii) scrupulously assure equality of facilities, instruction and curricula opportunities throughout the district; (iii) utilize their authority to draw attendance zones to promote integration; and (iv) locate new schools, close old ones, and determine the size and grade categories with this same objective in mind. Where school authorities decide to undertake the transportation of students, this also must be with integrative opportunities in mind.

The foregoing prescription is not intended to be either definitive or all-inclusive, but rather an indication of the contour characteristics of an *integrated school system* in which all citizens and pupils may justifiably be confident that racial discrimination is neither practiced nor tolerated. An integrated school system does not mean—and indeed could not mean in view of the residential patterns of most of our major metropolitan areas—that *every school* must in fact be an integrated unit. A school which happens to be all or predominantly white or all or predominantly black is not a "segregated" school in an unconstitutional sense if the system itself is a genuinely integrated one.

Having school boards operate an integrated school system provides the best assurance of meeting the constitutional requirement that racial discrimination, subtle or otherwise, will find no place in the decisions of public school officials. Courts judging past school board actions with a view to their *general integrative effect* will be best able to assure an absence of such discrimination while avoiding the murky, subjective judgments inherent in the court's search for "segregatory intent." Any test resting on so nebulous and elusive an element as a school board's segregatory "intent" provides inadequate assurance that minority children will not be shortchanged in the decisions of those entrusted with the nondiscriminatory operation of our public schools.

Public schools are creatures of the state, and whether the segregation is state-created or state-assisted or merely state-perpetuated should be irrelevant to constitutional principle. The school board exercises pervasive and continuing responsibility over the long-range planning as well as the daily operations of the public school system. It sets policies on attendance zones, faculty employment and assignments, school construction, closings and consolidations, and myriad other matters. School board decisions obviously are not the sole cause of segregated school conditions. But if, after such detailed and complete public supervision, substantial school segregation still persists, the presumption is strong that the school board, by its acts or omissions, is in some part responsible. Where state action and supervision are so pervasive and where, after years of such action, segregated schools continue to exist within the district to a substantial degree, this court is justified in finding a prima facie case of a constitutional violation. The burden then must fall on the school board to demonstrate it is operating an "integrated school system." . . .

The court today does move for the first time toward breaking down past sectional disparities, but it clings tenuously to its distinction. It searches for *de jure* action in what the Denver School Board has done or failed to do, and even here the court does not rely upon the results or effects of the board's conduct but feels compelled to find segregatory intent . . . . I can discern no basis in law or logic for holding that the motivation of school board action is irrelevant in Virginia and controlling in Colorado. . . . The net result of the court's language, however, is the application of an *effect* test to the actions of southern school districts and an *intent* test to those in other sections, at least until an initial *de jure* finding for those districts can be made. Rather than straining to perpetuate any such dual standard, we should hold forthrightly that significant segregated school conditions in whatever section of the country are a prima facie violation of constitutional rights.

B

There is thus no reason as a matter of constitutional principle to adhere to the *de jure/de facto* distinction in school desegregation cases. In addition, there are reasons of policy and prudent judicial administration which point strongly toward the adoption of a uniform national rule. The litigation heretofore centered in the South already is surfacing in other regions. The decision of the court today, emphasizing as it does the elusive element of segregatory intent, will invite numerous desegregation suits in which there can be little hope of uniformity of result. . . .

This court has recognized repeatedly that it is "extremely difficult for a court to ascertain the motivation, or collection of different motivations, that lie behind a legislative enactment." *Palmer v Thompson* 403 US 214, 224 (1971); *McGinnis v Royster* ____ US ____, ____ (1973); *US v O'Brien* 391 US 367, 381 (1968). Whatever difficulties exist with regard to a single statute will be compounded in a judicial review of years of administration of a large and complex school system.[16] Every act of a school board and school administration, and indeed every failure to act where affirmative action is indicated, must now be subject to scrutiny. . . .

III

As the court's opinion virtually compels the finding on remand that Denver has a "dual school system," that city will then be under an "affirmative duty" to desegregate its entire system "root and branch." *Green v County School Bd* 391 US at 438. Again, the critical question is what ought this constitutional duty to entail.

A

The controlling case is *Swann, supra,* and the question which will confront and confound the district court and Denver School Board is what indeed does *Swann* require. *Swann* purported to enunciate no new principles, relying heavily on *Brown 1* and *2* and on *Green.* Yet it affirmed a district court order which had relied heavily on "racial ratios" and sanctioned transportation of elementary as well as secondary pupils. Lower federal courts have often read *Swann* as requiring far-reaching transportation decrees[17] "to achieve the greatest possible

---

16. As one commentator has expressed it:

"If the courts are indeed prepared to inquire into motive, thorny questions will arise even if one assumes that racial motivation is capable of being proven at trial. What of the case in which one or more members of a school board, but less than a majority, are found to have acted on racial grounds? What if it appears that the school board's action was prompted by a mixture of motives, including constitutionally innocent ones that alone would have prompted the board to act? What if the members of the school board were not themselves racially inspired but wished to please their constituents, many of whom they knew to be so? If such cases are classified as unconstitutional de jure segregation, there is little point in preserving the de jure/de facto distinction at all. And it may well be that the difference between any of these situations and one in which racial motivation is altogether lacking is too insignificant, from the standpoint of both the moral culpability of the state officials and the impact upon the children involved, to support a difference in constitutional treatment." [Goodman, "De Facto Segregation: A Constitutional and Empirical Analysis," 60 *Calif L Rev* 275, 284-85 (1972).]

17. See, e.g., *Thompson v School Bd* ____ F2d ____, ____ (1972), where the Fourth Circuit *en banc,* upheld a district court assignment plan where "travel time, varying from a minimum of forty minutes and a maximum of one hour, each way, would be required for busing black students out of the old city and white students into the old city in order to achieve a racial balancing of the district." This transportation was decreed for children from the third grade up, involving children as young as eight years of age.

degree of actual desegregation." 402 US at 26. In the context of a large urban area, with heavy residential concentrations of white and black citizens in different—and widely separated—sections of the school district, extensive dispersal and transportation of pupils is inevitable if *Swann* is read as expansively as many courts have been reading it to date.

To the extent that *Swann* may be thought to require large-scale or long-distance transportation of students in our metropolitan school districts, I record my profound misgivings. Nothing in our Constitution commands or encourages any such court compelled disruption of public education. It may be more accurate to view *Swann* as having laid down a broad rule of reason under which desegregation remedies must remain flexible and other values and interests be considered. Thus the Court recognized that school authorities, not the federal judiciary, must be charged in the first instance with the task of desegregating local school systems. 402 US at 16. It noted that school boards in rural areas can adjust more readily to this task than those in metropolitan districts "with dense and shifting population, numerous schools, congested and complex traffic patterns." 402 US at 14. Although the use of pupil transportation was approved as a remedial device, transportation orders are suspect "when the time or distance of travel is so great as to either risk the health of the children or significantly impinge on the education process." 402 US at 31. Finally, the age of the pupils to be transported was recognized by the Court in *Swann* as one important limitation on the time of student travel. *Ibid.* . . .

Thus in school desegregation cases, as elsewhere, equity counsels reason, flexibility and balance. . . . I am aware, of course, that reasonableness in any area is a relative and subjective concept. But with school desegregation, reasonableness would seem to embody a balanced evaluation of the obligation of public school boards to promote desegregation with other, equally important educational interests which a community may legitimately assert. Neglect of either the obligation or the interests destroys the even-handed spirit with which equitable remedies must be approached.[19] Overzealousness in pursuit of any single goal is untrue to the tradition of equity and to the "balance" and "flexibility" which this court has always respected.

B

Where school authorities have defaulted in their duty to operate an integrated school system, district courts must insure that affirmative desegregative steps ensue. Many of these can be taken effectively without damaging state and paren-

In *Northcross v Memphis Bd of Educ* 466 F2d 890, 895 (1972), the Sixth Circuit affirmed a district court assignment plan which daily transported 14,000 children with "the maximum time to be spent on the buses by any child [being] thirty-four minutes. . . ," presumably each way. But as Judge Weick noted in dissent the Sixth Circuit instructed the district judge to implement yet further desegregation orders. Plans presently under consideration by that court call for the busing of 39,085 and 61,530 children respectively, for undetermined lengths of time. 466 F2d at 895-986.

19. The relevant inquiry is "whether the costs of achieving desegregation in any given situation outweigh the legal, moral and educational considerations favoring it. . . . It is clear . . . that the Constitution should not be held to require any transportation plan that keeps children on a bus for a substantial part of the day, consumes significant portions of funds otherwise spendable directly on education, or involves a genuine element of danger to the safety of the child." "School Desegregation After Swann: A Theory of Government Responsibility," 39 *U Chi L Rev* 421, 422-43 (1972).

tal interests in having children attend schools within a reasonable vicinity of home. Where desegregative steps are possible within the framework of a system of "neighborhood education," school authorities must pursue them. For example boundaries of neighborhood attendance zones should be drawn to integrate, to the extent practicable, the school's student body. Construction of new schools should be of such a size and at such a location as to encourage the likelihood of integration. . . . Faculty integration should be attained throughout the school system. . . . An optional majority to minority transfer program, with the state providing free transportation to desiring students, is also a helpful adjunct to a desegregated school system. . . . It hardly need be repeated that allocation of resources within the school district must be made with scrupulous fairness among all schools.

The above examples are meant to be illustrative, not exhaustive. The point is that the overall integrative impact of such school board decisions must be assessed by district courts in deciding whether the duty to desegregate has been met. For example, "neighborhood school plans are constitutionally suspect when attendance zones are superficially imposed upon racially defined neighborhoods, and when school construction preserves rather than eliminates the racial hegemony of given schools." . . . This does not imply that decisions on faculty assignment, attendance zones, school construction, closing and consolidation, must be made to the detriment of all neutral, nonracial considerations. But these considerations can, with proper school board initiative, generally be met in a manner that will enhance the degree of school desegregation.

C

A *constitutional requirement* of extensive student transportation solely to achieve integration presents a vastly more complex problem. It promises on the one hand a greater degree of actual desegregation, while it infringes on what may fairly be regarded as other important community aspirations and personal rights. Such a requirement is further likely to divert attention and resources from the foremost goal of any school system: the best quality education for all pupils. The equal protection clause does indeed command that racial discrimination not be tolerated in the decisions of public school authorities. But it does not require that school authorities undertake widespread student transportation solely for the sake of maximizing integration.

This obviously does not mean that bus transportation has no place in public school systems or is not a permissible means in the desegregative process. The transporting of school children is as old as public education, and in rural and some suburban settings it is as indispensable as the providing of books. It is presently estimated that approximately half of all American children ride buses to school for reasons unrelated to integration. At the secondary level in particular, where the schools are larger and serve a wider, more dispersed constituency than the elementary school, some form of public or privately financed transportation is often necessary. There is a significant difference, however, in transportation plans voluntarily initiated by local school boards for educational purposes and those imposed by a federal court. The former usually represent a necessary or convenient means of access to the school nearest home; the latter often require lengthy trips for no purpose other than to further integration. . . . The neighborhood school does provide greater ease of parental and student access and convenience, as well as greater economy of public administration. These are obvious and distinct advantages, but the legitimacy of the neighborhood concept rests on more basic grounds.[26]

Neighborhood school systems, neutrally administered, reflect the deeply felt desire of citizens for a sense of community in their public education. Public schools have been a traditional source of strength to our nation, and that strength may derive in part from the identification of many schools with the personal features of the surrounding neighborhood. Community support, interest and dedication to public schools may well run higher with a neighborhood attendance pattern: distance may encourage disinterest. Many citizens sense today a decline in the intimacy of our institutions—home, church, and school—which has caused a concomitant decline in the unity and communal spirit of our people. I pass no judgment on this viewpoint, but I do believe that this court should be wary of compelling in the name of constitutional law what may seem to many a dissolution in the traditional, more personal fabric of their public schools.

Closely related to the concept of a community and neighborhood education, are those rights and duties parents have with respect to the education of their children. The law has long recognized the parental duty to nurture, support, and provide for the welfare of children, including their education. In *Pierce v Society of Sisters* 268 US 510, 534, 535, a unanimous court held that:

> Under the doctrine of *Meyer v Nebraska* 262 US 390, we think it entirely plain that the Act of 1922 unreasonably interferes with the liberty of parents and guardians to direct the upbringing and education of children under their control. . . . The child is not the mere creature of the state; those who nurture him and direct his destiny have the right, coupled with the high duty, to recognize and prepare him for additional obligations.

And in *Griswold v Connecticut* 381 US 479, 482 (1965), the court noted that in *Pierce,* "the right to educate one's children as one chooses is made applicable to the states by the force of the First and Fourteenth Amendments." I do not believe recognition of this right can be confined solely to a parent's choice to send a child to public or private school. Most parents cannot afford the luxury of a private education for their children, and the dual obligation of private tuitions and public taxes. Those who may for numerous reasons seek public education for their children should not be forced to forfeit all interest or voice in the school their child attends. It would, of course, be impractical to allow the wishes of particular parents to be controlling. Yet the interest of the parent in the enhanced parent-school and parent-child communication allowed by the neighborhood unit ought not to be suppressed by force of law.

In the commendable national concern for alleviating public school segregation, courts may have overlooked the fact that the rights and interests of children affected by a desegregation program also are entitled to consideration. Any child, white or black, who is compelled to leave his neighborhood and spend significant time each day being transported to a distant school suffers an impairment of his liberty and his privacy. . . .

---

26. I do not imply that the neighborhood concept must be embodied in every school system. But where a school board has chosen it, federal judges should accord it respect in framing remedial decrees.

The argument for student transportation also overlooks the fact that the remedy exceeds that which may be necessary to redress the constitutional evil. Let us use Denver as an example. The Denver School Board, by its action and nonaction, may be legally responsible for some of the segregation that exists. But if one assumes a maximum discharge of constitutional duty by the Denver Board over the past decades, the fundamental problem of residential segregation would persist. It is indeed a novel application of equitable power—not to mention a dubious extension of constitutional doctrine—to require so much greater a degree of forced school integration than would have resulted from purely natural and neutral nonstate causes.

The compulsory transportation of students carries a further infirmity as a constitutional remedy. With most constitutional violations, the major burden of remedial action falls on offending state officials. Public officials who act to infringe personal rights of speech, voting, or religious exercise, for example, are obliged to cease the offending act or practice and, where necessary, institute corrective measures. It is they who bear the brunt of remedial action, though other citizens will to varying degrees feel its effects. School authorities responsible for segregation must, at the very minimum, discontinue segregatory acts. But when the obligation further extends to the transportation of students, the full burden of the affirmative remedial action is borne by children and parents who did not participate in any constitutional violation.

Finally, courts in requiring so far-reaching a remedy as student transportation solely to maximize integration, risk setting in motion unpredictable and unmanageable social consequences. No one can estimate the extent to which dismantling neighborhood education will hasten an exodus to private schools, leaving public school systems the preserve of the disadvantaged of both races. Or guess how much impetus such dismantlement gives the movement from inner city to suburb, and the further geographical separation of the races. Nor do we know to what degree this remedy may cause deterioration of community and parental support of public schools, or divert attention from the paramount goal of quality in education to a perennially devisive debate over who is to be transported where....

.... It is time to return to a more balanced evaluation of the recognized interests of our society in achieving desegregation with other educational and societal interests a community may legitimately assert. This will help assure that integrated school systems will be established and maintained by rational action, will be better understood and supported by parents and children of both races, and will promote the enduring qualities of an integrated society so essential to its genuine success.

Mr. Justice Rehnquist, dissenting.

.... Underlying the court's entire opinion is its apparent thesis that a district judge is at least permitted to find that if a single attendance zone between two individual schools in the large metropolitan district is found by him to have been "gerrymandered," the school district is guilty of operating a "dual" school system, and is apparently a candidate for what is in practice a federal receivership. Not only the language of the court in the opinion, but its reliance on the case of *Green v County School Bd* 391 US 430, 437-38 (1968), indicates that such would be the case. It would therefore presumably be open to the district court to require, *inter alia,* that pupils be transported great distances throughout the district to and from schools whose attendance zones have not been gerrymandered. Yet unless the equal protection clause of the Fourteenth Amendment now be held to embody a principle of "taint," found in some primitive legal systems but discarded centuries ago in ours, such a result can only be described as the product of judicial fiat.

Green . . . represented a marked extension of the principles of *Brown v Board of Education*. . . . The drastic extension of *Brown* which *Green* represented was barely, if at all, explicated in the latter opinion. To require that a genuinely "dual" system be disestablished, in the sense that the assignment to a child of a particular school is not made to depend on his race, is one thing. To require that school boards affirmatively undertake to achieve racial mixing in schools where such mixing is not achieved in sufficient degree by neutrally drawn boundary lines is quite obviously something else.

The court's own language in *Green* makes it unmistakably clear that this significant extension of *Brown's* prohibition against discrimination, and the conversion of that prohibition into an affirmative duty to integrate, was made in the context of a school system which had for a number of years rigidly excluded Negroes from attending the same schools as were attended by whites. Whatever may be the soundness of that decision in the context of a genuinely "dual" school system, where segregation of the races had once been mandated by law, I can see no constitutional justification for it in a situation such as that which the record shows to have obtained in Denver. . . .

Notes and Questions

1. The De Jure/De Facto Distinction

The court retains the distinction between de facto segregation, which is unintentional, and de jure segregation, which is purposeful or intentional.

a. What Is Intentional Segregation? Does the court adopt the *Bell* or the *Guinn* approach to de jure segregation? Does it implicitly favor the latter when it quotes from the district court opinion, stating that often a school location and size decision is made "with conscious knowledge that the result would be a segregated school . . ."? What of the court's reference to student transfer, student transportation, and faculty assignment policies that have the "effect" of creating a dual school system? Is the meaning of the reference changed by the notation that these decisions were made on "racially identifiable bases"? What evidence does the court cite for this proposition? Does the court simply rely on the factual conclusions of the district court?

b. Proving Intentional Segregation. How should a court determine whether school segregation was racially motivated? Suppose some members of the board of education admitted that they voted to close a school to avoid integration, but others joined in the vote for unrelated reasons? Is it enough that any single member of a decision-making body was improperly motivated? What if a board member was influenced only in part by racial considerations? Is this sufficient for a finding of de jure segregation? What impact will the *Keyes* decision have on the willingness of board members to reveal their motivations? Will courts be compelled to imply motive from the segregatory decisions themselves? If so, what is left of the de facto/de jure distinction?

c. Proving Intentional Segregation in Keyes. What proof did the plaintiff offer in *Keyes* to demonstrate unlawful intent to segregate? Are there any references in the court's opinion to specific racial pronouncements by board members? Does the decision to build a small elementary school in the middle of the Negro community necessarily indicate a discriminatory intent? If parents in some areas were given a choice of more than one school, and black parents chose predominantly black schools and white parents chose predominantly white schools, is this proof that school authorities had adopted the policy with the purpose of fostering segregation? Does the "excessive" use of mobile classrooms reveal segregatory intent?

d. Relevancy of Intention to Discriminate. Why is intentional segregation unconstitutional, while other forms of segregation are not? If segregation is stigmatizing, harmful, or otherwise undesirable as a matter of public policy, how do the good or bad motivations of governmental decision makers alter the equation? Is Justice Powell correct when he asserts: "Public schools are creatures of the state, and whether the segregation is state-created or state-assisted or merely state-perpetuated should be irrelevant to constitutional principle"?

e. Burden of Proof. In the court's view, which party must prove intentional segregation? Does the burden shift once some intentional discrimination has been proven?

f. De Jure Segregation: North and South. Justice Powell stated in *Keyes* that he could discern "no basis in law or logic for holding that the motivation of school board action is irrelevant in Virginia and controlling in Colorado." Is this a fair statement of the majority's position? Is not the enactment of compulsory segregation laws in the South the clearest example of an intention to discriminate? Is intention to discriminate simply more difficult to prove in the North? What might Justice Powell have had in mind when he referred to a dual constitutional standard for the North and South? Is Powell objecting to the fact that in the South a segregationist law is sufficient to show an intention to discriminate *in futuro*, while in the North a present intention to discriminate must be shown?

2. What Is a Segregated School?

a. The Numbers Game. Is a school segregated when it has more than 70 to 75 percent blacks? When the ratio of blacks to whites is greater than the ratio in the entire student population of the school district? If desegregation is premised on the denial of equal educational opportunity to blacks, should the courts determine at what point the school becomes sufficiently segregated to injure black students? Does this suggest that there is an underlying assumption "that whites are better [educational] resources than blacks"? (Dimond, "School Segregation in the North: There Is But One Constitution," 7 *Harv Civil Rights—Civil Liberties Rev* 1, 16 (1972).) Might this be true?

Psychologist Thomas Pettigrew has testified that a 70 : 30 or 60 : 40 ratio of white to black students creates the ideal learning environment. See *Beckett v School Bd* 302 F Supp 18 (ED Va 1969), 308 F Supp 1274 (ED Va 1969), *rev'd*, 434 F2d 408 (4th Cir 1970), *cert denied*, 399 US 929 (1970). Compare *Brunson v Board of Trustees of School Dist No 1* 429 F2d 820 (4th Cir 1970); *Bradley v School Bd* 338 F Supp 67 (ED Va 1972), *rev'd*, 462 F2d 1058 (4th

Cir 1972), *aff'd* 36 L Ed2d 771 (1973). Does this imply that if blacks constitute more than 60 percent of a school's student population, the school is segregated? What if there are not enough white students to make a 60 : 40 ratio in each school? Is the Pettigrew thesis consistent with *Swann*? See *Swann v Charlotte-Mecklenburg Board of Educ* 402 US 1, 24 n8 (1971).

b. Mexican-Americans. Should Mexican-Americans be treated as an identifiable class for purposes of determining whether a school or school system is segregated? See *Cisneros v Corpus Christi Independent School Dist* 467 F2d 142 (5th Cir 1972); *US v Texas* 467 F2d 848 (5th Cir 1972). Is it sufficient to say that both blacks and Mexican-Americans have been discriminated against? That they both presently suffer educational inequities? That both are economically and culturally deprived? That both groups do less well in schools than whites? Is the extension of *Brown* and its progeny to Mexican-Americans consistent with the underlying purposes of the Fourteenth Amendment? Is this simply another instance of a problem that the draftsmen of that amendment never addressed? If the court had focused only on blacks and whites, would this discriminate against the only other substantial racial or ethnic minority in Denver? Does *Keyes* portend the extension of *Brown* to other minorities? Do *Keyes* and *Swann,* read together, mean that every, or nearly every, school in a school system must be ethnically and racially balanced?

3. Relationship between Racially Motivated Acts and Obligation to Desegregate

a. Past Discrimination and Present Segregation. The court notes that "if the actions of school authorities were to any degree motivated by segregative intent and the segregation resulting from those actions continues to exist, the fact of remoteness does not make those actions any less 'intentional.' " How close must the relationship be between the past segregatory acts and the present segregation in Denver? Must the plaintiffs prove that racially motivated decisions with respect to school location and size resulted in segregated neighborhoods, which in turn led to a segregated school system? Is the burden on the defendants? What does it mean to say that past school segregation policies "may have been a factor in creating a natural environment for the growth of further segregation"? Does the court's emphasis on broadly construing the causal relationship between past segregatory acts and present school segregation, combined with the shifting of the burden of persuasion to the defendants, preordain the results in northern desegregation cases? Has the court, without being explicit, adopted Justice Powell's view that there is an affirmative obligation to integrate the public schools, whether or not the segregation is de jure?

b. De Jure Segregation in Part of the System

i. The Issue. The court frames the issue for decision in limited terms: when there is substantial segregation in part of a school system, is the entire system a dual school system that must be wholly desegregated? Why did the court frame the issue in these terms? The district court had ordered the desegregation of schools outside Park Hill on the theory that a segregated school, irrespective of racial motivation or state action, deprived minority children of an equal educational opportunity. Is that finding relevant here? Could the court have passed on the district court's determination without deciding whether de facto segregation was constitutional? (See Goodman, "De Facto Segregation: A Constitutional and Empirical Analysis," 60 *Calif L Rev* 275, 276 n 6 (1972).) Without reviewing the social science evidence of the effect of segregation and integration on achievement?

ii. Resolving the Issue. The court treats the issue of substantial segregation in a part of the system as relevant in two ways to a system-wide determination of de jure segregation. First, the court notes that de jure segregation in part of the system may determine the racial composition of other neighborhoods within a metropolitan area, thereby causing the segregation of schools outside the tainted area of the city. This is particularly true since the decision to maintain segregated schools in one area necessarily limits the possibilities for integration in other areas. The court admits that sometimes this will not be the case, but intimates that such occasions are rare. Second, the court holds that intentional segregation in a portion of a school system creates a presumption that segregation elsewhere in the system is racially motivated, shifting the burden of proof to the defendants.

iii. Result. Can the court's treatment of less than system-wide discrimination be accurately described as a sort of "catch 22?" If a substantial amount of racially motivated segregation is found, lower courts usually will find that the entire system has been tainted. If the school district does convince the court that the de jure practices are isolated episodes, there is still a presumption that any other segregation in the system is racially motivated. Consider also the burden of proof borne by the district. It must prove that "segregative intent was not among the factors that motivated their actions." Does the court's elaboration of evidentiary rules largely obliterate the de facto/de jure distinction?

4. The Remedy

The majority reaffirms the court's position in *Green* and *Swann* that there is an affirmative duty to integrate and create a unitary school system once there has been a determination that the school authorities have engaged in unlawful segregation. Does the court place this obligation in a remedial context, as in *Swann*? Does it suggest that the extent of the integration remedy is within the discretion of the lower courts? Does the majority adequately respond to Justice Rehnquist's contention that *Brown* required only the elimination of racial classifications? Would Justice Powell characterize the duty to integrate as substantive rather than remedial? What should one make of his statement that integration will best "assure an absence of . . . discrimination while avoiding the murky, subjective judgments inherent in the court's search for 'segregatory intent' "?

5. Costs of Integration

Justice Powell, in his separate concurring and dissenting opinion, raises an issue rarely addressed by the Supreme Court in desegregation cases: what cost limitations should be placed on the accomplishment of the goal of integration? See Glazer, "Is Busing Necessary," 53 *Commentary* 39 (March 1972); Mondale, "Busing in Perspective," *The New Republic*, 4 March 1972, at 18-19. How much busing should be required? What age children may be bused? When should the integration of faculties be given precedence over traditional methods of faculty assignment according to seniority, education, or union contract? What of convenience and safety? What of the liberty of parents to make educational choices for their children? What of the value of the sense of community fostered by neighborhood schools? In short, how should conflicting goals be resolved and what weight should each receive in determining the scope of the desegregation obligation? How does Justice Powell weigh the costs of integration against other social goals? What is the meaning of "balanced recognition of the recognized interests of our society in achieving desegregation with other educational and societal interests a community may legitimately assert"? Consider Justice Powell's description of an integrated school system:

> A system would be integrated in accord with constitutional standards if the responsible authorities had taken appropriate steps to (i) integrate faculties and administration; (ii) scrupulously assure equal facilities, instruction and curricula opportunities throughout the district; (iii) utilize their authority to draw attendance zones to promote integration; and (iv) locate new schools, close old ones, and determine the size and grade categories with this same objective in mind. Where school authorities decide to undertake the transportation of students, this also must be with integrative opportunities in mind. 93 S Ct at 2706.

In what way does this description strike the balance for Justice Powell between integration and other values? Why does he reject extensive busing? Is it fair to say that a limitation on busing is as much a matter of political necessity, in the light of popular opposition, as a dispassionate analysis of the costs? Or is popular opposition itself a cost? In urban areas, how much integration is likely to occur as a result of the remedies advocated by Justice Powell?

If the likelihood of symbolic or real benefits from integration is unclear, and the causal relationships between integration, segregation, and social satisfaction are speculative, how can the costs of integration be reasonably computed? In economic terms, the question is not simply the cost of integration, but rather the marginal costs of integration to achieve a particular, desirable social outcome. Does this imply that rational decisions about integration cannot be made without a more advanced social science? Do we already possess that degree of certainty about the impact of integration? Does this analysis suggest that the computation of marginal costs is itself an ethical decision?

6. Impact of *Keyes*

If *Swann* was widely interpreted as requiring racial balance and extensive busing, may not *Keyes* be popularly viewed as extending *Swann* to the North? As this book goes to press, *Keyes* has not given rise to any of the public outcry which accompanied *Brown* or *Swann*. How do you explain the mildness of the public reaction?

7. Aftermath of Desegregation

Integration advocates hoped that once the de jure elements of school segregation were eliminated "root and branch," the problems associated with school desegregation would disappear. That hope has proved overly optimistic. In both

North and South desegregation has given rise to what sociologist Nathan Glazer calls "a second generation of problems affecting both students and teachers." Violence and disruptive behavior is more common in integrated schools than in either all-black or all-white schools. Havighurst, Smith, and Wilder, "A Profile of the Large-City High School," *NASSP Bull,* January 1971, p 76. One Mississippi commentator notes:

> Every effort is being made to beat down the spirits of black children. Individual teachers who had tried to give their classes some sense of their black culture have been told to stop. In some cases, the brightest children are tracked separately from other black children, alienating them from their own communities. Resegregation is another way that black children are reminded of "their place." Although black and white children attend school under the same roof in many systems, the roof is literally all they share. Separate, labeled water fountains can still be found. One system has even gone so far as to install "white" and "colored" bells. White children change classes on the hour and black children change on the half-hour. Although it is difficult to document, it appears that one by one the older, brighter, and more self-assured black students are being forced to leave school through strict enforcement of rules on length of hair, on tardiness, or on other noneducational matters. (Barber, "Swann Song from the Delta: From Intransigence to Compliance Is Two Steps Forward and Two Steps Back," *Inequality in Education,* June 1970, pp 13, 14.)

a. Students. Conflicts over virtually every aspect of school identity—from the selection of football players and cheerleaders to the appropriateness of flying the confederate flag—have characterized the desegregation experience. The courts have repeatedly been asked to intervene and resolve them. See, e.g., *Dunn v Tyler Independent School Dist* 460 F2d 137 (5th Cir 1972); *Tate v Board of Educ* 453 F2d 975 (8th Cir 1972); *Caldwell v Craighead* 432 F2d 213 (6th Cir 1970), *cert denied,* 402 US 953 (1971). Conflict has provoked harsher disciplinary policies, and blacks allege that the policies are applied more rigidly and harshly to them than to white students. School administrators respond that blacks are more inclined to physical aggression, particularly as they are removed from their neighborhoods and placed in an unfamiliar, if not hostile, school environment. See, e.g., *Tillman v Dade County School Bd* 327 F Supp 930 (SD Fla 1971); *Blount v Ladue School Dist* 321 F Supp 1245 (ED Mo 1970).

This litigation has taxed the patience and the competence of the courts, both because it is so frequent, and because it concerns minor—if symbolically significant—incidents. The frequency of disputes (including many that never reach the courts) suggests that in at least some districts educators have not sought diligently to make integration work; it also serves as a reminder that in many parts of the country integration signals a social revolution that inevitably causes considerable dislocation and strife.

b. Teachers and Administrators. The retention and placement of school teachers and administrators in desegregating school districts has also provoked dispute. Frequently, black teachers, who had taught for many years in all-black schools, were fired by districts that viewed them as unacceptable teachers for white students. Rims Barber observes:

Black teachers are being emasculated and stripped of their standing before their own communities. Teachers with years of experience are being assigned as teacher aides or assistants to white teachers. New job categories are created; black Mississippians will explain to you that "Coprincipal is short for colored principal."

Black teachers are being fired. We estimate that more than 15 percent of the 9,500 black teachers in the state will be out of work next fall. Ruses like requiring teachers to score 1,000 or more on the Graduate Record Exam are common, even though the test was designed to find good graduate students, not good teachers. ("Swann Song from the Delta.")

As black schools were closed, black principals were often demoted to assistant principal positions in the new integrated schools. The courts have reacted sharply against such practices. See, e.g., *Moore v Board of Educ* 448 F2d 709 (8th Cir 1971); *Sparks v Griffin* 460 F2d 433 (5th Cir 1972); *Armstead v Starkville Munic Separate School Dist* 325 F Supp 560 (ND Miss 1971); *Baker v Columbus Munic Separate School Dist* 329 F Supp 706 (ND Miss 1971). But see *Christian v Board of Educ* 440 F2d 608 (8th Cir 1971).

c. Problem: Battle of the Songs. Because Alvin Afro refused to toot his clarinet when the band played "Old Black Joe" during a pep rally, he was suspended from newly desegregated Jefferson Davis High School's marching band. Two weeks later, Afro's mother claimed that the school administration discharged her from her job as a teacher's aide at J.D. in retaliation for her support of her son's action. Alvin and his mother brought a class action, on behalf of themselves and all blacks in the state, alleging discrimination based on race and a denial of their First Amendment rights. The attorneys for J.D.'s administration answered that (1) Alvin's expulsion from band activities was a legitimate disciplinary dismissal made pursuant to a valid band regulation, (2) in any event, Alvin has now graduated from J.D. so his claim is moot, (3) Mrs. Afro's services were terminated due to her "unsatisfactory" work, and (4) the particular fact pattern here does not present an appropriate issue for a class action since Alvin and his mother are really trying to enforce individual rights arising out of a unique chain of events, not the rights of all blacks in the entire state.

While the case was pending, J.D.'s principal, Colonel Plantation, suddenly died. Despite much protest by the board of education, Rhoda Reform, the black vice-principal, assumed Plantation's post in accordance with an old rule that called for the vice-principal to fill the principalship of any school left vacant during a school year. (When J.D. was first integrated during the previous year, the board began a study of administrative rules it considered to be "obsolete"— the rule governing temporary principalships was one of these, but since it had not yet been revised, it remained in effect during the time of Plantation's sudden death.) Reform's first official action in her new capacity (after changing the name of the school from "Jefferson Davis" to "Angela Davis") was to ban the playing or singing of "Old Black Joe" on the entire campus. When Wendell Wasp was caught after several warnings playing that tune on his violin during orchestra practice, Reform advised him that he could no longer be a member of the orchestra. Wendell argued that "Old Black Joe" had musical and poetic merit, that the singing and playing of Stephen Foster tunes was an expression of pride in the South and not an expression of racism, and that Reform's decision was a denial of his First Amendment rights. When Reform refused to reinstate him in the orchestra, Wendell sued on these grounds.

The same judge heard *Afro v Jefferson Davis High School* and *Wasp v Angela Davis High School*. What result in each case? (See *Caldwell v Craighead* 432 F2d 213 (6th Cir 1970), *cert denied*, 402 US 953 (1971); *Melton v Young* 328 F Supp 88 (ED Tenn 1971).)

d. One-way Busing. Finally, many school districts, either voluntarily or under the aegis of a court order, have sought to desegregate by closing schools in black neighborhoods and transporting black children to schools located in white neighborhoods. On occasion such practices have been challenged by black parents concerned that their children are bearing more than their fair share of the burdens of desegregation. To that argument, one court responded: "that the 'burdens,' if any, of busing and attendance at a nonneighborhood school, although statistically related to race, actually stem from a valid administrative decision against the continued location and building of educational facilities in areas of underprivileged minority group concentration because of the detrimental effects on quality education which might result." *Norwalk CORE v Norwalk Bd of Educ* 298 F Supp 213 at 222 (D Conn 1969), *aff'd*, 423 F2d 121 (2d Cir 1970). But see *Brice v Landis* 314 F Supp 974 (ND Cal 1969). See generally Recent Cases, "Equal Protection of the Laws—Schools," 83 *Harv L Rev* 1434 (1970); Note, "School Decentralization: Legal Paths to Local Control," 57 *Geo LJ* 992 (1969). One-race busing poses a number of questions. Are schools in white neighborhoods somehow better than schools in black neighborhoods? Is it less expensive to bus blacks only, particularly where they represent only a minority of the district's student population? Is one-race busing a stigmatizing racial classification that should be overturned regardless of the short-term costs? To what extent should the courts take into account the desire of the black community to keep its neighborhood schools open and to control what goes on in those schools? See generally Kirp, "Community Control, Public Policy, and the Limits of the Law," 68 *Mich L Rev* 1355, 1384-87 (1970).

C. Racial Segregation and School District Boundaries

WRIGHT v COUNCIL OF EMPORIA
407 US 451 (1972).

Mr. Justice Stewart:

I

The city of Emporia lies near the center of Greensville County, Virginia, a largely rural area located on the North Carolina border. Until 1967, Emporia was a "town" under Virginia law, which meant that it was a part of the surrounding county for practically all purposes, including the purpose of providing public education for children residing in the county.

In 1967, Emporia, apparently dissatisfied with the county's allocation of revenues from the newly enacted state sales tax, successfully sought designation as a "city of the second class." As such, it became politically independent from the surrounding county, and undertook a separate obligation under state law to

provide free public schooling to children residing within its borders. To fulfill
this responsibility, Emporia at first sought the county's agreement to continue
operating the school system on virtually the same basis as before, with Emporia
sharing in the administration as well as the financing of the schools.[6] When the
county officials refused to enter into an arrangement of this kind, Emporia
agreed to a contract whereby the county would continue to educate students
residing in the city in exchange for Emporia's payment of a specified share of
the total cost of the system. Under this agreement, signed in April 1968, Emporia had a formal voice in the administration of the schools only through its
participation in the selection of the Superintendent. The city and county were
designated as a single school "division" by the State Board of Education[7] and
this arrangement was still in effect at the time of the district court's order challenged in this case.

This lawsuit began in 1965, when a complaint was filed on behalf of Negro
children seeking an end to state-enforced racial segregation in the Greensville
County school system. Prior to 1965, the elementary and high schools located in
Emporia served all white children in the county, while Negro children throughout
the county were assigned to a single high school or one of four elementary
schools, all but one of which were located outside the Emporia town boundary.
In January, 1966, the district court approved a so-called freedom-of-choice plan
that had been adopted by the county in April of the previous year. *Wright v
School Bd* 252 F Supp 378. No white students ever attended the Negro schools
under this plan, and in the 1968-69 school year only 98 of the county's 2,510
Negro students attended white schools. The school faculties remained completely
segregated.

Following our decision in *Green v County School Bd* 391 US 430, holding
that a freedom-of-choice plan was an unacceptable method of desegregation
where it failed "to provide prompt and effective disestablishment of a dual
system," (391 US at 438), the petitioners filed a motion for further relief. The
district court ordered the county to demonstrate its compliance with the holding
in *Green*, or to submit a plan designed to bring the schools into compliance.
After various delays, during which the freedom-of-choice system remained in
effect, the county submitted two alternative plans. The first would have preserved the existing system with slight modifications, and the second would have
assigned students to schools on the basis of curricular choices or standardized
test scores. The district court promptly rejected the first of these proposals, and
took the second under advisement. Meanwhile, the petitioners submitted their
own proposal, under which all children enrolled in a particular grade level would
be assigned to the same school, thus eliminating any possibility of racial bias in

6. Emporia was entitled under state law to establish an independent school system when it
became a city in 1967, but it chose not to do so because, according to the testimony of the
chairman of the city school board, a separate system did not seem practical at the time. In a
letter to the county board of supervisors in July 1969, the Emporia city council stated that it
had authorized a combined system in 1968 because it believed that "the educational interest of
Emporia citizens, their children and those of the citizens and children of Greensville County,
could best be served by continuing a combined city-county school division, thus giving students
from both political subdivisions full benefits of a larger school system."

7. Under Virginia law as it stood in 1969, the school "division" was the basic unit for the
purpose of school administration. See Virginia Code Ann. §§22-30, 22-34, 22-100.1.

pupil assignments. Following an evidentiary hearing on June 23, 1969, the district court rejected the county's alternative plan, finding that it would "substitute . . . one segregated school system for another segregated school system." By an order dated June 25, the court ordered the county to implement the plan submitted by the petitioners, referred to by the parties as the "pairing" plan, as of the start of the 1969-70 school year.

Two weeks after the district court entered its decree, the Emporia city council sent a letter to the county board of supervisors announcing the city's intention to operate a separate school system beginning in September. The letter stated that an "in-depth study and analysis of the directed school arrangement reflects a totally unacceptable situation to the citizens and city council of the city of Emporia." It asked that the 1968 city-county agreement be terminated by mutual consent, and that title to school property located within Emporia be transferred to the city. The letter further advised that children residing in the county would be permitted to enroll in the city schools on a tuition basis. At no time during this period did the city officials meet with the county council or school board to discuss the implementation of the pairing decree, nor did they inform the district court of their intentions with respect to the separate school system.

The county school board refused either to terminate the existing agreement or to transfer school buildings to Emporia, citing its belief that Emporia's proposed action was "not in the best interest of the children in Greensville County." The city council and the city school board nevertheless continued to take steps toward implementing the separate system throughout the month of July. Notices were circulated inviting parents to register their children in the city system, and a request was made to the state board of education to certify Emporia as a separate school division. This request was tabled by the state board at its August meeting, "in light of matters pending in the federal court."

According to figures later supplied to the district court, there were 3,759 children enrolled in the unitary system contemplated by the desegregation decree, of whom 66 percent were Negro and 34 percent were white. Had Emporia established a separate school system, 1,123 of these students would have attended the city schools, of whom 48 percent were white. It is undisputed that the city proposed to operate its own schools on a unitary basis, with all children enrolled in any particular grade attending the same school.

On August 1, 1969, the petitioners filed a supplemental complaint naming the members of the Emporia city council and the city school board as additional parties defendant, and seeking to enjoin them from withdrawing Emporia children from the county schools. At the conclusion of a hearing on August 8, the district court found that the establishment of a separate school system by the city would constitute "an impermissible interference with and frustration of" its order of June 25, and preliminarily enjoined the respondents from taking "any action which would interfere in any manner whatsoever with the implementation of the court's order heretofore entered. . . ."

. . . . At a further hearing in December, the respondents presented an expert witness to testify as to the educational advantages of the proposed city system, and asked that the preliminary injunction be dissolved. On March 2, 1970, the district court entered a memorandum opinion and order denying the respondents' motion and making the injunction permanent. 309 F Supp 671. The Court of

Appeals for the Fourth Circuit reversed, 442 F2d 570, but stayed its mandate pending action by this court on a petition for certiorari, which we granted. 404 US 820.

II

Emporia takes the position that since it is a separate political jurisdiction entitled under state law to establish a school system independent of the county, its action may be enjoined only upon a finding either that the state law under which it acted is invalid, that the boundaries of the city are drawn so as to exclude Negroes, or that the disparity of the racial balance of the city and county schools of itself violates the Constitution. As we read its opinion, the district court made no such findings, nor do we.

The constitutional violation that formed the predicate for the district court's action was the enforcement until 1969 of racial segregation in a public school system of which Emporia had always been a part. That finding has not been challenged, nor has Emporia questioned the propriety of the "pairing" order of June 25, 1969, which was designed to remedy the condition that offended the Constitution. Both before and after it became a city, Emporia educated its children in the county schools. Only when it became clear—fifteen years after our decision in *Brown v Board of Educ* 347 US 483—that segregation in the county system was finally to be abolished, did Emporia attempt to take its children out of the county system. Under these circumstances, the power of the district court to enjoin Emporia's withdrawal from that system need not rest upon an independent constitutional violation. The court's remedial power was invoked on the basis of a finding that the dual school system violated the Constitution, and since the city and the county constituted but one unit for the purpose of student assignments during the entire time that the dual system was maintained, they were properly treated as a single unit for the purpose of dismantling that system. . . .

The court of appeals apparently did not believe this case to be governed by the principles of *Green* . . . . It held that the question whether new school district boundaries should be permitted in areas with a history of state-enforced racial segregation is to be resolved in terms of the "dominant purpose of [the] boundary realignment."

> If the creation of a new school district is designed to further the aim of providing quality education and is attended secondarily by a modification of the racial balance, short of resegregation, the federal courts should not interfere. If, however, the primary purpose for creating a new school district is to retain as much of separation of the races as possible, the state has violated its affirmative constitutional duty to end state-supported school segregation. (442 F2d at 572.)

Although the district court had found that "in a sense, race was a factor in the city's decision to secede," 309 F Supp at 680, the court of appeals found that the primary purpose of Emporia's action was "benign," and was not "merely a cover-up" for racial discrimination. 442 F2d at 574.

This "dominant purpose" test finds no precedent in our decisions. It is true that where an action by school authorities is motivated by a demonstrated discriminatory purpose, the existence of that purpose may add to the discriminatory effect of the action by intensifying the stigma of implied racial inferiority. And where a school board offers nonracial justifications for a plan that is less effective than other alternatives for dismantling a dual school system, a demonstrated racial purpose may be taken into consideration in determining the weight to be given to the proffered justification. . . . But as we said in *Palmer v Thompson* 403 US 217, 225, it "is difficult or impossible for any court to determine the 'sole' or 'dominant' motivation behind the choices of a group of legislators," and the same may be said of the choices of a school board. In addition, an inquiry into the "dominant" motivation of school authorities is as irrelevant as it is fruitless. The mandate of *Brown 2* was to desegregate schools, and we have said that "the measure of any desegregation plan is its effectiveness." *Davis v Board of School Comm'rs* 402 US 33, 37. Thus, we have focused upon the effect—not the purpose or motivation—of a school board's action in determining whether it is a permissible method of dismantling a dual system. The existence of a permissible purpose cannot sustain an action that has an impermissible effect. . . .

III

. . . . The district court noted that the effect of Emporia's withdrawal would be a "substantial increase in the proportion of whites in the schools attended by city residents, and a concomitant decrease in the county schools." 309 F Supp at 680. In addition, the court found that the departure of the city's students, its leadership, and its financial support, together with the possible loss of teachers to the new system, would diminish the chances that transition to unitary schools in the county would prove "successful."

Certainly, desegregation is not achieved by splitting a single school system operating "white schools" and "Negro schools" into two new systems, each operating unitary schools within its borders, where one of the two new systems is, in fact, "white" and the other is, in fact, "Negro." Nor does a court supervising the process of desegregation exercise its remedial discretion responsibly where it approves a plan that, in the hope of providing better "quality education" to some children, has a substantial adverse effect upon the quality of education available to others. In some cases, it may be readily perceived that a proposed subdivision of a school district will produce one or both of these results. In other cases, the likelihood of such results may be less apparent. This case is of the latter kind, but an examination of the record shows that the district court's conclusions were adequately supported by the evidence.

Data submitted to the district court at its December hearing showed that the school system in operation under the "pairing" plan, including both Emporia and the county, had a racial composition of 34 percent white and 66 percent Negro. If Emporia had established its own system, and had total enrollment remained the same, the city's schools would have been 48 percent white and 52 percent Negro, while the county's schools would have been 28 percent white and 72 percent Negro.

We need not and do not hold that this disparity in the racial composition of the two systems would be a sufficient reason, standing alone, to enjoin the creation of the separate school district. The fact that a school board's desegregation plan leaves some disparity in racial balance among various schools in the system does not alone make that plan unacceptable. We observed in *Swann, supra,* that "the constitutional command to desegregate schools does not mean that every school in every community must always reflect the racial composition of the school system as a whole." 402 US at 24.

But there is more to this case than the disparity in racial percentages reflected by the figures supplied by the school board. In the first place, the district court found that if Emporia were allowed to withdraw from the existing system, it "may be anticipated that the proportion of whites in county schools may drop as those who can register in private academies," 309 F Supp at 680, while some whites might return to the city schools from the private schools in which they had previously enrolled. Thus, in the judgment of the district court, the statistical breakdown of the 1969-70 enrollment figures between city residents and county residents did not reflect what the situation would have been had Emporia established its own school system.

Second, the significance of any racial disparity in this case is enhanced by the fact that the two formerly all-white schools are located within Emporia, while all the schools located in the surrounding county were formerly all-Negro. The record further reflects that the school buildings in Emporia are better equipped and are located on better sites than are those in the county. We noted in *Swann* that factors such as these may in themselves indicate that enforced racial segregation has been perpetuated:

> Independent of student assignments, where it is possible to identify a "white school" or a "Negro school" simply by reference to the racial composition of teachers and staff, the quality of school buildings and equipment, or the organization of sports activities, a prima facie case of violation of substantive constitutional rights under the equal protection clause is shown. (402 US at 18.)

Just as racial balance is not required in remedying a dual system, neither are racial ratios the sole consideration to be taken into account in devising a workable remedy.

The timing of Emporia's action is a third factor that was properly taken into account by the district court in assessing the effect of the action upon children remaining in the county schools. While Emporia had long had the right under state law to establish a separate school system, its decision to do so came only upon the basis of—and, as the city officials conceded, in reaction to—a court order that prevented the county system from maintaining any longer the segregated system that had lingered for fifteen years after *Brown 1*. In the words of Judge Winter, dissenting in the court of appeals, "if the establishment of an Emporia school district is not enjoined, the black students in the county will watch as nearly one-half the total number of white students in the county abandon the county schools for a substantially whiter system." 442 F2d at 590. The message of this action, coming when it did, cannot have escaped the Negro children in the county. As we noted in *Brown 1:* "To separate [Negro school children] from others of similar age and qualifications, solely because of their race generates a feeling of inferiority as to their status in the community that may affect their hearts and minds in a way unlikely ever to be undone." 347 US at 494. We think that, under the circumstances, the district court could rationally have concluded that the same adverse psychological effect was likely to result from Emporia's withdrawal of its children from the Greensville County system.

The weighing of these factors to determine their effect upon the process of desegregation is a delicate task that is aided by a sensitivity to local conditions, and the judgment is primarily the responsibility of the district judge. . . . Given the totality of the circumstances, we hold that the district court was justified in its conclusion that Emporia's establishment of a separate system would actually impede the process of dismantling the existing dual system.

IV

Against these considerations, Emporia advances arguments that a separate system is necessary to achieve "quality education" for city residents, and that it is unfair in any event to force the city to continue to send its children to schools over which the city, because of the character of its arrangement with the county, has very little control. These arguments are entitled to consideration by a court exercising its equitable discretion where they are directed to the feasibility or practicality of the proposed remedy. See *Swann v Charlotte-Mecklenburg Bd of Educ, supra,* at 31. But as we said in *Green v County School Bd, supra,* the availability of "more promising courses of action" to dismantle a dual system "at the least . . . places a heavy burden upon the board to explain its preference for an apparently less effective method." 391 US at 439. . . .

At the final hearing in the district court, the respondents presented detailed budgetary proposals and other evidence demonstrating that they contemplated a more diverse and more expensive educational program than that to which the city children had been accustomed in the Greensville County schools. These plans for the city system were developed after the preliminary injunction was issued in this case. In August 1969, one month before classes were scheduled to open, the city officials were intent upon operating a separate system despite the fact that the city had no buildings under lease, no teachers under contract, and no specific plans for the operation of the schools. Thus, the persuasiveness of the "quality education" rationale was open to question. More important, however, any increased quality of education provided to city students would, under the circumstances found by the district court, have been purchased only at the price of a substantial adverse effect upon the viability of the county system. The district court, with its responsibility to provide an effective remedy for segregation in the entire city-county system, could not properly allow the city to make its part of that system more attractive where such a result would be accomplished at the expense of the children remaining in the county.

A more weighty consideration put forth by Emporia is its lack of formal control over the school system under the terms of its contract with the county. . . .

We do not underestimate the deficiencies, from Emporia's standpoint, in the arrangement by which it undertook in 1968 to provide for the education of its children. Direct control over decisions vitally affecting the education of one's children is a need that is strongly felt in our society, and since 1967 the citizens of Emporia have had little of that control. But Emporia did find its arrangement with the county both feasible and practical up until the time of the desegregation decree issued in the summer of 1969. While city officials testified that they were dissatisfied with the terms of the contract prior to that time, they did not attempt to change it. . . . Under these circumstances, we cannot say that the enforced continuation of the single city-county system was not "reasonable, feasible, and workable."

The district court explicitly noted in its opinion that its injunction does not have the effect of locking Emporia into its present circumstances for all time. . . . Once the unitary system has been established and accepted, it may be that Emporia, if it still desires to do so, may establish an independent system without such an adverse effect upon the students remaining in the county, or it may be able to work out a more satisfactory arrangement with the county for joint operation of the existing system. We hold only that a new school district may not be created where its effect would be to impede the process of dismantling a dual system. . . . In this case, we believe that the district court did not abuse its discretion. For these reasons, the judgment of the court of appeals is

Reversed.

Mr. Chief Justice Burger, with whom Mr. Justice Blackmun, Mr. Justice Powell, and Mr. Justice Rehnquist join, dissenting.

If it appeared that the city of Emporia's operation of a separate school system would either perpetuate racial segregation in the schools of the Greensville County area or otherwise frustrate the dismantling of the dual system in that area, I would unhesitatingly join in reversing the judgment of the court of appeals and reinstating the judgment of the district court. However, I do not believe the record supports such findings and can only conclude that the district court abused its discretion in preventing Emporia from exercising its lawful right to provide for the education of its own children.

By accepting the district court's conclusion that Emporia's operation of its own schools would "impede the dismantling of the dual system," the court necessarily implies that the result of the severance would be something less than unitary schools, and that segregated education would persist in some measure in the classrooms of the Greensville County area. The court does not articulate the standard by which it reaches this conclusion, and its result far exceeds the contemplation of *Brown v Board of Educ* 347 US 483 (1954), and all succeeding cases, including *Swann v Charlotte-Mecklenburg Bd of Educ* 402 US 1 (1971).

If the severance of the two systems were permitted to proceed, the assignment of children to schools would depend solely on their residence. County residents would attend county schools, and city residents would attend city schools. Assignment to schools would in no sense depend on race. Such a geographic assignment pattern is prima facie consistent with the equal protection clause. See *Spencer v Kugler* 326 F Supp 1235 (NJ 1971), *aff'd,* 404 US 1027 (1972).

However, where a school system has been operated on a segregated basis in the past, and where ostensibly neutral attendance zones or district lines are drawn where none have existed before, we do not close our eyes to the facts in favor of theory. In *Green v County School Bd* 391 US 430 (1968), the court ruled that dual school systems must cease to exist in an objective sense as well as under the law. It was apparent that under the freedom-of-choice plan before the court in *Green,* the mere elimination of mandatory segregation had provided no meaningful remedy. *Green* imposed on school boards the responsibility to "fashion steps which promise realistically to convert promptly to a system without a 'white' school and a 'Negro' school, but just schools." 391 US at 442. That, I believe, is precisely what would result if Emporia were permitted to operate its own school system—schools neither Negro nor white, "but just schools." As separate systems, both Emporia and Greensville County would have a majority of

Negro students, the former slightly more than half, the latter slightly more than two-thirds. In the words of the court of appeals, "[t]he Emporia city unit would not be a white island in an otherwise black county." 442 F2d at 573. Moreover, the Negro majority in the remaining county system would only slightly exceed that of the entire county area including Emporia. It is undisputed that education would be conducted on a completely desegregated basis within the separate systems. Thus the situation would in no sense be comparable to that where the creation of attendance zones within a single formerly segregated school system leaves an inordinate number of one-race schools, such as were found in *Davis v School Comm'rs* 402 US 33 (1971). Rather than perpetuating a dual system, I believe the proposed arrangement would completely eliminate all traces of state-imposed segregation.

It is quite true that the racial ratios of the two school systems would differ, but the elimination of such disparities is not the mission of desegregation. . . . It can no more be said that racial balance is the norm to be sought, than it can be said that mere racial imbalance was the condition requiring a judicial remedy. The pointlessness of such a "racial-balancing" approach is well illustrated by the facts of this case. The district court and the petitioners have placed great emphasis on the approximate 6 percent increase in the proportion of Negro students in the county schools that would result from Emporia's withdrawal. I do not see how a difference of one or two children per class would even be noticed, let alone how it would render a school part of a dual system. We have seen that the normal movement of populations could bring about such shifts in a relatively short period of time. Obsession with such minor statistical differences reflects the gravely mistaken view that a plan providing more consistent racial ratios is somehow more unitary than one which tolerates a lack of racial balance. Since the goal is to dismantle dual school systems rather than to reproduce in each classroom a microcosmic reflection of the racial proportions of a given geographical area, there is no basis for saying that a plan providing a uniform racial balance is more effective or constitutionally preferred. School authorities may wish to pursue that goal as a matter of policy, but we have made it plain that it is not constitutionally mandated. See *Swann v Charlotte-Mecklenburg Bd of Educ* 402 US at 16. . . .

It is argued that even if Emporia's operation of its own unitary school system would have been constitutionally permissible, it was nevertheless within the equitable discretion of the district court to insist on a "more effective" plan of desegregation in the form of a countywide school system. In *Brown v Board of Educ* 349 US 294 (1955) (*Brown 2*), the court first conferred on the district courts the responsibility to enforce the desegregation of the schools, if school authorities failed to do so, according to equitable remedial principles. While we have emphasized the flexibility of the power of district courts in this process, the invocation of remedial jurisdiction is not equivalent to having a school district placed in receivership. It has been implicit in all of our decisions from *Brown 2* to *Swann,* that if local authorities devise a plan that will effectively eliminate segregation in the schools, a district court must accept such a plan unless there are strong reasons why a different plan is to be preferred. A local school board plan that will eliminate dual schools, stop discrimination and improve the quality of education ought not to be cast aside because a judge can evolve some other plan that accomplishes the same result, or what he considers a preferable result, with a 2 percent, 4 percent or 6 percent difference in racial composition. Such an approach gives controlling weight to sociological theories, not constitutional doctrine.

This limitation on the discretion of the district courts involves more than polite deference to the role of local governments. Local control is not only vital to continued public support of the schools, but it is of overriding importance from an educational standpoint as well. The success of any school system depends on a vast range of factors that lie beyond the competence and power of the courts. Curricular decisions, the structuring of grade levels, the planning of extracurricular activities, to mention a few, are matters lying solely within the province of school officials who maintain a day-to-day supervision that a judge cannot. A plan devised by school officials is apt to be attuned to these highly relevant educational goals; a plan deemed preferable in the abstract by a judge might well overlook and thus undermine these primary concerns.

The discretion of a district court is further limited where, as here, it deals with totally separate political entities. This is a very different case from one where a school board proposes attendance zones within a single school district or even one where a school district is newly formed within a county unit. Under Virginia law, Emporia is as independent from Greensville County as one state is from another. . . . This may be an anomaly in municipal jurisprudence, but it is Virginia's anomaly; it is of ancient origin, and it is not forbidden by the Constitution. To bar the city of Emporia from operating its own school system, is to strip it of its most important governmental responsibility, and thus largely to deny its existence as an independent governmental entity. It is a serious step and absent the factors that persuade me to the contrary in *Scotland Neck,* decided today, I am unwilling to go that far. . . .

Although acknowledging Emporia's need to have some "[d]irect control over decisions vitally affecting the education of its children," the court states that since Emporia found the contractual arrangement tolerable prior to 1969, it should not now be heard to complain. However, the city did not enter that contract of its own free choice. From the time Emporia became a city, consideration was given to the formation of a separate school system, and it was at least thought necessary that the city participate in administration of the county school system. After the county rejected the city's proposal for joint administration, the county threatened to terminate educational services for city children unless the city entered an agreement by April 30, 1968. Only then—under virtual duress—did the city submit to the contractual arrangement. It was not until June of 1969 that the city was advised by its counsel that the agreement might be illegal. Steps were then taken to terminate the strained relationship.

Recognizing the tensions inherent in a contractual arrangement put together under these conditions, the court indicates that Emporia might be permitted to operate a separate school system at some future time. The court does not explain how the passage of time will substantially alter the situation that existed at the time the district court entered its injunction. If, as the court states, desegregation in the county was destined to fail if Emporia established its own school system in 1969, it is difficult to understand why it would not be an undue risk to allow separation in the future. The more realistic view is that there was never such a danger, and that the district court had no cause to disregard Emporia's desire to free itself from its ties to Greensville County. However, even on the court's terms, I assume that Emporia could go back to the district court tomorrow and renew its request to operate a separate system. The countywide plan has been in effect for the past three years, and the city should now be relieved of the court-imposed duty to purchase whatever quality of education the county sees fit to provide.

Finally, some discussion is warranted of the relevance of discriminatory purpose in cases such as these. It is, of course, correct that "the measure of a desegregation plan is its effectiveness" (*Davis v Board of Comm'rs* 402 US 33, 37 (1971)), and that a plan that stops short of dismantling a dual school system cannot be redeemed by benevolent motives. But it is also true that even where a dual system has in fact been dismantled, as it plainly has been in Emporia, we must still be alert to make sure that ostensibly nondiscriminatory actions are not designed to exclude children from schools because of their race. We are well aware that the progress of school desegregation since 1954 has been hampered by persistent resistance and evasion in many places. Thus the normal judicial reluctance to probe the motives or purposes underlying official acts must yield to the realities in this very sensitive area of constitutional adjudication. Compare *Griffin v County School Bd* 377 US 218 (1964), with *Palmer v Thompson* 403 US 217 (1971).

There is no basis for concluding, on this record, that Emporia's decision to operate a separate school system was the manifestation of a discriminatory purpose. The strongest finding made by the district court was that race was "in a sense" a factor in the city's decision; read in context, this ambiguous finding does not relate to any invidious consideration of race. The district court relied solely on the following testimony of the chairman of the city school board: "Race, of course, affected the operation of the schools by the county, and I again say, I do not think, or we felt that the county was not capable of putting the monies in and the effort and the leadership into a system that would effectively make a unitary system work . . . ," 309 F Supp at 680. I cannot view this kind of consideration of race as discriminatory or even objectionable. The same doubts about the county's commitment to the operation of a high-quality unitary system would have come into play even if the racial composition of Emporia were precisely the same as that of the entire county area, including Emporia.

Nor is this a case where we can presume a discriminatory purpose from an obviously discriminatory effect. Cf *Gomillion v Lightfoot* 364 US 399 (1960). We are not confronted with an awkward gerrymander or striking shift in racial proportions. The modest difference between the racial composition of Emporia's proposed separate school system and that of the county as a whole affords no basis for an inference of racial motivation. And while it seems that the more cumbersome features of the district court's plan hastened the city's inevitable decision to operate a separate unitary school system, this was not because of any desire to manipulate the racial balance of its schools.

Read as a whole this record suggests that the district court, acting before our decision in *Swann*, was reaching for some hypothetical perfection in racial balance, rather than the elimination of a dual school system. To put it in the simplest terms, the court, in adopting the district court's approach, goes too far.

Notes and Questions

1. *Emporia* and *Scotland Neck*

On the same day that it decided *Emporia,* the court unanimously reversed the court of appeals in *US v Scotland Neck Bd of Educ* 407 US 484 (1972). Both cases involved an attempt to create a "splinter district," and an allegation by the plaintiffs that both the effect and the purpose of such school district reorganization were inconsistent with the constitutional duty to dismantle the dual school system. In *Scotland Neck,* the county population was 77 percent black and splintering would have left the county schools 80 percent black.

Justices Burger, Blackmun, Powell, and Rehnquist concurred in the *Scotland Neck* result, contending that *Emporia* was distinguishable: if Scotland Neck were permitted to sever its schools from those in Halifax County, North Carolina, several "racially identifiable" schools would exist. Moreover, Burger argued, Scotland Neck had never been an independent governmental entity, and the splintering was racially motivated. Are these distinctions tenable? Should they be controlling?

2. Racial Motivation

In *Keyes,* the court held that the de facto/de jure distinction was based on the absence or presence of a discriminatory motive in the adoption of school policies leading to segregation. Why does the majority in *Emporia* examine only the effects of the decision to create a new splinter district and not the purpose or intention of school officials? Is the court implying an improper motive from the effects of the decision? Is this consistent with its assertion that "an inquiry into the 'dominant' motivation of school authorities is as irrelevant as it is fruitless?" Does the justification for different standards in *Keyes* and *Emporia* lie in the nature of the different questions presented in each case? That is, in *Keyes* the court was asked to determine whether Denver had unlawfully segregated its schools, and the question, as formulated by the court, turned on the extent of state responsibility for the segregation of the schools. In *Emporia,* a finding of de jure segregation had been made and was not disputed, but the court was called on to determine the adequacy of the remedy in dismantling the dual school system. Or does *Emporia* lend support to Justice Powell's assertion in his concurring opinion in *Keyes* that the court is applying different standards to northern and southern school segregation?

3. Unitary School System

Does the dispute between the majority and the dissent in *Emporia* turn on the definition of a unitary school system? Is the majority implicitly holding that the creation of a unitary school system requires a racial balance in each school? If so, was the new splinter district racially balanced in the sense that each school reflected the proportion of whites and blacks in the whole student population? Has the majority gone beyond racial balance, requiring that the number of whites in each desegregated school be maximized? Is this a bold application of the universalist ethic, or an endorsement of Professor Pettigrew's thesis that whites must predominate in each school in order to promote learning?

4. Desegregation and School District Boundaries

The two opinions in *Emporia* differ markedly in the weight they give to preserving school district boundaries. How much importance should courts attach to the prior existence of separate governmental units in assessing school desegregation issues? What scrutiny should the court give to the allegation that the maintenance of school district boundaries by the state—with the knowledge that they will promote racial isolation in the schools—is unconstitutional? Should a distinction be drawn between judicial disapproval of a unit that secedes in order to further segregation and a judicial demand for the fusion of two previously unrelated units in order to further desegregation? These and other related questions are raised by *Bradley.*

BRADLEY v SCHOOL BOARD
462 F2d 1058 (4th Cir 1972), *aff'd by an equally divided court,*
36 L Ed 2d (1973)

Craven, Circuit Judge:

May a United States District Judge compel one of the states of the Union to restructure its internal government for the purpose of achieving racial balance in the assignment of pupils to the public schools? We think not, absent invidious discrimination in the establishment or maintenance of local governmental units, and accordingly reverse.

This is a new aspect of an old school case begun in 1961. Neither the parties to this appeal nor the numerous amici permitted to file briefs question the duty of the Richmond School Board to achieve a unitary school system. . . . Indeed, it is virtually conceded and established beyond question that, albeit belatedly, Richmond has at this juncture done all it can do to disestablish to the maximum extent possible the formerly state-imposed dual school system within its municipal boundary.

What is presented on appeal is whether the district court may compel joinder with Richmond's unitary school system two other school districts (also unitary) in order to achieve a greater degree of integration and racial balance. The district judge felt compelled to order consolidation of the three school units partly because of his concern with what seemed to him an unfortunate racial balance in the three separate systems and partly because he felt this racial balance was the result of invidious state action. In his concern for effective implementation of the Fourteenth Amendment he failed to sufficiently consider we think a fundamental principle of federalism incorporated in the Tenth Amendment and failed to consider that *Swann v Charlotte-Mecklenburg Bd of Educ* 402 US 1 (1971), established limitations on his power to fashion remedies in school cases.

I

. . . . Under the [original court] approved plan . . . it was projected that the percentage of whites in high schools would range from 21 percent to 57 percent and the percentage of blacks from 43 percent to 79 percent, that the range in middle schools would be 19 percent to 61 percent whites and 39 percent to 81 percent black, and the elementary range would be from 20 percent to 66 percent white and from 34 percent to 80 percent black. Such arithmetic pointed up the obvious: that if the heavily white school population of the adjoining counties could be combined with the majority black school population of Richmond a "better" racial mix would result. Thus, on November 4, 1970, the city filed a "motion to compel joinder of parties needed for just adjudication under Rule 19." The court allowed the motion and the filing of an amended complaint directed toward relief against these new respondents: the board of supervisors of Chesterfield County, the board of supervisors of Henrico County, the school board of Chesterfield County, the school board of Henrico County, the state board of education, and the superintendent of public instruction. On January 10, 1972, came judgment: all defendants, including the state board of education, the state superintendent of public instruction, the school boards of the two counties and the city, the boards of supervisors of the two counties, and the city council of the city, were enjoined to create a single school division composed of the city and the two counties. . . . [see 338 F Supp 67 (ED Va 1972)]

II

Were we to sustain this injunctive decree, the result would be one of the largest school districts in America. In the fall of 1970 the Richmond school district had 47,824 pupils and was the third largest school district in Virginia. The Henrico school division had 34,080 and was the fifth largest in Virginia, and the Chesterfield school district had 24,069 pupils and was the twelfth largest in Virginia. Richmond has a geographical area of 63 square miles, Henrico 244 square miles, and Chesterfield 445 square miles. The mandated school consolidation would thus create a district containing over 750 square miles and in excess of 100,000 pupils. . . .

For the school year 1970-71, the Richmond City School Board operated fifty-seven schools, and the racial composition of the pupil population was approximately 64 percent black and 36 percent white. Henrico operated forty-three schools, and the racial composition was approximately 92 percent white and 8 percent black. Chesterfield operated twenty-eight schools, and the racial composition was approximately 91 percent white and 9 percent black.

. . . [T]he district judge [set] out in some detail the theory advanced by various witnesses of a "viable racial mix." In order to effect such a mix, the court approved, subject to trial and error, a lottery program similar to the national draft.

> Under the lottery program developed by the Richmond officials, whether a child is among those normally assigned to the school in his attendance zone who would be transported elsewhere is determined by birth date. A single birthday or 366 might be picked out of a hat. Then, starting with the first picked and taking all born subsequently, or following the list of 366 in order drawn, sufficient pupils are chosen to meet the quota of those to be transported out. After the child's status is determined according to the lottery, he would remain with his fellows during his tenure at each level of school. A new lottery would be conducted for him as he moved into middle school and later into high school.

In his concern to achieve a "viable racial mix," the district court did not rule out the possibility of joining additional counties and indeed ventured the opinion that "due to the sparsity of population in some of the adjoining counties, the task will not be difficult."

It is not clear from the district court's decision the weight given to the testimony of various witnesses. Some importance, however, undoubtedly attaches to the testimony of Dr. Pettigrew adopted in part by the court below.

> To achieve "integration," in Dr. Pettigrew's terms one must have the "mix plus positive interaction as we would want to say, between whites and blacks." Current research indicates that in order to achieve these benefits there is an optimum racial composition which should be sought in each school. Dr. Pettigrew placed this at from 20 to 40 percent black occupancy. These figures are not at all hard and fast barriers, but merely indicate the racial composition range in which interaction of a positive sort is the more likely to occur. Social science is not such an exact science that the success or failure of integration depends upon a few percentage points. The low level of 20 percent fixes the general area below which the black component takes on the character of a token presence. Where only a few black students are in the particular school, there simply are insufficient numbers for them to be represented in most areas of school activities. Such participation would be crucial to the success of integration. The high level of 40 percent is linked not to the likely behavior of the students so much as it is to the behavior of their parents. When the black population in a school rises substantially above 40 percent, it has been Dr. Pettigrew's experience that white students tend to disappear from the school entirely at a rapid rate, and the court so finds. . . .

The district court also emphasized the fact that without consolidation, very few pupils in the city or the counties would attend schools whose racial mix corresponded to that considered "viable" by Dr. Pettigrew, while with consolidation under the proposed plan,

> Ninety-seven percent of the black students in the area would attend schools in the range of 20 to 40 percent black; the remainder would be in 15 to 20 percent black schools. Under that plan 92.5 percent of the white students in the area would be in schools of the optimum mix determined by Dr. Pettigrew, and 7.5 percent would be in schools with a 15 to 20 percent black enrollment. . . .

III

The boundaries of the three school districts, Richmond, Chesterfield and Henrico, have always been (for more than 100 years) coterminous with the political subdivision of the city of Richmond, the county of Chesterfield and the county of Henrico. The boundaries have never been changed except as occasioned by annexation of land within the two counties caused by the expansion and growth of the city of Richmond. The most recent annexation has resulted in adding to the school population of Richmond 10,240 pupils, of which approximately 9,867 are white. It is not contended by any of the parties or by amici that the establishment of the school district lines more than 100 years ago was invidiously motivated. We have searched the 325-page opinion of the district court in vain for the slightest scintilla of evidence that the boundary lines of the three local governmental units have been maintained either long ago or recently

for the purpose of perpetuating racial discrimination in the public schools.
. . .

It is urged upon us that within the city of Richmond there has been state
(also federal) action tending to perpetuate apartheid of the races in ghetto patterns throughout the city, and that there has been state action within the adjoining counties also tending to restrict and control the housing location of black
residents. We think such findings are not clearly erroneous, and accept them. Just
as all three units formerly operated dual school systems, so likewise all three are
found by the district court to have in the past discriminated against blacks with
respect to places and opportunity for residence. But neither the record nor the
opinion of the district court even suggests that there was ever joint interaction
between any two of the units involved (or by higher state officers) for the
purpose of keeping one unit relatively white by confining blacks to another.
What the district court seems to have found, though this is not clear, is that
there has been in the past action by the counties which had a tendency to keep
blacks within the boundaries of the city of Richmond and excluded them from
the counties. In arriving at this conclusion, the district court seemed to place
great reliance on the selection of new school construction sites over the years,
racially restrictive covenants in deeds, the nonparticipation of the counties in
federally assisted low-income housing, and testimony concerning private acts of
discrimination in the sale of housing. If the district court's theory was that the
counties were thus keeping blacks in Richmond schools while allowing whites to
flee to relatively white sanctuaries, the facts do not support this theory. . . .

We think that the root causes of the concentration of blacks in the inner
cities of America are simply not known and that the district court could not
realistically place on the counties the responsibility for the effect that inner city
decay has had on the public schools of Richmond. We are convinced that what
little action, if any, the counties may seem to have taken to keep blacks out is
slight indeed compared to the myriad reasons, economic, political and social, for
the concentration of blacks in Richmond and does not support the conclusion
that it has been invidious state action which has resulted in the racial composition of the three school districts. Indeed this record warrants no other conclusion
than that the forces influencing demographic patterns in New York, Chicago,
Detroit, Los Angeles, Atlanta and other metropolitan areas have operated in the
same way in the Richmond metropolitan area to produce the same result. . . .

IV

[N]either under the old constitution and statutes in effect prior to July 1,
1971, nor under the new constitution and statutes in effect after that date, could
the state board of education, acting alone, have effected the consolidation of the
school systems of Richmond, Henrico and Chesterfield into a single system under
the control of a single school board.

But even if we were to ignore Virginia law, as we are urged to do, there are
practicalities of budgeting and finance that boggle the mind. Each of the three
political subdivisions involved here has a separate tax base and a separate and
distinct electorate. The school board of the consolidated district would have to
look to three separate governing bodies for approval and support of school budgets. . . .

V

By the Tenth Amendment to the Constitution of the United States it is provided that: "The powers not delegated to the United States by the Constitution, nor prohibited by it to the states, are reserved to the states respectively or to the people."

One of the powers thus reserved to the states is the power to structure their internal government.

> Municipal corporations are political subdivisions of the state, created as convenient agencies for exercising such of the governmental powers of the state as may be entrusted to them. . . . The number, nature and duration of the powers conferred upon these corporations and the territory over which they shall be exercised rests in the absolute discretion of the state. (*Hunter v Pittsburgh* 207 US 161, 198 (1907).)

Because we are unable to discern any constitutional violation in the establishment and maintenance of these three school districts, nor any unconstitutional consequence of such maintenance, we hold that it was not within the district judge's authority to order the consolidation of these three separate political subdivisions of the commonwealth of Virginia. . . .

Reversed.

Winter, Circuit Judge (dissenting):

It was unfortunately predictable that a court which approved the dismantling of existing school districts so as to create smaller whiter enclaves,[1] now rejects the consolidation of school districts to make effective the mandate of *Brown 1* and its progeny. My view of this case is that the district court formulated appropriate relief and, indeed, that it decreed the only relief permissible under the Fourteenth Amendment. Nothing in the controlling decisions of the Supreme Court points to the contrary. I would affirm.

I

The city of Richmond and the surrounding counties of Henrico and Chesterfield each comprise a separate school district under existing Virginia law, although Virginia law would permit them to consolidate, provided that each consented to the consolidation.[3] The plan approved by the district court requires the consolidation of the Richmond board, composed of nine members with Richmond, Henrico and Chesterfield representation on a four, three, two basis,

---

1. *US v Scotland Neck City Bd of Educ* 442 F2d 575 (4th Cir 1971). . . . *Wright v Council of the City of Emporia* 442 F2d 570 (4th Cir 1971). . . . While the district court attempted to distinguish these cases, the fact is that they are simply the obverse of the same coin which is presented here. In each of *Scotland Neck* and *Emporia,* the effect of splitting the school district was further to delay and hinder the achievement of what would otherwise have been a unitary system in the original district, although arguably there were noninvidious reasons for subdividing. Here, as I view the case, the question is one of consolidating school districts *within the framework of state law* in order to eradicate the effects of past discrimination and to achieve a unitary system. Logically it is impossible to sustain the former and not condemn the converse. Were the case as simple as described in the opening paragraph of the majority opinion, I doubt that I would dissent.

3. . . . . It may be added that in all respects the order of the district court complied with the provisions of existing state law, save only that of the requirement of consent of the school boards and governing bodies of all of the affected political subdivisions.

respectively, to administer the district. The single consolidated district would be subdivided into six geographical subdivisions, each of which, except that known as subdivision six, comprising the southern area of Chesterfield County which has a relatively sparse population, would have a student population varying from approximately 17,000 to 20,000. Subdivision six would have a student population of approximately 9,000. . . .

Each of the subdivisions would have an overall racial composition substantially similar to that of the metropolitan area as a whole. . . .

Under the plan, the great majority of students would attend a school located within the particular subdivision in which they reside. In no case would there be an exchange between noncontiguous subdivisions. Approximately 36,000 students would be exchanged between the existing Richmond system and those of the two counties, with about 1,000 more white students than black students being involved in the exchange. . . .

Approximately 68,000 pupils are currently transported by bus within the existing three independent school districts. Under the plan approximately 78,000 pupils would be transported (from home to school, rather than from school to school as presently in Richmond)—approximately 10,000 more than at the present. The three school systems currently operate over 600 buses and a total of only 524 buses would be necessary to meet the transportation requirements under the metropolitan plan, even with school-to-home transportation of students who remain beyond the usual school day for extracurricular activities. The evidence shows that travel time and travel distance in each of the three presently independent school districts would not be appreciably changed when consolidation is effected.

II

. . . Over the last decade the overall racial composition of the three divisions has varied only .1 percent, yet, in Richmond, the racial composition has fluctuated from 57.9 percent white when *Brown 1* was decided, to a current figure of approximately 70 percent black, while the Henrico and Chesterfield systems over the corresponding period have experienced a decrease in the overall percentages of black student enrollment. Over 85 percent of the black students in the combined area are contained within the Richmond system alone.

The sordid history of Virginia's, and Richmond's, attempts to circumvent, defeat, and nullify the holding of *Brown 1* has been recorded in the opinions of this and other courts, and need not be repeated in detail here. It suffices to say that there was massive resistance and every state resource, including the services of the legal officers of the state, the services of private counsel (costing the state hundreds of thousands of dollars), the state police, and the power and prestige of the office of the governor, was employed to defeat *Brown 1*. In Richmond, as has been mentioned, not even freedom of choice became actually effective until 1966, *twelve years after the decision of Brown 1*. It is at once obvious that this is not a case in which there was a reasonably prompt, bona fide and sincere attempt to carry out the mandate of *Brown 1*, where, as a result of benign influences, a unitary system of schools has subsequently taken on a one-sided racial identity. It is a case in which the transition to a unitary system has been delayed, as a result of state action and state inaction, until the schools on either side of artificial political subdivision boundaries, when compared one to the other, can only be said to be racially identifiable and, within the community of interest extending beyond political subdivision boundaries, constitute a dual system.

Beyond mere delay—and the unmistakable message that the delay of the character practiced by Virginia carried to the black and to the white community—the district court found many other instances of state and private action contributing to the concentration of black citizens within Richmond and white citizens without. These were principally in the area of residential development. Racially restrictive covenants were freely employed. Racially discriminatory practices in the prospective purchase of county property by black purchasers were followed. Urban renewal, subsidized public housing and government-sponsored home mortgage insurance had been undertaken on a racially discriminatory basis. Henrico and Chesterfield Counties provided schools, roads, zoning and development approval for the rapid growth of the white population in each county at the expense of the city, without making any attempt to assure that the development that they made possible was integrated. Superimposed on the pattern of government-aided residential segregation, which the district court aptly characterized as "locking" the blacks into Richmond, had been a discriminatory policy of school construction, i. e., the selection of school construction sites in the center of racially identifiable neighborhoods manifestly to serve the educational needs of students of a single race.

The majority does not question the accuracy of these facts. I accept the findings of the district court in this regard as clearly correct. But the majority seeks to avoid their effect on the ground that evidence was lacking that the three subdivisions engaged in joint interaction to achieve the result . . . .

To me, the majority's statements simply beg the issue. First, . . . the mandate of the Fourteenth Amendment, as spelled out in *Brown 1,* is directed to the state of Virginia, not simply individually to its various subdivisions. The premise of the majority's statement is that each political subdivision is free to operate in its own orbit so long as it obeys the Fourteenth Amendment and does not undertake to conspire with others to defeat it. I do not conceive this to be the law; whether acting singly or in concert, action and inaction, by Richmond, Henrico and Chesterfield Counties in the several regards described are all *state* action and it is to overall state action that the Fourteenth Amendment is addressed. But for present purposes, what is more important is that when Richmond, Henrico and Chesterfield Counties are *finally* being brought into compliance with the Fourteenth Amendment, we are faced with the situation where there has occurred, at least in part as a result of state action, a marked segregation of the races, in that the vast majority of black citizens are concentrated within Richmond and the vast majority of white citizens are concentrated outside of Richmond, both the "within" and "without" constituting a single unified community and constituting a portion of a single state, not so large in geographical scope that a single system of schools is not feasible and practicable without undue hardship on the combined student population.

To decree a single system and interchange of students, notwithstanding historical political subdivision boundaries, represents no abuse of discretion under existing law. . . .

III

. . . . Of course, I do not suggest that the equal protection clause requires that there be an homogeneous racial mixture in all of the schools throughout the state of Virginia. Unquestionably, there comes a point when a school district becomes too large geographically, is too cumbersome administratively, and encompasses so many pupils that to eliminate racially identifiable schools within the district, transportation of pupils would be required to be undertaken in such magnitude of numbers and cost that unreasonable hardships would result. The direction to create such a district would be invalid, but the consolidated school district ordered here is not of that category. . . .

Therefore, as I view the application of the Fourteenth Amendment, *Brown 1* *requires* consolidation in this case. While discreetly exercised, the equitable jurisdiction of the district court was used to do no more than the Constitution directs. . . .

Notes and Questions

1. State Action

a. Involvement of State Authorities. Does the majority intend to suggest that the setting of school district boundaries is not state action? Is such a position tenable? Should each school district be treated as a separate governmental unit for the purpose of assessing the Fourteenth Amendment obligation to desegregate? Does your answer to this question depend on whether the district was created to avoid desegregation? How do *Griffin* and *Emporia* bear on the answers to these questions?

b. State Law. Of what relevance is state law to the resolution of the constitutional issues raised in *Bradley*? If state law carefully regulates and circumscribes the powers of local school districts to set educational and fiscal policies, does this strengthen the arguments for not treating each school district as a distinct entity for constitutional purposes? Both majority and dissent focus on the Virginia requirement that voters approve the alteration of school district boundaries. Of what relevance is this factor to the determination of the constitutional issues in *Bradley*? Does the majority intend to suggest that there is an inherent right to local government, embodied in Virginia law and in the Tenth Amendment, which has been transgressed by the lower court's decision? Is it unconstitutional, in the majority's view, to merge school districts without the popular consent of the constituents of each district involved in the merger? See generally F. Michelman and T. Sandalow, *Law in Urban Areas*, 179-85, 539-44 (1969).

c. Intention to Discriminate. Does the majority position rest on the assumption that district boundaries were not drawn with the purpose or intention of discriminating against blacks? Is this position sustainable in the light of *Keyes* (decided after *Bradley*)? Were not the boundary lines maintained with the "conscious knowledge" that they would perpetuate racial segregation in the schools? What is the relevance of the fact that there was extensive government-fostered discrimination in housing? Is this sufficient evidence of an intention to discriminate against blacks by "locking" them into Richmond? Must the plaintiffs prove that the three counties acted in concert to achieve this end? That the discrimination had an intercounty effect? If government policies accentuated the trend of black concentration in the inner city, is this a sufficient basis to hold the state responsible for the resultant intercounty segregation? Compare *Spencer v Kugler* 326 F Supp 1235 (DNJ 1971), *aff'd mem,* 404 US 1027 (1972).

2. Community

a. Which Community? The universal integrationist ethic does not demand uniform racial balance. The conceptual problem is the definition of the community within which the integration of the schools must take place. For example, one definition, albeit an impractical one, is that each school in a state must be racially integrated in accordance with the proportion of blacks and whites in the state as a whole. Alternatively, the school district or school attendance zones may be taken as the appropriate unit for integration purposes. Or the community may be defined by particular interest groups, not necessarily in territorial proximity, such as Catholics, or handicapped or vocational education children. Which of these communities is the appropriate one for purposes of the application of the Fourteenth Amendment's prohibition against racial discrimination? Should the state be free to define a community that makes integration impossible, e.g., the community of all blacks in Harlem? To what extent should the courts be bound by the state determination of community where that definition is not racially motivated? See generally Note, "Racial Imbalance and Municipal Boundaries—Educational Crisis in Morristown," 24 *Rutgers L Rev* 354 (1970).

b. Judicial Definition. Should the courts attempt to define the relevant community for school desegregation purposes? If many people living in Henrico and Chesterfield counties work in Richmond, attend cultural events in Richmond, and feel that they are a part of the larger Richmond community, may the courts treat the Richmond metropolitan area as a single unit even if the state has not chosen to do so? If the court defines the community in this fashion, has it intruded into the democratic processes in an undesirable way?

c. Communitarian Impulse. Consider Nathan Glazer's appraisal of the political consequences of boundary shifting for purposes of school desegregation:

> Perhaps the most serious constitutional issue in a line of cases erasing the distinction between de jure and de facto segregation and also erasing the political boundaries between school districts in order to achieve a racial balance in which every black student is a minority in every school (and presumably, as the cases develop, every Spanish-speaking student, and so on), is that all this makes impossible one kind of organization that a democratic society may wish to choose for its schools: the kind of organization in which the schools are the expression of a geographically defined community of the small scale and regulated in accordance with the democratically expressed views of that community.... [T]he new line of cases makes the school ever more distant from the community in which it is located and from the parents who send their children to it. Glazer, "Is Busing Necessary?" 53 *Commentary* 39, 47 (March 1972).

Do you agree with Professor Glazer's conclusions? Does your answer depend on whether school district boundaries describe "real" communities or whether they are "artificially" imposed on existing communities?

3. White Flight

To what extent were the district court and the appellate court dissent motivated by the fact that whites sought to escape school desegregation in Richmond by fleeing to the suburbs? Might whites have sought to escape from Richmond for unrelated reasons, such as better housing, less crime, or superior municipal services? Is it appropriate or feasible for courts to attempt to reverse a social trend of such massive proportions? See A. Bickel, *The Supreme Court and the Idea of Progress*, 103-51 (1970).

4. Merger of School Districts and Community Control

a. Merger for Pupil Assignment Only? If school districts are merged for the purpose of promoting integration, must they also be merged for governance, tax raising, or educational policy-making purposes? For example, could the district court have fashioned a plan that would have left the school board of each county in control of educational and fiscal decisions, while ordering the three counties to exchange pupils for purposes of their assignment to particular schools? Is this practical? What of the fact that under Virginia law boards of education do not have the power to raise revenues but must rely on city and county officials to finance public schools? What will be the result of giving a board of education control over the educational destinies of children whose parents do not live in the district from which the board members were selected? Is it less likely to be responsive to their needs? Will it be responsive because it fears retaliation from boards of education responsible for educating the children bused out of the district?

b. Bradley v Milliken. In *Bradley v Milliken* 468 F2d 902 (6th Cir 1973), the Court of Appeals for the Sixth Circuit upheld a decision requiring Detroit and surrounding suburban communities to submit a metropolitan desegregation plan. The Court attempted to distinguish *Bradley v School Bd:*

> In the instant case the district court has not ordered consolidation of school districts, but directed a study of plans for the reassignment of pupils in school districts comprising the metropolitan area of Detroit. In the Richmond case the court found that neither the Constitution nor statutes of Virginia, previously or presently in effect, would have permitted the state board of education, acting alone, to have effected a consolidation of the three school districts into a single system under the control of a single school board. The Fourth Circuit held that compulsory consolidation of political subdivisions of the state of Virginia was beyond the power of a federal court because of the Tenth Amendment to the Constitution of the United States. The decisions which now are under review did not contemplate such a restructuring.
>
> Furthermore, the court in the Richmond case cited provisions of the Constitution and statutes of Virginia in support of its holding that: "The power to operate, maintain and supervise public schools in Virginia is, and always has been, within the exclusive jurisdiction of the local school boards and not within the jurisdiction of the state board of education." 462 F2d at 1067.

The record in the present case amply supports the finding that the state of Michigan has not been subject to such limitations in its dealings with local school boards. 468 F2d 910.

Do you find these suggested distinctions persuasive? Does the *Milliken* Court imply that a metropolitan plan that merges school districts only for the purpose of pupil assignment is within the remedial discretion of the district court, but that a plan that merges them for governance and fiscal purposes would not be?

c. Black Power. Suppose an organization representing black voters made the following argument to the Detroit court: "Traditionally, the Detroit schools have been run by whites and for the benefit of white children. For the first time in the history of the city, blacks have made inroads into this white domination. As the city's black population increases, the board of education, city council, and other important political positions will be occupied by black community leaders. This will enable the schools to establish educational programs geared to the needs of black children. Just as the efforts to gain control of the Detroit schools are about to bear fruit, the white power structure, which has always opposed integration, reverses itself and seeks to merge Detroit with surrounding communities in order to promote integration. This is simply a device to prevent the black community from asserting a degree of control over the public schools that historically has been exercised by whites." How should the court respond to this argument?

VI. Equality of Opportunity and the Communitarian Impulse

Unhappiness with court-ordered desegregation is not limited to politicians and irate white parents. Since the late 1960s, some minority spokesmen have challenged policies and practices that ignore or submerge racial and ethnic differences, urging instead ghetto schools governed and staffed by the community. This section considers both the policy underpinnings and constitutional implications of this phenomenon.

A. Community Control: Policy Issues

The following excerpt explores the impetus for community control.

THE PRICE OF COMMUNITY CONTROL
David K. Cohen
48 Commentary 23 (July 1969)

Decentralization and community control refer to a variety of notions about schooling and school reform, not all of them related to the problem of disparities in achievement. One of these is that the potentially effective components of city school systems—parents, teachers, and inquisitive children—are walled off from each other by a Byzantine bureaucratic maze; before the elements can function to the children's best advantage, the argument runs, the walls must be broken down and the bureaucracy brought under control. Another view is that the entire educational system is racist, from the way it allocates resources, to the attitudes of its teachers and the character of its textbooks; according to this view the remedy is not to make the system more accessible but to transfer control of the enterprise altogether: until the schools are operated by the parents of their young black clients (or those who legitimately stand in loco parentis), they will not be responsive to the needs of Negro children. A third view is that the problem resides in the psychological consequences of powerlessness. As things now stand, it is argued, the central fact of life for black Americans is that they do not control their personal and collective destinies. All the significant ghetto institutions—schools, government, welfare, etc.—are controlled by whites. Unless these whites are replaced by Negroes, black children will lack a sense that the world will respond to their efforts, and their achievement will languish as a consequence. The last two ideas roughly comprise the meaning of community control, the first, decentralization.

Of the three, the notion that the root problem is bureaucracy probably has the broadest appeal. For one thing, the complexity and unresponsiveness of many big city school systems is legendary; no client of any class or color happily accepts the reign of the clerk, and increasing numbers reject the inflexible style and pedagogy of the schools. For another, we have long been accustomed to the idea that the very size of institutions inevitably produces a kind of social arteriosclerosis, and assume that the remedy lies not in reaming out the conduits, but in reducing the distance between the vital organs and the extremities. Finally, the antibureaucratic critique is almost always couched in irresistible contrasts between extreme situations—Scarsdale as opposed to Bedford-Stuyvesant, or Winnetka as opposed to the West Side of Chicago.

Unfortunately, however, there is no evidence that the level of parent participation in schools is related to students' achievement. It is true that parents in suburban communities are somewhat more likely to participate in school affairs than those in central cities, but this seems to have more to do with the consequences of affluence than with anything else; analysis of the data in the Coleman Report fails to reveal any association between the level of parental participation and achievement. Nor is there any evidence that smaller school districts—which we all presume to be less bureaucratized and more responsive to parents and children—produce higher levels of achievement than larger ones. With a few outstanding exceptions, public education in the US runs on the assumption that administrative decentralization, small and homey school districts, and local control are educational essentials; literally thousands of school jurisdictions stand as testimony to this creed, against only a handful of urban monoliths. Yet here again there appears to be no relation whatsoever between the size of a school district (or whether its board is elected or appointed) and the achievement of the students in its schools. . . .

Advocates of community control (as opposed to administrative decentralization) might raise the objection here that the source of underachievement is not bureaucratic inertia in the first place, but institutional racism. There is, in fact, no dearth of evidence that city school systems discriminate against the poor in general and Negroes in particular. Studies of resource allocation almost always reveal that predominantly black schools suffer by comparison with white schools, in terms of such things as teacher experience, tenure, and certification. In addition, the attitudes of many teachers are influenced by class and racial antagonisms; in the Coleman sample of northern urban elementary schools, between 10 and 20 percent of teachers in ghetto schools overtly expressed a preference for schools with all or nearly all white student bodies. . . .

Here it may be countered that it is not a teacher's racial attitudes which affect performance, but his expectations of his students' academic success. And indeed, this idea appears to make intuitive good sense. It seems reasonable to believe that bigoted white teachers—or Negroes who accept white stereotypes—will somehow communicate to their students the sense that black children are academically less capable. If that is so, then it might well follow that the most efficient way to deal with such teachers, short of large-scale psychotherapy, would be to sharpen dramatically their responsibility to the parents of Negro children, on the theory that they would then have to shape up or ship out.

Let us assume for the moment that this hypothesis is correct. Let us also grant that community control would transform academic expectations that have been distorted over the years by bigotry or brainwashing. Would it also eliminate underachievement in ghetto schools? The latter is unlikely, for most achievement differences appear to be related not to a student's race or to his school's racial composition, but to factors having to do with social class. . . .

Both of the theories that I have discussed so far suffer from the obvious defect of presuming that schools have an impact upon students' achievement, when most evidence on this point tends in the opposite direction. The third—the fact-control theory—does not so presume. Its premise is the notion that the central educational problem for black children is not poor pedagogy, but power-lessness, a political condition in the ghetto which is not at all unique to the schools. Now, it takes only a modicum of political insight to notice that Negroes do not control most of the institutions which directly affect their lives, and little ideological originality to argue that hence they are a subject people, dominated in colonial fashion by a foreign white ruling class. This argument has been advanced with increasing strength since World War II, but until publication of the Coleman Report there was no way to link the political fact of powerlessness with students' performance in school. One of that report's major findings, however, was that the extent to which black students felt they could master their destiny was a powerful determinant of their achievement, more important than all the measures of family, social, and economic status combined.

That provided the necessary link. If a student's sense of environment control strongly influenced his achievement, black control of ghetto schools, it seemed to follow, would produce a sense of personal efficacy which would in turn lead to improved performance. The idea now enjoys enormous popularity, primarily because it seems entirely consistent with reality. First of all, political and cultural emasculation has been a dominant element of the black experience in America. Secondly, all the precedents of American ethnic history are supposed to demonstrate that group political and economic solidarity is the touchstone of personal status and mobility. Finally, it seems to make eminent sense that people who feel in control of their destiny will be high achievers; the sense of mastery leads to mastery.

But try it the other way: mastery leads to the sense of mastery; high achievers are more likely to have a stronger sense of environment control than low achievers. It sounds just as persuasive one way as the other, a perplexity which is amply reflected in research. Some studies suggest that the sense of efficacy causes achievement, some suggest that it works the other way around, and others find no association whatsoever. We have no studies of the relationship between parents' political efficacy (or their sense thereof) and their children's test scores;

the few studies that relate parents' general sense of environment control to their children's achievement are inconclusive and contradictory. Here as elsewhere, the results of scientific research provide a firm basis for nothing but further research.

In summary: a good deal has been made of the various ways in which decentralization and community control will improve achievement, but a review of what we know turns up confused, contradictory, or discouraging evidence. This does not mean that greater participation, less bureaucracy, greater openness, and more accountability are not worthwhile goals; I happen to think they are crucial. In my view, however, these are essentially political and administrative issues, and one's assessment of their significance or desirability should be determined by theory and evidence particular to those realms of experience. The one thing my brief review of the educational evidence *does* mean is this: if one were guided solely by research on achievement and attitudes, one would not employ community control or decentralization as the devices most likely to reduce racial disparities in achievement. . . .

[There is] a profound crisis of authority in ghetto schools, a sense that these schools lack legitimacy as educational institutions. This feeling is strongest among Negroes—especially the young, the activists, and the professionals—but it is reinforced by the many middle- and upper-middle-class whites who reject the public schools' regimentation and authoritarianism for other reasons. For some blacks and whites, the notion that only parents and community residents are legitimately empowered to operate schools rests on what is taken to be the objective inadequacy of those in authority; scarcely anyone with access to print denies that the schools have failed to correct ghetto educational problems. Repeated for years, this assertion has led effortlessly to the idea that the established agencies lack the special competence upon which most educational authority is assumed to rest.

There is, however, more to the crisis of authority than that. The illegitimacy of ghetto education is more and more often proclaimed to reside not in the failure of that education to produce achievement equal to that of white schools— had it done so, according to the earlier logic, the criterion of legitimacy need never have been challenged—but in the defective nature of the social contract between black and white America. One manifestation of this position is the attack that has been launched on the instruments—achievement test results, rates of college acceptance, etc.—typically used to determine if the older, "rational" criterion of authority was being satisfied; not only that, but the intellectual and cultural content of those instruments has been dismissed as irrelevant or antithetical to the black community's political and cultural aspirations. A second, and politically more explosive, manifestation of this view is the assertion that school officials and teachers whose ideas or activities suggest the absence of political and cultural identification with the black community therefore also lack the qualifications requisite to educate black children. This is entirely consistent with the new criterion of authority, which assumes that the task of educators in the ghettos is to establish the basis for a valid social contract between Negroes and the institutions in their communities. Hence it becomes not at all strange to substitute for the old, "rational" tests of educational competence a subjective test of political consensus, for in a sense the situation is presumed to have reverted to the precontract state of nature, wherein the main issue is one of defining the body politic that is about to come into being, and deciding who shall be its citizens.

... [T] he crisis in urban education is passing into a phase in which only a change in the locus of authority will bring peace. How long the present transition period will last is hard to say, but the main elements of the domestic political situation appear to favor an increase rather than a diminishing of the anticolonial impulse. Those elements include: the inability of the liberal/labor/civil-rights coalition to secure legislation that would mount a broad and basic attack upon black-white disparities in income and occupation; an unprecedented (but hardly unheralded) upsurge of black nationalism; the emergence of a black professional class in Northern cities as a political force.

Since the collapse of the Johnsonian consensus on domestic affairs, which can be roughly dated to the 1966 White House conference "To Fulfill These Rights," these three elements have come into high relief, reinforcing one another. After the White House conference, it became increasingly clear that congressional liberals were light-years away from the political strength required to legislate fundamental change in the economic and social status of Negroes. The resources lost to the war effort in Vietnam were of course partly to blame, but there was more to it than that: as the White House conference report suggested, fundamental change would require social spending on an absolutely unprecedented scale. Even without a war in Vietnam the congressional struggle would have been titanic in its proportions; it was clearly impossible under conditions of large-scale defense spending.

In the cities, therefore, where no real effort has been made to deal with the underlying problems of jobs and income, attention remains where it has been since 1954. The schools are visible and accessible, in the sense that the political nexus of employment and housing is not; their performance has been obviously out of harmony with the ideology of education expounded by all moderates and liberals since *Brown v Board of Education*; and the inability in the last decade to effect widespread educational reforms has insured that existing frustrations would grow as performance fell farther and farther behind expectations. . . .

One commentator suggests that, in the long run, integration and community control may not be antithetical concepts:

COMMUNITY CONTROL
A. Altschuler
20-25 (1970)

[A] t present most black spokesmen whose long-run objective is integration are *also* supporters of community control . . . [They declare that] to proclaim full integration as one's immediate and only goal is idle rhetoric. Only a tiny minority of white Americans are prepared to have their own neighborhoods and schools integrated, except in token proportions and by black families that have adopted white life styles. . . .

By contrast, an overwhelming majority of blacks has supported integration in the past and continues to do so. . . .

Those who favor both community control and integration maintain that, if history has ever taught a lesson, it has taught that those few white liberals who genuinely desire full integration cannot deliver it—at least not in the foreseeable future. . . .

Black leaders, the "moderate" proponents of community control point out, have rarely opposed integration in practice, even though some have taken to rejecting it as a goal in their rhetoric. None propose denying individual blacks the right to move to predominantly white neighborhoods today. It is still *whites* who provide the political constituency for segregation. All the blacks have done is to change tactics. They have revived the distinction between integration and equality as objectives, and determined to concentrate for the time being upon the latter.

Essentially this decision has been pragmatic. They have judged that if integration ever came about it would do so only *after* black achievement equalled white. (The traditional view, of course, accepted by the Supreme Court in the *Brown* decision, had been that integration was a prerequisite of equal achievement.) They have judged that the real key to unlocking the black potential is self-respect, and that given white resistance to integration, the most feasible way for blacks to acquire it is to exercise responsibility in their own communities. . . .

The evidence available suggests that the calls for black pride and black power have struck responsive chords among the Negro masses, but without substantially altering the basic thrust toward equality and integration. . . .

What all this suggests is that Negroes and whites have radically different views as to whether black power and black pride need violate the traditionally acceptable limits of American ethnic pluralism. The rhetoric and the demands will probably change as and if white America becomes truly receptive to integration. In the long interim, it ill behooves white liberals to reject black-proposed ghetto improvement schemes out of hand. So, at least, the "moderate" supporters of community control maintain.

B. Community Control: Legal Issues

1. Is Community Control of Schools Constitutionally Permissible?

"COMMUNITY CONTROL, PUBLIC POLICY,
AND THE LIMITS OF LAW "
D. Kirp
68 *Mich L Rev* 1355, 1361-74 (1970)

. . . . The way in which *Brown* [2] is interpreted has important implications for community control. If the court meant to dismantle those dual educational systems which had previously existed through force of law, other forms of racial isolation—including, presumably, community control—are not proscribed. If, on the other hand, the court felt that racial segregation was constitutionally repugnant whether or not mandated by law, *Brown* makes integration an affirmative constitutional requirement.

While the debate about *Brown* has most frequently centered on whether de facto, as well as de jure, segregation is unconstitutional, two other elements of that decision merit attention in considering the constitutionality of community control. The segregation condemned in *Brown* was involuntary; the plaintiffs had been given no choice but to send their children to an all-black school. By striking down this restriction of individual choice, *Brown* clearly upholds the right of free association of individuals against irrational state curbs on that right. In that respect, it is less a case concerned with education than a pronouncement about general public behavior. If the *Brown* court's focus on uncoerced association is significant, it might enable a court to accept a community control arrangement which coupled neighborhood-run schools with a provision permitting children to opt for an integrated education outside the neighborhood.

The Supreme Court in *Brown* also noted the adverse effect of segregation on the quality of education afforded black children, suggesting that integration was not regarded as an end valued in itself, but as a means of ensuring equal educational outcomes. Such a reading of the case leaves extant the possibility that plausible alternatives to desegregation as means of promoting equality—such as community control—would be acceptable.

The *Brown* court focused on no single element of segregation as the basis of its proscription. In *Brown* the court appears to have posited integration, uncoerced association, and racially equal educational outcomes as aspects of the same end. Today that assumption lacks validity: racial integration by itself will not ensure free association or equalize educational outcomes. Moreover, the value of integration has been called into question by those who renounce racially heterogeneous schooling in favor of community control, asserting the inadequacy of any other solution. In light of the ambiguous legal doctrine, and in light of new questions of ideology, it seems appropriate to attempt to identify again the unconstitutional aspects of segregation and to reevaluate the means available for remedying these fatal defects.

The dimensions of the problem vary enormously between the North and the South, and even within different communities in each region. The complexity of issues, whether viewed as legal conundrums or as regional fact patterns susceptible to differing understandings, augurs ill for any effort at unitary solution. In the South, the courts continue to strive for an end to the dual system of schooling, which *Brown* clearly found unconstitutional. The push has been slow and costly, both in terms of judicial energy and, more notably, in terms of deferred educational promises. Southern school districts have shown considerable and lamentable ingenuity in evading *Brown*. They put forth a whole host of alternatives—such as massive resistance, freedom-of-choice plans, neighborhood schools (where neighborhoods were residentially segregated), and tuition voucher schemes—which effectively retained segregation under various guises. . . .

In the South . . . community control seems both an unlikely demand for the black community to make and, at least until the dismantling of separate schools has been fully accomplished, of doubtful constitutionality. The essence of southern segregation is domination: the imposition of a separate system of schools upon the black community, against the will of its leaders, unaccompanied by any transfer of power or control. Under such a system, choice is a chimera, rightly and forcefully condemned by the courts. Community control is a quite different, indeed antithetical, notion. It connotes an active choice of dominion over the community's schools by a group which defines itself as a community for the purpose of making the choice. The concept of community control further implies a transfer of significant power to the community in order to make meaningful the exercise of control. Advocates of community control argue that equal educational opportunity can be achieved through means other than integration, that the opportunity for a parent to exercise real and direct influence over his children's education—to be able to hold the school accountable for its failures—carries with it educational benefits. It is segregation without choice or control that southern schoolmen have proffered and black leaders oppose, and the southern black community has thus far been disinclined to propose the very different separation implicit in community control. Moreover, in order to eliminate state-imposed segregation, federal courts in the South have found it necessary to strike down all proposed alternatives to desegregation that would have operated to maintain the status quo. Until the vestiges of the dual school system are abandoned, courts are unlikely to embrace community control where communities are racially and socially defined.

In the North, on the other hand, black leaders have come to regard community control of schools as the most promising means of securing educational equality. Certain of the educational ends that they seek are similar to those sought by the integrationists: schools that can succeed in teaching basic cognitive skills, such as reading and ciphering, to poor and black school children; schools that can prepare children to cope with life in a complex and too often hostile environment. Community control advocates argue either that integration has not worked, or, more typically, that the political will to attempt it has been lacking. As a result, they contend, continuing reliance on integration as a means for achieving the desired educational ends no longer seems appropriate. Rather, in their view, control, and the educational, psychological, and political benefits that assertedly follow from such control, is a preferable means.

Judicial insistence that southern schools integrate "at once," coupled with the increasing willingness of northern courts to identify racially motivated practices of city school boards as illegitimate, makes evident the potential conflict between community control in the North and the *Brown* rule. The conflict may be simply put: decentralization promotes racial isolation; *Brown* inveighs against it. If *Brown* is read to disallow all racial separation, community control will be found to be unconstitutional; and no expression favoring separateness, even if made by the majority of a black community, will be able to cure the constitutional defect.

Yet that reading of *Brown* seems overly mechanical and is peculiarly unresponsive to different factual contexts and to the educational consequences of alternative arrangements. It also fuses two elements of the decision that merit separate analysis: *Brown*'s concern with *educational* consequences, and its concern with *associational* consequences. . . .

The *Brown* court apparently assumed that racial isolation causes racially different outcomes and that racial integration will yield racially identical results. Current social science evidence drastically qualifies that assumption. It suggests that race has only a modest effect on schooling success and that social class integration is more likely than is racial integration to lead to significant educational benefits for poor and black school children. Even more important, the limitations of the evidence from social science are also more plain today. . . .

In the face of such an educational dilemma, the court would be unwise to equate equality of educational opportunity—the constitutional standard—with equality of educational outcome; exhortations to do the impossible do not make good law. For the community control advocate, this seems fortunate, since the evidence suggesting the educational efficacy of community control is slim indeed. While there is substantial rhetoric to the contrary, little data exists which indicates that community control alone, without substantial infusions of dollars and resources, would significantly change educational outcomes. The notion of community control is at its heart a political statement, equally appropriate in the context of police or fire protection. But that often camouflaged fact should not in itself make community control any less acceptable to the courts; few contrary educational assertions carry much empirical weight. . . . [Professor Kirp next considers whether choice, unconstrained by "irrelevant barriers," such as race (*Deal v Cincinnati Bd of Educ* 369 F2d 55 (6th Cir 1966)), is crucial to the *Brown* decision.]

Unconstrained freedom of association is, at first blush, an arrestingly attractive judicial concept. It falls within the ambit of traditional equal protection decisions, and it removes the court from the troublesome business of reviewing discretionary acts, such as adherence to a neighborhood school policy, for which some educational justification can be shown. Indeed, it is "choice" that community control advocates favor in arguing that certain self-defined communities have a right to manage their own educational affairs.

Yet where the self-selected community is predominately black (or Puerto Rican or Mexican-American), the exercise of choice may yield constitutionally troubling consequences. The clear teaching of *Green v County School Bd* [391 US 430 (1968)] is that a politically dominant white community cannot opt for a nominally free-choice arrangement which in fact excludes black students from formerly all-white schools. Does community control, insofar as it promotes racially identifiable communities, fall within the category of discriminatory association condemned by *Brown* and *Green*? The question is more sharply posed in the context of a hypothetical lawsuit, brought by a black parent, challenging a community control arrangement on the grounds that the effect of such an arrangement is to deny his children the opportunity to associate with white school children. If the community is indeed racially defined, and if the arrangement offers the parent no option but to send his child to the neighborhood (and black) school, the parent's argument is appealing: his children do not have the chance to go to school with white children, and the source of that denial is the official policy of the school board, not just the happenstance of residence.

Certainly, there are differences between the rationale that prompts community control and the rationale for other forms of segregated schooling. But the effect is the same—state-promoted racial isolation. The remedy in such a situation, however, is not necessarily that community control be struck down in its entirety. If unconstrained choice is the value to be conserved, the parent's concern extends only to his children and to the class of children in the community who are prevented by the community control plan from attending integrated schools. If the arrangement were structured in such a manner as to attend, at public expense, a school in which his race is a minority, this constraint on choice would be removed. The arrangement might then, and only then, be constitutionally acceptable. The constitutional question has not, however, been posed to the courts in this form. Decisions striking down freedom-of-choice plans in the South assumed, quite rightly, that freedom of choice in that context was but a subterfuge to avoid disestablishing the dual educational system. Yet where such a system has not previously existed . . . , freedom of choice for the integration-minded, predicated on the wishes of the black community, might well be permissible.

But discussions of constitutional possibility do not foreclose the educational problems. Coupling community control with a "majority-to-minority transfer" provision places the burden of choosing an integrated education on the parent, rather than on the state; in so doing it implies that communitarianism is to be regarded as the norm and integration as the exception. Furthermore, it subjects the parent who prefers an integrated education for his children to considerable community pressure. Whether the burden and the pressure ought to rest with the integration-minded parent is a dilemma not easily resolved. . . .

Notes and Questions

1. *Keyes* and Community Control

Is community control, as Professor Kirp defines it, consistent with the *Keyes* decision? Suppose that after *Keyes* the Denver black community (or, more realistically, a segment of that community) persuaded the school board to permit it to run its own schools. Would such an arrangement survive constitutional challenge? Would the outcome of such a case differ if the school district was one that had, in the past, voluntarily desegregated its schools? If the district had never been held to be a de jure segregated district?

2. What Is "the Community?"

Professor Kirp identifies community control as connoting "an active choice of dominion over the community's schools by a group which defines itself as a community for the purpose of making the choice." How might a court determine whether the group did indeed "represent" the community? In assessing the constitutionality of a given governance arrangement, would a court be required to define "dominion?"

BRADLEY v MILLIKEN

433 F2d 897 (6th Cir 1970), *appeal after remand,*

438 F2d 945 (6th Cir 1971)

[In 1969, the state of Michigan adopted legislation mandating the decentralization of "any first class school district with more than 100,000 student membership . . . ." MCLA § § 388.171 et seq. Detroit is the only such Michigan district. The legislation divides the district into eight regions and creates a thirteen-member district board: five of its members are to be elected at large; eight are the chairmen of regional boards. Under the legislation, the chairman is the regional board member receiving the greatest number of votes in the regional board election. Regions are to be "as compact, contiguous, and nearly equal in population as practicable," and their board members are elected by those who reside in the region.

[Governance powers are allocated between the district and the regional boards. Regional boards, "subject to guidelines established by the first class district board," are authorized: (i) to employ a superintendent for the region, choosing from a list submitted by the district board; (ii) to employ, discharge, assign, and promote all teachers, subject to district board review; (iii) to determine curriculum, educational, and testing programs; and (iv) to determine the budget, based on the allocation of funds received from the district board.

[The statutory provision on which the *Bradley* court focuses was added to the statute as an amendment in 1970.]

Phillips, Chief Judge.

This case involves an effort by the Detroit board of education, as constituted on April 7, 1970, to effect a more balanced ratio of Negro and white students in twelve senior high schools. This effort was thwarted by an act of the Michigan legislature, Act No 48, effective July 7, 1970 . . . .

The appeal is under 28 USC § 1292(a) from the interlocutory order of the district court entered September 3, 1970, which, among other things, refused to grant a preliminary injunction.

The plaintiffs are pupils and parents of pupils who attend the Detroit public schools, and the Detroit branch of the National Association for the Advancement of Colored People. The defendants are the governor of Michigan, the attorney general of Michigan, the acting state superintendent of public instruction, the state board of education, the board of education of the city of Detroit, three members of the latter board,[1] and the superintendent of the Detroit public schools.

On April 7, 1970, the Detroit board of education adopted a plan which provided for changes in twelve high school attendance zones, designed to effect a more balanced ratio of Negro and white students at the senior high school level. The plan was applicable to twelve of the twenty-one high schools in Detroit that serve particular neighborhood or geographical areas. The April 7 plan was to take effect over a three-year period, applying initially to those students entering the tenth grade in September 1970 at the beginning of 1970-71 school year. In successive stages the eleventh grade was to have been affected at the opening of the 1971-72 school year, and the twelfth grade at the beginning of the 1972-73 school year.

Dr. Norman Drachler, the superintendent of the Detroit public schools, testified that the plan was adopted after an extended study. He described the purpose of the plan as follows:

Q What was the purpose of the plan as adopted?

A The purpose of the plan was, in addition to complying with the regulations of the State Act 244 [MCLA § § 388.171 et seq] to bring about a decentralized school system within the city which would allow for the election of regional boards which would bring about greater participation at the local level by the community. That it would undoubtedly, in the opinion of most of us, add towards the improvement of quality education, quality integrated education insofar as possible.

The board of education has, as long as I can recall, always accepted

---

1. The Detroit board of education normally consists of seven members. At the time the complaint was filed four of the members had been recalled in an election held August 4, 1970. On August 31, 1970, the governor appointed four new members to the vacancies created by the recall vote.

the premise that the task of improving education is a very complex one in a large city, but they have consistently held to the premise that wherever possible, wherever reasonably we can bring about integration in the process of developing our educational program, that this would enhance the opportunity of all children, black and white, both in terms of their educational achievement as well as their potential as responsible citizens in a democracy.

So in this plan the board saw an opportunity, the majority, that we could at the high school level in some twelve high schools bring about over a three-year period a certain amount of integration although it involved only the movement of some ten to twelve thousand children over the three-year period, nevertheless, that is, the transfer of 12,000 children in three years—nevertheless these children were in twelve schools which involved about 35,000 students, which is over 50 percent of our total high school enrollment.

We have certain high schools that are already integrated. Thus, we saw this as a step not only toward achieving a goal of the decentralization act but also the broader goal which the board has always had of quality integrated education.

The board of education adopted the plan by a vote of four to two, with one member absent because of illness. This seventh member, who is represented to have favored the plan but was unable to vote, has since died and his vacancy has been filled. . . .

Following adoption of the plan on April 7, 1970, Detroit school officials began to prepare procedures to carry it into effect at the beginning of the 1970-71 school year.

The Michigan legislature enacted, and on July 7, 1970, the governor of Michigan signed into law, Act No 48, Public Acts of 1970.

Section 12 of this Act is as follows:

Sec 12. The implementation of any attendance provisions for the 1970-71 school year determined by any first class school district board shall be delayed pending the date of commencement of functions by the first class school district boards established under the provisions of this amendatory act but such provision shall not impair the right of any such board to determine and implement prior to such date such changes in attendance provisions as are mandated by practical necessity. In reviewing, confirming, establishing or modifying attendance provisions the first class school district boards established under the provisions of this amendatory act shall have a policy of open enrollment and shall enable students to attend a school of preference but providing priority acceptance, insofar as practicable, in cases of insufficient school capacity, to those students residing nearest the school and to those students desiring to attend the school for participation in vocationally oriented courses or other specialized curriculum.

By its terms this statute applies only to "first class school districts." The Detroit school system is the only "first class school district" in Michigan. Although on its face the statute is a general act, it is applicable only to one local school system in the state.

Following enactment of Act 48, the superintendent of Detroit city schools requested an opinion from the attorney for the board of education as to the effect of this statute. This opinion, dated July 28, 1970, contains the following language with respect to §12:

> The answer to this question is found in Section 12 of Act 48. Section 12 says:
>
> "The implementation of any attendance provisions for the 1970-71 school year determined by any first class school district board shall be delayed pending the date of commencement of functions by the first class school district boards established under the provisions of this amendatory act * * * ."
>
> This quoted portion of section 12 obviously, albeit indirectly, addresses itself to the action taken by the board on April 7, 1970, with respect to establishing new high school attendance areas. In our opinion, the effect of this provision is to rescind—for at least one year—the attempt made by the board of education on April 7, 1970, to achieve integration in its high schools. While Act 48 itself purports only to delay implementation until January 1, 1971, it is well known that no implementation begun even on January 1, 1971, could be placed into operation earlier than the beginning of the fall semester in September, 1971. For these reasons we deem it unnecessary to recommend that the board's action on April 7, 1970, establishing high school attendance areas be rescinded.

Further, a movement was initiated by certain Detroit voters to recall the four members of the Detroit School Board who had voted in favor of the April 7, 1970, plan. The recall movement was resolved at the August 4, 1970, election, which resulted in the recall and removal from office of the four board members who voted in favor of the April 7 plan. As stated in footnote 1, these four positions were vacant at the time the complaint was filed and on August 31, 1970, were filled by appointment by the governor.

In accordance with the opinion of the attorney for the board of education quoted above, Detroit school officials did not put the April 7 plan into effect for the 1970-71 school year beginning in September 1970. The superintendent of city schools testified that he instructed regional superintendents that "we had to go back to the plan of April 6." The principals of the affected high schools sent out letters or otherwise notified students that regardless of any previous instructions to the contrary, they should attend the high school they would have attended prior to April 7. It is undisputed, that, obedient to the mandate of §12 of Act 48, the plan adopted by the board of education on April 7, has been suspended, or at least deferred to a time beyond January 1, 1971. The high schools in question have reverted to the attendance zones which were in effect prior to the April 7 action of the Board. The tenth grade students who would have attended a high school with an improved racial balance as determined by the board of education on April 7 have been deprived of that opportunity from the beginning of the 1970-71 school year until the time of the rendering of this opinion.

On August 18, 1970, plaintiffs filed their complaint in the present case as a class action, attacking the constitutionality of §12 of Act 48. . . .

We first consider the issue of the constitutionality of the statute.

As previously stated, the plan adopted by the Detroit board of education was designed to provide a better balance between students of the Negro and white races in twelve high schools. If this plan had come into existence under a judgment of the United States District Court for the Eastern District of Michigan, there could be no question that §12 of Act 48 would be void. The legislature of a state cannot annul the judgments nor determine the jurisdiction of the courts of the United States. *US v Peters* 9 US 115 (1809).

In the present case the April 7 plan came into being, not as the result of a judgment of a district court, but by the voluntary action of the Detroit board of education in its effort further to implement the mandate of the Supreme Court in *Brown v Board of Educ* 347 US 483, 349 US 294, and succeeding cases, such as *Alexander v Holmes County Bd of Educ* 396 US 19 and *Green v County School Bd* 391 US 430. The implementation of the April 7 plan was thwarted by State action in the form of the act of the legislature of Michigan.

In numerous decisions the Supreme Court and other federal courts have held that state action in any form, whether by statute, act of the executive department of a state or local government, or otherwise, will not be permitted to impede, delay or frustrate proceedings to protect the rights guaranteed to members of all races under the Fourteenth Amendment. See:

Hunter v Erickson 393 US 385, holding that the repeal by referendum of the fair housing ordinance previously adopted by the city council of Akron, Ohio, "discriminates against minorities, and constitutes a real, substantial, and invidious denial of the equal protection of the laws." (393 US at 393.)

Reitman v Mulkey 387 US 369, holding invalid a provision of the constitution of California, adopted by statewide referendum, which nullified previously enacted statutes regulating racial discrimination in housing and authorized "racial discrimination in the housing market." (387 US at 381.)

Griffin v County School Bd of Prince Edward County 377 US 218, and cases cited therein, invalidating the "massive resistance" legislation enacted by the Virginia legislature designed to prevent or delay school integration, and requiring reopening of public schools of Prince Edward County.

Cooper v Aaron 358 US 1, 9, nullifying a 1956 amendment to the constitution of Arkansas which commmanded the Arkansas legislature to oppose "in every constitutional manner the unconstitutional desegregation decisions" of the Supreme Court, and various state statutes enacted for that purpose.

Kelley v Board of Educ of Nashville 270 F2d 209 (6th Cir), *cert denied*, 361 US 924, holding a Tennessee statute authorizing separate segregated schools on a voluntary basis to be "patently and manifestly unconstitutional on its face." (270 F2d at 231.)

Lee v Nyquist 318 F Supp 710 (WDNY) (three-judge court, Sept 29, 1970), which held invalid under the equal protection clause of the Fourteenth Amendment § 3201(2) of the New York Education Law, McKinney's Consol Laws, c 16, which "prohibits state education officials and appointed school boards from assigning students, or establishing, reorganizing or maintaining school districts, school zones or attendance units for the purpose of achieving racial equality in attendance." (318 F Supp 713.)

Keyes v School Dist No One, Denver, Colo 313 F Supp 61, 303 F Supp 279, and 303 F Supp 289 (D Colo), 396 US 1215, involving a school desegregation plan adopted by a school board and an effort to rescind this plan made by the same board after changes in membership following a school board election. . . .

Defendants rely upon the decision of this court in *Deal v Cincinnati Bd of Educ* 369 F2d 55, *cert denied,* 389 US 847, 419 F2d 1387 (6th Cir). *Deal* is distinguishable on its facts from the present case. In *Deal* this court held that the school board of a long-established unitary non-racial school system had no constitutional obligation to bus white and Negro children away from districts of their residences in order that racial complexion be balanced in each of the many public schools in the city. In the present case the Detroit board of education in the exercise of its discretion took affirmative steps on its own initiative to effect an improved racial balance in twelve senior high schools. This action was thwarted, or at least delayed, by an act of the state legislature. No comparable situation was presented in *Deal.* . . .

We hold §12 of Act 48 to be unconstitutional and of no effect as violative of the Fourteenth Amendment. By this ruling on the invalidity of §12, we express no opinion at the present stage of the case as to the merits of the plan adopted by the school board on April 7, 1970, or as to whether it was the constitutional obligation of the school board to adopt all or any part of that plan. . . .

Notes and Questions

1. Discrimination

Is the court's conclusion, that the Michigan legislation is unconstitutionally discriminatory, correct? See *North Carolina State Bd of Educ v Swann* 402 US 43 (1971).

2. Legislative Purpose

The *Bradley* court views the challenged statute as designed to frustrate integration efforts. But the legislation might also have been intended to further the goal of community control, by giving regional boards some say in student assignment policy. That reading of the legislation sets the goals of community control and integration at odds with one another, and reveals a strong judicial preference for the latter goal. How does Professor Kirp's discussion of this issue, *supra* page 460, affect the analysis? See also F. Michelman and T. Sandalow, *Government in Urban Areas,* 1972 Supplement 48-57.

2. Is Community Control of Schools Constitutionally Required?

"COMMUNITY CONTROL, PUBLIC POLICY, AND THE LIMITS OF LAW"
D. Kirp
68 *Mich L Rev* 1355, 1374-84 (1970)

Those who would make community control a constitutional right develop two quite different arguments. The first, relied on in the New York litigation [*Oliver*

v Donovan 293 F Supp 958 (EDNY 1968)], insists that only through control
can equal educational opportunity be achieved, since any other form of school
governance inevitably disadvantages poor and black children. The second, the
basis of the Boston litigation [*Owens v School Comm* 304 F Supp 1327 (D Mass
1969)], draws on the reapportionment decisions to establish for groups of like-
minded individuals the general right to manage their own political affairs and the
specific right to manage their own schools.

The argument equating decentralization with equal opportunity for poor and
black children reflects the disillusionment of the black community with earlier
efforts at securing quality education, notably through busing black children to
white schools and developing "magnet schools" to draw children from all parts
of the city. For a variety of reasons, the most significant of which were minimal
financial support and insufficient political force, those measures proved less than
adequate to meet the needs of the affected communities. On the basis of that
particular educational and political failure, plaintiffs in the New York case . . . asserted that any educational effort managed by the city-wide board would inevitably harm poor and black urban school children. In a subsequent suit, arguing
for the right of the experimental school districts to survive a citywide redistrict-
ing, New York community groups presented the view that:

> As a result of the *past history* of educational deprivation out of which the
> demonstration projects grew, the immediate design of *this present plan* to
> eliminate the demonstration projects [described elsewhere in the complaint
> as "an attempt by the governmental agencies of the state to return mem-
> bers of the nonwhite communities to a status inferior to that of white
> communities; i.e. 'to keep them in their place,' in violation of the Thir-
> teenth Amendment"] and the *ultimate effect* of this plan for the educa-
> tional future of the nonwhite communities involved, the state's attempted
> withdrawal of the community-controlled education experiments, and the
> education benefits and experimental value inherent in those projects, vio-
> lates the constitutional mandates of the Thirteenth and Fourteenth Amend-
> ments. . . .

The argument is couched in terms of equal protection: when a right is "fundamental" (and it is asserted that education is such a right), state action which
discriminates even unintentionally against one group of citizens is unconstitutional unless that action is the only way of furthering a legitimate state interest.
School governance is an example of this situation, since a citywide school board,
by attempting to treat all children in the same fashion, benefits only its middle-
class constituency. Such differential consequences are viewed as an inevitable
concomitant of citywide educational governance. . . .

To argue that the failure of the present educational system makes decentralization a constitutional requirement is to oversimplify a vexing educational problem. While the argument obtains support from commonly held misgivings about
urban schooling, it proposes as the only acceptable remedy what is in fact only
one of several alternative and competing choices. The consequences of each competing choice are not altogether clear. Even after numerous academic skirmishes,
no one really knows what pedagogic consequences will follow from altering the
method of school governance. Nor is it self-evident that slackness in the central
school administration bears on or causes disasters in the classroom. Perhaps it

does; but that conclusion depends on speculations about human nature and political behavior, speculations not usually accorded constitutional recognition. . . .

A second line of constitutional argument focuses not on the quality of education that community-controlled schools would assertedly ensure, but on the community's political rights to govern its own schools. It challenges the practice of citywide elections for school board members, asserting that that practice ensures the election of an all middle-class board, thereby effectively disenfranchising the poor and black urban communities. . . .

The proponents [of that approach, which is embodied in *Owens v School Comm* 304 F Supp 1327 (D Mass 1969)] argue that black and poor parents have identifiable common interests in the education of their children, that those interests are distinguishable from middle-class concerns, and that those interests require recognition in a school district managed by and for the community. That view is, of course, inconsistent with the conventional philosophy of American schooling—a philosophy which insists that the mission of the schools is to Americanize, to make all children equal by making them all the same, a philosophy which has sought since the mid-nineteenth century to produce a common breed of men by socializing them in common public schools. In part, the control argument embodies a recognition of the failure of that conventional view. It demands that the common-schooling ideal be seen not as the exclusive method to provide schooling, but merely as one alternative solution embodying—like the "one man, one vote" reapportionment standard—one particular set of political and social value choices. The community control supporters argue that since the universal and common approach has failed, it is necessary to adopt an approach which emphasizes the particular and the different. . . .

[The constitutional implications of that approach are] profoundly troubling. [It] requires . . . elevat[ing] the single-member, community-based election district to constitutional status, the application of that principle to school board elections, and the extension of that doctrine to force decentralization. It binds the courts to a set of assumptions about group interests—and about the adequacy of group representation to secure those interests—that are rooted in assertion and ideology rather than in law. It commits the court to an almost constant search for a community entitled to a political recognition, even though a court is ill-equipped to make that search. It suggests that there is one set of standards for poor and black communities and another, thus far unarticulated, set for other sorts of communities. Moreover, it assumes that only through decentralization can group representation be achieved. By making that assumption, it preserves like-mindedness at the expense of heterogeneity and choice—attributes which, for schooling if not for electoral districts, are considered by some authorities to be virtues. The inadequacy of adjudication as a means of making this difficult set of decisions is likely to lead the courts not to insist on decentralization, but rather to defer to the body politic for guidance and political choice making. . . .

Notes and Questions

1. A Disappearing Phenomenon?

Aside from the dispute discussed in Note 3 (*infra* at 472), there has been little attention paid to community control by minority community leaders since 1970.

While some school districts, such as New York City, did "decentralize" during this period (each decentralized district in New York is the size of Providence, Rhode Island), in no school district has full authority to run schools been vested in a neighborhood or community. Has the issue disappeared? Why? Did community leaders conclude that the notion of control was not a sensible one? That it was politically unfeasible? Is the demise of community control a reflection of decreasing interest in educational policy? Does it indicate that the Supreme Court's decisions in *Swann* and *Keyes* have helped to restore the minority community's historic commitment to integration?

2. Further Reading

The community control movement has spawned a considerable literature. Much of it centers on the prolonged controversy in New York City over the fate of "experimental," Ford-Foundation-supported, community-controlled districts in Brooklyn and Harlem (an experiment which culminated in the decentralization of New York City's schools). For a general discussion of community control, see *Community Control of Schools* (H. Levin ed 1970) (Fein, "Community Schools and Social Theory: The Limits of Universalism" is a particularly noteworthy essay in that volume); *Education and Social Policy: Local Control of Education* (C. Bowers, I. Housego, and D. Dyke, eds 1970); M. Fantini, M. Gittell, and R. Magat, *Community Control and the Urban School* (1970); Kristol, "Decentralization for What?" 11 *Public Interest* 17 (Spring 1968). For a discussion of the New York City experience, see M. Berube and M. Gittell, *Confrontation at Ocean Hill-Brownsville* (1969).

3. Community Control: The Berkeley Experience

In 1971, the Berkeley, California, Unified School District created an Experimental Schools Program. That venture, funded by the National Institute for Education as part of a national program of the same name, includes twenty-four "alternative schools" within the public school system. Each school offers an education differing in method or content from traditional schooling. Each school draws from the citywide population, and each embodies what has been termed a "community of limited liability," see S. Greer, *The Emerging City: Myth and Reality* 107-37 (1962), rather than a neighborhood-based community. Two of the schools enroll students exclusively (or almost exclusively) from one racial or ethnic group: Black House admits black students and Casa de la Raza admits Chicano students. The following excerpt describes the two schools in some detail:

Comment, "ALTERNATIVE SCHOOLS FOR MINORITY STUDENTS:
THE CONSTITUTION, THE CIVIL RIGHTS ACT
AND THE BERKELEY EXPERIMENT,"
61 Calif L Rev 858, 859-64 (1973)

Berkeley's Black House—A Practical Adjustment to the Needs of the Black Student

Black House, now at its own site in Berkeley's industrial district, has a faculty of approximately sixteen teachers and a student body of seventy-five tenth, eleventh, and twelfth graders. Since over 1,400 blacks attend Berkeley high schools, the proportion of black high school students attending Black House is quite small.

Horace Upshaw, the present director of Black House, sees the school as a response to problems typically experienced by black students. Because many black students have been found deficient in basic developmental skills, the curriculum of Black House stresses such fundamental subjects as reading and mathematics. But, wherever possible, these remedial efforts attempt to develop skills through the use of ethnically oriented materials rather than through more traditional vehicles. In a sense, the student at Black House is not exposed to an appreciably different curriculum than that characteristic of an ordinary high school; the material simply is presented in a different fashion.

Nonetheless, Upshaw does see two significant ways in which an education at Black House differs from that available at other schools. First, the school attempts to present a more critical analysis of the role of democratic institutions in American society. . . .

Second, Upshaw believes that there is an educationally valuable relationship between student and teacher, when both are black, that cannot exist when that pair is racially mixed. Emphasizing that his conclusions are tentative and require additional study, Upshaw also suggests that, in their attempts to ingratiate themselves to their minority students and to demonstrate their lack of racial prejudice, white teachers often have difficulties that might be detrimental to the students' long-term educational interests. Alternatively, a black student can be educationally harmed in less subtle ways by an unsympathetic or racist white institution.

[N]o nonblack has ever attempted to gain admission. According to Upshaw, Berkeley High School and a variety of other alternative schools offer multicultural courses of study, including fairly comprehensive black studies programs. Hence, Upshaw can envision no reason why a nonblack would even want to attend Black House. The school's name, its all-black staff, and an unspoken understanding within the Berkeley community perhaps have created a "for-blacks-only" impression. But Upshaw prefers to attribute the lack of nonblack applicants to Black House's image as a remedial institution for students experiencing particular problems. If such problems arise from membership in a particular racial group, students from different racial groups would derive little benefit from the experiment.

In Upshaw's judgment, Black House has successfully accomplished its twin goals of heightening racial awareness among its students and remedying their deficiencies in developmental skills. . . .

Casa de la Raza—A School for the Chicano Community

According to Francisco Hernandez, Casa de la Raza's newly appointed director and principal, Casa and Black House share the same basic philosophy of education; they simply are designed to meet the needs of different segments of Berkeley's population. Like Black House, Casa attempts to develop "basic skills" among its students. Yet, while the substance of the educational program resembles that of other schools, Hernandez emphasizes that "the delivery" is different.

Chicano culture is the medium for transmission of knowledge, and most of Casa's curriculum is taught bilingually.

The most distinctive feature of Casa is its community orientation. The school includes the twelve academic grades plus a kindergarten class, whereas Black House operates solely as a high school. The governing body of Casa is composed of parents, students, and staff members. Community-related projects form a significant part of the educational program. In short, Casa's concept of an appropriate education for the Chicano student appears to be much broader than that envisioned by most other schools. Out of the 427 Chicano students in Berkeley public schools in the kindergarten through the twelfth grade, approximately 125 attend Casa.

In stressing Chicano culture and involvement with the Spanish-American community, Casa has limited its students and personnel to Chicanos. Although a handful of white students have attended Casa in the primary grades and a few white reading specialists have been instructors there, the participation of non-Chicanos has been minimal. Hernandez .... notes that there are twenty-three alternative schools in Berkeley, several of which offer multicultural programs; consequently, Casa would appear to have nothing unique to offer non-Chicanos.

Hernandez believes that if enthusiasm and interest are regarded as components of successful schooling, then Casa has been able to offer to its students an environment for learning that is superior to that available in the ordinary classroom. However, because the use of conventional testing devices would be particularly inappropriate in a school like Casa, Hernandez is unable to offer statistical evidence of Casa's educational success. Currently he is attempting to raise funds for developing tests that would afford appropriate measures of academic achievement among these students. . . .

Does the existence of either or both of these schools violate the equal protection clause? In answering that question, what is the relevance of (a) the racial or ethnic composition of student body; (b) the criteria for admission; (c) the racial or ethnic composition of the faculty; (d) the proportion of the minority group in the entire system; (e) the pedagogical rationale; (f) student performance; (g) the "experimental" nature of the program; (h) the role of the minority community in school governance; (i) the availability of similar programs in a nonsegregated setting; (j) the fact that, before the establishment of the experimental schools program, Berkeley voluntarily desegregated its school system; (k) the "benignity" of the motivation for creating the schools. Consider the following assessment, which follows a detailed treatment of these issues:

> The essential problem is the difficulty of establishing a legal precedent that would permit the kind of separate schooling undertaken in Berkeley without providing a loophole for school districts still attempting to evade *Brown*. While the two kinds of racial separation are distinguishable, delineating that distinction in case or statutory law would be difficult and potentially dangerous. For example, if blacks in New Kent County [where the Supreme Court rejected a freedom-of-choice plan that had not resulted in desegregation (*Green v County School Bd* 391 US 430 (1968))] now asked for a Black House, could a court infer truly free choice in 1973 if it

could not in 1968? On the other hand, if blacks in Berkeley are offered educational options, should blacks in New Kent County be denied such opportunities simply because whites discriminated against blacks there in the past.

Such anomalies exemplify the problem. Admittedly, public school desegregation already has encountered legal difficulties and public hostility. A community like Berkeley, openly dedicated to the concept of educational equality, appreciates the precarious position of desegregation in other parts of the nation and understands the possible impact of court-approved racial separation of any kind. Nonetheless, educational experimentation must not come to a standstill because of apprehensions that the legal justifications for it might be misused. Whatever the political merits of caution and compromise, the educational and social values promoted by Black House and Casa are of overriding importance. (61 *Calif L Rev* at 917-18.)

The constitutional issues presented by Black House and Casa de la Raza were not resolved. In April 1973 the Office of Civil Rights, HEW, responding to a complaint from Arkansas Senator John McClellan, found the two schools to be in "probable noncompliance" with the 1964 Civil Rights Act and Regulations, 45 CFR §§80.1-80.13 (1972). In making its determination, the Office of Civil Rights relied primarily on the racial and ethnic composition of the student bodies and faculties.

"Probable noncompliance" is a term found nowhere in the statutes or regulations; it is not a predicate for the administrative hearings that must precede fund cutoff. Nonetheless, the finding required Berkeley to develop a satisfactory compromise, close the schools, or seek judicial vindication.

Berkeley initially chose to pursue the first option. It proposed a multicultural umbrella school, called Alliance, which would include Black House, Casa de la Raza, a new Asian-American school, and Odyssey, whose students were drawn equally from the black and Mexican-American communities. The four subschools would be located on separate sites. Students would apply to Alliance and be assigned to one of the subschools on the basis of a matching of interests and needs. Admission would not be based on either race or ethnicity. Students would spend half their day in Alliance-wide programs and half in subschool programs.

In June 1973 the Office of Civil Rights rejected the proposal. It concluded that students could spend only 25 percent of their school day in racially or ethnically identifiable programs. Until such a proposal could be developed, Berkeley was required to close the two schools, or risk nonapproval of the new three million dollar, multiyear experimental school program contract. Berkeley chose to close the schools. In July 1973 the district decided not to pursue the legality of the Alliance proposal by seeking an informal administrative hearing; instead it requested the development of a proposal that would satisfy the Office of Civil Rights criteria. As this book went to press, the Casa de la Raza community board was considering filing a lawsuit to compel the reopening of its schools.

Assuming that the definition of discrimination under the Civil Rights Act is not broader than the equal protection requirement, how should a court have resolved the Office of Civil Rights-Berkeley dispute over the legality of the Alliance proposal? What additional facts, if any, are needed to answer that question? On what grounds might the Casa community group seek to reopen Casa de la Raza? Might they contend that community-controlled, culturally relevant education was constitutionally required?

VII. "Benign" Racial Classifications

The issues canvassed in the preceding section concerned efforts on the part of minority groups to isolate themselves and provide their own education. This section examines a quite different question: May schools whose primary purpose is not to remedy past de jure segregation take race into account in order to secure integration?

A. Benign Quotas

Several states, including Massachusetts and Illinois, have adopted statutes that require or encourage affirmative action to eliminate racial imbalance. Massachusetts, for example, declares:

> Whenever the state board of education finds that racial imbalance exists in a public school it shall notify in writing the school committee.... The school committee shall thereupon prepare a plan to eliminate such racial imbalance and file a copy of such plan with the board ... detail[ing] the changes in existing school attendance districts, the location of proposed school sites, the proposed additions to existing school buildings, and other methods for the elimination of racial imbalance.... [Racial imbalance is defined as] a ratio between nonwhite and other students in public schools which is sharply out of balance with the racial composition of the society in which nonwhite children study, serve and work .... [and] shall be deemed to exist when the percent of nonwhite students in any public school is in excess of 50 percent of the total number of students in such school. (Mass Gen Laws Ann ch 71, § 37D (West Supp 1973).)

These measures, evidencing little confidence that neutral assignment schemes will provide integration, take race into account; on that ground, they have been subject to attack by white parents. The claim that such racial classifications are unconstitutional has been rejected by the courts. See, e.g., *Offermann v Nitkowski* 378 F2d 22 (2d Cir 1967); *Tometz v Board of Educ* 39 Ill 2d 593, 237 NE2d 498 (1968); *School Comm v Board of Educ* 352 Mass 693, 227 NE2d 729 (1967) *appeal dismissed,* 389 US 572 (1967); *State ex rel Citizens Against Mandatory Bussing v Brooks* 80 Wash 2d 121, 492 P2d 536 (1972). As Professors Michelman and Sandalow note:

> Opinions in these cases tend to make one or more of the following points: (1) Since government is under a constitutional obligation not to foster segregation deliberately, it would be absurd and illogical to prevent government from taking steps to prevent or reduce segregation. (2) Government action in the form of boundary drawing, even if influenced by racial considerations, affects *groups* of persons and thus does not discriminate against any *individual person* on the ground of his race. (3) Race mixing is only one of several factors taken into account in fixing the boundary, so the

boundary is not strictly a racial classification. (4) Evidence exists from which a legislative body could reasonably infer that a mixture of races in the classroom is educationally beneficial. (Michelman and Sandalow, *Materials on Government in Urban Areas* 556 (1970).)

Do you find any of these reasons persuasive? Should racial classifications favoring blacks be treated differently from those which disfavor them? Is the former racism against whites?

B. Minority Preferential Admissions

DEFUNIS v ODEGAARD
82 Wash 2d 11, 507 P2d 1169 (1973)

Neill, Justice:

Defendants, who include the members of the Board of Regents of the University of Washington, the president of the university, and the dean and certain members of the Admissions Committee of the University of Washington School of Law, appeal from a judgment ordering them to admit plaintiff Marco DeFunis, Jr., as a first-year student to the University of Washington School of Law, as of September 22, 1971.

Broadly phrased, the major question presented herein is whether the law school may, in consonance with the equal protection provisions of the state and federal constitutions, consider the racial or ethnic background of applicants as one factor in the selection of students.

Marco DeFunis, Jr. (hereinafter plaintiff), his wife, and his parents commenced an action in the superior court, alleging that plaintiff, an applicant for admission to the University of Washington School of Law (hereinafter law school) for the class commencing September 1971, had been wrongfully denied admission in that no preference was given to residents of the state of Washington in the admissions process and that persons were admitted to the law school with lesser qualifications than those of plaintiff. The complaint asked that the court order the defendants to admit and enroll plaintiff in the law school in the fall of 1971 and, upon the failure of defendants to do so, that plaintiffs recover damages in the sum of not less than $50,000. . . .

Law school admissions pose a complex problem, and require a sensitive balancing of diverse factors. To gain insight into the complicated process of selecting first-year law students, and to better appreciate the essence of plaintiff's complaint against the law school, we turn first to the circumstances and operative facts—as delineated by the record—from which this litigation arises.

Under RCW 28B.20.130(3), the Board of Regents of the University of Washington has the power and duty to establish entrance requirements for students seeking admission to the university. The dean and faculty of the law school, pursuant to the authority delegated to them by the board of regents and the president of the university, have established a committee on admissions and readmissions to determine who shall be admitted to the law school. . . .

The number of qualified applicants to the law school has increased dramatically in recent years. In 1967, the law school received 618 applications; in 1968, 704; in 1969, 860; and in 1970, 1026 applications were received. The law school received 1601 applications for admission to the first-year class beginning September 1971. Under the university's enrollment limitation there were only 445 positions allotted to the law school, and of these the number available for the first-year class was between 145 and 150. The chairman of the admissions committee stated that most of these applicants would be regarded as qualified by admissions standards at this and other comparable law schools in recent years. Hence, the task of selection is difficult, time-consuming and requires the exercise of careful and informed discretion, based on the evidence appearing in the application files. While many applicants are relatively easy to select for admission because of very outstanding qualifications, and others are relatively easy to reject, the middle group of candidates is much more difficult to assess. Plaintiff was in this latter category.

Applicants for admission to the law school must have earned an undergraduate degree and taken the Law School Admission Test (LSAT) administered by the Education Testing Service of Princeton, New Jersey. They must also submit with their written application a copy of transcripts from all schools and colleges which they have attended prior to application for admission. . . . The application for admission gives the applicant the option to indicate his "dominant" ethnic origin.

For the purpose of a preliminary ranking of the applicants for the class of 1974, the junior-senior undergraduate grade point average and the Law School Admissions Test scores for each applicant were combined through a formula to yield a predicted first-year of law school grade average for the applicant. . . .

Ranking of applicants by PFYA (predicted first year average) was used to help organize the committee's processing of the applications. On the basis of the previous year's applicant group, the committee decided that most promising applicants for the class of 1974 would be defined as applicants with predicted first-year law school averages over 77. Applicants with PFYAs above 77 were reviewed and decided by the full committee as they came in, in order to reach an early decision as to the acceptance of such students. Each of these files was assigned to a committee member for thorough review and for presentation to the committee.

Applicants with PFYAs below 74.5 were reviewed by the chairman of the committee, and were either rejected by him, or placed in a group for later review by the full committee. . . .

Two exceptions were made in regard to applicants with PFYAs below 74.5. First, the law school had established a policy that persons who had been previously admitted but who were unable to enter, or forced to withdraw from, the law school because of induction into the military service, had a right to reenroll if they reapplied immediately upon honorable completion of their tour of duty. Second, all files of "minority" applicants (which the committee defined for this purpose as including black Americans, Chicano Americans, American Indians and Philippine Americans) were considered by the full committee as warranting their attention, regardless of the PFYA of the individual applicant.

Applicants with predicted first-year averages between 74.5 and 76.99 were accumulated and held until the applications deadline had passed and essentially all the applications were complete and ready for review, so that the critical decisions as to the remainder of the incoming class could be made with a relatively complete view of qualified applicants not therebefore admitted. Plaintiff's application, presenting a 76.23 predicted first-year average, was placed in this third category. Included for consideration at that time, in addition to the minority group and those with PFYAs between 74.5 and 77, were some applicants with PFYAs above 77 upon whom the committee had reserved judgment, feeling that such applicants were not as promising as their PFYAs seemed to indicate.

These "close cases,"—i.e., where the applicant was neither clearly outstanding nor clearly deficient—required the most effort of the committee. In selecting the applicants from this narrow range, the committee used the process described in its guide for applicants, a copy of which was sent to all applicants:

> We gauged the potential for outstanding performance in law school not only from the existence of high test scores and grade point averages, but also from careful analysis of recommendations, the quality of work in difficult analytical seminars, courses, and writing programs, the academic standards of the school attended by the applicant, the applicant's graduate work (if any), and the nature of the applicant's employment (if any), since graduation.
>
> An applicant's ability to make significant contributions to law school classes and the community at large was assessed from such factors as his extracurricular and community activities, employment, and general background. . . .
>
> An applicant's racial or ethnic background was considered as one factor in our general attempt to convert formal credentials into realistic predictions. . . .

In considering minority applicants, the committee was guided by a university-wide policy which sought to eliminate the continued effects of past segregation and discrimination against blacks, Chicanos, American Indians and other disadvantaged racial and ethnic minority groups. . . .

The law school sought to carry forward this university policy in its admission program, not only to obtain a reasonable representation from minorities within its classes, but to increase participation within the legal profession by persons from racial and ethnic groups which have been historically denied access to the profession and which, consequently, are grossly underrepresented within the legal system. In doing so, the admissions committee followed certain procedures which are the crux of plaintiff's claimed denial of equal protection of the laws.

First, in reviewing the files of minority applicants, the committee attached less weight to the PFYA in making a total judgmental evaluation as to the relative ability of the particular applicant to succeed in law school. Also, the chairman testifed that although the same standard was applied to all applicants (i.e., the relative probability of the individual succeeding in law school), minority applicants were directly compared to one another, but were not compared to applicants outside of the minority group. The committee sought to identify, within the minority category, those persons who had the highest probability of succeeding in law school. Thus, the law school included within its admitted group minority applicants whose PFYAs were lower than those of some other applicants, but whose entire record showed the committee that they were capable of successfully completing the law school program.

As a result of this process, the committee admitted a group of minority applicants, placed a group of such applicants on a waiting list, and rejected other minority applications. The dean of the law school testified that the law school has no fixed admissions quota for minority students, but that the committee sought a reasonable representation of such groups in the law school. He added that the law school has accepted no unqualified minority applicants, but only those whose records indicated that they were capable of successfully completing the law school program.

The admissions committee sent letters of acceptance to over 200 applicants. . . .

. . . . [T]he ultimate determination of applicants to whom admission was offered did not follow exactly the relative ranking of PFYAs. Of those invited, seventy-four had lower PFYAs than plaintiff; thirty-six of these were minority applicants, twenty-two were returning from military service, and sixteen were applicants judged by the committee as deserving invitations on the basis of other information contained in their files. Twenty-nine applicants with higher PFYAs than plaintiff's were denied admission. Of the thirty-six minority group students invited eighteen actually enrolled in the first-year class.

The trial court found that some minority applicants with college grades and LSAT scores so low that had they been of the white race their applications would have been summarily denied, were given invitations for admission; that some such students were admitted instead of plaintiff; that since no more than 150 applicants were to be admitted to the law school, the admission of less-qualified students resulted in a denial of places to those better qualified; and that plaintiff had better "qualifications" than many of the students admitted by the committee. The trial court also found that plaintiff was and is fully qualified and capable of satisfactorily attending the law school. . . .

II

The essence of plaintiff's Fourteenth Amendment argument is that the law school violated his right to equal protection of the laws by denying him admission, yet accepting certain minority applicants with lower PFYAs than plaintiff who, but for their minority status, would not have been admitted.

To answer this contention we consider three implicit, subordinate questions: (A) whether race can ever be considered as one factor in the admissions policy of a state law school or whether racial classifications are per se unconstitutional because the equal protection of the laws requires that law school admissions be "color-blind"; (B) if consideration of race is not per se unconstitutional, what is the appropriate standard of review to be applied in determining the constitutionality of such a classification; and (C) when the appropriate standard is applied does the specific minority admissions policy employed by the law school pass constitutional muster?

A

Relying solely on *Brown v Board of Educ* 347 US 483 (1954), the trial court held that a state law school can never consider race as one criterion in its selection of first-year students. . . .

Brown did not hold that all racial classifications are per se unconstitutional; rather, it held that invidious racial classifications—i.e., those that stigmatize a racial group with the stamp of inferiority—are unconstitutional. Even viewed in a light most favorable to plaintiff, the "preferential" minority admissions policy administered by the law school is clearly not a form of invidious discrimination. The goal of this policy is not to separate the races, but to bring them together. And, as has been observed, "Preferential admissions do not represent a covert attempt to stigmatize the majority race as inferior; nor is it reasonable to expect that a possible effect of the extension of educational preferences to certain disadvantaged racial minorities will be to stigmatize whites." O'Neil, "Preferential Admissions: Equalizing the Access of Minority Groups to Higher Education," 80 *Yale LJ* 699, 713 (1971).

While *Brown v Board of Educ, supra,* certainly provides a starting point for our analysis of the instant case, we do not agree with the trial court that *Brown* is dispositive here. Subsequent decisions of the United States Supreme Court have made it clear that in some circumstances a racial criterion *may* be used—and indeed in some circumstances *must* be used—by public educational institutions in bringing about racial balance. School systems which were formerly segregated de jure[10] now have an affirmative duty to remedy racial imbalance. [Citing *Green v County School Bd* 391 US 430 (1968); *Swann v Charlotte-Mecklenburg Bd of Educ* 402 US 1 (1971).]

Thus, the Constitution is color conscious to prevent the perpetuation of discrimination and to undo the effects of past segregation. . . .

However, plaintiff contends that cases such as *Green v County School Board, supra,* and *Swann v Charlotte-Mecklenburg Board of Education, supra,* are inapposite here since none of the students there involved were deprived of an education by the plan to achieve a unitary school system. It is questionable whether defendants deprived plaintiff of a legal education by denying him admission.[11] But even accepting this contention, arguendo, the denial of a "benefit" on the basis of race is not necessarily a per se violation of the Fourteenth Amendment, if the racial classification is used in a compensatory way to promote integration [citing *Porcelli v Titus* 431 F2d 1254 (3d Cir 1970); *cert denied,* 402 US 944 (1971)].

We proceed, therefore, to the question of what standard of review is appropriate to determine the constitutionality of such a classification.

B

Generally, when reviewing a state-created classification alleged to be in violation of the equal protection clause of the Fourteenth Amendment, the question

---

10. "De jure" segregation generally refers to "segregation directly intended or mandated by law or otherwise issuing from an official racial classification," *Hobson v Hansen* 269 F Supp 401, 492 (DDC 1967), *aff'd sub nom, Smuck v Hobson* 408 F2d 175 (DC Cir 1969), or, in other words, to segregation which has, or had, the sanction of law. In the context of public education the United States Supreme Court has expanded the meaning of the term *de jure* segregation "to comprehend any situation in which the activities of school authorities have had a racially discriminatory impact contributing to the establishment or continuation [of racial imbalance] . . . ." *State ex rel Citizens Against Mandatory Bussing v Brooks* 80 Wash 2d 121, 130, 492 P2d 536, 542 (1972).

Where the segregation is inadvertent and without the assistance or collusion of school authorities, and is not caused by any "state action," but rather by social, economic and other determinants, it will be referred to as "de facto" herein. See Fiss, "Racial Imbalance in the Public Schools: the Constitutional Concepts," 78 *Harv L Rev* 564, 565-66, 584, 598 (1965).

11. Plaintiff alleged in his complaint that he had previously applied to, and been accepted by, the law school at each of the following universities: University of Oregon, University of Idaho, Gonzaga University and Willamette University.

is whether the classification is reasonably related to a legitimate public purpose. . . .

However, where the classification is based upon race, a heavier burden of justification is imposed upon the state. . . .

It has been suggested that the less strict "rational basis" test should be applied to the consideration of race here, since the racial distinction is being used to redress the effects of past discrimination; thus, because the persons normally stigmatized by racial classifications are being benefited, the action complained of should be considered "benign" and reviewed under the more permissive standard. However, the minority admissions policy is certainly not benign with respect to nonminority students who are displaced by it. . . .

The burden is upon the law school to show that its consideration of race in admitting students is necessary to the accomplishment of a compelling state interest.

C

It can hardly be gainsaid that the minorities have been, and are, grossly underrepresented in the law schools—and consequently in the legal profession—of this state and this nation. We believe the state has an overriding interest in promoting integration in public education. In light of the serious underrepresentation of minority groups in the law schools, and considering that minority groups participate on an equal basis in the tax support of the law school, we find the state interest in eliminating racial imbalance within public legal education to be compelling.

Plaintiff contends, however, that any discrimination in this case has been de facto, rather than de jure. Thus, reasons plaintiff, since the law school itself has not actively discriminated against minority applicants, it may not attempt to remedy racial imbalance in the law school student body, and, consequently, throughout the legal profession. We disagree. . . .

Significantly, this case does not present for review a court order imposing a program of desegregation. Rather, the minority admissions policy is a voluntary plan initiated by school authorities. Therefore, the question before us is not whether the Fourteenth Amendment *requires* the law school to take affirmative action to eliminate the continuing effects of de facto segregation; the question is whether the Constitution *permits* the law school to remedy racial imbalance through its minority admissions policy. . . .

The de jure/de facto distinction is not controlling in determining the constitutionality of the minority admissions policy voluntarily adopted by the law school.[13] Further, we see no reason why the state interest in eradicating the continuing effects of past racial discrimination is less merely because the law school itself may have previously been neutral in the matter. . . .

The legal profession plays a critical role in the policy-making sector of our society, whether decisions be public or private, state or local. That lawyers, in making and influencing these decisions, should be cognizant of the views, needs and demands of all segments of society is a principle beyond dispute. The educa-

13. We do not, therefore, reach the question of whether there is an inherent cultural bias in the Law School Admission Test, or in the methods of teaching and testing employed by the law school, which perpetuates racial imbalance to such an extent as to constitute de jure segregation.

tional interest of the state in producing a racially balanced student body at the law school is compelling.

Finally, the shortage of minority attorneys—and, consequently, minority prosecutors, judges and public officials—constitutes an undeniably compelling state interest. If minorities are to live within the rule of law, they must enjoy equal representation within our legal system.

Once a constitutionally valid state interest has been established, it remains for the state to show the requisite connection between the racial classification employed and that interest. The consideration of race in the law school admissions policy meets the test of necessity here because racial imbalance in the law school and the legal profession is the evil to be corrected, and it can only be corrected by providing legal education to those minority groups which have been previously deprived.

It has been suggested that the minority admissions policy is not necessary, since the same objective could be accomplished by improving the elementary and secondary education of minority students to a point where they could secure equal representation in law schools through direct competition with nonminority applicants on the basis of the same academic criteria. This would be highly desirable, but eighteen years have passed since the decision in *Brown v Board of Educ, supra,* and minority groups are still grossly underrepresented in law schools. If the law school is forbidden from taking affirmative action, this underrepresentation may be perpetuated indefinitely. No less restrictive means would serve the governmental interest here. . . .

We hold that the minority admissions policy of the law school, and the denial by the law school of admission to plaintiff [does not violate] the equal protection clause of the Fourteenth Amendment to the United States Constitution. . . .

Justice Wright's separate concurrence is omitted.

Hale, Chief Justice (dissenting).

Racial bigotry, prejudice and intolerance will never be ended by exalting the political rights of one group or class over that of another. The circle of inequality cannot be broken by shifting the inequities from one man to his neighbor. To aggrandize the first will, to the extent of the aggrandizement, diminish the latter. There is no remedy at law except to abolish all class distinctions heretofore existing in law. For that reason, the constitutions are, and ever ought to be, color-blind. Now the court says it would hold the constitutions color-conscious that they may stay color-blind. I do not see how they can be both color-blind and color-conscious at the same time toward the same persons and on the same issues, so I dissent.

The court, as I see it, upholds palpably discriminatory law school admission practices of the state university mainly because they were initiated for the laudable purpose of enhancing the opportunities of members of what are described as "ethnic minorities." It thus suggests a new rule of constitutional interpretation to be applied here that, if the administrative intentions are adequately noble in purpose, Mr. DeFunis may be deprived of equal protection of the laws and certain special immunities and privileges may be granted to others which, on the same terms, are denied to him. One should keep in mind the wisdom of the old saying that the road to perdition is paved with good intentions.

The court holds that the university law school may give preferential treatment to persons who come from groups "which have been historically suppressed by encouraging their enrollment within the various programs offered at the university." But what seems to me to be a flagrant departure from the constitutions, ignored by the court, is epitomized in the statement that the admission policy was adopted by the law school "to increase participation within the legal profession by persons from racial and ethnic groups which have been historically denied access to the profession and which, consequently, are grossly underrepresented within the legal system." This assertion confesses to prior racial discrimination which I doubt existed, and fails to recognize, in a case where the demand for seats in the law school is much greater than the school's capacity, that the increased minority participation assured by such admission procedures inevitably produces a correlative denial of access to nonminority applicants. . . .

Mr. DeFunis supported his application for admission with every conceivable evidence of competence except possibly an astrological horoscope. . . .

The way things worked out, however, the law school failed to apply even its own vague, loose and whimsical admission standards. . . .

In deciding which particular groups should be classified as ethnic minorities, the committee on admissions first made an assumption supported by no evidence whatever, i.e., that all of the accepted minority students except Asian-Americans were of a lower economic status than Mr. DeFunis. No comparative investigation or study as to the financial condition or economic background was made to establish the relative economic and cultural condition of the students applying. It was thus categorically assumed that the ethnic minority applicants were, to use the descriptive term current in academic circles, culturally deprived—meaning, one must suppose, that the environmental factors surrounding a minority student and tending to affect his academic achievements were of a lower order than those surrounding white or majority students. This sweeping and unsupported assumption, derived from no real evidence whatever, that all of the admitted minority students were both poor and culturally deprived, supplied the modus vivendi for the scheme of preferences. It ignored the correlative assumption which inevitably had to be made that neither Mr. DeFunis nor any of the nonminority applicants had been equally culturally or economically deprived. . . .

Of the approximately 150 students actually enrolled in the class for which Petitioner DeFunis made his application, only some 42 admission files were placed in evidence. But an inspection of these files, in my judgment, fails to show any consistent policy on admissions at which a prelaw student could aim his career. If he is intelligent, works hard, and achieves high grades, his place in the law school class may be preempted by someone with lesser grades but who is engaged in what is described as "community activities," or is otherwise described as a student activist. Or, if he is engaged in community activities and still attains high grades through diligence and intelligence and long hours at the books, his position may be taken in the entering class by one who has neither engaged in "community activity" nor achieved high grades but, nevertheless, has made a high LSAT score. Or, even if he studied hard, is intelligent, and placed high in grades, LSAT and PFYA, and engaged in what are called community activities, his place might still be awarded to a minority student who has done none of these. All of these inequities are, I fear, bound to foster a spirit of anti-intellectualism in the heart of what should be an intellectual center. . . .

This method of selection operated to deprive Mr. DeFunis of his position in the entering law classes both in 1970 and again in 1971. Not being a member of a preferred ethnic minority, he found his place taken by others who not only possessed far lower credentials and qualifications but among whom were some who on the face of their records were unqualified. He was the victim of what in current parlance has come to be described as "affirmative action," which includes preferential treatment for the sake of creating a more equitable racial balance—a process which the court now finds constitutional.

If this be constitutional, then, of course, the constitutions are not color-blind; one racial group may be given political or economic preferment over another solely because of race or ethnic origin. Yet, this was the very thing that the Fourteenth Amendment was designed to prevent. All races, and all individuals, are entitled to equal opportunity to enter the law school. To admit some solely because of race or ethnic origin is to deny others that privilege solely for the same reasons, which in law amounts to a denial of equal protection to the one while granting special privileges and immunities to the other. . . .

The majority concedes and the record is indisputable that Petitioner DeFunis was ousted from the list of acceptable students solely because of preference accorded others, and that this preference was granted to many solely because of race and ethnic origin. Even though there are many areas of public endeavor where it would be deemed a valid and constitutional exercise of the police power to provide special assistance for those segments of our population described as disadvantaged or poor, or culturally deprived, such special assistance could not constitutionally deprive Mr. DeFunis of a seat in the law school and award it to a member of a group whose existence is defined or controlled by considerations of race or ethnic origin. When the seat in the law school is awarded on the basis of race or ethnic origin, the procedure necessarily falls within the constitutional principles prohibiting racial segregation or preference.

In referring to special aid and assistance, the fact remains that the committee on admissions and readmissions made no investigation whatever as to whether any of the minority students admitted were poorer, more disadvantaged or more culturally deprived than some of the students of higher educational and aptitude qualifications who had been turned down. The committee simply applied a theory and ipso facto assumed that every black American, Indian-American or Chicano, or Philippine-American, because of his ethnic origin of necessity had to be more disadvantaged, poorer and more culturally deprived than those of Asian, Caucasian, or other ethnic origin. . . .

. . . . [T]his court's decision in *State ex rel Citizens Against Mandatory Bussing v Brooks* 80 Wash 2d 121, 492 P2d 536 (1972), would tend to sustain DeFunis's position in the present case. There is no more than a coincidental parallel between the *Mandatory Bussing* case and Mr. DeFunis's case. There we sustained a modest program of compulsory busing initiated by the Seattle school district for the stated purpose of assuring higher quality of education for all students of whatever racial, religious or ethnic background. The policy of required busing has been adopted because the school board was of the opinion that racially segregated schools, even those where the segregation if de facto and not de jure, are inferior to integrated schools, and that a racially segregated student body will receive an education inferior to that of a racially integrated student body. This court held that the school board was acting within its lawful powers in reaching this conclusion and in implementing its views by a program of mandatory busing. In the *Mandatory Bussing* case, the Seattle school board did no more than act officially upon conclusions it had the authority to reach, and provide for racially integrated education while curtailing de facto segregation.

There is no genuine parallel between Mr. DeFunis's case and the case of the children required to ride the buses. There, we were dealing with a procedurally sound administrative determination that every child, under the plan and the constitution, would gain an integrated and thereby superior education at the expense of no other child. Providing one child with a better, i.e., integrated, education did not operate to deprive another of an equal, integrated education. Benefit to one would not be at the expense of another. Putting one child on a bus to ride to school did not operate to take away another's seat in the classroom. Ordering busing to eliminate segregated schools was no less compatible with the constitutions than the idea that children needing or requesting specialized training may have to ride buses to special schools because every department and facility of a school system, in the nature of things, cannot be equidistant from all children. In the *Mandatory Bussing* case, the Seattle school board was attempting to discharge its constitutional duty of providing equality of educational opportunity for all children within the district at the expense of no child or children.

Here we have precisely the opposite. Putting some applicants into the classroom deprived a qualified applicant of his seat there. It operated to deprive him thereby of the equal protection of the laws and at the same time granted to others privileges and immunities not available to him on equal terms. Thus, aside from the patently arbitrary and capricious method earlier delineated, by which Mr. DeFunis's position was given to a less-qualified applicant, his ouster fell explicitly within the constitutional principle that education must be provided to all students on equal terms and all public education programs must be conducted without regard to race, color or national origin. . . .

Are there methods by which a state-owned and operated law school may be fairly and constitutionally administered so as to comport with the constitutions? Although the courts have neither the power nor the aptitude to operate a university and should be without the inclination to do so, several possible methods come to mind which prima facie, at least, meet the fairness and equal protection standards of the constitutions. One would be a system of comprehensive competitive examinations in predesignated courses such as English, history, basic science, mathematics, economics and sociology, and with optional courses in other fields selected by the student.

Another method would be to work out a reasonably accurate mathematical correlation between grade values from different colleges or universities in preannounced prelaw courses and to compute those equivalent grades with admission granted the 150 students with the highest grades. This gives every student a fair chance to achieve his ambition.

Another possible solution—in case the faculty believes that high prelaw grades should not be the main criterion—prescribe a sound but not extraordinarily high prelaw grade standard and make a random selection by lot and chance of the 275 applicants to be admitted from among those qualifying. And the fairest way of all—but I doubt its efficacy—admit all applicants possessing a minimum prerequisite grade point in prescribed courses, conduct the law classes in the field house or stadium, if necessary, give frequent examinations, and let the better-qualified few survive on the basis of their grades in law school. There are, of course, other methods equally fair and impartial which may be readily developed, all of which will meet the constitutional tests of fair and impartial application. But whatever scheme is developed, one thing is certain: Keep it within the principles of the constitutions, no one can be preferred and no one can be disparaged because of race, color, creed, ethnic origin or domestic environment.

If it is the state policy—and I think it should be—to afford special training, guidance and coaching to those students whose domestic environment has deprived them of a fair chance to compete, or to provide financial assistance to students in economic straits, it is within the state's constitutional powers to do so, but once these students have reached the point of seeking admission to a professional or graduate school, no preference or partiality can or should, under the constitutions, be shown them. . . .

Mr. DeFunis came before the bar of the Superior Court much as did petitioners, parents of school children, in *Brown v Board of Educ* 347 US 483 (1954), asking that he not be denied admission to the university law school because of race or ethnic origin. The trial court properly ordered his admission. So, too, would I, and, therefore, I would affirm.

[Justice Hunter's separate dissent is omitted.]

Notes and Questions

1. *DeFunis:* Constitutional Basis

Does the *DeFunis* court find the law school's preferential admission policy constitutionally justifiable because it—like the integration plan ordered in *Swann* —is a means of remedying past wrongs? Is the remedial theory appropriately applied where the remedying agency has not also caused the wrong? Is *DeFunis* better read as finding constitutionally justifiable an affirmative action policy based not on prior wrongs but on present social needs? That is, is this the universalist ethic in its broadest judicial application?

2. Benign Quota Analogy

In several significant ways, preferential admissions differ from benign quotas, discussed in the previous section. Benign quotas do not deny any person access to an educational institution; preferential admission does. Benign quotas restrain the choices of both blacks and whites; by contrast, preferential admission restrains the choices only of white students. Benign quotas are designed only to provide primary and secondary school students with the opportunity to attend an integrated school; preferential admission is here intended to ensure an increased supply of minority lawyers. Should these considerations be constitutionally controlling?

3. Nature of "Compelling Interest"

The *DeFunis* majority suggests two highly provocative reasons for concluding that the state's interest in "eliminating racial imbalance in public legal education" is compelling: (1) Since lawyers are key policy makers, the court concludes that the legal profession "should be cognizant of the views, needs and demands of all segments of society." But does that justification require increasing the number of minority lawyers or increasing the sensitivity of all lawyers? (2) The court notes the acute shortage of minority lawyers. Is the court assuming that minority lawyers will in fact return to their communities? That minority lawyers can best represent minority communities? Are these assumptions valid?

Consider the following discussion of preferential admissions:

> While blacks comprise about 12 percent of the population of the United States, they represent only about 1 percent of the bar. [See Gellhorn, "The Law Schools and the Negro," 1968 *Duke LJ* 1069, 1073.] .... The sparse evidence available for other minority groups indicates a comparable or even more acute underrepresentation ....
>
> The problem defined by these figures is critical only if minority groups really need minority lawyers to serve their legal interests. Several factors do suggest a special role for the attorney who grew up in the ghetto or barrio and returns there to practice. First, the bar as presently structured simply does not meet the full range of the minority community's needs .... The need is particularly compelling where the cause of the minority client is an unpopular one.... Moreover, the white lawyer is far less likely to understand the background of the case, to be able to interview witnesses from the minority community ... or to be able to establish the necessary rapport with his client .... Other considerations reinforce the case. Minority attorneys suggest to youthful members of the community not only that there are ways of "making it," but also that there is some hope of changing the system through legal institutions rather than solely by self-help .... Increased minority group representation in such high-status professions as law and medicine constitutes by itself an important socioeconomic achievement certain to have multiplier effects in the next generation. Finally, increasing minority group representation in the bar fosters the development of responsible and articulate community leadership, thus facilitating the participation of minority groups in the processes and institutions of government. (O'Neil, "Preferential Admissions: Equalizing the Access of Minority Groups to Higher Education," 80 *Yale LJ* 699, 726-28 (1971).)

Do the factors recited by Professor O'Neil provide constitutionally persuasive reasons for upholding preferential admission policies?

4. Aptitude Testing, Law School Performance, and Lawyerly Performance

The *DeFunis* court explicitly avoids "the question of whether there is an inherent cultural bias in the Law School Admission Test, or in the methods of teaching and testing employed by the law school ...." The question is complex. Minority students do perform less well on law school aptitude tests than do whites. But it is far from clear that these tests inaccurately predict the law school performance of minority students; indeed, they may overpredict how well these students will do academically. Compare Austin, "Racial Considerations in Admissions," in *The Campus and the Racial Crisis* 113 (D. Nichols and O. Mills eds 1970). As Professor Gellhorn notes: "The ... test is a mirror image of the law schools. Thus, the cultural bias, if any, is not inherent in the test, but rather is in the law schools and in their teaching and testing methods." Gellhorn, "The Law Schools and the Negro," 1968 *Duke LJ* 1069, 1089. Does that statement suggest that law school curricula might be vulnerable to constitutional attack? The same question may be posed of bar examinations, required by almost all states as a means of certifying attorneys, since these too "were, of course, designed for the predominantly white, middle class students . . ." O'Neil, "Preferential Admissions: Equalizing the Access of Minority Groups to Higher Education," 80 *Yale LJ* 699, 734 (1971). Furthermore, no attempt has been made to correlate aptitude test scores, law school grades, or bar exam results with lawyerly competence. How should a court respond to a challenge to any of these screening devices? Might a white student challenge any of these devices as unconstitutionally arbitrary? Chapter 7 considers related issues in the public school context.

5. Unanswered Questions

Several questions of considerable relevance to the preferential admission issue are not directly confronted by the *DeFunis* court. (a) Does the special admission process in fact identify talented black applicants who fail to meet the regular admission criteria? (b) What is the impact of failing law school performance on the minority student admitted to law school under a preferential admission program? Compare *Chronicle of Higher Education,* 20 April 1970, p 2, col 1. (c) Will specially admitted minority students, once they become lawyers, represent their clients adequately or as well as other lawyers? (d) What other groups that are underrepresented in the legal profession will insist that they be treated as a minority group for law school admission purposes, and by what criteria should their claims be assessed?

In not addressing these issues, is the court implying: (i) that they are constitutionally unimportant; (ii) that their answers are intuitively obvious; (iii) that institutions other than courts—law schools and state bar examiners—will and should resolve them; or (iv) that they are premature? Are these responses plausible? For other discussions of this issue, see Symposium, "Disadvantaged Students and Legal Education—Programs for Affirmative Action," 1970 *Toledo L Rev* 277; Askin, "The Case for Compensatory Treatment," 24 *Rutgers L Rev* 65 (1969); Graglia, "Special Admission of the Culturally Deprived to Law School," 119 *U Pa L Rev* 351 (1970).

chapter five

Sex-Based Discrimination and Equal Educational Opportunity

As the previous chapter notes, governmental classification on the basis of race is constitutionally suspect, permissible only where the government can establish a compelling justification. But race is not the only immutable physical attribute on which the government has drawn distinctions. In many contexts—including public education—sex-based distinctions are made. Some are both readily apparent and legally mandated: the exclusion of women from school sports teams and many vocational programs, for example. Other and more subtle sex-based distinctions are condoned by law: for instance, many textbooks define male and female roles differently, and teachers may treat boys and girls differently. Are sex and race distinctions in education equally offensive in constitutional terms?

The simplest answers are, of course, doctrinaire. To the ardent women's liberationist any officially drawn male-female distinction is evidence of a chauvinistic attempt to preserve and maintain male domination. See Hodes, "Women and the Constitution: Some Legal History and a New Approach to the Nineteenth Amendment," 25 *Rutgers L Rev* 26 (1970). To the equally fervid traditionalist the sexual distinctions adopted by legislatures simply reflect the natural order. See *Bradwell v Illinois* 83 US (16 Wall) 130, 141 (1872) (Bradley, J, concurring) ("Man is, or should be, woman's protector and defender. . . . The paramount destiny of woman [is to be a] wife and mother."). Compare *Hoyt v Florida* 368 US 57, 61-62 (1961) ("Despite the enlightened emancipation of women from restrictions and protections of bygone years . . . woman is still regarded as the center of the home."). The constitutional implications of differentiated treatment—at least in the realm of public education—are more complex than either of these extreme positions admits.

This chapter examines classifications that clearly deprive one sex—usually, though not necessarily females—of a right or opportunity available to the other, or that purport to secure "separate but equal" treatment for each sex. The central issues of the chapter are (a) whether such inequality or separateness with respect to education is ever constitutionally appropriate, and (b) the policy consequences of judicial review of sex-based educational classifications.

I. Sex and Race Discrimination: Search for a Standard

A. Prevalence and Rationale for Sex-based Distinctions

Sex-distinguishing legislation is pervasive. Numerous state and federal laws treat women and men differently with respect to social conduct, familial responsibility, obligations of citizenship (e.g., to serve in the armed forces and on juries), access to jobs and public accommodations, labor regulations, and criminal sentencing. See Note, "Sex Discrimination, and the Constitution," 2 *Stan L Rev* 691 (1950); Kanowitz, "Sex-based Discrimination in American Law I: Law and the Single Girl," 11 *St Louis U LJ* 293 (1967); Kanowitz, "Sex-based Discrimination and America Law II: Law and the Married Woman," 12 *St Louis U LJ* 3 (1967). This legislation appears to be premised either on the need to protect women or on differences in ability. See Note, "Sex Discrimination and Equal Protection: Do We Need a Constitutional Amendment?" 84 *Harv L Rev* 1499, 1500 (1971).

Historically, judicial review of challenges to such sex distinctions was characterized "by two prominent features: a vague but strong substantive belief in women's 'separate place,' and an extraordinary methodological casualness in reviewing state legislation based on such stereotypical views of women." Brown, Emerson, Falk, and Freedman, "The Equal Rights Amendment: A Constitutional Basis for Equal Rights for Women," 80 *Yale LJ* 871, 876 (1971). In *Goesart v Cleary* 335 US 464 (1948), for example, the Supreme Court upheld a Michigan statute that barred a woman from being licensed as a bartender unless she was "the wife or daughter of a male owner." The *Goesart* court, finding that the subject "need not detain us long," applied the "reasonable classification" test, and virtually ignored the obvious effect of the statute, monopolization of the bartending profession for men. In *Hoyt v Florida* 368 US 57 (1961), the court adopted the same approach in upholding legislation that excluded women from jury service unless they voluntarily applied. "We cannot say that it is constitutionally impermissible for a state, acting in pursuit of the general welfare, to conclude that a woman should be relieved from the civic duty of jury service unless she herself determines that such service is consistent with her own special responsibilities." 368 US at 62.

Two recent decisions suggest that the court now takes more seriously the claim that differential treatment of women poses serious constitutional issues. In *Reed v Reed* 404 US 71 (1971), a unanimous court struck down an Idaho probate code provision that gave preference to men as administrators of the estates of those dying intestate. Two years later, in *Frontiero v Richardson* 93 S Ct 1764, 36 L Ed2d 583 (1973), the court held unconstitutional legislation that differentiated between servicemen and servicewomen in determining whether a spouse could be claimed as a "dependent" for the purpose of obtaining additional benefits.

In *Reed,* the court purported to apply the traditional reasonableness test, concluding that the sex-based differences served no rational purpose. The court ignored the state's assertion that "men [are] as a rule more conversant with business affairs than . . . women," (Brief for Appellee p12, 404 US 71 (1971)), disingenuously concluding that the state had made an "arbitrary legislative choice." 404 US at 76. See Gunther, "The Supreme Court, 1971 Term—Foreword: In Search of Evolving Doctrine on a Changing Court: A Model for a Newer Equal Protection," 86 *Harv L Rev* 1, 34 (1972).

In *Frontiero,* four members of the court announced that sex, like race and alienage, should be treated as a suspect classification, requiring a "compelling" justification. But the other four justices who concurred in the result would not go so far. To Justice Powell that issue had "far-reaching implications" and did not have to be reached, since in his judgment the classification was unreasonable. The fact that an equal rights amendment had been approved by Congress and submitted for ratification by the states also argued for judicial caution, since the fate of that amendment would "resolve the substance of this precise question." 36 L Ed2d at 595.

B. Race and Sex

Are the similarities between race and sex classification sufficient to warrant treating both as suspect? Four of the nine justices in *Frontiero* thought so:

There can be no doubt that our nation has had a long and unfortunate history of sex discrimination. Traditionally, such discrimination was rationalized by an attitude of "romantic paternalism" which, in practical effect, put women not on a pedestal, but in a cage. . . .

As a result of notions such as these, our statute books gradually became laden with gross, stereotypical distinctions between the sexes and, indeed, throughout much of the nineteenth century the position of women in our society was, in many respects, comparable to that of blacks under the pre-Civil War slave codes. Neither slaves nor women could hold office, serve on juries, or bring suit in their own names, and married women traditionally were denied the legal capacity to hold or convey property or to serve as legal guardians of their own children . . . . And although blacks were guaranteed the right to vote in 1870, women were denied even that right—which is itself "preservative of other basic civil and political rights"—until adoption [of] the Nineteenth Amendment half a century later.

It is true, of course, that the position of women in America has improved markedly in recent decades. Nevertheless, it can hardly be doubted that, in part because of the high visibility of the sex characteristic, women still face pervasive, although at times more subtle, discrimination in our educational institutions, on the job market and, perhaps most conspicuously, in the political arena. See generally, K. Amundsen, *The Silenced Majority: Women and American Democracy* (1971); The President's Task Force on Women's Rights and Responsibilities, *A Matter of Simple Justice* (1970).

Moreover, since sex, like race and national origin, is an immutable characteristic determined solely by the accident of birth, the imposition of special disabilities upon the members of a particular sex because of their sex would seem to violate "the basic concept of our system that legal burdens should bear some relationship to individual responsibility. . . ." *Weber v Aetna Cas & Sur Co* 406 US 164, 175 (1972). And what differentiates sex from such nonsuspect statutes as intelligence or physical disability, and aligns it with the recognized suspect criteria, is that the sex characteristic frequently bears no relation to ability to perform or contribute to society. As a result, statutory distinctions between the sexes often have the effect of invidiously relegating the entire class of females to inferior legal status without regard to the actual capabilities of its individual members.

We might also note that, over the past decade, Congress has itself manifested an increasing sensitivity to sex-based classifications. In Title VII of the Civil Rights Act of 1964, for example, Congress expressly declared that no employer, labor union, or other organization subject to the provisions of the act shall discriminate against any individual on the basis of "race, color, religion, *sex,* or national origin." Similarly, the Equal Pay Act of 1963 provides that no employer covered by the act "shall discriminate . . . between employees on the basis of *sex.*" And §1 of the Equal Rights Amendment, passed by Congress on March 22, 1972, and submitted to the legislatures of the states for ratification, declares that "equality of rights under the law shall not be denied or abridged by the United States or by any state on account of sex." Thus, Congress has itself concluded that classifications based upon sex are inherently invidious, and this conclusion of a coequal branch of government is not without significance to the question presently under consideration. . . .

With these considerations in mind, we can only conclude that classifications based upon sex, like classifications based upon race, alienage, or national origin, are inherently suspect, and must therefore be subjected to strict judicial scrutiny. . . . (93 S Ct at 1770-71, 36 L Ed2d at 590-92.)

The *Frontiero* opinion avowedly expands the scope of the equal protection clause—certainly well beyond what was envisioned when the Fourteenth Amendment was adopted. Its treatment of sex discrimination reflects and affirms a marked change in social attitudes. See also *Sail'er Inn v Kirby* 5 C3d 1, 485 P2d 529 (1971). In a constitution "fit for permanence" (in Professor Bickel's terms), should such expansion, without more, be cause for criticism? Justice Frankfurter's view of the process of constitutional adjudication, offered as one justification for the result in *Goesart*—"The constitution does not require legislatures to reflect sociological insight, or shifting social standards"—seems plainly at odds with the *Reed* and *Frontiero* decisions.

But the analogy between racial and sex-based classifications advanced in the *Frontiero* opinion warrants critical examination. Consider the following observations in Rossi, "Sex Equality: The Beginning of Ideology":

. . . [T]here are also fundamental differences between sex as a category of social inequality and the categories of race, religion, or ethnicity . . . .

1. Category Size and Residence. In the case of race, religion, and ethnicity, we are literally dealing with minority groups in the American population, whether Mexican, Indian, Jewish, Catholic, or black. This is not the case for sex, since women are actually a numerical majority in the population.

While the potential is present for numerical strength to press for the removal of inequalities, this is counterbalanced by other ways in which women are prevented from effectively utilizing their numerical strength. . . . [Because] women are for the most part *evenly distributed throughout the population* [, they] can exert political pressure in segmental roles as consumers, workers, New Yorkers, or the aged; but not as a cohesive political group based on sex solidarity.

2. Early Sex Role Socialization. Age and sex are the earliest social categories an individual learns. The differentiation between mother and father, or parent and child, is learned at a tender, formative stage of life; and consequently, we carry into adulthood a set of age and sex-role expectations that are extremely resistant to change.

As a result of early sex-role socialization, there is bound to be a lag between political and economic emancipation of women and the inner adjustment to equality of both men and women. Even in radical political movements, women have often had to caucus and fight for their acceptance as equal peers to men. Without such efforts on their own behalf, women are as likely to be "girl Friday" assistants in a radical movement espousing class and racial equality as they are in a business corporation, a labor union, or a conservative political party.

3. Pressures against Sex Solidarity. Racial, ethnic, and religious conflict can reach an acute stage of political strife in the movement for equality, without affecting the solidarity of the families of blacks, whites, Jews, or Gentiles. Such strife may, in fact, increase the solidarity of these family units. A "we versus them" dichotomy does not cut into family units in the case of race, religion, or ethnicity as it does in the case of sex. Since women typically live in greater intimacy with men than they do with other women, there is potential conflict within family units when women press hard for sex equality. Their demands are on predominantly male legislators and employers in the public domain—husbands and fathers in the private sector. A married black woman can affiliate with an activist civil rights group with no implicit threat to her marriage. For a married woman to affiliate with an activist women's rights group might very well trigger tension in her marriage. . . . A large proportion of married women [who] have not combated sex discrimination . . . fear conflict with men, or benefit in terms of a comfortable high status in exchange for economic dependence upon their husbands. There are many more women in the middle class who benefit from sex inequality than there are blacks in the middle class who benefit from racial inequality. (29 *The Humanist,* 3, 4-5 (Sept/Oct 1969).)

Do Professor Rossi's observations suggest that sex and race discrimination should be treated as constitutionally different phenomena? That they are politically different phenomena?

Two basic questions are left open after *Frontiero:*

1. Will (and should) any justification for different treatment of men and women, such as the existence of aggregate statistical differences between the sexes or the high administrative costs of a non-sex-based standard, survive judicial scrutiny? Compare *Korematsu v US* 323 US 214 (1944) (held that asserted administrative difficulty of identifying those Japanese-Americans who threatened national security justified mass internment).

2. Does nondiscrimination require identical treatment of men and women, or is the "separate but equal" standard—rejected in the racial context in *Brown v Board of Education*—constitutionally adequate to cure sex-based discrimination?

C. The Equal Rights Amendment

As *Frontiero* notes, the Equal Rights Amendment—not yet ratified when this book went to press—declares that "[e]quality of rights under the law shall not be denied or abridged by the United States or by any state on account of sex."

Does that amendment require the Supreme Court to adopt the same standard of review in sex classification and race classification cases—i.e., one which invalidates such classifications unless a "compelling" justification can be shown? Or does the amendment require an absolutist approach, barring all sex-based classifications, however justified they might be? One commentary, which supports the amendment, takes the latter position:

> ... the constitutional mandate must be absolute. The issue under the equal rights amendment cannot be different but equal, reasonable or unreasonable classification, suspect classification, fundamental interest, or the demands of administrative expediency. Equality of rights means that sex is not a factor. This at least is the premise of the equal rights amendment. Only privacy claims could justify any sex-based differentiation. ("The Equal Rights Amendment: A Constitutional Basis for Equal Rights for Women," 80 *Yale LJ* 871, 892-893 (1971).)

Professor Freund, on the other hand, opposes the amendment, largely because, in his view, it "attempts to impose a single standard of sameness on the position of the sexes in all of the multifarious roles regulated by law." Freund, "The Equal Rights Amendment Is Not the Way," 6 *Harv Civ Rights—Civ Lib L Rev* 234 (1971). Does the language of the amendment in fact demand that result? In reading this chapter, consider how each interpretation of the amendment would affect the outcome of each case.

D. On Novelty

Despite the pervasiveness of sex classification in education, relatively few of the issues canvassed in this chapter have been litigated. (Indeed, Leo Kanowitz's *Women and the Law: The Unfinished Revolution* (1969), the leading book in the field, makes no reference to education.) The absence of case law is in some respects surprising: it contrasts sharply with the race area, where many of the most significant constitutional decisions concern educational policy; it appears inconsistent with the claim that education is critical to the development of women's opportunities.

We can only speculate as to explanations:

1. Sex discrimination, while historic, is constitutionally novel; relatively few cases have been brought challenging any sex-based policy.

2. School officials often move to render moot the sex discrimination complaints that are brought, giving the individual student what she wants while avoiding the litigation. One student who sought to enroll in a shop course writes: "Dr. Larson [the school supervisor] passed on the request to the district superintendent, Dr. Russo [who sent it to the state education agency] .... Word was passed along to me that nobody in Albany wanted to touch the issue, and they finally sent down an edict that I could do what I wanted to do." Dvorkin, "The Suburban Scene," in *Sisterhood Is Powerful* 363, 364-65 (R. Morgan ed 1970).

3. Many women either do not recognize or are uninterested in sex-based education policies. As Kate Mueller notes: "Many women admittedly want nothing changed. . . ." Mueller, "Education: The Realistic Approach," in *The Challenge to Women,* 112, 117 (S. Farber and R. Wilson eds 1966).

4. Nonlawyers less concerned with such visible (and easily changed) sex discrimination practices in schools as the exclusion of pregnant students from

classes or women tennis players from the athletic team—issues that have already been litigated—than with more subtle sexual stereotyping, a process of socialization analogous in many ways to that described generally in chapter 2. Yet the latter issues—including, for example, the role models available to elementary school girls and the types of behavior for which women in school are praised— are, because of their subtlety, difficult to conceptualize in legal terms. Whether they can (or should) be so conceptualized is an issue that recurs throughout the discussion.

II. Constitutional and Policy Issues

A. Denial or Restriction of Educational Opportunity

In several areas, women are either excluded from or provided with less of a given educational opportunity than are men. Pregnant women, but not their impregnators, are barred from high school; certain courses, such as shop and vocational education, are open to men only; athletic competition is restricted to male students; admission criteria for selective academic high schools (a phenomenon of the East and West coasts) are higher for women than for men. While the contexts vary, each alleged discrimination poses the following questions (few of which are explicitly raised or fully explored by the courts):

1. Does the denial or restriction in fact harm women students? Is proof of such harm constitutionally necessary?

2. How might a school district justify a policy restricting the educational opportunities of women? Would such justifications pass judicial muster under the rationality test as applied by the Supreme Court in *Reed*? Under the stricter test urged by four members of the court in *Frontiero*?

3. In each case would (or should) the outcome of the case differ if the school's policy did not have a sex-specific effect? Is it the significance of the right being restricted or the sex-based nature of the restriction that is (or should be) controlling?

4. Assuming that the school's policy does discriminate against women students, what remedy is constitutionally appropriate (or mandated)? For example, if women have historically been excluded from shop classes, has the school district met its constitutional obligation by opening this courses to women on a freedom-of-choice basis? By opening it to all "qualified" students? Should a court treat significant deviations from the school's male/female ratio in shop classes as an indication of sex-based discrimination?

In each case, a separate but equal remedy is theoretically plausible. The constitutional validity of such a solution is more thoroughly assessed in section B, but these diverse situations should provoke consideration of when, if at all, such a solution might be valid in the sex discrimination context.

1. Pregnancy and Marriage

ORDWAY v HARGRAVES
323 F Supp 1155 (D Mass 1971)

Caffrey, District Judge.
This is a civil action brought on behalf of an eighteen-year-old pregnant,

unmarried senior at the North Middlesex Regional High School, Townsend, Massachusetts. The respondents are the principal of the high school, Robert Hargraves, the seven individual members of the North Middlesex Regional High School Committee, and the school committees of Pepperell and Townsend. The cause of action is alleged to arise under the Civil Rights Act, 42 USCA §1983, and jurisdiction of this court is invoked under 28 USCA §1343. The matter came before the court for hearing on plaintiff's application for preliminary injunctive relief in the nature of an order requiring respondents to readmit her to the regional high school on a full-time, regular-class-hour basis.

At the hearing, eight witnesses testified. On the basis of the credible evidence adduced at the hearing, I find that the minor plaintiff, Fay Ordway, resides at East Pepperell, Massachusetts, and is presently enrolled as a senior in the North Middlesex Regional High School; and that plaintiff informed Mr. Hargraves, approximately January 28, 1971, that she was pregnant and expected to give birth to a baby in June 1971. There is outstanding a rule of the regional school committee, numbered rule 821, which provides: "Whenever an unmarried girl enrolled in North Middlesex Regional High School shall be known to be pregnant, her membership in the school shall be immediately terminated." Because of the imminence of certain examinations and the fact that school vacation was beginning on February 12, Mr. Hargraves informed plaintiff that she was to stop attending regular classes at the high school as of the close of school on February 12. This instruction was confirmed in writing by a letter from Mr. Hargraves to plaintiff's mother, Mrs. Iona Ordway, dated February 22, 1971, in which Mr. Hargraves stated that the following conditions would govern Fay Ordway's relations with the school for the remainder of the school year:

(a) Fay will absent herself from school during regular school hours.

(b) Fay will be allowed to make use of all school facilities such as library, guidance, administrative, teaching, etc., on any school day after the normal dismissal time of 2:16 P.M.

(c) Fay will be allowed to attend all school functions such as games, dances, plays, etc.

(d) Participation in senior activities such as class trip, reception, etc.

(e) Seek extra help from her teachers during after school help sessions when needed.

(f) Tutoring at no cost if necessary; such tutors to be approved by the administration.

(g) Her name will remain on the school register for the remainder of the 1970-71 school year (to terminate on graduation day—tentatively scheduled for June 11, 1971).

(h) Examinations will be taken periodically based upon mutual agreement between Fay and the respective teacher.

Thereafter, plaintiff retained counsel, a hearing was requested, and was held by the school committee on March 3, 1971. The school committee approved the instructions and proposed schedule set out in Mr. Hargraves' letter of February 22, and a complaint was filed in this court on March 8. . . .

At the hearing, Dr. F. Woodward Lewis testified that he is plaintiff's attending physician and that she is in excellent health to attend school. He expressed the opinion that the dangers in attending school are no worse for her than for a nonpregnant girl student, and that she can participate in all ordinary school activities with the exception of violent calisthenics. An affidavit of Dr. Charles R. Goyette, plaintiff's attending obstetrician, was admitted in evidence, in which Dr. Goyette corroborated the opinions of Dr. Lewis and added his opinion that "there is no reason that Miss Ordway could not continue to attend school until immediately before delivery." . . .

Dr. Mary Jane England, a medical doctor and psychiatrist attached to the staff of St. Elizabeth's Hospital, expressed the opinion that young girls in plaintiff's position who are required to absent themselves from school become depressed, and that the depression of the mother has an adverse effect on the child, who frequently is born depressed and lethargic. She further testified that from a psychiatric point of view it is desirable to keep a person in the position of plaintiff in as much contact with her friends and peer group as possible, and that they should not be treated as having a malady or disease. . . .

Plaintiff testified that her most recent grades were an A, a B plus, and two C pluses, and that she strongly desires to attend school with her class during regular school hours. She testified that she has not been subjected to any embarrassment by her classmates, nor has she been involved in any disruptive incidents of any kind. She further testified that she has not been aware of any resentment or any other change of attitude on the part of the other students in the school. . . .

The remaining witness for plaintiff was Dr. Norman A. Sprinthall, chairman of the guidance program, Harvard Graduate School of Education, who testified that in his opinion the type of program spelled out in Mr. Hargraves' letter of February 22, for after-hours instruction, was not educationally the equal of regular class attendance and participation.

It is clear, from the hearing, that no attempt is being made to stigmatize or punish plaintiff by the school principal or, for that matter, by the school committees. It is equally clear that were plaintiff married, she would be allowed to remain in class during regular school hours despite her pregnancy. Mr. Hargraves made it clear that the decision to exclude plaintiff was not his personal decision, but was a decision he felt required to make in view of the policy of the school committee which he is required to enforce as part of his duties as principal. In response to questioning, Mr. Hargraves could not state any educational purpose to be served by excluding plaintiff from regular class hours, and he conceded that plaintiff's pregnant condition has not occasioned any disruptive incident nor has it otherwise interfered with school activities. Cf. *Tinker v Des Moines Independent Community School Dist* 393 US 503 (1969). . . .

Mr. Hargraves did imply, however, his opinion is that the policy of the school committee might well be keyed to a desire on the part of the school committee not to appear to condone conduct on the part of unmarried students of a nature to cause pregnancy. The thrust of his testimony seems to be: the regional school has both junior and senior high school students in its student population; he finds the twelve-to-fourteen age group to be still flexible in their attitudes; they might be led to believe that the school authorities are condoning premarital relations if they were to allow girl students in plaintiff's situation to remain in school.

It should be noted that if concerns of this nature were a valid ground for the school committee regulation, the contents of paragraph (b), (c) and (d) of Mr.

Hargraves' letter of February 22 to plaintiff's mother substantially undercut those considerations.

In summary, no danger to petitioner's physical or mental health resultant from her attending classes during regular school hours has been shown; no likelihood that her presence will cause any disruption of or interference with school activities or pose a threat of harm to others has been shown; and no valid educational or other reason to justify her segregation and to require her to receive a type of educational treatment which is not the equal of that given to all others in her class has been shown.

It would seem beyond argument that the right to receive a public school education is a basic personal right or liberty. Consequently, the burden of justifying any school rule or regulation limiting or terminating that right is on the school authorities. . . . On the record before me, respondents have failed to carry this burden. Accordingly, it is

Ordered:

1. Respondents are to re-admit plaintiff to regular attendance . . . .

Notes and Questions

1. Scope of the *Ordway* Decision

a. Importance of Education. Because, in the court's view, education is a "basic personal right or liberty," the court imposes on the school board the burden of justifying its policy concerning pregnant students. Would the result change if education were not a fundamental right? Compare *Rodriguez v San Antonio Independent School Dist* 93 S Ct 1278 (1973). Does the court's reliance on the importance of education suggest that if a less basic right were at issue it would adopt a more traditional allocation-of-burdens approach?

b. Evenhandedness. Is punishing pregnant students, but not their impregnators, constitutionally offensive? Would a policy that dealt evenhandedly with both sexes pass constitutional muster?

c. Harm. Is the student whose educational opportunities are limited or curtailed because of pregnancy more significantly injured than other students—for instance, the disruptive or seriously handicapped student—whom the school wishes to treat differently? See chapters 2 and 7.

The social science evidence cited in *Ordway* notes two types of harm assertedly specific to pregnancy exclusions: (i) the pregnant student is likely to become depressed; (ii) the child of such a mother "frequently is born depressed and lethargic." If the evidence is correct, does it suggest that the school district has a particular obligation to the mother? To the fetus? Must the school minimize the social opprobrium that attaches to the pregnancy of a single woman? Is the following observation correct?

> The unwed pregnancy policies lead to an indirect discrimination against illegitimate children as well, by impairing their mothers' ability to support them. In the last few years the Supreme Court has extended the benefits of equal protection law to illegitimate children; only a "legitimate state interest" can support discrimination against them. The effects of school policies

penalizing unwed mothers would appear to undermine the state's interest in strengthening the ability of its citizens to support themselves and their dependent children, in order to minimize welfare demands. The entire complex of state interests points in the direction of increased education for unwed mothers, not toward curtailing their access to public education. (Comment, "Marriage, Pregnancy, and the Right to Go to School," 50 *Tex L Rev* 1196, 1219 (1972).)

d. Justification. Denying pregnant women the right to attend regular classes is defended by school personnel on several grounds. Are any of the following persuasive?

i. Morality. Can such policies be defended as a means of punishing students who become pregnant and of allaying community fears that welcoming pregnant students in the classroom is an endorsement of immorality? See *Shull v Columbus Munic Separate School Dist* 338 F Supp 1376 (ND Miss 1972). Does a single pregnancy in fact demonstrate immorality? See *Perry v Grenada Munic Separate School Dist* 300 F Supp 748 (ND Miss 1969). Does the availability of what might be viewed as less onerous alternatives—for example, family living classes to inform students of the risks and harms of extramarital sex—oblige the board to use these alternatives rather than exclusion? Is the discussion in chapter 2 of permissible and impermissible means of socializing students relevant here?

ii. Health. Can the school argue that the hurly-burly of student life is dangerous to the pregnant student and that that fact justifies exclusion? *Ordway* suggests that medical evidence appears to rebut the argument. See A. Guttmacher, *Pregnancy and Birth,* 114 (2d ed 1962). Furthermore, "the typical regulation, which allows students, either explicitly or under a 'known-or-shows' rule, to remain in school until the fourth or fifth month, makes no medical sense. A woman generally experiences the greatest discomfort from pregnancy during the first three months, and three out of four miscarriages occur before the end of the third month." Comment, "Marriage, Pregnancy, and the Right to Go to School," 50 *Tex L Rev* 1196, 1223 (1972).

iii. Disruption. Might the school contend that the presence of pregnant students is likely to divert the attention of other students, thus disrupting the educational enterprise? What would have to be proven in order to support that contention? Who would bear the burden of proof? Assuming that disruption could be shown, does the fact that only women are affected by this policy differentiate the case from *Tinker?*

2. School Board Policy toward Pregnant Students

Most school districts exclude pregnant students from regular classes at some time during their pregnancy.

Some systems suspend immediately upon discovery of the pregnancy. Other systems require the pregnant student to withdraw in the third, fourth, fifth, sixth, seventh, or eighth month of pregnancy. Still other systems, less chronologically secure, suspend the student when the pregnancy becomes obvious. And other schools report that "every effort is made to retain students in school to a time the expectant mother and/or her doctor recommend absence for maternity." (Knowles, "High Schools, Marriage, and the Fourteenth Amendment," 11 *J Fam L* 711, 732 (1972).)

In some districts, pregnant students are assigned to special education programs that include both academic courses and "homemaker preparation" instruction. After *Ordway* is such assignment constitutionally permissible? Might the school district argue that the prenatal care and counseling provided in such programs make them better placements than the regular program for pregnant students? See Stine and Kelley, "Evaluation of a School for Young Mothers," 46 *Pediatrics* 581 (1970). Is the race-sex analogy controlling here? Is the school district's argument constitutionally different from the claim that a separate program for black students provides them a more useful educational opportunity? If a special program were offered to pregnant students who preferred special to regular class placement during pregnancy, would that freedom-of-choice arrangement withstand constitutional scrutiny? Compare the discussion of non-sex-based objections to special education in chapter 7.

3. Married Students

Many school districts restrict the educational opportunities available to married students. The exclusion of married students, premised on a desire to deter teenage marriage or to protect innocent teenagers from the company of young marrieds, has generally been overturned on nonconstitutional grounds. In *McLeod v State ex rel Colmer* 154 Miss 468, 475, 122 So 737, 738 (1929), for example, the Mississippi supreme court noted: "Marriage is a domestic relation highly favored by the law. When the relation is entered into with correct motives, the effect on the husband and wife is refining and elevating, rather than demoralizing. Pupils associating in school with a child occupying such a relation, it seems, would be benefited instead of harmed." See also *Alvin Independent School Dist v Cooper* 404 SW2d 76 (Tex Civ App 1966); *Anderson v Canyon Independent School Dist* 412 SW2d 387 (Tex Civ App 1967).

School districts more frequently bar married students from participating in extracurricular activities. The rationales for such rules include discouraging early marriage, preventing fraternization that might cause undue interest in sex among unmarrieds, freeing the individual student's time for marital responsibilities, and keeping schools free of interspousal jealousy. Assuming that such regulations apply equally to married male and female students, what constitutional issues, if any, do they pose? Are they a constitutionally impermissible invasion of the privacy of married couples? See Comment, "Marriage, Pregnancy, and the Right to Go to School," 50 *Tex L Rev* 1196, 1207-11 (1972). Compare *Romans v Crenshaw* 354 F Supp 868 (SD Tex 1972). For a nonconstitutional analysis, see *Cochrane v Board of Educ* 360 Mich 390, 103 NW2d 569 (1960); *Kissick v Garland Independent School Dist* 330 SW2d 708 (Tex Civ App 1959); Goldstein, "The Scope and Sources of School Board Authority to Regulate Student Conduct and Status: A Nonconstitutional Analysis," 117 *U Pa L Rev* 373 (1969).

4. An Unrecognized Right?

Although regulations pertaining to the status of pregnant students are nearly universal, legal challenges to exclusion are rare. Most pregnant students drop out of school; married students faced with the financial responsibilities of a new home are often forced to leave school. These students may also fear that a lawsuit will occasion personal retaliation. Consider the following story:

> In 1958 we expelled four students for skipping away from school and . . . getting married. We were sued by one parent, and the court ordered that we readmit one girl. The board, of course, had no choice but to honor the order. They stipulated numerous conditions for the girl to meet [which would force her into] being practically isolated from all other students. The girl then chose not to return to school. (Knowles, "High Schools, Marriage, and the Fourteenth Amendment," 11 *J Fam L* 711, 713-14 (1972).)

If the anecdote represents common practice, does it suggest that rules requiring identical treatment of pregnant and nonpregnant students are the only means of assuring that pregnant students will not be stigmatized and isolated? What are the policy costs of adopting such a rule?

5. Pregnant Teachers and the Law

Teachers who become pregnant are subject to a variety of employment limitations. In *LaFleur v Cleveland Bd of Educ* 465 F2d 1184 (6th Cir 1972), *cert granted,* 93 S Ct 1925 (1973), the court struck down a board rule requiring pregnant teachers to take unpaid leaves of absence five months before the expected birth of the child and to continue on unpaid status until the beginning of the first school term following the date when the child became three months old.

The principal social purpose claimed to be served by the Cleveland Board of Education rule is continuity of classroom instruction and relief of burdensome administrative problems. Yet any actual disability imposed on any teacher, male or female, poses the same administrative problems and many (including flu and the common cold) can't be anticipated or planned for at all. This rule may arguably make some administrative burdens lighter. But these are not the only values concerned. The Supreme Court reminds us: "The establishment of prompt efficacious procedures to achieve legitimate state ends is a proper state interest worthy of cognizance in constitutional adjudication. But the Constitution recognizes higher values than speed and efficiency . . . *Stanley v Illinois* 405 US 645 (1972). . . .

The three-month enforced unemployment after birth has no relation to the employer's interest at all. While having a mother with her infant for a period after birth may arguably be a question of general state concern, Ohio has not thus far expressed it in any general and nondiscriminatory statute.

Appellees also urge consideration of a view expressed by the author of this rule when in 1952 he suggested its adoption. Dr. Schinnerer testified that he thought that absent the rule, pregnant teachers would be subjected to "pointing, giggling and . . . snide remarks" by the students. Basic rights such as those involved in the employment relationship and other citizenship responsibilities cannot be made to yield to embarrassment. . . . Additionally, at the present time pregnant students are allowed to continue in the Cleveland schools without any apparent ill effects upon the educational system. . . .

Under no construction of this record can we conclude that the medical evidence presented supports the extended periods of mandatory maternity leave required by the rule both before and after birth of the child. (465 F2d at 1187-88.)

See also *Green v Waterford Bd of Educ* 473 F2d 629 (2d Cir 1973). But see *Cohen v Chesterfield City School Bd* 474 F2d 395 (4th Cir 1972), *cert granted*, 93 S Ct 1925 (1973).

2. Curriculum

a. Exclusion. In many school districts, women are barred from taking shop or vocational courses. The reasons for such exclusion are rarely articulated, but appear to include (i) tradition, (ii) the asserted inappropriateness of such courses for women, and (iii) concern that the allegedly less-coordinated female student might be more injury-prone than her male counterpart. Several intrepid women have successfully challenged such practices; in each instance, the case has been settled before judicial decision. See Note, "Teaching Woman Her Place: The Role of Public Education in the Development of Sex Roles," 24 *Hastings LJ* 1191 (1973). One woman student who litigated her way into a metal shop class subsequently won the outstanding student award for metalwork. West, "Women's Liberation, or Exploding the Fairy Princess Myth," *Scholastic Teacher* 6 (Nov 1971).

In these cases, is the student's claim stronger because she is a female? Might a male, denied admission to a home economics course, persuade a court to overturn that determination?

Is the fact that wood shop is closely linked to a woman student's career plans legally relevant? Or does exclusion from any course—whatever its relative importance to the student or class of students—demand searching judicial review if it is sex based? What justification, if any, should satisfy a court?

Both the exclusion of women from certain courses and the requirement that women take certain courses—home economics, for example—are designed to socialize women in particular ways; both also define the educational opportunities available to students in sexual terms. Are the two practices constitutionally distinguishable? See *Robinson v Washington* Civ No 9576 (WD Wash April 1971), cited in 2 *Women's Rights L Rep* 42 (1972).

b. Differential Treatment. In other and more subtle ways, elementary schools treat boys and girls differently. However, as the following excerpt suggests, the differences do not consistently favor boys or girls.

SEXISM IN SCHOOL AND SOCIETY
N. Frazier and M. Sadker 86-106 (1973)

Schools against Boys

Many educators feel that the cards are stacked against the elementary school boy. At age six when he enters the first grade, he may be twelve months behind his female classmate in developmental age, and by nine this discrepancy has increased to eighteen months. Thus he is working side by side with a female who may be not only bigger than he, but who seems able, as we shall see, to handle school more competently and more comfortably. Added to this handicap is the fact that the elementary school boy must function in an environment that is antithetical to the independent life style he has been encouraged to develop up until then. He is in a situation where neatness, good manners, and docility appear to be keys to success. Writers and cartoonists often depict him as a male misfit in a female world, a young bull whose every move seems to disrupt the delicate balance of the china shop.

Patricia Sexton is one educator who has frequently expressed concern for the development of the young boy in the "feminine" elementary school. In a *Saturday Review* article titled "Are Schools Emasculating Our Boys?" she has stated:

> Boys and the schools seem locked in a deadly and ancient conflict that may eventually inflict mortal wounds on both. . . . The problem is not just that teachers are too often women. It is that the school is too much a woman's world, governed by women's rules and standards. The school code is that of propriety, obedience, decorum, cleanliness, physical and, too often, mental passivity. [Sexton, "Are Schools Emasculating Our Boys," *Saturday Review*, 19 June 1965, p 57. See also Goldman, "Males: A Minority Group in the Classroom," *J Learning Disabilities* 276 (1970).] . . .

What does the young boy learn from this feminine environment that stresses passivity, neatness, and docility? For one thing, he may learn how to be more quiet, neat, and docile—although for many this is not likely. He may instead learn that school is a girl's world, one that has little appeal, meaning, or pertinence for him. In fact, one study has shown that elementary school children, both boys and girls, labeled school objects such as blackboard, book, page of arithmetic, and school desk, as feminine rather than neuter or masculine. [Kagan, "The Child's Sex Role Classification of School Objects," 25 *Child Development* 105 (1964).] . . .

. . . [T]he young boy must spend approximately a thousand hours a year at an institution that restrains and checks him. This lack of comfortable fit between the more active behavior allowed at home and the passivity demanded in school may force young boys into open rebellion. We can see how this happens as we take another look at boys in the elementary school.

> The scene is a restless and unruly afternoon in Miss Hodgkins' fifth-grade class. She has issued warning after warning trying to get the class to quiet down, but she has little success. Finally she explodes, "I've had just all I'm going to take! As usual, the boys are causing all the trouble, so, as usual, all the boys will stay after school. If only you boys could be nice and quiet like the girls, what a pleasure teaching would be."

How likely is it that this scene (or some reasonable facsimile) will occur in an elementary school? Educational research suggests that it is quite likely indeed. Those who study what goes on in classrooms have focused much attention on classroom interaction patterns, who talks with whom, how much of a lesson is teacher talk, who is criticized, who is praised and how often. One finding of these studies is that a different pattern of interaction emerges for boys than for girls.

Researchers studied how teachers dispensed reward and disapproval in three sixth-grade classrooms. Children in these classes were asked to nominate those classmates who received the teacher's approval and those who received her disapproval. Both classroom observers and the children themselves noted that the teachers expressed greater approval of girls and greater disapproval of boys. [Meyer and Thompson, "Teacher Interactions with Boys, as Contrasted with Girls," *Psychological Studies of Human Development* 510 (1963).] In another study it was found that boys receive eight-to-ten times as many prohibitory control messages (warnings like: "That's enough talking Bill. Put that comic book away, Joe.") as their female classmates. Moreover, this same researcher has also found that when teachers criticize boys, they are more likely to use harsh or angry tones than when talking with girls about an equivalent misdemeanor. [Jackson and Lohaderne, "Inequalities of Teacher-Pupil Contacts," in *The Experience of Schooling,* 123 (M. Silberman ed 1971).]

However, it has been found that teachers not only disapprove of boys more, but also interact with them more in general. [Similar findings with respect to Mexican-American students are reported in US Comm'n on Civil Rights, *The Excluded Student, Report III, Educational Practices Affecting Mexican-Americans in the Southwest* (1972).]

We have been discussing school as a feminine environment in which boys rebel against the network of restrictions imposed upon them. It also appears that boys view this feminine environment as an inappropriate arena for combat and achievement. . . . Elementary school boys appear to be quite unsuccessful when it comes to winning good grades. Among boys and girls of comparable IQ, girls are more likely to receive higher grades than boys. Also, boys who do equally as well as girls on achievement tests get lower grades in school. In fact, throughout elementary school two-thirds of all grade repeaters are boys. [Peltier, "Sex Differences in the School: Problem and Proposed Solution," 50 *Phi Delta Kappan* 182 (Nov 1968).] Reading is a subject that seems to be a good deal more difficult for boys than for girls. In a study of one thousand first graders in Maryland, it was found that for every girl with a reading problem, there were about two boys. [Bentzen, "Sex Ratios in Learning and Behavior Disorders," 46 *Nat'l Elem School Principal* 13 (Nov 1966).] Other researchers have found that three times more boys than girls have trouble with reading.

There is evidence that shows that this difficulty is not something inherently male, but rather one of the more pernicious examples of incidental learning. John McNeil studied seventy-two kindergarten boys and sixty kindergarten girls who were enrolled in a reading program that consisted of programed instruction. In this program, the children sat in individual cubicles; they were presented identical segments of reading material at a common pace, and they received the same number of taped comments of encouragement. The boys and girls were given equal opportunity to respond, and the same number of responses were demanded daily from all learners. On a word recognition test administered after the program had been in operation for four months, boys made significantly higher scores than girls did. After completing this program, the children were placed in a regular classroom situation where they received their reading instruction from female teachers. After four months of classroom reading, a similar test was administered. This time the boys did not do as well as the girls.

In an attempt to figure out reasons for the shift in test scores, McNeil asked the children to nominate those in their reading group who received negative comments from the teacher such as "Sit Up!" "Pay attention." The nominations indicated that boys not only received more negative admonitions, but also were given less opportunity to read. [E. Maccoty, *Women's Intellect*.] Thus it appears that boys may be taught reading in a more punitive manner, and these negative contacts may be associated with difficulties boys have in beginning reading. . . .

In many ways the experience of schooling reinforces the already partially formed sex-role stereotypes that boys bring to it. Often the nuclear family environment is a feminine one from which the father departs early in the morning and does not return until evening, possibly even after the youngster has gone to bed. Mother and child spend long unbroken hours in one another's company. Typically, the elementary school classroom is also a "feminine" environment organized and administered by a woman. A difference emerges in the way the young boy is treated in these two environments. At home an independent life style is fostered. In the classroom, where approximately thirty individuals are packed into close quarters, activity and independence are frowned upon. There, docility is the message of the hidden curriculum. Often boys rebel. This rebellion brings increased teacher disapproval, but also increased teacher attention in general. As they refuse to buy this message of docility, as they interact more directly and actively with teachers, their approach to learning becomes increasingly independent and autonomous.

That is a positive result of the boy's conflict with school. There are negative effects, too. School may become so distasteful that he drops out. He may do this literally, but he can also drop out in a less concrete fashion. Although he may remain a firmly entrenched figure in the second seat, fourth row, his thoughts and energy are everywhere but in the classroom. This kind of dropping out can be seen in high male failure rates, in bad grades, and in the expressed hatred of school.

School against Girls

Observant anthropologists have suggested that the basic values of the early grades are a stylized version of the feminine role in society, cautious rather than daring, governed by a ladylike politeness. . . . Girls in the early grades who learn to control their fidgeting earlier are rewarded for excelling in their feminine values. The reward can be almost too successful in that in later years it is difficult to move girls beyond the orderly virtues they learned in their first school encounters. The boys, more fidgety in the first grades get no such reward, and as a consequence may be freer in their approach to learning in the later grades. [J. Bruner, *Toward a Theory of Instruction*, 123-24 (1966).] . . . .

Owing to the teachers' bestowal and withdrawal of rewards and an environment that stresses docility, the elementary school directly reinforces the passivity that the young female student may bring with her from home. The result is a bizarre distortion of the learning process. Neatness, conformity, docility, these qualities for which the young girl receives good grades and teacher's praise have little to do with active intellectual curiosity, analytical problem solving, and the ability to cope with challenging material. For good grades and teachers' praise, the grade school girl relinquishes the courage that it takes to grapple with difficult material. . . .

By effectively reinforcing a passive approach to learning, the school runs the risk of decreasing the female student's ability. Ironically, while attempting to increase student potential, the school, in reality, may be likely to limit it. . . .

How does [the fact that 85 percent of all elementary school teachers, but only 21 percent of all elementary school principals are women (National Education Association, Research Division, *Estimates of School Statistics, 1971-72*, 14 (1971)] affect the elementary school girl? . . . [T]he male boss in the form of the principal does emerge as an important figure. Whenever an issue is too big or troublesome for the teacher (usually female) to handle, the principal (usually male) is called upon to offer the final decision, to administer the ultimate punishment or reward. . . . The teacher is the boss of the class; the principal is boss of the teacher. And the principal is a man. In the child's mind associations form. When a woman functions professionally, she takes orders from a man, and the image of female inferiority and subservience begins to come across. . . .

The dismissal of pregnant teachers also harms children, for pregnancy and birth can be presented and discussed in schools in a highly positive manner. . . .

[Such policies] deprive children as well, teaching them by omission that a pregnant woman is someone to giggle at or be embarrassed about and also denying them involvement in the fascinating process of birth.

Curricular materials as they now exist also harm elementary school children—particularly girls. . . .

It is not only the history books that deny the young elementary school child heroic and positive female role models. If she wishes to read a biography about a famous American, she can turn for inspiration to Henry Hudson, Lewis and Clark, Robert Peary, Kit Carson, Davy Crockett, Buffalo Bill, Abraham Lincoln, George Washington, Ben Franklin, Thomas Jefferson, Andrew Jackson, Woodrow Wilson, Mike Fink, and Albert Einstein, to name some of the more well-known figures. If for any reason she would like to read about a woman, she also has a choice: Annie Oakley, Amelia Earhart, and more recently, Shirley Chisholm. Of course other biographies about women do exist, but she will have to look a good deal harder to find them. [See Education Committee, National Organization of Women, *Report on Sex Bias in the Public Schools* (1971); Metzner, "Literary Voyages in American History," 66 *Elem School J* 235 (1966).] . . . .

[T]he major reading series used in almost all public and private schools across the country teach that being a girl means being inferior. In these texts, boys are portrayed as being able to do so many things: they play with bats and balls, they work with chemistry sets, they do magic tricks that amaze their sisters, and they show initiative and independence as they go on trips by themselves and get part-time jobs. Girls do things too: they help with the housework, bake cookies and sit and watch their brothers—that is, assuming they are present. In 144 texts studied, there were 881 stories in which the main characters are boys and only 344 in which a girl is the central figure. [Miles, "Harmful Lessons Little Girls Learn in School," 86 *Redbook* 168 (Mar 1971).] Furthermore, . . females are depicted as having less mental perseverance and moral strength than males. . . .

Adults in these readers are also characterized by stereotyped behavior. The men do a variety of exciting jobs; career possibilities include being an astronaut, explorer, inventor, scientist, writer, and so on. Occasionally, women in these texts work, but only in the sex-typed jobs of secretary, nurse, teacher, and librarian. Moreover, when women do fulfill the traditional role of housewife and mother, they are depicted as one-dimensional cardboard characters. . . .

Are the kinds of harm to which Frazier and Sadker refer constitutionally cognizable? How do they differ from the harms that segregated schools historically inflicted on black students? How should a court treat a challenge to (i) textbook selection, on grounds that the books chosen favor males, (ii) counseling policies that channel men and women into "appropriate" roles, or (iii) elementary school punishment, which falls more heavily on boys than girls? Is sex-role stereotyping as it affects both sexes amenable to judicial resolution?

Is it possible or useful to assess whether the elementary school experience is more harmful to one sex or the other?

Sex-role stereotyping carries over into the high school. History textbooks minimize the contributions of women; teachers have differing expectations of men and women students; counselors dichotomize professions into those "appropriate" for men and those "appropriate" for women. See Trecker, "Women in U.S. History High School Textbooks," 35 *Social Education* 249 (March 1971); Key, "Male and Female in Children's Books—Dispelling All Doubts," *Am Teacher* 17 (Feb 1971); U'Ren, "The Images of Woman in Textbooks," in *Woman in Sexist Society,* 218 (V. Gornick and B. Minar eds 1971); Thomas and Stewart, "Counselor's Response to Female Clients with Deviate and Conforming Career Goals," 18 *J Counseling Psychology* 352 (1971).

Secondary school stereotyping affects men as well as women, as the following excerpt from a hair regulation case indicates:

> The school authorities offer as justification for the haircut regulation the following reasons: boys' haircuts that do not conform to the regulation cause the boys to comb their hair in classes and to pass combs, both of which are distracting; cause the boys to be late for classes because they linger in the restrooms combing their hair; cause the boys to congregate at a mirror provided for girls to use while combing their hair; in some instances, cause an unpleasant odor, as hair of a length in excess of that provided by the regulation often results in the hair being unclean; cause some of the boys who do not conform to the haircut regulation to be reluctant about engaging in physical educational activities (presumably because they do not want to "muss" their hair); and, finally, cause resentment on the part of other students who do not like haircuts that do not conform to the school's haircut regulation. (*Griffin v Tatum* 300 F Supp 60-61 (MD Ala 1969), *aff'd,* 425 F2d 201 (5th Cir 1970).)

Would the school raise similar objections to long hair worn by women students? Is it hair length or some more basic understanding of appropriate sex roles that is really at issue here? Compare *Sims v Colfax Community School Dist* 307 F Supp 485 (SD Iowa 1970)(hair length regulation successfully challenged by woman student).

Consider the *Griffin* court's resolution of the controversy:

The school authorities' "justification," or the reasons they advance for the necessity for such a haircut rule, completely fail. If combing hair or passing combs in classes is distracting, the teachers, in the exercise of their authority, may stop this without requiring that the head be shorn. If there is congestion at the girls' mirrors, or if the boys are late for classes because they linger in the restrooms grooming their hair, appropriate disciplinary measures may be taken to stop this without requiring a particular hair style. If there is any hygienic or other sanitary problem in connection with those students who elect to wear their hair longer than that presently permitted by the regulation there are ways to remedy this other than by requiring their hair shorn. The same is true of their failure to participate in the physical educational programs. As to the fear that some students might take action against the students who wear hair longer than the regulation now permits, suffice it to say that the exercise of a constitutional right cannot be curtailed because of an undifferentiated fear that the exercise of that right will produce a violent reaction on the part of those who would deprive one of the exercise of that constitutional right. (300 F Supp at 63.)

Does the court imply that objections to particular behavior must apply to both sexes in order to withstand constitutional scrutiny? But see the *Griffin* decision on appeal, 425 F2d 201 (5th Cir 1970).

3. Admission to Selective High Schools

BRAY v LEE
337 F Supp 934 (D Mass 1972)

Caffrey, District Judge. . . .

Plaintiffs, who are female students in the Boston public school system, seek permanent injunctive and declaratory relief against respondents, the members of the Boston School Committee, the superintendent of schools, the headmaster of Boston Latin School, the headmistress of Girls Latin School, and the chief examiner of the Boston Board of Examiners.

Briefly stated, the plaintiffs, who bring this action through their next friends, are a group of girl students, each of whom took the examination in March 1970 for admission as seventh-grade students to the Girls Latin School for the academic year beginning in September 1970. Plaintiffs allege, and I find, that they are representatives of a class with an outside figure of 177 members, all of whom took the same examination for admission to Girls Latin School in September 1970, scored from 120 to 133, and, nevertheless, were not admitted in the fall of 1970. In their complaint plaintiffs allege that the various respondents illegally discriminated against them on the basis of their sex, for the reason that a boy who applied for admission to Latin School for the school year beginning September 1970 was admitted if he made a score on the examination of 120 or better out of a possible 200 points. Plaintiffs further allege that a girl who took the same examination was required to score 133 or better in order to gain admission at the same time to Girls Latin School. The accuracy of these factual representations is conceded by respondents. . . .

To further understand the working and application of the admissions test, it should be noted that the Boys Latin building has a seating capacity for approximately 3,000 students and the Girls Latin building has a seating capacity for approximately 1,500 students. Because of the disparity in the seating capacity of the two buildings, the Boston School Department, in evaluating the results of examinations in the past, first made a determination of how many seats were available in the boys building. They then counted down from the top possible score of 200 until they had accepted a number of boys equal to the number of available seats for the following September. This established the cutoff mark for the admission of boys which, in 1970, turned out to be a mark of 120 out of a possible 200. Any boy who scored 120 or higher was then admitted to Boys Latin school for the school year beginning in September 1970.

Using the same technique with reference to the number of seats available in Girls Latin School, the school department evaluated the result of the girls' examination by counting down from 200 until they reached a number equal to the number of seats available in September 1970 and thus determined that the cutoff mark for girls, because of the lesser number of seats available, was 133 out of a possible 200.

In response to a direction from the court, the school department made a computation, the accuracy of which has been stipulated to by counsel for the plaintiffs, that in September 1970 a combined total of 648 seats were filled by incoming seventh grade students at the Boys and Girls Latin schools, and a further determination was made that had the school department not used separate cutoff marks for boys and girls, but, on the contrary, had used one cutoff mark for both boys and girls measured by the available 648 seats, the cutoff for both boys and girls on a merged basis would have been a score of 127 out of the possible 200. . . .

On the basis of the foregoing, I rule that the use of separate and different standards to evaluate the examination results to determine the admissibility of boys and girls to the Boston Latin schools constitutes a violation of the equal protection clause of the Fourteenth Amendment, the plain effect of which is to prohibit prejudicial disparities before the law. This means prejudicial disparities between all citizens, including women or girls. I further find that on the basis of the record of this case female students seeking admission to Boston Latin School have been illegally discriminated against solely because of their sex, and that discrimination has denied them their constitutional right to an education equal to that offered to male students at the Latin school. . . .

Accordingly, respondents are permanently enjoined from hereafter using a different standard to determine the admissibility of boys and girls, and are affirmatively ordered to use the same standard for admission of boys and girls to any school operated by the city of Boston, including the Boston Latin School. . . .

Notes and Questions

1. Equal Scores or Equal Numbers?

The *Bray* court requires that the school district adopt a uniform test cutoff score for admission. Suppose that, as a result of applying such a standard, women outnumbered men by a 2:1 ratio (a somewhat hyperbolic but not implausible supposition, given the consistently superior performance of women on such tests)? See Smith, "He Only Does It to Annoy," in *Sex Differences and Discrimination in Education,* 28 (S. Anderson ed 1972); Achenbach, "Cue Learning, Associative Responding, and School Performance of Children," 1 *Developmental Psychology* 717 (1969). Would that "differential impact" pose constitutional problems? How does the problem differ from that posed when a school opens its shop course to all "qualified" students, regardless of sex, in response to a charge of discrimination against women students? Compare the discussion in chapter 7 of racial disproportionality in less advanced curricula.

Suppose the district chose to admit equal numbers of men and women to the Latin Schools in order to maintain "a balanced community representative of the population." Would that practice be vulnerable to constitutional scrutiny? On what grounds? See *Berkelman v San Francisco Unified School Dist No 73* 1686 (ND Cal 1972).

2. Sex-based Differences in Aptitude and Achievement

In *Berkelman,* school officials justified applying a higher admission standard for women than for men by arguing that "girls achieve better grades than boys in the first nine grades of school while boys catch up during high school or later." The justification suggests two questions: (1) do sex-based differences in aptitude and achievement exist? and (2) what are their causes? The following excerpts summarize the existing research:

a. Existence of Sex-based Differences

(1) *General intelligence.* Most widely used tests of general intelligence have been standardized to minimize or eliminate sex differences. Whether differences are found on any particular test will depend on the balance of the items—whether there are more items of a kind on which one sex normally excels. There is a tendency for girls to test somewhat higher on tests of general intelligence during the preschool years, boys during the high school years. There is a possibility that the latter finding is in part a function of differential school dropout rates; more boys drop out, leaving a more highly selected group of boys in high school. But some longitudinal studies in which the same children have been tested repeatedly through their growth cycle show greater gains for boys than girls. . . . The changes in tested intelligence that occur during late adolescence and adulthood appear to favor men somewhat; that is, women decline somewhat more, or gain somewhat less, depending on the test used.

(2) *Verbal ability.* Through the preschool years and in the early school years, girls exceed boys in most aspects of verbal performance. . . . By the beginning of school, however, there are no longer any consistent differences in vocabulary. Girls learn to read sooner, and there are more boys than girls who require special training in remedial reading programs; but by approximately the age of ten, a number of studies show that boys have caught up in their reading skills. Throughout the school years, girls do better on tests of grammar, spelling, and word fluency.

(3) *Number ability.* Girls learn to count at an earlier age. Through the

school years, there are no consistent sex differences in skill at arithmetical computation. During grade school years, some studies show boys beginning to forge ahead on tests of "arithmetical reasoning," although a number of studies reveal no sex differences on this dimension at this time. Fairly consistently, however, boys excel at arithmetical reasoning in high school, and the differences in mathematical skills are substantially in favor of men among college students and adults. . . .

(4) *Spatial ability.* While very young boys and girls do not differ on spatial tasks such as form boards and block design, by the early school years boys consistently do better on spatial tasks, and this difference continues through the high school and college years.

(5) *Analytic ability.* This term . . . is used to refer to the ability to respond to one aspect of a stimulus situation without being greatly influenced by the background or field in which it is presented. . . . On measures of this trait . . . boys of school age score consistently and substantially higher than girls. . . .

A related meaning of "analytic ability" is concerned with modes of grouping diverse arrays of objects or pictures. People who group "analytically"—put objects together on the basis of some selected element they have in common (e.g., all the persons who have a hand raised)—have been shown to be less influenced by background conditions in recognition tests, and hence are analytic in the [first] sense as well. Boys more commonly use analytic groupings than do girls. How early this difference emerges is still an open question. . . .

(6) *"Creativity."* There are relatively few studies comparing the sexes on aspects of creativity, and the outcome depends on the definition of the term. If the emphasis is on the ability to break set or restructure a problem, there is a tendency for boys and men to be superior, particularly if the problem involves a large perceptual component. Breaking set is involved in the tasks used to measure "analytic ability," discussed above, and in some of the tests that have a high loading on the space factor.

If creativity is thought of in terms of divergent, as distinct from convergent, thinking, the evidence appears to favor girls somewhat, although the findings are not consistent. A task requiring children to think of ways in which toys could be improved showed that in the first two grades of school, each sex was superior when dealing with toys appropriate to its own sex, but by the third grade, boys were superior on both feminine and masculine toys. On the other hand, girls and women do better on a battery of divergent tasks measuring the variety of ideas produced for the solution of verbally presented problems.

(7) *Achievement.* Girls get better grades than boys throughout the school years, even in subjects in which boys score higher on standard achievement tests. In adulthood, after graduation from school, men achieve substantially more than women in almost any aspect of intellectual activity where achievements can be compared—books and articles written, artistic productivity, and scientific achievements. A follow-up study of gifted children showed that while gifted boys tended to realize their potential in their occupations and creative output, gifted girls did not.

[S] ex differences in spatial ability and in some aspects of analytic ability are substantial from the early sschool years on, and . . . sex differences in mathematical reasoning by high school age are also substantial, while differences in verbal ability are less marked. But on all measures reported, there is considerable overlap between the distribution of scores of the two sexes. . . . (E. Maccoby, "Sex Differences in Intellectual Functioning," in *The Development of Sex Differences,* 25-27 (E. Maccoby ed 1966).)

Certain sex-related psychological attributes also correlate with high academic performance, as Professor Maccoby notes in "Sex Differences," pp 29-35:

Impulse control. . . . [I] mpulsiveness is a negative factor for at least some aspects of intellectual development in boys, but for girls it is a less negative— and perhaps even a positive—factor.

Impulse control is highly valued by teachers and is generally considered a "feminine" characteristic. Boys as boys seem to need more control; girls seem to need less if intellectual function is the criterion.

Fearfulness and anxiety. Correlations between measures of anxiety and measures of aptitude or achievement are substantially negative for girls and women, while the correlations are either low negative, zero, or positive for boys and men.

Fearfulness and anxiety are generally considered to be more feminine than masculine and are not too severely frowned upon by elementary teachers. It seems again that boys to succeed should maybe have a little more of the characteristics, girls less.

Aggression and competitiveness. . . . [A] ggressiveness appears to be more of an inhibitor, or less of a facilitator, for intellectual development among boys than among girls . . . competitiveness was found to correlate with IQ, and with progressive increases in IQ, for both sexes, but the correlations are higher for girls than boys.

Aggressiveness and competitiveness are usually considered masculine and are not favored in the elementary school culture. Once again it seems girls need more and boys need less.

Level of aspiration and achievement motivation. . . . [T] he bulk of the findings seem to indicate that boys are more likely to rise to an intellectual challenge, girls to retreat from one.

Once more, girls to succeed should show more of this "masculine" characteristic.

Dependency, passivity, and independence. For both sexes, there is a tendency for the more passive-dependent children to perform poorly on a variety of intellectual tasks, and for independent children to excel.

Passive dependency seems to be a positive value in the school culture; independence is often frowned upon by the teacher. Passive dependency is usually thought of, though perhaps wrongly, as feminine, independence as masculine. Girls to succeed should once again show more of the so-called masculine characteristics.

b. Causes of Sex-based Differences. It is, of course, easier to identify differences than to determine their causes. Some of the causes appear to be biological.

Some of the biological differences that might be influential include sex differences in reproductive functions, hormones, chromosomes, body build and other anatomical features, physiological functioning, and biochemical processes. These physical differences may function directly in shaping sex differences in activities, interests, and achievements in various fields and indirectly by influencing body image and self-concept, which might then serve to mediate a variety of psychological processes. Another possible biological basis for psychological sex differences may be found in the accelerated developmental timetable of girls, which leads them to develop language skills and certain cognitive abilities earlier than boys. There is also some indication of a partial biological underpinning for the pervasive difference in aggressiveness between males and females. The operation of such biological contributions, however, should not be taken to mean that the psychological variables in question would be unresponsive to cultural influences or social intervention. (Messick, "What Kind of Difference Does Sex Make?" in *Sex Differences and Discrimination in Education,* 2, 4 (S. Anderson ed 1972).)

To what extent are sex-based differences environmentally or culturally caused? One frequently noted environmental explanation is that:

members of each sex are encouraged in, and become interested in and proficient at, the kinds of tasks that are most relevant to the roles they fill currently or are expected to fill in the future. According to this view, boys in high school forge ahead in math because they and their parents and teachers know they may become engineers or scientists; on the other hand, girls know that they are unlikely to need math in the occupations they will take up when they leave school. . . . Undoubtedly, matters of opportunity and life setting play a very large role in the relative accomplishments of the two sexes. That this is not the whole story, however, is suggested by a study of Radcliffe Ph.D.'s, in which it was found that the women Ph.D.'s who had taken academic posts had published substantially less than their male counterparts, and that this was just as true of unmarried academic women as it was of married ones. . . .

Some of the major sex differences . . . do not appear to have any direct relevance to adult sex roles, actual or anticipated. Does a girl of nine do poorly on an embedded-figures test because she thinks that this kind of skill is not going to be important for her later on in life, and well on a spelling test because she thinks this kind of skill is going to be important? It is doubtful whether either children or adults see those ability areas where we have detected the greatest sex differences as sex-role specific. This is not to say that sex typing is irrelevant to intellectual development. But it is doubtful whether the sex differences in spatial ability, analytic style, and breaking set can be understood in terms of their greater direct relevance to the role requirements of one sex or the other. (Maccoby, "Sex Differences in Intellectual Functioning," in *The Development of Sex Differences* (E. Maccoby ed 1966).)

Similar analytic difficulties arise from the hypotheses that (i) sexes differ in their opportunities to learn different skills, and (ii) sex differences are attributable to the fact that children tend to model themselves on the same sex parent. Each factor has some explanatory power; each factor is in part inconsistent with what is known about sex differences in intellectual functioning.

Others have suggested that the greater conformity and dependency of women account for differences in intellectual success. See H. Witkin et al, *Psychological Differentiation* (1962). But that approach simply substitutes one unknown (why are women more dependent?) for another (why do women's intellectual performances differ from men's?).

The usual retreat from such dilemmas is to attribute differences to environmental and hereditary causes. But even that approach appears to oversimplify a vexing phenomenon. The same environmental input has different effects on boys and girls, and different inputs appear to provoke optimal performance from boys and girls. A childhood characterized by maternal warmth and protection may yield bright boys and dependent girls; a childhood characterized by relative independence may have the opposite result. See Hoffman, "Early Childhood Experiences and Women's Achievement Motives," 28 *J Social Issues* 129 (1972).

[E]nvironmental effects are not merely something added to, or superimposed upon, whatever innate temperamental differences there are that affect intellectual functioning. Rather, there is a complex interaction. The two sexes would appear to have somewhat different intellectual strengths and weaknesses, and hence different influences serve to counteract the weaknesses and augment the strengths. (Maccoby, "Sex Differences in Intellectual Functioning.")

Do these sex-based differences justify the sex quota standard approved in *Berkelman*? Do they suggest that some sex-specific educational policies might be educationally beneficial?

4. Athletics

Unequal treatment of women students extends to the athletic field. In many school districts, women are afforded no opportunity to engage in competitive events; women have no separate teams, nor can they compete for the all-male teams. This exclusionary policy has recently been challenged in court.

BRENDEN v INDEPENDENT SCHOOL DISTRICT 742
477 F2d 1292 (8th Cir 1973)

Before Lay, Heaney and Stephenson, Circuit Judges.
Heaney, Circuit Judge.
This is a civil rights action brought under 42 USC §1983 to enjoin enforcement of a rule promulgated by the Minnesota State High School League which bars females from participating with males in high school interscholastic athletics. The rule states:

Girls shall be prohibited from participation in the boys' interscholastic athletic program either as a member of the boys' team or a member of the girls' team playing the boys' team.

The girls' team shall not accept male members. ("Athletic Rules for Girls, Article III, Section 5," in *Minnesota State High School League Official Handbook, 1971-72.*)

The complaint charges that this rule discriminates against females in violation of the equal protection clause of the Fourteenth Amendment to the United States Constitution.

The plaintiffs are Peggy Brenden and Antoinette St. Pierre, female high school students at Minnesota public high schools. Brenden attends the St. Cloud Technical High School in Independent School District 742 and St. Pierre attends Hopkins Eisenhower High School in Independent School District 274. Neither school district has appealed the judgment below. The defendant and sole appellant, the Minnesota State High School League, is a nonprofit corporation which claims the membership of the state's 485 public high schools, including St. Cloud Technical High School and Hopkins Eisenhower High School.

The plaintiffs desired to participate in noncontact interscholastic sports: Brenden in tennis; St. Pierre in cross-country skiing and cross-country running. Neither of their schools provided teams for females in the respective sports. They did, however, provide such teams for males. Both plaintiffs would have liked to qualify for positions on the teams which have been established for males, but they were precluded from doing so on the basis of the above quoted rule. The trial court found that both were excellent athletes, and that neither would be damaged by competition with males.

The court, after a trial on the merits, granted relief. . . . We affirm the decision of the trial court.

Having stated what this case is about, we would also like to emphasize what it is not about. First, because neither high school provided teams for females in the sports in which Brenden and St. Pierre desired to participate, we are not faced with the question of whether the schools can fulfill their responsibilities under the equal protection clause by providing separate but equal facilities for females in interscholastic athletics. See generally, Note, "Sex Discrimination in High School Athletics," 57 *Minn L Rev* 339, 366-70 (1972). Second, because the sports in question are clearly noncontact sports, we need not determine if the High School League would be justified in precluding females from competing with males in contact sports such as football. See, *Morris v Michigan State Bd of Educ* 472 F2d 1207 (6th Cir 1973).

In evaluating a claim that state action violates the equal protection clause, the following three criteria must be considered: ". . . [I] the character of the classification in question; [II] the individual interests affected by the classification; [III] and the governmental interests asserted in support of the classification. . . ." *Dunn v Blumstein* 405 US 330, 335 (1972).

I. *Sex-Based Classifications. . . .*[1]

In recent years, Congress and the executive have acted to eliminate discrimination based on "stereotyped characterizations of the sexes," *Phillips v Marietta Corp* 400 US 542 (1971) (Marshall, J, concurring). See, Title VII of the Civil

---

1. See *American Women, The Report of the President's Commission on the Status of Women* (1963); *A Matter of Simple Justice, The Report of the President's Task Force on Women's Rights and Responsibilities* (April 1970); *Discrimination Against Women, Hearings Before the Special Subcommittee on Education of the House Committee on Education and*

Rights Act of 1964,[2] the Equal Pay Act,[3] and Title IX of the Education Amendments of 1972.[4] The jurisdiction of the Civil Rights Commission has been extended to include discrimination on the basis of sex.[5] Finally, Congress has passed the equal rights amendment and transmitted it to the states.

In recent years, courts, too, have become sensitive to the problems of sex-based discrimination. . . . There is no longer any doubt that sex-based classifications are subject to scrutiny by the courts under the equal protection clause and will be struck down when they provide dissimilar treatment for men and women who are similarly situated with respect to the object of the classification. . . . Furthermore, discrimination on the basis of sex can no longer be justified by reliance on "outdated images . . . of women as peculiarly delicate and impressionable creatures in need of protection from the rough and tumble of unvarnished humanity." *Seidenberg v McSorleys' Old Ale House* 317 F Supp 593, 606 (SDNY 1970). . . .

In this case, it is unnecessary for this court to determine whether classifications based on sex are suspect and, thus, can be justified only by a compelling state interest because the High School League's rule cannot be justified even under the standard applied to test nonsuspect classifications. See *Eisenstadt v Baird* 405 US 438 (1972).

II. *The Plaintiffs' Interest in Interscholastic Athletics.*

The High School League contends that relief under the Civil Rights Act is inappropriate because participation in interscholastic sports is a privilege and not a right. We disagree. The Supreme Court has rejected "the concept that constitutional rights turn upon whether a governmental benefit is characterized as a 'right' or as a 'privilege.'. . ." *Graham v Richardson* 403 US 365, 374 (1971). The question in this case is not whether the plaintiffs have an absolute right to participate in interscholastic athletics, but whether the plaintiffs can be denied the benefits of activities provided by the state for male students. See *Reed v Nebraska School Activities Ass'n* 341 F Supp 258, 262 (D Neb 1972).

Discrimination in education has been recognized as a matter of the utmost importance. . . . *Brown v Board of Educ* 347 US 483 (1954). In particular, "discrimination in education is one of the most damaging injustices women suffer. It denies them equal education and equal employment opportunity, contributing to a second class self-image." *A Matter of Simple Justice, The Report on the President's Task Force on Women's Rights and Responsibilities* 7 (April 1970). . . .

Discrimination in high school interscholastic athletics constitutes discrimination in education. The Supreme Court of Minnesota has stated that: ". . . interscholastic activities . . . are today recognized . . . as an important and integral facet of the . . . education process, see *Bunger v Iowa High School Athletic Ass'n* 197 NW2d 555 (1972); *Kelley v Metropolitan County Bd of Educ* 293 F Supp 485 (MD Tenn 1968) . . ." *Thompson v Barnes* 200 NW2d 921, 926 n11 (Minn 1972). . . .

Labor, 91st Cong, 2d Sess, (1970); L. Kanowitz, *Women and the Law* (1964); US Department of Labor, *1969 Handbook on Women Workers,* Women's Bureau Bulletin 294.

2. 42 USC §2000e, et seq.

3. 29 USC §206(d).

4. Sections 901-907, PL 92-318, 86 Stat 235 (June 23, 1972). [reprinted at pp 529-31].

5. Section 3, PL 92-496, 86 Stat 813 (October 14, 1972).

The importance of interscholastic athletics for females as part of the total educational process has been recently emphasized by the Minnesota State Board of Education. Its recent statement of policy and proposed action, *Eliminating Sex Bias in Education* (September 1972), states that:

[O]ur educational system has helped perpetuate the division of the sexes into predetermined roles and has failed to provide freedom from discrimination because of sex . . . .

The practice of stereotyping and socializing men and women into "masculine" "feminine" roles has resulted in prejudice, dominance, discrimination and segregation harmful to the human development of both sexes.

. . . .

The state board of education is concerned about four areas in particular: discrimination in hiring and promoting, *sex requirements for boys and girls to participate in sports and extra-curricular activities,* sex bias in curricular and teaching materials, and providing in-service training for administrators and teachers to overcome the habits and practices of teaching stereotyped social roles. (Emphasis added.)

In view of these circumstances, we must conclude that at the very least, the plaintiffs' interest in participating in interscholastic sports is a substantial and cognizable one. . . .

III. *The High School League's Interest.*

Because the defendant high schools have not provided teams for females in tennis and cross-country skiing and running, the effect of the High School League's rule is to completely bar Brenden and St. Pierre from competition in these noncontact interscholastic sports, despite their being fully qualified. The High School League argues, however, that its rule is justified in order to assure that persons with similar qualifications compete among themselves. They state that physiological differences between males and females make it impossible for the latter to equitably compete with males in athletic competition.[7]

In evaluating the High School League's justification for their rule, we will, as we have indicated, apply the equal protection standard for evaluating nonsuspect classifications. . . .

We recognize that because sex-based classifications may be based on outdated stereotypes of the nature of males and females, courts must be particularly sensitive to the possibility of invidious discrimination in evaluating them, and must be particularly demanding in ascertaining whether the state has demonstrated a substantial rational basis for the classification. Compare, *Reed v Reed, supra,* with Gunther, "The Supreme Court, 1971 Term—Foreword: In Search of Evolving Doctrine on a Changing Court: A Model for a Newer Equal Protection," 86 *Harv L Rev* 1, 34 (1972). . . . This is especially true where the classification involves the interest of females in securing an education.

---

7. ". . . As testified to by defendants' expert witnesses, men are taller than women, stronger than women by reason of a greater muscle mass; have larger hearts than women and a deeper breathing capacity, enabling them to utilize oxygen more efficiently than women, run faster, based upon the construction of the pelvic area, which when women reach puberty, widens, causing the femur to bend outward, rendering the female incapable of running as efficiently as a male. . . ." *Brenden v Independent School Dist 742* 342 F Supp 1224, 1233 (D Minn 1972).

We believe that in view of the nature of the classification and the important interests of the plaintiffs involved, the High School League has failed to demonstrate that the sex-based classification fairly and substantially promotes the purposes of the League's rule.

(A)

First, we do not believe the High School League has demonstrated a sufficient rational basis for their conclusion that women are incapable of competing with men in noncontact sports. The trial court specifically found that the plaintiffs were capable of such competition and the evidence indicates that the class of women, like the class of men, includes individuals with widely different athletic abilities.

Essentially, the testimony of those witnesses who concluded that females were wholly incapable of competing with men in interscholastic athletics was based on subjective conclusions drawn from the physiological difference between the sexes by individuals who were not themselves familiar with mixed competition. This subjective testimony is particularly susceptible to discrimination based on stereotyped notions about the nature of the sexes.

Furthermore, the High School League failed to show that it had established any objective nondiscriminatory minimum standards for evaluating qualifications for noncontact interscholastic athletics. The record indicates, in fact, that the schools had adopted no-cut policies allowing male students, no matter *how untalented,* to participate in the noncontact interscholastic sports involved here.

We note that there is at least one systematic study of mixed competition in noncontact sports. In 1969, a rule of the New York State Department of Education prohibiting competition between males and females in noncontact sports was challenged. The department reports:

> Faced with the need for valid supporting data, the Education Department gathered all the evidence it could find on the matter. Very little was reported in professional literature. In the limited number of experiences that came to its attention wherein girls competed on boys' teams (primarily at the college level), the only negative factor reported was that it was not yet socially acceptable for a girl to defeat a boy in athletic competition. Discussion with various medical personnel elicited a unanimous expression that there are no medical reasons to prohibit girls from competing on boys' teams in selected noncontact sports. Thus, it became clear that the department had little or nothing to support its traditional position. It was then suggested that a moratorium be declared on a decision until some evidence could be gathered through experience. Thus, the experimental project came into being. (University of the State of New York, The State Department of Education, Division of Health, Physical Education and Recreation, *Report on Experiment: Girls on Boys Interscholastic Athletic Teams, March 1969-June 1970,* 1 (February, 1972).)

The department then conducted an experiment in which 100 schools over a sixteen-month period maintained athletic teams on which both males and females participated. The results of the experiment were overwhelmingly favorable to continuing mixed competition:

> Should the practice of allowing girls to compete on boys' athletic teams be continued? Eighty percent of the principals, directors, women physical

educators, coaches, and physicians involved in the experiment voted in favor of continuing the practice, either as an experiment or as legal policy. Slightly more than 90 percent of the boy team members, girl participants, parents, coaches and opposing coaches also favored continuation of the practice. . . . Ibid at 4.

As a result of the experiment, New York amended its rules to allow females to compete with males.[8]

(B)

Second, even if we assume, arguendo, that, on the whole, females are unlikely to be able to compete with males in noncontact interscholastic sports, this fact alone would not justify precluding qualified females like Brenden and St. Pierre from such competition. *Reed v Reed, supra.* Cf., *Stanley v Illinois*, 405 US 645 (1972). . . .

[Females are entitled to] an individualized determination of their qualifications for a benefit provided by the state.

In the present case, the underlying purpose of the High School League's rule is, as we have indicated, to insure that persons with similar qualifications will compete with each other. Yet, females, whatever their qualifications, have been barred from competition with males on the basis of an assumption about the qualifications of women as a class. The failure to provide the plaintiffs with an individualized determination of their own ability to qualify for positions on these teams is, under *Reed,* violative of the equal protection clause. . . .

The High School League argues that invalidation of its rule will have an adverse impact on the future development of opportunities for females in interscholastic sports. This argument is too speculative to have merit. . . .

This argument certainly cannot be used to deprive Brenden and St. Pierre of their rights to equal protection of the law. With respect to these two females, the record is clear. Their schools have failed to provide them with opportunities for interscholastic competition equal to those provided for males with similar athletic qualifications. Accordingly, they are entitled to relief. . . .

Affirmed

---

8. New York has determined that: "(4) Girls may participate on the same team with boys in interscholastic competition in the sports of archery, badminton, bowling, fencing, golf, gymnastics, riflery, rowing (but only as coxswain), shuffleboard, skiing, swimming and diving, table tennis, tennis, and track and field, provided the school attended by a girl wishing to participate in any such sport does not maintain a girls' team in that sport. In exceptional cases, the principal or the chief executive officer of a school may permit a girl or girls to participate on a boys' team in a designated sport or sports, notwithstanding the fact that the school maintains a girls' team in that sport or sports." Section 135.4 of the Regulations of the Commissioner of Education.

New York is not alone in having concluded that mixed competition is feasible. A new Michigan statute states: "Female pupils shall be permitted to participate in all noncontact interscholastic athletic activities, including but not limited to archery, badminton, bowling, fencing, golf, gymnastics, riflery, shuffleboard, skiing, swimming, diving, table tennis, track and field and tennis. Even if the institution does have a girls' team in any noncontact interscholastic athletic activity, the female shall be permitted to compete for a position on the boys' team. Nothing in this subsection shall be construed to prevent or interfere with the selection of competing teams solely on the basis of athletic ability." MCLA 340.379(2), Pub Act No. 138 (Mich May 22, 1972). . . .

Notes and Questions

1. Standard of Review

Does *Brenden* apply the traditional standard of review in assessing whether plaintiffs have been denied equal protection? Is its treatment of defendants' claim that most women cannot compete with men on the athletic field consistent with that standard? If the issue were one of racial discrimination, would the judicial analysis be significantly different?

2. Importance of Education

The court notes that "discrimination in high school interscholastic athletics constitutes discrimination in education," and speaks of the constitutional significance of educational opportunity. If the team for which plaintiffs wanted to try out were not part of a public school athletic program (a community-sponsored tennis team, for example), would the outcome in the case be the same? Would plaintiffs have to demonstrate the constitutional importance of athletic competition? Is *Brenden* premised primarily on the importance of education or the invidiousness of sex classification? Compare *San Antonio Independent School Dist v Rodriguez* 93 S Ct 1278 (1973); see pp 583-607.

3. Scope of the Decision

Are the implications of *Brenden* limited by the fact that plaintiffs (i) want to participate in noncontact sports, or (ii) are "proven" athletes?

The court notes that: "the schools had adopted no-cut policies allowing male students, no matter how untalented, to participate in [tennis and cross-country skiing]. . . ." After *Brenden*, are all women eligible to participate in those sports? Would a rescission of the no-cut policy be constitutionally permissible?

The *Brenden* complaint sought "a declaration that the substantial disparity of tax funds allocated to boys' athletic programs as opposed to girls' programs is a . . . violation . . . of the Fourteenth Amendment." *Brenden v Independent School Dist No. 742* 342 F Supp 1224, 1228 (D Minn 1972). Neither the district nor the circuit court addressed that issue. How should it be decided? Suppose the school district concentrated all of its athletic budget on the upper 20 percent of its contact sport athletes—all of whom were men. Would such a policy raise constitutional problems? Would the outcome of such a suit differ if brought by athletically less-talented men?

4. Separate But Equal

Would the provision of a separate athletic team provide equal opportunities for a highly talented woman athlete? Are school systems obliged to provide different levels of athletic competition for men and women students?

5. Other Litigation

The availability of competitive athletic opportunities is one of the most frequently litigated sex discrimination issues. Most of the decisions strike down exclusionary rules; none have reached either the contact sports or the separate but equal issue. See, e.g., *Morris v Michigan State Bd of Educ* 472 F2d 1207 (6th Cir 1973); *Reed v Nebraska School Activities Ass'n* 341 F Supp 258 (D Neb 1972). But see *Bucha v Illinois High School Ass'n,* 351 F Supp 69 (ND Ill 1972). See generally Note, "Sex Discrimination in High School Athletics," 57 *Minn L Rev* 339 (1972).

B. Separate But Equal (or Equivalent) Educational Opportunity

WILLIAMS v MCNAIR
316 F Supp 134 (DSC 1970), *aff'd mem,* 401 US 951 (1971)

Russell, District Judge:

This is an action instituted by the plaintiffs, all males, suing on behalf of themselves and others similarly situated, to enjoin the enforcement of a state statute which limits regular admissions to Winthrop College, a state-supported college located at Rock Hill, South Carolina, to "girls". They assert that, except for their sex, they fully meet the admission requirements of the college.

The defendants are the present members of the board of trustees of Winthrop College, as constituted under its enabling legislation. . . .

It is clear from the stipulated facts that the state of South Carolina has established a wide range of educational institutions at the college and university level consisting of eight separate institutions, with nine additional regional campuses. The several institutions so established vary in purpose, curriculum, and location. Some are limited to undergraduate programs; others extend their offerings into the graduate field. With two exceptions, such institutions are coeducational. Two, by law, however, limit their student admissions to members of one sex. Thus the Citadel restricts its student admission to males and Winthrop, the college involved in this proceeding, may not admit as a regular degree candidate males. There is an historical reason for these legislative restrictions upon the admission standards of these two latter institutions. The first, the Citadel, while offering a full range of undergraduate liberal arts courses and granting degrees in engineering as well, is designated as a military school, and apparently, the Legislature deemed it appropriate for that reason to provide for an all-male student body. Winthrop, on the other hand, was designed as a school for young ladies, which, though offering a liberal arts program, gave special attention to many courses thought to be specially helpful to female students.[3]

The equal protection clause of the Fourteenth Amendment does not require "identity of treatment" for all citizens, or preclude a state, by legislation, from

---

3. See Section 401, Title 22, Code of South Carolina (1962):

"There shall be established an institution for the practical training and higher education of white girls which shall be known as Winthrop College . . . ."

In Section 408, Title 22, the purpose of Winthrop College was stated to be:

"The establishment, conduct and maintenance of a first-class institution for the thorough education of the white girls of this state, the main object of which shall be (1) to give to young women such education as shall fit them for teaching and (2) to give instruction to young women in stenography, typewriting, telegraphy, bookkeeping, drawing (freehand, mechanical, architectural, etc.), designing, engraving, sewing, dressmaking, millinery, art, needlework, cooking, housekeeping and such other industrial arts as may be suitable to their sex and conducive to their support and usefulness. Said trustees may add, from time to time, such special features to the institution and may open such new departments of training and instruction therein as the progress of the times may require."

making classifications and creating differences in the rights of different groups. It is only when the discriminatory treatment and varying standards, as created by the legislative or administrative classification are arbitrary and wanting in any rational justification that they offend the equal protection clause. Specifically, a legislative classification based on sex, has often been held to be constitutionally permissible. See *West Coast Hotel Co v Parrish* (1937) 300 US 379, 394-95 (statute providing minimum wages for women but not men). . . . Thus, the issue in this case is whether the discrimination in admission of students, created by the statute governing the operation of Winthrop and based on sex, is without rational justification.

It is conceded that recognized pedagogical opinion is divided on the wisdom of maintaining "single-sex" institutions of higher education but it is stipulated that there is a respectable body of educators who believe that "a single-sex institution can advance the quality and effectiveness of its instruction by concentrating upon areas of primary interest to only one sex." The idea of educating the sexes separately, the plaintiffs admit, "has a long history" and "is practiced extensively throughout the world." It is no doubt true, as plaintiffs suggest, that the trend in this country is away from the operation of separate institutions for the sexes, but there is still a substantial number of private and public institutions, which limit their enrollment to one sex and do so because they feel it offers better educational advantages. While history and tradition alone may not support a discrimination, the Constitution does not require that a classification "keep abreast of the latest" in educational opinion, especially when there remains a respectable opinion to the contrary; it only demands that the discrimination not be wholly wanting in reason. Any other rule would mean that courts and not legislatures would determine all matters of public policy. It must be remembered, too, that Winthrop is merely a part of an entire system of state-supported higher education. It may not be considered in isolation. If the state operated only one college and that college was Winthrop, there can be no question that to deny males admission thereto would be impermissible under the equal protection clause. But, as we have already remarked, these plaintiffs have a complete range of state institutions they may attend. They are free to attend either an all-male or, if they wish, a number of coeducational institutions at various locations over the state.[15] There is no suggestion that there is any special feature connected with Winthrop that will make it more advantageous educationally to them than any number of other state-supported institutions. They point to no courses peculiar to Winthrop in which they wish to enroll. It is true that, in the case of some, if not all, of the plaintiffs, Winthrop is more convenient geographically for them than the other state institutions. They, in "being denied the right to attend the state college in their home town, are treated no differently than are other students who reside in communities many miles distant from any state-supported college or university. The location of any such institution must necessarily inure to the benefit of some and to the detriment of

15. See *Heaton v Bristol* 317 SW2d 86 (Tex Civ App 1958), *cert denied*, 359 US 230 (1959), where the court said: "Such a plan (i.e., giving the student a choice of a "single-sex" and coeducational institutions) exalts neither sex at the expense of the other, but to the contrary recognizes the equal rights of both sexes to the benefits of the best, most varied system of higher education that the state can supply." 317 SW2d at 100.

others, depending upon the distance the affected individuals reside from the institution."

Under these circumstances, this court cannot declare as a matter of law that a legislative classification, premised as it is on respectable pedagogical opinion, is without any rational justification and violative of the equal protection clause. It might well be that if the members of this court were permitted a personal opinion on the question, they would reach a contrary conclusion. Moreover, it may be, as plaintiffs argue, that the experience of the college in admitting in its summer and evening classes male students, has weakened to some extent the force of the legislative determination that the maintenance of at least one all-female institution in the state system has merit educationally. The evaluation of such experience, however, is not the function or prerogative of the courts; that falls within the legislative province and the plaintiffs must address their arguments to that body and look to it for relief. After all, flexibility and diversity in educational methods, when not tainted with racial overtones, often are both desirable and beneficial; they should be encouraged, not condemned.

It is suggested by the plaintiffs that this conclusion is contrary to the ruling in *Kirstein v Rector and Visitors of Univ of Va* 309 F Supp 184 (DC Va 1970). The court there very pointedly remarked, however, that "We are urged to go further and to hold that Virginia may not operate any educational institution separated according to the sexes. We decline to do so." 309 F Supp at 187. There the women plaintiffs were seeking admission to the University of Virginia and it was conceded that the university occupied a preeminence among the state-supported institutions of Virginia and offered a far wider range of curriculum. No such situation exists here. It is not intimated that Winthrop offers a wider range of subject matter or enjoys a position of outstanding prestige over the other state-supported institutions in this state whose admission policies are coeducational.

Let judgment be entered for the defendants.

Notes and Questions

1. Scope of the *Williams* Decision

Does the court hold that men are not discriminated against by the admission policy of Winthrop college because (a) the state's one-sex colleges are "equal", (b) the state's one-sex colleges are "equivalent", or (c) it is "rational" for the state to provide one-sex colleges?

Would the court's decision be different if Winthrop and the Citadel were the only two state colleges? Would such separation produce "a strong inference . . . that the scheme reflected an assumption that women are inherently incapable of education on an equal basis with men. . . ."? Johnston and Knapp, "Sex Discrimination by Law: A Study in Judicial Perspective," 46 *NYU L Rev* 675, 724-25 (1971). If so, why does the existence of other coeducational institutions affect the outcome of the case?

Would the addition of Winthrop student plaintiffs, who alleged that they were harmed by the absence of male students, have affected the outcome of the case? Would (or should) a suit brought by women students challenging the exclusion from the Citadel have produced a different outcome? In such a suit, would the women's case have been strengthened had they asserted an interest in a military career?

2. Can Separate Be Equal?

In assessing whether sex-separated schools are in fact equal, what factors are relevant: (a) the availability of courses desired by a student barred from admission by virtue of his or her sex (see *Allred v Heaton* 336 SW2d 251 (Tex Civ App 1960), *cert denied,* 364 US 517 (1960)); (b) the proximity of a given school to a student's residence (or family) (see *Heaton v Bristol* 317 SW2d 86 (Tex Civ App 1958), *cert denied* 359 US 230 (1959); (c) the expenditure per student at each school (compare Boston Commission to Improve the Status of Women, "Discrimination on the Basis of Sex in Occupational Education in the Boston Public Schools" (1972), noting at p 5 that the per-pupil instructional expenditure at Boys Trade High School is $1477, compared with $886 spent on each girl enrolled in Trade High School for Girls); (d) the number and variety of courses available at each school; or (e) the "prestige" of each school? Would careful investigation of these factors produce many (or any) examples of schools that were sex separated and wholly equivalent?

3. Separate But Equal: the Race Analogy

Professor Emerson notes that "separate treatment of two groups, one of which has previously been treated by law as inferior, can never amount to equal treatment." Emerson, "In Support of the Equal Rights Amendment," 6 *Harv Civ Rights—Civ Lib L Rev* 225, 231 n19 (1971). Does Emerson's observation determine the constitutionality of sex-based, separate but equal schooling? In the case of racial separation, separation connotes stigma—a connotation appreciated by black and white alike. Further, as the *Plessy*-to-*Brown* history suggests, racially separate schools were also unequal in fact; blacks received fewer tangible resources than did whites. For those reasons, a per se condemnation of separate but equal in the race context seems appropriate. But is the argument equally fitting in the sex context?

Professor Freund thinks not. He views an assault on separate schools (such as Boston's Boys and Girls Latin Schools, noted in the previous section) as a quest for "a single standard of sameness ... a doctrinaire equality." Freund, "The Equal Rights Amendment Is Not the Way," 6 *Harv Civ Rights—Civ Lib L Rev* 234, 238 (1971). Freund rejects the full application of the race-sex analogy:

> It is sometimes said that a rigid requirement of equality is no less proper for the sexes than for the races, and no less workable. But the moral dimensions of the concept of equality are clearly not the same in the two cases. . . . A school system offering a triple option based on race—all-white, all-black, and mixed schools—would elevate freedom of choice over equal protection in an impermissible way. Are we prepared to pass that judgment as readily on a school system that offers a choice of boys', girls', and coeducational schools? (6 *Harv Civ Rights—Civ Lib L Rev* at 240.)

See also Moody, "The Constitution and the One-sex College," 20 *Cleve State L Rev* 465 (1971). Does Professor Freund indicate why the analogy is inappropriate? Is he suggesting that the society's views concerning race separation are clearer (or more fully formed) than its views concerning sex separation? Is the suggestion correct? Does it indicate that *Plessy v Ferguson* and *Brown v Board of Education* were both decided correctly?

Compare the following analysis of the race-sex analogy, specifically responding to the *Williams* decision:

> [S]uppose that South Carolina, in addition to operating one or more racially mixed institutions, should maintain two other colleges. One, Dred Scott Institute, would offer degrees in agriculture, music, dance and physical education; it would accept only black students. The other, Calhoun College, would offer degrees in nuclear physics, medicine, law, engineering and business administration; only whites need apply. Even assuming that all of these studies were available at a biracial institution in the state, would such a scheme survive constitutional scrutiny?

> It is difficult to see how; indeed, any other answer is unthinkable. And yet, the maintenance of two institutions for the sexes in South Carolina, one for male warriors and the other for female domestics, is different only in that the assumptions it reflects about individual capabilities and aspirations are more widely shared. The role of a housewife or a secretary is an honorable and productive one; so of course is the role of a champion athlete or a tenant farmer. To attack the attitudes reflected in the *Williams* decision is not to denigrate the individuals for whom such stereotypes happen to be accurate; it is to attack the arrogant assumption that merely because these stereotypes are accurate for some individuals, the state has a right to apply them to all individuals—and, indeed, to shape its official policy toward the end that they shall *continue* to be accurate for all individuals. (Johnston and Knapp, "Sex Discrimination by Law: A Study in Judicial Perspective," 46 *NYU L Rev* 675, 725-26 (1971).)

Do Professors Johnston and Knapp overemphasize the distinction between the Citadel and Winthrop? Are they correct in stating that the maintenance of these two schools, in an otherwise coeducational system, applies sex stereotypes "to all individuals"?

4. Sex Separation and Racial Desegregation

In a number of desegregation cases, school districts have proposed to integrate racially, while separating students according to sex. See, e.g., *Moore v Tangipahoa Parish School Bd* 304 F Supp 244 (ED La 1969) (authorizing sex separation as a transitional measure); *Smith v Concordia Parish School Bd* 331 F Supp 330 (WD La 1971) (declaring unconstitutional sex segregation). Should sex segregation in the context of a racial desegregation plan be treated differently from other sex segregation situations? Is such a plan likely to be racially motivated, to reinforce racial stereotypes concerning the sexuality of blacks, or to cause psychological harm to black students? See generally Note, "The Constitutionality of Sex Separation in School Desegregation Plans," 37 *U Chi L Rev* 296 (1970).

5. Separateness: Justifications

Separate schooling for men and women has been justified on two quite different grounds: as a means of preventing immorality and as a way of securing the fullest intellectual development of each group.

a. Morality. The argument that sex separation prevents immorality and promiscuous behavior has most frequently been advanced by Catholic spokesmen. In his encyclical *The Christian Education of Youth,* Pope Pius XI defended sex separation in education and referred to coeducation as "false" and "harmful," based on "a deplorable confusion of ideas that mistake a leveling promiscuity and equality for the legitimate association of the sexes." He concluded: "there is not in nature itself, which fashions the two quite different in organism, in temperament, in abilities, anything to suggest that there can or ought to be promiscuity, and much less equality, in the training of the two sexes." Pope Pius XI, "The Christian Education of Youth," in *Five Great Encyclicals,* 37, 56-57 (G. Treacy ed 1939).

If this position were to be empirically validated, would it provide constitutionally sufficient justification for sex-separated, but equal schools?

b. Intellectual Benefit. Relatively little research on the effects of single-sex education on achievement have been undertaken. The differential development of boys and girls is asserted to require separate instruction. N. McCluskey, *Catholic Viewpoint on Education,* 97-98 (1959); Levine, "Coeducation—A Contributing Factor in the Miseducation of the Disadvantaged," 46 *Phi Delta Kappan* 126 (1964). Discipline problems are said to be fewer in single-sex schools. Lyles, "Grouping by Sex," 46 *Nat'l Elem Principal* 38 (1966). Single-sex schools may also be less competitive. Herman and Criscuolo, "Sex Grouping," 77 *The Instructor* 97 (March 1968). As in almost all areas of education research, however, the findings are inconsistent. See Fisher and Waetjen, "An Investigation of the Relationship between the Separation by Sex of Eighth Grade Boys and Girls and English Achievement and Self-concept," 59 *J Ed Research* 409 (1966).

One scholar, concerned that sex stereotyping in the public schools may adversely affect the potential of boys and girls, suggests that "maybe, just maybe, all-boy and all-girl classes might help":

"HE ONLY DOES IT TO ANNOY" in
SEX DIFFERENTIATION IN EDUCATION
Smith
28, 42-43 (S. Anderson ed 1972)

The Fairfax County, Virginia, School Board in the early 1960s sponsored experiments with all-boy and all-girl classes in the third, fifth, and sixth grades. No special curricular changes were made in the way of "masculine" or "feminine" materials, nor were special teachers assigned. Nevertheless, J. F. Hurley reports that in achievement the one-sex classes consistently tended to do better than matched controls. . . . [Hurley, "Report of Project Evaluation: A Study of All-boy and All-girl Groups at the Third and Fifth Grade Levels and on Evaluation after Two Years in Same Sex Classes," (Office of Psychological Services, Fairfax County School Dist, Fairfax, Va, 1965).] One group was studied that had same-sexed classes in both the fifth and sixth grades. The boys in the second year group continued their considerable advantage over the controls. The girls did not. Hurley points out that boys were more eager for the second year than the girls. Perhaps this was because the girls at 11-12 years of age were rapidly approaching puberty while the boys were still well away.

In the fifth-grade one-sex classes, boys were noisier, more enthusiastic, more experimental, and more imaginative than girls—a result to be expected if the early grades had done well their job of making the girls "nice." Boys seemed to be less inhibited than boys in mixed classes in displaying girl-type interests. Similarly girls seemed more ready to express interest in boy-type subjects and activities. Girls became somewhat less worried about grades and less concerned about covering up deficiencies than did girls in mixed classes. . . . [I]t was the boys of lower aptitude that benefited most from all-boy classes. It is just these boys that become, in regular classes, the behavior problems and the dropouts.

The data on which these behaviors are based are not firm enough to be quantified, but they do suggest a need for examining the possibilities of same-sex classes, not only to promote academic achievement, but also to free our children of stereotypes.

R. W. Strickler in a preliminary report cites enthusiastic support among teachers, parents, and children for one-sex classes. His early data indicate considerable reading gains by boys in all-boy classes compared with boys in mixed classes. [Strickler, "Thomas Coeburn Elementary School Kindergarten Primary Masculinization Project 1968-72 and Kindergarten-Primary Masculinization Project 1970-1971" (Penn-Delco School Dist, Ashton, Pa, 1972).]

Some of Strickler's informal observations are intriguing:

> Several girls in the all-girl class assumed the more aggressive roles usually played by boys.
>
> Girls became more critical of mistakes made by other girls.
>
> Girls became more active and had less regard for the "good girl" role which they usually play in a mixed group.
>
> The usual "prime-year" work was quickly exhausted by the all-girl group.
>
> Boys suffered fewer kindergarten adjustment problems when separated from girls.
>
> A masculinized program was appropriate for girls, too. Girls related well to male resource persons and helpers, and enjoyed boy-oriented stories as well.
>
> Boys developed more realistic self-concepts and more positive attitudes toward school when they were separated from girls.

It is hard to see these children as hurting. Strickler's program was designed specifically to "masculinize" the boys' school experience in order to foster their learning and improve their perception of the school. Things seem to be happening to the girls, too. Maybe Strickler, in searching for the boys, has discovered the girls.

These data should be treated extremely cautiously. The studies are small and subject to substantial methodological criticism. If sex-segregated, but equal, schools were proved to be both academically better and less likely to provoke sexual stereotyping than coeducational schools, would such a finding provide constitutionally sufficient justification for a separate but equal policy? Compare Note, "The Constitutionality of Sex Separation in School Desegregation Plans," 37 *U Chi L Rev* 296, 323-26 (1970).

6. Separateness: Women's Liberation Argument

Women have argued that sex-separate educational institutions were needed in order to overcome the sex stereotyping perpetrated by men on women in coeducational institutions. Compare Tobias, "How Coeducation Fails Women," in *Sex Differences in Education,* 83 (S. Anderson ed 1973). Might such an argument provide constitutional justification of sex-separate schools? Require that such schools be created? Might men advance a similar claim? Is the analogy to minority-controlled community schools appropriate?

III. Sex Discrimination: The Federal Role

Title IX of the Education Amendments of 1972, Public Law 92-318, prohibits certain forms of sex discrimination.

1972 EDUCATION AMENDMENTS (20 USC § § 1681-86)
TITLE IX—PROHIBITION OF SEX DISCRIMINATION
SEX DISCRIMINATION PROHIBITED

Sec 901. (a) No person in the United States shall, on the basis of sex, be excluded from participation in, be denied the benefits of, or be subjected to discrimination under any education program or activity receiving federal financial assistance, except that:

(1) in regard to admissions to educational institutions, this section shall apply only to institutions of vocational education, professional education, and graduate higher education, and to public institutions of undergraduate higher education;

(2) in regard to admissions to educational institutions, this section shall not apply (A) for one year from the date of enactment of this act, nor for six years after such date in the case of an educational institution which has begun the process of changing from being an institution which admits only students of one sex to being an institution which admits students of both sexes, but only if it is carrying out a plan for such a change which is approved by the commissioner of education or (B) for seven years from the date an educational institution begins the process of changing from being an institution which admits only students of only one sex to being an institution which admits students of both sexes, but only if it is carrying out a plan for such a change which is approved by the commissioner of education, whichever is the later;

(3) this section shall not apply to an educational institution which is controlled by a religious organization if the application of this subsection would not be consistent with the religious tenets of such organization;

(4) this section shall not apply to an educational institution whose primary purpose is the training of individuals for the military services of the United States, or the merchant marine; and

(5) in regard to admissions this section shall not apply to any public institution of undergraduate higher education which is an institution that traditionally and continually from its establishment has had a policy of admitting only students of one sex.

(b) Nothing contained in subsection (a) of this section shall be interpreted to require any educational institution to grant preferential or disparate treatment to the members of one sex on account of an imbalance which may exist with respect to the total number or percentage of persons of that sex participating in or receiving the benefits of any federally supported program or activity, in comparison with the total number or percentage of persons of that sex in any community, state, section, or other area: *Provided,* That this subsection shall not be construed to prevent the consideration in any hearing or proceeding under this title of statistical evidence tending to show that such an imbalance exists with respect to the participation in, or receipt of the benefits of, any such program or activity by the members of one sex.

(c) For purposes of this title an educational institution means any public or private preschool, elementary, or secondary school, or any institution of vocational, professional, or higher education, except that in the case of an educational institution composed of more than one school, college, or department which are administratively separate units, such term means each such school, college, or department.

FEDERAL ADMINISTRATIVE ENFORCEMENT

Sec 902. Each federal department and agency which is empowered to extend federal financial assistance to any education program or activity, by way of grant, loan, or contract other than a contract of insurance or guaranty, is authorized and directed to effectuate the provisions of section 901 with respect to such program or activity by issuing rules, regulations, or orders of general applicability which shall be consistent with achievement of the objectives of the statute authorizing the financial assistance in connection with which the action is taken. No such rule, regulation, or order shall become effective unless and until approved by the president. Compliance with any requirement adopted pursuant to this section may be effected (1) by the termination of or refusal to grant or to continue assistance under such program or activity to any recipient as to whom there has been an express finding on the record, after opportunity for hearing, of a failure to comply with such requirement, but such termination or refusal shall be limited to the particular political entity, or part thereof, or other recipient as to whom such a finding has been made, and shall be limited in its effect to the particular program, or part thereof, in which such noncompliance has been so found, or (2) by any other means authorized by law: *Provided, however,* That no such action shall be taken until the department or agency concerned has advised the appropriate person or persons of the failure to comply with the requirement and has determined that compliance cannot be secured by voluntary means. In the case of any action terminating, or refusing to grant or continue, assistance because of failure to comply with a requirement imposed pursuant to this section, the head of the federal department or agency shall file with the committees of the House and Senate having legislative jurisdiction over the program or activity involved a full written report of the circumstances and the grounds for such action. No such action shall become effective until thirty days have elapsed after the filing of such report. . . .

INTERPRETATION WITH RESPECT TO LIVING FACILITIES

Sec 907. Notwithstanding anything to the contrary contained in this title, nothing contained herein shall be construed to prohibit any educational institution receiving funds under this act, from maintaining separate living facilities for the different sexes.

Notes and Questions

1. Scope of Coverage

How would each of the issues canvassed in this chapter—differential treatment with respect to curriculum; access to selective high schools; differential treatment of pregnant and married students; separate and assertedly equivalent treatment of men and women—be decided under Title IX?

Do the distinctions that the legislation draws between (a) traditionally one-sex public institutions and other public institutions; (b) public and private institutions; and (c) private vocational institutions and private undergraduate higher education institutions pose problems under the equal protection clause (as "incorporated" in the Fifth Amendment, see *Bolling v Sharpe* 347 US 497 (1954))? What is the policy rationale for each of those distinctions?

2. Sex and Religion

Does §901(a)(3), in deferring to sectarian beliefs, violate the First Amendment's establishment of religion clause? Would §901(a)(3) be constitutional after the adoption of the equal rights amendment?

3. Sex and Race

The language of §901(a) barring exclusion, denial of benefits, or discrimination on the basis of sex mirrors the language of the 1964 Civil Rights Act (42 USC §1983). Does this suggest that—with the exceptions enumerated in §§901(1)-(5) and 907—Congress views sex and race discrimination as requiring similar forms of redress? Do not the "exceptions" indicate a very different "rule"?

4. Enforcement

As this book went to press, the Office of Civil Rights, Department of Health, Education and Welfare, had yet to issue guidelines or regulations. Groups such as the National Organization for Women (NOW) and the Women's Equity Action League (WEAL) pushed for prompt release and strict enforcement of regulations concerning, among other matters, nonstereotyped treatment of women in textbooks and open access to athletic and vocational programs.

Does the enforcement history of racial segregation guidelines, discussed in chapter 4, suggest the sorts of organizational and political difficulties that HEW is likely to encounter? Or are the politics of race and sex discrimination so different as to render such analogies misleading?

chapter six
Equal Educational Opportunity: Educational Resources and School Outcomes

I. Introduction

The denial of equal educational opportunity is, as we have seen, one doctrinal source for objection to discriminations based on race or sex. But the concept also has other meanings, both for policy makers and courts.

Historically, educational opportunity was defined primarily in resource (or input) terms: its elements included a universally available and free education; a common curriculum; equality of resources—teachers, texts, and the like—within a given school district. See Coleman, "The Concept of Equality of Educational Opportunity," in *Equal Educational Opportunity* 9, 13 (Harvard Educational Review ed 1969). As Professor Coleman notes, a host of alternative definitions are conceivable:

> One type of inequality may be defined in terms of differences of the community's input to the schools, such as per-pupil expenditure. . . .
>
> A [second] type of inequality would include various intangible characteristics of the school as well as the factors directly traceable to the community inputs to the school [see *Sweatt v Painter* 339 US 629 (1950)]. Yet such a definition gives no suggestion of where to stop, or just how relevant these factors might be for school quality.
>
> Consequently, a [third] type of inequality may be defined in terms of consequences of the school for individuals with equal backgrounds and abilities. In this definition, equality of educational opportunity is equality of results, given the same individual input. With such a definition, inequality might come about from differences in the school inputs and/or racial composition and/or from more intangible things. . . .
>
> A [fourth] type of inequality may be defined in terms of consequences of the school for individuals of unequal backgrounds and abilities. In this definition, equality of educational opportunity is equality of results given *different* individual inputs. The most striking examples of inequality here would be children from households in which a language other than English . . . is spoken. . . .
>
> Such a definition taken in the extreme would imply that educational equality is reached only when the results of schooling (achievement and attitudes) are the same for racial and religious minorities as for the dominant group. (Coleman, "Equality of Educational Opportunity," 18-19.)

532

This chapter considers several definitions of equal opportunity: equal outcomes, equal resources, nondiscrimination in the distribution of resources, and nonexclusion from education. Each definition raises three discrete issues: (1) Is this kind of equality *accomplishable*, given what is known about the distribution of schooling resources and the relationship between those resources and educational success; (2) as a matter of policy is it *desirable*; and (3) in the light of institutional and doctrinal limitations, should the courts declare that a given definition of equal opportunity is *constitutionally required*? The issues are, of course, interrelated: for example, the sweep of the equal protection clause gives courts considerable latitude in defining its bounds, and policy consequences are—indeed, should be—factors that courts consider in assessing whether a given inequality has constitutional dimensions. But the distinctions between these questions are useful and should be kept in mind while assessing the alternative theories of equal educational opportunity.

II. Equal Educational Opportunity: Needs and Outcomes

A. The Judicial Response

McINNIS v SHAPIRO
293 F Supp 327 (ND Ill 1968), *aff'd sub nom, McINNIS v OGILVIE,*
394 US 322 (1969)

Before Hastings, Circuit Judge, and Decker and Marovitz, District Judges.
Decker, District Judge.

This is a suit filed by a number of high school and elementary school students attending school within four school districts of Cook County, Illinois, on behalf of themselves and all others similarly situated challenging the constitutionality of various state statutes dealing with the financing of the public school system.

Plaintiffs claim that these statutes violate their fourteenth amendment rights to equal protection and due process because they permit wide variations in the expenditures per student from district to district, thereby providing some students with a good education and depriving others, who have equal or greater educational need. Plaintiffs claim to be members of this disadvantaged group.

To correct this inequitable situation, they seek a declaration that the statutes are unconstitutional and a permanent injunction forbidding further distribution of tax funds in reliance on these laws.

The defendants are state officials charged with the administration of the legislation which allegedly permits this discrimination. . . .

II. The Financing of Illinois' Public Schools. The general assembly has delegated authority to local school districts to raise funds by levying a tax on all property within the district. In addition, the school districts may issue bonds for constructing and repairing their buildings. Legislation limits both the maximum indebtedness and the maximum tax rate which localities may impose for educational purposes. In 1966-67, the approximately 1300 districts had roughly $840 per pupil with which to educate their students, of which about 75 percent came from local sources, 20 percent was derived from state aid, and 5 percent was supplied by the federal government. Since the financial ability of the individual districts varies substantially, per pupil expenditures vary between $480 and $1,000. State statutes which permit such wide variations allegedly deny the less fortunate Illinois students of their constitutional rights. . . .

III. The Fourteenth Amendment: Equal Protection and Due Process. The underlying rationale of the complaint is that *only* a financing system which apportions public funds according to the educational needs of the students satisfies the Fourteenth Amendment.[11] Plaintiffs assert that the distribution of school revenues to satisfy these needs should not be limited by such arbitrary factors as variations in local property values or differing tax rates.

Clearly, there are wide variations in the amount of money available for Illinois' school districts, both on a per pupil basis and in absolute terms. Presumably, students receiving a $1000 education are better educated than those acquiring a $600 schooling. While the inequalities of the existing arrangement are readily apparent, the crucial question is whether it is unconstitutional. Since nearly three-quarters of the revenue comes from local property taxes, substantially equal revenue distribution would require revamping this method of taxation, with the result that districts with greater property values per student would help support the poorer districts.

A. Social Policy. While the state common school fund tends to compensate for the variations in school districts' assessed valuation per pupil, variation in actual expenditures remains approximately 3.0 to 1, 2.6 to 1, and 1.7 to 1 for elementary, high school and unit districts respectively. Though districts with lower property valuations usually levy higher tax rates, there is a limit to the amount of money which they can raise, especially since they are limited by maximum indebtedness and tax rates. Plaintiffs argue that state statutes authorizing these wide variations in assessed value per student are irrational, thus violating the due process clause. Moreover, under the equal protection clause, the students contend that the importance of education to the welfare of individuals and the nation requires the courts to invalidate the legislation if potential, alternative statutes incorporating the desirable aspects of the present system can also achieve substantially equal per pupil expenditures.

Illustrating how the school financing could be improved, plaintiffs suggest two alternatives: (1) all students might receive the same dollar appropriations, or (2) the state could siphon off all money in excess of $ X per pupil which was produced by a given tax rate, in effect eliminating variations in local property values while leaving the districts free to establish their own tax rate.[15]

---

11. Although plaintiffs stress the alleged denial of equal protection, they seek relief resembling substantive due process. Surely, quality education for all is more desirable than uniform, mediocre instruction. Yet if the Constitution only commands that all children be treated equally, the latter result would satisfy the Fourteenth Amendment. Certainly, parents who cherish education are constitutionally allowed to spend more money on their children's schools, be it by private instruction or higher tax rates, than those who do not value education so highly. Thus, the students' goal is presumably a judicial pronouncement that each pupil is entitled to a minimum level of educational expenditures, which would be significantly higher than the existing $400.

15. For example, if a district only levied a 1 percent tax rate, it could keep only $400 per pupil, regardless of absolute dollars produced. On the other hand, the state would also

Without doubt, the educational potential of each child should be cultivated to the utmost, and the poorer school districts should have more funds with which to improve their schools. But the allocation of public revenues is a basic policy decision more appropriately handled by a legislature than a court. To illustrate, the following considerations might be relevant to a financing scheme: statewide variations in costs and salaries, the relative efficiency of school districts, and the need for local experimentation. . . .

In the instant case, the general assembly's delegation of authority to school districts appears designed to allow individual localities to determine their own tax burden according to the importance which they place upon public schools. Moreover, local citizens must select which municipal services they value most highly. While some communities might place heavy emphasis on schools, others may cherish police protection or improved roads. The state legislature's decision to allow local choice and experimentation is reasonable, especially since the common school fund assures a minimum of $400 per student.[20]. . .

B. Plaintiffs' Legal Precedent. The complaining students rely upon recent Supreme Court decisions in the fields of school desegregation, voting rights and criminal justice. Specifically, they contend that "equal educational opportunity," however that term may be defined, is constitutionally compelled because (1) state discrimination in education may not be based on color, (2) the state may not employ arbitrary geographical lines to establish electoral units within local governments, and (3) wealth may not be used to differentiate among criminal defendants if such discrimination is adverse to the indigent.

But the plaintiffs' conclusion does not follow so readily from the preceding building blocks. The decided cases established significant, but limited principles. To illustrate, *Brown v Board of Education* was primarily a desegregation case. Although placed in the context of public schools, it does not undermine the validity of Illinois' public financing. . . . The holding in *Douglas v California* 372 US 353 (1963), derived primarily from its criminal justice setting, rather than the poverty of the defendant. Moreover, *Reynolds v Sims* 377 US 533 (1964), strengthened citizens' voting rights because the Constitution specifically enfranchises all citizens equally, not as a result of general antipathy to historical geographical divisions. . . .

---

guarantee $400 per pupil to units imposing the 1 percent. At higher rates, such as 4 percent, the state would thus substantially aid districts with low valuations, deriving most of its funds from wealthy districts which produced far more than $400 per pupil by a 1 percent rate.

20. While condemning the present distribution system, plaintiffs concede the virtue of decentralization, as follows: "Decentralized administration and decision making are desirable for administrative and political reasons. A division of the state into local school districts is therefore necessary. The voters in any particular area are best able to weigh convenience, the desired degree of homogeneity in the student body, and other factors. These voters are the best able to draw school district boundaries. Once these boundaries are drawn, the administrators or residents of the district, being closest to the problem, are best able to determine the educational needs of the district's children. That decision takes the form of support for a certain tax rate. Sometimes, this decentralized decision making in creating districts or in adopting a tax rate will result in insufficient distribution of educational services. When that occurs the state in recognition of its ultimate responsibility provides sufficient funds to purchase 'basic' education for each child. Four hundred dollars per pupil is the figure necessary to support a 'basic' educational program. Of course, any disadvantage is outweighed by the values of decentralized administration and decision making."

IV. Lack of Judicially Manageable Standards. Even if the Fourteenth Amendment required that expenditures be made only on the basis of pupils' educational needs, this controversy would be nonjusticiable. While the complaint does not present a "political question" in the traditional sense of the term, there are no "discoverable and manageable standards" by which a court can determine when the Constitution is satisfied and when it is violated.[34]

The only possible standard is the rigid assumption that each pupil must receive the same dollar expenditures. Expenses are not, however, the exclusive yardstick of a child's educational needs. Deprived pupils need more aid than fortunate ones.[35] Moreover, a dollar spent in a small district may provide less education than one used in a large district. As stated above, costs vary substantially throughout the state. The desirability of a certain degree of local experimentation and local autonomy in education also indicates the impracticability of a single, simple formula. Effective, efficient administration necessitates decentralization so that local personnel, familiar with the immediate needs, can administer the school system. As new teaching methods are devised and as urban growth demands changed patterns of instruction, the only realistic way the state can adjust is through legislative study, discussion and continuing revision of the controlling statutes. Even if there were some guidelines available to the judiciary, the courts simply cannot provide the empirical research and consultation necessary for intelligent educational planning. As early as 1919 Mr. Justice Holmes explained that "the Fourteenth Amendment is not a pedagogical requirement of the impracticable." *Dominion Hotel v Arizona* 249 US 265, 268 (1919).

V. Conclusion. The present Illinois scheme for financing public education reflects a rational policy consistent with the mandate of the Illinois Constitution. Unequal educational expenditures per student, based upon the variable property values and tax rates of local school districts, do not amount to an invidious discrimination. Moreover, the statutes which permit these unequal expenditures on a district to district basis are neither arbitrary nor unreasonable.

There is no constitutional requirement that public school expenditures be made only on the basis of pupils' educational needs without regard to the financial strength of local school districts. Nor does the Constitution establish the rigid guideline of equal dollar expenditures for each student.

Illinois' general assembly has already recognized the need for additional educational funds to provide all students a good education. Furthermore, the legislative school problems commission assures a continuing and comprehensive study of the public schools' financial problems. If other changes are needed in the present system, they should be sought in the legislature and not in the courts. Plaintiffs have stated no grounds for judicial relief, and this cause must be dismissed.

---

34. Illustrating the lack of standards, plaintiffs' original complaint sought to have this court "order defendants to submit . . . a plan to raise and apportion all monies . . . in such a manner that such funds available to the school districts wherein the class of plaintiffs attend school will . . . assure that plaintiff children receive the same educational opportunity as the children in any other district . . . ."

35. Ideally, disadvantaged youth should receive more than average funds, rather than equal expenditures, so their potential can be fully developed. A rule coercing equal expenditures for all, especially if raised to a constitutional plane, would completely frustrate this ideal. See generally Kurland, "Equal Educational Opportunity: The Limits of Constitutional Jurisprudence Undefined," 35 *U Chi L Rev* 583, 591 (1968).

Notes and Questions

McInnis was affirmed without opinion by the Supreme Court (394 US 322 (1969)); a "scarcely distinguishable" case (*Burruss v Wilkerson* 310 F Supp 572 (WD Va 1969), *aff'd mem*, 397 US 44 (1970)) received similarly curt judicial treatment.

1. Local Control

The *McInnis* court assumes that local school districts are essential, both to promote educational experimentation and to maintain educational efficiency. Granting the court's assumption, does it necessarily follow that school financing must also be decentralized? Are the fiscal inequities of which the court speaks the necessary price for local control over public education?

Professor Kurland observes:

[T]he [*McInnis*] argument, in essence, demands the elimination of local governmental authority to choose the ways in which it will assess, collect, and expend its tax funds. To the extent that the argument is valid with reference to education, it is equally applicable to the small host of activities that are still left to local government control... [T]his prospect... calls for a more fundamental change in our notions of local governmental authority than any that the Supreme Court has yet compelled. (Kurland, "Equal Educational Opportunity: The Limits of Constitutional Jurisprudence Undefined," 35 *U Chi L Rev* 583, 589 (1968).

Is Professor Kurland correct in his assessment of the effect of the *McInnis* plaintiffs' argument? See Levin and Cohen, *Levels of State Aid Relating to State Restrictions on Local School District Decision Making* (1973).

2. Necessity for Legislative Supervision

The court treats financing issues as questions of policy that the legislature is particularly competent to resolve. Is the court suggesting that no remedy requiring reallocation of resources should be ordered by a court? Is education finance so complex a policy question or so politically explosive that judicial involvement is unfeasible?

Consider the following discussion of the process of budget making:

The general problem of allocating a public budget may be considered a problem of constrained maximization; that is, the budgetary decision maker tries to maximize certain goals (or values)... subject to budgetary and other constraints....

The problem of maximization can be stated as a rule: the last dollar spent on each program should yield the same return [as the first]....

The heart of the budgetary process is the selection of values to be maximized. Even a small change in the value (or goal) that the decision maker is trying to maximize can change program allocations....

Specific budgetary allocations require not only the selection of a value for maximization, but also a compromise between that value and others. .... In the case of education, for example, the budget serves, among other goals, those of efficiency, equality, and consumption. Helping disadvantaged children is only one budgetary goal. (Schoettle, "The Equal Protection Clause in Public Education," 71 *Colum L Rev* 1355, 1389-92 (1971).)

How would the remedy proposed in *McInnis,* if judicially adopted, have affected the budgetary process with respect to education? With respect to public services generally?

3. Educational Needs

The court rejects as "judicially unmanageable" the requirement that expenditures be made only on the basis of students' educational needs. Is it suggesting that the means proposed by plaintiffs to effectuate the needs standard would not in fact accomplish that end? How might the court determine whether in fact a student's needs were satisfied? Consider the following situations: (a) a blind student seeks instruction in braille; (b) a student performing two years below the national average for his grade wants "catch-up" help; (c) a budding Picasso demands the services of a highly talented art teacher to develop his artistic potential. Could each assert that his educational needs were not being met? Would the financing schemes proposed by the *McInnis* plaintiffs satisfy these students? Were they designed to do so?

How adequately does the following excerpt respond to these questions? (While the excerpt treats intradistrict practices and should be assessed again in the context of section III, the analysis relies on cases analyzing state-created or state-tolerated inequalities, and so is pertinent to the present discussion.)

"UNSEPARATE BUT UNEQUAL—THE EMERGING FOURTEENTH
AMENDMENT ISSUE IN PUBLIC SCHOOL EDUCATION"
H. Horowitz
13 UCLA L Rev 1147, 1166 (1966)

. . . . Can there be a denial of equal educational opportunity to some children in a school district even if the school board provides an identical quality of facilities, programs, and services in all of the schools in the district? Should the equal protection clause be interpreted to require more than such "equality" for children whose preparation for education is such that they cannot achieve to the full extent of their capacities under the programs and services normally provided by the schools in the district? The factual basis for this inquiry is provided by research findings on markedly lower educational achievement by children in schools in "disadvantaged" areas, the close correlation between socioeconomic status and educational achievement, and the progressively lower achievement of culturally deprived children as they advance through the school grades·coupled with developing data concerning significant improvement in achievement when special programs, adapted to the specific needs of these children, are provided. There are indications that provision, particularly at the primary level, of significantly smaller classes, specially designed approaches to the curriculum, and supportive health, welfare, and counselling personnel can bring about higher achievement by such children. If these factual premises are established, does the equal protection clause require that a school board, in administering a compulsory educational system, provide, or at least make reasonable effort to provide, such "compensatory" programs?

A possible constitutional inequality would be found in the fact that a school board was providing to some (and probably most) but not all, children within its district an educational program geared to their preparation for education and relatively well designed to result in their achieving to the maximum extent of their capacities.... [F]ailure to provide compensatory programs [to the disadvantaged] would be violative of the equal protection clause unless the board could show that there was no available rationally based way to do so. And in most situations there would be a rationally based alternative available: expending funds for compensatory programs—if necessary, by reducing expenditures for other purposes or by increasing the total funds available for expenditure.

Analysis of this suggested principle should begin with an apparent distinction between failure to provide the same educational programs to all children and failure to provide different programs to children with different preparation for education. The distinction is found in the degree of immediate state responsibility for, or contribution to, the total effect of inequality in a specific fact situation. In the compensatory education problem the bases for the constitutional inquiry are the facts that children with equal capacity to achieve at a given level actually attain different levels of achievement, and that the school board does not provide educational programs which respond to the varying needs of all children. The child's degree of preparation for education, to a great extent a direct function of his socioeconomic status, is one of the causal factors for the level of educational achievement which he attains. The question then arises as to the obligation of the state under the Fourteenth Amendment, in carrying forward a governmental program, to compensate for inequalities among individuals, not directly caused by the state, which lead to unequal benefit from the governmental program.

Can the state, then, in its public education programs, take children as it finds them? Is the equal protection requirement satisfied if there are differences in educational achievement which would be significantly eliminated by different educational programs?...

It should not be a controlling argument...—against the principle suggested here—that unequal achievement of some children is the result not just of the failure of the schools to provide them with adequate programs, but also of their inadequate preparation for the programs provided, the latter a factor which the state has not immediately caused. *Griffin* and *Douglas* rejected this argument, where the state sought to impose criminal sanctions on the defendant. [In these cases the state was required by the Fourteenth Amendment to compensate for inequalities in economic resources by providing transcripts and counsel to indigent defendants. See *Griffin v Illinois* 351 US 12 (1956); *Douglas v California* 372 US 353 (1963).] The argument should be rejected in the public education area as well. The public school has a meaningful degree of responsibility for the ultimate result of unequal educational achievement by children with equal capacity, because it does not provide to some children, as it does to others, educational programs designed to permit them to achieve to the full extent of their capacities. And the state has *compelled* these children to participate in the educational programs. Where the state seeks to deprive a person of his life, liberty, or property, or requires him to participate in a governmental program, the fact that the state is not the sole cause of inequalities in the opportunity of individuals to defend, or to benefit from the program, should not be permitted to obscure the fact that the state was the motive force in placing the individual ultimately in a position of inequality. The degree of state responsibility in *Griffin* and *Douglas* and in the compensatory education case is so significant as to lead to the conclusion that the state has failed to comply with the Fourteenth Amendment's principle of equality in governmental action.

An analogous question might be raised about the apparent scope of the reading of the equal protection clause suggested in this article. It might be said that this reading places an "affirmative duty" on a state to eliminate *all* economic inequalities between individuals, so that, for example, the state would be required to make monetary grants to individuals in order to make substantially equal the financial status of all persons. It is important, therefore, to point out that whatever may be the merits of the contention that under some circumstances a state has an "affirmative duty" under the Fourteenth Amendment to extend legal "protection" to an individual, the broader aspects of that contention are not involved in the compensatory education problem. The problem here deals only with a governmental program in which the recipients of the benefits of the program are compelled to participate, and in which the consequences of comparatively lower quality benefits to some persons are of the most serious magnitude. . . .

The principle contended for in this article is that a school board denies disadvantaged children the equal protection of the laws if, having a "rational basis" to do so, it fails to provide them with an educational program as well designed to permit achievement to the full extent of their capacities as it provides to other children. There would be no unique problem for a court in applying such a principle: the question would be whether there were any rationally based alternatives which the school board had not utilized, and, if there were, the issuance of a decree requiring the board (not the court, it should be noted) to develop a plan for utilization of such alternatives. . . .

Is there any difference between requiring compensatory education "unless there was no available rationally based way to do so"—the standard proposed by Professor Horowitz—and the "needs" standard rejected in *McInnis*? If the relationship between resources and outcomes were less clear-cut than Professor Horowitz posits, how would his constitutional argument be affected? Does Horowitz persuade you that the judgments he would have courts make are "no different in nature from those courts are customarily called upon to make"?

4. Judicial Enforceability

Could a decision upholding the needs standard have been enforced? Consider the following excerpt, written before the case was decided.

"EQUAL EDUCATIONAL OPPORTUNITY: THE LIMITS OF
CONSTITUTIONAL JURISPRUDENCE UNDEFINED"
Kurland
35 U Chi L Rev 583, 592, 598-600 (1968)

I suggest that the ingredients for success of any fundamental decision based on the equal protection clause are three, at least two of which must be present each time for the court's will to prevail beyond its effect on the immediate parties to the lawsuit. The first requirement is that the constitutional standard be a simple one. The second is that the judiciary have adequate control over the means of effectuating enforcement. The third is that the public acquiesce—there is no need for agreement, simply the absence of opposition—in the principle and its application. . . .

Complex problems—and the deficiencies of our educational system are certainly those—do not lend themselves to ready solution by judicial fiat. . . .

Are there values to be achieved by a Supreme Court decision that would merely state the goal to which we aspire, even if it did not help to achieve it? Certainly there are arguments to be made for such a decision. "The public has come to expect the court to intervene against gross abuses. And so the court must intervene.". . .

It might be said that some part of our government certainly should seek a solution to the deplorable educational conditions that exist. A display of national conscience by those who have appointed themselves to display the national conscience could supply the symbol or banner round which men of good will could rally forces to fight the good fight.

It might be argued that the Supreme Court of the United States is really the schoolmaster of the Republic and if it cannot command, it can at least educate the American people about what they need to do to improve the educational systems of the country.

Finally, it might be said that if the evils of the present system are not reduced by such a Supreme Court decision, they are not likely to be aggravated by such a judgment, so there is everything to gain and nothing to lose.

There are, however, difficulties with these propositions as well . . . [R]eal harm can come from a futile display of morality by the court by raising expectations that cannot be met. . . .

A court that has used up much of its credit in the bank of public confidence is not likely to provide such leadership. Much of the civil strife that has wracked the nation in recent years has been blamed on the failure of government to keep its promises . . . . [D]isrespect for law is mounting. An empty Supreme Court decision would certainly not help.

Finally, one of the difficulties with resort to litigation to solve such problems as confront us is that we thereby tend to absolve from responsibility those more competent and appropriate to afford solutions. The federal and state executives have the resources for the necessary research to develop appropriate answers. . . . The national and state legislatures have the capacities to supply the wherewithal to put the plans into effect. The judiciary has neither. Responsibility is a concomitant of power. Let's place the responsibility where it belongs. Let's permit the states an opportunity to experiment with different answers to these difficult problems and free them to undertake the experiment. Perhaps after a consensus has been developed as to what the right answer is, or the right answers are, the Supreme Court will be in a position to put them into effect. As of now, I think it is too early for the court to announce the doctrine of equal educational opportunity. . . .

Who appears to have the better of the Kurland-Horowitz argument with respect to implementation? Professor Kurland suggests that an "empty" court decision—*i.e.* one that does not "solve" the problem it addresses—is not useful judicial activity. What might be the effects of a constitutionally mandated "needs" standard? Even if such a standard were unenforceable in full, what impact might its declaration have on educational budget making? On popular perceptions of the schools' responsibility? On the "equality" and "rising expectations" revolutions? Do these effects justify adoption of the "needs" approach?

B. The Policy Problem

1. Is a Needs/Outcomes Standard Desirable?

As the preceding section suggests, defining "needs" is a tricky business, a fact that may suggest the wisdom of judicial nonintervention. But does it make sense in terms of educational policy to define educational opportunity in "needs" terms? Consider the following excerpt:

a. The "Outcomes" Model

SCHOOLS AND INEQUALITY
J. Guthrie, G. Kleindorfer, H. Levin, and R. Stout
219-221 (1971)

Defining Equality of Educational Opportunity. In our society's present race for "spoils" not all runners begin at the same starting line . . . [C]hildren from higher SES [socioeconomic status] circumstances presently begin life with many advantages. Their home environment, health care, nutrition, material possessions, and geographic mobility provide them with a substantial headstart when they begin schooling at age five or six. Lower SES children begin school with more physical disabilities and less psychological preparation for adjusting to the procedures of schooling. This condition of disadvantage is then compounded by having to attend schools characterized by fewer and lower-quality services.

What must we do to compensate for these disparities and provide equality of opportunity? What actions are implied in such a goal? In responding to these questions it is important from the outset to make clear that we are *referring to equality of opportunity among groups of individuals,* that is, by race, socioeconomic status, residence in city or suburb, and so on. We recognize fully that genetic differences and variations in other characteristics among individuals *within* such groups will continue to promote intragroup differences in attainment. However, we reject explicitly the idea of inevitable differences *among* groups with regard to the equality of their opportunity. Equality of opportunity implies strongly that a representative individual of any racial or social grouping has the same probability of success as a representative individual of any other racial or social grouping. Stated in another way, given equality of opportunity, there should be a random relationship between the social position of parents and the lifetime attainments of their offspring.

We believe strongly that the task of the school is to equalize opportunities among different social groupings by the end of the compulsory schooling period. This belief is reinforced by the fact that Michigan requires all minors to attend schools until age sixteen. Implied in this mandate is the view that formal schooling will enable representative youngsters from all social and racial groups to begin their postschool careers with equal chances of success. . . . Our society would wish that representative children of each social grouping begin their adult lives with equal chance of success in matters such as pursuing further schooling, obtaining a job, and participating in the political system. It would seem that equality of educational opportunity could be interpreted in no other way.

The excerpt from *Schools and Inequality* focuses on schooling *outcomes,* while our previous analysis has assessed the appropriateness of a *needs* standard. Are the two functionally distinguishable? The needs standard nominally directs our attention to educational resources, suggesting that these must vary in accord with the varying characteristics of students. But how does one know whether needs have been satisfied until one determines the effects of such resource variation on outcomes? Professor Horowitz specifies, on pp 538-40, the needs-outcomes nexus: his proffered constitutional standard would require an educational program designed to assure that children achieve "to the full extent of their capacities." 13 *UCLA L Rev* at 1171. That approach does not carry us as far as that of *Schools and Inequality*: Professor Horowitz presumably would accept variations among class and racial groups if the educational program satisfied his criterion. In both instances, however, educational outcomes are the standard against which the success of a policy (or court decision) is measured.

b. The "Classic" Model. The argument advanced by the authors of *Schools and Inequality* differs notably from the historic view of equality. As Daniel Bell notes:

> The principle of equality of opportunity derives from a fundamental tenet of classic liberalism: that the individual—and not the family, the community, or the state—is the basic unit of society, and that the purpose of societal arrangements is to allow the individual the freedom to fulfill his own purposes. . . . It was assumed that individuals will differ—in their natural endowments, in their energy, drive, and motivation, in their conception of what is desirable—and that the institutions of society should establish procedures for regulating fairly the competition and exchanges necessary to fulfill these diverse desires and competences. (Bell, "On Meritocracy and Equality," *The Public Interest* 29, 40 (Fall 1972).)

Does the historic approach describe the way in which society has operated? Does it pay too little attention to the desire—and capacity—of high-status parents to pass on their positions to their children? Does it ignore the function of luck as a determinant of success? Does it instill in society a competitive feeling that damages those who succeed and, even more so, those who fail? See generally C. Jencks, *Inequality: A Reassessment of the Effect of Family and Schooling in America* (1972).

What are the consequences—in education and more generally with respect to the distribution of social goods—of choosing one or the other approaches as a basis for social policy?

c. Assessing the "Outcomes" Model. Consider the following discussion of the outcomes or "socialist model" of educational policy.

"EQUAL EDUCATIONAL OPPORTUNITY AND THE COURTS"
M. Yudof
51 *Tex L Rev* 411, 420-22 (1973)

The socialist model views schooling as a process designed to sever what is deemed to be an illegitimate relationship between family background—race and class—and educational success. The model assumes that the capacity to learn is randomly distributed between races and socioeconomic groups, and cites the nonrandom distribution of success and failure in public school as proof that poor and minority group children are not performing to their full capacities. A properly functioning educational system is one in which failure—poor achievement and lack of access to further schooling—cannot be correlated with race, class, or wealth. Significantly, an educational system that treated all students shabbily would satisfy the socialist model. The target evil is discrimination and not the deprivation of an essential right.

The socialist model further assumes that everyone accepts a single definition of educational success. Test scores measure educational performance, high test scores allow access to additional years of schooling, and both are prerequisites to the good life—that is, status and income. In the words of one commentator, "the value of education is seen as instrumental, leading to ends extrinsic from the processes of formal instruction itself. We get an education *now* so that at some *later* time we can earn money, vote intelligently, raise children, serve our country and the like." The socialist model rejects a healthy pluralism of educational ends in favor of a single goal—improved achievement as measured by tests. Arguments about the possible cultural bias of the most commonly used tests and about the efficacy of school performance as a predictor of life performance are disregarded. The untestable aims of education—instilling a sense of community, maximizing individual liberty, creating self-respect, and fostering intellectual growth—are ignored.

The boldest assumptions of the socialist model, the ones most directly affecting judicial intervention, are as follows: first, that our technology can identify precisely what factors affect schooling outcomes; second, that there are experts who can and will perform this function; and third, that society is obliged to heed the advice of these experts in formulating the scope of constitutional rights. Defining the ideal school system as one that eliminates differences in achievement arising from racial and socioeconomic background factors, the socialist model assumes that we know how to intervene in the schooling process to bring about that result.

Professor Yudof cites the passage from *Schools and Inequality* as representative of the socialist model. Is his description fair? Does that model necessarily insist on outcome equalization as the "single goal" of education? If the socialist model also attended to other educational goals, would Professor Yudof's objections be met? Would yours?

Assume that the educational technology required to carry out the goal of the socialist model—equalization of schooling outcomes, across racial and class lines—does exist. As a matter of policy, if not of constitutional law, should the model be implemented? What costs does the model impose in terms of state coercion of child behavior demanded to attain the desired outcome? Does the socialist model imply that cultural differences must be obliterated? Recall Frances Wright's proposed universal nursery, discussed in chapter 1. Do the two suggestions raise analogous problems?

2. Is a Needs/Outcomes Standard Feasible: the Coleman Report and the Critics

Several of the scholars whose views were assessed in the preceding two notes assume that, in Professor Yudof's words, "Our technology can identify precisely what factors can affect schooling outcomes" (51 *Tex L Rev* 411 at 422); that there is a known relationship between resources and outcomes. As the following materials suggest, that relationship is not well understood; and the effect of school resources (teacher experience, textbooks, and the like) on outcomes seems minimal when compared with the effect of extraschool resources (family social background and the social class of fellow students).

a. The Coleman Report. In 1964, pursuant to §402 of the 1964 Civil Rights Act, the US Office of Education undertook a "survey . . . concerning the lack of availability of equal educational opportunities. . . ." It was the second largest social science research project in history: background and achievement test data for some 570,000 pupils, information concerning some 60,000 teachers and 4,000 school facilities was gathered by a group headed up by sociologist James S. Coleman.

The conclusions of *Equality of Educational Opportunity Survey* (1966) (usually referred to, and hereafter cited, as the Coleman Report) are surprising on several counts. First, the differences in resources available to minority and white students are small, and while on balance the differences favor the whites, that is not always the case. This pattern seems to hold true in the South—still largely segregated at the time of the report—as well as elsewhere in the nation. Some notable differences between minority and white schools do, however, emerge: minority schools have less academic and accelerated instruction, were less likely to be accredited, and the teachers of minorities had lower verbal test scores than the teachers of whites. And regional differences in resource availability persist: Southern schools are generally less well endowed than schools elsewhere. Professors Mosteller and Moynihan, commenting on this data, observe: "in 1966 the nation had come much closer to achieving [the] classical notion of equality of educational opportunity [equality of resources] than most of us realized then or realize now." Mosteller and Moynihan, "A Pathbreaking Report," in *On Equality of Educational Opportunity*, 3, 11-12 (1972)(hereafter referred to as Mosteller and Moynihan).

Second, and even more interesting, the Coleman Report analyzed "the relation of variation in school facilities to variation in levels of academic achievement. It reported *so little relation as to make it almost possible to say there was none.*" *Coleman Report*, 15 (emphasis added). School expenditures, exposure to schooling, facilities (rooms per teacher, laboratories and the like), access to libraries or textbooks, class size, teacher background and training—none of these input measures had much effect on student outcomes. Pupil-teacher ratio showed so little relationship to achievement that it was dropped from the final analysis. District per pupil instructional expenditure for grades six, nine, and twelve accounted for a mere .09 percent of the "variance" in educational achievement of Negro students in the North, and .29 percent for white northerners.

What do these findings mean? The popular, but incorrect, reading of the Coleman Report is that schools "don't make any difference." As Professors Mosteller and Moynihan rightly note: "This is absurd. Schools make a very great difference to children. Children don't think up algebra on their own. . . . But given that schools have reached their present levels of quality, the observed variation in schools were reported by EEOR to have little affect upon school achievement." Mosteller and Moynihan, 21.

Certain resources do affect school achievement. The student's home background (including region, degree of urbanization, socioeconomic status, and ethnic group) was found to be the primary determinant of school success; that variable, however, is largely unreachable by any school policy. Student achievement also varied with the social class of other students in the school: children of low socioeconomic status appeared to benefit significantly from exposure to more affluent and more highly motivated peers. But the general picture that emerged from the Coleman Report was clear and discouraging. "[S]chools receive children who already differ widely in their levels of educational achievement. The schools thereafter do not close the gaps between students aggregated into ethnic/racial groups. Things end much as they begin." Mosteller and Moynihan, 21. The following table reporting achievement test scores, drawn from the summary of the Coleman Report, illustrates the point.

b. Responses to Coleman Report. The chief finding of the Coleman Report—that "the schools are remarkably similar in the way they relate to the achievement of their pupils when the socioeconomic background of the students is taken into account," (*Coleman Report*, 21)—was viewed as "literally of revolutionary significance." Nichols, "Schools and the Disadvantaged," 154 *Science* 1312, 1314 (December 9, 1966). The report challenged the basic assumptions of many professional educators whose concern has generally focused on school achievement, and for that reason it aroused significant professional opposition. Scholars criticized the report on methodological grounds: it was suggested that the way in which input/outcome relationships were calculated was structured to minimize the importance of school factors; the sample was not properly done; there were too many nonresponses and too many districts that refused to cooperate with the survey. The most detailed criticism concluded:

> We have attempted to show that both the measurement of school resources and the control of social background of the student were inadequate, and that the statistical techniques used were inappropriate. By no means do we wish to suggest that the actual relations are the opposite of what the report concludes or that further research will not substantiate some of the report's findings; but until better evidence is found, we will have to remain agnostic about which relationships prevail. (Bowles and Levin, "The Determinants of Scholastic Achievement—An Appraisal of Some Recent Evidence," 3 *J Human Resources* 3, 23 (1968).)

The Coleman Report data was reanalyzed over a four-year period by a group of Harvard social scientists. Christopher Jencks, who examined resource/outcome relationships for northern urban schools, noted:

Nationwide median test scores for first- and twelfth-grade pupils

Test	Racial or ethnic group					
	Puerto Ricans	Indian-Americans	Mexican-Americans	Oriental-Americans	Negro	Majority
First grade:						
Nonverbal	45.8	53.0	50.1	56.6	43.4	54.1
Verbal	44.9	47.8	46.5	51.6	45.4	53.2
Twelfth grade:						
Nonverbal	43.3	47.1	45.0	51.6	40.9	52.0
Verbal	43.1	43.7	43.8	49.6	40.9	52.1
Reading	42.6	44.3	44.2	48.8	42.2	51.9
Mathematics	43.7	45.9	45.5	51.3	41.8	51.8
General information	41.7	44.7	43.3	49.0	40.6	52.2
Average of 5 tests	43.1	45.1	44.4	50.1	41.1	52.0

(1) Eliminating all school-to-school differences in mean achievement would only reduce the overall inequality of sixth-grade academic outcomes by 16 to 22 percent in the urban North. [In other words, 78 to 84 percent of the differences lie within, not among, schools.]

(2) Only a handful of the school policies and resources measured in the EEOS were appreciably related to the racial and socioeconomic backgrounds of urban sixth graders. [In other words, there is little correspondence between school resources and student characteristics, thus making it impossible to disentangle the effects of the two types of factors.]

(3) Differences in achievement among students from the same socioeconomic and racial background were not related to most of the school characteristics measured in the EEOS. This was especially true of reading and math achievement. Where achievement was associated with a school characteristic, the nature and direction of causality were almost always in doubt. [Some resources, such as library books, appear to be associated with *lower* achievement.]

(4) Ninety percent of the variation in northern urban elementary schools' mean verbal achievement, 85 percent of the variation in their mean math achievement, and 80 percent of the variation in their mean reading achievement were accounted for by region, racial composition, and socioeconomic composition. An additional 2 or 3 percent could probably be accounted for by variations in initial ability. (Jencks, "The Coleman Report and the Conventional Wisdom," in *On Equality of Educational Opportunity,* 69, 104-5 (F. Mosteller and D. Moynihan eds 1972).

c. The Needs/Outcome Standard Reconsidered. The Coleman Report and its reanalyses do not—indeed, could not—resolve all questions about the relationship between school resources and academic success. Its methodology has been faulted, but the reanalysis, which took into account many of the criticisms leveled at the original statistical approaches, reached conclusions generally consistent with the report's findings. Since the report is a snapshot of the resource-outcomes relationship at a single point in time, it could not examine gains over time as might be done by comparing resources and performance over a number of grades. The report does not closely examine variations in resources *within* schools where, as Professor Jencks notes, most achievement variation occurs; one such resource variation, the ability grouping of students, is discussed in chapter 7. Finally, a full understanding of the nexus between outcomes and resources may well depend on large-scale experiments conducted with rigid controls, a politically unlikely prospect.

What further research on the resource-outcomes relationship should be conducted? Professor Coleman himself suggests one approach: he distinguishes between "inputs as disbursed by the school system and inputs as received by the child."

[A] school board can spend identical amounts on textbooks in two different schools . . . so that inputs as disbursed by school boards are identical. But if texts depreciate more rapidly, through loss and lack of care, in one school or one system than the other, then the text as received by a given child [in a later year] constitutes a *lesser* input of educational resources to him than if he were in the other school. . . . Thus even the apparently simple study of input resources becomes a rather complex one if it is viewed as it should be—neither solely from the viewpoint of the administrator as distributor of resources, nor solely from the viewpoint of the child as recipient, but from the viewpoints of both. (Coleman, "The Evaluation of *Equality of Educational Opportunity*," in *On Equality of Educational Opportunity*, 146, 151-52 (F. Mosteller and D. Moynihan eds 1972).)

What other issues are left unanswered by the Coleman Report and its reanalyses? In light of what is presently known about the resources-outcomes relationship, does the needs-outcome standard seem simply unimplementable? For further discussion of these questions, see (in addition to the references cited earlier in this note) *Equal Educational Opportunity* (Harvard Educational Review eds 1969); Cain and Watts, "Problems in Making Policy Inferences from the Coleman Report," 35 *Am Soc Rev* 228 (1970); H. Averch et al, *How Effective Is Schooling?* (1971).

Is it clear that disparities in income and job status would be reduced, if educational outcomes were equalized across race and social class lines? Christopher Jencks concludes his reanalysis of the Coleman Report data by observing: "If and when we develop a comprehensive picture of inequality in American life, we will find that educational inequality is of marginal importance. Such things as control over capital, occupational specialization, and the traditions of American politics will turn out to be far more important." Jencks, "The Coleman Report and the Conventional Wisdom," in *On Equality of Educational Opportunity*, 69, 105 (1972); cf. R. Herrnstein, *IQ in the Meritocracy* (1973). If equalizing educational outcomes turns out to have little effect on other measures of social success, does that suggest that policy research should focus primarily on intraschool, rather than interschool inequalities? That educational policy decisions are simply inconsequential?

C. The Judicial Response Revisited

SERNA v PORTALES MUNICIPAL SCHOOLS
351 F Supp 1279 (DNM 1972)

Mechem, J.

Plaintiffs are minors of Spanish-surnamed heritage represented by their parents in this suit which they have brought as a class action. They seek declaratory and injunctive relief, invoking jurisdiction here under 28 USC §1343, 2201 and 2203. Plaintiffs assert that defendants have discriminated against them and the members of the class they claim to represent in failing to provide learning opportunities which satisfy both their educational and social needs. They claim deprivation of due process and equal protection guaranteed by the Fourteenth Amendment of the United States Constitution and of their statutory rights under Title VI of the Civil Rights Act of 1964, specifically §601 (42 USC §2000(d)).

The city of Portales is divided by railroad tracks. The Spanish-surnamed population is concentrated on the north side of these tracks. One of the city's four elementary schools, Lindsey School, is located in that area. For the 1971-1972 school year Lindsey School had a student enrollment of 86.7 percent Spanish-surnamed students. The ethnic composition of the three elementary schools south of the tracks, Brown, James and Steiner, during the same year was predominately Anglo, with 78 percent to 88 percent Anglo enrollment. Spanish-surnamed children comprise 34.5 percent of the student population of the four elementary schools in the Portales school district. There is one junior high school and one senior high school in the district. The junior high school enrollment is 70.2 percent Anglo and 28.8 percent Spanish-surnamed. In the senior high school, 82 percent of the students are Anglo and slightly over 17 percent are Spanish-surnamed.

The focal point of this action pivots around the education offered in the Lindsey School where the Spanish-surnamed children comprise a large majority. While plaintiffs assert that educational discrimination exists throughout the Portales school system, it is alleged to be most evident at Lindsey. Plaintiffs claim discrimination is the result of an educational program within the Portales school system which is tailored to educate the middle-class child from an English-speaking family without regard for the educational needs of the child from an environment where Spanish is the predominant language spoken. Such a program, it is claimed, is a denial of equal educational opportunity to the Spanish-surnamed children.

Plaintiffs do not claim that the program in the Lindsey School is inferior to that offered in any other school within the district. In fact plaintiffs contend that the educational program at Lindsey is substantially the equivalent of that offered at the Brown, James and Steiner schools. It is the similarity of these programs which is the crux of plaintiffs claim of inequality of educational opportunity. . . .

Defendant school district asserts that the [pilot bilingual-bicultural] programs which have been established at Lindsey and the increase in the number of teachers with a Spanish surname indicate its awareness of the needs of the Spanish-surnamed children and constitutes sufficient affirmative action to remedy whatever deficiencies may have existed. The evidence presented, however, indicates that the achievement of children at Lindsey is consistently lower than that of the children attending the other three elementary schools. IQ tests administered to fifth-grade students in the four Portales municipal elementary schools reveal that the children at Lindsey scored approximately 13 percent lower than children at James and approximately 8 percent lower than children at Steiner. In language expression, Lindsey students were two and one-half years behind James students and 1.3 years behind the national norm. . . .

Testimony by an educational psychologist established that in his opinion language difficulties accounted for 80 percent to 85 percent of the differences indicated in achievement testing. He stated that the reading ability of the average child at Lindsey was 1.7 years behind the national norm.

Evidence relating to IQ test scores of children in the Portales school system was admitted at the trial with the recognition that such scores are not conclusive indicia of student achievement or failure. What becomes apparent from an examination of these scores, however, is that the performance of the children at every level at Lindsey School is not what it should be when compared with the performance of students at the other schools. Coupled with the testimony of educational experts regarding the negative impact upon Spanish-surnamed children when they are placed in a school atmosphere which does not adequately reflect the educational needs of this minority, as is found to be the situation in the Portales schools, the conclusion becomes inevitable that these Spanish-surnamed children do not in fact have equal educational opportunity and that a violation of their constitutional right to equal protection exists.

The administrators of the Portales school district are aware of these conditions, have taken some steps to alleviate the problem, and have made positive improvements. These corrections, however, are not adequate. Under these circumstances, it is incumbent upon the school district to reassess and enlarge its program directed to the specialized needs of its Spanish-surnamed students at Lindsey and also to establish and operate in adequate manner programs at the other elementary schools where no bilingual-bicultural program now exists. . . .

[I] t would be a deprivation of equal protection for a school district to effectuate a curriculum which is not tailored to the educational needs of minority students. . . . The promulgation and institution of a program by the Portales school district which ignores the needs of such students does constitute state action.

Defendant school district also contends that it is seriously restricted by its operating budget in expanding its bilingual-bicultural programs. Evidence at the trial established that there are sources of funds [from both the federal government and the state of New Mexico] available to implement and maintain such programs. . . . Defendant school district is directed to investigate and utilize wherever possible the sources of available funds to provide equality of educational opportunity for its Spanish-surnamed students.

It is also claimed that an obstacle to expanding bilingual-bicultural programs in the Portales school system is the absence of qualified teachers. Defendant school district has made an effort to recruit and has recruited Spanish-speaking teachers. It points to the fact that it has received few applications from such teachers and that the teacher turnover in the Portales Municipal Schools is relatively low. However great the effort, this is not an acceptable justification for not providing specialized programs where the deprivation of them violates a constitutional right and where funding is available. It is incumbent upon the school district to increase its recruiting efforts and, if those recruiting efforts are unsuccessful, to obtain sufficient certification of Spanish-speaking teachers to allow them to teach in the district.

Jurisdiction over this action will be retained for ninety days from the date of entry of this memorandum opinion so as to enable the Portales school district to submit to the court its plans for remedial action to be undertaken by the defendant in compliance with the requirements set forth in this opinion.

Notes and Questions

1. Needs and Outcomes

Serna was decided three years after the the Supreme Court affirmed the *McInnis* decision; no intervening decisions had reversed the court's ruling on "needs." What is the constitutional justification for *Serna*?

The court identifies "harm" by examining achievement and IQ test scores—

both outcome measures. How can the court implement its order to undo this harm? Suppose that five years after implementation of a bilingual-bicultural program Mexican-American students in Portales still do not do as well as their white counterparts. Do those students have a cause of action?

2. Discrimination

Is the fact that plaintiffs are Mexican-Americans pertinent to the decision? Is *Serna* premised on discrimination against a defined ethnic group? Compare *Keyes v Denver School District #1*, 93 Sup Ct 2686 (1973). If so, do the facts justify the premise?

3. Problem: the Nonachieving Student

While in school, Johnny Jones is never left back and never receives failing grades. His parents, who are concerned about Johnny's success, are assured by the school system that his performance is adequate. After graduation from high school, Johnny applies for a job but is denied the position because he scores at the fifth-grade level on a standard reading test administered by the prospective employer. Applicable state laws require that all high school graduates attain at least an eighth-grade reading ability. Does Johnny have a cause of action against the school system on either statutory or constitutional grounds? See *Doe v San Francisco Unified School Dist*, Civil No 653-312 (Sup Ct San Francisco, filed November 20 1972); Saretsky and Mecklenburger, "See You in Court?" *Saturday Review* 50 (November 1972).

D. The Congressional Response: Title I of the Elementary and Secondary Education Act of 1965 (20 USC § 241)

Historically, the federal government has played a limited role in financing public instruction. As late as 1959-60, Washington provided only 649 million dollars in educational support. The passage of the Elementary and Secondary Education Act of 1965 dramatically changed the pattern. See generally G. Eidenberg and R. Morey, *An Act of Congress* (1969); P. Meranto, *The Politics of Federal Aid to Education in 1965: A Study in Political Innovation* (1967). While the federal government still provides only 6.6 percent of all school aid, its absolute contribution almost quadrupled to 2.545 billion dollars (1969-70). Johns, "The Development of State Support for the Public Schools" in *Status and Impact of Educational Finance Programs*, 1, 4 (R. Johns, K. Alexander, and D. Stollar eds 1971) (National Educational Finance Project, vol. 14). See generally *Hearings Before the Select Senate Committee on Equal Educational Opportunity*, 92d Cong, pt 17 (October 7, 1971).

Over half of this money—1.6 billion dollars—is committed to Title I of ESEA. Title I is intended to provide additional resources to meet the particular educational needs of poor and "educationally handicapped" children; its aspirations are in many respects similar to those of the *McInnis* plaintiffs. The following excerpt describes the workings of Title I.

"THE NEW DELUDER ACT: A TITLE I PRIMER"
M. Yudof
2 Inequality in Education 1 (December 5, 1969)

Purposes of Title I

In enacting a novel federal statute which imposed federal educational priorities upon existing state and local structures, Congress, not surprisingly, created a law with diverse and, at times, inconsistent objectives. However, taking the broadest perspective, the purposes of Title I may be accurately represented as those set forth in the declaration of policy which precedes the substantive provisions of the act:

> In recognition of the special educational needs of children of low-income families and the impact that concentrations of low-income families have on the ability of local educational agencies to support adequate educational programs, the Congress hereby declares it to be the policy of the United States to provide financial assistance . . . to local educational agencies serving areas with concentrations of children from low-income families to expand and improve their educational programs by various means (including preschool programs) which contribute particularly to meeting the special educational needs of educationally deprived children. (20 USC §241a)

In other words, while the act was enacted in recognition of the special needs of low-income children and of districts with concentrations of such children, the purpose was to provide financial assistance to districts of high poverty concentration in order to meet the needs of *all educationally deprived children*. This means that a school district establishes its eligibility for Title I funds on the basis of the number of low-income children residing in the district, but that the programs financed by these grants are open to all students whose achievement levels fall below that "appropriate for children of their age," even if they are not poor. Congress apparently assumed a high correlation between educational failure and poverty, and, in order to attack this conjunction, designed the act so that the greater the overlap in a school or a district of poor children and educationally disadvantaged children, the greater the federal expenditure per eligible child.

The Basic Aid Formula

The maximum amount which a local school district is eligible to receive is an amount equal to 50 percent of the average per-pupil expenditure in the state multiplied by the number of children, ages five to seventeen, whose families have an annual income of less than $2000, or whose families have an income in excess of $2000 due to payments from an approved aid to dependent children program, or who are "living in institutions for neglected or delinquent children." (20 USC §241d) The formula may be expressed by the following equation:

$$.50P \ (I+D+N) = E$$

Where: P=Per-pupil expenditure in the state
I=Number of children in families with less than $2000 in income

D=Number of children in families receiving aid to dependent children with incomes in excess of $2000

N=Number of neglected or delinquent children in institutions

E=Maximum entitlement of a local school district

The allocation to which a state is entitled is the sum of the entitlements of the local school districts within a state. While maximum entitlement is calculated according to the above formula, Congress has never appropriated a sum of money for Title I which even approaches the authorized level of expenditure of $2.7 billion. Under these circumstances, the act provides that the allocation to each local district should be "reduced ratably" such that each will receive the same proportionate share of its maximum entitlement. (20 USC §241h) Furthermore, Congress has inserted in recent Title I appropriation bills the proviso that no district may receive less than 92 percent of the amount of Title I payments it received the previous year.

Statutory Criteria for the Approval of Title I Applications

While the state educational authorities have the responsibility of approving or disapproving the local Title I project applications, the states must make their determinations on the basis of criteria established by the act itself and such "basic criteria as the commissioner may establish." (20 USC §241e) Indeed, the state educational agency's application to the commissioner of education must contain assurances that Title I payments are being used for programs which have been approved pursuant to these criteria, and it must "provide for such fiscal control and fund accounting procedures [including state audits] as may be necessary for the proper disbursement of funds paid to the state and to local educational agencies..." (45 CFR §116.48) The commissioner of education may suspend payments to any state which fails to comply substantially with these provisions. (20 USC §241j)

There are eleven requirements for Title I projects stated in the act itself. The most important are:

The projects must be "designed to meet the special educational needs of educationally deprived children in the school attendance areas having high concentrations of children from low-income families," and "of sufficient size, scope, and quality to give reasonable promise of substantial progress toward meeting those needs..."

The local educational agency must make provision for providing educationally deprived children in private schools, including parochial schools, with "special educational services and arrangements." However, the control of funds for private schools and the title to all property purchased with the funds must be in a public agency.

In the case of applications for funds for planning, the planning must be directly related to Title I programs, and the funds must be needed because of "the innovative nature of the program" or "because the local educational agency lacks the resources necessary to plan adequately."

Provision must be made for evaluating the effectiveness of the program in meeting the special educational needs of the eligible children.

The local educational agency must make periodic reports and keep records which will enable the state educational agency to verify the reports and to fulfill its obligations to the commissioner of education.

Procedures must be adopted for acquiring and disseminating information to teachers and administrators with regard to "promising educational practices" developed in the course of Title I projects. (20 USC §241e)

Administrative Criteria for the Approval of Title I Projects

While the statutory criteria embodied in Title I for the approval of projects are useful as broad articulations of federal policy, the politically sensitive task of drawing up concrete standards, which would relate federal priorities to the states and to local school districts, fell to the commissioner of education. . . .

1. Supplement, Not Supplant

The most significant criterion which the commissioner of education promulgated for Title I projects is the requirement that federal appropriations supplement existing state and local expenditures for education, and that the federal funds not be used as a substitute for local funds in order to provide services which would or should be provided without federal assistance. In other words, federal payments must be additive, and purchase educational services for the underprivileged which are not available to the local school population at large. These principles are embodied in a guideline, which, although hardly a model for clarity, is crucial to the achievement of the act's purposes:

> The instructional and ancillary services provided with state and local funds for children in the project areas should be comparable to those provided for children in the nonproject areas, particularly with respect to class size, special services, and the number and variety of personnel. Title I funds, therefore, are not to be used to supplant state and local funds which are already being expended in the project areas or which would be expended in those areas if the services in those areas were comparable to those for nonproject areas. This means that services that are already available or will be made available for children in the nonproject areas should be provided on an equal basis in the project areas with state and local funds, rather than with Title I funds . . . .*

2. Concentration of Funds per Child

The regulations and guidelines provide that Title I resources must be concentrated "on those children who are most in need of assistance," and that "decisions should be made in terms of the effectiveness of providing comprehensive services to a limited number of children in a few groups as opposed to the ineffectiveness of spreading diluted services over all eligible children in all groups." Thus:

---

*The comparability requirement was subsequently written into the Title I legislation: "A local education agency may receive a grant under [Title I] for any fiscal year only upon application therefor approved by the appropriate state educational agency, upon its determination (consistent with such basic criteria as the commissioner may establish) that state and local funds will be used in the district of such agency to provide services in project areas which, taken as a whole, are at least comparable to services being provided in areas in such district which are not receiving funds under [Title I]." 20 USC §241e(a)(3)(C).

The greater the concentration of effort, as indicated by investment per child, the greater the likelihood that the program will have a significant impact on the children in the program. *The investment per child on an annual basis for a program of compensatory educational services which supplement the child's regular school activities should be expected to equal about one-half the expenditures per child from state and local funds for the applicant's regular school program....*

3. Concentration of Funds on Target Areas

The guidelines provide that the attendance areas selected by local educational authorities as sites for Title I programs, the so-called target school populations, should be those areas in which the concentration of children from low-income families is as high or higher than the percentage of such children for the district as a whole. The statutory basis for this requirement is §105(a)(1) of Title I, which provides that the projects must be "designed to meet the special educational needs of educationally deprived children in school attendance areas having high concentrations of children from low-income families." (20 USC §241e) Presumably, this statutory provision was enacted because Congress felt that it was more expensive to educate a low-income child in a school largely composed of low-income children than it was to educate the same child in a school in which most of the students are from a higher socioeconomic background, and that school districts with high concentrations of poor students were likely to have a lower tax base and therefore to have less funds available for educational services. Under both theories, schools in such districts would be in greater need of financial assistance.

The approach adopted by the commissioner of education for identifying attendance areas with high concentrations of low-income children [requires that target areas be] selected on the basis of an intradistrict standard which disregards the vast differences between student populations in urban, suburban, and rural areas. For example, a school located in an urban district in which 50 percent of the students are economically underprivileged may not qualify as a target area if the percentage of such children for the whole district is greater. Conversely, a school located in a suburban area, which is attended by only ten low-income children, comprising barely 1 percent of the student body, is entitled to a Title I program if the percentage for the whole district is no higher. (Ten is the minimum number permitted for a Title I program under the act.) ... [Since] all "educationally deprived children who are in need of the special educational services," regardless of the income levels of their families, may participate in Title I programs, ... the hypothetical suburban school, having identified its small group of low-income children for purposes of entitlement and target designation, may dilute its expenditures per low-income child by opening its program to all the "educational failures" in the target area....

4. Construction Projects and Equipment Purchases

The commissioner of education has determined that Title I programs should be conducted in existing facilities wherever possible since the construction of new school facilities is deemed to be the responsibility of the local school districts. Nonetheless, in instances of extreme need, Title I funds may "be used for construction . . . [in order to] meet the highest priority needs of educationally deprived children. . . ." Furthermore, purchases of equipment are limited "to the minimum required to implement approved Title I activities or services." Evidently, this emphasis on operational expenditures is a corollary to the per-pupil concentration; its thrust is to prevent local districts from making equipment and construction purchases which are likely to benefit the whole student population rather than only the educationally deprived. . . .

Notes and Questions

1. Policy

Is Title I ESEA a legislative effort to define equal opportunity in "needs" terms? Is this effort more appropriate to the Congress than to the courts? Does the preceding section suggest that Title I is doomed to failure? Or is the resources-outcomes data simply too scanty a basis on which to make such judgments? How might one evaluate the success of this program? See J. Wholey, B. White, L. Vogt, and R. Zamoff, *Title I Evaluation and Technical Assistance: Assessment and Prospects* (1971).

Title I requires that funds be "targeted" to schools with high concentrations of poor children. Is that requirement inconsistent with school desegregation policy? With the social science data suggesting that students of a higher socioeconomic status are really the poor child's best "resource"? See *George v O'Kelly* 448 F2d 148 (5th Cir 1971).

Any school district with ten or more poor children—as defined by the statute —is eligible for Title I assistance; in practice, that has meant that almost all school districts receive some Title I aid. As a result, large cities with high concentrations of poor children receive less funds than if this eligibility requirement were more stringent. Are there policy justifications—or political explanations—for the present standard?

2. Noncompliance by School Districts

Within three years of the passage of Title I, reports of noncompliance—produced by both the Office of Education and by outside investigators—were commonplace. School districts were using Title I money for construction, teacher salaries, libraries, and the like—all of which had previously been paid for by state and local funds. Those practices violated supplanting prohibitions and comparability requirements. In many areas, particularly in the South, Title I payments provided predominantly black schools with facilities and services that had been provided (with nonfederal money) to predominantly white schools. Responding to political pressures and a desire to help as many children as possible, school districts spread Title I funds over large groups of eligible children, or over the district at large, violating the concentration requirement. Construction of school buildings and equipment purchases, well beyond the "highest priority needs of educationally deprived children," were commonplace. See Washington Research Project of the Southern Center for Studies in Public Policy and the NAACP Legal Defense and Educational Fund, *Title I of ESEA: Is It Helping Poor Children?* (1969); National Advisory Council on the Education of Disadvantaged Children, Fourth Annual Report, *Title I-ESEA: A Review and a Forward Look*

(1967). For a similar analysis of federal Indian education programs, see NAACP Legal Defense and Educational Fund, with the cooperation of the Center for Law and Education, Harvard University, *An Even Chance* (1971).

Noncompliance with the comparability requirement has been most abundantly and most recently documented. In a 1972 survey of eighty school systems receiving Title I funds, all but one of them had one or more noncomparable schools; one quarter lacked comparability in 80 percent or more of their schools. Over half of the districts surveyed had not even developed a comparability plan for submission to the Office of Education. And the comparability reports that were submitted were often deficient, disorganized, and erroneous. Confusion with respect to which schools should be compared in order to satisfy federal regulations (45 CFR §116.26(d)) also limited the utility of the district reporting. One Nebraska administrator stated: "We do not have a lucid grasp of what comparability entails." More basically, however, objections to the purpose of comparability—assertions that it is unrealistic and limits flexibility—appear to explain noncompliance with this provision. See Lawyers' Committee for Civil Rights Under Law, *Title I Comparability: A Preliminary Evaluation* (1972).

3. Causes of Noncompliance

The following excerpt examines the behavior of federal and state education officials charged with enforcing the Title I, ESEA, requirements. To what extent does it explain the pattern of noncompliance?

"THE EDUCATION BUREAUCRACIES IMPLEMENT NOVEL POLICY:
THE POLITICS OF TITLE I OF ESEA, 1965-72,"
in POLICY AND POLITICS IN AMERICA
JEROME MURPHY
161, 172-183 (A. Sindler ed 1973)

. . . . Federal Administration of Title I: 1965-69

USOE: A State-Oriented Agency. [R]eformers read Title I's intent as assigning resources for the educationally deprived, particularly the poor, while others understood it as providing general aid to education. This disagreement, of course, would have to be "resolved" during the program's administration, and primarily by personnel who had not pushed for Title I in the first place. The executive branch reformers who promoted the passage of ESEA were largely uninvolved in its implementation; they continued to develop and propose new policies in other areas. It fell to USOE officials to administer the program, so that Title I's effectiveness would depend heavily on the USOE's inclination to act aggressively on the managerial and political dimensions of its task.

Federal administration of ESEA was turned over to lower levels in the ninety-eight-year-old USOE. This staff had not influenced the development of Title I, and would have preferred general aid. Lacking experience with grants-in-aid of the size and scope of Title I, the agency had never been called on to write "basic criteria" governing the approval of projects. Herculean efforts to bring in new blood and to be responsive to its ESEA responsibilities produced some changes within USOE. But the "old guard," if not always controlling policy, continued to staff the program and to make the day-to-day decisions setting the tone and much of the substance of the federal operations.

Even if USOE had been less rigid in its attitudes, it did not have enough people to monitor the program effectively. Title I was administered by the Division of Compensatory Education in the Bureau of Elementary and Secondary Education of USOE. Monitoring was carried out by area desk officers, generally professional educators, in the operations branch. . . . By the end of 1969, there were some thirty professionals working on all facets of Title I—technical assistance, accounting, program support—but only three area desk officers for the entire nation. The one dealing with Massachusetts, for example, also had sole responsibility for twenty-three other states. . . .

In addition, the USOE staff had traditionally taken a passive role with respect to the states. USOE's job was to write checks, not to meddle in state and local affairs. "Everything in the bureau was assistance and state-oriented," commented a Title I staffer. "Anytime you mentioned compliance in [bureau chief] Lessinger's presence, he would have a fit.". . . . The area desk officer viewed his job as one of trouble-shooting, answering complaints, and providing service. He did not want to provide leadership, nor did he view himself as a program "monitor" in the sense of being an enforcement officer. He readily admitted that he did not have the time to know what was going on in his states, and thus was dependent on information supplied by state officials as to whether they were enforcing the law. He found the limited staff situation frustrating, not because he was unable to monitor the states, but because he could not give them assistance. . . .

Inaction on Audits of Abuses. Federal audit reviews, conducted by the HEW Audit Agency, constituted another important area of federal responsibility. . . .

These audits disclosed numerous violations of the law across the country. Title I supplied general aid for *all* children in some school districts, rather than focusing on the special needs of the disadvantaged. Title I was used *in place of* state and local funds, rather than adding *supplementary* services in others. In addition, a variety of questionable, if not illegal, purchases were made: classroom carpeting, bedroom sets, football jerseys, air conditioners, and even swimming pools. In the judgment of HEW auditors, the misuse of funds was "severe"; they estimated that it was "substantially greater" than 15 percent of Title I's total allocation. . . . Despite these documented abuses, USOE virtually ignored the audit findings. In the winter of 1969, a backlog of more than thirty audits existed, some of them more than three years old, with no action yet taken and little prospect of reduction.

USOE's Timidity. Why was USOE so hesitant to administer Title I aggressively and to follow up on the audits? Its limited staff and its overall service orientation are important parts of the answer, but other complicating factors also came into play. First, the pressure was on in the early days of Title I for the program to move quickly, to get federal-state relations off on the right foot. Hence there was little disposition to inject conflict by striking at alleged misuses. Second, the administration's need to demonstrate the program's success to the public and the Congress meant that program administrators were obliged to generate favorable statistics on the number of schools involved, the number of children affected, and so forth. Third, there was confusion among Title I staffers as to what stance they should take with the states. Those who wanted to enforce Title I usually received little support from their bureau-level bosses, many of whom believe that Congress "really" meant Title I as general aid. Not coincidentally, many of these officials were philosophically committed to that same goal and viewpoint. Finally, other Title I staffers feared that if USOE pushed too hard, Congress would indeed replace Title I with general aid, in which case USOE would have even less influence over the schooling of the poor. . . .

The states recognized these constraints on USOE's exercise of its authority and realized that orders or threats from USOE were not likely to be backed up with penalties. With USOE's limited influence based on its capacity to persuade and with its small staff almost totally reliant on the states for information about local programs, the states knew it was essential for USOE to maintain cordial relations with them. Exploiting these bargaining conditions, the states could exact a price for their good will. Consequently, USOE was willing to overlook and therefore sanction state/local deviations from the statute in exchange for retention of open communications. Given its dependency position, USOE's service orientation and its deference to local officials can be understood as strategic behavior designed to achieve the greatest possible influence in an environment unsupportive of a more aggressive stance on its part. USOE's problem, then, was not only lack of staff, but primarily the reinforcing weaknesses of lack of will and of political muscle. Like other politicians in similar circumstances, many key federal education administrators were unwilling to take risky actions unless pressure persuaded them that their failure to do so might be no less risky.

Resisting USOE's Initiative: Concentrating the Funds. . . . One of the critical issues addressed in the original draft guidelines was the concentration of limited resources for a limited number of students. Title I officials believed that if the program was to have significant impact, the money could not be spread thin. The original provision in the draft guidelines (fall 1965) stated that the number of children served had to be approximately the same as the number of children counted under the formula for allocating funds. This meant that each of about 5.4 million students would receive about $200 extra for the cost of their education.

This standard came under fire from congressmen and professional interest groups opposed to this effort to concentrate funds. They argued that the standard was inconsistent with congressional intent; the number of children counted for purposes of distributing money had nothing to do with the number of children to be served. They also reminded Commissioner Keppel of the language in the 1965 Senate report which directed USOE not to go beyond the criteria written in the law. In November 1965, the word came down from Commissioner Keppel to "slenderize" the guidelines, and the concentration provision subsequently was removed. More than 8 million children participated the first year with an average expenditure of just under $120. This early defeat of the Division of Compensatory Education's attempt to exert leverage made it clear that federal guidelines and criteria were "fair game" for political intervention in the future.

More than two years after the law was passed, USOE issued the first set of "basic criteria" on April 14, 1967, responding to what the memorandum described as a "definite need" for states to apply specific criteria in approving local projects. Twelve criteria were proposed, backed up by a "supporting statement of the types of evidence or indications that the applicant's proposal should contain. . ." The critera regarding concentration simply stated: "Title I services will be programed so that the services provided will be concentrated on a limited number of children." The supporting discussion, however, established a new standard: "The investment per child on an annual basis for a program of compensatory educational services which supplement the child's regular school activities should be expected to equal about one-half the expenditure per child from state and local funds for the applicant's regular school program." Suppose, for example, that Bayside School District spends $600 each year per pupil. Under the standard, each Title I student would receive an extra $300 in services, making a total of $900 per participating disadvantaged child.

Exactly ten days later, under congressional pressure, the USOE issued a "clarifying" memorandum, which read in part: "The criteria statements are the requirements to be met, whereas the discussion matter *provides guidance* in meeting the criteria. It should be expected, of course, that the discussion guides *may not be fully applicable to every project application.*" [Emphasis added.] Translated, then, the "clarifying" memorandum meant simply that the new standard had been rendered impotent.

Some nineteen months later, not satisfied that funds were being adequately concentrated and disturbed by several evaluations showing Title I's failure to raise achievement test scores, USOE issued another memorandum (November 20, 1968) focused on improving the quality of Title I programs. The draft memorandum that went to Commissioner Harold Howe's desk for signature specifically called for the implementation by 1970 of the initial concentration standard of 1967. At the last minute, the draft was pulled back by the USOE Bureau of Elementary and Secondary Education and revised. Bureau officials, sympathetic to their public school lobbyist friends, were reluctant to impose precise standards on the states. Instead, a hastily drawn statement was inserted: "Plan the program so that by 1970 the average Title I expenditure per child ... *is raised to a significant level*" (emphasis added). Nowhere in the memorandum was "significant level" discussed or the previous standard mentioned. Thus, a memorandum which had begun in the Division of Compensatory Education as an attempt to accomplish greater concentration of resources emerged from the USOE bureaucracy with no standard even as "guidance." In the meantime, dollar expenditures per Title I child were decreasing each year, and 30 percent of the students participating in 1968 were neither educationally nor economically disadvantaged while several million eligible students went unaided. . . .

State Administration of Title I

Despite USOE's failure to gain control over Title I, federal priorities theoretically could be met by state departments of education, which had major responsibility for administering the law and guaranteeing that educationally deprived children benefited from Title I. As noted earlier, the states were authorized to review and approve local projects, monitor and audit ongoing activities, evaluate results and provide leadership in the development of program improvements. Title I's effectiveness, then, depended in large measure on the strength of these state agencies and on their relationships with both federal and local governmental units.

But in 1965 state education agencies varied widely in their capacity to carry out their Title I tasks. A few states had the administrative structure and staff capable of establishing state education priorities and, occasionally, the political support and the will to go beyond federal priorities in implementing Title I vigorously. For most states, however, the administrative apparatus was weak and unable to exercise significant leverage over local school policies. Inadequate staff capability and a strong tradition of localism promoted a general pattern of limited state educational leadership.

The Massachusetts Department of Education certainly was no exception to this pattern of weakness. A 1970 study found: "The department of education, for many reasons, continues to carry out a wide variety of mandated functions, most of which have little to do with educational leadership or which have any visible impact on improving quality of education for students in our schools." While Massachusetts' handling of Title I may not necessarily be typical, an examination of its problems highlights important political, bureaucratic, and intergovernmental barriers to Title I's implementation that are found in many states.

Management of Massachusetts' Title I. Each year from 1966 to 1969 Massachusetts school districts received approximately $16 million to support about 420 Title I projects in some 325 school districts. An average of about 100,000 children participated annually in these locally determined projects. The overall program was administered by a Title I unit in the Bureau of Elementary and Secondary Education in the Massachusetts Department of Education.

Although the state had major responsibility for administering the law, the Title I unit adopted an essentially passive attitude, leaving almost total program discretion to local school districts. Robert L. Jefferey, Massachusetts' Title I director, saw his job mainly as that of a consultant providing technical assistance and service to local schoolmen. This entailed regional meetings, workshops, and "helpful" visits to local Title I projects. But it did not entail an insistence on strict adherence to the law. In effect, Jeffery was . . . reluctant to interfere with local prerogatives . . .; he saw his role vis-à-vis local districts—a service role—the same way that his federal counterparts perceived their role toward Massachusetts. . . .

[L]axity at the local level sometimes came to light through state visits to schools. State officials selectively monitored projects, especially those receiving more than $100,000 a year under Title I. But state officials often were reluctant to take strong action, even when they knew that the law and regulations were being loosely "interpreted." For example, Boston was permitted to spend Title I on *all* children in some target schools, despite a regulation that the money must be expended for supplementary services for those children identified as most in need. This was "blatant general aid," noted one unusually outspoken state official. Subtler violations of law were either ignored or never uncovered by the state. Some Boston schools, for instance, did go through the ritual of identifying the neediest educationally deprived children. According to the Boston criteria, a child had to perform below the so-called sixth stanine to be eligible for Title I assistance. This sounded objective, official, and educationally sound. But, in fact, this criterion opened the program to students performing *above* average for the nation, hardly those most in need. In short, the state's project approval procedures and subsequent monitoring were not effective in preventing local misuse of funds. Localities could pursue their own priorities, even if the law was stretched in the process, without fear of being called to account by the state.

The department's financial management procedures were equally weak. A 1969 HEW audit report on Massachusetts found that for the fiscal years 1966,

1967, and 1968 the department allowed Title I allotments of more than $1 million to lapse each year because of ineffective management. The audit concluded that "significant improvements in procedures and practices are needed at both the state and local levels. . . ."

The absence of adequate state audit procedures also precluded close scrutiny of the program. Although three auditors were paid with Title I funds, only one actually audited local projects. Working slowly without written procedures, he was unable to cope with the backlog of unaudited projects. As of November of 1968, less than one-third of the 1967 projects and none of the 1968 projects had ever been audited. . . .

A similar pattern existed in the state's execution of its responsibilities for program evaluation. Title I required local districts to make annual evaluation reports to the states, including "appropriate objective measurements of educational achievement." Unlike previous federal programs, this provision called for the public disclosure of information which schoolmen knew might be used against them in the enforcement of new priorities. It also strained many local and state education units which had little evaluation experience or capability. Not surprisingly, persistent resistance to providing full and objective evaluation was evident. After all, in the absence of evaluation, local districts could meet their own priorities without being subject to challenge based on evidence of failure.

A 1970 study found that less than half of the local projects sampled had an evaluation design at all and that two of every three had made little effort to analyze their evaluation data. In keeping with that pattern, the Title I director did not turn down projects because of failure to show success. On evaluation standards as with enforcement, then, the Massachusetts department related to local districts as the federal level related to the states: little direction.

An Explanation of the Massachusetts Pattern. The weakness in Massachusett's management of Title I implementation by local school districts—in project approvals, monitoring, auditing, and program evaluation—can be traced to several factors. Title I was a new and complicated program thrust on a weak department, unfamiliar with managing large-scale programs. . . .

The root causes of Massachusetts' limited attempt to impose federal priorities go deeper than even these severe management problems. In America's federal system, states are independent entities with their own sources of political support. They have no incentive to enforce federal directives conflicting with state priorities unless they are suitably penalized or rewarded for such action. But such penalties and rewards were not part of the Title I program. The states received their full entitlement of funds by simply "assuring" USOE that the law would be followed, as opposed to having to submit an approvable plan, produce some specified result, or do a good job by some agreed-on measures. Although *legally* USOE could cut off funds for violations of the law, state officials knew that USOE *politically* was reluctant to do so.

Not only were compliance incentives missing, but the states received mixed signals from Washington on what they were expected to comply with. Whether USOE saw Title I as a program providing supplementary services for the disadvantaged or really as general aid to education remained unclear. . . . Knowing that USOE directives would not likely be enforced stringently, Jeffery and other

Massachusetts education administrators felt free, in turn, to follow those policies helpful to the state department and to slight the others.

The Massachusetts department was no more able or willing to impose its priorities on local districts than USOE was to dictate to Massachusetts. The formula grant system, by eliminating competition for Title I funds, weakened the state's bargaining position as it did USOE's. And the kind of individuals administering the state program were like USOE's veteran staffers. They viewed themselves as professional educators assisting their professional colleagues on the local firing line. The role of an enforcer or a regulator, of monitoring and reviewing the judgment of their local peers, was repugnant to them.

The historical dedication in Massachusetts to local school autonomy also constricted state action, whether in the form of implementing federal priorities or their own. Local school control is *"The Battle Hymn of the Republic of New England educators,"* noted Jeffery. In the absence of strong pressure from USOE, the Massachusetts department could not buck local autonomy even if it wanted to. Consequently, the department was virtually deprived of leverage to control local Title I expenditures. Implementation depended on local priorities which often differed from those of the federal and state governments. . . .

4. Pressure for Compliance: Inside and Outside the Office of Education

HEW responded to reports of noncompliance by creating an internal task force. In their final (still unpublished) report, the task force found "considerable evidence" that the Office of Education was not "meeting its management responsibilities." At the task force's urging, thirty new federal positions were authorized for Title I. Between July 1970 and July 1972, the Title I staff visited every state, an unprecedented undertaking; the visits were followed by letters calling for specific "corrective actions." The Title I office also requested the return of almost ten million dollars in misspent funds; as of late 1972, less than 1 percent had been returned. For further discussion of the Office of Education's role in implementing Title I, see S. Bailey and E. Mosher, *ESEA: The Office of Education Administers a Law* (1968).

The noncompliance data also encouraged community groups, as well as their attorneys, to press for educational programs that were both consistent with legal mandate and, more importantly, responsive to parent-perceived needs. Two sources of pressure—parent involvement in Title I program planning, required by Title 1 guidelines, and litigation—were employed, sometimes in tandem.*

Title I guidelines permitted local school districts to develop their own framework for parental involvement. Community groups pressed for parent advisory councils with limited success; Massachusetts made such councils mandatory in 1970, but its example was not taken up by other states. A proposed congressional amendment to the legislation mandating such councils was rejected in 1970; one influential guardian of local school autonomy, Congresswoman Edith Green (D, Ore), led the fight to have the "extremely obnoxious" provision deleted. The revised legislation did authorize the commissioner to promulgate guidelines for

*Similar attention was focused on the National School Lunch Act, 42 USC §1751, et seq. See *Briggs v Kerrigan* 431 F2d 967 (1st Cir 1970); *Davis v Robinson* 346 F Supp 847 (DRI 1972); Note, "The National School Lunch Program, 1970: Mandate to Feed the Children," 60 *Geo LJ* 711 (1972).

parent involvement. A broad coalition—ranging from the League of Women Voters to the National Welfare Rights Organization—was able to counter the views of state and local school agencies; largely as a result of that coalition's efforts system-wide parent advisory councils were made mandatory, and their members were guaranteed broad rights of access to Title I project information (36 Fed Reg 20015, 20016 (1971); 45 CFR 116.1-116.26).

It is unclear, however, whether that legal mandate has generally been carried out. In Massachusetts, for example, a report issued several months after the adoption of parent participation guidelines found that "election procedures were determined solely by local school officials, that elections were rigged, that information and technical assistance were not being provided, and that, as a general proposition, the state department of education was not monitoring compliance with the law." League of Women Voters of Massachusetts in Cooperation with the Massachusetts Title I Task Force, "Unkept Promises to the Children of the Poor," 10 (1971).

The community groups also turned to their lawyers in attempting to promote compliance with Title I. A host of cases were filed—in Maine, Rhode Island, New York, New Mexico, and Washington, among other states—and most of these were settled out of court, on terms favorable to the plaintiffs. For example, in *Cantu v Saunders,* Civ No 2773 (ED Wash, settlement filed July 1973), the school district agreed to limit Title I participation to eligible children, to use Title 1 funds only for approved activities, to limit equipment purchases, to accept a state audit of the local program, and to create a parents' advisory committee. The committee—whose members are to be nominated by Title I parents—is given broad authority to recommend educational programs, including the authority to appeal disagreements between parents and school administrators to the state superintendent of public instruction. The few court decisions concerning Title I violations have generally accepted the plaintiff's position. See, e.g., *Community School Bd, Dist 3 v Board of Educ* 321 NYS2d 949, 66 Misc 2d 739 (NYC Sup Ct 1971); *Natonabah v Board of Educ* 355 F Supp 716 (DNM 1973). See generally Note, "Public Education—ESEA—Parent Participation—Title I ESEA," 1972 *Wisc L Rev* 583.

Title I litigation was directly linked to attempts to increase parent participation. The decision to file a lawsuit, Professor Yudof declared, "must be made in terms of whether the litigation will enable parents and the community to gain some power over educational decisions. The prospect of such power must be the primary purpose of Title I litigation." "Title I and Empowerment: A Litigation Strategy," *Inequality in Education,* 16 March 1970, p 16.

Did the efforts of OE reformers and outside groups succeed in creating a program that was both law-abiding and able to benefit the children it was designed to serve? We can give no adequate answer to that question, because we have neither the necessary data concerning compliance nor a consensus concerning the legislative goals. Jerome Murphy, whose discussion of federal and state enforcement of Title I regulations is excerpted above, offers a gloomy appraisal:

[T]he initial burst of energy accompanying the Martin-McClure report [*Title I of ESEA: Is It Helping Poor Children?* (1969)] has subsided. The Title I coalition and USOE have both let down. The momentum of change and the crusading atmosphere at the federal level have all but disappeared. The current mood is one of uncertainty about Title I's future. Hence, if the Martin-McClure report was a turning point in the implementation of Title I, the turn has been less than enduring. And even with the improvements that have been made, the question is whether they can be sustained. As one new-breed area desk officer noted somewhat sadly, "That's the question we all talk about at lunch." (Murphy, "The Education Bureaucracies Implement Novel Policy: The Politics of Title I of ESEA, 1965-72," in *Policy and Politics in America,* 161, 193 (A. Sindler ed 1973).)

5. Title I: Reassessment

a. Courts. The few court decisions concerning Title I mandate changes in the practices of a particular district; they do not address state or national practices. What impact would you expect such decisions to have in the district whose conduct was judicially reviewed? Would you anticipate any more generalized effects?

b. Parents. Those who advocated increased parent participation in Title I decision making argued in part that parents were the only effective monitors of district behavior. Would you suspect that parents' primary concern would be enforcement of the legislation's requirements? In several communities, parent groups sought to use Title I funds in order to purchase school clothing and hot breakfasts for poor children. They asserted that unless a child were adequately clothed and fed, he would be unable to profit from schooling. Does the argument make sense? Is it consistent with the legislative purposes of Title I?

c. OE Strategists. Almost a decade after its passage, many of Title I's promises appear not to have been fulfilled. In a letter to former Secretary of Health, Education, and Welfare, Elliot L. Richardson, Senator Jacob Javits (R, NY) expressed what has become the conventional viewpoint: "It [Title I] has been used as a means of increasing teachers' salaries and other forms of general assistance; it has not succeeded in the aggregate in improving poor children's educational performance"—the primary goal of those who urged the adoption of the legislation.

Given the considerable political problems that have confronted both the Office of Education and state education departments, is it conceivable that the legal requirements—to say nothing of the primary goals—of Title I could ever be fully implemented? Would the federal government be better advised to abandon its hope of determining educational program priorities and leave resource allocation decisions wholly to states and local districts? If such an approach—usually termed "block grants"—were adopted, which children would you expect to benefit from the federal aid?

d. Beyond Title I. The Nixon administration has promoted block grant legislation for education, see HR 5823 (introduced March 20, 1973), and a national "value-added" or sales tax to finance federal aid. See Advisory Commission on Intergovernmental Relations, *Financing Schools and Property Tax Relief* (1973); Kirp and Yudof, "Revenue Sharing and Its Effect on the Poor," 5 *Clearinghouse Rev* 496 (1972). Whatever the merits of these proposals, they represent a shift away from federal policy designed explicitly to provide extra resources to meet the educational needs of poor children.

III. Equal Educational Opportunity: Equal Resources

HOBSON v HANSEN
269 F Supp 401 (DDC 1967), *aff'd en banc sub nom, SMUCK v HOBSON,*
408 F2d 175 (DC Cir 1969)

[The court considered three related constitutional problems: the segregation of students in the District of Columbia school system; the tracking scheme by which students were assigned to different educational programs on the basis of tested aptitude*; and inequities in the distribution of resources within the District. This last issue is of concern here.

The court sought to determine (1) whether the distribution of educational resources favored white over black students, and (2) if so, whether such discrimination was legally justifiable. A host of inputs were considered: the age, physical condition, and educational adequacy of school buildings; library books and facilities; school congestion; such factors assertedly relevant to assessing faculty quality as teacher experience, faculty education, and reliance on temporary (noncertified) teachers; textbooks and supplies, curricula and special programs; and per-pupil expenditures. In each area, the court identified inequities which favored white students. Predominantly black schools, for example, were filled to 115 percent of capacity, while predominantly white schools had 23 percent of their space unfilled; teachers at white schools were better educated, more experienced, and were more typically certified than their counterparts at black schools. Financial disparities were notable, as the following table, taken from the court's findings of fact, suggest:

Median for schools with percent Negro students

85-100%	$292
67-85%	$292
33-67%	$273
15-33%	$325
0-15%	$392

The court then proceeded to consider the constitutional consequences of these findings.]

... Taking what has been called "a 'new' approach to litigation over racial imbalance," the court considers whether these documented inequalities in the predominantly Negro schools deny the children who are assigned by defendants to attend them equal educational opportunity and equal protection of the law. However the Supreme Court ultimately decides the question of a school board's duty to avoid pupil-assignment policies which lead to *de facto* segregation by race and class, it should be clear that if whites and Negroes, or rich and poor, are to be consigned to separate schools pursuant to whatever policy, the minimum the Constitution will require and guarantee is that for their objectively measurable

---

*The portion of the *Hobson* opinion concerning student classification appears at pages 674-83.

aspects these schools be run on the basis of real equality, at least unless any inequalities are adequately justified.

To invoke a separate but equal principle is bound to stir memories of the bygone days of *Plessy v Ferguson* 163 US 537 (1896). To the extent that *Plessy's* separate but equal doctrine was merely a condition the Supreme Court attached to the states' power deliberately to segregate school children by race, its relevance of course does not survive *Brown*. Nevertheless, to the extent the *Plessy* rule, as strictly construed in cases like *Sweatt v Painter* 339 US 629 (1950), is a reminder of the responsibility entrusted to the courts for ensuring that disadvantaged minorities receive equal treatment when the crucial right to public education is concerned,[165] it can validly claim ancestry for the modern rule the court here recognizes. It was in the latter days of *Plessy* that the rule of actual equality began regularly to be applied. At that time de jure segregation was of very shaky status, morally, socially and constitutionally; so it is with de facto segregation today. If in either circumstance school boards choose not to integrate, it is just and right that courts hold these segregated schools to standards of material equality. Of course, however, there are important differences between the doctrines old and new. Under *Plessy's* provisions once a court discovered a substantial inequality between white and Negro schools its inquiry apparently came to an end: even strong justification underlying the inequality could not deprive the Negro student of his right to judicial relief. No court would advance so absolutist an approach outside the de jure framework.

The constitutional principle from which this modern separate but equal rule draws its sustenance is, of course, equal protection. Orthodox equal protection doctrine can be encapsulated in a single rule: government action which without justification imposes unequal burdens or awards unequal benefits is unconstitutional. The complaint that analytically no violation of equal protection vests unless the inequalities stem from a deliberately discriminatory plan is simply false. Whatever the law was once, it is a testament to our maturing concept of equality that, with the help of Supreme Court decisions in the last decade, we now firmly recognize that the arbitrary quality of thoughtlessness can be as disastrous and unfair to private rights and the public interest as the perversity of a willful scheme.

Theoretically, therefore, purely irrational inequalities even in two schools in a culturally homogeneous, uniformly white suburb would raise a real constitutional question. But in cases not involving Negroes or the poor, courts will hesitate to enforce the separate but equal rule rigorously. Through use of a generous de minimis rule or of a relaxed justification doctrine, or simply in the name of institutional comity, courts will tolerate a high degree of inequality-producing play and delay, in the joints of the educational system. But the law is too deeply committed to the real, not merely theoretical (and present, not deferred) equality of the Negro's educational experience to compromise its diligence for any of these reasons when cases raise the rights of the Negro poor. . . .

---

165. The crime which *Plessy* committed was that in applying its standard it concluded that de jure segregated facilities were or could be equal. The court, ruling in *Brown* that deliberately segregated schools were *inherently* unequal, implicitly accepted the separate but equal frame of reference, exploding it from the inside so far as its application to de jure schools was concerned.

In any event the particular inequalities which have been uncovered in the course of this very long trial easily suffice to lay the predicate for an equal protection violation;... they may well spell the margin between "superior and inferior education".... If any countervailing advantages favor the predominantly Negro schools, defendants have failed to highlight them.

And here, too, there is an absence of convincing justification for the discriminations. The school system's failure to keep up with burgeoning population in the Negro neighborhoods explains several of the inequalities, thereby showing that the board cannot be charged with having schemed their eventuation. But the element of deliberate discrimination is, as indicated above, not one of the requisites of an equal protection violation; and, given the high standards which pertain when racial minorities and the poor are denied equal educational opportunity, ... justification must be in terms not of excusing reasons of this stripe but of positive social interests protected or advanced. A related line of defense is that the school administration, through its six-year building plan, is moving to close at least the most glaring inequalities. But that a party is in process of curing illegality, although that circumstance may affect the relief which equity finally grants, does not oust the court from its jurisdiction to declare the constitutional wrong. . . .

The failure to justify the teacher inequalities can also be confirmed. The attributes of individual schools' faculties are natural outgrowths of the methods by which teachers are assigned to the schools. And the court has already found that teacher assignment has been characterized by unconstitutional racial considerations. Absent strong evidence, the court will not assume that the superiorities in the qualifications of the predominantly white schools' faculties are unrelated to the infirmities in the appointment process.

The final question concerns the remedy to be administered for relief of the inequalities here identified. Once the showing of inequality is completed, it may be that until it is eliminated the Negro student has the right to transfer to one of the advantaged white schools, as he did during *Plessy*'s reign under similar circumstances. See *Missouri ex rel Gaines v Canada* 305 US 337 (1938). He certainly is entitled to appropriate injunctive relief directed at phasing out the inequality. These two considerations coalesce in the remedy the court is ordering for overcrowding: that the board transport volunteering Negro students from the city's overcrowded elementary schools into the partly vacant white schools west of the park. . . .

The teacher inequalities need no direct rectification at this time. Pursuant to one section of this court's order entered for reasons apart from separate but equal, the school system will soon be integrating its faculties. Compliance with this provision will necessarily encompass the reassignment of a number of white teachers currently serving at predominantly white schools. Since in general these are the best-educated, longest-experienced and highest-salaried teachers in the system, integration will also serve as a vehicle for equalizing faculty. The court will therefore defer formulation of specific provisions for faculty equalization at least until the dust surrounding this fall's "substantial" teacher integration settles. . . .

HOBSON v HANSEN
327 F Supp 844 (DDC 1971)

J. Skelly Wright, Circuit Judge. . . .

In its 1967 decree, the court attacked de jure segregation in the District directly, ordering the track system and optional attendance zones abolished and calling for integration of school faculties. The court held further that per-pupil expenditure is a measure which summarizes most other relevant distributions of educational resources. But on the assumption that compliance with other items of the 1967 decree would have the secondary effect of equalizing overall resource distribution, the court deferred any more specific remedy for the inequality in per-pupil expenditures. The thrust of plaintiffs' 1970 amended motion for further relief and enforcement was that this hoped for secondary effect of the original decree has not occurred. Plaintiffs returned to the court asking for further relief in view of the fact that the spread in total expenditures per pupil at various District elementary schools had increased by over 100 per cent since 1964, the last year for which complete figures were available at the time of the original litigation. Plaintiffs requested a more specific remedy to alleviate these inequalities.

After a year of discovery and argument by memoranda, the record now before the court indicates that a striking differential in per-pupil expenditures for teachers' salaries and benefits exists between schools east and west of the park and that the differential is greater in fiscal 1971 than it was in fiscal 1970. The area west of the Park, where despite voluntary busing the public school population is today 74 percent white, is decidedly favored over the rest of the city where the school population is 98 percent black, and is especially favored over Anacostia, one of the most poor and black sections of the city. The following tables show the extent of existing inequities by comparison of pupil-teacher ratios, average cost per teacher, and average teacher cost per child for both fiscal 1970 and fiscal 1971.

Differences between west of the park elementary schools
and schools in the remainder of the city (excluding special schools)

	West of Park	Remainder of City	West of Park Advantage
Fiscal 1970			
Pupil-teacher ratio	21.4/1	22.9/1	7.0% smaller
Average teacher cost	$11,734	$10,167	15.4% greater
Teacher expenditures per pupil	$552	$444	24.3% greater
Fiscal 1971			
Pupil-teacher ratio	18.1/1	20.9/1	15.5% smaller
Average teacher cost	$12,118	$11,048	9.7% greater
Teacher expenditures per pupil	$669	$528	26.7% greater

Differences between west of the park elementary schools
and anacostia elementary schools

Fiscal 1970

	West of Park	Anacostia	West of Park Advantage
Pupil-teacher ratio	21.4/1	24.6/1	14.9% smaller
Average teacher cost	$11,734	$10,046	16.8% greater
Teacher expenditures per pupil	$552	$413	33.7% greater

Fiscal 1971

Pupil-teacher ratio	18.1/1	22.6/1	24.9% smaller
Average teacher cost	$12,118	$10,775	12.5% greater
Teacher expenditures per pupil	$669	$478	40.0% greater

Particularly in view of the 1967 opinion and decree in this case, these figures make out a compelling prima facie case that the District of Columbia school system operates discriminatorily along racial and socioeconomic lines. As the Fifth Circuit taught us in *Brooks v Beto* 366 F2d 1, 9 (1966), "figures speak and when they do, courts listen." If plaintiffs' strong prima facie case of racial discrimination in the administration of the District school system is not rebutted, then these results can only be justified by a "compelling state interest." The thrust of the defense in this case has not, however, been with the demonstration of such compelling interests, but rather with various attempts to undermine the preliminary finding of discrimination in the dispensation of educational opportunity. . . .

[T]he court has considered and rejected defendants' argument that the observed wide discrepancies in teacher expenditures per pupil favoring schools west of the park are random and do not favor any particular racial group or economic class of children. The court has also rejected defendants' position that, even if an objective pattern of discrimination exists, it does so solely or primarily for technological reasons (i. e., economics of scale [cost differences due solely to school size]) which are beyond defendants' control and which cannot be remedied by a court order. Now the court comes to defendants' ultimate defense: that even if a pattern of unequal expenditures does exist, and even if the differential expenditures per pupil are within defendants' control, the resulting real resource differentials are nonetheless inconsequential as they relate to equal educational opportunity.

Teacher expenditure per pupil is a sum, of course, which reflects both the size of the class in which a given student finds himself and the salary paid his teacher. With regard to the average teacher salary component of teacher expenditures per pupil, defendants take the position that the different salaries paid teachers are primarily rewards for experience, and that experience has not been shown to have a significant correlation with a teacher's productivity measured by student achievement tests. The short response to this position is that defendants are seeking to reopen and relitigate an issue which has already been decided in the 1967 *Hobson* opinion.

It is almost an affront to common sense to say, as do defendants, that a pattern of spending so discriminatory on its face as the one which exists in the District reflects no discrimination in "educational opportunity." To overcome the heavy burden against them, defendants lean in part on an argument by their expert, Dave O'Neill, that only teacher experience of six years and less has educational consequence. But even if this assumption, which O'Neill admits is really an "intuitive hunch," were true, the west of the park school is still favored in that it has a higher percentage of teachers with six years or more experience than schools in the rest of the city. Moreover, as the court reads them the rather inconclusive educational studies tell us only that teachers seem to be *over*compensated for experience relative to their productivity. That is, researchers consistently find some relationship between experience and achievement, though not so great as is traditionally paid for. In the absence of more conclusive studies, large differentials such as exist in the District of Columbia cannot be condoned.

Moreover, the board cannot be allowed in one breath to justify budget requests to the Congress and to the District of Columbia City Council by stressing the connection between longevity and quality teaching, and then in the next breath to disavow any such connection before the court. Speaking before the city council on the subject of teacher salary legislation, the chairman of the school board said:

> The board recognizes that to achieve quality education in the District of Columbia public schools it is imperative that students must be housed in educational facilities conducive to learning and be taught by a highly motivated and well-trained teaching staff. It believes that in order to accomplish this objective, it must begin to offer a salary schedule attractive enough to retain its experienced master teachers. . . .

Under these circumstances, where teacher experience has not been proved to be unrelated to educational opportunity, where the administration itself has chosen to reward experience, and where a pattern of racial and socioeconomic discrimination in expenditures continues in the District, the law requires either that experienced teachers be distributed uniformly among the schools in the system or that some offsetting benefit be given to those schools which are denied their fair complement of experienced teachers.[22]

---

22. At the same time they argue that the longevity component of teachers' salaries is unrelated to the effectiveness of their performance—an argument which I reject for the reasons outlined above—defendants seek to justify the current spending pattern and to prove themselves innocent of discriminatory intent by giving several alternative reasons why a policy which rewards longevity might be employed. In this regard, defendants seek first to "explain" the presence of the most experienced and most educated teachers in the schools west of the park as being merely "historical. . . ."

[D]efendants [also] maintain that there are at least three sound theoretical economic reasons why length of service might be compensated in excess of its associated productivity increases. According to defendants:

"(1) Turnover costs supply a rationale for an age-earnings profile that starts with earnings below productivity and, as experience accumulates, begins to pay wages in excess of productivity. . . .

"(2) The market for teachers' services has a supply side as well as a demand side. Union pressures are another possible explanation for salary patterns. If more experienced teachers

Defendants have also alleged that the observed variations in pupil-teacher ratios—the second and larger component of the widely disparate teacher expenditures per pupil—are of no consequence in terms of educational performance or opportunity. Without here going into this contention exhaustively, the court rejects it for much the same reasons as those given in the discussion of the value of teacher experience. The outside studies referred to in the Michelson and O'Neill reports [reports submitted by expert witnesses for plaintiffs and defendants, respectively] are themselves inconclusive. There are so many other variables to be controlled in a study of the relationship between teacher-pupil ratio and educational product that the indefiniteness of the studies made to date is not the least bit surprising. To give only one example, the studies upon which O'Neill relies all concern achievement test results, and we do not know what the consequences of smaller class sizes might be on other measures of school outcomes. O'Neill himself has computed that "about two-thirds of the children in the DC system are in classes with pupil classroom teacher ratios of between 24.4 and 28.4. No empirical studies of school inputs could isolate any effect within this range of class size on educational quality." But even accepting his findings arguendo, the negative implication would seem to be that a third of the children in the system, or approximately 30,000 children, are in schools outside this pupil-teacher range, and that at least some empirical studies have found a discriminatory effect outside this range. In the absence of more knowledge about the effect of class size on productivity, the large variation which still exists in the sizes of classes in the District of Columbia cannot be condoned.

In the end the court finds itself most persuaded, once again, by defendants' own words, uttered before the lawyerly rationalization process began in earnest. . . . [I]n the program justification for the 1972 fiscal budget we read that "class size is one of the most important factors in maximizing education achievement. . . . Thus do defendants put themselves in the awkward position of asking

---

control the union, they will use negotiations to get high salaries for themselves relative to new teachers. . . .

"(3) A third reason why the relative pay of experienced teachers may be higher than their relative productivity has to do with costs which are the same for all teachers, regardless of experience. Examples of such costs are hiring costs and the cost of providing a classroom for the teacher. . . ."

Any worry that shifts in teaching personnel necessitated by an equalization order "would breach the contract which has been effected with the Washington Teachers Union" (Benjamin Henley, Acting Superintendent of Schools, Supplemental Affidavit of August 12, 1970) is quickly allayed by reference to the contract itself which provides that "the fundamental transfer policy shall take into consideration the following factors: . . . legal requirements as ordered by the courts or Congress. . . ."

The other alternative reasons offered by defendants for rewarding experience without regard to productivity smack of post hoc rationalization, are extremely speculative, and are essentially makeweights. Without pursuing them in detail in this opinion, the court rejects them. . . .

[In its 1967 *Hobson* opinion which set] a *minimum* standard, the court did not wish to preclude the school administration from focusing, if it saw fit, on equality of output, in terms of giving each student an equal opportunity to attain his own unique potential, rather than on equality of inputs. But the minimum required was that there be an equality of inputs in terms of objective resources. Under injunction to refrain from further discrimination, defendants have failed to comply with this "minimum." The court having found that an unequal distribution of the most experienced and highly paid teachers in favor of the predominantly white west of the park area *does* favor this area as well in educational opportunity, no excuse for this continuing racial discrimination short of a "compelling state interest" is worthy of this court's attention at this late date in the history of the case.

to be applauded for their expensive efforts to reduce class sizes generally and of requesting funds for further reduction of class sizes under the rationale of productivity, while inconsistently maintaining for purposes of this litigation that no discrimination results when class sizes remain significantly smaller in west of the park schools as compared with those in the rest of the city.

Plaintiffs' prima facie case of discrimination in the provision of educational opportunity, based upon the pattern of unequal expenditures which favors the schools west of the park, is strongly buttressed by further evidence in the record concerning the results of citywide sixth grade reading achievement tests. The record shows that the west of the park elementary schools produced an average reading achievement test score that was significantly higher—indeed 2.4 grades higher—than the average for the rest of the city. Obviously, these results tend to corroborate the presumption created by the pattern of expenditures that the city provides a better educational opportunity to its richer, white students....

These achievement test results suggest that not only are the children in schools east of the park being denied an educational opportunity equal to those west of the park, but also they in fact are not being as well educated. Thus these test scores reflect the result of the discrimination against the east of the park children in per-pupil expenditure. The burden of establishing that these test results reflect something other than the proven discriminatory distribution of educational opportunity falls upon defendants. And once again defendants have failed to meet their burden.

. . . .

As has already been documented, the record now before the court shows a current differential in teacher expenditures per pupil every bit as striking as the differential in total expenditures per pupil noted in the 1967 opinion. The record also shows that this differential, which favors the schools west of the park, has increased in percentage terms from fiscal 1970 to fiscal 1971. Today in Washington the 74 percent white schools west of the park enjoy a 27 percent advantage in teacher expenditures per pupil over the 98 percent black elementary schools in the rest of the city.

Four years after this court's first *Hobson* opinion, defendants have by their own admission failed to equalize the access of all students to dollar resources for teachers' salaries and benefits. Although defendants have argued strenuously that there is no proven connection between the showing that black students have unequal access to dollars and the crucial constitutional showing that black students are denied equal educational opportunity, the court has found otherwise....

The court finds further that defendants have failed to offer the legal justification or compelling state interest necessary to overcome the presumptive invalidity of awarding benefits which affect the fundamental interests of and results in discrimination against a racial minority. Defendants argue, citing *Dandridge v Williams* 397 US 471 (1970), and *McInnis v Shapiro* 293 F Supp 327 (ND Ill 1968), *aff'd sub nom, McInnis v Ogilvie* 394 US 322 (1969), that the rational relationship test should be applied to this case. But whatever the restrictive impact of *Dandridge* and *McInnis* on the reach of the equal protection clause with regard to the *poor*, the law is clear beyond doubt that, where a racial minority is treated in a discriminatory fashion, there is a presumptive constitutional violation demanding exacting scrutiny by the court and imposing a heavy burden of justification on defendants.[27] Compare *James v Valtierra* 402 US 137, 91 S Ct 1331, 28 L Ed 2d 678 (April 26, 1971), with *Hunter v Erickson* 393 US 385 (1969), in which the court specifically stated: "Because the core of the Fourteenth Amendment is the prevention of meaningful and unjustified official distinctions based on race, . . . racial classifications are 'constitutionally suspect' . . . and subject to the 'most rigid scrutiny' . . . . They 'bear a far heavier burden of justification' than other classifications . . . ." 393 US at 391-92. Moreover, as the cases establish, the court's duty to scrutinize alleged discrimination against a racial minority is especially high when the right of the minority affected is the right to equal educational opportunity. . . . It is precisely the *Brown* requirement that public education be made available to racial minorities on equal terms which plaintiffs seek to effect in *Hobson.* 347 US at 493.

Whatever may be the differences in constitutional concern between purely de facto and purely de jure segregation, it is too late for defendants to suggest that discrimination of constitutional dimension does not arise where a school board has knowingly favored in an unjustified and substantial way predominantly white schools over predominantly black schools. Since 1967, following the rationale of *Hobson,* several of the circuits have rejected the rational relationship test in finding a violation of the equal protection clause where the state has acted affirmatively and where the direct *effect* of the challenged state action was inescapably discriminatory to the enjoyment of an important right by a racial minority. See, e. g., *Hawkins v Shaw* 437 F2d 1286, 1291-92 (5th Cir 1971); *Kennedy Park Homes Ass'n v Lackawanna* 436 F2d 108, 114-15 (2d Cir 1970); *Southern Alameda Spanish Speaking Organization v Union City* 424 F2d 291, 295-96 & n9 (9th Cir 1970); *Norwalk CORE v Norwalk Redevelopment Agency* 395 F2d 920, 931-32 (2d Cir 1968); *Keyes v School Dist No 1* 313 F Supp 61, 82-83 (D Colo 1970). Unlike these cases, defendants here are already under an injunction to refrain from discrimination. Thus defendants' burden of justification here is greater, and the court's duty to scrutinize defendants' actions is even more exacting.

. . . .

For reasons already discussed, the court finds that plaintiffs' initially requested relief requiring equalization of total expenditures per pupil across the system would sweep too broadly and would require the school administration to equalize some inputs which have little or nothing to do with educational opportunity. But upon careful consideration, the court does find that the equalization order approach is a good one, provided it is focused upon expenditures per pupil

---

27. Both *Dandridge* and *McInnis* involved challenges to programs of statewide application. In *McInnis* a three-judge court upheld a statewide educational resource allocation formula which permitted school districts with a higher dollar value of taxable property per pupil to raise more money to support education than poor school districts. In addition to the crucial distinction that neither *Dandridge* nor *McInnis* involved allegations of racial discrimination, the court also notes that *McInnis* did involve the difficult problem of balancing a request for interdistrict equality against a rational justification of inequality based upon the existence of local, interdistrict diversity and the need for autonomy as among local political subdivisions. The *Hobson* case is easier because it involves a single district and a request for intradistrict equality only. In granting plaintiffs' request for relief, the court follows what has been the law of the land at least since *Plessy v Ferguson* 163 US 537 (1896). See Wertz, "Equal Opportunity in the Allocation of Public School Faculties," 39 *Geo Wash L Rev* 341, 365-66 (1971).

for teachers' salaries and benefits, so as to cover only inputs which do have a direct bearing on the quality of a child's education.

Having found continuing substantial discrimination, the court cannot agree with defendants' expert that an equalization order would amount to "much ado about nothing." Defendants stress that implementation of the proposed order would result merely in an increase of $3.39 per black child across the city. . . . Defendants' figure of $3.39 per child masks the fact that some individual black schools are shockingly far below the citywide average expenditure per pupil level. Thus, to take one of many possible examples, if teacher expenditures per pupil in fiscal 1971 at the Draper School (actually $362) had been at the citywide average ($497), they would have increased by $135 per pupil. The increase in total teacher expenditures would then have been approximately $147,000. Under salary scales currently in effect, this would have permitted the addition of perhaps fifteen new teachers at Draper. This addition would have reduced the pupil-teacher ratio from the present 25 to 1 to 18 to 1. Even defendants' expert seems to concede that such a reduction has a beneficial effect on school outcomes when measured by achievement test scores.

A review of relevant cases reveals that many courts have ordered equalization of per-pupil expenditures in all schools within a single school district, and that such an order provides a judicially manageable standard.

See, e.g., *US v Jefferson County Bd of Educ* 372 F2d 836, 899-900 (5th Cir 1966), *aff'd per curiam on rehearing en banc,* 380 F2d 385, *cert denied,* 389 US 840 (1967) . . . . And see also the Department of Health, Education and Welfare Memorandum to Chief State School Officers: "Subject: Advisory Statement on the Development of Policy on Comparability," regarding implementation of the 1970 amendments to the Elementary and Secondary Education Act, September 18, 1970, p7, et seq.

Under all these circumstances, the court believes it should now use its broad equitable powers to set a standard for expenditures which will not interfere with the successful operation of the school system but which will ensure that it operates in a substantially nondiscriminatory fashion.

Wherefore it is ordered, adjudged and decreed that

1. On and after October 1, 1971, per-pupil expenditures for all teachers' salaries and benefits from the regular District of Columbia budget (excluding . . . all funds not from the regular congressional appropriation) in any single elementary school (*not* "administrative unit") shall not deviate by more than 5 percent from the mean per-pupil expenditure for all teachers' salaries and benefits at all elementary schools in the District of Columbia school system as that mean is defined in this paragraph. The 5 percent limit may be exceeded only for adequate justification on an individual school basis shown to this court in advance. "Adequate justification" shall include provision of compensatory education for educationally deprived pupils at certain schools or provision of special educational services for the mentally retarded or physically handicapped at certain schools or for other "exceptional" students. It shall also include a showing that variance above or below the 5 percent limit is accounted for *solely* on the basis of economies or diseconomies of scale. For purposes of this order, the "mean" shall be computed *after* excluding from the computation total expenditures for all teachers' salaries and benefits and total average daily membership at all

schools for which permission to exceed the 5 percent limitation because of compensatory education or education of "exceptional" students is sought and granted. . . .

Notes and Questions

1. Politics of Educational Decision Making

Until recently, politics was a dirty word to school men, redolent of the nepotism and graft that they had historically fought. That view has changed considerably: school administrators openly speak of themselves as political actors, actively developing strategies that will help them accomplish their policy goals (and ensure their job survival). See M. Nunnery and R. Kimbrough, *Politics, Power, Polls, and School Elections* (1971).

How do education policy decisions actually get made? The classic view asserts that local school boards—composed of lay community members, either elected or appointed to their posts—make rational decisions concerning curriculum, facilities, personnel, and the like, relying in part on the expressed sentiments of the community; these judgments are conveyed to and carried out by board-appointed school administrators. That model, while consistent with the statutory mandates of school boards, appears inconsistent with political fact. One administrator, writing pseudononymously, notes that: "School boards chiefly perform the function of *legitimating* the politics of the school system to the community, rather than *representing* the various segments of the community to the school administration. . . ." Kerr, "The School Board as an Agency of Legitimation," in *Governing Education* 137, 139 (A. Rosenthal ed 1969).

To the extent that boards do exercise decision-making power, rationality is not always, and perhaps not usually, the primary criterion. In school boards, as in other public agencies, decisions emerge from bargaining. The bargaining process may be based wholly on the interests of the community majority; it may take into account the needs of education interest groups, such as the teachers' union and civil rights organizations; or it may be ideological in nature; but most likely it will combine all these elements. There are, of course, attempts to do what is educationally most enlightened, but as we have seen, such enlightenment evades precise definition.

Even when the school board reaches a decision, its implementation is by no means secured. School organizations are highly structured, hierarchical bureaucracies with their own organizational needs. See generally *State, School, and Politics* (M. Kirst ed 1972); *The Politics of Education at the Local, State, and Federal Levels* (M. Kirst ed 1970). A board decision that appears to upset these needs may well be resisted either openly or, more likely, covertly. See *The Politics of Urban Education* (M. Gitell and B. Hevesi eds 1969); M. Gittell, *Participants and Participation* (1967). The response of New York's school administrators to the student rights code promulgated by the board of education (see chapter 2) is one example of such behavior.

2. Politics of Educational Budget Making

The allocation of the education budget is the most crucial issue to confront the school board. As Professor Thomas Eliot notes: "Schools cannot be built, equipped, or staffed without money. The problems of financing are inherent in virtually all [education policy] issues. . . ." Eliot, "Toward an Understanding of School Politics," in *Governing Education* 3, 19 (A. Rosenthal ed 1969). The budget is prepared by the superintendent and his staff and presented to the board; it is a document that reflects internal bureaucratic bargaining. Teachers and noncertificated service personnel present their demands—either through union representatives or informally—to the superintendent before formal submission. Depending on his style of operation, the superintendent may choose to involve board of education members at this preliminary stage or to present a formal budget recommendation to the board; he may provide detailed supporting data or simply budget figures. However the budget is presented, the administrative staff "has in mind a definite dollar amount, or percentage figure, which they believe the board will accept." James, Kelly, and Garms, "The School Budget Process in Large Cities," in *The Politics of Education* 74, 82 (M. Kirst ed 1970). In large cities, the power of the school bureaucracy over the budget is countered to some extent by various interest groups—unions, taxpayers' groups, and the like—who rely on their own professional research staffs to prepare "counter-budgets." As a consequence, the school board typically finds itself balancing a variety of conflicting pressures: middle-class parents seeking better (and more costly) educational programs; school personnel seeking more money for higher salaries and better working conditions; and taxpayers' groups anxious to keep costs and taxes as low as possible.

While specifics may vary, the bargaining that characterizes education budget making is a general organizational phenomenon. See A. Wildavsky, *The Politics of the Budgetary Process* (1964). Two effects of the process are worth noting: (1) the give and take that characterizes decisions over dollars makes dramatic change unlikely from one year to the next, for budgetary increases or cutbacks are likely to arouse strong political opposition; (2) individuals and groups who are both outside the system and unable to wield considerable political pressure are in essence shut out of the budgetary bargaining. The historic powerlessness of these groups—notably poor and minority communities—has meant that their educational needs, translated into budget terms, are considered last. That political pattern has changed noticeably, but as Harold Baron notes in writing about Chicago's schools:

> "Prior to the advent of the mass northern civil rights movement in 1961, the allocation of educational funds on a per pupil basis clearly demonstrated preferential treatment on the basis of both race and status. . . . [Although political] protest [by minority groups] paid off somewhat [in terms of reordered budgetary priorities] . . . . monetary flows do not always correspond to the real allocation of resources to educational purposes. Some schools, because of traditions of effectiveness or prestige, are able to attract excellent staffs on the basis of nonpecuniary satisfactions and therefore can pay less for high-quality services. On the other hand, funds can be spent on goods and services as a form of conspicuous consumption or to serve certain ritualistic social purposes other than pedagogic results. . . . [Although such spending did close the gap between black-white school expenditures in Chicago between 1961 and 1966,] the evidence strongly shows

[that] the high-status white groups are able to sustain their preferred position by securing larger investments in the education of their children. (Baron, "Race and Status in School Spending: Chicago, 1961-66," 6 *J Human Resources* 3, 19-21 (1971). See also P. Sexton, *Education and Income* (1962).)

Does this discussion suggest a possible explanation for the black-white resource disparities noted in both *Hobson* opinions? Does it indicate what difficulties might beset the implementation of the second *Hobson* decision?

3. *Hobson 1*

a. Why did the *Hobson* court choose to examine some, but not all, inputs in assessing whether blacks receive fewer educational resources than do whites? Is the court tacitly assuming that these inputs affect educational outcomes? That they are perceived as important by the black community? That taken together, they constitute the bulk of the district's school budget? Should the court distinguish between such factors as age of school buildings and teacher experience? On what constitutional basis? Can any of the disparities in resources examined in *Hobson* be justified on demographic or other nondiscriminatory grounds? Would assignment of teachers by seniority constitute such a ground?

b. After discussing "the range of inequities" in resources provided to black and white students, the court ignores all of them except teacher inequalities. The court further suggests that the desegregation of Washington's teachers (ordered earlier in the opinion) will cure this particular inequality. On what evidence is that statement based? Had the court chosen to equalize distribution of each of the factors discussed in the opinion, how would it have gone about the task?

c. The court's examination of resource inequities is predicated on the presence of segregation. Does that fact suggest that *Plessy v Ferguson*'s insistence on equality remains good law? Does the court's analysis apply only in situations where minority students receive fewer resources than do whites? Would the decision be the same if the district was 100 percent white? 100 percent black? Would it be the same if resources were randomly distributed, adversely affecting no definable group but accomplishing no educationally defensible end? Is the latter situation representative of what the court terms "the arbitrary quality of thoughtlessness"?

4. *Hobson 2*: The Court's Analysis

a. The *Hobson 2* opinion focuses exclusively on black-white inequities in teacher expenditure. Is the court suggesting that money spent on teachers is somehow "most important?" Does the educational research support this contention? Is the court's attention focused on teachers' salaries and benefits because they are the biggest items in the school budget?

b. Once disparities in teacher salaries and pupil-staff ratios between "white" and "black" schools were demonstrated, the court placed the burden on the school district either to rebut the inference of discrimination or to offer "compelling" justification for the disparities. Given the state of knowledge about the effectiveness of various school inputs, does the placement of the burden decide the outcome? If so, is the approach constitutionally justifiable? Are there policy reasons that support the standard of review adopted by the court? See Hornby and Holmes, "Equalization of Resources within School Districts," 48 *Va L Rev* 1119, 1143-55 (1972).

c. The *Hobson 2* court never heard the oral testimony of witnesses. Instead, an exchange of memoranda—drafted in part by social scientists representing the parties—assessed the plausibility of the school district's justifications for salary inequalities. While the court makes ample use of this material (see, e.g., footnotes 21 and 22), it criticizes both parties' presentations:

> The reports by the experts—one noted economist plus assistants for each side—are less helpful than they might have been for the simple reason that they do not begin from a common data base, disagree over crucial statistical assumptions, and reach different conclusions. . . . [T]he studies by both experts are tainted by a vice well known in the statistical trade—data shopping and scanning to reach a preconceived result; and the court has had to reject parts of both reports as unreliable because biased. . . . [T]he court has been forced back to its own common sense approach to a problem which, though admittedly complex, has certainly been made more obscure than was necessary. The conclusion I reach is based upon burden of proof, and upon straightforward moral and constitutional arithmetic. 327 F Supp at 859.

Precisely what does "straightforward moral and constitutional arithmetic" mean? Are the factual issues in *Hobson*—determining, for example, whether teacher experience improves classroom effectiveness—best resolved by adversary presentation? Would the court have been better served had it appointed its own expert? How might such an expert have resolved the methodological disputes that continue to divide economists? Do these issues bear at all on the discussion of social science evidence in the context of racial discrimination (see chapter 4)? For further discussion of the *Hobson* economists' debate, see Michelson, "For the Plaintiffs—Equal Resource Allocation," 7 *J Human Resources* 283 (1972); O'Neil, Gray, and Horowitz, "For the Defendants—Educational Equality and Expenditure Equalization Orders," 7 *J Human Resources* 307 (1972).

d. In their legal memoranda to the court, plaintiffs focused on the fact that poor students had fewer teacher-dollars spent on them than did middle-class students. The *Hobson* opinion, however, adheres to the racial discrimination issue, even though over 95 percent of the Washington, D.C., student population was black at the time of the litigation. Is the court suggesting that discrimination against the poor does not raise constitutional questions analogous to those presented by discrimination against minorities? See *Dandridge v Williams* 397 US 471 (1970) (per-household ceilings on welfare grants); *James v Valtierra* 402 US 137 (1971) (referendum requirement for low cost housing construction); *San Antonio Independent School Dist v Rodriguez* 411 US 1 (1973). Has the court misdescribed the facts of the case in order to reach what it regards as a desirable policy outcome? In order to avoid appellate reversal?

e. Does *Hobson* imply that the Title I, ESEA, comparability provisions (see section II above) are constitutionally required in all districts?

5. *Hobson 2*: Remedy and Aftermath

a. The *Hobson* remedy requires expenditure equalization within 5 percent of mean expenditure. If, for example, the district spends an average of $600 per student on teachers' salaries, expenditures between $570 and $630 require no justification. What is the practical justification for this limited flexibility?

The court permits expenditure deviations greater than 5 percent with "adequate justification." Is justification limited to instances where additional help is provided on a "catch-up" basis to slow or handicapped students? Could a program for the gifted be justified to the court? Is the court converting into constitutional doctrine what philosopher John Rawls has termed "the difference principle": "All social primary goods—liberty and opportunity, income and wealth, and the bases of self-respect—are to be distributed equally unless an unequal distribution of any or all of these goods is to the advantage of the least favored." J. Rawls, *A Theory of Justice*, 303 (1971).

b. Recall that, in analyzing patterns of discrimination, *Hobson* focuses on black-white disparities. Is the appropriate cure for such discrimination equalization of expenditures for black and white students? How does the Court justify a remedy which also bars expenditure inequalities among schools attended exclusively by black (or white) students?

c. The court in *McInnis v Shapiro*, 293 F Supp 327, characterized an equal dollars standard as "rigid," and rejected the approach: "Expenditures are not . . . the exclusive yardstick of a child's educational needs." See also Kurland, "Equal Educational Opportunity: The Limits of Constitutional Jurisprudence Undefined," 35 *U Chi L Rev* 583 (1968). Is the *Hobson 2* remedy subject to the same criticism? Are the differences between *Hobson* and *McInnis* analytically reconcilable?

Is it easier—as a matter of either law or policy—for a court to remedy disparities within a given school district than to remedy interdistrict disparities? Consider the following comment, contrasting the two issues:

> Since partition of the municipal budget has already occurred, the court [assessing intradistrict inequalities] need not consider the entire budgetary process. . . . Moreover, action by the court will not entail substantial interference with the political process. Most intradistrict allocation decisions are administrative in character and therefore somewhat isolated from electoral control. Finally, the protection of students from excessive discrimination would seem to be a function for which the courts have peculiar institutional competence. (Schoettle, "The Equal Protection Clause in Public Education, 71 *Colum L Rev* 1355, 1412 (1971).)

d. The Washington, D.C., school system was sharply divided over *Hobson*. While one school board member declared that "everything in the order we should want to do anyhow," the representative of the only predominantly white section of the city assailed Judge Wright as a "mush-headed super-superintendent." School Superintendent Hugh J. Scott felt that the order did not constitute "sound educational policy." And the school board president, Anita F. Allen, noted: "I am very much disappointed—and astounded—that the judge expects us to move teachers wholesale. I think people, both black and white, will question the wisdom of moving teachers because they are either too old or too young for a particular school building." Yet ten days later, the board of education voted eight to one not to appeal the ruling. "Wholesale" teacher transfer is indeed one way of complying with the equalization order; are there fiscally feasible alternatives?

e. The school district's own analysis of teacher expenditure data, undertaken nine months after the decision and after some effort at equalization had been made, found that only 67 of the 136 schools were in compliance with the *Hobson 2* order; 6 schools deviated by more than 20 percent from the district mean expenditure level. Hornby and Holmes, "Equalization of Resources within Districts," 58 *Va L Rev* 1119, 1156, n202 (1972). Are there noninvidious explanations for these facts? What further steps, if any, might the court take to ensure compliance?

IV. Equal Educational Opportunity: "Fiscal Neutrality"

The Supreme Court's affirmance of the *McInnis* decision (see section II above) did not mark the demise of interest in a constitutional assault on interdistrict resource inequality. If such an assault were to succeed, it was important to design a judicially manageable constitutional standard for review to replace the discredited "needs" approach. Professors John Coons, William Clune, and Stephen Sugarman proposed an alternative "fiscal neutrality" standard in *Private Wealth and Public Education* (1970): the quality of education (defined in dollar terms) may not be a function of wealth, other than the wealth of the state as a whole. The prevailing system violated this fiscal neutrality standard, Coons and his colleagues argued, by creating wealth disparities among districts and making the dollars spent on a child's schooling a function of where he lived. Unlike the "needs" standard, the "fiscal neutrality" approach asked only that courts reject existing financing schemes as arbitrary and unfair, leaving the states free to adopt any of a variety of alternative funding arrangements consistent with its negative command.

In August 1971 the California Supreme Court accepted the "fiscal neutrality" approach. Its landmark opinion, *Serrano v Priest* 5 C3d 584, 487 P2d 1241, 96 Cal Rptr 601 (1971), technically reversed the state trial court's summary dismissal of plaintiffs' complaint and remanded the case for trial. But the court's opinion left little doubt as to its ultimate views on the dispute:

> The California public school financing system . . . . conditions the full entitlement to [education] on wealth, classifies its recipients on the basis of their collective affluence and makes the quality of a child's education depend upon the resources of his school district and ultimately upon the pocketbook of his parents. We find that such financing system as presently constituted is not necessary to the attainment of any compelling state interest. Since it does not withstand the requisite "strict scrutiny," it denies to the plaintiffs and others similarly situated the equal protection of the laws. 487 P2d at 1263.

Reaction in California was swift and varied: superintendents in wealthy districts expressed concern that "educational mediocrity" would result from the ruling, while their counterparts in poor districts were jubilant. Elsewhere, several states, including New York and Wisconsin, established special commissions to consider the educational finance question. Sidney Marland, then US commissioner of education, called the ruling a "very fundamental breakthrough in the concept of state educational systems," and the then HEW secretary, Elliot Richardson, praised it as "the American ideal of labor rewarded." Lawyers in some thirty-eight states, ably assisted by the Lawyers' Committee for Civil Rights under Law, pressed similar suits. In most instances, plaintiffs' claim was upheld. See *Van Dusartz v Hatfield* 334 F Supp 870 (D Minn 1971); *Robinson v Cahill* 118 NJ Super 223, 287 A2d 187 (1972); cf. *Sweetwater County Planning Comm'n v Hinkle* 491 P2d 1234 (Wyo 1971), *juris relinquished*, 493 P2d 1050 (Wyo 1972). But see *Spano v Board of Educ* 68 Misc 2d 804, 328 NYS2d 229 (Sup Ct 1972). Compare *Parker v Mandel* 344 F Supp 1068 (D Md 1972). For a more detailed discussion of the background of the school finance litigation, see Kirp, "Judicial Policy-making: Inequitable Public School Financing and the *Serrano* Case (1971)," in *Policy and Politics in America*, 83, 97-104 (A. Sindler ed 1973). The first "fiscal neutrality" suit to reach the Supreme Court was *San Antonio Independent School Dist v Rodriguez.*

SAN ANTONIO INDEPENDENT SCHOOL DISTRICT v RODRIGUEZ
411 US 1 (1973)

Mr. Justice Powell delivered the opinion of the court.

This suit attacking the Texas system of financing public education was initiated by Mexican-American parents whose children attend the elementary and secondary schools in the Edgewood Independent School District, an urban school district in San Antonio, Texas. They brought a class action on behalf of school children throughout the state who are members of minority groups or who are poor and reside in school districts having a low property tax base. Named as defendants[2] were the state board of education, the commissioner of education, the state attorney general, and the Bexar County (San Antonio) Board of Trustees. The complaint was filed in the summer of 1968 and a three-judge court was impaneled in January 1969. In December 1971[4] the panel rendered its judgment in a per curiam opinion holding the Texas school finance system unconstitutional under the equal protection clause of the Fourteenth Amendment.[5] The state

---

2. The San Antonio Independent School District, whose name this case still bears, was one of seven school districts in the San Antonio metropolitan area that were originally named as defendants. After a pretrial conference, the district court issued an order dismissing the school districts from the case. Subsequently, the San Antonio Independent School District joined in the plaintiffs' challenge to the state's school finance system and filed an amicus curiae brief in support of that position in this court.

4. The trial was delayed for two years to permit extensive pretrial discovery and to allow completion of a pending Texas legislative investigation concerning the need for reform of its public school finance system. 337 F Supp 280, 285 n11 (WD Tex 1971).

5. 337 F Supp 280. The district court stayed its mandate for two years to provide Texas an opportunity to remedy the inequities found in its financing program. The court, however, retained jurisdiction to fashion its own remedial order if the state failed to offer an acceptable plan. 337 F Supp at 286.

appealed, and we noted probable jurisdiction to consider the far-reaching constitutional questions presented. . . . For the reasons stated in this opinion we reverse
the decision of the district court. . . .

[The court summarizes the early evolution of Texas' school financing scheme.
It notes the failure of earlier schemes to take into account wealth disparities
among school districts.]

Recognizing the need for increased state funding to help offset disparities in
local spending and to meet Texas' changing educational requirements, the state
legislature in the late 1940s undertook a thorough evaluation of public education
with an eye toward major reform. In 1947 an eighteen-member committee, composed of educators and legislators, was appointed to explore alternative systems
in other states and to propose a funding scheme that would guarantee a minimum or basic educational offering to each child and that would help overcome
interdistrict disparities in taxable resources. The committee's efforts led to the
passage of the Gilmer-Aiken bills, named for the committee's cochairmen, establishing the Texas Minimum Foundation School Program. Today this program
accounts for approximately half of the total educational expenditures in Texas. . . .

The design of [the new] complex system was twofold. First, it was an attempt to assure that the Foundation Program would have an equalizing influence
on expenditure levels between school districts by placing the heaviest burden on
the school districts most capable of paying. Second, the program's architects
sought to establish a local fund assignment that would force every school district
to contribute to the education of its children but that would not by itself
exhaust any district's resources. . . .

The school district in which appellees reside, the Edgewood Independent
School District, has been compared throughout this litigation with the Alamo
Heights Independent School District. This comparison between the least and
most affluent districts in the San Antonio area serves to illustrate the manner in
which the dual system of finance operates and to indicate the extent to which
substantial disparities exist despite the state's impressive progress in recent years.
Edgewood is one of seven public school districts in the metropolitan area. Approximately 22,000 students are enrolled in its twenty-five elementary and secondary schools. The district is situated in the core-city sector of San Antonio in
a residential neighborhood that has little commercial or industrial property. The
residents are predominantly of Mexican-American descent: approximately 90 percent of the student population is Mexican-American and over 6 percent is Negro.
The average assessed property value per pupil is $5,960—the lowest in the metro-
politan area—and the median family income ($4,686) is also the lowest. At an
equalized tax rate of $1.05 per $100 of assessed property—the highest in the
metropolitan area—the district contributed $26 to the education of each child for
the 1967-68 school year above its local fund assignment for the Minimum Foundation Program. The Foundation Program contributed $222 per pupil for a state-
local total of $248. Federal funds added another $108 for a total of $356 per
pupil.[32]

32. While federal assistance has an ameliorating effect on the difference in school budgets
between wealthy and poor districts, the district court rejected an argument made by the
state in that court that it should consider the effect of the federal grant in assessing the
discrimination claim. 337 F Supp at 284. The state has not renewed that contention here.

Alamo Heights is the most affluent school district in San Antonio. Its six schools, housing approximately 5,000 students, are situated in a residential community quite unlike the Edgewood District. The school population is predominantly Anglo, having only 18 percent Mexican-Americans and less than 1 percent Negroes. The assessed property value per pupil exceeds $49,000 and the median family income is $8,001. In 1967-68 the local tax rate of $.85 per $100 of valuation yielded $333 per pupil over and above its contribution to the Foundation Program. Coupled with the $225 provided from that program, the district was able to supply $558 per student. Supplemented by a $36 per-pupil grant from federal sources, Alamo Heights spent $594 per pupil....

Although the 1967-68 school year figures provide the only complete statistical breakdown for each category of aid, more recent partial statistics indicate that the previously noted trend of increasing state aid has been significant. For the 1970-71 school year, the Foundation School Program allotment for Edgewood was $356 per pupil, a 62 percent increase over the 1967-68 school year. Indeed, state aid alone in 1970-71 equaled Edgewood's entire 1967-68 school budget from local, state, and federal sources. Alamo Heights enjoyed a similar increase under the Foundation Program, netting $491 per pupil in 1970-71 . . . .[35]

Despite these recent increases, substantial interdistrict disparities in school expenditures found by the district court to prevail in San Antonio and in varying degrees throughout the state still exist. And it was these disparities, largely attributable to differences in the amounts of money collected through local property taxation, that led the district court to conclude that Texas' dual system of public school financing violated the equal protection clause. . . .

We must decide, first, whether the Texas system of financing public education operates to the disadvantage of some suspect class or impinges upon a fundamental right explicitly or implicitly protected by the Constitution, thereby requiring strict judicial scrutiny. If so, the judgment of the district court should be affirmed. If not, the Texas scheme must still be examined to determine whether it rationally furthers some legitimate, articulated state purpose and therefore does not constitute an invidious discrimination in violation of the equal protection clause of the Fourteenth Amendment.

II

The district court's opinion does not reflect the novelty and complexity of the constitutional questions posed by appellees' challenge to Texas' system of school financing. In concluding that strict judicial scrutiny was required, that court relied on decisions dealing with the rights of indigents to equal treatment in the criminal trial and appellate processes,[45] and on cases disapproving wealth restrictions on the right to vote.[46] Those cases, the district court concluded, established

---

35. Although the Foundation Program has made significantly greater contributions to both school districts over the last several years, it is apparent that Alamo Heights has enjoyed a larger gain. The sizable difference between the Alamo Heights and Edgewood grants is due to the emphasis in the state's allocation formula on the guaranteed minimum salaries for teachers. Higher salaries are guaranteed to teachers having more years of experience and possessing more advanced degrees. Therefore, Alamo Heights, which has a greater percentage of experienced personnel with advanced degrees, receives more state support. In this regard the Texas program is not unlike that presently in existence in a number of other states. . . .

45. E.g., *Griffin v Illinois* 351 US 12 (1956); *Douglas v California* 372 US 353 (1963).

46. *Harper v Virginia Bd of Elections* 383 US 663 (1966); *McDonald v Board of Election*

wealth as a suspect classification. Finding that the local property tax system discriminated on the basis of wealth, it regarded those precedents as controlling. It then reasoned, based on decisions of this court affirming the undeniable importance of education, that there is a fundamental right to education and that, absent some compelling state justification, the Texas system could not stand.

We are unable to agree that this case, which in significant aspects is *sui generis,* may be so neatly fitted into the conventional mosaic of constitutional analysis under the equal protection clause. Indeed, for the several reasons that follow, we find neither the suspect classification nor the fundamental interest analysis persuasive.

A

The wealth discrimination discovered by the district court in this case, and by several other courts that have recently struck down school financing laws in other states,[48] is quite unlike any of the forms of wealth discrimination heretofore reviewed by this court. . . .

The case comes to us with no definitive description of the classifying facts or delineation of the disfavored class. . . . The Texas system of school financing might be regarded as discriminating (1) against "poor" persons whose incomes fall below some identifiable level of poverty or who might be characterized as functionally "indigent," or (2) against those who are relatively poorer than others, or (3) against all those who, irrespective of their personal incomes, happen to reside in relatively poorer school districts. Our task must be to ascertain whether, in fact, the Texas system has been shown to discriminate on any of these possible bases and, if so, whether the resulting classification may be regarded as suspect.

The precedents of this court provide the proper starting point. The individuals or groups of individuals who constituted the class discriminated against in our prior cases shared two distinguishing characteristics: because of their impecunity they were completely unable to pay for some desired benefit, and as a consequence, they sustained an absolute deprivation of a meaningful opportunity to enjoy that benefit. In *Griffin v Illinois* 351 US 12 (1956), and its progeny, the court invalidated state laws that prevented an indigent criminal defendant from acquiring a transcript, or an adequate substitute for a transcript, for use at several stages of the trial and appeal process. The payment requirements in each case were found to occasion de facto discrimination against those who, because of their indigency, were totally unable to pay for transcripts. . . .

Williams v Illinois 399 US 235 (1970), and *Tate v Short* 401 US 395 (1971), struck down criminal penalties that subjected indigents to incarceration simply because of their inability to pay a fine. Again, the disadvantaged class was composed only of persons who were totally unable to pay the demanded sum. Those cases do not touch on the question whether equal protection is denied to persons with relatively less money on whom designated fines impose heavier burdens. . . .

Finally, in *Bullock v Carter* 405 US 134 (1972), the court invalidated the Texas filing fee requirement for primary elections. Both of the relevant classify-

---

Comm'rs 394 US 802 (1969); *Bullock v Carter* 405 US 134 (1972); *Goosby v Osser* 409 US 512 (1973).

48. *Serrano v Priest* 5 Cal3d 584, 487 P2d 1241 (1971); *Van Dusartz v Hatfield* 334 F Supp 870 (DC Minn 1971); *Robinson v Cahill* 118 NJ Super 223, 287 A2d 187 (1972); *Milliken v Green* 203 NW2d 457 (Mich SC 1972), rehearing granted January 1973.

ing facts found in the previous cases were present there. The size of the fee, often running into the thousands of dollars and, in at least one case, as high as $8,900, effectively barred all potential candidates who were unable to pay the required fee. . . .

Only appellees' first possible basis for describing the class disadvantaged by the Texas school finance system—discrimination against a class of definably "poor" persons—might arguably meet the criteria established in these prior cases. Even a cursory examination, however, demonstrates that neither of the two distinguishing characteristics of wealth classifications can be found here. First, in support of their charge that the system discriminates against the "poor," appellees have made no effort to demonstrate that it operates to the peculiar disadvantage of any class fairly definable as indigent, or as composed of persons whose incomes are beneath any designated poverty level. Indeed, there is reason to believe that the poorest families are not necessarily clustered in the poorest property districts. A recent and exhaustive study of school districts in Connecticut concluded that "it is clearly incorrect . . . to contend that the 'poor' live in 'poor' districts . . . . Thus, the major factual assumption of *Serrano*—that the educational financing system discriminates against the 'poor'—is simply false in Connecticut."[53] Defining "poor" families as those below the Bureau of the Census "poverty level," the Connecticut study found, not surprisingly, that the poor were clustered around commercial and industrial areas—those same areas that provide the most attractive sources of property tax income for school districts. . . .

Second, neither appellees nor the district court addressed the fact that, unlike each of the foregoing cases, lack of personal resources has not occasioned an absolute deprivation of the desired benefit. The argument here is not that the children in districts having relatively low assessable property values are receiving no public education; rather, it is that they are receiving a poorer quality education than that available to children in districts having more assessable wealth. Apart from the unsettled and disputed question whether the quality of education may be determined by the amount of money expended for it, a sufficient answer to appellees' argument is that at least where wealth is involved the equal protection clause does not require absolute equality or precisely equal advantages. . . .[57]

For these two reasons—the absence of any evidence that the financing system discriminates against any definable category of "poor" people or that it results in the absolute deprivation of education—the disadvantaged class is not susceptible of identification in traditional terms.[60]

---

53. Note, "A Statistical Analysis of the School Finance Decisions: On Winning Battles and Losing Wars," 81 *Yale LJ* 1303, 1328-29 (1972).

57. E. g., *Bullock v Carter* 405 US 134, 137, 149 (1972); *Mayer v Chicago* 404 US 189, 194 (1971); *Draper v Washington* 372 US 487, 495-96 (1963); *Douglas v California* 372 US 353, 357 (1963).

60. An educational financing system might be hypothesized, however, in which the analogy to the wealth discrimination cases would be considerably closer. If elementary and secondary education were made available by the state only to those able to pay a tuition assessed against each pupil, there would be a clearly defined class of "poor" people—definable in terms of their inability to pay the prescribed sum—who would be absolutely precluded from receiving an education. That case would present a far more compelling set of circumstances for judicial assistance than the case before us today. After all, Texas has undertaken to do a

As suggested above, appellees and the district court may have embraced a second or third approach, the second of which might be characterized as a theory of relative or comparative discrimination based on family income. Appellees sought to prove that a direct correlation exists between the wealth of families within each district and the expenditures therein for education. That is, along a continuum, the poorer the family the lower the dollar amount of education received by the family's children. . . .

[A] survey of approximately 10 percent of the school districts in Texas . . . [shows] only that the wealthiest few districts in the sample have the highest median family incomes and spend the most on education, and that the several poorest districts have the lowest family incomes and devote the least amount of money to education.[63] For the remainder of the districts—96 districts composing almost 90 percent of the sample—the correlation is inverted, i. e., the districts that spend next to the most money on education are populated by families having next to the lowest median family incomes while the districts spending the least have the highest median family incomes. It is evident that, even if the conceptual questions were answered favorably to appellees, no factual basis exists upon which to found a claim of comparative wealth discrimination.

This brings us, then, to the third way in which the classification scheme might be defined—*district* wealth discrimination. Since the only correlation indicated by the evidence is between district property wealth and expenditures, it may be argued that discrimination might be found without regard to the individual income characteristics of district residents. . . .

However described, it is clear that appellees' suit asks this court to extend its most exacting scrutiny to review a system that allegedly discriminates against a large, diverse, and amorphous class, unified only by the common factor of residence in districts that happen to have less taxable wealth than other districts.[66] The system of alleged discrimination and the class it defines have none of the traditional indicia of suspectness: the class is not saddled with such disabilities,

---

good deal more than provide an education to those who can afford it. It has provided what it considers to be an adequate base education for all children and has attempted, though imperfectly, to ameliorate by state funding and by the local assessment program the disparities in local tax resources.

63. Market Value of Taxable Property Per Pupil	Median Family Income from 1960	Percent Minority Pupils	State & Local Expenditures Per Pupil
Above $100,000 (10 districts)	$5,900	8%	$815
$100,000-$50,000 (26 districts)	$4,425	32%	$544
$50,000-$30,000 (30 districts)	$4,900	23%	$483
$30,000-$10,000 (40 districts)	$5,050	31%	$462
Below $10,000 (4 districts)	$3,325	79%	$305

66. Appellees, however, have avoided describing the Texas system as one resulting merely in discrimination between districts per se since this court has never questioned the state's power to draw reasonable distinctions between political subdivisions within its borders. *Griffin v County School Bd* 377 US 218, 230-231 (1964); *McGowan v Maryland* 366 US 420, 427 (1961); *Salsburg v Maryland* 346 US 545, 552 (1954).

or subjected to such a history of purposeful unequal treatment, or relegated to such a position of political powerlessness as to command extraordinary protection from the majoritarian political process.

We thus conclude that the Texas system does not operate to the peculiar disadvantage of any suspect class. But in recognition of the fact that this court has never heretofore held that wealth discrimination alone provides an adequate basis for invoking strict scrutiny, appellees have not relied solely on this contention. They also assert that the state's system impermissibly interferes with the exercise of a "fundamental" right and that accordingly the prior decisions of this court require the application of the strict standard of judicial review. . . .[68]

B

In *Brown v Board of Educ* 347 US 483 (1954), a unanimous court recognized that "education is perhaps the most important function of state and local governments. . . ." This theme, expressing an abiding respect for the vital role of education in a free society, may be found in numerous opinions of justices of this court writing both before and after *Brown* was decided. . . .

Nothing this court holds today in any way detracts from our historic dedication to public education. We are in complete agreement with the conclusion of the three-judge panel below that "the grave significance of education both to the individual and to our society" cannot be doubted. But the importance of a service performed by the state does not determine whether it must be regarded as fundamental for purposes of examination under the equal protection clause. . . . [The Court discusses *Shapiro v Thompson* 394 US 618 (1969), which struck down welfare residence requirements as an infringement on the constitutionally guaranteed "right to interstate travel." It distinguishes *Lindsey v Normet* 405 US 56 (1972), which rejected a constitutional challenge to procedural limitations on tenants in suits brought by landlords, and *Dandridge v Williams* 397 US 471 (1970), which rejected a constitutional challenge to Maryland's setting a welfare ceiling for families, as cases involving no explicitly constitutionally guaranteed right.]

The lesson of these cases in addressing the question now before the court is plain. It is not the province of this court to create substantive constitutional rights in the name of guaranteeing equal protection of the laws. Thus the key to discovering whether education is "fundamental" is not to be found in comparisons of the relative societal significance of education as opposed to subsistence or housing. Nor is it to be found by weighing whether education is as important as the right to travel. Rather, the answer lies in assessing whether there is a right to education explicitly or implicitly guaranteed by the Constitution. . . .

Education, of course, is not among the rights afforded explicit protection under our federal Constitution. Nor do we find any basis for saying it is implicitly so protected: As we have said, the undisputed importance of education will

---

68. See . . . J. Coons, W. Clune, and S. Sugarman, [*Private Wealth and Public Education* 339-93 (1970)]; Goldstein, ["Interdistrict Inequalities in School Financing: A Critical Analysis of *Serrano v Priest* and Its Progeny," 12 *U Pa L Rev* 504, 534-41 (1972)]; Vieira, ["Unequal Educational Expenditures: Some Minority Views on *Serrano v Priest*," 37 *Mo L Rev* 617, 618-24 (1972); Comment, "Educational Financing, Equal Protection of the Laws, and the Supreme Court," 70 *Mich L Rev* 1324, 1335-42 (1972); Note, "The Public School Financing Cases: Interdistrict Inequalities and Wealth Discrimination," 14 *Ariz L Rev* 88, 120-24 (1972).

not alone cause this court to depart from the usual standard for reviewing a state's social and economic legislation. It is appellees' contention, however, that education is distinguishable from other services and benefits provided by the state because it bears a peculiarly close relationship to other rights and liberties accorded protection under the Constitution. Specifically, they insist that education is itself a fundamental personal right because it is essential to the effective exercise of First Amendment freedoms and to intelligent utilization of the right to vote. In asserting a nexus between speech and education, appellees urge that the right to speak is meaningless unless the speaker is capable of articulating his thoughts intelligently and persuasively. The "marketplace of ideas" is an empty forum for those lacking basic communicative tools. Likewise, they argue that the corollary right to receive information becomes little more than a hollow privilege when the recipient has not been taught to read, assimilate, and utilize available knowledge.

A similar line of reasoning is pursued with respect to the right to vote. Exercise of the franchise, it is contended, cannot be divorced from the educational foundation of the voter. The electoral process, if reality is to conform to the democratic ideal, depends on an informed electorate: a voter cannot cast his ballot intelligently unless his reading skills and thought processes have been adequately developed.

We need not dispute any of these propositions. The court has long afforded zealous protection against unjustifiable governmental interference with the individual's rights to speak and to vote. Yet we have never presumed to possess either the ability or the authority to guarantee to the citizenry the most *effective* speech or the most *informed* electoral choice. That these may be desirable goals of a system of freedom of expression and of a representative form of government is not to be doubted. These are indeed goals to be pursued by a people whose thoughts and beliefs are freed from governmental interference. But they are not values to be implemented by judicial intrusion into otherwise legitimate state activities.

Even if it were conceded that some identifiable quantum of education is a constitutionally protected prerequisite to the meaningful exercise of either right, we have no indication that the present levels of educational expenditure in Texas provide an education that falls short ... [N]o charge fairly could be made that the system fails to provide each child with an opportunity to acquire the basic minimal skills necessary for the enjoyment of the rights of speech and of full participation in the political process.

Furthermore, the logical limitations on appellees' nexus theory are difficult to perceive. How, for instance, is education to be distinguished from the significant personal interests in the basics of decent food and shelter? Empirical examination might well buttress an assumption that the ill-fed, ill-clothed, and ill-housed are among the most ineffective participants in the political process and that they derive the least enjoyment from the benefits of the First Amendment. If so appellees' thesis would cast serious doubt on the authority of *Dandridge v Williams* ... and *Lindsey v Normet*. ...

C

We need not rest our decision, however, solely on the inappropriateness of the strict scrutiny test. A century of Supreme Court adjudication under the equal protection clause affirmatively supports the application of the traditional standard of review, which requires only that the state's system be shown to bear some rational relationship to legitimate state purposes. This case represents far more than a challenge to the manner in which Texas provides for the education of its children. We have here nothing less than a direct attack on the way in which Texas has chosen to raise and disburse state and local tax revenues. We are asked to condemn the state's judgment in conferring on political subdivisions the power to tax local property to supply revenues for local interests. In so doing, appellees would have the court intrude in an area in which it has traditionally deferred to state legislatures. . . .

[T]he justices of this court lack both the expertise and the familiarity with local problems so necessary to the making of wise decisions with respect to the raising and disposition of public revenues. Yet we are urged to direct the states either to alter drastically the present system or to throw out the property tax altogether in favor of some other form of taxation. No scheme of taxation, whether the tax is imposed on property, income, or purchases of goods and services, has yet been devised which is free of all discriminatory impact. In such a complex arena in which no perfect alternatives exist, the court does well not to impose too rigorous a standard of scrutiny lest all local fiscal schemes become subjects of criticism under the equal protection clause.[85]

In addition to matters of fiscal policy, this case also involves the most persistent and difficult questions of educational policy, another area in which this court's lack of specialized knowledge and experience counsels against premature interference with the informed judgments made at the state and local levels. . . . On even the most basic questions in this area the scholars and educational experts are divided. Indeed, one of the major sources of controversy concerns the extent to which there is a demonstrable correlation between educational expenditures and the quality of education[86]—an assumed correlation underlying virtually

85. Those who urge that the present system be invalidated offer little guidance as to what type of school financing should replace it. The most likely result of rejection of the existing system would be statewide financing of all public education with funds derived from taxation of property or from the adoption or expansion of sales and income taxes. See Simon, *supra*, n62. The authors of *Private Wealth and Public Education*, *supra*, n13, at 201-242, suggest an alternative scheme, known as "district power equalizing." In simplest terms, the state would guarantee that at any particular rate of property taxation the district would receive a stated number of dollars regardless of the district's tax base. To finance the subsidies to "poorer" districts, funds would be taken away from the "wealthier" districts that, because of their higher property values, collect more than the stated amount at any given rate. This is not the place to weigh the arguments for and against "district power equalizing," beyond noting that commentators are in disagreement as to whether it is feasible, how it would work, and indeed whether it would violate the equal protection theory underlying appellees' case. President's Comm'n on School Financing, *Schools, People & Money* 32-33 (1972); Bateman and Brown, "Some Reflections on *Serrano v Priest*," 49 *J Urban L* 701, 706-8 (1972); Brest, Book Review, 23 *Stan L Rev* 591, 594-96 (1971); Goldstein, *supra*, n38, at 542-43; Wise, "School Finance Equalization Lawsuits: A Model Legislative Response," 2 *Yale Rev L & Soc Action* 123, 125 (1971); Silard and White, "Intrastate Inequalities in Public Education: The Case for Judicial Relief Under the Equal Protection Clause," 1970 *Wis L Rev* 7, 29-30.

86. The quality-cost controversy has received considerable attention. Among the notable authorities on both sides are the following: C. Jencks, *Inequality* (1972); C. Silberman, *Crisis in the Classroom* (1970); Office of Education, *Equality of Educational Opportunity* (1966) (The Coleman Report); *On Equality of Educational Opportunity* (Moynihan and Mosteller

every legal conclusion drawn by the district court in this case. Related to the questioned relationship between cost and quality is the equally unsettled controversy as to the proper goals of a system of public education. . . . In such circumstances the judiciary is well advised to refrain from imposing on the states inflexible constitutional restraints that could circumscribe or handicap the continued research and experimentation so vital to finding even partial solutions to educational problems and to keeping abreast of ever changing conditions.

It must be remembered also that every claim arising under the equal protection clause has implications for the relationship between national and state power under our federal system. . . . [I] t would be difficult to imagine a case having a greater potential impact on our federal system than the one now before us, in which we are urged to abrogate systems of financing public education presently in existence in virtually every state.

The foregoing considerations buttress our conclusion that Texas' system of public school finance is an inappropriate candidate for strict judicial scrutiny. These same considerations are relevant to the determination whether that system, with its conceded imperfections, nevertheless bears some rational relationship to a legitimate state purpose. It is to this question that we next turn our attention. . . .

The Texas system of school finance . . . , [w] hile assuring a basic education for every child in the state, . . . permits and encourages a large measure of participation in and control of each district's schools at the local level. . . .

The persistence of attachment to government at the lowest level where education is concerned reflects the depth of commitment of its supporters. In part, local control means, as Professor Coleman suggests, the freedom to devote more money to the education of one's children. Equally important, however, is the opportunity it offers for participation in the decision-making process that determines how those local tax dollars will be spent. . . .

Appellees do not question the propriety of Texas' dedication to local control of education. To the contrary, they attack the school financing system precisely because, in their view, it does not provide the same level of local control and fiscal flexibility in all districts. Appellees suggest that local control could be preserved and promoted under other financing systems that resulted in more equality in educational expenditures. While it is no doubt true that reliance on local property taxation for school revenues provides less freedom of choice with respect to expenditures for some districts than for others,[107] the existence of

eds 1972); J. Guthrie, G. Kleindorfer, H. Levin, and R. Stout, *Schools and Inequality* (1971); President's Comm'n on School Finance, *supra*, n85; Swanson, "The Cost-Quality Relationship, in The Challenge of Change in School Finance," *10th Nat'l Educational Ass'n Conf on School Finance* 151 (1967).

107. Mr. Justice White suggests in his dissent that the Texas system violates the equal protection clause because the means it has selected to effectuate its interest in local autonomy fail to guarantee complete freedom of choice to every district. He places special emphasis on the statutory provision that establishes a maximum rate of $1.50 per $100 valuation at which a local school district may tax for school maintenance. Tex Educ Code §20.04(d) (1972). The maintenance rate in Edgewood when this case was litigated in the district court was $.55 per $100, barely one-third of the allowable rate. (The tax rate of $1.05 per $100, see p584, *supra*, is the equalized rate for maintenance and for the retirement of bonds.) Appellees do not claim that the ceiling presently bars desired tax increases in Edgewood or in any other Texas district. Therefore, the constitutionality of that statutory provision is not

"some inequality" in the manner in which the state's rationale is achieved is not alone a sufficient basis for striking down the entire system.... The people of Texas may be justified in believing that other systems of school financing, which place more of the financial responsibility in the hands of the state, will result in a comparable lessening of desired local autonomy. That is, they may believe that along with increased control of the purse strings at the state level will go increased control over local policies.[109]

Appellees further urge that the Texas system is unconstitutionally arbitrary because it allows the availability of local taxable resources to turn on "happenstance." They see no justification for a system that allows, as they contend, the quality of education to fluctuate on the basis of the fortuitous positioning of the boundary lines of political subdivisions and the location of valuable commercial and industrial property. But any scheme of local taxation—indeed the very existence of identifiable local governmental units—requires the establishment of jurisdictional boundaries that are inevitably arbitrary....

Moreover, if local taxation for local expenditures were an unconstitutional method of providing for education then it might be an equally impermissible means of providing other necessary services customarily financed largely from local property taxes, including local police and fire protection, public health and hospitals, and public utility facilities of various kinds. We perceive no justification for such a severe denigration of local property taxation and control as would follow from appellees' contentions....

In sum, to the extent that the Texas system of school financing results in unequal expenditures between children who happen to reside in different districts, we cannot say that such disparities are the product of a system that is so irrational as to be invidiously discriminatory. Texas has acknowledged its shortcomings and has persistently endeavored—not without some success—to ameliorate the differences in levels of expenditures without sacrificing the benefits of local participation. The Texas plan is not the result of hurried, ill-conceived legislation. It certainly is not the product of purposeful discrimination against any group or class....

IV

The complexity of these [school finance] problems is demonstrated by the lack of consensus with respect to whether it may be said with any assurance that the poor, the racial minorities, or the children in overburdened core-city school districts would be benefitted by abrogation of traditional modes of financing education. Unless there is to be a substantial increase in state expenditures on

before us and must await litigation in a case in which it is properly presented. Cf. *Hargrave v Kirk* 313 F Supp 944 (MD Fla 1970), *vacated,* 401 US 476 (1971).

109. This theme—that greater state control over funding will lead to greater state power with respect to local educational programs and policies—is a recurrent one in the literature on financing public education. Professor Simon, in his thoughtful analysis of the political ramifications of this case, states that one of the most likely consequences of the district court's decision would be an increase in the centralization of school finance and an increase in the extent of collective bargaining by teacher unions at the state level. He suggests that the subjects for bargaining may include many "nonsalary" items, such as teaching loads, class size, curricular and program choices, questions of student discipline, and selection of administrative personnel—matters traditionally decided heretofore at the local level. Simon, ["The School Finance Decisions: Collective Bargaining and Future Systems," 82 *Yale LJ* 409, 434-37 (1973)] ....

education across the board—an event the likelihood of which is open to considerable question—these groups stand to realize gains in terms of increased per-pupil expenditures only if they reside in districts that presently spend at relatively low levels, *i. e.,* in those districts that would benefit from the redistribution of existing resources. Yet recent studies have indicated that the poorest families are not invariably clustered in the most impecunious school districts. Nor does it now appear that there is any more than a random chance that racial minorities are concentrated in property-poor districts. Additionally, several research projects have concluded that any financing alternative designed to achieve a greater equality of expenditures is likely to lead to higher taxation and lower educational expenditures in the major urban centers, a result that would exacerbate rather than ameliorate existing conditions in those areas.

These practical considerations, of course, play no role in the adjudication of the constitutional issues presented here. But they serve to highlight the wisdom of the traditional limitations on this court's function. . . . We hardly need add that this court's action today is not to be viewed as placing its judicial imprimatur on the status quo. The need is apparent for reform in tax systems which may well have relied too long and too heavily on the local property tax. And certainly innovative thinking as to public education, its methods and its funding, is necessary to assure both a higher level of quality and greater uniformity of opportunity. These matters merit the continued attention of the scholars who already have contributed much by their challenges. But the ultimate solutions must come from the lawmakers and from the democractic pressures of those who elect them.

Reversed.

Mr. Justice Stewart, concurring.

The method of financing public schools in Texas, as in almost every other state, has resulted in a system of public education that can fairly be described as chaotic and unjust. It does not follow, however, and I cannot find, that this system violates the Constitution of the United States. I join the opinion and judgment of the court because I am convinced that any other course would mark an extraordinary departure from principled adjudication under the equal protection clause of the Fourteenth Amendment. . . .

Mr. Justice White, with whom Mr. Justice Douglas and Mr. Justice Brennan join, dissenting. . . .

I cannot disagree with the proposition that local control and local decision making play an important part in our democratic system of government. Cf. *James v Valtierra* 402 US 137 (1971). Much may be left to local option, and this case would be quite different if it were true that the Texas system, while insuring minimum educational expenditures in every district through state funding, extended a meaningful option to all local districts to increase their per-pupil expenditures and so to improve their children's education to the extent that increased funding would achieve that goal. The system would then arguably provide a rational and sensible method of achieving the stated aim of preserving an area for local initiative and decision.

The difficulty with the Texas system, however, is that it provides a meaningful option to Alamo Heights and like school districts but almost none to Edgewood and those other districts with a low per-pupil real estate tax base. In these latter districts, no matter how desirous parents are of supporting their schools with greater revenues, it is impossible to do so through the use of the real estate property tax. In these districts the Texas system utterly fails to extend a realistic choice to parents, because the property tax, which is the only revenue-raising mechanism extended to school districts, is practically and legally unavailable. . . .

If the State aims at maximizing local initiative and local choice, by permitting school districts to resort to the real property tax if they choose to do so, it utterly fails in achieving its purpose in districts with property tax bases so low that there is little if any opportunity for interested parents, rich or poor, to augment school district revenues. Requiring the state to establish only that un-equal treatment is in furtherance of a permissible goal, without also requiring the state to show that the means chosen to effectuate that goal are rationally related to its achievement, makes equal protection analysis no more than an empty gesture. In my view, the parents and children in Edgewood, and in like districts, suffer from an invidious discrimination violative of the equal protection clause. . . .

There is no difficulty in identifying the class that is subject to the alleged discrimination and that is entitled to the benefits of the equal protection clause. I need go no farther than the parents and children in the Edgewood district, who are plaintiffs here and who assert that they are entitled to the same choice as Alamo Heights to augment local expenditures for schools but are denied that choice by state law. This group constitutes a class sufficiently definite to invoke the protection of the Constitution . . . [I]n the present case we would blink reality to ignore the fact that school districts, and students in the end, are differentially affected by the Texas school financing scheme with respect to their capability to supplement the Minimum Foundation School Program. At the very least, the law discriminates against those children and their parents who live in districts where the per-pupil tax base is sufficiently low to make impossible the provision of comparable school revenues by resort to the real property tax which is the only device the state extends for this purpose.

Mr. Justice Marshall, with whom Mr. Justice Douglas concurs, dissenting.

The court today decides, in effect, that a state may constitutionally vary the quality of education which it offers its children in accordance with the amount of taxable wealth located in the school districts within which they reside. The majority's decision represents an abrupt departure from the mainstream of recent state and federal court decisions concerning the unconstitutionality of state educational financing schemes dependent upon taxable local wealth. More unfortunately, though, the majority's holding can only be seen as a retreat from our historic commitment to equality of educational opportunity and as unsupportable acquiescence in a system which deprives children in their earliest years of the chance to reach their full potential as citizens. The court does this despite the absence of any substantial justification for a scheme which arbitrarily channels educational resources in accordance with the fortuity of the amount of taxable wealth within each district. . . .

I

The court acknowledges that "substantial interdistrict disparities in school expenditures" exist in Texas . . . and that these disparities are "largely attributable to differences in the amounts of money collected through local property taxation". . . . But instead of closely examining the seriousness of these disparities and the invidiousness of the Texas financing scheme, the court undertakes an elaborate exploration of the efforts Texas has purportedly made to close the gaps between its districts in terms of levels of district wealth and resulting educational funding. Yet, however praiseworthy Texas' equalizing efforts, the issue in this case is not whether Texas is doing its best to ameliorate the worst features of a discriminatory scheme, but rather whether the scheme itself is in fact unconstitutionally discriminatory in the face of the Fourteenth Amendment's guarantee of equal protection of the laws. When the Texas financing scheme is taken as a whole, I do not think it can be doubted that it produces a discriminatory impact on substantial numbers of the school-age children of the state of Texas.

[Justice Marshall reviews the workings of the Texas school finance scheme. He notes that: "The necessary effect of the Texas local property tax is . . . to favor property rich districts and to disfavor property poor ones." That disparity, he adds: "cannot be dismissed as the result of lack of local effort—that is, lower tax rates—by property poor districts. To the contrary, the data presented below indicate that the poorest districts tend to have the highest tax rates and the richest districts tend to have the lowest tax rates." Justice Marshall then turns to other sources of school revenues. Federal funds, which pay for some 10 percent of the total cost of public education in Texas, do not "ameliorate significantly the widely varying consequences for Texas school districts and children of the local property tax element of the state financing scheme." And state funds, which pay half of Texas' education bill tend "to subsidize the rich at the expense of the poor." The allocation criteria enable property rich districts to claim a larger share of educational costs than property poor districts; the economic index upon which state aid is calculated includes factors which are not "predictive of a district's relative ability to raise revenues through local property taxes."]

B

The appellants do not deny the disparities in educational funding caused by variations in taxable district property wealth. They do contend, however, that whatever the differences in per-pupil spending among Texas districts, there are no discriminatory consequences for the children of the disadvantaged districts. . . .

In my view, though, even an unadorned restatement of this contention is sufficient to reveal its absurdity. Authorities concerned with educational quality no doubt disagree as to the significance of variations in per pupil spending. . . . We sit, however, not to resolve disputes over educational theory but to enforce our Constitution. It is an inescapable fact that if one district has more funds available per pupil than another district, the former will have greater choice in educational planning than will the latter. In this regard, I believe the question of discrimination in educational quality must be deemed to be an objective one that looks to what the state provides its children, not to what the children are able to do with what they receive. . . .

Hence, even before this court recognized its duty to tear down the barriers of state-enforced racial segregation in public education, it acknowledged that inequality in the educational facilities provided to students may be discriminatory state action as contemplated by the equal protection clause. As a basis for striking down state enforced segregation of a law school, the court in *Sweatt v Painter* 339 US 629, 633-34 (1950), stated:

[W]e cannot find substantial equality in the educational opportunities offered white and Negro law students by the state. In terms of number of the faculty, variety of courses and opportunity for specialization, size of the student body, scope of the library, availability of law review and similar activities, the [white only] law school is superior. . . . It is difficult to believe that one who had a free choice between these law schools would consider the question close.

See also *McLaurin v Oklahoma State Regents* 339 US 637 (1950). Likewise it is difficult to believe that if the children of Texas had a free choice, they would choose to be educated in districts with fewer resources, and hence with more-antiquated plants, less-experienced teachers, and a less-diversified curriculum. In fact, if financing variations are so insignificant to educational quality, it is difficult to understand why a number of our country's wealthiest school districts, which have no legal obligation to argue in support of the constitutionality of the Texas legislation, have nevertheless zealously pursued its cause before this court. . . .

At the very least, in view of the substantial interdistrict disparities in funding and in resulting educational inputs shown by appellees to exist under the Texas financing scheme, the burden of proving that these disparities do not in fact affect the quality of children's education must fall upon the appellants. Cf. *Hobson v Hansen* 327 F Supp 844, 860-61 (DCDC 1971). Yet appellants made no effort in the district court to demonstrate that educational quality is not affected by variations in funding and in resulting inputs. . . .

Nor can I accept the appellants' apparent suggestion that the Texas Minimum Foundation School Program effectively eradicates any discriminatory effects otherwise resulting from the local property tax element of the Texas financing scheme. Appellants assert that, despite its imperfections, the program "does guarantee an adequate education to every child." The majority, in considering the constitutionality of the Texas financing scheme, seems to find substantial merit in this contention. . . . But I fail to understand how the constitutional problems inherent in the financing scheme are eased by the Foundation Program. . . .

The suggestion may be that the state aid received via the Foundation Program sufficiently improves the position of property poor districts vis-à-vis property rich districts—in terms of educational funds—to eliminate any claim of interdistrict discrimination in available educational resources which might otherwise exist if educational funding were dependent solely upon local property taxation. . . . But as has already been seen, we are hardly presented here with some *de minimis* claim of discrimination resulting from the play necessary in any functioning system; to the contrary, it is clear that the Foundation Program utterly fails to ameliorate the seriously discriminatory effects of the local property tax.

Alternatively, the appellants and the majority may believe that the equal protection clause cannot be offended by substantially unequal state treatment of persons who are similarly situated so long as the state provides everyone with some unspecified amount of education which evidently is "enough." The basis for such a novel view is far from clear. . . . The Equal Protection Clause is not addressed to the minimal sufficiency but rather to the unjustifiable inequalities of state action. It mandates nothing less than that "all persons similarly circumstanced shall be treated alike." *F. S. Royster Guano Co v Virginia* 253 US 412, 415 (1920).

Even if the equal protection clause encompassed some theory of constitutional adequacy, discrimination in the provision of educational opportunity would certainly seem to be a poor candidate for its application. Neither the majority nor appellants inform us how judicially manageable standards are to be derived for determining how much education is "enough" to excuse constitutional discrimination. One would think that the majority would heed its own fervent affirmation of judicial self-restraint before undertaking the complex task of determining at large what level of education is constitutionally sufficient. . . .

C

Despite the evident discriminatory effect of the Texas financing scheme, both the appellants and the majority raise substantial questions concerning the precise character of the disadvantaged class in this case. . . .

[W]hile on its face the Texas scheme may merely discriminate between local districts, the impact of that discrimination falls directly upon the children whose educational opportunity is dependent upon where they happen to live. Consequently, the district court correctly concluded that the Texas financing scheme discriminates, from a constitutional perspective, between school children on the basis of the amount of taxable property located within their local districts. . . .

A number of theories of discrimination have, to be sure, been considered in the course of this litigation. Thus, the district court found that in Texas the poor and minority group members tend to live in property poor districts, suggesting discrimination on the basis of both personal wealth and race. . . . Although I have serious doubts as to the correctness of the court's analysis in rejecting the data submitted below,[56] I have no need to join issue on these factual disputes.

I believe it is sufficient that the overarching form of discrimination in this

---

56. The court rejects the district court's finding of a correlation between poor people and poor districts with the assertion that "there is reason to believe that the poorest families are not necessarily clustered in the poorest property districts" in Texas. . . . In support of its conclusion the court offers absolutely no data—which it cannot on this record—concerning the distribution of poor people in Texas to refute the data introduced below by appellees; it relies instead on a recent law review note concerned solely with the state of Connecticut, Note, "A Statistical Analysis of the School Finance Decisions: On Winning Battles and Losing Wars," 81 *Yale LJ* 1303 (1972). Common sense suggests that the basis for drawing a demographic conclusion with respect to a geographically large, urban-rural, industrial-agricultural state such as Texas from a geographically small, densely populated, highly industrialized state such as Connecticut is doubtful at best.

Furthermore, the article upon which the court relies to discredit the statistical procedures employed by Professor Berke to establish the correlation between poor people and poor districts, see n11, *supra*, based its criticism primarily on the fact that only 4 of the 110 districts studied were in the lowest of the five categories, which were determined by relative taxable property per pupil, and most districts clustered in the middle three groups. See Goldstein, "Interdistrict Inequalities in School Financing: A Critical Analysis of *Serrano v Priest* and Its Progeny," 120 *U Pa L Rev* 504, 524 n67 (1972). But the court fails to note that the four poorest districts in the sample had over 50,000 students which constituted 10 percent of the students in the entire sample. It appears, moreover, that even when the richest and the poorest categories are enlarged to include in each category 20 percent of the students in the sample, the correlation between district and individual wealth holds true.

Finally, it cannot be ignored that the data introduced by appellees went unchallenged in the district court. The majority's willingness to permit appellants to litigate the correctness

case is between the school children of Texas on the basis of the taxable property wealth of the districts in which they happen to live. To understand both the precise nature of this discrimination and the parameters of the disadvantaged class it is sufficient to consider the constitutional principle which appellees contend is controlling in the context of educational financing. In their complaint appellees asserted that the Constitution does not permit local district wealth to be determinative of educational opportunity. This is simply another way of saying, as the district court concluded, that consistent with the guarantee of equal protection of the laws, "the quality of public education may not be a function of wealth, other than the wealth of the state as a whole." . . . Under such a principle, the children of a district are excessively advantaged if that district has more taxable property per pupil than the average amount of taxable property per pupil considering the state as a whole. By contrast, the children of a district are disadvantaged if that district has less taxable property per pupil than the state average. . . . Whether this discrimination, against the school children of property poor districts, inherent in the Texas financing scheme is violative of the equal protection clause is the question to which we must now turn.

II . . . .

A

To begin, I must once more voice my disagreement with the court's rigidified approach to equal protection analysis. See *Dandridge v Williams* 397 US 471, 519-21 (1970) (dissenting opinion); *Richardson v Belcher* 404 US 78, 90 (1971) (dissenting opinion). The court apparently seeks to establish today that equal protection cases fall into one of two neat categories which dictate the appropriate standard of review—strict scrutiny or mere rationality. But this court's decisions in the field of equal protection defy such easy categorization. A principled reading of what this court has done reveals that it has applied a spectrum of standards in reviewing discrimination allegedly violative of the equal protection clause. This spectrum clearly comprehends variations in the degree of care with which the court will scrutinize particular classifications, depending, I believe, on the constitutional and societal importance of the interest adversely affected and the recognized invidiousness of the basis upon which the particular classification is drawn. . . .

I therefore cannot accept the majority's labored efforts to demonstrate that fundamental interests, which call for strict scrutiny of the challenged classification, encompass only established rights which we are somehow bound to recognize from the text of the Constitution itself. To be sure, some interests which the court has deemed to be fundamental for purposes of equal protection analysis are themselves constitutionally protected rights. . . .

[But] I would like to know where the Constitution guarantees the right to procreate, *Skinner v Oklahoma ex rel Williamson* 316 US 535, 541 (1942), or the right to vote in state elections, e. g., *Reynolds v Sims* 377 US 533 (1964), or the right to an appeal from a criminal conviction, e. g., *Griffin v Illinois* 351 US 12 (1956). These are instances in which, due to the importance of the interests at stake, the court has displayed a strong concern with the existence of discriminatory state treatment. But the court has never said or indicated that these are interests which independently enjoy full-blown constitutional protection. . . .

of those data for the first time before this tribunal—where effective response by appellees is impossible—is both unfair and judicially unsound.

The majority is, of course, correct when it suggests that the process of determining which interests are fundamental is a difficult one. But I do not think the problem is insurmountable. And I certainly do not accept the view that the process need necessarily degenerate into an unprincipled, subjective "picking-and-choosing" between various interests or that it must involve this court in creating "substantive constitutional rights in the name of guaranteeing equal protection of the laws." . . . Although not all fundamental interests are constitutionally guaranteed, the determination of which interests are fundamental should be firmly rooted in the text of the Constitution. The task in every case should be to determine the extent to which constitutionally guaranteed rights are dependent on interests not mentioned in the Constitution. As the nexus between the specific constitutional guarantee and the nonconstitutional interest draws closer, the nonconstitutional interest becomes more fundamental and the degree of judicial scrutiny applied when the interest is infringed on a discriminatory basis must be adjusted accordingly. . . .

[Justice Marshall next discusses several cases which, while assertedly testing the constitutionality of legislation against the traditional equal protection "rationality" standard, in fact reject the "two tier" review approach. In *Eisenstadt v Baird* 405 US 438 (1972), the court struck down a Massachusetts statute which denied unmarried persons access to contraceptive devices on the same basis as married persons. ". . . [A]lthough there were conceivable state interests intended to be advanced by the statute—e.g., deterrence of premarital sexual activity; regulation of the dissemination of potentially dangerous articles—the court was not prepared to accept these interests on their face, but instead proceeded to test their substantiality by independent analysis." A similar standard of review was applied in *James v Strange* 407 US 128 (1972), which held unconstitutional a state statute providing for recoupment from indigent convicts of legal defense fees paid by the state, and in *Reed v Reed* 404 US 71 (1971), which struck down a statute which gave men preference over women when persons of equal entitlement apply for assignment as administrator of a particular estate. To Justice Marshall, "*James* and *Reed* can only be understood as instances in which the particularly invidious character of the classification caused the court to pause and scrutinize with more than traditional care the rationality of state discrimination." And, notes Justice Marshall, *Weber v Aetna Cas & Sur Co* 406 US 164 (1972), which held unconstitutional a portion of a state workman's compensation statute that relegated unacknowledged illegitimate children of the deceased to a lesser status with respect to benefits than that enjoyed by legitimate children of the deceased, is the clearest recent example of the "court's sensitivity to the invidiousness of the basis for discrimination. . . ."]

In summary, it seems to me inescapably clear that this court has consistently adjusted the care with which it will review state discrimination in light of the constitutional significance of the interests affected and the invidiousness of the particular classification. . . . The majority suggests, however, that a variable standard of review would give this court the appearance of a "superlegislature." . . . I cannot agree. Such an approach seems to me a part of the guarantees of our Constitution and of the historic experiences with oppression of and discrimination against discrete, powerless minorities which underlie that document. In truth, the court itself will be open to the criticism raised by the majority so long as it continues on its present course of effectively selecting in private which cases will be afforded special consideration without acknowledging the true basis of its action.[67]

Opinions such as those in *Reed* and *James* seem drawn more as efforts to shield rather than to reveal the true basis of the court's decisions. Such obfuscated action may be appropriate to a political body such as a legislature, but it is not appropriate to this court. Open debate of the bases for the court's action is essential to the rationality and consistency of our decision-making process. Only in this way can we avoid the label of legislature and ensure the integrity of the judicial process.

Nevertheless, the majority today attempts to force this case into the same category for purposes of equal protection analysis as decisions involving discrimination affecting commercial interests. By so doing, the majority singles this case out for analytic treatment at odds with what seems to me to be the clear trend of recent decisions in this court, and thereby ignores the constitutional importance of the interest at stake and the invidiousness of the particular classification, factors that call for far more than the lenient scrutiny of the Texas financing scheme which the majority pursues. . . .

B

. . . [T]he fundamental importance of education is amply indicated by the prior decisions of this court, by the unique status accorded public education by our society, and by the close relationship between education and some of our most basic constitutional values.

The special concern of this court with the educational process of our country is a matter of common knowledge. [citing *Brown v Board of Educ* 347 US 483, 493 (1954): "Today, education is perhaps the most important function of state and local governments"; *Wisconsin v Yoder* 406 US 205, 213 (1972): "Providing public schools ranks at the very apex of the function of a state."] . . .

Education directly affects the ability of a child to exercise his First Amendment interest both as a source and as a receiver of information and ideas, whatever interests he may pursue in life. . . .

Of particular importance is the relationship between education and the political process. . . . Education serves the essential function of instilling in our young an understanding of and appreciation for the principles and operation of our governmental processes. Education may instill the interest and provide the tools necessary for political discourse and debate. Indeed, it has frequently been suggested that education is the dominant factor affecting political consciousness and participation. . . .[72] But of most immediate and direct concern must be the demonstrated effect of education on the exercise of the franchise by the electorate.

---

67. See generally Gunther, The Supreme Court, 1971 Term: Foreword, In Search of Evolving Doctrine on a Changing Court: A Model for a Newer Equal Protection, 86 *Harv L Rev* 1 (1972). [cf. Note, "Legislative Purpose, Rationality, and Equal Protection," 82 *Yale L J* 123 (1972).]

72. That education is the dominant factor in influencing political participation and awareness is sufficient, I believe, to dispose of the court's suggestion that, in all events, there is no indication that Texas is not providing all of its children with a sufficient education to enjoy the right of free speech and to participate fully in the political process. . . . There is, in short, no limit on the amount of free speech or political participation that the Constitution guarantees. Moreover, it should be obvious that the political process, like most other aspects of social intercourse, is to some degree competitive. It is thus of little benefit to an indi-

The right to vote in federal elections is conferred by Art I, §2, and the Seventeenth Amendment of the Constitution, and access to the state franchise has been afforded special protection because it is "preservative of other basic civil and political rights," *Reynolds v Sims* 377 US 533, 562 (1964). Data from the presidential election of 1968 clearly demonstrates a direct relationship between participation in the electoral process and level of educational attainment; and, as this court recognized in *Gaston County v US* 395 US 285, 296 (1969), the quality of education offered may influence a child's decision to "enter or remain in school." It is this very sort of intimate relationship between a particular personal interest and specific constitutional guarantees that has heretofore caused the court to attach special significance, for purposes of equal protection analysis, to individual interests such as procreation and the exercise of the state franchise.[74]

While ultimately disputing little of this, the majority seeks refuge in the fact that the court has "never presumed to possess either the ability or the authority to guarantee to the citizenry the most *effective* speech or the most *informed* electoral choice." . . . This serves only to blur what is in fact at stake. With due respect, the issue is neither provision of the most *effective* speech nor of the most *informed* vote. Appellees do not now seek the best education Texas might provide. . . . The issue is . . . one of discrimination that affects the quality of the education which Texas has chosen to provide its children; and, the precise question here is what importance should attach to education for purposes of equal protection analysis of that discrimination. . . . The factors just considered, including the relationship between education and the social and political interests enshrined within the Constitution, compel us to recognize the fundamentality of education and to scrutinize with appropriate care the bases for state discrimination affecting equality of educational opportunity in Texas' school districts[75]—a conclusion which is only strengthened when we consider the character of the classification in this case.

---

vidual from a property poor district to have "enough" education if those around him have more than "enough."

74. I believe that the close nexus between education and our established constitutional values with respect to freedom of speech and participation in the political process makes this a different case from our prior decisions concerning discrimination affecting public welfare, see, e.g., *Dandridge v Williams* 397 US 471 (1970), or housing, see, e.g., *Lindsey v Normet* 405 US 56 (1972). There can be no question that, as the majority suggests, constitutional rights may be less meaningful for someone without enough to eat or without decent housing . . . . But the crucial difference lies in the closeness of the relationship. Whatever the severity of the impact of insufficient food or inadequate housing on a person's life, they have never been considered to bear the same direct and immediate relationship to constitutional concerns for free speech and for our political processes as education has long been recognized to bear. Perhaps, the best evidence of this fact is the unique status which has been accorded public education as the single public service nearly unanimously guaranteed in the constitutions of our states . . . . Education, in terms of constitutional values, is much more analogous in my judgment, to the right to vote in state elections than to public welfare or public housing. . . .

75. The majority's reliance on this court's traditional deference to legislative bodies in matters of taxation falls wide of the mark in the context of this particular case. . . . The decisions on which the court relies were simply taxpayer suits challenging the constitutionality of a tax burden in the face of exemptions or differential taxation afforded to others. See, e.g., *Allied Stores v Bowers* 358 US 522 (1959) . . . . There is no question that from the perspective of the taxpayer, the equal protection clause "imposes no iron rule of equality,

C

. . . . This court has frequently recognized that discrimination on the basis of wealth may create a classification of a suspect character and thereby call for exacting judicial scrutiny. . . . The majority, however, considers any wealth classification in this case to lack certain essential characteristics which it contends are common to the instances of wealth discrimination that this court has heretofore recognized. We are told that in every prior case involving a wealth classification, the members of the disadvantaged class have "shared two distinguishing characteristics: because of their impecunity they were completely unable to pay for some desired benefit, and as a consequence, they sustained an absolute deprivation of a meaningful opportunity to enjoy that benefit." . . . .

I cannot agree. . . .

In *Harper*, the court struck down as violative of the equal protection clause an annual Virginia poll tax of $1.50, payment of which by persons over the age of twenty-one was a prerequisite to voting in Virginia elections. In part, the court relied on the fact that the poll tax interfered with a fundamental interest—the exercise of the state franchise. In addition, though, the court emphasized that "[l]ines drawn on the basis of wealth or property . . . are traditionally disfavored." 383 US at 668. Under the first part of the theory announced by the majority the disadvantaged class in *Harper,* in terms of a wealth analysis, should have consisted only of those too poor to afford the $1.50 necessary to vote. But the *Harper* court did not see it that way. In its view, the equal protection clause "bars a system which excludes [from the franchise] those unable to pay a fee to vote or who *fail to pay.*" . . . So far as the court was concerned, the "degree of the discrimination [was] irrelevant.". . . . Thus, the court struck down the poll tax in toto; it did not order merely that those too poor to pay the tax be exempted; complete impecunity clearly was not determinative of the limits of the disadvantaged class, nor was it essential to make an equal protection claim.

Similarly, *Griffin* and *Douglas* refute the majority's contention that we have in the past required an absolute deprivation before subjecting wealth classifications to strict scrutiny. The court characterizes *Griffin* as a case concerned simply with the denial of a transcript or an adequate substitute therefor, and *Douglas* as involving the denial of counsel. But in both cases the question was in fact whether "a state that [grants] *appellate review* can do so in a way that discriminates against some convicted defendants on account of their poverty." *Griffin v Illinois* 351 US at 18 . . . . In that regard, the court concluded that inability to purchase a transcript denies "the poor an adequate *appellate review* accorded to all who have money enough to pay the costs in advance," . . . and that "the type of an *appeal* a person is afforded . . . hinges upon whether or not he can pay for the assistance of counsel," *Douglas v California* 372 US at 355-56 . . . . The right of appeal itself was not absolutely denied to those too poor to pay; but because of the cost of a transcript and of counsel, the appeal was a substantially less

---

prohibiting the flexibility and variety that are appropriate to reasonable schemes of state taxation.". . . But in this case we are presented with a claim of discrimination of an entirely different nature—a claim that the revenue-producing mechanism directly discriminates against the interests of some of the intended beneficiaries; and in contrast to the taxpayer suits, the interest adversely affected is of substantial constitutional and societal importance. Hence, a different standard of equal protection review than has been employed in the taxpayer suits is appropriate here.

meaningful right for the poor than for the rich. It was on these terms that the court found a denial of equal protection, and those terms clearly encompassed degrees of discrimination on the basis of wealth which do not amount to outright denial of the affected right or interest.[77]

This is not to say that the form of wealth classification in this case does not differ significantly from those recognized in the previous decisions of this court. Our prior cases have dealt essentially with discrimination on the basis of personal wealth. Here, by contrast, the children of the disadvantaged Texas school districts are being discriminated against not necessarily because of their personal wealth, or the wealth of their families, but because of the taxable property wealth of the residents of the district in which they happen to live. The appropriate question, then, is whether the same degree of judicial solicitude and scrutiny that has previously been afforded wealth classifications is warranted here. . . .

Discrimination on the basis of group wealth in this case likewise calls for careful judicial scrutiny. First, it must be recognized that while local district wealth may serve other interests, it bears no relationship whatsoever to the interest of Texas school children in the educational opportunity afforded them by the state of Texas. Given the importance of that interest, we must be particularly sensitive to the invidious characteristics of any form of discrimination that is not clearly intended to serve it, as opposed to some other distinct state interest. Discrimination on the basis of group wealth may not, to be sure, reflect the social stigma frequently attached to personal poverty. Nevertheless, insofar as group wealth discrimination involves wealth over which the disadvantaged individual has no significant control, it represents in fact a more serious basis of discrimination than does personal wealth. For such discrimination is no reflection of the individual's characteristics or his abilities. . . .

The disability of the disadvantaged class in this case extends as well into the political processes upon which we ordinarily rely as adequate for the protection and promotion of all interests. Here legislative reallocation of the state's property wealth must be sought in the face of inevitable opposition from significantly advantaged districts that have a strong vested interest in the preservation of the status quo, a problem not completely dissimilar to that faced by underrepresented districts prior to the court's intervention in the process of reapportionment, see *Baker v Carr* 369 US 186, 191-92 (1962).

Nor can we ignore the extent to which, in contrast to our prior decisions, the state is responsible for the wealth discrimination in this instance. . . . The means for financing public education in Texas are selected and specified by the state. It is the state that has created local school districts, and tied educational funding to the local property tax and thereby to local district wealth. . . . In short, this case, in contrast to the court's previous wealth discrimination decisions, can only be seen as "unusual in the extent to which governmental action *is* the cause of the wealth classifications."

---

77. Even if I put aside the court's misreading of *Griffin* and *Douglas*, the court fails to offer any reasoned constitutional basis for restricting cases involving wealth discrimination to instances in which there is an absolute deprivation of the interest affected. As I have already discussed, . . . the equal protection clause guarantees equality of treatment of those persons who are similarly situated; it does not merely bar some form of excessive discrimination between such persons.

D

The only justification offered by appellants to sustain the discrimination in educational opportunity caused by the Texas financing scheme is local educational control. . . .

I do not question that local control of public education, as an abstract matter, constitutes a very substantial state interest. [Citing *Wright v Council of Emporia* 407 US 451 (1972).] The state's interest in local educational control—which certainly includes questions of educational funding—has deep roots in the inherent benefits of community support for public education. Consequently, true state dedication to local control would present, I think, a substantial justification to weigh against simply interdistrict variations in the treatment of a state's school children. But I need not now decide how I might ultimately strike the balance were we confronted with a situation where the state's sincere concern for local control inevitably produced educational inequality. For on this record, it is apparent that the state's purported concern with local control is offered primarily as an excuse rather than as a justification for interdistrict inequality.

In Texas statewide laws regulate in fact the most minute details of local public education. For example, the state prescribes required courses. All textbooks must be submitted for state approval, and only approved textbooks may be used. The state has established the qualifications necessary for teaching in Texas public schools and the procedures for obtaining certification. The state has even legislated on the length of the school day.

Moreover, even if we accept Texas' general dedication to local control in educational matters, it is difficult to find any evidence of such dedication with respect to fiscal matters. It ignores reality to suggest . . . that the local property tax element of the Texas financing scheme reflects a conscious legislative effort to provide school districts with local fiscal control. If Texas had a system truly dedicated to local fiscal control one would expect the quality of the educational opportunity provided in each district to vary with the decision of the voters in that district as to the level of sacrifice they wish to make for public education. In fact, the Texas scheme produces precisely the opposite result. Local school districts cannot choose to have the best education in the state by imposing the highest tax rate. Instead, the quality of the educational opportunity offered by any particular district is largely determined by the amount of taxable property located in the district—a factor over which local voters can exercise no control. . . .

If for the sake of local education control, this court is to sustain interdistrict discrimination in the educational opportunity afforded Texas school children, it should require that the state present something more than the mere sham now before us.

III

In conclusion it is essential to recognize that an end to the wide variations in taxable district property wealth inherent in the Texas financing scheme would entail none of the untoward consequences suggested by the court or by the appellants.

First, affirmance of the district court's decisions would hardly sound the death knell for local control of education. It would mean neither centralized decision making nor federal court intervention in the operation of public schools.

Clearly, this suit has nothing to do with local decision making with respect to educational policy or even educational spending. It involves only a narrow aspect of local control—namely, local control over the raising of educational funds. In fact, in striking down interdistrict disparities in taxable local wealth, the district court took the course which is most likely to make true local control over educational decision-making a reality for *all* Texas school districts.

Nor does the district court's decision even necessarily eliminate local control of educational funding. The district court struck down nothing more than the continued interdistrict wealth discrimination inherent in the present property tax. Both centralized and decentralized plans for educational funding not involving such interdistrict discrimination have been put forward.[98] The choice among these or other alternatives would remain with the state, not with the federal courts. . . .

Still, we are told that this case requires us "to condemn the state's judgment in conferring on political subdivisions the power to tax local property to supply revenues for local interests." . . . Yet no one in the course of this entire litigation has ever questioned the constitutionality of the local property tax as a device for raising educational funds. The district court's decision, at most, restricts the power of the state to make educational funding dependent exclusively upon local property taxation so long as there exists interdistrict disparities in taxable property wealth. But it hardly eliminates the local property tax as a source of educational funding or as a means of providing local fiscal control.

The court seeks solace for its action today in the possibility of legislative reform. The court's suggestions of legislative redress and experimentation will doubtless be of great comfort to the school children of Texas' disadvantaged districts, but considering the vested interests of wealthy school districts in the preservation of the status quo, they are worth little more. The possibility of legislative action is, in all events, no answer to this court's duty under the Constitution to eliminate unjustified state discrimination. . . .

---

98. Centralized educational financing is, to be sure, one alternative. . . . Central financing would leave in local hands the entire gamut of local educational policy making—teachers, curriculum, school sites, the whole process of allocating resources among alternative educational objectives.

A second possibility is the much discussed theory of district power equalization put forth by Professors Coons, Clune, and Sugarman in their seminal work, *Private Wealth and Public Education* 201-42 (1970). Such a scheme would truly reflect a dedication to local fiscal control. Under their system, each school district would receive a fixed amount of revenue per pupil for any particular level of tax effort regardless of the level of local property tax base. Appellants criticize this scheme on the rather extraordinary ground that it would encourage poorer districts to overtax themselves in order to obtain substantial revenues for education. But under the present discriminatory scheme, it is the poor districts that are already taxing themselves at the highest rates, yet are receiving the lowest returns.

District wealth reapportionment is yet another alternative which would accomplish directly essentially what district power equalization would seek to do artificially. . . .

A fourth possibility would be to remove commercial, industrial, and mineral property from local tax rolls, to tax this property on a statewide basis, and to return the resulting revenues to the local districts in a fashion that would compensate for remaining variations in the local tax bases.

None of these particular alternatives are necessarily constitutionally compelled; rather, they indicate the breadth of choice which would remain to the state if the present interdistrict disparities were eliminated.

I would therefore affirm the judgment of the district court.
[Justice Brennan's dissenting opinion is omitted.]
[Appendices omitted.]

Notes and Questions

1. State School Finance Systems

The following excerpt describes the workings of a "typical" school finance system, which differs only in details from the Texas legislation whose constitutionality was assessed in *Rodriguez*.

"JUDICIAL POLICY-MAKING: INEQUITABLE PUBLIC SCHOOL
FINANCING AND THE *SERRANO* CASE (1971)"
in *POLICY AND POLITICS IN AMERICA*
D. Kirp
83, 86-91 (A. Sindler ed 1973)

The Historical Pattern. Ever since the Massachusetts Bay Colonies were settled, America has maintained publicly supported primary and secondary schools. The Northwest Ordinance of 1787 made the provision of public education national policy, declaring that "schools and the means of education shall forever be encouraged," and requiring the new territories to set aside land for school construction. Until the nineteenth century, however, education was chiefly financed by individual contribution. The rich went to private academies. The poor generally attended charity and rate-bill schools (the latter charging minimal tuition) whose inadequacy evoked demands for reform from those who, echoing Massachusetts Education Commissioner Horace Mann, saw public education as "the balance wheel of the social machinery." A general tax, administered by the state, was urged. Instead, all states chose to permit (and ultimately to require) local communities to tax their residents, set up and run their own schools.

The minimal state role implicit in such a policy persists. . . . Although states now make substantial contributions to the cost of public instruction, local school districts still foot most of the $43 billion annual bill. In 1970-71, 52 percent of school revenue was provided by local sources, 41 percent came from state sources, and the remaining 7 percent from the federal government. . . .

The Price of Local Hegemony. Because school districts raise the bulk of educational revenues from their own taxable resources, [there exist] great fiscal disparities among districts. By any measure of wealth, some communities are richer than others: they contain more wealthy people or fancier homes or bigger industries. Since school districts raise 98 percent of their revenues through the property tax, a district's real property (the value of its buildings and land) effectively defines its wealth. [Taxation of personal property in law or practice, is relatively rare.] Thus, the presence of valuable real property, or, more accurately a high ratio of valuable property to the number of schoolchildren, makes a community "wealthy," in educational finance terms.

Consider for example, districts A and B. Both have 1,000 schoolchildren. District A, with $10 million of taxable property, has a $100,000 tax base for each child; district B, with $1 million of taxable property, has only $10,000.

District A is ten times wealthier—has ten times more taxable resources per child to draw upon—than district B. . . .*

The tenfold wealth difference between districts A and B is not just hypotheti-' cal. In California, the richest school district (the district with the highest proper- ty valuation per pupil) is twenty-five times wealthier than the poorest. In Michi- gan, the ratio is 30 : 1, in Illinois 20 : 1.[†] For that reason, the poorest California school district would have to fix a tax rate twenty-five times higher than the richest—in economists' terms, would have to make twenty-five times greater tax effort—in order to raise an equal number of dollars. Not surprisingly, poor dis- tricts have not made such Sisyphean demands on their residents. Rich districts consistently raise more money for schools than poor ones, even though poor districts typically set higher tax rates than rich ones. . . .

The State [and Federal Government] as "Equalizer." During the past seventy years, states have markedly increased their financial contribution to education. The intent of these grants, as Ellwood Cubberley, the most influential of the early school finance reformers noted, is "to secure for all as high a minimum of good instruction as possible . . . to equalize the advantages to all as nearly as can be done with the resources at hand." Yet in fact, state aid policies only slightly mitigate the consequences of community wealth variations.

Most states provide basic and/or "flat grants"—a fixed number of dollars per schoolchild—to all school districts, rich and poor. California, for example, pro- vides $125 for each pupil. But because these grants are both relatively small and are distributed to all districts, they do nothing to reduce the wealth disparities among districts.

State "equalizing grants" are ostensibly designed to satisfy Cubberley's goal of "equalizing the advantages to all." In calculating a district's equalizing aid, the state first determines how much local property tax revenue would be generated if the district levied a hypothetical property tax (in California, the tax rate used in the calculation is $1 per $100 assessed valuation for elementary school districts). To that figure, the state adds the flat grant. If the sum of these two figures is less than a minimum per-student "foundation," the state contributes the differ- ence. In California, the foundation guarantee per child is $355 for elementary school districts and $488 for high school districts.

The workings of this formula may be better understood by considering its effect on our hypothetical districts A and B. District A, with $100,000 tax base

---

*One complicating factor, which this analysis does not treat, is the typical practice of assessing property at a fraction of its real or market value, and applying tax rates to this assessed valuation. If assessment practices differ from district to district, relative wealth may be difficult to determine, since an apparently poor district may simply be underassessing its real property relative to other districts. In considering district wealth, this analysis assumes that assessment variations do not explain district wealth discrepancies; available data are consistent with that assumption. See generally Yudof, "The Property Tax in Texas under State and Federal Law," 51 *Tex L Rev* 885 (1973).

†The data on wealth disparities, presented in the text, based on data gathered by the President's Commission on School Finance, includes only consolidated districts (which have both elementary and high schools). When one considers all California districts, property valuation per child ranges from $952,156 to $103, a ratio of nearly 10,000 : 1. The range diminishes considerably if one compares not the wealthiest and poorest districts, but districts at the 95th and 5th wealth percentile. In California, that wealth ratio is 5.9 : 1; in Michigan, 3.4 : 1; in Illinois 2.4 : 1.

per child, receives a flat grant of $125. If it taxes itself at $1 per $100 assessed valuation (i.e., at 1 percent), it will raise $1,000. Since $1,125 is greater than the equalizing grant of $355, district A receives no foundation aid money. District B also receives the $125 flat grant. The 1 percent tax on its $10,000 tax base per child yields only $100. Thus, district B is entitled to $130 for each elementary school child ($355 foundation grant minus both $125 flat grant and the $100 which its taxes raise) and $263 for each high school student.

While combining flat and equalizing grants could equalize schooling resources among rich and poor districts, it has not done so. In many states flat grant funds are subtracted from the foundation guarantee, and hence aid only the rich districts which would not receive foundation grant support in any case. The equalizing grant has almost invariably been set at a level lower than what politicians and schoolmen recognize as necessary to maintain an educational system. . . . [T]he ten *poorest* California school districts spent an average of $609 for each school-age child, $254 more than the elementary school foundation grant and $121 more than the high school foundation grant. While the formula by which foundation support is calculated varies from state to state, the inadequacy of state assistance to poor school districts is universally true. In Cubberley's terms, the "resources at hand" have never been sufficient.

"Categorical" state grants provide additional dollars for the education of children whom the state deems particularly needy: the physically handicapped, the retarded, and, in a few states, poor and "educationally disadvantaged" children. But these programs account for only a small proportion of state aid and their impact on the problem of fiscal inequity has been minimal; they are not designed to address that problem.

The consolidation of school districts, reducing their number from 150,000 to [17,000] during the past fifty years, has succeeded in eliminating some of the most glaring inequities by combining rich and poor districts. But the legal and political feasibility of district consolidation varies from state to state. And while the broad effect of consolidation has been to reduce resource disparities, it cannot eliminate them. Many poor districts simply do not have rich neighbors with whom they can merge.

Federal educational monies have had a marginal equalizing effect. The largest federal program, Title I of the Elementary and Secondary Education Act, initiated in 1965, annually provides $1.6 billion for the schooling of poor and educationally disadvantaged children. But the federal contribution is simply too small—about 6 percent of school expenditures—seriously to upset the pattern of inequity. Throughout the nation, inequities similar to those in California prevail. . . .

2. The Property Tax

As Justice Marshall observes in his dissent, the *Rodriguez* plaintiffs did not challenge the constitutionality of reliance on the property tax to raise school revenues: they attempted to keep separate the revenue raising and benefit distribution functions. But since the property tax both provides 98 percent of all locally raised education dollars, and causes interdistrict inequalities, it is likely, although not necessary, that tax reform and amelioration of expenditure inequities will go hand in hand. For example, states cannot provide equalizing grants to poor school districts until they determine which districts are poor, and this would necessitate some uniformity in assessment reporting practices. The following excerpt discusses the workings of property taxation and provides an economic evaluation of its strengths and weaknesses.

THE ECONOMICS OF PUBLIC EDUCATION
C. Benson
107-25 (1968)

Property Taxes

The property tax is based on the value of taxable property and is collected from owners of that property. Theoretically, all kinds of taxable property, unless specially noted to the contrary, are subject to assessment (i.e., valuation for tax purposes) at a uniform ratio and to tax at a single uniform rate, or at classified rates, by the jurisdiction in which they are located. No consideration is given in the levy to the amount of the owner's equity in the property, that is, the legal owner is taxed according to the value of the property with no regard, say, to any mortgages that are secured by it.

Such a description of the property tax raises a number of questions. What is taxable property? On what bases are properties assessed? How is the tax rate determined? We will take these up in order.

Though the property tax is administered primarily by local governments, the legal bases of its existence are found in state constitutions and statutes. Definitions of taxable property show diversity among states but uniformity within them. Because of the differences among the states, certain general comments must suffice.

Practically all *real property* (land and improvements thereon) is subject to the tax. However, twenty-seven states in 1966 allowed partial exemptions of value of real property before application of the general tax rates. The main categories of exemptions are "homestead" and "veterans," with the homestead category being the more important. The exempt portion of locally assessed real property amounted to $15 billion, which was 2.9 percent of the total value of locally assessed real property....

The third major category of taxable property is *intangibles*: bank deposits, stocks, bonds, accounts receivable, and other monies or claims to ownership or control. It has long been recognized that intangibles are difficult to locate and assess. For this reason, taxation of intangibles has been dropped or modified in a number of states....

[A]ssessment [of property for tax purposes] is mainly a local matter. In a majority of states, assessors are county officials (western and southern region) or district government (eastern region). Cities often have the right to make their own assessments independently of county or township officials, primarily in order to increase their taxing and borrowing power under statutory tax and debt limits. This is to say that they seek to raise the average level of assessment, not to correct individual inequities. County, town, and district assessors are commonly elected officials, while assessors in large cities are likely to be appointed.

Assessment involves two processes: (1) the placing of property on the tax rolls and (2) the assigning of a value to it.

To get *personal property* (tangible and intangible) on the tax rolls, heavy reliance is placed on the initiative of the taxpayer. Because of the substantial premium on evasion, underreporting of personal property is to be expected. . . .

Real property is much easier to place on the tax rolls. Deeds and building permits are available in central offices for inspection. Aerial photographs can be compared with tax maps, etc.

Conceptually, the harder task in assessment is the valuation of properties. About valuation of *personal property*, little can be said in general, given the diversity in kind of these properties and the diversity in philosophy of their assessment. Self-appraisal by the owner and rule of thumb by an assessor are the two most common practices.

Valuation of *real property* is a matter of greater practical importance. . . . In all states the general property tax is the subject of specific statute and sometimes of constitutional provision. To describe value, the most frequently used phrases are "true cash value," "fair cash value," "fair market value," "true value," "full value," "fair value," and "actual value." These phrases do not give a clear guide to valuation. In general the courts have construed them to mean "market value." "Market value" is further defined as the price that would prevail in a free sale between a willing buyer and a willing seller. Commonly, courts have accepted values which were determined, say, on the basis of replacement cost minus depreciation if the figure was not markedly different from their own estimate of market value. . . .

The only available measure of uniformity in assessment is the relation between assessed value and measurable sales price. Because urban properties are not assessed on the basis of market value wholly, because large elements of personal judgment enter into appraisal of properties for tax purposes, and because of the preference of assessors to report properties at some fraction of full value (to be discussed below), differences in the ratio of assessed valuation to sales price may be expected, whether comparisons are being made among states, among different types of real property (residential and industrial, for example), or among and within tax jurisdictions with respect to the same type of property in a given state. Such differences do appear to exist. . . .

In no state is real property assessed, on the average, at current market value. Fractional assessment is not necessarily a bad thing. For instance, if real properties are equitably assessed within individual counties, if state distributions to local governments are not based on local property assessments, and if state-imposed tax limits do not severely cramp local expenditures, then fractional assessment per se should have no harmful consequences. A low ratio of assessment would imply simply higher tax rates, and vice versa. However, tax limits imposed on assessments *do* restrict needed local expenditures in a number of states. Often state aid *is* adjusted to the standing of districts in terms of their locally assessed valuations, used as a measure of relative ability to support services from local sources.

Finally, there is reason to believe that fractional assessment increases inequities. Under fractional assessment an aggrieved taxpayer cannot be certain that a board of appeal of a court will not see fit to raise instead of lower his assessment. With full-value assessment cases of inequity would be much easier for the taxpayer to detect and to demonstrate to the authorities. At present, appeals of assessment are rather infrequent in most states. It is hard to believe that this is the case because of any conviction of equity in valuation of property.

Why do local assessors prefer fractional assessment? Among the reasons are these: First, the officials feel they cultivate good will by underassessing. This is to say that the taxpayer can be hoodwinked, since low assessment almost inevitably implies a high tax rate. Second, full-value assessment would put the assessor's skill to a much more severe test. Taxpayers' appeals of assessment would surely increase. Third, in some states (twenty-two) the amount of state funds that a district receives varies inversely with the size of locally determined valuation. It pays to have a lower ratio in your own district than exists in neighboring districts. (Formerly, state governments levied a tax on local assessments, a practice that gave additional support to fractional valuation. By and large, this type of state taxation has been discarded.) Fourth, low assessment may be seen as a means to promote local economy in government, either through the operation of state-imposed tax and debt limits that are based on a maximum ratio to local valuations or through the fictional importance that citizens may attach to the tax rates as distinct from per capita tax levy. Fifth, fractional assessments may "just happen." Under a prolonged period of rising real estate values, failure to reassess will cause older properties to become substantially undervalued for tax purposes. Few jurisdictions make a serious attempt at thoroughgoing annual reassessment, though most state laws require it.

Once assessment is complete, i.e., once properties have been placed on the tax rolls and assessed, the total valuation in each jurisdiction is obtained by adding up the individual assessments. Through its budgetary processes each jurisdiction determines the amount of money to be raised from the property tax levy. That is, the various expenditure items are cast up and the revenue from sources other than property tax is subtracted from the estimate of total expenditures. The remainder is the "amount to be raised from local taxation."

Each jurisdiction determines its own rate by dividing the figure of total assessed valuation for the area into the sum to be collected from the property tax. Thus, the rate is a percentage. On the tax bill it is usually expressed as so many mills per dollar of assessed valuation, or so many dollars per $1,000 of valuation. . . .

The "impact" of the property tax is on the owner of the property; it is he who pays the tax bill to the tax jurisdiction. However, the owner may be able to "shift" the tax to someone else. For example, the owner of the apartment house may shift the tax to his tenants. In such a case the "incidence" of tax rests on the tenant, not the landlord.

Taxes can be shifted only through the market. That is, the person on whom the impact falls must be able *on account of the tax levy* to charge someone a higher price for something he sells (his products if he is a factory owner; otherwise the services of resources at his command, such as those of an apartment house, but including his own labor resources) or to pay a lower price for something he buys. If he can do one or the other of these things, he can pass the tax burden to someone else. . . .

What theoretical justification is there for the property tax? At various times it has been defended in terms of the ability-to-pay principle, as a benefit tax, and as an instrument to absorb "unearned increments." As we will now see, none of the three arguments can be strongly stated. In short, the property tax has no theoretical justification and must finally be defended in terms of expediency or tradition.

In a rural society where farmers owned their lands in fee simple, the property tax could truly be regarded as one based on ability to pay. Nowadays, when the levy is defended on ability grounds, the tendency is to concentrate on that part of the tax that is levied on housing. Even here, however, the case is weak. A family with many young children requires a large house. It may have less taxable capacity than a small family in a small house. Presumably, the larger house will carry a higher assessment. More damaging, the tax takes no account of the taxpayer's equity. . . . One family may have its house mortgaged practically to full value. Another in a similar house may own it outright. The two pay the same amount of tax, but it is hard to believe their taxable capacity is the same.

The argument is identical with respect to rental housing. The owners of two similar apartment houses will pay like taxes, but one may hold a much greater equity in his house than the other. When we come to the property tax on other types of income-producing properties, the defense of the instrument is weak indeed. For industrial properties, if the tax is shifted to the consumers, the levy is neither more nor less equitable than the general sales tax, an instrument which is seldom praised on grounds of fairness. If the tax is borne by stockholders, there is no necessary connection between amount of tax and rate of profit. Insofar as the tax cannot be shifted, it penalizes those industries, such as farming, that are forced to carry the major part of their capital in real or other tangible property.

In recent years it has become common to defend the tax in benefit terms. There are two approaches in this exercise. First, one may seek to relate the amount of the tax to the amount of services—education, protection, use of streets, etc.—that a given taxpayer receives. There is an enormous problem in the valuation of these benefits, however. Second, (and a more workable approach), one may seek to relate the taxpayer's contribution to the costs that his existence imposes on the community. There are the costs of education of his dependents, if he has any, and his protection. Further, his existence may add costs to protect others from him.

Let us consider the second form of the argument. Under this concept, vacant land would be exempt from taxation. Going on from there, it implies, under the present legal interpretation of assessment, that a house with a market value ten times as high as that of another imposes ten times as much cost on the community. It is hard to see why this is the case. People who live in a rich neighborhood may send their children to private schools, and they require less police and sanitation service than households in a poor neighborhood.

Industrial plants typically impose less burden on the community relative to the taxes they pay than do households. The reason is simply that factories have no children, and education represents over a third of local budgets. This is why so many places are eager to increase the size of their industrial tax base. The tax does not discriminate well *among* income-producing properties with regard to the burden they impose on the community. . . .

With respect to equity it has long been recognized that the tax is probably regressive in incidence [i.e., falls most heavily on those least able to pay] . . . .

It is sometimes claimed that high-priced houses are assessed at lower ratios to market value than low-priced ones. . . .

It is hard to obtain evidence on the extent, if any, to which high-priced properties are underassessed (in the relative sense) or new properties overassessed. Statewide averages reveal only slight distortions of these kinds, though many local observers have indicated that they do occur. However, there is still a major reason why one would expect the property tax to be regressive. That part of the tax which is levied on residential properties is by definition a tax on housing expenditure. The percentage of income that households spend on housing is greater in low-income groups than in high. . . . Since the millage rate is uniform by income groups, it follows that the tax must be regressive.

A third cause for regressivity is found in geographic differentials in tax burden. To a certain extent, rich households cluster in certain school districts and poor households in others. It is not uncommon to find that poorer households have more children in public schools than do the rich; further, the poorer households may demand vocational and technical programs for their children, and these are expensive. The upshot is that the tax burden relative to income is greater in the school district of the poor families.

The matter of regressivity is sometimes dismissed as being of little consequence. If regressive local taxes are overweighted in dollar value by progressive (income and corporation) federal taxes, what difference does the "wrong" kind of burden at the local level make? If one is concerned only with equity in taxation, the point is valid. However, regressive taxes are generally more unpopular with large numbers of the population than other kinds are. If important services, such as education, are financed to a significant degree by highly unpopular taxes, the expansion of these important services can be handicapped, with a loss in social welfare.

With regard to neutrality, there are two points to be made. First, the property tax can be considered an excise on housing. It has been estimated that the levy represents, on the average, a 25 percent excise on shelter. . . . Viewed as an excise, the tax cannot be defended on conventional grounds. Excessive consumption of housing, unlike liquor, is not socially harmful. Housing is not a luxury. And, as we have seen, there are serious weaknesses in treating the property tax as a benefit levy.

Economic reasoning would lead one to conclude that the tax restricts the consumption of housing. When an excise is imposed on a commodity, its price to the consumer will tend to rise. Unless the act of imposing the tax changes the tastes (or preferences) of the consumers, they will buy relatively less of this article and relatively more of other things. . . .

Curiously, tax levies to support education in order that today's children may have a better life are exactly those levies that serve to contract and make meager the physical character of the home environment, this also being important in the development of the child's interests and capabilities.

The second point about neutrality has to do with the taxation of business.

The problem is particularly noticeable in manufacturing. The land and capital requirements of industry vary markedly by type of economic activity. The petroleum industry, paper and pulp companies, primary metals manufacturers, and electric utilities all have vast needs for physical capital as compared with textile, instrument, and electrical machinery companies. The property tax arbitrarily bears much more heavily on the former type of activity than the latter. Further, the existence of the property tax accentuates local competition for industry and, hence, among other harmful results, produces uneconomic locational patterns. . . .

What, now, of costs of administration and compliance? Superficially, the property tax is not difficult to administer. To administer it *well* is another matter. [See Advisory Commission on Intergovernmental Relations, *The Role of States in Strengthening the Property Tax* (1963)] Local administration is concerned mainly with real properties. It is easy to identify the person who is to pay the tax, because ownership is a matter of legal record. It is easy to determine in what district the property is, so jurisdictional disputes on tax *sites* are rare. It is relatively easy to forecast yield from one year to the next. These are all very real advantages in local administration. But *assessment* is a complicated business, often beyond the capacity of local officials. There would appear to be only two solutions to the problem of poor assessment. One is to hire state authorities to do the work. This would not involve any serious loss of local autonomy. Another is to merge small units of local government into larger units to obtain efficient administration. . . .

It is with respect to costs of compliance that the property tax comes into its own. They are practically nil. Whether the tax is paid by homeowner or industrial plant manager, the procedure is the same: a tax bill is received once (or twice) a year and all one need do is write out a check to pay it.

What, finally, of yield? Earlier it was indicated that the yield of the property tax is relatively inelastic [i.e., stable over time].

The Suitability of the Property Tax for Local Use

In spite of its patent disadvantages, the case *for* the property tax is essentially the case for local government. That is, no other tax has the unique combination of features that make it as suitable for major local use. . . .

The prime case for the property tax rests upon its stability of yield. This has been commented upon for many years. It is not unlikely that the stability of property tax yields is different in periods of rising income and of falling income. The latter stability is most important for local governments; it would be expected on general grounds to be high, probably higher than in the times of increasing prosperity. When national population is rising, many localities can anticipate an increase in their own population, an increase in income, an increase in tax base and yield. In small districts, large upward changes in these variables can occur in a short time period. However, the reverse does not hold. Once property improvements have been put in place, they stand for many years. Except in the event of a major natural catastrophe, no community can expect to see its tax base dwindle sharply overnight. Even if factories and houses become vacant, they are still in place and owned by someone. In short, tax liability, once established, does not vanish. . . .

Why is stability in tax yield important for local governments? What is at stake is local autonomy itself. Local governments are not sovereign powers. The only alternative to strict state control of local expenditures is local control that operates under a set of rules. Experience indicates a necessary rule: that local governments shall not borrow extensively to meet deficits from current operations. Borrowing in anticipation of taxes is one thing, but when local governments incur debt to meet unplanned deficits the results have generally been disastrous. Abuses develop that may lead to municipal bankruptcy; then state control of spending usually follows. Thus, large downward fluctuations in tax revenue cannot be made up by resort to the banks. . . .

For a contrary view of the regressivity of the property tax, see Baffney, "The Property Tax Is a Progressive Tax," in *Proceedings of 64th Annual Conference* (National Tax Association 1971). The practice of assessing property between and within districts at different assessment ratios raises substantial constitutional issues. See *Weissinger v Boswell* 330 F Supp 615 (MD Ala 1971); Yudof, "The Property Tax in Texas under State and Federal Law," 51 *Tex L Rev* 885 (1973); Note, "Inequality in Property Tax Assessments: New Cures for an Old Ill," 75 *Harv L Rev* 1374 (1962).

3. *Rodriguez:* Scope of the Decision

The two major opinions in *Rodriguez* discuss at considerable length both policy and constitutional issues posed by the "fiscal neutrality" standard. The reader seeking more extensive background on those issues is referred to the numerous legal and policy analyses cited by Justices Powell and Marshall. The winter 1971 issue of *The Yale Review of Law and Social Action* (vol 2, no 2) is devoted to the subject of "Who Pays for Tomorrow's Schools: The Emerging Issue of School Finance." This note is intended to highlight certain of the disputes reflected in the opinions.

a. Poverty. Who is injured by existing school finance schemes: those who live in property poor districts? Poor people? Poor people who live in property poor districts? Racial and ethnic minorities (see footnote 63 in the majority opinion)? What legal consequences, if any, follow from identifying the injured class? Is the court's reluctance to grant relief to a nebulous class of claimants well founded? Consistent with earlier decisions?

The majority concludes that in its earlier poverty discrimination cases, the disadvantaged class "shared two distinguishing characteristics: because of their impecunity they were completely unable to pay for some desired benefit, and as a consequence, they sustained an absolute deprivation of a meaningful opportunity to enjoy that benefit." 411 US at 20. Is the court correctly construing its prior poverty cases? Should *complete* inability to pay and *absolute* deprivation be the only bases for judicial concern? Might the standard of judicial review of asserted discrimination against the poor vary with (i) the nature of the burden placed on them by the state of their poverty and (ii) the nature of the state's justification for imposing that burden? See Brest, Book Review, 23 *Stan L Rev* 591 (1971).

In a portion of Justice White's opinion not reprinted in the text, he notes that because Texas places a ceiling on the tax rate, which a local district is permitted to set, poor districts are "precluded in law, as well as in fact, from achieving a yield even close to that of some other districts." 411 US at 67. Is elimination of the tax rate constitutionally required after *Rodriguez*? See *Hargrave v Kirk* 313 F Supp 944 (MD Fla 1970), *vacated,* 401 US 476 (1971). Is there a theoretical "right" to raise equal education revenues, which the state may not infringe, but not a "right" to the fiscal capacity to raise such revenues?

Both the majority and dissenting opinions assume that the property base of a local district is the primary determinant of its capacity to raise education revenues. Yet school districts and local government units are also "poor" in ways not discussed in *Rodriguez*. Some localities have high noneducation municipal expenditures (e.g., for police and fire protection) which would constrain their ability to tax for education even if tax bases were "equalized." Also, the average family wealth in school districts appears to exert an influence on school revenues of roughly the same magnitude as that of property assessments; the wealthy appear more willing to tax themselves for schooling than do the poor. See Note, "A Statistical Analysis of the School Finance Decisions: On Winning Battles and Losing Wars," 81 *Yale LJ* 1303 (1972); Weiss, *Existing Disparities in Public School Finance and Proposals for Reform* (1970). Would equalization of these factors—municipal overburden and differential wealth-based taste for education—be required to satisfy the "fiscal neutrality" standard? Does the very existence of such complicating factors suggest the wisdom of judicial noninvolvement?

b. Education

i. Justices Powell and Marshall both concede the importance of education as a basic social good. Yet the majority declines to treat education as a "fundamental" interest, whose unequal provision requires "strict judicial scrutiny." The court equates fundamental interests with rights "explicitly or implicitly guaranteed in the constitution." Is that standard consistent with prior opinions? What might an "implicit" constitutional guarantee be?

ii. Although the majority recognizes the nexus between education and the freedoms of speech and franchise, it nonetheless rejects plaintiffs' claim. "[W]e have never presumed to possess either the ability or the authority to guarantee to the citizenry the most *effective* speech or the most *informed* electoral choice." Does that statement aptly characterize the plaintiff's complaint in *Rodriguez*? Is Justice Marshall's description of the issue—"one of discrimination that affects the quality of education"—more accurate?

Justices Powell and Marshall both assume that increased expenditures make effective participation in the electoral process more likely. Available data suggest, however, that to the extent that schools influence political development (and the school's influence is limited), they do so quite uniformly. Once students' political ideas take shape—usually around the end of elementary school—they undergo little subsequent change. One study compared two Los Angeles area school districts: one spent $150 more per student and more vigorously engaged in devising and promoting educational innovation. At grades nine and twelve there were only trivial differences between the two districts in students' political thought and knowledge. The study concludes: "[V]ariations in educational inputs have little effect on those democratic values that demand the most rigorous thought." R. Merelman, *Political Socialization and Educational Climates,* 104 (1971). See also

A. Greely and P. Rossi, *The Education of Catholic Americans* (1966); Jennings and Miemi, "Patterns of Political Learning," 38 *Harv Educ Rev* 444 (1968). Does that finding bear on the constitutional analysis of education's significance? Or is education's significance to be taken as given, impervious to research findings?

iii. Justice Powell's opinion frequently notes the "considerable dispute among educators" about the relationship between school resources and outcomes. Is the court suggesting that, unless such a relationship be established, existing inequalities are invulnerable to constitutional attack? Is Hobson v Hansen overruled? Is such an approach correct? Is it consistent with the court's decision in *Sweatt v Painter* 339 US 629 (1950)? In the absence of provable "harm" with respect to academic achievement are there no policy reasons to support the eradication of discriminatory allocation schemes? See Yudof, "Equal Educational Opportunity and the Courts, 51 *Tex L Rev* 411, 504 (1973).

iv. Justice Powell distinguishes the Texas financing scheme from an instance of "absolute denial of educational opportunities," noting that "no charge fairly could be made that the system fails to provide each child with an opportunity to acquire the basic minimal skills necessary for the enjoyment of the rights of speech and of full participation in the political process." 411 US at 37. Is the court implying that some minimum level of educational services is constitutionally required? That the state must guarantee to all its children some minimum educational success? How might that question be tested? Is a "minimum" standard more or less difficult for a court to develop than a "fiscal neutrality" standard? More or less attuned to the policy problems? How would you phrase such a standard?

Professor Michelman addresses some of these issues in "The Supreme Court 1968 Term—Foreword: On Protecting the Poor through the Fourteenth Amendment," 83 *Harv L Rev* 7 (1969):

> [T]he judicial "equality" explosion of recent times has largely been ignited by reawakened sensitivity, not to equality, but to a quite different sort of value or claim which might better be called "minimum welfare." In the recent judicial handiwork which has been hailed (and reviled) as an "egalitarian revolution," a particularly striking and propitious note has been sounded through those acts whereby the court has directly shielded poor persons from the most elemental consequence of poverty; lack of funds to exchange for needed goods, services, or privileges of access. . . . [T]hese events in particular can, with profit to the understanding, be approached through systematic resistance to the notions that economic inequality as such is repugnant to constitutional values (if the state is in any manner implicated by its activities in that inequality), and that the court's interventions are mainly designed to move us toward a condition of economic equality. Certainly these notions are uneasy ones, given a society which on the whole continues to be individualistic, competitive, and market oriented.
>
> Of course, the court's "egalitarian" interventions are often occasioned by problems which would not exist but for economic inequality. *Yet I hope to make clear that in many instances their purposes could be more soundly and satisfyingly understood as vindication of a state's duty to protect against certain hazards which are endemic in an unequal society,*

rather than vindication of a duty to avoid complicity in unequal treatment. . . .

[D]ifferences of consequence [between two approaches] may ensue from a theoretical distinction between a duty to protect against certain severe consequences of economic inequality and a duty to avoid hyperoffensive inequalities in treatment [the traditional equal protection approach]. Two obvious differences are that a duty to extend protection against certain hazards need not entail or suggest any "equalization" of treatment or circumstances beyond that necessary to obviate the hazard and, more important, that such a duty may obtain even where the state would choose to remain quiescent and to "treat" everyone equally by not according any relevant treatment whatsoever. If offensive and demoralizing discrimination generally be taken as the target evil, and if an empirical assumption be made that the affairs in which government is visibly involved are ipso facto likely to be popularly invested with special meaning, then there is a certain kind of sense in a "state action" qualification upon government's duties to relieve against hazards of poverty. But it is less easy to be reconciled to the "state action" notion when alleviation of certain, specially poignant hardships or crushing disadvantages is thought to be the object. If we can see and feel that the hardship is poignant or the disadvantage dire, the government's noninvolvement then may come not as relief but as reproach. . . . (83 *Harv L Rev* at 9-11.)

Professor Michelman recognizes the difficulties a court would encounter in adopting his approach:

There is to begin with, the language of the Constitution. The due process clause inveighs only against certain "deprivations" by the "state," occurrences which seemingly cannot occur by mere default. On the other hand, the equal protection clause's injunction against "denying" the "equal protection of the laws" is not so clearly void of a requirement that the quiescent state must "act" (i.e., cease denying protection) in certain circumstances when it would choose not to. Moreover, possibly because of unhappy connotations associated with "substantive due process" as well as because equal protection remains an empty conundrum without some frank infusion of judicially "sculpted" values, the court seems currently more comfortable in staking out and valuing "fundamental" interests under the aegis of equal protection than it could well feel under due process.

But to the extent that the court were disposed to exploit the equal protection clause to enforce some affirmative duties of protection, it could hardly help noticing that it would be "equal," not minimum protection which had to be extended. X, it seems, would be entitled to protection only insofar as Y was protected. By the same token, X would be entitled to just as much protection as Y enjoyed. Therefore, if the situation were one which obligated the state to extend protection to X at all, it would also be one which required that X's "treatment" be made "equal" to Y's. The rhetoric of equality would be injected by the preferred constitutional text.

But apart from the texts, there is an independent problem of standards which would be likely to induce reliance (even if spurious) on equality. How could the court . . . defend in suitably judicial terms the abstract proposition that some particular risk associated with poverty is one of those relatively few risks against which the state must protect? Even after the risk had been so identified, how could the court say when "enough" protection had been furnished? "As much as" seems to provide just the certainty of measure which "enough of" so sorely lacks. . . .

Finally, it must be noted that while the idea of "just wants" or "severe deprivations" expresses an ethical precept distinct from that of "equality," detecting a failure to provide the required minimum may nonetheless depend in part upon the detection of inequalities; and elimination or reduction of inequality may be entailed in rectifying such a failure, insofar as the just minimum is understood to be a function (in part) of the existing maximum. Such an understanding could grow out of a residue of indissoluble interpenetration of the felt evils of relative deprivation and poignant hardship. Thus if the extent of society's obligation to tax itself for support of the needy depends in part upon its overall level of affluence, widening inequalities become increasingly suggestive of failure to furnish the just minimum. Or again, insofar as the components of the required (or "a decent") minimum are affected by what others have—by prevailing tastes and expectations, or by emulation—then extremity of inequality is suggestive. Standing on a quite different ground is the relevance of what others have when the want in question is deemed specially significant—as education, for example, might be—because of its importance for success in competitive activities. . . . (83 *Harv L Rev* at 16-19.)

How would Professor Michelman apply the "minimum protection" approach to the problem of education financing? He notes that the "minimum protection" standard—unlike the fiscal neutrality approach advanced in *Rodriguez*—would not be satisfied by a remedy that permitted a district to opt entirely out of providing publicly supported schooling; the "arcana of 'state action'," would not limit its scrutiny. In other ways, a minimum protection would be more conservative than fiscal neutrality:

For the demands of minimum protection can, in principle, be satisfied by a state aid system of "flat" or "foundation" grants which assure to each district an acceptable minimum resource per pupil at a tolerable sacrifice level, but leave each district free to repair to its own unequalized tax base for some additional level of funding as long as the competitive-inequality gap does not grow too large. But this can never satisfy an equal protection doctrine which is offended by the state's involvement in any wealth favoritism in the educational field. . . . (83 *Harv L Rev* at 57.)

Yet Professor Michelman concludes that the two standards might indeed lead to similar constitutional conclusions:

It happens that educational inequality and educational deprivation are so closely intertwined that minimum protection thinking about the educational-finance problem may lead to a statement of grievance in a justiciable form resembling that of more conventional equal protection disputation.

The flow of thought might go something like this. First, in a market-oriented and technological society justice demands minimum educational assurances, and the minimum is significantly a function of the maximum and to that extent calls for equalization. Second, there are gross disparities in educational expenditure (which may correlate with other plausible indices of equality), and also evidence of the relationships among these disparities and the other crucial factors of wealth and effort, sufficient to raise a strong suspicion that lack of money is resulting in severe educational deprivation. Third, a system of family power equalizing, if embracing all educational spending in the state, can provide assurances against such deprivation without trenching significantly on subsidiarity. . . . (83 *Harv L Rev* at 58.)

Did the *Rodriguez* court in effect apply or misapply Professor Michelman's approach? Does the court suggest that education is not the sort of "basic" good to which the minimum protection standard is properly applied? Does this approach seem analytically preferable to "fiscal neutrality?" Is it more directly responsive to the policy problem posed by education finance inequities? Does it provide the basis for defining an appropriate remedy?

c. Equality. Plaintiffs in *Rodriguez* sought to limit the principle of fiscal neutrality to education, arguing that its relationship to constitutionally guaranteed rights was unique among state-supported goods. The majority, however, was not persuaded: "Empirical examination might well buttress an assumption that the ill-fed, ill-clothed, and ill-housed are among the most ineffective participants in the political process and that they derive the least enjoyment from the benefits of the First Amendment." 411 US at 37. Is education constitutionally distinguishable from other public goods? Fiscal neutrality—as argued in *Rodriguez*—would permit wide disparities in the provision of health, welfare, and housing, while challenging any wealth-based educational disparity. Does that seem a sensible policy outcome for the court to reach?

Professor Michelman suggests that the minimum protection approach offers a more useful way to determine which inequalities merit careful judicial scrutiny:

An additional effect of minimum protection thinking may be to help the decision maker understand how to differentiate education from other goods, say opera and golf, which persons will have to continue to pay for out of their own means or do without. Evenhandedness tends to be an all-encompassing value, to become an end in itself, to be "not easily cabined" once loosed. Education, golf, and opera may tend to seem but fungible objects upon which evenhandedness can work, or vehicles through which evenhandedness can realize itself. The distinctive psychic and moral evils of relative deprivation may not seem significantly less present when golf or opera is made available through a governmental facility, but only to those who can and will pay, than when schooling is similarly offered. . . . The notion of protection against severe deprivation may seem helpfully selective when laid beside that of evenhandedness. It is insistent upon getting what is basic, but is outspokenly explicit in claiming nothing more. It reacts more hospitably than evenhandedness to the question: why education and not golf? (83 *Harv L Rev* at 59.)

Would "minimum protection" provide a useful limiting principle for judicial involvement?

d. Alternative Legal Principles

i. Inequality of Budgetary Options. A quite different approach to the school finance issue holds that the constitutional wrong is the unequal distribution of tax bases within a given state, which assures that some taxpayers will bear a greater tax burden than others in order to provide similar services. That approach, advanced by Professor Schoettle in "The Equal Protection Clause in Public Education," 71 *Colum L Rev* 1355 (1971), draws its constitutional support from the reapportionment (one man, one vote) cases and the pre-*Rodriguez* school finance cases. The standard advanced by Schoettle—a municipal financing system is unconstitutional where "irrational allocations of taxable property . . . afford the taxpayers and voters of different school districts unequal budgetary options, solely because of their place of residence," 71 *Colum L Rev* at 1407—would apply not only to education but also to all services wholly or partly financed by local governments. In light of *Rodriguez*, does the Schoettle approach have continuing constitutional vitality? Could it in fact be implemented? With what policy consequences? See also Carrington, "On Egalitarian Overzeal: A Polemic against the Local School Property Tax Cases," 1972 *U Ill LF* 232 (viewing Professor Schoettle's approach as constitutionally more modest than the "fiscal neutrality" standard).

ii. Rationality. Yet another treatment of the school finance issue would require "that the state may not discriminate against any child in the allocation of public funds for education without a substantial and rational justification. The criteria for distributing the resources must relate to . . . the children, or to the costs of the programs required to meet their needs as the state perceives them." Yudof, "Equal Educational Opportunity and the Courts," 51 *Tex L Rev* 411, 491 (1973). Does *Hobson v Hansen* support Professor Yudof's approach? Do Justice White and Professor Yudof define "rationality" in the same way? Is the logic of this approach limited to education? Does it countenance local control over schooling as a "rational justification?" See Horowitz and Neitring, "Equal Protection Aspects of Inequalities in Public Education and Public Assistance Programs from Place to Place Within a State," 15 *UCLA L Rev* 787 (1968).

4. The "Free Textbooks" Case

In *Johnson v New York State Educ Dep't* 449 F2d 871 (2d Cir 1971), the court of appeals upheld legislation that permitted local school boards to charge a textbook fee to public school students, rejecting the claim that the legislation discriminated against poor children. It found "rational" the state's interest in promoting certain subjects—secondary school science, mathematics, and foreign languages—by distributing free texts in those subjects. While "sound argument can be made that children in the formation years in grades one to six should have books and of a value far in excess of $7.50 [the state allotment for elementary texts] if a maximum of educational opportunity is to be achieved, the legislature was not required to address itself to this argument where the action it did take was clearly justified in terms of the goals it sought thereby to advance." The assertion "that wherever the state undertakes to provide education, there is a duty to provide free textbooks," was curtly dismissed. 449 F2d at 877-78. "Unless the courts are to take over legislative functions and to decree that all children in all grades are to have free textbooks, the judgment of the legislature should control." 449 F2d at 880.

Judge Kaufman, in dissent, found that: "[T]he legislative scheme here creates two classes of children, not physically separate yet unequal—the poor suffer while the rich receive the full benefits of the state's educational program." 449 F2d at 883. "It will not do to say, as does the majority, that in this case 'public funds are distributed equally.' The same argument would apply if schools charged a toll to defray the cost of operating public school buses. Were indigent children denied entry to the bus that passed their doors each morning because they could not bear their share of the cost—and thus were barred from public schools attended by their richer neighbors—would the answer also be 'equal expenditures and an offer on equal terms to each child is sufficient?' " 449 F2d at 884.

The Supreme Court, 409 US 75 (1972), vacated and remanded the case to determine whether it had been rendered moot by a change in local practice. In the light of *Rodriguez,* how should the case now be decided? Are the two suits distinguishable?

Suppose the legislation under attack permitted local school districts to suspend students whose parents neither paid the requisite textbook fee nor established their indigency. What constitutional problems would be presented? See *Chandler v South Bend Community School Corp* Civil No 71-S-51 (ND Ind August 26, 1971).

The constitutionality of school fees for various activities has also been challenged. See *Williams v Page* 309 F Supp 814 (ND Ill 1970); *Bond v Public Schools* 18 Mich App 506, 171 NW2d 557 (Mich Ct App 1969)(state constitutional grounds); *Granger v Cascade County School Dist* 499 P2d 780 (Mont 1972) (state constitutional grounds). In assessing such claims, should courts distinguish between "required" and "optional" activities, requiring free supplies only for required activities (if at all)?

5. Higher Education: Tuition Fees

Justice Powell suggests that a tuition scheme for financing public schools that effectively excluded those too poor to pay would raise constitutional questions. 411 US at 25 n60. Are similar problems posed by tuition fees charged by public universities? Does Justice Powell's comment suggest that the state has a constitutional obligation to provide scholarships to indigent students?

If a state may charge tuition for higher education, may it distinguish between in-state and out-of-state students, charging higher fees to the latter group? See *Starns v Malkerson* 326 F Supp 234 (D Minn 1970), *aff'd,* 401 US 985 (1971). May the state establish an "irrebuttable presumption" that students residing elsewhere before enrolling in a state institution are out-of-state students for the duration of their stay at that institution? See *Vlandis v Kline* 412 US 441 (1973).

6. Future of School Finance Reform

a. Alternatives. In recent years, attention to interdistrict school finance inequities has not been limited to the courts. States have begun actively to explore a variety of alternatives to the present system. These include:

i. Full State Funding of Elementary and Secondary Education. A state tax levy would raise all education revenues. These could be distributed (a) on an equal per-pupil basis to school districts; or (b) according to some measure of educational needs developed by the state, and/or (c) according to a formula taking account of the varying costs—based on such factors as cost of living differentials—of providing schooling within a given district. A fourth alternative would provide education vouchers directly to all children (see chapter 1). See generally President's Comm'n on School Finance, *Schools, People and Money* (1972); J. Berke, A. Campbell, R. Goettel, et al., *Report of the New York State Comm'n on the Quality Cost and Financing of Elementary and Secondary Education* (1972).

ii. State-Local Funding. The alternatives summarized above would take from school districts all authority to raise educational revenues. "District power equalizing," by contrast, would preserve this authority but would guarantee to each district a given revenue yield for any tax rate a district chose to impose on itself. If two districts, whatever their relative wealth and tax base, set identical property tax rates, the per-pupil revenue in the two districts will be equal. This approach, first developed by J. Coons, W. Clune, and S. Sugarman, *Private Wealth and Public Education* (1970), may be better understood with an illustration:

How District Power Equalizing Might Work

District	Tax Rate Selected	Guaranteed Yield			Actual Yield		Difference Between Actual and Guaranteed Yield	
		.1%	3% (plan 1)	3% (plan 2)	.1%	3%	Plan 1	Plan 2
Rich	3%	$30	$900	$750	$35	$1050	+$130	+$300
Poor	3%	$30	$900	$750	$15	$ 450	-$450	-$300

Under either power-equalizing plan (1 or 2), the rich district owes its "surplus" revenues—i.e., revenues that exceed the guaranteed level for 3 percent—to the state, while the poor district is entitled to receive the difference between what it has collected and the guaranteed rate. Plan 1 assumes a uniform tax rate/revenue guarantee ratio, i.e., thirty dollars for each .1 percent (one mill), while under plan 2 the ratio is not uniform; a tax increment above a certain point (say 2 percent) would yield less than thirty dollars for each additional mill. Plan 2 permits the state to induce districts to limit their tax rates. As long as a given tax effort produces the same revenue, the effort/revenue ratio may vary in a district power equalizing scheme.

A similar plan, called "family power equalizing," gives the family, not the school district, the power to set its own tax rate; the state would reward a given level of tax effort with a guaranteed amount of dollars, distributed to the family in the form of an education voucher. See Coons and Sugarman, "Family Choice in Education: A Model State System for Vouchers," 59 *Cal L Rev* 321 (1971); cf. Center for the Study of Public Policy, *Education Vouchers* (1971).

iii. Mixed Models. It is, of course, possible to combine several of these schemes. For example, the state could provide school districts with $600 grants for each child, as well as supplemental grants for particular categories of "child need" (e.g., educationally disadvantaged or mentally retarded) or "district need" (e.g., cost of living differentials); in addition, the state could permit, for example, the district to "power equalize" up to an additional $200 per child.

b. Choosing Among Alternatives. The several models described above attempt to maximize different values: equality, attention to children's or district's needs and "subsidiarity" (concern for local or family choice making). One's policy preference depends in part on one's view of how these factors should be weighted. Is the resource-outcomes research discussed in section II above relevant to making such choices?

Is each of the alternatives consistent with the "fiscal neutrality" principle? With the "minimum protection" principle? With the "rationality" approach?

c. Political Outlook. Even before the Supreme Court's decision in *Rodriguez,* the outlook for major reforms in school financing was questionable. See Kirp and Yudof, Book Review, 6 *Harv Civ Rights—Civ Lib L Rev* 619 (1971). The "fiscal neutrality" approach neither pressed for a particular alternative nor provided the political muscle significantly to alter the seemingly immovable system. The supporters of finance reform were typically weak and politically divided; the issue was not the political first priority of any group. By contrast, the opposition—taxpayers' groups, wealthy districts—was generally united and politically skilled, able to play on legislators' concerns for "wasted" educational dollars. See A. Meltsner, G. Kast, J. Kramer, and R. Nakamura, *Political Feasibility of Reform in School Financing: The Case of California* (1973).

The *Rodriguez* decision makes the prognosis for reform even more gloomy. Despite the court's concluding statement—"We need hardly add that this court's action today is not to be viewed as placing its judicial imprimatur on the status quo" (411 US at 58)—the decision is likely to be viewed by the public and state officials as approving current state financing practices.

7. School Finance Reform and State Courts

Rodriguez concludes that existing school finance legislation does not violate the equal protection clause of the US Constitution. But most state constitutions contain their own version of the equal protection clause; they also include guarantees that the state will provide a "thorough and efficient" or a "thorough and uniform" public education. The following case, decided after *Rodriguez,* offers one interpretation of such a state constitutional provision.

ROBINSON v CAHILL
62 NJ 473, 303 A2d 273 (1973)

The opinion of the court was delivered by Weintraub, CJ.

[The opinion begins by describing the New Jersey education finance system, similar in pertinent respects to the Texas legislation reviewed in the *Rodriguez* decision.]

The question whether the equal protection demand of our state constitution is offended remains for us to decide. Conceivably a state constitution could be

more demanding. For one thing, there is absent the principle of federalism which
cautions against too expansive a view of a federal constitutional limitation upon
the power and opportunity of the several states to cope with their own problems
in the light of their own circumstances. . . .

We hesitate to turn this case upon the state equal protection clause. The
reason is that the equal protection clause may be unmanageable if it is called
upon to supply categorical answers in the vast area of human needs, choosing
those which must be met and a single basis upon which the state must act. The
difficulties become apparent in the argument in the case at hand. [The court
rejects constitutional arguments premised either on wealth being a suspect classification, or education meriting treatment as a fundamental interest.]

The remaining question is whether certain provisions of our state constitution . . . [are violated by the current system of financing public education in New
Jersey].

The provisions relating to public education were added to the constitution of
1844 by amendments adopted in 1875. Art IV, §7, ¶6, was amended by adding
this sentence: "The legislature shall provide for the maintenance and support of a
thorough and efficient system of free public schools for the instruction of all the
children in this state between the ages of five and eighteen years." This provision
is now Art VIII, §4, ¶1, of the 1947 constitution. The other amendment in
1875 added Art IV, §7, ¶11, which prohibits "private, local or special laws" in
"enumerated cases," among which appears: "Providing for the management and
support of free public schools." The quoted provision is item (7) in Art IV, §7,
¶9, of the 1947 constitution, with the word "control" substituted for the word
"support." . . . [I] t cannot be said the 1875 amendments were intended to ensure statewide equality among taxpayers. But we do not doubt that an equal
educational opportunity for children was precisely in mind. The mandate that
there be maintained and supported "a thorough and efficient system of free
public schools for the instruction of all the children in the state between the ages
of five and eighteen years" can have no other import. Whether the state acts
directly or imposes the role upon local government, the end product must be
what the constitution commands. A system of instruction in any district of the
state which is not thorough and efficient falls short of the constitutional command. Whatever the reason for the violation, the obligation is the state's to
rectify it. If local government fails, the state government must compel it to act,
and if the local government cannot carry the burden, the state must itself meet
its continuing obligation. . . .

The trial court found the constitutional demand had not been met and did so
on the basis of discrepancies in dollar input per pupil. We agree. We deal with
the problem in those terms because dollar input is plainly relevant and because
we have been shown no other viable criterion for measuring compliance with the
constitutional mandate. The constitutional mandate could not be said to be
satisfied unless we were to suppose the unlikely proposition that the lowest level
of dollar performance happens to coincide with the constitutional mandate and
that all efforts beyond the lowest level are attributable to local decisions to do
more than the state was obliged to do.

Surely the existing statutory system is not visibly geared to the mandate that
there be "a thorough and efficient system of free public schools for the instruction of all the children in this state between the ages of five and eighteen years."

Indeed the state has never spelled out the content of the educational opportunity the constitution requires. Without some such prescription, it is even more difficult to understand how the tax burden can be left to local initiative with any hope that statewide equality of educational opportunity will emerge. . . .

On its face the [1970] statutory scheme has no apparent relation to the mandate for equal educational opportunity. . . .

We have outlined the formula of the 1970 act to show . . . it is not demonstrably designed to guarantee that local effort plus the state aid will yield to all the pupils in the state that level of educational opportunity which the 1875 amendment mandates. We see no basis for a finding that the 1970 act, even if fully funded, would satisfy the constitutional obligation of the state. . . .

[I]f the state chooses to assign its obligation under the 1875 amendment to local government, the state must do so by a plan which will fulfill the state's continuing obligation. To that end the state must define in some discernible way the educational obligation and must *compel* the local school districts to raise the money necessary to provide that opportunity. The state has never spelled out the content of the constitutionally mandated educational opportunity. Nor has the state *required* the school districts to raise moneys needed to achieve that unstated standard. Nor is the state aid program designed to compensate for local failures to reach that level. It must be evident that our present scheme is a patchy product reflecting provincial contests rather than a plan sensitive only to the constitutional mandate. . . .

Upon the record before us, it may be doubted that the thorough and efficient system of schools required by the 1875 amendment can realistically be met by reliance upon local taxation. The discordant correlations between the educational needs of the school districts and their respective tax bases suggest any such effort would likely fail. . .

Although we have dealt with the constitutional problem in terms of dollar input per pupil, we should not be understood to mean that the state may not recognize differences in area costs, or a need for additional dollar input to equip classes of disadvantaged children for the educational opportunity. Nor do we say that if the state assumes the cost of providing the constitutionally mandated education, it may not authorize local government to go further and to tax to that further end, provided that such authorization does not become a device for diluting the state's mandated responsibility.

The present system being unconstitutional, we come to the subject of remedies. We agree with the trial court that relief must be prospective. The judiciary cannot unravel the fiscal skein. Obligations incurred must not be impaired. And since government must go on, and some period of time will be needed to establish another statutory system, obligations hereafter incurred pursuant to existing statutes will be valid in accordance with the terms of the statutes. . . .

Subject to the modifications expressed in this opinion and the matters reserved in the preceding paragraph, the judgment of the trial court is affirmed.

Notes and Questions

1. The "Thorough and Efficient" Standard

Robinson concludes that New Jersey's financing scheme is not a "thorough and efficient" system. Does a "thorough and efficient" system require equal expenditures per pupil? No wealth discrimination? Rationality? Minimum sufficiency? What plan would satisfy the court? Is the constitutional standard against which such a plan would be tested more intrusive on legislative policy making than the "fiscal neutrality" approach? Would such an intrusion be more justifiable when imposed by a state rather than a federal court?

2. Effects of *Robinson*

The *Robinson* decision—like the earlier *Serrano v Priest* decision—is likely to spur similar litigation in other state courts. The outcome of these cases may well vary from state to state, as different courts struggle to interpret the seldom-tested state constitutional guarantees respecting education. Is the projected lack of uniform results in these cases undesirable?

V. Equal Educational Opportunity: Exclusion and "Functional Exclusion"

The Supreme Court's opinion in *Rodriguez* distinguishes interdistrict financing inequities from a state "financing system [that] occasioned an absolute denial of educational opportunities to any of its children." 411 US at 37. The court also notes that a tuition assessment plan that "absolutely precluded [poor children] from receiving an education . . . would present a far more compelling set of circumstances for judicial assistance than the case before us today." 411 US at 25 n60.

Those statements raise two related constitutional questions: (1) under what circumstances, if any, is exclusion of a class of children from the public schools—or, more broadly, from publicly supported educational services—constitutionally justifiable; and (2) is it constitutionally plausible to extend a principle of non-exclusion to certain children enrolled in public schools who are "functionally excluded": effectively denied meaningful access to school services? One such category of children is those whose native language is not English, but who are nonetheless compelled to attend schools where only English is spoken. Implicit in these constitutional questions are policy problems concerning the just allocation of educational resources to different types of children. Both constitutional and policy questions are posed by the materials in this section.

A. Exclusion

HOSIER v EVANS
314 F Supp 316 (DVI 1970)

Christian, District Judge.

The plaintiffs herein are minor children of school age, each of whom has brought this action by "next friend," one of his parents. They are all aliens and the children of alien parents. They are all lawfully in the Virgin Islands as "nonimmigrant" visitors. . . .

Plaintiffs pray for declaratory and injunctive relief for themselves, and on behalf of all other noncitizen children, similarly situated. They ask that the court adjudge that they, as well as all members of the class on whose behalf they sue, are entitled to attend the public schools of the Virgin Islands, and that the court also enjoin defendants to refrain from excluding plaintiffs and the members of their class from the said public schools.... They ground their joint claim for relief on violations of §3 of the Revised Organic Act of the Virgin Islands which extends to that territory, among other articles and amendments, or portions of them, the "due process" and "equal protection" clauses of the Fourteenth Amendment of the Constitution of the United States. . . .

Following in the footsteps of our federal government, we too "must consider public education in the light of its full development and its present place in American life." *Brown v Board of Educ* 347 US 483, 492 (1954). With like perception we must recognize that:

> Today, education is perhaps the most important function of state and local governments. Compulsory school attendance laws and the great expenditures for education both demonstrate our recognition of the importance of education to our democratic society. . . . Today it is the principal instrument in awakening the child to cultural values, in preparing him for later professional training, and in helping him to adjust normally to his environment. In these days, it is doubtful that any child may reasonably be expected to succeed in life if he is denied the opportunity of an education. . . . 347 US at 493.

The foregoing, it will be remembered, was said by the Supreme Court of the United States with respect to black children, citizens of the United States, in striking down the separate but equal, so-called, system of public education. Here we address ourselves to the problem of alien children in this territory, worse in plight, for they are offered no free, public education at all. As did the court in *Brown v Board of Education, supra,* I hold that public education, "where the state has undertaken to provide it, is a right which must be made available to all on equal terms. . . ."

[T]he conclusion is inescapable that alien children, lawfully within this territory, in the status of these plaintiffs, are unquestionably "persons" within the Equal Protection Clause of the Fourteenth Amendment. . . .

Defendants contend that the legislature of the Virgin Islands is authorized to establish categories or classes of persons who may be admitted or excluded from the public schools so long as such classes or categories bear a reasonable relation to the power of the legislature to enact laws for the protection of the public welfare. With this general principle, so well settled, none can quarrel, and it must be admitted that in this effort, a legislature is to be given great latitude. . . . This legislative power is not without its limitations, however, especially where basic civil rights are concerned, *Skinner v Oklahoma* 316 US 535 (1942), and those classifications which invade or restrain fundamental rights are to be "closely scrutinized and carefully confined." *Harper v Virginia State Bd of Elections* 383 US 663, 670 (1966).

Defendants make much of the influx of aliens into the territory over the last few years and suggest that the cost of admitting these plaintiffs and all others in the class to the public schools would create an undue burden on the government of the Virgin Islands. They would cover themselves with the cloak of "already severely inadequate" facilities which, by the granting of the relief here prayed for, would be rendered "so chaotic as to totally destroy public education for all so entitled." The short answer to that argument is that fundamental rights guaranteed by the Constitution may be neither denied nor abridged solely because their implementation requires the expenditure of public funds. For such purposes, the government must raise the funds. *Griffin v County School Bd* 377 US 218 (1964). . . . What defendants advance as an inescapable conclusion—that relief must be denied—"until such time as the educational facilities are adequate," I reject out of hand as constitutionally impermissible, once the plaintiffs' right be established. These litigants may not be relegated to such a state of neglect, "benign" or otherwise.

Defendants stress that it is in the interest of the public weal that plaintiffs be debarred from the public schools, except upon such special conditions as they may prescribe. They would bottom this position with unbending reliance on the police power of the government. But what is in the public interest cannot be permanently catalogued on some motion of what was deemed best at a given time. The public's best interest inevitably changes with changing conditions and changing times. If ever sound public policy dictated that noncitizens be barred from the public schools, it can hardly be argued that the criteria and conditions which then dictated such policy still persist. . . .

It cannot be gainsaid that it is manifestly contrary to the public good in this territory to develop and foster a ghetto of ignorance, with countless numbers of untrained, untutored and perhaps untended children (since their parents are bonded workers) roaming the streets, this with the concomitant evils of crime, immorality and general social degeneracy. In the public interest a generation of illiterates is to be avoided, whatever the financial cost. I am of the opinion that the most compelling of public concern militates in favor of the prompt admission of these plaintiffs, and all others of their class, to the public schools. . . .

[T] he plaintiffs' motion for summary judgment should be granted.

MILLS v BOARD OF EDUCATION
348 F Supp 866 (DDC 1972)*

Waddy, District Judge.

This is a civil action brought on behalf of seven children of school age by their next friends in which they seek a declaration of rights and to enjoin the defendants from excluding them from the District of Columbia Public Schools and/or denying them publicly supported education and to compel the defendants to provide them with immediate and adequate education and educational facilities in the public schools or alternative placement at public expense. They also seek additional and ancillary relief to effectuate the primary relief. They allege that although they can profit from an education either in regular classrooms with supportive services or in special classes adopted to their needs, they have been labeled as behavioral problems, mentally retarded, emotionally disturbed or hyperactive, and denied admission to the public schools or excluded therefrom after admission, with no provision for alternative educational placement or periodical review. . . .

---

*The portion of the *Mills* opinion concerning procedural remedies appears at pages 706-8.

The Problem

The genesis of this case is found (1) in the failure of the District of Columbia to provide publicly supported education and training to plaintiffs and other "exceptional" children, members of their class, and (2) the excluding, suspending, expelling, reassigning and transferring of "exceptional" children from regular public school classes without affording them due process of law.

The problem of providing special education for "exceptional" children (mentally retarded, emotionally disturbed, physically handicapped, hyperactive and other children with behavioral problems) is one of major proportions in the District of Columbia. The precise number of such children cannot be stated because the District has continuously failed to comply with §31-208 of the District of Columbia Code which requires a census of all children aged three to eighteen in the District to be taken. Plaintiffs estimate that there are "22,000 retarded, emotionally disturbed, blind, deaf, and speech or learning disabled children, and perhaps as many as 18,000 of these children are not being furnished with programs of specialized education." According to data prepared by the Board of Education, Division of Planning, Research and Evaluation, the District of Columbia provides publicly supported special education programs of various descriptions to at least 3,880 school age children. However, in a 1971 report to the Department of Health, Education and Welfare, the District of Columbia Public Schools admitted that an estimated 12,340 handicapped children were not to be served in the 1971-72 school year.

Each of the minor plaintiffs in this case qualifies as an "exceptional" child. . . .

Although all of the named minor plaintiffs are identified as Negroes the class they represent is not limited by their race. They sue on behalf of and represent all other District of Columbia residents of school age who are eligible for a free public education and who have been, or may be, excluded from such education or otherwise deprived by defendants of access to publicly supported education. . . .

Plaintiffs Are Entitled to Relief

Plaintiffs' entitlement to relief in this case is clear. The applicable statutes and regulations and the Constitution of the United States require it.

Statutes and Regulations

Section 31-201 of the District of Columbia Code requires that:

Every parent, guardian, or other person residing in the District of Columbia who has custody or control of a child between the ages of seven and sixteen years shall cause said child to be regularly instructed in a public school or in a private or parochial school or instructed privately during the period of each year in which the public schools of the District of Columbia are in session. . .

Under §31-203, a child may be "excused" from attendance only when

. . . upon examination ordered by . . . [the board of education], [the child] is found to be unable mentally or physically to profit from attendance at school: Provided, however, that if such examination shows that such child may benefit from specialized instruction adapted to his needs, he shall attend upon such instruction."

Failure of a parent to comply with §31-201 constitutes a criminal offense. DC Code 31-207. The court need not belabor the fact that requiring parents to see that their children attend school under pain of criminal penalties presupposes that an educational opportunity will be made available to the children. The board of education is required to make such opportunity available. . . .

The Constitution—Equal Protection and Due Process

. . . .

In *Hobson v Hansen* 269 F Supp 401 (DC Cir 1967) Circuit Judge J. Skelly Wright . . . stated that "the court has found the due process clause of the Fourteenth Amendment elastic enough to embrace not only the First and Fourth Amendments, but the self-incrimination clause of the Fifth, the speedy trial, confrontation and assistance of counsel clauses of the Sixth and the cruel and unusual clause of the Eighth." (269 F Supp 401, 493, citations omitted.) Judge Wright concluded "from these considerations the court draws the conclusion that the doctrine of equal educational opportunity—the equal protection clause in its application to public school education—is in its full sweep a component of due process binding on the district under the due process clause of the Fifth Amendment."

In *Hobson v Hansen, supra,* Judge Wright found that denying poor public school children educational opportunities equal to that available to more affluent public school children was violative of the due process clause of the Fifth Amendment. *A fortiori,* the defendants' conduct here, denying plaintiffs and their class not just an equal publicly supported education but all publicly supported education while providing such education to other children, is violative of the due process clause. . . .

The Defense

The answer of the defendants to the complaint contains the following:

These defendants say that it is impossible to afford plaintiffs the relief they request unless:

(a) The Congress of the United States appropriates millions of dollars to improve special education services in the District of Columbia; or

(b) These defendants divert millions of dollars from funds already specifically appropriated for other educational services in order to improve special educational services. These defendants suggest that to do so would violate an act of Congress and would be inequitable to children outside the alleged plaintiff class.

This Court is not persuaded by that contention.

The defendants are required by the Constitution of the United States, the District of Columbia Code, and their own regulations to provide a publicly-supported education for these "exceptional" children. Their failure to fulfill this clear duty to include and retain these children in the public school system, or otherwise provide them with publicly supported education, and their failure to afford them due process hearing and periodical review, cannot be excused by the claim that there are insufficient funds. In *Goldberg v Kelly* 397 US 254 (1969) the Supreme Court, in a case that involved the right of a welfare recipient to a hearing before termination of his benefits, held that constitutional rights must be afforded citizens despite the greater expense involved. The court stated . . . that "the state's interest that his [welfare recipient] payments not be erroneously terminated, clearly outweighs the state's competing concern to prevent any increase in its fiscal and administrative burdens." Similarly the District of Columbia's interest in educating the excluded children clearly must outweigh its interest in preserving its financial resources. If sufficient funds are not available to finance all of the services and programs that are needed and desirable in the system then the available funds must be expended equitably in such a manner that no child is entirely excluded from a publicly supported education consistent with his needs and ability to benefit therefrom. The inadequacies of the District of Columbia public school system, whether occasioned by insufficient funding or administrative inefficiency, certainly cannot be permitted to bear more heavily on the "exceptional" or handicapped child than on the normal child.

Implementation of Judgment. . . .

Inasmuch as the board of education has presented for adoption by the court a proposed "order and decree" embodying its present plans for the identification of "exceptional" children and providing for their publicly supported education, including a time table, and further requiring the board to formulate and file with the court a more comprehensive plan, the court will not now appoint a special master as was requested by plaintiffs. . . .

Judgment and Decree

[I]t is hereby ordered, adjudged and decreed that summary judgment in favor of plaintiffs and against defendants be, and hereby is, granted, and judgment is entered in this action as follows:

1. That no child eligible for a publicly supported education in the District of Columbia public schools shall be excluded from a regular public school assignment by a rule, policy, or practice of the board of education of the District of Columbia or its agents unless such child is provided (a) adequate alternative educational services suited to the child's needs, which may include special education or tuition grants, and (b) a constitutionally adequate prior hearing and periodic review of the child's status, progress, and the adequacy of any educational alternative. . . .

3. The District of Columbia shall provide to each child of school age a free and suitable publicly supported education regardless of the degree of the child's mental, physical or emotional disability or impairment. Furthermore, defendants shall not exclude any child resident in the District of Columbia from such publicly supported education on the basis of a claim of insufficient resources. . . .

5. Defendants shall provide each identified member of plaintiff class with a publicly supported education suited to his needs within thirty days of the entry of this order. . . .

9. a. Defendants shall utilize public or private agencies to evaluate the educational needs of all identified "exceptional" children and, within twenty days of the entry of this order, shall file with the clerk of this court their proposal for each individual placement in a suitable educational program, including the provision of compensatory educational services where required. . . .

10. a. Within forty-five days of the entry of this order, defendants shall file with the clerk of the court, with copy to plaintiffs' counsel, a comprehensive plan which provides for the identification, notification, assessment, and placement of class members. Such plan shall state the nature and extent of efforts which defendants have undertaken or propose to undertake to

(1) describe the curriculum, educational objectives, teacher qualifications, and ancillary services for the publicly supported educational programs to be provided to class members; and

(2) formulate general plans of compensatory education suitable to class members in order to overcome the present effects of prior educational deprivations. . .

11. The defendants shall make an interim report to this court on their performance within forty-five days of the entry of this order. Such report shall show:

(1) The adequacy of defendants' implementation of plans to identify, locate, evaluate and give notice to all members of the class.

(2) The number of class members who have been placed, and the nature of their placements.

(3) The number of contested hearings before the hearing officers, if any, and the findings and determinations resulting therefrom.

12. Within forty-five days of the entry of this order, defendants shall file with this court a report showing the expunction from or correction of all official records of any plaintiff with regard to past expulsions, suspensions, or exclusions effected in violation of [plaintiff's] procedural rights . . . together with a plan for procedures pursuant to which parents, guardians, or their counsel may attach to such students' records any clarifying or explanatory information which the parent, guardian or counsel may deem appropriate. . . .

Notes and Questions

1. Hosier v Evans

Is *Hosier* consistent with *Rodriguez*? Could defendants respond to the *Hosier* order by opening the public school to all children, while reducing the school day from six to four hours? By ceasing to offer eleventh- and twelfth-grade instruction?

2. Problem: Sparsely Settled Community

Because population in the state of Wasteland is so widely scattered, the state has established two kinds of secondary schools: regular high schools, in areas whose population is sufficient to sustain them; and boarding schools, which enroll students from the hinterlands. One group of hinterlanders, unhappy with boarding school treatment, refused to be removed from their homes to attend school. They argue a constitutional entitlement to have a secondary education where they live, and that any other arrangement excludes them from school.

What result? See *Sage v State Bd of Educ (Alas)* Civil No 71-1245, settlement approved, May 5, 1971.

3. *Pennsylvania Ass'n for Retarded Children (PARC) v Commonwealth*
334 F Supp 1257 (ED Pa 1971), 343 F Supp 279 (ED Pa 1972).

A consent order in *PARC*, subsequently affirmed by the court, required Pennsylvania to provide a "free, public program of education and training appropriate to the child's capacity, within the context of a presumption that, among the alternative programs of education and training required by statute to be available, placement in a regular public school class is preferable to placement in a special public school class [i.e., a class for "handicapped" children] and placement in a special public school class is preferable to placement in any other type of program of education and training. . . ." 334 F Supp at 1260. The basis for that requirement was the court's statement that: "Having undertaken to provide a free public education to all of its children, including its exceptional children, the Commonwealth of Pennsylvania may not deny any mentally retarded child access to a free public program of education and training." Compare *Flaherty v Connors* 319 F Supp 1284 (D Mass 1970).

Does *PARC* follow logically from *Hosier*? Are the two classes of plaintiffs—aliens and retardates—similar in constitutional status? What justification might the state offer for denying retardates a publicly supported education. To what kind of education are retardates constitutionally entitled?

4. *Mills v Board of Education*

The class of plaintiffs in *Mills* is considerably broader than in *PARC*; it includes not only retarded children, but all children excluded from publicly supported instruction. By holding such exclusions unconstitutional, does *Mills* suggest that all children have a right to attend public schools? A right to publicly supported instruction? Would the outcome in *Mills* differ if a school district sought to cut off all public funds for schooling (recall the discussion of "minimum protection").

In *Mills*, what is the nature of the education to which previously excluded children are entitled? Does the school district satisfy its constitutional obligation if it places all children in something that is called an "educational setting," regardless of the appropriateness of that setting to the child's needs? If not, how can *Mills* be reconciled with *McInnis v Shapiro* (293 F Supp 327)? Is the distinction between a constitutional standard and the judicial remedy adopted to implement that standard pertinent here? Is the *Mills* requirement—education "suited to the child's needs" (348 F Supp at 878)—equivalent to the "minimal" standard suggested in *Rodriguez*? Compare *Tidewater Soc'y for Autistic Children v Commonwealth* (ED Va 1972) (unpublished opinion); *Harrison v Michigan* 350 F Supp 846 (ED Mich 1972).

In *Mills* one not atypical plaintiff, Janice King, is described by the court as "brain damaged and retarded, with right hemiplegia." 348 F Supp at 870. Suppose the cost of providing her a "suitable" education is five times the cost of providing the "normal" student with an education. Assuming that no additional money is forthcoming from nonlocal sources, must the district reduce its expenditures for other students in order to provide Miss King a "suitable" education?

How would a court respond to the argument that such reductions deny "suitable" instruction to the nonhandicapped student?

For certain children, notably the profoundly retarded (those with IQ scores below 30), "education" may mean learning to use the bathroom and tie one's shoes. Is that the sort of education that publicly supported instruction should provide? If not, on whom should the burden of providing such instruction fall?

Mills links "handicapped" children with those excluded for disciplinary or other reasons. Does that linkage make constitutional sense? Do the problems of implementing the *Mills* decree differ for the two classes of litigants? The implications of *Mills* have been widely discussed. See, Herr, "Retarded Children and the Law: Enforcing the Constitutional Rights of the Mentally Retarded," 23 *Syr L Rev* 995 (1972); Weintraub and Abeson, "Appropriate Education for all Handicapped Children: A Growing Issue," 23 *Syr L Rev* 1037 (1973); Murdoch, "Civil Rights of the Mentally Retarded: Some Critical Issues," 48 *Notre Dame Lawyer* 133 (1972).

In *Knight v Board of Educ* 48 FRD 115 (EDNY 1969), the federal court required the New York City school system to readmit students stricken from school rolls for nonattendance and to provide them with catch-up help equivalent to the education they had been denied. If the *Mills* and *PARC* exclusions were wrongful, are plaintiffs entitled to similar help? How might equivalency be defined, in either the *Knight* or *Mills/PARC* contexts?

B. "Functional Exclusion"

LAU v NICHOLS
483 F2d 791 (9th Cir 1973), *cert. granted*, 412 US 938 (1973)

[This opinion, formerly 472 F2d 909, was officially withdrawn by the Ninth Circuit Court of Appeals after the United States Supreme Court granted certiorari in June 1973.]

Trask, Circuit Judge:

This appeal is from the district court's adverse disposition of a civil rights class action filed by appellants to compel the San Francisco Unified School District to provide all non-English-speaking Chinese students attending district schools with bilingual compensatory education in the English language. The defendants-appellees are the superintendent and members of the board of education of the school district, and members of the board of supervisors of the city and county of San Francisco.

Two classes of non-English-speaking Chinese pupils are represented in this action. The first class, composed of 1,790 of the 2,856 Chinese-speaking students in the district who admittedly need special instruction in English, receive no such help at all. The second class of 1,066 Chinese-speaking students receive compensatory education, 633 on a part-time (one hour per day) basis, and 433 on a full-time (six hours per day) basis. Little more than one-third of the fifty-nine teachers involved in providing this special instruction are fluent in both English and Chinese, and both bilingual and English-as-a-Second Language (ESL) methods are used. As of September 1969, there were approximately 100,000 students attending district schools, of which 16,574 were Chinese.

Appellants' complaint states seven causes of action, alleging violations of the United States Constitution, the California Constitution,[2] §601 of the Civil

---

2. The right to an education is claimed under the Fifth (due process), Ninth (reserved powers), and Fourteenth (equal protection clause) Amendments to the Constitution of the

Rights Act of 1964, 42 USC §2000d, and provisions of the California Education Code. Essentially, appellants contend that appellees have abridged their rights to an education and to bilingual education, and disregarded their rights to equal educational opportunity among themselves and with English-speaking students. They pray for declaratory judgment and for preliminary and permanent injunctive relief mandating bilingual compensatory education in English for all non-English-speaking Chinese students. . . .

As hereinbefore stated, the district court denied appellants all relief, and found for appellees on the merits. The court expressed well-founded sympathy for the plight of the students represented in this action, but concluded that their rights to an education and to equal educational opportunities had been satisfied, in that they received "the same education made available on the same terms and conditions to the other tens of thousands of students in the San Francisco Unified School District . . . ." Appellees had no duty to rectify appellants' special deficiencies, as long as they provided these students with access to the same educational system made available to all other students.

As applied to the facts of this case, appellants reason, *Brown* [*v Board of Educ* 347 US 483 (1954)] mandates consideration of the student's responses to the teaching provided by his school in determining whether he has been afforded equal educational opportunity. Even though the student is given the same course of instruction as all other school children, he is denied education on "equal terms" with them if he cannot understand the language of instruction and is, therefore, unable to take as great an advantage of his classes as other students. According to appellants, *Brown* requires schools to provide "equal" opportunities to all, and equality is to be measured not only by what the school offers the child, but by the potential which the child brings to the school. If the student is disadvantaged with respect to his classmates, the school has an affirmative duty to provide him special assistance to overcome his disabilities, whatever the origin of those disabilities may be.

Appellants' reading of *Brown* is extreme, and one which we cannot accept. . . . *Brown* concerned affirmative state action discriminating against persons because of their race. . . . Appellants have neither alleged nor shown any such discriminatory actions by appellees. The evidence, that English is and has been uniformly used as the language of instruction in all district schools, does not evince the requisite discrimination in the maintenance of this otherwise proper policy.

Neither can appellants invoke the teachings of cases like *Gaston County v US* 395 US 285 (1969) . . . . In those cases, facially neutral policies were held unconstitutional not simply because the burdens they created fell most heavily upon blacks, but because the states' actions perpetuated the ill effects of past de jure segregation.

[A]ppellants have alleged no past de jure segregation. More importantly, there is no showing that appellants' lingual deficiencies are at all related to any such past discrimination. This court, therefore, rejects the argument that appellees have an affirmative duty to provide language instruction to compensate for appellants' handicaps, because they are carry-overs from state-imposed segregation. *See Swann v Board of Educ* 402 US 1, 15 (1971). If there are any such remnants, that appellants' primary language is Chinese has not been shown to be one of them.

United States; and under Article IX, §5 of the Constitution of the State of California (provision for system of common schools).

It is with this reasoning in mind that we consider, and distinguish, *U S v Texas* [342 F Supp 24 (ED Tex 1971)] ... [I]n that order the court mandated bilingual education for Mexican-American and Anglo-American students in the San Felipe-Del Rio Consolidated Independent School District. However, the basis for that order was the court's prior determination ... that there had been de jure segregation. The purpose of the order was, therefore, to " 'eliminate discrimination root and branch,' *Green v New Kent County Bd of Educ* 391 US 430 (1968), and to create a unitary school system with no [Mexican] schools and no white schools but just schools." *US v Texas*. ... [such] a rationale for requiring compensatory bilingual instruction is not applicable under the facts of this case.
. . .

Every student brings to the starting line of his educational career different advantages and disadvantages caused in part by social, economic and cultural background, created and continued completely apart from any contribution by the school system. That some of these may be impediments which can be overcome does not amount to a "denial" by the board of educational opportunities within the meaning of the Fourteenth Amendment should the board fail to give them special attention, this even though they are characteristic of a particular ethnic group. Before the board may be found to unconstitutionally deny special remedial attention to such deficiencies there must first be found a constitutional duty to provide them.

However commendable and socially desirable it might be for the school district to provide special remedial educational programs to disadvantaged students in those areas, or to provide better clothing or food to enable them to more easily adjust themselves to their educational environment, we find no constitutional or statutory basis upon which we can mandate that these things be done.
. . .

Because we find that the language deficiency suffered by appellants was not caused directly or indirectly by any state action, we agree with the judgment of the district court and distinguish this case from *Brown v Board of Educ* 347 US 483 (1954), and its progeny of de jure cases. Under the facts of this case, appellees responsibility to appellants under the equal protection clause extends no further than to provide them with the same facilities, textbooks, teachers and curriculum as is provided to other children in the district. There is no evidence that this duty has not been discharged. ... The classification claimed invidious is not the result of laws enacted by the state presently or historically, but the result of deficiencies created by the appellants themselves in failing to learn the English language. For this the Constitution affords no relief by reason of any of the Constitutional provisions under which appellants have sought shelter.

Furthermore, the determination of what special educational difficulties faced by some students within a state or school district will be afforded extraordinary curative action, and the intensity of the measures to be taken, is a complex decision, calling for significant amounts of executive and legislative expertise and nonjudicial value judgments. As with welfare (to which these claims are closely akin), the needs of the citizens must be reconciled with the finite resources available to meet those needs. ...

As long as there is no discrimination by race or national origin, as has neither been alleged nor shown by appellants with respect to this issue, the states should be free to set their educational policies, including special programs to meet special needs, with limited judicial intervention to decide among competing demands upon the resources at their commands, subject only to the requirement that their classifications be rationally related to the purposes for which they are created. . . .

Judged by this standard, the administration of the compensatory education program for non-English-speaking Chinese children in the San Francisco Unified School District passes constitutional muster. Prior to the institution of this litigation, remedial instruction was provided as part of a pilot program. As such, emphasis would quite reasonably be on experimentation. Therefore, some children were given all their academic instruction within the program, and some were taken out of the regular school structure only part-time; some pupils were taught by bilingual teachers, and some received their instruction by the more intensive ESL method. Because of limited finances and the exploratory nature of the efforts, not all lingually deficient Chinese children took part.

With due regard to the nature of the school district's efforts, nothing before this court would indicate that the program has been managed so as to invidiously discriminate against appellants. We find that appellees have not violated appellants' rights to equal protection in the administration of the compensatory program for non-English-speaking Chinese students within the District.

The judgment is affirmed.

Hill, District Judge, dissenting:

I dissent.

In my view, the majority's construction of the equal protection clause is too narrow. They fail to assign sufficient value and importance to the rights plaintiffs assert in this case. A child's right to an equal educational opportunity is of the greatest importance and should not be abridged without persuasive justification. . . .

I would reverse the judgment and remand the case to the trial court for the taking of further evidence on defendants' justification, if any, for their failure to provide the bilingual teaching which plaintiffs seek. The facts already adduced show, in my opinion, that the San Francisco school system withholds from a readily identifiable segment of an ethnic minority the minimum English language instruction necessary for that segment to participate in the educational processes with any chance of success. I view such a deprivation as being prima facie within the ambit of the equal protection clause.

The plaintiffs, and the class they represent, are grade school children of Chinese parents who have recently immigrated to this country. The law requires these children to attend school; so, they come. But they enter the San Francisco School System unable to speak or understand the English language. All the instruction they receive is in English as are all of the books and all of the visual materials which are used. As the *amicus* brief from the Harvard University Center for Law and Education puts it, education for these children becomes "mere physical presence as audience to a strange play which they do not understand." These *amici* correctly stress the fact that the essence of education is communication: a small child can profit from his education only when he is able to understand the instruction, ask and answer questions, and speak with his classmates and teachers. When he cannot understand the language employed in the school, he cannot be said to have an educational opportunity in any sense. As against his English-speaking classmates, his educational opportunity is manifestly unequal even though there is an illusion of equality since the facilities, books, and teachers made available to him are the same as those made available to the rest of the students. It seems clear to me that a pupil knowing only a foreign language cannot be said to have an educational opportunity equal to his fellow students unless and until he acquires some minimal facility in the English language. . . .

The majority misapprehend the nature of the relief sought in this case. They characterize plaintiffs as seeking "bilingual education." Plaintiffs have carefully and repeatedly abjured any such objective. . . .

[T]hey seek only that "defendants . . . provide special instruction in English and that such instruction . . . be taught by bilingual teachers." When the majority emphasize that this is an "English-speaking nation" and that English is the "language of instruction" in all public schools, they set up a straw man which they have clothed in irrelevant truisms. Plaintiffs do not seek to be taught in Chinese, in whole or in part. They seek only to learn English. They claim, with apparent justification, that they cannot learn English effectively unless it is taught to them by persons who have a facility in the only language they understand, i.e., Chinese. It seems abundantly clear that as soon as the plaintiffs have achieved enough proficiency in English to understand their teachers and classmates and participate somewhat in the course of instruction, they will expect no further Chinese to be uttered in their classes. They do not seek instruction in the Chinese language or to be taught anything in Chinese except how to speak English. . . .

When government action particularly affects or burdens a given class or group, it is often called "discrimination." It is important to remember that no intent to discriminate is required in order to invoke the equal protection clause. One can deal with an apparently neutral and nondiscriminatory statute or scheme which is applied or enforced without any intent to discriminate (or even without knowledge that the effect is a discriminatory one) and still run afoul of the equal protection clause if illegal discrimination in fact results. When such action particularly affects or burdens one of the classes or groups mentioned above, it is presumptively illegal discrimination. However, not all discrimination is illegal. Discrimination which is apparently illegal may be excused by a showing that the discrimination or classification is justified by overriding governmental objectives and necessities. . . .

The strength of the justification needed to overcome a prima facie violation of the equal protection clause will vary depending on the nature of the right involved. When the right involved is a fundamental one, only a compelling state interest will justify its abridgment, and the discrimination must be necessary to the achievement of the overriding governmental interest. . . .

Turning now to the rights involved in this case, it cannot be doubted that the right to equal educational opportunity is one of the most vital and fundamental of all of the rights enjoyed by Americans. . . .

Thus, when defendants are given the opportunity to present their justification, their showing would necessarily be required to be persuasive in the extreme.

The defendants could be allowed to show, in the resumed trial, the limits of their resources, the conflicting demands made upon those resources, and their judgment as to the priorities to be applied to those resources and demands. And the court would then decide whether the defendants are justified in their refusal to provide bilingual instruction for the teaching of English to all of the Chinese-speaking pupils who require it.

The majority apparently foreclose plaintiffs from relief under the equal protection clause because their language deficiency was not "caused directly or indirectly by any state action." In other words, the majority see the equal protection clause as available only when the inequality or discrimination results from some present intent to discriminate or from some past or historical governmental discriminatory conduct for which the state can be blamed. The majority cite no previous decision which so limits the scope of the equal protection clause. . . .

In another group of cases it is clear that relief is granted under the equal protection clause where no historical blame can be placed upon the state. These cases deal with the obligation of the state to provide special services to criminal defendants who are unable to pay for those services themselves. . . . These cases stand for the proposition that a person's poverty may not be the basis for denying him the same facilities and aids in combating criminal charges against him as are enjoyed by those who can pay for such facilities and aids with their own funds. Affirmative state action is required to redress the inequality, and the state's duty to redress is imposed without reference to whether or not it can be said that the state in some way caused the inequality in the first place. The state's duty to take affirmative action does not arise because it can be said that the state is primarily responsible for making a poor man poor. Rather, the duty arises because the state must put justice within reach of every man if the state chooses to provide a system of criminal justice at all. Similarly, when the state chooses to provide education and makes attendance at school compulsory, it has a duty to grant to each child an equal educational opportunity and a duty to avoid illegal discrimination. That duty does not arise because of the existence of either a present intent to discriminate or past historical discrimination. Rather, the duty arises because once the state chooses to put itself in the business of educating children, it must give each child the best education its resources and priorities allow.

One last word. The plaintiffs in this case are small, Chinese-speaking children who sue on their own behalf and on behalf of others similarly situated. The majority describe the plight of these children as being "the result of deficiencies created by the appellants themselves in failing to learn the English language." To ascribe some fault to a grade school child because of his "failing to learn the English language" seems both callous and inaccurate. If anyone can be blamed for the language deficiencies of these children, it is their parents and not the children themselves. Even if the parents can be faulted (and in many cases they cannot, since they themselves are newly arrived in a strange land and in their struggle for survival may have had neither the time nor opportunity to study any English), it is one of the keystones of our culture and our law that the sins of the fathers are not to be visited upon the children.

Notes and Questions

1. Functional Exclusion

Is the plight of the *Lau* plaintiffs similar to the plight of children who are in fact excluded from school? What does "functional exclusion" mean? Does the concept apply both to non-English-speaking Chinese students receiving *no* special help and to those receiving some (assertedly insufficient) help?

2. Discrimination

Is *Lau* more aptly considered in the context of racial discrimination cases (see chapter 4)? If non-Chinese students were unable to understand English because little English was spoken in their homes, would the nature of their constitutional claim to special instruction differ from that advanced by the *Lau* plaintiffs?

3. Remedy

What remedy is being sought by the *Lau* plaintiffs: access to instruction designed to improve their comprehension of the English language? Access to instruction that in fact improves such comprehension? If the former remedy is what is being pressed, might the school district argue that an "English only" instruction program was its equivalent to the "Berlitz" or total language immersion method of teaching a foreign language? What additional facts concerning the educational careers of students who commence school not speaking English would you need in order to evaluate the "Berlitz" argument?

4. Educational Needs

In what way do plaintiffs' contentions in *Lau* differ from the "educational needs" approach, rejected in *McInnis v Shapiro*? Is the *Lau* demand for "special instruction in English," constitutionally distinguishable from the demand pressed in *Serna v Portales Municipal Schools* for "bilingual-bicultural" instruction? In short, has this chapter gone full circle, revisiting and rephrasing here issues previously analyzed in section II?

If "functional exclusion" seems distinguishable from "needs," what is the scope of the doctrine? How would the "functional exclusion" approach treat the following cases?

a. X, a polio victim, is in all other respects just like his peers. Because the school to which he has been assigned has four flights of stairs which X cannot mount, he is unable to go to school.

b. Y speaks no English; his native language is Hungarian, a tongue spoken by no one else in the school system (and indeed by only twelve others in the state). Because the school to which he has been assigned provides no special program for non-English-speaking Hungarian students, Y can understand nothing that is said in school.

c. Z is completely turned off by school. His interests lie in the occult and supernatural, spheres which the school to which he is assigned does not reach (indeed, tacitly discourages). Since Z does not communicate in words, but rather by signs, he understands nothing that is said in school.

5. Nonconstitutional Issues

The Civil Rights Act of 1964, 42 USC §2000d, states that no person "on the ground of race, color, or national origin," shall "be denied the benefits of, or be subjected to discrimination under any program or activity receiving federal financial assistance." Pursuant to this statute, the United States Department of Health, Education and Welfare has issued guidelines requiring that: "Where inability to speak and understand the English language excludes national origin-minority group children from effective participation in the educational program offered by a school district, the district must take affirmative steps to rectify the language deficiency in order to open its instructional program to these students." 35 Fed Reg 11595 (July 18, 1970), App, p 26a.

Does the HEW guideline resolve the issues posed by *Lau*? By *Serna v Portales*? By the "student Y" hypothetical? Is the guideline consistent with the statute?

Is there a difference between a "denial of benefits" and "discrimination," under the statute? Is *Lau* a case concerning "denial of benefits," but not "discrimination"?

chapter seven
Equal Educational Opportunity and Student Classification

The classification (or sorting) of students by schools—that is, differentiations among students, ostensibly premised on intellectual performance or potential—is a relatively new area of inquiry both for policy makers and lawyers.* Until recently concern with national, state, or districtwide issues has had precedence over the internal workings of schools. While courts have struggled to define equality of educational opportunity, and to demarcate the liberties that students retain while attending public school, they have generally been unwilling to review essentially pedagogical judgments.

This chapter examines particular school classifications: ability grouping (or tracking) and assignment to special classes for handicapped (or special or exceptional) children.† It also assesses the devices that facilitate classification: testing, grading, and counseling. The inquiry is organized around the chief criticisms that have been leveled at present practice: that it misidentifies or misclassifies significant numbers of students, that it is racially discriminatory, and that it denies some students an equal educational opportunity. It then reviews a variety of remedies—some couched in terms of better policy, others posed as plausible constitutional requirements—that have been proposed to rectify the asserted shortcomings of classification. Throughout, the chapter examines the appropriateness of applying constitutional concepts developed in other contexts to the issues of student classification.

Perhaps more than any of the issues previously canvassed, student classification presses at the limits of judicial competence to affect educational policy. The minuteness of many within-school and within-class decisions makes it difficult to conceive of them as posing legally manageable problems. Such decisions are complex, interrelated, and numerous. For that reason, a court that undertook routinely to review them might well find itself acting as schoolmaster in an uncomfortably literal sense. Furthermore, these practices lie at the heart of the school official's claim to professional competence; any challenge may be perceived as a threat to that competence and for that reason strenuously resisted. Whether such resistance is indeed proper—whether, for some or all of the questions considered

---

*The legitimacy of certain bases of classification—e.g., race, sex, and wealth—is, of course, the question that courts routinely entertain in determining whether legislation violates the equal protection guarantee of the Fourteenth Amendment. In this chapter, the term is given a different and rather more precise meaning.

†The legal and policy issues posed by the exclusion of severely handicapped 'ineducable' children, another form of classification, are treated in chapter 6, pp. 628-36.

in this chapter, judicial involvement is inappropriate—is a critical and unresolved issue.

I. Introduction: Nature and Purpose of Classification

"SCHOOLS AS SORTERS: THE CONSTITUTIONAL AND POLICY
IMPLICATIONS OF STUDENT CLASSIFICATION"
D. Kirp
121 *U Pa L Rev* 705, 710-17 (1973)

. . . . Public schools regularly sort students in a variety of ways. [See survey data reported in W. Findley and M. Bryan, *Ability Grouping: 1970* (1971).] They test them when they first arrive at school and at regular intervals thereafter in order to identify aptitude—i.e., capacity to learn. Although such capacity may not in fact be measured, and may indeed be unsusceptible to measurement, what is important for descriptive purposes is the fact that schools act on the assumption that tests can measure aptitude.

From primary school until graduation, most schools group (or track) students on the basis of estimated intellectual ability, both within classrooms—the brighter "tigers" separated from the less intelligent "clowns"—and in separate classes. In primary school grouping, the pace of instruction, but typically not its content, is varied. Grouping decisions may be made for each school subject—the cleverest in arithmetic may be dullards at spelling—or a given group may stay intact for the entire curriculum. During the school year, students are graded. Those grades, combined with aptitude and achievement test results and teacher recommendations, determine whether a child is promoted to the next grade level and into which ability group he is placed.

In secondary school, variations among educational "tracks" reflect both interest and ability. There, for the first time in his educational career, the student may be offered choices. As the process actually works, however, grammar school success usually means college track or academic high school assignment while mediocre grade school performance leads frequently to placement in a general (noncollege preparatory), business, or vocational program. It is counselors, and not students, who frequently make these decisions, by matching school offerings to their own estimates of each student's ability and potential. [See A. Cicourel and J. Kitsuse, *The Educational Decision Makers* (1963).] That classification determines both the nature of the secondary school education—Shakespeare, shorthand or machine shop—and the gross choices—college or job—available after the twelfth grade.

Students whom the school cannot classify in this manner are treated as "special" or "exceptional" children.* These students by no means resemble one

---

*"Special education" refers to classes for students with particular and acute learning disabilities. The disability may be defined in terms of test scores, physical impediments (i.e., classes for the blind, deaf and dumb, or perceptually handicapped), or psychological disturbance (i.e., classes for the emotionally disturbed). Special education classes are a relatively recent and increasingly common phenomenon. A recent national estimate of enrollment in special education concludes that 2,106,100 children (35 percent of those who "need" such help) are enrolled in some special program. Retarded children are somewhat better served than other children in need of special education—based on a prevalence estimate of 2.3

another. They may have intellectual, physical or emotional handicaps; they may not speak English as their native language; they may simply be hungry, or unhappy with their particular school situation. These students share only their differentness. The number and variety of differentiating characteristics is large; overlapping among the characteristics (multiple differentnesses) further complicates the pattern. Yet the school, in part because its resources are scarce, cannot tailor individual programs to satisfy individual needs. Instead, it develops classifications which attempt to reconcile the variations among "exceptional" children with the limitations of school resources. When a school or school district provides only a single "special education" program, the classroom may resemble a Noah's Ark of deviations from the school norm: the retarded, the crippled, and the emotionally disturbed. The teacher assigned to such a class cannot hope to do much more than maintain order. A more amply endowed school district may offer several "special" programs, differentiating both among levels of retardation ("educable," "trainable," "profound") and between retardation and such other school handicaps as "learning disabilities" and "emotional disturbance." . . .

C. School Classification and School Needs

1. Historical Development of Classification. While, as one testing manual contends, "the original [classification] was when God . . . looked at everything he made and saw that it was *very good*," [W. Mehrens and I. Lehmann, *Standardized Tests in Education*, 3 (1969)] only during the past sixty years have schools devoted considerable effort to classifying and sorting students. The prototypal common school, energetically promoted by Horace Mann and Henry Barnard, was designed to provide a common educational experience for all comers—all, that is, who could afford to stay in school for an extended period of time. Through the nineteenth century, the shared curriculum was characteristic of schools which, at least in theory, respected neither class nor caste.

The arrival of significant numbers of immigrants from Eastern and Southern Europe late in the nineteenth century obliged school officials to provide instruction for children who spoke no English and had little, if any, previous schooling. It made no sense to place these students in regular classes; they needed assistance of a kind that schools had not previously been asked to provide. Urban school systems created "opportunity classes," special programs designed to overcome the students' initial difficulties and to prepare them for regular schoolwork.

Other societal factors served to promote the need for differentiation among students. The insistence that schools be "businesslike" and efficient was increasingly heard, and American educators began to adopt the modern business corporation's complex organizational structure as their model. [See R. Callahan, *Education and the Cult of Efficiency* (1962); G. Counts, *The Social Composition of Boards of Education: A Study in the Social Control of Public Education* (1927).] Further, the increasingly complex American economy and society demanded a differentiation of skills that a common education simply couldn't provide. As Boston's superintendent of schools argued in 1908: "Until very recently [the schools] have offered equal opportunity for all to receive *one kind* of education, but what will make them democratic is to provide opportunity for

---

percent, close to one-half of retarded children are in special classes. R. Mackie, *Special Education in the United States: Statistics 1948-1966*, 39 (1969).

all to receive such education as will fit them *equally well* for their particular life work." [Brooks, "Twenty-Eighth Annual Report of the Superintendent of Public Schools," in School Committee, City of Boston, *Documents of the School Committee, 53*, (1908).] Varied curricula were developed for students of varying ability. [See generally L. Cremin, *The Transformation of the School* (1961); C. Greer, *The Great School Legend* (1972).]

The advent of standardized aptitude testing early in the twentieth century provided a useful means of identifying and placing those students. [See generally R. Herrnstein, *I.Q. in the Meritocracy* (1973).] As Ellwood Cubberly, one of the most influential educators of that time, maintained:

> The educational significance of the results to be obtained from careful measurements of the intelligence of children can hardly be overestimated. Questions relating to the choice of studies, vocational guidance . . . the grading of pupils, promotional schemes . . . all alike acquire new meaning and significance when viewed in the light of the measurement of intelligence. [L. Terman, *The Measurement of Intelligence*, vii-viii (1916).]

Intelligence tests were increasingly used by American educators because they accorded with the educators' demand for categorization and efficiency. Tests offered scientific justification for the differentiated curriculum, enabling it to function with some rationality. [See Schudson, "Organizing the 'Meritocracy': A History of the College Entrance Examination Board," 42 *Harv Educ Rev* 34, 51 (1972).]

Today ability grouping claims widespread adherence among nonrural school districts.[44] Federal and state support has made particular specialized programs—notably industrial and agricultural trade courses—financially attractive to school districts. Differentiated special education programs, also given impetus by state and federal legislation, have expanded with similar speed (if not quite the same universality) since the 1920s. [See R. Mackie, *Special Education in the United States: Statistics 1948-1966* (1969) for data concerning the growth of differentiated special education.]

2. Current School Needs . . . Grouping, special education assignment, and exclusion have significant and similar school purposes. They: (1) provide mechanisms for differentiating among students; (2) offer rewards and sanctions for school performance; (3) ease the tasks of teachers and administrators by restricting somewhat the range of ability among students in a given classroom; and (4) purportedly improve student achievement.[49]

Interestingly, the first two purposes—sorting and rewarding-punishing—are seldom mentioned by school officials. The sorting function is self-evident: where previously there existed just students, classification permits the parceling out of

44. . . . . A 1958-59 survey undertaken by the National Education Association Research Division reported that among school districts with more than 2500 pupils, 77.6 percent grouped by ability in the primary grades and 90.5 percent utilized ability grouping in secondary schools . . . A similar pattern was reported seven years later. [Research Division, National Education Association, *Ability Grouping*, 12, 15-17 (1968).]

49. Classifications serve an additional purpose, one not directly related to the public schools: they provide a means for *other* public and private institutions (universities, employers, etc.) to distinguish among students, thus serving—for better or worse—the demands of the larger society.

students among different educational programs.[51] That certain of these classifications reward and others punish is apparent from investigations of the effects of
grouping on students' self-perception. [See J. Barker Lunn, *Streaming in the
Primary School* (1970); W. Borg, *Ability Grouping in the Public Schools* (1966)
[originally appeared in 34 *J Experimental Educ,* Winter 1965, at 1]; Mann,
"What Does Ability Grouping Do to the Self-Concept?" 36 *Childhood Educ* 356
(1960); cf. M. Goldberg, A. H. Passow and J. Justman, *The Effects of Ability
Grouping* (1966).] The reward-punishment facet of classification represents one
aspect of the school's stress on intellectual competition, with praise accompanying only performance that the school or teacher defines as successful.

The third and fourth purposes—easing the tasks of teachers and administrators,
and improving the education of students—are more commonly advanced. These
purposes—one emphasizing benefits to teachers and administrators, the other
emphasizing benefits to students—permit school officials to view classification as
an unmixed blessing. There is little recognition that classification may have decidedly limited educational benefits for schoolchildren and that certain sorting
practices may even do educational injury. The belief that classification helps
everyone is significant for two reasons. It partially explains the popularity that
grouping enjoys among teachers: only 18.4 percent of teachers surveyed by the
National Education Association preferred to teach nongrouped classes. [Research
Division, National Education Association, *Teachers' Opinion Poll: Ability
Grouping,* 57 *NEA J* 53 (Feb 1968).] It also underscores the problems that
reformers—whether pedagogues or lawyers—unhappy with present classification
practices are likely to encounter in seeking to restructure them. . . .

II. Legal and Policy Issues: Misclassification, Race and Class Discrimination, and Equal Educational Opportunity

A. Misclassification

Any sorting decision—for example, assignment to an advanced track or to a
class for the mildly retarded—is typically based both on certain nominally objective criteria, such as aptitude tests, and on more subtle judgments of ability and
potential, such as teacher evaluations.

Misclassification can mean several quite different things. It may denote the
misapplication of approved criteria. If the criteria are objective, the issue may be
relatively simple to resolve, but if the criteria are judgmental, resolution becomes
more difficult. Consider two disputes over the just grade in a multiple choice
test: (1) the student alleges that the teacher miscounted the number of correct
answers; (2) the student alleges that a given question is sufficiently ambiguous
that either "true" (the teacher's answer) or "false" (the student's answer) is
correct.

Misclassification may also denote disputes over the criteria themselves. For
example, a student may assert that IQ tests are incapable of measuring intellectual potential, and for that reason should not be used to assign students to

---

51. Certain critics charge that sorting is indeed all that schools do, see Lauter and Howe,
"How the School System is Rigged for Failure," *NY Rev Books,* 18 June 1970, 14, and
perhaps all that they have ever done. C. Greer, *The Great School Legend* (1972). See also
Stein, "Strategies for Failure, 41 *Harv Educ Rev* 158 (1971).

tracks. One study of 378 educable mentally retarded students from thirty-six school districts in the Philadelphia area notes such misclassification. The researchers tested mildly handicapped students with a battery of tests, rather than the single IQ test typically used by school systems; they found the diagnosis for 25 percent of the youngsters to be clearly erroneous, while, for an additional 43 percent, the diagnosis was questionable. Garrison and Hammill, "Who Are the Retarded?" 38 *Exceptional Children*, 13 (1971). The judgment of system-made error is premised on the assumption that the researchers' multiple criteria are better classifying instruments than the districts' single criterion.

In *Hobson v Hansen* 269 F Supp 401, 490 (DDC 1967), the district court noted an instance of this type of misclassification:

> In 1965 Dr. Hansen announced a change in official policy: thenceforth, no student was to be assigned to the special academic track without first being evaluated by a clinical psychologist and, if necessary, undergoing an individual test of ability. In September of that year 1,272 students, either already in the special academic track or about to be enrolled in it on the recommendations of their teachers and principals, were reevaluated by the psychologists under the new order. As a result of this reevaluation approximately 820, almost two-thirds, were discovered to have been improperly judged as requiring assignment to the special academic curriculum. . . .

Does either type of misclassification pose issues of constitutional dimension? Would a parent have a constitutional right to have his child reclassified (1) on the basis that the school had incorrectly scored the aptitude test which was administered; (2) on the basis that the retesting of the child by an independent psychologist yielded a score considerably higher than that recorded by the school, or (3) on the basis that the aptitude test did not in fact measure the child's aptitude?

CONNELLY v UNIVERSITY OF VERMONT AND STATE AGRICULTURAL COLLEGE
244 F Supp 156 (D Vt 1965)

Gibson, District Judge.

The substance of the plaintiff's complaint is as follows: He is a third year student at the defendant's college of medicine, and during the months of March through June of 1964, he was enrolled in a twelve-week course in pediatrics-obstetrics. He states that due to illness he missed a portion of the course from May 11 to June 7, 1964, that he made up this lost time from July 1 to July 16, 1964, and that he believes his grades prior to his illness were 82 and 87 in the pediatrics and obstetrics parts of the course respectively. He further states that on July 17, 1964 he was advised that he had failed the pediatrics-obstetrics course and could not advance to his fourth year by reason of having failed 25 percent or more of the major courses of his third year, this under a rule of the college of medicine. The plaintiff then petitioned the college's committee on advancement for permission to repeat his third year's work. His petition was denied and he was subsequently dismissed from school. He alleges that his teacher during the period from July 1 to July 16, 1964 decided early in that period "that he would not give plaintiff a passing grade in said pediatrics-obstetrics course regardless of his prior work in the spring and regardless of the quality of his work in said makeup period." The plaintiff alleges that his work was of passing quality, and that his dismissal was wrongful, improper, arbitrary, summary and unjust. He prays that it be rescinded by the mandate of this court. . . .

Where a medical student has been dismissed for a failure to attain a proper standard of scholarship, two questions may be involved; the first is, was the student in fact delinquent in his studies or unfit for the practice of medicine? The second question is, were the school authorities motivated by malice or bad faith in dismissing the student, or did they act arbitrarily or capriciously? In general, the first question is not a matter for judicial review. However, a student dismissal motivated by bad faith, arbitrariness or capriciousness may be actionable.

In *Barnard v Inhabitants of Shelburne* 216 Mass 19, 102 NE 1095 (1913) a high school student was dismissed for failure to attain a proper standard of scholarship. The trial court submitted the case to the jury on the theory that it had power to question whether in fact the plaintiff was delinquent in his studies, and the jury found that he was not. In reversing, the Supreme Judicial Court of Massachusetts said,

> So long as the school committee act in good faith their conduct in formulating and applying standards and making decisions touching this matter is not subject to review by any other tribunal. It is obvious that efficiency of instruction depends in no small degree upon this feature of our school system. It is an educational question, the final determination of which is vested by law in the public officials charged with the performance of that important duty.

The only issue for the jury, said the court, was "whether the exclusion of the plaintiff from the high school was an act of bad faith by the school committee." . . .

The effect of . . . [such] decisions is to give the school authorities absolute discretion in determining whether a student has been delinquent in his studies, and to place the burden on the student of showing that his dismissal was motivated by arbitrariness, capriciousness or bad faith. The reason for this rule is that in matters of scholarship, the school authorities are uniquely qualified by training and experience to judge the qualifications of a student, and efficiency of instruction depends in no small degree upon the school faculty's freedom from interference from other noneducational tribunals. It is only when the school authorities abuse this discretion that a court may interfere with their decision to dismiss a student. . . .

In *Eddie v Columbia Univ* 8 Misc2d 795, 168 NYS2d 643 (1957), a candidate for the degree of doctor of philosophy at Columbia University whose dissertation had been rejected conditionally, with the proviso that he could revise it, sought a court order to reinstate him as a certified candidate for the degree, "and to have him finally examined on the basis of his dissertation as it now stands." The New York Supreme Court, after noting that it was not established that the rejection of the dissertation was arbitrary, capricious or unreasonable, said, "The court may not substitute its own opinion as to the merits of a doctoral dissertation for that of the faculty members whom the university has selected to make a determination as to the quality of the dissertation."

The rule of judicial nonintervention in scholastic affairs is particularly applicable in the case of a medical school. A medical school must be the judge of the qualifications of its students to be granted a degree; Courts are not supposed to be learned in medicine and are not qualified to pass opinion as to the attainments of a student in medicine. *People ex rel Pacella v Bennett Medical College* 205 Ill App 324. In the instant case, the plaintiff Connelly alleges on information and belief

> ... that, on the basis of his work in the pediatrics-obstetrics course during the spring of 1964 and the continued sixteen-day makeup period in July 1964, he either received, or, in the alternative, should have received a passing grade therein and that his work in said course was comparable to and in many instances superior to the work of other students who received a passing grade in that course.

Whether the plaintiff should or should not have received a passing grade for the period in question is a matter wholly within the jurisdiction of the school authorities, who alone are qualified to make such a determination. The subject matter of this count of the complaint is not a subject for judicial review and this count of the complaint fails to state any claim for which relief can be granted.

However, to the extent that the plaintiff has alleged his dismissal was for reasons other than the quality of his work, or in bad faith, he has stated a cause of action. He has alleged "that the agent of defendant's college of medicine who taught plaintiff from July 1 to July 16, 1964, decided early in said period that he would not give plaintiff a passing grade in said pediatric-obstetrics course regardless of his prior work in the spring and regardless of the quality of his work in said makeup period." The plaintiff has also alleged that the action of defendant in dismissing him was "summary and arbitrary." The allegation that the plaintiff was failed by an instructor who had made up his mind to fail him before he completed the course is equivalent, in this court's opinion, to an allegation of bad faith, arbitrariness, and capriciousness on the part of the said instructor, and if proven, this court would be justified in affording the plaintiff appropriate relief. . . .

It should be emphasized that this court will not pass on the issue of whether the plaintiff should have passed or failed his pediatrics-obstetrics course, or whether he is qualified to practice medicine. This must and can only be determined by an appropriate department or committee of the defendant's college of medicine. . . . Therefore, should the plaintiff prevail on the issue of whether the defendant acted arbitrarily, capriciously or in bad faith, this court will then order the defendant university to give the plaintiff a fair and impartial hearing on his dismissal order.

ORDER

Therefore it is ordered that the motions of defendant to dismiss and for summary judgment under Rule 56, FRCP be and hereby are denied. The case is to be set for hearing on the limited issue of whether the defendant university acted arbitrarily, capriciously, or in bad faith in dismissing the plaintiff.

Notes and Questions

1. Nature of the Objection

Is Connelly objecting to the practice of grading? To the grade which he received? To the basis on which his grade was calculated? Which type of misclassification does he assert? For a critical discussion of grading, see H. Kirschenbaum, S. Simon, and R. Napier, *Wad-ja-get?* (1971).

2. Standard of Review

The court notes that, while it "will not pass on the issue of whether the aggrieved student should have passed or failed his pediatric-obstetrics course, or whether he is qualified to practice medicine," it will consider whether "the [medical professor] acted arbitrarily." Are the two questions so readily distinguishable? How can the student demonstrate the requisite arbitrariness without at the same time attempting to prove that he was entitled to a passing grade in the course? Compare *Mustell v Rose* 211 So2d 489 (Ala Sup Ct 1968). Is arbitrariness equivalent to bad faith? Discriminatory motive? Why is it relevant to the court's decision?

3. Remedy

If the court concludes that plaintiff's grade was indeed arbitrarily awarded, why does the court propose to let the university determine whether or not plaintiff should graduate, rather than ordering the university to give the plaintiff a passing grade? Of what use is a hearing? Is the *Connelly* issue in fact one of procedure, not substance?

4. Graduation

Disputes between students and educational institutions concerning the number of credits and nature of courses required for graduation are commonplace. Most, however, are resolved in the registrar's office and not in court. But courts have been willing to review the bases of registrar's determinations. See *In re Blank v Board of Higher Educ* 51 Misc2d 724, 273 NYS2d 796 (Sup Ct 1966); *Carr v St. John's Univ* 12 NY2d 802, 235 NYS2d 834, 187 NE2d 18 (1962).

ACKERMAN v RUBIN
35 Misc2d 707, 231 NYS2d 112 (Sup Ct 1962)

Newman, Justice.

Petitioner seeks an order of the court . . . compelling respondents to admit his son, who has completed his sixth grade and is now eligible to enter the Junior High School Division, to a two-year special progress class in September of 1962, to be conducted at his Junior High School in The Bronx.

Respondents readily concede that the pupil is academically well qualified, but have denied him admission to the special class on the grounds (a) that he is not of the required age (11.3 years), and (b) that he had been previously "accelerated" in school. These grounds for refusal are in accordance with respondents' established criteria for admission to the special progress class. The latter objection was waived in several similar situations, and hence the respondents' refusal must be predicated on the former ground, viz., that the pupil is younger than the requisite age. Petitioner contends that this criterion applicable to his son (10.7 years of age) is arbitrary, capricious and without legal foundation.

It appears that the board of education initiated special progress classes more than forty years ago. Indeed, it has been the experience of the board and of educators throughout the country that special progress classes and enriched program classes are of great benefit to gifted students, enabling them the better to develop their potential. From time to time the board has revised the requirements for entrance to such special classes.

The last revision was promulgated by a board of education directive in July of 1962—after decades of study and trial by experienced eduators—and the board now offers three different courses comprising the junior high school curriculum: (a) regular three-year classes; (b) three-year special progress classes, embodying a specially enriched curriculum; (c) two-year special progress classes, accelerated to cover the regular three-year course in two years. The directive limits eligibility to the b and c courses to pupils with superior scholarship grades. Petitioner's son has been admitted to b, but has been denied admission to c, primarily because of the fact that he will be 10.7 years of age in September—the date of admission—as against the 11.3-year age requirement. The board freely acknowledges that the pupil meets all the other detailed requirements; but insists that the norms adopted are not arbitrary, and that the additional year required for younger students will serve to develop them emotionally, socially, and physiologically at the adolescent stage so as to eliminate stress and aid the child's development.

Petitioner, in effect, desires to substitute the judgment of a justly proud parent for that of experienced educators, who seek to apply their observations and experience for the benefit of his son. Contrary to petitioner's contentions, the standards adopted by respondents are based, not on whim or caprice, but on years of study and trial; they are derived from the experience of day-to-day dealings with children and their problems.

In the instant proceeding, it appears to be the considered opinion of those educators who are in close contact with petitioner's son that, although he is a gifted child, nevertheless for reasons specifically outlined in the board's answering papers, further acceleration might be detrimental to this student's best interests. Indeed, the pupil's teacher for the last two years graciously avers that the pupil "has a great potential and will develop into an exceptional student, if his development is allowed to take a natural course."

Certainly, the court may not hold as arbitrary or capricious the respondent's determination that chronologically determined physical, social, and emotional maturity are vital and proper factors to be considered in the development and education of a child. To thrust a youngster into an environment where all his classmates are older may well result in the consequent impairment of the necessary social integration of the child with his classmates. The court proceeds from the hypothesis that these respondents are dedicated to the proper educational development of the whole child; and nothing has been shown to cast the slightest doubt upon the validity of this assumption. It may be that respondents, in the exercise of their continuing concern for the proper development of all their charges, including petitioner's son, will find it possible to afford him all or some of the additional benefits of the accelerated special progress classes. It may be that continuing examination of the emotional, physiological and social maturity of petitioner's son will afford respondents, in the future, a basis for review of their determination challenged herein. Our educational system continually changes and reexamination of procedures and policies is a constant process. In the course of this process, perhaps the respondents will afford intellectually gifted, but chronologically younger children, such as petitioner's son, opportunities for advancement and enrichment supplementing those afforded in the three-year special progress program described above. However, the court will not attempt to invade that area; nor may the court seek to substitute its judgment in that area for respondents' expertise.

Consequently, the court finds the board's directive (to which petitioner objects) to be proper and in accord with the applicable law.... And the court sincerely believes that petitioner, upon objective reflection, will agree that respondents, in adopting these regulations, have acted in the best interests of his son and all other school children. Furthermore, it is axiomatic that a reasonable administrative determination will not be disturbed by the court.... Plainly, then, the directive comes within the familiar rule that the courts will apply the presumption of reasonableness to the acts of public officials taken for the general welfare....

Accordingly, the application is denied and the petition is dismissed.

Notes and Questions

1. Nature of the Objection

Is Ackerman contending that the minimum age rule is arbitrary on its face? Arbitrary as applied to him? Should school officials be required to render individualized judgments with respect to each student? Could a student argue that a grade of 78 should have a different meaning with respect to him than to other students? Does this make any policy sense? Compare the discussion of *Bongart* and *Massa* in chapter 1.

2. *Connelly* and *Ackerman*

Are *Connelly* and *Ackerman* distinguishable? Is *Connelly* a challenge to the application of approved criteria while *Ackerman* disputes the critera themselves? Does the difference lie in the fact that Connelly alleged bad faith and Ackerman did not? Could Ackerman have legitimately raised the issue of bad faith in relation to the requirement of no past acceleration? Do the remedies sought distinguish the cases?

3. Uniformity

The *Ackerman* court held that the refusal to admit the plaintiff to the special progress class could not be predicated on his previous acceleration since the board had waived this requirement in several cases. Why is this so? Could not the board argue that it should have the discretion to waive this requirement? Is such an argument inconsistent with its position in relation to the age rule? If the board confessed that it had erred in granting waivers to the no-acceleration rule and promised not to do so in the future, might it successfully argue that past errors should not be used as a basis for an erroneous waiver in the *Ackerman* case?

4. Impact

How might the use of classifying criteria be affected if courts undertook to scrutinize individual cases closely? Might school officials be tempted to apply more subjective—and more difficult to review—standards? Might the number of classifications diminish in an effort to avoid student unhappiness and judicial review?

5. Aptitude Tests

a. Test Construction. Aptitude or IQ tests are the primary basis for determining into which educational program a given student should be placed. In *Ackerman* it is probable that the plaintiff would have had no claim to a special progress class unless he had achieved a superior score on an IQ test. But, are IQ tests in fact appropriate classifying instruments? Do they predict educational success? Do they accurately measure ability? Do they distinguish between students in need of different types of education? As Judge Irving Goldberg has noted, "[a] sorting device would be invalid to the extent that it does not measure aptitude for a group of students . . . the basis for separation is simply irrational." *Allen v City of Mobile* 466 F2d 122, 127 (5th Cir 1972) (Goldberg, J, dissenting).

R. J. Herrnstein, a staunch defender of IQ tests, has summarized the advantages of the IQ test in the following terms:

> The IQ cuts across the fine structure of the various theories, coming up with what is a weighted average of a set of abilities. Any modern intelligence test battery samples so broadly that most of the abilities get tapped. And since the abilities themselves tend to be intercorrelated, an omission here and there will have little effect. The high correlations among full test scores for different sorts of intelligence tests bear this out. When the task is to get a single number measuring a person's intellectual power, the IQ still does the job. . . .
>
> [The test] must satisfy common expectations as well as be reliable and practical. In the case of intelligence, common expectations center around the common purposes of intelligence testing—predicting success in school, suitability for various occupations, intellectual achievement in life. By this standard, the conventional IQ test does fairly well. The more complex measures, such as Thurstone's PMA's or Guilford's three-dimensional taxonomy, add predictive power that is sometimes essential. As for what intelligence "really" is, the concept still has ragged edges where convenience and sheer intuition set boundaries that will no doubt change from time to time. The undisputed territory has, however, become formidable. (R. J. Herrnstein, *I.Q. in the Meritocracy*, 106-8 (1973).)

While, as Professor Herrnstein would readily admit, the predictive power of IQ tests is far from perfect, "the correlation between elementary school test scores and eventual educational attainment [years of schooling completed] seems to have hovered just under 0.60 for some decades." C. Jencks, *Inequality*, 144 (1972). Thus, the IQ test appears to be a reasonably objective predictor of school performance. Moreover, when contrasted with school grades or teacher recommendations—the other plausible criteria for school classifications—the IQ test appears to be better able to estimate future academic performance. The former criteria are limited in their utility by their subjectivity and the likelihood that teacher biases and prejudices will be reflected in the results.

Yet IQ tests, while useful, have several asserted shortcomings:

(1) Their questions are ambiguous, a trap for the overly thoughtful who rightly recognize that more than one answer may be correct.

(2) They treat intelligence (or more accurately, school intelligence) in aggregate terms, failing to recognize that a given student is likely to be competent at some things but not at others, and that combining those strengths and weaknesses into a single score necessarily misdescribes and oversimplifies the notion of intelligence.

(3) They fail to measure "adaptive behavior," the capacity to survive in society, and place too high a premium on school intelligence.

(4) The tests do not indicate why a given student did poorly in a particular subject. That a child scored in the fortieth percentile in mathematics aptitude, for example, does not tell the teacher what he did not understand or why he did not understand it. It provides no basis for educational intervention to improve performance.

(5) So-called intelligence tests treat a highly mutable phenomenon—aptitude—as a given with which the school can work. They identify intelligence as static and not dynamic, and fail to account for the uneven growth patterns of individual children.

See B. Hoffman, *The Tyranny of Testing* (1962); Heber, "A Manual on Terminology and Classification in Mental Retardation," *Am J Ment Deficiency* (Monograph Supp 1961); J. Franseth and R. Koury, *Survey of Research Grouping as Related to Pupil Learning* (US Office of Education, HEW 1966); Stodolsky and Lesser, "Learning Patterns in the Disadvantaged," 37 *Harv Educ Rev* 540 (1967).

b. Test use. Many of the asserted shortcomings of IQ tests relate more to the use made of test results than to the basic construction of the test instrument. Often school officials and teachers view test scores punitively rather than remedially: they are used to label students as "smart" or "dumb" or to distinguish "college material" from future blue-collar workers. In that sense, IQ test results become self-fulfilling prophecies.

Test results can be used in a number of useful ways. Schools can disaggregate test scores to determine whether an overall score conceals marked variations in performance; they can supplement IQ test scores with other measures of the child's ability; most importantly, they can use test scores to develp educational strategies to remedy a student's deficiencies, and retest often to check on his (and their) progress.

c. IQ Tests and Judicial Review. Are the debates over IQ test construction or use appropriate for judicial review in the context of a suit challenging a particular classification decision? Should courts give deference to the judgment of school officials with regard to the appropriateness of the testing instrument? Do *Ackerman* and *Connelly* shed any light on these issues? See D. Goslin, *The Search for Ability*, 71-72 (1963); Note, "Legal Implications of the Use of Standardized Ability Tests in Employment and Education," 68 *Colum L Rev* 691 (1968).

B. Racial Overrepresentation

Few schools sort students explicitly on the basis of race. Classification in large systems is routinely handled by a school official who knows nothing about a given student except his academic record. When counselors discuss appropriate track placement with their students, their recommendations are not prompted by racial considerations, but are premised on estimates of student ability and school needs. The grounds on which school administrators defend sorting—its alleged benefits to both students and teachers—reveal no apparent racial motivation. And while prevailing sorting practices are widely and vigorously criticized, it is usually their inefficacy and not their racial effect that is noted.

Yet school sorting does in fact have significant racial consequences. It isolates —or, more accurately, tends to concentrate—minority children in certain less-advanced school programs. While racial disproportionality does not characterize programs for students with readily identifiable handicaps—classes for the trainable mentally retarded or blind, for example—the proportion of minority students in school classifications whose efficacy has been questioned—assignment to special programs for the educable mentally retarded; placement in slow learners' classes and nonacademic high school programs—is typically two or three times greater than their proportion of the school-age population. The following table illustrates this phenomenon.

	%-school population	%-physically handicapped	%-trainable mentally retarded	%-educable mentally retarded
Black Students	9.3	13.1	12.4	26.7
Mexican-American Students	16.0	14.6	19.2	23.9

Source, California State Dep't of Education, *Racial and Ethnic Distribution of Pupils in California Public Schools* (1972).

See also A. H. Passow et al, *Toward Creating a Model Urban School System* (1967).

Such racial overrepresentation has been a cause of considerable political concern. It has encouraged some blacks and radical whites to view classification as a means of race and class oppression. See Lauter and Howe, "How the School System Is Rigged for Failure," *New York Review of Books*, 18 June 1970. It has led California's legislature to assert "that there should not be disproportionate enrollment of any socioeconomic, minority, or ethnic group pupils in classes for the mentally retarded...." Cal Educ Code §6902.06 (West Supp 1972).

The policy implications of racial overrepresentation in less-advanced school programs are difficult to assess. If blacks are proportionately in greater need of special educational services, then there appears to be nothing illegitimate in providing those services—even if some degree of racial isolation becomes inevitable. Educators would be responding to the assertion often made by black spokesmen that the regular curriculum is not geared to the educational needs and experiences of the black community. But, if the mechanisms of classification are racially biased, if the special programs do not meet the special needs of black children, or if the classification scheme is a disguised effort to segregate the races, racial overrepresentation in less-advanced programs may give rise to legitimate policy concerns. In the legal context, challenges to classification schemes that assertedly discriminate on the basis of race have occurred in two situations: (1) challenges to efforts by formerly dual school systems to adopt new classification schemes; and (2) challenges to particular classifications—notably, special classes for the mildly (or educable) mentally retarded—in districts that lack a history of de jure segregation.

1. Student Classification in the South

Lemon v Bossier Parish School Board
444 F2d 1400 (5th Cir 1971)

Before Gewin, Goldberg, and Dyer, Circuit Judges.

Per Curiam:

This is an appeal from an order of the district court approving a school board plan for the operation of the public schools in Plain Dealing, Louisiana. The plan in question provides that students in grades 4-12 will be assigned to one of the two schools in the system on the basis of scores made on the California Achievement Test. Plaintiffs appeal, contesting the validity of the board's plan.

We think it obvious that the plan approved by the district court, insofar as it provides for the assignment of students on the basis of achievement test scores, is not in compliance with previous orders of this court in school desegregation cases. In *Singleton v Jackson Munic Separate School Dist* 419 F2d 1211 (5th Cir 1969), *rev'd in part on other grounds,* 396 US 290, this court sitting en banc said: "This suit seeks to desegregate two school districts, Marshall County and Holly Springs, Mississippi. The district court approved plans which would assign students to schools on the basis of achievement test scores. We pretermit a discussion of the validity per se of a plan based on testing except to hold that testing cannot be employed in any event until unitary school systems have been established." 419 F2d at 1219.

Since *Singleton* we have repeatedly rejected testing as a basis for student assignments, *U S v Sunflower County School Dist* 430 F2d 839 (5th Cir 1970); *U S v Tunica County School Dist* 421 F2d 1236 (5th Cir 1970), and we see no occasion to depart from this rule in the present case. The Plain Dealing school system has been a unitary system for only one semester. This is insufficient to even raise the issue of the validity of testing itself. In *Singleton* we made it clear that regardless of the innate validity of testing, it could not be used until a school district had been established as a unitary system. We think at a minimum this means that the district in question must have for several years operated as a unitary system. . . .

Vacated and remanded with direction.

Notes and Questions

1. Basis of Decision

What is the constitutional basis for the *Lemon* decision? If the court is simply asserting that a formerly dual school system has an obligation to remedy all vestiges of de jure segregation, why is an ability-grouping plan necessarily inconsistent with that objective? Is the court suggesting that the prior discrimination may have caused lower black achievement and thus, despite its neutral gloss, assignment according to ability is discriminatory? Does that proposition depend on empirical proof of educational harm caused by segregation? See Yudof, "Equal Educational Opportunity and the Courts," 51 *Texas L Rev* 411, 451 (1973). Is the court assuming that black students will predominate in the lower track, whites in the upper track? If so, why is that of constitutional concern? Is the court suggesting that the motive for adopting ability grouping is racial? In this regard, would the district's past grouping practices be relevant? See Ely, "Legislative and Administrative Motivation in Constitutional Law," 79 *Yale LJ* 1205 (1970).

2. Testing.

The *Lemon* court views the constitutionality of "testing per se" as a "complex and troubling question." What might be legally troubling about testing? The use of tests? The ability of tests to identify student ability? The likelihood that test use will yield racial overrepresentation in less-advanced school programs?

3. Interschool grouping.

Would the result in the case have changed if defendants proposed grouping within schools rather than between them? Does this give away their true motivation? Should there be any difference in legal standards between intraschool and interschool grouping?

COPELAND v SCHOOL BOARD
464 F2d 932 (4th Cir 1972)

Before Haynsworth, Chief Judge, and Winter, Craven, Butzner, Russell and Field, Circuit Judges, sitting en banc.

Per Curiam:

This is a school desegregation case. Both the plaintiffs and the school board have appealed from an order establishing a plan for the operation of the schools as a unitary system. We shall consider first the appeal of the plaintiffs. . . .

The plaintiffs take exception to the operation of two special schools located in two formerly black-identified schools. One of these special schools (Mt. Hermon School) is for retarded children, both white and black. The children assigned to this school, the defendants testified, are those who test at between 30 and 75 on the standardized tests, thereby qualifying as "mentally retarded" but "trainable and educable" in special facilities. There was no inquiry into the reliability or relevance of such tests in ascertaining retardation. The argument of the plaintiffs centered primarily on the results of the assignments made on the basis of the tests administered. They argued that the fact that because 75 per cent of the students tested and assigned are black, the school should be disapproved.

The plaintiffs level a like argument against the operations of the Riddick Weaver School. This facility is for students who are "mentally normal" but with "individualized learning problems", such as "a reading deficiency or a mathematical deficiency". In essence, this is a school where the normal child who has developed some particular deficiency may, through individualized instruction in that deficiency, overcome his deficiency and resume his normal school schedule. It was testified without any serious contradiction that modern educational practices sustain this method of correcting a learning problem in the normal student. It was stated in argument, though there was no proof in the record of the fact, that the experience of the school has been good, and that, in general, those assigned are enabled within a reasonable period of specialized instruction to overcome their deficiencies and to resume successfully their normal school schedule. There was testimony by the defendants, too, that assignments to this school —even as the assignments to the Mt. Hermon School—were free of any racial discrimination. They are made, it was testified, on the basis of "psychological examinations" conducted by a professionally trained staff at the "Diagnostic, Adjustive and Corrective Center". The fairness of these examinations and the professional competency of the examiners were not specifically inquired into. Again, the plaintiffs raised primarily the point that simply because more blacks than whites are assigned to this school, the operation of the school should be disallowed in the approved plan.

It was testified by the defendants that both of the schools, to the operation of which the plaintiffs object, were designed, without any reference to race, to benefit the student with special problems. Both are stated to be sound educationally. It is obvious that a mentally retarded child, whether he be black or white, is better served by assignment to a special school where he can be given a form of education adapted to his capacity. Similarly, a perfectly normal child, again either white or black, who develops a learning deficiency, is manifestly given a better advantage to succeed educationally if taken out of a school, where, because of his deficiency he cannot succeed and will inevitably fall farther behind, and assigned to a special school where, along with his other work, he may be given individualized instruction in his deficiency. When assignments are made to achieve such salutary educational objectives and are in no sense the product of racial discrimination, nothing in *Brown,* or any subsequent precedents enlarging on *Brown,* would invalidate such assignments. *Brown* did not proscribe sound educational practices intended to maximize educational opportunities, when applied in a nondiscriminatory manner. Merely because there may be in any school system more mentally retarded black children than there are white, or vice-versa, is no reason for the discontinuance of a special school particularly designed to meet the needs of such children. Any other rule would mean the sacrifice of the student and his education to the single goal of absolute, inflexible racial balance. Such a result is not constitutionally required. But it is essential that the record establish that the tests and examinations used in making assignments are relevant, reliable and free of discrimination. *Griggs v Duke Power Co* [401 US 424 (1972).] Unfortunately, the testimony as to the character of tests and examinations used in making the assignments to these two schools is sparse and incomplete. The proceeding is accordingly remanded to the district court for the purpose of determining whether the tests and examinations used are relevant, reliable and free of discrimination. If they are, then it is of no moment that, as a result of the use of such fair and nondiscriminatory tests, more blacks than whites proportionately are assigned to these schools. On the other hand, if the assignments are made on the basis of irrelevant or unreliable tests, then it is the duty of the court to take appropriate corrective action. . . .

Reversed in part, affirmed in part.

Notes and Questions

1. *Copeland* and *Lemon*

In *Lemon*, the Fifth Circuit barred an ability-grouping scheme before it began to operate. In *Copeland*, the Fourth Circuit upheld the constitutionality of two special education programs—even though a disproportionate number of blacks had been assigned to them. How can these two cases be distinguished? Is special education more educationally sound than ability grouping? Is it relevant that in *Lemon* there were only two schools, both of which would have been segregated, while in *Copeland* a much larger system was completely integrated with the exception of the two special programs? Was there evidence of a discriminatory motive in *Lemon* absent in *Copeland*?

2. Misclassification

Under what circumstances would the *Copeland* court deny the school district permission to operate the two special education programs? Suppose plaintiffs demonstrated that, while the tests used to assign students to those programs were nondiscriminatory, the programs themselves provided no educational benefits to the students. Would that evoke a different decision?

3. Integration

Is *Copeland* correctly decided in the light of *Keyes v School Dist No 1* 93 Sup Ct 2686 (1973)? Does *Copeland* raise the issue discussed by Justice Powell in *Keyes* (see chapter 4) as to the need to weigh values other than integration in determining whether a dual school system has been disestablished?

2. Student Classification in the North

LARRY P. v RILES
343 F Supp 1306 (ND Cal 1972)

Peckham, Judge.

Plaintiffs in this case have asked the court to issue a preliminary injunction restraining the San Francisco Unified School District from administering IQ tests for purposes of determining whether to place black students in classes for the educable mentally retarded. Named plaintiffs, who remain anonymous for their own protection, are black San Francisco elementary school children who have been placed in EMR (Educable Mentally Retarded) classes because, *inter alia,* they scored below 75 on the defendant school district's IQ tests. They claim that they are not mentally retarded, and that they have been placed in EMR classes on the basis of tests which are biased against the culture and experience of black children as a class, in violation of their Fourteenth Amendment rights. In fact, plaintiffs have presented evidence, in the form of affidavits from certain black psychologists, that when they were given the same IQ tests but with special attempts by the psychologists to establish rapport with the test takers, to overcome plaintiffs' defeatism and easy distraction, to reword items in terms more consistent with plaintiffs' cultural background, and to give credit for nonstandard answers which nevertheless showed an intelligent approach to problems in the context of that background, plaintiffs scored significantly above the cutting-off point of 75.

Irreparable injury is alleged to flow from plaintiffs' placement in EMR classes because the curriculum is so minimal academically, teacher expectations are so low, and because other students subject EMR students to ridicule on account of their status. Furthermore, EMR students allegedly acquire severe feelings of inferiority. . . . To add to this alleged irreparable harm, the fact of placement in EMR classes is noted on a student's permanent school record, for colleges, prospective employers, and the armed forces to see. . . .

Defendants justify the EMR program by noting that the curriculum, pace, and increased attention available in its classes are designed to be beneficial to retarded students, and that in San Francisco the classes are labeled "ungraded" or "adjustment" in order to minimize any stigma. . . . However, defendants do not seem to controvert plaintiffs' assertion that a student who does not belong in an EMR class is harmed by being placed there. Rather, defendants claim that since students are permitted to achieve their way out of EMR classes on the basis of yearly evaluations, plaintiffs can be suffering only negligible harm as a result of their placement in such classes, even if it is true that they are not mentally retarded. The court finds this contention to be specious. For even if a student remains in an EMR class for only one month, that placement is noted on his permanent record, his education is retarded to some degree, and he is subjected to whatever humiliation students are exposed to for being separated into classes for the educable mentally retarded.

This court is thus of the view that for those students who are wrongfully placed in EMR classes, irreparable harm ensues. The more troublesome question, however, is whether some students, including named plaintiffs, are in fact being wrongfully placed in such classes, in violation of their constitutional rights. . . .

Plaintiffs contend that they are being deprived of equal protection of the laws. In order to establish a prima facie case that such a constitutional violation has occurred, plaintiffs claim that they need only demonstrate that the method of classification being used by defendants (the IQ test), although not one based explicitly on race, nevertheless leads to a racial imbalance in the EMR classes. Thus, they reject the traditional equal protection test, which states that the burden is on the plaintiff to prove that no rational relationship exists between the method of classification used and the outcome of the classification. See, e.g., *Williamson v Lee Optical Co* 348 US 483 (1955). Instead they assert that once their prima facie case has been made, the burden of proof shifts to defendants to demonstrate the rationality of the mode of classification.

The conceptual scheme which plaintiffs have proposed is one borrowed from cases involving employment discrimination under Title VII of the Civil Rights Act of 1964, jury selection, and school desegregation. For example, if a job qualification test is given which results in a greatly disproportionate number of blacks failing in relation to the percentage of blacks in the job-seeking community, then the burden shifts to the employer to explain how the test is valid for purposes of selecting employees. *Griggs v Duke Power Co* 401 US 424

(1971) . . . Similarly, when qualification tests for jury service lead to a disproportionately low number of blacks on grand and petit juries, the burden shifts to the state to explain why passing such a test is a necessary prerequisite to being an effective juror. *Carmical v Craven* 457 F2d 582 (9th Cir 1971) (Hufstedler, J). And finally, when a school district's methods for delineating school boundaries result in student bodies being predominantly of one race or another, the burden shifts to the school district to demonstrate that its methods serve valid and educationally relevant purposes. See, e.g., *US v School Dist 151* 286 F Supp 786 (N D Ill 1968), *aff'd,* 404 F2d 1125 (7th Cir 1968). The court believes that this same approach should be utilized in analyzing plaintiffs' contention that the use of I Q tests to determine placement in EMR classes violates their right to equal protection of the laws. There are several reasons why the burden is shifted in employment discrimination, jury selection, and school desegregation cases; and all of them dictate that the same process be followed in the instant case.

First, shifting of the burden is a reflection of the strong judicial and constitutional policy against racial discrimination. Of all the evils the equal protection clause was designed to eliminate, racial discrimination is the one we are most certain the drafters contemplated. Indeed, race has been declared by the Supreme Court to be a "suspect classification"; and there is little doubt that if the San Francisco Unified School District were to classify students explicitly on the basis of race for purposes of EMR placement, it would have a near impossible burden to sustain in attempting to justify it. See, e.g., *Loving v Virginia* 388 US 1 (1967). In the de facto race classification cases where the burden has been shifted, courts have manifested this same distrust of laws which harm blacks as an identifiable class. But since the classifications in these cases are not explicitly on the basis of race, these courts have lightened the burden placed on defendants, and have required defendants merely to come forward with evidence that a rational relationship exists between the seemingly neutral method of classification used and the valid purpose of the classification; they have not, as in the explicit racial classification cases, demanded that defendants provide a compelling justification for the classification.

Insofar as the cases which have shifted the burden of proof rely for their support on this general distrust of classifications which harm blacks as an identifiable group, then this court feels compelled to shift the burden in the instant case if plaintiffs can demonstrate that the IQ tests are in fact the primary basis for placing students in EMR classes and that in fact there is a disproportionately high number of black students in the EMR classes. . . .

A second reason for shifting the burden of proof in de facto racial classification cases has been the existence of a positive duty to avoid racial imbalance in certain of our institutions. Thus the justification for doing so in jury selection cases is the fact that the Supreme Court "has charged state officials with an affirmative duty to seek, and include within the jury selection process, all persons qualified under state law." *Carmical v Craven* 457 F2d 582, 586 (9th Cir 1971). While this legal duty does not demand that each jury exactly reflect the racial breakdown of the community, it does establish a sufficiently strong policy in favor of representative juries that the burden of proof must be shifted to the defendants when a method of jury selection leads to a significant racial imbalance in jury composition. . . .

A third rationale for shifting the burden of proof is the one which seems to underlie the employment discrimination cases. In such cases there seems to be an empirical assumption that for most unskilled or semiskilled jobs, an ample pool of qualified or potentially qualified workers of both races exists; and if racial imbalance in the work force nevertheless occurs, it is likely to be the consequence of racial discrimination. The analogous assumption in the instant case would be that there exists a random distribution among all races of the qualifications necessary to participate in regular as opposed to EMR classes. Since it does not seem to be disputed that the qualification for placement in regular classes is the innate ability to learn at the pace at which those classes proceed . . . such a random distribution can be expected if there is in turn a random distribution of these learning abilities among members of all races. . . .

Accordingly, this court is of the opinion that if plaintiffs can demonstrate that the IQ tests challenged herein are the primary determinant of whether a child is placed in an EMR class, and that racial imbalance exists in the composition of such classes, then the burden must shift to the defendants to demonstrate the rational connection between the tests and the purpose for which they allegedly are used. The fact of racial imbalance is demonstrated by plaintiffs' undisputed statistics, which indicate that while blacks constitute 28.5 percent of all students in the San Francisco Unified School District, 66 percent of all students in San Francisco's EMR program are black. . . . Certainly these statistics indicate that there is a significant disproportion of blacks in EMR classes in San Francisco. . . .

Having concluded that racial imbalance exists in the EMR classes, this court must then determine whether the result of an IQ test forms the principal basis for a decision to place a child in an EMR class. In August 1971, a new scheme for selecting students for EMR classes was instituted statewide by the California legislature. Also in August of that year, the California Department of Education issued a special education memorandum establishing policies and procedures for "the identification, assessment, and placement of minors" in EMR programs, in order to implement the new sections of the Education Code. These new laws require the administration of IQ tests after a student has been referred to a counselor by his teacher because he has demonstrated "a general pattern of low academic achievement, maladaptive or immature behavior, poor social relationships, and consistently low standardized test scores." No tests may be given, however, unless there is parental consent, after an explanation by the school psychologist of the nature and purpose of the tests.

IQ test results, however, are not the only basis for determining whether the student is to be placed in an EMR class. Section 6902.085 of the Education Code states,

> No minor may be placed in a special education program for the mentally retarded . . . unless a complete psychological examination by a credentialed school psychologist investigating such factors as developmental history, cultural background, and school achievement substantiates the retarded intellectual development indicated by the . . . individual test scores. This examination shall include estimates of adaptive behavior. Until adaptive behavior scales are normed and approved by the state board of education, such

adaptability testing shall include, but is not limited to, a visit, with the consent of the parent or guardian, to the minor's home by the school psychologist or a person designated by the chief administrator of the district, upon the recommendation of the school psychologist, and interviews of the minor's family at their home.

The regulations elaborate on the requirement of adaptive behavior tests, specifying investigations of the child's home language skills as well as consideration of family mobility, occupational history and status of parent, sibling relationships, isolation of home, family, and child within the environment, developmental materials present in the home, and other home and environmental factors influential upon the educational process. Similarly, the regulations are very particular about the requirement of a developmental history, and provide plainly that "In order to establish mental retardation, the developmental records should reveal significant delays and/or retarded development in such behavior as walking, talking, appropriate effective responses, assumption of responsibility, obedience within the family structure, play activities, and peer relationships within the home and in the community." Such developmental measures are to be taken by means of standardized instruments.

Thus, the IQ test is not the only type of psychological assessment that results in the placement of a student in an EMR class; and it is stated in the regulations that "recommendations for appropriate educational placement shall be made after a full review of all the information available on the minor." In addition, the statute provides that no student may be placed in an EMR class without the consent of his parent or guardian, and that no parental consent shall be obtained until the parent is given an exact description of the special education program and is informed that the program is for pupils who have retarded intellectual development.

Is it to be concluded, then, that the IQ test is but one criterion among many leading to placement of students in EMR classes, and not a very important criterion at that? . . .

In the instant case there is . . . evidence in the record to indicate that the San Francisco Unified School District places substantial emphasis on IQ test results. Such evidence includes the statement in the recently enacted Education Code that a child will not be placed in an EMR class unless other evidence "substantiates" the IQ test scores, a statement which suggests that the IQ score is the primary standard. Furthermore, there is evidence in the instant record that IQ test scores influence teacher evaluation. . . .

Thus, the fact that adaptive behavior tests and teacher evaluations are considered in conjunction with IQ test scores in determining whether to place a child in an EMR class need not preclude the finding that IQ test scores loom as a most important consideration in making assignments to EMR classes. Defendants' contention that IQ tests are not responsible for the racial imbalance in EMR classes because parental consent is a necessary prerequisite to placement in such classes can be analyzed similarly. Clearly, if fully informed parental consent is sought in every case, plaintiffs have nothing to complain of. However, parents are likely to be overawed by scientific-sounding pronouncements about IQ; and if their decisions whether to provide their consent are so colored by IQ results, then the IQ tests again appear as the prime determinants of EMR placement. Furthermore, if the IQ tests are found in fact to be biased against the culture and experience of black children, any consent which is obtained from the parents of such children absent communication of full information to that effect is not effective consent.

This court is left to conclude, then, that all the prerequisites to shifting the burden of proof to the defendants to justify the use of IQ tests are present in this case. What facts can they muster in defense of that means of classification? Defendants do not seem to dispute the evidence amassed by plaintiffs to demonstrate that the IQ tests in fact are culturally biased. Indeed, defendants have stated that they are merely awaiting the development of what they expect will be a minimally biased test. This test currently is being standardized; but the final product is not expected to be available for more than a year.

Instead of denying the bias inherent in the IQ tests, defendants argue either that the tests are not the cause of the racial imbalance in EMR classes, or that the tests, although racially biased, are rationally related to the purpose for which they are used because they are the best means of classification currently available. Their attempts to explain the racial imbalance as the result of location of EMR classes in predominantly black schools prior to desegregation of the San Francisco Unified School District or as the result of more white parents than black parents placing their mentally retarded children in private schools must fail for lack of substantiation in the record. And their attempts to justify use of a racially biased IQ test in the name of lack of alternatives must meet with similar lack of success. Admittedly, there is a strong need to treat truly mentally retarded children specially and to isolate them from regular classes. That need does not, however, justify depriving black children of their right to equal protection of the laws. Indeed, the absence of any rational means of identifying children in need of such treatment can hardly render acceptable an otherwise concededly irrational means, such as the IQ test as it is presently administered to black students.

At the same time, there exist alternatives which seem to the court to be at least as useful to defendants in addressing this need. Plaintiffs have provided this court with evidence of how the New York City and Massachusetts school systems have attempted to minimize greatly the importance of IQ tests. . . . New York City relies heavily on achievement test results and teacher evaluation; group IQ tests have been banned there. Massachusetts requires "psychological assessment" of potential EMR students, but does not specify IQ testing as part of that assessment. In addition, Massachusetts has instituted an elaborate system for reviewing decisions to place students in such classes. Other alternatives include administering the IQ tests to black children in the same manner as IQ tests were administered to named plaintiffs in this case by representatives of the Bay Area Association of Black Psychologists, or instituting thorough-going parental consent requirements . . . .

Accordingly, this court concludes that defendants have not sustained their burden of demonstrating that IQ tests are rationally related to the purpose of segregating students according to their ability to learn in regular classes, at least insofar as those tests are applied to black students. . . .

Accordingly, it is hereby ordered that defendants be restrained from placing black students in classes for the educable mentally retarded on the basis of criteria which place primary reliance on the results of IQ tests as they are currently administered, if the consequence of use of such criteria is racial imbalance in the composition of such classes.

Notes and Questions

1. De Facto-De Jure

In *Johnson v San Francisco Unified School Dist* 339 F Supp 1315 (ND Cal 1971), the federal district court concluded that there was *de jure* segregation in San Francisco and ordered system-wide relief. Is that history relevant to *Larry P.*? Does it suggest that the mode of analysis adopted in *Lemon* (or *Copeland*) is appropriate to this setting?

The final order in *Johnson* enjoined the district from "authorizing, permitting or using tracking systems or other educational techniques or innovations without effective provisions to avoid segregation." 339 F Supp at 1325. Does that provision resolve the *Larry P.* issue?

2. Constitutional Standard

a. Existence of Racial Overrepresentation. Is the *Larry P.* court suggesting that a showing of racial disproportionality in less-advanced school programs is sufficient to require some justification? If so, would such a standard of review be appropriately applied to a program with a racially disproportionate impact such as a sickle cell anemia research program? The establishment of municipal bus routes, some of which served more whites than blacks?

In *Jefferson v Hackney* 406 US 535 (1972), the Supreme Court was confronted with the claim that Texas' welfare policy was constitutionally suspect because it provided a less-adequate subsidy for a welfare program whose beneficiaries were primarily black than for a welfare program whose beneficiaries were primarily white. The contention was characterized and dismissed as a "naked statistical argument." 406 US at 548. How does the *Larry P.* contention differ? In the nature of the interest sought to be protected? In the nature of the justification required (or sought to be required)?

b. Rational Relationship Standard. In assessing the school district's justification for racial overrepresentation, *Larry P.* purports to apply the traditional rational relationship equal protection standard. Is that standard in fact applied? Is the burden of proof typically shifted to the school district under the rational relationship test? The school district claimed that "the tests, although racially biased, are rationally related to the purpose for which they are used because they are the best means of classification currently available." Why is this not sufficient to meet its burden of proof? Under the rationality test, is it necessary for the district to demonstrate that reliance on aptitude tests is the *most* reliable way to classify students? Is the existence of other bases for grouping students—achievement tests, teacher recommendations, and psychological evaluations—constitutionally relevant?

3. Racially Specific Harm

As section C below suggests, assignment to a less-advanced program may give rise to a claimed denial of equal educational opportunity, premised on the assertion that such placement secures no educational benefit—and may even cause injury. But assuming that the motivation for placement is not discriminatory, what does the fact of racial overrepresentation add to the constitutional argument? Are minority students more likely to be harmed by such placement than are their white peers?

Fragmentary evidence suggests a positive answer. Although few studies have examined the racially specific harm of sorting, one reanalysis of *Equality of Educational Opportunity* did attempt to assess the impact of intraschool segregation on the verbal achievement of black students. It concluded that while *school* integration does not benefit blacks, *classroom* integration does improve black students' test scores. Since proportionately more whites than blacks are assigned to higher tracks, advanced track placement does influence student success. But the differences in verbal achievement between Negro students in mostly white classes and those in mostly Negro classes cannot simply be explained by selection processes that operate within the school. Classroom segregation itself causes harm for black students in fast as well as slow classes; classroom desegregation has racially specific benefits. See McPartland, "The Relative Influences of School and of Classroom Desegregation in the Academic Achievement of Ninth Grade Negro Students," *J Social Issues,* Summer 1969, p 93. Compare Zito and Bardon, "Achievement Motivation among Negro Adolescents in Regular and Special Education Programs," 74 *Am J Ment Deficiency* 20 (1969).

The United States Civil Rights Commission's reexamination of the Coleman data noted a subtler (and difficult to document) effect of intraschool segregation: black students in nominally integrated schools, "accorded separate treatment, with others of their race, in a way which is obvious to them as they travel through their classes, felt inferior and stigmatized." 2 US Comm'n on Civil Rights, *Racial Isolation in the Public Schools* 86-87 (1967). The harm caused by interschool segregation appeared to the commission far less substantial than the harm caused by intraschool segregation: while interschool segregation resulted from the relatively impersonal criterion of neighborhood residence, intraschool segregation was clearly caused by personal and pejorative judgments of ability. See also Jones, Erickson, and Crowell, "Increasing the Gap between Whites and Blacks: Tracking as a Contributory Source," 4 *Educ & Urban Soc'y* 339 (1972).

Does such evidence justify the *Larry P.* result in the absence of a history of de jure segregation? Compare Goodman, "De Facto Segregation: A Constitutional and Empirical Analysis," 60 *Cal L Rev* 275 (1972).

4. Aptitude Testing and Minority Students

Criticism of aptitude tests as a basis for student classification, discussed in section A, acquires particular force when these tests become the basis for racial disproportionality in school programs. Aptitude tests and their use by schools are condemned on several grounds: (a) aptitude tests reward white and middle-class values and skills, especially the ability to speak standard English, and thus penalize minority children because of their backgrounds; (b) the impersonal environment in which aptitude tests are given depresses the scores of minority students, who become anxious or apathetic in such situations; (c) aptitude tests, standardized (or "normed") for white, middle-class children, cannot determine the intelligence of minority children whose backgrounds differ notably from those of the normed population. See *Hobson v Hansen* 269 F Supp 401, 473-88 (DDC 1967), *aff'd sub nom, Smuck v Hobson* 408 F2d 175 (DCC 1969).

Such arguments, while partially true, oversimplify complex phenomena. Available evidence does not wholly support the critics' contentions. The conditions under which aptitude tests are administered appear to have only slight effects on student performance. Minority children perform poorly even on so-called culture-free tests, which are structured to avoid class and cultural biases. See Rosenblum, Keller, and Papania, "Davis-EELLS ("Culture-Fair") Test Performance of Lower-class Retarded Children," 19 *J Consulting Psych* 51 (1955); Angelino and Shedd, "An Initial Report of a Validation Study of the Davis-EELLS Tests of General Intelligence or Problem-solving Ability," 40 *J Psych* 35 (1955). Similarly, when psychologists have looked at different students' aptitude test performance on a question-by-question basis, they have found that poor and minority children do no better on culture-free questions. See Chase and Pugh, "Social Class and Performance on an Intelligence Test," 8 *J Educ Measurement* 197 (1971).

Whatever may be the shortcomings of aptitude tests, they do not reveal, but merely confirm, that non-middle-class and minority children fare badly in schools as they presently are organized; for if tests are culturally biased, so too are school curricula and employer expectations. Using a culturally neutral (or culturally relevant) test for minority students might well be an academic exercise, unless such tests were accompanied by drastic alterations in schooling and hiring practices.

5. Race and Intelligence

School officials might seek to defend overrepresentation in less-advanced programs on the grounds that blacks are genetically inferior to whites. That viewpoint is seldom asserted publicly, but may in fact be the rationale for some classification practices. As Dean Schwebel notes:

> The most direct evidence of a school system's stand on ability is the way it educates the mass of its children. If it believes that the postnatal determinants are significant, then it will mobilize its services to overcome learning defects, and it will function as if the vast majority of children, with appropriate help, will be intellectually equipped for successful learning during the period of required attendance. Only the school system which regards the genetic factor as paramount, and the environmental as so insignificant would . . . rightly subdivide its population in accordance with the native ability revealed by achievement tests and would proffer a curriculum suitable to the talents of each group. The decision whether it is wise to group children by ability depends upon one's view of the origin of intelligence. (M. Schwebel, *Who Can Be Educated?* 75 (1968).)

a. Empirical Evidence: Pro and Con. Since the publication of Professor Arthur Jensen's article, "How Much Can We Boost IQ and Scholastic Achievement," in the Winter 1969 issue of the *Harvard Education Review*, a controversy has raged over the degree to which intelligence is genetically determined. The focus of the debate is whether inherited elements of intelligence are responsible for the substantially lower IQ scores of lower social class groups (including most blacks) and whether these differences provide pedagogical justification for elaborate classification schemes in the public schools. Not surprisingly, the debate has often been more acrimonious than scholarly. See generally R. J. Herrnstein, *I.Q. in the Meritocracy,* 3-59 (1973).

Professor Jensen's argument asserts that IQ tests, while culturally bound, measure a general ability which underlies surface skills. This quality, commonly referred to as *g*, Jensen asserts, is largely inherited. Since IQ highly correlates with social class and race, he concludes that these IQ differences between populations reflect real genetic variation between social strata. Finally, Jensen claims that the schools fail to educate poor children properly because they assume that all children have "average ability" and teach them as though they were average. Pointing to the well-documented failure of compensatory education programs, he urges school officials to create programs more sensitive to the varying ability levels of children.

Jensen's basic assumption that intelligence is largely inherited is drawn from data concerning the "variance components and heritability coefficients" "among individuals of different degrees of kinship." Jensen, "How Much Can We Boost I.Q. and Scholastic Achievement," 39 *Harv Educ Rev* 1, 48 (1969). A number of studies have been done over the years comparing the IQ scores of siblings, parents and children, twins, foster children and parents, and so on. Close relatives share various proportions of their genetic makeups, and if intelligence were determined largely from genetic factors, the IQ scores between relatives would vary roughly in the same proportion as the proportion of genes they hold in common. This would be especially true of related children who were not raised by the same parents since they would not share a common environment. First cousins share .14 of their genes, siblings .52 of their genes, parents and children .49 of their genes, dizygotic twins .50 of their genes, and monozygotic twins share 1.00 of their genes. 39 *Harv Educ Rev* at 49.

A compilation of family intelligence studies shows that, indeed, relatives tend to score very close to the genetic prediction of how similar their IQs should be if it is highly heritable. Monozygotic twins reared apart correlate .75 in their IQs while those reared together correlate .87. Siblings reared apart correlate .47 while those reared together correlate .55. Despite tremendous differences in subject populations, tests used, and other conditions that one would expect to muddy the results, kinsmen score surprisingly close to their predicted level. In addition, studies of foster children show that their intelligence has little relationship to that of their adoptive parents but closely matches the predicted similarities to their true parents' IQs. Summarizing the kinship studies, Jensen concluded that at least .75 of the variation in IQ test performance is due to heritability. 39 *Harv Educ Rev* at 50. Thus, Jensen argues, much of the disparity in IQ scores between black and whites must be attributed to inherited differences in intelligence.

Professor Herrnstein, reviewing the same evidence, was somewhat more modest in his conclusions:

Although there are scraps of evidence for a genetic component in the black-white difference [in IQ scores], the overwhelming case is for believing that American blacks have been at an environmental disadvantage. To the extent that variations in the American social environment can promote or retard IQ, blacks have probably been held back. But a neutral commentator (a rarity these days) would have to say that the case is simply not settled, given our present stage of knowledge. (Herrnstein, "I.Q.," *Atlantic Monthly* September 1971, p 43.)

Critics of Professors Jensen and Herrnstein do not deny that an individual's intelligence is highly influenced by his genetic background. As both Jensen and Herrnstein make clear, the overwhelming evidence supports this assumption. Nor do the critics deny the undeniable: that the IQ test scores of children from low socioeconomic backgrounds, including most blacks, are substantially lower than those of middle-class white children. Rather the critics challenge the interpretation of the evidence, which asserts that the differences in IQ scores between racial and socioeconomic groups are largely genetic and not environmental in origin. Underlying the critics' objections is the often expressed fear that Professor Jensen's theories will be relied on by racists to relegate blacks to an inferior position in American society and by educators to demonstrate that the academic failures of black children are inevitable and not attributable to institutional shortcomings.

Professor Lee J. Cronbach, a prominent psychometrician, argues that the Jensen inherited intelligence theory is inconsistent with what is known about human development:

> Dr. Jensen has girded himself for a holy war against "environmentalists" and his zeal leads him into over-statements and misstatements. . . .
>
> I do not doubt that performance—intellectual, physical, and social—is developed from a genotypic inherited base. The organism, as it evolves prenatally and postnatally incorporates energy and information. What the person does with an experience, and what it does to him, depends on physical structures that were laid down during the previous years, or days, of his existence. Human development is a cumulative, active process of utilizing environmental inputs, not an unfolding of genetically given structures. (Cronbach, "Heredity, Environment and Educational Policy," 39 *Harv Educ Rev* 338-39 (1969).)

Cronbach's environmentalist position is supported by a reevaluation by Light and Smith of the data relied on by Professor Jensen:

> First, we accept (for argument's sake) Professor Jensen's estimate of the proportion of IQ variability explained by hereditary versus environmental factors. Using his proportions, with no interaction effects, we show that more than half of the fifteen-point difference in mean IQ between races is explained by the differential allocation of the races to social conditions. Second, we demonstrate that if the interaction between genetic and environmental effects accounts for only 1 percent of the total IQ variance, then a fifteen-point difference between means occurs even if the racial genetic distributions were identical. Since Jensen's data suggest that the proportion of interaction variance is 1 percent, this analysis is entirely consistent with his data. Third, we present the results of computer simulations which establish the instability of doubt on the reliability of his parameter estimates. We conclude that if the usual statistical criteria for significance are used, Jensen's data are not inconsistent with the presence of a moderate amount of genetic-environmental interaction. Fourth, we show that if moderate amounts of interaction exist, mean IQs of blacks and whites could easily differ by more than fifteen points; despite identical genetic distributions in the two races.

In summing up they state: "Finally, the inconsistencies of the data in their additive behavior, together with the complete lack of any data at all on black twins, in our judgment wrecks the credibility of even a tentative assertion of genetic differences in intelligence between races." Light and Smith, "Social Allocation Models of Intelligence: A Methodological Inquiry," 39 *Harv Educ Rev* 2-3, 25 (1969).

A broader, and probably more damaging attack on the genetic position is made by Professors Cole and Bruner, who challenge the assumption that testing is "situation blind and culture blind." That assumption yields inevitable mistakes in the assessment of mental abilities:

> The psychological status of the concept of competence (or capacity) is brought deeply into question when one examines conclusions based on standard experiments. Competence so defined is both situation blind and culture blind. If performance is treated (as it often is by linguists) only as a shallow expression of deeper competence, then one inevitably loses sight of the ecological problem of performance. For one of the most important things about any "underlying competence" is the nature of the situations in which it expresses itself. Herein lies the crux of the problem. One must inquire, first, whether a competence is expressed in a particular situation and, second, what the significance of that situation is for the person's ability to cope with life in his own mileu. . . [W] hen we systematically study the situational determinants of performance, we are led to conclude that cultural differences reside more in differences in the situations to which different cultural groups apply their skills than to differences in the skills possessed by the groups in question. (Cole and Bruner, "Cultural Differences and Inferences about Psychological Processes," 57 *Amer Psychologist* 10, 874 (1971).

Cole and Bruner argue that standard intelligence tests, adapted to use in schools, are effective for certain well-established organizational purposes and are fairly effective measures of the performance of certain subcultural groups, particularly the white upper-middle class in America. It is questionable, in their view, whether they give accurate indications of the abilities of poor and minority children because the demands of their lives are so different from those of middle-class children. These children learn, through personal experience and from neighborhood socialization, that school is a threatening place and that its skills will not be useful to them. They score poorly on IQ tests because they have not developed many of the skills demanded by schools and tests.

b. Constitutional Implications. With rare exception, courts have eschewed discussion or reliance on data suggesting that the inherited intelligence of blacks is less than that of whites. See *Stell v Savannah-Chatham County Bd of Educ* 220 F Supp 667, 672 (SD Ga 1963), *rev'd*, 333 F2d 55 (5th Cir 1964). Is this wise as a matter of judicial policy? Does *Brown* in fact foreclose the issue? Is the evidence clear enough to permit conclusions to be drawn from it? How might courts employ such data in deciding a case in which a classificatory scheme is attacked because of the overrepresentation of blacks in less-advanced educational programs? Might a court decide that the racial isolation attributable to classification decisions is unconstitutional notwithstanding the lower test scores of blacks—whether those scores are genetically or environmentally determined?

6. Remedy

Assuming that a significant racial overrepresentation in the less-advanced school programs is unconstitutional, what remedy is appropriate? What are the costs and benefits of the following remedies: (1) abolish all classifications; (2) establish racial quotas so that the racial composition of the entire student body is reflected in each program; or (3) make classification assignments randomly? What are the policy implications of each approach? Can a court do much more than to exhort school officials to be more flexible and conscious of the racial ramifications of classification decisions? Is "flexibility" a legally meaningful concept? See Kirp, "Schools as Sorters: The Constitutional and Policy Implications of Student Classification," 121 *U Pa L Rev* 705, 773-74 (1973).

Other remedial issues are considered in section III below.

C. Class Discrimination

Poor children are also overrepresented in less-advanced school programs. Patricia Sexton's study of Detroit's schools, *Education and Income* (1961), concluded that children from higher social strata usually enter the "higher-quality" groups, and those from lower strata the "lower" ones; the child whose family earned less than $7,000 was almost ten times less likely than the child whose family earned more than $7,000 to be identified as a gifted child. Sexton, *Education and Income* at 60. Another study of two midwestern high schools found that 83 percent of students from white collar homes, but only 48 percent of students from blue collar homes, were assigned to the advanced track. Schafer, Olexa, and Polk, "Programmed for Social Class: Tracking in High School," *Transaction,* October 1970, p 39. Do these data give rise to constitutional issues akin to those considered in the discussion of racial discrimination? Should schools be required to justify overrepresentation of the poor in less-advanced programs? How does *Rodriguez* bear on this issue? See pp 583-607.

A recent study asked eighteen school counselors to evaluate a hypothetical case: a nine-year-old boy described as defiant, disruptive, aggressive, and a poor achiever. Half of the counselors were told that the child came from an upper-middle-class family; the others heard that the total family income was $320 per month. The counselors' reactions differed notably. In the case of the upper-class child, the counselors expressed a desire to pursue the facts further—through home visits, personal involvement with the family, and the like—before making judgments. In the case of the lower-class child, the counselors took a more punitive attitude, urging that the child be retained in his present grade; they considered delinquency and "dropping out" inevitable. Garfield, Weiss, and Pollack, "Effects of the Child's Social Class on School Counselor's Decision Making," 20 *J Counseling Psych* 166 (1973). Do you suspect that the reactions reported by Garfield and his colleagues are typical of school counselors? That such reactions account for a significant amount of the overrepresentation of poor children in less-advanced programs? Assume that proof of such differentiated reactions could be fashioned. Would the poor child have a constitutional cause of action?

D. Equal Educational Opportunity

1. Constitutional Context. The basic premise of school classification is that treating children who have identifiably different needs differently will increase the educational opportunities available to all. That premise has been questioned by critics who assert that particular classifications diminish, rather than enhance, educational opportunity.

Alleged diminution of educational opportunity may rest on three quite different grounds: (1) students assigned to certain programs receive fewer tangible resources than students assigned to other programs; (2) certain programs, because of their structural rigidity or inefficacy, restrict the educational potential of students assigned to them; and (3) certain programs unnecessarily stigmatize students.

Outside the racial discrimination context, no court has assessed whether particular classifications deny equal educational opportunity. *Hobson v Hansen,* the most famous of the classification cases, focuses primarily on the race and class discrimination that tracking assertedly fosters. Yet *Hobson* raises questions broader than race and class discrimination; it suggests that other nonracial aspects of classification might be the subject of constitutional challenge. For that reason, the case is reconsidered here.

HOBSON v HANSEN

269 F Supp 401 (DDC 1967), *aff'd sub nom, Smuck v Hobson*

408 F2d 175 (DC Cir 1969) (en banc)*

Judge Wright:

IV.

. . . . The District of Columbia school system employs a form of ability grouping commonly known as the track system, by which students at the elementary and secondary level are placed in tracks or curriculum levels according to the school's assessment of each student's ability to learn. . . . As the evidence in this case makes painfully clear, ability grouping as presently practiced in the District of Columbia school system is a denial of equal educational opportunity to the poor and a majority of the Negroes attending school in the nation's capital, a denial that contravenes not only the guarantees of the Fifth Amendment but also the fundamental premise of the track system itself. What follows, then, is a discussion of that evidence—an examination of the track system: in theory and in reality. . . .

Purpose and Philosophy. Dr. Hansen [Superintendent of Schools] believes that the comprehensive high school (and the school system generally) must be systematically organized and structured to provide differing levels of education for students with widely differing levels of academic ability. This is the purpose of the track system. In expressing the track system's philosophy Dr. Hansen has said, "Every pupil in the school system must have the maximum opportunity for self-development and this can best be brought about by adjusting curriculum offerings to different levels of need and ability as the pupil moves through the stages of education and growth in our schools." . . . And he has identified as the

---

*The portion of the *Hobson* opinion concerning resource inequality appears at pp 567-69.

two objectives on which the track system is founded: "(1) The realization of the doctrine of equality of education and (2) The attainment of quality education."

Student Types. Within the student body Dr. Hansen sees generally four types of students: the intellectually gifted, the above-average, the average, and the retarded. He assumes that each of these types of students has a maximum level of academic capability and, most importantly, that that level of ability can be accurately ascertained. The duty of the school is to identify these students and provide a curriculum commensurate with their respective abilities. Dr. Hansen contends that the traditional school curriculum—including the usual two-level method of ability grouping—does a disservice to those at either end of the ability spectrum.

The gifted student is not challenged, so that he becomes bored, lazy, and perhaps performs far below his academic potential; his intellectual talents are a wasted resource. The remedy lies in discovering the gifted student, placing him with others of his own kind, thereby stimulating him through this select association as well as a rigorous, demanding curriculum to develop his intellectual talent. Indeed, "the academically capable student should be required as a public necessity to take the academically challenging honors curriculum."

On the other hand, continues Dr. Hansen, the retarded or "stupid" student typically has been forced to struggle through a curriculum he cannot possibly master and only imperfectly comprehends. Typically he is slow to learn and soon falls behind in class; he repeatedly fails, sometimes repeating a grade again and again; he becomes isolated, frustrated, depressed, and—if he does not drop out before graduation—graduates with a virtually useless education. Here the remedy is seen as separating out the retarded student, directing him into a special curriculum geared to his limited abilities and designed to give him a useful "basic" education—one which makes no pretense of equalling traditionally taught curricula.

In short, Hansen views the traditional school curriculum as doing too little for some students and expecting too much of others. As for the latter type, whom Dr. Hansen characterizes as "the blue-collar student," going to school—a "white-collar occupation"—can be an artificial experience. "Twelve years of white-collar experience is unrealistic preparation for the young man or woman who will suddenly make the change into work clothes for jobs in kitchens, stockrooms, street maintenance or building construction. . . . ."

Tracking. In order to tailor the educational process to the level appropriate to each student, Dr. Hansen adopted the track system. Each track is intended to be a separate and self-contained curriculum, with the educational content ranging from the very basic to the very advanced according to the track level. In the elementary and junior high schools three levels are used: Basic or Special Academic (retarded students), General (average and above-average), and Honors (gifted). In the senior high school a fourth level is added: the Regular Track, a college-preparatory track intended to accommodate the above-average student.

The significant feature of the track system in this regard is its emphasis on the ability of the student. A student's course of instruction depends upon what the school system decides he is capable of handling. . . .

Flexibility. Dr. Hansen, while assuming that some students can be educated to their maximum potential in one of the four curricula, also anticipates that not all students will neatly or permanently fit into a track. Thus a second important assumption underlying the track system is that tracking will be a flexible process. Flexibility encompasses two things: First, although a student today may demonstrate an ability level which calls, for example, for placement in the General Track, a constant and continuing effort must be made to assure that he is at his true ability level. This calls for instruction directed toward correcting any remediable educational problems which account for the student's present poor performance; and it calls for close analysis and counseling to determine whether these remediable deficiencies exist and when they have been sufficiently corrected. When the latter is determined, the student is to be upgraded to the next higher track. Second, even though a student may not be in a position to make an across-the-board move from one track to another, his ability level may be such that he needs to take courses in two track levels on a subject-by-subject basis. This process, known as cross-tracking, is critical: it is the mechanism the system relies upon to assure that students whose ability levels vary according to particular subjects are not thwarted in developing their strong areas because their weak areas result in their being placed in a lower curriculum level. It also serves as a way of selectively raising the intensity of instruction on a subject-matter basis as a part of the process of gradually upgrading a student.

Fundamental Assumptions. To summarize, the track system's approach is twofold. The separate curriculum levels are for some the maximum education their abilities permit them to achieve. For others, a track is supposed to be a temporary assignment during which a student's special problems are identified and remedied in whatever way possible. The express assumptions of this approach are three: *First,* a child's maximum educational potential can and will be accurately ascertained. *Second,* tracking will enhance the prospects for correcting a child's remediable educational deficiencies. *Third,* tracking must be flexible so as to provide an individually tailored education for students who cannot be pigeonholed in a single curriculum. . . .

[The court discusses differences in purpose, criteria for admission, and curriculum among the four tracks. It then analyzes the overrepresentation of poor and minority students in lower tracks.]

Flexibility in Pupil Programming. The importance of flexibility to the proper operation of the track system has been adverted to earlier in this opinion.

[However] flexibility in pupil programming in the District of Columbia school system is an unkept promise.

Movement Between Tracks: Upgrading. . . . [A]t least 85 percent of those assigned to the special academic track—and it appears that something over 90 percent is more typical—remain at the lowest achievement level. Although it cannot be said that an assignment to the special academic track inevitably is permanent, neither can it be said that the chances of progressing into a more challenging curriculum are very high.

Plaintiffs have charged that this lack of movement is attributable to a complex of causes: the simplified curriculum, coupled with the absence of variety in the students' levels of ability, does not stimulate the special academic student; reme- dial training is inadequate; special academic teachers are not formally trained for special educational problems; teachers underestimate the potential of their stu- dents and therefore undereducate them. None of these reasons can be either isolated or proved with absolute certainty. Nonetheless, there is substantial evi- dence . . . that the cause of limited upgrading in the special academic track lies more with faults to be found in the system than with the innate disabilities of the students. And certainly the results . . . do not support the thesis that tracking is flexible.[80] . . .

. . . [T]he pattern observed with respect to upgrading from the special aca- demic track is repeated in all track levels. Movement between tracks borders on the nonexistent. . . .

Thus in the 1963-64 school year, where the figures show the highest amount of intertrack movement, almost 92 percent of the senior high students did not leave their assigned track. Moreover, 44 percent of the students who did move, moved downward.

What is most important, however, is the miniscule amount of movement from the lower tracks to the college preparatory tracks. Of the approximately 7,800 general track students, only 404—about 5 percent—moved up a level, none going into the honors curriculum. Although five special academic students were able to jump ahead two levels to the regular track, the number not moving at all remains by far predominant. In sum, then, of all the students in the two lower tracks —constituting almost 60 percent of the student body—only 4.8 percent ad- vanced to the college preparatory curriculum. And at the same time, it should be noted, 320 students—or 4.8 percent—from the regular or honors track fell back to the lower tracks.

Viewed as a whole, the evidence of overall movement between tracks conclu- sively demonstrates the defendants' failure to translate into practice one of the most critical tenets of the track system: "Pupil placement in a curriculum must never be static or unchangeable. Otherwise, the four-track system will degenerate into a four-rut system." The tragedy has occurred.

Movement Between Tracks: Cross-Tracking. . . . [C]ross-tracking is track terminol- ogy for electing courses above or below an assigned curriculum level. . . . The purpose of cross-tracking is to assure flexibility in meeting individual students' needs, allowing students who cannot qualify for—or who do not require or desire —full-time assignment to a higher or lower track (upgrading or downgrading) to take one or more courses at an advanced or simplified level.

In practice cross-tracking of the sort described is confined to the senior high

---

80. Interestingly enough, however, Dr. Hansen characterized the 1962-63 data for the secondary schools, showing 347 (8.2 percent) students upgraded in junior high and 175 (9.7 percent) in senior high, as "a sizable number of students." . . . From these data he con- cluded: "1. The search for the more talented low-achievers continues throughout the six years of the basic curriculum in the secondary schools. *Pupils, rather than being permanently 'tracked' or pigeonholed at a low academic level, are challenged to move up the ladder of accomplishment.*

"*Those who charge that ability grouping makes the lowest group a 'dumping' ground for the problem learners where they are forgotten and unstimulated are not conversant with the facts.* . . .

level, there being structural reasons why elementary and junior high pupils do not really "cross-track." And. . . . even at the senior high school level cross-tracking proves to be the exception, not the rule. . . .

In the special academic track containing 9.0 percent of the District's high school students almost 89 percent did not take courses outside the basic curriculum. And in the general track, in which half the students were located, two-thirds (66.2 percent) did no cross-tracking. Together, these two lower tracks accounted for 58.6 percent of the high school student body, and 70 percent of those students did not cross-track.

Defendants have not explained why so few students in the three lower curricula (special academic, general, and regular) do any cross-tracking. However, there is substantial evidence, some of it already discussed in relation to upgrading, pointing to several reasons.

The first is that students are being denied permission to cross-track—or discouraged from seeking that permission—on the assumption that they cannot handle a more difficult assignment. . . .

Another reason, related to the first is that many students do not obtain effective, individual counseling on programs, counseling that is obviously necessary if a student is to be directed to a curricular program fitted to his needs and abilities. . . . Absent this close attention, the student will remain locked into his assigned curriculum, unless the student or his parents are disposed to question the merits of that continued assignment.

A third reason for limited cross-tracking, . . . is the inability to qualify for the more advanced courses either for lack of the prerequisite fundamental courses or because of continuing academic deficiencies. . . . A fourth reason is the substantial possibility that some school principals, or their staffs, take a very restrictive view of cross-tracking. . . .

Causes of Discrimination and the Collapse of Track Theory. Having seen how the track system in practice has become a relatively rigid form of class separation, the court now turns to a discussion of the principal causes of this result. In the preceding section some of the probable reasons for inflexibility were identified. Here the focus will be on the major institutional shortcomings that not only thrust the disadvantaged student into the lower tracks but tend to keep him there once placed. The first area of concern is the lack of kindergartens and honors programs in certain [predominantly black] schools; the second relates to remedial and compensatory programs for the disadvantaged and educationally handicapped student; and the third, and most important, involves the whole of the placement and testing process by which the school system decides who gets what kind of education. . . .

[The court finds that disadvantaged students have less access to kindergarten programs (which, the court asserts, may be "indispensable to their success in the whole of their academic career") and to honors track instruction.]

Remedial and Compensatory Education. One purpose of the track system is to facilitate remedial education for students who are temporarily handicapped in basic academic skills. In addition, the school system has recognized that it must provide a substantial number of its students with special compensatory education programs for there to be any real hope of their becoming qualified for the more advanced tracks. There is substantial evidence, however, that neither the remedial nor the compensatory education programs presently in existence are adequate; rather the disadvantaged student consigned to the lower track tends simply to get the lesser education, not the push to a higher level of achievement.

Remedial Programs: Curricular.

Special Academic Track. . . . Defendants have made it quite clear that a child placed in a special academic class will receive a slower-paced, simplified course of instruction.

General Track. . . . [T] here is within the overall framework of the general track a certain amount of further subgrouping. . . . Presumably, given the commitment to homogeneity in grouping, this permits teachers to concentrate on a class of children of like ability levels; however, there is no indication that the low pupil-teacher ratio found in the special academic track prevails. Moreover, although there is testimony suggesting that special remedial programs may be adopted in the lower ability groupings in this track—at least in elementary schools . . . —there is no evidence of a systematized remedial program being included within the general curriculum itself. Instead, as with the special academic track, the prevailing philosophy is to teach children at existing ability levels; those that indicate potential for a more advanced curriculum must be approved for cross-tracking or upgrading. . . . And again, as with the special academic track, evidence of such intertrack movement shows relatively few moving up. . . . What has not been made clear, however, is how a student given a steady diet of simplified materials can keep up, let alone catch up, with children his own age who are proceeding in a higher curriculum at a faster pace and with a more complex subject-matter content. While much has been made of the "enriched" honors curriculum . . . nothing has been said to indicate that the slow learner—who almost certainly is in some degree slow due to a disadvantaged background—is also given an enriched curriculum to stimulate him to higher achievement. . . . Rather the pervading spirit of the special academic track—captured in the general track as well—seems to be essentially a negative one: slow the pace, teach less, and hope that what is learned will be "useful." But what the disadvantaged child needs most—by defendants' own admission—is not just instruction watered down to his present level of ability; he needs stimulation, enrichment and challenge to assure that his present temporary handicaps do not by educational conditioning become permanent. That this stimulation has not been forthcoming from the basic curriculum is clear from the lack of upward movement from that track. . . .

Special Remedial and Compensatory Education Programs. It is because of the high proportion of disadvantaged children in the district school system that it is imperative that special programs outside the regular school curriculum be adopted so that the disadvantaged child has a real opportunity to achieve at his maximum level of ability. . . .

Defendants, fully aware of the importance of remedial and compensatory education and professing to be committed to developing such programs in order to assure equal educational opportunity, have attempted to show that the District is indeed possessed of a substantial number of such programs. . . .

A review of defendants' evidence in this regard does reveal a substantial number of projects which run the gamut from physical fitness and breakfast programs, art and music programs, work-study programs, to various remedial and cultural enrichment projects. . . . Most of them are of very recent vintage, many having been instituted since 1965 as a result of various federal and foundation fundings. Nonetheless, upon close examination it becomes painfully obvious that few if any of these programs have as yet been able to reach with any intensity the great number of disadvantaged children enrolled in the District schools. . . .

[T]hese programs are of course commendable; indeed they are vital to the future of Washington's public school system. But as yet they have not gone far enough. They cannot obscure the sad fact that the vast majority of the disadvantaged school children in this school system, if not altogether untouched by remedial and compensatory programs, are at best touched only in passing. It is true that the schools alone cannot compensate for all the handicaps that are characteristic of the disadvantaged child; but it is the schools that must—as defendants admit—lead the attack on the verbal handicaps which are the major barrier to academic achievement. . . .

The track system adds to that obligation, however, because tracking translates ability into educational opportunity. When a student is placed in a lower track, in a very real sense his future is being decided for him; the kind of education he gets there shapes his future progress not only in school but in society in general. Certainly, when the school system undertakes this responsibility it incurs the obligation of living up to its promise to the student that placement in a lower track will not simply be a shunting off from the mainstream of education, but rather will be an effective mechanism for bringing the student up to his true potential. Yet in the District the limited scope of remedial and compensatory programs, the miniscule number of students upgraded, and the relatively few students cross-tracking make inescapable the conclusion that existing programs do not fulfill that promise. . . .

[The court examines what it terms "the most important single aspect of the track system . . . the process by which the school system goes about sorting students into the different tracks. This importance stems from the fact that the fundamental premise of the sorting process is the keystone of the whole track system: that school personnel can with reasonable accuracy ascertain the maximum potential of each student and fix the content and pace of his education accordingly." 269 F Supp at 473-74. The court concludes that aptitude tests are the primary basis for sorting; that "there is substantial evidence that defendants presently lack the techniques and the facilities for ascertaining the innate learning abilities of a majority of district schoolchildren . . . [and that] lacking these techniques and facilities, defendants cannot justify the placement and retention of these children in lower tracks on the supposition that they could do no better, given the opportunity to do so." 269 F Supp at 488.]

The Self-fulfilling Prophecy. The real tragedy of misjudgments about the disadvantaged student's abilities is, as described earlier, the likelihood that the student will act out that judgment and confirm it by achieving only at the expected level. Indeed, it may be even worse than that, for there is strong evidence that performance in fact *declines.* . . . And while the tragedy of misjudgments can occur even under the best of circumstances, there is reason to believe the track system compounds the risk.

First, the fundamental commitment of the track system is to educate *ability*, not just the student. By assuming the responsibility of deciding who gets what kind of educational opportunity, the school system places a dear price on teacher misjudgments. Thus, when a misjudgment does occur, the result will be institutionally to shunt the student into a curriculum paced to his presumed abilities, where he is likely to progress only at the speed at which he is taught.[146] A sixth-grade student nourished on third-grade instruction is apt to finish the year with a third-grade education; yet the haunting question: could he have done better?

Another aspect of the track system's emphasis on ability is the distinctly competitive atmosphere injected into the curriculum. Indeed, competition is the intent, for it is competition that Dr. Hansen relies upon as the spur to individual efforts to achieve and rise up. But in a school system such as the District's where well over half of the students come from improvished backgrounds and 90 percent are born into a world where the color of their skin makes life an inevitable struggle simply to obtain equality, turning the pursuit of education into yet another competition is just unfair. As might be expected, in such a setting the race goes to the swift; and to the child disadvantaged only by birthright can go a second-class education.

The third feature of the track system is its tendency to reinforce the psychological impact of being adjudged of low ability. By consigning students to specifically designated curricula, the track system makes highly visible the student's status within the school structure. To the unlearned, tracks can become pejorative labels, symptomatic of which is the recent abandonment of the suggestive "basic" for the more euphemistic "special academic" as the nomenclature of the lowest track. And even if a student may be unaware of labels, he cannot ignore the physical fact of being separated from his fellow students.

None of this is to suggest either that a student should be sheltered from the truth about his academic deficiencies or that instruction cannot take account of varying levels of ability. It is to say that a system that presumes to tell a student what his ability is and what he can successfully learn incurs an obligation to take account of the psychological damage that can come from such an encounter between the student and the school; and to be certain that it is in a position to decide whether the student's deficiencies are true, or only apparent. The District of Columbia school system has not shown that it is in such a position.

OPINION OF LAW

Plaintiffs' attack on the track system, Superintendent Hansen's special form of ability grouping, touches yet another phase of the District's administration of the public schools, here the concern being specifically the kind of educational opportunities existing within the classroom. The evidence amassed by both parties with regard to the track system has been reviewed in detail [and] ... the court has already had occasion to note the critical infirmities of that system. The sum result of those infirmities, when tested by the principles of equal protection and due process, is to deprive the poor and a majority of the Negro students in the District of Columbia of their constitutional right to equal educational opportunities.

---

146. ... [A]nother risk of reinforcing a child's present disabilities [is] the lack of contact with students having a command of standard English. The homogeneous class, by grouping students similarly handicapped, removes a source of stimulation available in a mixed ability setting.

At the outset it should be made clear that what is at issue here is not whether defendants are entitled to provide different kinds of students with different kinds of education. Although the equal protection clause is, of course, concerned with classifications which result in disparity of treatment, not all classifications resulting in disparity are unconstitutional. If classification is reasonably related to the purposes of the governmental activity involved and is rationally carried out, the fact that persons are thereby treated differently does not necessarily offend.

Ability grouping is by definition a classification intended to discriminate among students, the basis of that discrimination being a student's capacity to learn. Different kinds of educational opportunities are thus made available to students of differing abilities. Whatever may be said of the concept of ability grouping in general, it has been assumed here that such grouping can be reasonably related to the purposes of public education. Plaintiffs have eschewed taking any position to the contrary. Rather the substance of plaintiffs' complaint is that in practice, if not by design, the track system—as administered in the District of Columbia public schools—has become a system of discrimination founded on socioeconomic and racial status rather than ability, resulting in the undereducation of many District students. . . .

These are, then, the significant features of the track system: separation of students into rigid curricula, which entails both physical segregation and a disparity of educational opportunity; and, for those consigned to the lower tracks, opportunities decidedly inferior to those available in the higher tracks. . . .

All of these circumstances, and more, destroy the rationality of the class structure that characterizes the track system. Rather than reflecting classifications according to ability, track assignments are for many students placements based on status. Being, therefore, in violation of its own premise, the track system amounts to an unlawful discrimination against those students whose educational opportunities are being limited on the erroneous assumption that they are capable of accepting no more. . . .

REMEDY

As to the remedy with respect to the track system, the track system simply must be abolished. In practice, if not in concept, it discriminates against the disadvantaged child, particularly the Negro. Designed in 1955 as a means of protecting the school system against the ill effects of integrating with white children the Negro victims of de jure separate but unequal education, it has survived to stigmatize the disadvantaged child of whatever race relegated to its lower tracks—from which tracks the possibility of switching upward, because of the absence of compensatory education, is remote.

Even in concept the track system is undemocratic and discriminatory. Its creator admits it is designed to prepare some children for white-collar, and other children for blue-collar, jobs. Considering the tests used to determine which children should receive the blue-collar special, and which the white, the danger of children completing their education wearing the wrong collar is far too great for this democracy to tolerate. Moreover, any system of ability grouping which, through failure to include and implement the concept of compensatory education for the disadvantaged child or otherwise, fails in fact to bring the great majority of children into the mainstream of public education denies the children excluded equal educational opportunity and thus encounters the constitutional bar. . . .

PARTING WORD

It is regrettable, of course, that in deciding this case this court must act in an area so alien to its expertise. It would be far better indeed for these great social and political problems to be resolved in the political arena by other branches of government. But these are social and political problems which seem at times to defy such resolution. In such situations, under our system, the judiciary must bear a hand and accept its responsibility to assist in the solution where constitutional rights hang in the balance. . . .

DECREE

It is further ordered, adjudged and decreed that the defendants be, and they are hereby, permanently enjoined from operating the track system in the District of Columbia public schools . . .

Notes and Questions

1. Scope of the Decision

Hobson declares that the tracking system "simply must be abolished." What is the basis for that conclusion: the fact that black and poor students are assigned in disproportionate numbers to the lowest tracks? The inadequacy of aptitude tests as a means of assigning these students to tracks? The inflexibility of the classification system? The inadequacy of eduation provided for lower track students? Which of these factors does the court identify as denying plaintiffs an equal educational opportunity?

The *Hobson* decision was affirmed on appeal. *Smuck v Hobson* 408 F2d 175 (DC Cir 1969)(en banc). The court held:

> The district court's decree must be taken to refer to the "track system" as it existed at the time of the decree . . . [Neither] the school board nor Superintendent Hansen were satisfied with the track system as it was or desired a freeze in its features. . . .
>
> Therefore, the provision of the decree below directing abolition of the track system will not be modified. We conclude that this directive does not limit the discretion of the school board with full recognition of the need to permit the school board latitude in fashioning and effectuating the remedies for the ills of the District school system. . . . The simple decree enjoining the "track system" does not interpose any realistic barrier to flexible school administration by a school board genuinely committed to attainment of more quality and equality of educational opportunity. (408 F2d at 189-90.)

Does the appellate court's interpretation undercut the force of Judge Wright's conclusion? Or is it consistent with Judge Wright's statement that: "What is at issue here is not whether defendants are entitled to provide different kinds of students with different kinds of education. . . . [I]t has been assumed here that [ability] grouping can be reasonably related to the purposes of public education [and thus be found constitutionally valid]." 269 F Supp at 511-12.

2. Rigidity

Hobson notes that relatively few students change their track assignment. This phenomenon is not unique to Washington. One study of urban school systems found that fewer than 10 percent of all students assigned to special education classes ever returned to the regular program. Gallagher, "The Special Education Contract for Mildly Handicapped Children," 38 *J Exceptional Children* 527, 529 (1972).

The court of appeals opinion in *Hobson* observes: "In some cases statistics are ineluctably ambiguous in their import—the fact that only a small percentage of pupils are reassigned may indicate either general adequacy of initial assignments or inadequacy of review." *Smuck v Hobson* 408 F2d 175, 187 (DC Cir 1969). Does any of the evidence reviewed by the trial court suggest which of these hypotheses might in fact be correct?

Professor Sorenson reports that classification schemes can differ in several ways: with respect to their *inclusiveness,* the number of opportunities assumed to be available at different educational levels; *electivity,* the degree to which students' own decisions are allowed to be a determining factor in classification; *selectivity,* the amount of homogeneity that school authorities intend to produce through classification; and *scope,* the extent to which a given group of students will be members of the same classroom over time. Sorenson, "Organizational Differentiation of Students and Educational Opportunity," 43 *Sociology of Educ* 355 (1970). How would Sorenson characterize the District of Columbia's tracking system?

Sorenson speculates on the effects of these organizational characteristics:

> . . . [T]he higher the inclusiveness of an educational system, the greater the probability that an individual student will aspire for a higher level of education. To the extent that variations in aspirations produce variations in achievement, a direct effect of inclusiveness on achievement will obtain. . . .
>
> Coleman and his colleagues found that a student's belief that he could control his own environment had a stronger positive correlation with achievement than any other noncognitive characteristics of the student [J. Coleman et al, *Equality of Educational Opportunity* (1966)]. . . . High electivity allows a students own preferences to determine which educational activities he will engage in, perhaps in turn increasing the student's subjective feeling of control. . . .
>
> High scope . . . precludes a high degree of congruence between specific abilities, interests, and activities. . . . Low scope should conversely enhance congruence, especially if combined with high electivity. . . .
>
> The greater the selectivity the greater the likelihood that a student's classmates will be alike in terms of noncognitive characteristics relevant for learning. The greater the selectivity the greater the probability that student characteristics relevant for learning will change toward the typical level of the class as a result of within-classroom social interaction. Increasing selectivity, therefore, may be expected to increase the general effect of a vertical differentiation on between-classroom variation in achievement. (43 *Sociology of Educ* at 363-70.)

Does this discussion suggest that organizational rigidity limits educational opportunities? What additional evidence would be useful in responding to that query? See also Coleman, "The Concept of Equality of Educational Opportunity," in *Equal Educational Opportunity,* 9 (Harv Educ Rev ed 1969). Compare A. Rosenthal, *Pygmalion in the Classroom* (1969). What school organizational needs do you suspect promote rigidity? For example, does rigidity enable the school to function as "the principal channel of selection" in a society which reveals a "general trend to structural differentiation?" Parsons, "The School Class as a Social System: Some of Its Functions in American Society," 29 *Harv Educ Rev* 297 (1959). Compare Bettelheim, "Segregation, New Style," 66 *School Rev* 251 (1958). How, if at all, might a court address itself to the issue of rigidity? What remedial standard should it impose?

3. Resources

a. Unequal Resources and Services. One effect of classification may be a differential allocation of resources or services among the different groups. Evidence on this point is scanty. For example, there exist no data concerning the allocation of direct educational expenditures among tracks. The Coleman Report does indicate that teachers with the greatest verbal ability, a resource that has some influence on student achievement, were consistently assigned to those students classified as brightest. One reanalysis of the Coleman Report data found that upper track students had consistently greater access to guidance counsellors, Heyns, "Social Selection and Stratification within the Schools," *Amer J Soc* (in press), although the explanation of this phenomenon is unclear. Is the differential allocation of resources suggested by these studies justifiable in policy terms? Is the concept of different education programs for different types of students inconsistent with resource equality? Are intraschool inequities and intradistrict inequities in resource allocation constitutionally distinguishable? See pp 567-82.

b. Compensatory Resources. *Hobson* asserts that: "[A]ny system of ability grouping which, through failure to include and implement the concept of compensatory education for the disadvantaged child or otherwise, fails in fact to bring the great majority of children into the mainstream of public education denies the children excluded equal educational opportunity...." 269 F Supp at 515. Is the court suggesting that lower-track children have a constitutional right not just to equivalent resources, but to additional resources?

4. Educational Outcomes

a. Social Science Evidence. *Hobson* notes that classification may affect student achievement. "A sixth-grade student nourished on third-grade instruction is apt to finish the year with a third-grade education; yet the haunting question: could he have done better?" 269 F Supp at 492.

There have been numerous studies of the educational efficacy of ability grouping and special education. These studies attempt to answer a question slightly different from the one posed in *Hobson*: is a given student likely to learn more in an ability-grouped system than he would in a heterogeneously grouped system? The following excerpt summarizes the research findings:

"SCHOOLS AS SORTERS: THE CONSTITUTIONAL AND POLICY
IMPLICATIONS OF STUDENT CLASSIFICATION"
D. Kirp
121 U Pa L Rev 705, 725-29 (1973)

With respect to internal school classifications—special education programs and ability grouping—abundant research has been undertaken. The diligent reader has available to him studies of every sort: survey data and single school studies; "natural" and "experimental" research; studies undertaken in this country and abroad.

The research is, however, flawed by a host of methodological difficulties: some studies are too short in time, and thus do not take into account the possibility that children behave differently because they are part of an exciting (or at least novel) experiment; "experimental" groups, assigned to particular classifications, are not adequately matched with "control" groups, so that performance variation may be explained by initial student differences; measures of change and growth vary from study to study; responses to questionnaires prove inadequate to reckon with the subtleties of sorting; most important, the definition of what constitutes ability grouping or an educable mentally retarded program varies from study to study.

Despite these problems, the consistency of result among all the studies (and particularly among those most carefully executed) is impressive: it indicates that most school classifications have marginal and sometimes adverse impact on both student achievement and psychological development. . . .

The research concerning the efficacy of special education programs is best treated as two sets of data. Studies of programs for children with profound problems—for example, autistic children or those whose IQ is below 25—reveal that careful intervention can secure substantial benefits. Of course, the measure of benefit differs for these children: the ability to tie one's own shoes or to talk is a major success. But the benefits are real, and for the most part unquestioned.

Research concerning classes for children with etiologically more ambiguous handicaps—the educable mentally retarded, mildly emotionally disturbed and perceptually handicapped—reach quite different conclusions. Those programs do not tangibly benefit their students, whose equally handicapped counterparts placed in regular school classes perform at least as well and without apparent detriment to their "normal" classmates.

> It is indeed paradoxical that mentally handicapped children having teachers especially trained, having more money (per capita) spent on their education, and being enrolled in classes with fewer children and a program designed to provide for their unique needs, should be accomplishing the objectives of their education at the same or at a lower level than similar mentally handicapped children who have not had these advantages and have been forced to remain in the regular grades. . . . [Johnson, "Special Education for the Mentally Handicapped—A Paradox," 29 *Exceptional Children* 62, 66 (1962).]

That finding has led one psychologist to term such programs "the 'human waste disposal authority'—dead places," and another to suggest that he would go to court before permitting his child to be placed in a self-contained special school or class.

The methodological difficulties, noted earlier, suggest one reason for treating these findings with some caution. Where, for example, "special education" is a euphemism for a day-sitting room staffed by an unqualified teacher, as is too often the case, any benefits that it yielded would be remarkable. Yet the philosophy of isolated special class treatment also makes the failure of such ventures understandable. These programs typically adopt a "passive-acceptant" approach, reflecting the assumption that

> the retarded individual is essentially unmodifiable and, therefore, that his performance level as manifested at a given stage of development is considered as a powerful prediction of his future adaptation. . . . Strategies aiming at helping him to adapt . . . will consist of molding the requirements and activities of his environment to suit his level of functioning, rather than making the necessary efforts to raise his level of functioning in a significant way. *This, of course, is doomed to perpetuate his low level of performance.*

Thus, even if a child performs admirably in the special class, he inevitably falls further behind his counterparts in the regular program. Only an "active-modificational" approach—which rejects the eductional isolation and early labeling of retarded children—is likely to reverse this pattern. [See Feuerstein, "A Dynamic Approach to the Causation, Prevention, and Alleviation of Retarded Performance," in *Sociocultural Aspects of Mental Retardation,* 341, 343, 345 (C. Haywood ed 1970) (emphasis added).]

In sum, the research conclusion about special education programs is consistent, if modest: programs for the severely handicapped do benefit children, while classes for the mildly retarded and mildly emotionally disturbed do not serve those children better than regular class placement. Nor, it should be pointed out, do those classes markedly impair academic performance: if the empirical findings are correct, special education assignment has little effect on student achievement.

Studies of ability grouping generally reach a similar conclusion: differentiation on the basis of ability does not improve student achievement. It improves the performance of the brightest only slightly (and only for some academic subjects), while slightly impairing the school performance of average and slow students. Professor Borg, whose tracking study is perhaps the most careful yet undertaken, found that "neither ability grouping with acceleration nor random grouping with enrichment is superior for all ability levels of elementary school pupils. In general, the relative achievement advantages of the two grouping systems were slight, but tended to favor ability grouping for superior pupils and random grouping for slow pupils." [W. Borg, *Ability Grouping in the Public Schools,* 30 (1966).] The National Education Association, surveying the tracking literature, concludes: "Despite its increasing popularity, there is a notable lack of empirical evidence to support the use of ability grouping as an instructional arrangement in the public schools." [National Education Association, *Research Summary: Ability Grouping,* 44 (1968).]

For studies of the efficacy of ability grouping, see M. Goldberg, A. H. Passow, and J. Justman, *The Effects of Ability Grouping* (1966); Heathers, "Grouping," in *Encyclopedia of Educational Research,* 559 (4th ed, 1969); W. Findley and M. Bryan, *Ability Grouping: 1970* (1971); J. Barker Lunn, *Streaming in the Primary School* (1970). For studies of the efficacy of special classes for the mildly handicapped, see H. Goldstein, J. Moss, and L. Jordan, *The Efficacy of Special Class Training on the Development of Mentally Retarded Children* (1965); E. Rubin, C. Simpson, and M. Betwee, *Emotionally Handicapped Children in the Elementary School* (1966); Dunn, "Special Education for the Mildly Retarded: Is Much

of It Justified?" in *Problems and Issues in the Education of Exceptional Children*
(R. L. Jones, ed 1971).

b. The Constitutional Issue

i. Needs. Does this discussion suggest that classification does in fact deny some
students—those placed in slower tracks and special classes for the mildly handicapped—equal educational opportunity? In assessing such a claim, which party
should bear the burden of proof of harm (or lack of harm)? What should the
nature of that burden be? See *Rodriguez v San Antonio Independent School
Dist,* 411 US 1 (1973). Compare *Wyatt v Stickney* 344 F Supp 387 (MD Ala
1972).

Is a constitutional challenge to particular school classifications on the ground
that they do not benefit (and may in fact harm students) but another way of
stating that particular programs do not meet the educational needs of children
assigned to them? If so, how might *McInnis v Shapiro,* 293 F Supp 327, be
distinguished? Is it constitutionally relevant that the needs argument requires the
creation of additional school programs, while the no-benefit argument would
probably restrict the number of permissible classifications?

ii. Functional Exclusion. Some special education classes include children with a
bewildering variety of handicaps; not surprisingly, little is taught or learned in
such classes. See H. Goldstein, J. Moss, and L. Jordan, *The Efficacy of Special
Class Training on the Development of Mentally Retarded Children* (1965). Is a
child placed in such a class "functionally excluded" from school? Recall the
discussion of *Lau v Nichols,* pp 636-43.

5. Stigma

Hobson notes the stigma that attaches to placement in a slow track or special
education class. "By consigning students to specifically designated curricula, the
track system makes highly visible the student's status within the school structure.
To the unlearned, tracks can become pejorative labels, symptomatic of which is
the recent abandonment of the suggestive 'Basic' for the more euphemistic
'Special Academic' as the nomenclature of the lowest track." 269 F Supp at
492.

a. Process of Stigmatization. The following excerpt describes in greater detail the
process of stigmatization:

"SCHOOLS AS SORTERS: THE CONSTITUTIONAL AND POLICY
IMPLICATIONS OF STUDENT CLASSIFICATION"
D. Kirp
121 U Pa L Rev 705, 733-37 (1973)

Many of the classifications that schools impose on students are stigmatizing.
However well-motivated the decision or complex the factual bases leading to a
particular classification, the classification lends itself to simplified labels. . . .

These adverse school classifications [e.g., placement in slow learner tracks or
special education classes] reduce both the individual's sense of self-worth and his
value in the eyes of others. For many children, this process is particularly painful

because it is novel. It represents the first formal revelation of differentness. The school's inclination to cope with a particular learning or social problem by isolating those who share that problem reinforces the child's sense of stigma.

[T]he more the child is "handicapped" the more likely he is to be sent to a special school [or to a special program within the school] for persons of his kind, and the more abruptly he will have to face the view which the public at large takes of him. He will be told that he will have an easier time of it among "his own," and thus learn that the own he thought he possessed was the wrong one, and that this lesser own is really his. [E. Goffman, *Stigma*, 33 (1963).]

The stigmatized child, who tends to hold the same beliefs about identity that others do, comes to learn, through contact with the school, that he has in effect been devalued by both the school and the society. [See L. A. Dexter, *The Tyranny of Schooling* (1964).]

Children perceive all too well what the school's label means. Jane Mercer observes that those assigned to special education classes "were ashamed to be seen entering the MR room because they were often teased by other children about being MR . . . [and] dreaded receiving mail that might bear compromising identification. As one black mother, whose own son is in a special class, reported:

Let's face it, children can be real cruel. I feel for the most part the youngsters that are in those classes and retained suffer a great emotional handicap. It's as if they have a sign around their neck for everyone to read. Bill is being retarded in special education. He doesn't like being labeled as retarded. It's affecting him. He begs us to have him removed from that class . . . . The only reason he consents to go [to school] is because we have been promised that he'll be taken out of that EMR class. [Mercer, "Sociocultural Factors in the Education of Black and Chicano Children," *10th Annual Conference on Civil and Human Rights of Educators and Students* (NEA, 1972).]

Students assigned to the general or slow learner track described similar feelings: "General teachers make kids feel dumb. Their attitude is, 'Well, nobody's been able to do anything with you, and I can't do better.'" [Harvard Center for Law and Education, "Putting the Child in Its Place," 41 (1971).]

Differences among school children clearly exist, and it would be folly to ignore them: to treat everyone in exactly the same fashion typically benefits no one. Yet even with that qualification, the consequentiality of the school's classification is an awesome fact with which the child must cope. Its psychological ramifications extend beyond the child; they reach his family, and those with whom the child has contact. [See Iano, "Social Class and Parental Evaluation of Educable Retarded Children," 5 *Educ & Training of the Mentally Retarded* 62 (1970); Vogel & Bell, "The Emotionally Disturbed Child as the Family Scapegoat," in *A Modern Introduction to the Family*, 382 (1960).] The child assigned to a special education class or a slow learners group discovers that his society is totally altered. His differentness is what matters most to the school. [Compare L. Webb, *Children with Special Needs in the Infants' School* (1967).]

The stigma is further exacerbated, at least in part, by the school's curriculum. The curriculum offered to the "slow" or "special" child is less demanding than that provided for "normal" children; even if the child assigned to the special class does creditable work, he falls further behind the school norm. The initial assignment becomes a self-fulfilling prophesy; the child's belief in his inferiority is reinforced by the knowledge that he is increasingly unable to return to the regular school program. In addition, because his classmates and teachers make fewer demands on him (for by definition less can be expected of the handicapped than the normal), he comes to accept their judgment of acceptable progress as his own. . . .

The effects of school-imposed stigmas do not cease at the time the child leaves school, for schools significantly are society's most active labelers. "The schools label more persons as mentally retarded, share their labels with more other organizations, and label more persons with IQ's above 70 and with no physical disabilities than any other formal organization in the community." [Mercer, "Sociological Perspectives on Mild Mental Retardation," in *Sociocultural Aspects of Mental Retardation*, 287 (C. Haywood ed 1970).] Slow track assignment makes college entrance nearly impossible and may discourage employers from offering jobs; assignment to a special education program forecloses vocational options. . . . While many children labeled retarded by the school do come to lead normal lives, the stigma persists. Robert Edgerton, who interviewed one hundred formerly institutionalized retardates, reports:

> To find oneself regarded as a mental retardate is to be burdened by a shattering stigma, . . . the ultimate horror. . . . These persons cannot both believe that they are mentally retarded and still maintain their self-esteem. Yet they must maintain self-esteem. . . . [T]he stigma of mental retardation dominates every feature of the lives of these former patients. Without an understanding of this point, there can be no understanding of their lives. [R. Edgerton, *The Cloak of Competence* (1967). See also D. Braginsky and B. Braginsky, *Hansels and Gretels* (1971).]

It overstates the point, but not by much, to suggest that through adverse classifications schools can manage not only the lives of children but the lives of adults as well.

Stigma is not a phenomenon that admits of ready empirical confirmation. While some studies of student self-perception suggest that students in less advanced school programs typically refer to themselves as "dumb" or "lazy," other studies reach inconclusive or inconsistent results. A summary of this research suggests that "the impact of ability grouping on the affective development of children is to build (inflate?) the egos of the high groups and reduce the self-esteem of average and low groups in the total student population." W. Findley and M. Bryan, *Ability Grouping: 1970*, 40 (1971). See also Mann, "What Does Ability Grouping Do to the Self-concept?" 36 *Childhood Educ* 356 (1960); Borg and Pepich, "Grouping of Slow Learning High School Pupils" 41 *J Secondary Educ* 231 (1966); Jones, "Labels and Stigma in Special Education," 38 *J Exceptional Children* 553 (1972). Few of these studies attempt to relate stigma to student achievement.

Does differential treatment always imply some stigmatization? Is the issue better conceptualized as a balancing of benefits and injuries to the child—the degree of stigmatization versus the extent of educational progress? Are courts the appropriate institution to draw this balance?

b. Legal Implications. What is the constitutional relevance of stigma? Professor Burt suggests that certain labels, such as "mentally retarded," so regularly invoke state stigmatization that they should be treated as constitutionally suspect.

"BEYOND THE RIGHTS TO TREATMENT: STRATEGIES FOR JUDICIAL ACTION TO AID THE RETARDED"
R. Burt
(President's Comm'n on Mental Retardation and Project on Classification of Exceptional Children, Vanderbilt Univ., 1973)

There are important analogs between [judicially] disfavored categories—blacks, aliens, illegitimates—and retarded persons.... The compelling similarities are found in the historical social reality. A group of persons labelled "retarded" have in this society been subjected to discriminations as brutal and dehumanizing as have been imposed on the slave population....

[A] legal theory can be drawn that will lead courts [to rule that present patterns of state segregation of retarded persons, as such, for "treatment" or "educational" purposes are in themselves impermissible].... That theory posits, first, that special state categorization of "retarded persons" is (or comes perilously close to) a constitutionally suspect classification, and, second, that state use of such classification for placement in socially and geographically isolated institutions is excessively harmful and unjustified.

[The difficulty with this argument is that] judges and others can too easily argue that differences between . . . most . . . retarded and normal persons reflect true differences in endowment and potential rather than prejudiced social artifact.... [Further, the argument would appear to bar] the vast range of state classifications based on intelligence—such as school grades, admission to state universities, state employment, and so forth....

There is a response to this argument, however. State grading decisions, admissions decisions, employment decisions—do not usually carry consequences so far-reaching or disastrous to those labeled "unintelligent" as the consequences imposed by the "retardation" label....

The fact that this state classification affects children, and segregates them from regular public educational facilities, is a further reason for judicial intervention....

A powerful case can . . . be mounted that courts should command states to spend extraordinary effort to avoid institutionalizing retarded children.... Why is separate treatment for the retarded necessary? Is not separate, in this context, inherently unequal just as racially segregated education was found inherently unequal in *Brown v Board of Education*? ... This constitutional principle would not forbid special provision for the special educational problems of the retarded. But . . . a powerful case would be required to prove that this special assistance necessarily required separating retarded students from daily classroom contact with others....

Is retardation in fact analogous to other characteristics—e.g., race and alienage —which have evoked special judicial solicitude? What constitutional consequences would follow from treating retardation as a suspect classification? Is the need of retarded children for special services a compelling state interest that justifies the suspect classification? Does the argument that retardation is a suspect classification imply that the state may never attach that label to a group of its citizens? What would be the impact of a court decision adopting Professor Burt's position?

6. Intraclass Classification

Schools sort students within classes as well as among them. One sociologist observed the process, following the same class of children through their first three grades of school. He notes:

> [T]he development of expectations by the kindergarten teacher as to the differential academic potential and capability of any student was significantly determined by a series of subjectively interpreted attributes and characteristics of that student. The argument may be succinctly stated in five propositions. First, the kindergarten teacher possessed a roughly constructed "ideal type" as to what characteristics were necessary for any given student to achieve "success" both in the public school and in the larger society. These characteristics appeared to be, in significant part, related to social class criteria. Secondly, upon first meeting her students at the beginning of the school year, subjective evaluations were made of the students as to possession or absence of the desired traits necessary for anticipated "success." On the basis of the evaluation, the class was divided into groups expected to succeed (termed by the teacher "fast learners") and those anticipated to fail (termed "slow learners"). Third, differential treatment was accorded to the two groups in the classroom, with the group designated as "fast learners" receiving the majority of the teaching time, reward-directed behavior, and attention from the teacher. Those designated as "slow learners" were taught infrequently, subjected to more frequent control-oriented behavior, and received little if any supportive behavior from the teacher. Fourth, the interactional patterns between the teacher and the various groups in her class became rigidified, taking on caste-like characteristics, during the course of the school year, with the gap . . . widening as the school year progressed. Fifth, a similar process occurred in later years of schooling, but the teachers no longer relied on subjectively interpreted data as the basis for ascertaining differences in students. Rather, they were able to utilize a variety of informational sources related to past performance as the basis for classroom grouping. (Rist, "Student Social Class and Teacher Expectations," 40 *Harv Educ Rev* 411, 413-14 (1970).)

Imagine a student, assigned to the slowest group within the kindergarten for the class reasons Rist suggests, bringing suit against the school system, claiming that the "caste-like" treatment he received represented a denial of equal educational opportunity. If one adds to Rist's description the fact that relatively few students were reassigned from group to group within the class, what differentiates this situation from *Hobson*? What difficulties might a court encounter in devising relief?

7. Judicial Competence

Hobson was a widely criticized decision. One law review note scored its "unclear basis in precedent, its potentially enormous scope, and its imposition of responsibilities which may strain the resources and endanger the prestige of the judiciary. . . ." Note, "Hobson v Hansen, Judicial Supervision of the Color-blind School Board," 81 *Harv L Rev* 1511, 1525 (1968). See also Note, "Hobson v Hansen: The De Facto Limits on Judicial Power," 20 *Stan L Rev* 1249 (1968).

Is the criticism justified? What might be the basis for the conclusion that the *Hobson* opinion exceeds the bounds of judicial competence: the nature of the evidence the court is obliged to evaluate? The seemingly intractable problems associated with affecting educational achievement through manipulation generally regarded as professional prerogatives?

8. Problem: Yankee's Grouping System

The Yankee Public School System, a northern system (50 percent black, 50 percent white; median family income $6,500) which maintains racially and economically "balanced" schools, utilizes the following grouping system:

In kindergarten, children are tested for "reading readiness" by the school psychologist. Those whom the tester concludes are ready to read begin with the elementary text. Those who are found unready to read continue to play classroom games until, on some subsequent retesting, readiness to read is determined. Under this system 75 percent of all children are given reading instruction in the first grade. A handful of children are not given reading instruction until the third grade. Of the 25 percent who do not take first grade reading, 90 percent are black.

In grades one through three, children are grouped within each class. Those assignments are made by the classroom teacher, who (according to the Yankee teachers' manual) relies on "aptitude test results, classroom academic performance, and attitude conducive to learning" in making assignments. Miss Upright's class—thirty students, half of them black/half of them boys—is divided into three groups of ten. The Aces (the most advanced group) include 8 white children, and 7 girls; the Melons (the least advanced group) include 1 white child, and 8 boys. During the course of the year, two students have moved up from the Melons to the Hawks (the middle level group), and 1 student has moved from the Aces to the Hawks group. One teachers' aide, paid for under Title I, ESEA, is assigned to each classroom in grades one through three. The Yankee system assigns aides to all such classrooms in the system, arguing that since all schools are racially and economically balanced, no "concentration" of funds is possible. The teachers' aides spend most of their time working with the slowest group in each class.

Grades four through eight are grouped formally, by ability, into three groups, termed High, Middle, and Low. Grouping assignments are initially made on the basis of standard aptitude and achievement test scores, intraschool grades and teacher recommendations. The group assignment is a full-day assignment; students within each group take all their classes, including lunch and gym, together. The most recent data from Yankee's planning office indicates that 10 percent of all students are reassigned, either up or down, at the end of any given academic year; there is no reassignment during the year. The three groups contain an equal number of students, and the average racial and sex breakdown of the groups is as follows: High, 70 percent white, 60 percent female; Middle, 60 percent white, 60 percent female; Low, 20 percent white, 30 percent female. It should be noted that, at certain schools (notably Enlightened Grade School), the three groups are balanced in terms of race and sex; at other schools, the disparities are substantially greater (one school, Benighted Normal, has several 100 percent black Low groups).

In grades nine through twelve, the curriculum is diversified. In addition to the High (college prep), Regular and Low courses—each of which uses different curricular materials—there also exist vocational and secretarial programs. While students are theoretically free to choose whichever of the five programs they desire, there are operational constraints. First, any student wishing to move to a more advanced academic curriculum, i.e., from Regular to college prep, must write an essay explaining his reasons for wanting to make the change; the essay is then graded by the counselor. Second, reassignment upward, when approved, is for a semester trial period only. Third, unless a student specifically requests a different program, he is placed at the same level as the previous year.

The vocational program, open only to boys, prepares students for trades in the local community; the secretarial program, open only to girls, prepares students for careers as secretaries. An analysis of postschool choices of students reveals that, in fact, as many students from the low and regular academic tracks acquire these jobs as students from the specialized programs. The specialized programs do, however, differ in terms of resources allocated to them: classes in vocational education are smaller, and the availability of special federal funds for equipment purchase means that more dollars are spent on each student in these programs than in the regular school program. The racial breakdown of the five programs is as follows: vocational education, 70 percent black; secretarial, 60 percent black; low academic, 90 percent black; regular, 40 percent black; high, 20 percent black. While 80 percent of the college prep group and 50 percent of the regular group go on to higher education, virtually none of the other students do so.

What changes in classification policy and practice would you suggest to Yankee? What constitutional or other legal questions does this factual recital raise? What additional facts might you need to know in order more fully to answer those questions?

2. Nonconstitutional Context

TRAURIG v BOARD OF EDUCATION
New Jersey Commissioner of Education Decision (1971)

The parents of Jonathan Traurig, petitioner, allege that the proposed placement of their son in a special class in the school system of respondent Livingston Township Board of Education, hereinafter "board," for the 1970-71 school year was improper in that it failed to give individual attention to the needs of petitioner, hereinafter, "J.T." They request that the board be required to continue the former 1969-70 school year placement of petitioner during the 1970-71 year on a tuition-expense basis. The board denies that its proposed placement of J.T.

for the 1970-71 school year was improper, and maintains, instead, that the placement was in all respects a legal exercise of discretion on the part of the board and its administrative personnel.

A hearing on this matter was held . . . before a hearing examiner appointed by the commissioner. . . . The report of the hearing examiner follows:

J.T. is a child who, under normal academic progression, would now be enrolled in a fifth grade classroom. He was placed in a regular classroom during his first two full years of school and for at least part of the third. He was then classified as neurologically impaired, and assigned to a special class program during the 1968-69 school year. His progress during that year can best be described as minimal. . . .

[I]n the spring of 1969, the director [of the Livingston special education program], with the evident concurrence of the board's school administrators, and members of its child study team, assigned J.T. to a special class for neurologically impaired children located in the nearby Essex Fells School. This school was in another school district, and the distance from J.T.'s home to it was approximately three miles. The teacher of the class was Mrs. Rose DiRuggiero—a teacher with ten years of prior experience in teaching handicapped children and a master's degree from Columbia University.

In September 1969, J.T. began his attendance in this school with this teacher. According to the testimony of the teacher, J.T. was "bright" but extremely fearful—particularly of new situations—and frustrated over prior school experiences in which he had experienced failure, insecurity and apprehensiveness. This particular school situation was the fourth different school assignment for J.T. in a four-year period. The teacher testified that she freed J.T. from strict disciplinary demands, and tried patiently over a long period of time to establish mutual feelings of trust and friendship. She stated that these feelings slowly and gradually developed and that the boy—after midyear—began a period of more stable conduct. J.T. began to be interested in academic learning, and his progress from that point to the end of the year was one of marked improvement although it was punctuated by periods of retrogression.

In March of 1970, this teacher, who had observed J.T. daily, and who had guided this slowly developing progress, made a recommendation in writing for his placement for the school year 1970-71. It was that he be reassigned to her room. Her testimony was that she could not believe that he would not be so assigned, and she described J.T.'s actions at that time as still having the potential of a "keg of dynamite." In the opinion of this teacher, J.T. was not capable of going to a "new" situation in September of 1970—for the fifth time in five years—and at the same time continue the progress which he had made.

J.T.'s teacher for the 1969-70 school year submitted her recommendations for J.T.'s 1970-71 placement to the director of the West Essex Cooperative. This official had also observed J.T. on three or four occasions during the year and had previously conferred with the teacher, and probably, according to what appeared to be the custom, with the board's school official. In June of 1970, the director of the cooperative assigned J.T. to the classroom of Mrs. Rose DiRuggiero in the Essex Fells School for the 1970-71 school year. . . .

However, following this assignment, the board decided to establish its own class for neurologically impaired children for the 1970-71 school year and to assign J.T. to it. Accordingly, a new assignment letter was sent dated July 1970 directing J.T.'s parents to "disregard" the earlier announcement. The parents promptly appealed this reassignment, but the board deemed the matter as "administrative," in nature and would not intervene. The board's school officials would not countermand the reassignment unless the psychiatrist for the cooperative and for the board indicated, as the result of a new examination, that such a placement was definitely not advisable. This psychiatrist had previously addressed a letter to the board's Department of Special Services on July 10, 1970. This letter said: "Because of the above named student's significant neurological impairment and emotional disorder it is recommended that he continue his education in a special class. I understand that he had made excellent progress with a teacher he had last year. Therefore, it would be detrimental to his growth if he is not allowed to continue with her. I have received a written report from his teacher presenting his progress."

However, in August 1970, following a new office consultation with J.T. and after having been told by the board's director of special services that the "decision for placement was an educational one," the psychiatrist sent a new letter on August 28, 1970, to the board's director which concluded: "I feel you have to evaluate his placement as to what is best for him, as I do not feel I can make this decision."

The dialogue continued, and was still not really resolved by September. On September 3, 1970, the director of the West Essex Cooperative sent the following letter to the director of the board's child study team. The letter is quoted in part below:

> This letter is a follow-up on our telephone conversation of Wednesday, September 2, 1970, regarding the special education placement of J.T., 74 Sykes Avenue, Livingston. We placed this child last year in our class for neurologically impaired children at Essex Fells. Taking all factors into consideration, this was an ideal placement for J.T. who, up to this point, had developed severe negative reactions to school in general. Toward the end of the past year, J.T. began to show good signs of academic progress, however, his fear of failure and rejection as indicated by his lack of involvement and participation in group activities is still present. Any change in program at the present will have an intensifying effect on this child's feeling of inadequacy. His adjustment to this teacher, her program and the pressure-free environment existing indicate the need for this child to continue another year at Essex Fells School.
>
> In general and in many cases, the policy of the West Essex Special Education Cooperative has been to maintain a child for two years within a particular special education program particularly when the first year indicated productivity. . . .

However, the letter had no effect in changing respondent's opinion as to what J.T.'s assignment should be for the school year 1969-70. Despite this refusal of the board to reconsider the matter, J.T.'s parents reenrolled him in the Essex Fells School in September of 1970, and the boy continues his attendance there to the present time on a tuition basis. J.T.'s parents have privately assumed the payments. . . .

[T]he board maintains that its notice of a change of assignment, given in July

1970, was ample notice to J.T.'s parents, and that there is nothing contained in the education statutes or in rules of the state board of education by which such a notice could be adjudged untimely. Further, the board avers that in July 1970, it had obtained a qualified teacher, and was prepared to establish a suitable facility; therefore, the board maintains it had an unabridged autonomous right to assign its own students to this class as it saw fit. . . .

The hearing examiner also makes the following observations:

1. This dispute is not between a private school and privately engaged professionals and officials. It is a dispute instead that revolves around the contentions of two separate and distinct groups working within the public school framework.

On the one hand are the director of a cooperative, a public school teacher and a psychiatrist. These officials knew J.T. well. From the documents in evidence and from the testimony, it is clear that in the spring months of 1970, they were unanimous in strongly supporting the idea that J.T. should remain for a second year in a placement where he had at last found a measure of success. . . .

On the other hand there are the board's special services team and school administrator. During the 1969-70 school year there is no evidence that any of these officials saw J.T. even once. Nevertheless, they supported the decision to place him in Essex Fells for a second year in May and June of 1970. It was only later that J.T.'s needs and the recommendations of those who knew him best were ignored because of reasons that might be labelled administrative expediency. At that point J.T. was reassigned.

2. J.T. and his parents were the innocent victims of a jurisdictional dispute between these two groups. . . .

3. The placement of J.T. for a second year in the school in Essex Fells for the school year 1970-71 was clearly evident as the best for him. The question remains as to whether or not it was the only suitable placement. The hearing examiner holds that it was. The primary basis for this finding is the long and graphic description by the classroom teacher of J.T.'s problems and progress during the 1969-70 school year. . . .

In summary, the hearing examiner finds that the issue raised by this petition is not whether the facilities and program proposed to be provided by the board for the education of J.T. during the 1970-71 school year were "suitable" in the usual sense of that word, but whether in the important context of J.T.'s whole experience he should have been moved there by tardy reassignment in the summer of 1970. The examiner holds that the proposed reassignment was an arbitrary and callous act under the circumstances and that the imposition of such a transfer under the auspices of powers granted to boards of education that are clearly meant to protect individual children with handicaps represents a misuse of such power which should not be supported. . . .

Accordingly, the board is directed to reimburse J.T.'s parents for the expenses of such placement as were incurred by them for tuition and transportation costs for the 1970-71 school year.

Notes and Questions

1. Legal Basis

What is the legal basis of the commissioner's decision? What standard of review does he apply to the alleged misclassification? Does the commissioner have the power to make an independent determination as to what is in the best interests of the child? In this regard, consider Section 18A:6-9 of the New Jersey Education Code: "The commissioner shall have jurisdiction to hear and determine . . . all controversies . . . arising under the school laws . . . or under the rules of the state board or of the commissioner." What rules or laws did the commissioner invoke? Did he simply hold that school boards do not have the power to engage in "arbitrary and callous" acts with respect to handicapped children? Is this an accurate characterization of the school board's reassignment of the plaintiff? Would the standard of review have been any different in federal or state court?

2. Comparison of Administrative and Judicial Process

Traurig embodies a careful review of the adequacy of the alternative educational programs available to handicapped children. Does this suggest that an administrative officer within the New Jersey education system would be more competent than a court to review and set aside a particular school classification? Does the commissioner's decision have more political legitimacy than a court-made decision?

III. Remedies

The sources of concern with classification practice vary widely, and so do the remedies that would allay these concerns. Certain of these remedial proposals—for example, racial quotas to eliminate overrepresentation of minority students in less-advanced school programs—have already been discussed. This section considers three more general remedies: (1) procedural protection for students whom the school wishes to place in a less-advanced school program; (2) education vouchers that the parents of a child who cannot be placed in a regular school program can use at any state-approved private facility; and (3) integration or "mainstreaming" of mildly handicapped and slow pupils into the regular educational program.

Each of these remedies finds its counterpart elsewhere in this casebook. For example, a general voucher proposal has been assessed in some detail in chapter 1; and the applicability of procedural protection to students has been discussed in chapter 2. In the context of student classification, however, each of these remedies poses somewhat different problems, both of policy and of law, and for that reason merits separate consideration.

A. Due Process

Traditionally, procedural protection under the due process clause of the Fourteenth Amendment is provided to assure that official action is not arbitrary, but rather consistent with general guidelines for ensuring fairness in governmental decisions. In the student classification context, such protection might minimize misapplication of the school's own criteria for placing students; it would require both clarity of standard and administrative regularity. The latter is required if due process is to be a reality. As Professor Fuller has noted:

> [A]djudication must take place within the framework of accepted or imposed standards of decision before the litigant's participation in the deci-

sion can be meaningful. If the litigant has no idea on what basis the tribunal will decide the case, his . . . opportunity to present proofs and arguments becomes useless. . . . There must be an extralegal community, existent or in the process of coming into existence, from which principles of decision may be derived. (Fuller, "Adjudication and the Rule of Law," *1960 Proceedings of the American Society of International Law*, 1, 5-7.)

MADERA v BOARD OF EDUCATION
267 F Supp 356 (SDNY 1967)

Motley, District Judge.

Findings of Fact and Conclusions of Law

The minor plaintiff, Victor Madera, is a fourteen-year-old pupil enrolled in Public School 22, a junior high school in the New York City public school system. On February 2, 1967, Victor was suspended from school by the principal. He has been out of school since that date.

After Victor was suspended, the principal of his school notified the district superintendent of District No. 1, Miss Theresa Rakow, a defendant in this suit. Miss Rakow notified Victor's parents, the adult plaintiffs, that a conference would be held in her office on February 17, 1967, with regard to Victor's suspension. . . .

After Victor's parents received the notice, they secured an attorney who contacted Miss Rakow's office to notify her that the attorney would appear at the February 17 hearing. The attorney was advised that he could not attend the hearing. Circular No. 16 provides as follows: "Inasmuch as this is a guidance conference for the purpose of providing an opportunity for parents, teachers, counselors, supervisors, et al., to plan educationally for the benefit of the child, attorneys seeking to represent the parent or child may not participate."

Plaintiffs' constitutional contentions are: (1) the "no attorneys provision" of Circular No. 16 deprives them of protection for their right against self incrimination, right to counsel and right to due process guaranteed by the Fifth, Sixth and Fourteenth Amendments to the Constitution of the United States, since any statements made by them in, or as a part of, the guidance conference may be used against them in subsequent family court proceedings, where Victor's personal liberty will be in jeopardy, and (2) the minor plaintiff's right not to testify against himself must be preserved because one of the consequences of a Guidance Conference may also be loss of personal liberty. . . .

[P]laintiffs claim that as a result of a guidance conference, Victor may be suspended from school for an indefinite period of time, placed in a school for socially maladjusted children (formerly known as "600" schools), involuntarily incarcerated in an institution, or referred to the family court for appropriate action. . . .

Plaintiffs' constitutional contention with respect to these claims is that since the above-enumerated irreparable consequences can flow from a guidance conference, the "no attorneys provision" of Circular No. 16 may result in Victor being denied his right to attend the public schools granted him by the Constitution and Education Law of the state of New York, without due process of law guaranteed by the Fourteenth Amendment. . . .

Upon the hearing of plaintiffs' motion for preliminary injunction and upon the trial, which were consolidated, the following facts were established in addition to those set forth above . . . .

District Superintendent Rakow, in addition to having responsibility for the supervision of the educational program of the district, conducts hearings relating to the suspension of students, as required by New York Education Law, § 3214. Miss Rakow and the other school authorities choose to refer to these hearings as "guidance conferences". These conferences are conducted in cases where a student has been suspended by the principal. Once a principal has suspended a child and so notified the parents and Miss Rakow, it is Miss Rakow's duty to hold a "guidance conference", "to determine", to use her words, "what next educational step may be taken to help the child." There are two kinds of principal's suspensions. There is what is called a "principal suspense which means that the principal merely suspends the child from school service until such a time as he personally can confer with the parent and try to make the adjustment directly in the school." In such a case, the principal is limited to keeping the child from school for no more than five days. The principal generally meets with a parent before a suspension to try to adjust the problem. However, if there is some emergency where there is not time to meet with the parent, a principal might suspend immediately. After a principal's conference with the parent, the child is returned to school. A child does not *normally* go to the district superintendent's office immediately after the principal's suspension as was the case with Victor. If after the pupil has returned to school there continues to be a problem which the principal feels he cannot handle, then the principal can suspend the pupil and refer that suspension to the district superintendent. There is no evidence that Victor had been thus previously suspended by the principal.

When a suspended pupil is referred to the district superintendent this is known as an "administrative suspense." There is no hearing held by the principal before an "administrative suspense" takes place. When the district superintendent receives a copy of a letter from the principal to the parents stating that the child has been suspended, the district superintendent notifies the parent of the date of hearing. The principal's letter advises the parents that they will be so notified.

When a conference is held in the district superintendent's office, she invites the principal of the suspended child's school and the guidance counselor of that school. The members of the district superintendent's staff who attend are: her assistant, the guidance counselor assigned to her office, and the school-court coordinator assigned to the district. The bureau of attendance, an arm of the board of education, which enforces the state's compulsory school attendance law is also notified of the conference. . . .

The suspended child may have a representative from any social agency, to whom the family may be known, to attend a suspension hearing in the district superintendent's office.

At the conference, all school personnel present sit around a table in Miss Rakow's office and discuss the child's anecdotal record, supplied by the principal, and the child's problems. Usually the parents and the child wait outside until a decision is reached. The parents and child are then brought in and asked if they have anything to say as to what should be done with the child. If the child is old enough, he is asked to express an opinion. If a representative of a social agency is present, he or she contributes to the discussion. The decision is then given to the child and his parents.

The decisions which the district superintendent may reach are the following:

1. The suspended child might be reinstated in the same school.

2. The suspended child might be transferred to another school of the same level, e. g., a junior high school child to another junior high school.

3. The suspended child might be transferred to a special school for socially maladjusted children; there are two in District No. 1.

4. The district superintendent may refer the student's case to the bureau of child guidance (BCG) or other social agency for study and recommendations, including medical suspension, home instruction, or exemption.

5. The district superintendent may refer the case to the bureau of attendance for court action.

The BCG is the clinical arm of the board of education. Its employees are social workers, psychologists and psychiatrists. When the district superintendent refers a child to the BCG, it makes a study of the child "as seems indicated to help" the district superintendent or to advise her "of what may be best educational placement."

The BCG may make one of the following recommendations:

1. The child is able to attend school but should be sent to a school with a particular kind of program.

2. The child should be sent to a special day school for socially maladjusted pupils or a residential institution where defendant board of education operates such a school.

3. The child should be instructed at home.

4. The child should be temporarily exempted from school while his parents seek institutional help.

5. The child should receive a medical suspension or exemption.

6. The child should be exempt from school.

If the child has not been attending school or has been attending irregularly, the child may be referred by the district superintendent to the bureau of attendance. If the compulsory school attendance law is not being obeyed, it is the responsibility of the bureau of attendance to take the matter to the family court where the pupil may then be sent to an institution.

In administrative suspense matters it is the general practice of the district superintendent's office to notify the bureau of attendance of a guidance conference. The bureau sends an attendance teacher to the home of the child to notify the parents of the suspense conference and request their appearance at the arranged time.

When, after a guidance conference, the district superintendent decides that a child should be in a special day school for socially maladjusted children, the parents are notified by letter to report to the school with the child. In other words, the cooperation and consent of the parents is thus sought in placing a child in a special day school for socially maladjusted pupils. If the child and his parents do not report for admission and attendance, the principal of the special school notifies the bureau of attendance. The bureau of attendance then petitions the family court to take appropriate action. The defendant board of education maintains and operates seventeen such special day schools throughout New York City.

When there is a decision by the BCG and the district superintendent that a student should receive his schooling in a residential institution where the defendant board of education operates a special school for socially maladjusted children, again parental consent is first sought. The guidance counselor in the district superintendent's office contacts the parents and advises them that in the opinion of the BCG, the school authorities and in the opinion of any other interested social agency that happens to be involved, this child should be institutionalized for an extended period of time.

If the parents "voluntarily" accept the recommendation, steps are then taken for the placement of the child. If the parents do not consent, then the bureau of attendance petitions the family court to place the child in an institution. The defendant board of education does not operate the residential institutions, per se, but the board does operate schools in more than thirty such residential institutions, remand centers, psychiatric hospitals and treatment centers.

Consequences of District Superintendent's Conference

Schools for socially maladjusted pupils (formerly known as "600" schools because of their numerical designation) were established about eighteen years ago. In 1964, there were twenty-seven of these schools with fourteen annexes serving a pupil population of about 5,200. Fourteen of the twenty-seven schools in 1964 were day schools serving about 2,000 pupils from ten to eighteen years of age. The remaining schools were located in hospitals, treatment and remand centers, and residential institutions. Of the fourteen day schools, only one served girls. The other thirteen served boys "whose alleged common characteristics included repeated disruptive and aggressive behavior." The "600" schools located in hospitals, treatment and remand centers and residential institutions are staffed by defendant board of education personnel. These institutions are not owned or operated by the defendant board. The "600" schools are not schools for children with retarded mental development; these children are assigned to special classes known as classes for children with retarded mental development (CRMD). Children with high IQ may be assigned to "600" schools. [An evaluation of these schools, undertaken for the school board, concludes:]

> The present '600' school program attempts to protect regular teachers and students from undue or damaging disruption, and to provide a therapeutic milieu for the disturbed child. But this program *is,* however worthwhile, ethnically segregated, inconveniently located, undersupported, organizationally unstable, and unable to meet the needs of its student body.

If the BCG should recommend that the child be placed in an institution, every possible assistance is given a cooperative parent by the district superintendent to help the parent secure a place in an institution. However, there is a serious problem with respect to a recommendation for institutional placement. The available facilities are severely limited. This means that such placements take time. While the child is awaiting placement in an institution, the BCG may make one of the following recommendations: (1) That the child be given home instruction "if possible"; (2) That the child be suspended pending institutional placement; (3) That the child be exempted from school while he awaits institutional placement. Finally, the district superintendent testified: "if it isn't taking too long, the child *remains* on suspense" pending institutional placement. (Emphasis added). . . .

Statistical records produced by Miss Rakow (for her district only) for attendance periods covering the years 1965 and 1966 and the first month of 1967, show the following:

1. During 1965, some pupils awaited placement in a school for socially maladjusted pupils after being suspended for as long as four to six months.

2. During 1966, some pupils awaited placement in a school for socially maladjusted pupils after being suspended for as long as three months.

3. At the end of January 1967, three pupils were awaiting placement in a school for socially maladjusted pupils. One was in his third month of suspension.

4. During 1965, some students awaited placement in an institution and were on suspension from four to six months.

5. During 1966, some students awaited placement in an institution on suspension from seven to ten months.

6. On January 4, 1967, the records show, one student on suspension from seven to eight months was awaiting institutional placement.

7. On January 4, 1967, the records show, one student was returned to his original school upon being in his second month of suspension and one student was transferred to another school (not a school for socially maladjusted students) upon being on suspension for a period of seven to eight months.

8. In 1965, one student was returned to his original school after an elapse of nine to ten months on suspension. . . .

As a result of a review of the testimony, exhibits and records produced by the district superintendent, this court finds that a "guidance conference" can ultimately result in loss of personal liberty to a child or in a suspension which is the functional equivalent of his expulsion from the public schools or in a withdrawal of his right to attend the public schools. . . .

For the foregoing reasons, this court concludes that the due process clause of the Fourteenth Amendment to the federal constitution is applicable to a district superintendent's guidance conference. More specifically, this court concludes that enforcement by defendants of the "no attorneys provision" of Circular No. 16 deprives plaintiffs of their right to a hearing in a state initiated proceeding which puts in jeopardy the minor plaintiff's liberty and right to attend the public schools.

Due Process and the Right to a Hearing

Serious consequences flow for the juvenile involved in a district superintendent's guidance conference—in many cases without opportunity for subsequent court hearing in which the right to counsel would be present. Proceedings which involve the loss of liberty and the loss of education are of "critical importance" both to the persons involved and to our system of justice. Any such proceeding must meet federal constitutional standards of fairness. . . .

The valuable right to a public school education which New York has made available to all children of the state should not be invaded or denied an individual child without the proper safeguards of procedural fairness. New York has recognized a similar obligation in disciplinary proceedings for state employees . . . and in revocation of state licenses proceedings. . . . How can obligations or procedural fairness be any the less applicable when a child's education is at stake? . . .

Defendants have objected that the presence of an attorney would change a "therapeutic" conference into an adversary proceeding, to the great detriment of any children involved. This court does not agree that this is the necessary consequence of having an attorney present. This court does not by this decision say that a full, judicial style hearing with cross-examination of child witnesses and strict application of the rules of evidence is required. There should be latitude for the board in conducting such a hearing. But this latitude should not be so wide as to preclude the child and parents from exercising their constitutionally protected right to be represented at such a hearing by counsel. . . .

An injunction will, therefore, issue restraining defendants from refusing to proceed immediately with the previously scheduled district superintendent's guidance conference and restraining them from enforcing the "no attorneys provision" of Circular No. 16 (1965-1966) or any similar provisions barring the attendance of attorneys at such conferences if the attorney is selected by the child or his parents as their spokesman.

MADERA v BOARD OF EDUCATION
386 F2d 778 (2d Cir 1967)

Moore, Circuit Judge:
The court below found that "a 'guidance conference' can *ultimately* result in loss of personal liberty to a child or in a suspension which is the functional equivalent of his expulsion from the public schools or in a withdrawal of his right to attend the public schools." . . . The difficulty with this holding is, of course, the word "ultimately." The trial court by a series of hypothetical assumptions, in effect, turned a mere guidance conference relating to Victor's future educational welfare into a quasi-criminal adversary proceeding. The possibilities of Youth House, the Psychiatrist Division of Kings County Hospital or Bellevue Hospital, institutionalization, or attendance enforcement proceedings were mentioned . . . . When, as and if, in the future, Victor or his parents find themselves faced with charges in the family court, there would seem to be adequate safeguards in the law for preservation of their constitutional rights, including the right to counsel. . . . At the most, the guidance conference is a very preliminary investigation, if it can be considered an investigation at all. After the conference, aside from a school reassignment, if any, a whole series of further investigations, hearings and decisions must occur before the child is subjected to any of the "serious consequences" which the district court suggested "flow for the juvenile involved in a district superintendent's guidance conference." . . . The real question is at what point along this chain is the full panoply of due process safeguards to apply. . . .

While it is arguable that in view of the limited character of the action that may be taken, a guidance conference cannot result in a deprivation of "liberty" within the meaning of the Fourteenth Amendment, the contrary will be assumed for present purposes and the question whether the due process clause requires the presence of counsel at such a conference will be considered forthwith. . . .

If due process is applicable to such a conference, it would not follow that the school must permit the presence of counsel. The "differing rules of fair play" encompassed by the concept of due process "[vary] according to specific factual contexts . . . and differing types of proceedings." *Hannah v Larche* 363 US 420, 442 (1960). . . .

What due process may require before a child is expelled from public school or is remanded to a custodial school or other institution which restricts his freedom to come and go as he pleases is not before us.

Appellees here argue that the presence of a lawyer is necessary because it is he "who has the communicative skill to express the position of the student's parents when—because of lack of education, inarticulateness, or simply awe at the array of highly educated and articulate professionals in whose presence they find themselves—they may themselves be unable to do so." . . . However, it does not appear that a lawyer could solve this communication problem. Actually the trial record supports the view, despite some testimony to the contrary . . . , that the social worker, who is allowed to attend the guidance conference, would provide more adequate counsel to the child or the parents than would a lawyer.

Appellees also argue that the presence of counsel is necessary because the decision of the guidance conference depends to a certain degree on the school's statement of the child's misbehavior and that this statement may be incorrect. In the present case there were eleven incidents of misbehavior reported by seven different teachers. The mere attendance of counsel at the conference would do little to aid this problem without also granting the other rights accorded in adversary proceedings—calling of witnesses, cross-examinations, etc. To do so would be destructive of the original purpose of the guidance conference—to provide for the future education of the child. The conference is not a judicial or even a quasi-judicial hearing. Neither the child nor his parents are being accused. In saying that the provision against the presence of an attorney for the pupil in a district superintendent's guidance conference "results in depriving plaintiffs of their constitutionally protected right to a hearing" . . . . The trial court misconceives the function of the conference and the role which the participants therein play with respect to the education and the welfare of the child. Law and order in the classroom should be the responsibility of our respective educational systems. The courts should not usurp this function and turn disciplinary problems, involving suspension, into criminal adversary proceedings—which they definitely are not. The rules, regulations, procedures and practices disclosed on this record evince a high regard for the best interest and welfare of the child. The courts would do well to recognize this. . . .

Judgment reversed; injunction vacated and complaint dismissed.

Notes and Questions

1. Application of Due Process Standards

The trial and appellate courts assess the consequences of a guidance conference quite differently. Which assessment seems more fully to correspond to the facts? Do the two courts apply the same standard in determining whether or not a guidance conference may lead to sufficient injury to warrant the invocation of due process procedures?

For what disputes is it appropriate to require school officials to hold a hearing in which various procedural safeguards are provided: assignment to an art class, when a student preferred mechanical drawing? Seating assignments? Objections to grades? Is it responsive to argue that due process protections apply to all of these situations, but that the nature of the hearing will vary with the gravity of the issue?

2. The Educational-Punitive Distinction

The trial court treats the guidance conference as analogous to a criminal proceeding; the court of appeals views such treatment as misconceiving "the function of the conference and the role which the participants therein play with respect to the education and welfare of the child." 386 F2d at 789. Who has the better of that argument? Is this an argument over the motivation of school officials?

However the guidance conference is described, its consequences vary for the parties at interest—what is best for one may not be suitable for the others. Is not the question for decision simply whether educational opportunities have been diminished and the student needlessly stigmatized? Is the educational-punitive distinction helpful in making this determination?

3. Role of Legal Counsel

Due process is, as the court of appeals' opinion notes, an elastic concept, whose dimensions vary with the nature of the alleged right involved, the nature of the proceeding, and the possible burden of the proceeding. In the student classification context, what might be the role of the lawyer? Will the presence of a lawyer necessarily convert the proceeding into an adversarial hearing? Is the conference in fact adversarial in nature?

Professor Kirp suggests that:

> The utility of a lawyer in classification hearings will depend upon the nature of the issues raised. If the sources of evidence are varied, the evidence itself ambiguous, and the issues complicated or confused, a person with lawyerly qualities can usefully present such evidence in an orderly fashion. The competency and qualifications of the decision maker and the need for lawyer-type advocacy skills are also related: the better the advocacy, the less demanding the decision-making function; the more amateurish the advocacy, the greater the need for control by a competent decision maker, capable of imposing clear ground rules for the proceedings. (Kirp, "Schools as Sorters: The Constitutional and Policy Implications of Student Classification," 121 *U Pa L Rev* 705, 789 (1973).)

Does this variable standard seem sensible? Does it overemphasize the skills of lawyers and underestimate those of other student advocates, *e.g.*, parents or social workers? How might a court employ it, in determining whether a particular classification dispute would be more satisfactorily resolved with a lawyer present? Compare W. Stapleton and L. Teitelbaum, *In Defense of Youth* (1972).

MILLS v BOARD OF EDUCATION
348 F Supp 866 (D D C 1972)*

Waddy, District Judge:

[M]any [of the children excluded from school by the District of Columbia]

---

*The portion of the *Mills* opinion dealing with the substantive constitutional rights of excluded children appears at pp 630-34.

are suspended or expelled from regular schooling or specialized instruction or reassigned without any prior hearing and are given no periodic review thereafter. Due process of law requires a hearing prior to exclusion, termination or classification into a special program. . . .

13. Hearing procedures.

a. Each member of the plaintiff class is to be provided with a publicly supported educational program suited to his needs, within the context of a presumption that among the alternative programs of education, placement in a regular public school class with appropriate ancillary services is preferable to placement in a special school class.

b. Before placing a member of the class in such a program, defendants shall notify his parent or guardian of the proposed educational placement, the reasons therefor, and the right to a hearing before a hearing officer if there is an objection to the placement proposed. . . .

c. Hereinafter, children who are residents of the District of Columbia and are thought by any of the defendants or by officials, parents or guardians, to be in need of a program of special education, shall neither be placed in, transferred from or to, nor denied placement in such a program unless defendants shall have first notified their parents or guardians of such proposed placement, transfer or denial, the reasons therefor, and of the right to a hearing before a hearing officer if there is an objection to the placement, transfer or denial of placement. . . .

e. Whenever defendants take action regarding a child's placement, denial of placement, or transfer . . . the following procedures shall be followed.

(1) Notice required hereinbefore shall be given in writing by registered mail to the parent or guardian of the child.

(2) Such notice shall:
   (a) describe the proposed action in detail;
   (b) clearly state the specific and complete reasons for the proposed action, including the specification of any tests or reports upon which such action is proposed;
   (c) describe any alternative educational opportunities available on a permanent or temporary basis;
   (d) inform the parent or guardian of the right to object to the proposed action at a hearing before the hearing officer;
   (e) inform the parent or guardian that the child is eligible to receive, at no charge, the services of a federally or locally funded diagnostic center for an independent medical, psychological and educational evaluation and shall specify the name, address and telephone number of an appropriate local diagnostic center;
   (f) inform the parent or guardian of the right to be represented at the hearing by legal counsel; to examine the child's school records before the hearing, including any tests or reports upon which the proposed action may be based, to present evidence, including expert medical, psychological and educational testimony; and, to confront and cross-examine any school official, employee, or agent of the school district or public department who may have evidence upon which the proposed action was based

(3) The hearing shall be at a time and place reasonably convenient to such parent or guardian.

(4) The hearing shall be scheduled not sooner than twenty days waivable by parent or child, not later than forty-five days after receipt of a request from the parent or guardian.

(5) The hearing shall be a closed hearing unless the parent or guardian requests an open hearing.

(6) The child shall have the right to a representative of his own choosing, including legal counsel. If a child is unable, through financial inability, to retain counsel, defendants shall advise child's parents or guardians of available voluntary legal assistance. . . .

(7) The decision of the hearing officer shall be based solely upon the evidence presented at the hearing.

(8) Defendants shall bear the burden of proof as to all facts and as to the appropriateness of any placement, denial of placement or transfer.

(9) A tape recording or other record of the hearing shall be made and transcribed and, upon request, made available to the parent or guardian or his representative.

(10) At a reasonable time prior to the hearing, the parent or guardian, or his counsel, shall be given access to all public school system and other public office records pertaining to the child, including any tests or reports upon which the proposed action may be based.

(11) The independent hearing officer shall be an employee of the District of Columbia, but shall not be an officer, employee or agent of the public school system.

(12) The parent or guardian, or his representative, shall have the right to have the attendance of any official, employee or agent of the public school system or any public employee who may have evidence upon which the proposed action may be based and to confront, and to cross-examine any witness testifying for the public school system.

(13) The parent or guardian, or his representative, shall have the right to present evidence and testimony, including expert medical, psychological or educational testimony.

(14) Within thirty days after the hearing, the hearing officer shall render a decision in writing. Such a decision shall include findings of fact and conclusions of law and shall be filed with the board of education and the department of human resources and sent by registered mail to the parent or guardian and his counsel.

(15) Pending a determination by the hearing officer, defendants shall take no action described in paragraphs 13.b. or 13.c., above, if the child's parent or guardian objects to such action. Such objection must be in writing and postmarked within five days of the date of receipt of notification hereinabove described.

Jurisdiction of this matter is retained to allow for implementation, modification and enforcement of this judgment and decree as may be required.

Notes and Questions

1. Scope of Procedural Safeguards

What purpose is served by such procedural safeguards as an independent hearing officer? Access to records? The right to an independent evaluation? Should similar procedures be used in track placement disputes where, for example, a student assigned to a regular track prefers honors placement? In disputes over grading? How do these procedures differ from those that courts have required in student discipline cases? Should they differ?

What is the nature of the burden of proof that the school district bears? Does the district have to demonstrate that (a) X has scored below the IQ cutoff for special education assignment, and thus has been properly placed; (b) while Y might be better served in an intraschool special class, such classes are presently filled, and the district is therefore justified in assigning Y to a residential institution; or (c) Z will in fact benefit from placement in a special program or will benefit more than if assigned to a regular class? Given what is presently known about the efficacy of special programs for slow and mildly handicapped students (see pp 685-88), is the allocation of the burden of proof likely to be decisive? Should it be? Compare *Pennsylvania Ass'n for Retarded Children v Commonwealth* 334 F Supp 1257, 1260 (ED Pa 1971); *Marlega v Board of School Directors* Civil Action 70-C-8 (ED Wisc 1970)(reprinted in Harvard Center for Law and Education, *Classification Materials* (1972)).

2. Impact of Procedural Safeguards

a. Intraschool Impact. Which of these effects seem likely to follow from the adoption of procedural safeguards for student classification?

a. Adherence to formal criteria will increase.

b. Fewer borderline classification decisions will be made.

c. Teachers and special education personnel will resent the requirement that their judgments be subject to outside review.

d. Teachers and school officials will retaliate, in subtle ways, against students intrepid enough to challenge classification decisions.

e. In the face of the burden imposed by proceduralization, school officials will reconsider the general process of classification.

f. Middle class children with assertive and verbal parents will not be misclassified, but poor children with less active parents will receive no additional protection.

On what basis do you estimate these effects? What does your estimate suggest concerning the costs and benefits of proceduralization of student classification? Is your estimate constitutionally relevant?

3. Legitimization

Sociologist Michael Young notes: "Castes or classes are universal, and the measure of harmony that prevails within a society is everywhere dependent upon the degree to which stratification is sanctioned by its code of morality." M. Young, *The Rise of the Meritocracy,* 152 (1961). Does proceduralization in fact render intraschool classification (or stratification) politically more legitimate? If so, is this a good or bad consequence?

4. Legislative Remedies

In 1972, Massachusetts adopted special education regulations that embody detailed procedural protection for students. Placement in special programs must be preceded by a detailed evaluation. Parents of such children are entitled to notice of this evaluation as well as an independent evaluation. If, at the conclusion of this evaluation, the district recommends special placement and the parent objects to the removal of his child from a regular class, the dispute is heard by regional officials of the state department of education. If, at the conclusion of that hearing, the parent continues to reject a recommended special class placement, the student remains in his regular class unless the state trial court finds (after a showing by the school board) that such placement would seriously endanger the health or safety of the child or substantially disrupt the regular program for the other students. If the parents reject the educational placement recommended by the regional officials of the state department of education and desire that their child be placed in a program other than the regular program, the matter is heard again by a state advisory commission on special education, half of whose members are parents. If the parents reject this determination, they may proceed to state trial court, which is empowered to order the placement of the child in an appropriate education program.

In effect, the Massachusetts legislation gives parents a veto power over attempts to remove their children from regular classes; if the parent is sufficiently persistent, only an extraordinary school order can accomplish that result. What is the justification for vesting such authority with parents: the parents' constitutional right to rear their children, noted in *Meyer v Nebraska,* 262 US 390? The policy conclusion that parents know their children's educational needs better than school officials? Why is the burden of persuasion altered when parents seek placement other than regular class assignment?

B. Vouchers

Several states have adopted voucher schemes that enable handicapped youngsters, whose educational needs cannot be adequately met by the public school system, to attend state-regulated private schools at public expense. Those who favor such schemes argue that vouchers may be the only way children with unusual handicaps will receive an education. Those whose interest lies more with vouchers than with the handicapped see these schemes as the beginning of a more general voucher plan, available to all children. Critics of vouchers for the handicapped view the voucher as a means by which the state can avoid what they view as an obligation to develop appropriate public facilities for all youngsters.

1. Legal Framework

McMILLAN v BOARD OF EDUCATION
430 F2d 1145 (2d Cir 1970)

Before Friendly, Smith and Hays, Circuit Judges.
Friendly, Circuit Judge:
[This] action was brought on behalf of three children, Larry McMillan, Steven Fournier and Teddy Sola, all of whom had been diagnosed as having suffered brain injuries.* The defendants were the board of education of New York City;

---

*During the pendency of the suit, plaintiffs Fournier and Sola were placed in special classes and plaintiffs Rodriguez and Earlick attempted to intervene. Rodriguez also was promptly placed in a special class.

Bernard Donovan, then the city's superintendent of schools; Marcus S. Arnold, the city's director of education for the physically handicapped; the New York State Department of Education; and Edward Nyquist, the state's acting commissioner of education. The complaint alleged that, as empowered by §4404 of the state's Education Law,[1] New York City had instituted some 132 classes serving approximately 745 brain-injured children, but that some 309 such children were on the waiting list and that children remained on this for substantial periods. The complaint then referred to §4407, subd. 1 of the Education Law:

§4407. Special provisions relating to instruction of certain handicapped children.

1. When it shall appear to the satisfaction of the department that a handicapped child, who, in the judgment of the department can reasonably be expected to benefit from instruction, is not receiving such instruction because there are no adequate public facilities for instruction of such a child within this state because of the unusual type of the handicap or combination of handicaps, the department is authorized to contract with an educational facility located within or without the state, which, in the judgment of the department, can meet the needs of such child, for instruction of such child in such educational facility, and the department is further authorized to expend for such purpose a sum of not to exceed two thousand dollars per annum for each such pupil. It alleged that Larry McMillan and Teddy Sola had been denied admission to the city's special classes for lack of available space; the complaint was less clear why Steven Fournier was not in a city class. But it did allege that all three plaintiffs had attended private schools; that the tuition was in the neighborhood of $3,000 a year; and that their parents lacked the means to provide the $1,000 required over and above the maximum state grant of $2,000 permitted by §4407.[2] The limit was alleged to deprive plaintiffs of their right to an elementary education in contravention of the equal protection clause of the Fourteenth Amendment. Plaintiffs sought to maintain the suit as a class action on behalf of all persons similarly aggrieved by the city's failure to provide classes adequate for educable brain-injured children and all poor persons similarly aggrieved by the $2,000 limit. The complaint sought temporary and permanent injunctions to prohibit the state department of education and the acting commissioner from enforcing the $2,000 limit, as well as injunctions requiring the three city defendants to provide an adequate number

---

1. The pertinent provisions are:
2. a. The board of education of each city and of each union free school district shall be required to furnish suitable education facilities for handicapped children by means of home teaching, transportation to school or by special classes. The need of the individual child shall determine which of such services shall be rendered. Where there are ten or more handicapped children who can be grouped homogeneously in the same classroom for instructional purposes such board shall establish such special classes as may be necessary to provide instruction adapted to the mental attainments and physical conditions of such children.

b. Provided, however, that in each city or union free school district in which schools for handicapped children exist or may hereafter be established, which are incorporated under the laws of the state and are found by the board of education to be adequate to provide instruction adapted to the mental attainments and physical conditions of such children, the board of education shall not be required to supply additional special classes for the children so provided for. The boards of education of such cities or union free school districts are hereby authorized and empowered to contract with such schools for the education of such children in special classes therein. . . .

2. Larry McMillan's parents receive public assistance.

of special classes and the usual accoutrement of declaratory relief. Since the request for injunctive relief against the state defendants was believed to fall within 28 USC §2281, the plaintiffs asked that a court of three judges be convened. . . .

[T]he [trial] judge concluded that the claim against the state defendants was unsubstantial. Accordingly he declined to ask for a three-judge court and dismissed the complaint as to them. . . .

We deal at the outset with the claim of lack of jurisdiction over the state defendants since if the state is right about this, it would end the matter. . . . There is indeed some difficulty in conceiving that a state officer "subjects" a citizen to the deprivation of constitutional rights within the meaning of the Civil Rights Act when he is not taking action against the citizen but simply is unable to pay him more than a state statute allows, and this seems rather a long way from what the Reconstruction Congress could have had in mind. But the Supreme Court evidently does not regard the point as even meriting discussion. See . . . *Shapiro v Thompson* 394 US 618 (1969); *Dandridge v Williams* 397 US 471 (1970). So we reach the question whether the court was justified in concluding that plaintiffs' claim was unsubstantial "either because it is obviously without merit or because its unsoundness so clearly results from the previous decisions of this court [the Supreme Court] as to foreclose the subject." *California Water Service Co v Redding* 304 US 252, 255 (1938). We do not think so.

We begin by agreeing with the district court that a state does not deny equal protection merely by making the same grant to persons of varying economic need, *Carmichael v Southern Coal & Coke Co* 301 US 495, 518 (1937). We add that if New York had determined to limit its financing of educational activities at the elementary level to maintaining public schools and to make no grants to further the education of children whose handicaps prevented them from participating in classes there, we would perceive no substantial basis for a claim of denial of equal protection. While at first blush the latter proposition might seem decisive in the state's favor, it is not. Nothing in the Constitution, for example, requires a state to provide any system of welfare payments for the indigent, yet if it does establish one, the equal protection clause prevents its discriminating against new residents, *Shapiro v Thompson, supra,* 394 US 618.

The plaintiffs assert that the $2,000 maximum established by §4407 of New York's Education Law on assistance for the private education of a handicapped child not receiving instruction in public schools "because there are no adequate public facilities for instruction of such a child within this state because of the unusual type of the handicap or combination of handicaps," has come to work unfairly[3] in various ways. The most glaring is in a situation like Larry McMillan's whose parents' means do not permit their making any supplementary payment at all. Since the state grant is available only if the child in fact attends a private class, the limitation thus has come to have the doubtless unintended result that the grant, fully available to those whose economic need is less, is unavailable as a practical matter to those whose economic need is greatest. The case differs in this respect from an equal grant to all handicapped children unable to attend public school classes, which is not conditioned on their attending private school.

---

3. We put it this way since it seems to be agreed that when the statute was enacted in 1957, the $2,000 figure was adequate to provide fully for almost all private school instruction of the handicapped.

Mitchell Garlick's mother has managed to eke out sufficient funds to use the grant, and we should not suppose that a substantial equal protection question was presented merely because this is harder on her than on a parent of larger means. But question is raised whether it is consistent with the equal protection clause that she should be required to pay $500 above the $2,000 limit when, as appellants claim in their brief, it would cost the state or its municipalities more than $2,000 to maintain Mitchell in a special class at a public school. Granted that a state which gives financial aid for the private education of handicapped children unable to attend classes in public schools may have to establish some maximum, cf. *Dandridge v Williams, supra,* 397 U S 471, since the cost of private education of a child with a particular constellation of handicaps might be astronomical, is there rational basis for a ceiling lower than the cost that would have been incurred in maintaining the child in the most closely related type of public school class?[5] Lurking behind all this is the unresolved claim that certain children who are qualified for the special classes, as the state asserts Larry and Mitchell are not, are being kept out for lack of space and thereby forced to seek private education at a substantial expense to their parents not entailed for those who have been admitted,[6] and the related issue whether the suit was maintainable as a class action.

In stating these questions, we are not suggesting that they will necessarily be resolved in plaintiffs' favor. The state may well be able to develop sufficient reasons to justify what it has done. We hold merely that the claims were sufficiently substantial to deserve exploration, possibly after the taking of evidence, before a court of three judges. This is a developing area of application of the equal protection clause and questions should not be deemed unsubstantial merely because they might have been so considered twenty years ago when the right-privilege distinction was more highly regarded than it is today.

The cause is remanded to the district judge with instructions that he vacate the judgment dismissing the complaint against the acting commissioner of education and request the chief judge of the circuit to convene a three-judge court.

Notes and Questions

1. The Constitutional Issue

a. Equal educational opportunity. The *McMillan* plaintiffs assert that it is irrational for an educational system to provide greater resources to handicapped students for whom there is space available in a public school program than to those

---

5. The state attempts to avoid this question by pointing out that it is the city's responsibility under §4404 to provide educational facilities and, if these are not provided, the city board of education may issue an order to provide private education, the cost of which is divided between the city and state under §4403. Thus, the state argues, §4407 is a "purely gratuitous remedy" and any disparity between the amount of the *state* grant thereunder and the cost of public school education to the *city* is legally irrelevant. But the point remains that the state has obligated itself under §4407 to provide educational aid for a certain class of handicapped children and there is still the question whether the entire scheme is consistent with the equal protection clause. Cf. *McInnis v Shapiro,* 394 US 322 (1969), *aff'g mem.,* 293 F Supp 327 (ND Ill 1968); Michelman, "On Protecting the Poor Through the Fourteenth Amendment," 83 *Harv L Rev* 7, 47-59 (1969).

6. The city contended that the children whom the complaint described as in this category were simply awaiting necessary examination and screening.

The considerations outlined in fn. 5 are applicable to this point also.

who must obtain private instruction. Would they be satisfied if all handicapped children were treated equally by the school district? Or are plaintiffs arguing that the school system must consider the special needs of all children and place them accordingly, regardless of financial constraints?

The court of appeals notes that: "If New York had determined to limit its financing of educational activities at the elementary level to maintaining public schools and to make no grants to further the education of children whose handicaps prevented them from participating in classes there, we would perceive no substantial basis for a claim of denial of equal protection." 430 F2d at 1149. Is the court's conclusion clearly correct? Is the court suggesting that a school district could exclude children who cannot be educated in regular classes? If so, is the court's conclusion consistent with *PARC* and *Mills* (see pp 630-36)? With *San Antonio Independent School District v Rodriguez* (see pp 583-607)?

b. Wealth Discrimination. The court notes that affluent parents can supplement the $2,000 voucher, but the poor cannot. Of what constitutional relevance is this inequality? The court also notes that the poor are not entitled to a $2,000 voucher unless (i) they can find a private school willing to accept their children for a $2,000 tuition fee, or (ii) they are able to supplement the voucher so that they can meet the higher tuition fee of a private school. How do these facts affect the constitutional issues posed in *McMillan*?

2. Half a Loaf?

Is the *McMillan* court suggesting that, once a state undertakes a tuition voucher program, the vouchers must be adequate to secure a private education? If so, is this sensible policy making? Is it wise to inflict further financial obligations on states that are experimenting with means of meeting the educational needs of the handicapped? Might it discourage states from experimenting with vouchers?

3. The Tactical Issue

The board of education found placements for three of the plaintiffs in *McMillan* shortly after they had filed their complaint. Might the board have done so in order to render the dispute moot? Do the newly placed plaintiffs still have a legal cause of action against the school board?

IN RE H.
66 Misc2d 1097, 323 NYS2d 302 (Fam Ct 1971)

Dachenhausen, Judge.

Marianne H., mother of Peter H., a physically handicapped child almost twelve years of age, seeks by petition . . . an order directing payment of her son's tuition at the Adams School, a nonpublic special educational facility located in New York City.

The yearly tuition at said school is in the sum of $3,600 and the state of New York, pursuant to the provisions of §4407 of the Education Law, paid $2,000 in the form of a tuition grant on behalf of said child for the school year 1970-71. In this proceeding petitioner seeks payment of the balance of the child's tuition for the 1970-71 school year ($1,600) plus the full tuition ($3,600) for the 1971-72 school year, or the total sum of $5,200.

The petition was opposed by the county attorney for Westchester County upon the grounds that special educational services of the type needed by this child were about to be offered by the city of Mt. Vernon Board of Education, commencing in the fall of 1971. . . .

The assistant principal of Adams School informed the court that the balance of the child's tuition for the school year 1970-71 ($1,600) had been covered by an Adams scholarship, leaving open the tuition for 1971-72 school year only.

A boarded psychiatrist, employed by the county of Westchester Community Mental Health Board, as associate director of its special childrens clinic, testified that upon examining the child the clinic diagnosis was entered as organic brain syndrome. This diagnosis indicates a functional impairment in the way the child's central nervous system is working; a disorder or abnormality in the manner he has developed. Since this testimony was not controverted, the court had no difficulty in determining Peter H. to be a physically handicapped child as defined in §232(b) of the Family Court Act.

Marianne H., the petitioner, a recipient of public assistance, testified that Peter had been enrolled for over three and one-half years in special education classes conducted by the Mt. Vernon public school system. . . . At one time or another, her child was placed in the same class with retarded children, emotionally disturbed children and other children who, for one reason or another were not educable in a regular classroom setting. Whether it was because these special classes lacked homogeneity or perhaps for other reasons which were not disclosed, Peter made practically no educational progress for the entire time he was attending public school in Mt. Vernon. This fact was readily admitted by the superintendent of special education for the city of Mt. Vernon, who also testified that his department had made plans to set up a special class for brain-damaged children in the fall of 1971. . . . [H]e could give only a few details of this program but he believed this special class would be adequate to meet Peter's needs.

In contrast to the foregoing, the testimony of the assistant principal of the Adams School, indicated that Peter has received remedial training in depth—had the services of a special reading teacher and a school psychologist on a regular basis; that he has come to like school, has made remarkable progress at school, has gained a great deal of self-confidence and now is much happier with himself.

Article 6, Section 13 of the New York State Constitution delineates the jurisdictional area of family court activity. Although there is no specific mention of proceedings relating to physically handicapped children, subdivision b(1), confers upon the family court jurisdiction over classes of actions and proceedings involving . . . "the protection, treatment, correction and commitment of those minors who are in need of the exercise of the authority of the court because of circumstances of neglect, delinquency or dependency, as the legislature may determine." . . .

The court was very favorably impressed with the testimony concerning the excellent progress the child has made over the past year at the Adams School, where for the first time it appears he may have finally found his niche.

It has been shown to the court's entire satisfaction that if this child is ever to be permitted to develop his intellectual potential and succeed in the academic area, it can be accomplished only in a special educational setting. It has been similarly shown that the Adams School can meet these needs. Whether or not the public school system in Mt. Vernon can do likewise in the coming year remains to be determined.

Realizing that the family court is under a mandate to act in the best interests of this child, the court cannot permit his entire future to be further jeopardized by gambling on a special educational system that has yet to prove itself. Unfortunately, three and a half precious years have already been wasted, which fact serves to further the court's resolve not to switch educational horses at this time. A year hence, upon a similar application, and after considering the conclusions and recommendations of a professional evaluation of this special educational program, it may well be that the court would decide this question against the petitioner. At this time, however, there appears no reasonable alternative to opting in favor of the child continuing his education in the school setting which is at hand and presently achieving good results.

Accordingly, the court sustains the petition and directs that the cost of providing for the special education of said child be paid pursuant to the provisions of § 4403 of the Education Law. Pursuant to this section, an order of the family court must be approved by the commissioner of education before funds will be applied. When so approved, one-half the cost ($1,800) shall be made a charge against the city of Mt. Vernon, wherein the handicapped child resides; the remaining cost ($1,800) shall be paid by the state of New York. Petitioner's inability to contribute to the cost of educating her child is obvious since she is presently receiving public assistance.

Submit order on notice.

Notes and Questions

1. Procedural Issue

The procedure by which the New York Family Court can order special educational services and allocate the cost of those services is "at best, cumbersome, and at worst, unclear and unnecessarily complex." *In re Leitner* 40 App Div 2d 38, 337 NYS2d 267, 272 (1972). As *H* notes, the New York Constitution delineates the general jurisdiction of the family court. The Family Court Act, § 232, gives the court jurisdiction over the special educational training of "a child with retarded mental development." A court order pursuant to that section must be approved by the commissioner of education, who then allocates the cost of providing educational services between the state and the county, each of whom assumes half of the cost "when not otherwise provided by parents, guardians, local authorities or by other sources, public or private." Education Law § 4403.

2. Substantive Issue

Plaintiff did not seek tuition reimbursement before enrolling her son in private school, as § 232 of the Family Court Act contemplates. On what basis does the court order tuition reimbursement after the fact of enrollment? Is the court suggesting that tuition reimbursement is legally appropriate whenever it can be demonstrated that the private school provides better education for handicapped youngsters than does the public school? Is such a holding consistent with the rationale for the New York voucher scheme, noted in *McMillan*? Does *H*. epitomize the appropriate manner for courts to handle classification decisions? That is, should the state courts be given broad discretion to devise a remedy in the child's best interest, rather than to review classification decisions in a constitutional framework?

2. *Voucher Plans in California.* The state of California provides tuition payments for private schooling for five classes of handicapped youngsters: (1) educationally handicapped (i.e., those with learning disabilities or emotional handicaps); (2) physically handicapped; (3) mentally retarded; (4) severely mentally retarded; and (5) multihandicapped. Cal Educ Code §6870. A parent seeking such a voucher must apply to the local school district for tuition payment. Tuition eligibility is determined by assessing the child's handicap and the fiscal feasibility of providing appropriate public educational services. The local district's decision may be appealed to the county superintendent of education and, ultimately, to the state department of education. At present, some 1,500 youngsters receive tuition reimbursement.

The California scheme is flawed in several respects:

a. The standards for eligibility and review are unclear. Thus, a child in district A may receive reimbursement while a child in district B—in all respects identical to the district A child—is denied reimbursement. The fact that one county in the state receives approximately 45 percent of all reimbursements suggests the lack of evenhanded application of criteria.

b. Parents are not informed by school districts of the availability of reimbursement funds; they must learn about the program on their own. Parents are also unrepresented at any stage of the reimbursement review proceeding.

c. The amount of reimbursement varies with the amount that the state and school district would spend on the handicapped child if he were attending public school. This creates two kind of inequities: (1) children from wealthy school districts receive larger reimbursements than do children from poor school districts; and (2) since reimbursement varies by handicap, those who would have relatively little spent on them if they were in public school may be unable to purchase any educational services with the voucher. The reimbursement payment appears to bear little if any relation to actual costs of private education.

d. The private schools that receive "reimbursement" children may charge whatever the traffic will bear, and may refuse admission to children whose handicaps are particularly acute.

How might a voucher scheme free of such defects be structured? Might a California parent legally challenge denial of a request for reimbursement? Denial for a full cost reimbursement? Denial of admission to a private school that accepts "reimbursement" children? On what grounds?

C. Integration (or Mainstreaming) of Slow and Mildly Handicapped Students

Many policy criticisms leveled at traditional classification practice suggest the need to reduce the kind of sorting that presently occurs. The abandonment of sorting seems both undesirable and quixotic: undesirable, because some students do need special help of one kind or another; quixotic, because differentiation among students—indeed, among individuals in the society—serves too many social purposes to admit of ready rejection. Nonetheless, there do exist a variety of educational strategies designed to limit the consequentiality of sorting decisions.

The fashionable educational innovations of the past twenty years—nongraded classes in which students of varied ages progress at their own rate working in small groups; team teaching, in which a given group of students is taught by two or more teachers, each of whom works with a portion of the class at any given time; "open classrooms" patterned after the Leicestershire model—all represent efforts to modify school classifications. None of these abandons the concept of sorting; indeed, the open classroom may well classify more frequently than does the traditional tracking system. But these approaches all afford greater flexibility than does the traditional tracking system. They make the educational program more diverse, while rendering any particular classification less significant and less likely to endure over time. See J. Featherstone, *Schools Where Children Learn* (1971); J. Goodlad and R. Anderson, *The Nongraded Elementary School* (1959); C. Silberman, *Crisis in the Classroom* (1970).

These innovations focus on the so-called normal school population. But, as the pedagogical and social consequences of segregating the mildly handicapped are increasingly questioned, educators have begun to consider means of integrating the mildly handicapped and normal students. Simply abolishing special classes is likely to yield disaster: the students in them need both catch-up help and special help with their particular problems. But that help can be offered as a supplement to the regular program, permitting the student to spend most of his day in the regular classroom. Even for the more seriously handicapped—the trainable mentally retarded, for example—classes such as gym and art can be shared with regular class students. See K. Beery, *Models for Mainstreaming* (1971); *New Directions in Special Education* (R. Jones, ed 1970); Cormany, "Returning Special Education Students to Regular Classes," 48 *Personnel and Guidance J* 641 (1970).

The chief difficulty with this form of integration is that it may not work: it will be resisted by special teachers concerned about their professional security and by regular teachers who lack the skills (or feel that they do) to deal with mildly handicapped youngsters. Professor Gallagher has proposed one modification, thus far untested. Under his scheme, placement of primary school age students in special education classes would require a contract signed between parents and educators. The contract, which would specify clear goals, would run for a maximum of two years, after which time the student would return to regular classes. It would be nonrenewable, or renewable only after full due process hearing. If the contract's goals were not met, parents would be eligible for a special education voucher, provided by the school district. Gallagher, "The Special Education Contract for Mildly Handicapped Children," 38 *Exceptional Children* 527 (1972). Professor Gallagher's proposal borrows from each of the remedies considered in this section: due process, vouchers, and integration. What reactions to such a scheme might be anticipated?

D. Judicial Role

Does the above discussion of remedies suggest that there are judicially manageable remedies for some of the problems considered earlier in this chapter? Do the problems associated with classification seem likely to be impervious to judicial relief?

Judge Bazelon, speaking about judicial competency in the mental health area, has noted:

[D]iffidence in the face of scientific expertise is conduct unbecoming a court. Very few judges are psychiatrists. But equally few are economists, aeronautical engineers, atomic scientists, or marine biologists. For some reason, however, many people seem to accept judicial scrutiny of, say, the effect of a proposed dam on fish life, while they reject similar scrutiny of the effect of psychiatric treatment on human lives. Since it can hardly be that we are more concerned for the salmon than the schizophrenic, I suspect the explanation must lie in our familiarity with judicial supervision of [nonpsychiatric matters] . . . [I] n the law as in all other areas we tend to accept the accustomed and fear the new. . . .

It is often unclear precisely what scope of review is appropriate, or what result such review demands. But the principle of a division of responsibility between administrators skilled in their area and judges skilled in the law is clear and has proved workable. . . . Psychiatrists' disagreements . . . while admittedly of epic proportions . . . do not seem qualitatively different from those among experts in other fields. . . . Nor do judges seem necessarily more ignorant and uneducable in psychiatry than in other fields. The more relevant question is whether judges can hope to learn enough within the narrow compass of cases brought before them to reach constructive decisions. (Bazelon, "Implementing the Right to Treatment," 36 *U Chi L Rev* 742, 743-45 (1969).)

In this context, can education be analogized to mental health? Is Judge Bazelon's defense of the judicial role correct? Are fields such as mental health or education similar to areas where courts have traditionally resolved disputes? Is the knowledge basis—or the nature of "constructive decisions"—different?

Notes and Questions

1. Problem: Midlothian's Special Programs

To a casual visitor, Midlothian seems singularly benighted. The point can be made more gently, but the blunt truth is this: Midlothianites are dumb. Perhaps the problem began a century ago, when the Kallikak and Jukes families moved into town; but whatever the origin of the problem, today the average IQ of a Midlothian school child hovers around 80. The school district—entirely managed by outsiders—has tried valiantly to cope with the problem, creating special programs for every conceivable type of educational shortcoming. The costs of the placement process and the special class program have mushroomed; a taxpayer rebellion suggests that drastic measures are called for. The director of special education has suggested the following possibilities:

(1) To reduce identification and placement costs, all children named Kallikak or Jukes, as well as siblings of all children who have been assigned to special programs, shall be labeled "special program children." The director justifies this measure by noting that, in fact, 85 percent of the children do turn out to be retarded after going through the elaborate screening process; the sibling percentage is 60 percent.

(2) To reduce the cost of maintaining special education programs, the director proposes: (a) to create a single program for all retarded children, whatever their degree of retardation (enrollment predictably would include students with IQs 20-80); (b) to limit enrollment to students who apply, on a first-come, first-served basis, to the existing number of classroom seats set aside for such programs; (c) to put the remainder of the students (a group presently estimated at 5 per cent of the student population) on a waiting list, and excuse them from attending school. Alternatively, the director (a would-be lawyer as well as a social scientist)

proposes that the school district sue the state, demanding that the state—responsible under its constitution for maintaining a "fair and equitable and universal system of public schools, to mold the minds, hearts and spirits of the young"—assume the financial and/or educational burden of educating the retarded of Midlothian.

What legal problems, if any, are raised by the director's proposal? What are its policy implications?

Appendix:
United States Constitution

PREAMBLE

We the People of the United States, in Order to form a more perfect Union, establish Justice, insure domestic Tranquility, provide for the common defence, promote the general Welfare, and secure the Blessings of Liberty to ourselves and our Posterity, do ordain and establish this Constitution for the United States of America.

ARTICLE I

Section 1.   All legislative Powers herein granted shall be vested in a Congress of the United States, which shall consist of a Senate and House of Representatives.

Section 2.   The House of Representatives shall be composed of Members chosen every second Year by the People of the several States, and the Electors in each State shall have the Qualifications requisite for Electors of the most numerous Branch of the State Legislature.

No Person shall be a Representative who shall not have attained to the Age of twenty five Years, and been seven Years a Citizen of the United States, and who shall not, when elected, be an Inhabitant of that State in which he shall be chosen.

Representatives and direct Taxes shall be apportioned among the several States which may be included within this Union, according to their respective Numbers, which shall be determined by adding to the whole Number of free Persons, including those bound to Service for a Term of Years, and excluding Indians not taxed, three fifths of all other Persons.   The actual Enumeration shall be made within three Years after the first Meeting of the Congress of the United States, and within every subsequent Term of ten Years, in such Manner as they shall by Law direct.   The Number of Representatives shall not exceed one for every thirty Thousand, but each State shall have at Least one Representative; and until such enumeration shall be made, the State of New Hampshire shall be entitled to chuse three, Massachusetts eight, Rhode Island and Providence Plantations one, Connecticut five, New York six, New Jersey four, Pennsylvania eight, Delaware one, Maryland six, Virginia ten, North Carolina five, South Carolina five, and Georgia three.

When vacancies happen in the Representatives from any State, the Executive Authority thereof shall issue Writs of Election to fill such Vacancies.

The House of Representation shall chuse their Speaker and other Officers; and shall have the sole Power of Impeachment.

Section 3.   The Senate of the United States shall be composed of two Senators from each State, chosen by the Legislature thereof, for six Years; and each Senator shall have one Vote.

Immediately after they shall be assembled in Consequence of the first Election, they shall be divided as equally as may be into three Classes. The Seats of the Senators of the first Class shall be vacated at the Expiration of the Second Year, of the second Class at the Expiration of the fourth Year, and of the third Class at the Expiration of the sixth Year, so that one third may be chosen every second Year; and if Vacancies happen by Resignation, or otherwise, during the Recess of the Legislature of any State, the Executive thereof may make temporary Appointments until the next Meeting of the Legislature, which shall then fill such Vacancies.

No Person shall be a Senator who shall not have attained to the Age of thirty Years, and been nine Years a Citizen of the United States, and who shall not, when elected, be an Inhabitant of that State for which he shall be chosen.

The Vice President of the United States shall be President of the Senate, but shall have no Vote, unless they be equally divided.

The Senate shall chuse their other Officers, and also a President pro tempore, in the Absence of the Vice President, or when he shall exercise the Office of President of the United States.

The Senate shall have the sole Power to try all Impeachments. When sitting for that Purpose, they shall be on Oath or Affirmation. When the President of the United States is tried, the Chief Justice shall preside: And no Person shall be convicted without the Concurrence of two thirds of the Members present.

Judgment in Cases of Impeachment shall not extend further than to removal from Office, and disqualification to hold and enjoy any Office of honor, Trust, or Profit under the United States: but the Party convicted shall nevertheless be liable and subject to Indictment, Trial, Judgment, and Punishment, according to Law.

Section 4.   The Times, Places and Manner of holding Elections for Senators and Representatives, shall be prescribed in each State by the Legislature thereof; but the Congress may at any time by Law make or alter such Regulations, except as to the Places of chusing Senators.

The Congress shall assemble at least once in every Year, and such Meeting shall be on the first Monday in December, unless they shall by Law appoint a different Day.

Section 5.   Each House shall be the Judge of the Elections, Returns, and Qualifications of its own Members, and a Majority of each shall constitute a Quorum to do Business; but a smaller Number may adjourn from day to day, and may be authorized to compel the Attendance of absent

Members, in such Manner, and under such Penalties as each House may provide.

Each House may determine the Rules of its Proceedings, punish its Members for disorderly Behavior, and, with the Concurrence of two thirds, expel a Member.

Each House shall keep a Journal of its Proceedings, and from time to time publish the same, excepting such Parts as may in their Judgment require Secrecy; and the Yeas and Nays of the Members of either House on any question shall, at the Desire of one fifth of those Present, be entered on the Journal.

Neither House, during the Session of Congress, shall, without the Consent of the other, adjourn for more than three days, nor to any other Place than that in which the two Houses shall be sitting.

Section 6.   The Senators and Representatives shall receive a Compensation for their Services, to be ascertained by Law, and paid out of the Treasury of the United States.   They shall in all Cases, except Treason, Felony and Breach of the Peace, be privileged from Arrest during their Attendance at the Session of their respective Houses, and in going to and returning from the same; and for any Speech or Debate in either House, they shall not be questioned in any other Place.

No Senator or Representative shall, during the Time for which he was elected, be appointed to any civil Office under the Authority of the United States, which shall have been created, or the Emoluments whereof shall have been increased during such time; and no Person holding any Office under the United States, shall be a Member of either House during his Continuance in Office.

Section 7.   All Bills for raising Revenue shall originate in the House of Representatives; but the Senate may propose or concur with Amendments as on other Bills.

Every Bill which shall have passed the House of Representatives and the Senate, shall, before it become a Law, be presented to the President of the United States; If he approve he shall sign it, but if not he shall return it, with his Objections to the House in which it shall have originated, who shall enter the Objections at large on their Journal, and proceed to reconsider it.   If after such Reconsideration two thirds of that House shall agree to pass the Bill, it shall be sent together with the Objections, to the other House, by which it shall likewise be reconsidered, and if approved by two thirds of that House, it shall become a Law.   But in all such Cases the Votes of both Houses shall be determined by yeas and Nays, and the Names of the Persons voting for and against the Bill shall be entered on the Journal of each House respectively.   If any Bill shall not be returned by the President within ten Days (Sundays excepted) after it shall have been presented to him, the Same shall be a Law, in like Manner as if he had signed it, unless the Congress by their Adjournment prevent its Return in which Case it shall not be a Law.

Every Order, Resolution, or Vote, to Which the Concurrence of the Senate and House of Representatives may be necessary (except on a question of Adjournment) shall be presented to the President of the United

States; and before the Same shall take Effect, shall be approved by him, or being disapproved by him, shall be repassed by two thirds of the Senate and House of Representatives, according to the Rules and Limitations prescribed in the Case of a Bill.

Section 8.   The Congress shall have Power To lay and collect Taxes, Duties, Imposts and Excises, to pay the Debts and provide for the common Defence and general Welfare of the United States; but all Duties, Imposts and Excises shall be uniform throughout the United States;

To borrow money on the credit of the United States;

To regulate Commerce with foreign Nations, and among the several States, and with the Indian Tribes;

To establish an uniform Rule of Naturalization, and uniform Laws on the subject of Bankruptcies throughout the United States;

To coin Money, regulate the Value thereof, and of foreign Coin, and fix the Standard of Weights and Measures;

To provide for the Punishment of counterfeiting the Securities and current Coin of the United States;

To Establish Post Offices and Post Roads;

To promote the Progress of Science and useful Arts, by securing for limited Times to Authors and Inventors the exclusive Right to their respective Writings and Discoveries;

To constitute Tribunals inferior to the supreme Court;

To define and punish Piracies and Felonies committed on the high Seas, and Offenses against the Law of Nations:

To declare War, grant Letters of Marque and Reprisal, and make Rules concerning Captures on Land and Water;

To raise and support Armies, but no Appropriation of Money to that Use shall be for a longer Term than two Years;

To provide and maintain a Navy;

To make Rules for the Government and Regulation of the land and naval Forces;

To provide for calling forth the Militia to execute the Laws of the Union, suppress Insurrections and repel Invasions;

To provide for organizing, arming, and disciplining, the Militia, and for governing such Part of them as may be employed in the Service of the United States, reserving to the States respectively, the Appointment of the Officers, and the Authority of training the Militia according to the discipline prescribed by Congress;

To exercise exclusive Legislation in all Cases whatsoever, over such District (not exceeding ten Miles square) as may, by Cession of particular States, and the Acceptance of Congress, become the Seat of the Government of the United States, and to exercise like Authority over all Places purchased by the Consent of the Legislature of the State in which the Same shall be, for the Erection of Forts, Magazines, Arsenals, dock-Yards, and other needful Buildings;—And

To make all Laws which shall be necessary and proper for carrying into Execution the foregoing Powers, and all other Powers vested by this Constitution in the Government of the United States, or in any Department or Officer thereof.

Section 9.   The Migration or Importation of Such Persons as any of the States now existing shall think proper to admit, shall not be prohibited by the Congress prior to the Year one thousand eight hundred and eight, but a Tax or duty may be imposed on such Importation, not exceeding ten dollars for each Person.

The privilege of the Writ of Habeas Corpus shall not be suspended, unless when in Cases of Rebellion or Invasion the public Safety may require it.

No Bill of Attainder or ex post facto Law shall be passed.

No Capitation, or other direct, Tax shall be laid, unless in Proportion to the Census or Enumeration herein before directed to be taken.

No Tax or Duty shall be laid on Articles exported from any State.

No Preference shall be given by any Regulation of Commerce or Revenue to the Ports of one State over those of another: nor shall Vessels bound to, or from, one State be obliged to enter, clear, or pay Duties in another.

No money shall be drawn from the Treasury, but in Consequence of Appropriations made by Law; and a regular Statement and Account of the Receipts and Expenditures of all public Money shall be published from time to time.

No Title of Nobility shall be granted by the United States: And no Person holding any Office of Profit or Trust under them, shall, without the Consent of the Congress, accept of any present, Emolument, Office, or Title, of any kind whatever, from any King, Prince, or foreign State.

Section 10.   No State shall enter into any Treaty, Alliance, or Confederation; grant Letters of Marque and Reprisal; coin Money; emit Bills of Credit; make any Thing but gold and silver Coin a Tender in Payment of Debts; pass any Bill of Attainder, ex post facto Law, or Law impairing the Obligation of Contracts, or grant any Title of Nobility.

No State shall, without the Consent of the Congress, lay any Imposts or Duties on Imports or Exports, except what may be absolutely necessary for executing it's inspection Laws: and the net Produce of all Duties and Imposts, laid by any State on Imports or Exports, shall be for the Use of the Treasury of the United States; and all such Laws shall be subject to the Revision and Controul of the Congress.

No State shall, without the Consent of Congress, lay any Duty of Tonnage, keep Troops, or Ships of War in time of Peace, enter into any Agreement or Compact with another State, or with a foreign Power, or engage in War, unless actually invaded, or in such imminent Danger as will not admit of delay.

Article II

Section 1.   The executive Power shall be vested in a President of the United States of America. He shall hold his Office during the Term of four Years, and, together with the Vice President, chosen for the same Term, be elected, as follows:

Each State shall appoint, in such Manner as the Legislature thereof may direct, a Number of Electors, equal to the whole Number of Senators and Representatives to which the State may be entitled in the Congress; but no Senator or Representative, or Person holding an Office of Trust or Profit under the United States, shall be appointed an Elector.

The Electors shall meet in their respective States, and vote by Ballot for two Persons, of whom one at least shall not be an Inhabitant of the same State with themselves. And they shall make a List of all the Persons voted for, and of the Number of Votes for each; which List they shall sign and certify, and transmit sealed to the Seat of the Government of the United States, directed to the President of the Senate. The President of the Senate shall, in the Presence of the Senate and House of Representatives, open all the Certificates, and the Votes shall then be counted. The Person having the greatest Number of Votes shall be the President, if such Number be a Majority of the whole Number of Electors appointed; and if there be more than one who have such Majority, and have an equal Number of Votes, then the House of Representatives shall immediately chuse by Ballot one of them for President; and if no Person have a Majority, then from the five highest on the List the said House shall in like Manner chuse the President. But in chusing the President, the Votes shall be taken by States the Representation from each State having one Vote; A quorum for this Purpose shall consist of a Member or Members from two thirds of the States, and a Majority of all the States shall be necessary to a Choice. In every Case, after the Choice of the President, the Person having the greater Number of Votes of the Electors shall be the Vice President. But if there should remain two or more who have equal Votes, the Senate shall chuse from them by Ballot the Vice President.

The Congress may determine the Time of chusing the Electors, and the Day on which they shall give their Votes; which Day shall be the same throughout the United States.

No person except a natural born Citizen, or a Citizen of the United States, at the time of the Adoption of this Constitution, shall be eligible to the Office of President; neither shall any Person be eligible to that Office who shall not have attained to the Age of thirty five Years, and been fourteen Years a Resident within the United States.

In case of the removal of the President from Office, or of his Death, Resignation or Inability to discharge the Powers and Duties of the said Office, the Same shall devolve on the Vice President, and the Congress may by Law provide for the Case of Removal, Death, Resignation or Inability, both of the President and Vice President, declaring what Officer shall then act as President, and such Officer shall act accordingly, until the Disability be removed, or a President shall be elected.

The President shall, at stated Times, receive for his Services, a Compensation, which shall neither be increased nor diminished during the Period for which he shall have been elected, and he shall not receive within that Period any other Emolument from the United States, or any of them.

Before he enter on the Execution of his Office, he shall take the following Oath or Affirmation: "I do solemnly swear (or affirm) that I will faithfully execute the Office of President of the United States, and will to the best of my Ability, preserve, protect and defend the Constitution of the United States."

Section 2.   The President shall be Commander in Chief of the Army and Navy of the United States, and of the militia of the several States, when called into the actual Service of the United States; he may require the Opinion, in writing, of the principal Officer in each of the Executive Departments, upon any Subject relating to the Duties of their respective Offices, and he shall have Power to grant Reprieves and Pardons for Offenses against the United States, except in Cases of Impeachment.

He shall have Power, by and with the Advice and Consent of the Senate to make Treaties, provided two thirds of the Senators present concur; and he shall nominate, and by and with the Advice and Consent of the Senate, shall appoint Ambassadors, other public Ministers and Consuls, Judges of the supreme Court, and all other Officers of the United States, whose Appointments are not herein otherwise provided for, and which shall be established by Law; but the Congress may by Law vest the Appointment of such inferior Officers, as they think proper, in the President alone, in the Courts of Law, or in the Heads of Departments.

The President shall have Power to fill up all Vacancies that may happen during the Recess of the Senate, by granting Commissions which shall expire at the End of their next Session.

Section 3. He shall from time to time give to the Congress Information of the State of the Union, and recommend to their Consideration such Measures as he shall judge necessary and expedient; he may, on extraordinary Occasions, convene both Houses, or either of them, and in Case of Disagreement between them, with Respect to the Time of Adjournment, he may adjourn them to such Time as he shall think proper; he shall receive Ambassadors and other public Ministers; he shall take Care that the Laws be faithfully executed, and shall Commission all the Officers of the United States.

Section 4. The President, Vice President and all civil Officers of the United States, shall be removed from Office on Impeachment for, and Conviction of, Treason, Bribery, or other high Crimes and Misdemeanors.

ARTICLE III

Section 1. The judicial Power of the United States, shall be vested in one supreme Court, and in such inferior Courts as the Congress may from time to time ordain and establish. The Judges, both of the supreme and inferior Courts, shall hold their Offices during good Behaviour, and shall, at stated Times, receive for their Services a Compensation, which shall not be diminished during their Continuance in Office.

Section 2.   The judicial Power shall extend to all Cases, in Law and Equity, arising under this Constitution, the Laws of the United States, and Treaties made, or which shall be made, under their Authority;—to all Cases affecting Ambassadors, other public Ministers and Consuls;—to all Cases of admiralty and maritime Jurisdiction;—to Controversies to which the United States shall be a Party;—to Controversies between two or more States;—between a State and Citizens of another State;—between Citizens of different States;—between Citizens of the same State claiming Lands under the Grants of different States, and between a State, or the Citizens thereof, and foreign States, Citizens or Subjects.

In all Cases affecting Ambassadors, other public Ministers and Consuls, and those in which a State shall be a Party, the supreme Court shall have original Jurisdiction. In all the other Cases before mentioned, the supreme Court shall have appellate Jurisdiction, both as to Law and Fact, with such Exceptions, and under such Regulations as the Congress shall make.

The trial of all Crimes, except in Cases of Impeachment, shall be by Jury; and such Trial shall be held in the State where the said Crimes shall have been committed; but when not committed within any State, the Trial shall be at such Place or Places as the Congress may by Law have directed.

Section 3.   Treason against the United States, shall consist only in levying War against them, or, in adhering to their Enemies, giving them Aid and Comfort. No Person shall be convicted of Treason unless on the Testimony of two Witnesses to the same overt Act, or on Confession in open Court.

The Congress shall have Power to declare the Punishment of Treason, but no Attainder of Treason shall work Corruption of Blood, or Forfeiture except during the Life of the Person attainted.

ARTICLE IV

Section 1. Full Faith and Credit shall be given in each State to the public Acts, Records, and judicial Proceedings of every other State. And the Congress may by general Laws prescribe the Manner in which such Acts, Records and Proceedings shall be proved, and the Effect thereof.

Section 2.   The Citizens of each State shall be entitled to all Privileges and Immunities of Citizens in the several States.

A Person charged in any State with Treason, Felony, or other Crime, who shall flee from Justice, and be found in another State, shall on demand of the executive Authority of the State from which he fled, be delivered up, to be removed to the State having Jurisdiction of the Crime.

No Person held to Service or Labour in one State, under the Laws thereof, escaping into another, shall, in Consequence of any Law or Regulation therein, be discharged from such Service or Labour, but shall be delivered up on Claim of the Party to whom such Service or Labour may be due.

Section 3.   New States may be admitted by the Congress into this

Union; but no new State shall be formed or erected within the Jurisdiction of any other State; nor any State be formed by the Junction of two or more States, or Parts of States, without the Consent of the Legislatures of the States concerned as well as of the Congress.

The Congress shall have Power to dispose of and make all needful Rules and Regulations respecting the Territory or other Property belonging to the United States; and nothing in this Constitution shall be so construed as to Prejudice any Claims of the United States, or of any particular State.

Section 4. The United States shall guarantee to every State in this Union a Republican Form of Government, and shall protect each of them against Invasion; and on Application of the Legislature, or of the Executive (when the Legislature cannot be convened) against domestic Violence.

ARTICLE V

The Congress, whenever two thirds of both Houses shall deem it necessary, shall propose Amendments to this Constitution, or, on the Application of the Legislatures of two thirds of the several States, shall call a Convention for proposing Amendments, which, in either Case, shall be valid to all Intents and Purposes, as part of this Constitution, when ratified by the Legislatures of three fourths of the several States, or by Conventions in three fourths thereof, as the one or the other Mode of Ratification may be proposed by the Congress; Provided that no Amendment which may be made prior to the Year One thousand eight hundred and eight shall in any Manner affect the first and fourth Clauses in the Ninth Section of the first Article; and that no State, without its Consent, shall be deprived of its equal Suffrage in the Senate.

ARTICLE VI

All Debts contracted and Engagements entered into, before the Adoption of this Constitution shall be as valid against the United States under this Constitution, as under the Confederation.

This Constitution, and the Laws of the United States which shall be made in Pursuance thereof; and all Treaties made, or which shall be made, under the Authority of the United States, shall be the supreme Law of the Land; and the Judges in every State shall be bound thereby, any Thing in the Constitution or Laws of any State to the Contrary notwithstanding.

The Senators and Representatives before mentioned, and the Members of the several State Legislatures, and all executive and judicial Officers, both of the United States and of the several States, shall be bound by Oath or Affirmation, to support this Constitution; but no religious Test shall ever be required as a Qualification to any Office or public Trust under the United States.

Article VII

The Ratification of the Conventions of nine States shall be sufficient for the Establishment of this Constitution between the States so ratifying the Same.

ARTICLES IN ADDITION TO, AND AMENDMENT OF, THE CONSTITUTION OF THE UNITED STATES OF AMERICA, PROPOSED BY CONGRESS, AND RATIFIED BY THE LEGISLATURES OF THE SEVERAL STATES PURSUANT TO THE FIFTH ARTICLE OF THE ORIGINAL CONSTITUTION.

Amendment I [1791]

Congress shall make no law respecting an establishment of religion, or prohibiting the free exercise thereof; or abridging the freedom of speech, or of the press; or the right of the people peaceably to assemble, and to petition the Government for a redress of grievances.

Amendment II [1791]

A well regulated Militia, being necessary to the security of a free State, the right of the people to keep and bear Arms, shall not be infringed.

Amendment III [1791]

No Soldier shall, in time of peace be quartered in any house, without the consent of the Owner, nor in time of war, but in a manner to be prescribed by law.

Amendment IV [1791]

The right of the people to be secure in their persons, houses, papers, and effects, against unreasonable searches and seizures, shall not be violated, and no Warrants shall issue, but upon probable cause, supported by Oath or affirmation, and particularly describing the place to be searched, and the persons or things to be seized.

Amendment V [1791]

No person shall be held to answer for a capital, or otherwise infamous crime, unless on a presentment or indictment of a Grand Jury, except in cases arising in the land or naval forces, or in the Militia, when in actual service in time of War or public danger; nor shall any person be subject for the same offence to be twice put in jeopardy of life or limb; nor shall be compelled in any criminal case to be a witness against himself, nor be deprived of life, liberty, or property, without due process of law; nor shall private property be taken for public use, without just compensation.

Amendment VI [1791]

In all criminal prosecutions, the accused shall enjoy the right to a speedy and public trial, by an impartial jury of the State and district wherein the crime shall have been committed, which district shall have been previously ascertained by law, and to be informed of the nature and cause of the accusation; to be confronted with the witnesses against him; to have compulsory process for obtaining witnesses in his favor, and to have the Assistance of Counsel for his defence.

Amendment VII [1791]

In Suits at common law, where the value in controversy shall exceed twenty dollars, the right of trial by jury shall be preserved, and no fact tried by jury, shall be otherwise re-examined in any Court of the United States, than according to the rules of the common law.

Amendment VIII [1791]

Excessive bail shall not be required, nor excessive fines imposed, nor cruel and unusual punishments inflicted.

Amendment IX [1791]

The enumeration in the Constitution, of certain rights, shall not be construed to deny or disparage others retained by the people.

Amendment X [1791]

The powers not delegated to the United States by the Constitution, nor prohibited by it to the States, are reserved to the States respectively, or to the people.

Amendment XI [1798]

The Judicial power of the United States shall not be construed to extend to any suit in law or equity, commenced or prosecuted against one of the United States by Citizens of another State, or by Citizens or Subjects of any Foreign State.

Amendment XII [1804]

The Electors shall meet in their respective states and vote by ballot for President and Vice-President, one of whom, at least, shall not be an inhabitant of the same state with themselves; they shall name in their ballots the person voted for as President, and in distinct ballots the person voted for as Vice-President, and they shall make distinct lists of all persons voted for as President, and of all persons voted for as Vice-President, and of the number of votes for each, which lists they shall sign and certify, and transmit sealed to the seat of the government of the United States, directed to the President of the Senate;—The President of the Senate shall, in the presence of the Senate and House of Representatives, open all the certificates and the votes shall then be counted;—The person having the greatest number of votes for President, shall be the President, if such number be a majority of the whole number of Electors appointed; and if no person have such majority, then from the persons having the highest numbers not exceeding three on the list of those voted for as President, the House of Representatives shall choose immediately, by ballot, the President. But in choosing the President, the votes shall be taken by states, the representation from each state having one vote; a quorum for this purpose shall consist of a member or members from two-thirds of the states, and a majority of all the states shall be necessary to a choice. And if the House of Representatives shall not choose a President whenever the right of choice shall devolve upon them before the fourth day of March next following, then the Vice-President shall act as President, as in the case of the death or other constitutional disability of the President.— The person having the greatest number of votes as Vice-President, shall be the Vice-President, if such number be a majority of the whole number of Electors appointed, and if no person have a majority, then from the two highest numbers on the list, the Senate shall choose the Vice-President; a quorum for the purpose shall consist of two-thirds of the whole number of Senators, and a majority of the whole number shall be necessary to a choice. But no person constitutionally ineligible to the office of President shall be eligible to that of Vice-President of the United States.

AMENDMENT XIII [1865]

Section 1. Neither slavery nor involuntary servitude, except as a punishment for crime whereof the party shall have been duly convicted, shall exist within the United States, or any place subject to their jurisdiction.

Section 2. Congress shall have power to enforce this article by appropriate legislation.

AMENDMENT XIV [1868]

Section 1. All persons born or naturalized in the United States, and subject to the jurisdiction thereof, are citizens of the United States and of the State wherein they reside. No State shall make or enforce any law which shall abridge the privileges or immunities of citizens of the United States; nor shall any State deprive any person of life, liberty, or property, without due process of law; nor deny to any person within its jurisdiction the equal protection of the laws.

Section 2. Representatives shall be apportioned among the several States according to their respective numbers, counting the whole number of persons in each State, excluding Indians not taxed. But when the right to vote at any election for the choice of electors for President and Vice President of the United States, Representatives in Congress, the Executive and Judicial officers of a State, or the members of the Legislature thereof, is denied to any of the male inhabitants of such State, being twenty-one years of age, and citizens of the United States, or in any way abridged, except for participation in rebellion, or other crime, the basis of representation therein shall be reduced in the proportion which the number of such male citizens shall bear to the whole number of male citizens twenty-one years of age in such State.

Section 3. No person shall be a Senator or Representative in Congress, or elector of President and Vice President, or hold any office, civil or military, under the United States, or under any State, who having previously taken an oath, as a member of Congress, or as an officer of the United States, or as a member of any State legislature, or as an executive or judicial officer of any State, to support the Constitution of the United States, shall have engaged in insurrection or rebellion against the same, or given aid or comfort to the enemies thereof. But Congress may by a vote of two-thirds of each House, remove such disability.

Section 4. The validity of the public debt of the United States, authorized by law, including debts incurred for payment of pensions and bounties for services in suppressing insurrection or rebellion, shall not be questioned. But neither the United States nor any State shall assume or pay any debt or obligation incurred in aid of insurrection or rebellion against the United States, or any claim for the loss or emancipation of any slave; but all such debts, obligations and claims shall be held illegal and void.

Section 5. The Congress shall have power to enforce, by appropriate legislation, the provisions of this article.

AMENDMENT XV [1870]

Section 1. The right of citizens of the United States to vote shall not be denied or abridged by the United States or by any State on account of race, color, or previous condition of servitude.

Section 2. The Congress shall have power to enforce this article by appropriate legislation.

AMENDMENT XVI [1913]

The Congress shall have power to lay and collect taxes on incomes, from whatever source derived, without apportionment among the several States, and without regard to any census or enumeration.

AMENDMENT XVII [1913]

The Senate of the United States shall be composed of two Senators from each State, elected by the people thereof, for six years; and each Senator shall have one vote. The electors in each State shall have the qualifications requisite for electors of the most numerous branch of the State legislatures.

When vacancies happen in the representation of any State in the Senate, the executive authority of such State shall issue writs of election to fill such vacancies: *Provided*, That the legislature of any State may empower the executive thereof to make temporary appointments until the people fill the vacancies by election as the legislature may direct.

This amendment shall not be so construed as to affect the election or term of any Senator chosen before it becomes valid as part of the Constitution.

Amendment XVIII [1919]

Section 1.   After one year from the ratification of this article the manufacture, sale, or transportation of intoxicating liquors within, the importation thereof into, or the exportation thereof from the United States and all territory subject to the jurisdiction thereof for beverage purposes is hereby prohibited.

Section 2.   The Congress and the several States shall have concurrent power to enforce this article by appropriate legislation.

Section 3.   This article shall be inoperative unless it shall have been ratified as an amendment to the Constitution by the legislatures of the several States, as provided in the Constitution, within seven years from the date of the submission hereof to the States by the Congress.

Amendment XIX [1920]

The right of citizens of the United States to vote shall not be denied or abridged by the United States or by any State on account of sex.

Congress shall have power to enforce this article by appropriate legislation.

Amendment XX [1933]

Section 1.   The terms of the President and Vice President shall end at noon on the 20th day of January, and the terms of Senators and Representatives at noon on the 3d day of January, of the years in which such terms would have ended if this article had not been ratified; and the terms of their successors shall then begin.

Section 2.   The Congress shall assemble at least once in every year, and such meeting shall begin at noon on the 3d day of January, unless they shall by law appoint a different day.

Section 3.   If, at the time fixed for the beginning of the term of the President, the President elect shall have died, the Vice President elect shall become President.   If the President shall not have been chosen before the time fixed for the beginning of his term, or if the President elect shall have failed to qualify, then the Vice President elect shall act as President until a President shall have qualified; and the Congress may by law provide for the case wherein neither a President elect nor a Vice President elect shall have qualified, declaring who shall then act as President, or the manner in which one who is to act shall be selected, and such person shall act accordingly until a President or Vice President shall have qualified.

Section 4.   The Congress may by law provide for the case of the death of any of the persons from whom the House of Representatives may choose a President whenever the right of choice shall have devolved upon them, and for the case of the death of any of the persons from whom the Senate may choose a Vice President whenever the right of choice shall have devolved upon them.

Section 5.   Sections 1 and 2 shall take effect on the 15th day of October following the ratification of this article.

Section 6.   This article shall be inoperative unless it shall have been ratified as an amendment to the Constitution by the legislatures of three-fourths of the several States within seven years from the date of its submission.

Amendment XXI [1933]

Section 1.   The eighteenth article of amendment to the Constitution of the United States is hereby repealed.

Section 2.   The transportation or importation into any State, Territory, or possession of the United States for delivery or use therein of intoxicating liquors, in violation of the laws thereof, is hereby prohibited.

Section 3.   This article shall be inoperative unless it shall have been ratified as an amendment to the Constitution by conventions in the several States, as provided in the Constitution, within seven years from the date of the submission hereof to the States by the Congress.

Amendment XXII [1951]

Section 1.   No person shall be elected to the office of the President more than twice, and no person who has held the office of President, or acted as President, for more than two years of a term to which some other person was elected President shall be elected to the office of President more than once.   But this Article shall not apply to any person holding the office of President when this Article was proposed by the Congress, and shall not prevent any person who may be holding the office of President, or acting as President, during the term within which this Article becomes operative from holding the office of President or acting as President during the remainder of such term.

Section 2.   This article shall be inoperative unless it shall have been ratified as an amendment to the Constitution by the legislatures of three-fourths of the several States within seven years from the date of its submission to the States by the Congress.

Amendment XXIII [1961]

Section 1.   The District constituting the seat of Government of the United States shall appoint in such manner as the Congress may direct:

A number of electors of President and Vice President equal to the whole number of Senators and Representatives in Congress to which the District would be entitled if it were a State, but in no event more than the least populous state; they shall be in addition to those appointed by the states, but they shall be considered, for the purposes of the election of President and Vice President, to be electors appointed by a state; and they shall meet in the District and perform such duties as provided by the twelfth article of amendment.

Section 2.   The Congress shall have power to enforce this article by appropriate legislation.

Amendment XXIV [1964]

Section 1. The right of citizens of the United States to vote in any primary or other election for President or Vice President, for electors for President or Vice President, or for Senator or Representative in Congress, shall not be denied or abridged by the United States or any State by reason of failure to pay any poll tax or other tax.

Section 2. The Congress shall have power to enforce this article by appropriate legislation.

Amendment XXV [1967]

Section 1. In case of the removal of the President from office or of his death or resignation, the Vice President shall become President.

Section 2. Whenever there is a vacancy in the office of the Vice President, the President shall nominate a Vice President who shall take office upon confirmation by a majority vote of both Houses of Congress.

Section 3. Whenever the President transmits to the President pro tempore of the Senate and the Speaker of the House of Representatives his written declaration that he is unable to discharge the powers and duties of his office, and until he transmits to them a written declaration to the contrary, such powers and duties shall be discharged by the Vice President as Acting President.

Section 4. Whenever the Vice President and a majority of either the principal officers of the executive departments or of such other body as Congress may by law provide, transmit to the President pro tempore of the Senate and the Speaker of the House of Representatives their written declaration that the President is unable to discharge the powers and duties of his office, the Vice President shall immediately assume the powers and duties of the office as Acting President.

Thereafter, when the President transmits to the President pro tempore of the Senate and the Speaker of the House of Representatives his written declaration that no inability exists, he shall resume the powers and duties of his office unless the Vice President and a majority of either the principal officers of the executive department or of such other body as Congress may by law provide, transmit within four days to the President pro tempore of the Senate and the Speaker of the House of Representatives their written declaration and the President is unable to discharge the powers and duties of his office. Thereupon Congress shall decide the issue, assembling within forty-eight hours for that purpose if not in session. If the Congress, within twenty-one days after receipt of the latter written declaration, or, if Congress is not in session, within twenty-one days after Congress is required to assemble, determines by two-thirds vote of both Houses that the President is unable to discharge the powers and duties of his office, the Vice President shall continue to discharge the same as Acting President; otherwise, the President shall resume the powers and duties of his office.

Amendment XXVI [1971]

Section 1.   The right of citizens of the United States, who are eighteen years of age or older, to vote shall not be denied or abridged by the United States or by any State on account of age.

Section 2.   The Congress shall have power to enforce this article by appropriate legislation.

[Equal Rights Amendment]

[Ratified by the House of Representatives, October 12, 1971; by the Senate, March 22, 1972. Must be ratified by 38 states by March 22, 1979; as of November 1973, has been ratified by 29 states.]

[Section 1.   Equality of rights of any person under the law shall not be denied or abridged by the United States or by any State on account of sex.

[Section 2.   This article shall not impair the validity of any law of the United States which exempts a person from compulsory military service or any other law of the United States or of any State which reasonably promotes the health and safety of the people.

[Section 3.   The Congress shall have the power to enforce, by appropriate legislation, the provisions of this article.

[Section 4.   This amendment shall take effect two years after the date of ratification.]

Credits

738

511, 514   Excerpted from "Sex Differences in Intellectual Functioning," by Eleanor E. Maccoby, in *The Development of Sex Differences,* edited by Eleanor E. Maccoby, with the permission of the publishers (Stanford: Stanford University Press, 1966), pp 25, 26, 27, 29, 30, 31, 33, and 35.

514   Samuel Messick, "What Kind of Difference Does Sex Make?" in *Sex Differences and Discrimination in Education* (ed Scarvia B. Anderson 1972), pp 2-4. Copyright ©1972 by Charles A. Jones Publishing Co.

527   Marshall P. Smith, "He Only Does It To Annoy," in *Sex Differences and Discrimination in Education* (ed Scarvia B. Anderson 1972), pp 28, 42-43. Copyright ©1972 by Charles A. Jones Publishing Co.

528   R. W. Strickler, "Thomas Coebourn Elementary School Kindergarten-Primary Masculinization Project 1968-1972 and Kindergarten-Primary Masculinization Project 1970-1971," unpublished manuscript. Printed by permission of Richard W. Strickler, Principal, and the kindergarten-primary staff of Thomas Coebourn Elementary School, Brookhaven, Pennsylvania.

537   Philip B. Kurland, "Equal Educational Opportunity: The Limits of Constitutional Jurisprudence Undefined," *University of Chicago Law Review* vol 35, pp 583, 589. Copyright © 1968 by the University of Chicago Law Review.

538   Harold W. Horowitz, "Unseparate but Unequal—The Emerging Fourteenth Amendment Issue in Public Education," *UCLA Law Review* vol 13, pp 1147, 1166-68. Copyright ©1966 by the UCLA Law Review.

542   Reprinted from *Schools and Inequality* by James W. Guthrie, George B. Kleindorfer, Henry M. Levin, and Robert T. Stout. By permission of the M.I.T. Press, Cambridge, Massachusetts. Copyright © 1971 by the M.I.T. Press.

544   Mark Yudof, "Equal Educational Opportunity and the Courts," *Texas Law Review* vol 51, pp 411, 420-22. Copyright © 1973 by the Texas Law Review. Reprinted by permission of Fred B. Rothman and Co.

553   Mark Yudof, "The New Deluder Act: A Title I Primer," *Inequality in Education* vol 2, 5 December 1969, p 1. Copyright ©1969 by the Harvard Center for Law and Education.

558   From Jerome T. Murphy, "The Education Bureaucracies Implement Novel Policy: The Politics of Title I of ESEA, 1965-72," in *Policy and Politics in America: Six Case Studies,* ed Allan P. Sindler, pp 161, 172-83. Copyright ©1973 by Little Brown and Company (Inc.). Reprinted by permission.

607   David L. Kirp, "Judicial Policy-Making: Inequitable Public School Financing and the *Serrano* Case (1971)," in *Policy and Politics in America: Six Case Studies,* ed Allan P. Sindler, pp 83, 86-91. Copyright © 1973 by Little Brown and Company (Inc.). Reprinted by permission.

618   Frank L. Michelman, "The Supreme Court 1968 Term—Foreword: On Protecting the Poor Through the Fourteenth Amendment," *Harvard Law Review* vol 83, p 7. Copyright ©1969 by the Harvard Law Review Association.

645, 685   David L. Kirp, "Schools as Sorters: The Constitutional and Policy Implications of Student Classification," *University of Pennsylvania Law Review* vol 121, pp 705, 710-17, 725-29. Copyright © 1973 by the University of Pennsylvania Law Review. Reprinted by permission of Fred B. Rothman and Co.

Index

[Page references indicate the beginning of the discussion of each topic.]